Koren Talmud Bavli
THE NOÉ EDITION

ZEVAḤIM

Steinsaltz Center

KOREN

תלמוד בבלי

KOREN TALMUD BAVLI

THE NOÉ EDITION

זבחים

ZEVAḤIM

Daf 15b through Daf 36b

COMMENTARY BY

Rabbi Adin Even-Israel Steinsaltz

EDITOR-IN-CHIEF

Rabbi Dr Tzvi Hersh Weinreb

SENIOR CONTENT EDITOR

Rabbi Dr Shalom Z Berger

EXECUTIVE EDITOR

Rabbi Joshua Schreier

•

STEINSALTZ CENTER

KOREN PUBLISHERS JERUSALEM

Supported by the Matanel Foundation

Koren Talmud Bavli, The Noe Edition
Vol. 29b: Tractate Zevaḥim, Daf 15b through Daf 36b
Paperback, ISBN, 978-965-7767-18-4

First Hebrew/English paperback edition, 2021

Koren Publishers Jerusalem Ltd.
PO Box 4044, Jerusalem 91040, ISRAEL
PO Box 8531, New Milford, CT 06776, USA
www.korenpub.com

Steinsaltz Center

Steinsaltz Center is the parent organization of institutions established by Rabbi Adin Even-Israel Steinsaltz

PO Box 45187, Jerusalem 91450 ISRAEL
Telephone: +972 2 646 0900, Fax +972 2 624 9454
www.steinsaltz-center.org

This book was published in cooperation with the Israel Institute for Talmudic Publications.

הִנֵּה יָמִים בָּאִים, נְאֻם אֲדֹנָי יֱהֹוִה, וְהִשְׁלַחְתִּי רָעָב בָּאָרֶץ,
לֹא־רָעָב לַלֶּחֶם וְלֹא־צָמָא לַמַּיִם, כִּי אִם־לִשְׁמֹעַ אֵת דִּבְרֵי יהוה.

Behold, days are coming – says the Lord God – I will send a hunger to the land, not a hunger for bread nor a thirst for water, but to hear the words of the Lord. (AMOS 8:11)

The Noé edition of the Koren Talmud Bavli
with the commentary of Rabbi Adin Even-Israel Steinsaltz
is dedicated to all those who open its covers
to quench their thirst for Jewish Knowledge,
in our generation of Torah renaissance.

This beautiful edition is for the young, the aged,
the novice and the savant alike,
as it unites the depth of Torah knowledge
with the best of academic scholarship.

Within its exquisite and vibrant pages,
words become worlds.

It will claim its place in the library of classics,
in the bookcases of the Beit Midrash,
the classrooms of our schools,
and in the offices of professionals and business people
who carve out precious time to grapple with its timeless wisdom.

For the Student and the Scholar

DEDICATED BY LEO AND SUE NOÉ

Steinsaltz Center

Executive Director, Steinsaltz Center

Rabbi Meni Even-Israel

Managing Editor

Rabbi Jason Rappoport

Senior Content Editor

Rabbi Dr. Shalom Z. Berger

Editors

Rabbi Dr. Joshua Amaru, *Coordinating Editor*
Rabbi Yehoshua Duker, *Senior Editor*
Rabbi Yedidya Naveh, *Content Curator*
Rabbi Avishai Magence, *Content Curator*
Rabbi Yehonatan Eliav, *Hebrew Edition*
Rabbi Gershon Kitsis, *Hebrew Edition*
Menucha Chwat
Rabbi Yonatan Shai Freedman
Rabbi Ayal Geffon
Rabbi Uri Goldstein
Noam Harris
Yisrael Kalker
Rabbi Tzvi Chaim Kaye
Rabbi Yonatan Kohn
Sholom Licht
Catriel Lev
Elisha Loewenstern
Rafi Miller
Rabbi Jonathan Mishkin
Rabbi Eli Ozarowski
Rabbi David Sedley
Rabbi Jonathan Shulman
Rabbi Michael Siev
Avi Steinhart
Rabbi David Strauss

Copy Editors

Aliza Israel, *Coordinator*
Ita Olesker
Debbie Ismailoff
Shira Finson
Ilana Sobel
Deena Nataf
Eliana Kurlantzick Yorav
Erica Hirsch Edvi
Sara Henna Dahan
Oritt Sinclair

Language Consultants

Dr. Stéphanie E. Binder, *Greek & Latin*
Rabbi Yaakov Hoffman, *Arabic*
Dr. Shai Secunda, *Persian*
Shira Shmidman, *Aramaic*

Technical Staff

Tani Bednarsh
Adena Frazer
Yaakov Shmidman
Shaltiel Shmidman
Nava Wieder

KOREN

Design & Typesetting

Dena Landowne Bailey, *Typesetting*
Tani Bayer, *Jacket Design*
Raphaël Freeman, *Design & Typography*

Images

Eliahu Misgav, *Illustration & Image Acquisition*
Daniel Gdalevich, *Illustration & Image Acquisition*

Introduction by the Publisher

The Talmud has sustained and inspired Jews for thousands of years. Throughout Jewish history, an elite cadre of scholars has absorbed its learning and passed it on to succeeding generations. The Talmud has been the fundamental text of our people.

Beginning in the 1960s, Rabbi Adin Even-Israel Steinsaltz שליט״א created a revolution in the history of Talmud study. His translation of the Talmud, first into modern Hebrew and then into other languages, as well the practical learning aids he added to the text, have enabled millions of people around the world to access and master the complexity and context of the world of Talmud.

It is thus a privilege to present the *Koren Talmud Bavli*, an English translation of the talmudic text with the brilliant elucidation of Rabbi Steinsaltz. The depth and breadth of his knowledge are unique in our time. His rootedness in the tradition and his reach into the world beyond it are inspirational.

Working with Rabbi Steinsaltz on this remarkable project has been not only an honor, but a great pleasure. Never shy to express an opinion, with wisdom and humor, Rabbi Steinsaltz sparkles in conversation, demonstrating his knowledge (both sacred and worldly), sharing his wide-ranging interests, and, above all, radiating his passion. I am grateful for the unique opportunity to work closely with him, and I wish him many more years of writing and teaching.

Our intentions in publishing this new edition of the Talmud are threefold. First, we seek to fully clarify the talmudic page to the reader – textually, intellectually, and graphically. Second, we seek to utilize today's most sophisticated technologies, both in print and electronic formats, to provide the reader with a comprehensive set of study tools. And third, we seek to help readers advance in their process of Talmud study.

To achieve these goals, the *Koren Talmud Bavli* is unique in a number of ways:

- The classic *tzurat hadaf* of Vilna, used by scholars since the 1800s, has been reset for great clarity, and opens from the Hebrew "front" of the book. Full *nikkud* has been added to both the talmudic text and Rashi's commentary, allowing for a more fluent reading with the correct pronunciation; the commentaries of *Tosafot* have been punctuated. Upon the advice of many English-speaking teachers of Talmud, we have separated these core pages from the translation, thereby enabling the advanced student to approach the text without the distraction of the translation. This also reduces the number of volumes in the set. At the bottom of each *daf*, there is a reference to the corresponding English pages. In addition, the Vilna edition was read against other manuscripts and older print editions, so that texts which had been removed by non-Jewish censors have been restored to their rightful place.
- The English translation, which starts on the English "front" of the book, reproduces the *menukad* Talmud text alongside the English translation (in bold) and commentary and explanation (in a lighter font). The Hebrew and Aramaic text is presented in logical paragraphs. This allows for a fluent reading of the text for the non-Hebrew or non-Aramaic reader. It also allows for the Hebrew reader to refer easily to the text alongside. Where the original text features dialogue or poetry, the English text is laid out in a manner appropriate to the genre. Each page refers to the relevant *daf*.

- Critical contextual tools surround the text and translation: personality notes, providing short biographies of the Sages; language notes, explaining foreign terms borrowed from Greek, Latin, Persian, or Arabic; and background notes, giving information essential to the understanding of the text, including history, geography, botany, archaeology, zoology, astronomy, and aspects of daily life in the talmudic era.
- Halakhic summaries provide references to the authoritative legal decisions made over the centuries by the rabbis. They explain the reasons behind each halakhic decision as well as the ruling's close connection to the Talmud and its various interpreters.
- Photographs, drawings, and other illustrations have been added throughout the text – in full color in the Standard and Electronic editions, and in black and white in the Daf Yomi edition – to visually elucidate the text.

This is not an exhaustive list of features of this edition, it merely presents an overview for the English-speaking reader who may not be familiar with the "total approach" to Talmud pioneered by Rabbi Steinsaltz.

Several professionals have helped bring this vast collaborative project to fruition. My many colleagues are noted on the Acknowledgments page, and the leadership of this project has been exceptional.

RABBI MENACHEM EVEN-ISRAEL, DIRECTOR OF THE STEINSALTZ CENTER, was the driving force behind this enterprise. With enthusiasm and energy, he formed the happy alliance with Koren and established close relationships among all involved in the work.

RABBI DR. TZVI HERSH WEINREB שליט"א, EDITOR-IN-CHIEF, brought to this project his profound knowledge of Torah, intellectual literacy of Talmud, and erudition of Western literature. It is to him that the text owes its very high standard, both in form and content, and the logical manner in which the beauty of the Talmud is presented.

RABBI JOSHUA SCHREIER, EXECUTIVE EDITOR, assembled an outstanding group of scholars, translators, editors, and proofreaders, whose standards and discipline enabled this project to proceed in a timely and highly professional manner.

RABBI MEIR HANEGBI, EDITOR OF THE HEBREW EDITION OF THE STEINSALTZ TALMUD, lent his invaluable assistance throughout the work process, supervising the reproduction of the Vilna pages.

RAPHAËL FREEMAN, EXECUTIVE EDITOR OF KOREN, created this Talmud's unique typographic design which, true to the Koren approach, is both elegant and user friendly.

It has been an enriching experience for all of us at Koren Publishers Jerusalem to work with the Steinsaltz Center to develop and produce the *Koren Talmud Bavli*. We pray that this publication will be a source of great learning and, ultimately, greater *avodat Hashem* for all Jews.

Matthew Miller, Publisher
Koren Publishers Jerusalem
Jerusalem 5772

Contents

For the vocalized Vilna Shas layout, please open as a Hebrew book.

Introduction to **Perek II**

And the Lord spoke to Moses, saying: Speak to Aaron and to his sons, that they separate themselves from the sacred items of the children of Israel, which they consecrate to Me, and that they not profane My holy name: I am the Lord.

(Leviticus 22:1–2)

When they go into the Tent of Meeting, they shall wash with water, that they not die; or when they come near to the altar to minister, to cause an offering made by fire to smoke unto the Lord.

(Exodus 30:20)

But if the sacrifice of his offering be a vow, or a gift offering, it shall be eaten on the day that he offers his sacrifice; and on the morrow that which remains of it may be eaten. But that which remains of the flesh of the sacrifice on the third day shall be burned with fire. And if any of the flesh of his peace offerings be at all eaten on the third day, it shall not be accepted, neither shall it be credited to he who offers it; it shall be an abhorred thing [piggul], and the soul that eats of it shall bear his iniquity.

(Leviticus 7:16–18)

After the discussion in Chapter One of disqualifications caused by improper designation of an offering, this chapter discusses two other types of disqualification. The first type stems not from improper intent, but rather from the identity of the person performing the service or the manner in which one performs it. The second type consists of disqualifications caused by two specific improper intentions: Intent to consume or burn the offering beyond its designated time, and intent to do so outside its designated area. The primary objective of the Gemara in this chapter is to clarify the *halakhot* pertaining to these two types of disqualification and to identify the biblical sources for each.

The latter category is not explicitly mentioned in the Torah, but the rabbinic tradition identifies two passages in Leviticus collectively as the implicit source for both intent to consume or burn an offering outside its designated area and intent to do so beyond its designated time. Since disqualification through each of these intentions is derived from the same passage in the Torah, the *halakhot* pertaining to them are largely parallel. The primary difference between them is the severity of the consequences each intention incurs. Intent to sprinkle the blood on the altar, or to burn the offering's sacrificial portions on the altar, or to eat the offering's eaten portions, beyond the designated time for each act respectively, renders the offering *piggul*. Not only is such an offering disqualified, but one who consumes its meat is punished with excision from the World-to-Come [*karet*]. Intent to perform any of the above acts outside the offering's designated area disqualifies the offering, but does not render it *piggul*. Unlike improper designation, these two intentions can disqualify any offering, and they therefore constitute one of the primary subjects of tractates *Zevaḥim* and *Menaḥot*.

The ordering of the chapters is at first glance counterintuitive, since Chapter Three will resume the discussion of improper designation of an offering and is therefore more closely associated thematically with Chapter One than with this chapter. In fact, the chapters are organized in order of the offering's procedure rather than thematically. Chapter One opens with a reference to the offering's slaughter, while Chapters Two and Three open with references to the collection of the blood.

מתני׳ כָּל הַזְּבָחִים שֶׁקִּבְּלוּ דָּמָן זָר, אוֹנֵן, טְבוּל יוֹם, וּמְחוּסַּר כִּפּוּרִים, וּמְחוּסַּר בְּגָדִים, שֶׁלֹּא רָחַץ יָדַיִם וְרַגְלַיִם, עָרֵל, טָמֵא, יוֹשֵׁב, עוֹמֵד עַל גַּבֵּי כֵלִים, עַל גַּבֵּי בְהֵמָה, עַל גַּבֵּי רַגְלֵי חֲבֵרוֹ – פָּסַל.

MISHNA With regard to **all slaughtered offerings,** if the one **who collected their blood**[N] was **a non-priest;**[H] or a priest who was **an acute mourner,**[HB] i.e., one whose relative has died and has not yet been buried; or **one** who was ritually impure **who immersed that day**[NH] and is waiting for nightfall for the purification process to be completed; **or one who has not yet** brought **an atonement** offering,[NHB] e.g., a *zav* or leper after the seventh day of the purification process; **or** a priest **lacking** the requisite priestly **vestments;**[H] or one **who did not wash his hands and feet**[H] from the water in the Basin prior to performing the Temple service; or **an uncircumcised**[NH] priest; or **a ritually impure**[H] priest; or if the one who collected the blood was **sitting;** or if he was **standing** not on the floor of the Temple but **upon vessels,**[NH] or **upon an animal,** or **upon the feet of another,** he has **disqualified** the offering.

קִבֵּל בִּשְׂמֹאל – פָּסַל, רַבִּי שִׁמְעוֹן מַכְשִׁיר.

If **he collected** the blood **with his left** hand,[H] he **disqualified** the blood for offering. In this last case, **Rabbi Shimon deems** it **fit.**

BACKGROUND

Acute mourner – אוֹנֵן: The period of acute mourning is observed on the day of the death of one's spouse, father, mother, son, daughter, brother, or sister. The mourner is exempt from all positive mitzvot from the time of the death of the close relative until after the burial. At that point, or according to some opinions, the morning after the burial, his status changes from that of an acute mourner to that of a mourner. An ordinary priest is unfit to serve in the Temple while observing acute mourning. A High Priest serves in the Temple even when he is an acute mourner, and his service is valid.

One who has not yet brought an atonement offering – מְחוּסַּר כִּפּוּרִים: This category includes a man who experienced a gonorrhea-like discharge [*zav*], a leper, a woman who experienced an unexpected discharge of uterine blood [*zava*], and a woman after childbirth. There are five possible sets of offerings incumbent on one who lacks atonement: The purification process of a *zav* or *zava* includes bringing a pair of turtledoves or pigeons, one as a sin offering and one as a burnt offering. A wealthy leper brings lambs as a sin offering, a burnt offering, and a guilt offering. A poor leper brings a pair of turtledoves or pigeons, one as a sin offering and one as a burnt offering, and a lamb as a guilt offering. A wealthy woman after childbirth brings a bird as a sin offering and a lamb as a burnt offering, whereas a poor woman brings a pair of turtledoves or pigeons, one as a sin offering and one as a burnt offering.

NOTES

Who collected their blood – שֶׁקִּבְּלוּ דָּמָן: This *halakha* applies not only to the one who collects the blood but to one who performs any other sacrificial rite. The mishna is referring specifically to collection of the blood since it is the first sacrificial rite that must be performed by a fit priest (see 32a).

One who immersed that day – טְבוּל יוֹם: In many cases of ritual impurity, the purification process involves two steps: The first is immersion in a ritual bath, and the second is arrival of nightfall of the day of the individual's immersion. During the period between immersion and nightfall, a certain measure of impurity remains. Consequently, in most cases, it is prohibited for one who immersed himself during the day to partake of offerings, or *teruma* if he is a priest. It is permitted for him to partake of second tithe.

One who has not yet brought an atonement offering – מְחוּסַּר כִּפּוּרִים: In some cases of ritual impurity, e.g., the impurity contracted by a man who experiences a gonorrhea-like discharge [*zav*] or a leper, one must immerse in a ritual bath and bring an atonement offering the day after immersion in order to complete the purification process. If one has not yet brought his offering, even if he has already immersed and night has fallen, he disqualifies any offering for which he performs sacrificial rites. For most types of impurity, e.g., those resulting from contact with a human corpse or a carcass of a creeping animal, one is not required to bring an atonement offering, and in such cases one may perform sacrificial rites after immersing and waiting until nightfall.

Uncircumcised – עָרֵל: According to Rashi, this is referring to a priest who could not be circumcised since it was deemed dangerous to his health. If he was uncircumcised by choice, he would be tantamount to an apostate and this, in and of itself, would disqualify him from performing the Temple service (see *Tiferet Yisrael*). According to *Tosafot*, the mishna is referring to one who was uncircumcised only due to fear of the pain it would cause. Such a person is not tantamount to an apostate. Most authorities rule in accordance with Rashi's opinion.

Standing upon vessels – עוֹמֵד עַל גַּבֵּי כֵלִים: The floor of the Temple is sanctified, and all priests must stand directly on it when performing sacrificial rites (Rashi).

HALAKHA

Non-priest – זָר: If a non-priest, i.e., one who is not a descendant in the male line of Aaron the High Priest, performs sacrificial rites, the rites are disqualified (Rambam *Sefer Avoda, Hilkhot Biat HaMikdash* 9:1).

Acute mourner – אוֹנֵן: If an acute mourner performs sacrificial rites, the rites are disqualified (Rambam *Sefer Avoda, Hilkhot Biat HaMikdash* 2:6–7).

One who immersed that day – טְבוּל יוֹם: If one who is ritually impure immerses and then performs sacrificial rites before nightfall, the rites are disqualified (Rambam *Sefer Avoda, Hilkhot Biat HaMikdash* 4:4).

One who has not yet brought an atonement offering – מְחוּסַּר כִּפּוּרִים: If one who has not yet brought an atonement offering to complete his purification performs sacrificial rites, the rites are disqualified (Rambam *Sefer Avoda, Hilkhot Biat HaMikdash* 4:5).

Lacking vestments – מְחוּסַּר בְּגָדִים: If a High Priest performs sacrificial rites wearing fewer than his eight requisite priestly vestments, or if an ordinary priest performs rites wearing fewer than his requisite four, he is considered to be lacking vestments, and the rites are disqualified (Rambam *Sefer Avoda, Hilkhot Kelei HaMikdash* 10:4).

Who did not wash his hands and feet – שֶׁלֹּא רָחַץ יָדַיִם וְרַגְלַיִם: If a priest performs sacrificial rites without first washing his hands and feet, the rites are disqualified (Rambam *Sefer Avoda, Hilkhot Biat HaMikdash* 5:1).

Uncircumcised – עָרֵל: If one who is uncircumcised performs sacrificial rites, the rites are disqualified, even if he is a priest (Rambam *Sefer Avoda, Hilkhot Biat HaMikdash* 6:8).

Ritually impure – טָמֵא: If a ritually impure priest performs sacrificial rites, the rites are disqualified (Rambam *Sefer Avoda, Hilkhot Biat HaMikdash* 4:1).

Sitting, standing upon vessels, etc. – יוֹשֵׁב עוֹמֵד עַל גַּבֵּי כֵלִים וכו׳: If one performs sacrificial rites while sitting, the rites are disqualified. Everyone participating in the Temple service must be standing on the floor of the Temple. If anything interposes between his feet and the ground, e.g., if he was standing upon vessels, upon an animal, or upon the feet of another priest, all rites he performs are disqualified (Rambam *Sefer Avoda, Hilkhot Biat HaMikdash* 5:17).

Collected the blood with his left hand – קִבֵּל בִּשְׂמֹאל: All sacrificial rites must be performed with the right hand. If one performs such rites with his left hand, the rites are disqualified (Rambam *Sefer Avoda, Hilkhot Biat HaMikdash* 5:18).

BACKGROUND

Frontplate – **צִיץ**: The frontplate of the High Priest was a plate of gold on which the words: "Sacred to the Lord" (Exodus 28:36), were engraved. This plate was tied to the forehead of the High Priest, adjacent to where his hairline began. The frontplate was one of the eight priestly vestments that composed the raiment of the High Priest. It is one of the four vestments that are called the golden vestments. The High Priest would wear all eight vestments year round, except during part of the Yom Kippur service, when he would wear only the four white vestments that all priests wore. The Torah states that by wearing the frontplate on his forehead: "Aaron shall bear the sin committed with the sacred items, which the children of Israel shall consecrate, even all their sacred gifts" (Exodus 28:38). The Sages explain that the frontplate does not atone for all sins related to the offerings in the Temple service; with regard to some offerings, the Torah states explicitly that they are not accepted. Rather, the verse's statement applies to specific cases of ritual impurity.

Frontplate

גמ׳ זָר מְנָלַן? דְּתָנֵי לֵוִי: ״דַּבֵּר אֶל אַהֲרֹן וְאֶל בָּנָיו לֵאמֹר וְיִנָּזְרוּ מִקָּדְשֵׁי בְנֵי יִשְׂרָאֵל״ וגו׳, בְּנֵי יִשְׂרָאֵל לְמַעוּטֵי מַאי? אִילֵּימָא לְמַעוּטֵי נָשִׁים – קָרְבַּן נָשִׁים בְּטוּמְאָה קָרֵב?

GEMARA **From where do we** derive that **a non-priest** who performs sacrificial rites disqualifies an offering? **As Levi teaches:** The verse states: **"Speak to Aaron and to his sons, that they separate themselves from the sacred items of the children of Israel** [*benei Yisrael*]" (Leviticus 22:2). Levi continues: **"The children of Israel"** serves **to exclude what** from the prohibition against sacrificing an offering in a state of impurity? **If we say** that it serves **to exclude** the offerings of **women,** and the verse states "*benei*" in the masculine to indicate sons but not daughters, is it conceivable that **an offering of women is sacrificed in** a state of **impurity?**

אֶלָּא לְמַעוּטֵי גּוֹיִם – הָשְׁתָּא צִיץ לֹא מְרַצֶּה, דְּאָמַר מָר: וּבְגוֹיִם – בֵּין בְּשׁוֹגֵג בֵּין בְּמֵזִיד לֹא הוּרְצָה, בְּטוּמְאָה קָרֵב?

Rather, perhaps it serves **to exclude** offerings of **gentiles. Now,** if the **frontplate**[B] of the High Priest, which normally effects acceptance for offerings of Jews sacrificed in a state of impurity, **does not effect acceptance** for the offerings of gentiles, **as the Master said: And with regard to** an offering of **gentiles, whether** it was offered in a state of impurity **unintentionally or intentionally,** it **was not accepted;** can it be, then, that such an offering **is sacrificed in** a state of **impurity** *ab initio*?

אֶלָּא הָכִי קָאָמַר: ״וְיִנָּזְרוּ מִקָּדְשֵׁי בְּנֵי יִשְׂרָאֵל וְלֹא יְחַלְּלוּ״.

Rather, this is what the verse **is saying,** i.e., it should be read in the following manner: **That they separate themselves from the sacred items; the children of Israel, and that they not profane** My holy name. That is, the verse states that they, the priests, must separate themselves from the sacred items when they are ritually impure, and that the children of Israel must separate themselves from performing the sacrificial rites, so that they will not profane, i.e., disqualify, the offerings.

דְּבֵי רַבִּי יִשְׁמָעֵאל תָּנָא: אָתְיָא בְּקַל וָחוֹמֶר מִבַּעַל מוּם, מַה בַּעַל מוּם שֶׁאוֹכֵל, אִם עָבַד – חִילֵּל,

A *tanna* of the **school of Rabbi Yishmael taught:** The *halakha* of a non-priest who performs the sacrificial rites **is derived via an** ***a fortiori*** inference **from** the case of **a blemished** priest: **Just as** with regard to **a blemished** priest, **who may partake** of the meat of offerings, **if he performed** sacrificial **rites** he has nevertheless **desecrated** the service,

Perek **II**
Daf **16** Amud **a**

NOTES

A non-priest, who may not partake of the meat of offerings of the most sacred order – **זָר שֶׁאֵינוֹ אוֹכֵל**: A non-priest, unlike a blemished priest, may not eat meat from offerings of the most sacred order. Non-priests may partake of offerings of lesser sanctity.

זָר שֶׁאֵינוֹ אוֹכֵל, אֵינוֹ דִּין שֶׁאִם עָבַד חִילֵּל?

then with regard to **a non-priest, who may not partake** of the meat of offerings of the most sacred order,[N] **is it not right that if he performed** sacrificial **rites he has desecrated** the service?

מַה לְּבַעַל מוּם, שֶׁכֵּן עָשָׂה בּוֹ קָרֵב כְּמַקְרִיב!

The Gemara rejects the inference: One cannot draw an *a fortiori* inference from a blemished priest, as **what** is notable **about** the case **of a blemished** priest? It is notable **in that** the Torah **rendered** an animal that **is sacrificed like** the priest who **sacrifices** it, i.e., both blemished animals and blemished priests are disqualified. Since there is an added element of stringency with regard to the case of a blemished priest, one cannot draw an *a fortiori* inference from it.

טָמֵא יוֹכִיחַ. מַה לְּטָמֵא, שֶׁכֵּן מְטַמֵּא!

The Gemara suggests: The case of **an impure** priest **will prove** that this is no reason to reject the *a fortiori* inference. While an animal and the priest are not equated with regard to ritual impurity, as an animal cannot become impure while alive but a priest can, an impure priest desecrates the service. The Gemara rejects this as well: **What** is notable **about** the case of **an impure** priest? It is notable **in that** an impure priest **imparts impurity** to others.

בַּעַל מוּם יוֹכִיחַ. וְחָזַר הַדִּין: לֹא רְאִי זֶה כִּרְאִי זֶה, וְלֹא רְאִי זֶה כִּרְאִי זֶה, הַצַּד הַשָּׁוֶה שֶׁבָּהֶן – שֶׁמּוּזְהָרִין, וְאִם עָבְדוּ – חִילְּלוּ, אַף אֲנִי אָבִיא זָר, שֶׁהוּא מוּזְהָר, וְאִם עָבַד – חִילֵּל.

The Gemara responds: **A blemished** priest **will prove** that this is no reason to reject the inference, as he cannot impart his blemish to others. **And the inference has reverted** to its starting point. Therefore, one may derive the *halakha* of a non-priest from the combination of the case of a blemished priest and that of an impure priest: **The aspect of this** case **is not like the aspect of that** case, **and the aspect of that** case **is not like the aspect of this** case. **Their common element** is **that they are prohibited** from performing sacrificial rites **and if they performed** these **rites they have desecrated** the service. Therefore, **I will also include a non-priest, who is prohibited** from performing sacrificial rites, **and** conclude that **if he performed** sacrificial **rites he has desecrated** the service.

מְנָלַן דְּמוּזְהָר? אִי מִ״וְיִנָּזְרוּ״ – חִילּוּל בְּגוּפֵיהּ כְּתִיב בֵּיהּ! אֶלָּא מִ״וְזָר לֹא יִקְרַב אֲלֵיכֶם״.

The Gemara asks: **From where do we** derive **that** a non-priest **is prohibited** from performing sacrificial rites? **If** it is derived **from** the verse: "Speak to Aaron and to his sons, **that they separate themselves** from the sacred items of the children of Israel, and that they not profane My holy name" (Leviticus 22:2), then the *a fortiori* inference is unnecessary, since **profanation itself is written in** the verse. **Rather,** it must be that it is derived **from** the verse: "Keep the charge of the Tent of Meeting, whatever the service of the Tent may be; **but a common man shall not draw close to you**" (Numbers 18:4).

אִיכָּא לְמִיפְרַךְ: מַה לְּהַצַּד הַשָּׁוֶה שֶׁבָּהֶן, שֶׁכֵּן לֹא הוּתְּרוּ בְּבָמָה!

The Gemara asks: Still, the *a fortiori* inference drawn from the cases of a blemished priest and an impure priest **can be refuted: What** is notable **about their common element?** It is notable **in that** a blemished priest and an impure priest **were not permitted** to perform sacrificial rites **on** a private **altar** during times when there was no Temple or permanent Tabernacle. Since it was permitted for non-priests to perform rites on private altars, perhaps non-priests do not desecrate the sacrificial rites performed in the Temple.

לָא תֵּימָא טָמֵא יוֹכִיחַ, אֶלָּא אֵימָא: אוֹנֵן יוֹכִיחַ. מַה לְּאוֹנֵן שֶׁכֵּן אָסוּר בְּמַעֲשֵׂר! [בַּעַל מוּם] יוֹכִיחַ.

The Gemara responds: **Do not say** that the case of **an impure** priest **will prove** the *a fortiori* inference with the case of a blemished priest; **rather, say** that the case of **an acute mourner will prove** it, as it is prohibited for him to perform the service and, if he were to perform it, he would desecrate it. This, too, is rejected: **What** is notable **about** the case of **an acute mourner?** It is notable **in that** he **is prohibited from** partaking of second **tithe,**[N] whereas a non-priest may partake of second tithe. The Gemara responds: **A blemished** priest **will prove** the inference, as he may partake of second tithe.

וְחָזַר הַדִּין: לֹא רְאִי זֶה כִּרְאִי זֶה, הַצַּד הַשָּׁוֶה שֶׁבָּהֶן שֶׁמּוּזְהָרִין כו׳.

And the inference has reverted to its starting point. **The aspect of this** case **is not like the aspect of that** case. **Their common element** is **that they are prohibited** from performing sacrificial rites *ab initio*, and they desecrate the service if they do so. Therefore, with regard to a non-priest, who is prohibited from performing sacrificial rites, if he performed sacrificial rites he has desecrated the service.

הָכָא נַמִי לִפְרוֹךְ: מַה לְּהַצַּד הַשָּׁוֶה שֶׁבָּהֶן, שֶׁכֵּן לֹא הוּתְּרוּ בְּבָמָה! מַתְקִיף לָהּ רַב סַמָּא בְּרֵיהּ דְּרָבָא: וּמַאן לֵימָא לָן דְּאוֹנֵן אָסוּר בְּבָמָה? דִּלְמָא שָׁרֵי בְּבָמָה!

The Gemara asks: **Here, too, let one refute** the inference: **What** is notable **about their common element?** It is notable **in that** both an acute mourner and a blemished priest **were not permitted** to perform sacrificial rites **on** a private **altar,** unlike a non-priest. **Rav Samma, son of Rava, objects to this: And who shall say to us that an acute mourner** was **prohibited** from performing rites **on** a private **altar? Perhaps** it was **permitted** for him to perform the rites **on** a private **altar.**

רַב מְשָׁרְשִׁיָּא אָמַר: אָתְיָא קַל וָחוֹמֶר מִיּוֹשֵׁב, מַה יּוֹשֵׁב שֶׁאוֹכֵל, אִם עָבַד – חִילֵּל, זָר שֶׁאֵינוֹ אוֹכֵל – אֵינוֹ דִּין שֶׁאִם עָבַד חִילֵּל?

Rav Mesharshiyya says: The *halakha* that a non-priest desecrates the service **is derived** by **an** ***a fortiori*** inference **from** the case of a priest who performed sacrificial rites while **sitting: Just as** with regard to a priest who was **sitting, who may partake** of the meat of offerings, **if he performed** sacrificial **rites he has desecrated** the service, then with regard to **a non-priest, who may not partake** of the meat of offerings of the most sacred order, **is it not right that if he performed** sacrificial **rites he has desecrated** the service?

NOTES

Prohibited from partaking of second tithe – אָסוּר בְּמַעֲשֵׂר: The verse states that one who separates tithes must declare: "I have not eaten thereof in my mourning" (Deuteronomy 26:14). The Sages teach that this is a reference to acute mourning.

NOTES

Is it written, etc. – מִי כְּתִיב וכו׳: One need not infer from the verse that if an ordinary priest performs sacrificial rites while in acute mourning he disqualifies those rites. The verse may simply counter the notion that the High Priest, due to his special status, would disqualify rites he performs while an acute mourner (Rashi). According to the Ramban, the verse can be understood as a warning that if a High Priest in acute mourning interrupts the service, he disqualifies it, not as a reassurance that he will not disqualify it by continuing. If so, one need not infer that ordinary priests in acute mourning disqualify the service by continuing it.

מַה לְּיוֹשֵׁב, שֶׁכֵּן פָּסוּל לְעֵדוּת! מִיּוֹשֵׁב תַּלְמִיד חָכָם.

The Gemara rejects this: **What** is notable **about** the case of **a sitting** priest? It is notable **in that** one who sits **is disqualified from bearing witness**, as witnesses must stand when testifying. Since there is an added aspect of stringency with regard to the case of a sitting priest, one cannot derive the *halakha* with regard to a non-priest from it. The Gemara responds: Learn instead **from** the *halakha* of **a sitting Torah scholar**, as the court may allow a Torah scholar to sit while testifying.

מַה לְּשֵׁם יוֹשֵׁב, שֶׁכֵּן פָּסוּל לְעֵדוּת! שֵׁם יוֹשֵׁב לָא פָּרֵיךְ. וְאִם תִּמְצָא לוֹמַר פָּרֵיךְ – אָתְיָא מִיּוֹשֵׁב וּמֵחֲדָא מֵהָנָךְ.

The Gemara challenges: Still, one cannot derive the *halakha* from this, as **what** is notable about **the category of a sitting** priest? It is notable **in that** generally speaking, one who sits **is disqualified from bearing witness**, even though there are exceptions. The Gemara responds: **The category of a sitting** priest **cannot refute** the derivation. One can refute a derivation only from concrete cases, not general concepts. **And** even **if you say it can refute** the derivation, the *halakha* with regard to a non-priest **can be derived from** the case of **a sitting** priest **and from one of those** other cases, i.e., a blemished priest, an impure priest, or an acute mourner, all of whom may testify.

וְיוֹשֵׁב דְּכָשֵׁר בְּבָמָה מְנָלַן? אָמַר קְרָא: ״לַעֲמֹד לִפְנֵי ה׳ לְשָׁרְתוֹ״, לִפְנֵי ה׳ – וְלֹא לִפְנֵי בָּמָה.

The Gemara asks: **And from where do we** derive **that** one who is **sitting is fit** to perform sacrificial rites **on** a private **altar?** If he is not, one can refute the common element in the same manner as above. The Gemara responds: **The verse states:** "The Lord separated the tribe of Levi to bear the Ark of the Covenant of the Lord, **to stand before the Lord to minister to Him**" (Deuteronomy 10:8). The verse indicates that the sacrificial rites must be performed while standing only **before the Lord,** i.e., in the Temple, where the Divine Presence resides, **and not before** a private **altar,** which is a mere place of worship.

״אוֹנֵן״. מְנָלַן? דִּכְתִיב: ״וּמִן הַמִּקְדָּשׁ לֹא יֵצֵא וְלֹא יְחַלֵּל״, הָא אַחֵר שֶׁלֹּא יָצָא – חִילֵּל.

§ The mishna teaches that rites performed by **an acute mourner** are disqualified. The Gemara asks: **From where do we** derive this? **As it is written** with regard to a High Priest who is an acute mourner: **"And he shall not leave the Sanctuary, and he will not profane** the Sanctuary of his God" (Leviticus 21:12). One can infer: **But** any **other** ordinary priest **who did not leave** the Sanctuary while he was an acute mourner and continued to perform the service **has desecrated** the rites he performed.

רַבִּי אֶלְעָזָר אָמַר, מֵהָכָא: ״הֵן הִקְרִיבוּ״? אֲנִי הִקְרַבְתִּי! מִכְּלָל דְּאִי אִינְהוּ אַקְרִיב – שַׁפִּיר אִישְׁתְּרוּף.

Rabbi Elazar says: One can derive it **from here** instead: When Moses asked Aaron why the sin offering that was sacrificed on the day that Nadav and Avihu died was burned and not eaten, he suspected that Aaron's other sons, Eleazar and Itamar, had sacrificed the sin offering while acute mourners, which disqualified it and forced them to burn it. Aaron responded to Moses: "This day have **they offered** their sin offering?" (Leviticus 10:19). Rather, **I offered** it. As High Priest, I do not desecrate the Temple service even when I am an acute mourner; I burned it only because, as acute mourners, my sons and I are prohibited from partaking of the meat. Rabbi Elazar continues: **By inference,** one can derive **that if they had offered** the sin offering they would have disqualified it, and it would have been **proper** that **it was burned.**

וְרַבִּי אֶלְעָזָר מַאי טַעְמָא לָא אָמַר מִ״וּמִן הַמִּקְדָּשׁ לֹא יֵצֵא״? אָמַר לָךְ: מִי כְּתִיב הָא אַחֵר שֶׁלֹּא יָצָא חִילֵּל?

The Gemara asks: **And what is the reason** that **Rabbi Elazar does not say** that this *halakha* is derived **from** the verse: **"And he shall not leave the Sanctuary"?** The Gemara responds: He could have **said to you: Is it written:**[N] **But** any **other** ordinary priest **that did not leave** the Sanctuary **has desecrated** the rites he performed? It is only an inference, and so it is not conclusive.

וְאִידָךְ, מַאי טַעְמָא לָא אֲמַר מֵ״הֵן הִקְרִיבוּ״? קָסָבַר: מִפְּנֵי טוּמְאָה נִשְׂרְפָה.

The Gemara asks: **And the other** Sage, who derives it from the verse: "And he shall not leave the Sanctuary," **what is the reason** that **he did not say** to derive it **from** the verse: "This day have **they offered** their sin offering?" The Gemara responds: He **holds** that the sin offering **was burned because** it became **ritually impure,** not because Aaron and his sons were acute mourners.

דְּבֵי רַבִּי יִשְׁמָעֵאל תָּנָא: אָתְיָא בְּקַל וָחוֹמֶר מִבַּעַל מוּם, וּמָה

A *tanna* of the **school of Rabbi Yishmael taught:** The *halakha* **is derived by** an ***a fortiori*** inference **from** the case of **a blemished** priest: **And just as**

בַּעַל מוּם שֶׁאוֹכֵל, אִם עָבַד – חִילֵּל, אוֹנֵן שֶׁאֵין אוֹכֵל – אֵינוֹ דִּין שֶׁאִם עָבַד חִילֵּל?

with regard to **a blemished** priest, **who may partake** of the meat of offerings, **if he performed** sacrificial **rites he has desecrated** the service, then with regard to **an acute mourner, who may not partake** of the meat of offerings,[N] **is it not right that if he performed** sacrificial **rites he has desecrated** the service?

מַה לְּבַעַל מוּם, שֶׁכֵּן עָשָׂה בּוֹ קְרֵיבִין כִּמַקְרִיבִין!

The Gemara rejects the inference: One cannot derive this *halakha* from the case of a blemished priest, as **what** is notable **about a blemished** priest? It is notable **in that** the Torah **rendered** animals that **are sacrificed like** the priests who **sacrifice** them. Since this stringency does not exist with regard to acute mourning, perhaps an acute mourner may perform sacrificial rites as well.

זָר יוֹכִיחַ. מַה לְּזָר, שֶׁכֵּן אֵין לוֹ תַּקָּנָה!

The Gemara responds: The case of **a non-priest will prove** that this is no reason to reject the *a fortiori* inference, since there is no equivalence between priest and sacrifice in this regard, yet a non-priest desecrates the service. The Gemara rejects this as well: One cannot cite a proof from the case of a non-priest, as **what** is notable **about** the case of **a non-priest?** It is notable **in that he has no remedy,** i.e., a non-priest may never perform the sacrificial rites. By contrast, an acute mourner will eventually become permitted to perform the service.

בַּעַל מוּם יוֹכִיחַ. וְחָזַר הַדִּין, לֹא רְאִי זֶה כִּרְאִי זֶה וְלֹא רְאִי זֶה כִּרְאִי זֶה, הַצַּד הַשָּׁוֶה שֶׁבָּהֶן – שֶׁהֵן מוּזְהָרִין, וְאִם עָבְדוּ חִילְּלוּ, אַף אֲנִי אָבִיא אוֹנֵן שֶׁמּוּזְהָר, וְאִם עָבַד – חִילֵּל.

The Gemara responds: **A blemished** priest **will prove** that this is no reason to reject the inference, as even though the priest may perform the service if the blemish is healed, he desecrates the service so long as he remains blemished. **And the inference has reverted** to its starting point. Therefore, one learns the *halakha* from the combination of the cases of a blemished priest and a non-priest: **The aspect of this case is not like the aspect of that** case, **and the aspect of that** case **is not like the aspect of this** case. **Their common element is that they are prohibited** from performing sacrificial rites, **and if they performed** such **rites they have desecrated** the service. Therefore, **I will also include an acute mourner, who is prohibited** from performing sacrificial rites, **and** conclude that **if he performed** sacrificial **rites he has desecrated** the service.

הֵיכָן מוּזְהָר? אִילֵימָא מִ״וּמִן הַמִּקְדָּשׁ לֹא יֵצֵא״ – חִילּוּל בְּגוּפֵיהּ כְּתִיב בֵּיהּ! אֶלָּא מֵ״הֵן הִקְרִיבוּ״, וְקָסָבַר: מִפְּנֵי אֲנִינוּת נִשְׂרְפָה.

The Gemara clarifies: **Where is** an acute mourner **prohibited** from performing sacrificial rites, as asserted in the inference? **If we say** that it is derived **from** the verse: **"And he shall not leave the Sanctuary,** and he will not profane the Sanctuary of his God" (Leviticus 21:12), then the above *a fortiori* inference is unnecessary, since **profanation itself is written in** the verse. **Rather,** it must be that it is derived **from** the verse: "This day have **they offered**[N] their sin offering?" (Leviticus 10:19), **and** this *tanna* **holds** that the sin offering brought by Aaron **was burned because** Aaron and his sons were in **acute mourning.**

אִיכָּא לְמִפְרַךְ: מַה לְּהַצַּד הַשָּׁוֶה שֶׁבָּהֶן, שֶׁכֵּן לֹא הוּתְּרָה מִכְּלָלוֹ!

The Gemara challenges: The inference from the common element of the cases of a blemished priest and a non-priest **can be refuted: What** is notable **about their common element?** It is notable **in that** there are **no** circumstances in which **its general prohibition was permitted.** There is an exception to the prohibition against an acute mourner performing the Temple service, namely the High Priest, who may perform the sacrificial rites while an acute mourner.

טָמֵא יוֹכִיחַ.

The Gemara responds: The case of **an impure** priest **will prove** that this is no reason to reject the inference, as there is an exception to the prohibition against performing the service while impure, namely that the prohibition against performing the Temple service in a state of impurity is permitted in cases involving the public, yet an impure priest desecrates the service.

NOTES

Acute mourner, who may not partake of the meat of offerings – אוֹנֵן שֶׁאֵין אוֹכֵל: According to Rashi, this prohibition is derived from the declaration of one who separates tithes: "I have not eaten thereof in my mourning" (Deuteronomy 26:14). If an acute mourner may not eat tithes, *a fortiori* he may not eat the meat of offerings, which bears even greater sanctity.

From the verse: This day have they offered, etc. – מֵהֵן הִקְרִיבוּ וכו׳: The Gemara understands this derivation as indicating that an acute mourner may not perform rites *ab initio*, but not necessarily that rites they perform are disqualified. The offering may have been burned because, as acute mourners, Aaron and his sons were not permitted to eat of its meat, not because the offering was disqualified (Rashi).

NOTES

The category of impurity, at least, is permitted – **שֵׁם טוּמְאָה מִיהָא אִישְׁתְּרַאי**: Communal offerings may be sacrificed in a state of ritual impurity if necessary (see *Pesaḥim* 77a). This applies even to individual offerings that must be offered at set times, e.g., the Paschal offering or the High Priest's griddle-cake offering (see *Menaḥot* 50a).

HALAKHA

With regard to a communal offering – **בְּקָרְבַּן צִבּוּר**: If an ordinary priest hears of the death of an immediate relative while serving in the Temple, he is not required to leave the Temple, but he may not participate in the service in a state of acute mourning. If he performed rites in this state they are disqualified, in accordance with the opinion of Rava bar Ahilai (Rambam *Sefer Avoda, Hilkhot Biat HaMikdash* 2:6).

LANGUAGE

Ordinary [*hedyot*] – **הֶדְיוֹט**: From the Greek ἰδιώτης, *idiotēs*, denoting a simple person with no title. In the Talmud this word is used to denote ordinary priests as opposed to the High Priest, a common citizen as opposed to a king, or property of an individual as opposed to that of the Temple treasury.

מַה לְּטָמֵא, שֶׁכֵּן מְטַמֵּא! הָנָךְ יוֹכִיחוּ, וְחָזַר הַדִּין כו׳, הַצַּד הַשָּׁוֶה שֶׁבָּהֶן שֶׁמּוּזְהָרִין כו׳.

The Gemara asks: **What** is notable **about** the case of **an impure** priest? It is notable **in that he imparts impurity** to others. Perhaps it is only for this reason that an impure priest desecrates the service. The Gemara responds: **Those** other cases, i.e., a blemished priest and a non-priest, **will prove** that this does not reject the inference, since they do not impart their status to others. **And the inference has reverted** to its starting point. Therefore, one can derive the *halakha* from the combination of the cases of an impure priest, a blemished priest, and a non-priest: The aspect of this case is not like the aspect of that case; **their common element is that they are prohibited** from performing sacrificial rites and they desecrate the service. Therefore, I will also conclude that since an acute mourner is prohibited from performing sacrificial rites, he desecrates the service.

וְלִפְרוֹךְ: מַה לְּהַצַּד הַשָּׁוֶה שֶׁבָּהֶן, שֶׁכֵּן לֹא הוּתְּרוּ מִכְּלָלָן אֵצֶל כֹּהֵן גָּדוֹל בְּקָרְבַּן יָחִיד! שֵׁם טוּמְאָה מִיהָא אִישְׁתְּרַאי.

The Gemara asks: **But let one refute** this as well: **What** is notable **about their common element?** It is notable **in that its general prohibition was not permitted,** even **in the case of a High Priest** performing rites **for an individual's offering.** By contrast, a High Priest in acute mourning may perform rites even for individual offerings. The Gemara responds: **The category of impurity, at least, is permitted**[N] in the case of communal offerings. Therefore, one cannot claim that an impure priest, a non-priest, and a blemished priest all share a lack of exemptions.

רַב מְשָׁרְשִׁיָּא אָמַר: אָתְיָא בְּקַל וָחוֹמֶר מִיּוֹשֵׁב, וּמַה יּוֹשֵׁב שֶׁאוֹכֵל – אִם עָבַד חִילֵּל, אוֹנֵן שֶׁאֵינוֹ אוֹכֵל – אֵינוֹ דִּין שֶׁאִם עָבַד חִילֵּל?

Rav Mesharshiyya says: The *halakha* with regard to an acute mourner **is derived by *a fortiori*** inference **from** the case of **a sitting** priest: **And just as** with regard to **a sitting** priest, **who may partake** of the meat of offerings, **if he performed** sacrificial **rites he has desecrated** the service, then with regard to **an acute mourner, who may not partake** of the meat of offerings, **is it not right that if he performed** sacrificial **rites he has desecrated** the service?

מַה לְּיוֹשֵׁב, שֶׁכֵּן פָּסוּל לְעֵדוּת! מִיּוֹשֵׁב תַּלְמִיד חָכָם.

The Gemara rejects this: **What** is notable **about** the case of **a sitting** priest? It is notable **in that** one who sits **is disqualified from bearing witness,** as witnesses must stand when testifying. The Gemara responds: Learn instead **from** the *halakha* of **a sitting Torah scholar,** as the court may allow a Torah scholar to sit while testifying.

מַה לְּשֵׁם יוֹשֵׁב, שֶׁכֵּן פָּסוּל לְעֵדוּת! שֵׁם יוֹשֵׁב לָא פָּרֵיךְ. וְאִם תִּימְצֵי לוֹמַר פָּרֵיךְ, אָתְיָא מִיּוֹשֵׁב וּמֵחֲדָא מֵהָנָךְ.

The Gemara challenges: Still, one cannot derive from this, as **what** is notable **about the category of a sitting** priest? It is notable **in that** generally speaking, one who sits **is disqualified from bearing witness,** even though there are exceptions. The Gemara responds: **The category of a sitting** priest **cannot refute** the derivation. One can refute a derivation only from concrete cases, not general concepts. **And** even **if you say it can refute** the derivation, the *halakha* with regard to a non-priest **can be derived from** the case of **a sitting** priest **and from one of those** other cases, i.e., a non-priest, an impure priest, or a blemished priest, through their common element.

״אוֹנֵן פָּסוּל״. אָמַר רָבָא: לֹא שָׁנוּ אֶלָּא בְּקָרְבַּן יָחִיד, אֲבָל בְּקָרְבַּן צִבּוּר – מְרַצֶּה, קַל וָחוֹמֶר מִטּוּמְאָה.

§ The mishna teaches that if **an acute mourner** collects the blood of an offering, the offering is **disqualified. Rava says: They taught** this **only with regard to an individual's offering. But with regard to a communal offering,**[H] a rite performed by an acute mourner does **effect acceptance.** One can derive this by ***a fortiori*** inference **from ritual impurity.**

מַה טּוּמְאָה שֶׁלֹּא הוּתְּרָה מִכְּלָלָהּ אֵצֶל כֹּהֵן גָּדוֹל בְּקָרְבַּן יָחִיד – הוּתְּרָה אֵצֶל הֶדְיוֹט בְּקָרְבַּן צִבּוּר, אֲנִינוּת שֶׁהוּתְּרָה מִכְּלָלָהּ אֵצֶל כֹּהֵן גָּדוֹל בְּקָרְבַּן יָחִיד – אֵינוֹ דִּין שֶׁהוּתְּרָה אֵצֶל כֹּהֵן הֶדְיוֹט בְּקָרְבַּן צִיבּוּר?

Just as the prohibition against performing rites in a state of **ritual impurity, whose general prohibition was not permitted in** the case of **a High Priest** performing rites **for an individual's offering,** as no individual offering may be sacrificed in a state of impurity, **was nevertheless permitted in** the case of **an ordinary** [*hedyot*][L] priest performing rites **for a communal offering,** as communal offerings may be sacrificed by an impure priest when necessary; then so too, with regard to the prohibition against performing rites while in a period of **acute mourning, whose general prohibition was permitted in** the case of **a High Priest** performing rites **for an individual's offering,** as the High Priest may perform all rites while an acute mourner, **is it not right that** this prohibition **was permitted in** the case of **an ordinary priest** performing rites **for a communal offering?**

מַתְקִיף לַהּ רָבָא בַּר אֲהִילַאי: לֹא תּוּתַּר אֲנִינוּת אֵצֶל כֹּהֵן גָּדוֹל בְּקָרְבַּן יָחִיד מִקַּל וָחוֹמֶר: וּמַה טוּמְאָה שֶׁהוּתְּרָה אֵצֶל כֹּהֵן הֶדְיוֹט בְּצִבּוּר – לֹא הוּתְּרָה אֵצֶל כֹּהֵן גָּדוֹל בְּקָרְבַּן יָחִיד, אֲנִינוּת שֶׁלֹּא הוּתְּרָה אֵצֶל כֹּהֵן הֶדְיוֹט בְּקָרְבַּן צִבּוּר – אֵינוֹ דִּין שֶׁלֹּא תּוּתַּר אֵצֶל כֹּהֵן גָּדוֹל בְּקָרְבַּן יָחִיד?

Rava bar Ahilai objects to this: On the contrary, if such an inference can be made, then perhaps one can make the following mistaken inference: The performance of rites in a state of **acute mourning should not be permitted in** the case of **a High Priest** performing rites **for an individual's offering,** by *a fortiori* inference: **And just as** the prohibition against performing rites in a state of **ritual impurity,** whose general prohibition **was permitted in** the case of **an ordinary priest** performing rites **for a communal offering, was not permitted in** the case of **a High Priest** performing rites **for an individual's offering;** then so too, with regard to the prohibition against performing the rites during a period of **acute mourning,** whose general prohibition **was not permitted in** the case of **an ordinary priest** performing rites **for a communal offering, is it not right that** this prohibition **should not be permitted in** the case of **a High Priest** performing rites **for an individual's offering?**

וְתוּתַּר טוּמְאָה אֵצֶל כֹּהֵן גָּדוֹל בְּקָרְבַּן יָחִיד מִקַּל וָחוֹמֶר: וּמָה אֲנִינוּת שֶׁלֹּא הוּתַּר אֵצֶל כֹּהֵן הֶדְיוֹט בְּקָרְבַּן צִבּוּר – הוּתְּרָה אֵצֶל כֹּהֵן גָּדוֹל בְּקָרְבַּן יָחִיד, טוּמְאָה שֶׁהוּתְּרָה אֵצֶל כֹּהֵן הֶדְיוֹט בְּקָרְבַּן צִבּוּר – אֵינוֹ דִּין שֶׁהוּתְּרָה אֵצֶל כֹּהֵן גָּדוֹל בְּקָרְבַּן יָחִיד?

And similarly, one may claim: The performance of rites in a state of **ritual impurity should be permitted in** the case of **a High Priest** performing rites **for an individual's offering, by** *a fortiori* inference: **And just as** the prohibition against performing rites in a state of **acute mourning,** whose general prohibition **was not permitted in** the case of **an ordinary priest** performing rites **for a communal offering,** still **was permitted in** the case of **a High Priest** performing rites **for an individual's offering;** then so too, with regard to the prohibition against performing the rites in a state of **ritual impurity,** whose general prohibition **was permitted in** the case of **an ordinary priest** performing rites **for a communal offering, is it not right that** this prohibition **was permitted in** the case of **a High Priest** performing rites **for an individual's offering?**

וְלֹא תּוּתַּר טוּמְאָה אֵצֶל כֹּהֵן הֶדְיוֹט בְּקָרְבַּן צִבּוּר מִקַּל וָחוֹמֶר: וּמָה אֲנִינוּת שֶׁהוּתְּרָה אֵצֶל כֹּהֵן גָּדוֹל בְּקָרְבַּן יָחִיד – לֹא הוּתְּרָה אֵצֶל כֹּהֵן הֶדְיוֹט בְּקָרְבַּן צִבּוּר, טוּמְאָה שֶׁלֹּא הוּתְּרָה אֵצֶל כֹּהֵן גָּדוֹל בְּקָרְבַּן יָחִיד – אֵינוֹ דִּין שֶׁלֹּא תּוּתַּר בְּכֹהֵן הֶדְיוֹט בְּקָרְבַּן צִבּוּר?

And similarly, one may claim: The performance of rites in a state of **ritual impurity should not be permitted in** the case of **an ordinary priest** performing rites **for a communal offering, by** *a fortiori* inference: **And just as** the prohibition against performing rites in a state of **acute mourning,** whose general prohibition **was permitted in** the case of **a High Priest** performing rites **for an individual's offering,** still **was not permitted in** the case of **an ordinary priest** performing rites **for a communal offering;** then so too, with regard to the prohibition against performing the rites in a state of **ritual impurity,** whose general prohibition **was not permitted in** the case of **a High Priest** performing rites **for an individual offering, is it not right that** this prohibition **should not be permitted in** the case of **an ordinary priest** performing rites **for a communal offering?**

(וְלֹא תּוּתַּר, וְלֹא תּוּתַּר, אֲנִינוּת, וְטוּמְאָה, טוּמְאָה, יָחִיד, וְיָחִיד, צִבּוּר, סִימָן.)

The Gemara provides **a mnemonic** for recalling the above rejections of Rava bar Ahilai: **And should not be permitted, and should not be permitted, acute mourning, and ritual impurity, ritual impurity, individual, and individual, communal.**

Perek **II**
Daf **17** Amud **a**

אֶלָּא אִיכָּא לְמִיפְרַךְ הָכִי, וְאִיכָּא לְמִיפְרַךְ הָכִי – כָּל חֲדָא וַחֲדָא תֵּיקוּ בְּדוּכְתֵּיהּ.

Rather, one **can derive this way**[N] **and** one **can derive that** way. Since these derivations contradict one another, **each and every** *halakha* **shall stand in its place** and not modify the other by *a fortiori* inference.

NOTES

One can derive [*lemifrakh*] this way, etc. – אִיכָּא לְמִיפְרַךְ הָכִי וכו׳: The word *lemifrakh* usually denotes a refutation of a suggested inference. Here, and in some other instances, it denotes derivation by *a fortiori* inference. The Gemara means that since here one can formulate *a fortiori* inferences that contradict each other, none can be considered sound. The prohibitions against service in acute mourning and in a state of impurity must therefore stand alone and not modify each other.

״טְבוּל יוֹם״. מְנָלַן? דְּתַנְיָא, רַבִּי סִימָאי אוֹמֵר: רֶמֶז לִטְבוּל יוֹם שֶׁאִם עָבַד חִילֵּל, מִנַּיִן? תַּלְמוּד לוֹמַר: ״קְדֹשִׁים יִהְיוּ...וְלֹא יְחַלְּלוּ״,

§ The mishna teaches that sacrificial rites performed by **one who immersed that day** are disqualified. The Gemara asks: **From where do we** derive this *halakha*? The Gemara answers: It is derived **as it is taught** in a *baraita* that **Rabbi Simai says: From where** in the Torah is the **allusion** with regard **to** a priest **who immersed that day,**[N] **that if he performed** the Temple **service he desecrated** that service? It is derived from a verse, as **the verse states: "They shall be sacred to their God and they shall not desecrate** the name of their God" (Leviticus 21:6).

אִם אֵינוֹ עִנְיָן לְטָמֵא דְּנָפֵיק מִ״וְיִנָּזְרוּ״, תְּנֵהוּ עִנְיָן לִטְבוּל יוֹם.

If this verse **is not** written with regard to the **matter of an impure** priest who performed the Temple service, **as** that *halakha* is **derived for us from** the verse: **"That they separate themselves** from the sacred items of the children of Israel" (Leviticus 22:2), then **apply it** to the **matter of** a priest **who immersed that day** who performed the Temple service. Although he is no longer impure in every sense, the priest remains impure in the sense that he is prohibited from partaking of *teruma* and sacrificial food, and from entering the Temple.

אֵימָא: תְּנֵהוּ עִנְיָן לְקוֹרֵחַ קׇרְחָה וּלְמַשְׁחִית פְּאַת זָקָן!

The Gemara asks: Why must the verse be applied to the matter of one who immersed that day? **Say** that one should **apply it** to the **matter of one who creates a bald spot**[B] upon his head **or** to the matter of **one who destroys** his **beard,**[B] as these matters are discussed in the preceding verse.

טְבוּל יוֹם דְּאִם עָבַד – בְּמִיתָה, מְנָא לָן? דְּגָמַר חִילּוּל חִילּוּל מִתְּרוּמָה; דְּפָסֵיל בִּתְרוּמָה – מַחֵיל עֲבוֹדָה, דְּלָא פָּסֵיל בִּתְרוּמָה – לָא מַחֵיל עֲבוֹדָה.

The Gemara responds: This verse is already used to indicate another *halakha* relating to one who immersed that day: **From where do we** derive **that if one who immersed that day performed** sacrificial **rites,** he is liable to receive the punishment of **death** at the hand of Heaven? **As** it is **derived** by verbal analogy between **profanation** mentioned in this context and **profanation from** ***teruma,*** as the verse states in this context: "And not profane the name of their God" (Leviticus 21:6), and the verse states with regard to *teruma*: "Lest they bear sin for it, and die therein, if they profane it" (Leviticus 22:9). It can be inferred from this verbal analogy that one **who disqualifies** ***teruma,*** i.e., one who immersed that day, **profanes** the Temple **service,** and one **who does not disqualify** ***teruma,*** i.e., one who creates a bald spot or one who destroys his beard, **does not profane** the **service.**

אֲמַר רַבָּה: לָמָּה לִי דִּכְתַב רַחֲמָנָא טָמֵא וּטְבוּל יוֹם וּמְחוּסַּר כִּפּוּרִים?

§ **Rabba said: Why do I** need **that** which **the Merciful One wrote,** i.e., that **an impure** priest, **and one who immersed that day, and one who has not yet** brought **an atonement** offering[N] all disqualify the rites they perform? Wouldn't it have been enough to teach the *halakha* in only one case?

צְרִיכִי; דְּאִי כְּתַב רַחֲמָנָא טָמֵא – שֶׁכֵּן מְטַמֵּא. בִּטְבוּל יוֹם – מְחוּסַּר כִּפּוּרִים לָא אָתֵי מִינֵּיהּ, שֶׁכֵּן פָּסוּל בִּתְרוּמָה. בִּמְחוּסַּר כִּפּוּרִים – טְבוּל יוֹם לָא אָתֵי מִינֵּיהּ, שֶׁכֵּן מְחוּסָּר מַעֲשֶׂה.

Rabba explains: All three **are necessary,** as in each case there is a stringency not present in the others. Therefore, **had the Merciful One written** only that **an impure** priest desecrates the service, one might say that this is **because he imparts impurity** to others, and since the other two cases do not, one cannot derive them from the case of an impure priest. And had the Merciful One written the *halakha* only **with regard to one who immersed that day,** then the case of **one who has not yet** brought **an atonement** offering **could not be derived from it, since** the former **is unfit to** partake of ***teruma*** while the latter is not. And had the Merciful One written the *halakha* only **with regard to one who has not yet** brought **an atonement** offering, then the case of **one who immersed that day could not be derived from it, since** only the former **has not yet** performed a necessary **action,** while one who immersed that day must simply wait for nightfall in order to become fully pure.

מֵחֲדָא לָא אָתֵי, תֵּיתֵי חֲדָא מִתַּרְתֵּי!

The Gemara asks: Still, why are all three necessary? Granted, **from one** of these cases the other two **cannot be derived,** but **let one be derived from** the other **two.**

NOTES

Allusion to a priest who immersed that day, etc. – רֶמֶז לִטְבוּל יוֹם וכו׳: In most cases, the term allusion is a reference to inconclusive evidence from a verse concerning a *halakha* whose actual force is by rabbinic law. The Ramban writes that sometimes the word may be a reference to a real proof from a verse, in which case the *halakha* has the status of Torah law.

An impure priest and one who immersed that day and one who has not yet brought an atonement offering – טָמֵא וּטְבוּל יוֹם וּמְחוּסַּר כִּפּוּרִים: These three cases all share an aspect of impurity. One who is impure can impart his impurity to other people, vessels, or food. One who was impure but immersed that day has second-degree ritual impurity, and while he does not impart impurity to non-sacred food, he disqualifies *teruma* and offerings by contact with them. One who has immersed but has not yet brought the necessary atonement offering disqualifies offerings but not *teruma*.

BACKGROUND

One who creates a bald spot – קוֹרֵחַ קׇרְחָה: The Torah prohibits tearing out one's hair as an act of mourning (see Leviticus 21:5). If violation of this prohibition is witnessed and the perpetrator was warned beforehand, lashes are administered for each act of tearing that results in a bean-sized exposure of the scalp.

One who destroys his beard – מַשְׁחִית פְּאַת זָקָן: The Torah prohibits shaving the edges of one's beard with a razor (see Leviticus 19:27, 21:5). There are five places on one's face that may not be shaved with a blade: The upper and lower cheek on each side of the face, and the chin.

בְּהֵי לָא לִכְתּוֹב רַחֲמָנָא? לָא לִכְתּוֹב בִּמְחוּסַּר כִּפּוּרִים וְתֵיתֵי מֵהָנָךְ – מָה לְהָנָךְ שֶׁכֵּן פְּסוּלִים בִּתְרוּמָה!

The Gemara asks: **Which of the three should the Merciful One not write?** If one suggests: **Let** the Merciful One **not write** the *halakha* **with regard to one who has not yet brought an atonement** offering **and derive it from these** other two, an impure priest and one who immersed that day, one can reply: **What** is notable **about these?** They are notable **in that they are unfit to** partake of ***teruma***. Since one who has not yet brought an atonement offering may partake of *teruma*, perhaps he does not disqualify rites he performs.

אֶלָּא: לָא לִכְתּוֹב רַחֲמָנָא בִּטְבוּל יוֹם, וְתֵיתֵי מֵהָנָךְ; דְּמַאי פָּרְכַתְּ? מָה לְהָנָךְ שֶׁכֵּן מְחוּסָּרִים מַעֲשֶׂה – סוֹף סוֹף קְלִישָׁא לַהּ טוּמְאָתָן!

Rather, say: **Let the Merciful One not write** the *halakha* **with regard to one who immersed that day and derive** it **from these** other two, an impure priest and one who has not yet brought an atonement offering. **As, what can you** say to **refute** this? One cannot reply: **What** is notable **about these;** they are notable **since they have not yet** performed a necessary **action,** because **ultimately their impurity,** i.e., the impurity of one who has not yet brought an atonement offering, **is weak**[N] when compared to one who immersed that day, and relatively speaking, one who has not yet brought an atonement offering is not considered to be lacking the performance of an action.

NOTES

Ultimately their impurity is weak – סוֹף סוֹף קְלִישָׁא לַהּ טוּמְאָתָן: According to Rashi, this can be referring only to one who has not yet brought an atonement offering. Since night has already fallen following his immersion, his impurity is weaker than one who immersed that day. An impure priest has not yet immersed, and his impurity must be stronger than one who has already immersed. Still, since at least one of the two cases has weaker impurity than one who has immersed that day, one cannot claim that both share a stringent aspect that the third case lacks. See *Shita Mekubbetzet* for a discussion concerning how this statement of the Gemara accords with the previous statement that one who has not yet brought an atonement offering is considered to be lacking an action.

Perek **II**
Daf **17** Amud **b**

קָסָבַר: מְחוּסַּר כִּפּוּרִים דְּזָב כְּזָב דָּמֵי.

The Gemara responds: Rabba **holds** that **a man who experiences a gonorrhea-like discharge** [***zav***][B] **who has not yet** brought **an atonement** offering[H] is still **considered** to have the impure status of **a *zav*.**[N] The impurity of one who has immersed but has not yet brought an atonement offering is therefore considered stronger than that of one who immersed that day but requires no atonement.

BACKGROUND

Zav – זָב: The term *zav* refers to a man suffering from a gonorrhea-like condition. The *halakhot* relating to the severe ritual impurity caused by this condition are detailed in the Torah (Leviticus 15:1–15) and in tractate *Zavim*. One becomes ritually impure as a *zav* due to the secretion of a white, pus-like discharge from his penis. A man who experiences a discharge of this kind on one occasion becomes ritually impure for one day, like a man who has emitted semen. If he experiences a second discharge on the same day or the following day, or a prolonged initial discharge, he contracts the more severe ritual impurity of a *zav*, which lasts seven days. If he experiences a third discharge within the next day, he is obligated to bring a pair of doves, one for a sin offering and one for a burnt offering, as part of his purification process. Not only does the man himself become ritually impure, but he imparts ritual impurity through contact with vessels or people, moving or being moved by them, lying or sitting on them, or through the medium of a large stone that he lies on while it is positioned over them. His bodily fluids, i.e., his spittle, urine, and semen, impart ritual impurity, and any item on which he sits or lies becomes a primary source of ritual impurity and can itself impart ritual impurity to other items.

HALAKHA

A *zav* who has not yet brought an atonement offering – מְחוּסַּר כִּפּוּרִים דְּזָב: It is prohibited for a *zav* to enter the Temple courtyard. If a *zav* who has immersed but not yet brought an atonement offering to complete his purification process enters the Temple courtyard, he is not liable to receive lashes by Torah law, but he receives lashes for rebelliousness. In this the Rambam rules in accordance with the opinion that a *zav* who has not yet brought an atonement offering is not considered a full-fledged *zav*, since one finds elsewhere that this is the opinion of Rabbi Yoḥanan (Mahari Kurkus). According to the Ra'avad, however, a *zav* who has not yet brought an atonement offering who enters the Temple courtyard is liable to receive the punishment of *karet* (Rambam *Sefer Avoda*, *Hilkhot Biat HaMikdash* 3:9 and *Hilkhot Pesulei HaMukdashin* 8:14).

NOTES

A *zav* who has not yet brought an atonement offering is still considered a *zav* – מְחוּסַּר כִּפּוּרִים דְּזָב כְּזָב דָּמֵי: Rashi explains that this principle also applies to a leper who has immersed but has not yet brought an atonement offering. Although one has immersed and night has fallen, so long as one has not yet brought the necessary atonement offering he retains his previous impure status in certain respects. For example, one who has not yet brought an atonement offering transmits impurity to offerings and is liable to receive the punishment of excision from the World-to-Come [*karet*] for entering the Temple or eating offerings, as though he were still impure (see *Tosafot*).

HALAKHA

If an acute mourner or one who has not yet brought an atonement offering burned the red heifer – שְׂרָפָהּ אוֹנֵן וּמְחוּסַּר כִּפּוּרִים: If an acute mourner or one who has not yet brought an atonement offering burned the red heifer, it is fit, in accordance with the opinion of the first *tanna* (Rambam *Sefer Tahara, Hilkhot Para Aduma* 4:14).

One who immersed that day is fit to participate in the rite of the red heifer – טְבוּל יוֹם שֶׁכָּשֵׁר בְּפָרָה: One who immersed that day is fit to participate in the rite of the red heifer and the preparation and sprinkling of the water of purification (Rambam *Sefer Tahara, Hilkhot Para Aduma* 1:13).

וּמְחוּסַּר כִּפּוּרִים דְּזָב כְּזָב דָּמֵי תַּנָּאֵי הִיא, דְּתַנְיָא: שְׂרָפָהּ אוֹנֵן וּמְחוּסַּר כִּפּוּרִים – כְּשֵׁרָה. יוֹסֵף הַבַּבְלִי אוֹמֵר: אוֹנֵן – כְּשֵׁרָה, מְחוּסַּר כִּפּוּרִים – פְּסוּלָה; מַאי לָאו בְּהָא קָמִיפַּלְגִי, מָר סָבַר: מְחוּסַּר כִּפּוּרִים דְּזָב כְּזָב דָּמֵי, וּמָר סָבַר: לָאו כְּזָב דָּמֵי?

The Gemara notes: **And** the matter of whether **a *zav* who has not** yet brought **an atonement** offering is still **considered a *zav*** is a dispute between ***tanna'im*, as it is taught** in a *baraita*: **If an acute mourner or one who has not yet** brought **an atonement** offering **burned** the red heifer,[HN] it is **fit. Yosef the Babylonian says:** If **an acute mourner** burned it, it is **fit,** but if **one who has not yet** brought **an atonement** offering burned it, it is **disqualified. What, is it not that they disagree with regard to this:** One Sage, Yosef the Babylonian, **holds** that **a *zav* who has not yet** brought **an atonement** offering **is considered** a full-fledged ***zav*** and therefore disqualifies the red heifer, **and one Sage,** the first *tanna*, **holds** that a *zav* who has not yet brought an atonement offering **is not considered a *zav*,** but is instead considered like one who immersed that day, who is fit to burn the red heifer?

לָא, דְּכוּלֵּי עָלְמָא כְּזָב דָּמֵי, וְהָכָא בְּהָא קָמִיפַּלְגִי, דִּכְתִיב: ״וְהִזָּה הַטָּהֹר״ – מִכְּלָל שֶׁהוּא טָמֵא, לִימֵּד עַל טְבוּל יוֹם שֶׁכָּשֵׁר בְּפָרָה;

The Gemara responds: **No, everyone** agrees that he **is considered a *zav*, and here** the *tanna'im* **disagree with regard to this** matter, **as it is written** with regard to the rite of the red heifer: **"And the pure person shall sprinkle"** the water of purification (Numbers 19:19). The preceding verse already states that the one performing the service must be ritually pure. Therefore, by stating "pure" this verse emphasizes that he needs be pure enough only to perform the rite of the red heifer specifically. **By inference,** one derives **that he** may **be impure** in some way that disqualifies him for other rites. This **teaches that one who immersed that day is fit** to participate **in** the rite of the red **heifer.**[H]

מָר סָבַר: טוּמְאָה דְּכָל הַתּוֹרָה כּוּלָּהּ, וּמָר סָבַר: טוּמְאָה דְּהָךְ פָּרָשָׁה.

The *tanna'im* disagree as to the extent of this *halakha*: One **Sage,** the first *tanna*, **holds** that it is referring to any state of **impurity** mentioned **in the entire Torah,**[N] i.e., anyone who immersed that day due to any impurity may participate in the rite of the red heifer. **And** one **Sage,** Yosef the Babylonian, **holds** that it is referring specifically to one who was in the state of **impurity** mentioned **in this passage,** i.e., impurity contracted from a corpse, which the red heifer purifies.

הִלְכָּךְ, אוֹנֵן וּטְבוּל יוֹם דִּטְמֵא שֶׁרֶץ דְּקִילִי – אָתוּ בְּקַל וָחוֹמֶר מִטְּבוּל יוֹם דְּמֵת, אֲבָל מְחוּסַּר כִּפּוּרִים דְּזָב דַּחֲמִיר, שֶׁכֵּן טוּמְאָה יוֹצְאָה עָלָיו מִגּוּפוֹ – לָא.

Therefore, according to Yosef the Babylonian, with regard to **an acute mourner**[N] **and one who immersed that day** after becoming **impure** due to contact with the carcass of **a creeping animal, since** they **are** treated more **leniently, they are derived *a fortiori* from** the case of **one who immersed that day** to remove impurity contracted from **a corpse,** and they are fit to participate in the rite of the red heifer. **But** with regard to **a *zav* who has not** yet brought **an atonement** offering, **who** is treated more **stringently, since** his **impurity emerges onto him from his body**[N] rather than being imparted from without, one does **not** derive that he is fit to participate in the rite of the red heifer.

NOTES

If an acute mourner or one who has not yet brought an atonement offering burned the red heifer, etc. – שְׂרָפָהּ אוֹנֵן וּמְחוּסַּר כִּפּוּרִים וכו׳: According to Rashi, the red heifer is not considered a true offering, and therefore standard restrictions on the Temple service do not apply to it. According to *Tosafot*, the language of the Torah and various aspects of the rite of the red heifer indicate that it is a true offering. Standard restrictions do not apply to it only because the Torah itself issued a special dispensation to permit one who immersed that day to participate in the rite. One infers *a fortiori* that acute mourners and those who have not yet brought atonement offerings may also participate in the rite.

Any state of impurity mentioned in the entire Torah – טוּמְאָה דְּכָל הַתּוֹרָה כּוּלָּהּ: This includes all those who immersed that day, no matter the original source of their impurity. It also includes a *zav* or a leper who has already immersed but still requires an atonement offering to complete their purification process.

Therefore an acute mourner, etc. – הִלְכָּךְ אוֹנֵן וכו׳: The cases of an acute mourner and of one who came into contact with the carcass of a creeping animal are treated more leniently than the case of one who came into contact with a corpse, who requires a week-long purification process. If the latter is permitted to participate in the rite of the red heifer, the former two certainly may as well. One who has not yet brought an atonement offering to complete his purification process is treated more stringently in that he must still perform a given action. Therefore, one cannot infer that he too is permitted to participate in the rite of the red heifer.

The reference to an acute mourner is difficult to understand, since acute mourning is not a stage in the purification process and cannot be rightly considered stringent or lenient in comparison to one who immersed that day or has not yet brought an atonement offering. Rashi's version of the text omits this reference altogether.

Impurity emerges onto him from his body – טוּמְאָתוֹ יוֹצֵאת עָלָיו מִגּוּפוֹ: Most types of impurity mentioned in the Torah are imparted from without, e.g., those imparted by another impure person or object, corpse, animal carcass, or dead creeping animal. The impurities of a *zav* and leper are unique among the cases discussed here in that they originate in the body of the individual, who becomes impure when the symptoms of his condition emerge onto the surface of his body. Therefore, these two impurities require the added step of an atonement offering to complete the purification process.

"מחוסר בגדים". מנלן? אמר רבי אבוה אמר רבי יוחנן, ומטו בה משמיה דרבי אלעזר ברבי שמעון, דאמר קרא: "וחגרת אותם אבנט אהרן ובניו וחבשת להם מגבעת והיתה להם כהנה לחקת עולם", בזמן שבגדיהם עליהם – כהונתם עליהם, אין בגדיהם עליהם – אין כהונתם עליהם.

§ The mishna teaches that a priest **lacking** the requisite priestly **vestments** disqualifies the rites he performs. The Gemara asks: **From where do we** derive this? **Rabbi Avuh says that Rabbi Yoḥanan says, and** some **determined it** to be stated[N] **in the name of Rabbi Elazar, son of Rabbi Shimon: As the verse states: "And you shall gird them with belts, Aaron and his sons, and bind mitres on them; and they shall have the priesthood by a perpetual statute"** (Exodus 29:9). The verse indicates that **when their vestments are on them,**[H] **their priesthood is upon them,** but if **their vestments are not on them, their priesthood is not upon them** and their rites are disqualified.

והא מהכא נפקא? מהתם נפקא, דתניא: מנין לשתויי יין שאם עבד חילל? תלמוד לומר: "יין ושכר אל תשת וגו׳ ולהבדיל בין הקדש ובין החל"; מחוסר בגדים ושלא רחוץ ידים ורגלים, מנין?

The Gemara asks: **But is this** *halakha* **derived from here? It is derived from there, as it is taught** in a *baraita*: **From where** is it derived **that if those who drank wine performed** sacrificial **rites**[H] **they have desecrated** the service? **The verse states** with regard to the priests: **"Drink no wine or strong drink,** you, nor your sons with you, when you go into the Tent of Meeting, so that you not die; it shall be a statute forever throughout your generations. **That you may put difference between the holy and the common"** (Leviticus 10:9–10). The *baraita* continues: With regard to **one lacking** the requisite **vestments and one whose hands and feet are not washed, from where** is it derived that their rites are disqualified as well?

NOTES

And some determined it to be stated – ומטו בה: This phrase denotes an extension of the statement's attribution, i.e., that Rabbi Yoḥanan did not himself formulate the statement but rather transmitted it in the name of a *tanna* who lived earlier.

HALAKHA

When their vestments are on them, etc. – בזמן שבגדיהם עליהם וכו׳: If the High Priest performs sacrificial rites wearing fewer than his eight requisite priestly vestments, or if an ordinary priest does so wearing fewer than his requisite four, he is considered to be lacking vestments and his rites are disqualified. He is liable to receive the punishment of death at the hand of Heaven, like a non-priest who performed sacrificial rites (Rambam *Sefer Avoda*, *Hilkhot Kelei HaMikdash* 10:4).

If those who drank wine performed sacrificial rites – שתויי יין שאם עבד: A priest who has drunk a quarter-*log* of wine at once may not enter the Temple past the place of the altar. If he did so and performed sacrificial rites, the rites are disqualified (Rambam *Sefer Avoda*, *Hilkhot Biat HaMikdash* 1:1).

Perek **II**
Daf **18** Amud **a**

תלמוד לומר: "חוקה" "חוקה" לגזירה שוה!

The verse states "statute" with regard to those who drank wine, and it likewise states **"statute"** with regard to the priestly vestments (Exodus 28:43) and with regard to the washing of the hands and feet (Exodus 30:21). One therefore derives **by verbal analogy** that the *halakha* in all three cases is the same. If so, there is already a source for the *halakha* that one who lacks the requisite priestly vestments disqualifies the service.

אי מהתם, הוה אמינא: הני מילי – עבודה דזר חייב עליה מיתה, אבל עבודה דאין זר חייב עליה מיתה – אימא לא, קא משמע לן.

The Gemara responds: **If** one derived the *halakha* only **from there, I would say: This matter,** i.e., that the rites of one who lacks the requisite vestments are disqualified, applies only to **a rite for which a non-priest is liable**[N] to receive the punishment of **death** at the hand of Heaven, since that is the topic of the passage discussing those who drank wine. **But** with regard to **a rite for which a non-priest is not liable** to receive **death** at the hand of Heaven, **I will say** that they are **not** subject to this *halakha*. Therefore, the verse (Exodus 29:9) **teaches us** that the *halakha* applies to all rites.

אשכחן מחוסר בגדים, שתויי יין מנלן? אתיא "חוקה" "חוקה" ממחוסר בגדים.

The Gemara asks: **We found** a source for the *halakha* that **one lacking** the requisite **vestments** disqualifies all rites, even those for which a non-priest is not liable to receive the punishment of death at the hand of Heaven; **from where do we** derive that the *halakha* is the same for **those who drank wine,** as the passage in Leviticus (10:9–10) addresses only rites for which a non-priest receives the death penalty? The Gemara responds: It **is derived** by verbal analogy between the word **"statute"** used there and the word **"statute" from** the verses discussing **one lacking** the requisite **vestments.**

והא תנא "ולהבדיל בין" וגו׳ קא נסיב לה! מקמי דליקום גזירה שוה.

The Gemara asks: **But doesn't the *tanna*** of the aforementioned *baraita* **derive** that the rites of those who drank wine are disqualified from the verse: **"That you may put difference between** the holy and the common" (Leviticus 10:10), and not by verbal analogy to a priest lacking the requisite vestments? The Gemara responds: "That you may put difference between the holy and the common" is the source of this *halakha* only **before** the **verbal analogy stands.** Once the verbal analogy is derived, it is the source of the *halakha* with regard to those who drank wine as well.

NOTES

Rite for which a non-priest is liable, etc. – עבודה דזר חייב וכו׳: The verse that discusses those who drank wine also states: "That you not die," indicating that the passage applies only to rites that incur death at the hand of Heaven if one performed them after drinking wine. The scope of applicability of the death penalty for service by anyone unfit is derived from the case of service by a non-priest, who, although prohibited from performing all rites, incurs the death penalty for performing only one of the following four: Sprinkling the blood, burning the offering on the altar, pouring libations of wine, and pouring libations of water on *Sukkot*. These rites are treated especially stringently because they involve application of the offering to the altar and are the final stages of the sacrificial service (Rashi; see *Yoma* 24a).

וְהָא תַּנָּא, מְחוּסַּר בְּגָדִים הוּא דְּקָא יָלֵיף מִשְּׁתוּיֵי יַיִן! הָכִי קָאָמַר: מִנַּיִן שֶׁלֹּא נֶחְלְקוּ בֵּין מְחוּסַּר בְּגָדִים לִשְׁתוּיֵי יַיִן וְשֶׁלֹּא רְחוּץ יָדַיִם וְרַגְלַיִם – תַּלְמוּד לוֹמַר: ״חוּקָּה״ ״חוּקָּה״ לִגְזֵירָה שָׁוָה.

The Gemara challenges: **But doesn't the** *tanna* of the *baraita* **derive** the *halakha* with regard to **one lacking** the requisite **vestments** itself **from** the case of **those who drank wine?** The Gemara responds: Actually, the disqualification of rites performed by one who drank wine is derived from the case of one lacking vestments. And **this** is what the *tanna* **is saying: From where** is it derived **that there is no distinction between one lacking** the requisite **vestments and those who drank wine and one whose hands and feet are not washed,** and that all three disqualify all rites? **The verses state** the word: **"Statute," "statute,"** in order **to** derive **a verbal analogy.**

אֶלָּא ״לְהַבְדִּיל״ לָמָּה לִי? לְכִדְרַב, דְּרַב לָא מוֹקִים אָמוֹרָא עֲלֵיהּ מִיּוֹמָא טָבָא לְחַבְרֵיהּ, מִשּׁוּם שִׁכְרוּת.

The Gemara asks: **But** if the *halakha* that one who drank wine disqualifies the service is derived from the verbal analogy, **why do I** need the verse: **"That you may put difference** between the holy and the common"? The Gemara responds: The verse is necessary **in accordance with** the custom **of Rav, as Rav** would **not place an interpreter before him,**[H] i.e., he would not lecture in public, **from** the time that he drank wine on **one Festival** day **until** the **other,** the second Festival day, **due to drunkenness.** Rav was concerned that he would not issue a proper ruling, because it was customary to drink wine on the Festivals, and the verse states: "And that you may put difference between the holy and the common, and between the impure and the pure. And that you may teach the children of Israel all the statutes which the Lord has spoken" (Leviticus 10:10–11), indicating that one who drank wine may not issue a halakhic ruling.

אַכַּתִּי, מֵהָכָא נָפְקָא? מֵהָתָם נָפְקָא: ״וְנָתְנוּ בְּנֵי אַהֲרֹן הַכֹּהֵן״ – בִּכְהוּנּוֹ, לִימֵּד עַל כֹּהֵן גָּדוֹל שֶׁלָּבַשׁ בִּגְדֵי כֹּהֵן הֶדְיוֹט וְעָבַד – עֲבוֹדָתוֹ פְּסוּלָה!

The Gemara asks: **Still,** is the disqualification of rites performed by one lacking the requisite vestments **derived from here,** i.e., from the verse: "And you shall gird them with belts, Aaron and his sons" (Exodus 29:9)? **It is derived from there: "And the sons of Aaron the priest shall put** fire upon the altar" (Leviticus 1:7). The superfluous term "the priest" serves to indicate that he may serve only **in his priestly state.** The verse therefore **teaches** that **with regard to a High Priest who wore the vestments of an ordinary priest**[H] **and performed** sacrificial **rites, his service is disqualified.**

אִי מֵהָתָם, הֲוָה אָמִינָא: הָנֵי מִילֵּי – עֲבוֹדָה דִּמְעַכְּבָא כַּפָּרָה, אֲבָל עֲבוֹדָה דְּלָא מְעַכְּבָא כַּפָּרָה – לָא.

The Gemara responds: **If** one derived the *halakha* only **from there,**[N] **I would say: This matter** applies only to **service that is indispensable for** effecting **atonement. But service that is not indispensable for** effecting **atonement,**[N] e.g., putting fire upon the altar, is **not** subject to the *halakha*. Therefore, the verse (Leviticus 1:7) indicates that the *halakha* applies even to rites that are not indispensable.

וְאַכַּתִּי, מֵהָכָא נָפְקָא? מֵהָתָם נָפְקָא: ״וְעָרְכוּ בְּנֵי אַהֲרֹן הַכֹּהֲנִים אֵת הַנְּתָחִים״ וגו׳, ״הַכֹּהֲנִים״ – בִּכְהוּנָּן, מִכָּאן לְכֹהֵן הֶדְיוֹט שֶׁלָּבַשׁ בִּגְדֵי כֹּהֵן גָּדוֹל וְעָבַד – עֲבוֹדָתוֹ פְּסוּלָה!

The Gemara asks: **But still,** is the *halakha* **derived from here,** i.e., from all of the previous sources? **It is derived from there: "And the sons of Aaron, the priests, shall lay the pieces,** and the head, and the fat, in order upon the wood that is on the fire, which is upon the altar" (Leviticus 1:8). The superfluous term **"the priests"** serves to indicate that the priests may serve only **in their priestly state. From here** one derives that **with regard to an ordinary priest who wore the vestments of** the **High Priest and performed** sacrificial **rites, his service is disqualified.**

אִי מֵהָתָם, הֲוָה אָמִינָא: הָנֵי מִילֵּי חִיסּוּר, אֲבָל יִיתּוּר – לָא, קָא מַשְׁמַע לַן.

The Gemara responds: **If** one derived the *halakha* only **from there, I would say: This matter** applies only to **a lack** of vestments, e.g., a High Priest who wore fewer than his requisite eight vestments, **but an excess** of vestments, e.g., an ordinary priest who wore more than his requisite four, is **not** subject to the *halakha*. This verse therefore **teaches us** that the *halakha* applies even to an excess of vestments.

תָּנוּ רַבָּנַן: הָיוּ מְרוּשָּׁלִין, מְסוּלָּקִין, מְשׁוּחָקִים, וְעָבַד – עֲבוֹדָתוֹ כְּשֵׁירָה. לָבַשׁ שְׁנֵי מִכְנָסַיִם, שְׁנֵי אַבְנֵטִים, חָסֵר אַחַת, יָתֵר אַחַת, אוֹ שֶׁהָיְתָה לוֹ רְטִיָּה עַל מַכַּת בְּשָׂרוֹ תַּחַת בִּגְדוֹ, אוֹ שֶׁהָיוּ

§ **The Sages taught:** If the priest's vestments **were dragging** on the ground, or **raised up** [*mesulakin*][NL] far from the ground, or **frayed, and** the priest **performed** sacrificial **rites** while wearing them, **his service is valid.**[N] If **he wore two** pairs of **trousers**[H] or **two belts,** or if he was **lacking one** of his requisite vestments, or if he wore **one extra** vestment, **or** in a case **where** a priest **had a bandage on a wound on his body under his vestment** such that the bandage acted as an interposition between the vestments and his skin, **or** if he wore vestments **that were**

HALAKHA

Would not place an interpreter before him, etc. – לָא מוֹקִים אָמוֹרָא עֲלֵיהּ וכו׳: Just as a priest may not enter the Temple under the influence of alcohol, so too no one, priest or non-priest, may issue halakhic rulings while drunk, in accordance with the verse: "And that you may teach the children of Israel" (Leviticus 10:11). Despite this, one is permitted to issue rulings on matters that are stated explicitly in the Torah, or teach Torah generally, including *halakhot*, as long as he does not issue practical rulings. If one is a recognized halakhic authority, he may not teach Torah generally while drunk, since his statements are regarded as halakhic rulings, in accordance with the practice of Rav and the Gemara in tractate *Karetot* 13b (Rambam *Sefer Avoda, Hilkhot Biat HaMikdash* 1:3–4; see *Shulḥan Arukh, Yoreh De'a* 242:13 and in the comment of Rema, and *Ḥoshen Mishpat* 7:5 and commentaries there).

High Priest who wore the vestments of an ordinary priest – כֹּהֵן גָּדוֹל שֶׁלָּבַשׁ בִּגְדֵי הֶדְיוֹט: If the High Priest performed the Temple service wearing fewer than his eight requisite vestments, it is considered as though a non-priest had performed the service. He is liable to receive the punishment of death at the hand of Heaven, and the rites he performed are disqualified. So too with regard to an ordinary priest who performed the service wearing extra vestments, e.g., if he wore the eight vestments of the High Priest; his rites are disqualified and he liable to die at the hand of Heaven, in accordance with the Gemara here (Rambam *Sefer Avoda, Hilkhot Kelei HaMikdash* 10:4–5).

Two pairs of trousers, etc. – שְׁנֵי מִכְנָסַיִם וכו׳: If a priest wore extra garments, e.g., two tunics or two belts, and performed sacrificial rites, he desecrated the service and is liable to die at the hand of Heaven (Rambam *Sefer Avoda, Hilkhot Kelei HaMikdash* 10:5).

NOTES

If one derived the *halakha* only from there, etc. – אִי מֵהָתָם וכו׳: Here, in a departure from the Gemara's normal usage, the word: There, is referring to the source that is the primary subject of discussion, Exodus 29:9, rather than the source raised in contradistinction, Leviticus 1:7. The Gemara explains why the former verse alone would be insufficient. It goes without saying that the latter verse alone would be insufficient, as Exodus 29:9 is necessary to teach that priesthood only fully inheres while the priest is wearing the requisite vestments (Rashi).

Service that is not indispensable for atonement – עֲבוֹדָה דְּלָא מְעַכְּבָא כַּפָּרָה: Putting fire on the altar is not indispensable for effecting atonement because there is always a heavenly fire on the altar (Rashi).

Raised up – מְסוּלָּקִין: This is referring to a case where the vestments were positioned higher on the body than appropriate. Rashi indicates that the vestments must properly reach the ground, but according to the Rambam they must only reach the heel. Some suggest that according to both Rashi and the Rambam the vestments should ordinarily reach the ground, but it is to be expected that at times they will be slightly raised; still, they should not rise above the level of the heel *ab initio* (*Ḥiddushei Batra*).

His service is valid – עֲבוֹדָתוֹ כְּשֵׁירָה: The vestments must be exactly fitted to the priest *ab initio* (see *Pesaḥim* 65b). If one serves in poorly fitted vestments, the service is valid after the fact.

LANGUAGE

Raised up [*mesulakin*] – מְסוּלָּקִין: The root *samekh, lamed, kuf* is used here in its Aramaic sense to denote rising or raising.

מְטוּשְׁטָשִׁין אוֹ מְקוֹרָעִין, וְעָבַד – עֲבוֹדָתוֹ פְּסוּלָה.

soiled or ripped,[HN] **and he performed** sacrificial rites, **his service is disqualified.**

אָמַר רַב יְהוּדָה אָמַר שְׁמוּאֵל: מְרוּשָּׁלִין – כְּשֵׁרִין, מְסוּלָּקִין – פְּסוּלִין. וְהָתַנְיָא: מְסוּלָּקִין – כְּשֵׁרִין! אָמַר רָמִי בַּר חָמָא, לָא קַשְׁיָא: כָּאן שֶׁסִּילְּקָן עַל יְדֵי אַבְנֵט, כָּאן דְּלֵיתְנֵיהוּ מֵעִיקָּרָא כְּלָל.

Rav Yehuda says that **Shmuel says:** If the vestments are **dragging** on the ground, **they are fit,** but if they are **raised up**[H] above the ground, **they are unfit.** The Gemara asks: **But isn't it taught** in the above *baraita* that even if the vestments were **raised up they are fit? Rami bar Ḥama says:** This is **not difficult. Here,** the *baraita* deems them fit in a case **where** the priest **raised them up by** his **belt,** although they were initially the proper length; **there,** Shmuel deems them unfit in a case where **they do not initially** cover the priest's feet **at all.**

רַב אָמַר: אֶחָד זֶה וְאֶחָד זֶה – פְּסוּלִין.

Rav says: In **both this** case **and that** case, whether they were dragging or raised up, **they are unfit.**

רַב הוּנָא אִיקְּלַע לְאַרְגִּיזָא, רְמָא לֵיהּ בַּר אוּשְׁפִּיזְכָנֵיהּ: מִי אָמַר שְׁמוּאֵל: מְרוּשָּׁלִין כְּשֵׁרִין, וּמְסוּלָּקִין פְּסוּלִין? וְהָתַנְיָא: מְסוּלָּקִין – כְּשֵׁרִין! אֲמַר לֵיהּ: בַּר מִינָּהּ דְּהַהִיא, דְּשַׁנְיֵיהּ רָמִי בַּר חָמָא.

The Gemara recounts: **Rav Huna happened** to come **to Argiza. The son of his innkeeper** [*oshpizekhaneih*][L] **raised a contradiction before him: Did Shmuel** actually **say** that if the vestments are **dragging** on the ground, **they are fit, but** if they are **raised up** above the ground, **they are unfit? But isn't it taught** in the *baraita* that even if the vestments were **raised up they are fit?** Rav Huna **said to him:** Raise a contradiction from any source **apart from this** *baraita*, **as Rami bar Ḥama** already **answered** that it does not contradict Shmuel's statement, as it applies only to vestments that were initially the proper length.

אֶלָּא לְרַב קַשְׁיָא! וְכִי תֵּימָא: מַאי מְרוּשָּׁלִין – מְסוּלָּקִין עַל יְדֵי אַבְנֵט, וְאַבְנֵט מֵיגַז אַגֵּיז; אֶלָּא מְסוּלָּקִין קַשְׁיָא!

The Gemara asks: **But** doesn't the *baraita* pose **a difficulty for Rav,** who deems the vestments unfit even if they were dragging? **And if you would say: What** is the meaning of the word: **Dragging,** in the *baraita*? It means that they would initially drag but were **raised up by a belt** to the proper length, **and** they are fit since the **belt** effectively **trims** them, **but** then the term: **Raised up,** in the *baraita* poses **a difficulty.** Why should the *baraita* deem raised vestments fit? If the *baraita* is referring to vestments that were initially the proper length and were then raised up by a belt, then shouldn't they be unfit as the belt trims them?

אָמַר רַבִּי זֵירָא: רַב חֲדָא תָּנֵי: מְרוּשָּׁלִין שֶׁסִּילְּקָן עַל יְדֵי אַבְנֵט – כְּשֵׁרִין.

Rabbi Zeira says: Rav taught the *baraita* not as referring separately to both dragging and raised vestments, but as **one** statement referring to vestments that are simultaneously dragging and raised, i.e., **dragging** vestments **that** the priest **raised up by** his **belt** to the proper height **are fit.** But if they were above or below their proper height for any reason, they are unfit.

אָמַר רַבִּי יִרְמְיָה מִדִּיפְתִּי: מְרוּשָּׁלִין שֶׁלֹּא סִילְּקָן – תַּנָּאֵי הִיא. דְּתַנְיָא: ״עַל אַרְבַּע כַּנְפוֹת כְּסוּתְךָ״ – אַרְבַּע וְלֹא שָׁלֹשׁ. אוֹ אֵינוֹ אֶלָּא אַרְבַּע וְלֹא חָמֵשׁ? כְּשֶׁהוּא אוֹמֵר: ״אֲשֶׁר תְּכַסֶּה בָּהּ״ – הֲרֵי בַּעֲלַת חָמֵשׁ אָמוּר, הָא מָה אֲנִי מְקַיֵּים ״אַרְבַּע״ – אַרְבַּע וְלֹא שָׁלֹשׁ. וּמָה רָאִיתָ לְרַבּוֹת בַּעֲלַת חָמֵשׁ וּלְהוֹצִיא בַּעֲלַת שָׁלֹשׁ? מְרַבֶּה אֲנִי בַּעֲלַת חָמֵשׁ – שֶׁיֵּשׁ בִּכְלַל חָמֵשׁ אַרְבַּע, וּמוֹצִיא אֲנִי בַּעֲלַת שָׁלֹשׁ – שֶׁאֵין בִּכְלַל שָׁלֹשׁ אַרְבַּע.

§ **Rabbi Yirmeya of Difti says:** The case of **dragging** vestments **that** the priest **did not raise** is the subject of a dispute between *tanna'im*. **As it is taught** in a *baraita*: The verse states: **"On the four corners of your garment"** (Deuteronomy 22:12), from which it can be inferred: **Four, but not three,**[H] i.e., a three-cornered garment is exempt from the obligation of ritual fringes.[B] One may ask: **Or perhaps it is only** specifying **four, but not five? When it says** in the same verse: **"With which you cover yourself,"**[N] a garment **of five** corners **is mentioned** as obligated. If so, **how do I realize** the meaning of: **"Four** corners"? It means **four, but not three. And what did you see** that led you **to include** a garment **of five** corners **and to exclude** a garment **of three** corners? **I include** a garment **of five** corners **as four is included in five, and I exclude** a garment **of three** corners **as four is not included in three.**

HALAKHA

Soiled or ripped – מְטוּשְׁטָשִׁין אוֹ מְקוֹרָעִין: The priestly vestments must be new, beautiful, and fitted like the clothes of nobles, as it is written: "For splendor and for beauty" (Exodus 28:2). If they were soiled or ripped they are unfit, and rites performed in them are disqualified (Rambam *Sefer Avoda, Hilkhot Kelei HaMikdash* 8:4).

Dragging…raised up – מְרוּשָּׁלִין...מְסוּלָּקִין: If the priestly vestments were too long or too short, or if the priest raised them up by his belt higher than appropriate, rites performed in them are disqualified. If the vestments were too long and the priest raised them up by his belt to adjust them to the appropriate length, his rites are valid, in accordance with the opinion of Rav and the interpretation of Rabbi Zeira (Rambam *Sefer Avoda, Hilkhot Kelei HaMikdash* 8:4).

Four but not three, etc. – אַרְבַּע וְלֹא שָׁלֹשׁ וכו׳: One places ritual fringes on a garment with four corners. Garments that have only three corners are exempt. Garments that have five or more corners are obligated, in accordance with the first *baraita*. Still, one should place fringes only on the four corners that are farthest apart. Some say that five-cornered garments are exempt (Rabbeinu Simḥa). Therefore, one should not create a many-cornered garment *ab initio* (Rambam *Sefer Ahava, Hilkhot Tzitzit* 3:3; *Shulḥan Arukh, Oraḥ Ḥayyim* 10:1 and *Mishna Berura* there).

BACKGROUND

Ritual fringes – צִיצִית: This is referring to the positive biblical mitzva to attach fringes to the four corners of a garment (Numbers 15:37–41). Only garments with at least four corners are obligated, and the garment must be large enough to wrap around the person wearing it. Each fringe comprises four, generally wool, threads; the threads are folded in half, making eight ends on each fringe. The upper part of the fringe [*gedil*] is knotted in a prescribed manner, and the eight half-threads hang down from it. Customs vary with regard to how precisely to knot the fringes. Originally, ritual fringes included three white threads and one thread dyed blue [*petil tekhelet*]. One is obligated in the mitzva of ritual fringes only when he is wearing a garment to which the mitzva applies; there is no obligation to wear such a garment *ab initio*. Nevertheless, it is customary to wear a large four-cornered garment [*tallit*] during the morning prayers and a smaller four-cornered garment [*tallit katan*] throughout the day. The mitzva of ritual fringes applies during the day, but not at night. Because it is a time-bound mitzva, its fulfillment is incumbent upon men but not women, who are generally exempt from this category of mitzvot.

LANGUAGE

His innkeeper [*oshpizekhaneih*] – אוּשְׁפִּיזְכָנֵיהּ: From the Middle Persian word aspini, meaning an inn.

NOTES

Ripped – מְקוֹרָעִין: Even if the vestments are new, a tear disqualifies them because they do not satisfy the Torah's requirement that they be: "For splendor and for beauty" (Exodus 28:2).

With which you cover yourself – אֲשֶׁר תְּכַסֶּה בָּהּ: This phrase in the verse appears to be referring to all garments that are used as covering. It is therefore interpreted as amplifying the scope of the mitzva to include certain cases not clearly included by the verses' other wording: Either a five-cornered garment or the garment of a blind person.

וְתַנְיָא אִידָּךְ: ״עַל אַרְבַּע כַּנְפוֹת כְּסוּתְךָ״ – אַרְבַּע וְלֹא שָׁלֹשׁ, אַרְבַּע וְלֹא חָמֵשׁ. מַאי לָאו בְּהָא קָמִיפַּלְגִי: דְּמָר סָבַר: יָתֵר כְּמַאן דְּאִיתֵיהּ דָּמֵי, וּמָר סָבַר: כְּמַאן דְּלֵיתֵיהּ דָּמֵי?

And it is taught in **another** *baraita* that the verse states: **"On the four corners of your garment,"** from which it may be inferred: **Four, but not three,** and also **four, but not five,** i.e., only a four-cornered garment is obligated in the mitzva of ritual fringes. Rabbi Yirmeya continues: **What, is it not** that these *tanna'im* **disagree with regard to this: That** one **Sage,** who deems a five-cornered garment exempt, **holds** that **an extra** item **is considered as though it exists** and cannot be ignored, **and** one **Sage,** who deems it obligated, **holds** that it **is considered as though it does not exist** and the garment has only four corners? Accordingly, the first Sage deems a dragging priestly vestment unfit, since one cannot ignore the extra fabric, while the second Sage deems it fit since the extra fabric is treated as immaterial.

לָא, דְּכוּלֵּי עָלְמָא כְּמַאן דְּאִיתֵיהּ דָּמֵי. וְשָׁאנֵי הָכָא, דְּרַבֵּי רַחֲמָנָא – ״אֲשֶׁר תְּכַסֶּה בָּהּ״.

The Gemara responds: **No, everyone** agrees that an extra piece of a garment **is considered as though it exists,** and therefore dragging vestments are unfit. **And** according to the *tanna* of the second *baraita,* it **is different here,** with regard to ritual fringes, **as the Merciful One amplifies** the *halakha* to obligate even five-cornered garments with the words **"with which you cover yourself."**

וְאִידָּךְ, הַאי ״אֲשֶׁר תְּכַסֶּה בָּהּ״ מַאי עָבֵיד לֵיהּ? מִיבָּעֵי לֵיהּ לְכִדְתַנְיָא: ״וּרְאִיתֶם אֹתוֹ״ – פְּרָט לִכְסוּת לַיְלָה. אוֹ אֵינוֹ אֶלָּא פְּרָט לִכְסוּת סוּמָא? כְּשֶׁהוּא אוֹמֵר: ״אֲשֶׁר תְּכַסֶּה בָּהּ״ – הֲרֵי כְּסוּת סוּמָא אָמוּר, הָא מָה אֲנִי מְקַיֵּים ״וּרְאִיתֶם אֹתוֹ״? פְּרָט לִכְסוּת לַיְלָה.

The Gemara asks: **And the other** Sage, who deems five-cornered garments exempt, **what does he do with this** verse: **"With which you cover yourself"?** The Gemara responds: **He requires it for that which is taught** in a *baraita*: The verse states: "And it shall be unto you for a fringe, **that you may look upon it"** (Numbers 15:39). The phrase: "That you may look upon it," serves to **exclude a night garment**[H] from the obligation of ritual fringes, as the fringes on such a garment cannot be seen. One might ask: **Or is it only** to **exclude the garment of a blind person,**[H] who is unable to see the ritual fringes? **When it states** in the verse: **"With which you cover yourself"** (Deuteronomy 22:12), the obligation of ritual fringes for **the garment of a blind person is mentioned. If so, how do I realize** the meaning of the phrase: **"That you may look upon it"?** It serves to **exclude a night garment.**

וּמָה רָאִיתָ לְרַבּוֹת כְּסוּת סוּמָא וּלְהוֹצִיא כְּסוּת לַיְלָה? מְרַבֶּה אֲנִי כְּסוּת סוּמָא – שֶׁיֶּשְׁנָהּ בִּרְאִיָּה אֵצֶל אֲחֵרִים, וּמוֹצִיא אֲנִי כְּסוּת לַיְלָה – שֶׁאֵינָהּ בִּרְאִיָּה אֵצֶל אֲחֵרִים.

The *baraita* continues: **And what did you see** that led you **to include the garment of a blind person and to exclude a night garment** and not the reverse? **I include the garment of a blind person because it is** at least **visible to others, and I exclude a night garment because it is not visible,** even **to others.**

[וְאִידָּךְ? נָפְקָא לֵיהּ מֵ״אֲשֶׁר״. וְאִידָּךְ? ״אֲשֶׁר״ לָא דָּרֵישׁ.]

The Gemara asks: **And the other** Sage, who derives that a five-cornered garment requires ritual fringes from the phrase: "With which you cover yourself," from where does he derive that the garment of a blind person requires ritual fringes? The Gemara responds: **He derives it from** the word **"which"**[N] in the phrase, as that term itself connotes an amplification of the *halakha*. The Gemara asks: **And** what does **the other** Sage do with this word? The Gemara responds: **He does not interpret** the word **"which"** as an amplification.

HALAKHA

To exclude a night garment – פְּרָט לִכְסוּת לַיְלָה: The obligation of ritual fringes applies only during the day, but not at night, in accordance with the *baraita*. According to the Rambam, all garments are exempt at night, but according to the Rosh, garments normally worn during the day are obligated even at night, while garments normally worn at night are exempt even during the day. The Rema writes that since one rules leniently in matters of uncertainty with regard to blessings, one should not recite a blessing when donning ritual fringes at night, or even during the day if the garment is normally worn at night (Rambam *Sefer Ahava, Hilkhot Tzitzit* 3:7; *Shulḥan Arukh, Oraḥ Ḥayyim* 18:1).

Garment of a blind person – כְּסוּת סוּמָא: A blind person is obligated to wear ritual fringes. Although the verse stipulates that one must see the fringes, others see his fringes, in accordance with the *baraita* (Rambam *Sefer Ahava, Hilkhot Tzitzit* 3:7; *Shulḥan Arukh, Oraḥ Ḥayyim* 17:1).

NOTES

He derives it from the word which – נָפְקָא לֵיהּ מֵאֲשֶׁר: Since the phrase "with which you cover yourself" is apparently superfluous, one Sage holds that each word in the phrase, including "which," indicates an additional *halakha*. The other Sage treats the phrase as one unit, teaching only one additional *halakha*.

תָּנוּ רַבָּנַן: "בַּד" – שֶׁיִּהְיוּ שֶׁל בּוּץ, "בַּד" – שֶׁיְּהוּ חֲדָשִׁים, "בַּד" – שֶׁיְּהוּ שְׁזוּרִים, "בַּד" – שֶׁיְּהוּ חוּטָן כָּפוּל שִׁשָּׁה, "בַּד" – שֶׁלֹּא יִלְבַּשׁ שֶׁל חוֹל עִמָּהֶן.

§ **The Sages taught** with regard to the priestly vestments that the term: "Linen [*bad*]" (Leviticus 6:3), used in the verse indicates several properties of the garments: The verse states **"linen"** to indicate **that they** must be made **of fine linen** [*butz*];[HL] **"linen," that they** must be **new;**[H] **"linen," that** their thread must **be twisted**[H] of several plies; **"linen," that their thread** must **be folded six** times; **"linen," that** the priest may **not wear non-sacred** clothes along **with them.**

אֲמַר לֵיהּ אַבַּיֵי לְרַב יוֹסֵף: בִּשְׁלָמָא שֶׁיְּהוּ שֶׁל בּוּץ – הָא קָא מַשְׁמַע לַן: בּוּץ – אִין, מִידֵי אַחֲרִינָא – לָא; אֶלָּא "בַּד" שֶׁיְּהוּ חֲדָשִׁים; חֲדָשִׁים – אִין, שְׁחָקִין – לָא? וְהָתַנְיָא: מְשׁוּחָקִין – כְּשֵׁרִים!

Abaye said to Rav Yosef: Granted, the statement **that they** must **be of fine linen** is understood; **this** requirement **teaches us** that if they are of **fine linen** they **are** fit, but if they are of **something else** they are **not. But** with regard to the statement: **Linen, that they** must **be new,** one can infer that if they are **new** they **are** fit but if they are **frayed** they are **not. But isn't it taught** in the *baraita* (18a) that even if they were **frayed** they **are fit?**

HALAKHA

Linen [*bad*], that they must be made of fine linen – בַּד שֶׁיִּהְיוּ שֶׁל בּוּץ: In any instance where the Torah uses the words *shesh*, *bad*, or *butz* to indicate linen, it means material made of flax (Rambam *Sefer Avoda, Hilkhot Kelei HaMikdash* 8:13).

That they must be new – שֶׁיְּהוּ חֲדָשִׁים: Priestly vestments must be new and beautiful. If they were faded and a priest performed rites while wearing them, the service is valid, in accordance with the conclusion of the Gemara (Rambam *Sefer Avoda, Hilkhot Kelei HaMikdash* 8:4).

That their thread must be twisted – שֶׁיְּהוּ שְׁזוּרִים: In any instance that the Torah mentions the words *shesh*, meaning linen, or *shesh mashzar*, meaning twined linen, the thread must be six-ply thread. If the verse uses the word *bad*, the thread should be six ply *ab initio*, but is fit after the fact even if it had only one ply. According to Rashi, the requirement of six plies is indispensable with regard to all vestments (Rambam *Sefer Avoda, Hilkhot Kelei HaMikdash* 8:14).

LANGUAGE

Fine linen [*butz*] – בּוּץ: There are many words in the Torah for flax, *Linum usitatissimum*, and the materials made from it. The plant is called *pishtim* in the Bible, or *pishtan* in rabbinic Hebrew, and in the Talmud it is called *kittana*. The latter word was later adapted to refer to cotton, which is called *kutena* in modern Hebrew. Material made from flax has several different Hebrew names, which are derived from different languages. For example, the word *shesh* derives from ancient Egyptian, while *butz* was widespread in Semitic languages. It is possible that the word *butz* in biblical Hebrew refers specifically to a high-quality fine weave, while *bad* refers to a coarser, more common weave. From the language of the *baraita* here, as well as the Aramaic translations of the Torah, it seems that the Sages used the word *butz* to denote linen. The images here illustrate some of the implements and processes by which flax is prepared to be spun.

Breaking the flax stalks

Flax stalks

Scutching, i.e., beating the stalks

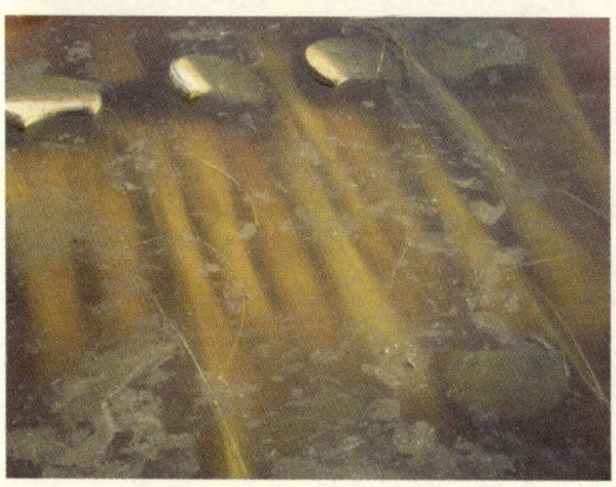

Retting, i.e., soaking the stalks to weaken them

Hackling, i.e., combing the flax

HALAKHA

They shall not gird themselves in a place in which people sweat – לֹא יַחְגְּרוּ בְּמָקוֹם שֶׁמְּזִיעִין: It is written explicitly in the Prophets that a priest may not gird himself with the belt in any place that one sweats. Rather, he must fasten it opposite the heart (Rambam *Sefer Avoda, Hilkhot Kelei HaMikdash* 10:2).

אֲמַר לֵיהּ: וְלִיטַעֲמֵיךְ, ״בַּד״ שֶׁיְּהוּ חוּטָן כָּפוּל שִׁשָּׁה, ״בַּד״ – חַד חַד לְחוּדֵיהּ מַשְׁמַע! אֶלָּא הָכִי קָאָמַר: בְּגָדִים שֶׁנֶּאֱמַר בָּהֶן ״בַּד״ – צְרִיכִין שֶׁיְּהוּ שֶׁל בּוּץ, חֲדָשִׁים, שְׁזוּרִין, שֶׁיְּהֵא חוּטָן כָּפוּל שִׁשָּׁה, יֵשׁ מֵהֶן לְמִצְוָה יֵשׁ מֵהֶן לְעַכֵּב.

Rav Yosef **said to him: And according to your reasoning** that the *baraita* intends to derive all of these requirements from the word linen, such that all of these requirements are indispensable, how can one understand the requirement: **Linen, that their thread** must **be folded six** times? The word ***bad*** itself **means each one on its own** (see Exodus 30:34). **Rather, this** is what the *baraita* **is saying:** Those **garments with regard to which it is stated: Linen, must be** made **of fine linen,** and they must be **new** and **twisted,** and **their thread** must **be folded six** times. **Some of** these requirements constitute **a mitzva**[N] *ab initio*, and **some of them are indispensable.**

מִמַּאי דְּהַאי ״בַּד״ כִּתָּנָא הוּא? אָמַר רַבִּי יוֹסֵף בְּרַבִּי חֲנִינָא: דָּבָר הָעוֹלֶה מִן הַקַּרְקַע בַּד בְּבַד.

The Gemara asks: **From where** is it known **that this** material ***bad*** **is** produced from the **flax** plant? **Rabbi Yosef, son of Rabbi Ḥanina, says:** The verse is referring to **an item that grows from the ground** with **each** stalk growing **on its own** [***bad bevad***], i.e., it does not split into multiple stalks. The flax plant fulfills this criterion.

אֵימָא עַמְרָא! עַמְרָא מִיפְּצַל. כִּיתָּנָא נַמִּי מִיפְּצַל! עַל יְדֵי לְקוּתָא מִיפְּצִיל.

The Gemara asks: Why not **say** that it is **wool?** The Gemara responds: The individual **wool** fibers **split** into smaller fibers. The Gemara rejects this: But **flax also splits.** The Gemara responds: **It splits** only **by being struck.**[N] Wool, by contrast, splits naturally.

רָבִינָא אָמַר, מֵהָכָא: ״פַּאֲרֵי פִשְׁתִּים יִהְיוּ עַל רֹאשָׁם וּמִכְנְסֵי פִשְׁתִּים יִהְיוּ עַל מָתְנֵיהֶם לֹא יַחְגְּרוּ בַּיָּזַע״.

Ravina says that the identity of *bad* is derived **from here:** The verse states with regard to the priestly vestments: **"They shall have linen [*pishtim*] crowns upon their heads, and shall have linen breeches upon their loins; they shall not gird themselves with *yaza*"** (Ezekiel 44:18). The word *pishtim* is clearly referring to flax.

אֲמַר לֵיהּ רַב אַשִׁי לְרָבִינָא: וְהָא עַד דַּאֲתָא יְחֶזְקֵאל מְנָלַן? וּלְטַעֲמֵיךְ, הָא דְּאָמַר רַב חִסְדָּא: דָּבָר זֶה מִתּוֹרַת מֹשֶׁה רַבֵּינוּ לֹא לָמַדְנוּ, מִדִּבְרֵי יְחֶזְקֵאל בֶּן בּוּזִי לָמַדְנוּ: ״כָּל בֶּן נֵכָר עֶרֶל לֵב וְעֶרֶל בָּשָׂר לֹא יָבֹא אֶל מִקְדָּשִׁי לְשָׁרְתֵנִי״, עַד שֶׁבָּא יְחֶזְקֵאל מְנָלַן? אֶלָּא גְּמָרָא גְּמִירִי לָהּ וַאֲתָא יְחֶזְקֵאל וְאַסְמְכֵיהּ אַקְּרָא; הָכָא נַמִּי, גְּמָרָא גְּמִירִי לָהּ כו׳.

Rav Ashi said to Ravina: But before Ezekiel came, from where did we derive the identity of *bad*? Ravina responded: **And according to your reasoning,** one could ask the same of **that which Rav Ḥisda said** with regard to the prohibition against Temple service by one who is uncircumcised or an apostate: **We did not learn this** following **matter from the Torah of Moses, our teacher; we learned** it **from the words of Ezekiel, son of Buzi: "No stranger, uncircumcised in heart or uncircumcised in flesh, shall enter into My Sanctuary to serve Me"** (Ezekiel 44:9). **Until Ezekiel came, from where did we** derive this? **Rather,** this *halakha* **is learned as a tradition** and therefore was observed for generations, **and Ezekiel came and gave it support by writing a verse. Here too, it is learned as a tradition,** and Ezekiel came and gave it support by writing a verse.

מַאי ״לֹא יַחְגְּרוּ בַּיָּזַע״? אֲמַר אַבַּיֵי: לֹא יַחְגְּרוּ בְּמָקוֹם שֶׁמְּזִיעִין. כְּדְתַנְיָא: כְּשֶׁהֵם חוֹגְרִין – אֵין חוֹגְרִין לֹא לְמַטָּה מִמָּתְנֵיהֶם, וְלֹא לְמַעְלָה מֵאַצִּילֵיהֶן, אֶלָּא

The Gemara asks: **What** is the meaning of the phrase in the verse: **"They shall not gird themselves with *yaza*"?**[N] **Abaye said: They shall not gird themselves in a place** in which people **sweat** [***mezi'in***].[H] **As it is taught** in a *baraita*: **When they gird** themselves with the belt, **they may not gird** themselves **below their loins nor above their elbows,** but **rather**

NOTES

Some of these requirements constitute a mitzva, etc. – יֵשׁ מֵהֶן לְמִצְוָה וכו׳: According to Rashi, all of the requirements in the *baraita* are derived from verses and are indispensable, except for the requirement that the vestments be new. The requirement that the thread be twisted is derived from another verse, which specifies "fine twined linen" with regard to certain vestments (see Exodus 39:28 and *Yoma* 71b). According to the Rambam, this requirement is indispensable only with regard to those vestments about which the term "twined linen" is stated expressly. With regard to vestments described simply as: Linen, the requirement applies only *ab initio*.

It splits only by being struck – עַל יְדֵי לְקוּתָא מִיפְּצִיל: Rashi explains that fibers of the flax stalk do not separate until beaten as part of the process of preparing linen. According to the commentary of Rabbi Shimshon of Saens on *Torat Kohanim*, the Gemara means that the stalks split only as a result of being stricken by disease.

They shall not gird themselves with *yaza* – לֹא יַחְגְּרוּ בַּיָּזַע: According to Rashi, the word *yaza* denotes sweat [*zei'a*]. Therefore, the priests may not gird themselves in places where the body folds, e.g., above the elbows or below the loins. Rav Hai Gaon interprets *yaza* as denoting movement [*za'azua*]. Therefore, the priests may not gird themselves in any place where the belt might shift and come undone, in upper or lower areas of the body.

כְּנֶגֶד אַצִּילֵי יְדֵיהֶן.

at the level of their elbows.

אָמַר רַב אַשִׁי, אֲמַר לִי הוּנָא בַּר נָתָן: זִימְנָא חֲדָא הֲוָה קָאֵימְנָא קַמֵּיהּ דְּאִיזְגַּדַּר מַלְכָּא, וַהֲוָה מַדְלֵי לִי הֶמְיָינַאי, וְתִיתְּיֵיהּ נִיהֲלֵיהּ, וַאֲמַר לִי: ״מַמְלֶכֶת כֹּהֲנִים וְגוֹי קָדוֹשׁ״ כְּתִיב בְּכוּ. כִּי אֲתַאי קַמֵּיהּ דְּאַמֵּימָר, אֲמַר לִי: אִקַּיֵּים בָּךְ ״וְהָיוּ מְלָכִים אוֹמְנַיִךְ״.

Rav Ashi says: Huna bar Natan[P] **said to me: Once, I was standing before Izgadar, king** of **Persia,**[P] **and my belt was raised** above its appropriate height, **and he lowered it** into place **and said to me: "A kingdom of priests, and a holy nation"** (Exodus 19:6), **is written about you;** therefore, you should always look dignified. **When I came before Ameimar** and recounted this incident, **he said to me:** With regard **to you,** God's promise to Israel: **"And kings shall be your foster fathers"** (Isaiah 49:23), **was fulfilled.**

תְּנַן הָתָם: כֹּהֵן שֶׁלָּקָה בְּאֶצְבָּעוֹ – כּוֹרֵךְ עָלֶיהָ גֶּמִי בַּמִּקְדָּשׁ, אֲבָל לֹא בַּמְּדִינָה. וְאִם לְהוֹצִיא מִמֶּנָּה דָּם – כָּאן וְכָאן אָסוּר.

§ With regard to the priestly vestments, **we learned** in a mishna **elsewhere** (*Eiruvin* 103b): **A priest who was injured on his finger**[H] on Shabbat may temporarily **wrap it**[B] **with a reed**[BN] so that his wound is not visible while he is serving in the Temple. This leniency applies **in the Temple, but not in** the rest of **the country,**[NH] as the reed also heals the wound, and medical treatment is prohibited on Shabbat by rabbinic decree. **But if** his intention is **to draw blood from** the wound,[B] **it is prohibited** both **here and there.**[N]

אָמַר רַבִּי יְהוּדָה בְּרֵיהּ דְּרַבִּי חִיָּיא: לֹא שָׁנוּ אֶלָּא גֶּמִי, אֲבָל צִילְצוּל קָטָן – הָוֵי יִתּוּר בְּגָדִים. וְרַבִּי יוֹחָנָן אָמַר: לֹא אָמְרוּ יִתּוּר בְּגָדִים אֶלָּא בִּמְקוֹם בְּגָדִים, אֲבָל שֶׁלֹּא בִּמְקוֹם בְּגָדִים – לָא הָוֵי יִתּוּר.

Rabbi Yehuda, son of Rabbi Ḥiyya, says: They taught only that **a reed** is permitted. **But a small sash** [*tziltzul*][L] as a bandage **is** considered **an extra garment** and is therefore forbidden, since it is prohibited for a priest to add to the priestly vestments prescribed by the Torah. **And Rabbi Yoḥanan says: They said** that wearing **extra garments** is prohibited **only** if the extra garment is worn **in a place** on the priest's body where the requisite **vestments** are worn.[H] **But** if the sash is **in a place** on his body where the **vestments** are **not** worn,[H] e.g., on his hand, it **is not** considered **an extra** garment.

PERSONALITIES

Huna bar Natan – הוּנָא בַּר נָתָן: Huna bar Natan was the Exilarch and a contemporary of Rav Ashi. He was a student of Rava, Rav Naḥman bar Yitzḥak, Ameimar, and Rav Pappa, and was also a close friend of Rav Ashi. He was himself a renowned Torah scholar, and his statements appear in several places in the Talmud. It is possible that he was a relative, or even a brother, of Mareimar, who occasionally served as a substitute for Rav Ashi according to *Iggeret Rav Sherira Gaon*.

As Exilarch and political leader of the Babylonian Jews on the one hand, and a great Sage on the other, Rav Huna bar Natan was referred to as: Torah and greatness in one place. As mentioned here, he had the favor of the king of Persia at that time. Still, he considered himself to be subject to Rav Ashi and made this clear publicly.

Some hold that when Rav Ashi died, Rav Huna bar Natan served for a short time as head of the yeshiva in Rav Ashi's place.

Izgadar, king of Persia – אִיזְגַּדַּר מַלְכָּא: This is the Persian king Yazdegerd I, who ruled 399–420 CE. Yazdegerd was a peaceful king who maintained good relations with Rome and exhibited great tolerance to his Christian and Jewish subjects, causing the Zoroastrian priests to label him a sinner. He accorded great respect to the Jews and the Exilarch. According to a tradition, his wife was the daughter of the Exilarch. The period of peace the Jews enjoyed under his rule may have been one of the factors that led to the compilation of the Talmud.

NOTES

Wrap it with a reed – כּוֹרֵךְ עָלֶיהָ גֶּמִי: In addition to the reed's medicinal purpose, one might wish to cover the wound during the Temple service for aesthetic reasons (Rashi).

In the Temple, but not in the country – בַּמִּקְדָּשׁ אֲבָל לֹא בַּמְּדִינָה: It is prohibited to apply a reed to a wound on Shabbat outside the Temple. The same applies to all other acts of healing, which are prohibited on Shabbat by rabbinic decree lest one desecrate Shabbat by crushing herbs to produce medicine (Rashi). According to *Tosafot*, the prohibition against applying a reed is a rabbinic decree lest one come to draw blood (see also *Sefer HaAgudda*). *Tosafot* concede that the language of the Jerusalem Talmud appears to support Rashi's interpretation.

It is prohibited both here and there – כָּאן וְכָאן אָסוּר: The drawing of blood is considered the creation of a wound, which is one of the labors prohibited by Torah law on Shabbat. Only prohibitions that are by rabbinic law do not apply in the Temple.

LANGUAGE

Sash [*tziltzul*] – צִילְצוּל: Instances of this word in other contexts suggest that it denotes a decorated ribbon worn as a belt. Some suggest that the word is related to the Hebrew *shalshelet*, meaning chain. This would indicate that a *tziltzul* was a thin chain. Alternatively, it was in the shape of a braid.

BACKGROUND

Wrap it – כּוֹרֵךְ עָלֶיהָ: The Sages prohibited any act of healing on Shabbat, including taking medicine, exercise, and bathing. This restriction applies only when one is suffering pain that is not life-threatening. One's health overrides Shabbat in any situation where his life might be in danger or in cases of serious illness; in such circumstances, all forms of treatment are permitted. Acts of healing were prohibited lest one grind and prepare medicines, which would be a violation of grinding, one of the principal categories of prohibited labor on Shabbat. Due to this concern, all forms of healing were prohibited, including those that do not involve grinding. The type of restriction described here is categorized as a *shevut*, a prohibition by rabbinic law. These prohibitions did not apply in the Temple.

Reed – גֶּמִי: The reed referred to in this context is probably an umbrella term for items produced from the papyrus sedge plant, *Cyperus papyrus* L. This plant, which grows in streams and swamps, was used in various industries. Its outer, harder section was used in the weaving of mats, while paper was manufactured from its inner part in ancient Egypt and other countries. These soft inner parts were also converted into strips with which items could be tied, and occasionally as a bandage for a wound, as in this case.

To draw blood from the wound – לְהוֹצִיא מִמֶּנָּה דָּם: Slaughtering or killing an animal is prohibited on Shabbat as one of the thirty-nine principal labors. Causing a wound to an animal or to a person is also prohibited as a subcategory of the prohibition against killing. This is so only when the wound results in bleeding; striking without breaking the skin, e.g., on the shoulder, would not constitute an infraction of this type. It is permitted to prevent a dangerous animal from attacking a person on Shabbat even if that requires taking the animal's life.

HALAKHA

Priest who was injured on his finger, etc. – כֹּהֵן שֶׁלָּקָה בְּאֶצְבָּעוֹ וכו׳: If a priest's finger is injured, he may wrap it with a reed or garment smaller than three fingerbreadths by three fingerbreadths on Shabbat, and he may participate in the Temple service. This is the *halakha* provided that the reed or garment does not interpose between his skin and the sacred vessel during the service. The priest may not dress the wound with the intention of drawing blood (Rambam *Sefer Avoda*, *Hilkhot Kelei HaMikdash* 10:9).

But not in the country – אֲבָל לֹא בַּמְּדִינָה: One whose finger is injured may not wrap it with a reed on Shabbat, since this is considered an act of healing (Rambam *Sefer Zemanim*, *Hilkhot Shabbat* 21:25; *Shulḥan Arukh*, *Oraḥ Ḥayyim* 328:24 in the comment of Rema).

In a place where vestments are worn – בִּמְקוֹם בְּגָדִים: By Torah law, the priestly vestments must be in direct contact with the priest's skin. Therefore, if even a thread, a dead louse, or dirt interposes between the priest's garment and his skin, his rites are disqualified (Rambam *Sefer Avoda*, *Hilkhot Kelei HaMikdash* 10:6).

In a place where vestments are not worn – שֶׁלֹּא בִּמְקוֹם בְּגָדִים: If a priest wrapped a garment that was three fingerbreadths by three fingerbreadths or larger around a part of his body where the priestly vestments are not worn, e.g., his finger or heel, his rites are disqualified. If the garment was smaller than this, his rites are not disqualified, in accordance with the opinion of Rabbi Yoḥanan and Rava (Rambam *Sefer Avoda*, *Hilkhot Kelei HaMikdash* 10:8).

NOTES

If the fabric is three fingerbreadths by three fingerbreadths it interposes – שָׁלֹשׁ עַל שָׁלֹשׁ חוֹצְצוֹת: This cannot be referring to an interposition between the priest's vestments and his body, since in such a case Rava says that even one thread constitutes an interposition. It also cannot be referring to interposition between the priest's hand and the sacred vessel, since there is no reason that the measure in such a case should be any different from that of an interposition between the priest's body and vestments. Rather, it means that if the cloth is three fingerbreadths by three fingerbreadths, it constitutes an extra garment, which disqualifies the service even if it does not actually interpose between the priest and his vestments or vessels (Rashi). According to the Sages, three fingerbreadths by three fingerbreadths is the smallest measure for a piece of cloth to be considered a garment for purposes of ritual impurity as well.

HALAKHA

A small sash is different – שָׁאנֵי צִילְצוּל קָטָן: If a priest wore a small sash, his rites are disqualified, even if it is smaller than three fingerbreadths by three fingerbreadths, since it is considered an independent garment. This is in accordance with the opinion of Rabbi Yehuda, son of Rabbi Ḥiyya, and the conclusion of the Gemara that this is the opinion of Rava as well (Rambam *Sefer Avoda, Hilkhot Kelei HaMikdash* 10:8).

If a gust of wind entered his vestment, etc. – נִכְנְסָה לוֹ רוּחַ בְּבִגְדוֹ וכו׳: A priest must take care not to allow dirt or lice, even live lice, to interpose between his skin and vestments. He should not allow a gust of wind to enter his vestment during the service, separating the vestment from him; he should not touch his chest under his clothes; he should not allow his hair to extend into his vestment; and there should be no thread dangling from the vestment. This is because the *halakha* in all these cases is left unresolved in the Gemara. If one of these circumstances occurred, the rites he performed are valid after the fact. One should not rule stringently and deem the offering disqualified due to uncertainty, because the replacement offering one would bring in such a case is possibly unnecessary, and by bringing it one would violate the prohibition against bringing non-consecrated animals into the Temple courtyard (Rambam *Sefer Avoda, Hilkhot Kelei HaMikdash* 10:7 and *Kesef Mishne* there).

וְתֵיפוֹק לֵיהּ מִשּׁוּם חֲצִיצָה! בִּשְׂמֹאל. אִי נָמֵי, שֶׁלֹּא בִּמְקוֹם עֲבוֹדָה.

The Gemara challenges: And let Rabbi Yoḥanan **derive** that a sash is prohibited **because** it acts as **an interposition** between the priest's hand and the sacred vessel he grips, which disqualifies the service. The Gemara rejects this: Rabbi Yoḥanan is referring to a case where the wound is **on** the priest's **left** hand. Since the entire service is performed exclusively with his right hand, a bandage on his left hand is not an interposition. **Alternatively,** the wound is on the priest's right hand, but **not in a place** used for the **service,** such that the bandage does not interpose between his hand and the sacred vessel.

וּפְלִיגָא דְּרָבָא, דְּאָמַר רָבָא אָמַר רַב חִסְדָּא: בִּמְקוֹם בְּגָדִים – אֲפִילּוּ נִימָא אַחַת חוֹצֶצֶת, שֶׁלֹּא בִּמְקוֹם בְּגָדִים – שָׁלֹשׁ עַל שָׁלֹשׁ חוֹצְצוֹת, פָּחוֹת מִכָּאן אֵינָן חוֹצְצוֹת.

And Rabbi Yoḥanan **disagrees** with the opinion **of Rava, as Rava says** that **Rav Ḥisda says: In a place** on the priest's body where the **vestments** are worn, **even one** extra **thread interposes** and is prohibited, whereas **in a place** on his body where the **vestments** are **not** worn, if the fabric is **three** fingerbreadths **by three** fingerbreadths **it interposes,**[N] but if it is **less than that it does not interpose.**

אַדְּרַבִּי יוֹחָנָן וַדַּאי פְּלִיגָא, אַדְּרַבִּי יְהוּדָה בְּרֵיהּ דְּרַבִּי חִיָּיא מִי לֵימָא דִּפְלִיגָא?

The Gemara notes: Rava **certainly disagrees with** the opinion **of Rabbi Yoḥanan,** who holds that fabric of any size that is in a place on his body where the vestments are not worn is not considered an interposition. **Shall we say** that **he** also **disagrees with the opinion of Rabbi Yehuda, son of Rabbi Ḥiyya,** who deems any sash an interposition, even one smaller than three by three fingerbreadths?

שָׁאנֵי צִילְצוּל קָטָן דַּחֲשִׁיב.

The Gemara responds: Even according to Rava, **a small sash is different,**[H] **as it is significant,** and it is therefore considered a garment even if it is less than three by three fingerbreadths.

לִישָּׁנָא אַחֲרִינָא אָמְרִי לַהּ, אָמַר רַבִּי יְהוּדָה בְּרֵיהּ דְּרַבִּי חִיָּיא: לֹא שָׁנוּ אֶלָּא גֶּמִי, אֲבָל צִילְצוּל קָטָן – חוֹצֵץ. וְרַבִּי יוֹחָנָן אָמַר: לֹא אָמְרוּ חֲצִיצָה בְּפָחוֹת מִשָּׁלֹשׁ עַל שָׁלֹשׁ אֶלָּא בִּמְקוֹם בְּגָדִים, אֲבָל שֶׁלֹּא בִּמְקוֹם בְּגָדִים – שָׁלֹשׁ עַל שָׁלֹשׁ חוֹצְצוֹת, פָּחוֹת מִיכָּן – אֵינָהּ חוֹצֶצֶת. וְהַיְינוּ דְּרָבָא אָמַר רַב חִסְדָּא.

Some say that there is **another version** of the dispute: **Rabbi Yehuda, son of Rabbi Ḥiyya, says** that **they taught only** that **a reed** is permitted, **but a small sash interposes. And Rabbi Yoḥanan says: They said** that an item acts as **an interposition when** it is **less than three by three** fingerbreadths **only in a place** on the priest's body where the **vestments** are worn. **But in a place** on his body where the **vestments** are **not** worn, the following distinction applies: If the fabric is **three** fingerbreadths **by three** fingerbreadths, **it interposes,** but if it is **less than this, it does not interpose. And this is** the same ruling **that Rava** says that **Rav Ḥisda says.**

לֵימָא פְּלִיגָא אַדְּרַבִּי יְהוּדָה בְּרֵיהּ דְּרַבִּי חִיָּיא? שָׁאנֵי צִילְצוּל קָטָן דַּחֲשִׁיב.

The Gemara suggests: **Let us say** that Rava **disagrees with** the opinion **of Rabbi Yehuda, son of Rabbi Ḥiyya,** who deems any sash an interposition, even one smaller than three fingerbreadths by three fingerbreadths. The Gemara rejects this: This is not necessarily so, as **a small sash is different, since it is significant.** It is therefore like a vestment, even if it is smaller than three fingerbreadths by three fingerbreadths.

וּלְרַבִּי יוֹחָנָן מַאי אִירְיָא גֶּמִי? לַשְׁמוֹעִינַן צִילְצוּל קָטָן! מִילְּתָא אַגַּב אוֹרְחֵיהּ קָא מַשְׁמַע לַן, דְּגֶמִי מַסֵּי.

The Gemara raises a question: **And according to** the opinion of **Rabbi Yoḥanan, why** does the mishna teach the *halakha* **specifically** with regard to **a reed? Let** the mishna **teach us** that a priest may wrap his wounded finger with **a small sash,** since this would teach the greater novelty that although a sash is significant, it does not constitute an interposition. The Gemara responds: **It teaches us a matter in passing, that a reed heals.**

בְּעֵי רָבָא: נִכְנְסָה לוֹ רוּחַ בְּבִגְדוֹ, מַהוּ? ״עַל בְּשָׂרוֹ״ בָּעֵינַן – וְהָא לֵיכָּא, אוֹ דִּלְמָא דֶּרֶךְ לְבִישָׁה בְּכָךְ?

§ **Rava raises a dilemma:** If a gust of **wind entered** the priest's **vestment,**[H] raising it slightly off his body, **what is the** *halakha*? Do **we require** that the vestment be: **"Upon his body"** (Leviticus 6:3), in a literal sense, **and this is not** the case when the wind raises his vestment? **Or perhaps** the service is valid because **this** is the normal **manner of wearing** clothes.

כִּינָּה מַהוּ שֶׁתָּחוֹץ?

Furthermore, **what is the** *halakha* with regard to **a louse** found under the priest's vestments? **Does it interpose** between the vestments and his body, disqualifying the service?

מֵתָה לָא תִּבָּעֵי לָךְ, דְּוַדַּאי חָיְיצָא. חַיָּה מַאי? מִי אָמְרִינַן: כֵּיוָן דְּאָתְיָא וְאָזְלָא – רְבִיתָא הִיא וְלָא חָיְיצָא, אוֹ דִּלְמָא כֵּיוָן דְּקָפֵיד עֲלָהּ – חָיְיצָא.

The Gemara clarifies: **Do not raise a dilemma** with regard to **a dead** louse, **as it certainly interposes,** like any other item. Rather, **what is** the *halakha* with regard to **a live** louse? **Do we say that since it comes and goes,** i.e., it moves around on his body, **it is like a growth and does not interpose? Or perhaps, since he objects to its** presence,[N] **it interposes?**

עָפָר מַהוּ שֶׁיָּחוֹץ? עָפָר וַדַּאי חָיֵיץ! אֶלָּא, אֲבַק עָפָר מַהוּ?

Furthermore, **what is** the *halakha* with regard to **dirt** found under the priest's vestments? **Does it interpose?** The Gemara objects: But **dirt certainly interposes.** The Gemara clarifies: **Rather,** the question is: **What is** the *halakha* with regard to **dust of dirt,**[N] i.e., a minute amount of dust?

בֵּית הַשֶּׁחִי מַהוּ שֶׁיָּחוֹץ? "עַל בְּשָׂרוֹ" בָּעֵינַן – וְהָא לֵיכָּא, אוֹ דִּלְמָא דֶּרֶךְ לְבִישָׁה בְּכָךְ?

Furthermore, **what is** the *halakha* with regard to the gap between the underarm of the vestment and the priest's **armpit?**[N] **Does it interpose?** Do we **require** that the vestment is **"upon his body"** in a literal sense, **and this is not** the case? **Or perhaps** the service is valid since **this** is the normal **manner of wearing** clothes.

הִכְנִיס יָדוֹ לְתוֹךְ חֵיקוֹ, מַהוּ? גּוּפוֹ מִי חָיֵיץ אוֹ לָא?

Furthermore, if the priest **inserted his hand into** his vestments and touched **his chest, what is** the *halakha*? **Does his body interpose**[N] **or not?**

נִימָא מַהוּ שֶׁתָּחוֹץ? נִימָא וַדַּאי חָיְיצָא! אֶלָּא נִימָא מְדוּלְדֶּלֶת, מַהוּ?

Furthermore, **what is** the *halakha* with regard to **a thread** [*nima*]?[L] **Does it interpose?** The Gemara interjects: But **a thread certainly interposes. Rather,** the question is: **What is** the *halakha* with regard to **a thread** that **hangs** off the vestment itself and will soon fall off? Is such a thread considered as though it has already detached from the vestment, in which case it interposes?

בָּעֵי מָר בַּר רַב אַשִׁי: יָצָא שְׂעָרוֹ בְּבִגְדוֹ, מַהוּ? שְׂעָרוֹ כְּגוּפוֹ דָּמֵי, אוֹ לָאו כְּגוּפוֹ דָּמֵי?

Mar bar Rav Ashi raises a dilemma: If **his hair emerged** from his head and extended **into his vestment** and separated it from his skin, **what is** the *halakha*? **Is his hair considered like his body,** in which case it does not interpose, **or is it not considered like his body?**

בָּעֵי רַבִּי זֵירָא: תְּפִילִּין מַהוּ שֶׁיָּחוֹצוּ? אַלִּיבָּא דְּמַאן דְּאָמַר: לַיְלָה לָאו זְמַן תְּפִילִּין הוּא – לָא תִּבָּעֵי לָךְ, כֵּיוָן דְּלַיְלָה חָיְיצִי – יוֹם נַמִי חָיְיצִי. כִּי תִּיבָּעֵי לָךְ – לְמַאן דְּאָמַר: לַיְלָה זְמַן תְּפִילִּין, מַאי? מִצְוָה דְּגוּפֵיהּ חָיֵיץ, אוֹ לָא חָיֵיץ?

Rabbi Zeira raises a dilemma: What is the *halakha* with regard to **phylacteries?**[N] **Do they interpose?** The Gemara clarifies: **According** to the opinion **of one who says** that **night is not** an appropriate **time** to don **phylacteries, do not raise the dilemma. Since they interpose** at **night, they also interpose** during the **day.** Rather, **when you raise the dilemma,** do so **according to the one who says** that **night is** an appropriate **time** to don **phylacteries.** According to this opinion, **what is** the *halakha*? **Does a mitzva** that one fulfills **with his body**[N] **interpose, or does it not interpose?**

אִיגַּלְגַּל מִילְּתָא וּמְטָא לְקַמֵּיהּ דְּרַבִּי אַמִּי. אֲמַר לֵיהּ: תַּלְמוּד עָרוּךְ הוּא בְּיָדֵינוּ: תְּפִילִּין חוֹצְצוֹת.

This **matter circulated** and eventually **came before Rabbi Ami,** who **said to him: It is a settled tradition in our possession** that **phylacteries interpose.**

מֵיתִיבֵי: כֹּהֲנִים בַּעֲבוֹדָתָן, וּלְוִיִּם בְּדוּכָנָן, וְיִשְׂרָאֵל בְּמַעֲמָדָן – פְּטוּרִין מִן הַתְּפִלָּה וּמִן הַתְּפִילִּין; מַאי לָאו אִם הִנִּיחָן – אֵינָן חוֹצְצוֹת? לָא, אִם הִנִּיחָן חוֹצְצוֹת.

The Gemara **raises an objection** from a *baraita*: **Priests in their service; and Levites on their platform** in the Temple, where they recite songs; **and Israelites at their watches,**[N] where they observe the sacrifice of the daily offering, **are** all **exempt from prayer**[H] **and from** donning **phylacteries. What, is it not** that the term: Exempt, indicates that **if they donned** phylacteries anyway, **they do not interpose?** Apparently, priests may wear phylacteries while performing the Temple service. The Gemara responds: **No, if they donned** phylacteries, **they interpose.**

NOTES

Since he objects to its presence – דְּקָפֵיד עֲלָהּ: Any item whose presence on a person's body is typically objectionable constitutes an interposition. Parts of one's body do not interpose, even if they are considered objectionable, e.g., an extra finger. Although lice are not, strictly speaking, part of one's body, they were considered an inseparable aspect of a person's existence.

Dust of dirt – אֲבַק עָפָר: This is referring to tiny amounts of dirt that are not visible, and the presence of which is not objectionable, but are still not part of one's body.

Armpit – בֵּית הַשֶּׁחִי: This question is distinct from the previous question with regard to a wind that created a gap between the vestment and the priest's body, since the gap under the armpit is always present.

Does his body interpose – גּוּפוֹ מִי חָיֵיץ: Although one's body generally cannot be considered an interposition, this case may be an exception, since one does not typically insert his hand under his clothing.

What is the *halakha* with regard to phylacteries – תְּפִילִּין מַהוּ: Rashi explains that the issue here is not literally interposition but the prohibition against wearing an extra vestment. According to *Tosafot*, the Gemara is suggesting that phylacteries may constitute an interposition between the priest's body and his vestments.

Mitzva that one fulfills with his body – מִצְוָה דְּגוּפֵיהּ: Since this mitzva is performed with the body, it is conceivable that the item used to perform the mitzva is considered part of the body itself and not an interposition or extra vestment.

Israelites at their watches – יִשְׂרָאֵל בְּמַעֲמָדָן: As explained in tractate *Ta'anit* (27a), Israelites had representatives who would be present in Jerusalem to witness the sacrifice of the communal offerings on behalf of the entire Jewish people. For this purpose, the population of Israelites was divided into twenty-four watches, corresponding to the twenty-four watches of the priests. Every week a new watch would arrive in Jerusalem, stand in the Temple at the time communal offerings were sacrificed, pray, and read from the Torah.

LANGUAGE

Thread [*nima*] – נִימָא: From the Greek νῆμα, *nēma*, meaning thread.

HALAKHA

Priests in their service…are exempt from prayer – כֹּהֲנִים בַּעֲבוֹדָתָן...פְּטוּרִין מִן הַתְּפִלָּה: Priests performing the service in the Temple, Levites singing on their platform, and Israelites standing at their watch in the Temple are all exempt from prayer and from donning phylacteries (Rambam *Sefer Ahava*, *Hilkhot Tefillin UMezuza VeSefer Torah* 4:13).

HALAKHA

This is of the hand, that is of the head – **הָא דְּיָד הָא דְּרֹאשׁ**: A priest may not wear the phylacteries of the hand while performing the service in the Temple, since they interpose between his skin and vestments. Phylacteries of the head do not interpose, and the priest may wear them while performing the service in the Temple even though he is exempt (Rambam *Sefer Avoda*, *Hilkhot Kelei HaMikdash* 10:6).

BACKGROUND

Between the frontplate and the mitre – **בֵּין צִיץ לַמִּצְנֶפֶת**: Between the High Priest's frontplate and mitre was a vacant spot just above the hairline on his forehead, where he would don his phylacteries.

אִי הָכִי, פְּטוּרִים? אֲסוּרִים מִיבָּעֵי לֵיהּ! כֵּיוָן דְּאִיכָּא לְוִיִּם וְיִשְׂרָאֵל דְּלָא מָתְנוּ לֵיהּ אָסוּר, מִשּׁוּם הָכִי תָּנָא פְּטוּרִין.

The Gemara asks: **If so,** why does the *baraita* use the word: **Exempt? It should have** used the word: **Prohibited,** since wearing phylacteries disqualifies the priests' service. The Gemara responds: **Since there are** also **Levites and Israelites** mentioned in the *baraita*, **concerning whom** the *baraita* could **not teach** the word: **Prohibited,** as it is permitted for them to don phylacteries, **due to that** reason the *baraita* **taught** the word: **Exempt,** which is applicable to all.

וְהָתַנְיָא: אִם הִנִּיחָן אֵינָן חוֹצְצוֹת! לָא קַשְׁיָא, הָא – דְּיָד, הָא – דְּרֹאשׁ.

The Gemara challenges: **But isn't it taught** in a *baraita*: **If** a priest **donned** phylacteries **they do not interpose?** The Gemara responds: That is **not difficult. This** *baraita*, which teaches that phylacteries interpose is referring to the phylacteries **of the hand,** whereas **that** *baraita*, which teaches that they do not is referring to the phylacteries **of the head.**[H]

מַאי שְׁנָא דְּיָד? דִּכְתִיב: "יִלְבַּשׁ עַל בְּשָׂרוֹ", שֶׁלֹּא יְהֵא דָּבָר חוֹצֵץ בֵּינוֹ לִבְשָׂרוֹ – דְּרֹאשׁ נָמֵי כְּתִיב: "וְשַׂמְתָּ הַמִּצְנֶפֶת עַל רֹאשׁוֹ"!

The Gemara asks: **What is different** about the phylacteries **of the hand** that only they interpose? The verse indicates the difference, **as it is written** with regard to the vestments covering the body: **"Shall he put upon his body"** (Leviticus 6:3), indicating **that nothing may interpose between** the vestment **and his body.** The Gemara challenges: But there is **also** a verse **written with regard to the head: "And you shall set the mitre upon his head"** (Exodus 29:6), indicating that there must be no interposition between the mitre and the head. If so, the phylacteries of the head should be considered an interposition as well.

תָּנָא: שְׂעָרוֹ הָיָה נִרְאֶה בֵּין צִיץ לַמִּצְנֶפֶת,

The Gemara responds: The Sages **taught: The hair of** the High Priest **was visible between the frontplate and the mitre.**[B] The frontplate was set on the forehead, below the hairline, while the mitre was set above it;

שֶׁשָּׁם מַנִּיחִין תְּפִילִּין.

it was **there that** the High Priests would **don** their **phylacteries.**[N] Consequently, the phylacteries of the head did not interpose between the mitre and the priest's head.

"מְחוּסַּר כִּיפּוּרִים". מְנָלַן? אָמַר רַב הוּנָא, אָמַר קְרָא: "וְכִפֶּר עָלֶיהָ הַכֹּהֵן וְטָהֵרָה" – טְהֵרָה מִכְּלָל שֶׁהִיא טְמֵאָה.

§ The mishna teaches that rites performed by **one who has not yet** brought **an atonement** offering to complete the purification process are disqualified. The Gemara asks: **From where do we** derive this? **Rav Huna says: The verse states** with regard to the offering brought by a woman who has given birth: **"And the priest shall make atonement for her, and she shall be pure"** (Leviticus 12:8). Since the verse states: "And **she shall be pure,**" one learns **by inference that she is ritually impure** to some extent until she brings her offering, even though she has already immersed. Anyone who has not yet brought an atonement offering is likewise impure to some extent, and rites performed by one who is impure are disqualified (see 17a).

NOTES

It was there that they would don phylacteries – **שֶׁשָּׁם מַנִּיחִין תְּפִילִּין**: Therefore, the phylacteries do not interpose between the vestments and the priest's skin, nor do they constitute an extra vestment, since phylacteries are not considered garments (Rashi). It is possible that this is in accordance with Rabbi Zeira's opinion that a mitzva performed with the body is considered part of the body. According to the Rashba, phylacteries are not considered an extra vestment because the prohibition against donning extra vestments applies only in places on the body where the priest's vestments are normally worn. Therefore the prohibition does not apply to phylacteries, which are worn between the place of the frontplate and the mitre.

וְ״שֶׁלֹּא רְחוּץ יָדַיִם וְרַגְלַיִם״. אָתְיָא ״חוּקָּה״ ״חוּקָּה״ מִמְּחוּסַּר בְּגָדִים.

§ The mishna teaches that rites performed by **one whose hands and feet are not washed** are disqualified. The Gemara explains: This *halakha* **is derived** by verbal analogy between **"statute"** mentioned in this context and **"statute" from** the case of **one lacking** the requisite **vestments,**[N] whose rites are disqualified (see 17b).

תָּנוּ רַבָּנַן: כֹּהֵן גָּדוֹל שֶׁלֹּא טָבַל וְשֶׁלֹּא קִידֵּשׁ בֵּין בֶּגֶד לְבֶגֶד וּבֵין עֲבוֹדָה לַעֲבוֹדָה, וְעָבַד – עֲבוֹדָתוֹ כְּשֵׁירָה. וְאֶחָד כֹּהֵן גָּדוֹל וְאֶחָד כֹּהֵן הֶדְיוֹט שֶׁלֹּא קִידֵּשׁ יָדָיו וְרַגְלָיו שַׁחֲרִית וְעָבַד – עֲבוֹדָתוֹ פְּסוּלָה.

The Sages taught: With regard to **a High Priest who did not immerse**[H] **or did not sanctify** his hands and feet during the Yom Kippur service **between** donning the golden **garments and** the white linen **garments, or between** performance of one **rite and** another **rite, and he performed** the **service** in this state, **his service is valid** after the fact. **But** with regard to **either a High Priest or an ordinary priest who did not sanctify his hands and feet** at all in the **morning**[H] **and performed the service, his service is disqualified.**

אֲמַר לֵיהּ רַב אַסִי לְרַבִּי יוֹחָנָן: מִכְּדִי חָמֵשׁ טְבִילוֹת וַעֲשָׂרָה קִדּוּשִׁין דְּאוֹרַיְיתָא, וְ״חוּקָּה״ כְּתִיב בְּהוּ, לִיעַכְּבוּ!

Rav Asi said to Rabbi Yoḥanan: Now, there are **five immersions and ten sanctifications** of the hands and feet during the Yom Kippur service **by Torah law, and** the word: **"Statute"** (Leviticus 16:34), **is written with regard to them.** Accordingly, **they should be indispensable** and should disqualify the service if not performed.

אֲמַר לֵיהּ, אָמַר קְרָא: ״וּלְבֵשָׁם״ – לְבִישָׁה מְעַכֶּבֶת, וְאֵין דָּבָר אַחֵר מְעַכֵּב.

Rabbi Yoḥanan **said to him:** After stipulating that the High Priest must wear the requisite vestments before performing the Yom Kippur service, **the verse states: "And put them on"** (Leviticus 16:4). This superfluous term serves to indicate that **wearing** the requisite vestments **is indispensable, but nothing else is indispensable.**

צָהֲבוּ פָּנָיו. אֲמַר לֵיהּ: וי״ו אַאוּפְתָּא כְּתַבִי לָךְ, אִי הָכִי דְּצַפְרָא נַמִי!

Rav Asi's **face lit up** with joy after hearing this response. Rabbi Yoḥanan **said to him: I have** merely **written** the letter ***vav* on a piece of wood**[N] **for you,** i.e., I have not given you a satisfactory answer. As, **if that is so,** that only the wearing of the vestments is indispensable, then failure to sanctify the hands and feet **in the morning** should **also** not disqualify the service, yet according to the *baraita* it disqualifies the service.

אָמַר חִזְקִיָּה, אָמַר קְרָא: ״וְהָיְתָה לָהֶם חָק עוֹלָם לוֹ וּלְזַרְעוֹ לְדֹרֹתָם״, דָּבָר הַמְעַכֵּב בְּזַרְעוֹ – מְעַכֵּב בּוֹ, דָּבָר שֶׁאֵינוֹ מְעַכֵּב בְּזַרְעוֹ – אֵין מְעַכֵּב בּוֹ.

Ḥizkiyya says there is an alternative answer: **The verse states** with regard to sanctification of the hands and feet: **"And it shall be a statute forever to them, even to him and to his seed throughout their generations"** (Exodus 30:21). From the comparison of Aaron to his children one may derive that **anything that is indispensable with regard to his seed,** the priests, **is indispensable with regard to him,** the High Priest during the Yom Kippur service, which only he may perform. But **anything that is not indispensable with regard to his seed is not indispensable with regard to him.** Therefore, the sanctification of the hands and feet between each rite, which is unnecessary for priests during the daily service, does not disqualify the High Priest's Yom Kippur service if not done.

רַבִּי יוֹנָתָן אָמַר, מֵהָכָא: ״וְרָחֲצוּ מִמֶּנּוּ מֹשֶׁה וְאַהֲרֹן וּבָנָיו״, דָּבָר הַמְעַכֵּב בְּבָנָיו – מְעַכֵּב בּוֹ, דָּבָר שֶׁאֵינוֹ מְעַכֵּב בְּבָנָיו – אֵין מְעַכֵּב בּוֹ.

Rabbi Yonatan says: The principle is derived **from here:** The verse states with regard to the Basin in the Temple: **"That Moses and Aaron and his sons might wash their hands and their feet from it"** (Exodus 40:31). One may derive from the verse that **anything that is indispensable with regard to his sons is indispensable with regard to him. But anything that is not indispensable with regard to his sons is not indispensable with regard to him.**

NOTES

Statute and statute from the case of one lacking vestments – חוּקָּה חוּקָּה מִמְּחוּסַּר בְּגָדִים: With regard to the priestly vestments, the verse states: "And they shall have the priesthood by a perpetual statute" (Exodus 29:9). With regard to the sanctification of the hands and feet, it is written: "And it shall be a statute forever to them" (Exodus 30:21).

***Vav* on a piece of wood – וי״ו אַאוּפְתָּא:** Rashi and the *Arukh* offer two interpretations of this idiom. First, the letter *vav* is not discernable if written on a piece of wood covered with grooves; likewise, Rabbi Yoḥanan's answer is ineffective. Second, the grooves on a piece of wood look like a *vav*, but are not really letters at all; so too, the answer provided is not an answer at all. The latter interpretation is also suggested by Rabbeinu Gershom Meor HaGola.

HALAKHA

High Priest who did not immerse, etc. – כֹּהֵן גָּדוֹל שֶׁלֹּא טָבַל וכו׳: If the High Priest did not immerse or sanctify his hands and feet between wearing each set of vestments during the Yom Kippur service, his service is valid (Rambam *Sefer Avoda, Hilkhot Biat HaMikdash* 5:7 and *Hilkhot Avodat Yom HaKippurim* 2:3).

Who did not sanctify his hands and feet in the morning – שֶׁלֹּא קִידֵּשׁ יָדָיו וְרַגְלָיו שַׁחֲרִית: If a priest performed the service without having sanctified his hands and feet that morning, he is liable to receive the punishment of death at the hand of Heaven, as it is stated: "They shall wash with water, that they not die" (Exodus 30:20). His service is disqualified, whether he is an ordinary priest or the High Priest (Rambam *Sefer Avoda, Hilkhot Biat HaMikdash* 5:1).

BACKGROUND

Basin – כִּיּוֹר: The Basin in the Temple was composed of a body and a base, both of which were made of copper (Exodus 30:18). In the Second Temple, the High Priest ben Katin installed twelve spigots on the Basin, so twelve priests would be able to sanctify their hands and feet simultaneously.

Basin in the Second Temple and the mechanism for raising and lowering it

NOTES

He lays both his hands, etc. – מַנִּיחַ שְׁתֵּי יָדָיו וכו׳: This would fulfill the literal meaning of the verse, which mentions the washing of hands and feet as one act of sanctification (Rashi).

Standing with support from the side – עֲמִידָה מִן הַצַּד: This term denotes standing in such a way that requires aid to maintain balance, as Rabbi Yosei, son of Rabbi Yehuda, describes (Rashi). This principle is significant in other contexts in which one is required to stand, e.g., bearing witness or reading from the Torah (*Tosafot*). *Tosefot Rabbeinu Peretz* cites Rabbeinu Yeḥiel of Paris, who holds that if one is theoretically able to stand unassisted, assistance in practice does not disqualify the service (*Shita Mekubbetzet*).

רַבִּי יוֹנָתָן מַאי טַעְמָא לָא אָמַר מִדְּחִזְקִיָּה? אָמַר לָךְ: הַהוּא לְדוֹרוֹת הוּא דִּכְתִיב.

The Gemara asks: **What is the reason** that **Rabbi Yonatan did not say** to derive this **from** the verse cited **by Ḥizkiyya?** The Gemara responds: Rabbi Yonatan could have **said to you: That** verse cited by Ḥizkiyya **is written** to teach that the *halakha* applies even **for** future **generations,** not to draw a parallel between the High Priest and ordinary priests.

וְאִידָךְ, מַאי טַעְמָא לָא אָמַר מֵהַאי? מִיבָּעֵי לֵיהּ לְכִדְרַבִּי יוֹסֵי בְּרַבִּי חֲנִינָא. דְּאָמַר רַבִּי יוֹסֵי בְּרַבִּי חֲנִינָא: כָּל כִּיּוֹר שֶׁאֵין בּוֹ כְּדֵי לְקַדֵּשׁ אַרְבָּעָה כֹּהֲנִים מִמֶּנּוּ – אֵין מְקַדְּשִׁין בּוֹ, שֶׁנֶּאֱמַר: ״וְרָחֲצוּ מִמֶּנּוּ מֹשֶׁה וְאַהֲרֹן וּבָנָיו״.

The Gemara asks: **And the other** Sage, Ḥizkiyya, **what is the reason** that **he did not say** to derive the *halakha* **from that** verse cited by Rabbi Yonatan? The Gemara responds: **He requires** that verse **for** the *halakha* taught **by Rabbi Yosei, son of Rabbi Ḥanina. As Rabbi Yosei, son of Rabbi Ḥanina, says:** With regard to **any** circumstance in **which** the **Basin**[B] **does not contain**[H] **enough** water **for four priests to sanctify** their hands and feet **from it,** the priests **may not sanctify** their hands and feet **with it, as it is stated: "That Moses and Aaron and his sons might wash** their hands and their feet **from it."** Moses, Aaron, and Aaron's two sons total four.

תָּנוּ רַבָּנַן: כֵּיצַד מִצְוַת קִידּוּשׁ? מַנִּיחַ יָדוֹ הַיְּמָנִית עַל גַּבֵּי רַגְלוֹ הַיְּמָנִית, וְיָדוֹ הַשְּׂמָאלִית עַל גַּבֵּי רַגְלוֹ הַשְּׂמָאלִית, וּמְקַדֵּשׁ. רַבִּי יוֹסֵי בְּרַבִּי יְהוּדָה אוֹמֵר: מַנִּיחַ שְׁתֵּי יָדָיו זוֹ עַל גַּב זוֹ, וְעַל גַּבֵּי שְׁתֵּי רַגְלָיו זוֹ עַל גַּבֵּי זוֹ, וּמְקַדֵּשׁ. אָמְרוּ לוֹ: הִפְלַגְתָּה, אִי אֶפְשָׁר לַעֲשׂוֹת כֵּן.

§ **The Sages taught: How is the mitzva of sanctification**[H] of the hands and feet performed? The priest **lays his right hand on top of his right foot, and his left hand on top of his left foot, and sanctifies** them with the water flowing from the Basin. **Rabbi Yosei, son of Rabbi Yehuda, says: He lays both his hands**[N] **one on top of the other, and** lays them together **on top of both his feet,** themselves laid **one on top of the other, and sanctifies** them. **They said to him: You have gone too far; it is impossible to do so.**

שַׁפִּיר קָאָמְרִי לֵיהּ! אָמַר רַב יוֹסֵף: וַחֲבֵירוֹ מְסַיְּיעוֹ.

The Gemara notes: **They speak well to him;** it seems impossible to assume such a position without losing one's balance. **Rav Yosef says:** Rabbi Yosei, son of Rabbi Yehuda, meant that the priest would assume the position **while another** priest would **help him** maintain his balance.

מַאי בֵּינַיְיהוּ? אָמַר אַבַּיֵי: עֲמִידָה מִן הַצַּד אִיכָּא בֵּינַיְיהוּ.

The Gemara asks: **What** is the difference **between** the reasoning of the Sages and that of Rabbi Yosei, son of Rabbi Yehuda? **Abaye says:** The difference **between them is** their opinion with regard to **standing** with support **from the side.**[N] According to the Sages, this is not considered standing and the priest may not sanctify his hands and feet while in such a position.

אֲמַר לֵיהּ רַב סַמָּא בְּרֵיהּ דְּרַב אַשִׁי לְרָבִינָא: וְלֵיתֵיב מֵיתָב וּלְקַדֵּשׁ! אָמַר קְרָא: ״לְשָׁרֵת״, וְשֵׁירוּת מְעוּמָּד הוּא.

Rav Samma, son of Rav Ashi, said to Ravina: And let him sit and sanctify his hands and feet while seated, and in this manner he may sanctify them all at once. Ravina said to him: **The verse states:** "When they go into the Tent of Meeting, they shall wash with water, that they not die; or when they come near to the altar **to minister"** (Exodus 30:20), **and ministration is** performed while **standing,**[H] as the verse states: "To stand to minister" (Deuteronomy 18:5). Therefore, sanctification must also be performed while standing.

HALAKHA

Any circumstance in which the Basin does not contain, etc. – כָּל כִּיּוֹר שֶׁאֵין בּוֹ וכו׳: The Basin in the Temple must contain at least enough water for four priests to sanctify their hands and feet, as the verse mentions Aaron together with Eleazar, Itamar, and Pinehas (Rambam *Sefer Avoda*, *Hilkhot Biat HaMikdash* 5:13 and Mahari Kurkus there).

How is the mitzva of sanctification – כֵּיצַד מִצְוַת קִידּוּשׁ: In performing the mitzva of sanctification of the hands and feet, the priest must lay his right hand on top of his right foot and his left hand on top of his left foot, and sanctify them from the water of the Basin, in accordance with the opinion of the first *tanna* in the *baraita* (Rambam *Sefer Avoda*, *Hilkhot Biat HaMikdash* 5:16).

Ministration is performed while standing – שֵׁירוּת מְעוּמָּד הוּא: One may not sanctify his hands and feet while seated, since it is considered a part of the service, and the entire service must be performed standing (Rambam *Sefer Avoda*, *Hilkhot Biat HaMikdash* 5:16).

תָּנוּ רַבָּנַן: קִידֵּשׁ יָדָיו וְרַגְלָיו בַּיּוֹם – אֵין צָרִיךְ לְקַדֵּשׁ בַּלַּיְלָה, בַּלַּיְלָה – צָרִיךְ לְקַדֵּשׁ בַּיּוֹם, דִּבְרֵי רַבִּי. שֶׁהָיָה רַבִּי אוֹמֵר: לִינָה מוֹעֶלֶת בְּקִידּוּשׁ יָדַיִם וְרַגְלַיִם. רַבִּי אֶלְעָזָר בְּרַבִּי שִׁמְעוֹן אוֹמֵר: אֵין לִינָה מוֹעֶלֶת בְּקִידּוּשׁ יָדַיִם וְרַגְלַיִם.

§ **The Sages taught:** If a priest **sanctified his hands and feet during the day,**[H] **he does not need to sanctify** them that **night,**[N] but if he sanctified them **at night, he must sanctify** them **during the** following **day.** This is **the statement of Rabbi** Yehuda HaNasi, as **Rabbi** Yehuda HaNasi **would say:** The disqualification of being **left overnight is determinative**[N] **with regard to sanctification**[H] **of the hands and feet,** like any sacrificial item that is sanctified. Accordingly, once night has passed, the priest must sanctify them again. **Rabbi Elazar, son of Rabbi Shimon, says:** The disqualification of being **left overnight is not determinative with regard to sanctification of the hands and feet.** Therefore, as long as the priest continues to serve, he need not sanctify them again.

תַּנְיָא אִידָּךְ: הָיָה עוֹמֵד וּמַקְרִיב עַל גַּבֵּי מִזְבֵּחַ כׇּל הַלַּיְלָה, לָאוֹרָה טָעוּן קִידּוּשׁ יָדַיִם וְרַגְלַיִם, דִּבְרֵי רַבִּי. רַבִּי אֶלְעָזָר בְּרַבִּי שִׁמְעוֹן אוֹמֵר: כֵּיוָן שֶׁקִּידֵּשׁ יָדָיו וְרַגְלָיו מִתְּחִילַּת עֲבוֹדָה, אֲפִילּוּ מִיכָּן וְעַד עֲשָׂרָה יָמִים – אֵינוֹ צָרִיךְ לְקַדֵּשׁ.

It is taught in **another** *baraita*: If the priest **was standing and sacrificing** offerings **on top of the altar all night,**[H] **in the morning he requires sanctification of** the **hands and feet** again. This is **the statement of Rabbi** Yehuda HaNasi. **Rabbi Elazar, son of Rabbi Shimon, says: Once he sanctified his hands and feet at the beginning of** the **service, even** if he continues to perform rites **for the next ten days, he does not need to sanctify** them again.

וּצְרִיכָא, דְּאִי אַשְׁמְעִינַן קַמַּיְיתָא – בְּהַהִיא קָאָמַר רַבִּי, דִּפְסַק לֵיהּ מֵעֲבוֹדָה לַעֲבוֹדָה, אֲבָל בְּהָא דְּלָא פְּסַק לֵיהּ – אֵימָא מוֹדֵי לֵיהּ רַבִּי לְרַבִּי אֶלְעָזָר בְּרַבִּי שִׁמְעוֹן; וְאִי אַשְׁמְעִינַן בְּהָא – בְּהָא קָאָמַר רַבִּי אֶלְעָזָר בְּרַבִּי שִׁמְעוֹן, אֲבָל בְּהָא – אֵימָא מוֹדֵי לֵיהּ לְרַבִּי, צְרִיכָא.

The Gemara notes: **And** both of the above *baraitot* are **necessary,** though they seem to present the same dispute. **As, if it had taught us** only **the first** *baraita*, one might have thought that **Rabbi** Yehuda HaNasi **stated** his opinion only **with regard to that** case, as there the priest **paused between** one **rite** and another **rite. But in this** case, i.e., the second *baraita*, **where he did not pause** between rites, **say** that **Rabbi** Yehuda HaNasi **concedes to Rabbi Elazar, son of Rabbi Shimon,** that the priest need not sanctify his hands and feet again. **And** conversely, **if it had taught us** only **with regard to that** case, i.e., the second *baraita*, one might have thought: **Rabbi Elazar, son of Rabbi Shimon, stated** his opinion only **in that** case. **But in this** case, **say that he concedes to Rabbi** Yehuda HaNasi. Therefore, both *baraitot* are **necessary.**

מַאי טַעְמָא דְּרַבִּי? דִּכְתִיב: ״בְּגִשְׁתָּם״. מַאי טַעְמָא דְּרַבִּי אֶלְעָזָר בְּרַבִּי שִׁמְעוֹן? דִּכְתִיב: ״בְּבוֹאָם״.

The Gemara asks: **What is the reasoning of Rabbi** Yehuda HaNasi? **As it is written:** The priests must sanctify their hands and feet: **"When they come near** to the altar to minister" (Exodus 30:20), i.e., when they begin the service in the morning. And **what is the reasoning of Rabbi Elazar, son of Rabbi Shimon? As it is written** in the same verse: **"When they go into** the Tent of Meeting," indicating that one sanctification suffices for the duration of a priest's service in the Tent of Meeting.

וְאִידָּךְ נָמֵי, הָא כְּתִיב: ״בְּבוֹאָם״! אִי כְּתִיב ״בְּגִשְׁתָּם״ וְלָא כְּתִיב ״בְּבוֹאָם״ הֲוָה אָמֵינָא עַל כׇּל גִּישָׁה וְגִישָׁה, כְּתַב רַחֲמָנָא: ״בְּבוֹאָם״.

The Gemara asks: **But** according to **the other** Sage, Rabbi Yehuda HaNasi, **as well, isn't it written: "When they go into** the Tent of Meeting"? How does he interpret this term? The Gemara responds: **If** only **"when they come near" had been written, and "when they go into" had not been written, I would say** that the priest must sanctify his hands and feet **for each and every approach,** i.e., every rite. Therefore **the Merciful One wrote: "When they go into,"** to indicate that it is necessary only once a day.

HALAKHA

Sanctified his hands and feet during the day, etc. – **קִידֵּשׁ יָדָיו וְרַגְלָיו בַּיּוֹם וכו׳**: If a priest sanctified his hands and feet in the morning, he need not sanctify them again that day to perform another service. Rather, he may continue to perform the Temple service all day and through the night, as the *halakha* is in accordance with the opinion of Rabbi Yehuda HaNasi in disputes between him and his colleagues. This applies only if the priest did not exit the Temple, sleep, urinate, or become distracted in the interim. If one of these occurred, the priest must sanctify his hands and feet again (Rambam *Sefer Avoda, Hilkhot Biat HaMikdash* 5:5).

The disqualification of being left overnight is determinative with regard to sanctification – **לִינָה מוֹעֶלֶת בְּקִידּוּשׁ**: One who sanctified his hands and feet in the morning must do so again the next morning, even if he did not sleep at all that night, in accordance with the opinion of Rabbi Yehuda HaNasi (Rambam *Sefer Avoda, Hilkhot Biat HaMikdash* 5:8).

Standing and sacrificing…all night – **עוֹמֵד וּמַקְרִיב...כׇּל הַלַּיְלָה**: If a priest sanctified his hands and feet at night and was engaged in the Temple service all night, he must still sanctify them again in the morning to participate in that day's service (Rambam *Sefer Avoda, Hilkhot Biat HaMikdash* 5:8).

NOTES

He does not need to sanctify them that night – **אֵין צָרִיךְ לְקַדֵּשׁ בַּלַּיְלָה**: For purposes of the Temple service, the night is considered part of the preceding day, rather than part of the following day, which is the norm with regard to the Jewish calendar. Therefore, one who sanctifies his hands and feet in the morning may continue to perform the Temple service into the night.

The disqualification of being left overnight is determinative – **לִינָה מוֹעֶלֶת**: Generally, the service for a given offering must begin and end on the same day (see 56a). The consumption of the portions of an offering burned on the altar may last through the night until the next morning (see *Berakhot* 2a). Therefore, any offering whose service has begun is disqualified if left until dawn the next morning. One could suggest that this *halakha* applies to sanctification of the hands and feet as well.

NOTES

For an entrance with no purpose – **אביאה ריקנית**: For example, a priest might enter the Temple courtyard to pray or witness the offerings being sacrificed by others. Some hold that in any event, a priest must sanctify his hands and feet before entering the Sanctuary, per the Jerusalem Talmud (*Yoma* 3:3). According to the Rambam, this requirement has the status of rabbinic law.

All concede – **הכל מודים**: During the Yom Kippur service, each time the High Priest changes between the golden vestments and the white vestments, he must sanctify his hands and feet, immerse in a ritual bath, and sanctify his hands and feet again. A disagreement is cited in tractate *Yoma* (34b) as to whether the first of the two sanctifications should be performed before or after he removes the vestments he was wearing. Rav Aḥa bar Ya'akov states that there is no disagreement with regard to the second sanctification; it must be performed after the High Priest has already the put on vestments he will now wear.

ואידך נמי, הא כתיב "בגשתם"! אי כתיב "בבואם" ולא כתיב "בגשתם", הוה אמינא אפילו אביאה ריקנית.

The Gemara asks: But according to **the other** Sage, Rabbi Elazar, son of Rabbi Shimon, **as well, isn't it written: "When they come near"**? How does he interpret this term? The Gemara responds: **If** only **"when they go into" had been written, and "when they come near" had not been written, I would say** that **even for an entrance with no purpose,**[N] i.e., where the priest has no intention of performing rites, he must sanctify his hands and feet. Therefore, the Merciful One wrote: "When they come near."

אביאה ריקנית?! הא כתיב: "לשרת"! אלא, "בגשתם" מיבעי ליה לכדרב אחא בר יעקב, דאמר רב אחא בר יעקב: הכל מודים בקידוש שני כשהוא לבוש מקדש, דאמר קרא: "או בגשתם" – מי שאינו מחוסר אלא גישה בלבד, יצא זה שמחוסר לבישה וגישה.

The Gemara rejects this: How could one have thought that the priest must sanctify his hands and feet **for an entrance with no purpose? Isn't is written** in the same verse: **"To minister"? Rather,** according to Rabbi Elazar, son of Rabbi Shimon, **"when they come near" is necessary for the** *halakha* taught **by Rav Aḥa bar Ya'akov. As Rav Aḥa bar Ya'akov says: All concede**[N] **with regard to the second sanctification** performed by the High Priest on Yom Kippur after each immersion that he must **sanctify** his hands and feet **while he is dressed** in the priestly vestments, **as the verse states: "Or when they come near** to the altar to minister." The verse indicates that **one who is lacking only to come near** to the altar, i.e., one who is in all other ways prepared for the service, may perform this sanctification. **Excluded is this one, who is lacking** both **dressing and coming near.**

"להקטיר אשה" למה לי?

The Gemara asks: **Why do I** need the continuation of the verse: **"To cause an offering by fire to smoke"?**

Perek **II**
Daf **20** Amud **a**

NOTES

Since it is sanctified in a service vessel – **כיון דקדוש להו בכלי שרת**: In general, the disqualification of being left overnight applies to an offering only once its service has begun, e.g., once a meal offering or libation has been sanctified in a service vessel. Since sanctification of the hands and feet is considered part of the service, perhaps this principle applies to the water in the Basin as well.

מהו דתימא, הני מילי – עבודה דמעכבא כפרה, אבל עבודה דלא מעכבא כפרה – לא, קא משמע לן.

The Gemara responds: **Lest you say** that **this matter,** sanctification of the hands and feet, applies only to **a rite that is indispensable** for effecting **atonement,** e.g., sprinkling the blood on the altar; **but a rite that is not indispensable** for effecting **atonement,** e.g., placing the fats and sacrificial portions of the offering on the altar, does **not** require prior sanctification of the hands and feet, therefore this verse **teaches us** that even such rites require sanctification of the hands and feet.

כי אתא רב דימי אמר רבי יוחנן, בעי אילפא: לדברי האומר אין לינה מועלת בקידוש ידים ורגלים, מי כיור מהו שיפסלו? מי אמרינן: הני למאי – לקידוש ידים ורגלים, קידוש ידים ורגלים גופייהו לא פסול בהו לינה. או דלמא: כיון דקדוש להו בכלי שרת, מיפסלי?

§ **When Rav Dimi came** from Eretz Yisrael to Babylonia, he said that **Rabbi Yoḥanan says: Ilfa raises a dilemma: According to the statement of** Rabbi Elazar, son of Rabbi Shimon, **who says** that the disqualification of being **left overnight is not determinative with regard to sanctification of** the **hands and feet, what is** the *halakha* with regard to **the water** in the **Basin? Is it disqualified** by being left overnight? **Do we say: For what** purpose is **this** water? It is **for the sanctification of** the **hands and feet,** and since **sanctification of** the **hands and feet itself is not disqualified** by being **left overnight,** the *halakha* should be the same concerning the water. **Or perhaps, since** the water **is sanctified in a service vessel,**[N] i.e., the Basin, **it is disqualified** by being left overnight, like all other items sanctified in service vessels.

כי אתא רבין אמר רבי ירמיה אמר רבי אמי אמר רבי יוחנן: הדר פשיט אילפא – כמחלוקת בזו כך מחלוקת בזו.

When Ravin came from Eretz Yisrael to Babylonia, he said: **Rabbi Yirmeya says** that **Rabbi Ami says** that **Rabbi Yoḥanan says: Ilfa then resolved** the dilemma: Just **as** there is **a dispute** between Rabbi Yehuda HaNasi and Rabbi Elazar, son of Rabbi Shimon, **with regard to that** issue, i.e., whether sanctification of the hands and feet is disqualified overnight, **so** too there is **a dispute** between the two **with regard to this** issue, i.e., the water in the Basin. Accordingly, Rabbi Elazar, son of Rabbi Shimon, holds that the water is not disqualified by being left overnight.

אָמַר לְפָנָיו רַבִּי יִצְחָק בַּר בִּיסְנָא: רַבִּי, אַתָּה אוֹמֵר כֵּן? אֶלָּא הָכִי אָמַר רַבִּי אַסִּי אָמַר רַבִּי יוֹחָנָן [מִשְּׁמֵיהּ דְּאִילְפָא]: כִּיּוֹר שֶׁלֹּא שִׁקְעוּ מִבָּעֶרֶב – מְקַדֵּשׁ מִמֶּנּוּ לַעֲבוֹדַת לַיְלָה, וּלְמָחָר אֵינוֹ מְקַדֵּשׁ;

Ravin continued: **Rabbi Yitzhak bar Bisna said before** Rabbi Yirmeya: **My teacher, do you say so? But this is what Rabbi Asi** says that **Rabbi Yoḥanan says in the name of Ilfa:** With regard to **a Basin that they did not sink** into its pit **at night,** which would have prevented the water from being disqualified by being left overnight, a priest **sanctifies** his hands and feet **from it for the service of** that **night, and the next day he does not sanctify** his hands and feet from it.

וְהָוֵינַן בָּהּ: לְמָחָר אֵינוֹ מְקַדֵּשׁ – דְּלָא צְרִיךְ לְקִדּוּשׁ, אוֹ דִּלְמָא אִיפַּסְלוּ בְּלִינָה? וְלָא פְּשֵׁיט לָן, וּמָר קָא פָּשֵׁיט לֵיהּ מִיפְשִׁיט.

And we discussed it:[N] When Ilfa said that **the next day he does not sanctify** his hands and feet from it, did he mean **that he does not require sanctification** the next day, since sanctification is not disqualified overnight? **Or perhaps** Ilfa meant that it is prohibited to sanctify one's hands and feet from the Basin since the water **was disqualified by** being **left overnight? And** Rabbi Asi **did not resolve** the issue **for us. But you, Master, are resolving** the issue by claiming that Ilfa ruled explicitly with regard to the opinion of Rabbi Elazar, son of Rabbi Shimon.

תָּא שְׁמַע: בֶּן קָטִין עָשָׂה שְׁנֵים עָשָׂר דַּד לַכִּיּוֹר. אַף הוּא עָשָׂה מוּכְנִי לַכִּיּוֹר שֶׁלֹּא יִהְיוּ מֵימָיו נִפְסָלִין בְּלִינָה; מַאי לָאו רַבִּי אֶלְעָזָר בְּרַבִּי שִׁמְעוֹן הִיא? לָא, רַבִּי הִיא.

The Gemara attempts to resolve the issue: **Come** and **hear** a proof from a mishna (*Yoma* 37a): The High Priest **ben Katin made twelve spigots**[H] **for the Basin** so that several priests could sanctify their hands and feet at once. **He also made a mechanism** [*mukhani*][NL] for sinking **the Basin**[H] into water during the night so **that its water would not be disqualified by** being **left overnight. What, is it not** that this mishna **is** in accordance with the opinion of **Rabbi Elazar, son of Rabbi Shimon?** If so, he holds that water of the Basin is disqualified by being left overnight. The Gemara responds: **No, it is** in accordance with the opinion of **Rabbi** Yehuda HaNasi.

וְהָא מִדְּרֵישָׁא רַבִּי אֶלְעָזָר בְּרַבִּי שִׁמְעוֹן, סֵיפָא נַמִי רַבִּי אֶלְעָזָר בְּרַבִּי שִׁמְעוֹן!

The Gemara challenges: **But from** the fact **that the first clause** of the mishna is in accordance with the opinion of **Rabbi Elazar, son of Rabbi Shimon,** one should infer that **the latter clause is also** in accordance with the opinion of **Rabbi Elazar, son of Rabbi Shimon.**

דְּקָתָנֵי רֵישָׁא: בָּא לוֹ אֵצֶל פָּרוֹ, וּפָר הָיָה עוֹמֵד בֵּין הָאוּלָם וְלַמִּזְבֵּחַ, רֹאשׁוֹ לַדָּרוֹם וּפָנָיו לַמַּעֲרָב, וְהַכֹּהֵן עוֹמֵד בַּמִּזְרָח וּפָנָיו לַמַּעֲרָב. מַאן שָׁמְעַתְּ לֵיהּ דְּאָמַר: בֵּין הָאוּלָם וְלַמִּזְבֵּחַ – צָפוֹן, רַבִּי אֶלְעָזָר בְּרַבִּי שִׁמְעוֹן.

The Gemara elaborates: **As the first clause teaches** (*Yoma* 35b): At one point during the Yom Kippur service, the High Priest would **come** and stand **next to his bull,**[HB] **and** his **bull was standing between the Entrance Hall and the altar** with **its head to the south**[N] **and its face to the west.**[B] **And the priest stands** to the east of the bull, **and his face points to the west.** This is where he would slaughter the bull. **Whom have you heard** who **says** that **between the Entrance Hall and the altar** is considered part of the **north** of the courtyard, where it is permitted to slaughter offerings of the most sacred order? It is **Rabbi Elazar, son of Rabbi Shimon.**

NOTES

And we discussed it – וְהָוֵינַן בָּהּ: Ilfa's statement and the subsequent discussion before Rav Asi must have been with regard to the opinion of Rabbi Elazar, son of Rabbi Shimon. It is clear that according to Rabbi Yehuda HaNasi, who holds that sanctification of the hands and feet is disqualified overnight, the same applies to the water in the Basin (Rashi). Accordingly, since Ilfa's statement is ostensibly unresolved, Rabbi Yirmeya's statement is problematic. According to Rabbeinu Peretz, Ilfa's statement certainly means that the water in the Basin is disqualified overnight; the question unresolved by Rav Asi is whether this statement should be understood in accordance with the opinion of Rabbi Yehuda HaNasi or that of Rabbi Elazar, son of Rabbi Shimon.

Mechanism – מוּכְנִי: According to most commentaries, the mechanism was a wheel used to lower the Basin into a pit where water flowed. The Rambam explains that the machine described here was a type of barrier surrounding the Basin, and the wheel filled the area surrounded by the barrier with water from the pit. In this way the water was not disqualified because it remained contiguous with the water in the pit.

Its head to the south, etc. – רֹאשׁוֹ לַדָּרוֹם וכו׳: Consequently, both the High Priest and the bull are facing the Sanctuary. The bull would not be positioned with its back facing the Sanctuary, so that if it defecated it would not constitute disrespect (see *Yoma* 36a).

HALAKHA

Ben Katin made twelve spigots – בֶּן קָטִין עָשָׂה שְׁנֵים עָשָׂר דַּד: The Basin in the Temple had twelve spigots, such that all of the priests participating in the service of the daily offering could sanctify their hands and feet at once (Rambam *Sefer Avoda, Hilkhot Beit HaBeḥira* 3:18).

Made a mechanism for the Basin – עָשָׂה מוּכְנִי לַכִּיּוֹר: A mechanism was made for the Basin to prevent its water from being disqualified by being left overnight. The Rambam, the Ra'avad, and others disagree with regard to the nature of this mechanism (Rambam *Sefer Avoda, Hilkhot Beit HaBeḥira* 3:18 and *Hilkhot Biat HaMikdash* 5:14).

Come and stand next to his bull – בָּא לוֹ אֵצֶל פָּרוֹ: When the High Priest comes to place his hands on his bull and slaughter it during the Yom Kippur service, or for any other offering of the most sacred order, the bull must stand between the Entrance Hall and the altar, with its head to the south and face turned west. The High Priest stands to the east of the bull, facing west, and places his hands on the bull and recites his confession (Rambam *Sefer Avoda, Hilkhot Avodat Yom HaKippurim* 4:1 and *Hilkhot Ma'aseh HaKorbanot* 3:14).

LANGUAGE

Mechanism [*mukhani*] – מוּכְנִי: From the Greek μηχανή, *mēchanē*, meaning machine.

BACKGROUND

He would come next to his bull – בָּא לוֹ אֵצֶל פָּרוֹ: On Yom Kippur, the High Priest sacrifices a bull as a sin offering for himself, his family, and all the members of the priesthood (Leviticus 16:3, 6). The bull's slaughter, the burning of its flesh, and the sprinkling of its blood resemble the procedures of those offerings of bulls that are burned outside Jerusalem. Its blood is also sprinkled between the staves of the Ark in the Holy of Holies. The blood of this bull is first sprinkled separately. Afterward it is mixed with the blood of the goat sacrificed as a sin offering for the entire people, and the mixture is sprinkled on the golden incense altar.

Its head to the south and its face to the west – רֹאשׁוֹ לַדָּרוֹם וּפָנָיו לַמַּעֲרָב: The image depicts the High Priest preparing to place his hands on the bull. The head of the bull is toward the south while its face is turned toward the west.

Priest placing his hands on the bull

NOTES

What is the north – אֵיזֶהוּ צָפוֹן: The verse specifies that offerings of the most sacred order must be slaughtered: "On the side of the altar northward before the Lord" (Leviticus 1:11). The Sages disagree as to the exact area delineated by this phrase. All agree that the area behind the Entrance Hall is not included, as the Entrance Hall interposes between it and the altar (Rashi).

HALAKHA

What is the north – אֵיזֶהוּ צָפוֹן: The north of the courtyard is the area bounded by the courtyard's north wall, the courtyard's east wall, the altar, and the wall of the Entrance Hall, in accordance with the opinion of Rabbi Yehuda HaNasi. This is the area fit for slaughter of offerings of the most sacred order (Rambam *Sefer Avoda, Hilkhot Beit HaBeḥira* 5:15–16).

LANGUAGE

Knives [*ḥalifot*] – חֲלִיפוֹת: *Ḥalaf* is an Aramaic word for knife. This was the common word in many Jewish communities for a knife used for ritual slaughter.

דְּתַנְיָא: אֵיזֶהוּ צָפוֹן – מִקִּיר מִזְבֵּחַ צְפוֹנִי וְעַד כּוֹתֶל עֲזָרָה צְפוֹנִי, וּכְנֶגֶד כָּל הַמִּזְבֵּחַ כּוּלּוֹ – צָפוֹן, דִּבְרֵי רַבִּי יוֹסֵי בְּרַבִּי יְהוּדָה. רַבִּי אֶלְעָזָר בְּרַבִּי שִׁמְעוֹן מוֹסִיף: אַף בֵּין הָאוּלָם וְלַמִּזְבֵּחַ. רַבִּי מוֹסִיף: אַף מְקוֹם דְּרִיסַת רַגְלֵי הַכֹּהֲנִים וּמְקוֹם דְּרִיסַת רַגְלֵי יִשְׂרָאֵל. אֲבָל מִן הַחֲלִיפוֹת וְלִפְנִים – הַכֹּל מוֹדִים שֶׁפָּסוּל.

This is **as it is taught** in a *baraita*: **What is the north?**[NHB] It is the area **from the northern wall of the altar until the northern wall of the Temple courtyard. And opposite the entire altar** is considered the **north;** this is **the statement of Rabbi Yosei, son of Rabbi Yehuda. Rabbi Elazar, son of Rabbi Shimon, adds even** the area **between the Entrance Hall and the altar** to the area that is considered north. **Rabbi** Yehuda HaNasi **adds** that **even** the areas to the north in **the place where the priests walk, and** the areas to the north in **the place where the Israelites walk. But all concede that** the area **from** the Chamber of **the Knives** [*haḥalifot*][L] **and inward,** which is an area to the side, is **unfit** for slaughtering offerings of the most sacred order, as it is not visible from the altar.

וְתִסְבְּרָא, רַבִּי אֶלְעָזָר בְּרַבִּי שִׁמְעוֹן הִיא וְלָא רַבִּי? [הָשְׁתָּא רַבִּי] אַדְּרַבִּי יוֹסֵי בְּרַבִּי יְהוּדָה מוֹסִיף, אַדְּרַבִּי אֶלְעָזָר בְּרַבִּי שִׁמְעוֹן לָא מוֹסִיף?

The Gemara rejects the proof: **And must you understand** that the first clause of the mishna **is** in accordance with the opinion of **Rabbi Elazar, son of Rabbi Shimon, and not** the opinion of **Rabbi** Yehuda HaNasi? **Now,** does **Rabbi** Yehuda HaNasi **add** only **to** the statement **of Rabbi Yosei, son of Rabbi Yehuda,** but **not add to** the statement **of Rabbi Elazar, son of Rabbi Shimon?** The area deemed north according to Rabbi Elazar, son of Rabbi Shimon, is included in the area deemed north by Rabbi Yehuda HaNasi. Accordingly, since the first clause of the mishna can also be in accordance with the opinion of Rabbi Yehuda HaNasi, perhaps the mishna offers no proof at all with regard to the opinion of Rabbi Elazar, son of Rabbi Shimon.

אֲנַן הָכִי קָאָמְרִינַן: אִי סָלְקָא דַּעְתָּךְ רַבִּי הִיא – לוֹקְמָהּ בִּמְקוֹם דְּרִיסַת רַגְלֵי כֹּהֲנִים וּבִמְקוֹם דְּרִיסַת רַגְלֵי יִשְׂרָאֵל.

The Gemara reformulates its suggestion: **This is what we are saying: If it enters your mind** to say that the mishna **is** in accordance with the opinion of **Rabbi** Yehuda HaNasi, then **let him stand** the bull **in the place where the priests walk and in the place where the Israelites walk,** since Rabbi Yehuda HaNasi holds that those areas are also considered north. Why is the bull placed specifically between the Entrance Hall and the altar?

אֶלָּא מַאי, רַבִּי אֶלְעָזָר בְּרַבִּי שִׁמְעוֹן הִיא? לוֹקְמָהּ מִקִּיר מִזְבֵּחַ צְפוֹנִי עַד כּוֹתֶל עֲזָרָה צְפוֹנִי! אֶלָּא מַאי אִית לָךְ לְמֵימַר – מִשּׁוּם חוּלְשָׁא דְּכֹהֵן גָּדוֹל, הָכָא נַמִי מִשּׁוּם חוּלְשָׁא דְּכֹהֵן גָּדוֹל.

The Gemara rejects this: **Rather, what** shall you say? Will you say that the mishna **is** only in accordance with the opinion of **Rabbi Elazar, son of Rabbi Shimon?** But if so, **let him stand** the bull anywhere **from the north wall of the altar to the north wall of the Temple courtyard,** as everyone agrees that this area is considered north. **Rather, what have you to say** to explain why the bull is positioned specifically between the Entrance Hall and the altar? It is **due to the weakness of** the **High Priest,** so that he need not exert himself and walk long distances on Yom Kippur. **Here too,** the mishna may be in accordance with the opinion of Rabbi Yehuda HaNasi, and **due to the weakness of** the **High Priest** the bull is positioned there.

BACKGROUND

What is the north – אֵיזֶהוּ צָפוֹן:

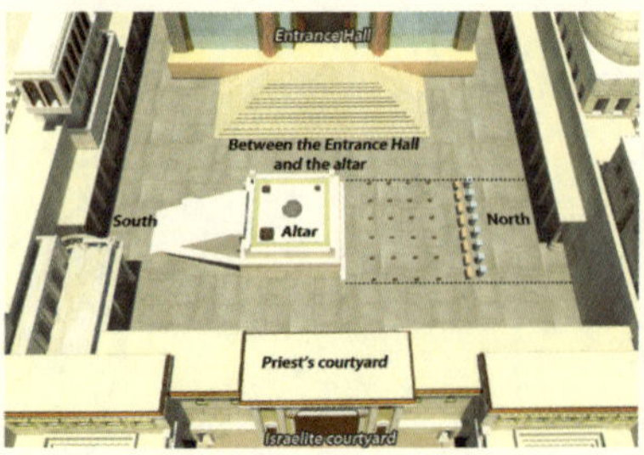

Opinion of Rabbi Yosei, son of Rabbi Yehuda

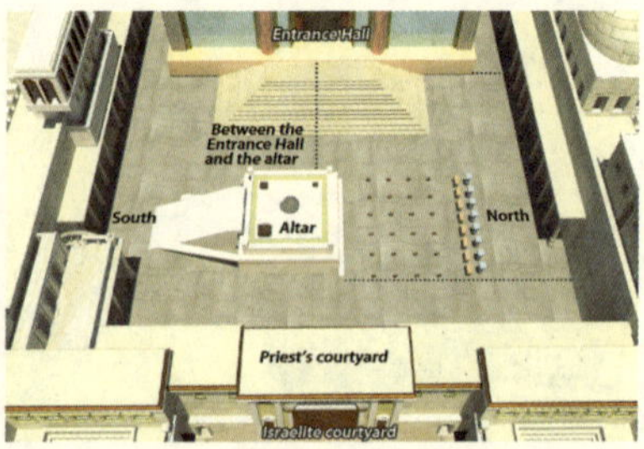

Opinion of Rabbi Elazar, son of Rabbi Shimon

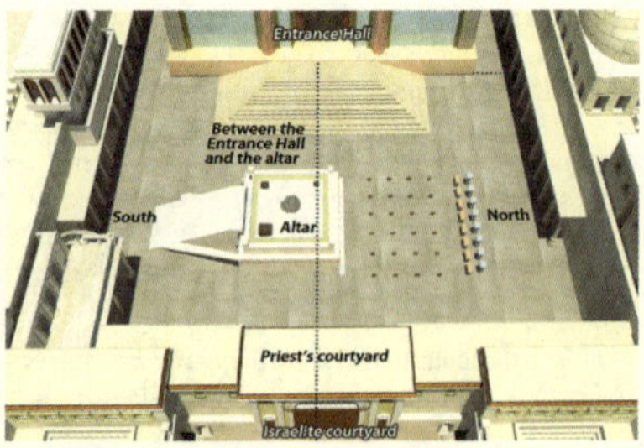

Opinion of Rabbi Yehuda HaNasi

אָמַר רַבִּי יוֹחָנָן: קִידֵּשׁ יָדָיו וְרַגְלָיו לִתְרוּמַת הַדֶּשֶׁן – לְמָחָר אֵינוֹ צָרִיךְ לְקַדֵּשׁ, שֶׁכְּבָר קִידֵּשׁ מִתְּחִילַּת עֲבוֹדָה.

§ **Rabbi Yoḥanan says:** If a priest **sanctified his hands and feet** in preparation **for the removal of the ashes,**[NH] the first service performed every day in the Temple, which was performed before dawn, then **the next day,** i.e., after dawn, **he does not need to sanctify** them again, **as he already sanctified** them at **the beginning of** the day's **service.**

לְמַאן? אִי לְרַבִּי – הָאָמַר: פָּסְלָה לִינָה, אִי לְרַבִּי אֶלְעָזָר בְּרַבִּי שִׁמְעוֹן – הָאָמַר: אֵין צָרִיךְ לְקַדֵּשׁ אֲפִילּוּ מִיכָּן וְעַד עֲשָׂרָה יָמִים!

The Gemara asks: **In accordance with whose** opinion is this statement? **If** it is **in accordance with** the opinion of **Rabbi** Yehuda HaNasi, **doesn't he say** that being **left overnight disqualifies** sanctification of the hands and feet? If so, one should be required to sanctify them again after dawn. And **if** it is **in accordance with** the opinion of **Rabbi Elazar, son of Rabbi Shimon, doesn't he say** that if the priest sanctified his hands and feet at the beginning of the service, **he does not need to sanctify** them again **even** if he continues to perform rites **for the next ten days?** Why, then, does Rabbi Yoḥanan state only that one who sanctified his hands and feet before the removal of the ashes is not required to do so after dawn?

אָמַר אַבַּיֵי: לְעוֹלָם לְרַבִּי, וְלִינָה דְּרַבָּנַן הִיא, וּמוֹדֵי דְּמִקְּרוֹת הַגֶּבֶר וְעַד צַפְרָא לָא פָּסְלָה לִינָה.

Abaye says: Actually, the statement is **in accordance with** the opinion of **Rabbi** Yehuda HaNasi, **and** the disqualification of sanctification of the hands and feet by being **left overnight is by rabbinic law. And** although the Sages mandate that a priest must sanctify his hands and feet every morning, **they concede that** during the period **from the rooster's crow** before dawn **until morning,** being **left overnight does not disqualify** his sanctification. Therefore, one who sanctifies his hands and feet at the rooster's crow may continue to perform rites after dawn.

רָבָא אָמַר: לְעוֹלָם רַבִּי אֶלְעָזָר בְּרַבִּי שִׁמְעוֹן [הִיא, וְרָאָה רַבִּי יוֹחָנָן דְּבָרָיו] בִּתְחִילַּת עֲבוֹדָה וְלֹא בְּסוֹף עֲבוֹדָה.

Rava says: Actually, the statement **is** in accordance with the opinion of **Rabbi Elazar, son of Rabbi Shimon. And Rabbi Yoḥanan saw the statement of** Rabbi Elazar, son of Rabbi Shimon, as correct **with regard to the beginning of** the **service,** i.e., that a priest may serve during the day on the strength of sanctification performed before dawn. **But** he did **not** agree **with regard to the end of the service.** Rather, Rabbi Yoḥanan holds that if a priest sanctified his hands and feet before participating in the day's final rites, he must sanctify them again the next morning. According to the opinion of Rabbi Yehuda HaNasi, one who sanctified his hands and feet before sunrise must do so again afterward.

מֵיתִיבֵי: רָאוּהוּ אֶחָיו הַכֹּהֲנִים שֶׁיָּרַד, וְהֵם רָצוּ וּבָאוּ, מִיהֲרוּ וְקִידְּשׁוּ יְדֵיהֶם וְרַגְלֵיהֶם מִן הַכִּיּוֹר.

The Gemara **raises an objection** from a mishna (*Tamid* 28b) that describes the daily service: **His priestly brethren,** members of the patrilineal family, **saw**[H] **that** the priest who removed the ashes **descended** from the altar with the coal pan in his hands, **and they ran and arrived** at the Basin. **They hurried and sanctified their hands and their feet** with water **from the Basin.**

Perek **II**
Daf **20** Amud **b**

בִּשְׁלָמָא לְאַבַּיֵי דְּמוֹקֵים לָהּ כְּרַבִּי, וּמוֹדֵי רַבִּי דְּמִקְּרוֹת הַגֶּבֶר עַד צַפְרָא לָא פָּסְלָה לִינָה, הָא מַנִּי? רַבִּי הִיא.

Assuming that these priests had all been serving in the Temple through the night, one can ask: **Granted, according to Abaye, who interprets** the statement of Rabbi Yoḥanan **in accordance with** the opinion of **Rabbi** Yehuda HaNasi, **and Rabbi** Yehuda HaNasi **concedes that** during the period **from the rooster's crow** before dawn **until morning,** being **left overnight does not disqualify** sanctification, in accordance with **whose** opinion **is this** mishna? **It is** in accordance with the opinion of **Rabbi** Yehuda HaNasi, who holds that although they served through the night, the previous day's sanctification was disqualified and they must sanctify their hands and feet again in the morning, but they may do so before dawn.

NOTES

For the removal of the ashes – לִתְרוּמַת הַדֶּשֶׁן: The removal of the ashes is prescribed in the Torah (see Leviticus 6:1–3). At the beginning of the service, one priest removes a small amount of ashes from the sacrificial portions of the previous day's offerings in a coal pan and places it on the ground next to the altar. The removal of the ashes would take place before dawn, usually at the rooster's crow. On Festivals, when the Temple service was more lengthy, it might occur even before midnight. After this was performed, the other priests would concentrate the excess ash on the altar onto the large pile of ashes at its center, or remove it from the Temple entirely.

HALAKHA

In preparation for the removal of the ashes – לִתְרוּמַת הַדֶּשֶׁן: If a priest sanctified his hands and feet in preparation for the removal of the ashes, even if he did so before sunrise, he need not sanctify them again to continue to participate in the Temple service that day, in accordance with the statement of Rabbi Yoḥanan (Rambam *Sefer Avoda, Hilkhot Biat HaMikdash* 5:9).

His priestly brethren saw, etc. – רָאוּהוּ אֶחָיו הַכֹּהֲנִים וכו׳: After the priest who removed the ashes from the altar descends, his priestly brethren hurry to sanctify their hands and feet. They take shovels and ascend onto the altar to put back all the portions of the offerings that had not been consumed. They then shovel the ashes from the sides of the altar into a pile in the altar's center (Rambam *Sefer Avoda, Hilkhot Temidin UMusafin* 2:13).

אֶלָּא לְרָבָא, דְּמוֹקֵים לַהּ כְּרַבִּי אֶלְעָזָר בְּרַבִּי שִׁמְעוֹן, אֲבָל לְרַבִּי – מִקְּרוֹת הַגֶּבֶר עַד צַפְרָא פָּסְלָה לִינָה, הָא מַנִּי? אִי רַבִּי – פָּסְלָה לִינָה, אִי רַבִּי אֶלְעָזָר בְּרַבִּי שִׁמְעוֹן – הָא אָמַר: אֲפִילּוּ מִיכָּן וְעַד עֲשָׂרָה יָמִים אֵינוֹ צָרִיךְ לְקַדֵּשׁ!

But according to Rava, who interprets the statement in accordance with the opinion of Rabbi Elazar, son of Rabbi Shimon, but who holds that according to Rabbi Yehuda HaNasi, during the period from the rooster's crow until morning being left overnight disqualifies sanctification, in accordance with whose opinion is this mishna? If it is in accordance with the opinion of Rabbi Yehuda HaNasi, then the priests' sanctification described therein is useless, since being left overnight disqualifies it at dawn. And if it is in accordance with the opinion of Rabbi Elazar, son of Rabbi Shimon, doesn't he say that even if the priest continues to perform rites for the next ten days, he does not need to sanctify his hands and feet again? If so, since the priests were serving throughout the night, they should not require sanctification.

לְעוֹלָם כְּרַבִּי אֶלְעָזָר בְּרַבִּי שִׁמְעוֹן, וְהָכָא בְּמַאי עָסְקִינַן – בְּכָהֲנֵי חֲדַתֵּי.

The Gemara responds: Actually, the mishna is in accordance with the opinion of Rabbi Elazar, son of Rabbi Shimon, and here we are dealing with new priests, who did not serve in the Temple that night. Since they are beginning their service now, they must sanctify their hands and feet.

אִיבַּעֲיָא לְהוּ: יְצִיאָה מַהוּ שֶׁתּוֹעִיל בְּקִידּוּשׁ יָדַיִם וְרַגְלַיִם? אִם תִּימְצֵי לוֹמַר לִינָה לָא פָּסְלָה – דְּלָא פָּרֵישׁ, אֲבָל יְצִיאָה דְּפָרֵישׁ – אַסּוּחֵי מַסַּח דַּעְתֵּיהּ, אוֹ דִּלְמָא כֵּיוָן דְּבִידוֹ לַחֲזוֹר – לָא מַסַּח?

§ A dilemma was raised before the Sages: What is the *halakha* with regard to leaving the Temple? Is it effective to disqualify sanctification of the hands and feet such that the priest must sanctify them again when he reenters the Temple? The Gemara elaborates: If you say that being left overnight does not disqualify it, perhaps that is only because he does not separate[N] from the Temple; but when leaving the Temple, where the priest separates from the Temple, it is possible that the priest becomes distracted from the service. If so, he must sanctify his hands and feet again. Or perhaps, since it is in his power to return to the Temple at any point, he does not become distracted, in which case he does not need to sanctify them again.

תָּא שְׁמַע: קִידֵּשׁ יָדָיו וְרַגְלָיו וְנִטְמְאוּ – מַטְבִּילָן, וְאֵין צָרִיךְ לְקַדֵּשׁ. יָצְאוּ – הֲרֵי הֵן בִּקְדוּשָּׁתָן.

The Gemara suggests: Come and hear a proof from a *baraita*: If a priest sanctified his hands and feet and his hands then became impure,[N] he may immerse them to purify them, and he does not need to sanctify them again. If he sanctified his hands and they then left[H] the Temple, they retain their sanctity. Apparently, leaving the Temple does not disqualify sanctification.

יָצְאוּ יָדָיו לָא קָמִיבַּעֲיָא לַן, כִּי קָמִיבַּעֲיָא לַן יָצָא כׇּל גּוּפוֹ, מַאי?

The Gemara responds: We do not raise the dilemma with regard to a case where only his hands left the Temple. In such a case, he certainly does not need to sanctify them again. When we raise the dilemma, it is with regard to a case where his entire body left the Temple; what is the *halakha* in such a case?

תָּא שְׁמַע: שֶׁלֹּא רְחוּץ יָדַיִם וְרַגְלַיִם מְקַדֵּשׁ בִּכְלִי שָׁרֵת בִּפְנִים. קִידֵּשׁ בִּכְלִי שָׁרֵת בַּחוּץ, אוֹ בִּכְלִי חוֹל בִּפְנִים, אוֹ שֶׁטָּבַל בְּמֵי מְעָרָה וְעָבַד – עֲבוֹדָתוֹ פְּסוּלָה. טַעְמָא, דְּקִידֵּשׁ בִּכְלִי שָׁרֵת בַּחוּץ, הָא קִידֵּשׁ בִּפְנִים וְיָצָא – עֲבוֹדָתוֹ כְּשֵׁירָה.

The Gemara suggests: Come and hear another proof from a *baraita*: One whose hands and feet are not washed must sanctify them with a service vessel inside[H] the Temple. If he sanctified them with a service vessel outside the Temple, or with a non-sacred vessel inside, or if he immersed in cave water[NH] and performed the service, his service is disqualified. The Gemara infers: The reason his service is disqualified is that he sanctified his hands and feet with a service vessel outside,[N] but if he sanctified them inside and then left, his service is valid.

NOTES

Does not separate – דְּלָא פָּרֵישׁ: According to Rashi, this means that the priest did not cease to perform the service. The *Baḥ* explains that the Gemara means that he did not leave the Temple.

Sanctified his hands and feet and they became impure – קִידֵּשׁ יָדָיו וְרַגְלָיו וְנִטְמְאוּ: This must be referring to impurity of the hands only, which is by rabbinic law and can be rectified by simply immersing the hands in a ritual bath (Rashi). Impurity of the entire body, which is by Torah law, requires one to wait until nightfall after immersion to become pure.

Cave water – מֵי מְעָרָה: This includes all water fit for ritual immersion. The *baraita* mentions cave water specifically since it was common practice to immerse in water collected in cave.

With a service vessel outside – בִּכְלִי שָׁרֵת בַּחוּץ: If leaving the Temple disqualifies the service, it would be unnecessary to teach that one who sanctifies his hands and feet outside the Temple is not considered to have sanctified them at all (Rashi). Rather, it must be that the *baraita* teaches this case specifically because it is only in this case that the service is disqualified.

HALAKHA

They left – יָצְאוּ: If a priest's hands leave the boundaries of the Temple courtyard, he does not need to sanctify them again, in accordance with the *baraita* (Rambam *Sefer Avoda, Hilkhot Biat HaMikdash* 5:5).

Must sanctify them with a service vessel inside – מְקַדֵּשׁ בִּכְלִי שָׁרֵת בִּפְנִים: It is a mitzva to sanctify one's hands from the Basin, but if one sanctified his hands with water from another service vessel, the sanctification is valid after the fact. One may not do so with a non-sacred vessel. If one used a non-sacred vessel even inside the Temple, or a sacred vessel outside the Temple, his service is disqualified (Rambam *Sefer Avoda, Hilkhot Biat HaMikdash* 5:10).

Immersed in cave water – טָבַל בְּמֵי מְעָרָה: If one immerses his hands and feet in a ritual bath or natural spring, this is not considered valid sanctification for service in the Temple, which must be performed with water from a vessel. Immersing one's entire body in a ritual bath is also insufficient (Rambam *Sefer Avoda, Hilkhot Biat HaMikdash* 5:11; see *Likkutei Halakhot*).

דִּלְמָא קִידֵּשׁ בִּכְלִי שָׁרֵת בַּחוּץ הֵיכִי דָּמֵי – כְּגוֹן דְּאַפֵּיק יָדָיו לְבָר וְקִידֵּשׁ; הָא קִידֵּשׁ בִּפְנִים וְיָצָא, דְּאַפֵּיק יְדֵיהּ לְבָר – כְּשֵׁירָה. אֲבָל יָצָא כָּל גּוּפוֹ תִּיבָּעֵי לָךְ!

The Gemara responds: **Perhaps** one can say: **What are the circumstances** of the case where one **sanctified** them **with a service vessel outside?** It is a case **where he removed** only **his hands** and placed them **outside** the Temple **and sanctified** them there. **Consequently,** one can infer only that if **he sanctified** them **inside and** then **left,** i.e., specifically **where he removed** only **his hand** and placed it **outside,** his service is **valid. But** with regard to a case where **his entire body left** the Temple, **you should raise the dilemma.**

אֲמַר לֵיהּ רַב זְבִיד לְרַב פַּפָּא: תָּא שְׁמַע, יָצָא חוּץ לִמְחִיצַּת חוֹמַת הָעֲזָרָה, אִם לִשְׁהוֹת – טָעוּן טְבִילָה, אִם לְפִי שָׁעָה – טָעוּן קִידּוּשׁ יָדַיִם וְרַגְלַיִם!

Rav Zevid said to Rav Pappa: Come and hear a proof from another *baraita*: In a case where a priest **left the boundary of the wall of the Temple courtyard,**[H] if he left long enough **to remain**[N] there for a time, **he requires immersion. If** he left only **for a moment, he requires sanctification of** the **hands and feet.** Apparently, one who leaves even for a brief time requires sanctification.

אֲמַר לֵיהּ: הָכָא בְּמַאי עָסְקִינַן – כְּגוֹן שֶׁיָּצָא לְהָסֵךְ רַגְלָיו וּלְהַטִּיל מַיִם.

Rav Pappa **said to him: Here we are dealing with** a case **where** the priest **left** the Temple **to cover his legs,** a euphemism for defecating, **or to urinate.** It is only for this reason that he must sanctify his hands and feet when reentering the Temple.

הָא בְּהֶדְיָא קָתָנֵי לָהּ: כָּל הַמֵּיסֵךְ רַגְלָיו – טָעוּן טְבִילָה, וְכָל הַמַּטִּיל מַיִם – טָעוּן קִידּוּשׁ יָדַיִם וְרַגְלַיִם! תָּנֵי וַהֲדַר מְפָרֵשׁ.

The Gemara challenges: **But** the mishna (*Yoma* 28a) already **teaches it explicitly: Anyone who covers his legs**[H] **requires immersion** afterward; **and anyone who urinates requires sanctification of** the **hands and feet** with water from the Basin afterward. The Gemara responds: The redundancy is not difficult. The *tanna* **teaches** the principle **and then explains it**[N] again.

תָּא שְׁמַע: פָּרָה, רַבִּי חִיָּיא בַּר יוֹסֵף אָמַר: מְקַדֵּשׁ בִּכְלִי שָׁרֵת בִּפְנִים וְיוֹצֵא, וְרַבִּי יוֹחָנָן אָמַר: אֲפִילּוּ בַּחוּץ, וַאֲפִילּוּ בִּכְלִי חוֹל, וַאֲפִילּוּ בִּמְקֵידָה שֶׁל חֶרֶס.

The Gemara suggests: **Come** and **hear** a proof from the following dispute: With regard to the priest who performs the service of the red **heifer,** which takes place outside the Temple, **Rabbi Ḥiyya bar Yosef says:** In preparation, he must **sanctify** his hands and feet **with a service vessel inside** the Temple, as he must before any other service, **and** afterward he **leaves** the Temple to perform the service. **And Rabbi Yoḥanan says:** He may sanctify his hands **even outside** of the Temple, **and even with a non-sacred vessel, and even with an earthenware bowl** [***bimkeida***].[L] Apparently, leaving the Temple does not disqualify sanctification of the hands and feet.

אֲמַר רַב פַּפָּא: שָׁאנֵי פָּרָה, הוֹאִיל וְכָל מַעֲשֶׂיהָ בַּחוּץ לָא פָּסְלָה בָּהּ יְצִיאָה. אִי הָכִי, לָמָּה לִי דִּמְקַדֵּשׁ? כְּעֵין עֲבוֹדָה פְּנִים.

Rav Pappa said: The rite of the red **heifer is different, since all of its acts are** performed **outside** the Temple, unlike other rites. Therefore, **leaving** the Temple **does not disqualify** sanctification of the hands and feet **with regard to it.** The Gemara asks: **If so, why do I require that** the priest **sanctify** his hands and feet at all for the service of the red heifer? The Gemara responds: The service of the red heifer must be **similar to the service** of offerings performed **inside**[N] the Temple.

HALAKHA

Left the boundary of the wall of the Temple courtyard – יָצָא חוּץ לִמְחִיצַּת חוֹמַת הָעֲזָרָה: If a priest leaves the Temple courtyard in order to remain outside for a long time, he must immerse before he returns to the Temple. If he left with the intention of returning immediately, he need only sanctify his hands and feet. If he neither immersed nor sanctified his hands and feet, his service is valid after the fact provided that he did not become distracted or urinate or defecate outside the Temple. The Rambam deems the service valid after the fact, even though the question is unresolved in the Gemara, because the replacement offering one would bring if the service were disqualified is itself possibly unnecessary, and bringing it would constitute transgression of the prohibition against bringing unsanctified animals into the Temple courtyard (Rambam *Sefer Avoda, Hilkhot Biat HaMikdash* 5:5 and *Kesef Mishne* there).

Anyone who covers his legs – כָּל הַמֵּיסֵךְ רַגְלָיו: A priest who defecates must immerse afterward and sanctify his hands and feet, and a priest who urinates must sanctify his hands and feet (Rambam *Sefer Avoda, Hilkhot Biat HaMikdash* 5:5; see *Likkutei Halakhot*).

LANGUAGE

Bowl [*mekeida*] – מְקֵידָה: A *mekeida* is a vessel usually made of earthenware. According to the *ge'onim*, it was identical to the earthenware or wooden vessel known as a *kod*. The *mekeida* was used primarily for storing drink when traveling, and some say it was constructed so as to be easily separated into two pieces that could be used separately.

NOTES

If he left long enough to remain – אִם לִשְׁהוֹת: Any priest who leaves the Temple courtyard in the middle of the service must immerse before reentering the Temple, even if he is pure (see *Yoma* 30a). One who leaves the Temple for a long time will almost certainly be distracted from the service. When he reenters, it is as though he is arriving at the beginning of his service, and therefore he requires immersion. One who leaves for only a short time does not require immersion, but he still must sanctify his hands and feet for having left the courtyard at all.

Teaches the principle and then explains it – תָּנֵי וַהֲדַר מְפָרֵשׁ: This explanation is invoked in instances where a general expression appearing in one mishna is interpreted as referring to a specific case that is taught explicitly in the following mishna. Here, the use of this explanation is unusual because the general expression appears in a *baraita* and the explicit case in a mishna. Rashi therefore understands that the latter text, generally understood to be a mishna, is actually the next clause of that *baraita*.

Similar to the service performed inside – כְּעֵין עֲבוֹדָה פְּנִים: Although the red heifer is different from proper offerings in several ways, it is still referred to as a sin offering in the Torah, and many of the requirements particular to offerings apply to it as well, including sanctification of the hands and feet. Nevertheless, sanctification specifically from the Basin is required only for service inside the Temple (see Exodus 30:18–20). Since the service of the red heifer is performed outside of the Temple, Rabbi Yoḥanan holds that sanctification of the hands and feet in preparation for it may be done from any vessel. It may even be preferable to sanctify one's hands and feet from a vessel that is unfit for sanctification in the Temple, in order to emphasize this distinction.

NOTES

What is the *halakha* with regard to ritual impurity – טוּמְאָה מַהוּ: This question proves that the aim of sanctification of the hands and feet is not to purify the priest, because if that were the goal, impurity would certainly disqualify it. Rather, sanctification is a form of demonstrating honor for service in the Temple.

Since he needs to allow the sun to set – כֵּיוָן דְּבָעֵי לְמֶעֱבַד הֶעֱרֵב שֶׁמֶשׁ: This is referring to one who is ritually impure by Torah law, who must immerse and then wait until nightfall to be permitted to enter the Temple and perform the service. One who is impure by rabbinic law, e.g., one who consumes impure food or drink, may return to service immediately following his immersion (see *Para* 11:5 and commentaries there).

HALAKHA

Sanctified his hands and feet and they became impure – קִידֵּשׁ יָדָיו וְרַגְלָיו וְנִטְמְאוּ: If a priest sanctified his hands and feet, and afterward his hands contracted ritual impurity, he may immerse them and thereby render them pure. He is not required to sanctify them again (Rambam *Sefer Avoda, Hilkhot Biat HaMikdash* 5:6).

His entire body became impure – נִטְמָא כָּל גּוּפוֹ: If one contracts impurity by rabbinic law, e.g., if he ate impure food, he may immerse and immediately sanctify his hands and feet and continue to serve. If he did not sanctify his hands and feet, his service is not disqualified provided that he did not become distracted in the interim. Likewise, if one contracts impurity by Torah law immediately before sunset, such that he may immerse and return to service immediately, he must sanctify his hands and feet *ab initio*. If he did not do so, his service is valid after the fact, provided that he was not distracted. The Rambam deems the service valid after the fact, even though the question is unresolved in the Gemara, because the replacement offering one would bring if the service were disqualified is itself possibly unnecessary (Rambam *Sefer Avoda, Hilkhot Biat HaMikdash* 5:6 and *Kesef Mishne* there).

אִיבַּעְיָא לְהוּ: טוּמְאָה מַהוּ שֶׁתּוֹעִיל לְקִידּוּשׁ יָדַיִם וְרַגְלַיִם? אִם תִּימְצֵי לוֹמַר יְצִיאָה לָא פָּסְלָה – דְּגַבְרָא חֲזִי, אֲבָל הָכָא דְּגַבְרָא לָא חֲזִי אַסּוּחֵי מַסַּח דַּעְתֵּיהּ. אוֹ דִּלְמָא כֵּיוָן דַּהֲדַר חֲזִי – [דַּק לֵיהּ] וְלָא מַסַּח דַּעְתֵּיהּ?

§ **A dilemma was raised before** the Sages: **What is the** *halakha* with regard to a priest who contracts **ritual impurity**[N] during the service? Is this **effective to** disqualify the **sanctification of** his **hands and feet** such that he must sanctify them again when he becomes pure? **If you say** that **leaving** the Temple **does not disqualify** sanctification, perhaps this is **because the person** remains **fit** to serve; **but here, where the person is unfit** for service, perhaps **he becomes distracted. Or perhaps, since he** will become **fit again** when he becomes pure, **he takes care not to become distracted.**

תָּא שְׁמַע: קִידֵּשׁ יָדָיו וְרַגְלָיו וְנִטְמְאוּ – מַטְבִּילָן, וְאֵין צָרִיךְ לְקַדֵּשׁ.

The Gemara suggests: **Come** and **hear** a proof from a *baraita*: If a priest **sanctified his hands and feet and they became impure,**[H] **he** may **immerse them, and he does not need to sanctify** them again.

נִטְמְאוּ יָדָיו – לָא מִיבַּעְיָא לָן, [כִּי מִיבַּעְיָא לָן] נִטְמָא כָּל גּוּפוֹ. כָּל גּוּפוֹ, תֵּיפוֹק לִי כֵּיוָן דְּבָעֵי לְמֶעֱבַד הַעֲרֵב שֶׁמֶשׁ – אַסּוּחֵי מַסַּח דַּעְתֵּיהּ! כְּגוֹן דְּאִיטְּמֵי סָמוּךְ לִשְׁקִיעַת הַחַמָּה.

The Gemara responds: **We do not raise the dilemma** with regard to a case where only **his hands became impure. When we raise the dilemma** it is with regard to a case where **his entire body became impure.**[H] The Gemara challenges: But if **his entire body** contracted impurity, **let me derive** that the sanctification is disqualified **since he needs to allow the sun to set**[N] in order to become pure after immersing, and **he** certainly **becomes distracted** in the interim. The Gemara responds: The dilemma concerns a case **where he became impure adjacent to sunset,** so that he does not need to wait long after immersing and will not become distracted.

תָּא שְׁמַע: פָּרָה, רַבִּי חִיָּיא בְּרַבִּי יוֹסֵף אָמַר: מְקַדֵּשׁ בִּכְלִי שָׁרֵת בִּפְנִים וְיוֹצֵא, וְרַבִּי יוֹחָנָן אָמַר: אֲפִילּוּ בַּחוּץ, וַאֲפִילּוּ בִּכְלִי חוֹל, וַאֲפִילּוּ בִּמְקֵידָה שֶׁל חֶרֶס.

The Gemara suggests: **Come** and **hear** a proof from the following dispute: With regard to the priest who performs the rite of the red **heifer, Rabbi Ḥiyya, son of Rabbi Yosef, says:** He must **sanctify** his hands and feet **with a service vessel inside** the Temple, **and** afterward he **leaves** the Temple to perform the service. **And Rabbi Yoḥanan says:** He may sanctify his hands **even outside** of the Temple, **and even with a non-sacred vessel, and even with an earthenware bowl.**

Perek **II**
Daf **21** Amud **a**

HALAKHA

They would render the priest who burns the heifer ritually impure – מְטַמְּאִין הָיוּ הַכֹּהֵן הַשּׂוֹרֵף אֶת הַפָּרָה: During the Second Temple period, the priest who burned the red heifer would be intentionally rendered impure by contact with the carcass of a creeping animal or a similar source of impurity, and he would then immerse and perform the ritual immediately. This was done to counter the opinion of the Sadducees, who deemed such a priest unfit to perform the ritual before nightfall (Rambam *Sefer Tahara, Hilkhot Para Aduma* 1:14).

NOTES

One who immersed that day is not unfit – טְבוּל יוֹם לָא פְּסִיל: This exception is derived from the verses describing the service of the red heifer (see 17b). Rashi explains that due to this exception, the service of the red heifer cannot serve as evidence to prove a point about the Temple service generally. Alternatively, one may explain that since one who immersed that day is considered pure with regard to the red heifer ritual, one cannot draw any parallel between him and those who are impure with regard to the service generally.

וְהָא פָּרָה, דְּטַמּוּיֵי מְטַמְּינַן לֵיהּ, דִּתְנַן: מְטַמְּאִין הָיוּ הַכֹּהֵן הַשּׂוֹרֵף אֶת הַפָּרָה וּמַטְבִּילִין אוֹתוֹ, לְהוֹצִיא מִלִּבָּן שֶׁל צְדוֹקִין, שֶׁהָיוּ אוֹמְרִים בִּמְעוֹרְבֵי שֶׁמֶשׁ הָיְתָה נַעֲשֵׂית; שְׁמַע מִינַּהּ, לָא פָּסְלָה בָּהּ (מַחֲשֶׁבֶת) טוּמְאָה!

And in preparation for the rite of the red **heifer, we** intentionally **impart impurity to** the priest after he has already sanctified his hands and feet, **as we learned** in a mishna (*Para* 3:7): **They would render the priest who burns the heifer ritually impure**[H] **and immerse him** immediately, **to remove** a misconception **from the hearts of** the **Sadducees** by means of a public display of disregard for their ruling. **As the Sadducees would say:** Only **by those for whom the sun set was** the heifer ritual **performed.** The Sadducees believed that it is prohibited for an impure priest who immersed that day to burn the red heifer until sunset, when the purification process is completed. The Gemara concludes: Since this impurity does not disqualify the sanctification of his hands and feet, **learn from it** that **impurity does not disqualify** sanctification of the hands and feet in general.

שָׁאנֵי פָּרָה, הוֹאִיל דִּטְבוּל יוֹם לָא פְּסִיל בָּהּ. אִי הָכִי, לָמָּה לִי דִּמְקַדֵּשׁ? כְּעֵין עֲבוֹדָה [בָּעֵינַן].

The Gemara responds: The service of the **heifer is different, as one who immersed that day is not unfit**[N] for performing **it,** unlike any other rite. Likewise, impurity does not disqualify the sanctification of hands and feet preceding the service of the heifer. The Gemara asks: **If so, why do I** require **that** the priest **sanctify** his hands and feet at all for the service of the red heifer? The Gemara responds: **We require** that the service of the red heifer be **similar to** the **service** of offerings performed inside the Temple.

אִיבַּעְיָא לְהוּ: מַהוּ לְקַדֵּשׁ יָדָיו [וְרַגְלָיו] בַּכִּיּוֹר? ״מִמֶּנּוּ״ אָמַר רַחֲמָנָא – וְלֹא בְּתוֹכוֹ, אוֹ דִּלְמָא אֲפִילּוּ בְּתוֹכוֹ?

§ **A dilemma was raised before** the Sages: **What is** the *halakha* with regard to a priest who wishes **to sanctify his hands and feet** by dipping them **in the Basin**[H] rather than letting the water run from it onto them? Must one say that the priest may not do so, since **the Merciful One states:** "And Aaron and his sons shall wash their hands and their feet **from it**" (Exodus 30:19), **and not inside it? Or perhaps** the priest may **even** use water still **inside it.**[N]

אֲמַר רַב נַחְמָן בַּר יִצְחָק, תָּא שְׁמַע: אוֹ שֶׁטָּבַל בְּמֵי מְעָרָה וְעָבַד – עֲבוֹדָתוֹ פְּסוּלָה. הָא מֵי כִּיּוֹר דּוּמְיָא דְּמֵי מְעָרָה וְעָבַד – עֲבוֹדָתוֹ כְּשֵׁרָה.

Rav Naḥman bar Yitzḥak said: Come and hear a proof from a *baraita*: **Or if** a priest **immersed in cave water and performed** the **service, his service is disqualified,** since this is not adequate sanctification of the hands and feet. From the *baraita* one infers: **But if** he used **water from the Basin** in a manner **similar to cave water,**[N] i.e., by immersing his hands, **and performed** the **service, his service is valid.**

לָא, מֵי מְעָרָה אִיצְטְרִיכָא לֵיהּ, שֶׁלֹּא תֹּאמַר: כׇּל גּוּפוֹ טוֹבֵל בָּהֶן, יָדָיו וְרַגְלָיו לֹא כׇּל שֶׁכֵּן?

The Gemara responds: **No,** it is possible that immersing one's hands in the Basin is insufficient as well. Nevertheless, it **was necessary** for the *baraita* to mention **cave water so that you shall not say:** If one **may immerse his entire body in** cave water to purify himself, **all the more so** is it **not** clear that he may sanctify **his hands and feet** by immersing them in cave water? The *baraita* therefore teaches that despite being fit for immersion of the entire body, cave water is unfit for sanctification of the hands and feet.

אָמַר רַבִּי חִיָּיא בַּר יוֹסֵף: מֵי כִּיּוֹר נִפְסָלִין לְמַתִּירִין כְּמַתִּירִין, לְאֵבָרִים כְּאֵבָרִים.

§ **Rabbi Ḥiyya bar Yosef says: The water in the Basin is disqualified** by being left out, at different times of day for different rites. **For** rites that are **permitting factors** for an offering, i.e., that must be performed before the meat of the offering may be eaten, the water is disqualified at sunset, **like the permitting factors**[N] themselves, which may be performed only during the day. For example, if a priest wishes to sprinkle an offering's blood on the altar, he may not sanctify his hands and feet from the Basin unless it was sunk into its pit at sunset on the previous day, preventing the water from being disqualified. Similarly, **for** the burning of the offering's **limbs** on the altar, which may be performed all night, the water in the Basin is disqualified at dawn, **like the limbs** themselves.

רַב חִסְדָּא אָמַר: אַף לְמַתִּירִין אֵין נִפְסָלִין אֶלָּא בְּעַמּוּד הַשַּׁחַר, כְּאֵבָרִין. וְרַבִּי יוֹחָנָן אָמַר: כִּיּוֹר, כֵּיוָן שֶׁשִּׁיקְּעוֹ – שׁוּב אֵין מַעֲלֵהוּ.

Rav Ḥisda says: Even for the performance of **permitting factors,** the water **is disqualified only at dawn,**[N] **as** it is for the burning of the **limbs. And Rabbi Yoḥanan says: Once** one **has sunk** the Basin into its pit at the end of the day's service, reconnecting the water in the Basin to flowing water to prevent it from being disqualified, **he may not raise it up again** the entire night.

HALAKHA

To sanctify his hands…by dipping them in the Basin – לְקַדֵּשׁ יָדָיו...בַּכִּיּוֹר: A priest may not sanctify his hands and feet in the Basin itself or in any other service vessel; he must do so in water running from it. The dilemma is unresolved in the Gemara, and therefore the Rambam deems the practice prohibited *ab initio*. After the fact, rites performed are deemed valid, so as to avoid the possibility of bringing an unjustified replacement offering (Rambam *Sefer Avoda, Hilkhot Biat HaMikdash* 5:11 and *Kesef Mishne* there).

NOTES

Or perhaps even inside it – אוֹ דִּלְמָא אֲפִילּוּ בְּתוֹכוֹ: According to this opinion, the term "from it" may be interpreted to exclude water from another vessel, rather than excluding water still inside the Basin. It may also be interpreted as teaching only that it is permitted to sanctify one's hands with water running from the Basin, on the assumption that immersion is more obviously permitted as it is mandated for purification of the entire body in a ritual bath.

Water from the Basin in a manner similar to cave water, etc. – מֵי כִּיּוֹר דּוּמְיָא דְּמֵי מְעָרָה וכו׳: If immersion of the hands and feet in the Basin were insufficient, the *baraita* should have listed it and allowed the *halakha* with regard to cave water to be inferred *a fortiori*, since it is clearly less preferable than the water of the Basin itself.

For rites that are permitting factors, the water is like the permitting factors – לְמַתִּירִין כְּמַתִּירִין: In such a case, the Basin must be sunk into its pit before sunset to connect its water to the underground spring, so it will not be considered to have remained in the vessel at sunset. Moreover, the water in the Basin is disqualified with regard to permitting factors if it was raised at any point during the night, since the entire night is unfit for performance of the offering's permitting factors. If the Basin is raised during the day, this does not disqualify the water with regard to the burning of limbs on the altar, since this service may be performed during the day as well. The water is disqualified in this respect only at dawn itself.

Rabbi Ḥiyya bar Yosef's reasoning is as follows: Since the water in the Basin is not itself an offering but is necessary in order to allow the performance of particular rites, it is disqualified by being left out only insofar as the respective rites would themselves have been disqualified.

Even for permitting factors, it is disqualified only at dawn, etc. – אַף לְמַתִּירִין אֵין נִפְסָלִין אֶלָּא בְּעַמּוּד הַשַּׁחַר וכו׳: The reasoning behind this claim is as follows: Since the water in the Basin is not designated in preparation for any specific rite, it is disqualified only after the time for the day's entire service has elapsed, at dawn the following day. According to the *Shita Mekubbetzet*, the reason is that since the water in the Basin is in a service vessel, it is disqualified at dawn like any offering placed in a service vessel.

NOTES

Is this to say, etc. – לְמֵימְרָא וכו׳: The Gemara assumes at this point that according to Rabbi Yoḥanan, raising the Basin at any point during the night would disqualify the water in it, even for sanctification in preparation for the night's service.

לְמֵימְרָא דְּלַעֲבוֹדַת לַיְלָה נַמִּי לָא חֲזֵי? וְהָאָמַר רַבִּי אַסִּי אָמַר רַבִּי יוֹחָנָן מִשְּׁמֵיהּ דְּאִילְפָא: כִּיּוֹר שֶׁלֹּא שִׁקְּעוֹ מִבָּעֶרֶב – מְקַדֵּשׁ מִמֶּנּוּ לַעֲבוֹדַת לַיְלָה, וּלְמָחָר אֵינוֹ מְקַדֵּשׁ!

The Gemara asks: **Is this to say**[N] **that** if the Basin was not sunk before sunset the water inside is **unfit for the night's service as well? But doesn't Rabbi Asi say that Rabbi Yoḥanan says in the name of Ilfa:** With regard to **a Basin that** the priests **did not sink** into its pit **at night,** a priest **sanctifies** his hands and feet **from it for the service of** that **night, and the next day he does not sanctify** from it? Apparently, for purposes of the night's service, the water in the Basin is not disqualified at sunset.

מַאי "אֵינוֹ מַעֲלֵהוּ" נַמִּי דְּקָאָמַר – לַעֲבוֹדַת יוֹם, אֲבָל לַעֲבוֹדַת לַיְלָה חֲזֵי.

The Gemara responds: **What** does it mean **when it says: He may not raise it up** again? It means that he may not raise it to sanctify his hands and feet in preparation **for the day's service; but** the water **is fit** for sanctification **for the night's service.**

[אִי הָכִי], הַיְינוּ דְּרַבִּי חִיָּיא בַּר יוֹסֵף!

The Gemara asks: **If so, this is** the same as the opinion **of Rabbi Ḥiyya bar Yosef,** i.e., that for purposes of the day's service the water in the Basin is disqualified at sunset, and for purposes of the night's service it is disqualified at dawn.

Perek **II**
Daf **21** Amud **b**

NOTES

Decree of sinking – גְּזֵירַת שִׁיקּוּעַ: The commentaries disagree with regard to the nature of this decree. The translation here follows the explanation of Rashi, who holds that Rabbi Yoḥanan agrees in principle with Rav Ḥisda that the water in the Basin is only ever disqualified at dawn. His opinion differs in that the Basin must remain sunk all night by rabbinic decree, lest it be inadvertently left raised at dawn. Others understand that Rabbi Yoḥanan agrees in principle with Rabbi Ḥiyya bar Yosef that if the Basin is raised at night the water is disqualified for sanctification prior to rites performed during the day, but not for rites that may be performed at night. Still, Rabbi Yoḥanan holds that if the Basin is raised at night the water may not be used even in the latter capacity due to rabbinic decree, lest the priests come to use it in preparation for the day's rites, or lest the Basin be inadvertently left raised at dawn.

Some understand that the rabbinic decree not only prohibits the raising of the Basin at night *ab initio*, but renders the water inside disqualified entirely by rabbinic law (see *Tosafot*).

אִיכָּא בֵּינַיְיהוּ: גְּזֵירַת שִׁיקּוּעַ.

The Gemara responds: The difference **between them** is that according to Rabbi Ḥiyya bar Yosef, if the water is raised at any point throughout the night, it is disqualified for sanctification prior to the day's services. According to Rabbi Yoḥanan, the water is not disqualified unless the Basin is raised at the break of dawn, but the Sages issued a rabbinic **decree of sinking**[N] the Basin into its pit all night *ab initio*, so that it would not be raised at dawn accidentally.

וְהָאָמַר רַבִּי יוֹחָנָן: קִידֵּשׁ יָדָיו לִתְרוּמַת הַדֶּשֶׁן – לְמָחָר אֵין צָרִיךְ לְקַדֵּשׁ, שֶׁכְּבָר קִידֵּשׁ מִתְּחִילַּת עֲבוֹדָה!

The Gemara asks: Does Rabbi Yoḥanan really hold that the Basin must be sunk all night? **But doesn't Rabbi Yoḥanan say:** If a priest **sanctified his hands** and feet in preparation **for the removal of the ashes** before dawn, then **the next day he does not need to sanctify** them again, **as he already sanctified** them **at the beginning of** the day's **service?** Evidently, the Basin is raised before dawn.

בִּשְׁלָמָא לְרָבָא דְּמוֹקֵים לְהַהִיא כְּרַבִּי אֶלְעָזָר בְּרַבִּי שִׁמְעוֹן – הָא כְּרַבִּי.

The Gemara elaborates: **Granted, according to Rava, who interprets that** statement **in accordance with** the opinion of **Rabbi Elazar, son of Rabbi Shimon,** that sanctification of the hands and feet is not disqualified overnight (see 20a), **this** statement that the Basin must be sunk all night is **in accordance with** the opinion of **Rabbi** Yehuda HaNasi, who holds that sanctification of the hands and feet is disqualified at dawn. Accordingly, he holds that the water in the Basin is disqualified as well.

אֶלָּא לְאַבָּיֵי דְּמוֹקֵים לַהּ כְּרַבִּי – קַשְׁיָא דְּרַבִּי אַדְּרַבִּי: מַאי שְׁנָא הָתָם דִּמְשַׁקַּע לֵיהּ, וּמַאי שְׁנָא הָכָא דְּלָא מְשַׁקַּע לֵיהּ?

But according to Abaye, who interprets that statement **in accordance with** the opinion of **Rabbi** Yehuda HaNasi, the first statement **of Rabbi** Yehuda HaNasi is **difficult** to reconcile **with** this other statement **of Rabbi** Yehuda HaNasi: **What is different there that** one must **sink** the Basin all night, **and what is different here,** with regard to sanctification prior to removal of the ashes, **that** one does **not** need to **sink it?**

דִּמְסַלֵּק לֵיהּ וַהֲדַר מְשַׁקַּע לֵיהּ.

The Gemara responds: There is no contradiction. Prior to removal of the ashes, one **raises** the Basin **and then sinks it again** so that it will not remain raised at dawn and render the water disqualified.

אִי הָכִי, לְמָחָר אֵינוֹ מְקַדֵּשׁ, [אַמַּאי? אֵין צָרִיךְ לְקַדֵּשׁ].

The Gemara asks: **If so, why** does Rabbi Yoḥanan say that the priest does **not sanctify** his hands and feet again **the next day?** If the water has not been disqualified, why would the priest need to avoid sanctifying his hands and feet with it? The Gemara responds: Rabbi Yoḥanan means to say that **he does not need to sanctify** them again for service on the same day, not that he is prohibited from doing so.

לְמֵימְרָא דִּלְמַתִּירִין מִיחֲזָא חֲזִי – הַיְינוּ דְּרַב חִסְדָּא!

The Gemara asks: **Is this to say that** according to Rabbi Yoḥanan, if one raised the Basin at night and sank it again before dawn, it remains **fit** for sanctification prior to performing the offering's **permitting factors** that day? If so, Rabbi Yoḥanan's opinion **is** the same as that **of Rav Ḥisda.**

אִיכָּא בֵּינַיְיהוּ: מִצְוַת שִׁיקּוּעַ.

The Gemara responds: The difference **between them** is that according to Rav Ḥisda, there is no **mitzva of sinking**[N] the Basin into its pit throughout the night, whereas Rabbi Yoḥanan holds that there is a mitzva of sinking the Basin into its pit all night *ab initio*.

מֵיתִיבֵי: לֹא הָיוּ רוֹאִין אוֹתוֹ וְלֹא שׁוֹמְעִין אֶת קוֹלוֹ, עַד שֶׁשּׁוֹמְעִים קוֹל שֶׁל עֵץ שֶׁעָשָׂה בֶּן קָטִין מוּכָנִי לַכִּיּוֹר, וְהֵן אוֹמְרִים: הִגִּיעַ [עֵת] קִידּוּשׁ יָדַיִם וְרַגְלַיִם מִן הַכִּיּוֹר; מַאי לָאו דִּמְסַלֵּק לֵיהּ? אַלְמָא מְשַׁקַּע לֵיהּ!

The Gemara **raises an objection** to the opinion of Rav Ḥisda from a mishna (*Tamid* 28b): The priests **would not see** the priest performing the removal of the ashes, **nor would they hear his voice.** Rather, they were unaware of his actions **until they would hear the sound of the wood** with **which ben Katin made a mechanism for** sinking **the Basin** into water during the night. **And** when they heard the sound of the mechanism, **they would say** to each other: **The time for sanctifying hands and feet from the Basin has come.** The Gemara asks: **What, is it not that** they heard the mechanism **raising** the Basin? **Apparently,** the mechanism would **sink it** during the night, in contradiction to the opinion of Rav Ḥisda, who holds that there was no need to sink it overnight.

לָא, דִּמְשַׁקַּע לֵיהּ. אִי דִּמְשַׁקַּע לֵיהּ, מִי מִשְׁתַּמַּע קָלֵיהּ? מְשַׁקַּע לֵיהּ בְּגִילְגְּלָא.

The Gemara responds: **No,** they heard the mechanism **sinking** the Basin, which had been raised all night. The Gemara asks: **If** the mechanism were **sinking it, would its sound be audible?** No mechanism is necessary to lower the Basin; it can simply be lowered with a chain. The Gemara responds: The priest would still **sink it by** using **a wheel,** which would make a sound.

לִישָּׁנָא אַחֲרִינָא: דִּמְשַׁקַּע לֵיהּ בְּחוּמְרָתֵיהּ, כִּי הֵיכִי דְּלִישְׁתַּמַּע קָלֵיהּ וְלִשְׁמְעֵי וְלֵיתֵי. וְהָא הֲוָה גְּבִינִי כָּרוֹז! בֵּי תְּרֵי הֶיכֵּרֵי הָווּ עָבְדִי, דְּשָׁמַע מֵהַאי – אָתֵי, וְשָׁמַע מֵהַאי – אָתֵי.

The Gemara presents **another version** of the answer: The priest would deliberately **sink it by its wheel**[N] **so that its sound would be audible, and** the other priests **would hear and come** to begin the service. The Gemara asks: **But wasn't there Gevini** the **crier,**[B] who would notify the priests of the beginning of the service? The Gemara responds: **They would make two conspicuous markers** for the beginning of the service: The sound of the wheel and the crier. Anyone **who heard from this** marker **would come, and** anyone who **heard from that** marker **would come.**

גּוּפָא, אָמַר רַבִּי יוֹסֵי בְּרַבִּי חֲנִינָא: כׇּל כִּיּוֹר שֶׁאֵין בּוֹ כְּדֵי לְקַדֵּשׁ אַרְבָּעָה כֹּהֲנִים מִמֶּנּוּ – אֵין מְקַדְּשִׁין בּוֹ, שֶׁנֶּאֱמַר: ״וְרָחֲצוּ מִמֶּנּוּ מֹשֶׁה וְאַהֲרֹן וּבָנָיו״ וגו׳.

§ Having mentioned a *halakha* earlier (19b), the Gemara addresses **the** matter **itself: Rabbi Yosei, son of Rabbi Ḥanina, says:** With regard to **any Basin that does not contain enough** water **for four priests to sanctify** their hands and feet **from it,** the priests **may not sanctify** their hands and feet **with it, as it is stated: "That Moses and Aaron and his sons might wash** their hands and their feet **from it"** (Exodus 40:31).

מֵיתִיבֵי: כׇּל הַכֵּלִים מְקַדְּשִׁין, בֵּין שֶׁיֵּשׁ בָּהֶן רְבִיעִית,

The Gemara **raises an objection** from a *baraita*: The priests may **sanctify** their hands and feet from **all vessels, whether they can hold a quarter-*log***[N] of water

BACKGROUND

Crier – כָּרוֹז: The crier was responsible for keeping time in the Temple. He or one of his men would announce, at the proper time: Arise, priests to your services, Levites to your platforms, and Israelites to your posts. It is recounted that the crier's voice could be heard at a distance of three parasangs.

NOTES

Mitzva of sinking – מִצְוַת שִׁיקּוּעַ: Although Rav Ḥisda agrees that the Basin must be sunk before dawn, Rabbi Yoḥanan holds that it must be sunk all night (Rashi). According to *Tosefot Rabbeinu Peretz*, Rav Ḥisda concedes even that the Basin must be sunk at the beginning of the night. His opinion differs from that of Rabbi Yoḥanan only in that he holds that if raised during the night, the Basin need not be lowered again immediately, but may remain raised until soon before dawn.

Sink it by its wheel – מְשַׁקַּע לֵיהּ בְּחוּמְרָתֵיהּ: According to Rashi, there is no difference in the content of the two answers, which merely use two different words to describe the wheel. According to *Tosafot*, the second answer posits that the mechanism would make a sound as it lowered the Basin, while according to the first answer, the Basin would be lowered on a wheel only so that it would make a sound when raised again.

Quarter-*log* – רְבִיעִית: This is a liquid measure, held by some to be the equivalent of 86 cc and by others 150 cc. It is certainly less than the amount necessary for four priests to sanctify their hands and feet. In several contexts, a quarter-*log* serves as a standard unit of measurement. For example, it is the minimum amount of wine over which *kiddush* may be recited; it is the amount of wine for which a nazirite receives lashes if he drinks it; and it is the minimum amount of certain foods which, if one transfers them from one domain to another on Shabbat, render one liable for transgressing the prohibition against carrying on Shabbat.

NOTES

Drills [*kode'ah*] – קוֹדֵחַ: Rashi interprets the word *kode'ah* as meaning to drill, referring to one who drills a hole in the Basin and attaches a small service vessel to it. The Basin itself must hold enough water for four priests, but the small vessel need not. According to *Tosafot*, the word *kode'ah* means to draw water from the Basin using a small service vessel. The word is used in both senses in other contexts.

From it, etc. – מִמֶּנּוּ וכו׳: Rashi interprets this challenge as directed not at Rav Adda bar Aha's statement but at the *baraita* itself, which states that one may sanctify the hands and feet from any service vessel.

A fortiori from the base of the Basin – קַל וָחוֹמֶר מִכַּנּוֹ: The base of the Basin was shaped like an overturned bowl or box and could contain water (see *Tosafot* and *Hok Natan*).

I have equated [*hikkashtiv*] – הִקַּשְׁתִּיו: In halakhic midrash, this term usually denotes the juxtaposition of two subjects in the Torah in order to indicate that they share some feature. Here, the equation of the Basin and its base with regard to their material is explicit in the verse (Rashi). According to the *Sefat Emet*, it is the redundant repetition of the word "copper" in the verse that teaches that this is the only feature that the Basin and its base must share.

בֵּין שֶׁאֵין בָּהֶן רְבִיעִית, וּבִלְבַד שֶׁיְּהוּ כְּלֵי שָׁרֵת!

or they cannot hold a quarter-*log* of water, provided that they are service vessels. Apparently, the Basin need not hold so much water.

אָמַר רַב אַדָּא בַּר אַהֲבָה: בְּקוֹדֵחַ בְּתוֹכוֹ.

Rav Adda bar Aha says: The *baraita* is referring to a case **where one drills**[N][H] a hole **in** the Basin and places a much smaller vessel at the hole as a conduit for the water. Even if that vessel is very small, the priest may sanctify his hands and feet from it, provided that there is enough water in the Basin for four priests.

וְהָא "מִמֶּנּוּ" אָמַר רַחֲמָנָא! "יִרְחֲצוּ" – לְרַבּוֹת כְּלֵי שָׁרֵת.

The Gemara asks: **But doesn't the Merciful One state** that the priests must wash their hands and feet **"from it,"**[N] i.e., from the Basin and not from another vessel? The Gemara responds: The following verse repeats the phrase **"they should wash," to include** any **service vessel.**

אִי הָכִי, כְּלִי חוֹל נָמֵי! אָמַר אַבָּיֵי: כְּלִי חוֹל לָא מָצֵית אָמְרַתְּ, מִקַּל וָחוֹמֶר מִכַּנּוֹ: וּמָה כַּנּוֹ שֶׁנִּמְשַׁח עִמּוֹ – אֵינוֹ מְקַדֵּשׁ, כְּלִי חוֹל שֶׁאֵינוֹ נִמְשַׁח עִמּוֹ – אֵינוֹ דִּין שֶׁאֵינוֹ מְקַדֵּשׁ?

The Gemara challenges: **If so,** then it should be permitted for a priest to use **a non-sacred vessel as well. Abaye says: You cannot say** that a priest may sanctify his hands and feet from **a non-sacred vessel,** since the matter may be derived **by *a fortiori*** inference **from** the *halakha* concerning **the base of** the Basin:[N] **And just as its base, which was anointed along with it** (see Exodus 40:11), **is** still **not** fit for a priest to **sanctify** his hands and feet with water from it, then with regard to **a non-sacred vessel, which was not anointed along with** the Basin, **is it not right that it is not** fit for a priest to **sanctify** his hands and feet with water from it?

וְכַנּוֹ מְנָלַן? דְּתַנְיָא, רַבִּי יְהוּדָה אוֹמֵר: יָכוֹל יְהֵא כַּנּוֹ מְקַדֵּשׁ כְּדֶרֶךְ שֶׁהַכִּיּוֹר מְקַדֵּשׁ – תַּלְמוּד לוֹמַר: "וְעָשִׂיתָ כִּיּוֹר נְחֹשֶׁת וְכַנּוֹ נְחֹשֶׁת" – לִנְחֹשֶׁת הִקַּשְׁתִּיו וְלֹא לְדָבָר אַחֵר.

The Gemara clarifies: **And from where do we** derive that water from **the base of** the Basin is unfit? **As it is taught** in a *baraita* that **Rabbi Yehuda says:** One **might** have thought that water from **its base should be** fit for priests to **sanctify** their hands and feet **just as** water from **the Basin** itself is fit to **sanctify** their hands and feet. Therefore, **the verse states: "You shall also make a Basin of copper, and the base thereof of copper"** (Exodus 30:18). The verse indicates that **I have equated**[N] the base and the Basin only **with regard to** the requirement that they both be made of **copper, but not for another matter.** Rather, the base, unlike the Basin, is unfit for sanctification.

אָמַר לֵיהּ מָר זוּטְרָא בְּרֵיהּ דְּרַב מָרִי לְרָבִינָא: מָה לְכַנּוֹ – שֶׁאֵין עָשׂוּי לְתוֹכוֹ, תֹּאמַר בִּכְלִי חוֹל שֶׁעָשׂוּי לְתוֹכוֹ! אֶלָּא: "מִמֶּנּוּ" – לְמַעוּטֵי כְּלִי חוֹל.

Mar Zutra, son of Rav Mari, said to Ravina: The *a fortiori* inference can be refuted: **What** is notable **about its base?** It is notable **in that its inside is not made for** use, as it is to be used only as a stand. Will **you say** that the *halakha* is the same **for a non-sacred vessel,** concerning **which its inside is made for** use? **Rather,** one must say that the term **"from it"** serves **to exclude a non-sacred vessel.**[H]

אִי הָכִי, כְּלִי שָׁרֵת נָמֵי! הָא רַבֵּי רַחֲמָנָא "יִרְחֲצוּ".

The Gemara challenges: **If so,** "from it" should exclude **a service vessel as well.** The Gemara responds: **But the Merciful One amplifies** the *halakha* with the term **"they should wash,"** to include a service vessel.

וּמָה רָאִיתָ? זֶה טָעוּן מְשִׁיחָה כְּמוֹהוּ, וְזֶה אֵין טָעוּן מְשִׁיחָה כְּמוֹהוּ.

The Gemara asks: **And what did you see** that led you to include a service vessel and exclude a non-sacred vessel, rather than the reverse? The Gemara responds: **This,** a service vessel, **requires anointing like** the Basin when the Tabernacle is raised (see Exodus, chapter 40), **and that,** a non-sacred vessel, **does not require anointing like** the Basin.

HALAKHA

Where one drills – בְּקוֹדֵחַ: One may sanctify his hands and feet from any service vessel, even one that does not hold a quarter-*log* of water. The Ra'avad writes that this applies only when one draws the water into that vessel from the Basin, which must contain enough water for four priests to sanctify their hands and feet (Rambam *Sefer Avoda, Hilkhot Biat HaMikdash* 5:11, and see *Kesef Mishne* there).

To exclude a non-sacred vessel – לְמַעוּטֵי כְּלִי חוֹל: It is a mitzva to sanctify the hands and feet from water in the Basin. If one sanctified them from another service vessel, the sanctification is valid. One may not use a non-sacred vessel (Rambam *Sefer Avoda, Hilkhot Biat HaMikdash* 5:10).

אָמַר רֵישׁ לָקִישׁ: כׇּל הַמַּשְׁלִים לְמֵי מִקְוֶה מַשְׁלִים לְמֵי כִּיּוֹר, לִרְבִיעִית – אֵינוֹ מַשְׁלִים.

§ **Reish Lakish says: Any** liquid **that** may be used to **complete**[H] the requisite measure of **water for a ritual bath**[B] **may complete** the requisite measure of **water for the Basin.** But **it may not complete** the **quarter-*log*** required for ritual washing of the hands.

לְמַעוּטֵי מַאי? אִילֵימָא לְמַעוּטֵי טִיט הַנָּדוֹק; הֵיכִי דָּמֵי? אִי דְּפָרָה שׁוֹחָה וְשׁוֹתָה מִמֶּנּוּ – אֲפִילּוּ לִרְבִיעִית נָמֵי, וְאִי אֵין פָּרָה שׁוֹחָה וְשׁוֹתָה מִמֶּנּוּ – אֲפִילּוּ לְמִקְוֶה נָמֵי אֵין מַשְׁלִים!

The Gemara asks: This statement means **to exclude what** as unfit for completing the requisite measure for ritual washing of the hands? **If we say** that it means **to exclude liquefied clay,**[NH] there is a difficulty, as **what is this clay like? If** it is such **that a cow can kneel and drink from it,** it is considered water and should be fit **even to** complete the measure of **a quarter-*log*** for ritual washing of the hands. **And if a cow cannot kneel and drink from it,** it **should not even** be fit to **complete** the requisite measure for **a ritual bath.**

אֶלָּא לְמַעוּטֵי יַבְחוּשִׁין אֲדוּמִּין – אֲפִילּוּ בְּעֵינַיְיהוּ נָמֵי, דְּהָא תַּנְיָא, רַבָּן שִׁמְעוֹן בֶּן גַּמְלִיאֵל אוֹמֵר: כׇּל שֶׁתְּחִילַּת בְּרִיָּיתוֹ מִן הַמַּיִם – מַטְבִּילִין בּוֹ; וְאָמַר רַב יִצְחָק בַּר אַבְדִּימִי: מַטְבִּילִין בְּעֵינוֹ שֶׁל דָּג!

Rather, say that it means **to exclude red gnats** that originate and grow in water. This, too, is difficult, as **even by themselves** they may constitute the entire measure of the ritual bath, not only to complete a deficient measure of water; **as it is taught** in a *baraita*: **Rabban Shimon ben Gamliel says:** With regard to **anything that originates in the water,**[H] **one may immerse in it,** since it is considered as though it were water. **And Rav Yitzḥak bar Avdimi says: One may immerse** even **in** liquefied **fish eye** of sufficient volume.

אָמַר רַב פַּפָּא: לְמַעוּטֵי נָתַן סְאָה וְנָטַל סְאָה. דִּתְנַן: מִקְוֶה שֶׁיֵּשׁ בּוֹ אַרְבָּעִים סְאָה מְכוּוָּנוֹת, נָתַן סְאָה וְנָטַל סְאָה – הֲרֵי זֶה כָּשֵׁר. וְאָמַר רַב יְהוּדָה בַּר שֵׁילָא אָמַר רַב אַסִי אָמַר רַבִּי יוֹחָנָן: עַד רוּבּוֹ.

Rav Pappa says: The statement of Reish Lakish means **to exclude** a case where **one added a *se'a***[B] **and removed a *se'a*,**[H] **as we learned** in a mishna (*Mikvaot* 7:2): In the case of **a ritual bath that contains** the minimum measure of **exactly forty *se'a*** of water, and **one added a *se'a*** of liquid other than water, **and** then **removed a *se'a*** of the mixture, the ritual bath remains **fit.** The added liquid is considered nullified in the forty *se'a* of water, so that when one *se'a* of the mixture is removed, there still remain the requisite forty *se'a* of fit water. **And Rav Yehuda bar Sheila says** that **Rav Asi says** that **Rabbi Yoḥanan says** that this *halakha* applies **up to the greater part**[NH] of the measure of the ritual bath. Adding and removing such a liquid to the requisite measure for washing of the hands renders the water unfit.

אָמַר רַב פַּפָּא: אִם קָדַח בּוֹ רְבִיעִית – מַטְבִּילִין בּוֹ מְחָטִין וְצִינּוֹרִיּוֹת, הוֹאִיל וּמֵהֶכְשֵׁירָהּ דְּמִקְוֶה אָתְיָא.

Rav Pappa says: If one drilled[N] in the wall of a ritual bath, and the sides of the hole can hold **a quarter-*log*** of liquid, **one may immerse** small vessels such as **needles**[N] **and hooks**[B] **in** the hole, even though it constitutes a space separate from the ritual bath, **since** the fitness of the water in the hole **derives from the fitness of** the water in **the ritual bath.** This *halakha* is parallel to the one discussed with regard to the Basin.

HALAKHA

Any liquid that may be used to complete, etc. – **כׇּל הַמַּשְׁלִים וכו׳**: Any liquid that may constitute part of the requisite measure of water in a ritual bath may do so for the Basin as well, in accordance with the statement of Reish Lakish (Rambam *Sefer Avoda, Hilkhot Biat HaMikdash* 5:12).

Liquefied clay – **טִיט הַנָּדוֹק**: Liquefied clay from which a cow can drink is counted as part of the volume of a ritual bath, and one must immerse in the clear portion of the bath. It also counts toward the requisite volume of the Basin and toward the quarter-*log* required for washing of the hands. If the clay is so thick that a cow cannot drink from it, it is unfit for all these purposes. In citing this *halakha*, the *Shulḥan Arukh* makes reference to water that was polluted by clay, positing that it is fit to constitute the requisite volume for a ritual bath or washing of the hands provided that a dog is able to drink it (Rambam *Sefer Tahara, Hilkhot Mikvaot* 7:3, 8:9, 11:2; *Shulḥan Arukh, Oraḥ Ḥayyim* 160:9 and *Yoreh De'a* 201:32).

That originates in the water – **שֶׁתְּחִילַּת בְּרִיָּיתוֹ מִן הַמַּיִם**: One may immerse in any substance or item that originates in the water, e.g., red gnats. So too, one may immerse in liquefied fish eye. One may also wash one's hands with these substances. According to the Rema, both the gnats and fish eyes must be liquefied (Rambam *Sefer Tahara, Hilkhot Mikvaot* 8:11; *Shulḥan Arukh, Oraḥ Ḥayyim* 160:10 and *Yoreh De'a* 201:33).

Added a *se'a* and removed a *se'a* – **נָתַן סְאָה וְנָטַל סְאָה**: If a ritual bath contains exactly forty *se'a* of water, and one *se'a* of some other liquid, e.g., fruit juice, liquid in which foods have been pickled, or fermented mead, falls into it, and one then removes one *se'a* of the mixture, the remaining forty *se'a* remain fit as a ritual bath, in accordance with the statement of Rav Pappa (Rambam *Sefer Tahara, Hilkhot Mikvaot* 7:6; *Shulḥan Arukh, Yoreh De'a* 201:24).

Up to the greater part – **עַד רוּבּוֹ**: According to the Rambam, if a ritual bath contains exactly forty *se'a*, and one adds one *se'a* of drawn water and then removes one *se'a* from the mixture, the remainder is fit. One may repeat the procedure until the added water composes the greater part of the volume of liquid in the ritual bath. The *Shulḥan Arukh* rules in accordance with the opinion of the Rosh that this principle holds only with regard to fruit juice and other liquids not fit to constitute part of the ritual bath's volume, but one may add and remove drawn water *ad infinitum* (Rambam *Sefer Tahara, Hilkhot Mikvaot* 4:7; *Shulḥan Arukh, Yoreh De'a* 201:24).

BACKGROUND

Ritual bath – **מִקְוֶה**: Forty *se'a* is the minimum quantity of water necessary for a ritual bath, which is the equivalent of eighty *hin* or 5,760 egg-bulks. The forty-*se'a* measure serves as the basis for all modern calculations of the various talmudic measures of volume, since the Talmud teaches that the dimensions of a ritual bath must be three cubits by one cubit by one cubit; this is the equivalent of forty *se'a* in volume. Consequently, according to the standard method of converting talmudic measurements of Rav Ḥayyim Na'e, a ritual bath must contain 332 ℓ of water, and according to the *Ḥazon Ish*, it must contain 573 ℓ.

Se'a – **סְאָה**: A *se'a* is a measure of dry volume first mentioned in Genesis 18:6. It is used by the Sages as a point of reference for all measures of volume. Every *se'a* contains six *kav*, which equals twenty-four *log*. Estimates of the modern equivalent of a *se'a* range from 7.2 to 14.4 ℓ.

Hooks [*tzinoriyyot*] – **צִינּוֹרִיּוֹת**: This word denotes a long needle, usually made of metal. Some of these had straight ends, some were hooked, and some were forked. These implements were used for various purposes, e.g., knitting, spinning, as tongs, and for catching and holding other items such as hot coals or food. They could also be used as parts for jewelry, hooking rings onto the ear or nose, or as a means for fastening a load onto a wagon.

NOTES

Liquefied [*hannadok*] clay – **טִיט הַנָּדוֹק**: Rashi interprets this as clay watered down to the point of being a liquid, such that it can be poured between vessels. Many sources have a version of the text that reads *hannaruk*, literally meaning: Pourable.

Up to the greater part – **עַד רוּבּוֹ**: According to *Tosafot*, this limitation applies only to liquid not fit to constitute even part of the requisite measure of a ritual bath, e.g., clay. Drawn water, which may constitute part of the measure of a ritual bath, may be added and removed *ad infinitum*. According to the Rambam, this limitation applies specifically to drawn water. The *Kesef Mishne* explains that if it were permitted to add and remove drawn water indefinitely, one might receive the incorrect impression that a ritual bath composed entirely of drawn water is fit.

Drilled [*kadaḥ*] – **קָדַח**: As with regard to the Basin, Rashi interprets this word as denoting drilling, while *Tosafot* interpret it to mean drawing a small amount of water from the ritual bath.

One may immerse needles – **מַטְבִּילִין...מְחָטִין**: By Torah law, a quarter-*log* of water is a sufficient measure for the immersion of vessels, provided that they can be fully immersed in the water. The measure of forty *se'a* is required only for the immersion of people. The Sages decreed that even small vessels must be immersed in a full-sized ritual bath.

NOTES

Water of a ritual bath – **מֵי מִקְוֶה**: Any water that has collected naturally in one place, e.g., rainwater, is fit for use as a ritual bath. All impurity is purged by such water, except that for which the Torah explicitly requires flowing water (see Leviticus 15:13).

But didn't Rabbi Shmuel teach [*tanna*] – **וְהָא תָּנָא רַבִּי שְׁמוּאֵל**: The original context of this statement is unclear (Rashi). It seems that the text should read: *Tanna devei Shmuel*, i.e., the *tanna* of the school of Shmuel. In any event, the statement poses a challenge to the Gemara's reasoning, since it indicates that water dedicated for use in the Basin, which therefore has a modifier, i.e., Basin water, is undesirable, and perhaps even unfit, for rites concerning which the Torah specifies that water be used.

HALAKHA

Not with wine, etc. – **לֹא בְּיַיִן וכו׳**: One must wash the innards of the offerings with water. One may not do so with wine, wine mixed with water, or any other liquid. All types of water are fit (Rambam *Sefer Avoda, Hilkhot Ma'aseh HaKorbanot* 6:6).

אָמַר רַבִּי יִרְמְיָה אָמַר רֵישׁ לָקִישׁ: מֵי מִקְוֶה כְּשֵׁירִים לְמֵי כִּיּוֹר.

§ **Rabbi Yirmeya says** that **Reish Lakish says: Water of a ritual bath**[N] **is fit to** be used as **water of the Basin.**

לְמֵימְרָא, דְּלָא מַיִם חַיִּים נִינְהוּ? וְהָתַנְיָא: "בַּמָּיִם" – וְלֹא בְּיַיִן, "בַּמָּיִם" – וְלֹא בְּמָזוּג, "בַּמָּיִם" – לְרַבּוֹת שְׁאָר מַיִם, וְקַל וָחוֹמֶר לְמֵי כִּיּוֹר. מַאי קַל וָחוֹמֶר לְמֵי כִּיּוֹר? לָאו דְּמַיִם חַיִּים נִינְהוּ?

The Gemara asks: **Is this to say that** the water in the Basin **does not** need to be **flowing water,** i.e., spring water? **But isn't it taught** in a *baraita*: The verse indicates that the innards of an offering must be washed: **"With water"** (Leviticus 1:9), **and not with wine;**[H] **"with water,"** and **not with** wine **mixed** with water; **"with water," to include other** types of **water,** even those that are not spring water. **And** it can be inferred ***a fortiori*** that **the water** used **for the Basin** may be used to wash the innards. **What is** the basis of the ***a fortiori*** inference that **the water** used **for the Basin** may also be used? Is it **not that it is** from a source of **flowing water** and therefore obviously fit for washing the innards?

לָא, (לקדוש) דְּקָדֵישׁ. וְקַדִּישֵׁי מְעַלְּיוּתָא הִיא? וְהָא תָּנָא רַבִּי שְׁמוּאֵל: מַיִם שֶׁאֵין לָהֶם שֵׁם לְוַי,

The Gemara responds: **No,** the *a fortiori* inference is based on the fact **that** the water used for the Basin is **sanctified** for the service. The Gemara asks: **But is sanctified** water **preferable,** given that the Torah stipulates simply "water"? **But didn't Rabbi Shmuel teach:**[N] The word **"water"** used in the verse denotes specifically water **whose name has no modifier;**

Perek **II**
Daf **22** Amud **b**

יָצְאוּ מֵי כִּיּוֹר שֶׁיֵּשׁ לָהֶם שֵׁם לְוַי! אֶלָּא לָאו – דִּרְאוּיִין לְמֵי כִּיּוֹר; אַלְמָא מַיִם חַיִּים נִינְהוּ!

excluded is water of the **Basin, which has a modifier** in its name? **Rather,** since the *baraita* cannot be referring to the water of the Basin itself, as it is unfit for washing the innards, **is it not** referring to water **that is fit to be water of the Basin? Apparently,** the only reason such water could be preferable is because it **is flowing water.**

תַּנָּאֵי הִיא, דְּאָמַר רַבִּי יוֹחָנָן: מֵי כִּיּוֹר, רַבִּי יִשְׁמָעֵאל אוֹמֵר: מֵי מַעְיָן הֵן, וַחֲכָמִים אוֹמְרִים: שְׁאָר מֵימוֹת הֵן.

The Gemara responds: The issue **is** a dispute between ***tanna'im***, **as Rabbi Yoḥanan says:** With regard to **the water of** the **Basin, Rabbi Yishmael says:** It must be **spring water,** i.e., flowing water, **and the Rabbis say:** It may be **another** type of **water.**[H]

"עָרֵל". מְנָלַן? אָמַר רַב חִסְדָּא: דָּבָר זֶה מִתּוֹרַת מֹשֶׁה רַבֵּינוּ לֹא לָמַדְנוּ, מִדִּבְרֵי יְחֶזְקֵאל בֶּן בּוּזִי לָמַדְנוּ: "כָּל בֶּן נֵכָר עֶרֶל לֵב וְעֶרֶל בָּשָׂר לֹא יָבֹא אֶל מִקְדָּשִׁי לְשָׁרְתֵנִי".

§ The mishna teaches that a priest who is **uncircumcised**[H] disqualifies sacrificial rites he performs. The Gemara elaborates: **From where** do we derive this? **Rav Ḥisda says: We did not learn this matter from the Torah of Moses, our teacher;** rather, **we learned** it **from the words of** the prophet **Ezekiel, son of Buzi: "No stranger, uncircumcised in heart or uncircumcised in flesh, shall enter into My Sanctuary to serve Me"** (Ezekiel 44:9).

וּמְנָלַן דִּמְחַלֵּי עֲבוֹדָה? דִּכְתִיב: "בַּהֲבִיאֲכֶם אֶת בְּנֵי נֵכָר עַרְלֵי לֵב וְעַרְלֵי בָשָׂר לִהְיוֹת בְּמִקְדָּשִׁי לְחַלֵּל אֶת בֵּיתִי".

And from where do we derive **that he desecrates** the **service** after the fact? **As it is written: "In that you have brought in strangers, uncircumcised in heart or uncircumcised in flesh, to be in My Sanctuary, to profane My house"** (Ezekiel 44:7).

תָּנוּ רַבָּנַן: "בֶּן נֵכָר" – יָכוֹל בֶּן נֵכָר מַמָּשׁ? תַּלְמוּד לוֹמַר: "עֶרֶל לֵב". אִם כֵּן, מַה תַּלְמוּד לוֹמַר "בֶּן נֵכָר" – שֶׁנִּתְנַכְּרוּ מַעֲשָׂיו לְאָבִיו שֶׁבַּשָּׁמַיִם. וְאֵין לִי אֶלָּא עֶרֶל לֵב, עֶרֶל בָּשָׂר מִנַּיִן? תַּלְמוּד לוֹמַר: "וְעֶרֶל בָּשָׂר".

The Sages taught: The verse states **"stranger";** one **might** have thought that this is referring to **an actual stranger,** i.e., a gentile. Therefore, **the verse states: "Uncircumcised in heart,"** to indicate that it is referring to a priest rather than a gentile. **If so, what** is the meaning when **the verse states: "Stranger"?** It is referring to one **whose actions are** considered **estranged from his Father in Heaven,** i.e., an apostate, who sins regularly. **And I have** derived **only** that **one uncircumcised in heart** is unfit to serve; **from where** is it derived that **one uncircumcised in flesh** is unfit as well? **The verse states: "Or uncircumcised in flesh."**

HALAKHA

It may be another type of water – **שְׁאָר מֵימוֹת הֵן**: All types of water, whether flowing water or collected water, are fit for sanctification of the hands and feet, provided that its appearance is that of water. This ruling is in accordance with the opinion of the Rabbis and Reish Lakish (Rambam *Sefer Avoda, Hilkhot Biat HaMikdash* 5:12).

Uncircumcised – **עָרֵל**: One who is uncircumcised is considered as though he were a gentile, as it is written: "No stranger…or uncircumcised in flesh." Therefore, if one who is uncircumcised performs sacrificial rites, his service is disqualified and he is liable to receive lashes as though he were a non-priest who performed the sacrificial rites. However, he is not liable to be punished with death at the hand of Heaven (Rambam *Sefer Avoda, Hilkhot Biat HaMikdash* 6:8).

וּצְרִיכִי, דְּאִי כְּתַב רַחֲמָנָא "עָרֵל בָּשָׂר" – מִשּׁוּם דִּמְאִיס, אֲבָל עָרֵל לֵב דְּלָא מְאִיס – אֵימָא לָא; וְאִי אַשְׁמְעִינַן עָרֵל לֵב – מִשּׁוּם דְּאֵין לִבּוֹ לַשָּׁמַיִם, אֲבָל עָרֵל בָּשָׂר דְּלִבּוֹ לַשָּׁמַיִם – אֵימָא לָא, צְרִיכִי.

The Gemara notes: **And** both phrases in the verse **are necessary. As, had the Merciful One written** only: **"Uncircumcised in flesh,"** one might think that only he is unfit **because he is disgusting** in that he possesses a foreskin, **but** concerning **one uncircumcised in heart, who is not disgusting, I will say** that he is **not** unfit. **And had** the verse **taught us** only that one **uncircumcised in heart** is unfit, one might think that only he is unfit, **because his heart is not** directed **toward Heaven, but one uncircumcised in flesh, whose heart is** directed **toward Heaven, I will say** that he is **not** unfit. Therefore, both phrases **are necessary.**

"טָמֵא פָּסוּל". אָמְרוּ זִקְנֵי דָרוֹם: לֹא שָׁנוּ אֶלָּא טְמֵא שֶׁרֶץ. אֲבָל טְמֵא מֵת, מִתּוֹךְ שֶׁמְּרַצֶּה בְּצִיבּוּר – מְרַצֶּה נַמִּי בְּיָחִיד.

§ The mishna teaches that a ritually **impure** priest is **unfit** for Temple service and disqualifies rites he performs. **The Elders of the South**[P] **said: They taught** this **only** with regard to one who became **impure due to** contact with the carcass of **a creeping animal.**[N] **But** with regard to a priest who became **impure due to** contact with **a corpse,**[NHB] **since he can effect acceptance** of his rites **for communal** offerings[N] *ab initio* if the majority of the community has contracted impurity from a corpse, **he can effect acceptance**[N] of his rites **for individual** offerings **as well** after the fact.

אִי הָכִי, טְמֵא שֶׁרֶץ נַמִּי לֵיתֵי בְּקַל וָחוֹמֶר מִטְּמֵא מֵת: מַה טְּמֵא מֵת שֶׁטָּעוּן הַזָּאָה שְׁלִישִׁי וּשְׁבִיעִי – מְרַצֶּה, טְמֵא שֶׁרֶץ שֶׁאֵינוֹ טָעוּן הַזָּאָה שְׁלִישִׁי וּשְׁבִיעִי – אֵינוֹ דִּין שֶׁמְּרַצֶּה?

The Gemara asks: **If so, let** it **be derived** that **one impure due to** the carcass of **a creeping animal** can also effect acceptance for communal offerings in cases of communal impurity *ab initio*, and for individual offerings after the fact, **by *a fortiori*** inference **from one impure due to a corpse: Just as** a priest who is **impure due to a corpse, who requires sprinkling** of the water containing the ashes of the red heifer on the **third and seventh** day to be purified, still **effects acceptance,** then with regard to **one** who is **impure due to** the carcass of **a creeping animal, who does not require sprinkling** on the **third and seventh** day, **is it not right that he** should also **effect acceptance?**

קָסָבְרִי זִקְנֵי דָרוֹם: מְכַפְּרִין כְּמִתְכַּפְּרִין, מַה מִּתְכַּפְּרִין – טְמֵא מֵת אִין, טְמֵא שֶׁרֶץ לָא, אַף מְכַפְּרִין – טְמֵא מֵת – אִין, טְמֵא שֶׁרֶץ לָא.

The Gemara responds: **The Elders of the South hold** that the *halakha* with regard to **those who effect atonement** is **like those who achieve atonement: Just as** with regard to **those who achieve atonement** through communal offerings, i.e., the community, only if a majority is **impure due to a corpse may** the offering be sacrificed in a state of impurity, but if they are **impure due to** the carcass of **a creeping animal** it may **not, so too** with regard to **those who effect atonement,** i.e., the priests, if they serve when they are **impure due to a corpse, yes,** their service achieves atonement, but if they serve when they are **impure due to the carcass of a creeping animal,** it does **not.**

מַאי קָסָבְרִי? אִי קָסָבְרִי: אֵין שׁוֹחֲטִין וְזוֹרְקִין עַל טְמֵא שֶׁרֶץ – אַמַּאי לָא עָבְדִי צִיבּוּר בְּטוּמְאָה? הָא כָּל שֶׁבְּיָחִיד נִדְחֶה – צִיבּוּר עָבְדִי בְּטוּמְאָה!

The response of the Gemara assumes that communal offerings may not be brought when the majority of the community is impure due to a creeping animal. The Gemara therefore asks: **What do** the Elders of the South **hold** with regard to the Paschal offering? **If they hold** that **one may not slaughter** it **nor sprinkle** its blood on the altar **for** an owner who is **impure due to a creeping animal,** even though he can immerse and become pure in time to eat the offering that night, then one may ask: **Why can't the community perform** communal offerings **in** such a state of **impurity? Isn't** it a principle that for **any** impurity **for which an individual** may not sacrifice the Paschal offering and **is deferred** to the second *Pesaḥ*, the **community may perform** its offerings **in** such a state of **impurity?**

PERSONALITIES

Elders of the South – זִקְנֵי דָרוֹם: This is a group of Sages that lived in Judea, the South of Eretz Yisrael, especially in Lod and the surrounding area, during the amoraic period. During that period, the majority of the Jews in Eretz Yisrael lived in the Galilee, where the most important Torah centers were located as well. Still, despite the destruction of the Jewish communities of Judea in the revolts against the Romans, some Sages survived there, preserving their own traditions. These traditions are relayed by bar Kappara and Rabbi Yehoshua ben Levi.

NOTES

Impure due to a creeping animal – טְמֵא שֶׁרֶץ: This includes other impurities of the same severity, e.g., that of a leper or a *zav*. Only impurity due to a corpse was permitted for communal offerings.

Impure due to a corpse – טְמֵא מֵת: This is referring specifically to one who has not yet undergone sprinkling of the water of purification. Once the water has been sprinkled upon him on the third and seventh days of the purification process, the impurity is reduced to the level of that contracted from a creeping animal. He need only immerse and will be fully pure at nightfall (*Tosafot*).

Can effect acceptance for communal offerings – שֶׁמְּרַצֶּה בְּצִיבּוּר: The verse states: "Let the children of Israel keep the Passover in its appointed season" (Numbers 9:2), indicating that the Paschal offering must always be sacrificed at its appointed time, even if this means it will be done in a state of impurity. This *halakha* is extended to all offerings that have appointed times.

Additional details with regard to this *halakha* are derived from the continuation of the verses: "If any man of you or of your generations shall be impure by reason of a dead body, or be in a journey afar off, he shall perform the Paschal offering to the Lord. In the second month on the fourteenth day at dusk they shall perform it" (Numbers 9:10–11). From the phrase "any man" it is derived that only individuals are deferred to the second *Pesaḥ*; if the community becomes impure they are not deferred. The verse also indicates that this *halakha* applies only to impurity imparted by a corpse, and not to lesser impurities.

According to Rabbeinu Tam, this *halakha* applies to lesser impurities as well, but to a different extent. If the majority of the community has contracted impurity due to a corpse, they may bring their offerings and also partake of the meat. If they have contracted impurity from a creeping animal or equivalent source, they may sacrifice the Paschal offering but may not partake of its meat.

He can effect acceptance – מְרַצֶּה: This does not mean that he may perform rites for individual offerings *ab initio*; rather, if he transgresses the prohibition and does so, the offering is accepted after the fact. Although he performed the service in a state of impurity, the High Priest's frontplate effects acceptance for the offering.

HALAKHA

Impure due to a corpse, etc. – טְמֵא מֵת וכו׳: All offerings, individual or communal, that have an appointed time override the prohibition against performing service while impure. In other words, if the majority of the community, or of the priests, or the sacred vessels contracted impurity from a corpse, the necessary offering is performed anyway in a state of impurity, and both pure and impure priests may participate. This applies only to impurity imparted by a corpse (Rambam *Sefer Avoda, Hilkhot Biat HaMikdash* 4:9–11).

BACKGROUND

Ritual impurity imparted by a corpse – טוּמְאַת הַמֵּת: Corpses are the ultimate primary source of ritual impurity [*avi avot hatuma*]. A person or item rendered ritually impure by a corpse becomes ritually impure at the level of a primary source of ritual impurity [*av hatuma*] and imparts that ritual impurity to people and garments for a period of seven days. A corpse transfers ritual impurity by contact, by being carried, and, uniquely, by what is known as impurity imparted in a tent. The latter form of transference takes place if an individual enters a room that contains a human corpse. Ritual impurity is caused not only by a whole corpse but also by parts of it, though there are many complex details with regard to the parts of a body considered significant enough to impart this form of ritual impurity. Many authorities claim that only corpses of Jews impart this impurity. Another unusual feature of ritual impurity imparted by corpses is that a metal utensil or vessel that touches a corpse assumes the status of the corpse itself and causes anyone who touches it or comes under the same roof with it to become ritually impure at the level of a primary source of ritual impurity. The *halakhot* of ritual impurity imparted by a corpse appear primarily in tractate *Oholot*.

אֶלָּא קָסָבְרִי: שׁוֹחֲטִין וְזוֹרְקִין עַל טְמֵא שֶׁרֶץ.

Rather, they must **hold**[N] that **one may slaughter** the Paschal offering **and sprinkle** its blood **for** an owner who is **impure due to a creeping animal.** Accordingly, the community may not offer the Paschal offering in such a state of impurity.

אָמַר עוּלָּא, תְּקַע לְהוּ רֵישׁ לָקִישׁ לִדְרוֹמָאֵי: וְכִי אֵיזֶה כֹּחַ מְרוּבֶּה, כֹּחַ מְכַפְּרִין אוֹ כֹּחַ מִתְכַּפְּרִין? הֱוֵי אוֹמֵר – כֹּחַ מִתְכַּפְּרִין;

Ulla says: Reish Lakish shouted [*teka*][L] **to the Elders of the South: But which power is greater** to overcome impurity with respect to offerings, **the power of those who effect atonement,** i.e., the priests, **or the power of those who achieve atonement,** the offerings' owners? Since the Elders of the South hold that the Paschal offering may be sacrificed for an owner who is impure due to a creeping animal, while a priest who is similarly impure may not sacrifice any offering, **you must say** that **the power of those who achieve atonement** is greater.

וּמָה בְּמָקוֹם שֶׁנִּטְמְאוּ בְּעָלִים בְּשֶׁרֶץ מְשַׁלְּחִין קׇרְבְּנוֹתֵיהֶן – כֹּהֵן שֶׁנִּטְמָא בְּשֶׁרֶץ אֵינוֹ מְרַצֶּה, מָקוֹם שֶׁנִּטְמְאוּ בְּעָלִים בְּמֵת, שֶׁאֵין מְשַׁלְּחִין קׇרְבְּנוֹתֵיהֶן – כֹּהֵן שֶׁנִּטְמָא בְּמֵת אֵינוֹ דִּין שֶׁאֵינוֹ מְרַצֶּה?

If so, your initial statement that a priest who contracted impurity from a corpse can effect acceptance for individual offerings can be refuted *a fortiori*: **And just as in a case where** the **owner became impure due to a creeping animal,** he **may send his offerings**[H] for sacrifice, and yet **a priest who became impure due to a creeping animal cannot effect acceptance,** then in **a case where the owner became impure due to a corpse, where he may not send his offerings** for sacrifice, **is it not right that a priest who became impure due to a corpse cannot effect acceptance?**

קָסָבְרִי זִקְנֵי דָרוֹם: טְמֵא מֵת [נַמִי] מְשַׁלֵּחַ קׇרְבְּנוֹתָיו.

The Gemara responds: **The Elders of the South hold** that an owner who is **impure due to a corpse may also send his offerings,** even though he will not be able to partake of his Paschal offering. Therefore, the *a fortiori* inference does not stand.

וְהָכְתִיב: ״אִישׁ אִישׁ כִּי יִהְיֶה טָמֵא וְעָשָׂה פֶסַח בַּחֹדֶשׁ הַשֵּׁנִי״ וגו׳! לְמִצְוָה.

The Gemara protests: **But isn't it written: "If any man of you or of your generations shall be impure** by reason of a dead body, or be in a journey afar off, **he shall perform the Paschal offering** to the Lord. **In the second month** on the fourteenth day at dusk they shall perform it" (Numbers 9:10–11)? Apparently, one impure due to a corpse in the first month must defer his Paschal offering to the second month. The Gemara responds: The verse intends this **as a mitzva** *ab initio*. But if he sends his offering in the first month, it is accepted, and he is not required to sacrifice a Paschal offering in the second month.

וְהָא כְּתִיב: ״אִישׁ

The Gemara asks: **But isn't it written:** "And if the household be too little for a lamb, then shall he and his neighbor next to his house take one according to the number of the souls; **a man,**

Perek **II**
Daf **23** Amud **a**

לְפִי אׇכְלוֹ״! לְמִצְוָה.

according to his eating, you shall make your count for the lamb" (Exodus 12:4)? This teaches that one may bring the Paschal offering only if he is able to partake of it. The Gemara responds: This requirement is also meant **as a mitzva** *ab initio*; it does not disqualify the offering if not fulfilled.

וּלְעַכּוֹבֵי לָא? וְהָתַנְיָא: ״בְּמִכְסַת נְפָשׁוֹת״ – מְלַמֵּד שֶׁאֵין הַפֶּסַח נִשְׁחָט אֶלָּא לִמְנוּיָיו. שְׁחָטוֹ שֶׁלֹּא לִמְנוּיָיו יָכוֹל יְהֵא כְּעוֹבֵר עַל הַמִּצְוָה? תַּלְמוּד לוֹמַר: ״תָּכֹסּוּ״, הַכָּתוּב שָׁנָה עָלָיו לְעַכֵּב; וְאִיתְּקַשׁ אוֹכְלִין לִמְנוּיִין!

The Gemara asks: **And** is this requirement **not indispensable** even after the fact? **But isn't it taught** in a *baraita* that the phrase **"according to the number of the souls" teaches that the Paschal offering may be slaughtered only for those who registered for it**[H] in advance. If the Paschal offering was **slaughtered for** individuals **who did not register for it,** one **might** have thought that **it would** only **be like transgressing a mitzva,** but the offering would not be disqualified. Therefore, **the verse states: "You shall make your count"; the verse repeats** the issue of counting **to** stress that the *halakha* is **indispensable,** and if one slaughters the offering for one who is not registered, it is disqualified. The Gemara concludes: **And those who eat** the offering **are juxtaposed to those registered** for it, as the verse states: "According to the number of the souls; a man, according to his eating." Accordingly, if one slaughters the Paschal offering for one who cannot partake of it, the offering is disqualified.

NOTES

Rather they must hold, etc. – אֶלָּא קָסָבְרִי וכו׳: Since one impure due to a creeping animal can immerse and become pure in time to partake of the Paschal offering that night, he is not deferred to the second *Pesaḥ*. By extension, one infers that there is no communal exemption for this type of impurity; rather, those priests who are pure must perform the service, and the community must immerse and partake of the offering that night.

LANGUAGE

Shouted [*teka*] – תְּקַע: This translation follows the opinion of Rashi, who interprets the word to denote a blast [*tekia*] like that of a shofar (see *Bava Kamma* 18b). Exclamation may have been typical of Reish Lakish's personality, as one also finds in tractate *Kiddushin* (44a): Reish Lakish screamed at them like a crane.

HALAKHA

May send his offerings – מְשַׁלְּחִין קׇרְבְּנוֹתֵיהֶן: One who is impure due to a creeping animal or a source of impurity of similar severity, or one who is uncircumcised, may send his offerings to be sacrificed on his behalf. The Paschal offering may not be sacrificed for one impure due to a creeping animal until he immerses. If one is impure due to a corpse, no offering may be sacrificed for him until he is pure (Rambam *Sefer Avoda*, *Hilkhot Biat HaMikdash* 2:12 and *Sefer Korbanot*, *Hilkhot Korban Pesaḥ* 6:1).

HALAKHA

For those who registered for it – לִמְנוּיָיו: The Paschal offering may be slaughtered only for those who registered for it in advance (Rambam *Sefer Korbanot*, *Hilkhot Korban Pesaḥ* 2:1).

זִקְנֵי דָרוֹם לָא מַקְשִׁי. וְכִי לָא מַקְשִׁי נַמִי, מֵהָא נַמִי אִית לְהוּ פִּירְכָא: וּמַה בְּמָקוֹם שֶׁנִּטְמְאוּ בְּעָלִים בְּשֶׁרֶץ, שֶׁמְּשַׁלְּחִין קׇרְבְּנוֹתֵיהֶם לְכַתְּחִילָּה – כֹּהֵן שֶׁנִּטְמָא בְּשֶׁרֶץ אֵינוֹ מְרַצֶּה, מָקוֹם שֶׁנִּטְמְאוּ בְּעָלִים בְּמֵת, שֶׁאֵין מְשַׁלְּחִין קׇרְבְּנוֹתֵיהֶן לְכַתְּחִילָּה – כֹּהֵן שֶׁנִּטְמָא בְּמֵת אֵינוֹ דִּין שֶׁאֵינוֹ מְרַצֶּה?

The Gemara responds: **The Elders of the South do not juxtapose** the phrases, i.e., they do not interpret the verse's juxtaposition of the two phrases as significant. The Gemara asks: **But even if they do not juxtapose** the phrases, **there is a refutation to** their statement **from this inference as well: And just as in a case where the owner became impure due to a creeping animal, where he may send his offerings** for sacrifice *ab initio*, **a priest who became impure due to a creeping animal** nevertheless **cannot effect acceptance,** then in **a case where the owner became impure due to a corpse, where he may not send his offerings** *ab initio*, **is it not right**[N] **that a priest who became impure due to a corpse cannot effect acceptance?**

מֵיתִיבֵי: מִפְּנֵי שֶׁאָמְרוּ: נָזִיר וְעוֹשֶׂה פֶּסַח, הַצִּיץ מְרַצֶּה עַל טוּמְאַת דָּם וְאֵין הַצִּיץ מְרַצֶּה עַל טוּמְאַת הַגּוּף.

Furthermore, the Gemara **raises an objection** from a mishna (*Pesaḥim* 80b): **As** the Sages **said** that with regard to **a nazirite and one who performs** the rite of the **Paschal offering, the frontplate effects acceptance for** offerings sacrificed in a state of **impurity of the blood,**[H] **but the frontplate does not effect acceptance for** offerings sacrificed in a state of **impurity of the body**[N] of the individual bringing it.

בְּמַאי? אִילֵימָא בְּטוּמְאַת שֶׁרֶץ – הָאָמְרַתְּ: שׁוֹחֲטִין וְזוֹרְקִין עַל טוּמְאַת שֶׁרֶץ! אֶלָּא טוּמְאַת מֵת, וְקָתָנֵי: אֵין הַצִּיץ מְרַצֶּה, אַלְמָא: נִטְמְאוּ בְּעָלִים בְּמֵת – אֵין מְשַׁלְּחִין קׇרְבְּנוֹתֵיהֶם!

The Gemara continues: **To what** impurity is it referring? **If we say** that it is referring **to impurity due to a creeping animal, didn't you say** above that according to the Elders of the South, **one may slaughter** the Paschal offering **and sprinkle** its blood **for** an owner who is in a state of **impurity due to a creeping animal? Rather,** it must be referring to **impurity due to a corpse, and** the mishna **teaches: The frontplate does not effect acceptance. Evidently,** if the **owner became impure due to a corpse, he may not send his offerings** for sacrifice, contrary to the opinion ascribed to the Elders of the South.

לָא, אִי דְּאִיטְמוּ בְּעָלִים בְּמֵת – הָכִי נַמִי. הָכָא בְּמַאי עָסְקִינַן – כְּגוֹן שֶׁנִּטְמָא כֹּהֵן בְּשֶׁרֶץ.

The Gemara responds: **No, if the owner became impure due to a corpse,** the frontplate **indeed** effects acceptance for the offering. The mishna is not referring to the owners of the offerings at all; rather, **here we are dealing with** a case **where** the officiating **priest became impure**[N] **due to a creeping animal.**

אִי הָכִי, אֵימָא סֵיפָא: נִיטְמָא טוּמְאַת הַתְּהוֹם – הַצִּיץ מְרַצֶּה; הָא תָּנֵי רַבִּי חִיָּיא: לֹא אָמְרוּ טוּמְאַת הַתְּהוֹם אֶלָּא לְמֵת בִּלְבַד, לְמֵת – לְמַעוּטֵי מַאי? לָאו לְמַעוּטֵי טוּמְאַת הַתְּהוֹם דְּשֶׁרֶץ?

The Gemara asks: **If so, say the latter clause** of the mishna: If it became known after the offering was brought that he had **contracted ritual impurity** imparted **in the depths,**[NH] i.e., a source of impurity that had been unknown at the time, **the frontplate effects acceptance** for the offering. This clause cannot be reconciled with the suggested interpretation of the mishna, since **Rabbi Ḥiyya teaches: They stated** this *halakha* of **impurity** imparted **in the depths only with regard to** impurity due to **a corpse.**[H] Now, when he says that it applies only **to** impurity due to **a corpse,** he means **to exclude what?** Does he **not** mean **to exclude impurity** imparted by the carcass of **a creeping animal in the depths?** If so, the mishna cannot be referring to impurity due to a creeping animal.

NOTES

Is it not right, etc. – **אֵינוֹ דִּין וכו׳**: This inference differs from the one refuted on the previous *amud* in its inclusion of the term: *Ab initio*. Although the Elders of the South hold that one impure due to a corpse may send his offerings, they concede that *ab initio* he should not.

Impurity of the body – **טוּמְאַת הַגּוּף**: The Gemara initially assumes that this is referring to the body of the offering's owner, but this assumption will later be contested.

Where the priest became impure, etc. – **כְּגוֹן שֶׁנִּטְמָא כֹּהֵן וכו׳**: The Gemara specifies impurity due to a creeping animal because the Elders of the South hold that a priest who is impure due to a corpse can effect acceptance. According to this interpretation, the first clause of the mishna applies to all offerings, not only to the Paschal offering and those of the nazirite. The mishna specifies these cases only because the following clause applies to them exclusively (Rashi).

Impurity imparted in the depths – **טוּמְאַת הַתְּהוֹם**: This is impurity imparted by a source unknown to anyone at the time it was contracted, e.g., if one passed over a place below which, unbeknownst to anyone, there was a grave. Rashi interprets the term as referring to a case of uncertainty as to whether or not one contracted impurity, just as one can never know the depth of an abyss. It is a *halakha* transmitted to Moses from Sinai that if a nazirite or one who brings his Paschal offering does so in a state of ritual impurity imparted by a grave in the depths, and the offering has already been slaughtered when the impurity is discovered, the frontplate effects its acceptance and he is not required to bring a replacement offering.

HALAKHA

The frontplate effects acceptance for impurity of the blood – **הַצִּיץ מְרַצֶּה עַל טוּמְאַת דָּם**: The High Priest's frontplate effects acceptance for portions of an offering burned on the altar in an impure state. In the case of the Paschal offering, it also effects acceptance for an offering whose service was completed when the animal's meat was impure, i.e., if the meat contracted impurity and then the blood was unwittingly sprinkled on the altar, the offering is accepted after the fact. The frontplate does not effect acceptance for offerings sacrificed while their owners were impure. Even if the blood was unwittingly sprinkled in such a case, the offering is not accepted. Likewise, if a nazirite completes his period of naziriteship and brings his offerings and shaves, and only afterward he discovers that he had contracted impurity from a known source during his naziriteship, his naziriteship is negated. He must undergo the rite of the impure nazirite and undergo another period of naziriteship to fulfill his vow (Rambam *Sefer Avoda*, *Hilkhot Biat HaMikdash* 4:7; *Sefer Korbanot*, *Hilkhot Korban Pesaḥ* 4:2, 6:11–12; and *Sefer Hafla'a*, *Hilkhot Nezirut* 6:16).

Contracted ritual impurity imparted in the depths – **נִיטְמָא טוּמְאַת הַתְּהוֹם**: One who contracted ritual impurity imparted in the depths may slaughter and partake of this Paschal offering *ab initio*. Likewise, if a nazirite brings his final offerings and afterward discovers he had contracted impurity from a source unknown to all, his naziriteship is not negated. This is a *halakha* transmitted to Moses from Sinai (Rambam).

If a priest performs the service and later discovers that he had contracted impurity from a known source, all offerings he sacrificed are disqualified. If he had contracted impurity from an unknown source, the frontplate effects acceptance for all offerings he sacrificed. This applies even if he discovered his impurity prior to the sprinkling of the blood, since the frontplate effects acceptance even for offerings sacrificed intentionally in a state of impurity imparted in the depths (Rambam *Sefer Avoda*, *Hilkhot Biat HaMikdash* 4:6; *Sefer Korbanot*, *Hilkhot Korban Pesaḥ* 4:2; and *Sefer Hafla'a*, *Hilkhot Nezirut* 6:16).

Only with regard to a corpse – **לְמֵת בִּלְבַד**: Impurity imparted in the depths is impurity not known to anyone in the world. The term can apply only to impurity due to a corpse (Rambam *Sefer Hafla'a*, *Hilkhot Nezirut* 6:18).

לָא, לְמַעוּטֵי טוּמְאַת הַתְּהוֹם דְּזִיבָה.

The Gemara responds: **No,** Rabbi Ḥiyya means **to exclude impurity** imparted **by** a gonorrhea-like **discharge** [*ziva*] **in the depths.**[N] Impurity due to the corpse of a creeping animal, by contrast, is within the scope of the mishna.

וְאֶלָּא הָא דְּבָעֵי רָמִי בַּר חָמָא: כֹּהֵן הַמְרַצֶּה בְּקָרְבְּנוֹתֵיהֶם, הוּתְּרָה לוֹ טוּמְאַת הַתְּהוֹם אוֹ לֹא הוּתְּרָה לוֹ טוּמְאַת הַתְּהוֹם? תִּפְשׁוֹט דְּטוּמְאַת הַתְּהוֹם הוּתְּרָה לוֹ, דְּהָא הָכָא בְּכֹהֵן קָיְימִינָא!

The Gemara asks: **But** how is one to understand **this dilemma that Rami bar Ḥama raises:** With regard to **a priest who effects acceptance for the offerings of** the nazirite and the Paschal offering, **was impurity** imparted **in the depths permitted for him or was impurity** imparted **in the depths not permitted for him?** According to the Elders of the South, why not **resolve** the dilemma and conclude **that impurity** imparted **in the depths was permitted for him, since** they hold that **we interpret** the mishna **here** as referring **to** an impure **priest?**

דְּרָמִי בַּר חָמָא וַדַּאי פְּלִיגִי.

The Gemara responds: The premise of this dilemma **of Rami bar Ḥama certainly disagrees** with the opinion of the Elders of the South, and Rami bar Ḥama does not interpret the mishna in this manner.

תָּא שְׁמַע: ״וְנָשָׂא אַהֲרֹן אֶת עֲוֹן הַקֳּדָשִׁים״, וְכִי אֵיזֶהוּ עָוֹן נוֹשֵׂא?

The Gemara suggests: **Come** and **hear** a proof from a verse written about the frontplate: "And it shall be upon Aaron's forehead, **and Aaron shall bear the sin committed with the sacred** items, which the children of Israel shall consecrate, even all their sacred gifts; and it shall be always upon his forehead, that they may be accepted before God" (Exodus 28:38). **And** the Sages expounded: **Which sin does** Aaron **bear?**

NOTES

Impurity imparted by *ziva* in the depths – **טוּמְאַת הַתְּהוֹם דְּזִיבָה**: *Ziva* is treated more stringently than impurity due to a creeping animal, since it originates in the body of the impure person. Rashi explains how such a case of uncertain impurity may be imparted by *ziva*: As a rule, a man who experiences *ziva* once does not immediately become impure as a *zav*. Rather, he contracts the more lenient impurity of one who experiences a seminal emission, and he may immerse that day and become pure at nightfall. If he experiences *ziva* twice, or if his *ziva* continues from one day to the next, he assumes the status of a *zav* and becomes impure for seven days. The Gemara here is referring to one who experiences *ziva* at twilight between the thirteenth and fourteenth of Nisan, the day that the Paschal offering must be sacrificed. If this *ziva* is considered to have occurred only on the thirteenth or only on the fourteenth, he is not considered a *zav*. But if it is considered to have extended from the thirteenth into the fourteenth, he is considered a *zav*. He therefore cannot be certain whether or not he is a *zav*.

Rabbeinu Tam objects to Rashi's interpretation, claiming that it is insufficient that the impurity be uncertain; the impurity must be unknown entirely to all until after the offering has been sacrificed. Rather, the Gemara must be referring to one who experienced *ziva* once, on the thirteenth of Nisan, and immersed before sunset so as to be pure on the fourteenth. He then proceeded to bring the Paschal offering in a state of purity, but afterward experienced *ziva* again. Retroactively, he was impure as a *zav* at the time of the sacrifice, but neither he nor anyone else had any way of knowing this at the time (see also Rashi on *Pesaḥim* 80b).

Perek **II**
Daf **23** Amud **b**

אִם עֲוֹן פִּיגּוּל – הֲרֵי כְּבָר נֶאֱמַר: ״לֹא יֵחָשֵׁב״, אִם עֲוֹן נוֹתָר – הֲרֵי כְּבָר נֶאֱמַר: ״לֹא יֵרָצֶה״,

If the verse means that he bears **the sin of *piggul*,**[N] **it is already stated:** "And if any of the flesh of his peace offerings be at all eaten on the third day, it shall not be accepted, **neither shall it be credited** to he who offers it" (Leviticus 7:18). **If** he bears **the sin of *notar*,**[B] **it is already stated** in the same verse: **"It shall not be accepted."**

הָא אֵינוֹ נוֹשֵׂא אֶלָּא עֲוֹן טוּמְאָה שֶׁהוּתְּרָה מִכְּלָלָהּ בְּצִבּוּר;

Rather, the frontplate **bears only the sin**[H] **of impurity, whose general prohibition was permitted in** cases involving **the public.** The verse indicates that the frontplate effects acceptance for individual offerings sacrificed in a state of ritual impurity.

מַאי טוּמְאָה? אִילֵימָא מִטּוּמְאַת שֶׁרֶץ – הֵיכָא אִישְׁתְּרֵי? אֶלָּא טוּמְאַת מֵת, וְלָאו כְּגוֹן שֶׁנִּטְמְאוּ בְּעָלִים בְּמֵת? אַלְמָא: נִטְמְאוּ בְּעָלִים בְּמֵת מְשַׁלְּחִין קָרְבְּנוֹתֵיהֶן.

The Gemara clarifies: **What is the impurity** borne by the frontplate? **If we say** that it effects acceptance **for impurity due to a creeping animal, where** does one find that the general prohibition was **permitted**[N] in cases involving the public? **Rather,** it must be referring to **impurity due to a corpse. And is it not** referring to a case **where the owner**[N] of the offerings **became impure from a corpse? Evidently,** if **the owner became impure from a corpse, he may send his offerings** for sacrifice, as the frontplate effects acceptance for them.

BACKGROUND

Notar – **נוֹתָר**: This is referring to parts of an offering left over after their appointed time for consumption elapsed. One who eats the leftover portion of an offering is liable to receive the punishment of *karet*. The Sages decreed that the leftover portion be considered ritually impure, so that the priests would be prompt and meticulous in its removal.

HALAKHA

Bears only the sin, etc. – **אֵינוֹ נוֹשֵׂא אֶלָּא עֲוֹן וכו׳**: The frontplate effects acceptance for offerings of which the sacrificial portions were impure. However, it does not effect acceptance for those offerings of which the eaten portions were impure, or for impurity of the body contracted from a known source, except in a case of impurity permitted for the public (Rambam *Sefer Avoda*, *Hilkhot Biat HaMikdash* 4:7 and *Hilkhot Pesulei HaMukdashin* 1:34, 11:19).

NOTES

If the sin of *piggul*, etc. – **אִם עֲוֹן פִּיגּוּל וכו׳**: In general, the term *piggul* refers to offerings that one sacrificed with intent to eat or burn them beyond their appointed time, while *notar* refers to meat of an offering whose time for consumption has expired. Nevertheless, the Gemara states later (29a) that the word *notar* mentioned here denotes offerings sacrificed with intent to render the meat *notar*; in other words, *notar* here refers to what is generally known as *piggul*. Rashi therefore writes that the term *piggul* here refers to offerings that one sacrificed with intent to eat or burn them outside of their designated place, while *notar* refers to those that one sacrificed with intent to eat or burn them beyond their appointed time. Ra'avad on *Torat Kohanim* notes that actual *notar* is not something for which the frontplate effects acceptance either.

Where does one find it was permitted – **הֵיכָא אִישְׁתְּרֵי**: The communal exemption for impurity is derived from the passage in Exodus concerning the Paschal offering, where it is contrasted to an impure individual's deferral to the second *Pesaḥ*. Since the verse (Numbers 9:10) states that only individuals who are impure due to a corpse are deferred to the second *Pesaḥ*, it follows that the communal exemption likewise only applies to impurity due to a corpse.

The owner, etc. – **בְּעָלִים וכו׳**: The Gemara could have suggested that the statement is referring to impurity of the offering's blood. It does not because there is no communal exemption for impurity of the blood as there is for impurity of the owners (*Tosafot*).

ובמאי? אי בנזיר – "וכי ימות מת עליו" אמר רחמנא! אלא לעושה פסח (ולאו כגון שנטמאו בעלים במת?).

And to what offering is this statement referring? If it is referring to the offering of a nazirite, doesn't the Merciful One state: "And if any man die very suddenly beside him, and he defile his consecrated head" (Numbers 6:9)? The passage indicates that even if a nazirite contracts impurity against his will, he still cannot bring his offerings until he is pure. Rather, it must be referring to one who performs the rite of the Paschal offering. This proves the claim of the Elders of the South that one who is impure due to a corpse may send his Paschal offering for sacrifice.

לעולם בשרץ, ושם טומאה בעולם.

The Gemara responds: **Actually,** the statement is referring **to** impurity due to **a creeping animal,** not due to a corpse. **And** although the general prohibition with regard to impurity due to a creeping animal was not permitted in cases involving the public, nevertheless, one finds that **the category of impurity in general** was permitted in such cases.

ואיכא דדייק ומייתי הכי: עון הקדשים – אין, עון מקדישין – לא; מאי טומאה? אילימא טומאת שרץ – מי אישתריא בציבור? אלא לאו טומאת מת, ועון קדשים – אין, עון מקדישים – לא!

The Gemara notes: **And some infer** the opposite **and derive like this:** The verse states of the frontplate: "And it shall be upon Aaron's forehead, and Aaron shall bear the sin committed with the sacred items" (Exodus 28:38). That is, it **does** bear **the iniquity of the sacred items,** but it does **not** bear **the iniquity of those who consecrate**[N] or sacrifice them, i.e., the owners of the offering or the priests involved in its sacrifice. And to **what impurity** is this verse referring? **If we say** that it is referring to **impurity** due to **a creeping animal,** is such impurity **permitted in** cases involving the **public? Rather, is it not** referring to **impurity** due to **a corpse, and** the verse indicates that the frontplate **does** bear **the iniquity of the sacred items** but does **not** bear **the iniquity of those who consecrate** them? This refutes the opinion of the Elders of the South that owners who are impure due to a corpse may send their offerings.

לעולם טומאת שרץ, ושם טומאה בעולם.

The Gemara responds: **Actually,** the verse is referring to **impurity due to a creeping animal,**[N] **and** although the general prohibition with regard to impurity due to a creeping animal was not permitted in cases involving the public, **the category of impurity in general** was permitted in such cases.

"יושב". מנלן? אמר רבא אמר רב נחמן: אמר קרא: "לעמד לשרת" – לעמידה בחרתיו ולא לישיבה.

§ The mishna teaches that a priest who is **sitting**[H] disqualifies the rites that he performs. The Gemara asks: **From where do we** derive this? **Rava says** that **Rav Naḥman says: The verse states** with regard to the priests: "For the Lord your God has chosen him out of all your tribes, **to stand to minister**" (Deuteronomy 18:5). The verse indicates that **I have chosen him for standing and not for sitting.**

תנו רבנן: "לעמד לשרת" – מצוה, כשהוא אומר: "העמדים" – שנה עליו הכתוב לעכב.

The Sages taught: "To stand to minister," indicates that there is **a mitzva** to perform the service while standing. **When it says:** "Then he shall minister in the name of the Lord his God, as all his brethren the Levites do, **who stand** there before the Lord" (Deuteronomy 18:7), **the verse repeats** the matter **to invalidate** rites that are performed while not standing.

אמר ליה רבא לרב נחמן: מכדי יושב כזר דמי, ומחיל עבודה, אימא: מה זר במיתה – אף יושב במיתה; אלמה תניא: אבל ערל, אונן, יושב – אינן במיתה אלא באזהרה?

Rava said to Rav Naḥman: Now, one who is sitting is considered like a non-priest[N] **and desecrates the service. Therefore, I will say: Just as a non-priest** who performs a rite is liable **to receive death** at the hand of Heaven, **so too one who is sitting** should be liable **to receive death** at the hand of Heaven. If so, **why is it taught** in a *baraita*: **But one who is uncircumcised, an acute mourner,** and **one who is sitting are not** liable **to** receive **death** at the hand of Heaven if they performed rites; **rather,** they simply transgress a **prohibition?**

משום דהוי מחוסר בגדים ושלא רחוץ ידים ורגלים שני כתובין הבאין כאחד,

The Gemara responds: That is taught **because** the case of a priest **lacking** the requisite priestly **vestments and** that of **one whose hands and feet are not washed are two verses that come as one,**[B] as the verse states explicitly for each case that if they perform rites they are liable to receive death at the hand of Heaven.

NOTES

The iniquity of those who consecrate – עון מקדישין: This is referring to impurity of the body in general, whether of the owners or of the priests.

Actually, the verse is referring to impurity due to a creeping animal – לעולם טומאת שרץ: In such a case the frontplate atones only for impurity of the offering itself. With regard to impurity due to a corpse, it atones for impurity of the body as well. Therefore, one impure due to a corpse may send his Paschal offering, and if a priest impure due to a corpse performs sacrificial rites, they are valid after the fact. Rashi adds that even with regard to impurity due to a creeping animal, although the frontplate does not atone for impurity of the priest, it still atones for impurity of the owner, since he can immerse and become pure in time to eat of the offering.

One who is sitting is considered like a non-priest – יושב כזר דמי: Some commentaries hold that Rav Naḥman's statement: I have chosen him for standing and not for sitting, indicates that one who is sitting loses his chosen status and is considered a non-priest in all respects. Others explain that although one who is sitting is not truly considered a non-priest, the fact that his rites are disqualified like those of a non-priest might lead one to infer that they receive the same punishment.

HALAKHA

Sitting – יושב: If one performs rites while sitting, his service is disqualified, but he is not liable to receive lashes, since the prohibition is inferred from a positive mitzva (Rambam *Sefer Avoda*, *Hilkhot Pesulei HaMukdashin* 5:17).

BACKGROUND

Two verses that come as one – שני כתובין הבאין כאחד: This principle limits the application of an analogy. Ordinarily, a *halakha* stated in the context of one case in the Torah may be inferred to apply to analogous cases as well. If such a *halakha* appears in connection with two or more cases in the Torah, these instances constitute two verses that come as one, and there is a principle that any two verses that come as one do not teach their common aspect to apply to other cases, i.e., an analogy may not be derived from two analogous cases. This is because a *halakha* that it was necessary to mention in two different places cannot be treated as self-evident; the two explicit references must constitute exceptional cases. Some Sages maintain that only when a *halakha* appears in three places is it not possible to derive an analogy, such that only three verses that come as one do not teach their common aspect.

BACKGROUND

Those who drank wine – **שְׁתוּיֵי יַיִן**: It is prohibited to enter the Temple courtyard and perform the Temple service while drunk. Violation of this prohibition by a priest is a capital offense, though the sentence is meted out by the hand of Heaven and not by a human court (Leviticus 10:9). Anyone who drinks a quarter-*log* of wine is included in this category. If a priest serves in the Temple while drunk from wine his service is disqualified, but intoxication resulting from other substances does not disqualify the service.

Sage from the school of Rabbi Yishmael taught – **תָּנָא דְּבֵי רַבִּי יִשְׁמָעֵאל**: Even after the writing of the Oral Torah was permitted by the Sages, much of it was not recorded. Some say that the Mishna itself was not written at the time of its redaction. Therefore, many rabbinic statements, such as the contents of the *Tosefta* and other *baraitot*, were preserved and transmitted orally. Each Sage was expected to commit the entire Mishna as well as a significant number of other tannaitic statements to memory. Complete mastery of all of these sources was the province of the *tanna'im*, experts who memorized vast amounts of material and were capable of reciting it on demand. Often, the most prominent of these *tanna'im* were affiliated with the specific study hall of one of the Sages, where they served as living anthologies of this material.

NOTES

The floor sanctifies, etc. – **רִצְפָּה מְקַדֶּשֶׁת וכו׳**: According to *Tosafot*, the floor of the Temple courtyard sanctifies the priest in that it is prohibited for him to perform rites when he is not standing upon it. The term: Service vessels, is referring to the priestly vestments, without which the priest may not serve. The *Shita Mekubbetzet* presents a textual variant, which Rashi had: The floor is sanctified, and service vessels are sanctified. The floor was sanctified by King David, as explained in the Gemara, while the service vessels are sanctified with the anointing oil.

Necessary, etc. – **צְרִיכָא וכו׳**: Ostensibly, the mishna could have mentioned only the case of a priest standing on another's feet, and the previous two cases could be inferred *a fortiori*. Some commentaries claim that if the mishna had mentioned only that case, one might not have inferred the other two. One might reason that while other human beings are significant and therefore constitute an interposition, animals or vessels are less so and might not (*Tzon Kodashim*; *Panim Meirot*). Alternatively, the mishna may have presented all three cases to stress the extent to which the prohibition applies.

וְכָל שְׁנֵי כְתוּבִים הַבָּאִין כְּאֶחָד אֵין מְלַמְּדִין.

And any two verses that come as one do not teach their common aspect to similar cases. Therefore, one cannot assume that analogous prohibitions carry penalty of death at the hand of Heaven as well.

וּלְמַאן דְּאָמַר מְלַמְּדִין, שְׁתוּיֵי יַיִן הֲוָה לֵיהּ שְׁלִישִׁי, וּשְׁלֹשָׁה לְדִבְרֵי הַכֹּל אֵין מְלַמְּדִין.

And even **according to the one who says** that they do **teach** their common aspect, the prohibition against service by **those who drank wine**[B] also contains explicit mention of death at the hand of Heaven and **constitutes a third** verse. **And all agree** that **three** verses that come as one **do not teach** their common aspect.

״עוֹמֵד עַל גַּבֵּי כֵלִים, עַל גַּבֵּי בְהֵמָה, עַל גַּבֵּי רַגְלֵי חֲבֵירוֹ – פָּסוּל״. מְנָלַן? דְּתָנָא דְּבֵי רַבִּי יִשְׁמָעֵאל: הוֹאִיל וְרִצְפָּה מְקַדֶּשֶׁת וּכְלֵי שָׁרֵת מְקַדְּשִׁים, מַה כְּלֵי שָׁרֵת – לֹא יְהֵא דָּבָר חוֹצֵץ בֵּינוֹ לְבֵין כְּלֵי שָׁרֵת, אַף רִצְפָּה – לֹא יְהֵא דָּבָר חוֹצֵץ בֵּינוֹ לְבֵין רִצְפָּה.

§ The mishna teaches that one who is **standing upon vessels**, or **upon an animal**, or **upon the feet of another**, is **unfit** to perform rites. The Gemara elaborates: **From where do we** derive this? This is derived **as** the Sage **from the school of Rabbi Yishmael taught:**[B] **Since the floor** of the Temple courtyard **sanctifies**[NH] the priest to perform the service, **and service vessels**, i.e., priestly vestments, also **sanctify** him, one may draw a comparison between the two: **Just as** with regard to **service vessels, nothing may interpose between** the priest **and the service vessel, so too** with regard to the **floor, nothing may interpose between** the priest **and the floor.**

וּצְרִיכָא, דְּאִי אַשְׁמְעִינַן כְּלִי – מִשּׁוּם דְּלָאו מִינָא דְּבָשָׂר נִינְהוּ, אֲבָל בְּהֵמָה דְּמִינָא דְּבָשָׂר הוּא אֵימָא לָא; וְאִי אַשְׁמְעִינַן בְּהֵמָה – דְּלָאו מִינָא דְּאָדָם הוּא, אֲבָל חֲבֵירוֹ דְּאָדָם הוּא אֵימָא לָא, צְרִיכָא.

The Gemara adds: **And** each of the three cases mentioned in the mishna is **necessary.**[N] **As,** had the mishna **taught us** only that **a vessel** interposes between the priest's feet and the floor, one might have thought that this is only **because it is not a type of flesh, but** with regard to **an animal, which is a type of flesh, I will say** that it **does not** constitute an interposition. **And had it taught us** only that **an animal** interposes, one might have thought that this is only **because it is not of the human species, but another** person, **who is human, I will say** that he does **not** interpose. Therefore, each is **necessary.**

תַּנְיָא, רַבִּי אֱלִיעֶזֶר אוֹמֵר: רַגְלוֹ אַחַת עַל הַכְּלִי וְרַגְלוֹ אַחַת עַל הָרִצְפָּה, רַגְלוֹ אַחַת עַל הָאֶבֶן וְרַגְלוֹ אַחַת עַל הָרִצְפָּה – רוֹאִין, כָּל שֶׁאִילּוּ יִנָּטֵל הַכְּלִי וְתִנָּטֵל הָאֶבֶן יָכוֹל לַעֲמוֹד עַל רַגְלוֹ אַחַת וְיַעֲבוֹד – עֲבוֹדָתוֹ כְּשֵׁירָה, וְאִם לָאו – עֲבוֹדָתוֹ פְּסוּלָה.

It is taught in a *baraita* that **Rabbi Eliezer says: If one of** the priest's **feet was on a vessel**[H] **and one of his feet** was **on the floor,** or **if one of his feet** was **on a stone and one of his feet** was **on the floor,** one **sees: Any** case **where, were the vessel to be removed or the stone removed,** he would still be **able to stand on one foot and perform rites, his service is valid. But if** he would **not** be able to stand on one foot, **his service** is **disqualified.**

בָּעֵי רַבִּי אַמִי: נִדַּלְדְּלָה הָאֶבֶן וְעָמַד עָלֶיהָ, מַהוּ? הֵיכָא דְּאֵין דַּעְתּוֹ לְחַבְּרָהּ – לָא תִּיבָּעֵי לָךְ, דְּוַדַּאי חָיְיצָא, כִּי תִּיבָּעֵי לָךְ – דְּדַעְתּוֹ לְחַבְּרָהּ, מַאי? כֵּיוָן דְּדַעְתּוֹ לְחַבְּרָהּ – כִּמְחוּבְּרָא דָּמְיָא, אוֹ דִּילְמָא הַשְׁתָּא מִיהָא הָא תְּלִישָׁא?

Rabbi Ami raises a dilemma: If one of **the stone** tiles of the Temple floor **came loose**[H] and began to wobble, **and the priest stood on it, what is the** *halakha*? The Gemara elaborates: **Do not raise the dilemma** with regard to a case **where he does not intend to attach** the stone to the floor again, **as it certainly interposes** in such a case, since it is considered an item separate from the Temple. Rather, **when you raise this dilemma,** do so with regard to a case **where he intends to attach it** again. In such a case, **what** is the *halakha*? Does one say that **since he intends to attach it, it is considered like that which is already attached? Or perhaps now, at least, it is disconnected,** and it is considered a separate item.

HALAKHA

Since the floor sanctifies – **הוֹאִיל וְרִצְפָּה מְקַדֶּשֶׁת**: All those participating in the Temple service must be standing on the floor. If there is any interposition between the priest and the ground, e.g., if he is standing on vessels or an animal or the feet of another, the offering is disqualified. The same *halakha* applies if there is an interposition between the priest's hand and the service vessel in use (Rambam *Sefer Avoda*, *Hilkhot Kelei HaMikdash* 5:17).

One of his feet was on a vessel – **רַגְלוֹ אַחַת עַל הַכְּלִי**: If one of the priest's feet was on a vessel or a stone and the other foot was on the floor as he served, the following distinction applies: If the vessel or the stone were to be removed and the priest would still be capable of standing on his other foot, his service is valid. If he would not be capable of standing on his other foot, his service is disqualified (Rambam *Sefer Avoda*, *Hilkhot Kelei HaMikdash* 5:18).

If the stone came loose – **נִדַּלְדְּלָה הָאֶבֶן**: If one of the stones of the Temple floor came loose, the priest may not stand on it while serving until it is reattached. If he did, his service is valid after the fact, provided that the stone was still in its original location. Although the issue is not resolved in the Gemara, the Rambam does not deem offerings disqualified in such cases of uncertainty (*Kesef Mishne*). According to *Likkutei Halakhot*, if there is no intention of reattaching the stone, it is considered as though it were a separate item and constitutes an interposition between the priest and the ground, disqualifying the offering (Rambam *Sefer Avoda*, *Hilkhot Kelei HaMikdash* 5:19, and see Mahari Kurkus and *Kesef Mishne* there).

רַבָּה זוּטִי בָּעֵי לָהּ הָכִי, בָּעֵי רַבִּי אַמִי: נֶעֶקְרָה הָאֶבֶן וְעָמַד בִּמְקוֹמָהּ, מַהוּ?

Rabba Zuti raises this dilemma like this: Rabbi Ami raises a dilemma: If one of **the stone** tiles **was uprooted**[H] **and** the priest **stood in its** empty **place, what is the** *halakha*?

מַאי קָא מִיבַּעְיָא לֵיהּ? כִּי קַדֵּישׁ דָּוִד – רִצְפָּה עֶלְיוֹנָה קַדֵּישׁ, אוֹ דִּילְמָא עַד לְאַרְעִית דִּתְהוֹמָא קַדֵּישׁ? וְתִיבָּעֵי לֵיהּ כָּל הָעֲזָרָה כּוּלָּהּ!

The Gemara interjects: **What is the dilemma he is raising?** Perhaps this is the dilemma: **When** King **David sanctified** the site of the Temple, **did he sanctify** the **upper** level of the **floor** but nothing underneath it, **or perhaps he sanctified** it **to the depths of the earth? But** if this is the dilemma, **let him raise the dilemma** with regard to **the entire Temple courtyard,** i.e., what is the *halakha* if the entire floor is removed?

לְעוֹלָם פְּשִׁיטָא לֵיהּ דְּעַד אַרְעִית דִּתְהוֹמָא קַדֵּישׁ, וְהָכִי קָמִיבַּעְיָא לֵיהּ: דֶּרֶךְ שֵׁירוּת בְּכָךְ, אוֹ אֵין דֶּרֶךְ שֵׁירוּת בְּכָךְ? תֵּיקוּ.

The Gemara responds: **Actually,** it is **obvious to him that** King David **sanctified** the site of the Temple **to the depths of the earth, and this is the dilemma that he raised:** When a priest stands on an unfinished part of the Temple floor, **is this** a normal **manner of ministration, or is this not** a normal **manner of ministration?** Concerning the dilemma itself, the Gemara responds: The dilemma **shall stand** unresolved.

״קִיבֵּל בִּשְׂמֹאל – פָּסוּל, וְרַבִּי שִׁמְעוֹן מַכְשִׁיר״. תָּנוּ רַבָּנַן: ״בְּאֶצְבָּעוֹ וְלָקַח״ – מְלַמֵּד שֶׁלֹּא תְּהֵא קַבָּלָה אֶלָּא בְּיָמִין, ״בְּאֶצְבָּעוֹ וְנָתַן״ – מְלַמֵּד שֶׁלֹּא תְּהֵא נְתִינָה אֶלָּא בְּיָמִין.

§ The mishna teaches: If the priest **collected** the blood **with** his **left** hand, the service is **disqualified, and Rabbi Shimon deems it fit. The Sages taught:** The verse states: "And the priest shall take of the blood of the sin offering with his finger and put it upon the corners of the altar" (Leviticus 4:25). The conjunction of the term **"with his finger"** and the term **"and the priest shall take"**[N] **teaches that** the **collection** of the blood **may be** performed **only with** the **right** hand, since the word "finger" in the context of priesthood is always referring to the right hand. Likewise, the phrase **"with his finger and put it" teaches that** the **placing** of the blood **may be** performed **only with** the **right** hand.

אָמַר רַבִּי שִׁמְעוֹן: וְכִי נֶאֶמְרָה יָד בְּקַבָּלָה? אֶלָּא ״בְּאֶצְבָּעוֹ וְנָתַן״ – שֶׁלֹּא תְּהֵא נְתִינָה אֶלָּא בְּיָמִין; הוֹאִיל וְלֹא נֶאֶמְרָה יָד בְּקַבָּלָה, קִיבֵּל בִּשְׂמֹאל – כָּשֵׁר.

Rabbi Shimon said: But is the word: **Hand, stated with regard to** the **collection**[N] of the blood? **Rather,** the verse states only: **"With his finger and put it,"** teaching **that** the **placing** of the blood **may be** performed **only with the right** hand. **Since** the word: **Hand, is not stated with regard to** the **collection** of the blood, even if **one collected** the blood **with** his **left** hand, the offering **is fit.**

וְרַבִּי שִׁמְעוֹן, מִמַּה נַּפְשָׁךְ? אִי אִית לֵיהּ גְּזֵירָה שָׁוָה – כִּי לֹא נֶאֶמְרָה יָד בְּקַבָּלָה מַאי הָוֵי? וְאִי לֵית לֵיהּ גְּזֵירָה שָׁוָה – כִּי נֶאֶמְרָה יָד בְּקַבָּלָה מַאי הָוֵי?

The Gemara asks: **But** as for **Rabbi Shimon, whichever** way **you** look at it, his opinion is difficult. **If he holds** that one derives a **verbal analogy** from the passage discussing a leper (Leviticus, chapter 14), which indicates that all references to hands and fingers mean specifically the right hand, then even **if** the word: **Hand, is not stated with regard to** the **collection** of the blood, **what of it?** In any event, the word "finger" is stated. **And if he does not hold** that one derives this **verbal analogy,** then even **if** the word: **Hand, were stated with regard to** the **collection** of the blood, **what of it?** The word would have no significance.

אָמַר רַב יְהוּדָה: לְעוֹלָם לֵית לֵיהּ גְּזֵירָה שָׁוָה, וְהָכִי קָאָמַר: וְכִי נֶאֱמַר יַד יָמִין בְּקַבָּלָה? הוֹאִיל וְלֹא נֶאֱמַר יַד יָמִין בְּקַבָּלָה, קִבֵּל בִּשְׂמֹאל – כָּשֵׁר.

Rav Yehuda says: Actually, he does not hold that one derives this **verbal analogy. And this** is what Rabbi Shimon **is saying: But is** the phrase: **Right hand, stated with regard to** the **collection** of the blood? Rather, **since** the phrase: **Right hand, is not stated with regard to** the **collection** of the blood, even if **one collected** the blood **with** his **left** hand, the offering **is fit.**

HALAKHA

If the stone was uprooted – נֶעֶקְרָה הָאֶבֶן: If one of the stones of the Temple floor was uprooted, even if it stood in place, it is unfit, and the priest may not perform rites while standing on it until it is affixed to the ground (Rambam *Sefer Avoda, Hilkhot Beit HaBeḥira* 1:10, and see Ra'avad, *Kesef Mishne*, and *Leḥem Mishne* there).

NOTES

Shall take – לָקַח: The Gemara (48a) teaches that this is referring to the collection of the blood of the offering, because this is the first service mentioned in the verse after the animal's slaughter, and because in another verse: "And Moses took half of the blood and put it in basins" (Exodus 24:6), this is the clear meaning of the word (see also *Torat Kohanim* on Leviticus 7:37).

But is hand stated with regard to collection – וְכִי נֶאֶמְרָה יָד בְּקַבָּלָה: According to the first *tanna*, the word finger is used instead of hand because the placing of the blood on the altar immediately afterward can be accomplished only with the finger. Still, the word finger itself teaches that the act must be performed with the right hand.

אֲמַר לֵיהּ רַבָּה: אִי הָכִי, אֲפִילּוּ נְתִינָה נַמִּי! וְעוֹד, וְכִי לֵית לֵיהּ לְרַבִּי שִׁמְעוֹן גְּזֵירָה שָׁוָה? וְהָתַנְיָא, רַבִּי שִׁמְעוֹן אוֹמֵר: כָּל מָקוֹם שֶׁנֶּאֱמַר ״יָד״ – אֵינָהּ אֶלָּא יָמִין, ״אֶצְבַּע״ – אֵינָהּ אֶלָּא יָמִין!

Rabba said to him: If so, then **even** the rite of **placing** the blood should be valid when performed with the left hand, since the phrase: Right hand, does not appear with regard to it **as well. And furthermore, does Rabbi Shimon** really **not hold** that one derives this **verbal analogy? But isn't it taught** in a *baraita* that **Rabbi Shimon says:** In **every instance** in the Torah **that** the word **"hand" is stated,** the verse **is** referring **only** to the **right** hand, and whenever the verse mentions **"finger,"** it is referring **only** to a finger of the **right** hand?

אֶלָּא אָמַר רָבָא: לְעוֹלָם אִית לֵיהּ גְּזֵירָה שָׁוָה, וְהָכִי קָאָמַר: וְכִי נֶאֶמְרָה יָד בְּקַבָּלָה? הוֹאִיל וְלֹא נֶאֶמְרָה יָד בְּקַבָּלָה אֶלָּא אֶצְבַּע, וְאִי אֶפְשָׁר לְקַבָּלָה בְּאֶצְבַּע, קִיבֵּל בִּשְׂמֹאל – כָּשֵׁר.

Rather, Rava says: Actually, Rabbi Shimon **holds** that one derives this **verbal analogy, and this** is what he **is saying: But is** the word: **Hand, stated with regard to** the **collection** of the blood? **Since** the word: **Hand, is not stated with regard to** the **collection** of the blood, **but** the word **"finger"** is stated, **and collection cannot** be performed **with a finger** alone, one must conclude that the word "finger" must actually be referring to the placing of the blood. Therefore, while the placing of the blood must be performed with the right hand, if **one collected** the blood **with** his **left** hand, the offering is **fit.**

אֲמַר לֵיהּ רַב סַמָּא בְּרֵיהּ דְּרַב אַשִׁי לְרָבִינָא: אֶיפְשָׁר דְּזָהֵיד לֵיהּ אוֹגֶן לְשִׂפַת מִזְרָק וּמְקַבֵּל בָּהּ!

Rav Samma, son of Rav Ashi, said to Ravina: But **it is possible to fashion** a small **handle for the rim of** the **bowl,** and one could then hold the bowl with his finger **and collect** the blood **in it.** If so, it is possible for one to collect the blood with only his finger.

אֶלָּא אָמַר אַבַּיֵי:

Rather, Abaye says:

Perek **II**
Daf **24** Amud **b**

NOTES

A verse is interpreted based on the language preceding it, etc. – מִקְרָא נִדְרָשׁ לְפָנָיו וכו׳: Typically in Hebrew, descriptors modify the words preceding them. This is the straightforward meaning of the verse in question and the understanding of Rabbi Elazar, son of Rabbi Shimon. The Rabbis hold that since the descriptor appears only once in the verse, it modifies all of the actions described therein. Still others hold that a descriptor can modify even matters preceding those that appear immediately before it in the verse. Rabbi Shimon holds that in principle, whenever a descriptor may be understood as modifying the words preceding or following it, it should be interpreted as modifying those that follow it.

Not to the language before that which immediately precedes it – וְלֹא לִפְנֵי פָנָיו: This means that in Exodus 29:12, the word "finger" describes the placing of the blood, but not its collection.

בְּמִקְרָא נִדְרָשׁ לְפָנָיו וּלְאַחֲרָיו קָמִיפַּלְגִי.

They disagree with regard to whether **a verse is interpreted** based on juxtaposition to the language **preceding it**[N] **and** to the language **following it.** According to Rabbi Shimon, a verse is interpreted only based on the language following it. Therefore, when the verse states: "And the priest shall take of the blood of the sin offering with his finger and put it upon the corners of the altar," the word "finger" is referring only to the placing of the blood and not its collection. The Rabbis hold that the verse is also interpreted based on the language preceding it. Accordingly, they require that both rites be performed with the right hand.

אָמַר אַבַּיֵי: הָא דְּרַבִּי אֶלְעָזָר בְּרַבִּי שִׁמְעוֹן, מַפְקָא מִדַּאֲבוּהּ, וּמַפְקָא מִדְּרַבָּנַן. דְּתַנְיָא, רַבִּי אֶלְעָזָר בְּרַבִּי שִׁמְעוֹן אוֹמֵר: כָּל מָקוֹם שֶׁנֶּאֱמַר אֶצְבַּע בְּקַבָּלָה, שִׁינָּה בְּקַבָּלָה – פָּסוּל, בִּנְתִינָה – כָּשֵׁר. וְכָל מָקוֹם שֶׁנֶּאֱמַר אֶצְבַּע בִּנְתִינָה, שִׁינָּה בִּנְתִינָה – פָּסוּל, בְּקַבָּלָה – כָּשֵׁר.

Abaye says: This statement **of Rabbi Elazar, son of Rabbi Shimon, diverges from** the opinion **of his father, and it diverges from** the opinion **of the Rabbis: As it is taught** in a *baraita*: **Rabbi Elazar, son of Rabbi Shimon, says:** In **every instance** in the Torah **that** the word **"finger" is stated with regard to collection** of the blood and not with regard to placing of the blood on the altar, if the priest **deviated** from the proper method **of collection** and performed it with the left hand, the offering is **disqualified,** but if he deviated from the proper method **of placing** the blood, the offering remains **fit. And** in **every instance that** the word **"finger" is stated** only **with regard to placing** the blood, if the priest **deviated** from the proper method **of placing,** the offering is **disqualified,** but if he deviated from the proper method **of collection,** the offering remains **fit.**

וְהֵיכָן נֶאֱמַר אֶצְבַּע בִּנְתִינָה – דִּכְתִיב: ״וְלָקַחְתָּ מִדַּם הַפָּר וְנָתַתָּה עַל קַרְנֹת הַמִּזְבֵּחַ בְּאֶצְבָּעֶךָ״. וְקָסָבַר: מִקְרָא נִדְרָשׁ לְפָנָיו וְלֹא לִפְנֵי פָנָיו וּלְאַחֲרָיו.

And where is the word "finger" **stated** only **with regard to placing? As it is written: "And you shall take of the blood of the bullock and put it upon the corners of the altar with your finger"** (Exodus 29:12). **And he holds** that **a verse is interpreted** based on juxtaposition to the language immediately **preceding it and not** to the language **before that** which immediately **precedes it,**[N] **nor** to the language **following it.**

אָמַר רַבָּה בַּר בַּר חָנָה אָמַר רַבִּי יוֹחָנָן: כׇּל מָקוֹם שֶׁנֶּאֱמַר אֶצְבַּע וּכְהוּנָּה – אֵינָהּ אֶלָּא יָמִין.

§ **Rabba bar bar Ḥana says** that **Rabbi Yoḥanan says:** In **every instance** in the Torah **that it is stated** that an action is performed with **a finger and** by members of the **priesthood,** it may be performed **only** with the **right** hand.

קָא סָלְקָא דַּעְתִּין תַּרְתֵּי בָּעֵינַן, כִּדְכְתִיב: ״וְלָקַח הַכֹּהֵן מִדַּם הַחַטָּאת בְּאֶצְבָּעוֹ״, וְיָלֵיף מִמְּצוֹרָע, דִּכְתִיב: ״וְטָבַל הַכֹּהֵן אֶת אֶצְבָּעוֹ הַיְמָנִית״. וַהֲרֵי קְמִיצָה דְּלָא כְּתִיב בָּהּ אֶלָּא כְּהוּנָּה, וּתְנַן: קָמַץ בִּשְׂמֹאל פָּסוּל!

The Gemara comments: It might **enter our mind** to say that this means that **we require both** a finger and the priesthood to be stated together in the verse in order to mandate use of the right hand, e.g., **as it is written: "And the priest shall take of the blood of the sin offering with his finger"** (Leviticus 4:25). **And** the fact that this verse is referring to a finger from his right hand **is derived from a leper, as it is written: "And the priest shall dip his right finger"** (Leviticus 14:16). This cannot be correct, **as** there is the verse that addresses **the removal of a handful** from a meal offering, **in which only** the **priesthood is written, and** yet **we learned** in a mishna (*Menaḥot* 6a): If one **removed the handful with** his **left** hand, the meal offering is **disqualified.**

אֶלָּא אָמַר רָבָא: אוֹ אֶצְבַּע אוֹ כְּהוּנָּה.

Rather, Rava says: This statement means that if the verse mentions **either a finger or** the **priesthood,** only the right hand may be used.

אֲמַר לֵיהּ אַבַּיֵי: הֲרֵי הוֹלָכַת אֵבָרִים לַכֶּבֶשׁ, דִּכְתִיב בְּהוּ כְּהוּנָּה, דִּכְתִיב: ״וְהִקְרִיב הַכֹּהֵן אֶת הַכֹּל [וְהִקְטִיר] הַמִּזְבֵּחָה״, וְאָמַר מָר: זוֹ הוֹלָכַת אֵבָרִים לַכֶּבֶשׁ, וּתְנַן: הָרֶגֶל שֶׁל יָמִין בִּשְׂמֹאלוֹ, וּבֵית עוֹרָהּ לַחוּץ!

Abaye said to Rava: But this is contradicted by the verse discussing **the conveyance of** the **limbs** of the daily burnt offering **to the ramp** of the altar, as **priesthood is written with regard to it, as it is written: "And the priest shall sacrifice the whole** and make it smoke **upon the altar"** (Leviticus 1:13), **and the Master said** that **this** verse is referring to the **conveyance of** the **limbs to the ramp. And** yet **we learned** in a mishna (*Tamid* 31b): When the priest conveys the limbs to the ramp, **the foot of** the **right** side of the offering is carried **in the left** hand[H] of the priest, **and the place of its skin,** i.e., the side of the limb covered in skin, is held facing **outward.** Clearly, use of the left hand does not disqualify the conveyance of the limbs.

[כִּי אָמְרִינַן] אוֹ אֶצְבַּע אוֹ כְּהוּנָּה – בְּדָבָר הַמְעַכֵּב כַּפָּרָה, דּוּמְיָא דִּמְצוֹרָע.

The Gemara responds: **When we say** that if the verse states **either finger or priesthood** then the left hand is disqualified, this is only **with regard to a matter that precludes atonement,** i.e., a rite whose performance is indispensable to the atonement, **similar to** the sprinkling of the oil on the **leper** (see Leviticus 14:16). The conveyance of the limbs, by contrast, is not indispensable to atonement.

וַהֲרֵי קַבָּלָה, דִּכְתַב בְּהוּ כְּהוּנָּה, וְדָבָר הַמְעַכֵּב בְּכַפָּרָה הוּא, וּתְנַן: קִבֵּל בִּשְׂמֹאל – פָּסוּל, וְרַבִּי שִׁמְעוֹן מַכְשִׁיר!

The Gemara asks: **But** isn't there the **collection** of the blood in a service vessel, **about which priesthood is written**[N] **and** which **is a matter that precludes atonement? And** yet **we learned** in the mishna: If **one collected** the blood **with** his **left** hand, the blood is **disqualified** for offering, **and Rabbi Shimon deems it fit.**

רַבִּי שִׁמְעוֹן תַּרְתֵּי בָּעֵי.

The Gemara responds: **Rabbi Shimon requires** that **both** matters appear in the verse, i.e., both finger and priesthood.

מִי בָּעֵי רַבִּי שִׁמְעוֹן תַּרְתֵּי? וְהָתַנְיָא, רַבִּי שִׁמְעוֹן אוֹמֵר: כׇּל מָקוֹם שֶׁנֶּאֱמַר יָד – אֵינוֹ אֶלָּא יָמִין, אֶצְבַּע – אֵינוֹ אֶלָּא יָמִין!

The Gemara asks: **Does Rabbi Shimon** really **require both? But isn't it taught** in a *baraita* that **Rabbi Shimon says:** In **every instance** in the Torah **that** the word **"hand" is stated,** the verse **is** referring **only** to the **right** hand, and whenever the verse mentions **"finger,"** it is referring **only** to a finger of the **right** hand?

אֶצְבַּע לָא בָּעֲיָא כְּהוּנָּה, כְּהוּנָּה בָּעֲיָא אֶצְבַּע.

The Gemara responds: According to Rabbi Shimon, if the verse mentions only **"finger,"** then it **does not require** a mention of the **priesthood** as well for the limitation to apply. But if the verse mentions only the **priesthood,** it **requires** a mention of **"finger"** for the limitation to apply.

וְאֶלָּא כֹּהֵן לָמָּה לִי? בְּכִיהוּנָּן.

The Gemara asks: **But** according to Rabbi Shimon, if the mention of the priesthood alone does not suffice to disqualify the right hand, then **why do I need** the superfluous reference to **a priest** with regard to the collection of the blood? After all, the verse already states that the collection must be performed by the sons of Aaron. The Gemara responds: The additional mention of the priesthood indicates that the priests must perform the collection of the blood **in their priestly state,** i.e., while wearing the priestly vestments.

HALAKHA

The foot of the right side is carried in the left hand – **הָרֶגֶל שֶׁל יָמִין בִּשְׂמֹאלוֹ**: When the priests convey the limbs of the burnt offering to the altar to be burned, the priest must hold the right leg in his left hand, with the side covered in skin facing outward. Some learn from the Gemara here that all rites not indispensable for atonement are not disqualified if performed with the left hand (Rambam *Sefer Avoda, Hilkhot Ma'aseh HaKorbanot* 6:11 and Mahari Kurkus there; see *Hilkhot Pesulei HaMukdashin* 2:24).

NOTES

Collection, about which priesthood is written – **קַבָּלָה דִּכְתַב בְּהוּ כְּהוּנָּה**: The verse states: "And the sons of Aaron, the priests, shall present the blood" (Leviticus 1:5), and the Sages interpret this as referring to the collection of the blood (see 13a). This rite is indispensable to atonement, since one cannot sprinkle the blood on the altar without first collecting it in a vessel.

וַהֲרֵי זְרִיקָה, דְּלָא כְּתַב בְּהוּ אֶלָּא כְּהוּנָּה, וּתְנַן: זָרַק בִּשְׂמֹאל – פָּסוּל, וְלָא פָּלֵיג רַבִּי שִׁמְעוֹן!

The Gemara asks: **But** isn't there the **sprinkling** of the blood,[N] **concerning which only** the **priesthood is written** in the verse, **and we learned: If one sprinkled** the blood **with his left** hand it is **disqualified; and Rabbi Shimon does not disagree** with this ruling, indicating that Rabbi Shimon holds that a mention of the priesthood does not require a mention of "finger"?

אָמַר אַבַּיֵי: פָּלֵיג בְּבָרַיְיתָא, דְּתַנְיָא: קִיבֵּל בִּשְׂמֹאל – פָּסוּל, וְרַבִּי שִׁמְעוֹן מַכְשִׁיר. זָרַק בִּשְׂמֹאל – פָּסוּל, וְרַבִּי שִׁמְעוֹן מַכְשִׁיר.

Abaye says: He disagrees with this ruling **in a** ***baraita*****,**[B] **as it is taught** in a *baraita*: If **one collected** the blood **with his left** hand, it is **disqualified, and Rabbi Shimon deems** it **fit.** Additionally, if **one sprinkled** the blood **with his left** hand, it is **disqualified, and Rabbi Shimon deems** it **fit.**

אֶלָּא הָא דְּאָמַר רָבָא: "יָד" "יָד" לִקְמִיצָה, "רֶגֶל" "רֶגֶל" לַחֲלִיצָה, "אֹזֶן" "אֹזֶן" לִרְצִיעָה, לָמָּה לִי? מִדְּרַבָּה בַּר בַּר חָנָה נָפְקָא!

The Gemara asks: **But that which Rava says** with regard to the superfluous phrases in the passage discussing a leper: One derives a verbal analogy between **"hand"** and **"hand"**[N] mentioned with regard **to the removal of a handful**[B] from a meal offering, to indicate that the latter must also be performed with the right hand. Additionally, one derives a verbal analogy between **"foot"** and **"foot"** mentioned with regard **to the** ***halitza***[B] ritual. And one derives a verbal analogy between **"ear"** and **"ear"** mentioned with regard **to the piercing**[B] of a Hebrew slave's ear with an awl. One may ask: **Why do I** need the first analogy? The requirement that the handful be removed with the right hand can be **derived from** the statement **of Rabba bar bar Ḥana** above, since priesthood is mentioned in the verse describing it.

חַד לְקוֹמֶץ, וְחַד לְקִידּוּשׁ קוֹמֶץ.

The Gemara responds: Both derivations are necessary, **one for** the removal of the **handful** from a meal offering, **and one for the sanctification of the handful,**[N] i.e., placing it into a second service vessel. Both must be performed with the right hand.

NOTES

But isn't there the sprinkling, etc. – **וַהֲרֵי זְרִיקָה וכו׳**: Rashi writes that this is referring to offerings other than a sin offering, since, as mentioned, the verse in Leviticus 4:34 is interpreted even according to Rabbi Shimon as mandating that the blood of the sin offering be placed on the altar with the right hand.

Between hand and hand, etc. – **יָד יָד וכו׳**: In detailing the purification process of the leper, the verse states: "The priest shall take of the blood of the guilt offering, and the priest shall put it upon the tip of the right ear of him that is to be purified, and upon the thumb of his right hand, and upon the big toe of his right foot" (Leviticus 14:14). Afterward, the description continues: "And the priest shall put of the oil that is in his hand upon the tip of the right ear of him that is to be purified, and upon the thumb of his right hand, and upon the big toe of his right foot, upon the place of the blood of the guilt offering" (Leviticus 14:17). Since the verse mentions: "The place of the blood of the guilt offering," the mention of the individual places of application in the second verse is redundant. Therefore, Rava infers that these details teach *halakhot* about other cases by verbal analogy (see alternative interpretations in *Tosafot* and *Shita Mekubbetzet* on *Menahot* 10a).

For the sanctification of the handful – **לְקִידּוּשׁ קוֹמֶץ**: According to Rashi, the statement teaches that the vessel must be held in the priest's right hand when the handful is placed inside. The *Likkutei Halakhot* notes that even Rashi holds that the removal itself must also be performed with the right hand. Accordingly, two priests must participate in the rite, one to remove the handful and one to hold the vessel.

BACKGROUND

Baraita – **בָּרַיְיתָא**: The word *baraita* literally means external, and it is used to refer to tannaitic material that was not included in the final compilation of the Mishna. When Rabbi Yehuda HaNasi redacted the canon of tannaitic material it was necessary to exclude much of it from the Mishna. This material, some of which comprises other collections, is known as *baraitot*. These *baraitot* contain variant texts and other important material.

Handful – **קְמִיצָה**: For most meal offerings, a priest must remove a handful from the offering and burn it on the altar (see, e.g., Leviticus 2:2). This service, which parallels the slaughter of an animal sacrifice, may be performed only by a priest. According to many authorities, the priest would scoop the flour out with the three middle fingers of his right hand, using his thumb and little finger to remove any surplus flour. He would then consecrate the flour by placing it in a sacred vessel used in the Temple service. Since the priest was required to scoop out a precise handful of flour, no more and no less, removal of the handful was considered one of the more difficult services in the Temple to perform.

Ḥalitza – **חֲלִיצָה**: *Ḥalitza* is the ceremony that frees a *yevama*, the widow of a man who died childless, from the obligation to marry one of her deceased husband's brothers, thereby allowing her to remarry another man (see Deuteronomy 25:7–10). The term *ḥalitza* is derived from the central element of this ceremony, the removal [*ḥalitza*] by the widow of a special sandal from the foot of one of her deceased husband's brothers, known as the *yavam*. *Ḥalitza* must be performed before a rabbinical court. The *halakhot* governing this ceremony are discussed in detail in tractate *Yevamot*.

Piercing – **רְצִיעָה**: A Hebrew slave who does not wish to terminate his servitude after six years may remain with his master until the Jubilee Year or his master's death (see Exodus 21:6 and Leviticus 25:40). Only a slave who was given a maidservant as a wife by his master and has children with her may make this request. The master brings the slave to the court, and after they have investigated the matter, the slave stands next to a doorpost and an awl or similar metal instrument is driven though his ear. This may be done only if there is a strong bond of friendship between the slave and his master. A priest who was sold into slavery may not have his ear pierced, since doing so would render him blemished and unfit to perform the Temple service. The rite of piercing may be performed only on a slave sold by the court, not on one who sold himself into slavery.

וּלְרַבִּי שִׁמְעוֹן דְּלָא בָּעֵי קִידּוּשׁ קוֹמֶץ, וּלְמַאן דְּאָמַר: לְרַבִּי שִׁמְעוֹן נָמֵי בָּעֵי קִידּוּשׁ קוֹמֶץ – בִּשְׂמֹאל אַכְשׁוּרֵי מַכְשַׁר, "יָד" "יָד" דְּרָבָא לְמָה לִי?

The Gemara asks: **And according to Rabbi Shimon, who does not require sanctification of the handful,**[N] **or according to the one who says that Rabbi Shimon also requires** the **sanctification of the handful** but that **he deems** the sanctification **fit** when performed **with the left hand,**[N] **why do I need the verbal analogy of Rava** between **"hand"** and **"hand"?**

אִי לִקְמִיצָה עַצְמָהּ – מִדְּרַב יְהוּדָה בְּרֵיהּ דְּרַבִּי חִיָּיא נָפְקָא, דְּאָמַר רַב יְהוּדָה בְּרֵיהּ דְּרַבִּי חִיָּיא: מַאי טַעְמָא דְּרַבִּי שִׁמְעוֹן? [דְּאָמַר קְרָא:] "קֹדֶשׁ קָדָשִׁים הִיא כַּחַטָּאת וְכָאָשָׁם",

If one suggests that it is necessary **to** indicate that the **removal of** the **handful itself** must be performed with the right hand, this cannot be, since that is **derived from** the verse cited by **Rav Yehuda, son of Rabbi Ḥiyya. As Rav Yehuda, son of Rabbi Ḥiyya, says: What is the reason that Rabbi Shimon** does not require that the handful be sanctified in a service vessel? **As the verse states** with regard to the meal offering: **"It is most holy, as the sin offering, and as the guilt offering"** (Leviticus 6:10).

בָּא לְעׇבְדָהּ בְּיָד – עוֹבְדָהּ בְּיָמִין כְּחַטָּאת, בָּא לְעׇבְדָהּ בִּכְלִי – עוֹבְדָהּ בִּשְׂמֹאל כְּאָשָׁם!

The verse compares the meal offering to a sin offering and a guilt offering. Therefore, if the priest **comes to perform** the burning of the handful **with** his **hand,** then **he performs it with** his **right** hand, **like a sin offering,** whose blood is sprinkled by hand. And if he **comes to perform it with a vessel,** i.e., if he first sanctifies the handful in a service vessel, then **he** may **perform it with** his **left** hand, **like a guilt offering,**[N] whose blood is sprinkled from a vessel. Since the removal of the handful is performed by hand, the verse indicates that it must be performed with the right hand, and the verbal analogy is unnecessary.

לָא נִצְרְכָא [אֶלָּא] לְקוֹמֶץ מִנְחַת חוֹטֵא; סָלְקָא דַּעְתָּךְ אָמֵינָא: הוֹאִיל וְאָמַר רַבִּי שִׁמְעוֹן: שֶׁלֹּא יְהֵא קׇרְבָּנוֹ מְהוּדָּר, כִּי קָמֵיץ לַהּ בִּשְׂמֹאל נָמֵי תִּיתַּכְשַׁר – קָא מַשְׁמַע לַן.

The Gemara responds: The verbal analogy **is necessary only for the handful of a meal offering of a sinner,** to teach that it must be removed with the right hand. It might **enter your mind to say: Since Rabbi Shimon says** that this offering does not require oil and frankincense **so that his offering will not be of superior** quality, perhaps **when he removed the handful with** his **left** hand, which is an inferior manner, **it should be fit as well.** The verbal analogy therefore **teaches us** that the handful must always be removed with the right hand, even in the case of the meal offering of a sinner.

מתני׳ נִשְׁפַּךְ הַדָּם עַל הָרִצְפָּה וַאֲסָפוֹ – פָּסוּל.

MISHNA If **the blood spilled**[H] **on the floor**[N] before the priest managed to collect it into a vessel, **and** the priest then **collected it** from the floor into a vessel, it is **disqualified.**

גמ׳ תָּנוּ רַבָּנַן: "וְלָקַח הַכֹּהֵן הַמָּשִׁיחַ מִדַּם הַפָּר" – מִדַּם הַנֶּפֶשׁ, וְלֹא מִדַּם הָעוֹר, וְלֹא מִדַּם הַתַּמְצִית.

GEMARA The Sages taught: The verse states: **"And the anointed priest shall take from the blood of the bull** [*middam happar*]" (Leviticus 4:5). This means that the priest shall take **from the blood of the soul,**[B] i.e., the blood that flows from the place of slaughter as the animal dies, **but not from the blood of the skin,** which bleeds out when the skin is cut before the slaughter, **nor from the blood of exudate,** i.e., that exudes from the neck of the animal after the initial spurt of its slaughter concludes.

"מִדַּם הַפָּר" – דָּם מֵהַפָּר יְקַבְּלֶנּוּ. דְּאִי סָלְקָא דַּעְתָּךְ מִדַּם הַפָּר כִּדְכְתִיב: "מִדַּם" – וַאֲפִילּוּ מִקְצָת דָּם – וְהָאָמַר רַב: הַשּׁוֹחֵט צָרִיךְ שֶׁיְּקַבֵּל אֶת כׇּל דָּמוֹ שֶׁל פַּר, שֶׁנֶּאֱמַר: "וְאֶת כׇּל דָּמוֹ יִשְׁפֹּךְ".

The *baraita* continues: When the verse states: **"From the blood of the bull,"** it should be interpreted as if it is written: **He shall collect the blood from the bull,** i.e., if the blood spills onto the floor before it is collected in a service vessel, it is disqualified. **As, if it enters your mind** that **"from the blood of the bull"** should be interpreted **as it is written,** i.e., that **"from the blood"** means that the priest may collect **even** only **a portion of the blood,** that is difficult: **But doesn't Rav say: One who slaughters** the offering **must collect all the blood**[H] **of the bull, as it is stated: "And all the blood of the bull he shall pour out** on the base of the altar" (Leviticus 4:7)? The verse emphasizes that the priest must pour all the blood of the bull, which is possible only if he has collected all of it.

NOTES

Who does not require sanctification of the handful – דְּלָא בָּעֵי קִידּוּשׁ קוֹמֶץ: The *amora'im* disagree in tractate *Menaḥot* (26a) with regard to Rabbi Shimon's opinion on the matter. According to Rabbi Yannai, Rabbi Shimon holds that sanctification of the handful is not a service rite at all. Rather, the priest simply takes the handful of the meal offering in his hand and conveys it to the altar. Rav Naḥman bar Yitzḥak holds that Rabbi Shimon requires sanctification of the handful in a service vessel, but deems it fit if the priest removed it afterward and placed it on the altar with his hand.

He deems it fit when performed with the left hand – בִּשְׂמֹאל אַכְשׁוּרֵי מַכְשַׁר: Sanctification of the handful in a service vessel for a meal offering is the equivalent of the collection of the blood for an animal offering. Since Rabbi Shimon holds that the latter is fit if performed with the left hand, he holds likewise with regard to the former.

He may perform it with his left hand, like a guilt offering – עוֹבְדָהּ בִּשְׂמֹאל כְּאָשָׁם: The burning of the handful of a meal offering is the equivalent of the sprinkling of the blood of animal offerings. According to Rabbi Shimon, the blood of animal offerings, including a guilt offering, is fit if sprinkled with the left hand, as mentioned in a *baraita* on the previous *amud*.

The blood spilled on the floor – נִשְׁפַּךְ הַדָּם עַל הָרִצְפָּה: This is referring to a case where the blood spilled onto the floor directly from the animal's neck. If the blood spilled out of the service vessel and the priest is able to gather it back inside, it remains fit because it entered the service vessel directly from the animal (see mishna on 32a).

HALAKHA

The blood spilled – נִשְׁפַּךְ הַדָּם: If the blood spilled from the service vessel in which it was collected and was then gathered again, it remains fit to be sprinkled. But if it spilled from the neck of the animal onto the floor, it is disqualified even if gathered up again, in accordance with the mishna (Rambam *Sefer Avoda, Hilkhot Pesulei HaMukdashin* 1:25).

Must collect all the blood – צָרִיךְ שֶׁיְּקַבֵּל כׇּל דָּמוֹ: The priest must attempt to collect all the blood of the offering. After the fact, the offering is fit if enough blood was collected to sprinkle, in accordance with the Gemara in *Menaḥot* 7b (Rambam *Sefer Avoda, Hilkhot Ma'aseh HaKorbanot* 4:8).

BACKGROUND

Blood of the soul – דַּם הַנֶּפֶשׁ: When an animal is slaughtered, the first blood drawn is that in the system of blood vessels that supply the animal's skin. When the knife reaches the main veins it releases the blood of the soul, i.e., the blood driven out of the animal's body by force of its heartbeat. This is called the blood of the soul because it is the most important to sustaining the animal's life, and when it exits the heart stops beating and the animal dies. Still afterward, some blood continues to flow through the veins due to gravity, and this is referred to as blood of exudate, i.e., blood that exudes from the neck of the animal after the initial spurt of its slaughter concludes.

אֶלָּא ״מִדַּם הַפָּר״ – דָּם מֵהַפָּר יְקַבְּלֶנּוּ, וְקָסָבַר: גּוֹרְעִין וּמוֹסִיפִין וְדוֹרְשִׁין.

Rather, "from the blood of the bull" means that the priest **shall collect** the **blood from the bull. And** this Sage **holds** that the Sages **subtract and add and interpret homiletically,** i.e., one may take a letter from one word, insert it into a second word, and explain the phrase in that manner. In this case, the *mem* of *middam* is added to *happar*, so that the verse is interpreted as though it states: *Dam mehappar*, meaning: Blood from the bull.

גּוּפָא, אָמַר רַב יְהוּדָה אָמַר רַב: הַשּׁוֹחֵט צָרִיךְ שֶׁיְּקַבֵּל אֶת כָּל דָּמוֹ שֶׁל פָּר, שֶׁנֶּאֱמַר: ״וְאֵת כָּל דַּם הַפָּר יִשְׁפֹּךְ״. וְהָא בְּשִׁירַיִים כְּתִיב!

§ The Gemara turns to **the matter itself: Rav Yehuda says** that **Rav says: One who slaughters** the offering **must collect all the blood of the bull, as it is stated: "And all the blood of the bull he shall pour out** on the base of the altar." The Gemara asks: **But isn't** this verse **written with regard to the remainder** of the blood that is poured onto the base of the altar after the sprinkling? How, then, can a *halakha* with regard to the collection of the blood be derived from it?

אִם אֵינוֹ עִנְיָן לְשִׁירַיִים, דְּהָא לֵיתֵיהּ לְכוּלֵּיהּ דָּם – תְּנֵיהוּ עִנְיָן בְּקַבָּלָה.

The Gemara responds: **If** this verse **is not** referring **to the matter of the remainder** of the blood after sprinkling, **as not all of the blood is** present for that rite since some of it has already been sprinkled, **apply it instead to the matter of collection** of the blood from the animal.

אָמַר רַב יְהוּדָה אָמַר שְׁמוּאֵל: הַשּׁוֹחֵט צָרִיךְ שֶׁיַּגְבִּיהַּ סַכִּין לְמַעְלָה, שֶׁנֶּאֱמַר: ״וְלָקַח מִדַּם הַפָּר״ – וְלֹא מִדַּם הַפָּר וְדָבָר אַחֵר.

Rav Yehuda says that **Shmuel says: One who slaughters** the offering **must hold the knife up**[H] after slaughter, so that blood that is on the knife does not fall into the service vessel, **as it is stated: "And** the anointed priest **shall take from the blood of the bull,"** i.e., **and not from** a mixture of **the blood of the bull and something else,** such as the blood from the knife.

וְדַם סַכִּין בְּמַאי מְקַנֵּחַ לֵיהּ? אָמַר אַבָּיֵי: בִּשְׂפַת מִזְרָק, כְּדִכְתִיב: ״כְּפוֹרֵי זָהָב״.

The Gemara asks: **And with what does he wipe**[HN] the **blood** from the **knife? Abaye says:** He wipes it **with the rim of the bowl**[N] used to collect the blood, **as it is written** of the bowls used to collect the blood: **"Atoning-bowls [*keforei*]**[L] **of gold"** (Ezra 1:10). The root *kaf*, *peh*, *reish* can also mean to wipe.

אָמַר רַב חִסְדָּא אָמַר רַב יִרְמְיָה בַּר אַבָּא: הַשּׁוֹחֵט צָרִיךְ שֶׁיִּתֵּן

Rav Ḥisda says that **Rav Yirmeya bar Abba says: One who slaughters** the offering **must place**

HALAKHA

Must hold the knife up – צָרִיךְ שֶׁיַּגְבִּיהַּ סַכִּין: The slaughterer must hold the knife up so that blood from it does not fall into the bowl and mix with the blood from the offering's neck (Rambam *Sefer Avoda, Hilkhot Ma'aseh HaKorbanot* 4:8).

With what does he wipe – בְּמַאי מְקַנֵּחַ: The blood remaining on the knife must be wiped off with the rim of the bowl (Rambam *Sefer Avoda, Hilkhot Ma'aseh HaKorbanot* 4:8).

NOTES

Wipe – מְקַנֵּחַ: The remaining blood must be wiped off the knife so that it does not mix with the blood of the next offering to be slaughtered, and so that it does not congeal and interfere with the knife's function in the future. Some explain that the blood must be wiped with the bowl because of the requirement to collect all the blood of the offering (see *Ḥiddushei Batra*).

With the rim of the bowl – בִּשְׂפַת מִזְרָק: This must be done with the outside of the bowl's rim, so that the blood on the knife does not mix with the blood inside the bowl.

LANGUAGE

Keforei – כְּפוֹרֵי: Rashi notes that the root *kaf*, *peh*, *reish* in the sense of wiping appears in Aramaic in the Talmud itself. The root also means to atone, in the sense of wiping away sin. A parallel root also exists in Syriac, meaning both to wipe and to atone.

וְרִידִין לְתוֹךְ הַכְּלִי. אִיתְּמַר נַמִי, אָמַר רַב אַסִּי אָמַר רַבִּי יוֹחָנָן: וְרִידִין צָרִיךְ שֶׁיִּרְאוּ אֲוִיר כְּלִי.

the **veins** of the offering **into the vessel,**[HN] so that all the blood will empty into it. **It was also stated: Rav Asi says** that **Rabbi Yoḥanan says:** The **veins must see the airspace of the vessel.**

בְּעָא מִינֵּיהּ רַבִּי אַסִּי מֵרַבִּי יוֹחָנָן: הָיָה מְקַבֵּל, וְנִפְחֲתוּ שׁוּלֵי מִזְרָק עַד שֶׁלֹּא הִגִּיעַ דָּם לָאֲוִיר, מַהוּ? אֲוִיר שֶׁאֵין סוֹפוֹ לָנוּחַ כְּמוּנָּח דָּמֵי, אוֹ לָא כְּמוּנָּח דָּמֵי?

§ **Rabbi Asi raised a dilemma before Rabbi Yoḥanan:** If the priest **was collecting** the blood, **and the bottom of the bowl**[N] **broke before** the **blood reached the** bowl's **airspace, what is** the *halakha*? Is blood that enters the **airspace** of a bowl **that will not ultimately** allow it **to settle**[HN] inside nevertheless **considered as** though it **settled** inside the vessel, so that when it spills through the break it is considered to have already been collected in the bowl? If so, it remains fit for sprinkling. **Or** is it **not considered as** though it **settled,** but is instead considered to have spilled directly from the animal's neck onto the floor, and is therefore disqualified?

HALAKHA

Veins into the vessel – וְרִידִין לְתוֹךְ הַכְּלִי: The one who slaughters the offering must attempt to collect all its blood in the vessel. He does this by gripping the gullet and windpipe and pulling them outward toward the vessel and then slaughtering (Rambam *Sefer Avoda, Hilkhot Ma'aseh HaKorbanot* 4:8).

That will not ultimately allow it to settle – שֶׁאֵין סוֹפוֹ לָנוּחַ: The airspace of the vessel is considered part of the vessel. If one was collecting the blood of an offering, and the bottom of the bowl broke before the blood reached the airspace of the vessel, the blood was not sanctified, because an item that enters the airspace of a vessel in such a manner that it will not ultimately settle there is not considered to have settled (Rambam *Sefer Avoda, Hilkhot Ma'aseh HaKorbanot* 4:9).

NOTES

Veins into the vessel – וְרִידִין לְתוֹךְ כְּלִי: Rashi notes that it is impossible to physically place the veins into the vessel. Rather, the Gemara means that the vessel should be situated just below the veins so as to collect the blood flowing from them. This is also the straightforward meaning of the subsequent statement of Rabbi Yoḥanan.

Bottom of the bowl – שׁוּלֵי מִזְרָק: Rashi writes that this is referring to a case where the bottom of the bowl broke. The Griz explains that this cannot mean that the entire bottom broke off from the rest of the vessel, as if that were the case, it would cease to be considered a vessel at all. Rather, the Gemara is referring to a case where a small hole was formed in the bottom of the bowl from which the blood leaks. In such a case, the bowl is still considered a vessel.

That will not ultimately allow it to settle – שֶׁאֵין סוֹפוֹ לָנוּחַ: Rashi interprets this question as referring to blood that was in the air over the vessel when it broke, but which did not yet enter the airspace within the vessel's walls. The blood that was already within the airspace of the vessel before it broke is considered to have settled.

אָמַר לֵיהּ, תְּנֵיתוּהָ: חָבִית שֶׁמּוּנַּחַת תַּחַת הַזִּינּוּק – מַיִם שֶׁבְּתוֹכָהּ וְשֶׁבַּחוּצָה לָהּ פְּסוּלִין; צֵירֵף פִּיהָ לַזִּינּוּק, מַיִם שֶׁבְּתוֹכָהּ – פְּסוּלִין, וְשֶׁבַּחוּצָה לָהּ – כְּשֵׁירִין.

Rabbi Yoḥanan **said to him: You learned** the answer in a *baraita*: With regard to a **barrel that is placed**[N] **under a pipe** to catch water running from it, both the **water that** has already flowed **inside** the barrel **and** that **which is** still **outside it** but about to fall in are **unfit**[N] to be used as water of purification, which purify one who contracts impurity from a corpse. The water of purification must be flowing water, and all of this water is considered to have been collected in the barrel. But if one **joined the mouth of** the barrel **to the pipe,** the **water that is inside** the barrel **is unfit, but** water **that is** still **outside it is fit,** even though it will ultimately fall in, since it is still in the pipe and is not considered to be above the airspace of the barrel. One can infer from the *baraita* that all liquid that enters the airspace of a vessel is considered to have been collected in it.

הַאי מַאי? בָּעֵי מִינֵּיהּ אֲוִיר שֶׁאֵין סוֹפוֹ לָנוּחַ, וְקָא פָּשֵׁט לֵיהּ אֲוִיר שֶׁסּוֹפוֹ לָנוּחַ!

The Gemara rejects this: **What is this** comparison? Rabbi Asi **raises a dilemma before** Rabbi Yoḥanan with regard to a case where an item enters the **airspace** of a vessel **that will not ultimately** allow it **to settle** inside, **and** Rabbi Yoḥanan **resolves** the dilemma by citing a case where the item enters the **airspace** of a vessel **that will ultimately** allow it **to settle** inside.

תַּרְתֵּי קָא בָּעֵי מִינֵּיהּ, אִם תִּמְצֵי לוֹמַר: אֲוִיר שֶׁאֵין סוֹפוֹ לָנוּחַ לָאו כְּמוּנָּח דָּמֵי, אֲוִיר שֶׁסּוֹפוֹ לָנוּחַ מַאי?

The Gemara responds: Rabbi Asi **raises two dilemmas before** Rabbi Yoḥanan: First, what is the *halakha* with regard to an item that will not come to rest in the vessel? Second, **if you say** that an item that enters the **airspace** of a vessel **that will not ultimately** allow it **to settle** inside is **not considered as** though it **settled** inside the vessel, **what** is the *halakha* with regard to an item that entered the **airspace** of a vessel **that will ultimately** allow it **to settle** inside?

רַב יוֹסֵף מַתְנֵי הָכִי. רַב כָּהֲנָא מַתְנֵי: חָבִית בְּעָא מִינֵּיהּ, וּפְשַׁט לֵיהּ חָבִית.

The Gemara notes: **Rav Yosef teaches** the exchange in **this** manner, i.e., as recounted. **Rav Kahana teaches** it as follows: Rabbi Asi **raised the dilemma before** Rabbi Yoḥanan with regard to **a barrel,** asking whether the water in its airspace is fit to be used for the water of purification, **and** Rabbi Yoḥanan **resolved** the dilemma **for him** by citing the *baraita* mentioning **a barrel,** with which he was unfamiliar.

רַבָּה מַתְנֵי: חָבִית בְּעָא מִינֵּיהּ, וּפְשַׁט לֵיהּ מִזְרָק, אִי אַתָּה מוֹדֶה בְּמִזְרָק שֶׁאִי אֶפְשָׁר לוֹ בְּלֹא זִינּוּק?

Rabba teaches the exchange as follows: Rabbi Asi **raised the dilemma before** Rabbi Yoḥanan with regard to **a barrel, and** Rabbi Yoḥanan **resolved** the dilemma **for him** by citing the *halakha* concerning **a bowl** used to collect the blood in the Temple, saying: **Do you not concede with regard to the bowl that it is impossible to** collect the blood in **it without a stream** of blood flowing through the air from animal's neck? If the air above the bowl is not considered part of the bowl, the blood would be considered to have entered the bowl from the air above rather than directly from the animal's neck, and all collected blood would be unfit. Therefore, the airspace must be considered part of the bowl, and the same holds for the barrel with regard to the water of purification.

תְּנַן הָתָם: נָתַן יָדוֹ אוֹ רַגְלוֹ אוֹ עֲלֵי יְרָקוֹת כְּדֵי שֶׁיַּעַבְרוּ מַיִם לֶחָבִית – פְּסוּלִין, עֲלֵי קָנִים וַעֲלֵי אֱגוֹזִים – כְּשֵׁירָה. זֶה הַכְּלָל: דָּבָר הַמְקַבֵּל טוּמְאָה – פְּסוּלִין, דָּבָר שֶׁאֵינוֹ מְקַבֵּל טוּמְאָה – כְּשֵׁירִין.

The Gemara adds: **We learned** in a mishna **elsewhere** (*Para* 6:4) with regard to sanctifying the water of purification: If one **placed his hand**[H] **or his foot**[N] **or vegetable leaves**[N] **in order** to allow flowing **water to pass** through them **to the barrel,** the water **is disqualified.** But if the water passed through **leaves of reeds or leaves of nuts,**[N] the water remains **fit. This is the principle:** If the water passes through **an item that is susceptible to impurity,** it **is disqualified;** if it passes through **an item that is not susceptible to impurity,** it **is fit.**

מְנָא הָנֵי מִילֵּי? דְּאָמַר רַבִּי יוֹחָנָן מִשּׁוּם רַבִּי יוֹסֵי בַּר אַבָּא: אָמַר קְרָא "אַךְ מַעְיָן וּבוֹר מִקְוֵה מַיִם יִהְיֶה טָהוֹר", הֲוָיָיתָן עַל יְדֵי טָהֳרָה תְּהֵא.

The Gemara asks: **From where are these matters** derived? **As Rabbi Yoḥanan says in the name of Rabbi Yosei bar Abba: The verse states: "Nevertheless a fountain or a cistern wherein is a gathering of water shall be pure"** (Leviticus 11:36). The verse indicates that **their being must be by way of purity,** i.e., the gathering of the water must not be accomplished by way of items susceptible to impurity.

NOTES

Barrel that is placed, etc. – **חָבִית שֶׁמּוּנַּחַת וכו׳:** The verse states with regard to the water of purification: "Running water shall be put thereto in a vessel" (Numbers 19:17), indicating that the source of the water must be flowing, e.g., a stream, river, or natural spring. Water from such sources is still considered to be flowing even if it runs through a man-made aqueduct attached to the ground. The water must be collected in a designated vessel for use in the ritual. One may also collect such water in a vessel designated for collecting water of purification, and thereafter transfer it into the appropriate vessel. If the barrel was not designated as such, it disqualifies water that enters it by stopping its flow (see Rabbi Shimshon of Saens on *Para* 9:6 and *Ḥazon Ish*).

Both water that has flowed inside the barrel and that which is outside it are unfit – **מַיִם שֶׁבְּתוֹכָהּ וְשֶׁבַּחוּצָה לָהּ פְּסוּלִין:** That is, one may not place another vessel inside the airspace of the vessel, or above it, to collect the water, since it is already considered to have settled in the barrel (Rashi).

Placed his hand or his foot, etc. – **נָתַן יָדוֹ אוֹ רַגְלוֹ וכו׳:** According to Rashi, this describes a case in which the water is descending along an incline, and one inserts his hand in such a way as to cause a stream of water to rise through the air and land in the vessel, rather than flowing weakly into it. The Rambam understands the mishna as referring to a case where one places the vessel into flowing water and then directs the water with his hands or feet into the vessel, or in which he uses his hands and feet to raise the water level, causing water to flow into the vessel.

Vegetable leaves – **עֲלֵי יְרָקוֹת:** This is referring to edible vegetable leaves, e.g., onion leaves or lettuce, which are susceptible to impurity because they are considered food. They disqualify the water even if they are not themselves impure.

Leaves of nuts – **עֲלֵי אֱגוֹזִים:** The Rambam's Commentary on the Mishna explains that this is referring to the green outer layer that surrounds the nut's shell. Although it is hollow, it is not considered a vessel, and it is therefore not susceptible to impurity.

HALAKHA

Placed his hand, etc. – **נָתַן יָדוֹ וכו׳:** If one placed a barrel in water and shoved the water with his hands or feet or vegetable leaves to move it into the barrel, the water is unfit to be used as water of purification. Likewise, if he sank such items in the water so the water level would rise, allowing the water to spill into the barrel, the water is unfit. If he did so with leaves of reeds or leaves of nuts, the water is fit. This is the principle: If one helped the water into the vessel with an item that is susceptible to impurity, the water is disqualified; if he did so with an item that is not susceptible to impurity, it is fit (Rambam *Sefer Tahara*, *Hilkhot Para Aduma* 6:8).

אָמַר רַבִּי חִיָּיא אָמַר רַבִּי יוֹחָנָן: זֹאת אוֹמֶרֶת אֲוִיר כְּלִי כִּכְלִי דָּמֵי.

Rabbi Ḥiyya says that Rabbi Yoḥanan says: Since this mishna states that water that flows over one's hand through the air into the barrel is disqualified, **that is to say** that the **airspace** above **a vessel is considered as** though it were part of the **vessel** itself. If it were not, the water would not be considered to have flowed directly from the hand to the vessel, but rather from the air above the vessel. Since air is not susceptible to impurity, the water would not be disqualified.

אֲמַר לֵיהּ רַבִּי זֵירָא לְרַבִּי חִיָּיא בַּר אַבָּא: וְדִילְמָא בְּשׁוֹתֵת? אֲמַר לֵיהּ: תְּרָדָא, "כְּדֵי שֶׁיַּעַבְרוּ מַיִם לֶחָבִית" תְּנַן!

Rabbi Zeira said to Rabbi Ḥiyya bar Abba: But perhaps the mishna is referring to a case **where** the water **flows weakly** straight from the hand into the vessel itself, since the hand is situated directly on the edge of the vessel, with no air separating them? Rabbi Ḥiyya bar Abba **said to him: Imbecile, we learned** in the mishna: **In order** to allow flowing **water to pass** through them **to the barrel.** This indicates that the water is traveling in a stream and will pass through the air before reaching the barrel.

וְאָמַר רַבִּי חִיָּיא בַּר אַבָּא אָמַר רַבִּי יוֹחָנָן: מֵעֵדוּתוֹ שֶׁל רַבִּי צָדוֹק נִשְׁנֵית מִשְׁנָה זוֹ, דִּתְנַן: הֵעִיד רַבִּי צָדוֹק עַל הַזּוֹחֲלִין שֶׁקִּילְּחָן בַּעֲלֵי אֱגוֹזִין – שֶׁהֵן כְּשֵׁירִין, זֶה הָיָה מַעֲשֶׂה בְּאוֹהָלְיָיא, וּבָא מַעֲשֶׂה לִפְנֵי חֲכָמִים בְּלִשְׁכַּת הַגָּזִית, וְהִכְשִׁירוּ.

And Rabbi Ḥiyya bar Abba says that **Rabbi Yoḥanan says: This mishna** concerning the barrel **was taught from the testimony of Rabbi Tzadok, as we learned** in a mishna (*Eduyyot* 7:4): **Rabbi Tzadok testified with regard to rivulets that one diverted** by way of a pipe made **with leaves of nuts**[H] **that** their water is **fit** to be used as water of purification. **This was an incident in** the town of **Ohalya,**[B] **and** an account of the **incident came before the Sages in the Chamber of Hewn Stone** in the Temple, **and they deemed** the water **fit.**

אָמַר רַבִּי זֵירָא אָמַר רַבִּי: הַצּוֹרֵם אֹזֶן הַפָּר וְאַחַר כָּךְ קִיבֵּל דָּמוֹ – פָּסוּל, שֶׁנֶּאֱמַר: "וְלָקַח מִדַּם הַפָּר", פָּר שֶׁהָיָה כְּבָר.

§ **Rabbi Zeira says** that **Rabbi** Yehuda HaNasi **says:** In the case of **one who slits the ear of the bull**[H] with the knife after slaughter, creating a blemish, **and thereafter collected its blood** from the neck, the offering is **disqualified, as it is stated: "And** the anointed priest **shall take from the blood of the bull"** (Leviticus 4:5). By referring to the animal as a bull even after its slaughter, the verse indicates that the **bull** must be at the time of collection of the blood as **it already was** before slaughter, without a blemish.

אַשְׁכְּחַן קׇדְשֵׁי קֳדָשִׁים, קֳדָשִׁים קַלִּים מְנָלַן?

The Gemara asks: **We found** a source for this *halakha* with regard to **offerings of the most sacred order,** since the verse is referring to such an offering; **from where do we** derive that the same holds for **offerings of lesser sanctity?**

אָמַר רָבָא: תַּנְיָא, "שֶׂה תָמִים זָכָר בֶּן שָׁנָה" – שֶׁיְּהֵא תָּמִים וּבֶן שָׁנָה בִּשְׁעַת שְׁחִיטָה; בְּקַבָּלָה, בְּהוֹלָכָה, בִּזְרִיקָה מִנַּיִן? תַּלְמוּד לוֹמַר "יִהְיֶה" – כׇּל הֲוָיוֹתָיו לֹא יִהְיוּ אֶלָּא תָּם וּבֶן שָׁנָה.

Rava says: It is taught in a *baraita* with regard to the Paschal offering, an offering of lesser sanctity: The verse states: **"A lamb without blemish, a male of the first year** it shall be for you" (Exodus 12:5), indicating **that it shall be unblemished and in its** first **year at the time of slaughter.**[N] **From where** is it derived that it must also be without blemish **at** the time of **collection** of the blood, **at** the time of **conveying** the blood to the altar, and **at** the time of the **sprinkling** of the blood? **The verse states: "It shall be,"** emphasizing that **all its happenings shall be only** when it is **unblemished and in its** first **year.**

אֵיתִיבֵיהּ אַבָּיֵי: רַבִּי יְהוֹשֻׁעַ אוֹמֵר: כׇּל הַזְּבָחִים שֶׁבַּתּוֹרָה, שֶׁנִּשְׁתַּיֵּיר מֵהֶן כַּזַּיִת בָּשָׂר אוֹ כַּזַּיִת חֵלֶב – זוֹרֵק אֶת הַדָּם!

Abaye raised an objection to this from a *baraita*: **Rabbi Yehoshua says:** With regard to **any of the** types of **offerings that** are mentioned **in the Torah from which there remains** either **an olive-bulk**[H] **of flesh or an olive-bulk of fat,** the *halakha* is that the priest **sprinkles the blood** of that offering. Apparently, one may sprinkle the blood even if much of the offering is damaged or missing.

תַּרְגּוּמָא אַבֶּן שָׁנָה.

The Gemara responds: **Interpret**[N] the verse as referring only **to** the requirement that the animal be **in its first year** until after the sprinkling. It may have a blemish at the time of sprinkling.

וּמִי אִיכָּא מִידֵּי דְּבִשְׁעַת שְׁחִיטָה בֶּן שָׁנָה, בִּשְׁעַת הוֹלָכָה וּזְרִיקָה בֶּן שְׁתַּיִם?

The Gemara challenges this: **But is there any** case **where** the animal is **in its first year at the time of slaughter,** but **at the time of conveying** the blood to the altar **and sprinkling** the blood it is **in its second** year?

אָמַר רָבָא: זֹאת אוֹמֶרֶת שָׁעוֹת פּוֹסְלוֹת בְּקׇדָשִׁים.

Rava says: That is to say that **hours disqualify sacrificial** animals,[H] i.e., one measures the age of the offering from the exact time of its birth. It is therefore possible that the animal reaches its second year between its slaughter and the conveying of its blood to the altar.

HALAKHA

Rivulets that one diverted with leaves of nuts – זוֹחֲלִין שֶׁקִּילְּחָן בַּעֲלֵי אֱגוֹזִין: If one diverted flowing water by way of nut leaves, it remains fit, since nut leaves are not considered vessels, in accordance with the testimony of Rabbi Tzadok (Rambam *Sefer Tahara, Hilkhot Mikvaot* 9:15; *Shulḥan Arukh, Yoreh De'a* 201:14).

One who slits the ear of the bull – הַצּוֹרֵם אֹזֶן הַפָּר: If a limb was removed from an offering after slaughter and before collection of the blood, the offering is disqualified. Likewise, if one slit the offering's ear before collection of the blood, he may not collect the blood, and if he collected and sprinkled it, it is disqualified, in accordance with the statement of Rabbi Zeira (Rambam *Sefer Avoda, Hilkhot Pesulei HaMukdashin* 1:29).

Any of the offerings…from which there remains an olive-bulk – כׇּל הַזְּבָחִים...שֶׁנִּשְׁתַּיֵּיר מֵהֶן כַּזַּיִת: In a case where the blood of any offering is collected in a vessel, and afterward the flesh of the offering is lost or burned before the blood has been sprinkled, if an olive-bulk of the flesh or of the portions to be burned on the altar remains, the blood may be sprinkled. If not, the blood may not be sprinkled, in accordance with Rabbi Yehoshua's statement (Rambam *Sefer Avoda, Hilkhot Pesulei HaMukdashin* 1:30).

Hours disqualify sacrificial animals – שָׁעוֹת פּוֹסְלוֹת בְּקׇדָשִׁים: With regard to offerings, one counts age even to the level of the hour. For example, if an offering must be in its first year, and it is slaughtered at its exact hour of birth, and the blood is sprinkled afterward, the offering is disqualified, in accordance with the statement of Rava (Rambam *Sefer Avoda, Hilkhot Ma'aseh HaKorbanot* 1:13).

BACKGROUND

Ohalya – אוֹהָלְיָיא: The location of this town is unknown. Some hold that it is the town of Helio, near modern-day Beit Shemesh.

NOTES

At the time of slaughter – בִּשְׁעַת שְׁחִיטָה: The language of the verse itself does not clearly refer specifically to the time of slaughter. Rashi explains that the verse is assumed to relate to the verse preceding it, which is understood by the Sages as referring to slaughter (see 23a).

Interpret, etc. – תַּרְגּוּמָא וכו׳: Since the term "it shall be" immediately follows the phrase "in its first year," it can be understood as applying only to this requirement.

אָמַר רַבִּי אַמִּי אָמַר רַבִּי אֶלְעָזָר: הָיְתָה בִּפְנִים וְרַגְלֶיהָ בַּחוּץ, חָתַךְ וְאַחַר כָּךְ שָׁחַט – כְּשֵׁרָה.

§ **Rabbi Ami says** that **Rabbi Elazar says:** In a case where the animal is standing **inside** the Temple courtyard **but its legs** are planted **outside** it, if one **severed** its legs **and thereafter slaughtered** it, the offering is **fit**, since all the blood collected in the bowl is from the portion of the animal standing in the courtyard.

Perek **II**
Daf **26** Amud **a**

שָׁחַט וְאַחַר כָּךְ חָתַךְ – פְּסוּלָה.

But if he **slaughtered** the animal **and thereafter severed** its legs,[H] the offering is **disqualified** because some of the blood collected is from the legs, which are outside the courtyard.

חָתַךְ וְאַחַר כָּךְ שָׁחַט – כְּשֵׁרָה? בַּעַל מוּם קָא מַקְרִיב! אֶלָּא אֵימָא: [חָתַךְ וְאַחַר כָּךְ קִיבֵּל – כְּשֵׁרָה]; קִיבֵּל וְאַחַר כָּךְ חָתַךְ – פְּסוּלָה.

The Gemara asks: If he **severed** its legs **and thereafter slaughtered** it, is the offering **fit**? But isn't **he sacrificing a blemished**[B] animal? **Rather, say:** If one slaughtered the animal while it stood wholly in the courtyard, and afterward its legs moved beyond the edge of the courtyard, and then he **severed** its legs **and thereafter collected**[H] the blood, the offering is **fit.** But if he **collected** the blood **and thereafter severed**[H] the animal's legs, the offering is **disqualified,** since the blood from the legs is mixed with the other blood of the animal.

חָתַךְ וְאַחַר כָּךְ קִיבֵּל כְּשֵׁרָה? וְהָא אָמַר רַבִּי זֵירָא: הַצּוֹרֵם אֹזֶן בִּבְכוֹר וְאַחַר כָּךְ קִיבֵּל דָּמוֹ – פָּסוּל, שֶׁנֶּאֱמַר: "וְלָקַח מִדַּם הַפָּר", פַּר שֶׁהָיָה כְּבָר!

The Gemara challenges: If he **severed** its legs **and thereafter collected** the blood, is the offering **fit? But doesn't Rabbi Zeira say:** If one **slits the ear of a firstborn** animal with the knife after slaughter, creating a blemish, **and thereafter collected its blood** from the neck, the offering is **disqualified, as it is stated: "And** the anointed priest **shall take from the blood of the bull"** (Leviticus 4:5)? The verse indicates that the **bull** must be at the time of collection of the blood as **it already was** before slaughter, without a blemish.

אָמַר רַב חִסְדָּא אָמַר אֲבִימִי: חוֹתֵךְ בָּאֵבֶר עַד שֶׁמַּגִּיעַ לָעֶצֶם.

Rav Ḥisda says that **Avimi says:** Rabbi Ami is not referring to a case where one severs the entire leg. Rather, one **cuts** the flesh **of the limb until he reaches the bone,** leaving the bone intact. This is not considered a blemish, and the animal remains fit for sacrifice.

קִיבֵּל וְאַחַר כָּךְ חָתַךְ – פְּסוּלָה; שְׁמַעְתְּ מִינַּהּ: דָּם הַמּוּבְלָע בָּאֵבָרִים – דָּם הוּא?

The Gemara suggests: Given that if he **collected** the blood **and thereafter severed** the animal's legs, the offering is **disqualified,** perhaps **you** can **conclude from it** that **blood absorbed in the limbs** of an animal **is** considered **blood,** such that it disqualifies the offering because this blood left the Temple courtyard.

דִּלְמָא מִשּׁוּם שַׁמְנוּנִית.

The Gemara responds: **Perhaps** the offering is disqualified **because of** the animal's **fat** that is mixed with the blood in the legs. This is considered to be like meat of the offering that has left the Temple courtyard, which also disqualifies the offering.

שְׁמַעְתְּ מִינַּהּ: בְּשַׂר קָדָשִׁים קַלִּים שֶׁיָּצָא לִפְנֵי זְרִיקַת דָּם – פָּסוּל?

The Gemara suggests: If so, perhaps **you** can **conclude** another *halakha* **from it:** In the case of **meat of offerings of lesser sanctity that left**[H] the Temple courtyard **before the sprinkling of** the **blood,** the offering is **disqualified,** even though the meat of such offerings may be eaten outside the Temple after the blood has been sprinkled.

דִּלְמָא בְּקָדְשֵׁי קָדָשִׁים.

The Gemara responds: **Perhaps** the *halakha* was stated only **with regard to offerings of the most sacred order,** whose meat must be eaten inside the Temple courtyard. It proves nothing about offerings of lesser sanctity.

HALAKHA

Slaughtered and thereafter severed its legs – שָׁחַט וְאַחַר כָּךְ חָתַךְ: If the offering's body was located inside the Temple courtyard with its legs outside, and one slaughtered it, it is disqualified (Rambam *Sefer Avoda, Hilkhot Pesulei HaMukdashin* 1:14).

Severed its legs and thereafter collected – חָתַךְ וְאַחַר כָּךְ קִיבֵּל: If one slaughtered the offering while its entire body was inside the Temple courtyard and then one of its legs moved outside the courtyard, one cuts the flesh until he reaches the bone, and then he collects the blood, in accordance with the statement of Rav Ḥisda in the name of Avimi. With regard to offerings of lesser sanctity, there is no need to sever the limbs. Rather, one moves the leg back into the Temple courtyard and collects the blood, since meat of offerings of lesser sanctity remains fit even if it leaves the Temple courtyard before the sprinkling of the blood, in accordance with the Gemara here (Rambam *Sefer Avoda, Hilkhot Pesulei HaMukdashin* 1:15, and see Ra'avad there).

Collected and thereafter severed – קִיבֵּל וְאַחַר כָּךְ חָתַךְ: If an offering's leg moved outside the Temple courtyard after the slaughter, and one collected the blood and only afterward severed its legs, the offering is disqualified due to its containing fat of the offering that left the Temple courtyard, in accordance with the Gemara's explanation (Rambam *Sefer Avoda, Hilkhot Pesulei HaMukdashin* 1:15).

In the case of meat of offerings of lesser sanctity that left, etc. – בְּשַׂר קָדָשִׁים קַלִּים שֶׁיָּצָא וכו׳: If meat of offerings of lesser sanctity left the Temple courtyard before the blood was sprinkled, the offering remains fit, even if the blood was sprinkled while the meat remained outside the courtyard, since the meat will ultimately leave the courtyard anyway. Still, it is prohibited to consume the meat, and it must be burned (Rambam *Sefer Avoda, Hilkhot Pesulei HaMukdashin* 1:32, and see *Kesef Mishne* there).

BACKGROUND

Blemished – בַּעַל מוּם: The blemishes that render an animal prohibited for sacrifice are enumerated in the Torah (see Leviticus 22:17–25) and explained in detail in tractate *Bekhorot*. There is a distinction between permanent blemishes and temporary blemishes: Permanent blemishes, e.g., when an animal is missing a leg, disqualify an animal permanently from being sacrificed as an offering. Temporary blemishes, such as certain types of boils, disqualify an animal only as long as it suffers from the condition.

תָּנוּ רַבָּנַן: קׇדְשֵׁי קֳדָשִׁים שְׁחִיטָתָן בַּצָּפוֹן וְקִבּוּל דָּמָן בִּכְלִי שָׁרֵת בַּצָּפוֹן. עָמַד בַּדָּרוֹם וְהוֹשִׁיט יָדוֹ לַצָּפוֹן וְשָׁחַט – שְׁחִיטָתוֹ כְּשֵׁרָה. קִיבֵּל – קַבָּלָתוֹ פְּסוּלָה, הִכְנִיס רֹאשׁוֹ וְרוּבּוֹ – כְּאִילּוּ נִכְנַס כּוּלּוֹ. פִּרְכְּסָה, וְיָצְתָה לַדָּרוֹם, וְחָזְרָה – כְּשֵׁרָה.

The Gemara suggests: Come and hear a proof from that which **the Sages taught** in a *baraita*: With regard to **offerings of the most sacred order, their slaughter is in the north**[H] of the Temple courtyard, **and collection of their blood in a service vessel** is **in the north.** If one **stood in the south and extended his hand**[H] into **the north and slaughtered** the offering there, **his slaughter** is **valid.** If he **collected** the blood in a similar manner, **his collection** is **not valid. If he inserted his head and most of his** body into the north of the courtyard and collected the blood there, it is **as if his entire** body **entered** the north. If he slaughtered the animal and it then **convulsed and left** the north **to the south**[H] **and** then **returned**[N] to the north, it remains **fit.**

קׇדָשִׁים קַלִּים – שְׁחִיטָתָן בִּפְנִים וְקִיבּוּל דָּמָן בִּכְלִי שָׁרֵת בִּפְנִים. עָמַד בַּחוּץ וְהִכְנִיס יָדוֹ לִפְנִים וְשָׁחַט – שְׁחִיטָתוֹ כְּשֵׁרָה. קִיבֵּל – קַבָּלָתוֹ פְּסוּלָה, וְהִכְנִיס רֹאשׁוֹ וְרוּבּוֹ – כְּאִילּוּ לֹא נִכְנַס. פִּרְכְּסָה וְיָצְתָה לַחוּץ וְחָזְרָה – פְּסוּלָה. שְׁמַע מִינַּהּ: בְּשַׂר קׇדָשִׁים קַלִּים שֶׁיָּצָא לִפְנֵי זְרִיקַת דָּמִים – פְּסוּלִים!

The *baraita* continues: With regard to **offerings of lesser sanctity, their slaughter is** anywhere **inside**[H] the Temple courtyard, **and collection of their blood in a service vessel** is anywhere **inside** the Temple courtyard. If one **stood outside and inserted his hand into** the courtyard **and slaughtered** the offering there, **his slaughter** is **valid.** If he **collected** the blood in a similar manner, **his collection is not valid. And** if he **inserted his head and most of his** body into the courtyard and collected the blood, it is **as if he had not entered** it at all. If he slaughtered the animal and it then **convulsed and left to the outside**[H] of the courtyard **and returned,** it is **disqualified.** The Gemara infers: **Conclude from** this *baraita* that in cases of **meat of offerings of lesser sanctity that left** the Temple courtyard **before the sprinkling of** the **blood,** the offerings **are disqualified.**

דִּילְמָא בְּאַלְיָה וְיוֹתֶרֶת הַכָּבֵד וּשְׁתֵּי כְלָיוֹת.

The Gemara responds: **Perhaps** the *baraita* is referring **to** the **tail,** the **diaphragm, and** the **two kidneys** of offerings of lesser sanctity, which are all burned on the altar. Since these portions are never meant to leave the Temple courtyard, they are disqualified if they leave even momentarily. It may still be that the remaining meat of such offerings is not disqualified.

בְּעָא מִינֵּיהּ אֲבוּהּ דִּשְׁמוּאֵל מִשְּׁמוּאֵל: הִיא בִּפְנִים וְרַגְלֶיהָ בַּחוּץ, מַהוּ?

§ **Shmuel's father raised a dilemma before Shmuel:** If the offering was standing **inside** the Temple courtyard **and its legs** were **outside,**[H] **what is the** *halakha*? May one slaughter it?

אֲמַר לֵיהּ, כְּתִיב: "וֶהֱבִיאוּם לַה'" – עַד שֶׁתְּהֵא כּוּלָּהּ לִפְנִים.

Shmuel **said to him: It is written: "That they may bring them to the Lord"** (Leviticus 17:5), indicating that the offering may not be slaughtered **unless all of it is inside.**

תְּלָה וְשָׁחַט, מַהוּ? אֲמַר לֵיהּ: כְּשֵׁרָה. אֲמַר לֵיהּ: אִישְׁתַּבַּשְׁתְּ, בָּעֵינַן שְׁחִיטָה עַל יֶרֶךְ, וְלֵיכָּא.

His father asked him further: If one **suspended** the animal in the air **and slaughtered**[H] it, **what is the** *halakha*? Shmuel **said to him:** It is **valid.** His father **said to him: You are mistaken. We require** that the **slaughter** occur **on the side** of the altar (see Leviticus 1:11), **and** this is **not** considered to fulfill that requirement.

נִתְלָה וְשָׁחַט, מַהוּ? אֲמַר לֵיהּ: פְּסוּלָה. אֲמַר לֵיהּ: אִישְׁתַּבַּשְׁתְּ, שְׁחִיטָה עַל יֶרֶךְ וְלֹא שׁוֹחֵט עַל יֶרֶךְ.

His father asked him further: If the one slaughtering the animal **was suspended** in the air **and slaughtered**[H] the offering while it was on the ground, **what is the** *halakha*? Shmuel **said to him:** It is **not valid.** His father **said to him: You are mistaken.** We require only that the **slaughter** occur **on the side** of the altar, **but not** that the **one who slaughters** be **on the side** of the altar.

נִתְלָה וְקִבֵּל, מַהוּ? אֲמַר לֵיהּ: כְּשֵׁרָה. אֲמַר לֵיהּ: אִישְׁתַּבַּשְׁתְּ, אֵין דֶּרֶךְ שֵׁירוּת בְּכָךְ.

His father asked him further: If the priest **was suspended** in the air **and collected**[NH] the blood of the offering in that position, **what is the** *halakha*? Shmuel **said to him:** It is **valid.** His father **said to him: You are mistaken. This is not** a normal **manner of ministration.**

NOTES

Left to the south and then returned – יָצְתָה לַדָּרוֹם וְחָזְרָה: Although the slaughter and collection of the blood of offerings of the most sacred order must be performed in the north of the courtyard, such offerings are not disqualified if they moved to the south of the courtyard. Still, they are disqualified if they moved outside of the courtyard entirely, since the courtyard itself is delineated by a physical boundary.

Was suspended and collected, etc. – נִתְלָה וְקִבֵּל וכו׳: The offering is fit if the one who slaughters it is suspended in the air because the rite of slaughter is not considered one of the ministrations of the priests, as it may be performed by a non-priest as well. It is therefore not subject to the same restrictions of the other rites, i.e., the collection of the blood and the rites that follow it, which may be performed only by the priests.

HALAKHA

Their slaughter is in the north – שְׁחִיטָתָן בַּצָּפוֹן: The slaughter and collection of the blood of offerings of the most sacred order must occur in the north of the Temple courtyard. If these were performed in the south they are not valid (Rambam *Sefer Avoda, Hilkhot Pesulei HaMukdashin* 1:7).

Stood in the south and extended his hand – עָמַד בַּדָּרוֹם וְהוֹשִׁיט יָדוֹ: If one stood in the south of the Temple courtyard and extended his hand to slaughter an offering of the most sacred order in the north, the offering is fit. If he extended his hand to collect its blood, the collection is disqualified. If he inserted his head and the majority of his body into the north of the courtyard, it is as though he were standing in the north (Rambam *Sefer Avoda, Hilkhot Pesulei HaMukdashin* 1:8–10).

Convulsed and left to the south – פִּרְכְּסָה וְיָצְתָה לַדָּרוֹם: If one slaughtered an offering of the most sacred order in the north of the Temple courtyard and it then moved to the south, it remains fit. If it convulsed and moved to the south and then returned to the north and he collected its blood in the north, it remains fit (Rambam *Sefer Avoda, Hilkhot Pesulei HaMukdashin* 1:11).

Their slaughter is anywhere inside, etc. – שְׁחִיטָתָן בִּפְנִים וכו׳: If an offering of lesser sanctity stood within the Temple courtyard, and one standing outside extended his hand inside and slaughtered it, the slaughter is valid. If he extended his hand inside to collect the blood, the collection is invalid, even if he introduced his head and the majority of his body into the courtyard (Rambam *Sefer Avoda, Hilkhot Pesulei HaMukdashin* 1:11–12).

Convulsed and left to the outside – פִּרְכְּסָה וְיָצְתָה לַחוּץ: If an offering of lesser sanctity left the Temple courtyard after the collection of its blood, it remains fit. This is the *halakha* even if the portions of the offering to be burned on the altar left the courtyard, since the Rambam holds that these portions may still be burned on the altar if they return. This ruling is in accordance with the Gemara on 89b rather than the discussion here (Rambam *Sefer Avoda, Hilkhot Pesulei HaMukdashin* 1:13, 33).

The offering was inside and its legs were outside – הִיא בִּפְנִים וְרַגְלֶיהָ בַּחוּץ: If an offering is slaughtered as it stands inside the Temple courtyard with its legs outside, it is disqualified, as the verse states: "That they may bring them to the Lord," teaching that the offering may not be slaughtered unless all of it is inside, in accordance with the statement of Shmuel (Rambam *Sefer Avoda, Hilkhot Pesulei HaMukdashin* 1:14).

One suspended and slaughtered – תְּלָה וְשָׁחַט: If one suspended an offering in the air of the Temple courtyard and slaughtered it in that manner, it is disqualified, as the verse states: "On the side of the altar," teaching that it must be slaughtered on the ground (Rambam *Sefer Avoda, Hilkhot Pesulei HaMukdashin* 1:16).

Was suspended and slaughtered – נִתְלָה וְשָׁחַט: The Rambam writes: If the animal is on the ground, and one is suspended in the air and slaughters it in that manner, an offering of the most sacred order is disqualified, while offerings of lesser sanctity are fit. According to the *Kesef Mishne*, this is a scribal error, and the text should read: If the slaughterer was suspended and slaughtered, the offering is fit, but if the animal was suspended, an offering of the most sacred order is disqualified, while offerings of lesser sanctity are fit. This ruling would then be in accordance with the statement of Rava. In the same vein, the previous *halakha* of the Rambam should be emended as well to distinguish between offerings of the most sacred order and offerings of lesser sanctity (Rambam *Sefer Avoda, Hilkhot Pesulei HaMukdashin* 1:17).

Was suspended and collected – נִתְלָה וְקִבֵּל: If the priest was suspended in the air and collected the blood from an animal standing on the floor, the offering is disqualified, since this is not a normal manner of ministration (Rambam *Sefer Avoda, Hilkhot Pesulei HaMukdashin* 1:19).

תָּלָה וְקִיבֵּל מַהוּ? אֲמַר לֵיהּ: פְּסוּלָה. אֲמַר לֵיהּ: אִישְׁתַּבַּשְׁתְּ, שְׁחִיטָה עַל יֶרֶךְ וְלֹא קַבָּלָה עַל יֶרֶךְ.

His father asked him further: If the priest **suspended** the offering in the air after slaughter **and collected**[H] its blood, **what is the** *halakha*? Shmuel **said to him:** It is **not valid.** His father **said to him: You are mistaken.** We require only that the **slaughter** occur **on the side** of the altar, **but not** that **collection** of the blood occur **on the side** of the altar.

אֲמַר אַבַּיֵי: בְּקׇדְשֵׁי קֳדָשִׁים כּוּלָּן פְּסוּלוֹת, בַּר מִנִּתְלָה וְשָׁחַט. בְּקֳדָשִׁים קַלִּים – כּוּלָּן כְּשֵׁרוֹת, בַּר מִן נִתְלָה וְקִיבֵּל.

Abaye said: With regard to offerings of the most sacred order, in **all of** those cases the offerings **are disqualified, except for** the case where one **was suspended** in the air **and slaughtered** the animal. **With regard to offerings of lesser sanctity,** in **all of** those cases the offerings **are fit, except for** the case where the priest **was suspended** in the air **and collected** the blood.

אֲמַר רָבָא: מַאי שְׁנָא תָּלָה וְקִיבֵּל בְּקָדָשִׁים קַלִּים דִּכְשֵׁרָה – דַּאֲוִיר פְּנִים כִּפְנִים דָּמֵי, בְּקׇדְשֵׁי קֳדָשִׁים נַמִי – אֲוִיר צָפוֹן כְּצָפוֹן דָּמֵי!

Rava said: What is different about a case where one **suspended** the animal **and collected** the blood of an **offering of lesser sanctity,** such **that** the offering **is fit?** Perhaps it is **because the air inside** the Temple courtyard **is considered** to be **inside** the courtyard for purposes of the service. But if so, then **with regard to offerings of the most sacred order as well,** let one say that **air** in the **north** of the Temple courtyard **is considered** to be in the **north** for purposes of the service.

אֶלָּא אָמַר רָבָא: בֵּין בְּקׇדְשֵׁי קֳדָשִׁים בֵּין בְּקָדָשִׁים קַלִּים – כְּשֵׁרוֹת, בַּר מִן תָּלָה וְשָׁחַט בְּקׇדְשֵׁי קֳדָשִׁים, נִתְלָה וְקִיבֵּל – בֵּין בְּקׇדְשֵׁי קֳדָשִׁים בֵּין בְּקָדָשִׁים קַלִּים.

Rather, Rava says: Both with regard to offerings of the most sacred order and with regard to offerings of lesser sanctity, they **are fit** in all of those cases **except** where one **suspended** the animal **and slaughtered** it in the case of **offerings of the most sacred order,** because the Torah mandates that such offerings be slaughtered on the side of the altar. And the offerings are also disqualified where the priest **was suspended** in the air **and collected** the blood, **both with regard to offerings of the most sacred order and with regard to offerings of lesser sanctity,** since this is not a normal manner of ministration.

בְּעָא מִינֵּיהּ רַבִּי יִרְמְיָה מֵרַבִּי זֵירָא: הוּא בִּפְנִים וְצִיצִיתוֹ בַּחוּץ, מַהוּ? אֲמַר לֵיהּ: לָאו אָמְרַתְּ "וֶהֱבִיאוּם לַה'" – עַד שֶׁתָּבֹא כּוּלָּהּ לִפְנִים? הָכָא נַמִי, "בְּבוֹאָם אֶל אֹהֶל מוֹעֵד" – עַד שֶׁיָּבֹא כּוּלּוֹ לְאֹהֶל מוֹעֵד.

Rabbi Yirmeya raised a dilemma before Rabbi Zeira: If the priest was **inside and his fringes,** i.e., his hair, were **outside,**[H] and he collected the blood, **what is the** *halakha*? Rabbi Zeira **said to him: Did you not say** that the verse: **"That they may bring them to the Lord"** (Leviticus 17:5), indicates that an offering may not be slaughtered **unless all of it comes inside? Here, too,** the verse states with regard to the priests: **"When they go into the Tent of Meeting"** (Exodus 28:43), indicating that the priest may not perform rites **unless all of him comes into the Tent of Meeting.**

מתני׳ נְתָנוֹ עַל גַּבֵּי הַכֶּבֶשׁ, שֶׁלֹּא כְּנֶגֶד הַיְסוֹד, נָתַן אֶת הַנִּיתָּנִין לְמַטָּה לְמַעְלָה, וְאֶת הַנִּיתָּנִין לְמַעְלָה לְמַטָּה, וְאֶת הַנִּיתָּנִין בִּפְנִים בַּחוּץ, וְאֶת הַנִּיתָּנִין בַּחוּץ בִּפְנִים – פָּסוּל, וְאֵין בּוֹ כָּרֵת.

MISHNA If the priest **placed** the blood **upon the ramp**[HB] leading up to the altar, or if he placed it on the wall of the altar in an area **that is not opposite the base**[N] of the altar, i.e., in those parts of the altar where there is no foundation; or if **he placed** the blood **that is to be placed below**[B] the red line that runs along the middle of the altar, e.g., the blood of a burnt offering, **above** the red line, **or** if he placed the blood **that is** to be **placed above** the red line, e.g., the blood of a sin offering, **below** the red line; **or** if he placed the blood **that is** to be **placed inside** the Sanctuary, i.e., on the golden altar or in the Holy of Holies, **outside** the Sanctuary on the external altar, **or** if he placed the blood **that is** to be **placed outside** the Sanctuary **inside** the Sanctuary, in all these cases the offering is **disqualified.** Nevertheless, **there is no** liability for *karet* **for** one who partakes of these offerings.

HALAKHA

The priest suspended and collected – תָּלָה וְקִיבֵּל: If one was standing in the Temple courtyard and suspended the bowl from his hand so as to collect the blood in the air, or if he suspended the animal in the air and collected the blood from it, the offering is fit because the airspace of an area is considered to be part of it, in accordance with the statement of Rava. The Rambam interprets the term: Suspended, used here as applying not only to the animal but to the service vessel as well (Rambam *Sefer Avoda, Hilkhot Pesulei HaMukdashin* 1:20).

He was inside and his fringes were outside – הוּא בִּפְנִים וְצִיצִיתוֹ בַּחוּץ: Collection of the blood is valid only if the priest is standing completely inside the Temple courtyard. Even if he was standing inside the courtyard but his hair was outside, the service is disqualified, in accordance with the statement of Rabbi Zeira (Rambam *Sefer Avoda, Hilkhot Pesulei HaMukdashin* 1:12).

Placed the blood upon the ramp, etc. – נְתָנוֹ עַל גַּבֵּי הַכֶּבֶשׁ וכו׳: If one placed blood that ought to have been placed on the upper half of the altar on the lower half, or vice versa, or if one placed blood that ought to have been placed in the Sanctuary on the external altar, or vice versa, or if one placed blood on the ramp rather than on the altar proper, or if one placed blood on a portion of the altar not opposite the base, then the offering is disqualified, in accordance with the ruling of the mishna (Rambam *Sefer Avoda, Hilkhot Pesulei HaMukdashin* 2:10).

NOTES

That is not opposite the base – שֶׁלֹּא כְּנֶגֶד הַיְסוֹד: The blood of offerings must always be placed on a portion of the altar overlooking its foundation. The foundation did not surround the base of the entire altar; rather, it ran along its north and west sides, extending one cubit around the northeast corner onto the east side and one cubit around the southwest corner onto the south side (see 51a).

BACKGROUND

Ramp – כֶּבֶשׁ: The ramp used for ascending onto the altar was located on the altar's south side. It measured thirty-two cubits in length and sixteen cubits in width.

1. Ramp
2. Corner of the altar
3. Surrounding ledge
4. Red line
5. Base of the altar

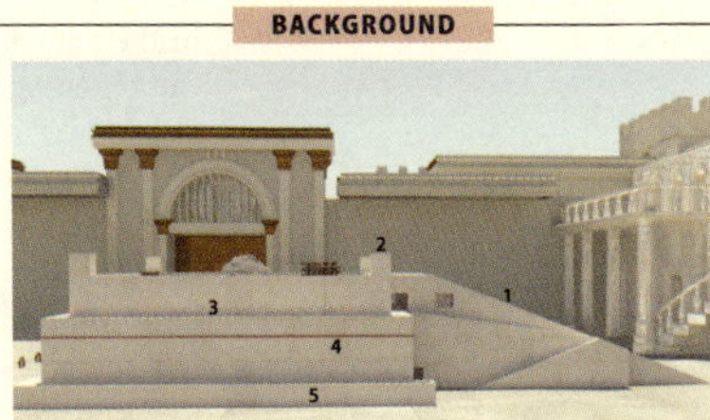

Altar

Blood that is placed below – הַנִּיתָּנִין לְמַטָּה: The blood of different offerings must be placed in different fashions on different sections of the altar, and sometimes inside the Sanctuary itself. The blood of a sin offering is unique in that it must be applied by the priest's finger on the upper section of the corners of the altar. The blood of many other offerings, e.g., burnt offerings, must be sprinkled from a bowl onto the bottom half of two corners of the altar, underneath the red line that marks half the altar's height, such that the blood reaches both sides of each corner.

גמ׳ אמר שמואל: פסול בשר, אבל בעלים נתכפרו. מאי טעמא? דאמר קרא: ״ואני נתתיו לכם על המזבח לכפר״, כיון שהגיע דם למזבח – נתכפרו בעלים.

GEMARA Shmuel says: When the mishna states that the offering is **disqualified,** it means that the **meat** is unfit for consumption. **But** the **owner** of the offering has **achieved atonement** through it. **What is the reason** for this? It is **as the verse states** with regard to the blood: **"And I have given it to you upon the altar**[N] **to atone** for your souls" (Leviticus 17:11), from which it is derived that **once the blood reaches** any location on **the altar,** the **owner** of the offering has **achieved atonement.**

אי הכי, בשר נמי! אמר קרא: ״לכפר״ – לכפרה נתתיו, ולא לדבר אחר.

The Gemara challenges: **If so,** the **meat** should be fit for consumption **as well.** The Gemara responds: **The verse states "to atone,"** emphasizing that **I have given it** to you **for atonement and for nothing else,** e.g., consumption of the meat.

אלמא קסבר: שלא במקומו – כמקומו דמי. תנן באידך פירקין: נתנו על הכבש, שלא כנגד היסוד, נתן את הניתנין למטה למעלה, ואת הניתנין למעלה למטה, ואת הניתנין בפנים בחוץ, ואת הניתנין בחוץ בפנים, אם יש דם הנפש – יחזור הכשר ויקבל;

The Gemara notes: **Apparently,** Shmuel **holds** that blood sprinkled **not in its proper place is considered as** though it were sprinkled in its proper **place.**[H] But **we learned** in a mishna **in another chapter** (32a): If an unfit person **placed** the blood **upon the ramp,** or on the wall of the altar **that is not opposite the base** of the altar; or if **he placed** the blood **that is** to be **placed below** the red line **above** the red line, **or** if he placed the blood **that is** to be **placed above** the red line **below** the red line; **or** if he placed the blood **that is** to be **placed inside** the Sanctuary **outside** the Sanctuary **or** the blood **that is** to be **placed outside** the Sanctuary **inside** the Sanctuary, then **if there is blood of the soul** that remains in the animal, **the** priest **fit** for Temple service **should collect** the blood **again** and sprinkle it on the altar.

ואי סלקא דעתך שלא במקומו כמקומו, למה לי יחזור הכשר ויקבל? וכי תימא: להתיר בשר באכילה – מי איכא זריקה דלא מכפרת ושריא בשר באכילה?

The Gemara continues: **And if** it would **enter your mind** to say **that** blood sprinkled **not in its** proper **place** is considered **as** though it were sprinkled in **its** proper **place, why do I** need **the fit** priest to **collect** the blood **again** and sprinkle it? **And if you would say** that although the first sprinkling already effected atonement, the second sprinkling is necessary **to permit the meat** of the offering **for consumption, is there** such a concept as **a sprinkling that does not** itself **effect atonement and** yet **permits** the **meat for consumption?** Rather, one must conclude that the first sprinkling did not effect atonement at all, since it was not sprinkled in its proper place.

אי דיהביה כשר – הכי נמי, הכא במאי עסקינן – דיהביה פסול.

The Gemara responds: **If a fit** priest **had** initially **placed** the blood improperly, the sprinkling would **indeed** have effected atonement after the fact and there would not be another sprinkling. But **here we are dealing with** a case **where an unfit** person **placed**[NH] the blood, so that it did not effect atonement at all.

וליהוי דחוי, דתנן: וכולן שקיבלו חוץ לזמנו וחוץ למקומו, אם יש דם הנפש – יחזור הכשר ויקבל; קיבלו – אין, זרקו – לא; מאי טעמא? לאו משום דהוי דחוי?

The Gemara asks: **But** if the mishna is dealing with a case where an unfit person placed the blood initially, then the offering **should be rejected**[N] permanently, **as we learned** in the same mishna: **And** with regard to **all** unfit people **who collected** the blood with the intent to offer it **beyond its** designated **time or outside its** designated **area, if there is blood of the soul** that remains in the animal, **the** priest **fit** for Temple service **should collect** the blood **again** and sprinkle it on the altar. Since the mishna states this *halakha* only with regard to collection of the blood, one can infer that specifically if an unfit person **collected** the blood with improper intent, a fit priest can **indeed** collect the blood again, but if they **sprinkled** the blood with improper intent he **cannot. What is the reason** for this? Is it **not because** the offering **is rejected** permanently when an unfit person sprinkles its blood?

NOTES

Upon the altar – על המזבח: These words seem unnecessary, since it is known that blood effects atonement when applied to the altar. This superfluous phrase, combined with the omission of any reference to a specific location on the altar, is therefore understood as teaching that the blood effects atonement if applied to any area on the altar (*Korban Aharon*).

Where an unfit person placed – דיהביה פסול: The fact that it was an unfit person is evident from the context in the mishna, which discusses only rites performed by an unfit person (Rashi). It is also clear from the clause: The priest fit for Temple service should collect the blood again, indicating the initial rites were performed by an unfit person.

Should be rejected – ליהוי דחוי: If one considers blood sprinkled on the wrong section of the altar as though it were sprinkled in its appropriate place, the offering should be disqualified permanently since one of its rites was performed by an unfit person (Rashi). If it is not considered to have been sprinkled in its appropriate place, it is as though the unfit person has done nothing, and it is reasonable that a fit priest would then be able to perform the rite correctly.

HALAKHA

Not in its proper place is considered as its proper place – שלא במקומו כמקומו דמי: If one placed blood on the bottom half of the altar when it should have been placed on the top half, or vice versa, or if one placed blood on the external altar when it should have been placed inside the Sanctuary, or vice versa, or if one placed blood on the ramp, not opposite the altar's foundation when it should have been placed on the altar, the meat of the offering is disqualified, but the owners achieve atonement, in accordance with Shmuel's statement (Rambam *Sefer Avoda, Hilkhot Pesulei HaMukdashin* 2:10).

Where an unfit person placed – דיהביה פסול: If a fit priest collected the blood of the offering and then gave it to an unfit person, who then placed it on the wrong section of the altar, or placed it in the Sanctuary when it should have been placed on the external altar, or vice versa, the meat of the offering is not disqualified. If some blood of the soul remains in the animal, a fit priest collects it and sprinkles it in its appropriate place (Rambam *Sefer Avoda, Hilkhot Pesulei HaMukdashin* 2:10).

לָא, מִשּׁוּם דְּפָסִיל בְּמַחְשָׁבָה.

The Gemara responds: **No,** the offering is rejected **because it is disqualified by** the improper **intent** of the person sprinkling the blood, not because that person is unfit.

אִי הָכִי, קַבָּלָה נַמִּי! וְעוֹד: מִי פָּסְלָה מַחְשָׁבָה? וְהָאָמַר רָבָא: אֵין מַחְשָׁבָה מוֹעֶלֶת אֶלָּא בְּמִי שֶׁרָאוּי לַעֲבוֹדָה, וּבְדָבָר הָרָאוּי לַעֲבוֹדָה, וּבְמָקוֹם הָרָאוּי לַעֲבוֹדָה!

The Gemara challenges: **If so,** then improper intent with regard to **collection** of the blood should disqualify the offering **as well. And furthermore, does intent disqualify** offerings in such cases? **But doesn't Rava say: Intent is effective** to disqualify an offering **only**[H] when it is expressed **by one who is fit for the** Temple **service, and with regard to an item that is fit for the** Temple **service,**[N] **and in a place that is fit for the** Temple **service?**[N] Here, the one collecting the blood is unfit.

לָא תֵּימָא: זָרְקוּ לָא, אֶלָּא אֵימָא: שָׁחֲטוּ לָא.

The Gemara responds: **Do not say** that one infers from the mishna that if an unfit person **sprinkled** the blood with improper intent a fit priest **cannot** collect it again. **Rather, say** that one infers that if an unfit person **slaughtered** the offering with improper intent the mistake **cannot** be rectified. Slaughter is valid if performed by one unfit for the Temple service, and therefore an unfit person's improper intent is effective to disqualify the offering. By contrast, collection and sprinkling of the blood must be performed by a fit priest. Consequently, an unfit person's intent with regard to those rites does not disqualify the offering.

מַאי קָא מַשְׁמַע לַן, דְּפָסְלָה מַחְשָׁבָה? תְּנֵינָא: לְפִיכָךְ הֵן פּוֹסְלִין בְּמַחְשָׁבָה!

The Gemara asks: According to this interpretation, **what is** the mishna **teaching us?** Can it mean to teach only **that** improper **intent** by an unfit person during slaughter **disqualifies** the offering? **We** already **learn** this in the same mishna (31b), which states: With regard to all those who are unfit for Temple service who slaughtered an offering, their slaughter is valid, and **therefore, these** unfit people **disqualify** the offering **with** improper **intent.**

הָא קָא מַשְׁמַע לַן: דְּמִקַּבָּלָה וְאֵילָךְ לָא פָּסְלָה מַחְשָׁבָה; מַאי טַעְמָא – כִּדְרָבָא.

The Gemara responds: **This** is what the mishna **teaches us: That** one who is unfit can disqualify the offering only during its slaughter, but **from** the rite of **collection** of the blood **onward**[H] the **intent** of an unfit person **does not disqualify** the offering. **What is the reason** for this? It is **like that which Rava** says: Intent is effective to disqualify an offering only when expressed by one who is fit for the service in question.

מֵיתִיבִי: חִישֵּׁב לִיתֵּן אֶת הַנִּיתָּנִין לְמַעְלָה לְמַטָּה, לְמַטָּה לְמַעְלָה, לְאַלְתַּר – כָּשֵׁר (לְמָחָר – פָּסוּל); חָזַר וְחִישֵּׁב

The Gemara **raises an objection** from a *baraita*: If one slaughtered an offering and **had intent to place** the blood **that is** to be **placed above** the red line **below** the red line, or to place the blood that is to be placed **below** the red line **above** the red line, and he had intent to do so **immediately,**[N] i.e., on the same day, the offering remains **fit.** Therefore, if **he subsequently had intent** when performing the other rites

Perek **II**
Daf **27** Amud **a**

חוּץ לִמְקוֹמוֹ – פָּסוּל וְאֵין בּוֹ כָּרֵת, חוּץ לִזְמַנּוֹ – פִּיגּוּל וְחַיָּיבִין עָלָיו כָּרֵת.

to burn or eat the offering or sprinkle its blood **outside its** designated **area,** the offering is **disqualified,**[H] **and there is no** liability for ***karet*** **for** burning or partaking **of it.** But if he had intent to perform one of those actions **beyond its** designated **time,** then it is rendered ***piggul,***[N] **and one is liable** to receive ***karet*** **for** burning or partaking **of it.**

HALAKHA

Intent is effective only, etc. – אֵין מַחְשָׁבָה מוֹעֶלֶת אֶלָּא וכו׳: Improper intent is effective to disqualify an offering only when expressed by one who is fit for the Temple service, and with regard to an item fit for the Temple service, and in a place that is fit for the Temple service. Consequently, if one unfit for the Temple service performed a sacrificial rite with improper intent, he does not disqualify the offering. Rather, if blood of the soul remains, a fit priest collects and sprinkles it appropriately and the offering is fit, in accordance with the statement of Rava (Rambam *Sefer Avoda, Hilkhot Pesulei HaMukdashin* 14:2–4).

Slaughtered, the mistake cannot be rectified – שָׁחֲטוּ לָא: If an unfit person slaughtered an offering with improper intent, the offering is disqualified because slaughter is valid if performed by non-priests (Rambam *Sefer Avoda, Hilkhot Pesulei HaMukdashin* 14:2).

Outside its designated area the offering is disqualified – חוּץ לִמְקוֹמוֹ פָּסוּל וכו׳: If one intended to place blood below the red line when it ought to be placed above, or had a similar improper intention that does not disqualify the offering, and he simultaneously intended to consume or burn the offering or sprinkle its blood beyond its designated time, the offering is rendered *piggul.* If instead he simultaneously intended to perform such an act outside its designated area, the offering is disqualified but not rendered *piggul* (Rambam *Sefer Avoda, Hilkhot Pesulei HaMukdashin* 16:5).

NOTES

And with regard to an item that is fit for the Temple service – וּבְדָבָר הָרָאוּי לַעֲבוֹדָה: The Ra'avad, in his commentary on *Torat Kohanim,* interprets this as referring to the animal, which would not be fit if blemished or otherwise disqualified. Yet the Gemara in tractate *Menahot* (5b) names the *omer* meal offering brought on Passover as an item unfit for Temple service. This indicates that the phrase: Unfit for Temple service, denotes an item that is sacrificed only in special circumstances, e.g., the *omer* meal offering, composed of barley, which is never otherwise offered as a meal offering. The *Shita Mekubbetzet* and *Tosafot* on tractate *Menahot* suggest in addition that the *omer* meal offering is exceptional because it is brought from the new year's grain, which is otherwise unfit for sacrifice until after *Shavuot.*

And in a place that is fit for the Temple service – וּבְמָקוֹם הָרָאוּי לַעֲבוֹדָה: If the altar is damaged, it is not fit for service until it is fixed (Rashi, citing *Menahot* 5b). The Ra'avad, in his commentary on *Torat Kohanim,* interprets the phrase in accordance with the Gemara here, as excluding a case where blood was sprinkled on the wrong section of the altar.

Immediately – לְאַלְתַּר: This means that if his intent was improper only with regard to where the blood would be placed, but he intended to perform the sprinkling at the appropriate time, the offering is not disqualified. Although failure to place the blood in its appropriate place renders the meat prohibited for consumption, the offering remains fit because improper intent disqualifies an offering only when it is expressed with regard to the timing or area of certain rites, or in some cases the designation of the offering (see 36a).

Beyond its designated time it is *piggul,* etc. – חוּץ לִזְמַנּוֹ פִּיגּוּל וכו׳: An offering is rendered *piggul* when the only impropriety in its sacrifice is intent to burn or consume it or sprinkle its blood beyond its appointed time. Only offerings designated as *piggul* carry the penalty of *karet* for their consumption.

HALAKHA

The next day the offering is disqualified – למחר פסול: If one intended to sprinkle the blood on the altar the following day and in the wrong place, e.g., above the red line as opposed to below it, the offering is disqualified, but it is not rendered *piggul*, because even without the improper intent with regard to the sacrifice's timing the meat would still be prohibited for consumption. This ruling is in accordance with Shmuel's opinion (Rambam *Sefer Avoda*, *Hilkhot Pesulei HaMukdashin* 16:6, and see Ra'avad and *Kesef Mishne* there).

למחר – פסול; חזר וחישב, בין חוץ לזמנו בין חוץ למקומו – פסול ואין בו כרת.

If he had intent to sprinkle the blood improperly **the next day,** beyond the permitted time, then the offering is **disqualified.**[H] Nevertheless, it is not rendered *piggul*, because he also had intent to sprinkle the blood improperly. Therefore, if **he subsequently had intent** to sacrifice the offering or consume its meat, **whether beyond its** designated **time or outside its** designated **area,** it is **disqualified and there is no** liability for ***karet*** **for** burning or partaking **of it,** because an offering can be rendered *piggul* only if it would have otherwise been fit.

ואי שלא במקומו כמקומו דמי, האי פסול? פיגול הוא!

The Gemara asks: **But if** blood sprinkled **not in its** proper **place** is considered **as** though it were sprinkled in **its** proper **place,** then in **this** case above, where he had intent to sprinkle the blood improperly the next day, is the offering merely **disqualified?** Since **it is** considered as though he had intent to sprinkle the blood properly the next day, shouldn't the offering be rendered ***piggul?***

אמר מר זוטרא: זריקה דשריא בשר באכילה – מייתא לידי פיגול, זריקה דלא שריא בשר באכילה – לא מייתא לידי פיגול.

Mar Zutra said: Intent with regard to **sprinkling that permits** the **meat for consumption** can **cause** the offering **to** become ***piggul.*** Intent with regard to **sprinkling that does not render** the **meat permitted for consumption does not cause** it **to** become ***piggul.*** Even Shmuel concedes that although the owner achieves atonement, if the blood is sprinkled in an improper place the meat may not be consumed. Accordingly, this offering is not rendered *piggul*.

אמר ליה רב אשי למר זוטרא: מנא לך הא? דכתיב: "ואם האכל יאכל מבשר זבח שלמיו...פגול יהיה" – מי שפיגולו גרם לו, יצא זה שאין פיגולו גרם לו, אלא איסור דבר אחר גרם לו.

Rav Ashi said to Mar Zutra: From where do you derive **this?** Mar Zutra replied: I derive it from a verse, **as it is written: "And if any of the flesh of his peace offerings be at all eaten** on the third day, it shall not be accepted, neither shall it be credited to he who offers it, **it shall be *piggul*"** (Leviticus 7:18). The verse indicates that only an offering **whose** intent of ***piggul*** alone **caused it** to be disqualified is considered *piggul*. **Excluded is this** case, **whose** intent of ***piggul*** alone **did not cause it** to be disqualified; **rather, the prohibition of something else,** i.e., the intent to sprinkle the blood in an improper location, **caused it** to be disqualified.

אי הכי, איפסולי נמי לא ליפסל!

The Gemara challenges: But **if so,** i.e., if blood applied not in its proper place is considered as though it were applied in its proper place, and the intent to sprinkle the blood the next day does not render the offering *piggul*, then **it should not even be disqualified** due to such an intention. Why, then, does the *baraita* rule that it is disqualified?

אמר רב נחמן בר יצחק: מידי דהוה אמחשבת הינוח, ואליבא דרבי יהודה.

Rav Naḥman bar Yitzḥak said: In general, intent to perform the rites of an offering beyond its designated time disqualifies the offering, even when it does not render it *piggul*, **just as is** the case **with regard to the intent to leave**[N] portions of the offering for the next day, as taught in a mishna in the next chapter (35b), **and according to** the opinion **of Rabbi Yehuda** there, that intent to leave the blood until the next day rather than sprinkling it on the altar disqualifies the offering even though it does not render it *piggul*.

NOTES

Just as is the case with regard to the intent to leave – מידי דהוה אמחשבת הינוח: According to the Rambam, the Gemara does not mean that the *tanna* of this mishna holds in accordance with the opinion of Rabbi Yehuda in that mishna, but instead he draws an analogy: Just as Rabbi Yehuda holds that intent to leave the blood until the next day disqualifies the offering without rendering it *piggul*, so too in this case one can hold that the intent to sprinkle the blood improperly beyond its appointed time disqualifies the offering without rendering it *piggul*. Therefore, the Rambam rules in accordance with the mishna here, although he rules against the opinion of Rabbi Yehuda with regard to intent to leave the blood until the next day (*Kiryat Sefer*; *Kesef Mishne*). Other later commentaries point out that a precise reading of the Gemara supports this interpretation (see *Sefat Emet*).

רֵישׁ לָקִישׁ אָמַר: לְעוֹלָם פָּסוּל מַמָּשׁ, וְשֶׁלֹּא בִּמְקוֹמוֹ כִּמְקוֹמוֹ דָּמֵי. וְלָא קַשְׁיָא: כָּאן – שֶׁנָּתַן בִּשְׁתִיקָה, כָּאן – שֶׁנָּתַן בַּאֲמִירָה.

§ The Gemara cites additional opinions with regard to the statement of the mishna that blood misapplied on the altar disqualifies the offering. **Reish Lakish says: Actually,** when the mishna states that the offering is **disqualified,** this is to be taken **literally,** i.e., that the owner does not even achieve atonement through it. **And** nevertheless, blood sprinkled **not in its proper place is considered as** though it were sprinkled in **its** proper **place,** and it effects atonement. **And** the apparent contradiction between these two claims is **not difficult: Here, where** misapplication of the blood effects atonement, it is a case **where he placed** it **in silence,** i.e., without specific intent; **there,** in the mishna, it is a case **where he placed** it **with a statement,**[N] i.e., intent to consume the offering beyond its appointed time.

תְּנַן: חִישֵּׁב לִיתֵּן אֶת הַנִּיתָּנִין לְמַטָּה לְמַעְלָה, לְמַעְלָה לְמַטָּה, עַד: מִידֵּי דַּהֲוָה אַמַּחֲשֶׁבֶת הִינּוּחַ וְאַלִּיבָּא דְּרַבִּי יְהוּדָה כּו׳.

Since Reish Lakish agrees with the statement of Shmuel that blood applied not in its proper place is considered as though it were applied in its proper place, the Gemara poses the same difficulties to the statement of Reish Lakish as posed above to Shmuel: **We learned** in a *baraita*: If one slaughtered an offering and **had intent to place** the blood **that is** to be **placed below** the red line **above** the red line, or to place the blood that is to be placed **above** the red line **below** the red line, etc., **until** the response of Rav Naḥman bar Yitzḥak: **Just as is** the case **with regard to the intent to leave** portions of the offering for the next day, **and according to** the opinion **of Rabbi Yehuda, etc.**

רַבִּי יוֹחָנָן אָמַר: אִידִי וְאִידִי שֶׁנָּתַן בִּשְׁתִיקָה, וְשֶׁלֹּא בִּמְקוֹמוֹ לָאו כִּמְקוֹמוֹ דָּמֵי. וְהָא – דְּאִיכָּא דַּם הַנֶּפֶשׁ, הָא – דְּלֵיכָּא דַּם הַנֶּפֶשׁ.

Rabbi Yoḥanan says: Both **here and there,** i.e., in the mishna here as well as in the mishna in the next chapter (32a), it is a case **where he placed** the blood **in silence. And** the mishna here rules that the offering is completely disqualified because blood applied **not in its** proper **place is not considered as** though it were applied in **its** proper **place. And that** mishna in the next chapter, which states that the blood may be collected and sprinkled again, is referring to a case **where there is blood of the soul** left in the animal to sprinkle again, while **this** mishna is referring to a case **where there is no blood of the soul** left.

תְּנַן: פָּסוּל וְאֵין בּוֹ כָּרֵת; בִּשְׁלָמָא לְרֵישׁ לָקִישׁ – הַיְינוּ דְּקָתָנֵי פָּסוּל וְאֵין בּוֹ כָּרֵת,

The Gemara challenges: **We learned** in the mishna that if the blood was misapplied on the altar, the offering is **disqualified, but there is no** liability for ***karet*** **for** one who partakes of the meat. **Granted, according to Reish Lakish,** who explains that the mishna is referring to one who expresses intent to sacrifice or consume the offering beyond its designated time, **this is** the reason **that** the *tanna* **teaches: Disqualified, but there is no** liability for ***karet*** **for** burning or partaking of **it,** to stress that although one sprinkled the blood with intent of *piggul,* since the sprinkling was performed improperly, his intent does not render the offering *piggul,* and one who partakes of it is not liable to receive *karet.*

אֶלָּא לְרַבִּי יוֹחָנָן מַאי אֵין בּוֹ כָּרֵת? קַשְׁיָא.

But according to Rabbi Yoḥanan, who explains that the mishna is referring to a case where the blood was sprinkled with no specific intent, of **what** necessity is the clause: **There is no** liability for ***karet*** **for** burning or partaking of **it?** Since the offering is disqualified because the blood was placed not in its proper place, and there was no intent of *piggul,* why would one think that there should be liability for *karet*? The Gemara responds: Indeed, this clause is **difficult** for Rabbi Yoḥanan.

וְלִשְׁמוּאֵל מַאי אֵין בּוֹ כָּרֵת? הָכִי קָאָמַר: אִם נָתַן בְּמַחֲשָׁבָה – פָּסוּל וְאֵין בּוֹ כָּרֵת.

The Gemara asks: **And according to Shmuel,**[N] of **what** necessity is the clause: **There is no** liability for ***karet*** **for** burning or partaking of **it?** The Gemara responds: **This** is what the mishna **is saying: If one placed** the blood improperly **with intent**[N] that would otherwise render the offering *piggul,* the offering is **disqualified, but there is no** liability for ***karet*** **for** burning or partaking of **it,** because such sprinkling would not have permitted the meat for consumption.

NOTES

There, where he placed it with a statement – כָּאן שֶׁנָּתַן בַּאֲמִירָה: Although Reish Lakish introduces a new element to the case not mentioned explicitly in the mishna, the ruling in the mishna seems appropriate to the case as he explains it.

And according to Shmuel – וְלִשְׁמוּאֵל: The Gemara's question is: Since Shmuel interprets the mishna as ruling that the offering successfully effects atonement, it cannot be that the priest sprinkled the blood with intent to consume or burn the offering beyond its appointed time; if so, why might it have occurred to anyone that the offering would be *piggul*?

If one placed the blood with intent – אִם נָתַן בְּמַחֲשָׁבָה: The expanded mishna would then read as follows: If the priest placed the blood that is placed below the red line above the red line, etc., the offering effects atonement, but its meat is disqualified. And if he did so with intent to consume or burn the offering beyond its appointed time, the offering is completely disqualified, and there is no liability for *karet* for one who partakes of it.

NOTES

He may not gather it up – לֹא יַאַסְפֶנּוּ: Although the sprinkling is invalid, Rabbi Yosei does not hold that it is as though the blood were spilled out on the floor, because it reaches the physical structure of the altar. Therefore, the blood may not be gathered up and sprinkled again.

וְרַבִּי יוֹחָנָן, אִי שֶׁלֹּא בִּמְקוֹמוֹ לָאו כִּמְקוֹמוֹ דָּמֵי, לֶיהֱוֵי כִּי נִשְׁפַּךְ מִן הַכְּלִי עַל הָרִצְפָּה, וְיַאַסְפֶנּוּ!

The Gemara challenges: **And** according to **Rabbi Yoḥanan, if** blood sprinkled **not in its** proper **place is not considered as** though it were sprinkled in **its** proper **place, it should be as if it spilled from the** service **vessel onto the floor, and let** the priest **gather it up** and sprinkle it again properly. Why, then, does the mishna rule that it is disqualified?

סָבַר לָהּ כְּמַאן דְּאָמַר: לֹא יַאַסְפֶנּוּ. דְּאָמַר רַב יִצְחָק בַּר יוֹסֵף אָמַר רַבִּי יוֹחָנָן: הַכֹּל מוֹדִים בַּנִּיתָּנִין לְמַעְלָה שֶׁנְּתָנָן לְמַעְלָה, לְמַטָּה שֶׁנְּתָנָן לְמַטָּה, שֶׁלֹּא כְּמִצְוָתָן – לֹא יַאַסְפֶנּוּ. לֹא נֶחְלְקוּ אֶלָּא בַּנִּיתָּנִין לְמַעְלָה שֶׁנְּתָנָן לְמַטָּה, לְמַטָּה שֶׁנְּתָנָן לְמַעְלָה, שֶׁרַבִּי יוֹסֵי אוֹמֵר: לֹא יַאַסְפֶנּוּ, וְרַבִּי שִׁמְעוֹן אוֹמֵר: יַאַסְפֶנּוּ,

The Gemara responds: The *tanna* of the mishna **holds in accordance with** the opinion of **the one who says: He may not gather it up. As Rav Yitzḥak bar Yosef says** that **Rabbi Yoḥanan says: All concede with regard to** the blood **that is** to be **placed above** the red line **that** if **one placed it above** the red line, and likewise with regard to the blood that is to be placed **below** the red line if one **placed it below** the red line, **not in accordance with** the procedure dictated by **its mitzva,** e.g., with the left hand or with improper intent, **he may not gather it up** again. **They disagree only with regard to** the blood **that is** to be **placed above** the red line **that one placed below** the red line, and blood that is to be placed below the red line **that one placed above** the red line, as **Rabbi Yosei says: He may not gather it up,**[N] **and Rabbi Shimon says: He may gather it up.**

Perek **II**
Daf **27** Amud **b**

וּמִשְׁנָתֵינוּ כְּדִבְרֵי הָאוֹמֵר: לֹא יַאַסְפֶנּוּ.

And our mishna is in accordance with the statement of the one who says: He may not gather it up.

וְרַב חִסְדָּא אָמַר אֲבִימִי: הַכֹּל מוֹדִין בַּנִּיתָּנִין לְמַטָּה שֶׁנְּתָנָן לְמַעְלָה – שֶׁלֹּא יַאַסְפֶנּוּ, וְכׇל שֶׁכֵּן בַּנִּיתָּנִין לְמַעְלָה שֶׁנְּתָנָן לְמַטָּה, הוֹאִיל וְדָמִים הָעֶלְיוֹנִים לְמַטָּה הֵן בָּאִין. לֹא נֶחְלְקוּ אֶלָּא בַּנִּיתָּנִין לִפְנִים שֶׁנְּתָנָן בַּחוּץ, בַּחוּץ שֶׁנְּתָנָן לִפְנִים, שֶׁרַבִּי יוֹסֵי אוֹמֵר: יַאַסְפֶנּוּ, וְרַבִּי שִׁמְעוֹן אוֹמֵר: לֹא יַאַסְפֶנּוּ.

And Rav Ḥisda says that **Avimi says: Everyone concedes with regard to** the blood **that is** to be **placed below** the red line **that** if **one placed it above** the red line **he may not gather it up** again. **And all the more so with regard to the** blood **that is** to be **placed above** the red line **that one placed below** the red line, **since the blood** placed **above** the red line will eventually run down the side of the altar and **reach below** the red line. **They disagree only with regard to** the blood **that is** to be **placed inside** the Sanctuary **that one placed outside** on the external altar, or blood that is to be placed **outside that one placed inside, as Rabbi Yosei says: He may gather it up,** as though it had spilled on the floor, **and Rabbi Shimon says: He may not gather it up,** because the blood was nevertheless placed on an altar.

אָמַר רַב נַחְמָן בַּר יִצְחָק: אַף אֲנַן נַמִי תָּנֵינָא, רַבִּי יְהוּדָה אוֹמֵר: ״זֹאת הִיא הָעוֹלָה״ – הֲרֵי אֵלּוּ מִיעוּטִין, פְּרָט לְנִשְׁחֲטָה בַּלַּיְלָה, וְשֶׁנִּשְׁפַּךְ דָּמָהּ, וְשֶׁיָּצָא דָּמָהּ חוּץ לַקְּלָעִים, אִם עָלְתָה – תֵּרֵד.

Rav Naḥman bar Yitzḥak says: We learn in a *baraita* **as well** that if the blood is misapplied on the altar it may not be gathered, in accordance with the opinion of Rabbi Yoḥanan: **Rabbi Yehuda says** that the verse states: **"This** is the law of the burnt offering: **It is that which goes up** [*ha'ola*] on the pyre upon the altar" (Leviticus 6:2), from which it is derived that a disqualified offering that ascended upon the altar shall not descend from it. **These** terms, i.e., "this," "it," and "that," **are** three terms of **exclusion,** which serve **to exclude** three cases of disqualified offerings from this *halakha*: An offering that **was slaughtered at night,**[H] one **whose blood was spilled, and** one **whose blood emerged outside the curtains,** i.e., the Temple courtyard. In these cases, even **if** the offering **ascended** upon the altar **it shall descend.**

HALAKHA

To exclude an offering that was slaughtered at night, etc. – פְּרָט לְנִשְׁחֲטָה בַּלַּיְלָה וכו׳: If a sacrificial animal was slaughtered at night, or if its blood was spilled, or if it left the Temple courtyard, and it then ascended onto the altar, it must descend, in accordance with the opinion of Rabbi Yehuda (Rambam *Sefer Avoda*, *Hilkhot Pesulei HaMukdashin* 3:6).

רַבִּי שִׁמְעוֹן אוֹמֵר: ״עוֹלָה״, אֵין לִי אֶלָּא עוֹלָה כְּשֵׁרָה, מִנַּיִן לְרַבּוֹת שֶׁנִּשְׁחֲטָה בַּלַּיְלָה, וְשֶׁנִּשְׁפַּךְ דָּמָהּ, וְשֶׁיָּצָא דָּמָהּ חוּץ לַקְּלָעִים, וְהַלָּן, וְהַיּוֹצֵא, וְהַטָּמֵא, וְשֶׁנִּשְׁחַט חוּץ לִזְמַנּוֹ וְחוּץ לִמְקוֹמוֹ, וְשֶׁקִּיבְּלוּ פְּסוּלִין וְזָרְקוּ אֶת דָּמָהּ, וְהַנִּיתָּנִין לְמַעְלָה שֶׁנְּתָנָן לְמַטָּה, וְהַנִּיתָּנִין לְמַטָּה שֶׁנְּתָנָן לְמַעְלָה, וְהַנִּיתָּנִין בִּפְנִים שֶׁנְּתָנָן בַּחוּץ, וְהַנִּיתָּנִין בַּחוּץ שֶׁנְּתָנָן בִּפְנִים, וְהַפֶּסַח וְהַחַטָּאת שֶׁשְּׁחָטָן שֶׁלֹּא לִשְׁמָן – מִנַּיִן?

Rabbi Shimon says: From the term **"burnt offering** [*ola*]**" I have** derived **only** that **a fit burnt offering** shall not descend. **From where** is it derived **that** the *halakha* **includes** an offering **that was slaughtered at night, or** one **whose blood was spilled, or** one **whose blood emerged outside the curtains, or** one **that was left overnight, or** one **that left** the courtyard, **or** one **that** became **impure,**[H] **or** one **that was slaughtered** with intent to consume it **beyond** its designated **time or outside** its designated **area, or** an offering for **which an unfit** person **collected and sprinkled its blood, or** a case where **one placed** the blood **that is** to be **placed above** the red line **below** it, **or** where **one placed** the blood **that is** to be **placed below** the red line **above** it, **or** where **one placed** the blood **that is** to be **placed inside** the Sanctuary **outside** on the external altar, **or** where **one placed** the blood **that is** to be **placed outside** the Sanctuary **inside** it, **or a Paschal offering or a sin offering that one slaughtered not for their sake? From where** is it derived that if these offerings ascended they shall not descend?

תַּלְמוּד לוֹמַר: ״תּוֹרַת הָעוֹלָה״ – רִיבָּה תּוֹרָה אַחַת לְכָל הָעוֹלִין, שֶׁאִם עָלוּ לֹא יֵרְדוּ.

The verse states: "The law of the burnt offering [*ha'ola*]**,"** literally: That which goes up. The verse **included** under **one law all** items **that ascend** upon the altar, teaching **that if they ascended** the altar, **they shall not descend.**

יָכוֹל שֶׁאֲנִי מְרַבֶּה אַף הָרוֹבֵעַ וְהַנִּרְבָּע, וְהַמּוּקְצֶה וְהַנֶּעֱבָד, וְהָאֶתְנַן, וְהַמְּחִיר, וְהַכִּלְאַיִם, וְהַטְּרֵיפָה, וְיוֹצֵא דוֹפֶן? תַּלְמוּד לוֹמַר: ״זֹאת״.

One **might** have thought **that I** should **include even an animal that** copulated with a person,[B] **or an animal that was the object of** bestiality, **or** an animal **that was set aside** for idol worship, **or** an animal **that was worshipped** as a deity, **or** an animal that was given as **payment** to a prostitute[B] **or** as **the price** of a dog, **or** an animal born of a mixture of **diverse kinds,**[B] **or** an animal that is **a** *tereifa*,[B] **or** an animal **born by caesarean section. The verse** therefore **states: "This,"** to exclude these animals from the *halakha*.

וּמָה רָאִיתָ לְרַבּוֹת אֶת אֵלּוּ וּלְהוֹצִיא אֶת אֵלּוּ? מְרַבֶּה אֲנִי אֶת אֵלּוּ – שֶׁהָיָה פְּסוּלָן בַּקּוֹדֶשׁ, וּמוֹצִיא אֲנִי אֶת אֵלּוּ – שֶׁלֹּא הָיָה פְּסוּלָן בַּקּוֹדֶשׁ.

The Gemara asks: **And what did you see** as the reason **to include** the former cases **and to exclude** the latter ones? The Gemara responds: **I include these** former cases, **whose disqualification occurred in sanctity,**[N] i.e., in the course of the Temple service, **and I exclude these** latter cases, **whose disqualification did not occur in sanctity** and were disqualified as offerings from the outset.

קָתָנֵי מִיהָא: הַנִּיתָּנִין לְמַטָּה שֶׁנְּתָנָן לְמַעְלָה וּלְמַעְלָה שֶׁנְּתָנָן לְמַטָּה, וְלָא פְּלִיג רַבִּי יְהוּדָה, מַאי טַעְמָא? לָאו מִשּׁוּם דְּקַלְטֵיהּ מִזְבֵּחַ? וּשְׁמַע מִינַּהּ: לֹא יַאַסְפֶנּוּ.

Rav Naḥman bar Yitzḥak continues: **In any event,** the *baraita* **teaches** that if **one placed** the blood **that is** to be **placed below** the red line **above** it, **or** if **one placed** the blood that is to be placed **above** the red line **below** it, the offering does not descend from the altar. **And Rabbi Yehuda does not disagree,** even though he holds that if the blood spilled on the ground the offering descends from the altar. **What is the reason** for this? Is it **not because** even if the blood was misapplied, **the altar has absorbed**[N] the blood and it is not considered to have been spilled on the floor? **Conclude from it** that if blood was misapplied on the altar, the priest **may not gather it up** again, in accordance with the statement of Rabbi Yoḥanan.

HALAKHA

That was left overnight, or that left the courtyard, or that became impure, etc. – הַלָּן וְהַיּוֹצֵא וְהַטָּמֵא וכו׳: Offerings whose blood, meat, or portions burned on the altar were left overnight, or became ritually impure, or were disqualified by improper intent with regard to the sacrifice's timing or location, or whose blood an unfit person collected or sprinkled, or whose blood was sprinkled out of place, and offerings of the most sacred order that were slaughtered or their blood collected in the south of the Temple courtyard, are all disqualified. Still, if any of these offerings ascended onto the altar, they shall not descend, as even Rabbi Yehuda concedes as much in such cases (Rambam *Sefer Avoda, Hilkhot Pesulei HaMukdashin* 3:7).

NOTES

Whose disqualification occurred in sanctity – שֶׁהָיָה פְּסוּלָן בַּקּוֹדֶשׁ: The meaning of this phrase is subject to dispute among the early commentaries. According to Rashi, it means that the animal was disqualified within the Temple, as opposed to an animal that copulated with a person or other animals disqualified before they arrived at the Temple. *Tosafot* interpret the term as denoting disqualified offerings that could theoretically be sacrificed in other circumstances, e.g., on a private altar before the Temple was built. Excluded are animals that could never be sacrificed under any circumstances (*Shita Mekubbetzet*).

Because the altar has absorbed – מִשּׁוּם דְּקַלְטֵיהּ מִזְבֵּחַ: One cannot suggest that according to Rabbi Yehuda, blood sprinkled not in its correct place is considered to have been sprinkled in its correct place and for this reason he does not say that an offering whose blood was misapplied must descend, since the *baraita* mentions only disqualified offerings that do not effect atonement (Rashi).

BACKGROUND

Animal that copulated with a person – רוֹבֵעַ: An animal that copulated with a person, or one that has been set aside to be used as an offering to an idol, or one that has been worshipped as an idol are all disqualified from being used as offerings, although it is permitted to derive benefit from them.

Payment to a prostitute – אֶתְנַן: The Torah prohibits the sacrifice of an animal used as payment to a prostitute or exchanged for a dog (see Deuteronomy 23:19). The Sages explain that the disqualification applies only to animals used directly for these purposes, but not to other items exchanged for those animals. Therefore, if money is given as payment to a prostitute, and she then uses it to purchase an animal, the animal is not disqualified. Likewise, only an animal that was directly exchanged for a dog is disqualified.

Diverse kinds – כִּלְאַיִם: The Torah prohibits crossbreeding different species of animals (Leviticus 19:19). This transgression is punishable by lashes. It is permitted to make use of the offspring of crossbreeding, e.g., a mule. The *halakhot* governing this prohibition are discussed in tractate *Kilayim*.

***Tereifa* – טְרֵיפָה:** Generally speaking, a *tereifa* is an animal that suffers from a condition that will cause it to die within twelve months. It is prohibited by Torah law to eat a slaughtered animal that had been injured or stricken with a disease of this nature, although the actual source for the prohibition is a matter of dispute. Some authorities cite Exodus 22:30: "You shall not eat any flesh that is torn of beasts in the field," while others suggest Deuteronomy 14:21: "You shall not eat of anything that died of itself." According to the *Minḥat Ḥinnukh* and others, both verses together serve as the source for the prohibition.

אָמַר רַבִּי אֱלִיעֶזֶר: מִזְבֵּחַ הַפְּנִימִי מְקַדֵּשׁ פְּסוּלִין.

§ Pursuant to the discussion of disqualified offerings that do not descend from the external altar, **Rabbi Eliezer says: The inner altar,**[B] i.e., the golden altar inside the Sanctuary, **sanctifies disqualified** offerings[H] such that if they ascended onto it, they do not descend.

מַאי קָא מַשְׁמַע לָן? תָּנֵינָא: הַנִּיתָּנִין בִּפְנִים כו׳!

The Gemara asks: **What is** this statement **teaching us? We** already **learn** this in the above *baraita*: If one placed the blood **that is** to be **placed inside** the Sanctuary outside on the external altar, or if one placed the blood that is to be placed outside the Sanctuary inside it, on the golden altar, the offering does not descend.

אִי מֵהָתָם, הֲוָה אָמִינָא: הָנֵי מִילֵּי – דָּם, דַּחֲזֵי לֵיהּ, אֲבָל קוֹמֶץ דְּלָא חֲזֵי לֵיהּ – אֵימָא לָא, קָא מַשְׁמַע לָן.

The Gemara responds: **If** one were to learn the *halakha* only **from there, I would say: This matter** applies only to **blood** mistakenly placed on the golden altar, **as it is fit to** be placed on that altar in certain contexts, i.e., the blood of the bull and goat sin offerings on Yom Kippur; **but** with regard to **a handful** from a meal offering, **which is not fit to** be placed on the golden altar in any context, **I will say** that it is **not** sanctified when placed on it. Rabbi Eliezer therefore **teaches us** that even a handful from a meal offering does not descend from it.

מֵיתִיבֵי: קְטֹרֶת זָרָה שֶׁעָלָה לְגַבֵּי מִזְבֵּחַ – תֵּרֵד, שֶׁאֵין לְךָ מְקַדֵּשׁ פְּסוּלִין אֶלָּא מִזְבֵּחַ הַחִיצוֹן בְּרָאוּי לוֹ; חִיצוֹן – אִין, פְּנִימִי – לָא!

The Gemara **raises an objection** from a *baraita*: If **strange incense,**[N] i.e., incense that it is prohibited to burn on the golden altar, **ascended onto the altar, it shall descend, as only the external altar sanctifies disqualified** offerings that are **suited for it.** One can infer that the **external** altar **does** sanctify disqualified offerings, but the **inner** altar does **not.**

תְּרֵיץ הָכִי: קְטֹרֶת זָרָה שֶׁעָלְתָה לַמִּזְבֵּחַ הַחִיצוֹן – תֵּרֵד, שֶׁאֵין מִזְבֵּחַ הַחִיצוֹן מְקַדֵּשׁ פְּסוּלִין אֶלָּא הָרָאוּי לוֹ, וְהַפְּנִימִי – בֵּין רָאוּי לוֹ בֵּין שֶׁאֵין רָאוּי לוֹ. מַאי טַעְמָא? הַאי – רִצְפָּה, וְהַאי – כְּלִי שָׁרֵת.

The Gemara responds: **Answer like this:** The *baraita* means that if **strange incense ascended onto the external altar, it shall descend, as the external altar sanctifies only disqualified** offerings **that are suited for it. But the inner** altar sanctifies everything, **whether it is suited for it or it is not suited for it. What is the reason** for this? **This,** the external altar, is considered part of the **floor,** since it is fixed to the floor of the Temple, **and that,** the inner altar, is considered **a service vessel** with a higher level of sanctity.

מתני׳ הַשּׁוֹחֵט אֶת הַזֶּבַח לִזְרוֹק דָּמוֹ בַּחוּץ אוֹ מִקְצָת דָּמוֹ בַּחוּץ, לְהַקְטִיר אֵימוּרָיו בַּחוּץ אוֹ מִקְצָת אֵימוּרָיו בַּחוּץ, לֶאֱכוֹל בְּשָׂרוֹ בַּחוּץ אוֹ כְּזַיִת מִבְּשָׂרוֹ בַּחוּץ, אוֹ לֶאֱכוֹל כְּזַיִת מֵעוֹר הָאַלְיָה בַּחוּץ – פָּסוּל, וְאֵין בּוֹ כָּרֵת.

MISHNA With regard to **one who slaughters the offering** with intent **to sprinkle its blood outside**[H] the Temple **or** to sprinkle **part of its blood outside** the Temple, **to burn its sacrificial portions outside** the Temple or to burn **part of its sacrificial portions outside** the Temple, **to partake of its meat outside** the Temple **or** to partake **of an olive-bulk**[B] **of its meat outside** the Temple, **or to partake of an olive-bulk of the skin of the tail outside** the Temple, in all of these cases the offering is **disqualified, and there is no** liability for ***karet*** for one who partakes of it.

לִזְרוֹק דָּמוֹ לְמָחָר, מִקְצָת דָּמוֹ לְמָחָר, לְהַקְטִיר אֵימוּרָיו לְמָחָר אוֹ מִקְצָת אֵימוּרָיו לְמָחָר, לֶאֱכוֹל בְּשָׂרוֹ לְמָחָר אוֹ כְּזַיִת מִבְּשָׂרוֹ לְמָחָר, אוֹ לֶאֱכוֹל כְּזַיִת מֵעוֹר הָאַלְיָה לְמָחָר – פִּיגּוּל, וְחַיָּיבִין עָלָיו כָּרֵת.

But if one had intent **to sprinkle its blood the next day**[H] or **part of its blood the next day, to burn its sacrificial portions the next day** or to burn **part of its sacrificial portions the next day, to partake of its meat the next day**[N] or to partake of an **olive-bulk of its meat the next day, or to partake of an olive-bulk of the skin of the tail the next day,** the offering is ***piggul*****, and one is liable** to receive ***karet*** **for** burning or partaking **of it.**[H]

גמ׳ סַבְרוּהָ: עוֹר אַלְיָה

GEMARA The students **assumed** that **the skin of the tail**

BACKGROUND

Inner altar – מִזְבֵּחַ הַפְּנִימִי: Also known as the golden altar or the incense altar, this small structure stood in the middle of the Sanctuary. It was one cubit long, one cubit wide, and two cubits high. This altar was overlaid with gold, and it had four protrusions, one on each corner. Incense was sacrificed every day on the inner altar, and on Yom Kippur the blood of the special Yom Kippur offerings was sprinkled on top of it and on the protrusions.

Olive-bulk – כְּזַיִת: An olive-bulk is one of the most significant halakhic units of volume. By Torah law, the act of eating is defined as consuming one olive-bulk, and every mitzva that either requires or prohibits eating is referring to this measure. The measure is defined in terms of the water displacement of a particular type of olive, and the precise size of this measurement is not clear. One talmudic passage indicates that it is almost half an egg-bulk, while another indicates that it is less than one-third of an egg-bulk. The opinions with regard to the measure of an olive-bulk range from 5 cc to 50 cc.

HALAKHA

The inner altar sanctifies disqualified offerings, etc. – מִזְבֵּחַ הַפְּנִימִי מְקַדֵּשׁ פְּסוּלִין וכו׳: The inner altar sanctifies disqualified offerings, whether or not they are suited for it. The external altar sanctifies disqualified offerings only if they are suited for it. For example, if disqualified animal offerings ascended onto the external altar, they do not descend. But if strange incense ascended on it, it must descend, because incense is never offered on the external altar. If the handful from a meal offering was placed on the inner altar, it shall not descend, even though meal offerings are never offered on the inner altar (Rambam *Sefer Avoda, Hilkhot Pesulei HaMukdashin* 3:18).

To sprinkle its blood outside, etc. – לִזְרוֹק דָּמוֹ בַּחוּץ וכו׳: If one slaughters an offering for its own sake, but with intention to sprinkle its blood or burn one of its sacrificial portions outside of the Temple courtyard, or to partake of one its eaten portions outside of its designated area, the offering is disqualified by this intent, but it is not rendered *piggul* (Rambam *Sefer Avoda, Hilkhot Pesulei HaMukdashin* 13:1, 16:1).

To sprinkle its blood the next day – לִזְרוֹק דָּמוֹ לְמָחָר: If one slaughters an offering for its own sake but with intention to sprinkle its blood after sunset, or to burn one of its sacrificial portions the next day, or to partake of one its eaten portions beyond its designated time, the offering is rendered *piggul* (Rambam *Sefer Avoda, Hilkhot Pesulei HaMukdashin* 13:1).

And one is liable to receive *karet* for it – וְחַיָּיבִין עָלָיו כָּרֵת: If an offering is rendered *piggul*, one who intentionally partakes of an olive-bulk or more of its meat is liable to receive *karet*. If he did so unintentionally, he is liable to bring a sin offering (Rambam *Sefer Avoda, Hilkhot Pesulei HaMukdashin* 18:6).

NOTES

Strange incense – קְטֹרֶת זָרָה: This is referring to any incense offered voluntarily, since no incense may be offered except at the time explicitly prescribed in the Torah as a communal obligation, every morning and afternoon (see *Menahot* 50a).

To partake of its meat the next day – לֶאֱכוֹל בְּשָׂרוֹ לְמָחָר: This is referring to offerings that may be eaten only on the day of the sacrifice and the following night, e.g., sin offerings. Other offerings, e.g., individual peace offerings, may be eaten the next day as well, and in such cases only intent to consume their meat after that time renders them *piggul*. In all cases, the sacrificial portions must be burned by the end of the first night, and intent to burn them beyond that time renders the offering *piggul* (Rashi).

כְּאַלְיָה דָּמֵי, וְהָא קָא מְחַשֵּׁב מֵאֲכִילַת מִזְבֵּחַ לְאָדָם!

is considered as though it were part of the **tail**[NB] itself. The tail of a sheep sacrificed as a peace offering is burned on the altar rather than eaten. **But** if so, one who slaughters the sheep with intent to consume the skin of its tail the next day **has intent** to shift its consumption **from consumption by** the **altar**, i.e., burning the offering, **to** consumption by **a person.** Since intent to consume part of an offering beyond its designated time renders an offering *piggul* only if that part is intended for human consumption, why does the mishna rule that such an offering is *piggul*?

אָמַר שְׁמוּאֵל: הָא מַנִּי – רַבִּי אֱלִיעֶזֶר הִיא, דְּאָמַר: מְחַשְּׁבִין מֵאֲכִילַת מִזְבֵּחַ לַאֲכִילַת אָדָם, וּמֵאֲכִילַת אָדָם לַאֲכִילַת מִזְבֵּחַ.

Shmuel says: In accordance with **whose** opinion **is this? It is** in accordance with the opinion of **Rabbi Eliezer, who says: One can have intent** to shift an item's consumption **from consumption by** the **altar to consumption by a person, or from consumption by a person to consumption by** the **altar,** and the offering will still be rendered *piggul*.

דִּתְנַן: הַשּׁוֹחֵט אֶת הַזֶּבַח לֶאֱכוֹל דָּבָר שֶׁאֵין דַּרְכּוֹ לֶאֱכוֹל, לְהַקְטִיר דָּבָר שֶׁאֵין דַּרְכּוֹ לְהַקְטִיר – כָּשֵׁר, וְרַבִּי אֱלִיעֶזֶר פּוֹסֵל.

This is **as we learned** in a mishna (35a): In a case of **one who slaughters the offering** with intent **to partake of an item whose** typical **manner** is such that one does **not** partake of it, or **to burn an item whose** typical **manner** is such that one does **not burn** it on the altar, beyond its designated time or outside its designated area, the offering is **fit. And Rabbi Eliezer deems it unfit.**

בְּמַאי אוֹקִימְתָּא – כְּרַבִּי אֱלִיעֶזֶר. אֵימָא סֵיפָא: זֶה הַכְּלָל, כָּל הַשּׁוֹחֵט, וְהַמְקַבֵּל, וְהַמּוֹלִיךְ, וְהַזּוֹרֵק, לֶאֱכוֹל דָּבָר שֶׁדַּרְכּוֹ לֶאֱכוֹל, וּלְהַקְטִיר דָּבָר שֶׁדַּרְכּוֹ לְהַקְטִיר;

The Gemara asks: **In accordance with which** opinion **did you interpret** the mishna here? You interpreted it **in accordance with** the opinion of **Rabbi Eliezer.** But if so, **say the latter clause,** i.e., the next mishna (29b): **This is the principle: Anyone who slaughters** the animal, **or who collects** the blood, **or who conveys** the blood, **or who sprinkles** the blood with the intent **to partake of an item whose** typical **manner** is such that one **partakes** of it, **or to burn an item whose** typical **manner** is such that one **burns** it on the altar, beyond its designated time, renders it *piggul*.

דָּבָר שֶׁדַּרְכּוֹ לֶאֱכוֹל – אִין, שֶׁאֵין דַּרְכּוֹ לֶאֱכוֹל – לָא, אֲתָאן לְרַבָּנַן. רֵישָׁא רַבִּי אֱלִיעֶזֶר וְסֵיפָא רַבָּנַן? אֲמַר לֵיהּ: אִין.

One can infer that intent to partake of **an item whose** typical **manner** is such that one **partakes** of it **does** render it *piggul*, while intent to partake of an item **whose** typical **manner** is such that one does **not partake** of it[H] does **not** render it *piggul*. In this clause, **we arrive at** the opinion of **the Rabbis.** Can it be that **the first clause** is in accordance with the opinion of **Rabbi Eliezer,** while **the latter clause** is in accordance with the opinion of **the Rabbis?** Shmuel **said to him: Yes.** That is how one must understand the mishna.

רַב הוּנָא אָמַר: עוֹר אַלְיָה לָאו כְּאַלְיָה דָּמֵי. אֲמַר רָבָא: מַאי טַעְמָא דְּרַב הוּנָא? ״חֶלְבּוֹ הָאַלְיָה״ – וְלֹא עוֹר הָאַלְיָה.

Rav Huna says: The skin of the **tail is not considered as** though it were the **tail**[H] itself. Unlike the tail itself, its skin is consumed. Consequently, both this mishna and the next can be understood in accordance with the opinion of the Rabbis. **Rava said: What is the reasoning of Rav Huna?** As the verse states: "And he shall present of the sacrifice of peace offerings an offering made by fire unto the Lord: **The fat thereof, the fat tail**" (Leviticus 3:9), indicating that the priest must offer the fat of the tail on the altar, **but not the skin of the tail.**

רַב חִסְדָּא אָמַר: לְעוֹלָם עוֹר הָאַלְיָה כְּאַלְיָה דָּמֵי, וְהָכָא בְּמַאי עָסְקִינַן – בְּאַלְיָה שֶׁל גְּדִי.

Rav Ḥisda says: Actually, the skin of the tail is considered as though it were the **tail** itself, and it is burned on the altar. **And here,** in the mishna, **we are dealing with the tail of a kid,** which is not burned on the altar but is consumed. Accordingly, intent to consume it outside its designated time renders it *piggul*.

כּוּלְּהוּ כִּשְׁמוּאֵל לָא אָמְרִי – רֵישָׁא רַבִּי אֱלִיעֶזֶר וְסֵיפָא רַבָּנַן לָא מוֹקְמִי. כְּרַב הוּנָא לָא אָמְרִי – עוֹר אַלְיָה כְּאַלְיָה דָּמֵי קָא מַשְׁמַע לְהוּ.

The Gemara notes: **All of them,** Rav Huna and Rav Ḥisda, **do not say as Shmuel** says, since **they do not** wish to **interpret** that **the first clause** is in accordance with the opinion of **Rabbi Eliezer and the latter clause** is in accordance with the opinion of **the Rabbis.** And Shmuel and Rav Ḥisda **do not say as Rav Huna** says, since **they heard** that the **skin of the tail is considered as** though it were the **tail** itself.

NOTES

Is considered as though it were part of the tail – **כְּאַלְיָה דָּמֵי:** The Torah (Leviticus 3:9) commands that when a sheep is sacrificed as a peace offering, the fatty area around its tail must be burned on the altar together with the portions that are burned in all other offerings. This does not apply to other animals such as goats, since only sheep possess a fat tail.

In general, the hide of an offering is not considered part of the flesh, and it is neither eaten nor burned on the altar. The skin of the tail is listed in tractate *Ḥullin* as being considered meat for purposes of ritual impurity, since it is soft and edible. The question therefore arises: Is it considered edible meat in the context of offerings as well, in which case intent to partake of it beyond its designated time would render the offering *piggul*? Alternatively, perhaps it is considered part of the fat tail itself, which must be burned rather than eaten, in which case only intent to burn it beyond its designated time would render the offering *piggul*.

BACKGROUND

Tail – **אַלְיָה:** This is referring to the long, thick, fatty tail characteristic of sheep found in Eretz Yisrael and its environs during talmudic times. The tail of this sheep would cover a large part of the animal's rear, such that the sex of an individual sheep was difficult to determine, particularly in lambs.

Fat-tailed sheep

HALAKHA

Whose typical manner is such that one does not partake of it – **שֶׁאֵין דַּרְכּוֹ לֶאֱכוֹל וכו׳:** If in the process one of the four sacrificial rites: Slaughter, collection of the blood, conveying the blood to the altar, and its sprinkling on the altar, one intends to partake of an item whose typical manner is such that one does not partake of it, or to burn an item whose typical manner is such that one does not burn it, outside its designated area or beyond its designated time, the offering remains fit (Rambam *Sefer Avoda, Hilkhot Pesulei HaMukdashin* 14:8).

The skin of the tail is not considered as though it were the tail – **עוֹר אַלְיָה לָאו כְּאַלְיָה דָּמֵי:** The skin of an animal is not one of the eaten portions of an offering, nor is it burned on the altar. The skin of the tail is considered an eaten portion. This ruling is in accordance with the opinion of Rav Huna, which is supported by a *baraita* and the straightforward understanding of the mishna (Rambam *Sefer Avoda, Hilkhot Pesulei HaMukdashin* 14:7; see *Likkutei Halakhot*).

כְּרַב חִסְדָּא מַאי טַעְמָא לָא אָמְרִי? מַאי קָא מַשְׁמַע לָן, עוֹר אַלְיָה כְּאַלְיָה דָּמֵי? תְּנֵינָא: וְאֵלּוּ שֶׁעוֹרוֹתֵיהֶן כִּבְשָׂרָן – עוֹר שֶׁתַּחַת הָאַלְיָה!

The Gemara asks: **What is the reason** that Shmuel and Rav Huna **do not say as Rav Ḥisda** says, that the mishna is referring to the tail of a kid? The Gemara responds that they reason: According to Rav Ḥisda, **what is** the mishna **teaching us**[N] by referring specifically to the skin of the tail? Does it mean to teach simply that the **skin of the tail is considered** edible, **like the tail** itself? **We** already **learn** this in another mishna (*Ḥullin* 122a): **These** are the entities **whose skin** has a halakhic status **like** that of **their meat,**[N] since it is soft and edible: The **skin beneath the tail.**[H]

וְרַב חִסְדָּא? אִיצְטְרִיךְ, סָלְקָא דַּעְתָּךְ אָמִינָא: הָנֵי מִילֵּי לְעִנְיַן טוּמְאָה, דְּרָכֵיךְ מִצְטָרֵף. אֲבָל הָכָא אֵימָא: ״לְמָשְׁחָה״ – לִגְדוּלָּה, כְּדֶרֶךְ שֶׁהַמְּלָכִים אוֹכְלִין, וְלָא עֲבִידִי מְלָכִים דְּאָכְלִי הָכִי – אֵימָא לָא, קָא מַשְׁמַע לָן.

The Gemara asks: **And Rav Ḥisda,** how would he respond? The Gemara answers: The reference here to the skin of the tail **was necessary,** as given only the mishna in tractate *Ḥullin,* it might **enter your mind to say: This matter,** the equation between the skin of the tail and the tail itself, applies only **with regard to the matter of ritual impurity,** as the skin of the tail is **soft** and edible, and it is therefore **counted** as part of the tail. **But here,** with regard to the matter of the Temple service, **I will say** that the verse states with regard to the gifts to which members of the priesthood are entitled: **"As a consecrated portion"** (Numbers 18:8), **to** indicate that they must be eaten in **greatness, in the way that the kings eat. And** since **kings do not generally eat** the skin of the tail, **I will say** that it is **not** considered an eaten portion of the offering. The mishna therefore **teaches us** that it is nevertheless considered like the tail itself.

מֵיתִיבֵי: הַשּׁוֹחֵט אֶת הָעוֹלָה לְהַקְטִיר כַּזַּיִת מֵעוֹר שֶׁתַּחַת הָאַלְיָה חוּץ לִמְקוֹמוֹ – פָּסוּל וְאֵין בּוֹ כָּרֵת, חוּץ לִזְמַנּוֹ – פִּיגּוּל וְחַיָּיבִין עָלָיו כָּרֵת.

The Gemara **raises an objection** from a *baraita*: **One who slaughters a burnt offering** with intent **to burn an olive-bulk of** the **skin beneath the tail outside its** designated **area** renders the offering **disqualified, but there is no** liability for ***karet*** **for** one who partakes of the offering. If his intent is to burn it **beyond its** designated **time,** it is rendered ***piggul,*** **and one is liable** to receive ***karet*** **for** eating **it.** This is the opinion of the Rabbis.

אֶלְעָזָר בֶּן יְהוּדָה אִישׁ אָבֵלִים אוֹמֵר מִשּׁוּם רַבִּי יַעֲקֹב, וְכֵן הָיָה רַבִּי שִׁמְעוֹן בֶּן יְהוּדָה אִישׁ כְּפַר עִיכוֹס אוֹמֵר מִשּׁוּם רַבִּי שִׁמְעוֹן: אֶחָד עוֹר בֵּית הַפְּרָסוֹת בְּהֵמָה דַּקָּה, וְאֶחָד עוֹר הָרֹאשׁ שֶׁל עֵגֶל הָרַךְ, וְאֶחָד עוֹר שֶׁתַּחַת הָאַלְיָה, וְכָל שֶׁמָּנוּ חֲכָמִים גַּבֵּי טוּמְאָה וְאֵלּוּ שֶׁעוֹרוֹתֵיהֶן כִּבְשָׂרָן, לְהָבִיא עוֹר שֶׁל בֵּית הַבּוֹשֶׁת, חוּץ לִמְקוֹמוֹ – פָּסוּל וְאֵין בּוֹ כָּרֵת, חוּץ לִזְמַנּוֹ – פִּיגּוּל וְחַיָּיבִין עָלָיו כָּרֵת;

Elazar ben Yehuda of Avelim[B] **says in the name of Rabbi Ya'akov, and so Rabbi Shimon ben Yehuda of Kefar Ikos**[B] **would say in the name of Rabbi Shimon: Whether** the **hide of the hooves**[N] **of small livestock, or the skin of the head of a young calf,**[N] **or** the **skin beneath the tail, or any** of the skins **that the Sages listed with regard to ritual impurity** under the heading: **These** are the entities **whose skin** has a halakhic status **like** that of **their meat,** which means **to include the skin of the womb,** if one has intent to burn one of them **outside its** designated **area,** the offering **is disqualified, but there is no** liability **for *karet*** **for** burning or partaking of **it,** and if one's intent is to burn it **beyond its** designated **time,** he renders it ***piggul,*** **and one is liable** to receive ***karet*** **for** burning or partaking of **it.**

NOTES

What is the mishna teaching us, etc. – מַאי קָא מַשְׁמַע לָן כו׳: According to Shmuel's opinion, the mishna's reference to the skin of the tail teaches that eaten portions and sacrificial portions are interchangeable with regard to improper intent, in accordance with the opinion of Rabbi Eliezer. According to Rav Huna's opinion, it teaches that the skin of the tail is considered an edible portion of the offering even though the tail itself must be burned on the altar. According to Rav Ḥisda, who holds that the tail in question is not a sheep tail, it is unclear why the mishna would single it out from any other portion of the offering that is not burned.

Whose skin is like their meat – שֶׁעוֹרוֹתֵיהֶן כִּבְשָׂרָן: The mishna is referring to matters of ritual impurity. When the skin of an animal is soft it is considered part of its meat rather than an independent entity. It can then be counted as part of the measure of meat required to impart ritual impurity.

Hooves – בֵּית הַפְּרָסוֹת: In tractate *Ḥullin* (122b), the Sages disagree as to whether this is referring only to the hide adjacent to the hooves, or to the hide covering the entire bottom part of the animal's leg.

Young calf – עֵגֶל הָרַךְ: In tractate *Ḥullin* (122b), the Gemara establishes that this is a calf less than one year old, or one that still nurses from its mother.

HALAKHA

Skin beneath the tail – עוֹר שֶׁתַּחַת הָאַלְיָה: The skin underneath the tail imparts ritual impurity as though it were the animal's meat. If one begins to process it into leather, it ceases to be susceptible to ritual impurity (Rambam *Sefer Tahara, Hilkhot She'ar Avot HaTumot* 1:9).

BACKGROUND

Avelim – אָבֵלִים: Avelim was a town in Eretz Yisrael and was called by other, similar names as well. The name is the plural form of the word *avel*, which can mean a place of pasture. This town was located in a particularly fertile area with many sources of water. The Arab village Avlin, located northeast of the town of Shefaram, preserves the old Hebrew name.

Avelim was significant because it was situated on the road from Egypt to Syria and Babylonia, which was an important commercial highway. Over the generations, a fort was built there to protect the road. It was also the home of several Sages, including Rabbi Elazar ben Yehuda and Rabbi Yosef ben Perida, who was visited there by his own rabbi, Rabbi Eliezer. The village today is the site of ancient ruins, including those of a talmudic-era synagogue with an Aramaic inscription over its entrance.

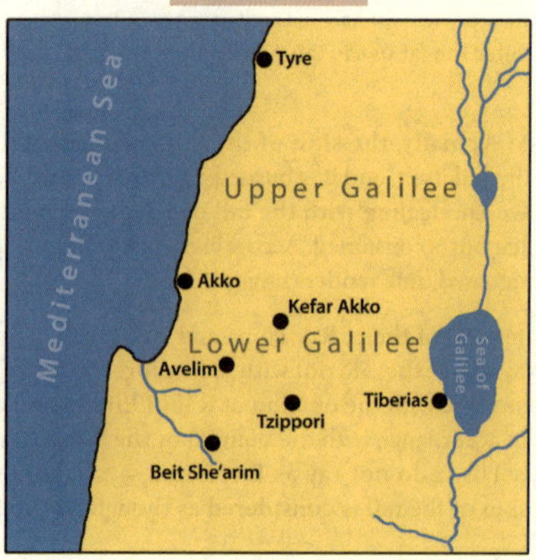

Locations of Avelim and Kefar Akko

Kefar Ikos – כְּפַר עִיכוֹס: Kefar Ikos is identified with the town of Kefar Akko, located in the Lower Galilee. Although it is not close to the city of Akko, from which its name is derived, it was considered part of the same province during the period of sparse Jewish population in the Galilee. At some point, perhaps during the time of Julius Caesar, the province of Akko was significantly reduced, and the town was associated with the province of the western Galilee.

The town is mentioned by Josephus Flavius in his account of the Great Revolt of 67 BCE as one of the forts of the Lower Galilee. In tractate *Ta'anit* (21a), the town as mentioned as a fortified place that could field five hundred foot soldiers, and it is possible that this is a reference to the number of soldiers it contributed to the Great Revolt. Based on this number, some estimate that the total population of the town at the time was approximately 2,500 people.

עוֹלָה – אִין, אֲבָל זֶבַח – לָא. בִּשְׁלָמָא לְרַב הוּנָא – הַיְינוּ דְּקָתָנֵי עוֹלָה, אֶלָּא לְרַב חִסְדָּא – מַאי אִירְיָא דְּתָנֵי עוֹלָה? לִיתְנֵי זֶבַח!

One can infer from the *baraita* that only with regard to **a burnt offering, yes,** the skin of the tail is burned on the altar like the tail itself. **But** with regard to another **offering,** this is **not** the *halakha*. **Granted, according to Rav Huna,** who holds that the skin of the tail of a peace offering is not considered as though it were the tail itself, and it is eaten rather than burned, **this is** the reason **that** the *tanna* **teaches** about a **burnt offering**[N] specifically, as all portions of a burnt offering are burned, even those that are eaten in the case of other offerings. **But according to Rav Ḥisda,** who holds that the skin of the tail is burned together with the tail, **why does** the *tanna* **specifically teach** about a **burnt offering?** If the skin of the tail is always considered as though it were the tail itself, **let** the *tanna* **teach** about any **offering.**

אָמַר לָךְ רַב חִסְדָּא: אִיבָּעֵית אֵימָא בְּאַלְיָה שֶׁל גְּדִי, וְאִיבָּעֵית אֵימָא: תְּנִי זֶבַח.

Rav Ḥisda could have **said to you: If you wish, say** that the *baraita* is referring **to the tail of a kid,** which is never burned on the altar except in the case of a burnt offering. **And if you wish, say** instead that one should emend the text of the *baraita* to **teach:** One who slaughters any **offering,** etc.

״פָּסוּל וְאֵין בּוֹ כָּרֵת״ כו׳. מְנָא הָנֵי מִילֵּי? אָמַר שְׁמוּאֵל: תְּרֵי קְרָאֵי כְּתִיבִי.

§ The mishna states that if one intends to consume the meat or sprinkle the blood outside its designated area, the offering is **disqualified, and there is no** liability for ***karet*** **for** one who partakes of it. If one intends to do so beyond its designated time, the offering is rendered *piggul*, and one is liable to receive *karet* for burning or partaking of it. The Gemara asks: **From where are these matters** derived? **Shmuel says: Two verses are written.**

מַאי הִיא? אָמַר רַבָּה: ״שְׁלִישִׁי״ – זֶהוּ חוּץ לִזְמַנּוֹ,

The Gemara asks: **What are** these verses? **Rabba said:** Shmuel is referring to two phrases from the verse: "And if any of the flesh of his peace offerings be at all eaten on the third day, it shall not be accepted, neither shall it be credited to he who offers it; it shall be *piggul*, and the soul that eats of it shall bear his iniquity" (Leviticus 7:18). The Sages taught that this verse is referring not to offerings actually eaten on the third day, but to one who performs one of the sacrificial rites with intent to eat the offering beyond its designated time. Now, when the verse states: "And if any of the flesh…be at all eaten on the **third** day," **this is** referring to intent to consume the meat **beyond its** designated **time.**

״פִּגּוּל״ – זֶהוּ חוּץ לִמְקוֹמוֹ, ״וְהַנֶּפֶשׁ הָאוֹכֶלֶת מִמֶּנּוּ״, אֶחָד וְלֹא שְׁנַיִם – זֶהוּ חוּץ לִזְמַנּוֹ, וּלְמַעוּטֵי חוּץ לִמְקוֹמוֹ.

When the verse states: "It shall be ***piggul***," **this is** referring to one who has intent to consume it **outside its** designated **area.**[N] And when the verse states: **"And the soul that eats of it** shall bear his iniquity," i.e., shall be liable to receive *karet*, "of it" indicates that only **one** of the above disqualifications carries the penalty of *karet* for one who partakes of it, **but not two** of them. And **this** included case **is** intent to consume the offering **beyond its** designated **time, to the exclusion of** intent to consume it **outside its** designated **area,** which carries no such penalty.

וְאֵימָא: ״וְהַנֶּפֶשׁ הָאוֹכֶלֶת מִמֶּנּוּ״ – זֶהוּ חוּץ לִמְקוֹמוֹ, וּלְמַעוּטֵי חוּץ לִזְמַנּוֹ! מִסְתַּבְּרָא חוּץ לִזְמַנּוֹ עֲדִיף, דְּפָתַח בֵּיהּ. אַדְּרַבָּה, חוּץ לִמְקוֹמוֹ עֲדִיף, דִּסְמִיךְ לֵיהּ!

The Gemara asks: **But** why not **say** the opposite, that when the verse states: **"And the soul that eats of it** shall bear his iniquity," **this is** referring to intent to consume the offering **outside its** designated **area, to the exclusion of** intent to consume it **beyond its** designated **time?** The Gemara responds: **It stands to reason** that intent to consume the offering **beyond its** designated **time** is the **preferable** candidate to carry the punishment of *karet*, as the verse **opened with it.** The Gemara rejects this: **On the contrary,** intent to consume the offering **outside its** designated **area** is **preferable, as** the clause that teaches liability for *karet* is **adjacent to it.**

אֶלָּא אָמַר אַבָּיֵי: כִּי אֲתָא רַב יִצְחָק בַּר אַבְדִּימִי [אָמַר רַב], סָמֵיךְ אַדְּתָנֵי תַּנָּא: כְּשֶׁהוּא אוֹמֵר ״שְׁלִישִׁי״ בְּפָרָשַׁת ״קְדֹשִׁים תִּהְיוּ״ – שֶׁאֵין תַּלְמוּד לוֹמַר, שֶׁהֲרֵי כְּבָר נֶאֱמַר: ״וְאִם הֵאָכֹל יֵאָכֵל מִבְּשַׂר זֶבַח הַשְּׁלָמִים בַּיּוֹם הַשְּׁלִישִׁי״,

Rather, Abaye said: When Rav Yitzḥak bar Avdimi came, he said that **Rav says:** Shmuel was actually referring to two separate verses. And he **relied on that which the** ***tanna*** **taught:** The verse is seemingly redundant **when it states:** "And if it be eaten at all on the **third** day, it is *piggul*; it shall not be accepted" (Leviticus 19:7), **in the** Torah **portion** that begins: **"You shall be holy"** (Leviticus 19:2), **as** there is **no** need for **the verse to state** this, **since it is already stated: "And if any of the flesh of his peace offerings be at all eaten on the third day**…it shall be *piggul*" (Leviticus 7:18).

NOTES

This is the reason that the *tanna* teaches about a burnt offering – הַיְינוּ דְּקָתָנֵי עוֹלָה: The skin of a burnt offering is not burned. The skin of the tail is not considered part of the skin, even though it is not considered part of the tail either. Rather, it is considered part of the animal's flesh, which is burned on the altar in the case of a burnt offering (Rashi).

***Piggul*, this is one who has intent to consume it outside its designated area – פִּגּוּל זֶהוּ חוּץ לִמְקוֹמוֹ:** Although the word *piggul*, which literally means a vile or abhorrent item, does not indicate intent to consume an offering outside its designated area any more than another disqualification, e.g., intent to spill out its blood on the floor, intent to consume an offering outside its designated area bears thematic resemblance to intent to consume it beyond its designated time, which is mentioned explicitly in the verse. It therefore stands to reason that the verse is referring to this disqualification in particular.

אִם אֵינוֹ עִנְיָן לְחוּץ לִזְמַנּוֹ – תְּנֵהוּ לְעִנְיַן חוּץ לִמְקוֹמוֹ; וּמִיעֵט רַחֲמָנָא גַּבֵּי נוֹתָר ״וְאֹכְלָיו עֲוֹנוֹ יִשָּׂא״ – לְמַעוּטֵי חוּץ לִמְקוֹמוֹ.

Therefore, if the verse **is not** referring **to the matter** of intent to consume the offering **beyond its** designated **time, apply it to the matter**[N] of intent to consume it **outside its** designated **area. And** as for the punishment of *karet*, **the Merciful One restricted** it to the prohibition of ***notar***,[N] i.e., actually partaking of the offering beyond its designated time, as the verse states: **"But whoever eats it shall bear his iniquity"** (Leviticus 19:8). This indicates that one is liable to receive *karet* for partaking of *notar*, **to the exclusion of** intent to consume the offering **outside its** designated **area.**

וְאֵימָא: ״וְאֹכְלָיו עֲוֹנוֹ יִשָּׂא״ – זֶהוּ חוּץ לִמְקוֹמוֹ, וּלְמַעוּטֵי נוֹתָר מִכָּרֵת!

The Gemara asks: **But** why not **say** instead that when the verse states: **"But whoever eats it shall bear his iniquity," this is** referring to intent to consume the offering **outside its** designated **area, and** the verse serves **to exclude *notar*** from the penalty of ***karet*?**

מִסְתַּבְּרָא נוֹתָר הֲוָה לֵיהּ לְאוֹקְמֵי בְּכָרֵת, לְמִגְמַר ״עָוֹן״ ״עָוֹן״ לְחוּץ לִזְמַנּוֹ דְּדָמֵי לֵיהּ בְּז״ב.

The Gemara responds: **It stands to reason** that ***notar* should be interpreted as** carrying the penalty of ***karet***, because this would allow one **to derive** by way of verbal analogy between **"iniquity"** and **"iniquity"**[N] stated with regard **to** the case of intent to consume the meat **beyond its** designated **time**, that the punishment of *karet* applies to the latter as well. The verbal analogy would be apt **since** one prohibition **is similar to** the other **in** that they share features that form the acronym ***zayin, beit***:[N] Both concern the offering's designated time [*zeman*], and both are applicable to an offering sacrificed on a private altar [*bama*].

אַדְּרַבָּה, חוּץ לִמְקוֹמוֹ הֲוָה לֵיהּ לְאוֹקְמֵי בְּכָרֵת, לְמִגְמַר ״עָוֹן״ ״עָוֹן״ לְחוּץ לִזְמַנּוֹ דְּדָמֵי לֵיהּ בְּמקד״ש!

The Gemara rejects this: **On the contrary**, intent to consume the offering **outside its** designated **area should be interpreted as** carrying the penalty of ***karet***, because this would allow one **to derive** by way of verbal analogy between **"iniquity"** and **"iniquity"** stated with regard **to** the case of intent to consume the meat **beyond its** designated **time**, that the punishment of *karet* applies to the latter as well. The verbal analogy would still be apt **since** one prohibition **is similar to** the other **in** that both share features that form the acronym ***mikdash***: Both concern intent [*maḥashava*]; both disqualify the entire offering even if one had intent with regard to only part [*ketzat*] of it; both occur while collecting or sprinkling the offering's blood [*dam*]; and with regard to both the verse contains an extraneous mention of the third [*shelishi*] day.

אֶלָּא אָמַר רַבִּי יוֹחָנָן, תָּנֵי זַבְדִּי בַּר לֵוִי: אָתְיָא ״קֹדֶשׁ״ ״קֹדֶשׁ״; כְּתִיב הָכָא: ״אֶת קֹדֶשׁ ה׳ חִלֵּל וְנִכְרְתָה״, וּכְתִיב הָתָם: ״וְשָׂרַפְתָּ אֶת הַנּוֹתָר בָּאֵשׁ״ וגו׳, מָה לְהַלָּן נוֹתָר – אַף כָּאן נוֹתָר.

Rather, Rabbi Yoḥanan says that **Zavdi bar Levi taught: It is derived** that the prohibition of *notar* carries the penalty of *karet* by way of verbal analogy between **"sacred"** and **"sacred."**[N] **It is written here:** "But whoever eats it shall bear his iniquity, because **he has profaned the sacred item of the Lord; and that soul shall be cut off** from his people" (Leviticus 19:8). **And it is written there:** "And if any of the flesh of the consecration, or of the bread, remain until the morning, **then you shall burn the remainder** [*notar*] **with fire;** it shall not be eaten, because it is sacred" (Exodus 29:34). **Just as** the verse **there** is referring **to *notar*, so too,** there verse **here** is referring to ***notar***.

וּמִיעֵט רַחֲמָנָא גַּבֵּי נוֹתָר ״וְאֹכְלָיו עֲוֹנוֹ יִשָּׂא״ – לְמַעוּטֵי חוּץ לִמְקוֹמוֹ מִכָּרֵת.

And consequently, when **the Merciful One restricted** the penalty of *karet* **to** the prohibition of eating ***notar***, as the verse states: **"But whoever eats it shall bear his iniquity,"** this restriction serves **to exclude** the case of intent to consume the offering **outside its** designated **area from** the penalty of ***karet***.

וּמַאי חָזֵית דִּקְרָא אֲרִיכָא בְּחוּץ לִזְמַנּוֹ, וּשְׁלִישִׁי דְּפָרָשַׁת ״קְדֹשִׁים תִּהְיוּ״ חוּץ לִמְקוֹמוֹ? אֵיפוּךְ אֲנָא!

The Gemara returns to the initial assumption that the statement of Shmuel is referring to two verses: **And what did you see** that led you to conclude **that the long verse** (Leviticus 7:18) is referring **to** intent to consume the offering **beyond its** designated **time, and** that the verse that mentions the **third** day (Leviticus 19:7) **in the** Torah **portion** that begins: **"You shall be holy,"** is referring to intent to consume it **outside its** designated **area? I** might just as well **reverse** the two.

NOTES

Apply it to the matter, etc. – **תְּנֵהוּ עִנְיָן וכו׳**: The verse's explicit reference to the third day is interpreted exegetically later in the Gemara (29a): The word "third" teaches that the *halakha* applies to three components of the offering: The blood, the meat, and the portions burned on the altar. The word "day" teaches that intent to consume the offering outside its designated area is comparable to intent to do so beyond its designated time (Ra'avad's commentary on *Torat Kohanim*).

The Merciful One restricted it to the prohibition of *notar* – **מִיעֵט רַחֲמָנָא גַּבֵּי נוֹתָר**: This passage in Leviticus reads: "It shall be eaten the same day you offer it, and on the morrow; and if any remain until the third day, it shall be burned with fire. And if it be eaten at all on the third day, it is *piggul*; it shall not be accepted. But whoever eats it shall bear his iniquity, because he has profaned the sacred item of the Lord; and that soul shall be cut off from his people" (Leviticus 19:6–8). The first verse refers explicitly to the prohibition of *notar*. Although the second verse is interpreted here as referring to intent to consume the offering outside its designated area, the third verse is nevertheless understood as referring to *notar* again, per the straightforward meaning of the verse (Rashi).

To derive by way of verbal analogy between iniquity and iniquity, etc. – **לְמִיגְמַר עָוֹן עָוֹן וכו׳**: The verse that discusses *piggul* (Leviticus 7:18) does not explicitly mention the punishment of *karet*. Rather, it is derived by verbal analogy from *notar*, as the verse states explicitly: "But whoever eats it shall bear his iniquity…and that soul shall be cut off [*venikhreta*] from his people" (Leviticus 19:8).

Zayin, beit – **ז״ב**: *Tosafot* explain that a tradition existed with regard to a verbal analogy between the word "iniquity" used in both verses, but it was unclear to what matter the first verse referred. The Gemara therefore posits *notar* as the more reasonable choice, since it is similar to *piggul* in two distinct ways. Comparisons of common features are often found where the Gemara attempts to decide between two possible verbal analogies, but this instance is slightly different, as the verbal analogy is a given and only the referent of the source verse is in question. Rashi suggests that the Gemara considers another verbal analogy altogether as possible, from the word "iniquity" used with regard to one who eats meat of an offering that has contracted ritual impurity. Since that offense does not carry the penalty of *karet*, such a verbal analogy would teach that neither does intent to consume the offering beyond its designated time (see *Shita Mekubbetzet*).

It is derived by verbal analogy between sacred and sacred – **אָתְיָא קֹדֶשׁ קֹדֶשׁ**: *Notar* can be called sacred, as it consists of meat of an offering that was sacrificed properly. The offense is only that it was eaten at the improper time. This is in contrast to an offering sacrificed with improper intent, which cannot be called sacred because it is instantly disqualified (Malbim).

מִסְתַּבְּרָא, אֲרִיכָא בְּחוּץ לִזְמַנּוֹ, דְּגָמַר ״עָוֹן״ ״עָוֹן״ מִנּוֹתָר דְּדָמֵי לֵיהּ בְּזו״ב.

The Gemara responds: **It stands to reason that the long** verse is referring **to** intent to consume the offering **beyond its** designated **time, as** this allows for one to **derive** by way of verbal analogy between **"iniquity"** and **"iniquity" from *notar*** that an offering sacrificed with such intent carries the penalty of *karet*. The verbal analogy is apt **since** one prohibition **is similar to** the other **in** that both share the features mentioned above that form the acronym: ***Zayin, beit.***

אַדְּרַבָּה, אֲרִיכָא בְּחוּץ לִמְקוֹמוֹ, וּשְׁלִישִׁי דִּ״קְדֹשִׁים תִּהְיוּ״ בְּחוּץ לִזְמַנּוֹ, מִשּׁוּם דְּדָמֵי לֵיהּ סַמְכֵיהּ, וְקָא מְמַעֵט לֵיהּ!

The Gemara rejects this: **On the contrary,** it stands to reason that **the long** verse is referring **to** intent to consume the offering **outside its** designated **area, and** that the verse that mentions the **third** day **in** the Torah portion that begins: **"You shall be holy,"** is referring **to** intent to consume it **beyond its** designated **time.** This is **due to** the fact **that** the latter intent is **similar to** *notar* in that both prohibitions share the features mentioned above that form the acronym: *Zayin, beit*, and it is therefore reasonable that the Torah **juxtaposed** the two in adjacent verses. **And** if so, when the verse states with regard to *notar*: "But whoever eats it shall bear his iniquity," this **excludes** intent to consume the offering beyond its designated time from the penalty of *karet*.

אֶלָּא אָמַר רָבָא: כּוּלְּהוּ מִקְּרָא אֲרִיכָא אָתְיָין. דִּכְתִיב: ״הֵאָכֹל יֵאָכֵל״ – בִּשְׁתֵּי אֲכִילוֹת הַכָּתוּב מְדַבֵּר, אֶחָד אֲכִילַת אָדָם וְאֶחָד אֲכִילַת מִזְבֵּחַ.

Rather, Rava says: One must accept the original interpretation of Shmuel's statement, that **all of** these *halakhot* with regard to intent to consume the offering beyond its designated time or outside its designated area **are derived from the long verse. As it is written:** "If any of the flesh of his peace offerings be at all eaten on the third day, it shall not be accepted, neither shall it be credited to he who offers it; it shall be *piggul*, and the soul that eats of it shall bear his iniquity" (Leviticus 7:18). When the verse states: **"Be at all eaten [*he'akhol ye'akhel*],"** using a doubled verb, **the verse speaks of** intent with regard to **two consumptions,**[H] **one consumption by a person, and one consumption by** the **altar,** i.e., burning the offering. Improper intent with regard to either of these acts renders the offering *piggul*.

״מִבְּשַׂר זֶבַח שְׁלָמָיו״ – מָה שְׁלָמִים מְפַגְּלִין וּמִתְפַּגְּלִין, אַף כֹּל מְפַגְּלִין וּמִתְפַּגְּלִין.

The phrase **"any of the flesh of his peace offerings"** indicates that **just as a peace offering** possesses that which **renders *piggul* and** that which **is rendered *piggul***, i.e., the blood, which renders the offering *piggul* through one's intent with regard to its rites, and the meat, which is rendered *piggul* through such intent, **so too** the verse is referring to **all** offerings that possess that which **renders** an offering ***piggul* and** that which **is rendered *piggul*.**[HN]

״שְׁלִישִׁי״ – זֶה חוּץ לִזְמַנּוֹ;

The term "on the **third** day" indicates that the verse is referring to intent to consume the offering **beyond its** designated **time,** as peace offerings may be eaten for only two days.

״לֹא יֵרָצֶה״ – כְּהַרְצָאַת כָּשֵׁר כֵּן הַרְצָאַת פָּסוּל, וּמָה הַרְצָאַת כָּשֵׁר עַד שֶׁיַּקְרִיבוּ כׇּל מַתִּירָיו – אַף הַרְצָאַת פָּסוּל עַד שֶׁיַּקְרִיבוּ כׇּל מַתִּירָיו.

The phrase **"it shall not be accepted"** indicates that an offering is deemed *piggul* following the stage of the service at which it would have otherwise effected atonement. Therefore, **like the acceptance of a fit offering, so is the acceptance of a disqualified** offering, **and just as the acceptance of a fit** offering does not occur **until one sacrifices all its permitting factors,** i.e., one sprinkles the blood properly, **so too the acceptance of a disqualified** offering does not occur **until one sacrifices all its permitting factors.**[H]

״הַמַּקְרִיב״ – בְּהַקְרָבָה הוּא נִפְסָל, וְאֵינוֹ נִפְסָל בַּשְּׁלִישִׁי. ״אוֹתוֹ״ – בַּזֶּבַח הַכָּתוּב מְדַבֵּר, וְאֵינוֹ מְדַבֵּר בַּכֹּהֵן.

The term **"he who offers"** indicates that *piggul* **is disqualified at** the time of **offering,** due to improper intent, **and it is not disqualified on the third day**[H] literally. And when the verse states **"it,"** this indicates that **the verse is speaking of** a disqualification of the **offering** only, **but it is not speaking of** the **priest,** who is not disqualified from the priesthood through such intent.

״לֹא יֵחָשֵׁב״,

The phrase **"neither shall it be credited [*yehashev*]"**

HALAKHA

The verse speaks of two consumptions – בִּשְׁתֵּי אֲכִילוֹת הַכָּתוּב מְדַבֵּר: It is learned by tradition that Leviticus 7:18 is referring to one who intends at the time of sacrifice to partake of the offering after its designated time, or to burn a sacrificial portion beyond its designated time. Such intent renders the offering *piggul* (Rambam *Sefer Avoda, Hilkhot Pesulei HaMukdashin* 13:2).

That which renders an offering *piggul* and that which is rendered *piggul* – מְפַגְּלִין וּמִתְפַּגְּלִין: One is liable to receive *karet* only for partaking of an item that had been rendered permitted for consumption or for burning on the altar by some other act involving a permitting factor, e.g., the blood of an animal offering. Items with no permitting factors, e.g., the flesh of sin offerings that are burned whole or meal offerings that are burned, cannot be rendered *piggul*. Partaking of such items is considered tantamount to partaking of a permitting factor itself, which does not carry the penalty of *karet* (Rambam *Sefer Avoda, Hilkhot Pesulei HaMukdashin* 18:7).

Until one sacrifices all its permitting factors – עַד שֶׁיַּקְרִיבוּ כׇּל מַתִּירָיו: In the case of any offering with permitting factors, one is not liable to receive *karet* for partaking of *piggul*, *notar*, or ritually impure meat unless he does so after all its permitting factors have otherwise been sacrificed properly, in accordance with the opinion of Rava (Rambam *Sefer Avoda, Hilkhot Pesulei HaMukdashin* 18:16).

Is not disqualified on the third day – אֵינוֹ נִפְסָל בַּשְּׁלִישִׁי: If an offering is sacrificed with proper intent and the blood is sprinkled properly, but its meat is left beyond its designated time, the meat is rendered *notar*, and it is prohibited to consume it. Still, the offering itself is accepted and effects atonement for its owner (Rambam *Sefer Avoda, Hilkhot Pesulei HaMukdashin* 13:3).

NOTES

And that which is rendered *piggul* – וּמִתְפַּגְּלִין: For example, the handful removed from a meal offering and burned on the altar is functionally equivalent to the blood of an animal offering. It too renders the offering *piggul* due to one's improper intent in the course of performing its rites. Since the rest of the meal offering is rendered *piggul* like the meat of an animal offering, one who partakes of it is liable to receive *karet*. The meal offering of priests is burned whole and has no permitting factor that renders the rest *piggul* during the course of its service. Therefore, the *halakha* of *piggul* does not apply to it (see 43a).

HALAKHA

Does not mix intentions, etc. – לא יערב בו מחשבות וכו׳: If one intends to partake of an offering or burn it beyond its designated time, it is rendered *piggul*. This applies only if he did not hold other improper intentions at the time. If he introduced other improper intentions along with the intention that disqualified the offering, e.g., intention to perform the offering's service in the wrong place or not for its sake, the offering is disqualified, but it is not rendered *piggul* (Rambam *Sefer Avoda*, *Hilkhot Pesulei HaMukdashin* 16:1).

לא יערב בו מחשבות אחרות;

indicates that to render an offering *piggul*, the priest **does not mix other** improper **intentions** [***mahashavot***][HN] **with** intent of *piggul*. If he has more than one type of improper intent, the offering is disqualified, but it is not rendered *piggul*.

״פגול״ – זה חוץ למקומו;

When the verse states: ***"Piggul,"* this is** referring to an offering that one had intent to consume **outside its** designated **area.**

״יהיה״ – מלמד שמצטרפין זה עם זה;

And since the verse states: **"It shall be,"** and not: They shall be, this **teaches that** intent to consume half an olive-bulk beyond its designated time and intent to consume half an olive-bulk outside its designated area **join together with one another** to constitute the minimum measure required to disqualify the offering.

״והנפש האכלת ממנו״ – אחד ולא שנים, ואיזה זה – חוץ לזמנו, דגמר ״עון״ ״עון״ מנותר, דדמי ליה בז״ב.

Finally, when the verse states: **"And the soul that eats of it** shall bear his iniquity," the term "of it" indicates that only **one** of the above disqualifications carries the penalty of *karet*, **but not two** of them. **And which is this?** It is intent to consume the offering **beyond its** designated **time, as** one **derives** by way of verbal analogy between **"iniquity"** and **"iniquity" from *notar*** (Leviticus 19:8), that "bear his iniquity" means that one is liable to receive *karet*. The comparison is apt **since** *notar* **is similar to** intent to consume the offering beyond its designated time **in** that both prohibitions share the features mentioned above that form the acronym: ***Zayin, beit.***

אמר ליה רב פפא לרבא: לדידך, ״שלישי״ דפרשת ״קדשים תהיו״ מאי דרשת ביה? ההוא מיבעי ליה למקום שיהא משולש, בדם בבשר ובאימורין.

Rav Pappa said to Rava: According to your opinion,[N] in **what** way do **you interpret** the reference to the **third** day (Leviticus 19:7) **in the** Torah **portion** that begins: **"You shall be holy"?** Rava responded: **That** verse is **necessary to** teach **that** a given **location** is considered to be outside the offering's designated area only if it **is** so **in three ways,**[N] i.e., outside the permitted limits **of** the **blood,** of the **meat, and of** the **sacrificial portions.**

תיפוק לי מקרא קמא ״אם האכל יאכל״, מדאפקיה רחמנא בלשון ״שלישי״!

The Gemara asks: Why not **let me derive** that *halakha* **from the first verse:** "And **if** any of the flesh of his peace offerings **be at all eaten** on the third day" (Leviticus 7:18), **since the Merciful One expresses** that verse as well **with the term "third"?** Since Rava derives the disqualification of intent to consume an offering outside its designated area from this verse, why not let him derive this *halakha* from the verse as well?

אמר רב אשי: אמריתה לשמעתא קמיה דרב מתנה, אמר לי: אי מהתם, הוה אמינא: ״שלישי״ – פרט, ״פגול״ – כלל, ונעשה כלל מוסף על הפרט, ואיתרבו שאר מקומות, קא משמע לן.

Rav Ashi said: I stated this *halakha* before Rav Mattana, and **he said to me: If** one were to derive this *halakha* only **from there** (Leviticus 7:18), **I would say:** The term **"third"** is **a detail,** and the term ***"piggul"*** is **a generalization, and** whenever a detail is followed by a generalization, **the generalization becomes an addition to the detail, and** consequently, all **other areas are included** as well. The additional verse **teaches us** that the *halakha* includes only those areas that are outside in three ways.

NOTES

Does not mix other improper intentions, etc. – לא יערב בו מחשבות אחרות וכו׳: The verse states *"lo yehashev,"* with the word *lo* spelled *lamed*, *alef*, meaning "no," with the phrase meaning "neither shall it be credited." This also alludes to the other meaning of the word *lo*, spelled *lamed*, *vav*, meaning "to him," in which case the phrase could be translated as: He shall not have intention, i.e., the offering is rendered *piggul* so long as the priest holds no other improper intentions. This principle is laid out explicitly in the mishna on the following *amud*, which states that an offering is rendered *piggul* only if its permitting factors are sacrificed properly in all other ways.

According to your opinion, etc. – לדידך וכו׳: According to Abaye's opinion, Leviticus 7:18 is referring to intent to consume the offering beyond its designated time, while Leviticus 19:7 is referring to intent to consume the offering outside its designated area. The phrase "the third day" is therefore necessary to define the conditions for intent outside a designated area. According to Rava, Leviticus 7:18 addresses both, and it is unclear why Leviticus 19:7 is necessary.

In three ways – משולש: According to Rashi, this means that one can disqualify an offering only when thinking of an area that, while not in the Temple courtyard, is nevertheless fit for consumption of the meat, burning of the sacrificial portions, and sprinkling of the blood. This includes areas outside the Temple courtyard, where these acts were performed before the construction of the Temple, in the era of private altars. It excludes the Sanctuary, in which offerings may never be burned. *Tosafot*, citing Rabbeinu Yom Tov, suggest that one disqualifies the offering only when thinking of an area unfit for all three. For example, one sacrificing a peace offering disqualifies it only if he intends to consume the meat outside the walls of Jerusalem, where the consumption of such an offering, its burning, and the sprinkling of its blood are all prohibited. This opinion is also ascribed to the Ra'avad in Rabbeinu Hillel's commentary on the *Sifra*.

תָּנוּ רַבָּנַן: "וְאִם הֵאָכֹל יֵאָכֵל מִבְּשַׂר זֶבַח שְׁלָמָיו", אָמַר רַבִּי אֱלִיעֶזֶר: כּוֹף אָזְנְךָ לִשְׁמוֹעַ: בִּמְחַשֵּׁב לֶאֱכוֹל מִזִּבְחוֹ בַּיּוֹם הַשְּׁלִישִׁי הַכָּתוּב מְדַבֵּר. אוֹ אֵינוֹ אֶלָּא בְּאוֹכֵל מִזִּבְחוֹ לְיוֹם שְׁלִישִׁי? אָמַרְתָּ: אַחַר שֶׁהוּא כָּשֵׁר – יַחֲזוֹר וְיִפָּסֵל?

§ **The Sages taught** with regard to the verse: **"And if any of the flesh of his peace offerings be at all eaten** on the third day, it shall not be accepted" (Leviticus 7:18): **Rabbi Eliezer said: Bend your ear to hear** the true meaning of the verse: **The verse is speaking of one who intends to partake of his offering on the third day. Or** perhaps it is referring **only to one who** actually **partakes of his offering on the third day**, per the straightforward meaning of the verse? But that cannot be; would **you say** that **after** the offering **is fit** for the first two days, **it should then be disqualified** retroactively by being eaten on the third day?

אָמַר לוֹ רַבִּי עֲקִיבָא: הֵן! מָצִינוּ בְּזָב וְזָבָה וְשׁוֹמֶרֶת יוֹם כְּנֶגֶד יוֹם, שֶׁהֵן בְּחֶזְקַת טָהֳרָה, וְכֵיוָן שֶׁרָאוּ – סָתְרוּ. אַף אַתָּה אַל תִּתְמַהּ עַל זֶה, שֶׁאַף עַל פִּי שֶׁהוּכְשַׁר – שֶׁיַּחֲזוֹר וְיִפָּסֵל!

Rabbi Akiva said to him: Yes, it could be disqualified retroactively. After all, **we find with regard to a man who experiences a gonorrhea-like discharge** [*zav*], **or a woman who experiences a discharge of uterine blood after her menstrual period** [*zava*],[BN] **or a woman who observes** a clean **day for a day**[N] when she experiences a discharge, **that they all have the presumptive status of purity** after immersing. **But once they have seen** another discharge the same day, **they have negated** this status retroactively, and everything they had touched after immersing becomes impure. Therefore, **you as well should not be surprised about this** offering consumed beyond its designated time, **that even though it was rendered fit, it may then be disqualified** retroactively.

אָמַר לֵיהּ: הֲרֵי הוּא אוֹמֵר "הַמַּקְרִיב" – בִּשְׁעַת הַקְרָבָה הוּא נִפְסָל, וְאֵינוֹ נִפְסָל בַּשְּׁלִישִׁי. אוֹ אֵינוֹ אוֹמֵר "הַמַּקְרִיב" – אֶלָּא זֶה כֹּהֵן הַמַּקְרִיב? כְּשֶׁהוּא אוֹמֵר "אֹתוֹ" – בְּזֶבַח הוּא מְדַבֵּר, וְאֵינוֹ מְדַבֵּר בַּכֹּהֵן.

Rabbi Eliezer **said to him: But** the same verse **says: "He who offers** it," indicating that the offering **is disqualified at the time of** its **offering, and it is not disqualified on the third** day. **Or** perhaps when the verse **says:**[N] **"He who offers** it," **this** is referring **only** to **the priest who sacrifices** the offering, indicating that he is disqualified. But if so, it would have been enough for the verse to state: He who offers shall not be credited. Therefore, **when it states** instead: "Neither shall it be credited to he who offers **it,"** this indicates that the verse **is speaking of the offering, and it is not speaking of the priest.**

בֶּן עַזַּאי אוֹמֵר: "אֹתוֹ" מַה תַּלְמוּד לוֹמַר? לְפִי שֶׁנֶּאֱמַר: "לֹא תְאַחֵר לְשַׁלְּמוֹ", יָכוֹל אַף מְאַחֵר נִדְרוֹ בְּ"לֹא יֵרָצֶה"? תַּלְמוּד לוֹמַר: "אֹתוֹ" – אוֹתוֹ בְּ"לֹא יֵרָצֶה", וְאֵין הַמְאַחֵר נִדְרוֹ בְּ"לֹא יֵרָצֶה".

Ben Azzai says: Why must **the verse state: "It"?** It is necessary **because** elsewhere **it is stated:** "When you shall vow a vow to the Lord your God, **you shall not delay paying it**; for the Lord your God will require it from you, and it will be sin in you" (Deuteronomy 23:22). One **might** have thought that **even** one who **is late** in fulfilling **his vow**[H] is included **in: "It shall not be accepted"** (Leviticus 7:18). Therefore, **the verse states: "It,"** to indicate that **it,** an offering rendered *piggul*, is included **in the** *halakha* of: **"It shall not be accepted," but** the animal of **one who is late** in fulfilling **his vow is not** included **in the** *halakha* of: **"It shall not be accepted."**

BACKGROUND

Zava – זָבָה: A *zava* is a woman who experiences a discharge of uterine blood on three consecutive days during a time of the month when she is not due to experience menstrual bleeding. The first discharge renders her ritually impure, but until the third discharge she need observe only one clean day, and she is not subject to all the halakhic rulings of a *zava*. After experiencing bleeding on the third day, the woman is considered a *zava* and becomes a primary source of impurity. She imparts ritual impurity as a *zav* does, through contact, being carried or moved, and through items that she sits or lies on. In addition, a man who engages in intercourse with her becomes a primary source of ritual impurity and imparts ritual impurity to others. Eventually the woman can be purified through immersion in a ritual bath. This is done following seven clean days without bleeding. The immersion of a *zava* takes place during the day. A *zava* is also obligated to bring an offering as part of her purification process.

HALAKHA

Late in fulfilling his vow, etc. – מְאַחֵר נִדְרוֹ וכו׳: Even if three Festivals pass after one vows to bring an offering, such that every day he violates the prohibition against delaying fulfillment of his vow, the offering still is fit and he may sacrifice it (Rambam *Sefer Avoda, Hilkhot Ma'aseh HaKorbanot* 14:15).

NOTES

With regard to a *zav* or a *zava*, etc. – בְּזָב וְזָבָה וכו׳: A *zav* or *zava* must count seven clean days after their discharge ceases before they immerse. If during these seven days they experience another discharge, they must wait until it ceases and count seven days anew. According to Rashi, the Gemara here is referring to this seven-day period, the beginning of which is retroactively nullified if the *zav* experiences another discharge. *Tosafot* note that during this period the *zav* is not presumed to be pure, since he has not yet immersed; consequently, the Gemara must instead be referring to a *zav* who immerses on the seventh day. Such a person is then presumably pure unless he experiences another discharge before nightfall, in which case his immersion is retroactively invalid.

A woman who observes a clean day for a day – שׁוֹמֶרֶת יוֹם כְּנֶגֶד יוֹם: If a woman experiences uterine bleeding at a time when she is not due to experience menstrual bleeding, she must wait one clean day and may then immerse. If she immerses before the clean day has finished she is presumed pure, but if she bleeds again before nightfall, her immersion is retroactively invalid and items she touched in the interim are ritually impure.

Or perhaps when the verse says, etc. – אוֹ אֵינוֹ אוֹמֵר וכו׳: According to Rashi, the Gemara here is suggesting that the priest himself might be disqualified by his own intent to consume the offering beyond its designated time. The *Shita Mekubbetzet* explains, citing Rashi, that in contrast to other uses of the term: Or perhaps, in the Talmud, the possibilities offered here are not mutually exclusive. Given that the verse teaches that the offering is disqualified by intention of the priest during the service, rather than at the time that the owners consume the offering, one could interpret it as referring in all ways to the priest, teaching that he disqualifies himself for service. In fact, it is difficult to understand the verse as referring to the priest while at the same time understanding that the offering is disqualified at the time of consumption, since peace offerings are eaten by their owners rather than by the priests.

The Ra'avad, in his commentary on *Torat Kohanim*, appears to interpret the Gemara as suggesting that the offering is disqualified at the time of consumption, and that the priests' consumption of the portions of the offering given to them is not considered a mitzva. The Malbim interprets the Gemara as suggesting that the priest disqualifies the offering by burning portions of it on the altar beyond their designated time. Consequently, the verse is referring to the priest while also referring to disqualification that occurs after the offering's designated time as opposed to during the service.

אֲחֵרִים אוֹמְרִים: "לֹא יֵחָשֵׁב" – בְּמַחֲשָׁבָה הוּא נִפְסָל, וְאֵינוֹ נִפְסָל בַּשְּׁלִישִׁי.

Aḥerim* say:** One can conclude that the verse (Leviticus 7:18) is referring to improper intention rather than improper consumption from the phrase **"neither shall it be credited** [yeḥashev***]**,"** which indicates that the offering **is disqualified by** improper **intention** [***maḥashava***], **and it is not disqualified** by consumption **on the third** day.

וּבֶן עַזַּאי, דִּבְזֶבַח הַכָּתוּב מְדַבֵּר וְאֵינוֹ בְּכֹהֵן, מְנָא לֵיהּ? אִי בָּעֵית אֵימָא – נָפְקָא לֵיהּ מִדַּאֲחֵרִים. וְאִיבָּעֵית אֵימָא: מִדִּכְתִיב "לֹא יֵרָצוּ" וְ"לֹא יֵרָצֶה" – זִיבְחָא הוּא.

The Gemara asks: **And ben Azzai,** who interprets the term "it" as excluding vows that were fulfilled late, **from where does he** derive **that the verse is speaking of** the **offering and not of** the **priest?** The Gemara responds: **If you wish, say** that **he derives it from** the statement **of *Aḥerim*** that the verse rules out disqualification on the third day itself. This would be necessary only if the verse is referring to the offering and not the priest. **Or, if you wish, say** instead: **From** the fact **that it is written: "They shall not be accepted"** (Leviticus 22:25), **and: "It shall not be accepted"** (Leviticus 7:18), it is evident that the verse **is** referring to **an offering,** which may be accepted or may not be accepted.

וּבֶן עַזַּאי, אוֹתוֹ בְּ"לֹא יֵרָצֶה" וְאֵין מְאַחֵר נִדְרוֹ בְּ"לֹא יֵרָצֶה", מֵהָכָא נָפְקָא? מִדַּאֲחֵרִים נָפְקָא! דְּתַנְיָא, אֲחֵרִים אוֹמְרִים: יָכוֹל יְהֵא בְּכוֹר שֶׁעִיבְּרָה שְׁנָתוֹ

The Gemara asks: **And** with regard to the statement of **ben Azzai** that one derives from the word "it" that **it,** i.e., *piggul*, is included **in** the *halakha* of: **"It shall not be accepted," but** the animal of one who **is late** in fulfilling **his vow is not** included **in** the *halakha* of: "It shall not be accepted," is this *halakha* **derived from here? It is derived from** the statement **of *Aḥerim*, as it is taught** in a *baraita*: ***Aḥerim* say:** One **might** have thought that **a firstborn** animal **whose** first **year passed,** during which time it ought to have been sacrificed, **should be**

Perek **II**
Daf **29** Amud **b**

HALAKHA

So too a firstborn is not disqualified, etc. – אַף בְּכוֹר אֵינוֹ נִפְסָל וכו׳: If one improperly delays the bringing of an unblemished firstborn animal to the Temple for more than a year, the animal is not disqualified even though the owner has transgressed a prohibition, and he may still sacrifice it. Likewise, if he delays the consumption of a blemished firstborn animal for more than a year, the priest may still slaughter it anywhere and eat it (Rambam *Sefer Korbanot, Hilkhot Bekhorot* 1:13).

כִּפְסוּלֵי הַמּוּקְדָּשִׁין וְיִפָּסֵל?

like disqualified consecrated animals, **and it should be disqualified** from being sacrificed, as though it had developed a blemish.

תַּלְמוּד לוֹמַר: "וְאָכַלְתָּ לִפְנֵי ה׳ אֱלֹהֶיךָ... מַעְשַׂר דְּגָנְךָ" וגו׳, מַקִּישׁ בְּכוֹר לְמַעֲשֵׂר, מָה מַעֲשֵׂר אֵינוֹ נִפְסָל מִשָּׁנָה לַחֲבֵירְתָּהּ – אַף בְּכוֹר אֵינוֹ נִפְסָל מִשָּׁנָה לַחֲבֵירְתָּהּ!

Therefore, **the verse states: "And you shall eat before the Lord your God,** in the place which He shall choose to place His name there, **the tithe of your grain,** of your wine, and of your oil, and the firstborns of your herds, and of your flocks" (Deuteronomy 14:23). The verse **juxtaposes a firstborn** animal **to the tithe** of grain to indicate that **just as the tithe is not disqualified** by being kept over **from** one **year to the next** (see Deuteronomy 14:28), **so too a firstborn** animal **is not disqualified**[H] by being kept over **from** one **year to the next.** If so, one already derives from this verse that an offering is not disqualified even if it is brought late.

אִיצְטְרִיךְ, סָלְקָא דַּעְתָּךְ אָמֵינָא: הָנֵי מִילֵּי – בְּכוֹר דְּלָאו בַּר הַרְצָאָה הוּא, אֲבָל קָדָשִׁים דִּבְנֵי הַרְצָאָה נִינְהוּ – אֵימָא לָא לִירְצוּ, קָא מַשְׁמַע לַן.

The Gemara responds: Nevertheless, the verse cited by ben Azzai **was necessary,** as without it, it might **enter your mind to say** that **this matter** applies only to **a firstborn, which is not for acceptance,** i.e., it does not serve to atone for any sin and is merely a gift for the priest, **but** with regard to other **sacrificial** animals **that are for acceptance, say** that **they shall not effect acceptance** when brought late. Therefore, the verse **teaches us** that even these others are not disqualified when brought late.

וְאַכַּתִּי, מֵהָתָם נָפְקָא: "וְהָיָה בְךָ חֵטְא" – וְלֹא בְּקָרְבָּנְךָ חֵטְא!

The Gemara asks further: **But still,** isn't this *halakha* **derived from** a *baraita* **elsewhere:** The verse states: "When you shall vow a vow to the Lord your God, you shall not delay paying it; for the Lord your God will require it from you; **and it will be sin in you"** (Deuteronomy 23:22), indicating that there is sin in you, **but** there is **no sin in your offering,** and therefore it is not disqualified due to the delay?

וּבֶן עַזַּאי: הַהוּא מִבְּעֵי לֵיהּ: ״וְהָיָה בְךָ חֵטְא״ – וְלֹא בְּאִשְׁתְּךָ חֵטְא; סָלְקָא דַּעְתָּךְ אָמֵינָא: הוֹאִיל וְאָמַר רַבִּי אֶלְעָזָר, וְאִיתֵּימָא רַבִּי יוֹחָנָן: אֵין אִשְׁתּוֹ שֶׁל אָדָם מֵתָה אֶלָּא אִם כֵּן מְבַקְּשִׁין מִמֶּנּוּ מָמוֹן וְאֵין לוֹ, שֶׁנֶּאֱמַר: ״אִם אֵין לְךָ לְשַׁלֵּם לָמָּה יִקַּח מִשְׁכָּבְךָ מִתַּחְתֶּיךָ״ – בְּהַאי עָוֹן דְּ״בַל תְּאַחֵר״ נַמִי מֵתָה, קָא מַשְׁמַע לָן.

The Gemara responds: **Ben Azzai requires that** verse to teach a different *halakha*: The phrase **"and it will be sin in you"** indicates that there will be sin in you, **but** there will **not be sin in your wife.** It might **enter your mind to say: Since Rabbi Elazar said, and some say** that it was **Rabbi Yoḥanan** who said: **A man's wife does not die unless** his creditors **ask him for money**[N] that he owes **and he does not have** it, **as it is stated: "If you do not have with what to pay, why should he take away your bed from under you?"** (Proverbs 22:27); therefore, one's wife **also dies for this transgression of** the prohibition: **You shall not delay,**[B] since one has failed to fulfill his commitment. Consequently, the verse **teaches us** that the sin is imputed to him alone.

אֲחֵרִים אוֹמְרִים: בְּמַחֲשָׁבָה הוּא נִפְסָל, וְאֵינוֹ נִפְסָל בַּשְּׁלִישִׁי. וְרַבִּי אֱלִיעֶזֶר, ״לֹא יֵחָשֵׁב״ מַאי עָבֵיד לֵיהּ?

§ The *baraita* stated that ***Aḥerim* say:** The phrase "neither shall it be credited" indicates that the offering **is disqualified by** improper **intention, and it is not disqualified** by consumption beyond its designated time **on the third** day. The Gemara asks: **And Rabbi Eliezer,** who derives this *halakha* from a different source, **what does he do with** the phrase **"neither shall it be credited"?**

מִיבְּעֵי לֵיהּ לְכִדְרַבִּי יַנַּאי, דְּאָמַר רַבִּי יַנַּאי: מִנַּיִן לְמַחְשָׁבוֹת שֶׁמּוֹצִיאוֹת זוֹ מִזּוֹ – שֶׁנֶּאֱמַר: ״לֹא יֵחָשֵׁב״, לֹא יְעָרֵב בּוֹ מַחְשָׁבוֹת אֲחֵרוֹת.

The Gemara responds: **He requires it for that which Rabbi Yannai** says, **as Rabbi Yannai says: From where** is it derived **with regard to intentions that they displace one another,** i.e., that an additional improper intention prevents the offering from being rendered *piggul*? **As it is stated: "Neither shall it be credited** [*yeḥashev*]," indicating that an offering is rendered piggul only if the priest does **not mix other** improper **intentions** [*maḥashavot*] **with** intent of *piggul*.

וְרַב מָרִי מַתְנֵי, אָמַר רַבִּי יַנַּאי: מִנַּיִן לִמְחַשֵּׁב בְּקָדָשִׁים שֶׁהוּא לוֹקֶה – תַּלְמוּד לוֹמַר: ״לֹא יֵחָשֵׁב״.

And Rav Mari teaches that **Rabbi Yannai says: From where** is it derived **that one who has** improper **intentions with regard to sacrificial** animals[H] **is flogged** like one who transgressed a prohibition? **The verse states: "Neither shall it be credited** [*lo yeḥashev*]," i.e., one reads the verse as if it states: One shall not have improper intention [*lo y'ḥashev*].

אֲמַר לֵיהּ רַב אָשֵׁי לְרַב מָרִי: לָאו שֶׁאֵין בּוֹ מַעֲשֶׂה הוּא, וְכׇל לָאו שֶׁאֵין בּוֹ מַעֲשֶׂה אֵין לוֹקִין עָלָיו! אֲמַר לֵיהּ: רַבִּי יְהוּדָה הִיא, דְּאָמַר: לָאו שֶׁאֵין בּוֹ מַעֲשֶׂה לוֹקִין עָלָיו.

Rav Ashi said to Rav Mari: But **it is a prohibition that does not involve an action,**[B] and the principle is that **for** transgressing **any prohibition that does not involve an action one is not flogged.** Rav Mari **said to him: It is** in accordance with the opinion of **Rabbi Yehuda, who says: For** transgressing **a prohibition that does not involve an action one is flogged.**

מתני׳ זֶה הַכְּלָל: כׇּל הַשּׁוֹחֵט, וְהַמְקַבֵּל, וְהַמְהַלֵּךְ, וְהַזּוֹרֵק, לֶאֱכוֹל דָּבָר שֶׁדַּרְכּוֹ לֶאֱכוֹל, וּלְהַקְטִיר דָּבָר שֶׁדַּרְכּוֹ לְהַקְטִיר, כַּזַּיִת, חוּץ לִמְקוֹמוֹ – פָּסוּל וְאֵין בּוֹ כָּרֵת, חוּץ לִזְמַנּוֹ – פִּגּוּל וְחַיָּיבִין עָלָיו כָּרֵת. וּבִלְבַד שֶׁיַּקְרִיב הַמַּתִּיר כְּמִצְוָתוֹ.

MISHNA **This is the principle:** With regard to **anyone who slaughters** the animal, **or who collects**[H] the blood, **or who conveys** the blood, **or who sprinkles** the blood, with intent **to partake of an item whose** typical **manner** is such that one **partakes** of it, e.g., the meat of the offering, **or to burn an item whose** typical **manner** is such that one **burns** it on the altar, if his intent was to partake of or to burn the measure of **an olive-bulk outside its** designated **area,** the offering is **disqualified, but there is no** liability for *karet* for burning or partaking **of it.** If his intent was to do so **beyond its** designated **time,** the offering is ***piggul* and one is liable** to receive ***karet* for** burning or partaking of **it, provided that the permitting factor,** the blood, **is sacrificed in accordance with its mitzva.**[H]

כֵּיצַד קָרַב הַמַּתִּיר כְּמִצְוָתוֹ? שָׁחַט בִּשְׁתִיקָה, קִבֵּל וְהִלֵּךְ וְזָרַק חוּץ לִזְמַנּוֹ; אוֹ שֶׁשָּׁחַט חוּץ לִזְמַנּוֹ, וְקִבֵּל וְהִלֵּךְ וְזָרַק בִּשְׁתִיקָה; אוֹ שֶׁשָּׁחַט וְקִבֵּל וְהִלֵּךְ וְזָרַק חוּץ לִזְמַנּוֹ – זֶהוּ שֶׁהִקְרִיב הַמַּתִּיר כְּמִצְוָתוֹ.

How is the permitting factor sacrificed in accordance with its mitzva? If one **slaughtered** the animal **in silence**[N] with no specific intent, and **he collected and conveyed and sprinkled** the blood with intent to burn or partake of the offering **beyond its** designated **time; or if** one **slaughtered** it with intent to burn or partake of the offering **beyond its** designated **time, and he collected and conveyed and sprinkled** the blood **in silence; or if** one **slaughtered** the animal **and collected and conveyed and sprinkled** the blood with intent to burn or partake of the offering **beyond its** designated **time, that is** the case **where** one **sacrifices the permitting factor in accordance with its mitzva.**

NOTES

Ask him for money – מְבַקְּשִׁין מִמֶּנּוּ מָמוֹן: Rashi interprets this as referring specifically to a case where restitution is demanded of a thief. *Tosafot* interpret it as referring to one who does not fulfill his vow.

Slaughtered in silence, etc. – שָׁחַט בִּשְׁתִיקָה וכו׳: Similarly, this would be the *halakha* if one slaughtered while expressing proper intent (Rambam).

BACKGROUND

You shall not delay – בַּל תְּאַחֵר: The source for this prohibition is Deuteronomy 23:22. One violates it when he fails to fulfill his commitment before three Festivals pass from the time it was pledged. The prohibition applies to all obligatory offerings, tithes, gifts, and pledges to the Temple treasury. It also applies to pledges of charity and the like.

Prohibition that does not involve an action – לָאו שֶׁאֵין בּוֹ מַעֲשֶׂה: This term describes a Torah prohibition that is transgressed by thought or speech and that does not involve a physical act, e.g., the prohibition against hating another Jew or bearing a grudge (see Leviticus 19:17–18). Generally, punishment is not administered for violating a prohibition of this kind, but exceptions are made in the following cases: One who curses another or himself by the name of God, one who attempts to substitute another animal for a sacrificial animal, one who takes a false oath, a defamer, and cases of conspiring witnesses.

HALAKHA

One who has improper intentions with regard to sacrificial animals – מְחַשֵּׁב בְּקָדָשִׁים: Anyone who holds improper intentions with regard to offerings transgresses a prohibition, as the verse states: "Neither shall it be credited [*yeḥashev*]." It is learned by tradition that this phrase teaches that one may not cause offerings to be disqualified due to improper intention, because this is similar to one who causes a blemish in an offering. Still, he does not receive lashes, because the offense does not involve an action. This ruling is in accordance with the Gemara here (Rambam *Sefer Avoda, Hilkhot Pesulei HaMukdashin* 18:1 and *Kesef Mishne* there).

Anyone who slaughters or who collects, etc. – כׇּל הַשּׁוֹחֵט וְהַמְקַבֵּל וכו׳: If one slaughters an offering for its own sake with the intention to sprinkle its blood or to burn its sacrificial portions outside the Temple courtyard, or to partake of the offering outside the area designated for its consumption, the offering is disqualified. If one slaughters an offering for its own sake with the intention to sprinkle its blood after sunset, i.e., after the time designated for sprinkling, or to burn its sacrificial portions after dawn, i.e., after the time designated for burning on the altar, or to partake of its eaten portions beyond the time designated for their consumption, this is the *piggul* mentioned in the Torah, which carries the penalty of *karet* for one who partakes of the offering (Rambam *Sefer Avoda, Hilkhot Pesulei HaMukdashin* 13:1).

In accordance with its mitzva – כְּמִצְוָתוֹ: *Piggul* applies only when one did not hold any other disqualifying intentions during the four sacrificial rites. If one combined improper intention with regard to the time of the offering's consumption with some other disqualifying intention, the offering is disqualified but not rendered *piggul* (Rambam *Sefer Avoda, Hilkhot Pesulei HaMukdashin* 16:1).

כֵּיצַד לֹא קָרֵב הַמַּתִּיר כְּמִצְוָתוֹ? שָׁחַט חוּץ לִמְקוֹמוֹ, קִבֵּל וְהָלַךְ וְזָרַק חוּץ לִזְמַנּוֹ; אוֹ שֶׁשָּׁחַט חוּץ לִזְמַנּוֹ, קִבֵּל וְהָלַךְ וְזָרַק חוּץ לִמְקוֹמוֹ; אוֹ שֶׁשָּׁחַט וְקִבֵּל וְהָלַךְ וְזָרַק חוּץ לִמְקוֹמוֹ (וְלִזְמַנּוֹ);

How is **the permitting factor not sacrificed in accordance with its mitzva?** If one **slaughtered** the animal with intent to burn it or partake of it **outside its** designated **area,** and **he collected and conveyed and sprinkled** the blood with intent to burn it or partake of it **beyond its** designated **time; or** if one **slaughtered** the animal with intent to burn it or partake of it **beyond its** designated **time,** and **collected and conveyed and sprinkled** the blood with intent to burn it or partake of it **outside its** designated **area; or** if one **slaughtered** the animal **and collected and conveyed and sprinkled** the blood with intent to burn it or partake of it **outside its** designated **area,** these are cases in which the permitting factor is not sacrificed in accordance with the mitzva.

הַפֶּסַח וְהַחַטָּאת שֶׁשְּׁחָטָן שֶׁלֹּא לִשְׁמָן, וְקִבֵּל וְהָלַךְ וְזָרַק חוּץ לִזְמַנּוֹ; אוֹ שֶׁשָּׁחַט חוּץ לִזְמַנּוֹ, קִיבֵּל וְהָלַךְ וְזָרַק שֶׁלֹּא לִשְׁמָן; אוֹ שֶׁשָּׁחַט וְקִבֵּל וְהָלַךְ וְזָרַק דָּמָן שֶׁלֹּא לִשְׁמָן – זֶהוּ שֶׁלֹּא קָרֵב הַמַּתִּיר כְּמִצְוָתוֹ.

Similarly, in the case of **the Paschal offering and the sin offering that one slaughtered not for their sake, and** one **collected and conveyed and sprinkled** the blood with intent to burn it or partake of it **beyond its** designated **time; or** if one **slaughtered** the Paschal offering or sin offering with intent to burn it or partake of it **beyond its** designated **time, and he collected and conveyed and sprinkled** the blood **not for their sake; or that one slaughtered** the Paschal offering or sin offering **and collected and conveyed and sprinkled their blood not for their sake, that is** the case of an offering **whose permitting factor is not sacrificed in accordance with its mitzva.**

לֶאֱכוֹל כַּזַּיִת בַּחוּץ כַּזַּיִת לְמָחָר, כַּזַּיִת לְמָחָר כַּזַּיִת בַּחוּץ, כַּחֲצִי זַיִת בַּחוּץ כַּחֲצִי זַיִת לְמָחָר, כַּחֲצִי זַיִת לְמָחָר כַּחֲצִי זַיִת בַּחוּץ – פָּסוּל וְאֵין בּוֹ כָּרֵת.

If one performed one of the sacrificial rites with the intent **to eat an olive-bulk outside** its designated area and **an olive-bulk the next day,**[H] or **an olive-bulk the next day** and **an olive-bulk outside** its designated area, or **half an olive-bulk outside** its designated area and **half an olive-bulk the next day,** or **half an olive-bulk the next day** and **half an olive-bulk outside** its designated area, the offering is **disqualified and there is no** liability **for** ***karet*** for burning or partaking **of it.**

אָמַר רַבִּי יְהוּדָה: זֶה הַכְּלָל, כָּל שֶׁמַּחֲשֶׁבֶת הַזְּמַן קָדְמָה לְמַחֲשֶׁבֶת הַמָּקוֹם – פִּגּוּל וְחַיָּיבִין עָלָיו כָּרֵת, וְאִם מַחֲשֶׁבֶת הַמָּקוֹם קָדְמָה לְמַחֲשֶׁבֶת הַזְּמַן – פָּסוּל וְאֵין בּוֹ כָּרֵת. וַחֲכָמִים אוֹמְרִים: זֶה וָזֶה פָּסוּל, וְאֵין בּוֹ כָּרֵת. לֶאֱכוֹל כַּחֲצִי זַיִת לְהַקְטִיר כַּחֲצִי כַּזַּיִת – כָּשֵׁר, שֶׁאֵין אֲכִילָה וְהַקְטָרָה מִצְטָרְפִין.

Rabbi Yehuda said that **this is the principle:** In **any** case **where the intent** with regard to **the time preceded the intent** with regard to **the area,** the offering is ***piggul*** **and one is liable** to receive ***karet*** for burning or partaking **of it. And if the intent** with regard to **the area preceded the intent** with regard to **the time,** the offering is **disqualified and there is no** liability **for** ***karet*** **for** burning or partaking **of it. And the Rabbis say:** In both **this** case **and that** case, the offering is **disqualified and there is no** liability **for** ***karet*** **for** burning or partaking **of it.** If his intent was **to eat half an olive-bulk** and **to burn**[H] **half an olive-bulk** not at the appropriate time or in the appropriate area, the offering is **fit because eating and burning do not join together.**

גמ׳ אָמַר אִילְפָא: מַחְלוֹקֶת בִּשְׁתֵּי עֲבוֹדוֹת, אֲבָל בַּעֲבוֹדָה אַחַת – דִּבְרֵי הַכֹּל עֵירוּב מַחֲשָׁבוֹת הָוֵי. וְרַבִּי יוֹחָנָן אָמַר: אַף בַּעֲבוֹדָה אַחַת מַחֲלוֹקֶת.

GEMARA With regard to the disagreement between Rabbi Yehuda and the Rabbis concerning a case where one has intent with regard to both time and area, **Ilfa says:** There is **a disagreement** only **with regard to two** sacrificial **rites,**[N] i.e., where each intent was held during a different rite, **but** if both were held **in the course of one rite, all agree** that **it constitutes a combination of intentions,** and the offering is not rendered *piggul*. **And Rabbi Yoḥanan says: Even** if the intentions were both held **in the course of one rite,**[N] there is still **a disagreement.**

HALAKHA

An olive-bulk outside and an olive-bulk the next day, etc. – **כַּזַּיִת בַּחוּץ כַּזַּיִת לְמָחָר וכו׳**: If, during one or more of the four sacrificial rites, one has intent to eat an olive-bulk of an eaten portion of the offering outside its designated area and another olive-bulk the next day, or vice versa, or if one intends to eat half an olive-bulk outside and half an olive-bulk the next day, or vice versa, the offering is disqualified and is not rendered *piggul*, in accordance with the opinion of the Rabbis in the mishna. The *halakha* is the same if one combined intentions with regard to burning the offering (Rambam *Sefer Avoda, Hilkhot Pesulei HaMukdashin* 16:2).

To eat half an olive-bulk and to burn, etc. – **לֶאֱכוֹל כַּחֲצִי זַיִת לְהַקְטִיר וכו׳**: If one eats or burns less than an olive-bulk, he is not considered to have eaten or burned anything. Therefore, if one intends to eat less than an olive-bulk of an eaten portion of the offering or to burn less than an olive-bulk of a sacrificial portion, the offering remains fit. Even if he held both intentions simultaneously, eating and burning do not join together (Rambam *Sefer Avoda, Hilkhot Pesulei HaMukdashin* 14:10).

NOTES

Disagreement with regard to two rites – **מַחְלוֹקֶת בִּשְׁתֵּי עֲבוֹדוֹת**: The Rabbis consider all of the offering's rites to be a single unit, such that any two intentions held at any point throughout the service interfere with each other. Rabbi Yehuda considers each rite a discrete entity. If a given rite was performed with intent to consume the offering beyond its designated time, the offering is rendered *piggul* regardless of another intention during a later rite. But if one had both intentions during a single rite, Rabbi Yehuda concedes that they interfere with each other (Rashi; see also Rashi on *Pesaḥim* 60a).

According to *Tosafot*, the phrase: Two rites, is not actually referring to two distinct rites but rather to the act of slaughter, which consists of two components, the severing of the gullet and of the windpipe. According to Rabbi Yehuda, even if one held one intention during one and another during the other, the two intentions do not interfere with each other.

Even in one rite – **אַף בַּעֲבוֹדָה אַחַת**: According to the Rabbis, two intentions in the course of one rite interfere with one another, while Rabbi Yehuda holds to the principle: Attend only to the first statement. The Meiri writes that this principle serves as the rationale for Rabbi Yehuda's opinion only in a case where both intentions were expressed in the course of the same rite. If they were expressed in the course of consecutive rites, the Meiri reasons simply that after improper intent during the first rite the offering is rendered *piggul* permanently, and no other intent can remove this status.

בִּשְׁלָמָא לְאִילְפָא, מִדְּרֵישָׁא בִּשְׁתֵּי עֲבוֹדוֹת – סֵיפָא נַמִי בִּשְׁתֵּי עֲבוֹדוֹת. אֶלָּא לְרַבִּי יוֹחָנָן, רֵישָׁא בִּשְׁתֵּי עֲבוֹדוֹת וְסֵיפָא בַּעֲבוֹדָה אַחַת?

The Gemara asks: **Granted,** the mishna is understandable **according to Ilfa, since the first clause** of the mishna: If one slaughtered the animal in silence with no specific intent and collected... beyond its designated time, etc., is referring to different intentions held **in** the course of **two** sacrificial **rites**, one can assume that **the latter clause** is referring **to two rites as well. But according to Rabbi Yoḥanan,** could it be that **the first clause** is referring **to two rites, and the latter clause** is referring to only **one rite?**

Perek **II**
Daf **30** Amud **a**

אִין, רֵישָׁא בִּשְׁתֵּי עֲבוֹדוֹת, סֵיפָא בֵּין בַּעֲבוֹדָה אַחַת בֵּין בִּשְׁתֵּי עֲבוֹדוֹת.

The Gemara responds: **Yes,** it can be explained that **the first clause** is referring **to two** sacrificial **rites,** while **the latter clause,** i.e., the disagreement between Rabbi Yehuda and the Rabbis, applies **to both one rite and two rites.**

תְּנַן, אָמַר רַבִּי יְהוּדָה: זֶה הַכְּלָל, אִם מַחְשֶׁבֶת הַזְּמַן קָדְמָה לְמַחְשֶׁבֶת הַמָּקוֹם – פִּיגּוּל, וְחַיָּיבִין עָלָיו כָּרֵת. בִּשְׁלָמָא לְרַבִּי יוֹחָנָן – הַיְינוּ דְּקָתָנֵי "זֶה הַכְּלָל", אֶלָּא לְאִילְפָא מַאי "זֶה הַכְּלָל"? קַשְׁיָא.

The Gemara suggests a proof: **We learned** in the mishna: **Rabbi Yehuda says** that **this is the principle: If the intent** with regard to **the time preceded the intent** with regard to **the area,** the offering is ***piggul* and one is liable** to receive ***karet*** for burning or partaking of it. **Granted, according to Rabbi Yoḥanan,** who says that the disagreement applies even to one rite, **this is** the reason **that** the *tanna* **teaches: This is the principle,** indicating that the principle is broad. **But according to Ilfa, what** is added by the phrase: **This is the principle?** The Gemara responds: This indeed poses **a difficulty** to the opinion of Ilfa.

תְּנַן הָתָם: "הֲרֵי זוֹ תְּמוּרַת עוֹלָה תְּמוּרַת שְׁלָמִים" – הֲרֵי זוֹ תְּמוּרַת עוֹלָה, דִּבְרֵי רַבִּי מֵאִיר.

§ **We learned** in a mishna **elsewhere** (*Temura* 25b): If one had two animals standing before him, one a burnt offering and one a peace offering, and he said with regard to another non-sacred animal of his: **This** animal **is hereby the substitute of** the **burnt offering, the substitute of** the **peace offering,**[H] then **that** animal **is the substitute of** the **burnt offering;** this is **the statement of Rabbi Meir.**

אָמַר רַבִּי יוֹסֵי: אִם לְכָךְ נִתְכַּוֵּון תְּחִילָּה, הוֹאִיל וְאִי אֶפְשָׁר לְהוֹצִיא שְׁתֵּי שֵׁמוֹת כְּאַחַת – דְּבָרָיו קַיָּימִין. וְאִם מִשֶּׁאָמַר: "הֲרֵי זוֹ תְּמוּרַת עוֹלָה" וְנִמְלַךְ וְאָמַר: "הֲרֵי זוֹ תְּמוּרַת שְׁלָמִים" – הֲרֵי זוֹ עוֹלָה.

Rabbi Yosei said: If that was his intent from the outset, i.e., his intent was that this animal be the substitute of both a burnt offering and a peace offering, **since it is impossible to produce two designations simultaneously** and one designation must precede the other, **his statement is effective,**[N] and the animal is the substitute of both a burnt offering and a peace offering. **But if** it was only **after he said: This** animal **is hereby the substitute of** the **burnt offering,** that **he reconsidered and said: This** animal **is hereby the substitute of** the **peace offering,** then **that** animal **is the substitute of a burnt offering** alone.

אִיבַּעְיָא לְהוּ: "הֲרֵי זוֹ תְּמוּרַת עוֹלָה וּשְׁלָמִים", מַהוּ? "לַחֲצוֹת", מַהוּ?

A dilemma was raised before the Sages: If one expressed the two intentions simultaneously and said: **This is hereby the substitute of a burnt offering and a peace offering,**[N] **what is** the *halakha*? Additionally, if one specified his intention **to split**[N] the animal between a burnt offering and a peace offering, but mentioned the burnt offering first, **what is** the *halakha*?

HALAKHA

The substitute of the burnt offering, the substitute of the peace offering – תְּמוּרַת עוֹלָה תְּמוּרַת שְׁלָמִים: In a case where one says: This is hereby a substitute for a burnt offering, a substitute for a peace offering, his statement is effective if he had intended to state that from the outset. The animal must be sold and half of the proceeds exchanged for a burnt offering and half for a peace offering. If he initially had intended that the animal be a burnt offering and changed his mind in the course of his declaration, his first expression is the decisive factor, even if he had already changed his mind while speaking. The animal is therefore a substitute for a burnt offering, in accordance with the opinion of Rabbi Yosei (Rambam *Sefer Korbanot, Hilkhot Temura* 2:4).

NOTES

His statement is effective – דְּבָרָיו קַיָּימִין: Since two types of sanctity apply simultaneously to the animal, one must wait until it acquires a blemish, and he should then sell it and use half of the proceeds to buy a burnt offering and half of the proceeds to buy a peace offering (Rashi).

Substitute of a burnt offering and a peace offering – תְּמוּרַת עוֹלָה וּשְׁלָמִים: Here, since the burnt offering and the peace offering are mentioned in the same clause, perhaps Rabbi Meir concedes in such a case that both sanctities apply to the animal. On the other hand, perhaps he maintains even then that the first expression is the decisive factor (Rashi).

To split [*lahatzot*] – לַחֲצוֹת: According to Rashi, here one says: This animal is hereby split into a burnt offering and a peace offering. This case is more extreme than the preceding one, since even before he named the first sanctity he specified that his intention was to split the offering, and this language should be given precedence. Still, one could claim that since the half-sanctity of a burnt offering takes effect first, it immediately expands to apply to the whole animal and leaves no room for any other type of sanctity.

Tosafot offer an alternative interpretation, citing Rabbeinu Ḥananel (*Pesaḥim* 63a): The word *lahatzot* here means: At noon. The sanctifier stipulates that the sanctity will take effect on the animal not immediately upon his declaration but later. If so, one can claim that since both intentions have already been stated at the time the sanctity takes effect, both will take effect equally. One may claim that nevertheless, the first expression is the decisive factor (see Rabbeinu Peretz).

אֲמַר אַבַּיֵי: בְּהָא וַדַּאי מוֹדֶה רַבִּי מֵאִיר. רָבָא אֲמַר: עֲדַיִין הִיא מַחֲלוֹקֶת.

Abaye said: In this case, **Rabbi Meir certainly concedes** that both types of sanctity apply to the animal. **Rava said: It is still a disagreement;** Rabbi Meir still holds in this case that since he mentioned the burnt offering first, only that sanctity applies to the animal.

אֲמַר רָבָא לְאַבַּיֵי: לְדִידָךְ, דְּאָמְרַתְּ: בְּהָא וַדַּאי מוֹדֶה רַבִּי מֵאִיר, הֲרֵי שְׁחִיטָה, דִּלְכִי לַחֲצוֹת דָּמֵי, וּפְלִיגִי!

Rava said to Abaye: According to your opinion, **as you say** that **in this** case **Rabbi Meir certainly concedes,** one may raise an objection from the mishna, which describes a case where one performs **slaughter** with intent to eat one olive-bulk of the offering beyond its time and one olive-bulk outside its area, **which is comparable to** a case where one says: **To split,**[N] since both intentions are held during the singular act of slaughter. **And** nevertheless, Rabbi Yehuda and the Rabbis **disagree,**[N] and Rabbi Yehuda, who holds that one attends only to the first statement, renders the animal *piggul*.

אֲמַר לֵיהּ: מִי סָבְרַתְּ אֵינָהּ לִשְׁחִיטָה אֶלָּא לְבַסּוֹף? יֶשְׁנָהּ לִשְׁחִיטָה מִתְּחִילָּה וְעַד סוֹף, וּמִשְׁנָתֵינוּ – דְּאָמַר: "סִימָן רִאשׁוֹן חוּץ לִזְמַנּוֹ, סִימָן שֵׁנִי חוּץ לִמְקוֹמוֹ".

Abaye **said to him: Do you hold** that **slaughter is** considered to have been performed **only at** its **end,** such that it takes effect in a single instant? Actually, **slaughter is** accomplished progressively, **from beginning to end,**[NH] **and our mishna** is referring to a case **where one says:** I slaughter the **first** ***siman***, the gullet or the windpipe, with intent to consume the offering **beyond its** designated **time,** and the **second** ***siman*** with intent to consume it **outside its** designated **area.**

הֲרֵי קְמִיצָה, דִּלְכִי לַחֲצוֹת דָּמֵי, וּפְלִיגִי!

The Gemara asks: **But** what about the **removal of a handful** from a meal offering with intent to eat one olive-bulk beyond its time and one outside of its area, **which is comparable to** a case where one says: **To split,** since both intentions are held during the removal, **and** nevertheless, Rabbi Yehuda and the Rabbis **disagree** with regard to it in tractate *Menaḥot* (12a)?

NOTES

Slaughter, which is comparable to a case where one says to split – שְׁחִיטָה דִּלְכִי לַחֲצוֹת דָּמֵי: Slaughter with intent to eat one olive-bulk outside its area and one olive-bulk beyond its time is considered one act because the two intentions do not contradict one another. By contrast, the statement: Substitute for a burnt offering, substitute for a peace offering, is an internal contradiction, since a burnt offering cannot be a peace offering, and it is therefore reasonable to suppose that the speaker changed his mind in the course of his declaration. Still, Rabbi Yehuda holds that the first expression is the decisive factor in the former case, and one may say likewise of Rabbi Meir with regard to the explicit intention of splitting the offering (Rashi). According to Rabbeinu Ḥananel's interpretation, the similarity between slaughter and the stipulation that the sanctity will take effect at noon is clear: Since slaughter takes effect only at the very end of the incision, both intentions have already been expressed at the exact time of the rite, and both apply simultaneously (see Rabbeinu Peretz).

And they disagree – וּפְלִיגִי: The Gemara assumes that the opinions of both Rabbi Yehuda and Rabbi Meir are undergirded by the principle that one always attends only to the first statement, as Rav Dimi states (Rashi).

From beginning to end – מִתְּחִילָּה וְעַד סוֹף: Rabbi Yehuda holds that one can render an offering *piggul* by improper intention during even half of a rite, e.g., the slaughtering of only one *siman*, and different intentions can therefore be assigned into a rite's different components. According to *Tosafot*, this is the *halakha* if one intention was expressed specifically during the first component of the slaughter and the other during the second. But if one simply expressed them both consecutively over the course of the slaughter, the offering is not rendered *piggul* according to the opinion of Rabbi Yehuda, since the two intentions did not take effect at different stages of the rite. In the course of conveying the blood to the altar, every step is considered a separate act, and therefore two consecutively expressed intentions may be assumed to apply to different components of the rite.

HALAKHA

From beginning to end – מִתְּחִילָּה וְעַד סוֹף: If one is slaughtering a consecrated animal, and he slaughters one of the *simanim* outside the Temple courtyard and finishes the slaughter inside, or if he slaughtered part of the *simanim* in the south of the Temple courtyard and finished the slaughter in the north, the offering is disqualified because slaughter takes effect from beginning to end. This ruling is in accordance with the opinion of Rabbi Yoḥanan in tractate *Ḥullin* (*Kesef Mishne*). *Tosafot* rule in accordance with the opinion of Reish Lakish that slaughter takes effect only at its end, since the Gemara here cites Rava as being of this opinion (Rambam *Sefer Avoda*, *Hilkhot Pesulei HaMukdashin* 1:18, and see *Sefer Kedusha*, *Hilkhot Sheḥita* 4:13).

הָתָם נַמִי, שֶׁהִקְטִיר קוֹמֶץ מִנְחָה חוּץ לִזְמַנּוֹ, קוֹמֶץ לְבוֹנָה חוּץ לִמְקוֹמוֹ.

The Gemara responds: Since the mishna does not state such a dispute explicitly, one can say that their disagreement is not with regard to the removal of the handful but with regard to the burning of the two permitting factors of the meal offering, the handful and the frankincense. Accordingly, **there too,** the case is such **that** the priest **burned the handful of** the **meal offering** with intent to eat it **beyond** its designated **time,** and he burned **the handful of frankincense**[B] with intent to eat the meal offering **outside its** designated **area.**

הֲרֵי קוֹמֶץ דְּמִנְחַת חוֹטֵא, דְּלֵיכָּא לְבוֹנָה בַּהֲדֵיהּ, וּפְלִיגִי!

The Gemara persists: **But** what about **the handful from a meal offering of a sinner, which has no frankincense with it, and** still Rabbi Yehuda and the Rabbis **disagree?**

לָא פְּלִיגִי. אָמַר רַב אַשִׁי: אִם תִּימְצֵי לוֹמַר פְּלִיגִי – פְּלִיגִי בִּפְסִיעוֹת.

The Gemara responds: In that case **they do not disagree. Rav Ashi says:** Even **if you say** that **they disagree** in that case, one may say that **they disagree** specifically **with regard to** a case where the priest had different intentions during his **steps** toward the altar while holding the handful. Consequently, even this rite is divisible into separate parts.

רַב שִׁימִי בַּר אַשִׁי מַתְנֵי כְּדְאַבַּיֵי, רַב הוּנָא בַּר נָתָן מַתְנֵי כִּדְרָבָא.

Rav Shimi bar Ashi would **teach in accordance with** the opinion **of Abaye** that in a case where one explicitly mentions both intentions at once, Rabbi Meir concedes that both sanctities apply to the animal. **Rav Huna bar Natan** would **teach in accordance with** the opinion **of Rava** that even in such a case, Rabbi Meir considers only the first sanctity mentioned.

כִּי אֲתָא רַב דִּימִי אֲמַר: רַבִּי מֵאִיר בְּשִׁיטַת רַבִּי יְהוּדָה אֲמָרָהּ, דְּאָמַר: תְּפוֹס לָשׁוֹן רִאשׁוֹן.

When Rav Dimi came from Eretz Yisrael to Babylonia, **he said:** When **Rabbi Meir** said that if one says: This animal is hereby the substitute of a burnt offering, the substitute of a peace offering, then the animal is the substitute of a burnt offering, he **said this according to the opinion of Rabbi Yehuda, who says** that in general, the *halakha* is to **attend** only to the **first statement.**

דִּתְנַן, אָמַר רַבִּי יְהוּדָה: זֶה הַכְּלָל, אִם מַחֲשֶׁבֶת הַזְּמַן קָדְמָה אֶת מַחֲשֶׁבֶת הַמָּקוֹם – פִּיגּוּל, וְחַיָּיבִין עָלָיו כָּרֵת.

As we learned in the mishna: **Rabbi Yehuda said** that **this is the principle: If the intent** with regard to **the time preceded the intent** with regard to **the area,** the offering is ***piggul*** **and one is liable** to receive ***karet*** **for** burning or partaking of **it.**

BACKGROUND

Boswellia sacra tree

Harvesting resin

Boswellia sacra resin

Frankincense pellets

Frankincense – לְבוֹנָה: Frankincense is an aromatic spice used in various Temple services. An addition to most of the meal offerings, except for the meal offering of a sinner and the meal offering of jealousy brought by a *sota*, it was sacrificed on the altar together with the handful of meal. Frankincense is derived from the resin of *Boswellia sacra* L., or frankincense trees.

אֲמַר לֵיהּ אַבַּיֵי: וְהָא רַבָּה בַּר בַּר חָנָה אָמַר רַבִּי יוֹחָנָן: כִּי מַגַּעַת לְהוּ, רַבִּי מֵאִיר וְרַבִּי יוֹסֵי בַּהֲדֵי הֲדָדֵי לָא פְּלִיגִי!

Abaye said to Rav Dimi: **But doesn't Rabba bar bar Ḥana say that Rabbi Yoḥanan says: When you consider their** opinions, **Rabbi Meir and Rabbi Yosei do not disagree with one another,** i.e., neither holds that one attends only to the first statement?

וְלָא פְּלִיגִי? וְהָא מִיפְלַג פְּלִיגִי! אֲמַר לֵיהּ: פְּלִיגִי בְּמַאי דִּפְלִיגִי, וְלָא פְּלִיגִי בְּמַאי דְּלָא פְּלִיגִי.

Rav Dimi objected: **And is it so that they do not disagree? But don't they disagree** explicitly in the mishna cited earlier? Abaye **said to him: They disagree where they disagree,**[N] i.e., that specific case, **but they do not disagree where they do not disagree,** i.e., the underlying principle. Accordingly, one must understand the basis of their dispute in another manner.

דְּאָמַר רַבִּי יִצְחָק בַּר יוֹסֵף אָמַר רַבִּי יוֹחָנָן: הַכֹּל מוֹדִים הֵיכָא דְּאָמַר ״תָּחוּל זוֹ וְאַחַר כָּךְ (אָמַר) תָּחוּל זוֹ״ – דִּבְרֵי הַכֹּל לָא חָיְילָא; ״לֹא תָּחוּל זוֹ אֶלָּא אִם כֵּן חָלָה זוֹ״ – דִּבְרֵי הַכֹּל חָיְילָא;

This is **as Rav Yitzḥak bar Yosef says** that **Rabbi Yoḥanan says: All,** i.e., Rabbi Meir and Rabbi Yosei, **concede that** in a case **where one says: Let this** sanctity of a burnt offering **take effect and afterward let that** sanctity of a peace offering **take effect, everyone agrees** that the sanctity of a peace offering **does not take effect,** because the sanctity of the burnt offering took effect first. Likewise, if one said: **This** sanctity **shall not take effect unless that** sanctity **applies, everyone agrees** that the sanctity of a peace offering **takes effect**[N] as well.

כִּי פְּלִיגִי – דְּאָמַר: ״תְּמוּרַת עוֹלָה תְּמוּרַת שְׁלָמִים״, רַבִּי מֵאִיר סָבַר: מִדַּהֲוָה לֵיהּ לְמֵימַר ״תְּמוּרַת עוֹלָה וּשְׁלָמִים״, וְאָמַר: ״תְּמוּרַת עוֹלָה תְּמוּרַת שְׁלָמִים״ – שְׁמַע מִינָּהּ מִיהֲדַר קָא הָדַר בֵּיהּ.

They disagree with regard to a case **where one says:** This animal is hereby **a substitute for a burnt offering, a substitute for a peace offering. Rabbi Meir holds: Since** if he wanted both sanctities to take effect, **he should have said: A substitute for a burnt offering and a peace offering, but he said** instead: **A substitute for a burnt offering, a substitute for a peace offering, learn from** his language that he originally intended for it to be a burnt offering, and he then **retracted** his first intention.[N]

וְרַבִּי יוֹסֵי: אִי אָמַר ״תְּמוּרַת עוֹלָה וּשְׁלָמִים״, הֲוָה אָמִינָא: פַּלְגָא תְּמוּרַת עוֹלָה וּפַלְגָא תְּמוּרַת שְׁלָמִים – לְהָכִי אָמַר ״תְּמוּרַת עוֹלָה תְּמוּרַת שְׁלָמִים״, לְמֵימְרָא דְּכוּלָּהּ עוֹלָה וְכוּלָּהּ שְׁלָמִים הָוְיָא.

And Rabbi Yosei holds that **if he had said: A substitute for a burnt offering and a peace offering, I would say**[N] that he means that **half** the animal should be **a substitute for a burnt offering and half a substitute for a peace offering. He therefore says: A substitute for a burnt offering, a substitute for a peace offering; that is to say that all of it is a burnt offering and all of it is a peace offering.** In any event, according to this explanation, Rabbi Meir does not necessarily hold that one attends only to the first statement.

אֲמַר לֵיהּ: הוּא אָמַר לָא פְּלִיגִי, וַאֲנָא אָמִינָא פְּלִיגִי.

Rav Dimi **said to** Abaye: **He,** Rabba bar bar Ḥana, **says that they do not disagree, but I say** that **they disagree,**[N] and Rabbi Meir holds that one attends only to the first statement, in accordance with the opinion of Rabbi Yehuda in the mishna.

אֲמַר עוּלָּא וְאִיתֵימָא רַב אוֹשַׁעְיָא: אֶפְשָׁר יָדְעִין חַבְרִין בַּבְלָאָה ״כַּזַּיִת״ ״כַּזַּיִת״ תְּנַן, אוֹ ״כַּזַּיִת וְכַזַּיִת״ תְּנַן?

§ The Gemara returns to discuss the mishna itself: **Ulla said, and some say** it was **Rav Oshaya who said: Perhaps our colleagues, the Babylonians, know** whether **we learn** the language of the improper intention in the mishna as: I hereby slaughter the animal with intent to consume **an olive-bulk** beyond its designated time, **an olive-bulk**[N] outside its designated area, **or we learn: An olive-bulk** beyond its designated time **and an olive-bulk** outside its designated area?

״כַּזַּיִת״ ״כַּזַּיִת״ תְּנַן, אֲבָל ״כַּזַּיִת וְכַזַּיִת״ – דִּבְרֵי הַכֹּל עֵירוּב מַחֲשָׁבוֹת הָוֵי. אוֹ דִּלְמָא: ״כַּזַּיִת וְכַזַּיִת״ תְּנַן, דִּלְרַבִּי יְהוּדָה פְּרָטָא הָוֵי, וְכׇל שֶׁכֵּן ״כַּזַּיִת כַּזַּיִת״?

The Gemara elaborates: Perhaps **we learn: An olive-bulk, an olive-bulk,** and it is only in this case that Rabbi Yehuda disagrees with the Rabbis. **But** if one said: **An olive-bulk and an olive-bulk, everyone agrees** that **it constitutes a combination of intentions,** and the animal is not rendered *piggul*. **Or perhaps we learn: An olive-bulk and an olive-bulk, where according to Rabbi Yehuda** each term **constitutes a separate** term despite the use of the conjunction: And, and he holds that one attends only to the first statement, **and all the more so** if one said: **An olive-bulk, an olive-bulk.**

NOTES

They disagree where they disagree, etc. – פְּלִיגִי בְּמַאי דִּפְלִיגִי וכו׳: If Rabbi Meir held that the first expression is always the decisive factor, there would be no case where one sanctity is mentioned first but both types of sanctity take effect. According to the statement of Rabbi Yoḥanan in the continuation of the discussion, Rabbi Meir seems to concede that if one says: A substitute for a burnt offering and a peace offering, both types of sanctity take effect upon the animal (Rashi).

Everyone agrees that it takes effect – דִּבְרֵי הַכֹּל חָיְילָא: Since the two types of sanctity are conditional upon one another, they both take effect simultaneously. The animal becomes a substitute for a burnt offering and a peace offering, but it cannot be sacrificed, because these two offerings must be sacrificed differently. Therefore, one must wait for the animal to develop a blemish, and then he must sell it and use half of the proceeds to purchase a burnt offering and half to purchase a peace offering.

Retracted his first intention – מִיהֲדַר קָא הָדַר בֵּיהּ: Since it is impossible to retract sanctity once effected, only the first sanctity takes effect with regard to the animal (Rashi).

I would say, etc. – הֲוָה אָמִינָא וכו׳: Whether one pronounces each sanctity on half the animal or intends that they both take effect with regard to the whole animal makes no practical difference. In both cases, one must wait for the animal to develop a blemish, and he must then sell the animal and split the proceeds. In this case, one assumes that the speaker was under the mistaken impression that if both sanctities take effect with regard to the whole animal it can be sacrificed. It is therefore assumed that he formulated his declaration deliberately, rather than changing his mind midsentence (Rashi).

But I say they disagree – וַאֲנָא אָמִינָא פְּלִיגִי: In this, Rav Dimi also disagrees with Rav Yitzḥak bar Yosef's statement in the name of Rabbi Yoḥanan that Rabbi Meir concedes in a case where one says: A substitute for a burnt offering and a peace offering. Rather, Rabbi Meir always holds that one attends only to the first statement.

An olive-bulk, an olive-bulk – כַּזַּיִת כַּזַּיִת: This is not simply a question with regard to the formulation of the mishna but rather an inquiry as to whether the addition of a conjunction in a clause unifies two separate terms. This question has ramifications for vows as well (see *Tosafot*).

תָּא שְׁמַע, דִּבְעָא מִינֵּיהּ לֵוִי מֵרַבִּי: חִישֵּׁב לֶאֱכוֹל כַּזַּיִת לְמָחָר בַּחוּץ, מַהוּ? אֲמַר לוֹ: זוֹ שְׁאֵילָה! עֵירוּב מַחֲשָׁבוֹת הָוֵי.

The Gemara suggests: **Come and hear** a proof from that **dilemma which Levi raised before Rabbi** Yehuda HaNasi: **If one had intent to consume an olive-bulk the next day outside** its designated area, **what is the** *halakha*? Rabbi Yehuda HaNasi **said to him: This** is an excellent **question.** The answer is that even Rabbi Yehuda concedes that this **constitutes a combination of intentions** and that the animal is not rendered *piggul*.

אָמַר לְפָנָיו רַבִּי שִׁמְעוֹן בְּרַבִּי: לֹא מִשְׁנָתֵינוּ הִיא? לֶאֱכוֹל כַּזַּיִת בַּחוּץ כַּזַּיִת לְמָחָר, כַּזַּיִת לְמָחָר כַּזַּיִת בַּחוּץ, כַּחֲצִי זַיִת בַּחוּץ כַּחֲצִי זַיִת לְמָחָר, כַּחֲצִי זַיִת לְמָחָר כַּחֲצִי זַיִת בַּחוּץ – פָּסוּל וְאֵין בּוֹ כָּרֵת; הָא אִידָּךְ – עֵירוּב מַחֲשָׁבוֹת הָוֵי!

Rabbi Shimon, son of Rabbi Yehuda HaNasi, **said before him:** How is this an excellent question; **is it not our mishna?** As we learned in the mishna: If one expressed intent **to eat an olive-bulk outside** its designated area and **an olive-bulk the next day,** or an **olive-bulk the next day** and **an olive-bulk outside** its designated area, or **half an olive-bulk outside** its designated area and **half an olive-bulk the next day,** or **half an olive-bulk the next day** and **half an olive-bulk outside** its designated area, the offering is **disqualified and there is no** liability **for** ***karet*** **for** burning or partaking of **it.** Rabbi Yehuda disagrees only with regard to these cases; **but** in **another** case, it could easily be inferred that he concedes that **it constitutes a combination of intentions.**

אֲמַר לֵיהּ: הוּא שָׁאַל בִּי דְּבַר חָכְמָה, וְאַתְּ אָמְרַתְּ מִשְׁנָתֵינוּ. לְדִידָךְ דְּאַתְנֵיתָךְ תַּרְתֵּי – לָא קַשְׁיָא לָךְ.

Rabbi Yehuda HaNasi **said to him:** Levi **asked me a matter of wisdom, and you say our mishna. For you, whom I taught two** phrasings of the mishna, both: An olive-bulk, an olive-bulk, and: An olive-bulk and an olive-bulk, the question is **not difficult,** since my omission of this other case allows you to infer its *halakha*.

לְדִידֵיהּ דְּלָא אַתְנִיתֵיהּ אֶלָּא חֲדָא, וְשַׁמְעִינְהוּ לְרַבָּנַן דְּקָא גָּרְסִי תַּרְתֵּי, וְסָבַר: דִּידִי דַּוְוקָא, וְדִידְהוּ עֵירוּב מַחֲשָׁבוֹת הָוֵי. אוֹ דִּלְמָא דִּידְהוּ דַּוְוקָא, וּלְדִידִי שַׁיּוּרֵי שַׁיֵּיר לִי, וּמִדְּשַׁיֵּיר לִי לְדִידִי הָא – שַׁיֵּיר לְהוּ לְדִידְהוּ נַמִי בְּהָךְ.

For him, whom I taught only one phrasing, **and** who **heard the Rabbis reciting two,** the question is excellent, since Levi **thought:** Perhaps **my** phrasing is **exact, and their** additional phrasing **constitutes a combination of intentions** according to all opinions. **Or perhaps their** phrasing is **exact, and my** phrasing **omitted** this case. **And if my phrasing omitted this** case, perhaps **their** phrasing **also omitted that** other case, even though it is subject to disagreement.

וְהֵי אַתְנְיֵיהּ? אִילֵימָא ״כַּזַּיִת וְכַזַּיִת״ אַתְנְיֵיהּ – הַאי לָאו שִׁיּוּרָא הוּא! אֶלָּא ״כַּזַּיִת כַּזַּיִת״ אַתְנְיֵיהּ.

The Gemara asks: **And which** phrasing **did** Rabbi Yehuda HaNasi **teach** Levi? **If we say** that **he taught him: An olive-bulk and an olive-bulk,** i.e., that Rabbi Yehuda still holds the terms to be distinct despite the conjunction, **this is not an omission,**[N] since one can infer *a fortiori* that the same applies to: An olive-bulk, an olive-bulk. **Rather,** it must be that **he taught him: An olive-bulk, an olive-bulk,** so that it was unclear to Levi what the *halakha* would be if one used the conjunction: And.

וְתִיבְּעֵי לֵיהּ ״כַּזַּיִת וְכַזַּיִת״?

The Gemara asks: If so, why did Levi raise the dilemma with regard to the phrasing: The next day outside? **Let him raise the dilemma** with regard to the phrasing: **An olive-bulk and an olive-bulk.**

סָבַר: אִיבְּעֵי מִינֵּיהּ חֲדָא דְּשַׁמְעָנָא תַּרְתֵּי. דְּאִי בָּעֵינָא ״כַּזַּיִת וְכַזַּיִת״, הָא נִיחָא אִי אָמַר לִי כְּלָלָא – כָּל שֶׁכֵּן ״כַּזַּיִת לְמָחָר בַּחוּץ״. אֶלָּא אִי אָמַר לִי פְּרָטָא – אַכַּתִּי ״כַּזַּיִת לְמָחָר בַּחוּץ״ קָא מִיבָּעֲיָא לִי.

The Gemara responds: Levi **thought: I will raise one dilemma before him so as to learn two** *halakhot*. **As, if I ask** only with regard to: **An olive-bulk and an olive-bulk, it will work out well if he says to me** that Rabbi Yehuda concedes that they constitute one **general** term, as this would apply **all the more so** if one said: **An olive-bulk the next day outside,** which is even more unified. **But if he says to me** that each term constitutes **a separate** term according to Rabbi Yehuda, then **I will still** need to **raise the dilemma** with regard to the case of: **An olive-bulk the next day outside.** I will therefore inquire with regard to the latter case.

אִי הָכִי, הַשְׁתָּא נַמִי, הָתֵינָח אִי אֲמַר לֵיהּ ״כַּזַּיִת לְמָחָר בַּחוּץ״ פְּרָטָא – כָּל שֶׁכֵּן ״כַּזַּיִת וְכַזַּיִת״. אֶלָּא אִי אֲמַר לֵיהּ כְּלָלָא – אַכַּתִּי ״כַּזַּיִת וְכַזַּיִת״ מִיבָּעֵי לֵיהּ!

The Gemara challenges: **If so, now too, it works out well if he says to him** that Rabbi Yehuda maintains that the wording: **An olive-bulk the next day outside,** is constituted of **separate** terms, as this would apply **all the more so** if one said: **An olive-bulk and an olive-bulk,** which is less unified. **But if he says to him** that it is one **general** term according to Rabbi Yehuda, then **he will still** need to **raise the dilemma** with regard to the case of: **An olive-bulk and an olive-bulk.**

NOTES

Omission – **שִׁיּוּרָא**: Usually, when a *tanna* presents a list of relevant cases, the initial assumption is that the list is comprehensive; cases not on the list are not subject to the *halakha* in question. There are several instances when a given case seems to be missing from the list, and the Gemara will then say that the *tanna*: Taught and omitted, i.e., did not intend to provide a comprehensive list. In such cases, the Gemara will frequently seek to justify this conclusion by inquiring after other omitted cases, asking: What else did he omit that he omitted this? The Gemara will also assume in such cases that the list was formulated as concisely as possible, omitting all cases that could be independently inferred. The omission of such cases can therefore not be taken as proof that the list is not comprehensive. These principles underlie Levi's reasoning as he attempts to deduce Rabbi Yehuda HaNasi's opinion.

אם כן מרתח רתח:

The Gemara responds: **If** Rabbi Yehuda HaNasi answered in **this** manner, i.e., that Rabbi Yehuda concedes that: An olive-bulk the next day outside, is considered one term, he would unwittingly provide the answer to the other question as well. As, if Rabbi Yehuda had also conceded with regard to: An olive-bulk and an olive-bulk, Rabbi Yehuda HaNasi would **become angry**[N] with Levi for asking the wrong question and say:

NOTES

Become angry – מרתח רתח: He would not have become truly angry, but rather put on a show of anger so that Levi would learn the additional *halakha* (*Shita Mekubbetzet*).

Perek **II**
Daf **31** Amud **a**

השתא "כזית וכזית" כללא, "כזית למחר בחוץ" מיבעיא?

Now that Rabbi Yehuda concedes that even: **An olive-bulk and an olive-bulk, is one general** term, **is it necessary** to inquire with regard to: **An olive-bulk the next day outside?**

לישנא אחרינא: "כזית למחר בחוץ" פרטא, "כזית כזית" מיבעיא?

The Gemara presents **another version** of this discussion: Rabbi Yehuda HaNasi might say that if Rabbi Yehuda maintains that even when one says: **An olive-bulk the next day outside,** each term is considered **separate, is it necessary** to inquire with regard to: **An olive-bulk, an olive-bulk?**

איתמר: חצי זית חוץ לזמנו חצי זית חוץ למקומו וחצי זית חוץ לזמנו – אמר רבא: "ויקץ כישן" הפיגול, ורב המנונא אמר: עירוב מחשבות הוי.

§ **It was stated:** If one had intent to eat **half an olive**-bulk **beyond its** designated **time, half an olive**-bulk **outside its** designated **area, and** another **half an olive**-bulk **beyond its** designated **time, Rava says:** In such a case, **the** ***piggul*****: "Awaked as one asleep"** (Psalms 78:65),[H] i.e., since one had intent to consume two halves of an olive-bulk beyond their designated time, these intentions are joined together. The middle thought is disregarded, since it constitutes only half the requisite measure, and the offering is rendered *piggul*. **And Rav Hamnuna says: It constitutes a combination of** improper **intentions.** The middle thought, although itself insufficient to disqualify the offering, is sufficient to interfere with the intention to consume it beyond its time, and the offering is not rendered *piggul*.

HALAKHA

The *piggul* awaked as one asleep, etc. – ויקץ כישן הפיגול וכו׳: If one intended to consume half an olive-bulk beyond its designated time and half an olive-bulk outside its designated area, and one then intended to consume another half olive-bulk beyond its designated time, the offering is rendered *piggul*, in accordance with the opinion of Rava, since Rav Ashi is also of this opinion (Rambam *Sefer Avoda, Hilkhot Pesulei HaMukdashin* 16:4).

If this portion fell by itself, etc. – נפל זה בעצמו וכו׳: If an egg-bulk of food with first-degree ritual impurity and an egg-bulk of food with second-degree ritual impurity are mixed together, the entire mixture is considered to have first-degree impurity. If one then split the mixture in half, each half is considered to have second-degree impurity, in accordance with the mishna in tractate *Teharot*. If either of the aforementioned halves of the mixture fell by itself onto a loaf of *teruma*, they disqualify it, such that it will not disqualify other *teruma* it touches. If they both fell at once, the *teruma* contracts second-degree impurity, in accordance with the mishna there (Rambam *Sefer Tahara, Hilkhot Tumat Okhalin* 4:13).

אמר רבא: מנא אמינא לה? דתנן: כביצה אוכל ראשון וכביצה אוכל שני שבללן זה בזה – ראשון. חלקן – זה שני וזה שני; הא חזר ועירבן – ראשון הוי.

Rava said: From where, i.e., based on what, **do I state** my ruling? **As we learned** in a mishna (*Teharot* 1:5): **An egg-bulk of food** with **first**-degree impurity **and an egg-bulk of food** with second-degree impurity **that one mixed together** are collectively considered to have **first**-degree impurity. If one **separated them** into two portions, each containing a homogenous mixture, **this** portion is considered to have **second**-degree impurity **and that** portion is considered to have **second**-degree impurity. Since neither of them contains the requisite amount of food with first-degree impurity, each mixture settles to the lower level of impurity between the two foods. Rava reasoned: **But** if one **mixed them again,** they revert to **be** of **first**-degree impurity.

ממאי? מדקתני סיפא: נפל זה בעצמו וזה בעצמו על ככר של תרומה – פסלוה, נפלו שניהן כאחת – עשאוה שניה.

From where do I know this? **From** the fact **that the latter clause** of that mishna **teaches:** If **this** portion **fell by itself**[H] **and that** portion fell **by itself onto a loaf of** ***teruma*****, it disqualifies it,** as would any food with second-degree impurity. But it does not render it impure, since only foods with first-degree impurity impart impurity to other foods. But if **they both fell simultaneously**[N] onto the loaf, **they render it** a food with **second**-degree impurity. Evidently, although the first-degree impurity lay dormant for lack of a requisite measure, it resurfaces when the rest of the measure is added, despite the fact that each portion was previously considered to have second-degree impurity. The *halakha* would be the same in the case of intent to consume the offering beyond its designated time, i.e., the intent to consume half an olive-bulk outside its area does not interfere with the intent of *piggul*.

NOTES

Both fell simultaneously – נפלו שניהן כאחת: The *halakha* would be the same even if they fall one after the other, as long as there is an instant where both are in contact with the loaf simultaneously (Rashi).

וְרַב הַמְנוּנָא אָמַר: הָתָם אִיכָּא שִׁיעוּרָא, הָכָא לֵיכָּא שִׁיעוּרָא.

And Rav Hamnuna says: The cases are different. **There,** in the case of ritual impurity, **there is** a requisite **measure** present at the outset, which is divided and then recombined. **Here,** in the case of the offering, **there is no** requisite **measure**[N] present at the outset to render it *piggul*.

אֲמַר רַב הַמְנוּנָא: מְנָא אָמִינָא לָהּ? דִּתְנַן: הָאוֹכֶל שֶׁנִּטְמָא בְּאַב הַטּוּמְאָה וְשֶׁנִּטְמָא בְּוָלַד הַטּוּמְאָה – מִצְטָרְפִין זֶה עִם זֶה לְטַמֵּא בַּקַּל שֶׁבִּשְׁנֵיהֶם; מַאי לָאו, אַף עַל גַּב דַּהֲדַר מַלְיֵיהּ?

Rav Hamnuna said: From where do I say my opinion? **As we learned** in another mishna (*Me'ila* 17b): **The food that became ritually impure** through contact **with a primary source of ritual impurity,**[BH] thereby assuming first-degree impurity, **and the** food **that became ritually impure** through contact **with a derivative source of ritual impurity,**[B] thereby assuming second-degree impurity, **join together** to constitute the requisite measure of an egg-bulk **to impart impurity in accordance with the** more **lenient of the two,** i.e., as a food of second-degree impurity. **What, is it not** that they retain second-degree impurity **even if one makes up** the requisite measure **again?** If so, it can be inferred that the first-degree impurity is lost, and it does not lie dormant or resurface. Here as well, the latter intent of *piggul* cannot restore the initial intent of *piggul,* as the intent to consume half an olive-bulk outside its area interfered.

דִּלְמָא דְּלָא הֲדַר מַלְיֵיהּ!

The Gemara responds: **Perhaps** the mishna is referring specifically to a case **where one does not complete** the requisite measure **again.**

כִּי אֲתָא רַב דִּימִי אֲמַר: חֲצִי זַיִת חוּץ לִמְקוֹמוֹ וַחֲצִי זַיִת חוּץ לִזְמַנּוֹ וַחֲצִי זַיִת חוּץ לִזְמַנּוֹ – תָּנֵי בַּר קַפָּרָא: פִּיגּוּל, אֵין חֲצִי זַיִת מוֹעִיל בִּמְקוֹם כַּזַּיִת.

The Gemara presents similar cases: **When Rav Dimi came** from Eretz Yisrael, **he said:** If one had intent to eat **half an olive-bulk outside its** designated **area, and half an olive-bulk beyond its** designated **time, and** then another **half an olive-bulk beyond its** designated **time, bar Kappara teaches** that the offering is rendered ***piggul,*** since the **half an olive-bulk** with regard to the area **is not effective**[NH] to interfere **where** the intent with regard to the time concerns a whole **olive-bulk.**

כִּי אֲתָא רָבִין אֲמַר: חֲצִי זַיִת חוּץ לִזְמַנּוֹ וַחֲצִי זַיִת חוּץ לִזְמַנּוֹ וַחֲצִי זַיִת חוּץ לִמְקוֹמוֹ – תָּנֵי בַּר קַפָּרָא: פִּיגּוּל, אֵין חֲצִי זַיִת מוֹעִיל בִּמְקוֹם כַּזַּיִת.

When Ravin came[N] from Eretz Yisrael, **he stated** a different formulation: If one had intent to eat **half an olive-bulk beyond its** designated **time, and** then another **half an olive-bulk beyond its** designated **time, and** then **half an olive-bulk outside its** designated **area, bar Kappara teaches** that the offering is rendered ***piggul,*** since the **half an olive-bulk is not effective** to interfere **where** the intent of *piggul* concerns a whole **olive-bulk.**

רַב אַשִׁי מַתְנֵי הָכִי: חֲצִי זַיִת חוּץ לִזְמַנּוֹ, וְכַזַּיִת חֶצְיוֹ חוּץ לִמְקוֹמוֹ וְחֶצְיוֹ חוּץ לִזְמַנּוֹ – תָּנֵי בַּר קַפָּרָא: פִּיגּוּל, אֵין חֲצִי זַיִת מוֹעִיל בִּמְקוֹם כַּזַּיִת.

Rav Ashi teaches[N] the *halakha* **in this** manner: If one had intent to eat **half an olive-bulk beyond its** designated **time, and** then intended with regard to a whole **olive-bulk** to eat **half of it**[H] **outside its** designated **area and half of it beyond its** designated **time, bar Kappara teaches** that the offering is rendered ***piggul,*** because the **half an olive-bulk is not effective** to interfere **where** the intent of *piggul* concerns a whole **olive-bulk.**

NOTES

There is no measure – לֵיכָּא שִׁיעוּרָא: Rashi explains that in the case of the offering there was no requisite measure at the outset to render the offering *piggul*. As soon as the second intention was expressed, the original intention was nullified and does not resurface when the second half of the measure is introduced. Here, by contrast, the requisite measure existed from the outset. Rabbeinu Tam challenges this interpretation, since the Gemara does not use the past tense: There was no measure, stating instead: There is no measure. Rather, he suggests that in the case of the food, the requisite measure exists at the moment, since the two halves of an egg-bulk have been reunited. In the case of the offering, the thought to consume half an olive-bulk outside its area pairs inseparably with the first thought to consume half an olive-bulk beyond its time, not allowing the second such thought to complete the measure. Rabbeinu Tam explains Rav Hamnuna's response in the continuation of the discussion in the same vein.

Half an olive-bulk is not effective, etc. – אֵין חֲצִי זַיִת מוֹעִיל וכו׳: Rather, the two parallel half olive-bulks join together while the third is ignored (Rashi). According to Rabbeinu Peretz, Rav Dimi is in agreement with Rav Hamnuna that insufficient intentions with regard to offerings do not lie dormant and resurface when the measure is completed. However, here the two insufficient intentions join together because they are expressed in immediate succession (*Shita Mekubbetzet*).

When Ravin came – כִּי אֲתָא רָבִין: Ravin's statement limits the scope of recombination of intentions more so than Rav Dimi's. According to Rav Dimi's statement, even if an improper intention with regard to the area is already established when the two intentions with regard to the time are expressed, they still join together to render the offering *piggul* despite the first improper intention. According to Ravin's statement, the two intentions with regard to the time can join together only in the absence of another intention, which will not interfere if expressed afterward.

Rav Ashi teaches – רַב אַשִׁי מַתְנֵי: Rav Ashi's opinion follows Rava's in that two insufficient intentions can join together again. It goes even further in claiming that even if one insufficient intention with regard to the time is expressly associated with the intention with regard to the area, it can still decouple from it and join together with another intention with regard to time (Rashi). The *Sefat Emet* suggests the opposite, i.e., that here even Rav Hamnuna would concede that the offering is rendered *piggul*, because the two latter intentions are expressed simultaneously and it is therefore considered as though the two intentions with regard to the time were expressed in immediate succession.

BACKGROUND

Primary source of ritual impurity – אַב הַטּוּמְאָה: This is the second most severe category of ritual impurity, after that of a corpse, which is considered the ultimate primary source of ritual impurity. An item with this status transmits ritual impurity to people and utensils. A person or a utensil that comes into contact with a primary source of impurity contracts first-degree ritual impurity. Any food or potable liquid that comes into contact with first-degree impurity contracts second-degree ritual impurity. Among the primary sources of impurity are: Creeping animals, i.e., the carcasses of any of the eight species of reptile or rodent listed in Leviticus 11:29–30; the carcass of an unslaughtered animal; semen; a leper; the water of purification mixed with the ashes of the red heifer; a menstruating woman; one who engaged in intercourse with a menstruating woman; a woman after childbirth; a *zav*; a *zava*; an item on which a *zav* or *zava* sits or lies; and one who has contacted ritual impurity from a corpse.

Derivative source of ritual impurity – וְלַד הַטּוּמְאָה: This is referring to an item that contracted first-degree ritual impurity by contact with a primary source of ritual impurity. Such an item imparts ritual impurity to foods or liquids with which it comes into contact. It does not impart ritual impurity to people or to utensils.

HALAKHA

With a primary source of ritual impurity, etc. – בְּאַב הַטּוּמְאָה וכו׳: No food can transmit ritual impurity unless it is of the volume of an egg-bulk. If foods of different levels of impurity join together to form an egg-bulk, they transmit the most lenient impurity that any one of them possessed (Rambam *Sefer Tahara, Hilkhot Tumat Okhalin* 4:12).

Half an olive-bulk is not effective, etc. – אֵין חֲצִי זַיִת מוֹעִיל וכו׳: If one intends to burn or partake of half an olive-bulk of an offering outside its area and an olive-bulk beyond its time, the offering is rendered *piggul*, no matter whether the intention with regard to the olive-bulk preceded or followed the intention with regard to the half olive-bulk, because the half an olive-bulk is given no weight to interfere with a whole olive-bulk (Rambam *Sefer Avoda, Hilkhot Pesulei HaMukdashin* 16:3).

Half of it, etc. – חֶצְיוֹ וכו׳: If one intended to consume half an olive-bulk beyond its designated time, and then intended with regard to a whole olive-bulk to consume half of it beyond its designated time and half outside its designated area, the offering is rendered *piggul*, in accordance with the statement of Rav Ashi (Rambam *Sefer Avoda, Hilkhot Pesulei HaMukdashin* 16:4).

NOTES

And the dogs shall eat Jezebel – וְאֶת אִיזֶבֶל יֹאכְלוּ הַכְּלָבִים: *Tosafot* suggest that although consumption of certain foods by animals is certainly considered eating, the verse proves this with regard to the consumption of meat specifically.

If one expressed it in terms of consumption – אִי דְּאַפְּקָהּ בִּלְשׁוֹן אֲכִילָה: This is a source for the claim of certain early commentaries that intention of *piggul* must be expressed verbally (see 2a) to be effective.

HALAKHA

If one expressed it in terms of consumption – אִי דְּאַפְּקָהּ בִּלְשׁוֹן אֲכִילָה: If one intended to eat half an olive-bulk beyond the time designated for eating and to burn half an olive-bulk beyond the time designated for burning on the altar, the offering remains fit, because eating and burning to not join together. If he expressed both intentions in the language of consumption, saying that he will consume half an olive-bulk and the fire will consume half an olive-bulk beyond its designated time, these two intentions join together, because the language of consumption is one. Likewise, if one intended that he eat half an olive-bulk and that an animal eat half an olive-bulk beyond its designated time, these intentions join together, because the language is the same, in accordance with the statement of Rabbi Yannai and the Gemara here (Rambam *Sefer Avoda, Hilkhot Pesulei HaMukdashin* 14:10).

אָמַר רַבִּי יַנַּאי: חִישֵּׁב שֶׁיֹּאכְלוּהוּ כְּלָבִים לְמָחָר – פִּיגּוּל, דִּכְתִיב: ״וְאֶת אִיזֶבֶל יֹאכְלוּ הַכְּלָבִים בְּחֵלֶק יִזְרְעֶאל״.

§ **Rabbi Yannai says:** If one **had intent that dogs would eat** the offering **the next day,** it is rendered ***piggul*, as it is written: "And the dogs shall eat Jezebel**[N] **in the portion of Jezreel"** (II Kings 9:10). The verse indicates that consumption by dogs is considered eating.

מַתְקִיף לַהּ רַבִּי אַמִי: אֶלָּא מֵעַתָּה, חִישֵּׁב שֶׁתֹּאכְלֵהוּ אֵשׁ לְמָחָר, דִּכְתִיב: ״תְּאָכְלֵהוּ אֵשׁ לֹא נֻפָּח״, הָכִי נַמִי דְּפִיגּוּל? וְכִי תֵּימָא הָכִי נַמִי – וְהָתְנַן: לֶאֱכוֹל כַּחֲצִי זַיִת וּלְהַקְטִיר חֲצִי כַּזַּיִת – כָּשֵׁר, שֶׁאֵין אֲכִילָה וְהַקְטָרָה מִצְטָרְפִין!

Rabbi Ami objects to this: If that is so, then if one **had intent that** non-sacred **fire would consume it the next day, as it is written: "A fire not blown shall consume him"** (Job 20:26), **this too** should be ***piggul*. And if you would say** that this is **indeed** so, that is difficult: **But didn't we learn** in the mishna: If his intent was **to eat half an olive-bulk and to burn half an olive-bulk** not at the appropriate time or in the appropriate area, the offering is **fit because eating and burning do not join together?**

אִי דְּאַפְּקָהּ בִּלְשׁוֹן אֲכִילָה – הָכִי נַמִי, הָכָא בְּמַאי עָסְקִינַן – דְּאַפְּקָהּ בִּלְשׁוֹן הַקְטָרָה, דִּלְשׁוֹן אֲכִילָה לְחוּד וּלְשׁוֹן הַקְטָרָה לְחוּד.

The Gemara responds: **If one expressed** his intention to burn the offering **in terms of consumption,**[NH] it would **indeed** join together with intention to eat. But in the mishna **here we are dealing with a case where he expressed it in terms of burning.** The two intentions do not join together **since terms of consumption and terms of burning are discrete** entities.

בָּעֵי רַב אַשִׁי: חִישֵּׁב לֶאֱכוֹל כַּזַּיִת בִּשְׁנֵי בְנֵי אָדָם, מַהוּ? בָּתַר מַחֲשָׁבָה אָזְלִינַן דְּאִיכָּא שִׁיעוּרָא, אוֹ בָּתַר אוֹכְלִין אָזְלִינַן וְלֵיכָּא שִׁיעוּרָא?

§ **Rav Ashi raises a dilemma:** If one **had intent that** two people would collectively **eat an olive-bulk, what is the** *halakha*? **Do we follow the intent,** in which case **there is** the requisite **measure** of an olive-bulk? **Or do we follow those who eat, and neither** eats the requisite **measure?**

אֲמַר אַבַּיֵי, תָּא שְׁמַע: לֶאֱכוֹל כַּחֲצִי זַיִת וּלְהַקְטִיר כַּחֲצִי זַיִת – כָּשֵׁר, שֶׁאֵין אֲכִילָה וְהַקְטָרָה מִצְטָרְפִין;

Abaye said: Come and **hear** a proof from the mishna: If his intent was **to eat half an olive-bulk and to burn half an olive-bulk** beyond the designated time or outside the designated area, the offering is **fit because eating and burning do not join together.**

Perek **II**
Daf **31** Amud **b**

HALAKHA

With two people the halves join together – בִּשְׁנֵי בְנֵי אָדָם מִצְטָרֵף: If one intended for two people to eat one olive-bulk together, the intentions with regard to the two halves of the olive-bulk join together, as Abaye infers from the mishna (Rambam *Sefer Avoda, Hilkhot Pesulei HaMukdashin* 14:10).

The time it takes to eat a half-loaf of bread – כְּדֵי אֲכִילַת פְּרָס: If one intended to eat an olive-bulk in more than the time it takes to eat a half-loaf of bread, the intention renders the offering *piggul*, in accordance with the opinion of Abaye (Rambam *Sefer Avoda, Hilkhot Pesulei HaMukdashin* 14:10, and see *Kesef Mishna* there).

BACKGROUND

The time it takes to eat a half-loaf of bread – כְּדֵי אֲכִילַת פְּרָס: Throughout the Torah, whether with regard to prohibitions against eating, e.g., during fasts, or obligations to eat, e.g., *matza* on Passover, the obligation is fulfilled or the prohibition is transgressed only if the requisite volume is eaten within the time it takes to eat a half-loaf of bread. A half-loaf of bread is equal to three or four egg-bulks, and it was calculated according to the loaves of bread baked in talmudic times to suffice for two meals. This measure is learned as a *halakha* transmitted to Moses from Sinai. Elsewhere, the Talmud specifies that this is the amount of time it takes to eat a loaf made from wheat, as opposed to barley, while reclining and eating it with a condiment, which takes less time than it would to eat it dry.

הָא לֶאֱכוֹל וְלֶאֱכוֹל דּוּמְיָא דְּלֶאֱכוֹל וּלְהַקְטִיר, וְהֵיכִי דָּמֵי – בִּשְׁנֵי בְנֵי אָדָם – מִצְטָרֵף, שְׁמַע מִינָּהּ.

It can be inferred **that** if one had intent **to eat and to eat** in a manner **similar to** a case of intent **to eat** half an olive-bulk **and to burn** half an olive-bulk; Abaye interjects: **And what are the circumstances** of such a case? It is a case **with two people,** i.e., where each one will consume half an olive-bulk. Abaye continues with the conclusion of his statement: Then the two halves **join together.**[H] The Gemara concludes: **Learn from it** that this is so.

בָּעֵי רָבָא: חִישֵּׁב לֶאֱכוֹל כַּזַּיִת בְּיָתֵר מִכְּדֵי אֲכִילַת פְּרָס, מַהוּ? לַאֲכִילַת גָּבוֹהַּ מְדַמִּינַן לֵיהּ, אוֹ לַאֲכִילַת הֶדְיוֹט מְדַמִּינַן לֵיהּ?

Rava raises a dilemma: If one **had intent to eat an olive-bulk in more than** the period of time it takes **to eat a half-loaf** of bread,[HB] **what is the** *halakha*? **Do we equate** the consumption of offerings **to the consumption of the Most High,** i.e., the burning of offerings on the altar, for which there is no maximum allotted time? **Or do we equate it to the consumption of an ordinary** person, for whom consumption slower than this rate is not considered eating?

אֲמַר אַבַּיֵי, תָּא שְׁמַע: לֶאֱכוֹל כַּחֲצִי זַיִת וּלְהַקְטִיר כַּחֲצִי זַיִת – כָּשֵׁר, שֶׁאֵין אֲכִילָה וְהַקְטָרָה מִצְטָרְפִין. טַעְמָא דְּלֶאֱכוֹל וּלְהַקְטִיר, הָא לֶאֱכוֹל וְלֶאֱכוֹל – מִצְטָרֵף; וְהָא הַקְטָרָה בְּיוֹתֵר מִכְּדֵי אֲכִילַת פְּרָס הוּא!

Abaye said: Come and **hear** a proof from the mishna: If his intent was **to eat half an olive-bulk and to burn half an olive-bulk** not at the appropriate time or in the appropriate area, the offering is **fit because eating and burning do not join together.** One may infer that the **reason** the offering is fit is that he had intent **to eat and to burn** the offering. **But** if he had intent **to eat** half an olive-bulk at the normal rate **and to eat** half an olive-bulk in the time it takes to burn half an olive-bulk, the two would **join together. But** the **burning** of an olive-bulk of an offering can take **more than** the time it takes **to eat a half-loaf** of bread. It therefore seems that there is no upper limit on the time in which one is considered to have consumed an offering.

דִּלְמָא בְּהֶיסֵּק גָּדוֹל.

The Gemara rejects the proof: **Perhaps** the mishna is referring to intent to burn half an olive-bulk **in a large fire,** which can consume it in the time it takes to eat a half-loaf of bread. Accordingly, one may draw the inference only with regard to a case where his intent was to consume the halves of an olive-bulk within this time.

״לֶאֱכוֹל כַּחֲצִי זַיִת וּלְהַקְטִיר כַּחֲצִי זַיִת – כָּשֵׁר״. טַעְמָא דְּלֶאֱכוֹל וּלְהַקְטִיר, הָא לֶאֱכוֹל וְלֶאֱכוֹל דָּבָר שֶׁאֵין דַּרְכּוֹ לֶאֱכוֹל – מִצְטָרֵף.

§ The mishna teaches: If one slaughtered the animal with intent **to eat half an olive-bulk and to burn half an olive-bulk** not at the appropriate time or in the appropriate area, the offering is **fit.** The Gemara infers: The **reason that** the two halves of an olive-bulk do not join together is because his intent was **to eat** half an olive-bulk **and to burn** half an olive-bulk. **But** if his intent was **to eat** half an olive-bulk of the meat **and to eat** half an olive-bulk of **an item whose** typical **manner** is such that one does **not partake** of it, then the halves do **join together** and disqualify the offering, as both intentions concern eating.

הָא קָתָנֵי רֵישָׁא: לֶאֱכוֹל אֶת שֶׁדַּרְכּוֹ לֶאֱכוֹל (מִצְטָרֵף); אֶת שֶׁדַּרְכּוֹ לֶאֱכוֹל – אִין, שֶׁאֵין דַּרְכּוֹ – לָא!

The Gemara notes an apparent contradiction: **But the first clause** of the mishna **teaches:** If one's intent was **to partake** of an item **whose** typical **manner** is such that one **partakes** of it, beyond its designated time, his intent **joins together** to disqualify the offering. One can infer that only if his intent was to partake of an item **whose** typical **manner** is such that one **partakes** of it, **does** his intent join together, but if his intent was to partake of an item **whose** typical **manner** is such that one does **not** to partake of it, then it does **not** join together.

אָמַר רַבִּי יִרְמְיָה: הָא מַנִּי – רַבִּי אֱלִיעֶזֶר הִיא, דְּאָמַר: מְחַשְּׁבִין מֵאֲכִילַת אָדָם לַאֲכִילַת מִזְבֵּחַ וּמֵאֲכִילַת מִזְבֵּחַ לַאֲכִילַת אָדָם. דִּתְנַן: הַשּׁוֹחֵט אֶת הַזֶּבַח לֶאֱכוֹל דָּבָר שֶׁאֵין דַּרְכּוֹ לֶאֱכוֹל, וּלְהַקְטִיר דָּבָר שֶׁאֵין דַּרְכּוֹ לְהַקְטִיר – כָּשֵׁר, וְרַבִּי אֱלִיעֶזֶר פּוֹסֵל.

Rabbi Yirmeya says: In accordance with **whose** opinion **is this** latter clause? **It is** in accordance with the opinion of **Rabbi Eliezer, who says: One can have intent** to shift an item's consumption **from consumption by a person to consumption by** the **altar, or from consumption by** the **altar to consumption by a person. As we learned** in another mishna (35a): In the case of **one who slaughters the offering** with intent **to partake of an item whose** typical **manner** is such that one does **not** to partake of it, **or to burn an item whose** typical **manner** is such that one does **not burn** it on the altar, beyond its designated time or outside its designated area, the offering is **fit, and Rabbi Eliezer deems** it **unfit.**

אַבַּיֵּי אָמַר: אֲפִילּוּ תֵּימָא רַבָּנַן; וְלָא תֵּימָא: הָא לֶאֱכוֹל וְלֶאֱכוֹל דָּבָר שֶׁאֵין דַּרְכּוֹ לֶאֱכוֹל, אֶלָּא אֵימָא: הָא לֶאֱכוֹל וְלֶאֱכוֹל דָּבָר שֶׁדַּרְכּוֹ לֶאֱכוֹל.

Abaye says: You may **even say** that the latter clause is in accordance with the opinion of **the Rabbis. And do not say** that one should infer from the mishna **that** if his intent was **to eat** half an olive-bulk of an item normally consumed **and to eat** half an olive-bulk of **an item whose** typical **manner** is such that one does **not partake** of it, then the offering is disqualified. **Rather, say** that one infers **that** if his intent was **to eat** half an olive-bulk **and to eat** another half an olive-bulk, both halves from **an item whose** typical **manner** is such that one **partakes** of it, then the halves join together to disqualify the offering.

מַאי קָא מַשְׁמַע לָן? אִי דָּבָר שֶׁדַּרְכּוֹ לֶאֱכוֹל קָא מַשְׁמַע לָן – מֵרֵישָׁא שְׁמַע מִינָּהּ: כַּחֲצִי זַיִת בַּחוּץ כַּחֲצִי זַיִת לְמָחָר – פָּסוּל, הָא כַּחֲצִי זַיִת לְמָחָר – פִּיגּוּל!

The Gemara asks: If so, **what** is this latter clause **teaching us? If it teaches us** that two half olive-bulks from **an item whose** typical **manner** is such that one **partakes** of it, join together, one can already **learn** this **from the first clause** of the mishna: If one has intent to consume **half an olive-bulk outside** its designated area and **half an olive-bulk the next day,** the offering is **disqualified.** One can infer **that** if his intent was to eat the first **half an olive-bulk the next day,** the offering would be rendered ***piggul.***

אֶלָּא אִי לֶאֱכוֹל וּלְהַקְטִיר – מִדּוּקְיָא דְּרֵישָׁא שְׁמַע מִינָּהּ: לֶאֱכוֹל דָּבָר שֶׁדַּרְכּוֹ לֶאֱכוֹל – אִין, שֶׁאֵין דַּרְכּוֹ לֶאֱכוֹל – לָא;

But if one will say that this term teaches its literal meaning, that intentions **to eat and to burn** two halves of an olive-bulk do not join together, one can already **learn** this **from the inference** drawn above **from the first clause** of the mishna, namely that intent **to partake** of **an item whose** typical **manner** is such that one **partakes** of it **does** disqualify the offering, but intent to partake of an item **whose** typical **manner** is such that one does **not partake** of it does **not.** By extension, intent to consume half an olive-bulk of such an item does not join to disqualify the offering.

הַשְׁתָּא וּמָה לֶאֱכוֹל וְלֶאֱכוֹל דָּבָר שֶׁאֵין דַּרְכּוֹ לֶאֱכוֹל – לָא מִצְטָרֵף, לֶאֱכוֹל וּלְהַקְטִיר מִיבָּעֵי?

Now, consider the following: **And just as** if when one has intent **to partake** of an item normally eaten **and to partake of an item whose** typical **manner** is such that one does **not partake** of it, his intentions **do not join together,** even though both intentions concern consumption, **is it necessary** for the mishna to teach that intentions **to consume and to burn** do not join together? The last clause therefore seems unnecessary.

לֶאֱכוֹל וּלְהַקְטִיר אִיצְטְרִיךְ; סָלְקָא דַּעְתָּךְ אָמִינָא: הָתָם הוּא דְּלָאו כִּי אוֹרְחֵיהּ קָא מְחַשֵּׁב, אֲבָל הָכָא דִּבְהַאי כִּי אוֹרְחֵיהּ וּבְהַאי כִּי אוֹרְחֵיהּ – אֵימָא לִיצְטָרֵף, קָא מַשְׁמַע לַן.

The Gemara responds: It **was necessary** for the mishna to explicitly address the case where one had intent **to eat and to burn,** as it might **enter your mind to say** that it **is** only **there,** where one's intentions are referring solely to consumption, that they do not join together, **since he has intent** to act in a way that is **not** consistent with **its** typical **manner** and consume an item not normally consumed. **But here, where** his intent is to both eat and burn the offering, such that **with regard to this** half he intends to act **in** a way consistent with **its** typical **manner, and with regard to that** half he intends to act **in** a way consistent with **its** typical **manner,** one might **say** that **they should join together.** Therefore, the mishna **teaches us** that intentions to eat and to burn do not join together.

הדרן עלך כל הזבחים שקבלו דמן

Summary of **Perek II**

This chapter clarified the primary *halakhot* pertaining to the disqualification of offerings due to improper actions or unfit people. The chapter did not address the varying severity of these disqualifications, some of which carry the penalty of death at the hand of Heaven, others lashes, and some which carry no punishment at all. Unfit people may be those inherently unfit to perform the service, e.g., a non-priest, a blemished priest, and an uncircumcised priest. Alternatively, their lack of fitness may be contingent on a temporary circumstance, as in the case of an acute mourner, an impure priest, one for whom the sun has not yet set after his immersion, one who still lacks atonement after his immersion, one who has not washed his hands and feet, or one who drank wine. Still others may disqualify the offering by dint of their actions, e.g., one sitting, standing on anything other than the Temple floor, or performing a rite with his left hand. Through all such acts, the offering is disqualified, but mere intent to perform any of them does not in itself disqualify the offering.

The Gemara explained several *halakhot* concerning the priestly vestments, the Basin in the Temple, the water it contains, and the matter of washing from it. Its primary conclusions are that the Basin is considered a service vessel whose contents are disqualified by being left overnight, and that washing from it is in many ways similar to a sacrificial rite.

The second major topic covered in the chapter concerned intentions to consume an offering beyond its designated time and outside its designated area, both of which disqualify the offering, and the former of which renders it *piggul* as well. These intentions can arise at any point during the four sacrificial rites of the service, but both can refer only to the eating of an olive-bulk of meat, the sprinkling of sufficient blood to sprinkle, or the burning of an olive-bulk of the offering's sacrificial portions. Although improper intentions with regard to eating and burning the offering both disqualify it, they cannot join together to complete the requisite measure of an olive-bulk. Furthermore, an offering can be rendered *piggul* only if its service, aside from the intent of *piggul*, was performed properly. If there were additional improper intentions or actions, the offering is disqualified but it is not rendered *piggul*.

Introduction to **Perek III**

And he shall slaughter the bull before the Lord, and Aaron's sons, the priests, shall present the blood, and sprinkle the blood roundabout against the altar that is at the door of the Tent of Meeting.

(Leviticus 1:5)

This chapter supplements the preceding chapter. While the previous chapter discussed individuals whose performance of the sacrificial rites renders those rites not valid and intentions that disqualify offerings, this chapter examines the exceptions to those *halakhot*. This includes cases in which individuals unfit to perform the Temple service do not render the offering unfit with their service, as well as cases in which improper intent does not disqualify an offering.

Three primary topics are addressed in this chapter, the first of which is the slaughter of the offering. Although the slaughter of an offering is one of the indispensable sacrificial rites, it may be performed by non-priests. The chapter enumerates the *halakhot* that pertain to slaughter performed by an individual unfit to perform the other sacrificial rites, including the technicalities of its performance, especially with regard to a ritually impure individual for whom it is prohibited to enter the Temple courtyard to slaughter the offering.

The second issue that is explored is the status of the later sacrificial rites, associated with the blood, that were performed by an individual unfit for the Temple service. Such rites can occasionally be rectified and redone properly, thereby preventing the offering from being rendered not valid. The chapter will discuss the specifics of this *halakha*, what can be corrected, and what cannot be.

The third issue analyzed in the chapter is that of improper intent with regard to the place and time of the offering. Various questions are raised in this context: Do all intentions to sacrifice or partake of the offering beyond its designated time render the offering *piggul*? Likewise, do all intentions to sacrifice or partake of the offering outside its designated area render the offering not valid? The chapter also discusses the *halakha* in situations where one had intent to perform other aspects of the sacrificial rites improperly.

The clarification of these issues, the presentation of the various differing opinions, and the citation of their biblical sources are the main topics of this chapter.

מתני׳ כָּל הַפְּסוּלִין שֶׁשָּׁחֲטוּ – שְׁחִיטָתָן כְּשֵׁרָה. שֶׁהַשְּׁחִיטָה כְּשֵׁרָה בְּזָרִים, וּבְנָשִׁים, וּבַעֲבָדִים, וּבִטְמֵאִים, וַאֲפִילּוּ בְּקָדְשֵׁי קָדָשִׁים, וּבִלְבַד שֶׁלֹּא יִהְיוּ טְמֵאִים נוֹגְעִין בַּבָּשָׂר. לְפִיכָךְ הֵן פּוֹסְלִין בְּמַחֲשָׁבָה.

MISHNA With regard to **all** those **who are unfit** for Temple service **who slaughtered**[H] an offering, **their slaughter is valid, as the slaughter** of an offering **is valid** *ab initio* when performed even **by non-priests, by women, by** Canaanite **slaves,**[B] **and by ritually impure** individuals. **And** this is the *halakha* **even with** regard to **offerings of the most sacred order, provided that the ritually impure will not touch the flesh** of the slaughtered animal, thereby rendering it impure. **Therefore,** these unfit individuals can **disqualify**[N] the offering **with** prohibited **intent,**[H] e.g., if one of them intended to partake of the offering beyond its designated time or outside its designated area.

HALAKHA

All those who are unfit who slaughtered – **כָּל הַפְּסוּלִים שֶׁשָּׁחֲטוּ:** Those who are unfit to perform the Temple service are permitted to slaughter offerings *ab initio*, even offerings of the most sacred order, except for a ritually impure individual; he may not perform the sacrificial rite of slaughter *ab initio*, lest he touch the flesh of the animal and render it ritually impure. If he did slaughter it and he did not render it ritually impure, the slaughter is valid (Rambam *Sefer Avoda, Hilkhot Pesulei HaMukdashin* 1:1).

Therefore they disqualify the offering with prohibited intent – **לְפִיכָךְ פּוֹסְלִים בְּמַחֲשָׁבָה:** If the individual who is unfit for performing the Temple service had a prohibited intention at the time of the slaughter, e.g., if he had intent to partake of the offering beyond its designated time or outside its designated area, or with regard to a sin offering or a Paschal offering, if it was sacrificed not for the sake of the offering or its owner, the offering is disqualified due to his intent, since the sacrificial rite of slaughter is valid when performed by those unfit for Temple service (Rambam *Sefer Avoda, Hilkhot Pesulei HaMukdashin* 14:2).

BACKGROUND

Canaanite slave – **עֶבֶד כְּנַעֲנִי:** A Canaanite slave is a gentile slave purchased by a Jew (see Leviticus 25:44–46). Such a slave must be immersed in a ritual bath and, if male, circumcised. These acts effect a change in the slave's status. Though not yet a Jew in all respects, a Canaanite slave must observe all of the Torah's prohibitions and must fulfill all positive mitzvot that are not dependent on a specific time for their performance. In many respects Canaanite slaves are their masters' property and may be sold and purchased like other possessions. A Canaanite slave's master can free him by giving him a bill of manumission, a document resembling a bill of divorce in its format, but there is a positive mitzva not to free a Canaanite slave without compelling reasons. A slave is automatically emancipated if his master blinds him, knocks out his tooth, or destroys any one of twenty-four extremities. This applies regardless of whether or not the master caused the damage intentionally (see Exodus 21:26–27).

NOTES

Therefore these unfit individuals disqualify – **לְפִיכָךְ הֵן פּוֹסְלִין:** Just as only a priest can disqualify an offering with prohibited intent during a sacrificial rite that is limited to performance by priests, as will be explained later in the mishna with regard to the sacrificial rite of blood collection, so too, anyone who is fit to perform the sacrificial rite of slaughter can disqualify the offering with prohibited intent during the slaughter.

וְכוּלָּן שֶׁקִּיבְּלוּ אֶת הַדָּם חוּץ לִזְמַנּוֹ וְחוּץ לִמְקוֹמוֹ, אִם יֵשׁ דַּם הַנֶּפֶשׁ – יַחֲזוֹר הַכָּשֵׁר וִיקַבֵּל.

And with regard to **all of them,** in a case **where they collected the blood**[H] with the intent to offer it **beyond its** designated **time**[N] **or outside its** designated **area, if there is blood of the soul** that remains in the animal, **the** priest **fit** for Temple service **should again collect** the blood and sprinkle it on the altar.

קִיבֵּל הַכָּשֵׁר וְנָתַן לַפָּסוּל – יַחֲזִיר לַכָּשֵׁר. קִיבֵּל בִּימִינוֹ וְנָתַן לִשְׂמֹאלוֹ – יַחֲזִיר לִימִינוֹ. קִיבֵּל בִּכְלִי קֹדֶשׁ וְנָתַן לִכְלִי חוֹל – יַחֲזִיר לִכְלִי קֹדֶשׁ. נִשְׁפַּךְ מִן הַכְּלִי עַל הָרִצְפָּה וַאֲסָפוֹ – כָּשֵׁר.

If **the** priest **fit** for Temple service **collected** the blood in a vessel **and gave** the vessel **to an unfit** person,[H] that person **should return** it **to the fit** priest. If the priest **collected** the blood in a vessel **in his right** hand **and moved** it **to his left** hand,[HN] **he should return** it **to his right** hand. If the priest **collected** the blood **in a sacred vessel**[N] **and placed it in a non-sacred vessel, he should return** the blood **to a sacred vessel.** If the blood **spilled from the vessel**[H] **onto the floor and he gathered it**[N] from the floor, it is **valid.**

נְתָנוֹ עַל גַּבֵּי הַכֶּבֶשׁ שֶׁלֹּא כְּנֶגֶד הַיְסוֹד, נָתַן אֶת הַנִּיתָּנִין לְמַטָּה לְמַעְלָן, וְאֶת הַנִּיתָּנִין לְמַעְלָן לְמַטָּה, וְאֶת הַנִּיתָּנִין בִּפְנִים בַּחוּץ, וְאֶת הַנִּיתָּנִין בַּחוּץ בִּפְנִים, אִם יֵשׁ דַּם הַנֶּפֶשׁ – יַחֲזוֹר הַכָּשֵׁר וִיקַבֵּל.

If an unfit person **placed** the blood **upon the ramp**[H] or on the wall of the altar **that is not opposite the base** of the altar, or if **he placed** the blood **that is** to be **placed below** the red line **above** the red line, **or** if he placed the blood **that is** to be **placed above** the red line **below** the red line, **or** if he placed the blood **that is** to be **placed inside** the Sanctuary **outside** the Sanctuary **or the** blood **that is** to be **placed outside** the Sanctuary **inside** the Sanctuary, then **if there is blood of the soul** that remains in the animal, **the** priest **fit** for Temple service **should again collect** the blood and sprinkle it on the altar.

גמ׳ ״שָׁחֲטוּ״, דִּיעֲבַד – אִין, לְכַתְּחִלָּה – לָא.

GEMARA The Gemara infers from the use of the past tense in the mishna: With regard to all those who are unfit for Temple service who **slaughtered,** that **after the fact, yes,** the slaughter is valid. But ***ab initio*, no,** those who are unfit may not slaughter an offering.

וּרְמִינְהוּ: ״וְשָׁחַט״ – שְׁחִיטָה בְּזָר כְּשֵׁרָה, שֶׁהַשְּׁחִיטָה כְּשֵׁרָה בְּזָרִים וּבְנָשִׁים וּבַעֲבָדִים וּבִטְמֵאִים, וַאֲפִילּוּ בְּקָדְשֵׁי קָדָשִׁים. אוֹ אֵינוֹ אֶלָּא בְּכֹהֲנִים?

And the Gemara **raises a contradiction** from what was taught in the halakhic midrash *Torat Kohanim*: The verse states with regard to a burnt offering: **"And he shall slaughter** the bull before the Lord" (Leviticus 1:5). The fact that the verse does not stipulate that a priest must slaughter the offering teaches that **slaughter is valid** if performed **by a non-priest,** as stated in the mishna: **As the** sacrificial rite of **slaughter is valid** when performed **by non-priests, by women, by** Canaanite **slaves, and by ritually impure** individuals, **and even with** regard to **offerings of the most sacred order. Or** perhaps the term "and he shall slaughter" in the verse is referring **only** to slaughter **by priests?**

HALAKHA

And with regard to all of them, where they collected the blood, etc. – וכולן שקיבלו את הדם וכו׳: Improper intent disqualifies an offering only if the rite is performed by someone who is fit to perform the Temple service. Consequently, if someone who is unfit for Temple service collected the blood and had the intent while performing the sacrificial rite to partake of the offering beyond its designated time or outside its designated area, he does not disqualify the offering with his intent, and the blood that he collected should be poured into the Temple courtyard drain. If blood of the soul remains, a priest fit for Temple service should collect it with the proper intent (Rambam *Sefer Avoda, Hilkhot Pesulei HaMukdashin* 14:2).

If the priest fit for Temple service collected the blood and gave it to an unfit person – קיבל הכשר ונתן לפסול: If a priest fit for Temple service collected the blood, and he gave it to an individual unfit for Temple service, and that individual did not walk with the blood, he should return it to the priest fit for Temple service, in accordance with the ruling of the mishna (Rambam *Sefer Avoda, Hilkhot Pesulei HaMukdashin* 1:27).

If he collected the blood in a vessel in his right hand and he moved it to his left hand – קיבל בימינו ונתן לשמאלו: If the priest collected the blood in his right hand and then transferred it into his left hand, he should return it to his right hand. If he collected the blood in a sacred vessel and placed it in a non-sacred vessel, he should return the blood to a sacred vessel, in accordance with the ruling of the mishna (Rambam *Sefer Avoda, Hilkhot Pesulei HaMukdashin* 1:24).

If the blood spilled from the vessel – נשפך מן הכלי: If the blood was collected in a vessel and then spilled from the vessel onto the floor, and it was gathered from the floor, it is valid. But if the blood spilled from the neck of the animal onto the floor, and it was gathered from the floor, even if the priest placed it into a sacred vessel the offering is disqualified, in accordance with the ruling of the mishna (Rambam *Sefer Avoda, Hilkhot Pesulei HaMukdashin* 1:25).

If he placed the blood upon the ramp – נתנו על גבי הכבש: If an individual unfit for Temple service placed the blood that is meant to be placed above the red line below the red line, or he placed the blood that is meant to be placed outside the Sanctuary inside the Sanctuary, or he placed the blood upon the ramp or on the wall of the altar that is not opposite the foundation of the altar, if there remains in the animal blood of the soul, the flesh of the offering has not been disqualified, and a priest fit for Temple service should place the blood properly (Rambam *Sefer Avoda, Hilkhot Pesulei HaMukdashin* 2:10).

NOTES

And with regard to all of them, where they collected the blood with the intent to offer it beyond its time, etc. – וכולן שקיבלו את הדם חוץ לזמנו וכו׳: Even if one who is not fit for Temple service collected the blood with the proper intent, the *halakha* is that if the blood of the soul remains in the animal the priest fit for Temple service should again collect the blood and place it on the altar. This is because if the individual is not fit for Temple service, the sacrificial rite of collecting the blood is not considered to have been performed. The reason this *halakha* was expressed in the scenario of improper intent is to teach that the improper intent of these individuals does not disqualify the offering, since the rite is not considered to have been performed in an improper manner, but rather to not have been performed at all.

If he collected the blood in his right hand and moved it to his left hand – קיבל בימינו ונתן לשמאלו: Had the priest collected the blood in his left hand, it would be disqualified, as taught in the previous chapter (15b). Although the priest is now holding the vessel in his left hand, and he must bring the blood to the altar and place it with his right hand (see 24a), merely holding the vessel in his left hand does not disqualify it. Therefore, he may return it to his right hand and continue performing the sacrificial rites.

If the priest collected the blood in a sacred vessel – קיבל בכלי קדש: Had the priest collected the blood in a non-sacred vessel, the blood would be disqualified (see *Tosefta* 1:5 and 97b).

If the blood spilled from the vessel…and he gathered it – נשפך מן הכלי...ואספו: It was taught in an earlier mishna (25a) that if the blood spilled from the neck of the animal onto the floor, the blood is disqualified.

אָמְרַתְּ: וְכִי מֵאַיִן בָּאתָה – מִכְּלָל שֶׁנֶּאֱמַר: "וְאַתָּה וּבָנֶיךָ אִתְּךָ תִּשְׁמְרוּ אֶת כְּהֻנַּתְכֶם לְכָל דְּבַר הַמִּזְבֵּחַ",

You can say in response: **From where did you come** to the idea that the verse is referring only to a priest? It is **from the fact that it is stated** to Aaron: **"And you and your sons with you shall keep your priesthood in everything that pertains to the altar"** (Numbers 18:7).

יָכוֹל אַף בִּשְׁחִיטָה? תַּלְמוּד לוֹמַר: "וְשָׁחַט אֶת בֶּן הַבָּקָר לִפְנֵי ה' וְהִקְרִיבוּ" וגו' – מִקַּבָּלָה וְאֵילָךְ מִצְוַת כְּהוּנָּה, לִימֵּד עַל הַשְּׁחִיטָה שֶׁכְּשֵׁרָה בְּכׇל אָדָם!

One **might** have thought that this is the *halakha* **even with** regard to **slaughter,** that only priests are fit to slaughter an offering. Therefore, **the verse states: "And he shall slaughter the bull before the Lord, and** Aaron's sons, the priests, **shall present** [***vehikrivu***] the blood" (Leviticus 1:5), from which it is inferred that specifically **from** the **collection** of the blood **and onward** it is **a mitzva** exclusively **of the priesthood.**[N] This **teaches about the** rite of **slaughter that it is valid** *ab initio* if performed **by any person.** This contradicts the inference from the mishna that slaughter of an offering by a non-priest is valid only after the fact.

הוּא הַדִּין דַּאֲפִילּוּ לְכַתְּחִילָּה נָמֵי, וּמִשּׁוּם דְּקָא בָּעֵי לְמִיתְנָא טְמֵאִים דִּלְכַתְּחִילָּה לָא, גְּזֵירָה שֶׁמָּא יִגְּעוּ בַּבָּשָׂר – תְּנָא: "שֶׁשָּׁחֲטוּ".

The Gemara answers: **The same is true that even** ***ab initio*** **as well**[H] it is permitted for those unfit for Temple service to slaughter an offering, **but because** the mishna **wants to teach** with regard to the **ritually impure that** they may **not** slaughter an offering *ab initio* due to a rabbinic **decree lest they touch the flesh** and render it ritually impure, therefore the mishna **taught** this *halakha* with the expression in the past tense: **Who slaughtered,** i.e., after the fact.

וְטָמֵא דִּיעֲבַד שַׁפִּיר דָּמֵי? וּרְמִינְהוּ: "וְסָמַךְ... וְשָׁחַט" מָה סְמִיכָה בִּטְהוֹרִים – אַף שְׁחִיטָה בִּטְהוֹרִים! מִדְּרַבָּנַן.

The Gemara asks: **And** in the case of **a ritually impure** individual who performed the slaughter, is it **permitted** even **after the fact? And** one can **raise a contradiction** from what is taught in the halakhic midrash: The Torah states two consecutive directives: **"And he shall place** his hand upon the head of the burnt offering… **And he shall slaughter** the bull before the Lord" (Leviticus 1:4–5). This juxtaposition indicates that both directives are referring to the same individual, which teaches that **just as placing hands** on the head of an offering may be performed only **by ritually pure** individuals, **so too,** the **slaughter** may be performed only **by ritually pure** individuals. The Gemara answers: **By rabbinic law,** an impure person is prohibited from slaughtering an offering lest he touch the flesh of the offering, but by Torah law the slaughter is valid.

מַאי שְׁנָא סְמִיכָה – דִּכְתִיב: "לִפְנֵי ה'", שְׁחִיטָה נָמֵי – הָכְתִיב: "לִפְנֵי ה'"! אֶפְשָׁר דַּעֲבֵיד סַכִּין אֲרוּכָּה וְשָׁחֵיט.

The Gemara asks: **What is different** about **placing hands** that it can be performed only by those who are ritually pure even by Torah law? It is **that it is written: "Before the Lord,"**[NH] which is referring to the Temple courtyard, and an impure person may not enter the Temple courtyard. With regard to **slaughter as well, isn't it written: "Before the Lord"** (Leviticus 1:5)? How can a ritually impure person enter the Temple courtyard to slaughter an offering? The Gemara answers: It is **possible,** in a case **where he fashions a long knife,** stands outside the Temple courtyard, **and slaughters** the offering that is inside the courtyard.

סְמִיכָה נָמֵי, אֶפְשָׁר דִּמְעַיֵּיל יְדֵיהּ וְסָמֵיךְ! קָסָבַר: בִּיאָה בְּמִקְצָת שְׁמָהּ בִּיאָה.

The Gemara asks: With regard to **placing hands also, it is possible,** in a case **where he inserts his hands** into the Temple courtyard **and places** them on the head of the offering. The Gemara answers: The *tanna* **holds** that **a partial entry,** in which only a part of the body enters the Temple courtyard, **is called entry.** Therefore, an impure individual may not insert even part of his body, such as his hands, into the Temple courtyard.

רַב חִסְדָּא מַתְנֵי אִיפְּכָא: "וְסָמַךְ... וְשָׁחַט", מָה שְׁחִיטָה בִּטְהוֹרִין – אַף סְמִיכָה בִּטְהוֹרִין. מַאי שְׁנָא שְׁחִיטָה – דִּכְתִיב: "לִפְנֵי ה'",

Rav Ḥisda taught the *baraita* in the **opposite** manner: **"And he shall place** his hand upon the head of the burnt offering… **and he shall slaughter** the bull" (Leviticus 1:4–5), teaches that **just as slaughter** may be performed only **by ritually pure** individuals, **so too, placing hands** may be performed only **by ritually pure** individuals.[H] The Gemara asks: **What is different** about **slaughter** that it may be performed only by those who are ritually pure? It is **that it is written** with regard to it: **"Before the Lord,"** which refers to the Temple courtyard, and a ritually impure person may not enter the Temple courtyard.

NOTES

From the collection of the blood and onward it is a mitzva of the priesthood – מִקַּבָּלָה וְאֵילָךְ מִצְוַת כְּהוּנָּה: Although the term *vehikrivu*, meaning: "And they shall present," does not literally mean collecting blood, nevertheless, it is referring to the subsequent sacrificial rite following the slaughter, which is collecting the blood. The verse used an expression of presenting the blood to indicate that conveying the blood to the altar is included in the rite of collecting it, and they therefore share the same *halakhot* (see 4a). Alternatively, it can be explained that the term *vehikrivu* means to turn the blood into an offering [*korban*]. This includes collecting the blood, carrying it to the altar, and presenting it on the altar (Ramban).

About placing hands that it is written: Before the Lord – סְמִיכָה דִּכְתִיב לִפְנֵי ה': The only place where it states explicitly "before the Lord" with regard to placing hands on the head of an offering is with regard to a bull sacrificed for an unwitting communal sin, where the verse states: "And the elders of the congregation shall lay their hands upon the head of the bull before the Lord" (Leviticus 4:15). Considering that this offering, which is one of the sin offerings that is sacrificed upon the inner altar, has a special stringency, the *halakha* cannot be derived from it to other offerings (see *Tosafot*). Rashi explains that the source of this *halakha* is from the verse cited with regard to a burnt offering: "And he shall slaughter the bull before the Lord" (Leviticus 1:5). Since the slaughter must immediately follow the placing of the hands, if the slaughter must be performed in the Temple courtyard, then the placing of the hands must also be done there. In the *Torat Kohanim*, the source cited for this *halakha* is the verse: "He shall sacrifice it, that he may be accepted, before the Lord, and he shall lay his hand upon the head of the burnt offering" (Leviticus 1:3–4), which indicates that the placing of the hands is performed in the same location as the slaughter, i.e., it is performed "before the Lord."

HALAKHA

Even *ab initio* as well – אֲפִילּוּ לְכַתְּחִילָּה נָמֵי: All those who are unfit for Temple service are permitted to slaughter offerings *ab initio*, even offerings of the most sacred order. A ritually impure individual may not perform the sacrificial rite of slaughter *ab initio* even if he stands outside the Temple courtyard and extends his hand inside to slaughter, as a precaution lest he touch the flesh of the animal and render it ritually impure, in accordance with the conclusion of the Gemara (Rambam *Sefer Avoda, Hilkhot Pesulei HaMukdashin* 1:1).

Placing hands…before the Lord – סְמִיכָה...לִפְנֵי ה': Placing hands on the head of an offering must be performed in the Temple courtyard, and if it was done outside the Temple courtyard, it must be performed again inside (Rambam *Sefer Avoda, Hilkhot Ma'aseh HaKorbanot* 3:11).

Placing hands by ritually pure individuals – סְמִיכָה בִּטְהוֹרִין: Only a ritually pure individual may perform the placing of hands on the head of an offering. If a ritually impure individual did so, it is valid after the fact. The *Leḥem Mishne* explains that since according to the opinion of the Rambam, partial entry into the Temple courtyard is not called an entry, although an impure individual may not perform the placing of the hands in the Temple courtyard *ab initio* lest he come to enter the courtyard entirely, if he did place his hands, it is a valid placing of the hands (Rambam *Sefer Avoda, Hilkhot Ma'aseh HaKorbanot* 3:11, and see *Sefer Korbanot, Hilkhot Meḥusrei Kappara* 4:2).

סְמִיכָה נַמִּי כְּתִיב: ״לִפְנֵי ה׳״! אֶפְשָׁר דִּמְעַיֵּיל יְדֵיהּ וְסָמֵיךְ. שְׁחִיטָה נַמִּי, אֶפְשָׁר דְּעָבֵיד סַכִּין אֲרוּכָּה וְשָׁחֵיט!

With regard to **placing hands** on the head of an offering **as well, it is written: "Before the Lord."** The Gemara answers that **it is possible,** in a case **where he inserts his hands** into the Temple courtyard **and places them**[N] on the head of the offering while he remains outside. The Gemara asks: But with regard to **slaughter also,** it is **possible,** in a case **where he fashions a long knife and slaughters** the animal while standing outside the Temple courtyard.

הָא מַנִּי – שִׁמְעוֹן הַתִּימְנִי הִיא. דְּתַנְיָא: ״וְשָׁחַט אֶת בֶּן הַבָּקָר לִפְנֵי ה׳״ – וְלֹא הַשּׁוֹחֵט לִפְנֵי ה׳. שִׁמְעוֹן הַתִּימְנִי אוֹמֵר: מִנַּיִן שֶׁיִּהְיוּ יָדָיו שֶׁל שׁוֹחֵט לִפְנִים מִן הַנִּשְׁחָט – תַּלְמוּד לוֹמַר: ״וְשָׁחַט אֶת בֶּן הַבָּקָר לִפְנֵי ה׳״, שׁוֹחֵט אֶת בֶּן הַבָּקָר יְהֵא לִפְנֵי ה׳.

The Gemara answers: In accordance with **whose** opinion **is this? It is** in accordance with the opinion of **Shimon HaTimni,** who holds that the one who slaughters an offering must stand inside the Temple courtyard. This is **as it is taught** in a *baraita*, that when the verse states: **"And he shall slaughter the bull before the Lord"** (Leviticus 1:5),[H] it teaches that the bull must be inside the Temple courtyard, **but the slaughterer** need **not** be **"before the Lord."** Therefore, he may stand outside the Temple courtyard and slaughter the offering that is inside. **Shimon HaTimni says: From where** is it derived **that the hands of** the **slaughterer must be** farther **inside** the Temple courtyard **than the** animal that is **slaughtered? The verse states: "And he shall slaughter the bull before the Lord,"** which teaches that the **slaughterer of the bull must be before the Lord.**[N]

אָמַר עוּלָּא אָמַר רֵישׁ לָקִישׁ: טָמֵא שֶׁהִכְנִיס יָדוֹ לִפְנִים – לוֹקֶה, שֶׁנֶּאֱמַר: ״בְּכָל קֹדֶשׁ לֹא תִגָּע״ וגו׳, מַקִּישׁ בִּיאָה לִנְגִיעָה, מַה נְּגִיעָה בְּמִקְצָת שְׁמָהּ נְגִיעָה, אַף בִּיאָה בְּמִקְצָת שְׁמָהּ בִּיאָה.

§ Apropos the question of whether partial entry into the Temple courtyard is considered entry, **Ulla says** that **Reish Lakish says: A ritually impure** individual **who inserted his hand inside**[H] the Temple courtyard **is flogged** for transgressing the prohibition of entering the Temple while impure, **as it is stated** with regard to the impurity of a woman who gave birth: **"Every consecrated item she shall not touch,** and to the Temple she shall not come, until the days of her purification are complete" (Leviticus 12:4). The verse **juxtaposes entry** into the courtyard **to touching** a sacred item. **Just as touching with** even **a part** of the body **is considered touching, so too, entry with part** of the body **is considered entry.**

אֵיתִיבֵיהּ רַב הוֹשַׁעְיָא לְעוּלָּא: מְצוֹרָע שֶׁחָל שְׁמִינִי שֶׁלּוֹ לִהְיוֹת בְּעֶרֶב הַפֶּסַח, וְרָאָה קֶרִי בּוֹ בַּיּוֹם וְטָבַל,

Rav Hoshaya raised an objection to Ulla from that which was taught in a *baraita*: There is the case of **a leper**[N] **whose eighth** day, on which he becomes ritually pure from his leprosy and performs the final stages of his purification process, **occurs on Passover eve,**[H] such that it would be possible to bring his offerings and be fit to partake of the Paschal offering that evening. **And he experienced a seminal emission**[B] **on that day** before he performed the final stages of his purification process, rendering him ritually impure and prohibited from entering the Temple. **And he** then **immersed** himself[N] in a ritual bath. The question is whether he may come to the gate of the Temple courtyard, which is necessary to complete his purification process and terminate his status as a leper.

NOTES

It is possible where he inserts his hands and places them – אֶפְשָׁר דִּמְעַיֵּיל יְדֵיהּ וְסָמֵיךְ: According to this opinion, partial entry of a ritually impure individual into the courtyard is not considered entry; therefore, without the juxtaposition to slaughtering it would have been understood that the placing of the hands on the head of an offering can be done by ritually impure individuals, as the individual can remain outside the courtyard and insert just his hands. The juxtaposition therefore teaches that ritually impure individuals may not place their hands on the heads of offerings (*Keren Ora*).

The slaughterer of the bull must be before the Lord – שׁוֹחֵט אֶת בֶּן הַבָּקָר יְהֵא לִפְנֵי ה׳: This does not mean that the slaughterer must stand specifically on the inner side of the animal. What is meant is that he must stand inside the courtyard (Ra'avad). Likewise, the *Shita Mekubbetzet* has a version of the text that reads: The slaughterer and the bull must be before the Lord (see *Korban Aharon*).

Leper – מְצוֹרָע: After his leprosy has healed, the leper allows seven days of purity to pass, immerses, and then comes to the Temple on the eighth day, brings his offerings, and achieves atonement. Before sacrificing his offerings, the leper is still considered to be lacking atonement. It is permitted for such a person to enter the Temple Mount, which is considered the Levite camp, but he is prohibited from entering the Temple courtyard, which is considered the camp of the Divine Presence. The priest must sprinkle some blood of his guilt offering and oil on the tip of the leper's ear and on his right thumb and big toe, and it must be done specifically inside the courtyard (see *Pesaḥim* 85b). Therefore, the leper stands within the Nicanor Gate, which is between the women's courtyard and the Temple courtyard and does not have the sanctity of the Temple courtyard, and he inserts his hands within the courtyard so that the priest can sprinkle the blood upon them.

And he experienced a seminal emission…and he immersed himself – וְרָאָה קֶרִי...וְטָבַל: Until sundown, he retains the status of one who immersed himself that day, and he is prohibited from entering the Temple or even the women's courtyard, since it has the status of the Levite camp. Consequently, this leper is prevented from reaching the Nicanor Gate to complete his purification process, and as long as he is lacking atonement he cannot partake of his Paschal offering. This is the *halakha* only for one who experienced a seminal emission, since his status is like that of a *zav*. One who is ritually impure due to coming in contact with the carcass of a creeping animal, an animal carcass, or even a corpse is permitted to enter the Temple Mount, and is prohibited only from entering the Temple courtyard, which has the status of the camp of the Divine Presence.

BACKGROUND

He experienced a seminal emission – רָאָה קֶרִי: Whether an emission of semen occurred involuntarily, intentionally, or during intercourse, the individual becomes ritually impure and cannot enter the Temple. To purify himself, he must immerse in a ritual bath, and after nightfall on the day of his immersion he again becomes ritually pure (see Leviticus 15:16–18).

HALAKHA

The bull before the Lord – בֶּן הַבָּקָר לִפְנֵי ה׳: In the case of offerings of lesser sanctity that were inside the Temple courtyard, with the person standing outside the courtyard and inserting his hand inside to perform the ritual slaughter, the slaughter is valid. If the animal was inside, aside from its leg, which was outside, and he slaughtered it, the offering is disqualified. This is in accordance with the opinion of the first *tanna* (Rambam *Sefer Avoda, Hilkhot Pesulei HaMukdashin* 1:11, 14).

A ritually impure individual who inserted his hand inside – טָמֵא שֶׁהִכְנִיס יָדוֹ לִפְנִים: A ritually impure individual who inserted his hand into the Temple is not flogged, since a partial entry is not considered an entry by Torah law. He does receive lashes for rebelliousness. The Ra'avad rules that a partial entry is considered an entry and he is therefore flogged for it (Rambam *Sefer Avoda, Hilkhot Biat HaMikdash* 3:18, and see *Kesef Mishne* and Mahari Kurkus there).

A leper whose eighth day occurs on Passover eve – מְצוֹרָע שֶׁחָל שְׁמִינִי שֶׁלּוֹ לִהְיוֹת בְּעֶרֶב הַפֶּסַח: In the case of a leper whose eighth day occurs on the fourteenth day of Nisan, and who experiences a seminal emission on that day, he immerses and enters the women's courtyard and brings his offerings. One who immersed that day is generally prohibited from entering the women's courtyard, but since that prohibition is by rabbinic law and the obligation to sacrifice the Paschal offering in its proper time is mandated by Torah law, and the failure to do so carries the punishment of *karet*, it overrides the prohibition of entering the women's courtyard, in accordance with the opinion of Rabbi Yoḥanan (Rambam *Sefer Korbanot, Hilkhot Korban Pesaḥ* 6:5).

אָמְרוּ חֲכָמִים: אַף עַל פִּי שֶׁאֵין טְבוּל יוֹם אַחֵר נִכְנָס – זֶה נִכְנָס, מוּטָב יָבוֹא עֲשֵׂה שֶׁיֵּשׁ בּוֹ כָּרֵת וְיִדְחֶה עֲשֵׂה שֶׁאֵין בּוֹ כָּרֵת.

The Sages said: Although any **other** individual who was ritually impure **who immersed that day** and is waiting for nightfall for the purification process to be completed **may not enter** the Temple mount until nightfall, **this one may enter.** The reason is that **it is better** for **a positive mitzva that has** a punishment of ***karet***, i.e., the bringing of the Paschal offering, to **come and override a positive mitzva for which there is no** liability to be punished with ***karet***,[N] i.e., the mitzva to remove individuals who are ritually impure from the Temple courtyard, than have the positive mitzva that has a punishment of *karet* not be performed.

וְרַבִּי יוֹחָנָן אָמַר: דְּבַר תּוֹרָה אֲפִילּוּ עֲשֵׂה אֵין בּוֹ, שֶׁנֶּאֱמַר: ״וַיַּעֲמֹד יְהוֹשָׁפָט בִּקְהַל יְהוּדָה וִירוּשָׁלַ͏ִם בְּבֵית ה׳ לִפְנֵי הֶחָצֵר הַחֲדָשָׁה״. מַאי ״חָצֵר הַחֲדָשָׁה״? אָמַר רַבִּי יוֹחָנָן: שֶׁחִידְּשׁוּ בָּהּ דְּבָרִים (הַרְבֵּה), וְאָמְרוּ: טְבוּל יוֹם אַל יִכָּנֵס לְמַחֲנֵה לְוִיָּה.

And Rabbi Yoḥanan says: By Torah law, there is not even a positive mitzva[N] that restricts from entering the Temple courtyard one who has immersed that day and will become pure only upon nightfall, **as it is stated: "And Jehoshaphat stood in the congregation of Judea and Jerusalem, in the House of the Lord, before the new courtyard"** (II Chronicles 20:5). **What is the meaning of "the new courtyard"? Rabbi Yoḥanan says:** This is referring to the place **in which they innovated many matters**[N] **and said** that **one who immersed that day may not enter the camp of the Levites,**[H] which in Jerusalem includes the entire Temple Mount. This indicates that the prohibition is of rabbinic origin, and by Torah law it is permitted for him to enter.

וְאִי אָמְרַתְּ בִּיאָה בְּמִקְצָת שְׁמָהּ בִּיאָה – הֵיכִי מְעַיֵּיל יְדֵיהּ בְּבְהוֹנוֹת? אִידֵי וְאִידֵי עֲשֵׂה שֶׁיֵּשׁ בּוֹ כָּרֵת הוּא!

Rav Hoshaya concludes his objection: **And if you say** that **partial entry** into the courtyard **is considered entry, how** does the leper who immersed himself that day **insert his hands** into the courtyard **so that** his right **thumb and big toe** will become purified? In this situation, both **this** mitzva to eat of the Paschal offering **and that** mitzva for an impure person to not enter the courtyard **are** each **a positive mitzva for which there is** liability to be punished with ***karet***, as someone who immersed himself that day who enters the Temple courtyard is liable to be punished with *karet*.

אֲמַר לֵיהּ: מִטּוּנָךְ, שָׁאנֵי מְצוֹרָע, הוֹאִיל וְהוּתַּר לְצָרַעְתּוֹ הוּתַּר לְקֶרְיוֹ.

Ulla **said to** Rabbi Hoshaya: A proof to my opinion can be brought **from your own burden,** i.e., from the question you asked. **A leper is different,** as the Torah permitted him to insert his right thumb and big toe into the courtyard in order to become purified despite the fact that he has not yet brought an atonement offering to complete the purification process, and **since he was permitted** to partially enter the courtyard **for** purification from **his leprosy, he was** also **permitted** with regard to his impurity due **to his seminal emission.** Nevertheless, a partial entry into the courtyard is in fact considered an entry.

אָמַר רַב יוֹסֵף, קָסָבַר עוּלָּא: רוּבָּן זָבִים וְנַעֲשׂוּ טְמֵאֵי מֵתִים, הוֹאִיל וְהוּתְּרוּ לְטוּמְאָתָן – הוּתְּרוּ לְזִיבָתָן.

Based on Ulla's previous comment, **Rav Yosef said: Ulla holds** that if **most of** the Jewish people were ***zavim***[N] on Passover eve, and were therefore prohibited from sacrificing the Paschal offering while impure, **and** then **they became ritually impure due to a corpse,** which allows them to sacrifice the Paschal offering despite their impurity as they are a majority of the Jewish people, **since they are permitted** to sacrifice the offering **with regard to their impurity** due to a corpse, **they are** also **permitted with regard to their *ziva*.**

אֲמַר לֵיהּ אַבָּיֵי: מִי דָּמֵי? טוּמְאָה אִישְׁתְּרַאי, זִיבָה לָא אִישְׁתְּרַאי!

Abaye said to him: Are the cases **comparable?** With regard to a leper who experienced a seminal emission, he was already permitted to partially enter the courtyard despite his initial impurity. Therefore, the subsequent impurity does not prohibit him from entering. By contrast, the *zavim* were originally prevented from sacrificing the Paschal offering. Therefore, even if he would be **permitted** to enter the courtyard despite becoming **impure** due to a corpse, he would **not** be **permitted** to enter due to the ***ziva*** that was previously present.

אֲמַר לֵיהּ: דִּלְמָא הָכִי קָאָמַר מָר: רוּבָּן טְמֵאֵי מֵתִים וְנַעֲשׂוּ זָבִים, הוֹאִיל וְהוּתְּרוּ לְטוּמְאָתָן – הוּתְּרוּ לְזִיבָתָן? אֲמַר לֵיהּ: אִין.

Furthermore, Abaye **said to him: Perhaps this** is what **the Master is saying:** If **most of** the Jewish people were initially **ritually impure due to a corpse, and they** subsequently **became *zavim*, since they are permitted with regard to their impurity** due to a corpse, **they are permitted with regard to their *ziva*** as well. Rav Yosef **said to him: Yes,** that was what I meant.

NOTES

And override a positive mitzva for which there is no *karet* – וְיִדְחֶה עֲשֵׂה שֶׁאֵין בּוֹ כָּרֵת: This is referring to the positive mitzva of: "They shall send out from the camp every leper and every *zav*, and whoever is unclean by the dead" (Numbers 5:2). The punishment of *karet* applies only to a ritually impure individual who enters the camp of the Divine Presence, which extends from the walls of the Temple courtyard and inward (see *Shevuot* 14a).

There is not even a positive mitzva – אֲפִילּוּ עֲשֵׂה אֵין בּוֹ: It would seem from Rashi's explanation that Rabbi Yoḥanan disagrees with the *baraita*. *Tosafot* hold that Rabbi Yoḥanan is not disagreeing with the *baraita*, but merely explaining it, saying that by Torah law one who immersed himself that day is not required to be sent out of the Levite camp.

In which they innovated many matters, etc. – שֶׁחִידְּשׁוּ בָּהּ דְּבָרִים וכו׳: Since it states in the verse that Jehoshaphat stood "in the congregation of Judea," it indicates that Jehoshaphat taught and spoke publicly before the congregation. Rabbi Yoḥanan explains that Jehoshaphat innovated a *halakha*, as it was common for the Sages to deliver a public address when they innovated a *halakha* (*Gilyonei HaShas*).

Most of the Jewish people were *zavim*, etc. – רוּבָּן זָבִים וכו׳: An individual or a minority of the congregation who are ritually impure due to a corpse are prohibited from sacrificing the Paschal offering on the fourteenth of Nisan, and it is postponed for them to the second Pesaḥ. If the majority of the congregation is impure, the bringing of the Paschal offering is not postponed until the second Pesaḥ; rather, it is brought on the first Pesaḥ while the people are impure (see 22b). This permission does not apply to all types of ritual impurity, but only to ritual impurity due to a corpse. Consequently, if a majority of the congregation are *zavim*, the Paschal offering may not be brought in Nisan.

HALAKHA

One who immersed that day in the Levite camp – טְבוּל יוֹם בְּמַחֲנֵה לְוִיָּה: One who was ritually impure and immersed that day may not enter the women's courtyard, but this *halakha* does not apply to one who is lacking atonement (Rambam *Sefer Avoda*, *Hilkhot Biat HaMikdash* 3:6).

NOTES

Ritual impurity is overridden, etc. – טומאה דחויה וכו׳: Rashi explains that it is with total permission that a leper is allowed partial entry into the courtyard. By contrast, sacrificing the Paschal offering while ritually impure is not entirely permitted, but rather the prohibition is overridden; it is facilitated through the frontplate worn by the High Priest, which atones for ritual impurity related to the Temple. Consequently, this reluctant allowance is limited in its scope.

What difference does it make to me if there is one impurity that is overridden, etc. – מה לי חד דחויא וכו׳: Since there is explicit permission for a leper to insert his right thumb and big toe into the courtyard, it is as though no prohibition exists. Consequently, this permission is not relevant to any other prohibition of ritual impurity. Conversely, with regard to ritual impurity in the case of the Paschal offering, since the prohibition is being overridden, this overriding force will function to override other ritual impurities as well (see *Keren Ora*).

ואכתי לא דמי, מצורע היתירא הוא, הואיל ואישתרי – אישתרי. טומאה דחויה היא, להא אידחאי, להא לא אידחאי!

The Gemara asks: **But still,** this is **not comparable** to the case of Ulla, since with regard to **a leper, it is** with total **permission** that he is allowed partial entry into the courtyard. And **since it was permitted** with regard to one impurity, **it was permitted** with regard to a second impurity. But the **ritual impurity** with regard to the sacrificing of the Paschal offering **is** only **overridden,**[N] and there is not a total permission. Perhaps **with regard to this,** i.e., ritual impurity due to a corpse, **it is overridden,** but **with regard to that,** i.e., the impurity of *ziva*, **it is not overridden.**

אמר ליה רבא: אדרבה, איפכא מסתברא: מצורע היתירא הוא, להא אישתראי ולהא לא אישתראי. טומאה דחויה הוא, מה לי חד דחויא מה לי שתי דחיות.

Rava said to him: On the contrary, the opposite is more **reasonable.** With regard to **a leper, it is** with specific **permission** that he was allowed by the Torah to insert his right thumb and big toe into the courtyard in order to become purified despite his ritual impurity, which was not granted for other impurities. Therefore, perhaps only **with regard to this** impurity **it is permitted, but with regard to that** impurity, i.e., due to a seminal emission, **it is not permitted.** But with regard to **ritual impurity,** since **it is overridden** in the case of ritual impurity due to a corpse, **what** difference does it make **to me** if there is **one** impurity that is **overridden,**[N] and **what** difference does it make **to me** if there are **two** impurities that are **overridden?**

Perek **III**
Daf **33** Amud **a**

HALAKHA

Impurity is overridden in cases involving the public – טומאה דחויה היא בצבור: In cases involving the public, ritual impurity is not permitted but is merely overridden. Therefore, in a case in which the priests of the priestly watch became ritually impure, if there is a priest from a different priestly watch that is pure, he should come and serve in the Temple so that the service should not be performed in impurity (Rambam *Sefer Avoda, Hilkhot Biat HaMikdash* 4:14–15).

Immediately following the placing of hands is slaughter – תכף לסמיכה שחיטה: In the same place where the hands are placed on the head of the offering the offering is slaughtered, and the slaughter immediately follows the placing of the hands. If it was slaughtered in a different place, or the slaughter was delayed, it is still valid (Rambam *Sefer Avoda, Hilkhot Ma'aseh HaKorbanot* 3:12).

Except for this case of a leper which was done in the Nicanor Gate – חוץ מזו שהיתה בשער נקנור: The priest waves the guilt offering of the leper and his *log* of oil, and then brings the guilt offering to the entrance of the courtyard. The leper inserts both of his hands into the Temple courtyard and places them on the head of his offering, and it is then immediately slaughtered. Partial entry into the courtyard is not considered an entry (Rambam *Sefer Korbanot, Hilkhot Mehusrei Kappara* 4:2 and Mahari Kurkus there).

מכלל דתרווייהו סבירא להו: טומאה דחויה היא בצבור.

The Gemara comments: It can be derived **by inference that both** Abaye and Rava **hold** that **impurity is overridden in** cases involving the **public**[H] and is not entirely permitted.

לימא מסייע ליה: כל הסמיכות שהיו שם, קורא עליהן אני: תכף לסמיכה שחיטה,

The Gemara returns to discussing Ulla's statement that partial entry of a ritually impure individual is considered entry: **Let us say** that a *baraita* (*Tosefta, Nega'im* 8:10) **supports** Ulla's opinion: Concerning **all the** cases of **placing hands that were there** in the Temple, **I say about them** that the principle: **Immediately** following the **placing of hands** on the head of an offering is its **slaughter,**[H] is applied, meaning that these acts must take place uninterruptedly and in the same location.

חוץ מזו שהיתה בשער נקנור, שאין מצורע יכול ליכנס לשם עד שמזין עליו מדם חטאתו ומדם אשמו; ואי אמרת ביאה במקצת לא שמה ביאה – ליעייל ידיה ולסמוך!

This is so **except for this** case of a leper who places hands on his guilt offering, **which was** done **in** the threshold of the **Nicanor Gate**[HB] and not in the Temple courtyard where the guilt offering was slaughtered. The reason for this is **that a leper cannot enter** the courtyard **until they sprinkle from the blood of his sin offering and from the blood of his guilt offering** on the altar **on his behalf.** The Gemara explains the proof: **And if you say** that **partial entry is not considered entry, let him insert his hands and place** them on the head of the offering, and the offering should then be slaughtered in that location next to the gate.

BACKGROUND

Nicanor Gate – שער נקנור: The Nicanor Gate, which was situated by the main entrance to the Temple courtyard, served many purposes in cases where it was necessary for someone to be as close as possible to the courtyard without actually entering it.

Depiction of Nicanor Gate

אָמַר רַב יוֹסֵף: הָא מַנִּי – רַבִּי יוֹסֵי בְּרַבִּי יְהוּדָה הִיא, דְּאָמַר: מְרַחֵק צָפוֹן.

Rav Yosef said: There is no proof from here, as in accordance with **whose** opinion **is this** *baraita*? **It is** in accordance with the opinion of **Rabbi Yosei, son of Rabbi Yehuda, who says** that the northern side of the courtyard in which it is permitted to slaughter offerings of the most sacred order, which includes a guilt offering, includes only the area to the north of the altar and not the entire northern section of the courtyard. This area is **far north** of the entrance to the courtyard, i.e., more than twenty-two cubits away. Consequently, even if the leper were to insert his hands into the courtyard and place them on the head of his guilt offering, it would not be permitted to slaughter it there.

וְלִיעֲבַד פִּישְׁפָּשׁ! אַבָּיֵי וְרָבָא דְּאָמְרִי תַּרְוַיְיהוּ: ״הַכֹּל בִּכְתָב מִיַּד ה׳ עָלַי הִשְׂכִּיל אֶת כֹּל מַלְאֲכוֹת הַתַּבְנִית״.

The Gemara suggests: **But let an opening** [*pishpash*][L] **be made** in the northern courtyard wall facing the altar, where the leper can insert his hands. The Gemara explains: **Abaye and Rava both say** that such structural changes cannot be made to the Temple, since the verse states with regard to the Temple construction: **"All in writing, as the Lord has made me wise by His hand upon me, even all the works of this pattern"** (I Chronicles 28:19).

אִיכָּא דְּאָמְרִי, אָמַר רַב יוֹסֵף: כׇּל הַסּוֹמֵךְ – רֹאשׁוֹ וְרוּבּוֹ מַכְנִיס, מַאי טַעְמָא – כׇּל כֹּחוֹ בָּעֵינַן, הִלְכָּךְ לָא אֶפְשָׁר.

There are those **who say** that **Rabbi Yosef said** another explanation as to why the leper cannot insert his hands into the courtyard and place them on the head of the offering: **Anyone who places hands** on the head of an offering must **insert his head and most of his** body into the courtyard. **What is the reason? We require** placing hands with **all of his force.**[H] **Therefore,** it is **not possible** for the leper to perform the placing of his hands properly without entering the courtyard, and the placing of hands on the offering is done instead in the threshold of the Nicanor Gate.

מַאי קָסָבַר? אִי קָסָבַר סְמִיכַת אֲשַׁם מְצוֹרָע דְּאוֹרָיְיתָא, וְתֵכֶף לִסְמִיכָה שְׁחִיטָה דְּאוֹרָיְיתָא – לֵיעוֹל וְלִסְמוֹךְ לְהֶדְיָא, דְּרַחֲמָנָא אָמַר!

The Gemara clarifies: **What** does the *tanna* of the *baraita* **hold? If he holds** that **placing hands** on the head of **a guilt offering of a leper** is **by Torah law, and** the principle that **immediately** following the **placing of hands** on the head of an offering must be its **slaughter** is also **by Torah law, let** the leper **openly insert** his hands into the courtyard **and place** them on the head of the offering, **as the Merciful One states** in the Torah that he must do so.

אָמַר רַב אַדָּא בַּר מַתְּנָה: גְּזֵירָה שֶׁמָּא יַרְבֶּה בִּפְסִיעוֹת. אִיכָּא דְּאָמְרִי, אָמַר רַב אַדָּא בַּר מַתְּנָה: סְמִיכַת אֲשַׁם מְצוֹרָע דְּאוֹרָיְיתָא, וְתֵכֶף לִסְמִיכָה שְׁחִיטָה לָאו דְּאוֹרָיְיתָא.

Rav Adda bar Mattana says: In principle that should be done. But the prohibition against the leper entering the courtyard is a rabbinic **decree,** due to the concern that **perhaps he will increase** his **steps,** enter the courtyard more than is necessary, and be liable for entering there in a state of impurity. **There are** those **who say** that **Rav Adda bar Mattana says** that **placing hands** on the head of **a guilt offering of a leper** is indeed **by Torah law, but** the requirement that **immediately** following the **placing of hands** is the **slaughter** is **not by Torah law.** Therefore, he places hands on the offering outside of the courtyard.

מֵיתִיבִי: ״וְסָמַךְ...וְשָׁחַט״ – מָה סְמִיכָה בִּטְהוֹרִין – אַף שְׁחִיטָה בִּטְהוֹרִין; וְאִי אָמְרַתְּ לָאו דְּאוֹרָיְיתָא, בִּטְמֵאִין נַמִי מַשְׁכַּחַתְּ לַהּ!

The Gemara **raises an objection** from a *baraita* cited previously (32a): The verse states: **"And he shall place** his hand upon the head of the burnt offering... **And he shall slaughter** the bull" (Leviticus 1:4–5). **Just as placing hands** may be performed only **by ritually pure** individuals, **so too,** the **slaughter** may be performed only **by ritually pure** individuals. **And if you say** that the requirement that placing hands must immediately precede the slaughter is **not by Torah law,** then **with regard to ritually impure** individuals **you also find** that placing hands may be performed, since they can do so outside the courtyard.

אֶלָּא, אֵיפוֹךְ: סְמִיכַת אֲשַׁם מְצוֹרָע לָאו דְּאוֹרָיְיתָא, וְתֵכֶף לִסְמִיכָה שְׁחִיטָה דְּאוֹרָיְיתָא.

Rather, reverse it and say that **placing hands** on the head of the **guilt offering of a leper** is **not by Torah law,**[N] and therefore the leper must do so outside the courtyard, **but** with regard to offerings that require placing of hands by Torah law, the requirement that **immediately** following the **placing of hands** must be the **slaughter** is **by Torah law.**

LANGUAGE

Opening [*pishpash*] – פִּשְׁפָּשׁ: This word also exists in Syriac Aramaic with the same meaning: A small door within a larger door. Some explain that the term derives from the Greek ψῆφος, *psēfos*, which refers to a stone that is embedded in a formation of stones that form a mosaic. From there the word was borrowed to describe a wicket embedded in a larger door.

Wicket in a large gate

HALAKHA

We require all of his force – כׇּל כֹּחוֹ בָּעֵינַן: The owner of the offering must place his hands on the head of the offering with both of his hands and all of his strength (Rambam *Sefer Avoda, Hilkhot Ma'aseh HaKorbanot* 3:13).

NOTES

Placing hands on the head of the guilt offering of a leper is not by Torah law – סְמִיכַת אֲשַׁם מְצוֹרָע לָאו דְּאוֹרָיְיתָא: If it is not required by Torah law, the leper may not place his hands on the head of the offering with all his strength, since it is considered as though he is performing labor with an offering. He may merely rest his hands on the head (*Tosafot*). Rashi explains that while other guilt offerings require placing of the hands although it is not mentioned explicitly in the Torah, it is derived from the juxtaposition: "As the sin offering and as the guilt offering" (Leviticus 6:10). The guilt offering of a leper is not included among other guilt offerings, since it does not serve to atone for a sin, but rather to purify him of his leprosy.

רָבִינָא אָמַר: לְעִנְיַן מַלְקוֹת אִיתְּמַר.

The Gemara returns to Ulla's statement in the name of Reish Lakish (32b) that an impure individual who inserted his hand into the Temple courtyard is flogged, as partial entry is considered entry. An objection was then raised from the case of the leper, where he is not liable to be punished with *karet* for partial entry, and Ulla offered one answer. **Ravina says** that there is another answer: It **was stated** only **with regard to lashes,** teaching that one is flogged for partially entering the courtyard while ritually impure. Reish Lakish agrees that there is no punishment of *karet* for partial entry as there is for a full entry.

כִּי אֲתָא רָבִין, אָמַר רַבִּי אַבָּהוּ: לְעִנְיַן טָמֵא שֶׁנָּגַע בְּקוֹדֶשׁ אִיתְּמַר.

When Ravin came from Eretz Yisrael to Babylonia, he said that **Rabbi Abbahu says** that the statement of Reish Lakish with regard to this verse **was stated with regard to a ritually impure** individual **who touched sacrificial food,** and not with regard to partial entry into the courtyard, as Ulla had said.

דְּאִיתְּמַר, טָמֵא שֶׁנָּגַע בְּקוֹדֶשׁ, רֵישׁ לָקִישׁ אָמַר: לוֹקֶה, רַבִּי יוֹחָנָן אָמַר: אֵינוֹ לוֹקֶה. רֵישׁ לָקִישׁ אָמַר: לוֹקֶה – ״בְּכׇל קֹדֶשׁ לֹא תִגָּע״. וְרַבִּי יוֹחָנָן אָמַר: אֵינוֹ לוֹקֶה – הַהוּא בִּתְרוּמָה כְּתִיב.

This is **as it was stated:** There is an amoraic dispute with regard to **an impure person who touched sacrificial** food.[H] **Reish Lakish says:** He is **flogged. Rabbi Yoḥanan says: He is not flogged.** The Gemara elaborates. **Reish Lakish says:** He is **flogged,** as it is written: **"Every consecrated item she shall not touch"** (Leviticus 12:4). **And Rabbi Yoḥanan says: He is not flogged,** as **that** verse **is written with regard to** touching **the portion of the produce designated for the priest** [*teruma*].[N]

וְרֵישׁ לָקִישׁ, הַאי קְרָא לְהָכִי הוּא דַּאֲתָא? הַאי מִיבְּעֵי לֵיהּ אַזְהָרָה לְאוֹכֵל בְּשַׂר קוֹדֶשׁ. דְּאִיתְּמַר, אַזְהָרָה לְאוֹכֵל בְּשַׂר קוֹדֶשׁ מִנַּיִן? רֵישׁ לָקִישׁ אָמַר: ״בְּכׇל קֹדֶשׁ לֹא תִגָּע״.

The Gemara asks: **But** does **Reish Lakish** actually hold that **this verse comes to** teach **this** *halakha*? **He requires this** verse to teach **a prohibition for** a ritually impure person **who eats sacrificial meat. As it was stated: From where is the prohibition for** a ritually impure person **who eats sacrificial meat**[H] derived? **Reish Lakish says** it is derived from the verse: **"Every consecrated item she shall not touch,"** which the Gemara will explain is referring to eating.

רַבִּי יוֹחָנָן אָמַר, תָּנֵי בַּרְדְּלָא: אָתְיָא ״טוּמְאָתוֹ״ ״טוּמְאָתוֹ״ מִבִּיאַת מִקְדָּשׁ, מָה לְהַלָּן עָנַשׁ וְהִזְהִיר – אַף כָּאן עָנַשׁ וְהִזְהִיר!

Rabbi Yoḥanan says: The Sage **Bardela**[P] **teaches** that this prohibition is **derived from** a verbal analogy of the term **"his impurity** [*tumato*]**"** written with regard to one who eats sacrificial meat while impure (Leviticus 7:20), and the term **"his impurity** [*tumato*]**"** written with regard to one who **enters** the **Temple** while impure (Numbers 19:13). **Just as there,** with regard to entering the Temple while impure, the Torah **prescribed** the **punishment** of *karet* **and** also explicitly **prohibited** doing so, **so too here,** with regard to eating sacrificial meat while impure, the Torah **prescribed** the **punishment** of *karet* **and** also explicitly **prohibited** doing so. Clearly, Reish Lakish understood this verse as referring to eating sacrificial meat, not merely touching it.

טָמֵא שֶׁנָּגַע בְּקוֹדֶשׁ – מִדְּאַפְקַהּ רַחֲמָנָא בִּלְשׁוֹן נְגִיעָה, אַזְהָרָה לְאוֹכֵל – מִדְּאִיתְקַשׁ קוֹדֶשׁ לְמִקְדָּשׁ.

The Gemara answers: Reish Lakish holds that both can be derived from Leviticus 12:4. The prohibition with regard to **a ritually impure** individual **who touched sacrificial** food is derived **from** the fact **that the Merciful One expressed** this prohibition **with a term of touching,**[N] while **the prohibition with regard to one who eats** sacrificial food while impure is derived **from** the fact **that** the Torah **juxtaposed** the prohibition of eating **sacrificial** food while impure **to** the prohibition of entering the **Temple** while impure in the verse: "Every consecrated item she shall not touch, and to the Temple she shall not come" (Leviticus 12:4).

תַּנְיָא כְּווֹתֵיהּ דְּרֵישׁ לָקִישׁ: ״בְּכׇל קֹדֶשׁ לֹא תִגָּע״ – אַזְהָרָה לְאוֹכֵל. אַתָּה אוֹמֵר: אַזְהָרָה לְאוֹכֵל, אוֹ אֵינוֹ אֶלָּא לְנוֹגֵעַ?

The Gemara comments: **It is taught** in a *baraita* **in accordance with** the opinion **of Reish Lakish.** It is written: **"Every consecrated item she shall not touch"**; this is a **prohibition for** an impure person who **eats** sacrificial food. **Do you say** that it is **a prohibition for** an impure person who **eats** sacrificial food, **or** perhaps **it is only** a prohibition **for** an impure person who **touches** sacrificial food?

HALAKHA

An impure person who touched sacrificial food – טָמֵא שֶׁנָּגַע בְּקוֹדֶשׁ: It is forbidden for a ritually impure individual to touch sacrificial food. One who did so is not flogged. This is in accordance with the opinion of Rabbi Yoḥanan, as the *halakha* is in accordance with his opinion in his disputes with Reish Lakish (Rambam *Sefer Avoda, Hilkhot Pesulei HaMukdashin* 18:12).

Prohibition for a ritually impure person who eats sacrificial meat – אַזְהָרָה לְאוֹכֵל מִן הַקֳּדָשִׁים בְּטוּמְאָה: With regard to anyone who is ritually impure with an impurity such that if he were to enter the Temple he would be liable to receive *karet* and who ate an olive-bulk of sacrificial food, whether pure or impure, if he did so intentionally he is liable to be punished with *karet*. This prohibition is derived from the verse: "Every consecrated item she shall not touch" (Leviticus 12:4). This is in accordance with the opinion of Reish Lakish (Rambam *Sefer Avoda, Hilkhot Pesulei HaMukdashin* 18:13–14 and *Kesef Mishne* there).

NOTES

That verse is written with regard to ***teruma*** **– הַהוּא בִּתְרוּמָה כְּתִיב:** Rashi explains that this is learned from the end of the verse, as it is written: "Every consecrated item she shall not touch, and to the Temple she shall not come, until the days of her purification be fulfilled" (Leviticus 12:4). This indicates that once her days of purification have been completed, it is permitted for her to touch consecrated items. This is the *halakha* only with regard to *teruma*, since with regard to sacrificial food it is permitted for her to touch it only after she has brought her offering of atonement. Consequently, it is concluded that the "consecrated item" referred to in the verse is not sacrificial food, but rather *teruma*, which she may touch once she is ritually pure.

From the fact that the Merciful One expressed this prohibition with a term of touching – מִדְּאַפְקַהּ רַחֲמָנָא בִּלְשׁוֹן נְגִיעָה: The meaning is that in conclusion the verse is explained as referring to eating sacrificial food while ritually impure, since the continuation of the verse, by comparing the touching to entering the Temple, a prohibition that is punishable with *karet*, indicates a more serious transgression than merely touching. The straightforward understanding of the verse is also taken into account, and it is explained as teaching a prohibition against touching.

PERSONALITIES

Bardela – בַּרְדְּלָא: It would seem that this is the same person mentioned in other places by his full name, Abba Kohen Bardela or Abba Kohen bar Dela. In the Jerusalem Talmud and in other places his name appears as Abba Kohen bar Dalia. He was apparently from the first generation of *amora'im*, as Rabbi Yoḥanan and Reish Lakish cite him. He is mentioned once in the halakhic midrash and a number of times in the aggadic midrash.

תַּלְמוּד לוֹמַר: ״בְּכׇל קֹדֶשׁ לֹא תִגָּע וְאֶל הַמִּקְדָּשׁ לֹא תָבֹא״, מַקִּישׁ קוֹדֶשׁ לְמִקְדָּשׁ, מָה מִקְדָּשׁ דָּבָר שֶׁיֵּשׁ בּוֹ

The verse states: "Every consecrated item she shall not touch, and to the Temple she shall not come" (Leviticus 12:4). The verse **juxtaposes** the matter pertaining to **sacrificial** food **to the** matter of entering the **Temple** while ritually impure. **Just as** entering the **Temple is a matter** that entails a punishment **that involves**

Perek **III**
Daf **34** Amud **a**

נְטִילַת נְשָׁמָה, אַף קוֹדֶשׁ – דָּבָר שֶׁיֵּשׁ בּוֹ נְטִילַת נְשָׁמָה; וְאִי בְּנוֹגֵעַ – נְטִילַת נְשָׁמָה מִי אִיכָּא? אֶלָּא בַּאֲכִילָה.

the taking of a life, i.e., *karet,* **so too,** the **matter** pertaining to **sacrificial** food entails a punishment **that involves the taking of a life.** The Gemara explains: **And if** the prohibition is **with regard to touching** sacrificial food, **is there** a punishment that entails **the taking of a life? Rather,** the prohibition is **with regard to eating.**

וְאַכַּתִּי מִיבְּעֵי לֵיהּ לְטָמֵא שֶׁאָכַל בְּשַׂר קוֹדֶשׁ לִפְנֵי זְרִיקָה. דְּאִתְּמַר, טָמֵא שֶׁאָכַל בְּשַׂר קוֹדֶשׁ לִפְנֵי זְרִיקָה, רֵישׁ לָקִישׁ אָמַר: לוֹקֶה, וְרַבִּי יוֹחָנָן אָמַר: אֵינוֹ לוֹקֶה.

The Gemara asks: **But** this verse is **still necessary for** Reish Lakish to teach the *halakha* **of a ritually impure** person **who ate sacrificial meat before** the **sprinkling** of the blood[H] of the offering on the altar, when the meat is not yet permitted. **As it was stated:** With regard to **an impure** individual **who ate sacrificial meat before** the **sprinkling** of the blood, **Reish Lakish says:** He **is flogged** for doing so, **and Rabbi Yoḥanan says: He is not flogged.**

HALAKHA

A ritually impure person who ate sacrificial meat before the sprinkling of the blood – טָמֵא שֶׁאָכַל בְּשַׂר קוֹדֶשׁ לִפְנֵי זְרִיקָה: A ritually impure individual who ate sacrificial meat before the sprinkling of the blood is not liable to be punished with *karet*. He is therefore also not flogged as an impure individual who ate sacrificial meat, in accordance with the opinion of Rabbi Yoḥanan (Rambam *Sefer Avoda, Hilkhot Pesulei HaMukdashin* 18:16).

רֵישׁ לָקִישׁ אָמַר: לוֹקֶה – ״בְּכׇל קֹדֶשׁ לֹא תִגָּע״, לֹא שְׁנָא לִפְנֵי זְרִיקָה, וְלֹא שְׁנָא לְאַחַר זְרִיקָה. רַבִּי יוֹחָנָן אָמַר: אֵינוֹ לוֹקֶה – כִּדְתָנֵי בַּרְדְּלָא: אָתְיָא ״טוּמְאָתוֹ״ ״טוּמְאָתוֹ״, וְכִי כְּתַב הַהוּא – לְאַחַר זְרִיקָה.

Reish Lakish says: He is **flogged,** as it is written: **"Every consecrated item she shall not touch,"** without limiting the prohibition to a specific time, indicating that it **is no different** if one eats the sacrificial meat **prior to sprinkling** the blood, **and** it **is no different** if one does so **after sprinkling** the blood. **Rabbi Yoḥanan says: He is not flogged,** as the Sage **Bardela teaches** that the prohibition **is derived** by means of the verbal analogy cited before, as the verse states **"his impurity"** with regard to an impure person who eats sacrificial food, and states **"his impurity"** with regard to an impure person entering the Temple. **And when** "his impurity" **is written,** it is with regard to partaking of sacrificial meat **after** the **sprinkling**[N] of the blood (see Leviticus 7:20).

אִם כֵּן, לֵימָא קְרָא ״בְּקֹדֶשׁ״, מַאי ״בְּכׇל קֹדֶשׁ״? שְׁמַע מִינַּהּ תַּרְתֵּי.

The Gemara answers for Reish Lakish: **If so,** that the verse was referring only to partaking of sacrificial meat after the sprinkling of the blood, **let the verse say: A consecrated item** she shall not touch. **What** is the reason for using the phrase **"every consecrated item"? Conclude two** conclusions **from it,** i.e., it also includes not eating sacrificial meat before the sprinkling of the blood.

גּוּפָא, טָמֵא שֶׁאָכַל בְּשַׂר קוֹדֶשׁ לִפְנֵי זְרִיקָה, רֵישׁ לָקִישׁ אָמַר: לוֹקֶה, רַבִּי יוֹחָנָן אָמַר: אֵינוֹ לוֹקֶה. אָמַר אַבָּיֵי: מַחֲלוֹקֶת בְּטוּמְאַת הַגּוּף, אֲבָל בְּטוּמְאַת בָּשָׂר – דִּבְרֵי הַכֹּל לוֹקֶה,

§ The Gemara discusses **the** matter **itself:** With regard to **an impure** individual **who ate sacrificial meat before the sprinkling** of the blood, **Reish Lakish says:** He **is flogged** for doing so, **and Rabbi Yoḥanan says: He is not flogged. Abaye says:** This **dispute** applies **with regard to** a case of **impurity of the body** of the one who eats the meat, **but with regard to impurity of the flesh** itself, i.e., if the sacrificial meat was ritually impure, **all agree** that he **is flogged.**

NOTES

And when "his impurity" is written, it is with regard to partaking of sacrificial meat after the sprinkling, etc. – וְכִי כְּתַב הַהוּא לְאַחַר זְרִיקָה וכו׳: As explained earlier (33b), the source of the prohibition to eat sacrificial meat while in a state of impurity is derived from a verbal analogy juxtaposing this prohibition to the prohibition against entering the Temple while in a state of impurity, based on the term "his impurity [*tumato*]." The punishment of *karet* for eating sacrificial meat while impure is limited to one who eats meat after the sprinkling of the blood, since the verse is discussing meat that is fit to be eaten, as it is written: "And the flesh, everyone that is pure may eat the flesh, but the soul that eats of the flesh…having his impurity upon him; that soul shall be cut off from his people" (Leviticus 7:19–20). This verse indicates that the meat referred to that an impure individual eats in this case is the same meat that is permitted to a pure individual (*Menaḥot* 25b). Consequently, the prohibition against eating sacrificial meat while in a state of impurity applies only to such meat as well.

דְּאָמַר קְרָא: "וְהַבָּשָׂר" – לְרַבּוֹת עֵצִים וּלְבוֹנָה דְּלָאו בְּנֵי אֲכִילָה נִינְהוּ, וַאֲפִילּוּ הָכִי רַבִּינְהוּ קְרָא.

This is **as the verse states:** "And the flesh that touches any impure item shall not be eaten; it shall be burned with fire; and the flesh, every one that is pure may eat the flesh" (Leviticus 7:19). The Sages derived that the extra term **"and the flesh"** serves **to include wood and frankincense, which are not fit for consumption, and even so the verse included them** as being susceptible to impurity, and one who eats them while he is impure is flogged. Therefore, sacrificial meat before the sprinkling of the blood, which is fit for consumption, is certainly included in the prohibition.

וְרָבָא אָמַר: מַחֲלוֹקֶת בְּטוּמְאַת הַגּוּף, אֲבָל בְּטוּמְאַת בָּשָׂר – דִּבְרֵי הַכֹּל אֵינוֹ לוֹקֶה, מַאי טַעְמָא? כֵּיוָן דְּלָא קָרֵינָא בֵּיהּ "וְטוּמְאָתוֹ עָלָיו וְנִכְרְתָה" – לָא קָרֵינָא בֵּיהּ "וְהַבָּשָׂר אֲשֶׁר יִגַּע בְּכָל טָמֵא לֹא יֵאָכֵל".

And Rava says: This **dispute** applies **with regard to** a case of **impurity of the body, but with regard to impurity of the meat all agree** that **he is not flogged.**[H] **What is the reason? Since** one **does not apply to** meat before the sprinkling of the blood the verse: "But the soul that eats of the flesh of the sacrifice of peace offerings of the Lord, **having his impurity upon him,** that soul **shall be cut off** from his people" (Leviticus 7:20), which is referring to meat after the sprinkling of the blood, so too, one **does not apply to it** the prohibition: **"And the flesh that touches any impure item shall not be eaten"** (Leviticus 7:19).

וְהָאָמַר מָר: "וְהַבָּשָׂר" – לְרַבּוֹת עֵצִים וּלְבוֹנָה!

The Gemara challenges the statement of Rava: **But doesn't the Master say** that the term **"and the flesh"** serves **to include wood and frankincense**[NH] that became impure as items that are forbidden to be eaten, despite the fact that they are not fit for consumption? Certainly, then, sacrificial flesh before the sprinkling of the blood should also be included in the category of items forbidden to be eaten.

הָכָא בְּמַאי עָסְקִינַן – כְּגוֹן שֶׁקְּדָשׁוֹ בִּכְלִי, דְּנַעֲשָׂה כְּמִי שֶׁקָּרְבוּ כָּל מַתִּירָיו.

The Gemara answers: **What are we dealing with here,** that one would be liable for eating wood and frankincense that are impure? It is a case **where** the wood and frankincense **were sanctified in a vessel,**[N] and the reason for the liability is **that** they are then **considered like** an item for **which all of its permitting factors were sacrificed,** such as flesh after the sprinkling of the blood, and only then is one liable for eating it while impure.

דִּתְנַן: כָּל שֶׁיֵּשׁ לוֹ מַתִּירִים – מִשֶּׁקָּרְבוּ מַתִּירָיו, כָּל שֶׁאֵין לוֹ מַתִּירִין – מִשֶּׁקָּדַשׁ בִּכְלִי.

This is **as we learned** in a mishna (*Me'ila* 10a): With regard to **anything that has permitting factors,**[H] i.e., rites that must be performed or items that must be sacrificed before the meat of the offering may be eaten, such as the meat of an offering that is permitted to be eaten by the sprinkling of the blood; one is liable for eating it while impure **from** the time **that its permitting factors were sacrificed.** With regard to **anything that does not have permitting factors,** such as the handful removed from a meal offering and the frankincense, which themselves render the rest of the meal offering permitted for consumption, one is liable for eating it while impure **from** the time **it is sanctified in a vessel.**

NOTES

And the flesh, to include wood and frankincense – וְהַבָּשָׂר לְרַבּוֹת עֵצִים וּלְבוֹנָה: The verse states: "And the flesh that touches any impure item shall not be eaten; it shall be burned with fire; and the flesh, every one that is clean may eat the flesh." According to Rashi, this *halakha* is derived from the second time the term "and the flesh" appears in the verse. In *Pesaḥim* 35a, Rashi explains that the term "the flesh," in and of itself, is not superfluous, and the *halakha* is derived from the addition of the conjunctive "and" (see *Pesaḥim* 24b).

A case where the wood and frankincense were sanctified in a vessel – כְּגוֹן שֶׁקְּדָשׁוֹ בִּכְלִי: The frankincense was inserted into a service vessel for it to be sacrificed. The question arises with regard to wood: With what sort of service vessel is wood sanctified? Rashi explains that refers to small chips of wood that entered the coal pan, which is a service vessel, when coals were scooped up from the altar during the removal of the ashes. *Tosafot* claim that this cannot be, as the wood was not removed, only the ashes of burned sacrifices were removed. They therefore explain that Rashi is referring to the coals removed by the High Priest on Yom Kippur for burning in the Holy of Holies. *Tosafot* offer another explanation, that when the wood was smoothed with an ax for it to be arranged on the altar, it was sanctified, despite an ax not being a service vessel (see *Tosafot* on *Menaḥot* 101a).

HALAKHA

With regard to impurity of the meat…he is not flogged – בְּטוּמְאַת בָּשָׂר...אֵינוֹ לוֹקֶה: A ritually pure individual who ate an olive-bulk of sacrificial meat that became impure is flogged, provided that he ate it after its permitting factors were sacrificed. One who eats impure sacrificial meat before its permitting factors were sacrificed is not flogged for eating impure sacrificial meat, in accordance with the opinion of Rava. Nevertheless, he receives lashes for rebelliousness (Rambam *Sefer Avoda, Hilkhot Pesulei HaMukdashin* 18:12).

To include wood and frankincense – לְרַבּוֹת עֵצִים וּלְבוֹנָה: The wood for the arrangement of wood on the altar, and frankincense, although they are not food, are nevertheless susceptible to impurity just like food, with regard to sacrifices. If they became ritually impure, the wood and frankincense become unfit for the altar, and they are not sacrificed. Likewise, a ritually pure individual who consumed an olive-bulk of frankincense from a meal offering that became impure after it was sanctified in a vessel is flogged (Rambam *Sefer Avoda, Hilkhot Pesulei HaMukdashin* 18:12 and *Hilkhot Issurei Mizbe'aḥ* 6:8).

Anything that has permitting factors, etc. – כָּל שֶׁיֵּשׁ לוֹ מַתִּירִים וכו׳: Concerning any item that has permitting factors, one is not liable for violating the prohibition of *piggul*, *notar*, or impurity, until the permitting factors were sacrificed properly. Concerning any item that does not have any permitting factors, once it was sanctified in a vessel, one is liable for impurity (Rambam *Sefer Avoda, Hilkhot Pesulei HaMukdashin* 18:16).

אִיתְּמַר, הַמַּעֲלֶה אֵבְרֵי בְּהֵמָה טְמֵאָה עַל גַּבֵּי הַמִּזְבֵּחַ, רֵישׁ לָקִישׁ אָמַר: לוֹקֶה, רַבִּי יוֹחָנָן אָמַר: אֵינוֹ לוֹקֶה. רֵישׁ לָקִישׁ אָמַר: לוֹקֶה, טְהוֹרָה – אִין, טְמֵאָה – לָא, וְלָאו הַבָּא מִכְּלַל עֲשֵׂה – לוֹקִין עָלָיו. וְרַבִּי יוֹחָנָן אָמַר: אֵין לוֹקִין עָלָיו, לָאו הַבָּא מִכְּלַל עֲשֵׂה – אֵין לוֹקִין עָלָיו.

§ **It was stated:** In the case of **one who offers up the limbs of a non-kosher animal**[H] **upon the altar, Reish Lakish says:** He **is flogged** for doing so, while **Rabbi Yoḥanan says: He is not flogged.** The Gemara explains the logic for each opinion: **Reish Lakish says** that he is **flogged,** because there is a positive mitzva to sacrifice an offering from the herd and the flock (see Leviticus 1:2), which are kosher animals. Therefore, it can be inferred that **a kosher** animal, **yes,** one may sacrifice, but **a non-kosher** animal one may **not** sacrifice, **and** one who transgresses **a prohibition that stems from a positive mitzva**[B] **is flogged for it. And Rabbi Yoḥanan says:** One is **not flogged for it,** as one who transgresses **a prohibition that stems from a positive mitzva is not flogged for it.**

מוֹתִיב רַבִּי יִרְמְיָה: ״אוֹתָהּ תֹּאכֵלוּ״ – וְלֹא בְּהֵמָה טְמֵאָה, וְלָאו הַבָּא מִכְּלַל עֲשֵׂה – עֲשֵׂה!

Rabbi Yirmeya raises an objection to the opinion of Reish Lakish from a *baraita* cited in *Torat Kohanim*: "Whatsoever parts the hoof, and is wholly cloven-footed, and chews the cud, among the beasts, **that may you eat"** (Leviticus 11:3).[H] One can infer: **But** you may **not** eat **a non-kosher animal;**[N] **and a prohibition that stems from a positive mitzva** has the status of **a positive mitzva.**

אֲמַר לֵיהּ רַבִּי יַעֲקֹב לְרַבִּי יִרְמְיָה בַּר תַּחְלִיפָא: אַסְבְּרָא לָךְ, בְּאֵבְרֵי בְּהֵמָה טְמֵאָה – דְּכוּלֵּי עָלְמָא לָא פְּלִיגִי, כִּי פְּלִיגִי – בְּחַיָּה. וְהָכִי אִיתְּמַר, רַבִּי יוֹחָנָן אָמַר: עוֹבֵר בַּעֲשֵׂה, רֵישׁ לָקִישׁ אָמַר: אֵינוֹ עוֹבֵר בְּלֹא כְלוּם.

Rabbi Ya'akov said to Rabbi Yirmeya bar Taḥlifa: I will explain it to you: With regard to one who sacrifices the **limbs of a non-kosher animal** upon the altar, **everyone agrees** that he is not flogged, as he violates only a positive mitzva. **When they disagree,** it is **with regard to** one who sacrifices a kosher **undomesticated animal**[H] on the altar, **and it was stated like this: Rabbi Yoḥanan says: He transgresses a positive mitzva. Reish Lakish says: He does not transgress anything.**

רַבִּי יוֹחָנָן אָמַר: עוֹבֵר בַּעֲשֵׂה, בְּהֵמָה – אִין, חַיָּה – לָא. רֵישׁ לָקִישׁ אָמַר: אֵינוֹ עוֹבֵר עָלָיו בְּלֹא כְלוּם, הַהוּא לְמִצְוָה.

The Gemara explains their reasoning: **Rabbi Yoḥanan says: He transgresses a positive mitzva,** since the Torah commanded that **a domesticated animal, yes,** should be sacrificed, from which it can be inferred that **an undomesticated animal** may **not** be sacrificed, and a prohibition that stems from a positive mitzva has the status of a positive mitzva. **Reish Lakish says: He does not transgress anything,** since **that** verse which instructs one to sacrifice offerings from the herd and the flock is referring **to** the optimal manner of fulfilling the **mitzva,** but if he sacrificed an undomesticated animal, he has not transgressed the mitzva.

מוֹתִיב רָבָא: אִילּוּ נֶאֱמַר ״קָרְבָּן לַה׳ בְּהֵמָה״ – הָיִיתִי אוֹמֵר: חַיָּה בִּכְלַל בְּהֵמָה, כְּעִנְיָן שֶׁנֶּאֱמַר: ״זֹאת הַבְּהֵמָה אֲשֶׁר תֹּאכֵלוּ שׁוֹר שֵׂה כְשָׂבִים וְשֵׂה עִזִּים אַיָּל וּצְבִי״ וגו׳ – תַּלְמוּד לוֹמַר: ״בָּקָר וְצֹאן״, בָּקָר וְצֹאן אָמַרְתִּי לְךָ, וְלֹא חַיָּה.

Rava raised an objection from a *baraita*: **Had** the verse (Leviticus 1:2) **stated** only: When any man of you brings **an offering to the Lord, animals** [*behema*], **I would say** that even **an undomesticated animal** is included **in the category of an animal** [*behema*], **like** that which **is stated: "These are the animals** [*behema*] **that you may eat: The ox, the sheep, and the goat, the deer, and the gazelle,** and the fallow deer, and the wild goat, and the oryx, and the aurochs, and the mountain sheep" (Deuteronomy 14:4–5), and, for example, the deer and gazelle are undomesticated animals. Therefore, **the verse states:** "From animals, from the **cattle and** from the **flock"** (Leviticus 1:2), which indicates that God says: **I have told you** to bring offerings from the **cattle and the flock, but not an undomesticated animal.**

יָכוֹל לֹא יָבִיא, וְאִם הֵבִיא כָּשֵׁר? הָא לְמָה זֶה דּוֹמֶה – לְתַלְמִיד שֶׁאָמַר לוֹ רַבּוֹ: ״הָבֵא לִי חִטִּים״ וְהֵבִיא לוֹ חִטִּים וּשְׂעוֹרִים, שֶׁאֵינוֹ כְּמַעֲבִיר עַל דְּבָרָיו אֶלָּא מוֹסִיף עַל דְּבָרָיו, וְכָשֵׁר?

One **might** have thought that one should **not bring** an undomesticated animal *ab initio*, **but if** one **did bring** it, it **is valid,** and **to what is this comparable? To a student whose teacher says to him: Bring me wheat,** and the student **brought him wheat and barley.** In this case, **it is not** as though the student is **disobeying the statement** of the teacher; **rather,** he is merely **adding to his statement, and** that should be **valid.**

NOTES

But you may not eat a non-kosher animal, etc. – וְלֹא בְּהֵמָה טְמֵאָה וכו׳: Rashi explains that the main proof is from the continuation of the *baraita* that appears in the *Torat Kohanim* on this verse, where the question is subsequently asked: Only a positive mitzva has been derived; from where do we derive a prohibition? The *Torat Kohanim* then mentions another verse. It is therefore clear that the deductive inference: A kosher animal but not a non-kosher animal, is not considered a prohibition but is considered a positive mitzva, for which one is not flogged (see *Tosafot* and *Shita Mekubbetzet*).

HALAKHA

One who offers up the limbs of a non-kosher animal, etc. – הַמַּעֲלֶה אֵבְרֵי בְּהֵמָה טְמֵאָה וכו׳: The Rambam writes: One who sacrifices the limbs of a non-kosher animal on the altar is flogged. Although the prohibition against sacrificing such limbs stems from a positive mitzva, the violation of which does not usually entail flogging, nevertheless, just as one is flogged for eating the meat of a non-kosher animal whose prohibition also stems from a positive mitzva, so too one is flogged for sacrificing it. The Ra'avad questions this, since this does not seem to be the conclusion of the Gemara here (Rambam *Sefer Avoda, Hilkhot Issurei Mizbe'aḥ* 5:6, and see Mahari Kurkus, Radbaz, and *Kesef Mishne* there).

That may you eat – אוֹתָהּ תֹּאכֵלוּ: From the fact that it states: "And every beast that parts the hoof, and has the hoof wholly cloven in two, and chews the cud" (Deuteronomy 14:6), one can derive that any animal that does not chew its cud and does not have split hooves is forbidden, and a prohibition that stems from a positive mitzva has the status of a positive mitzva. Concerning the camel, pig, hare, and rock badger it states: "Nevertheless, these you shall not eat" (Deuteronomy 14:7), although they possess one of the signs of being kosher. It can therefore be derived *a fortiori* that other non-kosher animals, which lack any signs of being kosher, are also prohibited. Consequently, one who eats an olive-bulk from the meat of a non-kosher animal, whether domesticated or undomesticated, is flogged. This is based on the *Torat Kohanim* (Rambam *Sefer Kedusha, Hilkhot Ma'akhalot Assurot* 2:1–2 and *Kesef Mishne* there).

When they disagree it is with regard to a kosher undomesticated animal – כִּי פְּלִיגִי בְּחַיָּה: One who sacrifices the limbs of a kosher undomesticated animal on the altar transgresses a positive mitzva but is not flogged, in accordance with the opinion of Rabbi Yoḥanan (Rambam *Sefer Avoda, Hilkhot Issurei Mizbe'aḥ* 5:6).

BACKGROUND

Prohibition that stems from a positive mitzva – לָאו הַבָּא מִכְּלַל עֲשֵׂה: This is an act prohibited implicitly by the Torah but which the Torah itself does not explicitly mention. Rather, it states a positive mitzva from which the prohibition is derived. For example, it is written concerning the Paschal offering: "And they shall eat the flesh during that night" (Exodus 12:18). This positive statement is interpreted by the Sages as a prohibition against eating the Paschal offering during the day (see *Pesaḥim* 41b). The violation of an implicit prohibition is considered like the violation of a positive mitzva. Accordingly, the court does not administer any punishment for its violation.

HALAKHA

I have told you to bring offerings from the cattle and the flock, etc. – בָּקָר וְצֹאן אָמַרְתִּי לָךְ וכו׳: All offerings of live animals may be brought from only five species: Cattle, sheep, goats, doves, and pigeons (Rambam *Sefer Avoda*, *Hilkhot Ma'aseh HaKorbanot* 1:1).

תַּלְמוּד לוֹמַר: ״בָּקָר וְצֹאן״ – בָּקָר וְצֹאן אָמַרְתִּי לָךְ, וְלֹא חַיָּה. הָא לְמָה זֶה דּוֹמֶה – לְתַלְמִיד שֶׁאָמַר לוֹ רַבּוֹ: ״אַל תָּבִיא לִי אֶלָּא חִיטִּין״ וְהֵבִיא לוֹ חִיטִּין וּשְׂעוֹרִים, שֶׁאֵינוֹ כְּמוֹסִיף עַל דְּבָרָיו אֶלָּא כִּמְעַבִיר עַל דְּבָרָיו,

Therefore, **the verse states** again: "From the **cattle**" (Leviticus 1:3), **and:** "From the **flock**" (Leviticus 1:10), to reiterate that God says: **I have told you** to bring offerings from the **cattle and the flock,**[H] **but not an undomesticated animal. To what is this comparable? To a student whose teacher told him: Bring me only wheat, and** the student **brought him wheat and barley. It is not as** though the student is **adding to the statement of** the teacher; **rather, it is as though he is disobeying his statement,** since his teacher instructed him to bring only wheat. Consequently, one who sacrifices an undomesticated animal does not merely add to a mitzva of the Torah, but also violates a prohibition,

Perek **III**
Daf **34** Amud **b**

NOTES

Does the fact that he presented some blood render the rest a remainder – שֶׁיַּעֲשֶׂה שִׁירַיִם: Although the Gemara mentions this question in connection with the clause of the mishna that addresses collecting the blood, Rashi explains that the question in fact concerns the presenting of the blood that was performed by an individual unfit for Temple service. The question is whether the presenting is significant and therefore renders the blood that remains in the neck of the animal a remainder, in which case a priest fit for service cannot subsequently collect it and present it on the altar. *Tosafot* explain that with regard to a case where blood was merely collected by an unfit individual, the mishna already teaches that a priest fit for service should collect more blood and present it.

As *Tosafot* point out, there is a difficulty with the explanation of Rashi. Reish Lakish himself holds (see 27a) that presentation of blood in an improper place is considered to have been presented in its proper place in terms of rendering the rest of the blood a remainder. It should therefore follow that the same *halakha* should apply if an individual unfit for service presented the blood (see *Shita Mekubbetzet* on 32a).

Tosafot, citing Rabbeinu Efrayim, explain that although the question of Reish Lakish concerns presenting the blood, it concerns not the blood remaining in the animal but rather the blood remaining in the vessel in which the blood was collected. Accordingly, his dilemma is that since it is taught (84a) that if an individual unfit for service collected and presented the blood and the portions of the sacrifice ascended the altar, they shall not descend, then is the blood that remains in the vessel considered a remainder and therefore poured onto the base of the altar, or is it rejected and poured down the Temple courtyard drain?

It appears that the Rambam understood the dilemma of Reish Lakish to be concerning the collecting of the blood, as follows: If an individual unfit for service collected the blood without improper intent, may a priest fit for service collect more blood, or does the individual unfit for service render the rest of the blood a remainder? (see *Ḥok Natan* and *Ḥiddushei HaGriz*).

It effects acceptance with regard to rendering the offering *piggul* – וּמְרַצֶּה לְפִיגּוּלוֹ: As long as the blood was not yet presented, the flesh is not rendered *piggul*, even if the previous sacrificial rites of slaughter, collecting, and conveying the blood were performed with intent to consume the offering beyond its designated time. Consequently, the fact that the Torah considers the sacrifice disqualified only after the blood was presented indicates that the presenting in this case is considered a significant rite.

וּפָסוּל. תְּיוּבְתָּא דְּרֵישׁ לָקִישׁ! תְּיוּבְתָּא.

and the offering is therefore **disqualified.** The Gemara concludes: **The refutation of** the opinion of **Reish Lakish** is indeed **a conclusive refutation.**

״וְכוּלָּן שֶׁקִּיבְּלוּ״ כו׳. בְּעָא מִינֵּיהּ רֵישׁ לָקִישׁ מֵרַבִּי יוֹחָנָן: פָּסוּל מַהוּ שֶׁיַּעֲשֶׂה שִׁירַיִם?

§ The mishna teaches: **And** with regard to **all of them,** in a case **where they collected** the blood with the intent to offer it beyond its designated time or outside its designated area, if there is blood of the soul that remains in the animal, the priest fit for Temple service should again collect the blood and sprinkle it on the altar. **Reish Lakish asked Rabbi Yoḥanan:** If an individual **unfit** for Temple service presented the blood, **what is** the *halakha* with regard to the blood that remains in the animal? Does the fact **that he** presented some blood **render** the rest of it **a remainder**[NH] and no longer fit to be presented, or perhaps the presenting performed by an unfit individual is not considered valid, and therefore a priest fit for Temple service may present the blood again?

אֲמַר לֵיהּ: אֵין עוֹשֶׂה שִׁירַיִם אֶלָּא חוּץ לִזְמַנּוֹ וְחוּץ לִמְקוֹמוֹ, הוֹאִיל וּמְרַצֶּה לְפִיגּוּלוֹ.

Rabbi Yoḥanan **said to him:** A not valid presenting **does not render** the rest of the blood **a remainder unless** it is a case where a priest fit for Temple service presented the blood with the intent to offer it **beyond its** designated **time or outside its** designated **area, since** it is only in that case that the presenting of the blood **effects acceptance,** i.e., it is considered a valid presenting, **with regard to** rendering the offering ***piggul*,**[N] i.e., an offering that was sacrificed with the intent to consume it after its designated time.

רַב זְבִיד מַתְנֵי הָכִי: בְּעָא מִינֵּיהּ רֵישׁ לָקִישׁ מֵרַבִּי יוֹחָנָן: כּוֹס פָּסוּל מַהוּ שֶׁיַּעֲשֶׂה שִׁירַיִם? אֲמַר לֵיהּ: פָּסוּל גּוּפֵיהּ מַאי סְבִירָא לָךְ? אִי פָּסוּל מְשַׁוֵּי שִׁירַיִם – כּוֹס פָּסוּל נַמִי מְשַׁוֵּי שִׁירַיִם, אִי פָּסוּל לָא מְשַׁוֵּי שִׁירַיִם – כּוֹס פָּסוּל נַמִי לָא מְשַׁוֵּי שִׁירַיִם!

Rav Zevid teaches the matter in **this** way: **Reish Lakish asked Rabbi Yoḥanan:** Concerning **a cup** of **disqualified** blood, e.g., one which had been taken out of the Temple courtyard and was then nevertheless presented on the altar, **what is** the *halakha* with regard to it **rendering** the remaining blood **a remainder** and unfit to be presented? Rabbi Yoḥanan **said to him:** In the case of **an unfit** individual who **himself** presented the blood, **what do you hold** to be the *halakha*? **If an unfit** individual who presented the blood **renders** the remaining blood **a remainder,** then **a cup** of **disqualified** blood should **also render** the remaining blood **a remainder. If an unfit** individual does **not render** the remaining blood **a remainder,** then **a cup** of **disqualified** blood should **also not render** the remaining blood **a remainder.**

HALAKHA

Does the fact that he presented some blood render the rest a remainder – שֶׁיַּעֲשֶׂה שִׁירַיִם: Individuals unfit for Temple service who presented blood of an offering do not render the rest of the blood a remainder, and a priest fit for service may collect the remaining blood of the soul and present it, in accordance with the opinion of Rabbi Yoḥanan. A ritually impure priest does render the blood a remainder, since he would be fit for Temple service in a case where an offering is sacrificed in a state of impurity (Rambam *Sefer Avoda*, *Hilkhot Pesulei HaMukdashin* 1:28 and Ra'avad and *Kesef Mishne* there, and see 14:2 and *Sefer Korbanot*, *Hilkhot Me'ila* 3:2).

רַב יִרְמְיָה מִדִּיפְתִּי מַתְנֵי הָכִי: בְּעָא מִינֵּיה אַבַּיֵי (מֵרָבָא) [מֵרַבָּה]: כּוֹס מַהוּ שֶׁיַּעֲשֶׂה אֶת חֲבֵירוֹ, דָּחוּי אוֹ שִׁירַיִם?

Rav Yirmeya of Difti teaches the discussion **this way: Abaye asked Rabba:** If the blood was collected in more than one cup and the presenting of the blood on the corners of the altar was performed with one **cup, what is the** *halakha*? Does the cup **render** the blood of **the other** cup **rejected,** and it is therefore poured into the drain running through the Temple courtyard, **or** does it render it **a remainder,** which is poured on the base of the altar?

אֲמַר לֵיהּ: פְּלוּגְתָּא דְּרַבִּי אֶלְעָזָר בְּרַבִּי שִׁמְעוֹן וְרַבָּנַן. דְּתַנְיָא: לְמַעְלָה הוּא אוֹמֵר: "אֶת דָּמוֹ יִשְׁפֹּךְ", לְמַטָּה הוּא אוֹמֵר: "וְאֶת כָּל דָּמָהּ יִשְׁפֹּךְ";

Rabba **said to him:** This is **a dispute between Rabbi Elazar, son of Rabbi Shimon, and the Rabbis. As it is taught** in a *baraita* with regard to the remainder of the blood of the external sin offering: In the verse **above,** discussing the sin offering of a *Nasi*, **it states: "And he shall pour its blood** out at the base of the altar of the burnt offering" (Leviticus 4:25). In the verse **below,** discussing the sin offering of an individual, **it states: "And he shall pour all its blood** out at the base of the altar" (Leviticus 4:30).

מִנַּיִן לְחַטָּאת שֶׁקִּיבֵּל דָּמָהּ בְּאַרְבָּעָה כּוֹסוֹת וְנָתַן מַתָּנָה אַחַת מִזֶּה, וּמַתָּנָה אַחַת מִזֶּה, שֶׁכּוּלָּן נִשְׁפָּכִין לַיְסוֹד – תַּלְמוּד לוֹמַר: "וְאֶת כָּל דָּמָהּ יִשְׁפֹּךְ".

The discrepancy between the first verse and the second verse, which contains the additional term "all," is explained as follows: **From where** is it derived **with regard to a sin offering which** the priest **collected its blood in four cups**[H] and **placed one placement** of blood onto the altar **from this** cup, **and one placement** of blood **from that** cup, and likewise for all four corners of the altar, **that** the remainder of blood from **all** the cups **are poured** out **onto the base** of the altar?[B] **The verse states: "And he shall pour all its blood."**

יָכוֹל נָתַן אַרְבַּע מַתָּנוֹת מִכּוֹס אֶחָד יְהוּ כּוּלָּן נִשְׁפָּכִין לַיְסוֹד? תַּלְמוּד לוֹמַר: "וְאֶת דָּמוֹ". הָא כֵּיצַד? הוּא נִשְׁפָּךְ לַיְסוֹד, וְהֵן נִשְׁפָּכִין לָאַמָּה.

One **might** have thought that if **he placed four placements** of blood of the sin offering **from one cup,** the blood in **all** the rest of the cups **should be poured onto the base** of the altar. Therefore, **the verse states: "And** he shall pour **its blood,"** and not all of its blood. **How so?** Only **that** blood in the cup from which blood was properly presented on the altar **is poured onto the base** of the altar, **and** the rest of the cups of blood are rejected and **are poured into the** Temple courtyard **drain.**

רַבִּי אֶלְעָזָר בְּרַבִּי שִׁמְעוֹן אוֹמֵר: מִנַּיִן לְחַטָּאת שֶׁקִּיבֵּל דָּמָהּ בְּאַרְבָּעָה כּוֹסוֹת וְנָתַן אַרְבַּע מַתָּנוֹת מִכּוֹס אֶחָד, שֶׁכּוּלָּן נִשְׁפָּכִין לַיְסוֹד – תַּלְמוּד לוֹמַר: "וְאֶת כָּל דָּמָהּ יִשְׁפֹּךְ". וְהָכְתִיב: "וְאֶת דָּמוֹ יִשְׁפֹּךְ"! אֲמַר רַב אַשִׁי: הַהוּא לְמַעוּטֵי שִׁירַיִם שֶׁבְּצַוַּאר בְּהֵמָה.

The *baraita* continues: **Rabbi Elazar, son of Rabbi Shimon, says: From where** is it derived **with regard to a sin offering which** the priest **collected its blood in four cups and** then **placed four placements from one cup, that** the blood from **all** the cups **are poured** out **onto the base** of the altar? **The verse states: "And he shall pour all its blood."** The Gemara asks: **But isn't it written: "And he shall pour its blood,"** which indicates that not all of the blood is poured? **Rav Ashi said: That** verse serves **to exclude** the **remainder that is in the throat of** the **animal** that was never collected in a vessel to be presented, which is not poured onto the base of the altar but into the Temple courtyard drain.

"קִיבֵּל הַכָּשֵׁר וְנָתַן לַפָּסוּל" כו'.

§ The mishna discussed three similar cases: If **the** priest **fit** for Temple service **collected** the blood in a vessel **and gave** the vessel **to an unfit** person, that person should return it to the fit priest. If the priest collected the blood in a vessel in his right hand and moved it to his left hand, he should return it to his right hand. If the priest collected the blood in a sacred vessel and placed it in a non-sacred vessel, he should return the blood to a sacred vessel.

וּצְרִיכָא, דְּאִי אַשְׁמְעִינַן פָּסוּל, הֲוָה אָמֵינָא: מַאי פָּסוּל – טָמֵא, דַּחֲזֵי לַעֲבוֹדַת צִיבּוּר, אֲבָל שְׂמֹאל – לָא.

The Gemara comments: **And** it was **necessary** to mention all of these cases, **as had** the mishna **taught us** only the case where he gave the blood to **an unfit** individual, **I would say: What** does the term: **Unfit,** mean? It means **an impure** priest, who is not completely unfit, **as he is fit for communal service** in the Temple when the priests or the entire community are impure, and that is why the blood is not disqualified; **but** if the priest moved the blood to his **left** hand, which under no circumstances may be used to perform the rite of collecting and carrying the blood, it is **no** longer valid.

HALAKHA

A sin offering which he collected its blood in four cups – חַטָּאת שֶׁקִּיבֵּל דָּמָהּ בְּאַרְבָּעָה כּוֹסוֹת וכו׳: If the blood of a sin offering was collected in four cups and one presentation was presented from each cup, the remaining blood in all four cups is poured onto the base of the altar. If all of the presentations were presented from one cup, the remaining blood in that cup is poured onto the base of the altar, and the blood in the other cups is poured into the Temple courtyard drain, in accordance with the opinion of the Rabbis (Rambam *Sefer Avoda, Hilkhot Pesulei HaMukdashin* 2:21).

BACKGROUND

Base of the altar – יְסוֹד הַמִּזְבֵּחַ:

The High Priest pouring blood on the base of the altar

NOTES

But let the blood be considered rejected – וְלֶיהֱוֵי לֵיהּ דָּחוּי: Rashi explains that this refers to the cases mentioned in the mishna, and the Gemara is questioning why the blood is not considered rejected and thereby disqualified, like any item that was once valid and subsequently rejected, as a rejected item cannot return to its former status of validity. *Tosafot* maintain that this principle cannot be applied to blood that was handed to an individual unfit for service or put in the left hand, since these actions are insignificant. They are comparable to when, as often occurred, a priest would place the vessel with the blood on a platform while waiting for the opportunity to present it. *Tosafot* explain that the question is limited to the case where the blood was put in a non-sacred vessel. See *Keren Ora*, which maintains that the discussion of the Gemara does not concern the cases where the blood was handed over improperly, but rather concerns the subsequent case in the mishna, where the blood spilled from the vessel onto the floor and was then gathered up.

BACKGROUND

Scapegoat – מִשְׁתַּלֵּחַ: The Torah requires that lots be drawn on Yom Kippur for two goats, one to be sacrificed as a sin offering in the Temple and one to be sent to Azazel (see Leviticus, chapter 16). This goat was thrown from a high desert cliff some 12–15 km from Jerusalem. Before sending the goat to its death, the High Priest would place his hands on the animal's head and confess the sins of the Jewish people, their intentional and inadvertent violations. During the confession, the High Priest would pronounce the ineffable name of God three times, leading all present to fall down to the ground in reverence. Afterward, he would send the goat to the wilderness with a person specifically designated for this task. The service associated with this goat, an essential part of the Yom Kippur ritual, atoned for sins that were not atoned for by any other offering.

Above: Lottery of the two goats conducted in the Temple on Yom Kippur

Top Right: High Priest confessing over the goat on Yom Kippur

Bottom Right: Scapegoat on its journey to the wilderness

Far Right: Scapegoat thrown from the cliff

וְאִי אַשְׁמַעִינַן שְׂמֹאל – דְּאִית לֵיהּ הֶכְשֵׁירָא בְּיוֹם הַכִּיפּוּרִים, אֲבָל כְּלִי חוֹל – לָא.

And had the mishna **taught us** only with regard to moving the blood to his **left** hand that he should return it to his right hand and present it, one would assume that the reason is **that** the left hand **has validity on Yom Kippur,** since the High Priest carries the spoon of incense with his left hand, **but** if he poured the blood into **a non-sacred vessel** then it is **not** valid.

וְאִי אַשְׁמַעִינַן כְּלִי חוֹל – מִשּׁוּם דַּחֲזוּ לְקִדּוּשִׁינְהוּ, אֲבָל הָנָךְ – אֵימָא לָא, צְרִיכָא.

And had the mishna **taught us** only with regard to **a non-sacred vessel** that the blood is not disqualified, one could suggest that perhaps it is **because** the vessels **are suitable to be consecrated, but** with regard to **these,** i.e., an unfit individual and the left hand, which have no possibility of becoming fit for service, **say** that the blood does **not** remain valid. Therefore, it is **necessary** for all of the cases to be mentioned.

וְלֶיהֱוֵי לֵיהּ דָּחוּי! אֲמַר לֵיהּ רָבִינָא לְרַב אַשִׁי, הָכִי אָמַר רַב יִרְמְיָה מִדִּיפְתִּי מִשְּׁמֵיהּ דְּרָבָא: הָא מַנִּי – חָנָן הַמִּצְרִי הוּא, דְּלֵית לֵיהּ דִּחוּיִין.

§ The Gemara questions the actual *halakha*: **But let** the blood **be** considered **rejected**[N] when placed in the hand of the unfit individual, the left hand, or the non-sacred vessel. **Ravina said to Rav Ashi: This is** what **Rav Yirmeya of Difti says in the name of Rava:** In accordance with **whose** opinion **is this mishna? It is** in accordance with the opinion of **Ḥanan the Egyptian, who does not** subscribe to the *halakha* of **rejection,** but holds that a sacrifice that was rejected temporarily is not rejected entirely.

דְּתַנְיָא, חָנָן הַמִּצְרִי אוֹמֵר: אֲפִילּוּ דָּם בַּכּוֹס – מֵבִיא חֲבֵירוֹ וּמְזַוֵּוג לוֹ.

This is **as it is taught** in a *baraita*: **Ḥanan the Egyptian says:** In the event that the scapegoat of Yom Kippur was lost, **even** if the **blood** of its partner that is sacrificed to God has already been collected **in the cup,** the blood is not rejected, but rather **he brings** another scapegoat as **its counterpart, and pairs it with** the goat that has already been slaughtered, and the blood is sprinkled.

רַב אַשִׁי אָמַר: כָּל שֶׁבְּיָדוֹ לָא הָוֵי דָּחוּי.

Rav Ashi says that there is another explanation to the mishna: **Anything that is in his power** to rectify **is not** considered **rejected,** as in these cases where he can simply return the blood to its proper place.

אֲמַר רַב שַׁיָּיא: כְּוָותֵיהּ דְּרַב אַשִׁי מִסְתַּבְּרָא; מַאן שָׁמְעַתְּ לֵיהּ דְּאִית לֵיהּ דִּחוּיִין – רַבִּי יְהוּדָה, דִּתְנַן: וְעוֹד אָמַר רַבִּי יְהוּדָה: נִשְׁפַּךְ הַדָּם – יָמוּת הַמִּשְׁתַּלֵּחַ, מֵת הַמִּשְׁתַּלֵּחַ – יִשָּׁפֵךְ הַדָּם.

Rav Shaya said: It **is reasonable** to explain the mishna **in accordance with** the opinion **of Rav Ashi,** as **whom have you heard who accepts** the reasoning of **rejection?** It is **Rabbi Yehuda, as we learned** in a mishna (*Yoma* 62a): **And furthermore, Rabbi Yehuda said:** If **the blood** of the goat sacrificed to God **spilled** from the cup before it was sprinkled, **the scapegoat**[B] is left to **die.** Similarly, if **the scapegoat died, the blood** of the goat sacrificed to God **should be spilled,** and two other goats are used. Consequently, Rabbi Yehuda holds that the scapegoat, or in the opposite case, the blood of the goat to be sacrificed to God, is totally rejected.

וְשָׁמְעִינַן לֵיהּ דְּאָמַר: כׇּל שֶׁבְּיָדוֹ – לָא הָוֵי דָּחוּי, דְּתַנְיָא, רַבִּי יְהוּדָה אוֹמֵר: כּוֹס אֶחָד הָיָה מְמַלֵּא מִדַּם הַתַּעֲרוֹבֶת וְזוֹרְקוֹ זְרִיקָה אַחַת כְּנֶגֶד הַיְסוֹד. שְׁמַע מִינָּהּ: כׇּל שֶׁבְּיָדוֹ לָא הָוֵי דָּחוּי, שְׁמַע מִינָּהּ.

And yet, **we have heard that** Rabbi Yehuda **says: Anything that is in his power** to rectify **is not rejected. As it is taught** in a *baraita*: **Rabbi Yehuda says:** A priest **would fill one cup with blood of the** many Paschal offerings brought that day that was now **mixed** together on the floor **and then sprinkle it** with **a single sprinkling against the base** of the altar. **Conclude from** the *baraita* that Rabbi Yehuda holds that although the blood originally spilled from the cup, **anything that is in his power** to rectify **is not rejected.** The Gemara affirms: **Conclude from it** that it is so.

גּוּפָא, תַּנְיָא, רַבִּי יְהוּדָה אוֹמֵר: כּוֹס אֶחָד הָיָה מְמַלֵּא מִדַּם הַתַּעֲרוֹבֶת, שֶׁאִם יִשָּׁפֵךְ אֶחָד מֵהֶם נִמְצָא שֶׁהוּא מַכְשִׁירוֹ. אָמְרוּ לוֹ לְרַבִּי יְהוּדָה: וַהֲלֹא לֹא נִתְקַבֵּל בִּכְלִי! מְנָא יָדְעִי? אֶלָּא, שֶׁמָּא לֹא נִתְקַבֵּל בִּכְלִי! אָמַר לָהֶן:

§ The Gemara discusses **the matter itself: It is taught** in a *baraita*: **Rabbi Yehuda says:** A priest **would fill one cup with the mixed blood,** so **that if one of** the cups with the collected blood of one of the Paschal offerings **were to spill,** it would be **found that this** cup of the mixed blood that was sprinkled **would render** the sacrifice **valid.** The Rabbis **said to Rabbi Yehuda: But** the mixed blood **was not collected in a vessel.** The Gemara asks: **From where do** the Rabbis **know** that the blood was not collected in a vessel? Perhaps it was collected and it spilled out. **Rather,** this is what they are saying: **Perhaps it was not collected in a vessel.** Rabbi Yehuda **said to them:**

Perek **III**
Daf **35** Amud **a**

אַף אֲנִי לֹא אָמַרְתִּי אֶלָּא כְּשֶׁנִּתְקַבֵּל בִּכְלִי. וְהוּא גּוּפֵיהּ מְנָא יָדַע? כֹּהֲנִים זְרִיזִין, וְעָבְדִין הַיָּיא וּמִשְׁתַּפְּכִין.

I too said that the blood should be sprinkled **only when it was collected in a vessel.** The Gemara asks: **But he,** Rabbi Yehuda, **himself, from where did he know** if the blood was indeed collected? The Gemara answers: He relies on the fact that **priests are vigilant,** and perform their service properly and collect all of the blood. **But they work swiftly, and** the blood therefore **spills** from the cup.

וַהֲלֹא דַּם הַתַּמְצִית מְעוֹרָב בּוֹ! רַבִּי יְהוּדָה לְטַעְמֵיהּ, דְּאָמַר: דַּם הַתַּמְצִית קְרִי דָּם.

The Gemara asks: **But isn't blood of exudate,**[H] which is unfit to be sprinkled upon the altar, **mixed with** the blood of the soul on the floor? The Gemara answers: **Rabbi Yehuda** conforms **to his** standard line of **reasoning, as he says** that **blood of exudate is considered blood.**

דְּתַנְיָא: דַּם הַתַּמְצִית בְּאַזְהָרָה, רַבִּי יְהוּדָה אוֹמֵר: בְּכָרֵת.

This is **as it is taught** in a *baraita*: **Blood of exudate** is **subject to a prohibition,** and one who consumes it receives lashes. This is not as severe as consuming blood of the soul, the blood that spurts out of an animal as it is being slaughtered, for which one is liable to receive *karet*. **Rabbi Yehuda says:** One who consumes blood of exudate is liable **to** receive ***karet***, as this blood is treated as proper blood.

וְהָאָמַר רַבִּי אֶלְעָזָר: מוֹדֶה רַבִּי יְהוּדָה לְעִנְיַן כַּפָּרָה שֶׁאֵינוֹ מְכַפֵּר, שֶׁנֶּאֱמַר: ״כִּי הַדָּם הוּא הַנֶּפֶשׁ״,

The Gemara challenges this answer: **But doesn't Rabbi Elazar say** that **Rabbi Yehuda concedes with regard to atonement that** presenting blood of exudate **does not effect atonement, as it is stated:** "For the soul of the flesh is in the blood; and I have given it to you upon the altar to make atonement for your souls; **for it is the blood** that makes atonement by reason **of the soul**" (Leviticus 17:11).

דָּם שֶׁהַנֶּפֶשׁ יוֹצְאָה בּוֹ – קָרוּי דָּם, שֶׁאֵין הַנֶּפֶשׁ יוֹצְאָה בּוֹ – אֵין קָרוּי דָּם!

This verse indicates that **blood with which the soul leaves** the animal, i.e., that spurts immediately upon slaughter, **is called blood;** but blood **with which the soul does not leave** the animal, i.e., blood of exudate, **is not called blood.** If so, even according to Rabbi Yehuda, blood of exudate is unfit for presenting upon the altar, and collecting blood from the floor should therefore be ineffective.

אֶלָּא רַבִּי יְהוּדָה לְטַעְמֵיהּ, דְּאָמַר: אֵין דָּם מְבַטֵּל דָּם.

Rather, Rabbi Yehuda conforms **to his** line of **reasoning, as he says: Blood does not nullify blood.**[N] Therefore, the blood in the cup that is fit for sprinkling on the altar is not nullified by the blood of exudate, and the entire mixture may be sprinkled on the altar.

HALAKHA

Blood of exudate – דַּם הַתַּמְצִית: One who consumes blood of exudate is not liable to receive *karet*, but he is flogged if he consumed an olive-bulk of blood, in accordance with the opinion of the first *tanna* (Rambam *Sefer Kedusha, Hilkhot Ma'akhalot Assurot* 6:4).

NOTES

Blood does not nullify blood – אֵין דָּם מְבַטֵּל דָּם: The opinion of Rabbi Yehuda with regard to the *halakhot* of nullification is that a substance is not nullified by another substance of the same type. Therefore, blood is not nullified when it mixes with other blood, and even if one sprinkles the blood of the soul together with blood of exudate, the blood of the soul is not nullified and still effects atonement.

אָמַר לָהֶם רַבִּי יְהוּדָה: לְדִבְרֵיכֶם, לָמָּה פּוֹקְקִין הָעֲזָרָה? אָמְרוּ לוֹ: שֶׁבַח הוּא לִבְנֵי אַהֲרֹן שֶׁיְּהַלְּכוּ עַד אַרְכּוּבוֹתֵיהֶן בְּדָם.

The Gemara cites the continuation of the *baraita*: **Rabbi Yehuda said to the Rabbis: According to your statement** that the mixed blood on the floor may not be used, **why do they plug** the drain of **the** Temple **courtyard** on Passover eve and not allow the blood to flow out through it? The **Rabbis said to him: It is a source of praise for the sons of Aaron**[N] **that they should walk in blood up to their ankles,** thereby demonstrating their love for the Temple service.

וְהָא דָּם הָוֵי חֲצִיצָה! לַח הוּא, וְלָא הָוֵי חֲצִיצָה. דִּתְנַן: הַדָּם, וְהַדְּיוֹ, וְהַדְּבַשׁ, וְהֶחָלָב, יְבֵישִׁין – חוֹצְצִין, לַחִין – אֵין חוֹצְצִין.

The Gemara challenges: **But the blood is an interposition** between the feet of the priests and the floor of the Temple, and this should invalidate the service. The Gemara explains: The blood **is moist and** is therefore **not an interposition, as we learned** in a *baraita*: With regard to **blood, ink,**[H] **honey, and milk,** when they are **dry they interpose,** but when they are **moist they do not interpose.**

וְהָא קָא מִיתַּוְּסֵי מָאנַיְיהוּ, וּתְנַן: הָיוּ בְּגָדָיו מְטוּשְׁטָשִׁין וְעָבַד – עֲבוֹדָתוֹ פְּסוּלָה! וְכִי תֵּימָא דְּמִדְלוּ לְהוּ – וְהָתַנְיָא: ״מִדּוֹ״ – כְּמִדָּתוֹ, שֶׁלֹּא יְחַסֵּר וְשֶׁלֹּא יוֹתִיר! בְּהוֹלָכַת אֵבָרִים לַכֶּבֶשׁ, דְּלָאו עֲבוֹדָה הִיא.

The Gemara asks further: **But don't their garments become soiled? And we learned** in a *baraita*: If a priest's **garments were soiled**[H] **and he performed** a Temple **rite** while wearing them, **his rite is disqualified. And if you would say that they raised** their garments so that they would stay clean, **but isn't it taught** in a *baraita*: "And the priest shall put on **his** linen **garment** [*middo vad*]" (Leviticus 6:3). The term *middo*, literally, his measure, teaches that his garment must be **according to his measure** [*kemiddato*], i.e., **that it should not be** too short **and that it should not be** too long. If the priest raises his garment, it will no longer be exactly his size. The Gemara answers that the priests would walk in the blood only **while carrying the** sacrificial **limbs to the ramp** of the altar, **which is not** actually **a rite,** but only preparation for a rite.

וְלָא? וְהָתַנְיָא: ״וְהִקְרִיב הַכֹּהֵן אֶת הַכֹּל״ – זוֹ הוֹלָכַת אֵבָרִים לַכֶּבֶשׁ. אֶלָּא בְּהוֹלָכַת עֵצִים לַמַּעֲרָכָה, דְּלָאו עֲבוֹדָה הִיא. וְלַעֲבוֹדָה הֵיכִי אָזְלִי? אָזְלִי אַאִיצְטָבֵי.

The Gemara asks: **And** is it **not** one of the rites? **But isn't it taught** in a *baraita*: **"And the priest shall bring it all** and burn it upon the altar" (Leviticus 1:13); **this is referring** to **the carrying of the limbs to the ramp? Rather,** the priests would walk in the blood only **while carrying wood to the arrangement** of wood on the altar, **which is not a rite.** The Gemara asks: **But** if the floor of the Temple was full of blood; **how did they walk to** perform **the** actual **rites** without soiling their garments? The Gemara answers: **They would walk on platforms** raised above the floor, so that the blood would not reach their garments.

מתני׳ הַשּׁוֹחֵט אֶת הַזֶּבַח לֶאֱכוֹל דָּבָר שֶׁאֵין דַּרְכּוֹ לֶאֱכוֹל, וּלְהַקְטִיר דָּבָר שֶׁאֵין דַּרְכּוֹ לְהַקְטִיר – כָּשֵׁר, וְרַבִּי אֱלִיעֶזֶר פּוֹסֵל.

MISHNA In the case of **one who slaughters an offering** with the intent **to eat,** beyond its designated time or outside its designated area, **an item whose** typical **manner** is such that one does **not partake** of it,[H] e.g., the portions of the offering consumed on the altar, **or** with the intent **to burn,** beyond its designated time or outside its designated area, **an item whose** typical **manner** is such that one does **not burn** it on the altar, e.g., the meat of the offering, the offering is **fit, and Rabbi Eliezer deems** it **unfit.**[N]

לֶאֱכוֹל דָּבָר שֶׁדַּרְכּוֹ לֶאֱכוֹל, וּלְהַקְטִיר דָּבָר שֶׁדַּרְכּוֹ לְהַקְטִיר פָּחוֹת מִכַּזַּיִת – כָּשֵׁר. לֶאֱכוֹל כַּחֲצִי זַיִת וּלְהַקְטִיר כַּחֲצִי זַיִת – כָּשֵׁר, שֶׁאֵין אֲכִילָה וְהַקְטָרָה מִצְטָרְפִין.

One who slaughters an offering with the intent **to eat,** beyond its designated time or outside its designated area, **an item whose** typical **manner** is such that one does **partake** of it, **or** with the intent **to burn,** beyond its designated time or outside its designated area, **an item whose** typical **manner** is such that one does **burn** it on the altar, but his intent was to partake or burn **less than an olive-bulk,**[H] the offering is **fit.** If his intent was **to eat half an olive-bulk and to burn half an olive-bulk**[H] beyond its designated time or outside its designated area, the offering is **fit, because eating and burning do not join together.**

HALAKHA

Blood, ink, etc. – הַדָּם וְהַדְּיוֹ וכו׳: Concerning ink, milk, honey, blood, the sap of figs, the sap of mulberries, the sap of carob, and the sap of the sycamore tree, while they are dry they interpose, but while they are moist they do not interpose. All other types of sap interpose even while moist. Likewise, blood that is stuck to the skin, even if it is moist, interposes (Rambam *Sefer Tahara, Hilkhot Mikvaot* 2:2 and *Kesef Mishne* there; *Shulḥan Arukh, Yoreh De'a* 198:15–16).

If his garments were soiled, etc. – הָיוּ בְּגָדָיו מְטוּשְׁטָשִׁין וכו׳: If while performing the Temple service a priest wore garments that were soiled or torn, were longer than his measure, or were shorter than his measure, the service is not valid, in accordance with the ruling of the *baraita* (Rambam *Sefer Avoda, Hilkhot Kelei HaMikdash* 8:4).

One who slaughters…with intent to eat an item whose typical manner is that one does not partake of it – הַשּׁוֹחֵט...לֶאֱכוֹל דָּבָר שֶׁאֵין דַּרְכּוֹ לֶאֱכוֹל: One who has intent during one of the four sacrificial rites to partake of an item that is not typically eaten, or to burn an item that is not typically burned on the altar, whether it was intent to partake of it or to burn it outside of its designated area, or intent to partake of it or to burn it beyond its designated time, the offering is valid, in accordance with the unattributed opinion in the mishna (Rambam *Sefer Avoda, Hilkhot Pesulei HaMukdashin* 14:8).

Partake of or to burn…less than an olive-bulk – לֶאֱכוֹל...וּלְהַקְטִיר...פָּחוֹת מִכַּזַּיִת: Eating less than an olive-bulk is not considered eating. Therefore, in a case where one has intent to eat less than an olive-bulk of part of an offering, even if it is a part that is typically eaten, or if one had intent to burn less than an olive-bulk of a part that is normally burned, whether it was intent to partake of it or to burn it beyond its designated time, or intent to partake of it or to burn it outside of its designated area, the offering is valid, in accordance with the ruling of the mishna (Rambam *Sefer Avoda, Hilkhot Pesulei HaMukdashin* 14:10).

To eat half an olive-bulk and to burn half an olive-bulk – לֶאֱכוֹל כַּחֲצִי זַיִת וּלְהַקְטִיר כַּחֲצִי זַיִת: If one had intent to eat half an olive-bulk and to burn half an olive-bulk outside its designated area, or if he had intent to eat half an olive-bulk and to burn half an olive-bulk beyond its designated time, the offering is valid, because eating and burning do not join together, in accordance with the ruling of the mishna. But if he expressed the intent to burn it employing a term of consumption, then they do join together (Rambam *Sefer Avoda, Hilkhot Pesulei HaMukdashin* 14:10).

NOTES

It is a source of praise for the sons of Aaron, etc. – שֶׁבַח הוּא לִבְנֵי אַהֲרֹן וכו׳: It would seem that the praise stems from two factors: First, that there are so many offerings, as all Jews brings Paschal offerings (see *Sefat Emet*); second, that the priests are undeterred by the blood and walk in it, demonstrating that since it is the blood of offerings they are not revolted by it.

Rabbi Eliezer deems it unfit – רַבִּי אֱלִיעֶזֶר פּוֹסֵל: In tractate *Menaḥot* (17a) it is explained that the reason for the opinion of Rabbi Eliezer is that he derives from the doubled verb in the verse: "And if it will be eaten [*he'akhol ye'akhel*]" (Leviticus 7:18), that improper intent can be effected from the parts of the offering that are eaten to parts of the offering that are burned, and the reverse. Rabbi Eliezer employs the term: Unfit, and not the term: Renders it *piggul*, because intent to eat or burn it beyond the designated area is included here as well, which does not render the offering *piggul* but simply disqualifies it. If he had intent to eat it or burn it beyond its designated time, then it would in fact be rendered *piggul*. There are opinions recorded in the Gemara in *Menaḥot* that Rabbi Eliezer deems it unfit only by rabbinic law.

הַשּׁוֹחֵט אֶת הַזֶּבַח לֶאֱכוֹל כַּזַּיִת מִן הָעוֹר, וּמִן הָרוֹטֶב, וּמִן הַקִּיפָה, וּמִן הָאָלָל, וּמִן הָעֲצָמוֹת, וּמִן הַגִּידִין, וּמִן הַקְּרָנַיִם, וּמִן הַטְּלָפַיִם, חוּץ לִזְמַנּוֹ וְחוּץ לִמְקוֹמוֹ – כָּשֵׁר, וְאֵין חַיָּיבִין עֲלֵיהֶן מִשּׁוּם פִּיגּוּל, וְנוֹתָר, וְטָמֵא.

In the case of **one who slaughters an offering** with the intent **to eat, beyond its** designated **time or outside its** designated **area, an olive-bulk from the hide,**[H] **or from the gravy, or from the spices** that amass at the bottom of the pot together with small amounts of meat, **or from a tendon in the neck,**[N] **or from the bones, or from the tendons,**[N] **or from the horns, or from the hooves,**[N] the offering is **fit and one is not liable** to receive *karet* **for it,** neither **due to** the prohibition of ***piggul,***[H] if the sacrificial rites were performed with the intent to partake of the offering beyond its designated time, **nor** due to the prohibition of **leftover** meat beyond the designated time, **nor** due to the prohibition against partaking of the meat while **ritually impure.**

הַשּׁוֹחֵט אֶת הַמּוּקְדָּשִׁין לֶאֱכוֹל שָׁלִיל אוֹ שִׁלְיָא בַּחוּץ – לֹא פִּיגֵּל. הַמּוֹלֵק אֶת הַתּוֹרִין לֶאֱכוֹל בֵּיצֵיהֶן בַּחוּץ – לֹא פִּיגֵּל.

In the case of **one who slaughters sacrificial** female animals with the intent **to eat the fetus**[H] of those animals **or** their **placenta outside** the designated area, **he has not rendered** the offering ***piggul.***[N] Likewise, in the case of **one who pinches**[B] **doves,** i.e., slaughters them for sacrifice by cutting the napes of their necks with his fingernail, with the intent **to eat their eggs** that are still in their bodies **outside** the designated area, **he has not rendered** the offering ***piggul.***[N] This is because the fetus, the placenta, and the eggs are not considered part of the body of the animal or the bird.

חֲלֵב מוּקְדָּשִׁין וּבֵיצֵי תוֹרִין – אֵין חַיָּיבִין עֲלֵיהֶן מִשּׁוּם פִּיגּוּל וְנוֹתָר וְטָמֵא.

For the same reason, one who consumes **the milk of sacrificial** female animals **or the eggs of doves**[HN] **is not liable** to receive *karet* for it, neither **due to the prohibition of *piggul,* nor** due to the prohibition of ***notar,* nor** due to the prohibition against partaking of the meat while **ritually impure.**

HALAKHA

To eat…an olive-bulk from the hide, etc. – לֶאֱכוֹל כַּזַּיִת מִן הָעוֹר וכו׳: One who has intent to eat or to burn an olive-bulk from the hide, the bones, the tendons, the gravy, or the flesh that remains attached to the hide after it is skinned, or from similar items that are not considered edible or fit for burning with regard to sacrifices, whether it was intent to partake of it or to burn it beyond its designated time, or intent to partake of it or to burn it outside of its designated area, the offering is valid, in accordance with the ruling of the mishna (Rambam *Sefer Avoda, Hilkhot Pesulei HaMukdashin* 14:7–8).

And one is not liable to receive *karet* for it due to the prohibition of *piggul* etc. – וְאֵין חַיָּיבִין עֲלֵיהֶן מִשּׁוּם פִּיגּוּל וכו׳: One who eats from the hide, the gravy, or the other parts listed in the mishna of an offering that was rendered *piggul* or *notar* is not liable to receive *karet*. Likewise, a ritually impure individual who ate one of these items from a valid offering is not liable to receive *karet*, but he is flogged for rebelliousness (Rambam *Sefer Avoda, Hilkhot Pesulei HaMukdashin* 18:22).

One who slaughters…with the intent to eat the fetus, etc. – הַשּׁוֹחֵט...לֶאֱכוֹל שָׁלִיל וכו׳: The fetus and the placenta are considered items that are inedible and are therefore irrelevant with regard to improper intent concerning sacrifices. Accordingly, if one had intent to partake of them or to burn them beyond their designated time, the offering is not rendered *piggul* (Rambam *Sefer Avoda, Hilkhot Pesulei HaMukdashin* 14:7).

Eggs of doves – בֵּיצֵי תוֹרִין: The eggs of birds are irrelevant with regard to improper intent concerning offerings. Accordingly, if one had intent to partake of them beyond their designated time, the offering is not rendered *piggul*. Likewise, with regard to a bird offering that was rendered *piggul* or *notar*, one who partakes of the eggs of the bird is not liable to receive *karet* due to the prohibition of *piggul* and *notar*, and the same applies if he ate them while ritually impure. This is in accordance with the ruling of the mishna. He is flogged for rebelliousness (Rambam *Sefer Avoda, Hilkhot Pesulei HaMukdashin* 14:7, 18:22).

NOTES

Tendon in the neck [*alal*] – אָלָל: Rashi explains in accordance with the opinion of Rabbi Yoḥanan in tractate *Ḥullin* (121a) that the word *alal* refers to a tendon in the neck that is very firm and inedible. The Rambam explains in accordance with the opinion of Reish Lakish in that Gemara that it is the flesh that remains attached to the hide after the hide is removed, and it is not considered to be edible (see *Tosafot*).

The tendons – הַגִּידִין: This is a general term for all of the tendons, ligaments, blood vessels, and nerves in the body (Rambam's Commentary on the Mishna).

The horns and the hooves – הַקְּרָנַיִם וְהַטְּלָפַיִם: This refers even to the soft parts that are next to the flesh and from which blood emerges when cut (Rambam's Commentary on the Mishna).

One who slaughters… to eat the fetus of those animals or their placenta…he has not rendered the offering *piggul* – הַשּׁוֹחֵט...לֶאֱכוֹל שָׁלִיל אוֹ שִׁלְיָא...לֹא פִּיגֵּל: The Rambam explains that these are considered substances that are not eaten by people. The Ra'avad, in his commentary on *Torat Kohanim*, agrees with that explanation with regard to the placenta. With regard to the fetus, he explains that according to this opinion a fetus does not become consecrated in its mother's womb but only once it is born, and it is therefore not considered part of the offering.

Outside, he has not rendered the offering *piggul* – בַּחוּץ לֹא פִּיגֵּל: This and the identical phrase in the previous sentence of the mishna are actually abbreviated statements. The intended meaning is that if the sacrifice was slaughtered with the intent to partake of it outside of its designated area then it is not disqualified, and if it was slaughtered with the intent to partake of it beyond its designated time, then it is not rendered *piggul* (Rambam's Commentary on the Mishna).

The milk of sacrificial female animals or the eggs of doves – חֲלֵב מוּקְדָּשִׁין וּבֵיצֵי תוֹרִין: In a case where an offering was slaughtered with the intent to partake of the mother animal beyond its designated time, one is not liable to receive *karet* due to the prohibition of *piggul* if one drank its milk or ate its eggs. This is because they are not at all part of the offering, as opposed to the *halakha* in the case of the fetus or the placenta (Rashi; *Keren Ora*).

BACKGROUND

One who pinches – הַמּוֹלֵק: Doves and young pigeons sacrificed as offerings in the Temple were not killed like other offerings by ritual slaughter with a knife, but rather by having the napes of their necks pinched. Performance of this task was especially difficult. The priest would hold the bird in his left hand with its legs and wings between his fingers, and the nape of its neck stretched out and facing upward. With his right fingernail, which he grew especially long for this purpose, the priest would cut the bird's neck and spine from the back until he reached and severed its windpipe and gullet. If the bird was to be sacrificed as a burnt offering, the priest would completely sever its head. If it was to be sacrificed as a sin offering, he would leave the head attached to the body. Only a priest was permitted to perform pinching, whereas animals brought as offerings in the Temple could be slaughtered even by a non-priest.

גמ׳ אָמַר רַבִּי אֶלְעָזָר: פִּיגֵּל בְּזֶבַח – נִתְפַּגֵּל הַשָּׁלִיל, בְּשָׁלִיל – לֹא נִתְפַּגֵּל הַזֶּבַח. פִּיגֵּל בְּאָלָל – נִתְפַּגְּלָה מוּרְאָה, בְּמוּרְאָה – לֹא נִתְפַּגֵּל אָלָל.

GEMARA **Rabbi Elazar says:** If one **renders an offering *piggul***[N] by slaughtering it with the intent to partake of it beyond its designated time, its **fetus is rendered *piggul*** as well,[H] and one who eats it is liable to receive *karet*. But if he intended to partake **of the fetus** beyond its designated time, **the offering has not been rendered *piggul*.** Likewise, if **he rendered** a bird offering ***piggul* by** having intent to partake of **a tendon in the neck,**[N] which is edible, beyond its designated time, then **the crop** of the bird **is rendered *piggul*** as well, although it is not considered an item that is usually eaten, since there are people who eat it. But if he intended to partake **of the crop** beyond its designated time, then **a tendon in the neck is not rendered *piggul*.**

פִּיגֵּל בָּאֵימוּרִין – נִתְפַּגְּלוּ פָּרִים, בַּפָּרִים – לֹא נִתְפַּגְּלוּ אֵימוּרִים.

If **he rendered** the offering ***piggul***, i.e., had improper intent **by** intending to burn **the sacrificial portions** that are consumed on the altar beyond their designated time, then **the** rest of the **bulls are rendered *piggul*.**[N] Therefore, if one partakes of their meat, he is liable to receive *karet* due to the prohibition of *piggul*. But if he intended to partake of the rest of **the bulls** beyond their designated time, since *piggul* does not apply to them, as they are not destined to be consumed on the altar or to be eaten, **the sacrificial portions** that are consumed on the altar **are not rendered *piggul*.**

לֵימָא מְסַיֵּיע לֵיהּ: וְשָׁוִים, שֶׁאִם חִישֵּׁב בַּאֲכִילַת פָּרִים וּבִשְׂרֵיפָתָן – לֹא עָשָׂה וְלֹא כְלוּם. מַאי לָאו, הָא חִישֵּׁב בָּאֵימוּרִים – נִתְפַּגְּלוּ פָּרִים? לָא,

The Gemara suggests: **Let us say** that the following *baraita* **supports** the opinion of Rabbi Elazar: **And** even those who hold that *piggul* applies to the bulls that are burned **agree that if he intended to partake of the bulls**[H] **or to burn them** beyond their designated time **he did not do anything.** This is because these bulls are not eaten or burned on the altar, and intentions can render an offering *piggul* only in the cases of offerings that are eaten or burned on the altar. The Gemara infers: **What, is it not** possible to infer **that** if **he intended with regard to the sacrificial portions** of the bulls that are consumed on the altar to burn them beyond their designated time, the **bulls are rendered *piggul*,** which is in accordance with the statement of Rabbi Elazar? The Gemara rejects this: **No,**

NOTES

If one renders an offering *piggul*, etc. – פִּיגֵּל בְּזֶבַח וכו׳: Rashi explains that according to the opinion of Rabbi Elazar, the fetus is considered a part of the offering, but it is not considered an item that is typically eaten. Therefore, if he had intent to eat the fetus beyond its proper time, it is as though he had intent with regard to an inedible item. By contrast, if the sacrifice was rendered *piggul*, the fetus is considered *piggul* as part of the offering because there are people who eat it.

If he rendered it *piggul* by intent to partake of a tendon in the neck [*alal*], etc. – פִּיגֵּל בְּאָלָל וכו׳: Although the *alal* was mentioned in the mishna as an item to which the *halakhot* of *piggul* do not apply, and Rashi explained there that it is firm and inedible, here Rashi explains that Rabbi Elazar is referring to a tendon of a bird that is soft and edible, and therefore the *halakhot* of *piggul* do apply to it just like flesh. There are those who explain that the term *alal* in the mishna is referring to the flesh that remains attached to the hide after the hide is removed. In this case, Rabbi Elazar is discussing a bird burnt offering, whose hide is not removed, and so the term must be referring to the part of the gullet that inevitably remains attached to the crop after the crop is removed. The gullet is analogized to the flesh, while the crop is analogized to the hide (*Tosafot*). The *Shita Mekubbetzet* explains that Rabbi Elazar is discussing a bird sin offering, which is eaten by the priests, and with regard to a bird burnt offering, the *halakhot* of *piggul* do not apply to the crop, since it is fit neither for eating nor for the altar.

The rest of the bulls are rendered *piggul* – נִתְפַּגְּלוּ פָּרִים: The Gemara here is referring to the bulls that are burned, which are sin offerings whose blood is sprinkled on the inner altar. The sacrificial portions of these offerings are burned on the altar, but the remaining flesh is not burned on the altar; rather, it is burned outside the Temple. Therefore, the sacrificial portions burned on the altar are subject to *piggul* if one intends to partake of them after the designated time, since they are fit for the altar, and the prohibition against consuming *piggul* then takes effect on all of the flesh of the bull as well. But if one had intent to partake of the flesh beyond its designated time, it does not render the flesh *piggul*, since the flesh is not fit for human consumption and it is not fit for the altar, as it is burned outside the Temple (Rashi; see *Tosafot*).

HALAKHA

If one renders an offering *piggul* its fetus is rendered *piggul* as well – פִּיגֵּל בְּזֶבַח נִתְפַּגֵּל הַשָּׁלִיל: With regard to an offering that was rendered *piggul*, if one partakes of the fetus or the placenta of the offering, he is liable to receive *karet* due to the prohibition of *piggul* like one who partakes of the rest of the animal, in accordance with the opinion of Rabbi Elazar. The same applies with regard to the prohibitions of *notar* and ritual impurity (Rambam *Sefer Avoda*, *Hilkhot Pesulei HaMukdashin* 18:23 and *Kesef Mishne* there).

If he intended to partake of the bulls, etc. – אִם חִישֵּׁב בַּאֲכִילַת פָּרִים וכו׳: If one had intent to partake of the flesh of the bulls or goats that are burned, outside of their designated area or beyond their designated time, they are still valid. Likewise, if he had intent to burn them beyond their designated time they are valid. This is in accordance with the ruling of the *baraita* (Rambam *Sefer Avoda*, *Hilkhot Pesulei HaMukdashin* 14:8 and *Kesef Mishne* there, and see 13:8).

הָא חִישֵּׁב בָּאֵימוּרִין – נִתְפַּגְּלוּ אֵימוּרִין עַצְמָן.

derive instead as follows: But if **he intended, with regard to the sacrificial portions** of the bulls, to burn them beyond their designated time, the **sacrificial portions themselves are rendered** ***piggul***, and one is liable to receive *karet* for eating them. The flesh of the bulls is never rendered *piggul*.

תָּא שְׁמַע: פָּרִים הַנִּשְׂרָפִים וּשְׂעִירִים הַנִּשְׂרָפִים – מוֹעֲלִין בָּהֶן מִשֶּׁהוּקְדְּשׁוּ, נִשְׁחֲטוּ – הוּכְשְׁרוּ לִיפָּסֵל בִּטְבוּל יוֹם, וּבִמְחוּסַּר כִּיפּוּרִים, וּבְלִינָה;

The Gemara suggests: **Come and hear** a proof from a mishna (*Me'ila* 9a): In the case of the **bulls that are burned**[HB] **and the goats that are burned,** one who derives benefit **from them** is liable for **misuse** of consecrated property **from the time that they were consecrated.** Once **they were slaughtered, they are susceptible to being rendered disqualified** for sacrifice **through** contact with **one who immersed that day, and through** contact with **one who has not yet** brought **an atonement** offering, **and through** being **left overnight** without the requirements of the offering having been fulfilled.

מַאי לָאו – לִינַת בָּשָׂר? וּשְׁמַע מִינָּהּ: מִגּוֹ דְּפָסְלָה בְּלִינָה – פָּסְלָה בָּהּ מַחֲשָׁבָה!

The Gemara derives: **What, is it not** referring to the **flesh** being **left overnight,**[H] which would render it not valid? **And conclude from** the mishna that **since** the flesh **is rendered disqualified by** being **left overnight,**[N] the flesh is also **rendered disqualified** by the **intention** to burn the sacrificial portions the next day, i.e., it is subject to *piggul*, which is in accordance with the statement of Rabbi Elazar.

לָא, לִינַת אֵימוּרִים. הָא מִדְּקָתָנֵי סֵיפָא: כּוּלָּן מוֹעֲלִין בָּהֶן עַל בֵּית הַדֶּשֶׁן עַד שֶׁיּוּתַּךְ הַבָּשָׂר, מִכְּלָל דְּרֵישָׁא לִינַת בָּשָׂר! מִידֵּי אִירְיָא? הָא כִּדְאִיתָא וְהָא כִּדְאִיתָא, רֵישָׁא אֵימוּרִים, וְסֵיפָא בָּשָׂר.

The Gemara responds: **No,** it is referring to **leaving overnight** the **sacrificial portions** of the offering, not the flesh. Likewise, only the sacrificial portions are rendered *piggul* by intent to eat them after their designated time. The Gemara asks: **But from** the fact **that the latter clause teaches:** One who derives benefit **from all of them by the place of the ashes**[B] where they are burned is liable for **misuse** of consecrated property **until the flesh is** completely **scorched, it may be inferred that the first clause** of the mishna is also referring to the **flesh** being **left overnight.** The Gemara answers: **Are the cases comparable? This** case is **as it is,** and **that** case is **as it is. The first clause** is referring to the **sacrificial portions** that are consumed on the altar, **and the latter clause** is referring to the **flesh.**

מוֹתִיב (רָבָא) [רַבָּה]: וְאֵלּוּ שֶׁאֵין מְפַגְּלִין וְאֵין מִתְפַּגְּלִין: צֶמֶר שֶׁבְּרָאשֵׁי כְבָשִׂים, וְשֵׂעָר שֶׁבִּזְקַן תְּיָישִׁים, וְהָעוֹר, וְהָרוֹטֶב, וְהַקִּיפָה, וְהָאָלָל, וְהַמּוּרְאָה, וְהָעֲצָמוֹת, וְהַגִּידִין, וְהַקְּרָנַיִם, וְהַטְּלָפַיִם, וְהַשָּׁלִיל, וְהַשִּׁלְיָא, וַחֲלֵב הַמּוּקְדָּשִׁין, וּבֵיצֵי תוֹרִין

Rabba raises an objection to the opinion of Rabbi Elazar from a *baraita*: **And these** are portions of the offering **that do not render** an offering ***piggul,*** **and they do not become** ***piggul***: **The wool that is on the head of the lambs,** the **hair that is in the beard of** the **goats, the hide, the gravy, the spices** that amass at the bottom of the pot together with small amounts of meat, **a tendon in the neck, the crop, the bones, the tendons, the horns, the hooves, the fetus, the placenta, the milk of sacrificial** animals, **and the eggs of doves.**

[כּוּלָּן] לֹא מְפַגְּלִין וְלֹא מִתְפַּגְּלִין, וְאֵין חַיָּיבִין עֲלֵיהֶן מִשּׁוּם פִּיגּוּל נוֹתָר וְטָמֵא, וְהַמַּעֲלֶה מֵהֶן בַּחוּץ – פָּטוּר;

The *baraita* continues: **All of these do not render** other items ***piggul*** in the case of intent to consume them after their designated time, **and they are not rendered** ***piggul,*** **and one is not liable** to receive *karet* **for them,** neither **due to** the prohibition of ***piggul,*** nor the prohibition of ***notar,*** **nor** the prohibition against partaking of the meat while **ritually impure. And one who offers up** one **of these outside** the Temple is **exempt,** since they are not fit to be sacrificed on the altar.

מַאי לָאו לֹא מְפַגְּלִין – הַזֶּבַח, וְלֹא מִתְפַּגְּלִין – מֵחֲמַת זֶבַח?

Rabba explains: **What,** does the *baraita* **not** mean that all of these items **do not render the offering** ***piggul*** if one intends to partake of them beyond the designated time, **and they** are also **not rendered** ***piggul*** **due to** the rest of the **offering** having been rendered *piggul*? This includes the fetus and placenta, and is therefore not in accordance with the statement of Rabbi Elazar that the rest of the offering does render them *piggul*.

HALAKHA

The bulls that are burned, etc. – **פָּרִים הַנִּשְׂרָפִים וכו׳**: With regard to the bulls and goats that are burned, one is liable for misuse of consecrated property if one derives benefit from them from the time that they are consecrated until they are entirely burned at the place of the ashes, in accordance with the ruling of the mishna in tractate *Me'ila* (Rambam *Sefer Avoda, Hilkhot Me'ila* 2:4).

Flesh being left overnight – **לִינַת בָּשָׂר**: With regard to the bulls and goats that are burned, there is an uncertainty (104b) as to whether being left overnight disqualifies their flesh as it does to the portions that are burned on the altar. Therefore, as a stringency they are deemed disqualified, and they are burned in the Temple courtyard (Rambam *Sefer Avoda, Hilkhot Pesulei HaMukdashin* 19:3).

BACKGROUND

Bulls that are burned – **פָּרִים הַנִּשְׂרָפִים**: There are two kinds of sin offerings: External sin offerings and inner sin offerings. An external sin offering is brought by an individual who unwittingly violated a prohibition that carries a punishment of *karet* for one who violates it intentionally. The blood of this offering is sprinkled on the corners of the external altar, and its fats and sacrificial portions are burned on that altar. The remainder of the meat is eaten by male priests. Inner sin offerings are brought by the High Priest or the community for following a mistaken halakhic ruling. In the first instance, the High Priest determined a mistaken ruling for himself and acted on it; in the second case the Sanhedrin issued a faulty judgment that led to the community sinning unwittingly. In the latter situation each tribe brings an offering to atone for its people's error. These inner sin offerings are bulls, and their blood is sprinkled toward the Curtain of the Holy of Holies and on the golden incense altar inside the Temple. Their organs are burned on the external altar, but their flesh, hides, and innards are burned outside the camp or outside the city of Jerusalem. The bull and goat sacrificed on Yom Kippur are also considered inner sin offerings.

Place of the ashes – **בֵּית הַדֶּשֶׁן**: This is a place outside Jerusalem where the ashes from the altar were deposited. The Yom Kippur sin offerings and other public sin offerings that were not eaten were burned there as well.

NOTES

Since the flesh is rendered disqualified by being left overnight, etc. – **מִגּוֹ דְּפָסְלָה בְּלִינָה**: Since the disqualification of being left overnight applies to the flesh despite its not being burned upon the altar, intent to leave it overnight also should disqualify it. This intent would be essentially identical to intent to consume it beyond its designated time. Although actual intent to eat the flesh beyond its designated time does not render the flesh *piggul*, as the flesh of the bulls and goats that are burned is not eaten by people or burned upon the altar, as explained previously (35a), nevertheless, since the disqualification of being left overnight is applicable to these offerings, it is logical that the flesh should also become *piggul* if the sacrificial portions were rendered *piggul*, in accordance with the opinion of Rabbi Elazar.

לא, לא מפגלין את הזבח, ולא מתפגלין – מחמת עצמן. אי הכי, הא דקתני סיפא: כולן לא מפגלין ולא מתפגלין, הא תו למה לי?

The Gemara responds: **No,** it means, that **they do not render the offering** ***piggul*****, and they are not rendered** ***piggul*** **due to themselves** if one had intent to partake of them beyond the designated time. But such intent with regard to the offering can render them *piggul*. The Gemara asks: **If so,** concerning **that which is taught in the latter clause: All of these do not render** other items ***piggul*** **and they are not rendered** ***piggul*****, why do I** also **need this?** Doesn't it teach that they are not rendered *piggul* due to the rest of the offering?

וליטעמיך, אין חייבין עליו משום פיגול, הא תו למה לי? אלא, איידי דבעי למיתנא נותר וטמא – תנא פיגול;

The Gemara answers: **And according to your reasoning** that the additional statement is necessary, then with regard to that which it says a third time: **One is not liable** to receive *karet* **for them due to** the prohibition of ***piggul*****, why do I** also **need this? Rather,** the third statement does not teach an additional *halakha*, but **since** the *tanna* **wants to teach** that one is not liable to receive *karet* due to violating the prohibition of ***notar*** **and** the prohibition against partaking of the meat while **ritually impure, he taught** the *halakha* with regard to ***piggul*** as well.

הכא נמי, איידי דבעי למיתני המעלה מהן בחוץ – תנא נמי: וכולן לא מפגלין ולא מתפגלין.

Here too, it can be explained similarly: **Since** the *tanna* **wants to teach** the *halakha* that **one who offers up** one **of these** items **outside** the Temple is exempt, **he also taught: And all of these do not render** other items ***piggul*** **and they are not rendered** ***piggul***. It may be that the rest of the offering does in fact render them *piggul*, as Rabbi Elazar stated.

רבא אמר: אף אנן נמי תנינא: השוחט את המוקדשים לאכול שליל או שיליא בחוץ – לא פיגל, והמולק את התורים לאכול ביציהם בחוץ – לא פיגל.

Rava says: We learn in accordance with the statement of Rabbi Elazar in the mishna **as well: One who slaughters sacrificial** female animals with the intent **to eat the fetus** of those animals **or** their **placenta outside** their designated area **has not rendered** the offering ***piggul*****. And one who pinches doves,** i.e., slaughters them for sacrifice by cutting the napes of their necks with his fingernail, with the intent **to eat their eggs** that are still in their bodies **outside** their designated area, **has not rendered** the offering ***piggul***.

והדר תני: חלב המוקדשין וביצי תורים – אין חייב עליהן משום פיגול נותר וטמא; הא שליל ושיליא – חייבים.

And then it is taught: One who consumes **the milk of sacrificial** female animals **or the eggs of doves is not liable** to receive *karet* **for** it **due to** the prohibition of ***piggul*****,** nor due to the prohibition of ***notar*****, nor** due to the prohibition against partaking of the meat while **ritually impure. But** it can be inferred that one who partakes of the **fetus or placenta,** which are not mentioned, is **liable**[H] to receive *karet* due to the prohibition of *piggul*.

אלא לאו שמע מינה: כאן – מחמת הזבח, כאן – מחמת עצמן, שמע מינה.

Rather, isn't it correct to **conclude from** the mishna that **here,** they are rendered *piggul* **due to the offering,** and **there, due to themselves,** i.e., if he had improper intent concerning them, then they are not rendered *piggul*. The Gemara affirms: **Conclude from** the mishna that it is so.

תנן התם: ובעלי מומין. רבי עקיבא מכשיר בבעלי מומים.

§ The *baraita* cited by Rabba is now discussed in a different context: **We learned** in a mishna **there** (84a) that if disqualified offerings are nevertheless brought upon the altar, they are removed, **and blemished** animals are also included in this *halakha*. **Rabbi Akiva deems blemished** animals **fit,** and if they were brought upon the altar they are not removed.

אמר רבי חייא בר אבא אמר רבי יוחנן: לא הכשיר רבי עקיבא אלא בדוקין שבעין, הואיל וכשירים בעופות. והוא שקדם הקדישה את מומה.

Rabbi Ḥiyya bar Abba says that **Rabbi Yoḥanan says: Rabbi Akiva deemed fit only** an animal with a blemish **on the cornea**[N] **of the eye**[N] and similar blemishes that are not noticeable, **since they are valid in** the case of **birds. And** in addition, **this is** the *halakha* provided **that its consecration preceded its blemish,** i.e., when the animal was consecrated it was still entirely fit.

אמר רבי חייא בר אבא: ומודה רבי עקיבא בעולת נקבה, דכמאן דקדם מומה להקדישה דמי.

Rabbi Ḥiyya bar Abba says: And Rabbi Akiva concedes with regard to a female burnt offering that was brought upon the altar **that** since a burnt offering may be only a male animal, **it is comparable** to a case **where its blemish preceded its consecration,** since the disqualifying factor was there from the outset. Therefore, if it was brought upon the altar it must be removed.

HALAKHA

One who partakes of the fetus or placenta is liable – שליל ושיליא חייבים: One who partakes of the fetus or the placenta is liable to receive *karet* due to the prohibition of *piggul*, *notar*, or ritual impurity, like one who partakes of the rest of the offering. This is in accordance with the opinion of Rabbi Elazar, and Rava's inference from the mishna (Rambam *Sefer Avoda, Hilkhot Pesulei HaMukdashin* 18:23).

NOTES

Cornea – דוקין: While some translate this term as cornea or some other part of the eye, Rashi seems to interpret it as referring specifically to some ailment in the eye's membranes that impairs vision, possibly cataracts. Others explain that it is a general term for various ailments of the eye. These ailments are listed more extensively in other places (see *Bekhorot* 28a).

Only an animal with a blemish on the cornea of the eye – אלא בדוקין שבעין: Since with regard to bird offerings this is not considered a blemish, with regard to animal offerings as well it is not considered a sufficiently significant blemish to require removal from the altar if it had already been brought upon it.

מְתִיב רַבִּי זֵירָא: הַמַּעֲלֶה מֵהֶן בַּחוּץ – פָּטוּר, הָא מֵאִימָּן – חַיָּיב, וְהֵיכִי מַשְׁכַּחַתְּ לָהּ – בְּעוֹלַת נְקֵבָה;

Rabbi Zeira raises an objection to this from the *baraita* cited by Rabba: **One who offers up** one **of these outside** the Temple is **exempt**, as they are not fit to be sacrificed on the altar. **But** it can be inferred that if he were to sacrifice **from** the flesh of the **mother of** one of **these** outside the Temple, he would be **liable. And how can you find these** circumstances? It is only **in the case of a female burnt offering.** This is because with regard to a peace offering, which may also be from a female animal, its flesh is not burned on the altar but is eaten. Therefore, there would be no liability for sacrificing it outside the Temple.

אִי אָמְרַתְּ בִּשְׁלָמָא קָסָבַר רַבִּי עֲקִיבָא עוֹלַת נְקֵבָה אִם עָלְתָה לֹא תֵּרֵד, הָא מַנִּי – רַבִּי עֲקִיבָא הִיא. אֶלָּא אִי אָמְרַתְּ אִם עָלְתָה תֵּרֵד – הָא מַנִּי?

Rabbi Zeira explains his objection: **Granted, if you say** that **Rabbi Akiva holds** with regard to **a female burnt offering** that **if it ascended** onto the altar **it does not descend,** in accordance with **whose** opinion **is this** *baraita*? It **is** that of **Rabbi Akiva.** This is because one is liable for sacrificing any offering outside the Temple that may be sacrificed on the altar, including one that was brought upon the altar inappropriately but is not removed. **But if you say** that with regard to a female burnt offering **if it ascended** the altar **it** must **descend,** and it entirely lacks the status of an offering fit to be sacrificed on the altar, in accordance with **whose** opinion **is this** *baraita*?

אֵימָא: הַמַּעֲלֶה מֵהֶן בַּחוּץ – פָּטוּר, הָא מֵאֵימוּרֵי אִימָּן – חַיָּיב.

The Gemara answers: **Say** that the inference should be as follows: **One who offers up** one **of** those items **outside** the Temple is **exempt, but** if he sacrificed **from the sacrificial portions** of the **mother of** one of **these,** he is **liable.** This *halakha* can apply to both a sin offering and a peace offering, for which a female may be brought and whose sacrificial portions are burned on the altar.

וְהָא "מֵהֶן" קָתָנֵי, וְאִימָּן דּוּמְיָא דִּידְהוּ! אֶלָּא אֵימָא: הַמַּעֲלֶה מֵאֵימוּרֵיהֶן בַּחוּץ – פָּטוּר, הָא מֵאֵימוּרֵי אִימָּן – חַיָּיב.

The Gemara challenges: **But** the *baraita* **teaches** this *halakha* with the term: **Of** one of **these,** indicating that it is referring to one who sacrifices the flesh, and not the sacrificial portions alone. **And** the case of **their mother** is **similar to** that of **them,** and is therefore referring to sacrificing the flesh of the mother outside the Temple, and not the sacrificial portions. **Rather, say** as follows: **One who offers up** part **of their sacrificial portions outside** the Temple is **exempt, but** one who offered up some **of the sacrificial portions of** the **mother of** one of **these** is **liable.**

מתני׳ שְׁחָטוֹ עַל מְנָת לְהַנִּיחַ אֶת דָּמוֹ אוֹ אֵימוּרָיו לְמָחָר, אוֹ לְהוֹצִיאָן לַחוּץ רַבִּי יְהוּדָה פּוֹסֵל, וַחֲכָמִים מַכְשִׁירִין. עַל מְנָת לִיתְּנָן עַל גַּבֵּי הַכֶּבֶשׁ שֶׁלֹּא כְּנֶגֶד הַיְּסוֹד, וְלִיתֵּן אֶת הַנִּיתָּנִים לְמַעְלָן לְמַטָּה, וְאֶת הַנִּיתָּנִים לְמַטָּה לְמַעְלָן, וְאֶת הַנִּיתָּנִים

MISHNA If one **slaughters** the animal **in order to leave its blood**[H] **or its sacrificial portions for the next day, or to remove them outside** the designated area, but not in order to sacrifice them the next day, **Rabbi Yehuda deems** the offering **unfit, and the Rabbis deem** it **fit.** In the case of one who slaughters the animal **in order to place** the blood **upon the ramp** or on the wall of the altar **that is not opposite the base** of the altar, **or** in order **to place** the blood **that is** to be **placed above** the red line **below** the red line, **or** to place the blood **that is** to be **placed below** the red line **above** the red line, **or** the blood **that is** to be **placed**

HALAKHA

One slaughters it in order to leave its blood, etc. – שְׁחָטוֹ עַל מְנָת לְהַנִּיחַ אֶת דָּמוֹ וכו׳: In a case where one has intent during the slaughter of the offering, the collection of the blood, the conveying of the blood, or the presenting of the blood, to leave over until the following day the blood of the offering or the portions that are burned on the altar, or to remove them from the Temple courtyard, or to place the blood on the ramp and not opposite the base of the altar, or to place the blood that is to be placed below the red line above the red line, or to place the blood that is to be placed above the red line below the red line, or to place the blood that is to be placed inside the Sanctuary outside the Sanctuary or vice versa, or to present the blood that is to be presented on the external altar on the inner altar or vice versa, in all of these cases the offering is valid. This is in accordance with the unattributed opinion in the mishna (Rambam *Sefer Avoda, Hilkhot Pesulei HaMukdashin* 13:8).

Perek **III**
Daf **36** Amud **a**

בִּפְנִים בַּחוּץ וְאֶת הַנִּיתָּנִין בַּחוּץ בִּפְנִים, שֶׁיֹּאכְלוּהוּ טְמֵאִים, שֶׁיַּקְרִיבוּהוּ טְמֵאִים, שֶׁיֹּאכְלוּהוּ עֲרֵלִים, וְשֶׁיַּקְרִיבוּהוּ עֲרֵלִים, לְשַׁבֵּר עַצְמוֹת הַפֶּסַח, לֶאֱכוֹל הֵימֶנּוּ נָא, וּלְעָרֵב דָּמוֹ בְּדַם הַפְּסוּלִים – כָּשֵׁר,

inside the Sanctuary **outside** the Sanctuary, **or** the blood **that is** to be **placed outside** the Sanctuary **inside** the Sanctuary; and likewise, if he slaughtered the animal with the intent **that ritually impure** people **will partake of it,**[H] or **that ritually impure** people **will sacrifice it,** or **that uncircumcised** people **will partake of it, or that uncircumcised** people **will sacrifice it;** and likewise, with regard to the Paschal offering, if he had intent during the slaughter **to break the bones of the Paschal offering,** or **to eat from** the meat of the Paschal offering **partially roasted, or to mix the blood of** an offering **with the blood of unfit** offerings, in all these cases, although he intended to perform one of these prohibited acts, some of which would render the offering unfit, the offering is **fit.**

HALAKHA

That ritually impure people will partake of it, etc. – שֶׁיֹּאכְלוּהוּ טְמֵאִים וכו׳: If one had intent concerning an offering that it will be eaten by ritually impure individuals or other individuals that are unfit to partake of it; or that it will be sacrificed by ritually impure individuals or other individuals that are unfit to sacrifice it; or intent to mix the blood of the offering with disqualified blood; or intent to break the bones of a Paschal offering or to eat it partially roasted; all of these intentions have no effect, and the offering is valid, in accordance with the ruling of the mishna (Rambam *Sefer Avoda, Hilkhot Pesulei HaMukdashin* 13:8).

שאין מחשבה פוסלת אלא בחוץ לזמנו וחוץ למקומו, והפסח והחטאת שלא לשמן.

The reason is **that intent does not render** the offering **unfit except in** cases of intent to eat or to burn the offering **beyond its** designated **time and outside its** designated **area, and** in addition, **the Paschal offering and the sin offering** are disqualified by intent to sacrifice them **not for their sake.**[H]

גמ׳ מאי טעמא דרבי יהודה? אמר רבי אלעזר: תרי קראי כתיבי בנותר, כתוב אחד אומר: ״לא תותירו ממנו עד בקר״, וכתוב אחד אומר: ״לא יניח ממנו עד בקר״, אם אינו ענין להניח – תנהו לענין מחשבת הינוח.

GEMARA The Gemara asks: **What is the reasoning of Rabbi Yehuda,** who deems the offering unfit if there was intent to leave it over until the next day or to take it out of its designated area? **Rabbi Elazar said:** There are **two verses** that **are written with regard to** ***notar*****. One verse states: "You shall let nothing of it remain until the morning,** and that which remains of it until the morning you shall burn with fire" (Exodus 12:10), **and one verse states: "He shall not leave any of it until the morning"** (Leviticus 7:15). **If** the additional verse **is not** necessary for **the matter of** the prohibition **against leaving** it overnight, which is already mentioned by the first verse, **apply it to the matter of intent of leaving** it overnight, which would therefore be prohibited as well.

ורבי יהודה, האי קרא להכי הוא דאתא? האי מיבעי ליה לכדתניא: ״ובשר זבח תודת שלמיו״ – למדנו לתודה שנאכלת ליום ולילה.

The Gemara asks: **But** according to the opinion of **Rabbi Yehuda, does this verse come to** teach **this** idea? **This** verse **is necessary for him to** derive **that which is taught** in a *baraita*: The verse states: "And the flesh of the sacrifice of his peace offerings for thanksgiving shall be eaten on the day of his offering; he shall not leave any of it until the morning" (Leviticus 7:15). From the words: **"And the flesh of the sacrifice of his peace offerings for thanksgiving," we learned with regard to a thanks offering that it is eaten for a day and a night.**[H]

חליפין וולדות תמורות מנין? תלמוד לומר: ״ובשר״. חטאת ואשם מנין? תלמוד לומר: ״זבח״.

With regard to animals **exchanged**[N] for thanks offerings, **and the offspring** of thanks offerings, and the **substitutes**[H] of thanks offerings, **from where** is it derived that they too are eaten for only a day and a night? **The verse states: "And the flesh [*uvesar*],"** and the additional "and" includes them. With regard to **a sin offering and a guilt offering, from where** is it derived[H] that they are eaten for only a day and a night? **The verse states: "Sacrifice,"** to include other types of offerings.

ומנין לרבות שלמי נזיר ושלמי פסח? תלמוד לומר: ״שלמיו״. לחמי תודה, וחלות ורקיקים שבנזיר מנין? תלמוד לומר: ״קרבנו״ – כולן קורא אני בהן ״לא יניח״.

The *baraita* continues: **And from where** is it derived **to include the peace offering of a nazirite,**[B] i.e., the ram that a nazirite brings at the close of his term of naziriteship, **and the peace offering of Passover?**[HN] **The verse** therefore **states: "His peace offerings,"** in the plural. With regard to **the loaves of the thanks offering, and the loaves and wafers that** are part of the offering brought by **a nazirite, from where** is it derived that they are eaten for only a day and a night? **The verse states: "His offering." With regard to all of them I** will **read** the phrase **"He shall not leave** any of it until the morning" as being applicable. Evidently, this verse is necessary to teach numerous *halakhot* concerning the allotted time to partake of offerings.

HALAKHA

And the Paschal offering and the sin offering not for their sake – והפסח והחטאת שלא לשמן: All offerings that were slaughtered not for their sake are fit, but they do not fulfill the obligation of the owner. Exceptions to this are the Paschal offering and the sin offering, which are unfit if they were slaughtered not for their sake (Rambam *Sefer Avoda, Hilkhot Pesulei HaMukdashin* 15:1).

A thanks offering is eaten for a day and a night – תודה נאכלת ליום ולילה: Despite its status of an offering of lesser sanctity, a thanks offering may be eaten only on the day that it is slaughtered and that following night (Rambam *Sefer Avoda, Hilkhot Ma'aseh HaKorbanot* 10:7).

The offspring and the substitutes – ולדות ותמורות: In the case of one who consecrated a thanks offering and it was lost, and he consecrated another animal in its place, and the first animal was then found and sacrificed, the second animal is sacrificed as a thanks offering as well. Likewise, the offspring of a thanks offering, and the substitute of a thanks offering, and the offspring of a substitute of a thanks offering are all sacrificed as a thanks offering. In all of these cases, the loaves of a thanks offering are not brought (Rambam *Sefer Avoda, Hilkhot Pesulei HaMukdashin* 12:8 and *Sefer Korbanot, Hilkhot Temura* 3:1, 4:1).

With regard to a sin offering and a guilt offering from where is it derived – חטאת ואשם מנין וכו׳: The ram of a nazirite, including both the portions that are eaten by the priests and the portions eaten by the owner, and the loaves that are brought with it, and a sin offering and a guilt offering, and communal peace offerings, and the leftovers of a meal offering may be eaten only on the day that the offerings are slaughtered and that following night (Rambam *Sefer Hafla'a, Hilkhot Nezirut* 8:12 and *Sefer Avoda, Hilkhot Ma'aseh HaKorbanot* 10:7).

Peace offering of Passover – שלמי פסח: The Festival peace offering of the fourteenth day of Nisan may be eaten for two days and one night, like all other peace offerings. This is in accordance with the ruling of the mishna in tractate *Pesaḥim*, and contrary to the *baraita* here (Rambam *Sefer Korbanot, Hilkhot Korban Pesaḥ* 10:13).

NOTES

Animals exchanged, etc. – חליפין וכו׳: An animal is exchanged in a situation where one consecrated as a thanks offering an animal that was then lost, and then another animal was consecrated as the offering, and subsequently the first animal was found. In that case, the second animal is also sacrificed as a thanks offering, despite the fact that it was initially intended to be a replacement for the first. A substitute animal is a non-sacred animal that one designated as the substitute of a thanks offering or another offering. In that case, the second animal is rendered a thanks offering while the first animal retains its consecrated status. The Sages derived from the verses cited that the *halakhot* of a thanks offering apply to these two cases as well as the offspring of a thanks offering, aside from the fact that the loaves of the thanks offering do not accompany them (see *Temura* 18b).

Peace offering of Passover – שלמי פסח: With regard to a standard peace offering, the verse explicitly states that it may be eaten for two days, i.e., the day it is sacrificed, the next day, and the intervening night. Rashi explains that the peace offering of Passover mentioned here is referring to the Festival peace offering of the fourteenth day of Nisan, which was sacrificed as a supplement to the Paschal offering in order to ensure that the Paschal offering would be consumed on a full stomach. See *Tosafot* (9a), who explain that it is referring to a leftover Paschal offering, i.e., an animal that was consecrated as a Paschal offering but was not actually sacrificed on the fourteenth of Nisan.

BACKGROUND

Nazirite – נזיר: A nazirite is an individual who takes a vow of naziriteship, as detailed in the Torah (see Numbers 6:1–21). A nazirite must refrain from eating or drinking products of the vine, especially wine. He must avoid contracting impurity from a corpse, and he must refrain from cutting his hair. A nazirite who violates any of these prohibitions is flogged. One can vow to be a nazirite for any period of time that he wishes, but the minimum term is thirty days. One who does not specify how long he wishes to be a nazirite assumes his obligations for thirty days. If a nazirite contracts impurity from a corpse, whether intentionally or not, he must first purify himself and then bring two pigeons or doves to the Temple as offerings, with one serving as a sin offering and the other as a burnt offering. He also brings a lamb as a guilt offering. After this, he must start his term of naziriteship anew. When the nazirite completes the term, he must bring two lambs as offerings, one female as a sin offering and one male as a burnt offering, as well as a ram for a peace offering. He shaves his hair and burns it beneath the pot in which the ram sacrificed as a peace offering is cooked. After these offerings have been sacrificed, his term of naziriteship ends.

אִם כֵּן לֵימָא קְרָא "לֹא תוֹתִירוּ", מַאי "לֹא יַנִּיחַ"? אִם אֵינוֹ עִנְיָן לְהִינּוֹחַ – תְּנֵהוּ עִנְיָן לְמַחְשֶׁבֶת הִינּוֹחַ.

The Gemara answers: **If so, let the verse state: And you shall let nothing** of it **remain** until the morning, as stated in the other verse. **What** is indicated by the phrase **"He shall not leave** any of it"? **If it is not** necessary for the **matter of** the prohibition **against leaving** it overnight, **apply it** to the **matter of intent** to **leave** it overnight.

הָתִינַח לְהַנִּיחַ, לְהוֹצִיא מַאי אִיכָּא לְמֵימַר?

The Gemara now questions the source cited by Rabbi Elazar: **This works out well** to explain the opinion of Rabbi Yehuda with regard to one who had intent **to leave** the sacrificial portions overnight. But with regard to disqualifying the offering due to one who had intent **to remove** them from the Temple, **what can be said** to explain the source of Rabbi Yehuda, as it cannot be derived from these verses?

וְעוֹד, טַעְמָא דְּרַבִּי יְהוּדָה סְבָרָא הוּא. דְּתַנְיָא, אָמַר לָהֶם רַבִּי יְהוּדָה: אִי אַתֶּם מוֹדִים שֶׁאִם הִנִּיחוֹ לְמָחָר שֶׁהוּא פָּסוּל? אַף חִישֵּׁב לְהַנִּיחוֹ לְמָחָר – פָּסוּל! אֶלָּא, טַעְמָא דְּרַבִּי יְהוּדָה סְבָרָא הוּא? וְנִיפְלוֹג נָמֵי רַבִּי יְהוּדָה בְּכוּלְּהוּ!

And furthermore, the statement of Rabbi Elazar can be questioned, as **the rationale of Rabbi Yehuda is** based on **logical reasoning** and is not derived from a verse. This is **as it is taught** in a *baraita*: **Rabbi Yehuda said to** the Rabbis: **Do you not concede that if he left it over until the next day that it is disqualified? So too,** if **he intended to leave it over**[N] **until the next day** it is **disqualified.** Clearly, Rabbi Yehuda bases his opinion on logical reasoning, as he equates intent with action. The Gemara asks: **Rather, is the rationale of Rabbi Yehuda** based on **logical reasoning** and not derived from the verse? **But** if so, **Rabbi Yehuda should also disagree with regard to all of** the other cases in the mishna due to the same reasoning.

בְּהֵי נִיפְלוֹג? בְּשׁוֹבֵר עַצְמוֹת הַפֶּסַח וְלֶאֱכוֹל מִמֶּנּוּ נָא – זִיבְחָא גּוּפֵיהּ מִי מִיפְּסִיל?

The Gemara rejects this: **With regard to which** case **should** Rabbi Yehuda **disagree?** Should he disagree **with regard to one who** slaughters the offering with intent to **break the bones of the Paschal offering, or** with intent **to partake of** the Paschal offering while it is **partially roasted?** Even had he actually realized such intent, **would the offering itself** thereby **be disqualified?** It presumably would not, as the presenting of the blood effects acceptance.

עַל מְנָת שֶׁיֹּאכְלוּהוּ טְמֵאִים וְשֶׁיַּקְרִיבוּהוּ טְמֵאִים – זִיבְחָא גּוּפֵיהּ מִי מִיפְּסִיל? שֶׁיֹּאכְלוּהוּ עֲרֵלִים וְשֶׁיַּקְרִיבוּהוּ עֲרֵלִים – זִיבְחָא גּוּפֵיהּ מִי מִיפְּסִיל? לִישָּׁנָא אַחֲרִינָא: כָּל כְּמִינֵּיהּ?

Likewise, if a rite was performed **on the condition that ritually impure** individuals **will partake of it, or that ritually impure** individuals **will sacrifice it,** i.e., burn the sacrificial portions on the altar, **would the offering itself be disqualified** if such actions occurred? Likewise, if it was done with the intent **that uncircumcised** individuals **will partake of it, or that uncircumcised** individuals **will sacrifice it, would the offering itself be disqualified** if this occurred? The Gemara presents **another version** of this question: **Is it in his** power to execute these actions that are contingent upon the will of others?

לְעָרֵב דָּמָן בְּדַם הַפְּסוּלִין – רַבִּי יְהוּדָה לְטַעְמֵיהּ, דְּאָמַר: אֵין דָּם מְבַטֵּל דָּם. לִיתֵּן אֶת הַנִּיתָּנִין לְמַעְלָה לְמַטָּה, לְמַטָּה לְמַעְלָה – רַבִּי יְהוּדָה לְטַעְמֵיהּ, דְּאָמַר: שֶׁלֹּא לִמְקוֹמוֹ נָמֵי מְקוֹמוֹ קָרֵינָא בֵּיהּ.

With regard to a case where one had intent **to mix their blood with the blood of unfit** offerings, where **Rabbi Yehuda** also does not disagree with the ruling of the mishna that the offering is valid, he conforms **to his** line of **reasoning, as he says: Blood does not nullify blood.** Therefore, even if one would actually mix the two types of blood, it would not be disqualified. Likewise, in cases where one had intent **to place** the blood **that is** to be **placed above** the red line **below** the red line, or those that are to be placed **below** the red line **above** the red line, **Rabbi Yehuda** conforms **to his** line of **reasoning, as he says:** Blood **that** was **not** placed **in its** proper **place** on the altar is **also considered** to be placed in **its** proper **place,** and it effects acceptance of the offering.

וְלִיפְלוֹג בְּנִיתָּנִין בִּפְנִים שֶׁנְּתָנָן בַּחוּץ, וְהַנִּיתָּנִין בַּחוּץ שֶׁנְּתָנָן בִּפְנִים!

The Gemara suggests: **And let him disagree with regard to** a case of blood that is to be **placed inside** the Sanctuary **that** was **placed outside, and** blood **that is** to be **placed outside** the Sanctuary **that** was **placed inside,** as the verse explicitly states that an external sin offering whose blood was sprinkled inside is disqualified (see Leviticus 6:23).

NOTES

So too if he intended to leave it over – אַף חִישֵּׁב לְהַנִּיחוֹ: Rabbi Yehuda infers the *halakha* from the *halakhot* of improper intent, where actually presenting the blood of an offering beyond its designated time or outside its designated area renders the offering not valid, and likewise intent to do so renders the offering not valid even if the intent was never actualized. If so, intent to leave over the offering should render the offering not valid, just as actually leaving over the offering would.

NOTES

That the intended place have threefold [*meshulash*] functionality – מָקוֹם שֶׁיְּהֵא מְשׁוּלָּשׁ: The explanation of *meshulash* here is in accordance with the opinion of Rashi. See 29a for other explanations of this term.

A sin offering whose blood went inside, etc. – חַטָּאת שֶׁנִּכְנַס דָּמָהּ לִפְנִים וכו׳: Since the verse states: "You shall not sacrifice [*tizbaḥ*] to the Lord…any evil thing" (Deuteronomy 17:1), and is therefore discussing the slaughter [*zeviḥa*] of the offering, it cannot be referring to one who actually brought the blood inside, but rather to one who slaughters the offering with the intent to do so (Rashi). *Tosafot* explain that Rabbi Yehuda homiletically interprets the term "evil thing [*davar ra*]" as though it were written: Evil word [*dibbur ra*], which would be referring to improper intent.

קָסָבַר רַבִּי יְהוּדָה: בָּעֵינַן מָקוֹם שֶׁיְּהֵא מְשׁוּלָּשׁ, בְּדָם בְּבָשָׂר וּבְאֵימוּרִין.

The Gemara explains: **Rabbi Yehuda holds** that in order to disqualify an offering with the intent to perform a rite outside its designated area, **we require that** the intended **place have threefold** functionality,[N] i.e., **for** the presenting of the **blood, for** the eating of the **meat, and for** the burning of the **sacrificial portions** on the altar, which is true only of the area outside the Temple courtyard, which was valid for these three activities during an era in which it was permitted to sacrifice offerings on private altars. Therefore, intent to present the blood in the Sanctuary, which lacks these three elements, does not disqualify the offering, as the meat and sacrificial portions are never eaten or burned there.

וּמִי אִית לֵיהּ לְרַבִּי יְהוּדָה הַאי סְבָרָא? וְהָתַנְיָא, רַבִּי יְהוּדָה אוֹמֵר: "דָּבָר רָע" – רִיבָּה כָּאן חַטָּאת שֶׁשְּׁחָטָהּ בַּדָּרוֹם. וְחַטָּאת שֶׁנִּכְנַס דָּמָהּ לִפְנִים – פְּסוּלָה!

The Gemara asks: **And does Rabbi Yehuda accept this reasoning** that it must be a place of threefold functionality? **But isn't it taught** in a *baraita*: **Rabbi Yehuda says** that the verse states: "You shall not sacrifice to the Lord your God an ox, or a sheep, that has a blemish, even any **evil thing**" (Deuteronomy 17:1). The verse **included here a sin offering that one slaughtered in the south** and not on the northern side of the Temple courtyard as required, **and** likewise **a sin offering whose blood entered inside,**[N] i.e., it was slaughtered with the intent that its blood would be brought inside the Sanctuary, that they are **disqualified.** This indicates that an offering slaughtered with improper intent with regard to a place that lacks threefold functionality nevertheless renders the offering not valid.

וְלֵית לְרַבִּי יְהוּדָה שְׁלִישִׁי? וְהָתְנַן, אָמַר רַבִּי יְהוּדָה: הִכְנִיס בְּשׁוֹגֵג – כָּשֵׁר; הָא בְּמֵזִיד – פָּסוּל, וְקַיְימָא לַן בְּשֶׁכִּיפֵּר;

The Gemara responds: **And** does **Rabbi Yehuda not accept** the requirement of a place of **three** functions? **But didn't we learn** in a mishna (82a) that **Rabbi Yehuda said:** If **he brought** the blood into the Sanctuary **unwittingly,** the blood remains **fit** for presenting, from which it may be inferred: **But** if he brought it in **intentionally,** it is **unfit. And we maintain** that Rabbi Yehuda deems it unfit only **where** one actually **effected atonement,** i.e., he presented the blood on the inner altar.

הַשְׁתָּא, וּמָה הָתָם עָיְילֵי עַיְּילָא, אִי כִּיפֵּר – אִין, אִי לָא כִּיפֵּר – לָא, הָכָא דְּחָשֵׁיב חֲשׁוּבֵי – לֹא כׇּל שֶׁכֵּן? תְּרֵי תַּנָּאֵי וְאַלִּיבָּא דְּרַבִּי יְהוּדָה.

Now, it stands to reason that **if there,** where one actually **brought** the blood inside, only **if he effected atonement, yes,** it is unfit, but **if he did not effect atonement** it is **not** unfit, then **here,** where he merely **thought** to bring it inside, **all the more so** is it **not** clear that it should be valid? The Gemara answers: There are **two *tanna'im*, and** they disagree **with regard to** the opinion **of Rabbi Yehuda** concerning a place with threefold functionality.

וְסָבַר רַבִּי יְהוּדָה, חַטָּאת שֶׁשְּׁחָטָהּ בַּדָּרוֹם

The Gemara asks: **And** does **Rabbi Yehuda hold** that with regard to **a sin offering that one slaughtered in the south,**

Perek **III**
Daf **36** Amud **b**

יְהֵא חַיָּיב?

the slaughterer **would be liable** to receive lashes?

וְהָתַנְיָא, רַבִּי יְהוּדָה אוֹמֵר: יָכוֹל חַטָּאת שֶׁשְּׁחָטָהּ בַּדָּרוֹם יְהֵא חַיָּיב? תַּלְמוּד לוֹמַר: "לֹא תִזְבַּח לַה׳ אֱלֹהֶיךָ שׁוֹר וָשֶׂה וגו׳ כֹּל דָּבָר רָע" – עַל דָּבָר רַע אַתָּה מְחַיְּיבוֹ, וְאִי אַתָּה מְחַיְּיבוֹ עַל חַטָּאת שֶׁשְּׁחָטָהּ בַּדָּרוֹם! תְּרֵי תַּנָּאֵי אַלִּיבָּא דְּרַבִּי יְהוּדָה.

But isn't it taught in a *baraita*: **Rabbi Yehuda says:** One **might** have thought that with regard to **a sin offering that one slaughtered in the south, he would be liable** for it. Therefore, **the verse states: "You shall not sacrifice to the Lord your God an ox, or a sheep,** that has a blemish, even **any evil thing"** (Deuteronomy 17:1), to teach that **for** slaughtering **an evil thing,** such as a blemished offering, **you deem him liable** to receive lashes, **but you do not deem him liable for a sin offering that he slaughtered in the south.** The Gemara answers: Here too, there are **two *tanna'im*,** and they disagree **with regard to** the opinion **of Rabbi Yehuda.**

אָמַר רַבִּי אַבָּא: וּמוֹדֶה רַבִּי יְהוּדָה, שֶׁחוֹזֵר וְקוֹבְעוֹ לְפִיגּוּל.

§ **Rabbi Abba says:** Although Rabbi Yehuda says that an offering is rendered not valid if it was slaughtered with the intent that its blood would be left over until the next day, **Rabbi Yehuda concedes that** if the priest subsequently collected, conveyed, or presented the blood with the intent to sacrifice or partake of the offering beyond its designated time, **he then establishes** the offering **as *piggul*.** The intent to leave it overnight does not prevent it from being rendered *piggul*, in contrast to intent to sacrifice or partake of it outside its designated area, or performing a sacrificial rite of the Paschal offering or a sin offering not for its own sake, which do prevent the offering from subsequently being rendered *piggul* (see 29b).

אָמַר רָבָא: תֵּדַע, דְּפִיגּוּל לִפְנֵי זְרִיקָה לָא כְּלוּם הוּא, וְאָתְיָא זְרִיקָה וְקָבְעָה לָהּ בְּפִיגּוּל.

Rava says: Know that this is so, **as** intent to sprinkle the blood the next day, which renders an offering ***piggul*** and which inherently includes the intent to leave the blood over until the next day so that he can then sprinkle it, **is nothing before** the **sprinkling** of the blood. And his intent during the slaughter to sprinkle the blood the next day does not render the offering *piggul* until the blood is sprinkled, **and** then the **sprinkling** of the blood **comes and establishes** the offering **as *piggul*.** Clearly, the intent to leave the blood over until the next day does not prevent the offering from subsequently being rendered *piggul*.

וְלָא הִיא, הָתָם הוּא חֲדָא מַחֲשָׁבָה הִיא, הָכָא – תְּרֵי מַחֲשָׁבוֹת.

The Gemara rejects Rava's proof: **But it is not so** that this is a valid proof, as **there,** with regard to standard *piggul* intent, **it is one intent** that is established with the sprinkling of the blood. By contrast, **here,** where he initially had intent to leave the blood until the next day and subsequently had intent to sprinkle it beyond its designated time, there are **two** separate **intents.** Therefore, since an improper intent already exists, the offering cannot thereafter be rendered *piggul*.

אֵיתִיבֵיהּ רַב הוּנָא לְרַבִּי אַבָּא: לִיתֵּן אֶת הַנִּיתָּנִין לְמַעְלָה לְמַטָּה, לְמַטָּה לְמַעְלָה, לְאַלְתַּר – כָּשֵׁר; חָזַר וְחִישֵּׁב חוּץ לִמְקוֹמוֹ – פָּסוּל וְאֵין בּוֹ כָּרֵת, חוּץ לִזְמַנּוֹ – פִּיגּוּל וְחַיָּיבִין עָלָיו כָּרֵת.

Rav Huna raised an objection to Rabbi Abba from a *baraita*: If one slaughtered an offering with the intent **to place** the blood **that is** to be **placed above** the red line **below** the red line, or to place the blood that is to be placed **below** the red line **above** the red line, and he had intent to do so **immediately,** i.e., on the same day, then it is **valid,** as such intent does not disqualify the offering. If **he then had intent** to sacrifice the offering **outside its** designated **area,** it is **disqualified, but there is no** liability to receive ***karet* for it.** If he had intent to sacrifice it **beyond its** designated **time,** then it is rendered ***piggul*, and one is liable** to receive ***karet* for it.**

לְמָחָר – פָּסוּל; חָזַר וְחִישֵּׁב, בֵּין חוּץ לִזְמַנּוֹ בֵּין חוּץ לִמְקוֹמוֹ – פָּסוּל, וְאֵין בּוֹ כָּרֵת. תְּיוּבְתָּא דְּרַבִּי אַבָּא! תְּיוּבְתָּא.

The *baraita* continues: If one had intent to place the blood that is to be placed above the red line below the red line or vice versa **the next day,** then it is **disqualified,** due to his intent to leave it overnight, in accordance with the statement of Rabbi Yehuda. In this case, if **he then had intent** to sacrifice the same offering **either beyond its** designated **time or outside its** designated **area,** it is **disqualified, and there is no** liability to receive ***karet* for it.** Evidently, intent to leave it overnight prevents the offering from subsequently being rendered *piggul*. The Gemara concludes: **The refutation of** the opinion of **Rabbi Abba** is indeed **a conclusive refutation.**

אָמַר רַב חִסְדָּא אָמַר רָבִינָא בַּר סִילָא: חִישֵּׁב שֶׁיֹּאכְלוּהוּ טְמֵאִים לְמָחָר – חַיָּיב. אָמַר רָבָא: תֵּדַע, דְּבָשָׂר לִפְנֵי זְרִיקָה לָא חֲזִי, וְכִי מְחַשֵּׁב בֵּיהּ – מִיפְּסִיל.

§ **Rav Ḥisda says** that **Ravina bar Sila says:** If one slaughtered an offering with **intent that impure** individuals **would eat** the meat of the offering **the next day,**[H] one is **liable** to receive *karet* due the prohibition of *piggul*. Although impure individuals are not fit to partake of the meat, this is nevertheless considered intent to partake of it beyond its designated time. **Rava says: Know** that this is so, **as meat prior to** the **sprinkling** of the blood is **not fit** to be eaten, **and when** one **has** improper **intent with regard to it,** it is **disqualified.** Clearly, intent to partake of a forbidden item beyond its designated time renders the offering *piggul*.

וְלָא הִיא, הָתָם – זָרֵיק וּמִיחֲזֵי, הָכָא – לָא מִיחֲזֵי כְּלָל.

The Gemara rejects Rava's proof: **But it is not so,** as **there,** with regard to standard *piggul* intent, **he sprinkles** the blood, **and** the meat **is rendered fit** to be eaten the next day. By contrast, **here,** it is **not rendered fit** to be eaten by impure individuals **at all.** Therefore, such intent is not considered significant intent to consume the meat after its designated time.

HALAKHA

That impure individuals would eat it the next day – שֶׁיֹּאכְלוּהוּ טְמֵאִים לְמָחָר וכו׳: If one had intent concerning an offering that it would be eaten by impure individuals or unfit individuals the next day, or that impure individuals or unfit individuals would sacrifice the portions that are fit to be sacrificed the next day, the offering is rendered *piggul*. This is in accordance with the statement of Rav Ḥisda, as while the proof that was brought to support his statement was rejected, his actual opinion was not rejected. In addition, there is another proof supporting his statement from the *halakha* of one who had intent that the offering would be eaten by dogs the next day (Rambam *Sefer Avoda, Hilkhot Pesulei HaMukdashin* 14:9 and *Kesef Mishne* there).

HALAKHA

Meat of a Paschal offering that was not roasted, etc. – **בְּשַׂר פֶּסַח שֶׁלֹּא הוּצְלָה וכו׳**: If one who was ritually impure ate the meat of a Paschal offering that was not roasted, or the loaves of a thanks offering from which the priests' portion was not separated, he is liable to receive *karet*, despite the fact that they are unfit to be eaten in any case. This is in accordance with the statement of Rav Ḥisda, because while the proof that was brought to support his statement was rejected, his actual opinion was not rejected (Rambam *Sefer Avoda*, *Hilkhot Pesulei HaMukdashin* 18:19 and *Kesef Mishne* there).

To include the sacrificial portions of offerings of lesser sanctity with regard to impurity – **לְרַבּוֹת אֵימוּרֵי קָדָשִׁים קַלִּים לְטוּמְאָה**: A ritually impure individual who partakes of the portions of the offering that are consumed on the altar is liable to receive *karet*, in accordance with the ruling of the *baraita* (Rambam *Sefer Avoda*, *Hilkhot Pesulei HaMukdashin* 18:18).

אָמַר רַב חִסְדָּא, מַרְגָּלָא בְּפוּמֵיהּ דְּרַב דִּימִי בַּר חִינָּנָא: בְּשַׂר פֶּסַח שֶׁלֹּא הוּצְלָה, וְלַחְמֵי תוֹדָה שֶׁלֹּא הוּרְמוּ – חַיָּיבִין עֲלֵיהֶן מִשּׁוּם טוּמְאָה.

Rav Ḥisda says that **Rav Dimi bar Ḥinnana was wont to say** the following *halakha*: With regard to **the meat of a Paschal offering that was not roasted,**[H] **and the loaves of a thanks offering** from **which** the priests' portion **was not separated,** although it is prohibited for them to be eaten, nevertheless **one is liable** to receive *karet* **due to** violating the prohibition against eating **them** in a state of **impurity.**

אָמַר רָבָא: תֵּדַע, דְּתַנְיָא: ״אֲשֶׁר לַה׳״ – לְרַבּוֹת אֵימוּרֵי קָדָשִׁים קַלִּים לְטוּמְאָה;

Rava said: Know that this is so, **as it is taught** in a *baraita*: The verse states: "But the soul that eats of the flesh of the sacrifice of peace offerings that pertain to the Lord, having his impurity upon him, that soul shall be cut off from his people" (Leviticus 7:20). The added words **"that pertain to the Lord"** serve **to include the sacrificial portions of offerings of lesser sanctity with regard to impurity,**[H] teaching that one who partakes of them while impure is liable to receive *karet*.

אַלְמָא, אַף עַל גַּב דְּלָאו בְּנֵי אֲכִילָה נִינְהוּ – וְחַיָּיבִין עֲלֵיהֶן מִשּׁוּם טוּמְאָה. הָכָא נַמִי – אַף עַל גַּב דְּלָאו בְּנֵי אֲכִילָה נִינְהוּ – חַיָּיבִין עֲלֵיהֶן מִשּׁוּם טוּמְאָה.

Apparently, even though they are not fit for consumption, one is liable to receive *karet* **due to** violating the prohibition against eating **them** in **ritual impurity. Here too,** with regard to the meat of a Paschal offering that was not roasted, and the loaves of a thanks offering from which the priests' portion was not separated, **even though they are not fit to be eaten, one is liable** to receive *karet* **due to** violating the prohibition against eating **them** in **impurity.**

וְלָא הִיא, הָתָם – אֵימוּרֵי קָדָשִׁים קַלִּים חֲזוּ לְגָבוֹהַּ, לְאַפּוֹקֵי בְּשַׂר פֶּסַח שֶׁלֹּא הוּצְלָה וְלַחְמֵי תוֹדָה שֶׁלֹּא הוּרְמוּ, דְּלָא חֲזוּ לֹא לְגָבוֹהַּ וְלֹא לְהֶדְיוֹט.

The Gemara rejects Rava's proof: **But it is not so,** as **there, the sacrificial portions of offerings of lesser sanctity** that are burned on the altar are at least **fit for** the **Most High,** i.e., for the consumption of the altar, and therefore one is liable to receive *karet* for eating them while ritually impure. This is **to the exclusion of the meat of a Paschal offering that was not roasted and** the **loaves of a thanks offering** from **which** the priests' portion **was not separated, which are not fit** at all, **not for** the **Most High, and not for an ordinary** person.

לִישָּׁנָא אַחֲרִינָא: הָא אֵימוּרִין לָא חֲזוּ. וְלָא הִיא, הָנָךְ חֲזוּ לְמִילְּתַיְיהוּ, וְהָנֵי לָא חֲזוּ כְּלָל.

The Gemara presents **another version** of the proof and its rejection: **But** the **sacrificial portions** are **not fit,** and yet one is liable if he consumes them while impure. The Gemara responds: **But it is not so,** since **these** sacrificial portions are **fit for their matters, and these,** i.e., the meat of a Paschal offering that was not roasted and the loaves of a thanks offering from which the priests' portion was not separated, **are not fit at all.**

הדרן עלך כל הפסולין

Summary of **Perek III**

With regard to the slaughter of an offering, it was concluded that individuals unfit to perform other sacrificial rites may nevertheless perform the slaughter even *ab initio*. A ritually impure individual may not perform the slaughter *ab initio*, lest he touch the flesh and render it impure.

If the collection, conveying, or presenting of the blood was performed inappropriately, e.g., in a case where it was done by one unfit to perform the sacrificial rite, if additional blood remains with which to perform the service, an individual who is fit to perform the Temple service performs the rite correctly, and the offering is valid and effects acceptance. The same *halakha* applies if the rite was performed in an improper manner, e.g., if the left hand was employed or the blood was presented in the wrong place, or if an individual unfit for Temple service had improper intent that would render the offering not valid or *piggul*. Likewise, if blood was collected in a vessel but subsequently spilled out onto the floor, if it is then gathered into the vessel, it is valid.

With regard to improper intent during the performance of the sacrificial rites, the Sages formulated the principle that any intent that does not disqualify an offering does not affect the offering at all. The cases of intent that render the offering not valid are improper intent with regard to the offering's type or owner, which negatively affects all offerings and renders a Paschal offering and sin offering not valid, and improper intent with regard to the designated time and place that the offering will be consumed. Therefore, intent to present the blood on the altar in the wrong place, to leave the meat and sacrificial portions of the animal overnight, or to perform a prohibited act with the offering, e.g., feeding the offering to an impure individual, does not affect the offering, and it remains valid. This is because the *halakhot* of improper intent are Torah edicts and are therefore limited to the scenarios explicated by the Torah; they are not extended to similar cases.

Image **Credits**

All images are copyright © Koren Publishers Jerusalem Ltd., except:

94 © **courtesy of the Temple Institute**; **p107** upper left, lower left, and center right images © uwgb admissions; **p107** upper right image © Anneli Salo; **p107** lower right image © Cordwainers Garden; **pp114–17** all images © **courtesy of the Temple Institute**; **p118** all images © HaRav Menachem Makover, courtesy of *Harenu Bevinyano*; **p145** © HaRav Menachem Makover, courtesy of *Harenu Bevinyano*; **p153** © Filip Maljkovic; **p165** upper left and lower left images © Mauro Raffaelli; **p165** upper right image © Mileli; **p165** lower right image © snotch; **p182** © HaRav Menachem Makover, courtesy of *Harenu Bevinyano*; **p183** © Meghan; **pp189–204** all images © **courtesy of the Temple Institute**.

My Notes

My Notes

My Notes

My Notes

תלמוד בבלי

— מהדורת נאה —

זבחים חלק ב

Steinsaltz Center

ירושלים

KOREN

Please note that the number ranges that appear at the bottom of each daf of the Vilna pages indicate the corresponding pages of the Koren Talmud Bavli translation and commentary.

תלמוד בבלי

הוצאת קורן ירושלים

— מהדורת נאה —

מסכת זבחים
דף טו: עד דף לו:

COMMENTARY BY

Rabbi Adin Even-Israel Steinsaltz

EDITOR-IN-CHIEF

Rabbi Dr Tzvi Hersh Weinreb

EXECUTIVE EDITOR

Rabbi Joshua Schreier

STEINSALTZ CENTER
KOREN PUBLISHERS JERUSALEM

לְאַמְטוּיֵיהּ. אֲמַר לֵיהּ א] רַב יִרְמְיָה לְרַב אַשִׁי: הָכִי אֲמַר רַב יִרְמְיָה מִדִּיפְתִּי, הָא צָרִיךְ לְאַמְטוּיֵיהּ – מַחֲלוֹקֶת רַבִּי (א) אֱלִיעֶזֶר וְרַבָּנַן. דִּתְנַן, ר"א אוֹמֵר: הַמְהַלֵּךְ בְּמָקוֹם שֶׁצָּרִיךְ לְהַלֵּךְ – מַחֲשָׁבָה פּוֹסֶלֶת, מָקוֹם שֶׁאֵין צָרִיךְ לְהַלֵּךְ – אֵין מַחֲשָׁבָה פּוֹסֶלֶת. וְאָמַר רָבָא: הַכֹּל מוֹדִים, קִבְּלוֹ בַּחוּץ וְהִכְנִיסוֹ בִּפְנִים – זֶהוּ הִילּוּךְ שֶׁצָּרִיךְ לְהַלֵּךְ. קִבְּלוֹ בִּפְנִים וְהוֹצִיאוֹ לַחוּץ – זֶהוּ הִילּוּךְ שֶׁאֵין צָרִיךְ לְהַלֵּךְ. *לֹא נֶחְלְקוּ ב] אֶלָּא כְּשֶׁהִכְנִיסוֹ וְחָזַר וְהוֹצִיאוֹ, *מָר סָבַר: הָא צָרִיךְ לְאַמְטוּיֵיהּ, וּמ"ס: לָאו כְּהִילּוּךְ הַצָּרִיךְ לַעֲבוֹדָה דָּמֵי. אֵיתִיבֵיהּ אַבַּיֵי, ר"א אוֹמֵר: הַמְהַלֵּךְ מָקוֹם שֶׁצָּרִיךְ לְהַלֵּךְ – מַחֲשָׁבָה פּוֹסֶלֶת, כֵּיצַד? קִבְּלוֹ ג] בַּחוּץ וְהִכְנִיסוֹ לִפְנִים – זֶהוּ הִילּוּךְ שֶׁצָּרִיךְ לְהַלֵּךְ, קִבְּלוֹ בִּפְנִים וְהוֹצִיאוֹ לַחוּץ – זֶהוּ הִילּוּךְ שֶׁאֵין צָרִיךְ לֵילֵךְ; ד] וְהָא חָזַר וְהִכְנִיסוֹ, הִילּוּךְ שֶׁצָּרִיךְ לְהַלֵּךְ הוּא! א"ל:* אִי תַּנְיָא – תַּנְיָא ה].§

הדרן עלך כל הזבחים

כָּל *הַזְּבָחִים (ג) ו] שֶׁקִּבְּלוּ דָּמָן אזָר, באוֹנֵן, גטְבוּל יוֹם, ז] *דוּמְחוּסַּר כִּפּוּרִים, הוּמְחוּסַּר בְּגָדִים, ושֶׁלֹּא רָחַץ יָדַיִם וְרַגְלַיִם, *זעָרֵל, חטָמֵא, טיוֹשֵׁב, *)יעוֹמֵד עַל גַּבֵּי כֵלִים, עַל גַּבֵּי בְהֵמָה, *עַל גַּבֵּי רַגְלֵי חֲבֵרוֹ – ח] פָּסַל. *כקִבֵּל בִּשְׂמֹאל – פָּסַל, ר"ש מַכְשִׁיר.§ **גמ'** זָר מְנָלַן? דְּתָנֵי לֵוִי: °"דַּבֵּר אֶל אַהֲרֹן וְאֶל בָּנָיו לֵאמֹר ט] וְיִנָּזְרוּ מִקָּדְשֵׁי בְנֵי יִשְׂרָאֵל" וגו', י] בְּנֵי יִשְׂרָאֵל לְמַעוּטֵי מַאי? אִילֵימָא לְמַעוּטֵי נָשִׁים – קָרְבַּן נָשִׁים בְּטוּמְאָה קָרֵב? אֶלָּא לְמַעוּטֵי גּוֹיִם – הַשְׁתָּא צִיץ לֹא מְרַצֶּה, דְּאָמַר מָר: *וּבְגוֹיִם – בֵּין בְּשׁוֹגֵג בֵּין בְּמֵזִיד לֹא הוּרְצָה, בְּטוּמְאָה קָרֵב? אֶלָּא הָכִי קָאָמַר: "וְיִנָּזְרוּ מִקָּדְשֵׁי בְנֵי יִשְׂרָאֵל וְלֹא יְחַלְּלוּ". *דְּבֵי רַבִּי יִשְׁמָעֵאל תָּנָא: יא] אָתְיָא בְּק"ו מִבַּעַל מוּם, (ג) מַה בַּעַל מוּם שֶׁאוֹכֵל, אִם עָבַד – חִילֵּל,

*) יומא נח.

(ויקרא כב)

רש"י

הָא צָרִיךְ לְאַמְטוּיֵיהּ. דְּקָאָמְרַתְּ לְמַחְשָׁבָה עֲבוֹדָה מֵהַאי יב] טַעַם, מַחֲלוֹקֶת ר' אֱלִיעֶזֶר וְרַבָּנַן (ד) בְּמַתְנִי'. בַּחוּץ. לְהַלָּן מִן הַמִּזְבֵּחַ, וְהִכְנִיסוֹ בִּפְנִים יג] לְצַד הַמִּזְבֵּחַ. וְהוֹצִיאוֹ לַחוּץ. כְּלוֹמַר, רִיחֲקוֹ מִן הַמִּזְבֵּחַ תּוֹךְ חוּץ וּפְנִים כּוּלְּהוּ בָּעֲזָרָה. הָא צָרִיךְ לְאַמְטוּיֵיהּ. יד] לִכְשֶׁיַּחֲזוֹר וְיַקְרִיבֶנּוּ לְצַד הַמִּזְבֵּחַ, אִם תְּהֵא אוֹתָהּ הוֹלָכָה בְּמַחֲשָׁבָה פְּסוּלָה טו]. לָאו כְּהִילּוּךְ הַצָּרִיךְ לַעֲבוֹדָה דָּמֵי. הוֹאִיל וְאֵלָּא לְצוֹרֶךְ הוֹלִיכוֹ, עַל חִנָּם הוּלַךְ לַחֲזוֹר וּלְהַכְנִיסוֹ. אִי תַּנְיָא. דְּמוֹדֶה בָּהּ ר' אֱלִיעֶזֶר, תַּנְיָא. וְאֵין מַחֲלוֹקֶת בֵּין ר"א לְת"ק, אֶלָּא טז] אַר"ש אֲבוּהּ קָאֵי וּפָלֵיג.

הדרן עלך כל הזבחים

כָּל הַזְּבָחִים. אוֹנֵן. כָּל זְמַן שֶׁלֹּא נִקְבַּר הַמֵּת. טְבוּל יוֹם. דְּשֶׁרֶץ, וּדְמֵת, יז] וּשְׁאָר טוּמְאוֹת שֶׁלֹּא הוּלְרְכוּ לְקָרְבָּן. מְחוּסַּר כִּפּוּרִים. זָב וּמְצוֹרָע שֶׁטָּבְלוּ, וְהֶעֱרִיב שִׁמְשָׁן, וְלֹא הֵבִיאוּ כַּפָּרָתָן. מְחוּסַּר בְּגָדִים. כֹּהֵן גָּדוֹל שֶׁשִּׁימֵּשׁ בְּפָחוֹת מִשְּׁמוֹנָה, וְכֹהֵן הֶדְיוֹט בְּפָחוֹת מִד'. וְשֶׁלֹּא רָחַץ יָדַיִם וְרַגְלַיִם. מִן הַכִּיּוֹר. עָרֵל. כֹּהֵן שֶׁמֵּתוּ אֶחָיו מֵחֲמַת מִילָה. יוֹשֵׁב אוֹ עוֹמֵד עַל גַּבֵּי כֵלִים. שֶׁיֵּשׁ חֲצִיצָה בֵּין רַגְלָיו לָרִצְפָּה. וְכוּלְּהוּ יָלֵיף בַּגְּמָ' דְּפָסְלִי בַּעֲבוֹדָה. **גמ'** וְיִנָּזְרוּ מִקָּדְשֵׁי וגו'. גַּבֵּי מַקְרִיבִים בְּטוּמְאָה כְּתִיב, דִּסְמִיךְ לֵיהּ: "כָּל אִישׁ אֲשֶׁר יִקְרַב מִכָּל זַרְעֲכֶם". (לְמַעוּטֵי מַאי) בְּנֵי יִשְׂרָאֵל לְמַעוּטֵי מַאי. קָרְבָּן שֶׁל מִי הוּא מְמַעֵט, מִלְּהַזְהִיר כֹּהֲנִים עַל הַטּוּמְאָה? אִילֵימָא לְמַעוּטֵי בְּנוֹת יִשְׂרָאֵל. קָרְבַּן נָשִׁים שֶׁלֹּא הוּזְהֲרוּ כֹּהֲנִים מִלְּהַקְרִיבוֹ בְּטוּמְאָה. קָרְבַּן נָשִׁים בְּטוּמְאָה קָרֵב. בִּתְמִיָּה, וְכִי יֵשׁ כֹּחַ יח] בְּקָרְבַּן נָשִׁים לִדְחוֹת הַטּוּמְאָה? אֶלָּא לְמַעוּטֵי קָרְבַּן גּוֹיִם. גּוֹי שֶׁשִּׁילַּח עוֹלָתוֹ יט] כִּדְתַנְיָא בְּ"הַכֹּל שׁוֹחֲטִין" (חולין דף יג:): "אִישׁ אִישׁ" – לְרַבּוֹת אֶת הַגּוֹיִם שֶׁנּוֹדְרִים נְדָרִים וּנְדָבוֹת כְּיִשְׂרָאֵל. הַשְׁתָּא צִיץ לֹא מְרַצֶּה. עַל טוּמְאַת עוֹלִין שֶׁבְּקָרְבָּנוֹ, כְּגוֹן נִטְמָא הַדָּם אוֹ הַחֵלֶב, כְּדֶרֶךְ שֶׁמְּרַצֶּה עַל שֶׁל יִשְׂרָאֵל. דְּאָמַר מָר. בִּמְנָחוֹת בְּ"הַקּוֹמֵץ רַבָּה" (דף כה.). לֹא הוּרְצָה. דִּכְתִיב: "לְרָצוֹן לָהֶם" – וְלֹא לַגּוֹיִם. בְּטוּמְאַת הַגּוּף יְהֵא קָרֵב. בִּתְמִיָּה, וַהֲלֹא כ] [אֲפִילּוּ] אֵצֶל קָרְבַּן יָחִיד דְּיִשְׂרָאֵל לֹא נִדְחֵת! אֶלָּא הָכִי קָאָמַר וְיִנָּזְרוּ מִקָּדְשֵׁי. יִתְרַחֲקוּ כא] בְּטוּמְאָה מִכָּל קֳדָשִׁים. בְּנֵי יִשְׂרָאֵל לֹא יְחַלְּלוּ. וְהַזָּרִים אַף הֵם יִנָּזְרוּ, כְּדֵי שֶׁלֹּא יְחַלְּלוּם. לִימֵּד עַל זָר שֶׁעָבַד, שֶׁחִילֵּל אֶת הַקֳּדָשִׁים וּפְסָלָם. בַּעַל מוּם שֶׁאוֹכֵל. אֶת קָדְשֵׁי קֳדָשִׁים, דִּכְתִיב (ויקרא כא): "מִקָּדְשֵׁי הַקֳּדָשִׁים וּמִן הַקֳּדָשִׁים יֹאכֵל". אִם עָבַד חִילֵּל. דִּכְתִיב כב]: "מוּם בּוֹ וְלֹא יְחַלֵּל אֶת מִקְדָּשַׁי" (שם). זָר

תוספות

זר ואונן. הא דלא תנא בעל מוס ושתויי יין *ופרועי ראש משום דכתיב בהן חילול בהדיא*. **טבול** יום. אע"ג תני טמא. ו"זו ואין לריך לומר זו" קתני, ומשום דאיכא תרי קראי תני תרוייהו. והא דלא תני טמא ברישא – דניחא ליה למיתני טמא בהדי ערל, כדאשכחן בפרק "הערל" (יבמות דף ע.) ובחגיגה (דף ד:). ועוד, איכא תנא דמרבי ליה לערל כי טמא. ומיהו סוגיא דגמ' דלא כוותיה, מדמלרכי ליה תרי קראי. וכי תימא: דאלטריך לערל בקרבן לבור, דאילו טמא שרי, כג] דהא כי מרבי *ר"ע לערל כי טמא – היינו כד] *בזב ומלורע, דמההוא קרא דריש, דכתיב: "איש איש מזרע אהרן והוא לרוע או זב" ואותה טומאה לא הותרה בלבור. **אלא** למעוטי גוים השתא ציץ לא מרצה. הקשה הרב רבי יוס טוב: דהכא משמע דהאי "בני ישראל" לא אתא למעוטי גוים. ולקמן אמרינן בפ' "ב"ש" (דף מה.): קדשי גוים אין חייבין עליהם משום נותר, דילפינן חילול מטומאה, ובטומאה כתיב "בני ישראל" ולא גוים! ואין לומר ד"מבני ישראל" דכתיב גבי אכילת קודש בטומאה קדרים, שזהו פסוק שני לו בפרשת "אמור אל הכהנים". דלא משמע הכי בתורת כהנים ובריש תמורה (דף ג.) דמייתי התם בהדיא קרא ד"וינזרו". ועוד, דגבי "וינזרו" כתיב חילול, ולא גבי אכילת קודש בטומאה! וי"ל: דקרא ד"וינזרו" מיירי בכל שימוש, בין בכהן טמא ששימש בין בזר ששימש, וגם איירי בכל טומאה, בין באכילת קדשים בטומאה בין בטמא ששימש. ופשיטא ליה דלמעוטי קדשי גוים מאכילה בטומאה לחודיה לא אתא, דמ"בני ישראל" דכתיב בתריה גבי אכילה בטומאה נפקא, ואתא למידרש זר מ"בני ישראל ולא יחללו", כה] ובאכילת טומאה דכתיב הכא לאשמועינן כו]דכתיב ביה חילול, לאגמורי אנותר. ואת"ת: א"כ במכות (דף יד:) ובשבועות (דף ז.) ובפרק "הערל" (יבמות דף עה.) אמאי דחק ר' יוחנן כז] אזהרה לאכילת קודש בטומאה? תיפוק לן מהכא? ויש לומר: משום דהאי קרא הוי לאו שבכללות, דאתא נמי לטמא ששימש. מיהו קשה, בפרק "אלו הן הנשרפין" (סנהדרין דף פג.) דיליף טמא ששימש במיתה מחילול תרומה. ופריך: נילף חילול חילול מנותר, דבכרת ולא במיתה! ומשני: חילול דרבים עדיף, ו"לא יחללו" מ"לא יחללו", אבל נותר כתיב "כי את קדש ה' חילל" בל' יחיד. והשתא אכתי הוה ליה למילף מאכילת טומאה דבכרת, דבהאי קרא גופיה! ועוד, כיון דמחד קרא נפקי – נקיט חילול דשימוש לחילול דאכילה! *ועוד, דלקמן שילהי פ' "בית שמאי" (דף מו.) אמרינן: "ולא יחללו" – בשני חלולין הכתוב מדבר, אחד פסול נותר ואחד פסול טומאה, ומקשי אהדדי. אם כן בנותר נמי איכא חילול דרבים "ולא יחללו"! וי"ל: דיליף טמא ששימש במיתה מחילול דכתיב בתרומה גבי מיתה "ומתו בו כי יחללוהו". ופריך: נילף כרת מחילול דנותר, דכתיב גבי כרת "כי את קדש ה' חלל ונכרתה"! ולכך משני: היינו חילול דיחיד. אבל "לא יחללו" דקרא ד"וינזרו", אע"ג דמיירי בטמא שאכל וגם בנותר – *ההוא חילול לא כתיב עונש בהדיה. ז"ה עיקר, ברו"ך. ועוד י"ל: דבהאי קרא ד"לא יחללו" משמע טמא ששימש, וזר ששימש, ואכילת קודש ונותר, ולא ידעינן להי מינייהו נקיט, אי לזר דבמיתה, או לאכילת קודש ונותר דבכרת – לכך לריך ג"ש. ומיהו, קשה לתנא דבי ר' ישמעאל דלא נפקא לן זר מהאי קרא! ועוד קשה: *אדנפקא לן ליה בעל מום ששימש במיתה מטמא ששימש – נילף מאכילת קודש דבכרת, וחילול דרבים! וקשה לרבינו ז"ל: דלקמן, דיליף דאין חייבין על קדשי גוים על עון דנותר, דיליף מחילול חילול דטומאה, דכתיב "בני ישראל" ולא גוים – הלא ההוא קרא גופיה בנותר מישתעי, כדתני לוי: בשני חילולין הכתוב מדבר! ועוד קשה לי: כח] מנלן ללוי דדריש שני חילולין, חילול נותר וחילול טומאה? הלא לוי גופיה בשמעתין מוקי לקרא בשני חילולין אחריני: חילול טומאה וחילול זרות! י"ל: כיון דטומאה וזרות כתיב בקרא, אפילו לא כתיב אלא חד חילול – ממילא הוה קאי אתרוייהו. ותימה לי: הא אלטריך חילול לשון רבים לאגמורי מיתה בטמא ששימש, פרק "הנשרפין" (סנהדרין דף פג.). ברו"ך.

אתיא בקל וחומר מבעל מום. מיושב שאוכל לא מצי למילף, דמה ליושב – שכן פסול לעדות, כדקאמר בסמוך. וממחוסר בגדים ושלא רחוץ ידים ורגלים נמי, דהני לא פסלי אלא מטעם זרות. כט] אבל קשה: דניליף בק"ו משתויי יין (דלקמן) ופרועי ראש (ועומד על גבי כלים)! [וי"ל:] דלא קשיא מידי משתויי יין. דלקמן מפיק שתויי יין מחילול מ"חוקה" "חוקה" ממחוסר בגדים, וממחוסר בגדים לא נפקא לן מחילול אלא מטעם זרות, וזר אכתי לא קמ"ל. וגם מפרועי ראש לא קשיא מידי, דשילהי פרק בן סנהדרין (דף כב:) אמרינן לפרועי ראש למיתה גמירי, אבל למיחל לא גמירי. ואפילו למאן דאמר התם דמחלל – היינו משום דאיתקש לשתויי יין דמחללי מטעם זרות. וצ"ע: אמאי לא יליף מק"ו דיושב דאינו במיתה, וגם זר דאינו במיתה בקבלה, לפי שאינה עבודה תמה, וממחללי – כל שכן פרועי ראש דבמיתה, דמחללי. ברו"ך.

מסורת הש"ס

הגהות הב"ח

(א) גמ' ומה יושב: (ב) רש"י ד"ה ה"ג מה וכו' תניא עלה. נ"ב סוף המסכת וע"ש: (ג) ד"ה קסבר וכו' והן היום הקריבו:

[קדושין כא. וש"נ]

זר שֶׁאֵינוֹ אוֹכֵל, אֵינוֹ דִּין שֶׁאִם עָבַד חִילֵּל? מַה לְּבַעַל מוּם, שֶׁכֵּן עָשָׂה בּוֹ קָרֵב כִּמְקָרִיב! טָמֵא יוֹכִיחַ. מַה לְּטָמֵא, שֶׁכֵּן מְטַמֵּא! בַּעַל מוּם יוֹכִיחַ. *וְחָזַר הַדִּין: לֹא רְאִי זֶה כִּרְאִי זֶה, וְלֹא רְאִי זֶה כִּרְאִי זֶה, הַצַּד הַשָּׁוֶה שֶׁבָּהֶן – שֶׁמּוּזְהָרִין, וְאִם עָבְדוּ – חִילְּלוּ, אַף אֲנִי אָבִיא זָר, שֶׁהוּא מוּזְהָר, וְאִם עָבַד – חִילֵּל. א] מְנָלַן דְּמוּזְהָר? אִי מִ"וְיִנָּזְרוּ" – חִילּוּל בְּגוּפֵיהּ כְּתִיב בֵּיהּ! אֶלָּא °מִ"וְזָר לֹא יִקְרַב אֲלֵיכֶם". (במדבר יח) אִיכָּא לְמִיפְרַךְ: מַה לְּהַצַּד הַשָּׁוֶה שֶׁבָּהֶן, שֶׁכֵּן לֹא הוּתְּרוּ בְּבָמָה! לָא תֵּימָא טָמֵא יוֹכִיחַ, אֶלָּא אֵימָא: אוֹנֵן יוֹכִיחַ. מַה לְּאוֹנֵן שֶׁכֵּן אָסוּר בְּמַעֲשֵׂר! [בַּעַל מוּם] יוֹכִיחַ. *וְחָזַר הַדִּין: לֹא רְאִי זֶה כִּרְאִי זֶה, ב] הַצַּד הַשָּׁוֶה שֶׁבָּהֶן שֶׁמּוּזְהָרִין כו'. ה"נ לִפְרוֹךְ: מַה לְּהַצַּד הַשָּׁוֶה שֶׁבָּהֶן, שֶׁכֵּן לֹא הוּתְּרוּ בְּבָמָה! מַתְקִיף לָהּ רַב סַמָּא בְּרֵיהּ דְּרָבָא: ג] וּמַאן לֵימָא לָן דְּאוֹנֵן אָסוּר בְּבָמָה? דִּלְמָא שָׁרֵי בְּבָמָה! רַב מְשַׁרְשְׁיָא אָמַר: אָתְיָא ק"ו מִיּוֹשֵׁב, (א) מַה יּוֹשֵׁב שֶׁאוֹכֵל, אִם עָבַד – חִילֵּל, זָר שֶׁאֵינוֹ אוֹכֵל – אֵינוֹ דִּין שֶׁאִם עָבַד חִילֵּל? ד] מַה לְּיוֹשֵׁב, שֶׁכֵּן פָּסוּל לְעֵדוּת! מִיּוֹשֵׁב ת"ח. מַה לְּשֵׁם יוֹשֵׁב, שֶׁכֵּן פָּסוּל לְעֵדוּת! שֵׁם יוֹשֵׁב לָא פָּרֵיךְ. וְאִם ת"ל פָּרֵיךְ – אָתְיָא מִיּוֹשֵׁב וּמֵחֲדָא מֵהָנָךְ. וְיוֹשֵׁב דְּכָשֵׁר בְּבָמָה מְנָלַן? אָמַר קְרָא: °"לַעֲמוֹד לִפְנֵי ה' לְשָׁרְתוֹ", (דברים י) לִפְנֵי ה' – וְלֹא לִפְנֵי בָּמָה. § "אוֹנֵן" ה]. § מְנָלַן? דִּכְתִיב: °"וּמִן הַמִּקְדָּשׁ לֹא יֵצֵא וְלֹא יְחַלֵּל", (ויקרא כא) הָא אַחֵר שֶׁלֹּא יָצָא – חִילֵּל. ו] רַבִּי אֶלְעָזָר אָמַר, מֵהָכָא: °"הֵן הִקְרִיבוּ"? (שם י) אֲנִי הִקְרַבְתִּי! מִכְּלָל דְּאִי אִינְהוּ אַקְרִיב – שַׁפִּיר אִישְׁתָּרוּף. וְרַבִּי אֶלְעָזָר מַאי טַעְמָא לָא אָמַר מִ"וּמִן הַמִּקְדָּשׁ לֹא יֵצֵא"? אָמַר לָךְ: מִי כְּתִיב הָא אַחֵר שֶׁלֹּא יָצָא חִילֵּל? וְאִידָךְ, מ"ט לֹא אָמַר מִ"הֵן הִקְרִיבוּ"? קָסָבַר: ז] *מִפְּנֵי טוּמְאָה נִשְׂרְפָה. (לקמן קא.) דְּבֵי רַבִּי יִשְׁמָעֵאל תָּנָא: אָתְיָא בְּק"ו מִבַּעַל מוּם, וּמַה בַּעַל

רש"י

זר שאינו אוכל. בקדשי קדשים. שכן עשה בו קרב כמקריב. המום פוסל בקרבן כדרך שפוסל בכהן. טמא יוכיח. שלא עשה בו קרב כמקריב, שאין בהמה מקבלת טומאה מחיים כשם שהכהן טמא מחיים. וכתיב: "וינזרו ולא יחללו", אלמא טמא שעבד חילל. שמוזהרין. שלא לעבוד, טמא מ"וינזרו", בעל מום מ"ולא יגש". היכא מוזהר. זר. אי נימא מוינזרו. ח] דדרשת ליה להאי קרא: "בני ישראל" – להזהיר זרים, כדאמר לעיל. חילול בגופיה כתיב. וק"ו למה לך? ה"ג: מה להצד כו' שכן לא הותרה בבמה. בבמת יחיד ט] (בבמה) בשעת היתר הבמות. דתנן בפ' בתרא (לקמן קיג.): הזמן והנותר והטמא שוין בזה ובזה. ובברייתא י] תניא (ב) עלה: דברים ששוותה במה קטנה לבמה גדולה: דם מתיר ומפגל ומותין. תאמר בזר שכשר בבמה, כדתנן התם: אלו דברים שבין במה גדולה לבמה קטנה, וקתני התם: כיהון ובגדי שרת. וקראי נמי יא] מוכחי, בגדעון ומנוח ושמואל שהקריבו בבמה. אונן. ילפינן לקמן מקראי אם עבד חילל. שכן אסור במעשר. דכתיב: "לא אכלתי באוני" (דברים כו). אונן מוזהר שלא יעבוד. דכתיב בכהן גדול: "ומן המקדש לא יצא ולא יחלל", הא אחר שלא יצא – חילל. דלמא שרי בבמה. דגבי אונן כתיב: "ומן המקדש". יושב אם עבד חילל. לקמן ילפינן לה בפירקין (כג:). שכן פסול לעדות. דאמרי' במס' שבועות (דף ל.): "ועמדו שני האנשים" – בעדים הכתוב מדבר. ומשני: מיושב תלמיד חכם. יב] *הכא מייתי לה, דכשר לעדות, כדאמרי' התם (שם) שבית דין חולקים לו כבוד ומושיבים אותו. יג] [שם יושב]. מצינו שם יושב בעלמא שפסול לעדות משום שם יושב, תאמר בשם זר שאינו נפסל לעדות משום שם זרות. שם יושב לא פריך. הואיל והוא יושב ת"ח דמייתי מיניה לק"ו כשר לעדות. ומחד מהנך. אונן או טמא או בעל מום. ויושב דכשר בבמה מנא לן. דלא נפרך: שכן לא הותרו בבמה. דהא מדשבקיה רב משרשיא לקל וחומר דלעיל דאונן וטמא ובעל מום, ונקט יושב – משום יד] הני פירכי שבקיה, דלא משכחת היתר בבמה בהדיא לחד מינייהו, הכא מנליה? לעמוד לפני ה'. במקדש הוא דבעי' עמידה. אונן מנלן. דפסול, כדקתני מתני'? ומן המקדש וגו'. לעיל מיניה כתיב: "לאביו ולאמו לא יטמא", ובכהן גדול משתעי, וסמיך ליה: "ומן המקדש" וגו' כלומר, אף ביום שמתו אביו ואמו אין צריך לצאת מן המקדש, אלא עומד ומקריב ולא יחלל, שאין הקדשים מתחללין בכך. הא הדיוט שלא יצא ועבד – חילל. הן הקריבו. "הן היום הקריבו" וגו'. מתשובתו של אהרן אתה לומד מה אמר לו משה: "מדוע לא אכלתם" כו' – שמא בניך הקריבוה באנינות, א) שהיו אוננים על נדב ואביהוא טו] *ופסלתיה, ולכך נשרפה? אמר לו אהרן: וכי הן הקריבו? והלא הדיוטות הן, ופסולין לעבודה! אני הקרבתי, שאמרת לי "ועשה את קרבן העם" וגו', ואני כהן גדול ומקריב אונן. מכלל דאי אינהו אקרוב – דשפיר אשתרוף, ולא היה משה אומר להם "מדוע לא אכלתם". מי כתיב הא אחר כו'. דלמא אחר נמי לא חילל. ובדידיה איצטריך ליה למישרייה, דלא תימא: מתוך טז] חישובו וקדושתו יתירה הוא פסול אונן. קסבר מפני טומאה. שנגע בה נשרפה, ולא הוזכר שם אנינות לענין הקרבה ו"הן (ג) הקריבו" ה"ק: הן היום – הלא עדיין יום הוא, *והיינו אסורין בקדשים לאכול עד הערב, יז] ומתוך כך אירע בה טומאה באונס. ואיכא תנאי דפליגי לקמן (דף קא.) בהא, חד אמר: מפני טומאה נשרפה, וחד אמר: מפני אנינות נשרפה, שלא היו יכולין לאוכלה אפילו לערב. דקסבר אנינות לילה נמי אסור ואפילו נקבר המת, ולפי שלא היו לה אוכלין נשרפה, וכדר' יוחנן בן ברוקה דאמר בפסחים (דף פב.) גבי נטמאו בעלים של פסח: אף זה ישרף מיד, שאין לו אוכלין, ואין טעון עבור צורה.

שאינו

א) עי' ל"ק ועי' ברמב"ן בחומש פרשת שמיני

תוספות

זר שאינו אוכל כו'. ואין לומר דטמא בקרבן צבור וכהן גדול אונן יח] יוכיח, שאינן אוכלין ועובדים. דמה להנך – שכן אינן מוזהרים, תאמר בזר דמוזהר. מה לטמא שכן מטמא. לא מצי למיפרך: שכן עשה בו קריבים כמקריבים [כדפי' בקונטרס].

אף אני אביא זר שמוזהר כו'. לכך צריך לטעמא דאזהרה, משום דלא תימא: טמא בקרבן צבור וכהן גדול אונן יוכיח, כדפרישית. ומהאי טעמא נמי צריך לקמן בערל הלכתא גמירי לה, דלא אתי בק"ו. היכן מוזהר. תימה: נימא מ"והקריבו בני אהרן" דדרשי' (לקמן דף לב.): מקבלה ואילך מצות כהונה! מיהו עדיפא יט] משני לאו גמור מ"וכל זר לא יקרב". הג"ה דלמא שרי בבמה. והאי דלא חשיב אונן לקמן בסוף מכילתין (דף קיג.) בדברים שבין במה גדולה לבמה קטנה, כדחשיב כיהון ובגדי שרת – דילמא תנא ושייר, דשייר נמי יושב. ומה יושב שאוכל. כגון במורם מקדשים כ] ובכור*. מה ליושב שכן פסול לעדות. צריך ליזהר שלא לדון ע"פ עדות דמיושב, ובגט אשה צריך ליזהר יותר. ושמא דיעבד אין לחוש, דאמר בירושלמי פרק "ד' מיתות" גבי מברך את השם: והדיינין עומדין על רגליהם – מיכן לדיינין שקבלו עדות מעומד שדנין על פי עדותן. ומשמע התם דכי היכי דאין עכובא בישיבת הדיינין, אע"פ שיש להם לישב מן התורה – ה"נ אין עכובא בעמידת העדים אע"פ שיש להם לעמוד מן התורה. הקשה ה"ר אפרים: כהן גזלן יהא פסול לעבודה, קל וחומר מבעל מום שכשר לעדות ואם עבד חילל, ולייתי מבעל מום ומחד מהנך! ולאו קושיא היא, דכיון דגזלן אינו מוזהר – לא אתי מינייהו, כדפרישית לעיל. מיושב תלמיד חכם. א"כ, הא דאמרי' (שבועות דף ל:) דתלמיד חכם לא ליזל אסהודי לקנייה דזוטר מיניה – לאו משום דצריך לעמוד, אלא משום זילותא, דהא אי אזיל לאסהודי (מנפשיה) מעיד מיושב. ותו: דאמרינן בפרק "שבועת העדות" (שם): הני מילי – לממונא, אבל לאיסורא – ילך להעיד, אין חכמה ואין תבונה לנגד ה'. ותימה: בסנהדרין (יט.) דאמרו לו לינאי: עמוד על רגליך ויעידו בך. והא מלך עדיף מתלמיד חכם, דמלך אין יכול למחול על כבודו, ותלמיד חכם יכול למחול! וי"ל: דלא דמי, דטעמא דמחיל תלמיד חכם – משום דתורה דידיה היא, אבל מלך – כתיב: שתהא אימתו עליך, אין זה שלו אלא של אחרים, ואין יכול למחול זה. ולגבי מלות יכול למחול, דאם מוחל על כבודו – כא] בשביל כך לא יניח שלא תהא אימתו עליך. ועוד יש לומר: דעובדא דינאי דיני נפשות הוה, ובדיני נפשות אפילו תלמיד חכם עומד. ואם תאמר: היכי גמר מיושב תלמיד חכם? מה ליושב תלמיד חכם שכן פסול לחליצה, דחליצה בעי מעומד, כדאמר שילהי "מצות חליצה" (יבמות קו.): בתי עמודי, וטעמא – משום דכתיב "ועמד ואמר"! ומיהו, כב] טעמא על כרחין דחליצה מעומד לאו משום "ועמד ואמר", דמי כתיב "ויעמד ויאמר"? כדדייק פ' בתרא דמועד קטן (דף כא.) גבי קריעה. אלמא טעמא משום דהוי כמו דין, ויכול תלמיד חכם ליסב, כג] ובדיעבד אם חלצה מיושב – כשרה. תדע, דהא תניא: חלצה, בין עומד בין יושב בין מוטה – כשרה. ואי מקרא ד"ועמד ואמר" בעינן מעומד – אם כן ליהוי עכובא מקרא ד"ככה". אלא מטעם דין הוי, כדפרישית. ובספרי דדריש עומד מקרא ד"ועמד ואמר" – אסמכתא הוא. כד] א). הגה"ה: ואם תאמר: מה ליושב שכן אסור בעזרה, כדאמר (יומא דף כה.): אין ישיבה בעזרה אלא למלכי בית דוד! ושמא אינו מן התורה. תדע, דאי דאורייתא – אמאי צריך קרא לקמן (דף כג:) ליושב למעוה? תיפוק ליה דאפילו כה] בלאו עבודה אין ישיבה. ב) ומיהו, איצטריך קרא לעובד בהשתחוואה ג).

קסבר מפני טומאה נשרפה. הוה מצי למימר כבדסמוך לתנא דבי רבי ישמעאל, דקסבר מפני אנינות נשרפה, ו"הן הקריבו" כו] אתי לאזהרה שאמר

א) [וע"ע תוס' יבמות קג. ד"ה בין עומד ותוספות שבועות ל. ד"ה מגוה] ב) עיין ל"ק מה שהביא בשם שו"ת אמונת שמואל ג) [ועי' היטב תוס' יומא כה. ד"ה אין ותוס' סוטה מ: ד"ה והאמר ועיין רש"י סנהדרין קא: ד"ה גמירי אין ישיבה וכו' הלכה למשה מסיני]

שיטה מקובצת

א] חילל היכן מוזהר אילימא מוינזרו: ב] זה כו' הצד: ג] ומאן לימא לן כו'. דכתיב ומן המקדש לא יצא ולא יחלל ודייקינן הא אחר שלא יצא חלל ודוקא במקדש כדקאמר קרא אבל בבמה לא וא"ת והיכי ס"ד הכי דאונן אסור בבמה והא מן המקדש כתיב בקרא וי"ל דס"ל משום רבותא דכה"ג נקטיה דלא יצא אפילו מן המקדש אבל לעולם ה"ה בבמה וא"ת והא מדלא תני ליה לקמן גבי חילוק דבמה גדולה לקטנה אלמא אסור בבמה וי"ל דתנא ושייר וכ"ת מאי שייר דהאי שייר שייר יושב. מהר"פ: ד] מה ליושב א) משמע מהכא דיושב פסול לעדות וא"כ צריך כו' עד עדותן כו' דכי היכי דאין כו' עד התורה כיון דמחד קרא נפקא לכך י"ל דפריך הכא מה ליושב שכן פסול לעדות לכתחלה. מהר"פ: ה] אונן (סנהדרין דף פד ע"א): ו] חילל וא"ת מאי קאמר אם איתא דאחר נמי לא חילל הוי ליה למכתב גבי כהן הדיוט ולא גבי כה"ג וי"ל דאי כתביה גבי כהן הדיוט הוי אמינא הא כה"ג אם עבד חילל דמתוך חשיבות הוא נפסל כך פי' הקונטרס: ז] מפני טומאה נשרפה. וקשה דמשמע דאם לא היתה טומאה היתה נאכלת והלא הם היו אוננים ואונן אסור בקדשים וי"ל דהיו יכולים לאכול בלילה וקסבר דאנינות לילה אינו אלא מדרבנן ומיהו קשה היאך אנו יכולים לומר דבשביל טומאה נשרפה הא משמע מקרא בפי' דמפני אנינות נשרפה מדכתיב ותקראנה אותי כאלה [וי"ל דהטומאה] אירעא להם בערב והיינו דקאמר אהרן היום לא היינו יכולים לאכול בשביל האנינות אבל בלילה היה פשוט לו למשה שלא היו יכולים לאכול בשביל הטומאה והיה שואל למה לא אכלו ביום באנינות כמו שאכלו את המנחה ואהרן אמר לו ואכלתי חטאת היום כלומר אם אמרו בקדשי שעה יאמרו בקדשי דורות וא"ת דנהי נמי מפני טומאה נשרפה מ"מ אין אנו יכולים למחוק את הפסוק (דמשמע הן) [דהן] הקריבו [דמשמע הא אי קריבו אינהו שפיר אישתרוף וי"ל דס"ל דהן הקריבו אינו בתמיה אלא הן (הנה) [הקריבו היום] בניחותא כלומר הן עדיין היה יום (בזרקו) [בזריקת] דמה והיינו אסורים לאכול בקדשים עד הערב ובתוך כך אירעה טומאה ועוד יש מפרשים כלומר אני הקרבתי [ולא] משום דאם הקריבו אותו בניו שהיה פסול אלא היה אומר לו האמת ותקראנה אותי כאלה שהיו בניו אוננים וגם אני הייתי אונן כמו כן ולכך לא אכלנוה דאונן אסור בקדשים ובלילה היינו יכולים לאכול לולי מפני הטומאה שאירעה בה וא"ת למה דחק עצמו לומר כו' דא"כ מאי היום דקאמר דמשמע דוקא יום בשלמא אי אמרינן מפני הטומאה נשרפה היינו דקאמר היום כלומר עדיין היום הוא ואנינות יום אסור בקדשים ובשביל כך לא אכלנו ובתוך כך בא (הטומאה) [טמאה] ר"ל ולא היה בו בר אחר רק מפני אנינות נשרפה ובשביל כך נתנו לאכול אפילו בלילה וא"ת ואידך דקאמר מפני אנינות נשרפה היאך מפרש [להן הקריבו] וי"ל דדריש ליה הכי הן הם הקריבו בתמי' ומתשובתו של

אהרן וכו' תוס' בסגנון אחר קסבר מפני טומאה שנגעה בה נשרפה ולא הוזכר שם אנינות לענין שריפה וכ"ת והלא אמת שהיו אוננין אבל מכל מקום בשביל זה לא היתה בשריפה דקסבר כמ"ד אנינות לילה לאו דאורייתא הלכך נהי דלא היו יכולים לאוכלה כל היום בשביל אנינות מ"מ בלילה היו יכולים לאוכלה דהוא נאכל ליום ולילה ואי מחמת ההקרבה שהיתה באנינות משום הכי לא מיפסלא ומפני מה שרפוה מפני שאירעה בו טומאה בתוך כך באונס ולא היו יכולים לאוכלה גם בלילה וכן הא דקאמר אהרן ותקראנה אותי כאלה שגם אני (היתה) [הייתי] אונן הטוב בעיני ה' אם היינו אוכלים אותה ביום שהיו אוננים על אחיהם וגם אני אונן הלכך לא אכלוה דאונן אסור בקדשים כל היום ופנחס נמי לא היה יכול לאוכלה דפנחס לא נתכהן עד שהרג לזמרי ובלילה היו יכולים לאכול אי לאו מפני טומאה שאירעה והשתא ר"ל הן היום בניחותא והא דקאמר הן היום אינו כמו הן הקריבו ובא לומר וכי הם הקריבו אלא הן כמו הנה וה"ק הן הקריבו היום אותם שהיה לו ליקרב ביום כלומר והלא היינו אסורים לאכול בקדשים עד הערב מחמת אנינות שאסור בקדשים ולא מחמת הקרבה ומה ששרפוה מפני הטומאה שאירעה וא"ת אם כן למה דחיק לתרץ מפני הטומאה נשרפה [שלא] הוזכר בפסוק לימא לעולם מפני אנינות נשרפה וקסבר אנינות לילה דאורייתא והן הקריבו בניחותא כמו הנה הקריבו כדפי' ולא תידוק מכלל דאינהו הקריבו וכו' וי"ל דאכתי [נפקא] לן מדכתיב בתר הכי ואכלתי חטאת היום דאנינות לילה לאו דאורייתא הלכך צריך לומר דמפני אנינות לילה לא שרפוה אלא מפני שאירעה בו טומאה וה"ל הן היום הלא יום הוא ואנינות יום אסור בקדשים ולכך לא אכלנוה ביום ובתוך כך בא הטומאה ולכך שרפוה אבל למ"ד מפני אנינות נשרפה מיירי קרא לענין הקרבת אנינות והן היום בתמי' וכי הן הקריבו ומתשובתו של אהרן אתה למד מה אמר לו משה מדוע לא אכלתם וגו' שמא בניך הקריבו באנינות שהיו אוננים ופסלוה ולכך נשרפה ואמר (ליה) [לו] אהרן וכי הם הקריבו שהן הדיוטים ומחללין עבודה כשהן אוננים אני הקרבתי שאני כה"ג ומותר לשמש באנינות ולכך קאמר הן היום הקריבו כלומר היום (שהן) [שהוא] משמיני למילואים והעבודה הוברירה בי כמו שאמרת לי קרב אל המזבח והאמת מפני אנינות נשרפה שלא היו לה אוכלים דקסבר אנינות לילה דאורייתא היא:

ח] מוינזרו דדרשת ליה להאי בני ישראל ותיבת קרא נמחק: ט] תיבת בבמה נמחק: י] ובברייתא תני עלה: יא] נמי מוכח הכי דגדעון ומנוח כו' בבמה שהיו זרים הס"ד: יב] תיבת הכא נמחק: יג] שם יושב כלומר מצינו שם יושב: יד] משום הך פירכא: טו] ופסלוה ולכך: טז] מתוך חשיבותו וקדושתו יתירא הוא דפסול אונן: יז] הערב ובתוך כך: יח] יוכיחו: יט] שני ליה לאו גמור מזר ס"א שני לאו גמור מן זר תיבת משני ל"ש: כ] מקדשים קלים ובכור דאי בשאר קדשים שאינם נאכלים אלא בעזרה הא אסור לישב בעזרה אי נמי אפילו בקדשי קדשים איירי וצורך קרבן שאני דכתיב למשחה נתתיו לך ודרשינן לקמן דרך גדולה כדרך שהמלכים אוכלין אותה: כא] בכבודו מפני המקום בשביל: כב] ומיהו דלמא טעמא דחליצה ותיבות על כרחין נמחק: כג] מתיבה ובדיעבד כו' עד תיבת כשרה נמחק: כד] הוא ע"כ אבל מה דקשה דאיכא למיפרך מה ליושב ת"ח שכן פסול לכתחלה הואיל והוא פרוך מלכתחלה לכתחלה כדפי' לעיל. מהר"פ: כה] דאפילו בלא עבודה: כו] הקריבו אתא אות י' נמחק:

א) כוונתו לדברי התוספות בד"ה מה ליושב ע"ש.

מפני

בעל מום שאוכל, אם עבד – חילל, אונן שאין אוכל – אינו דין שאם עבד חילל? מה לבעל מום, שכן עשה בו קריבין כמקריבין! זר יוכיח. מה לזר, שכן אין לו תקנה! בעל מום יוכיח. *וחזר הדין, לא ראי זה כראי זה ולא ראי זה כראי זה, הצד השוה שבהן – שהן מוזהרין, ואם עבדו חיללו, אף אני אביא אונן שמוזהר, ואם עבד – חילל. היכן מוזהר? אילימא מ"ומן המקדש לא יצא" – חילול בגופיה כתיב ביה! אלא °מ"הן (ויקרא י) הקריבו", וקסבר: א] *מפני אנינות נשרפה. איכא למפרך: מה להצד השוה שבהן, ב] שכן לא הותרה מכללו! טמא יוכיח. מה לטמא, שכן מטמא! הנך יוכיחו, וחזר הדין כו', הצד השוה שבהן שמוזהרין כו'. ולפרוך: מה להצד השוה שבהן, שכן לא הותרו מכללן אצל כהן גדול בקרבן יחיד! שם טומאה מיהא אישתראי. רב משרשיא אמר: ג] אתיא בקל וחומר מיושב, ומה יושב שאוכל – אם עבד חילל, אונן שאינו אוכל – אינו דין שאם עבד חילל? מה ליושב, שכן פסול לעדות! מיושב תלמיד חכם. מה לשם יושב, שכן פסול לעדות! שם יושב לא פריך. ואם תימצי לומר פריך, אתיא מיושב ומחדא מהנך. "אונן פסול". אמר ד] רבא: לא שנו אלא בקרבן יחיד, ה] אבל בקרבן צבור – מרצה, קל וחומר מטומאה: (א) מה טומאה שלא הותרה מכללה אצל כהן גדול בקרבן יחיד – הותרה אצל הדיוט בקרבן צבור, אנינות שהותרה מכללה אצל כהן גדול בקרבן יחיד – אינו דין שהותרה אצל כהן הדיוט בקרבן ציבור? מתקיף לה רבא בר אהילאי: לא תותר אנינות אצל כהן גדול בקרבן יחיד מקל וחומר: ומה טומאה שהותרה אצל כהן הדיוט בצבור – לא הותרה אצל כהן גדול בקרבן יחיד, אנינות שלא הותרה אצל כהן הדיוט בקרבן צבור – אינו דין שלא תותר אצל כהן גדול בקרבן יחיד? ותותר טומאה אצל כ"ג בקרבן יחיד מק"ו: ומה אנינות שלא הותר אצל כהן הדיוט בקרבן צבור – הותרה אצל כהן גדול בקרבן יחיד, טומאה שהותרה אצל כהן הדיוט בקרבן צבור – אינו דין שהותרה אצל כ"ג בקרבן יחיד? ולא תותר טומאה אצל כהן הדיוט בקרבן צבור מקל וחומר: ומה אנינות שהותרה אצל כ"ג בקרבן יחיד – לא הותרה אצל כהן הדיוט בקרבן צבור, טומאה שלא הותרה אצל כהן גדול בקרבן יחיד – אינו דין שלא תותר בכהן הדיוט בקרבן צבור? (ולא תותר ולא תותר אנינות וטומאה טומאה יחיד ויחיד ציבור, סימן)

אלא

שאינו אוכל. דכתיב: "לא אכלתי באוני". [אין לו תקנה]. ואונן יש לו תקנה למחר. בעל מום. יש לו תקנה כשיעבור מומו. חילול בגופיה כתיב. כיון דדייקת: הא אחר שלא יצא, ו] ק"ו תו למה לך? וקסבר מפני אנינות נשרפה. שלא היו לו אוכלין, וכדפרישית. וכשאמרו לו: מפני אנינות שרפנוה – טעה, כסבור שהקריבוה אוננים, ואמר להם: שמא באנינות הקריבוה. ומיהו, חילול לא יליף ר' ישמעאל מיניה, דאי לאו ז] (קרא אחרינא) הוה אמינא: האי דאמר להו שמא באנינות הקרבתם אותו – לאו למימרא דאי עביד הכי שפיר אשתרוף. אלא כשאמרו לו: מפני אנינות שרפנוה, אמר להם: שמא עברתם על האזהרה, והקרבתם ח] אוננין. ואמר לו אהרן: וכי הן הקריבו, דאסורים להקריב אוננין? אני הקרבתי שאין אנינות פוסל בי. לא הותרו מכללן. זר ובעל מום מכלל איסורן שנאסרו במקדש לא הותרו אצל שום קרבן ולא אצל שום אדם. תאמר באונן שהותר מכללו אצל כהן גדול. טמא יוכיח. שהותר מכללו אצל קרבן צבור, דכתיב: "במועדו" – ואפילו בטומאה. ואם עבד בקרבן יחיד חילל. ולפרוך מה להצד השוה. שבשלשתן, שכן לא הותרו בקרבן יחיד אפי' אצל כ"ג. אבל אונן הותר. שם טומאה מיהא הא אישתראי. כגון בצבור, הלכך לאו פירכא היא. ואי קשיא: למה לי למימר טמא יוכיח? בזר נמי משכחת לה, דהותר שם זרות בבמה! אין זה הותר מכללו, שהרי לא נאסר שם מעולם. אבל אונן הותר מכללו, שהרי נאסר במקדש אצל כהן [הדיוט]. מתקיף לה רבא בר אהילאי. ט] אדרבא פריך, דפשיטא ליה דטומאה לא הותרה לכהן גדול בקרבן יחיד, מדלא אשכחן דאישתראי אלא בצבור. ופשיטא ליה דהותרה בצבור אפילו אצל כהן הדיוט, מדאישתראי סתמא. ופשיטא ליה דאנינות הותרה אפילו בקרבן יחיד אצל כהן גדול, מדאשתראי סתמא. ובאיסור אנינות אצל כהן הדיוט בא לחלק על ידי ק"ו, ולומר: לא נאסר אלא ביחיד, ולא אמרי' סתמא איתסר. אם במה שלא חלקו הכתובים אתה בא לחלק על ידי קל וחומר – אמאי פשיטא לך בהנך דלעיל? יש לך לדרוש קל וחומר חילוף ולהחליף את כולן י]. לא תותר אנינות אצל כהן גדול ביחיד. וכי שרייה בצבור שרייה. מק"ו ומה טומאה שהותרה כו'. דהא סתמא אישתרי. לא הותרה כו'. דהא לא אשכחן דאישתראי ביחיד, דלא כתיב "במועדו" אלא בצבור, אנינות כו'. ותותר טומאה כו'. כלומר, אי נמי דריש הכי: ותותר טומאה אצל כ"ג יא] ביחיד, ואוקי איסורא בכהן הדיוט. ולא תותר טומאה אצל כהן הדיוט כו'. כלומר, א"כ החליף ודרוש בו. נמצא מסולק מכולן, ולא תדע מה תדרוש. אלא, יב] אל תחלוק במה שלא פירשו לך הכתובים.

דאיכא

שאמר להם משה: שמא עברתם על איסור הקרבת אנינות וטעיתם מחמת כך לשורפו? ומיהו לא יתול, כדפי' בקונטרס בסמוך. וסוגיא זו יג] לא כחד מהנך תנאי דפ' "טבול יום" (לקמן קא.). ואין לתמוה על זה, *דהנהו תנאי דרשי קראי דהתם לפי האמת, דקי"ל דאונן מחיל עבודה מקרא אחרינא, אבל אי לאו דנפקא לן מקרא אחרינא – מהתם לא הוה שמעינן, דהוה דרישנא לקרא כי הכא, וכדמפרש ליה בקונטרס.

והיכן מוזהר כו' אלא מהן הקריבו וקסבר מפני אנינות נשרפה. שלא היו* יד] אוכלין כל היום ולילה שאחרי כן, ולמחרתו יהיה טו] [נותר], ונשרף בו ביום בלא עבור צורה. דקסבר: אנינות לילה נמי אסור, ואפי' נקבר המת. וכשאמר לו אהרן: מפני אנינות נשרפה, טעה משה, שלא הבין מפני אנינות דקאמר אהרן שזהו שלא היו ראויין לאכול מחמת אנינותם. אלא טז] קסבר שהקריבו אוננים, ואמר להו משה: שמא יז] באנינות הקרבתוה. ומיהו, חילול לא יליף ר' ישמעאל מיניה, דאי לאו קרא אחרינא הוה אמינא דכי נמי יח] דאמר להם באנינות אקרבתוה – לא למימר דאי עבוד הכי שפיר אשתרוף. אלא כשאמרו לו: מפני אנינות שרפנוה, אמר להם: שמא עברתם על אזהרה והקרבתם אוננים? ואמר יט] אהרן: וכי הן הקריבו? כך פי' בקונט'. וקצת צריך להוסיף על פירושו, דכשאמר להם: שמא עברתם על אזהרה והקרבתם אוננים – כ] רוצה לומר: וטעיתם לשורפה על כך. כא] דאי לאו הכי – מה ענין זה אצל כב] (זה) שריפה? ועל זה השיב אהרן: הן הקריבו? אני הקרבתי. ומפני אנינות שאמרתי – לא מפני הקרבתם באנינות, אלא מפני שלא יכולנו לאכול מפני אנינות. וא"ת: בפ' "כיצד צולין" (פסחים פב.) ולקמן בפרק "התערובת" (דף פג.) דדרשינן: חטאת שנכנס דמה לפנים פסולה מ"הן לא הובא את דמה", כג] היכי דריש ליה? דלמא הכי קאמר ליה: שמא כד] טעית לשורפה, מפני שנכנס דמה לפנים! וי"ל: דלא דמי, דלמה היה לו להזכיר למשה הנך פסולין דיוצא ונכנס דמה לפנים? דבשלמא גבי אנינות – היה סבור שמא טעה, לפי שאמר לו אהרן מפני אנינות נשרפה. וה"ר חיים תירץ: דאנינות לא אמר לו משה בפירוש, אלא מתוך תשובתו של אהרן. אבל "הן לא הובא את דמה" אמר משה בפי', משמע בהדיא דאם הובא – שפיר אשתרוף. **שכן** לא הותרו מכללן. פירש בקונטרס: וזר דהותר בבמה – אין זה הותר מכללו, שהרי לא נאסר שם מעולם. והקשה ה"ר חיים: דב"הקומץ רבה" (מנחות כה.) קרי כה] עון יוצא הותר מכללו כו] בבמה! ותירץ: דשאני גבי ציץ, דכתיב "לרצון להם" – בכל מקום שמרצה. ועוד י"ל: דאפילו מיקרי הותר מכללו – מ"מ פרכינן הכא שפיר, שכן לא הותרו מכללן במקום שנאסרו. **שם** טומאה מיהא אישתראי. וא"ת: מה להנך, זר בעל מום טמא, שכן במיתה, תאמר באונן וכו'! וי"ל: דסבר לה כרבנן דאמרי (סנהדרין פג.): בעל מום ששימש באזהרה, ולא כרבי [דאמר] במיתה. וא"ת: מה להנך שכן פסולין בפרה, בעל מום זר וטמא, תאמר באונן (לקמן דף יז:)? וי"ל: טבול יום יוכיח. **אתיא** בק"ו מיושב. תימה: מה ליושב שכן לא הותר מכללו! **אבל** בקרבן צבור מרצה. תימה: הרי חטאת דאהרן דהיינו שעיר דר"ח, דקיימא לן פרק "טבול יום" (לקמן קא.) ובשמעתין דאם הקריבוה באנינות פסולה! וי"ל: כיון דלא ילפינן אלא מטומאה – דינו כטומאה, דאינו מרצה אלא כז] באימורין, אבל הקרבן אינו נאכל. ועוד, דבלאו הכי סתר ליה שפיר להאי ק"ו. **ומה** טומאה. תימה: אי אנינות לילה דאורייתא – איכא למיפרך: מה לטומאה שכן הותרה בפסח הבא בטומאה באכילה, תאמר באנינות שלא הותר. **ולא** תותר אנינות כו'. תימה: מה לטמא, שכן מטמא! כח] ויש לומר: דאינו ק"ו גמור, אלא סתירת דברים כט].

*) **כל** חדא וחדא תיקום בדוכתיה. ל] ל"ע פ"ק דחולין (דף כג:) גבי ק"ו דכשר בתורים פסול בבני יונה, וגבי כשר שבפרה פסול בעגלה (שם כג.), וגבי ויהיו כל הכלים מקבלין טומאה מאוירן מק"ו (שם כה.), ובפר' "ואלו מנחות" (מנחות עה.) גבי חלות ורקיקין, וכן פר' "כל המנחות" (שם דף סג:) גבי שלמי יחיד שטעונין סמיכה, ובפ' "השוכר את הפועלים" (ב"מ פח:) גבי שור אוכל במחובר, ובפרק "כיצד הרגל" (ב"ק כה:) דקאמר: ותהא שן חייבת ברשות הרבים מק"ו. ובפ"ק דקדושין (דף יד.) ותהא יבמה יוצאה בגט מקל וחומר, ובנזיר פרק "שלשה מינין" (דף מד.) גבי **)טמא כמיטמא, ובסוף "יש מותרות" (יבמות פז:) דנעשה מתים כחיים מק"ו. צריך לדקדק בכולן, אמאי לא אמר כל חדא וחדא תיקום בדוכתיה! ושמא שאני הכא, משום

*) שייך לדף שאחר זה **) נ"ל מטמא נ"ק

דהכי

[נ"ל ק"ו]

[קדושין כא. וש"נ]

[לקמן קא. פסחים פב:]

הגהות הב"ח

(א) גמרא ומה טומאה:

דהנהו תנאי דהתם דרשי קראי לפי האמת דקי"ל דאונן מחיל עבודה וילפינן מקרא אחרינא כו' אחרינא מהך קרא לא הוה כו' נ"ק

נ"א שלא היו יכולין לאכול כל היום ולילה שאחריו עד למחרתו והיו שורפין בו ביום כו' נ"ק

שיטה מקובצת

א] מפני אנינות נשרפה. וא"ת חילול נמי בגופיה כתיבא כדאמר לעיל הא אקריבו אינהו שפיר אשתרוף [וי"ל דאי] לאו קרא אחרינא הוי אמינא הא דאמר להו שמא באנינות הקרבתם אותה לאו למימרא דאי עבדי הכי שפיר אשתרוף כו' כפ"ה וא"ת בפרק התערובת כו' וי"ל דלא דמי לאנינות א) [דלא] אמר משה בפירוש אלא מתוך תשובתו של אהרן כדפי' אבל הן לא הובא את דמה כתוב בפירוש משמע בהדיא הא אם הובא שפיר אשתרוף. תוספות בסגנון אחר: ב] שכן לא הותרה מכללו. וא"ת הרי הותר מכללו בבמה וי"ל דהואיל ושם לא נאסר מעולם אין זה הותר מכללו דמכללו משמע ממקום שנאסר וכפ"ה והקשה הר"ר חיים כהן כו' וי"ל דה"פ מה לזר שכן לא הותר בבמת צבור תאמר באונן שכן הותר מכללן בבמת צבור. מהר"פ: ג] אתיא בקל וחומר מיושב. לא בא רב משרשיא לחלוק על דברי דבי רבי ישמעאל שהוא תנא אלא תנא דבי רבי ישמעאל אמר דבריו בקיצור אתיא מקל וחומר ולא יותר ופי' התלמוד לעיל מבעל מום ואונן ורב משרשיא פי' מיושב ויש לתמוה על הסוגיא דלעיל אמר לתנא דבי ר' ישמעאל קאתי זר מאונן ובעל מום דקאמר אונן יוכיח אלמא פשיטא ליה אונן מחלל יותר מזר והכא פשיט אונן מבעל מום וזר (אלא) [אלמא] פשיט ליה דזר מחלל יותר מאונן ואמר מורי דתנא דלעיל מיירי לפי אותה שיטה דקים לן דאונן מחלל עבודה מקרא דהן הקריבו או מן המקדש כו' הא אחר שלא יצא כו' אבל זר לא נפקא לן מוינזרו דלא מיירי כלל בזרות אלא בטומאה והכא איירי לפי אותה שיטה דזר מחלל עבודה מוינזרו ולא נפקא לן אונן לא מהן הקריבו ולא מן המקדש לא יצא. מהר"פ. אתיא מיושב כו' וא"ת מה ליושב שכן לא הותר מכללו במקדש אצל כה"ג בקרבן יחיד תאמר באונן כו' וי"ל דהוי פירכא כל דהו ופירכא כל דהו לא פרכינן על חדא מחדא ומיהו לבסוף דקאמר אתיא מיושב וחד מהנך קשה דאיכא למיפרך מה להצד השוה שבהן שכן לא הותר מכללן במקדש וי"ל דשם טומאה מיהא אישתראי ונילף מיושב ומטמא. מהר"פ: ד] אמר רבה אות א' נמחק: ה] אבל בקרבן צבור מרצה. תימה הא מדכתיב הן היום הקריבו משמע אי אקרבוה שפיר אשתרוף והתם קרבן צבור הוי וי"ל דנהי דמרצה מ"מ אינו נאכל דדיו לבא מן הדין [להיות] כנדון דמטומאה גמרינן לה והתם אינו נאכל אע"ג דמרצה ומיהו קשה דלא דמי לטומאה דהתם הא דאינו נאכל היינו משום דנטמא הבשר כשנוגע בה הלכך אע"ג דמרצה הבשר (טמאה) [טמא] אבל באנינות לא שייך למימר הכי לכך נראה דרבא סבר מפני טומאה נשרפה ומה שלא אכלוה היום מפני שהיו אוננים ולא היו להם אוכלים אבל ודאי אם היה שם כהנים שלא היו אוננים היו מותרים לאכול אף על פי שהאוננים הקריבוה כיון דקרבן צבור הוה וחילול עבודה דאונן נפקא ליה לרבא מלא יחלל וסבירא ליה דאנינות לילה לאו דאורייתא והיינו [הן] היום כדפי' לעיל ותדע דאי קסבר אנינות לילה דאורייתא א"כ היכא יליף דתותר אנינות מטומאה הא איכא למיפרך מה לטומאה שכן הותר מכללו אצל אכילת פסחים. מהר"פ: ו] יצא חילל ק"ו: ז] לאו ק"ו ותיבות קרא אחרינא נמחק: ח] אוננין. גליון כלומר טעיתם לשורפה על כך ואין בו אלא אזהרה: ט] אהילאי אדרבה פריך: י] כולן ודרוש לא והד"א: יא] כה"ג בקרבן יחיד ואוקי: יב] אלא לא תחלוק: יג] דלא כחד: יד] היו לה אוכלין: טו] יהיה נשרף בו ביום ולכן ישרף בלא עבור צורה: טז] קסבר מפני אנינות נשרפה שלא היו לה אוכלין וקסבר אנינות לילה דאורייתא מיהו לא יליף חילול ר' ישמעאל מיניה דאי לאו קרא אחרינא כו'. לשון מהר"פ: יז] שמא אקרבתוה באנינות ופסלתוה ומיהו חילול: יח] נמי אמר להם שמא: יט] ואמר לו אהרן וכי הן הקריבו דאסורים להקריב אוננים אני שאני כה"ג הקרבתים שאין אנינות פוסלת בי כך: כ] אוננים היה רוצה לומר משה שמא טעיתם לשורפה: כא] עיין בהשמטות בסוף המסכת: כב] תיבת זה נמחק: כג] דמה דמשמע הא אם הובאה דמה פסולה והיכי דריש ליה דלמא: כד] שמא עברת על האזהרה וטעית: כה] תיבת עון נמחק: כו] מכללו לפי שהותר בבמה: כז] אלא האימורין אבל: כח] מטמא ועוד הרבה איכא למיפרך על אלו קלים וחמורים: כט] דברים בעלמא הס"ד: ל] בדוכתיה. כלומר אם באתם לחלק בכתובים ולומר דלא מיירי בכל ענין א"כ תעשה קלים וחמורים להוציא מהם דברים שאינם אלא ודאי אין להוציא ולגרוע על המפורש בכתובים והא דשרי רחמנא אונן [בכה"ג] אין לחלק בין קרבן צבור בין קרבן יחיד וכשאסר רחמנא אונן כהן בכל ענין אמרו בין בקרבן יחיד בין בקרבן צבור וקרבן צבור דשרי רחמנא [בטומאה] בין בכהן גדול ובין בכהן הדיוט וכשאסר רחמנא קרבן יחיד בטומאה בין בכהן גדול ובין בכהן הדיוט כל חד וחד בדוכתיה. מהר"פ:

חדא

א) והוא תירוץ של ה"ר חיים בתוספות סוד"ה וזכן

נ"ל כלומר יש לדרוש ולהחליף ולא נדע כו' נ"ק

יא א מיי' פ"ב מהלכות ביאת מקדש הלכה ו:

אֶלָּא אִיכָּא לְמִיפְרַךְ הָכִי, וְאִיכָּא לְמִיפְרַךְ הָכִי – אֵכָל א] חֲדָא וַחֲדָא תֵּיקוּ בְּדוּכְתֵּיהּ.§ "טְבוּל יוֹם".§ מְנָלַן? *דְּתַנְיָא, רַבִּי סִימָאי אוֹמֵר: רֶמֶז לִטְבוּל יוֹם שֶׁאִם עָבַד חִילֵּל, מִנַּיִן? ת"ל: °"קְדוֹשִׁים יִהְיוּ וְלֹא יְחַלְּלוּ", אִם אֵינוֹ עִנְיָן לְטָמֵא דְּנָפֵיק ב] °מִ"וְיִנָּזְרוּ", תְּנֵהוּ עִנְיָן לִטְבוּל יוֹם. אֵימָא: תְּנֵהוּ עִנְיָן לְקוֹרֵחַ קָרְחָה וּלְמַשְׁחִית פְּאַת זָקָן! טְבוּל יוֹם דְּאִם עָבַד – בְּמִיתָה, מְנָא לָן? דְּגָמַר חִילּוּל חִילּוּל מִתְּרוּמָה; ג] *דְּפָסֵיל בִּתְרוּמָה – מַחֵיל עֲבוֹדָה, דְּלָא פָּסֵיל בִּתְרוּמָה – לָא מַחֵיל עֲבוֹדָה. אָמַר רַבָּה: לָמָּה לִי דִּכְתַב רַחֲמָנָא טָמֵא וּטְבוּל יוֹם וּמְחוּסַּר כִּפּוּרִים? צְרִיכִי; דְּאִי כָּתַב רַחֲמָנָא טָמֵא – שֶׁכֵּן מְטַמֵּא. בִּטְבוּל יוֹם – מְחוּסַּר כִּפּוּרִים לָא אָתֵי מִינֵּיהּ, שֶׁכֵּן ד] פָּסוּל בִּתְרוּמָה. בִּמְחוּסַּר כִּפּוּרִים – טְבוּל יוֹם לָא אָתֵי מִינֵּיהּ, שֶׁכֵּן מְחוּסָּר מַעֲשֶׂה. מֵחֲדָא לָא אָתֵי, תֵּיתֵי חֲדָא מִתַּרְתֵּי! בְּהֵי לָא לִכְתּוֹב רַחֲמָנָא? לָא לִכְתּוֹב בִּמְחוּסַּר כִּפּוּרִים וְתֵיתֵי מֵהָנָךְ – מַה לְּהָנָךְ שֶׁכֵּן ה] פְּסוּלִים בִּתְרוּמָה! אֶלָּא: לָא לִכְתּוֹב רַחֲמָנָא בִּטְבוּל יוֹם, וְתֵיתֵי מֵהָנָךְ; דְּמַאי פָּרְכַתְּ? מַה לְּהָנָךְ שֶׁכֵּן מְחוּסָּרִים מַעֲשֶׂה – ו] סוֹף סוֹף קְלִישָׁא לָהּ טוּמְאָתָן! קָסָבַר

ויקרא כא | שם כב | תורה אור

רש"י

ז] דְּאִיכָּא לְמִיפְרַךְ הָכִי כו'. *יֵשׁ לָדוּן (א) כו' וְיֵשׁ לְהַחֲלִיף, וְלֹא נֵדַע אֵיזֶה נִדְרוֹשׁ. הִלְכָּךְ כָּל חֲדָא תֵּיקוּ בְּדוּכְתָּהּ כִּכְתִיבָתָהּ סְתָם: כְּשֶׁהוּתְּרָה אֲנִינוּת לְכ"ג סְתָם – בֵּין בְּיָחִיד בֵּין בְּצִבּוּר הוּתְּרָה, וּכְשֶׁנֶּאֶסְרָה לְהֶדְיוֹט – בֵּין בְּיָחִיד בֵּין בְּצִבּוּר נֶאֶסְרָה, וּכְשֶׁהוּתְּרָה טוּמְאָה בְּצִבּוּר – הוּתְּרָה אַף לְכֹהֵן הֶדְיוֹט, וּכְשֶׁנֶּאֶסְרָה בְּקָרְבַּן יָחִיד – נֶאֶסְרָה אַף לְכ"ג. קְדוֹשִׁים יִהְיוּ. גַּבֵּי טוּמְאָה כְּתִיב בֶּ"אֱמוֹר": "וְלֹא יְחַלְּלוּ וגו' כִּי אֶת אִשֵּׁי ה' לֶחֶם" וגו' – בְּחִילּוּל קָדָשִׁים הַכָּתוּב מְדַבֵּר. דְּנָפְקָא לֵיהּ מִוַּיִּנָּזְרוּ. דִּכְתִיב בֵּיהּ חִילּוּל. ח] וְנֵימָא תְּנֵהוּ עִנְיָן וכו'. דְּמִינַּיְיהוּ סָלֵיק: "לֹא יִקְרְחוּ קָרְחָה", וְסָמֵיךְ לֵיהּ "קְדוֹשִׁים יִהְיוּ". "אֶלָּא" לֹא גָּרַס. ט] טְבוּל יוֹם דְּאִם עָבַד בְּמִיתָה. י] שִׁינּוּיָא הוּא. כְּלוֹמַר, לֹא מָצֵית לְמִיתְנֵי: תְּנֵהוּ עִנְיָן לְקוֹרֵחַ קָרְחָה, דְּמִיתָה גַּבֵּי טְבוּל יוֹם שֶׁעָבַד יא] יָלְפִינַן לָהּ בְּסַנְהֶדְרִין בְּ"אֵלּוּ הֵן הַנִּשְׂרָפִין" (דף פג:) יב] וְגָמַר חִילּוּל חִילּוּל מִתְּרוּמָה, וּמֵחִילּוּל דְּהַאי קְרָא יָלֵיף לָהּ: נֶאֱמַר כָּאן חִילּוּל, וְנֶאֱמַר בְּטָמֵא וּטְבוּל יוֹם שֶׁאָכְלוּ תְּרוּמָה חִילּוּל, "וּמֵתוּ בוֹ כִּי יְחַלְּלוּהוּ", מַה לְּהַלָּן בְּמִיתָה כו'. וְהִלְכָּךְ, הוֹאִיל וְהַאי קְרָא לִגְ"שׁ מִתְּרוּמָה אֲתָא, וְלֹא מְפָרֵשׁ בֵּיהּ בְּמַאי קָאֵי – לֹא תִּתְּנֵהוּ עִנְיָן אֶלָּא לִפְסוּלִין לִתְרוּמָה, יג] דְּיָלְפִי' מִינֵּיהּ דְּפָסוּל בִּתְרוּמָה מָחֵיל עֲבוֹדָה יד] כו'. לָמָּה לִי דִּכְתַב רַחֲמָנָא טָמֵא וּטְבוּל יוֹם כו'. אַטָּמֵא לֹא מִיבַּעְיָא לֵיהּ, דְּאִי לָאו כְּתַב טָמֵא – לֹא הֲוָה אָתֵי לָן חַד מִנַּיְיהוּ שֶׁיְּחַלֵּל עֲבוֹדָה, דְּהָא טְבוּל יוֹם בְּ"אִם אֵינוֹ עִנְיָן לְטָמֵא" טו] יָלְפִינַן, וְאִי לֹא הֲוָה כְּתַב טָמֵא בְּ"וְיִנָּזְרוּ" – הֲוָה אוֹקִימְנָא לִ"קְדוֹשִׁים יִהְיוּ" בְּטָמֵא. וְכֵן מְחוּסַּר כִּפּוּרִים נַמִי לֹא כְּתַב טז] בֵּיהּ חִילּוּל, אֶלָּא מִדְּאִיקְרֵי טָמֵא יָלְפִינַן לֵיהּ לְקַמָּן. (ב) וְכִי מִיבַּעֵי לֵיהּ לְרַבָּה, טְבוּל יוֹם וּמְחוּסַּר כִּפּוּרִים מִיבַּעְיָא יז]. בִּמְחוּסַּר כִּפּוּרִים טְבוּל יוֹם לֹא אָתֵי מִינֵּיהּ שֶׁכֵּן מְחוּסַּר מַעֲשֶׂה. הֲבָאַת קָרְבָּן. תֹּאמַר בִּטְבוּל יוֹם שֶׁאֵינוֹ מְחוּסָּר יח] הֲבָאַת קָרְבָּן, וְשִׁמְשָׁא מִמֵּילָא עָרְבָא. בְּטָמֵא לֵיכָּא לְמֵימַר דְּלֹא אָתְיָא מִינֵי', דְּהָא אִיהוּ נַמִי מְחוּסַּר טְבִילָה. וְעוֹד, דְּטָמֵא לֹא קָמִיבַּעְיָא לֵיהּ, מִדְּלָא קָאָמַר בְּסֵיפָא דְּמִילְּתָא: לֹא לִכְתּוֹב טָמֵא וְתֵיתֵי מֵהָנָךְ, דְּתוּ לֹא הֲוָה לֵיהּ לְשַׁנּוּיֵי עֲלָהּ מִידֵי. קְלִישָׁא לֵיהּ טוּמְאָתוֹ. דִּמְחוּסַּר כִּפּוּרִים, יט] שֶׁהֲרֵי הֶעֱרִיב שִׁמְשׁוֹ. וְתוּ לֵיכָּא פִּירְכָא דְּ"מַה כ] הַצַּד", דַּהֲוָה לֵיהּ חַד מִינַּיְיהוּ נַמִי שֶׁאֵינוֹ מְחוּסַּר מַעֲשֶׂה. קָסָבַר

סנהדרין פג. | בס"י למיתביה ענין

הגהות הב"ח

(א) רש"י ד"ה דאיכא וכו' יש לדון וכו' ויש להחליף וכו' נ"ב ר"ל לקמן דף יט ע"ב וכו' מיבעי וכו' קמיבעיא ליה הס"ד:

תוספות

דהכי ק"ו סתרי אהדדי, מה שאין כן בהנהו. כא] והטעם כמו שפירש בקונט': משום דנכתבו הכתובים סתם, דכשהותרה אנינות לכ"ג סתם – בין ביחיד בין בצבור הותרה, וכשנאסרה להדיוט – בין ביחיד בין בצבור נאסרה, וכשהותרה טומאה לצבור – הותרה אף לכהן הדיוט, וכשנאסרה בקרבן יחיד – נאסרה אף לכ"ג. ואם במה שלא חלקן הכתובים נדון לחלק על ידי ק"ו, אמאי פשיטא בהאי טפי מבהאי? דיש לדרוש חלוף ולהחליף את כולן, הלכך אמרינן כל חדא וחדא תיקום בדוכתיה כב]*. **טבול** יום מנא לן. תימה: תיפוק לי מדכתיב גבי טבול יום "ובא השמש וטהר" – מכלל שהוא טמא, כדדריש לקמן מחוסר כפורים: מדכתיב "וטהרה" מכלל שהיא טמאה! כג] ותירץ ה"ר חיים: דגבי טבול יום איכא למידרש "וטהר" – טהר יומא, כד] כדדרשינן בשמעתא קמייתא דברכות (דף ב:), אבל "וטהרה" לא שייך למידרש הכי. ואע"ג דבפ' "הערל" (יבמות עד:) דרשי' "וטהרה" כה] לטבולת יום ארוך – הואיל מחוסרת כפרה היא, ועל ידי "מכלל שהיא טמאה" לא אתי מיניה טבול יום גרידא. ומיהו קשה: דאיכא קרא אחרינא בקדשים – "לא יאכל עד אשר יטהר", דמוקמינן בפרק "הערל" (שם) בזב בעל שתי ראיות, דלאו בר קרבן הוא, ולענין תרומה. ונימא: מכלל שהוא טמא! ויש לומר: דרבי סימאי דדריש הכא טבול יום מקרא אחרינא, *סבר לה כתנא כו] [דפליג התם אתנא] דבי רבי ישמעאל, דמוקי ליה התם בזב בעל שלש ראיות, ומאי "עד אשר יטהר" – עד דמייתי כפרה. ומיהו קשה: דגבי כז] נגיעת כלי כתיב "במים יובא וטמא עד הערב וטהר" – כח] [מכלל שהוא טמא]! וצריך לומר: דאי לאו קרא דר' סימאי דהכא, דדריש טבול יום מ"ולא יחללו" – לא הוה דרשינן מחוסר כפרה מ"וטהרה" מכלל שהיא טמאה, ולא טבול יום מ"וטהר" מכלל שהוא טמא, משום דקלישא טומאתייהו. אבל מכיון דאשכחן קרא בהדיא לטבול יום, ואע"ג דקלישא טומאתיה – תו דרשינן שפיר מ"וטהרה" מחוסר כפרה. כט] ותימה: "במים יובא וטמא" הלא מפורש בהדיא ל] לטבול יום דאיקרי טמא! וי"ל: דצריך קרא גבי עבודה לא] ד"לא יחללו" דשמעתין, וגבי אכילת תרומה וקדשים קרא אחרינא בפרק "הערל" (שם), ולא ילפינן מהדדי. אבל "וטהרה" דכתיב גבי יולדת, לב] דרשינן מיניה מחוסר כפורים דאסור בקדשים פרק "הערל", וגבי דמחלל עבודה לקמן בפרקין, דאשה כשרה לשחוט קדשים, כדתנן ריש "כל הפסולין" – א"כ שייך בה חילול עבודה. ותימה: דגבי זב וזבה ובעל קרי ושכבת זרע כתיבי כמה פעמים: "ורחץ במים וטמא עד הערב" – אלמא טבול יום איקרי טמא, בין לעבודה בין לקדשים, דקראי סתמא כתיבי ואיקרי טמא לכל מילי! ועוד קשה: דבפ' "שלשה מינין" (נזיר מה.) ובפ' "אלו הן הגולין" (מכות דף ח:) אמרינן: "טמא יהיה" – לרבות טבול יום, "עוד טומאתו בו" – לרבות מחוסר כפורים לענין ביאת מקדש. והשתא ל"ל קרא? הא איקרי טמא לענין עבודה ואכילת קדשים! וכי תימא דלא נילף ביאת מקדש מנייהו (ועוד) – קשה, שהרי קרא ד"ורחץ במים וטמא עד הערב" סתמא כתיב, דטבול יום איקרי טמא לכל מילי, ואפי' לביאת מקדש! ועוד תימה: כיון דדרשי' טבול יום מ"טמא יהיה", למה איצטריך תו "עוד טומאתו" למחוסר כפורים? תיפוק לי מ"וכפר עליה הכהן וטהרה" כדדרשינן לקמן בפירקין: מכלל שהיא טמאה לענין עבודה! ובפ' "הערל" (יבמות דף עד:) לענין אכילת קדשים נדרוש נמי לענין ביאת מקדש, דקרא בכל מילי איירי, שהיא טמאה קודם כפרה! *ואין לתרץ נמי, דאי לאו אלא חד רבויא הוה מוקמינא ליה במחוסר כפורים משום דמחוסר מעשה, ולא בטבול יום משום דשמשא ממילא ערבא – דאם כן הוה ליה למימר איפכא: "טמא יהיה" – לרבות מחוסר כפורים, "עוד טומאתו בו" – לרבות טבול יום! ונראה לתרץ: דלענין ביאת מקדש לא הוה דרשנא מחוסר כפורים מ"וטהרה" מכלל שהיא טמאה, משום דבכרת דטומאת מקדש כתיב: "איש אשר יטמא ולא יתחטא" דמיירי בטומאת מת, אבל מחוסר כפרה דלא שייך במת – לא ליהוי בכרת.* ועוד י"ל: דצריך קרא לרבות טבול יום, לג] [משום דבכרת דטומאת מקדש כתיב "ולא יתחטא"], דמשמע: אבל נתחטא, שהזה ושנה וטבל, דלאו מחוסר מעשה הוא, כגון טבול יום – לא הוי בכרת. ומהני טעמי אתי שפיר, דליכא למימר למה לי קרא, הא איתקש קדש למקדש. דהא קרא דביאת מקדש מישתעי לפטורא. וקרא "ובא השמש וטהר" איצטריך משום דכתיב בשרץ, דקיל טפי מנדה ושכבת זרע לד]. **הג"ה:** ולמאי דפרישית, דמ"וטהרה" מכלל שהיא טמאה לא הוה מרבינן מחוסר כפורים, אי לאו דאשכחן טבול יום מקרא דרבי סימאי, קצת קשה הא דקאמר בסמוך דאי כתב רחמנא במחוסר כפורים טבול יום לא אתי מיניה, הא לא אתי לן מחוסר כפורים אי לאו דאשכחנא קרא בטבול יום! לה] וי"ל שרוצה לומר: אי כתב רחמנא מחוסר כפורים בפירוש. וכי האי גוונא לו] בפרק "כילד" (יבמות דף כג.) גבי שפחה ונכרית, ומיהו קשה: אי להאי אתיא, א"כ ניכתוב רחמנא טבול יום ומחוסר כפורים בהדיא, ולא ליכתוב טמא! וי"ל: דכיון דלא לז] משכחת לריכותא בהני לא חש לדקדק. **רמז** לטבול יום שאם עבד חילל מנין. הוה מצי למילף מיושב או מבעל מום וחד מהנך. **דגמר** חילול חילול מתרומה. הקשה ה"ר חיים: כיון דטבול יום יליף מתרומה, אם כן טבול יום שאכל תרומה יהא במיתה. ובפ' "הנשרפין" (סנהדרין פג.) לא חשיב טבול יום! ושמא הוא הדין. וא"ת: כי היכי דממעטי התם (דף פד.). רבנן בעל מום ששימש, מדכתיב "בו" ולא בעל מום – ה"ה "ומתו בו" דכתיב בתרומה – "בו" ולא בטבול יום. ומיהו, טמא ששימש אין למעט מדכתיב "בו", דלהכי אתי ג"ש דחילול חילול. וכן טבול יום ששימש נמי הוי במיתה, כדאיתא הכא והתם. והיינו טעמא, דדמי לטמא טפי מבעל מום. ונראה דה"ה לתרומה, דלא ממעטין טבול יום. וכן פירש בקונטרס בהדיא, דטבול יום שאכל תרומה – במיתה. ויש ליתן טעם דלא חשיב ליה התם – משום דטמא וטבול יום מחד קרא נפקי, דהכי כתיבי קראי בפרשת "אמור אל הכהנים": "ובא השמש וטהר ואחר יאכל מן הקדשים" וגו', והדר כתיב: "ולא ישאו עליו חטא ומתו בו כי יחללוהו". וקצת תימה: היכי יליף התם בסנהדרין מחוסר כפורים ששימש במיתה משום דאיקרי טמא, וטמא ילפינן חילול חילול מתרומה? לח] נימא דפסול בתרומה – במיתה, ודלא פסול בתרומה – לא, כדאמרינן הכא דפסול בתרומה מחיל עבודה כו'! ויש לומר: כיון דמחיל עבודה לט] *מטעמא דנפקא לן מ"וינזרו ולא יחללו", כל דאיקרי טמא – מ] [סברא היא, דגמרינן] בגזירה שוה ד"חילול" "חילול" מתרומה פרק "הנשרפין" דהוי במיתה אע"ג דטהור לתרומה. קסבר

[ועי' היטב תוס' מנחות סב: ד"ה ויהו זבחים וכו' ותוס' מנחות נט. ד"ה ונתת ותוס' חולין כו: ד"ה והכא]

[עי' תוס' לקמן כח: ד"ה מסתברא]

גי' נ"ק סבר (לאידך) [כאידך] תנא דבי ר"י ומוקי ליה כו'

בס"י ליתא

עי' בחדושי מהרש"א בסנהדרין שם ועיין נ"ק

עיין נ"ק נ"א

נ"א בטמאה

שיטה מקובצת

א] חדא וחדא. עיין מנחות (דף נט ע"א) תוס' [ד"ה ונתת] (ודף סב ע"ב) תוס' [ד"ה ויהו]: ב] דנפיק לן מוינזרו: ג] דפסיל בתרומה כו'. תימה הרי טבול יום דלא פסול בתרומה ומחיל העבודה וי"ל דלא קאמר דכל דלא פסיל לא מחיל העבודה דאה"נ דאם נוכל להוכיח מפסוק דמחלל עבודה שפיר ניחא אע"ג דלא פסיל בתרומה אבל הכא ה"ק לא ידעינן במאי מיירי קרא רק באם אינו ענין הלכך לית לן לאוקמי ולא יחלל רק במאן דפסיל בתרומה כיון דנפקא לן שזה שבא באם אינו ענין זה במיתה מחילול חילול דתרומה ולא בקורח קרחה דלא פסיל בתרומה ואע"ג דלא סליק [אלא] מיניה. ה"ג למה לי דכתב רחמנא טבול יום ומחוסר כפורים ול"ג טמא דאי לא כתיב טמא כו'. מהר"פ: ד] פוסל בתרומה: ה] שכן פוסלים בתרומה: ו] סוף סוף קלישא כו'. ותימה דלעיל קאמר במחוסר כפורים טבול יום לא אתי מיניה שכן מחוסר מעשה ואמאי לא קאמר דמ"מ קלישא ליה טומאתו דמחוסר כפורים דהכי קאמר ליה השתא אע"ג דמן הצד הוא כ"ש חדא מחדא וי"ל דלא דמי לעיל גבי מחוסר כפורים ר"ל מחוסר מעשה שמחוסר כפרה (מהו) [מה] שאינו כן בטבול יום אבל הכא מחוסר מעשה דקאמר אינו ר"ל מחוסר כפרה דהא טמא לאו מחוסר כפרה הוא כגון

דמי

טמא שרץ וטמא מת ומגע זוב אלא ר"ל שכן מחוסר מעשה יותר מטבול יום דשמשא ממילא ערבא הלכך קאמר שפיר דקלישא טומאתו דמחוסר כפורים כיון שטבל והעריב שמשו לא מקרי מחוסר מעשה אלא מחוסר כפרה מיקרי וטמא לאו מחוסר כפרה הוא הלכך לא שייך למפרך מידי. מהר"פ ז"ל: ז] מה"ד איכא למיפרך הכי כו' יש לדון וכן יש תיבת כו' נמחק: ח] מה"ד אימא: ט] לא גרס וה"ג טבול יום: י] דשנויא הוא כלומר לא מצית לאוקמי באם אינו ענין: יא] שעבד מינה ילפינן: יב] הנשרפין דגמר אות ו' נמחק: יג] לתרומה היינו טבול יום דילפינן: יד] עבודה ומינה דלא פסיל בתרומה לא מחיל עבודה הס"ד ותיבת כ' נמחק: טו] לטמא הוא דילפינן: טז] כתב ביה: יז] קמבעיא ליה הס"ד ומה"ד ה"ג במחוסר: יח] מחוסר מעשה דשמשא ממילא ערבא וטמא ליכא: יט] כפורים לענין קדשים: כ] דמה להצד דהו"ל חד מינייהו כמו שאינו: כא] שהטעם כאן כמו: כב] בדוכתיה ככתיבתה סתם הס"ד: כג] טמאה עד השתא ותירץ: כד] יומא ולא קאי וטהר אגברא כדדרשינן: כה] וטהרה לטבול יום שהיא טבולת יום ארוך כו' כפרה נמי היא: כן כתנא קמא דפליג התם אתנא דבי: כז] נגיעת כלי. ס"א תרומה בכלי: כח] וטהר. לשון הר"פ מכלל שהוא טמא אלמא דטבול יום איקרי טמא וי"ל דאי לאו קרא דרבי סימאי דדריש הכי דטבול יום מחלל עבודה ממה דטבול יום אקרי טמא לא נפקא ליה דאיכא למימר דקלישא טומאתיה לענין שלא יחלל העבודה וכ"ת והלא מחוסר כפרה נפקא לן דמחלל עבודה מוטהרה מכלל שהיא טמאה ולא אמרינן דקלישא טומאה וי"ל דלאחר הגלי לן ר' סימאי מקרא דלא יחללו דטבול יום מחלל עבודה אע"ג דקלישא כו' ע"כ: כט] מתיבת ותימה עד סוף הדבור מוקף חצי לבנה שהוא הג"ה: ל] בהדיא דטבול יום אקרי טמא: לא] עבודה ולא יחללו: לב] טבול יום משום דטמא הנכנס למקדש כתוב בטומאת מת ולא יתחטא דמשמע: לד] זרע ע"כ הג"ה: לה] בטבול יום דמחלל וי"ל: לו] גוונא איכא בפרק: לז] דלא אשכחנא צריכותא לא תיבת בהני נמחק: לח] מתרומה לימא: לט] תיבת מטעמא נמחק: מ] טמא סברא דגמרינן מתרומה דהוי חיובת בגז"ש דחילול חילול פרק הנשרפין נמחק:

יב א מיי' פ"ד מהל' פרה אדומה הלכה יז:
יג ב מיי' פ"ג מהלכות ביאת מקדש הלכה ט וע"ש בכ"מ ופי"ח מהל' פסה"מ הלכה יז:
ל"ל בכרת ל"ק
יד ג מיי' פ"א מהלכות פרה אדומה הלכה יג:
טו ד מיי' פ"י מהלכות כלי המקדש הלכה ז:
טז ה מיי' פ"א מהל' ביאת מקדש הל' ח:

קָסָבַר: *מְחוּסַּר כִּפּוּרִים דְּזָב כְּזָב דָּמֵי. א] וּמְחוּסַּר כִּפּוּרִים דְּזָב כְּזָב דָּמֵי תַּנָּאֵי הִיא, *דְּתַנְיָא: שְׂרֵפָה אוֹנֵן וּמְחוּסַּר כִּפּוּרִים – אכְּשֵׁרָה. יוֹסֵף הַבַּבְלִי אוֹמֵר: אוֹנֵן – כְּשֵׁרָה, מְחוּסַּר כִּפּוּרִים – פְּסוּלָה; מַאי לָאו בְּהָא קָמִיפַּלְגִי, מָר סָבַר: מְחוּסַּר כִּפּוּרִים דְּזָב כְּזָב דָּמֵי, וּמָר סָבַר: בלָאו כְּזָב דָּמֵי? לָא, דְּכוּלֵּי עָלְמָא כְּזָב דָּמֵי, וְהָכָא בְּהָא קָמִיפַּלְגִי, דִּכְתִיב: °"וְהִזָּה הַטָּהֹר" (במדבר יט) – *מִכְּלָל שֶׁהוּא טָמֵא, גלִימֵּד עַל טְבוּל יוֹם שֶׁכָּשֵׁר בְּפָרָה; מָר סָבַר: טוּמְאָה דְּכָל הַתּוֹרָה כּוּלָּהּ, •וּמָר סָבַר: טוּמְאָה דְּהָךְ פָּרָשָׁה. הִלְכָּךְ, (א) אוֹנֵן וּטְבוּל יוֹם דִּטְמֵא שֶׁרֶץ דְּקִילֵי – אָתוּ בְּקַל וָחוֹמֶר מִטְּבוּל יוֹם דְּמֵת, אֲבָל מְחוּסַּר כִּפּוּרִים דְּזָב דַּחֲמִיר, שֶׁכֵּן טוּמְאָה יוֹצְאָה עָלָיו מִגּוּפוֹ – לָא. § "מְחוּסַּר בְּגָדִים". § מְנָלַן? *אָמַר רַבִּי אֲבוּהּ אָמַר רַבִּי יוֹחָנָן, וּמָטוּ בָּהּ מִשְּׁמֵיהּ דְּרַבִּי אֶלְעָזָר בְּרַבִּי שִׁמְעוֹן, דְּאָמַר קְרָא: °"וְחָגַרְתָּ אוֹתָם אַבְנֵט (שמות כט) אַהֲרֹן וּבָנָיו וְחָבַשְׁתָּ לָהֶם מִגְבָּעוֹת וְהָיְתָה לָהֶם כְּהוּנָּה לְחֻקַּת עוֹלָם", דבִּזְמַן שֶׁבִּגְדֵיהֶם עֲלֵיהֶם – כְּהוּנָּתָם עֲלֵיהֶם, אֵין בִּגְדֵיהֶם עֲלֵיהֶם – אֵין כְּהוּנָּתָם עֲלֵיהֶם. וְהָא מֵהָכָא נָפְקָא? מֵהָתָם נָפְקָא, דְּתַנְיָא: מִנַּיִן לִשְׁתוּיֵי יַיִן השֶׁאִם עָבַד חִילֵּל? תַּלְמוּד לוֹמַר: °"יַיִן וְשֵׁכָר אַל תֵּשְׁתְּ (ויקרא י) וגו' °וּלְהַבְדִּיל בֵּין הַקֹּדֶשׁ וּבֵין הַחֹל" (שם); מְחוּסַּר בְּגָדִים וְשֶׁלֹּא רְחוּץ יָדַיִם וְרַגְלַיִם, מִנַּיִן? תַּלְמוּד

תורה אור

קָסָבַר. רַבָּה דְּדָרְשָׁהּ לְהַאי שְׁמַעְתָּא, לְמֵימַר דְּכוּלְּהוּ צְרִיכִי. מְחוּסַּר כִּפּוּרִים דְּזָב כְּזָב. ה"ה לִמְצוֹרָע, אֶלָּא חַד מִנַּיְיהוּ נָקַט. מְחוּסַּר כִּפּוּרִים דְּזָב כְּזָב דָּמֵי – לְעִנְיַן קָדָשִׁים שֶׁלֹּא הוּתַּר אֶצְלוֹ ב] הֲוָה לֵיהּ כְּאִילּוּ לֹא טָבַל, וְאִם אֲכָלוֹ – חַיָּיב כָּרֵת, אוֹ אִם נָגַע בְּהוּ – ג] טִמְּאָן לִמְנוֹת בָּהֶן רִאשׁוֹן וְשֵׁנִי, לְכָךְ לֹא קְלִישָׁה טוּמְאָה אֵצֶל קָדָשִׁים כְּלָל. שְׂרֵפָה אוֹנֵן כו'. בְּפָרָה אֲדוּמָּה קָאֵי. כְּשֵׁרָה. דְּקָדְשֵׁי בֶּדֶק הַבַּיִת הִיא, וְאֵין אוֹנֵן (ב) אָסוּר בָּהּ, דְּלָא כְּתִיבֵי הָנָךְ קְרָאֵי אֶלָּא בְּקָדְשֵׁי מִזְבֵּחַ. כְּזָב דָּמֵי. וַהֲוָה לֵיהּ טָמֵא, וּקְרָא כְּתִיב "אִישׁ טָהוֹר". לָאו כְּזָב דָּמֵי. וַה"ל כִּטְבוּל יוֹם, דְּקַיְימָא ד] [לָן] דְּכָשֵׁר בְּפָרָה. לָא דְּכ"ע כְּזָב דָּמֵי. ה] וּלְעִנְיַן שְׁאָר קָדָשִׁים, שֶׁטְּבוּל יוֹם אָסוּר בְּהוּ, ו] הֲוָה מְחוּסַּר כִּפּוּרִים דְּזָב חָמוּר מִטְּבוּל יוֹם דִּשְׁאָר טוּמְאוֹת שֶׁאֵין טְעוּנוֹת כַּפָּרָה. וְהָכָא. גַּבֵּי פָּרָה, בְּהַאי קְרָא קָמִיפַּלְגִי: "וְהִזָּה הַטָּהוֹר עַל הַטָּמֵא" – טָהוֹר כָּל דְּהוּא מַשְׁמַע, דְּהָא קְרָא יְתֵירָא הוּא, דִּכְתִיב לְעֵיל מִינֵּיהּ: "וְלָקַח אֵזוֹב וְטָבַל בַּמַּיִם אִישׁ טָהוֹר" וַהֲוָה לֵיהּ לְמִכְתַּב "וְהִזָּה עַל הַטָּמֵא", לִימֵּד עַל טְבוּל יוֹם שֶׁכָּשֵׁר בְּפָרָה, דְּאַשְׁכַּחַן טְבוּל יוֹם דְּאִיקְּרֵי טָהוֹר לְמַעֲשֵׂר, דִּכְתִיב: "וְרָחַץ בַּמַּיִם וְטָהֵר". מָר סָבַר טוּמְאָה דְּכָל הַתּוֹרָה. ת"ק סָבַר: הַאי טְבוּל יוֹם דְּאַכְשַׁר בֵּהּ קְרָא – אַטְּבוּל יוֹם דְּכָל הַטּוּמְאוֹת שֶׁבַּתּוֹרָה ז] קָאֵי, וְאַף טְבוּל יוֹם דְּזָב, שֶׁהוּא מְחוּסַּר כִּפּוּרִים. טוּמְאָה דְּאוֹתָהּ פָּרָשָׁה. וְהַיְינוּ דְּמֵת, טְבוּל יוֹם דְּטוּמְאַת מֵת אַכְשַׁר בֵּהּ. הִלְכָּךְ, טְבוּל יוֹם שֶׁל שְׁאָר טוּמְאוֹת דְּמַגָּע וּמַשָּׂא, כְּגוֹן שֶׁרֶץ וּנְבֵילָה (ג) וּמַגַּע ח] [זָב], אָתֵי לְהֶכְשֵׁירָא מִטְּבוּל יוֹם דְּמֵת מִק"ו: וּמַה טְבוּל יוֹם [דְּמֵת] דְּטוּמְאַת שִׁבְעָה – כָּשֵׁר, טְבוּל יוֹם דְּטוּמְאַת עֶרֶב – לֹא כ"ש. אֲבָל מְחוּסַּר כִּפּוּרִים ט] וכו'. וְהָיְתָה לָהֶם. הַלְּבִישָׁה הַזֹּאת (ד) לִכְהוּנָּה. אַלְמָא כְּהוּנָּתָן תְּלוּיָה בְּבִגְדֵיהֶן, וְאִי לָא – הָווּ לְהוּ זָרִים, וּבְזָר אַשְׁכַּחַן דְּמָחֵיל עֲבוֹדָה. וּבֵין הַחוֹל. עֲבוֹדָה שֶׁאַתָּה עוֹבֵד בְּשִׁכְרוּת קְרוּיָה חוֹל.

חוּקָּה

[כריתות י. עיין שם] · יבמות עג. תוספתא דפרה פ"ג · ל"ק · יומא מג: יבמות עג. · סנהדרין פג.

קסבר רבה מחוסר כפורים דזב כזב דמי. הכי נמי אית ליה פרק שני דכריתות (דף י.). ופירש בקונט': לענין קדשים שלא הותר י] אצלן הוה ליה כאילו לא טבל, ואם אכלן – חייב כרת, או אם נגע בהן – טמאן למנות בהן ראשון ושני. וקשה לפירושו: דאם כן, למ"ד לאו כזב דמי – לית ביה כרת. ובריש מסכת כלים תנן בהדיא דמחוסר כפורים שנכנס למקדש *חייב, יא] דתנן: עזרת ישראל מקודשת ממנה, שאין מחוסר כפורים נכנס לשם, וחייב חטאת. וכן בההיא דפרק "אלו הן הגולין" (מכות דף ח:) ו"שלשה מינין" (נזיר מה.): "טמא יהיה" – לרבות טבול יום, "עוד טומאתו בו" – לרבות מחוסר כפורים. וב"הקומץ רבה" (מנחות דף כז:): מחוסר כפרה שנכנס לפנים ממחילתו לעזרה, בשוגג – חייב חטאת, במזיד – ענוש כרת. ואיתקש קודש למקדש ב"הערל" (יבמות עה.) ובמכות (דף יד.) ובשבועות (דף ז.)! ודוחק לומר דכל הני אתיין כמאן דאמר מחוסר כפורים דזב כזב דמי. ועוד, דבההיא סוגיא דנזיר יב] "וטמא יהיה" לרבות טבול יום, דכ"ע מחוסר כפורים דזב לאו כזב דמי, ואפילו הכי מרבה התם כרת למקדש במחוסר כפורים. ומיהו, פלוגתא דאמוראי יג] איכא ריש פ' "כל הפסולין" (לקמן לב: לג:), אית דאמרי הא דאיתקש קודש למקדש – היינו אפילו לכרת, דביאה במקצת יד] שמה ביאה כמו נגיעה. ואית דאמרי לענין מלקות דוקא איתמר, ומוקי לה "בכל קדש לא תגע" – אזהרה לנוגע לקודש, דליכא אלא לאו, אע"ג ד"אל המקדש לא תבא" הוי בכרת. ועוד: מה שפי' בקונטרס לענין למנות בו ראשון ושני לקדש – *תימה: הלא טבול יום אין מונין בו ראשון ושני *לטומאה, טו] [וכ"ש מחוסר כפורים]! ועוד הא תנן במסכת מעילה (דף ח.): חטאת העוף כו' הוכשר ליפסל בטבול יום ובמחוסר כפורים. ודייק בגמ': ליפסל – אין, לטמויי – לא! ורבינו תם היה אומר: דלא נקט פסול במחוסר כפורים אלא אגב טבול יום. והקשה לו הרב רבינו חיים מהא דבסוטה פרק "כשם" (ד' כט.) אמרי': מנין לרביעי בקודש שהוא פסול? ומה מחוסר כפורים שמותר בתרומה – פסול בקודש. משמע: פסול – אין, טמא – לא. ועוד: אי מונין בו ראשון ושני – א"כ יעשה רביעי חמישי בקודש מק"ו! ומיהו, יש לומר בזה דחמישי אין ללמוד, דמן הדין הוה למימר דיו כתרומה, אי לאו משום דמפרך ק"ו, ודי לנו במעלה אחת יותר מתרומה שיעשה רביעי. ומיהו, עוד קשה מהא דתנן בפ' בתרא דנדה (דף עא:): היושבת על דם טוהר (היתה) מערה מים לפסח, חזרו לומר הרי היא כמגע טמא מת לקדשים. ומוקי לה בגמ' כאבא שאול דאמר טבול יום תחלה לקודש, משמע: אבל לרבנן – לא. טז] ודוחק לומר דכולהו, ההיא דמעילה ודסוטה ורבנן דאבא שאול, סברי כמ"ד מחוסר כפורים דזב לאו כזב דמי! •ומפרש הרב ר' חיים: דנפקא מינה *לענין פסח הבא בטומאה, דתנן (פסחים דף לה:): לא יאכלו ממנו זבין וזבות. דלמ"ד מחוסר כפורים דזב כזב דמי – אין שוחטין וזורקין עליו, דלא אישרתאי בצבור אלא טמא מת. וה"ה טמא שרץ, דאין טומאה יוצאה מגופו, בק"ו ממת, כדאיתא לקמן. ומ"ד לאו כזב דמי – שוחטין. והכי מוכח בהדיא בפרק שני דכריתות (דף י.). ועוד: דנפקא מינה לענין טומאה דחוייה בצבור יז] (לקמן דף לב:).

שרפה אונן ומחוסר כפורים כשרה. פי' בקונט': דפרה קדשי בדק הבית היא. וקשה: דמ"מ אית בה כל פסולין שבקרבן, כגון יח] שלא לשמה, דאמר ב"הקומץ רבה" (מנחות כז:): ושבע הזאות שבפרה שעשאן שלא לשמן – פסולות, ונפקא לן בסיפרי משום דחטאת קרייה רחמנא. ומהאי טעמא נמי אמרינן בפ"ק דחולין (דף יא.) דטרפות פוסל בה! ונראה דהיינו טעמא יט] הכא – משום דטבול יום כשר בפרה, ואתי אונן ומחוסר כפורים בק"ו מטבול יום שאסור בנגיעת תרומה ומותר בפרה. כ] ולמ"ד מחוסר כפורים דזב כזב דמי – לא אתי בק"ו, דמה לטבול יום דמת – שמותר לאכול בפסח הבא בטומאה, מה שאין כן *במחוסר כפורים. והאי כא] דטבול יום כשר מן התורה – אפשר דמדרבנן פסול, דהא אמרינן דאפי' בגדי אוכלי קודש מדרס לחטאת, כל שכן טבול יום. והא כב] [דאמרי' במסכת פרה (פ"ג) מטמאין היו כהן השורף את הפרה להוציא מלבן של צדוקים שאמרו] במעורבי שמש היתה נעשית – לאו היינו טבול יום ממש, אלא אחיו הכהנים היו מניחין ידיהם על ראשו ומאותה נגיעה היה טבול יום, כדתניא בתוספתא, ואיכא כג] בהו היכרא לצדוקים. ועוד יש לפרש: דטבול יום ממש היה כשר בה. והא דבגדי אוכלי קודש מדרס לחטאת – משום היסח הדעת דשאר טומאות. **והזה** הטהור. ואף על גב דהזאת מי חטאת כשרה בזר, ושרפה כד] פסול – מכל מקום יליף שרפה מהזאה.

אונן וטבול יום של טמא שרץ דקילי אתו מק"ו מטבול יום דמת. ואין להקשות: מה לטבול יום – שכן מותר במעשר, מה שאין כן באונן! דמנגיעה ילפינן, כדאמר בפ' "הערל" (יבמות עג:): ערל שהזה – הזאתו כשרה, מידי דהוה אטבול יום, שאע"פ שאסור בתרומה – כשר בפרה. ופריך: מה לטבול יום – שכן מותר במעשר! ומשני: אטו אנן לאכילה קאמרינן? לנגיעה קאמרינן: ומה טבול יום שאסור בנגיעה דתרומה – מותר בפרה, ערל שמותר בנגיעה דתרומה – אינו דין שמותר בפרה? וה"נ ילפינן אונן. וא"ת: מחוסר כפורים ובעל מום יוכיחו, שמותרין בתרומה ואסורין בפרה, אף אני אביא ערל ואונן! ומיהו, אאונן לא קשיא, דמה להנך – שכן לא הותרו מכללן, תאמר באונן שהותר מכללו אצל כ"ג. אבל אערל קשה! כה] ונראה לי: דמה למחוסר כפורים שאסור ליגע בקדשים, אבל ערל ואונן – מותרין. אבל מבעל מום קשה. ברו"ך. ועוד: מה לטבול יום – שכן אינו מחוסר מעשה, תאמר בערל. *אין בגדיהם עליהן אין כהונתן עליהם. מהכא ילפינן מיתה בפרק "הנשרפין" (סנהדרין דף פג:) דקאמר: אין בגדיהם עליהם – הוו להו זרים, ואמר מר: זר ששימש במיתה. והקשה הרב רבי יעקב מאורלינש: והא מיתה כתיבא בהדיא בפרשת "ואתה תצוה"! ותירץ דאף על גב דכולהו בגדים כתיבי התם, מכל מקום מיתה אמכנסיים דוקא כתיבא, כדמשמע פשטא דקרא. וקרא ד"וחגרת" דכתיב בפרשה שאחריה, דדרשינן מינה דאין בגדיהם עליהם אין כהונתן עליהם – איצטריך לשאר בגדים, ומיניה לא הוה ילפינן מכנסיים, דמכנסיים לא כתיבי התם. ועוד יש לומר: דקרא ד"וחגרת" צריך לחילול עבודה, דמקרי זר*. ברו"ך.

תלמוד

עי' ל"ק נ"א · נ"א לתרומה

נ"א לענין פסח הבא בטומאה דתנן פסח הבא בטומאה לא יאכלו ממנו זבין וזבות דלמ"ד כו' כזב דמי גם מחוסר כפורים לא יאכלו ממנו דלא אישתרא בצבור כו' ולמ"ד לאו כזב דמי יאכלו ממנו והכי מוכח בהדיא כו' ל"ק וע"ש

גירסת ל"ק במחוסר כפורים הס"ד ואח"כ מה"ד טבול יום כשר בפרה האי ט"י דכשר כו'

[עיין לקמן כד בתוספות ריש עמוד א']

[וע"ע תוס' סנהדרין פג ד"ה אין]

הגהות הב"ח

(א) גמ' דהך פרשה הלכך טבול יום דנבלה וטמא שרץ דקילי כצ"ל: (ב) רש"י ד"ה כשרה וכו' ואין אונן ומחוסר כפורים אסור בה: (ג) ד"ה טומאה וכו' ונבלה אתו כצ"ל ותיבת ומגע נמחק: (ד) ד"ה והיתה וכו' כהונה כצ"ל ואות ל' נמחק:

גליון הש"ס

גמ' ומ"ס טומאה דהך פרשה. עיין יומא דף ע"א תוס' ד"ה ריב"ג: **תום'** ד"ה קסבר וכו' ומפרש הר"ר חיים. עי' יבמות דף ז ע"ב תוד"ה רי"א:

שיטה מקובצת

א] דמי לימא מחוסר אות ו' נמחק: ב] אצלו והוה ליה: ג] בהו טימאן: ד] דקיימא לן: ה] דמי לענין שאר: ו] הוי מחוסר: ז] שבתורה קאמר ותיבת קאי נמחק: ח] ומגע הזב: ט] תיבת וכו' נמחק: י] הותר אצלו דהוה ליה: יא] חייב כרת: יב] דנזיר טמא יהיה: יג] דאמוראים היא ותיבת איכא ל"ש: יד] במקצת גופו: טו] לטומאה וכ"ש מחוסר כפורים ועוד הא תנן במסכת מעילה פרק שני חטאת: טז] לא אלמא טבול יום דיולדת לא מנינן בו ראשון ושני וכ"ש מחוסר כפורים: יז] בצבור דאם הן טמא מתים עושין בטומאה ואם הם זבים נדחין לשני: יח] כגון שרפה שלא: יט] טעמא. ס"א משום דילפינן מק"ו דטבול יום פסול בתרומה כשר בפרה כדבסמוך כ"ש אונן כו': כ] בפרה כ"ש אונן ומחוסר כפורים: כא] והאי. ס"א ושמא אע"ג דטבול כו': כב] והא דאמרינן במסכת פרה בפ"ג ומטמאין היו את הכהן השורף את הפרה מפני הצדוקין שלא יהיו אומרין: כג] ואיכא בהכי: כד] ושרפה בזר: כה] מתיבת ונראו לי עד תיבת ברוך מוקף בחצי לבנה:

יז א מיי' פ"ו מהלכות כלי המקדש הל' ד:
יח ב ג מיי' שם הל' ה:

מהתם, הוה אמינא: הני מילי — עבודה דזר חייב עליה מיתה, אבל עבודה דאין זר חייב עליה מיתה — אימא לא, קמ"ל. אשכחן מחוסר בגדים, שתויי יין מנלן? אתיא "חוקה" "חוקה" ממחוסר בגדים. והא תנא א] "ולהבדיל בין" וגו' קא נסיב לה! מקמי ב] דליקום גזירה שוה. והא תנא, מחוסר בגדים הוא דקא יליף משתויי יין! ה"ק: מנין שלא (א) ג] נחלקו בין מחוסר בגדים לשתויי יין ושלא רחוץ ידים ורגלים — תלמוד לומר: "חוקה" "חוקה" לגזירה שוה. אלא "להבדיל" למה לי? לכדרב, *דרב לא מוקים אמורא עליה מיומא טבא לחבריה, משום שכרות. ואכתי, מהכא נפקא? מהתם נפקא: °"ונתנו בני אהרן הכהן" — בכיהונו, אלימד על כהן גדול שלבש בגדי כהן הדיוט ועבד — עבודתו פסולה! אי מהתם, הוה אמינא: ה"מ — עבודה דמעכבא כפרה, ד] אבל עבודה דלא מעכבא כפרה — לא. ואכתי, מהכא נפקא? מהתם נפקא: °"וערכו בני אהרן הכהנים את הנתחים" וגו', הכהנים — בכיהונן, במכאן לכהן הדיוט שלבש בגדי כהן גדול ועבד — עבודתו פסולה! אי מהתם, הוה אמינא: הני מילי חיסור, ה] אבל ייתור — לא, קמ"ל. §*תנו רבנן: היו מרושלין, מסולקין, משוחקים, ועבד — עבודתו כשירה. גלבש שני מכנסים, שני אבנטים, חסר אחת, יתר אחת, או שהיתה לו רטיה על ו] מכת בשרו תחת בגדו, *או שהיו מטושטשין

(ויקרא י) (שמות כט) (ויקרא א) (שם)

רש"י

חוקה חוקה. בשתויי יין ז] [כתיב] "חוקת עולם", ובמחוסר בגדים כתיב כהונה "לחוקת עולם", וברחיצת יד ורגל כתיב "והיתה להם (ג) לחוקת עולם". אי מהתם. משתויי יין, הוה אמינא: ח] ה"מ דמתחלי עבודה [במחוסר בגדים] — בעבודה שהזר חייב עליה מיתה, כדכתיב בההוא קרא: "בבואכם אל אהל מועד ולא תמותו" — בעבודה שיש בה חיוב מיתה לפסולים הכתוב מדבר, ואינה אלא ט] ארבע עבודות: זריקה והקטרה וניסוך המים והיין, כדילפינן בפ"ב י] בסדר יומא (דף כד.) מ"ועבדתם עבודת מתנה וגו' והזר הקרב יומת" — עבודת מתנה ולא עבודת סילוק, "ועבדתם" — עבודה תמה ולא עבודה שיש אחריה עבודה, כגון קבלה והולכה וקמיצה. וכל חיוב מיתות יא] בפסולי עבודה מזרות גמרינן, כדתנן בפ' בתרא (לקמן קיב:): הקומץ והבולל והיוצק והמקבל דמים וכו', ואין בהם לא משום זרות, ולא משום טומאה, ולא משום מחוסר בגדים, ולא משום שלא רחץ ידים ורגלים — אלמא מזר גמרינן. אבל עבודה שאין זר חייב עליה מיתה אימא לא. מחלי לה מחוסר בגדים. להכי כתב "והיתה להם (ג) לכהונת עולם" — לשוינהו זרים כשאין בגדיהם עליהם. ובזר אשכחן חילול, ולא חלק בין עבודה שיש בה מיתה לעבודה שאין בה מיתה יב]. אשכחן מחוסר בגדים. בכל העבודות. שתויי יין מנלן. דפסלי עבודה שאין הזר חייב עליה מיתה. והא תנא מלהבדיל קנסיב לה. לשתויי יין, ולא גמר מגזירה שוה, ואמאי ניקו וניפלוג עלה למילף מקרא אחרינא? הני מילי מקמי דתיקו ליה גזירה שוה. לא הוה ליה למילף שתויי יג] יין אלא מ"להבדיל". ובמסקנא (ד) אידכר ליה גזירה שוה, ותנא (ליה) שבקיה לאורחיה קמייתא, ונקט גזירה שוה *למילף יד] משתויי יין מחוסר בגדים. והא תנא. נקטיה לגזירה שוה מחוסר בגדים הוא דיליף בה משתויי יין, ולא שבקיה לאורחיה. והכי קאמר מנין שלא טו] נחלקו כו'. לעולם לא למילף מחוסר בגדים משתויי יין אתא, אלא למילף שתויי יין ממחוסר בגדים. והכי קאמר: למדנו לעבודות של מיתה שמתחללות בשיכרות, מנין שלא טז] נחלוק בין מחוסר בגדים לשתויי יין דכי היכי דמחוסר בגדים כל עבודותיו פסולות אף שתויי יין ושלא רחץ כן? תלמוד לומר: "חוקה" "חוקה". אלא (ה) יז] בין החול למה לי. הואיל ולא ילפינן מיניה חילול לעבודה. לא מוקים אמורא עליה. למידרש (ו) בפירקין. מיומא טבא לחבריה. משעה שאכל ושתה ועשה יום טוב עד למחר. דהכי משמע קרא: יין ושכר אל תשת בבואכם וגו' וכן בשעה שאתה בא להבדיל ולהורות בין דבר קדושה לדבר חול — אל תהי שכרות. מהכא נפקא. מחוסר בגדים. מהתם נפקא. אכתי קרא אחרינא כתיב, ולמאי יח] איצטריך "הכהן" הכא גבי "ונתנו בני אהרן הכהן אש" לאשמועינן מחוסר בגדים? בכיהונו. בשעה שהוא מלובש בגדיו נקרא אהרן הכהן, ולא כשהוא לבוש בגדי הדיוט. אי מהתם. מ"והיתה להם כהונה", הוי מוקמינא ליה יט] היא בעבודה המעכבת כפרה. אבל נתינת אש של הדיוט, דמצוה בעלמא היא, שהרי יש שם אש שירדה מן השמים — אימא לא תיבעי בגדים, קא משמע לן "ונתנו בני אהרן הכהן אש". כ] להכי כתב הכא חסרון בגדים, למילף [דאף בעבודה שאינה מחוסר כפרה], דאי עבד אהרן בבגדי הדיוט — לאו שפיר עבד. והא ליכא למיפרך: לימא האי *)ולא תיבעי ההוא. דהכא לאו בגדים כתיבי, ואי לאו כא] דכתב "והיתה להם כהונה" [אלא "וחגרת אותם אבנט"] דשמעינן כהונה תלויה בבגדים — לא הוה ידעינן הכהן בכיהונו מאי היא. הכהנים. אבני" קאי, דהוו הדיוטים. בכיהונן. בראוין להן, שמתלית כהונתן בהן. אי מהתם. מ"והיתה להם כהונה". כב] [חיסור. כגון כה"ג בבגדי כהן הדיוט: אבל ייתור. כגון כהן הדיוט בבגדי כה"ג]. מרושלין. = נגררין בקרקע. מסולקין. מן הקרקע, מתוך שהם קצרים. משוחקים. = ישנים. כשרין. ואע"ג דכתיב: "מדו בד" שתהא כמדתו — מצוה בעלמא היא, ולא לעכב. חיסר אחת. כג] מכל הבגדים. ייתר אחת. הוסיף עליהם שום בגד בעולם. רטייה. *איפלסטר"א, שחוצץ בין בשרו לבגד, דבעינן "ילבש על בשרו".

*) ס"א ולא תיבעי ההוא קרא דוהיתה להם כהונה להכהל לאו כו'

מטושטשין

תוספות

תלמוד לומר חוקה חוקה לגזירה שוה. מכאן אומר ר"ת דהא דאמרינן במנחות (דף יט.): כל מקום שנאמר "תורה" ו"חוקה" אינו אלא לעכב — לאו חד טעמא נינהו, ד"חוקה" מגזירה שוה, ו"תורה" ממשמעות*. **אתיא** חוקה חוקה ממחוסר בגדים. בפ' "הנשרפין" (סנהדרין דף פד.) אמרינן דאונן באזהרה דכתיב: "ומן המקדש לא יצא ולא יחלל", הא אחר שלא יצא — חילל. ולא ילפי' שיהא במיתה [בג"ש] חילול חילול מתרומה, משום דחילול בגופיה לא כתיב, מכללא [דכ"ג] הוא דקאתי — הוי דבר הבא מן הכלל, וכל דבר הבא מן הכלל אין דנין אותו בגזירה שוה. וקשה מהך דשמעתין, דהא כד] אין בגדיהם עליהם אין כהונתן עליהן אינו כתיב בפי', וילפינן "חוקה" "חוקה" ממחוסרי בגדים. וכן בכל הנך דכתיב "ולא יחללו" דדייקינן: הא עבד חיללו, וילפינן מיתה חילול חילול מתרומה. ובתורס מן הרעה על היפה, דלא ילפינן דלהוי דחוחה בגזירה שוה ד"חטא" "חטא", תירץ ה"ר יעקב מאורלינ"ש: משום דהוי דבר הבא מן הכלל. כה] [וצריך לחלק אמאי הוי דבר שבכלל] טפי מהני. ותימה לי: דבפ' "הנשרפין" (שם פג:) בעי: שתויי יין ושלא רחוץ ידים ורגלים במיתה מנא לן? וקאמר דבגופייהו כתיב בהו מיתה בהדיא. והשתא למה לי למיכתב מיתה? תיפוק ליה מגזירה שוה ד"חוקה" "חוקה" ממחוסר בגדים, כדילפינן חילול בהו מהתם! מיהו, לקמן בפירקין (דף כד.) אמרינן דהוו שלשה כתובין הבאין כאחד ואין מלמדין: מחוסר בגדים, ושתויי יין, ושלא רחוץ ידים. והשתא אתי שפיר גם קושיית ה"ר יעקב, דהשתא בשלשתן כתיב מיתה מיותר, למימר בהני (זרים) דווקא דמקריין זרים בגזירה שוה ד"חוקה" — איכא מיתה. אבל יושב, אע"ג דקרוי זר — אינו במיתה. אבל שאר פסולין כגון ערל ואונן — לא איצטריך קרא למעוטינהו ממיתה, כיון דלא איקרו זרים. ברו"ך. כו] תוזרני לומר דקושית ה"ר יעקב קיימת, דהא למ"ד נמי דבעי' שלשה כתובין הבאין כאחד — ליכא מיותר כי אם השנים, ואחד הוי לגופיה, וא"כ תרי קראי במחוסר בגדים למה? ובתרוייהו כתיב "חקה" [א]. ומיהו "וחגרת" דדרשינן מינה חוקת עולם — אצטריך משום חילול. דאע"ג דממילא שמעינן, מדאיקרי כז] [זר — מ"מ] זר במכנסים לא כתיב. ולעולם בפרשה דלעיל קאי מיתה אכולהו בגדים כח]. **הג"ה:** כהן גדול שלבש בגדי כהן הדיוט ועבד עבודתו פסולה. ואם תאמר: הא דאמר רבי יוסי כט] (יומא דף יב:): שני אינו ראוי לא לכהן גדול ולא לכהן הדיוט, כהן גדול — משום איבה, כהן הדיוט — משום מעלין בקודש ולא מורידין. מדקאמר משום איבה — משמע דמן הדין כהן גדול הוא. וא"כ כהן הדיוט תיפוק ליה משום מחוסר בגדים! ואין לפרש דלאחר מיתת הראשון קאמר, דלא הוי כהן גדול משום איבה, דהא מודה ר' יוסי (שם יג.) דאם מת ראשון — שני חוזר לעבודתו. ויש לומר: דכהן גדול ל] נתמנה לעבודתו בפה ומסתלק בפה [ב](ובפ' קמא דיומא לא] (דף יב) דריש ליה מקרא, ובירושלמי) ומסתברא שהדבר תלוי במלך ואחיו הכהני', כמו שמצינו בפ' "הבא על יבמתו" (יבמות סא.) ביהושע בן גמלא דאוקמיה ינאי מלכא. ואמרינן לב] בירושלמי ובפ"ק דיומא (דף יב:) ובתוספתא (דיומא פ"א) ביוסף בן אלם מצפורי שאירע פסול בכה"ג ושימש תחתיו, וכשילא אמר למלך: אדוני המלך, פר ושעיר *)שקרבו היום משל מי, [משלי או משל כה"ג? א"ל המלך: לא דייך ששימשת שעה א' לפני מי שאמר והיה העולם] כו', וידע לג] שהוסר מן הכהונה.

*) נ"ל שקרבין

מסולקין

כריתות ז. [מס' סופרים פ' יח הל"ד] — פסחים סה: [לקמן לה.] — תוספתא דמנחות פ"א

[ע' תוס' מנחות יט. ד"ה תורה ותוס' חולין כג. ד"ה אמר]

עין משפט
נר מצוה

יט א ב ג ד מיי' פ"ח מהלכות כלי המקדש הלכה ד:
כ ה ו מיי' פ"ג מהלכות ציצית הלכה ג סמג עשין כו טוש"ע א"ח סי' י' סעיף א:
כא ז ח מיי' שם הל' ז סמג שם טוש"ע א"ח סימן יז סעיף א וסימן יח סעיף א:

נ"ל דלקמן נ"ק

כב ט מיי' פ"ח מהלכות כלי המקדש הל' יג:
כג י מיי' שם הל' ד:
כד כ ל מיי' שם הל' יד:
כה מ מיי' פ"י שם הלכה ב:

[ע' תוס' יומא יב: ד"ה ילבש]

נ"א דכל בגדים האמורים בתורה סתם היינו למר ופשתים לתנא דבי רבי ישמעאל וגם לרבנן דתנא דבי ר"א לא קשה מידי לפי מה דפי' בקונטרס כו' כן הוא בס"א

[וע"ע תוס' יומא עא: ד"ה ואימא וכו']

מסורת הש"ס

תורה אור

אמטושטשין או א] מקורעין, ועבד — עבודתו פסולה. אמר רב יהודה אמר שמואל: מרושלין — כשרין, מסולקין — פסולין. והתניא: מסולקין — כשרין! אמר רמי בר חמא, לא קשיא: כאן שסילקן על ידי אבנט, כאן דליתניהו מעיקרא כלל. רב אמר: באחד זה ואחד זה — פסולין.§ רב הונא איקלע לארגיזא, רמא ליה בר אושפיזכניה: מי אמר שמואל: מרושלין כשרין, ומסולקין פסולין? והתניא: מסולקין — כשרין! א"ל: בר מינה דההיא, דשנייה רמי בר חמא. אלא לרב קשיא! וכי תימא: מאי מרושלין — מסולקין על ידי אבנט, ב] גואבנט מיגז אגיז; אלא מסולקין קשיא! אמר רבי זירא: רב חדא תני: דמרושלין שסילקן ע"י אבנט — כשרין. אמר ר' ירמיה מדיפתי: מרושלין שלא סילקן — תנאי היא. *דתניא: °"על ארבע (דברים כב) כנפות כסותך" — ארבע הולא שלש. או אינו אלא ארבע ולא חמש? כשהוא אומר: °"אשר תכסה (שם) בה" — והרי בעלת חמש אמור, הא מה אני מקיים "ארבע" — ארבע ולא שלש. ומה ראית לרבות בעלת חמש ולהוציא בעלת שלש? מרבה אני בעלת חמש — שיש בכלל חמש ארבע, ומוציא אני בעלת שלש — שאין בכלל שלש ארבע. ותניא אידך: "על ארבע כנפות כסותך" — ארבע ולא שלש, ארבע ולא חמש. מאי לאו בהא קמיפלגי: דמר סבר: יתר כמאן דאיתיה דמי, ומר סבר: כמאן דליתיה דמי? לא, דכ"ע כמאן דאיתיה דמי. ושאני הכא, דרבי רחמנא — "אשר תכסה בה". ואידך, האי "אשר תכסה בה" מאי עביד ליה? מיבעי ליה לכדתניא: °"וראיתם אותו" (במדבר טו) — *פרט זלכסות לילה. או אינו אלא פרט לכסות סומא? כשהוא אומר: "אשר תכסה בה" — חהרי כסות סומא אמור, הא מה אני מקיים "וראיתם אותו"? פרט לכסות לילה. ומה ראית לרבות כסות סומא ולהוציא כסות לילה? מרבה אני כסות סומא — שישנה בראיה אצל אחרים, ומוציא אני כסות לילה — שאינה בראיה אצל אחרים. ג] [ואידך? נפקא ליה מ"אשר". ואידך? "אשר" לא דריש.] (רש"ק)§ תנו רבנן: ט"בד" — שיהיו של בוץ, י"בד" — שיהו חדשים, כ"בד" — שיהו שזורים, ל"בד" — שיהו חוטן כפול ששה, "בד" — שלא ילבש של חול עמהן. א"ל אביי לרב יוסף: בשלמא שיהו של בוץ — הא קמ"ל: בוץ — אין, מידי אחרינא — לא; אלא "בד" שיהו חדשים; חדשים — אין, שחקין — לא? והתניא: משוחקין — כשרים! אמר ליה: וליטעמיך, "בד" שיהו חוטן כפול ששה, "בד" — חד חד לחודיה משמע! אלא הכי קאמר: בגדים שנאמר בהן "בד" — צריכין שיהו של בוץ, חדשים, שזורין, שיהא חוטן כפול ששה, יש מהן למצוה יש מהן לעכב. *ממאי דהאי "בד" כיתנא הוא? אמר ד] רבי יוסף ברבי חנינא: דבר העולה מן הקרקע בד בבד. אימא עמרא! עמרא מיפצל. כיתנא נמי מיפציל! על ידי לקותא מיפציל. רבינא אמר, מהכא: °"פארי פשתים יהיו על ראשם ה] [ומכנסי פשתים יהיו על מתניהם לא יחגרו (יחזקאל מד) ביזע".] א"ל רב אשי לרבינא: והא עד דאתא יחזקאל מנלן? ולטעמיך, הא *דאמר רב חסדא: דבר זה מתורת משה רבינו לא למדנו, מדברי יחזקאל בן בוזי למדנו: °"כל (שם) בן נכר ערל לב וערל בשר לא יבא אל מקדשי *(לשרתני",) עד שבא יחזקאל מנלן? אלא גמרא גמירי לה ו] ואתא יחזקאל ואסמכיה אקרא; הכא נמי, גמרא גמירי לה כו'. מאי °"לא יחגרו ביזע"? אמר אביי: מלא יחגרו במקום שמזיעין. כדתניא: (שם) כשהם חוגרין — אין חוגרין לא למטה ממתניהן, ולא למעלה מאציליהן, אלא כנגד

מטושטשין. בטיט. מקורעין. ואפילו הן חדשים. דלאו בגד (א) ז] הוא הראוי לעבודה, דבעינן "לכבוד ולתפארת". כאן שסילקן ע"י אבנט. *משקורלייר בלע"ז, כדרך שהנשים עושות — כשרין, דהא איתנהו. אחד זה ואחד זה. אחד מרושלין ואחד מסולקין יותר מדאי שלא על ידי אבנט. והתניא. בברייתא דלעיל. אלא לרב קשיא. מרושלין. וכ"ת מאי מרושלין. דמכשר תנא, כגון שסילקן עד למדתו על ידי אבנט. וקמכשר ליה תנא, דקסבר אבנט מיגז ח] אגיז, כלומר, כל סלוק שע"י אבנט הוה ליה כחותך ונוטל היתר שבהן ומכשירו. אלא מסולקין קשיא. דקתני כשרין, וסתם מסולקין גבוהין מן הקרקע למעלה מרגליו משמע. ולרב ליכא לאוקומא כגון שסילקן ע"י אבנט ט] כדתרצה שמואל, דהא על כרחיך י] לרב דשני דסילוק אבנט מיגז יא] אגיז, והשתא הוו כולהו כקצרים מעיקרא. רב חדא תני. להנך מרושלין ומסולקין דברייתא, בחדא מילתא תני להו: מרושלין שסילק רישולן ע"י אבנט עד כדי מדתו — כשרין. אבל מסולקין יותר מדאי — פסולין אפילו ע"י אבנט. ולא שלש. לימד על טלית של בת שלש כנפות שפטורה מן הציצית. והיכי דמי — כגון שעיגל אחת מד' כנפיה. בת חמש. כגון שחתך מעט מן הכנף, ולא עיגל שני מורשי קרנתא (ב) יב] ממקום חתך, דנעשה כשתי כנפות. הרי בעלת חמש אמור. לחיוב דריבויא הוא. מר סבר. מאן דפטר בעלת חמש סבר: לא אמרינן יתר כמאן דליתיה דמי, אלא כמאן דאיתיה הוא, ולא קרינן לה בת ארבע. ומאן דמחייב ס"ל: יתר כמאן דליתיה דמי להאי חמישי. וגבי מרושלין נמי לא הוי ייתור בגדים. פרט לכסות לילה. °טלית העשויה לכסות לילה פטורה מן הציצית. שישנה בראיה כו'. וקרינן ביה "וראיתם אותו". בד. יג] (ג) שהוא מן בוץ, כדמפרש לקמן ממשמעותא. חדשים. כשעת שהיו יד] בבדי פשתן. שיהו שזורים וחוטן כפול ששה. ולקמן פריך: והא "בד" לחודיה משמע, כמו "לבדו". שלא ילבש של חול עמהם. דמשמע: לבדו ילבש. וליטעמיך. דילפת טו] לה *ממשמעותא (ד) מקראי, חוטן כפול ששה טז] מנא ליה? דברים שנאמר בהן בד צריכין כו' יש מהן למצוה. חדשים יז] לנוי, דלאו ממשמעותא אתי ויש מהן לעכב בוץ, ושזורים, וחוטן כפול ששה. בוץ — כדמפרש ואזיל: דבר העולה מן הקרקע בד בבד. שזורים — כיון דבד היינו בוץ, ובעלמא קרי להו "שש משזר". וחוטן כפול ששה — כדאמרינן בסדר יומא (דף עא:), יח] וילפינן בסדר יומא מקראי: דברים שנאמר בהן שש — חוטן כפול ששה, ויליף ליה לעיכובא. העולה מן הקרקע בד בבד. קנה יחידי מכל יט] *גיזעי, ואין ב' קנים עולים מגזע אחד. ואימא עמרא. שאף הצמר עולה מן הבהמה בד בבד, נימא נימא לבדה. מיפציל. הנימא מתפצלת ומתחלקת לשנים על גבי בהמה מאליה. כיתנא נמי מיפציל. לפני טוויתו כותשים הגבעול, והוא נחלק לנימין הרבה. אגב לקותא. שמכין אותו וחובטים אותו בעץ או בגלגל, הוא נכתש ונחלק. ומכנסי פשתים יהיו וגו'. ובעלמא כ] הרי הוא אומר "ומכנסי בד", ש"מ: בד היינו פשתים. דבר זה. כא] קאמר לה לקמן (דף כב:) אמתני' דקתני: ערל מחלל עבודה. בן נכר. שנתנכרו מעשיו מחמת ערלת לבו, שהוא ערל לב — רשע. וערל בשר. שמתו אחיו מחמת מילה, לא יבא אל מקדשי. ולקמן (דף כב:) יליף בה חילול בהדיא. במקום שמזיעין. במקום שהבשר נכפל על הבשר, ומתחמם ומזיע. כשהן חוגרין. אבנטיהם בשעת עבודה. למטה ממתניהם. מקום שנכפל ונופל שומן הבטן על הקילבוסת, שקורין אנק"א. ולא למעלה מאציליהן. למעלה כב] מנגד מרפקן, שקורא קוד"א לפי ששם *היד שוכב תמיד על הצלעות ומזיע. כנגד

מסולקין כשרין. הא דתניא בפ' "תמיד נשחט" (פסחים סה:) "מדו בד" — כמדתו, פי' הקונטרס: דהיינו למצוה, ולא לעכב.

ואידך אשר לא דריש. משמע הכא דאיכא דמרבה כסות דסומא ולא מרבה בעלת חמש. ומקשה ר"ת: דבפ' "התכלת" (מנחות דף מג.) גבי פלוגתא דר' שמעון, מרבי התם רבי שמעון כסות סומא מ"אשר תכסה" ובעלת חמש מ"אשר"! ולאו פירכא היא, דהיא סוגיא כמאן דמרבי הכא בעלת חמש. ומיהו, קשה כג] אההיא דמנחות,* ולקמן בפ' "בית שמאי" (דף מ.) אמרינן דר"ש "אשר" לא דריש! ויש לומר, דהכי אמרינן: "אשר" כי האי לא דריש. וטובא איכא כי האי גוונא בפ' קמא דבכורות (דף ו:) דדריש ר"ש "את הגמל", ובפ"ק דמנחות (דף יא:) לא דריש "את".

והתניא משוחקין כשרין. תימה: דביומא (דף יב:) דרשינן: מה ת"ל "ילבש" — לרבות את השחקין, ואמאי צריך רבוי?* ואימא עמרא. ה"ר אפרים היה מדקדק דקנבוס דתנן שיהי כלאים שמותר עם צמר — אין זה מה שאנו קורין קנב"א בלע"ז, מדלא פריך: ואימא קנבוס שעולה בד בבד. והיה אומר דקנבוס הוא כד] פשתן, ואסור עם הצמר משום כלאים. כה] והשיב לו רבינו חיים כהן, דהאי דלא פריך: ואימא קנבוס — משום דבגדי כהונה אי אפשר להיות אלא מצמר ופשתים, *דכל בגדים האמורים בתורה סתם היינו צמר ופשתים. כו] ועוד: דכל קנבוס אינו עולה בד בבד, דפריש בקונטרס: בד בבד — קנה יחידי מכל גרעין, ואין שני קנים עולים מגרעין אחד. ואפשר דקנבוס אינו כן. אלא כז] כמו חיטין שכמה שבלין עולין מחיטה אחת*.
כורך

הגהות הב"ח

(א) רש"י ד"ה מקורעין וכו' בגד הראוי הוא לבעינן: (ב) ד"ה בת חמש וכו' למקום: (ג) ד"ה בד שיהו מין בוץ: (ד) ד"ה ולטעמיך וכו' מקרא כו' ליה הס"ד ואח"כ מ"ה בגדים שנאמר:

מנחות מג:

מנחות שם. שבת כז:

[לקמן מ. מנחות מג:]

נ"א ממשמעותיה דקרא חוטן כפול ששה מי משמע ליה מקרא הס"ד נ"ק

[יומא עא:]

[לקמן כב: מ"ק ה.] יומא עא: תענית יז: סנהדרין כב: ודף פג:

ליתא בקרא

נ"א גרעין

גליון הש"ס

רש"י ד"ה פרט לכסות וכו' טלית העשויה. וכ"כ רש"י שבת דף כז ע"ב ד"ה לכסות ועי' מנחות דף מ ע"ב ברש"י ד"ה ה"ג:

נ"א הזרוע

שיטה מקובצת

א] מקורעין. פ"ה דלאו בגד הראוי הוא דבעינן לכבוד ולתפארת ולקמן גבי יש מהן למצוה פ"ה כגון חדשים דמשום נוי הוא וצ"ל דלא מלתפארת נפיק ליה דא"כ הו"ל לעכב כמו מקורעין דהכא כיון דממשמעות דקרא נפקית ליה אלא ודאי ר"ל משום הידור מצוה (כגון) כשאר מצות דעלמא דמלתפארת לא ממעטינן כי אם בגד שאינו ראוי כמו שמבואר בלשונו: ב] אלמא אבנט מיגז גאיז: ג] אחרים. ס"א ואידך מאשר דריש ואידך אשר לא דריש: ד] ר' יוסי: ה] ראשם ומכנסי פשתם יהיו על מתניהם לא יחגרו ביזע: ו] לה ס"א ואסמכוה רבנן אקרא: ז] בגד הראוי הוא לעבודה: ח] מיגז גאיז: ט] כדתרץ לשמואל נ"א דכיון דאמרינן דאבנט מיגז גאיז א"כ כשסילק ע"י אבנט יותר מכדינם היו פסולים מטעם דאבנט מיגז גייז להו מה דסילק כמאן דליתנהו מעיקרא כלל: י] דהא ע"כ שני לרב ס"א דבמרושלין דברייתא כשרישלן ע"י אבנט אם כן ש"מ דמסולקים דברייתא לאו דסילק ע"י אבנט הוא אלא בקצרים מעיקרא וקתני כשרים: יא] מיגז גאיז: יב] קרנתא דמקום: יג] בד שיהו של בוץ כדמפרש: יד] בבד פשתן: טו] דילפת ליה: טז] ששה מי משמע ליה מקראי הס"ד ומה"ד בגדים שנאמר בהן בד: יז] חדשים למצוה: יח] כדאמרינן בסדר יומא דילפינן מקראי דברים כו' כפול ששה ויליף לה: יט] מכל גרעין ותיבת גזעי נמחק: כ] ובעלמא קרי להו מכנסי בד: כא] זה לקמן קאמר לה: כב] ומכנגד הזרוע שוכב תמיד: כג] קשה אהדדי ותיבת אההיא ל"ש ונמחק: כד] הוא מין: כה] כלאים ושלח לר"ת תשובות מלאות שערות שתלש מזקנו על מנהג העולם מרוב צער: כו] ופשתים לתנא דבי ר' ישמעאל לא קשה מידי לפום מאי דפירש בקונטרס. ותיבות ועוד דכל קנבוס אינו עולה בד בבד נמחק: כז] אלא. ס"א כמה קנים יוצאים מגרעין אחד כמו:

כְּנֶגֶד אַצִּילֵי יְדֵיהֶם. עַל צַלְעוֹתֵיהֶן כְּנֶגֶד הַמַּרְפֵּק. אִיזְגַּדַר מַלְכָּא. כָּךְ שְׁמוֹ, וַהֲוָה מִדְלֵי הֶמְיָינַאי וְתִיתְיֵיהּ נִיהֲלֵיהּ. אַבְנֵטוֹ הָיָה גָּבוֹהַּ חָגוּר לְמַעְלָה מִכְּנֶגֶד אַצִּילֵי יָדָיו, וְהִפְשִׁיטוֹ לְמַטָּה כְּדֵי לְנַאוֹתוֹ. אָמַר מַמְלֶכֶת כֹּהֲנִים כְּתִיב בְּכוּ. וּצְרִיכִין אַתֶּם לִנְהוֹג עַצְמְכֶם בְּתִפְאֶרֶת שֶׁל כֹּהֲנִים, דִּכְתִיב בְּהוּ: "לֹא יַחְגְּרוּ בַּיָּזַע". כּוֹרֵךְ עָלֶיהָ

כְּנֶגֶד אַצִּילֵי יְדֵיהֶן. אָמַר רַב אַשִׁי, אָמַר לִי הוּנָא בַּר נָתָן: זִימְנָא חֲדָא הֲוָה קָאֵימְנָא קַמֵּיהּ דְּאִיזְגַּדַר מַלְכָּא, וַהֲוָה מַדְלֵי לִי הֶמְיָינַאי, וְתִיתְיֵיהּ נִיהֲלֵיהּ, וַאֲמַר לִי: °"מַמְלֶכֶת כֹּהֲנִים וְגוֹי קָדוֹשׁ" כְּתִיב בְּכוּ. כִּי אֲתַאי קַמֵּיהּ דְּאַמֵּימָר, א"ל: אִקַּיֵּים בָּךְ °"וְהָיוּ מְלָכִים אוֹמְנַיִךְ". § *תְּנַן הָתָם: אכֹּהֵן שֶׁלָּקָה בְּאֶצְבָּעוֹ — א] כּוֹרֵךְ עָלֶיהָ גֶּמִי בַּמִּקְדָּשׁ, באֲבָל לֹא בַּמְּדִינָה. וְאִם לְהוֹצִיא מִמֶּנָּה דָּם — כָּאן וְכָאן אָסוּר. *אָמַר ר' יְהוּדָה בְּרֵיהּ דְּרַבִּי חִיָּיא: לֹא שָׁנוּ אֶלָּא גֶּמִי, אֲבָל צִילְצוּל קָטָן — הָוֵי יִתּוּר בְּגָדִים. וְרַבִּי יוֹחָנָן אָמַר: לֹא אָמְרוּ יִתּוּר בְּגָדִים אֶלָּא בִּמְקוֹם בְּגָדִים, אֲבָל שֶׁלֹּא בִּמְקוֹם בְּגָדִים — לָא הָוֵי יִתּוּר. (א) ב] וְתֵיפּוֹק לֵיהּ מִשּׁוּם חֲצִיצָה! בִּשְׂמֹאל. א"נ, שֶׁלֹּא בִּמְקוֹם עֲבוֹדָה. וּפְלִיגָא דְּרָבָא, ג] דְּאָמַר רָבָא אָמַר רַב חִסְדָּא: גבִּמְקוֹם בְּגָדִים — אֲפִי' נִימָא אַחַת חוֹצֶצֶת, דשֶׁלֹּא בִּמְקוֹם בְּגָדִים — שָׁלֹשׁ עַל שָׁלֹשׁ ד] חוֹצְצוֹת, פָּחוֹת מִכָּאן אֵינָן חוֹצְצוֹת. אַדְּרַבִּי יוֹחָנָן וַדַּאי פְּלִיגָא, אַדְּר' יְהוּדָה בְּרֵיהּ דְּרַבִּי חִיָּיא מִי לֵימָא דִּפְלִיגָא? השָׁאנֵי צִילְצוּל קָטָן דַּחֲשִׁיב. לִישָּׁנָא אַחֲרִינָא אָמְרִי לָהּ, אָמַר ר' יְהוּדָה בְּרֵיהּ דְּרַבִּי חִיָּיא: לֹא שָׁנוּ אֶלָּא גֶּמִי, אֲבָל צִילְצוּל קָטָן — חוֹצֵץ. וְרַבִּי יוֹחָנָן אָמַר: לֹא אָמְרוּ חֲצִיצָה בְּפָחוֹת מִשָּׁלֹשׁ עַל שָׁלֹשׁ אֶלָּא בִּמְקוֹם בְּגָדִים, אֲבָל שֶׁלֹּא בִּמְקוֹם בְּגָדִים — שָׁלֹשׁ עַל שָׁלֹשׁ חוֹצְצוֹת, ה] פָּחוֹת מִכָּאן — אֵינָהּ חוֹצֶצֶת. וְהַיְינוּ דְּרָבָא אָמַר רַב חִסְדָּא. לֵימָא פְּלִיגָא אַדְּר' יְהוּדָה בְּרֵיהּ דְּרַבִּי חִיָּיא? שָׁאנֵי צִילְצוּל קָטָן דַּחֲשִׁיב. וּלְר' יוֹחָנָן מַאי אִירְיָא גֶּמִי? לַשְׁמוּעִינַן צִילְצוּל קָטָן! (ג) מִילְּתָא אַגַּב אוֹרְחֵיהּ קמ"ל, דְּגֶמִי מַסֵּי. בָּעֵי רָבָא: ונִכְנְסָה לוֹ רוּחַ בְּבִגְדוֹ, מַהוּ? "עַל בְּשָׂרוֹ" בָּעֵינַן — וְהָא לֵיכָּא, אוֹ דִּלְמָא דֶּרֶךְ לְבִישָׁה בְּכָךְ? זכִּינָּה מַהוּ שֶׁתָּחוֹץ? חמֵתָה לָא תִּבָּעֵי לָךְ, דְּוַדַּאי חָיְיצָא. חַיָּה מַאי? מִי אָמְרִינַן: כֵּיוָן דְּאָתְאָ וְאָזְלָא — רְבִיתָא הִיא וְלָא חָיְיצָא, אוֹ דִּלְמָא כֵּיוָן דְּקָפֵיד עֲלָהּ — חָיְיצָא. עָפָר מַהוּ שֶׁיָּחוֹץ? טעָפָר וַדַּאי חָיֵיץ! אֶלָּא, יאֲבַק עָפָר מַהוּ? כבֵּית הַשֶּׁחִי מַהוּ שֶׁיָּחוֹץ? "עַל בְּשָׂרוֹ" בָּעֵינַן — וְהָא לֵיכָּא, אוֹ דִּלְמָא דֶּרֶךְ לְבִישָׁה בְּכָךְ? להִכְנִים יָדוֹ לְתוֹךְ חֵיקוֹ, מַהוּ? גּוּפוֹ מִי חָיֵיץ אוֹ לָא? נִימָא מַהוּ שֶׁתָּחוֹץ? נִימָא וַדַּאי חָיְיצָא! אֶלָּא מנִימָא מְדוּלְדֶּלֶת, מַהוּ? בָּעֵי מָר בַּר רַב אַשִׁי: נִיָּצָא שְׂעָרוֹ בְּבִגְדוֹ, מַהוּ? *שְׂעָרוֹ כְּגוּפוֹ דָּמֵי, אוֹ לָאו כְּגוּפוֹ דָּמֵי? בָּעֵי רַבִּי זֵירָא: תְּפִילִּין מַהוּ שֶׁיָּחוֹצוּ? אַלִּיבָּא דְּמַאן דְּאָמַר: *)לַיְלָה לָאו זְמַן תְּפִילִּין הוּא — לָא תִּבָּעֵי לָךְ, כֵּיוָן דְּלַיְלָה חָיְיצִי — יוֹם נַמִּי חָיְיצִי. כִּי תִּיבָּעֵי לָךְ — לְמ"ד: לַיְלָה זְמַן תְּפִילִּין, מַאי? מִצְוָה דְּגוּפֵיהּ חָיֵיץ, אוֹ לָא חָיֵיץ? אִיגַּלְגַּל מִילְּתָא וּמְטָא לְקַמֵּיהּ דְּרַבִּי אַמִּי. א"ל: תַּלְמוּד עָרוּךְ הוּא בְּיָדֵינוּ: תְּפִילִּין חוֹצְצוֹת. מֵיתִיבֵי: סכֹּהֲנִים בַּעֲבוֹדָתָן, וּלְוִיִּם בְּדוּכָנָן, וְיִשְׂרָאֵל בְּמַעֲמָדָן — פְּטוּרִין מִן הַתְּפִלָּה וּמִן הַתְּפִילִּין; מַאי לָאו אִם הִנִּיחָן — אֵינָן חוֹצְצוֹת? לָא, אִם הִנִּיחָן חוֹצְצוֹת. א"ה, פְּטוּרִים? אֲסוּרִים מִיבָּעֵי לֵיהּ! כֵּיוָן דְּאִיכָּא לְוִיִּם וְיִשְׂרָאֵל דְּלָא מִתְנוּ לֵיהּ אָסוּר, מִשּׁוּם הָכִי תְּנָא פְּטוּרִין. וְהָתַנְיָא: אִם הִנִּיחָן אֵינָן חוֹצְצוֹת! לָא קַשְׁיָא, עהָא — דְּיַד, הָא — דְּרֹאשׁ. מַאי שְׁנָא דְּיַד? דִּכְתִיב: °"יִלְבַּשׁ עַל בְּשָׂרוֹ", שֶׁלֹּא יְהֵא דָּבָר חוֹצֵץ בֵּינוֹ לִבְשָׂרוֹ — דְּרֹאשׁ נַמִּי כְּתִיב: °"וְשַׂמְתָּ הַמִּצְנֶפֶת עַל רֹאשׁוֹ"! ***)תָּנָא: פשְׂעָרוֹ הָיָה נִרְאֶה בֵּין צִיץ לְמִצְנֶפֶת, שֶׁשָּׁם

*) [עירובין צו. מנחות לו:] **) [ערכין ג:] ***) [שם.]

עין משפט נר מצוה

לו א מיי' פ"ה מהלכות ביאת מקדש הלכה ז ופ"ב מהלכות עבודת יוה"כ הלכה ג:

לז ב מיי' פ"ה מהלכות ביאת מקדש הלכה טז:

עיין נ"ק

לח ג מיי' שם הלכה ג:

לט ד ה מיי' שם הלכה ח:

גי' הנ"ק לאותו שהלך לתרום המזבח היה מהלך יחידי והיה מהלך ידיו ורגליו והיה פליגא או היה שום דבר כו' כנ"ל

ועי' היטב בתוס' דיומא כה. ד"ה אין ישיבה

לקמן כח:

וחוקה כתיב בהו ליעכבו. אפי' למאן דאמר (יומא דף ס.) דלא כתיבא "חוקה" אלא יח] [בדברים הנעשים] בבגדי לבן בפנים, לכל הפחות קידוש דהוי בין בגדי זהב לבגדי לבן ליעכב. דלורך פנים כפנים, כדאמר שילהי "הוציאו לו" (שם דף ס:) דקטרת שחפנה קודם שחיטת הפר – פסולה, דלורך פנים כפנים דמי. **אי הכי דצפרא נמי.** *תימה: מאי קושיא? כיון דהוי במיתה, אתי בקל וחומר מיושב, שאינו במיתה ואם עבד חילל. וכי תימא: מה ליושב כו', ונילף מיושב וחד מהנך! ועוד: דהא יושב לא פריך, ואמאי חשיב ליה וי"ו אאופתא!

וחבירו מסייעו יט] – במסכת תמיד (דף כח. פרק א מ"ד) משמע *דאותו [שהיה הולך לתרומת הדשן] היה כ] מהלך יחידי. והיא פליגא. או היה שם דבר שהיה מסייעו.

עמידה מן הצד איכא בינייהו. לרבנן לא שמיה עמידה מן הצד. ונראה, כא] כשקורין בתורה – שלא לסמוך, משום דאמר (רבי) במגילה פרק "הקורא את המגילה עומד" (דף כא.) דבתורה בעי עמידה. ובירושלמי נמי אמרינן דאסור לסמוך, משום דכשם שניתנה באימה – כך נוהגין אותה באימה.

וליתב מיתיב וליקדש. לאו ישיבה ממש קאמר, דאין ישיבה בעזרה, אלא סמיכה*.

אלא כב] האי בגשתם מיבעי ליה לכדרב אחא בר יעקב. אף על גב דיומא משמע דרבי נמי אית ליה דרב אחא בר יעקב, כג] דקסבר דתרתי שמע מינה.

מיתיבי

שֶׁשָּׁם (א) מַנִּיחִין תְּפִילִּין.§ "מְחוּסַּר כִּיפּוּרִים". מְנָלַן? אָמַר רַב הוּנָא, אָמַר קְרָא: °"וְכִפֶּר עָלֶיהָ הַכֹּהֵן וְטָהֵרָה" (ויקרא יב) — *טְהֵרָה מִכְּלָל שֶׁהִיא טְמֵאָה.§ וְ"שֶׁלֹּא רְחוּץ יָדַיִם וְרַגְלַיִם".§ אָתְיָא "חוּקָּה" "חוּקָּה" מִמְּחוּסַּר בְּגָדִים.§ ת"ר: *אכֹּהֵן גָּדוֹל שֶׁלֹּא טָבַל וְשֶׁלֹּא קִידֵּשׁ בֵּין בֶּגֶד לְבֶגֶד וּבֵין עֲבוֹדָה לַעֲבוֹדָה, וְעָבַד — עֲבוֹדָתוֹ כְּשֵׁרָה. וְאֶחָד כֹּהֵן גָּדוֹל וְאֶחָד כֹּהֵן הֶדְיוֹט שֶׁלֹּא קִידֵּשׁ יָדָיו וְרַגְלָיו שַׁחֲרִית וְעָבַד — עֲבוֹדָתוֹ פְּסוּלָה. א"ל רַב אַסִּי לְרַבִּי יוֹחָנָן: מִכְּדִי *חָמֵשׁ טְבִילוֹת וַעֲשָׂרָה קִידּוּשִׁין דְּאוֹרַיְיתָא, וְ"חוּקָּה" כְּתִיב בְּהוּ, לִיעַכְּבוּ! א"ל, אָמַר קְרָא: °"וּלְבֵשָׁם" (שם טז) — לְבִישָׁה מְעַכֶּבֶת, וְאֵין דָּבָר אַחֵר מְעַכֵּב. צָהֲבוּ פָּנָיו. *אָמַר לֵיהּ: וָי"ו אַאוּפְתָּא כְּתַבִי לָךְ, א] אִי הָכִי דְּצִפְּרָא נָמֵי! אָמַר חִזְקִיָּה, אָמַר קְרָא: °"וְהָיְתָה לָהֶם חָק עוֹלָם (שמות ל) לוֹ וּלְזַרְעוֹ לְדוֹרוֹתָם", ב] דָּבָר הַמְעַכֵּב בְּזַרְעוֹ — מְעַכֵּב בּוֹ, דָּבָר שֶׁאֵינוֹ מְעַכֵּב בְּזַרְעוֹ — אֵין מְעַכֵּב בּוֹ. רַבִּי יוֹנָתָן אָמַר, מֵהָכָא: °"וְרָחֲצוּ מִמֶּנּוּ מֹשֶׁה (שם מ) וְאַהֲרֹן וּבָנָיו", דָּבָר הַמְעַכֵּב בְּבָנָיו — מְעַכֵּב בּוֹ, דָּבָר שֶׁאֵינוֹ מְעַכֵּב בְּבָנָיו — אֵין מְעַכֵּב בּוֹ. רַבִּי יוֹנָתָן מ"ט לָא אָמַר מִדְּחִזְקִיָּה? אָמַר לָךְ: הַהוּא לְדוֹרוֹת הוּא דִּכְתִיב. וְאִידָךְ, מ"ט לָא אָמַר מֵהַאי? מִיבָּעֵי לֵיהּ לְכִדְרַבִּי יוֹסֵי בְּרַבִּי חֲנִינָא. *דְּאָמַר רַבִּי יוֹסֵי בְּרַבִּי חֲנִינָא: כָּל כִּיּוֹר *שֶׁאֵין בּוֹ כְּדֵי לְקַדֵּשׁ אַרְבָּעָה כֹּהֲנִים מִמֶּנּוּ — אֵין מְקַדְּשִׁין בּוֹ, שֶׁנֶּאֱמַר: "וְרָחֲצוּ מִמֶּנּוּ ג] מֹשֶׁה וְאַהֲרֹן וּבָנָיו".§ ת"ר: כֵּיצַד מִצְוַת קִידּוּשׁ? במַנִּיחַ יָדוֹ הַיְמָנִית עַל גַּבֵּי רַגְלוֹ הַיְמָנִית, וְיָדוֹ הַשְּׂמָאלִית עַל גַּבֵּי רַגְלוֹ הַשְּׂמָאלִית, וּמְקַדֵּשׁ. רַבִּי יוֹסֵי בְּרַבִּי יְהוּדָה אוֹמֵר: מַנִּיחַ שְׁתֵּי יָדָיו זוֹ עַל גַּב זוֹ, וְעַל גַּבֵּי שְׁתֵּי רַגְלָיו זוֹ עַל גַּבֵּי זוֹ, וּמְקַדֵּשׁ. אָמְרוּ לוֹ: הִפְלַגְתָּה, אִי אֶפְשָׁר לַעֲשׂוֹת כֵּן. שַׁפִּיר קָאָמְרִי לֵיהּ! אָמַר רַב יוֹסֵף: וַחֲבֵירוֹ מְסַיְּיעוֹ. מַאי בֵּינַיְיהוּ? אָמַר אַבַּיֵי: ד] עֲמִידָה מִן הַצַּד אִיכָּא בֵּינַיְיהוּ. א"ל רַב סַמָּא בְּרֵיהּ דְּרַב אַשִׁי לְרָבִינָא: וְלֵיתִיב מֵיתָב וּלְקַדֵּשׁ! אָמַר קְרָא: °"לְשָׁרֵת", (שם ל) וְשֵׁירוּת מְעוּמָּד הוּא.§ ת"ר: גקִידֵּשׁ יָדָיו וְרַגְלָיו בַּיּוֹם — אֵין צָרִיךְ לְקַדֵּשׁ בַּלַּיְלָה, דבַּלַּיְלָה — צָרִיךְ לְקַדֵּשׁ בַּיּוֹם, דִּבְרֵי רַבִּי. שֶׁהָיָה רַבִּי אוֹמֵר: לִינָה מוֹעֶלֶת בְּקִידּוּשׁ יָדַיִם וְרַגְלַיִם. רַבִּי אֶלְעָזָר בְּרַבִּי שִׁמְעוֹן אוֹמֵר: אֵין לִינָה מוֹעֶלֶת בְּקִידּוּשׁ יָדַיִם וְרַגְלַיִם. תַּנְיָא אִידָךְ: *הָיָה העוֹמֵד וּמַקְרִיב עַל גַּבֵּי מִזְבֵּחַ כָּל הַלַּיְלָה, ה] לָאוֹרָה טָעוּן קִידּוּשׁ יָדַיִם וְרַגְלַיִם, דִּבְרֵי רַבִּי. רַבִּי אֶלְעָזָר בְּרַ"שׁ אוֹמֵר: כֵּיוָן שֶׁקִּידֵּשׁ יָדָיו וְרַגְלָיו מִתְּחִילַּת עֲבוֹדָה, אֲפִילּוּ מִיכָּן וְעַד עֲשָׂרָה יָמִים — אֵינוֹ צָרִיךְ לְקַדֵּשׁ. וּצְרִיכָא, דְּאִי אַשְׁמְעִינַן קַמַּיְיתָא — בְּהַהִיא קָאָמַר רַבִּי, דִּפְסַק לֵיהּ מֵעֲבוֹדָה לַעֲבוֹדָה, אֲבָל בְּהָא דְּלָא פְּסַק לֵיהּ — אֵימָא מוֹדֵי לֵיהּ רַבִּי לְרַבִּי אֶלְעָזָר בְּרַבִּי שִׁמְעוֹן; וְאִי אַשְׁמְעִינַן בְּהָא — בְּהָא קָאָמַר רַבִּי אֶלְעָזָר בְּרַבִּי שִׁמְעוֹן, אֲבָל בְּהָא — אֵימָא מוֹדֵי לֵיהּ לְרַבִּי, צְרִיכָא. מַאי טַעְמָא דְּרַבִּי? דִּכְתִיב: °"בְּגִשְׁתָּם". (שם) מ"ט דְּרַבִּי אֶלְעָזָר בְּרַ"שׁ? דִּכְתִיב: °"בְּבוֹאָם". (שם) וְאִידָךְ נָמֵי, הָא כְּתִיב: "בְּבוֹאָם"! אִי כְּתִיב "בְּגִשְׁתָּם" וְלָא כְּתִיב "בְּבוֹאָם" הֲוָה אָמִינָא עַל כָּל גִּישָׁה וְגִישָׁה, כְּתַב רַחֲמָנָא: "בְּבוֹאָם". וְאִידָךְ נָמֵי, הָא כְּתִיב "בְּגִשְׁתָּם"! אִי כְּתִיב "בְּבוֹאָם" וְלָא כְּתִיב "בְּגִשְׁתָּם", והֲוָה אָמִינָא אֲפִילּוּ אַבִּיאָה רֵיקָנִית. אַבִּיאָה רֵיקָנִית?! הָא כְּתִיב: "לְשָׁרֵת"! אֶלָּא, "בְּגִשְׁתָּם" מִיבָּעֵי לֵיהּ לְכִדְרַב אַחָא בַּר יַעֲקֹב, *דְּאָמַר רַב אַחָא בַּר יַעֲקֹב: הַכֹּל מוֹדִים בְּקִידּוּשׁ שֵׁנִי כְּשֶׁהוּא לָבוּשׁ מְקַדֵּשׁ, דְּאָמַר קְרָא: "אוֹ בְגִשְׁתָּם" — מִי שֶׁאֵינוֹ מְחוּסָּר אֶלָּא גִּישָׁה בִּלְבַד, יָצָא זֶה שֶׁמְּחוּסָּר לְבִישָׁה וְגִישָׁה. °"לְהַקְטִיר אִשֶּׁה" (שם) לָמָּה לִי?

מַהוּ

תורה אור

שֶׁשָּׁם מַנִּיחַ תְּפִילִין. הִלְכָּךְ לֵיכָּא חֲצִיצָה. וְתַנָּא דְּאִיצְטְרִיךְ לְאַשְׁמוּעִינַן אִם הִנִּיחָן אֵין חוֹצְצוֹת – מִשּׁוּם יִיתּוּר בְּגָדִים הוּא דְּאִיצְטְרִיךְ, ו] לְאַשְׁמוּעִינַן דְּלָאו בֶּגֶד הוּא. מִכְּלָל שֶׁהִיא טְמֵאָה. עַד עַכְשָׁיו, וְטָמֵא כְּתִיב בֵּיהּ: "וְיִנָּזְרוּ וְלֹא יְחַלְּלוּ". אָתְיָא חוּקָּה חוּקָּה. מַה לְּהַלָּן אִם עָבַד חִילֵּל – אַף כָּאן אִם עָבַד חִילֵּל. כֹּהֵן גָּדוֹל כו'. כְּגוֹן בְּחָמֵשׁ עֲבוֹדוֹת שֶׁל יוֹם הַכִּפּוּרִים, דְּיָלְפִינַן בְּסֵדֶר יוֹמָא (דף לב.) שֶׁהוּא מְשַׁנֶּה מִבִּגְדֵי זָהָב לְבִגְדֵי לָבָן וּמִבִּגְדֵי לָבָן לְבִגְדֵי זָהָב, וְצָרִיךְ לְכָל חִילּוּף טְבִילָה וּשְׁנֵי קִידּוּשִׁין מִן הַמִּקְרָא. אִם לֹא טָבַל וְלֹא קִידֵּשׁ – עֲבוֹדָתוֹ כְּשֵׁרָה. שַׁחֲרִית. בֵּין בְּיוֹם הַכִּפּוּרִים בֵּין בְּכָל הַשָּׁנָה – עֲבוֹדָתוֹ פְּסוּלָה, כִּדְיָלְפִינַן "חוּקָּה" "חוּקָּה" מִמְּחוּסַּר בְּגָדִים. דְּאוֹרַיְיתָא. דִּכְתִיב: "וְרָחַץ אֶת בְּשָׂרוֹ בַּמַּיִם וּלְבֵשָׁם". וְהָתָם יָלֵיף לְכוּלָּהּ מִילְּתָא. וְחוּקָּה כְּתִיב בְּהוּ. לְאַחַר שֶׁגָּמַר כָּל הַפָּרָשָׁה כְּתִיב: "וְהָיְתָה לָהֶם לְחוּקַּת עוֹלָם בַּחֹדֶשׁ הַשְּׁבִיעִי בֶּעָשׂוֹר" וגו'. אָמַר קְרָא וּלְבֵשָׁם. שִׁינָּה הַכָּתוּב בִּלְבִישָׁה לְעַכֵּב, דִּכְתִיב: "יִלְבַּשׁ" "וּלְבֵשָׁם". וּלְהָכִי כְּתִיב ז] הָכָא עִכּוּבָא – לְמַעוּטֵי עִכּוּבָא דְּחוּקָּה, דְּלָא קַיְימָא אַהַאי קְרָא דְּאַיְירֵי בִּרְחִילָה וּלְבִישָׁה, אֶלָּא אַשְּׁאָר ח] (שְׁנֵי) דְּבָרִים הָאֲמוּרִים בַּפָּרָשָׁה. וְאֵין דָּבָר אַחֵר. ט] בְּפָסוּק זֶה מְעַכֵּב. צָהֲבוּ פָּנָיו. שֶׁל ר' אַסִּי מִפְּנֵי שִׂמְחָה, כְּסָבוּר טַעַם הָגוּן שָׁמַע. וָי"ו אַאוּפְתָּא כְּתִיבֵי לָךְ. כָּתַבְתִּי לְךָ וָי"ו עַל הַבְּקַעַת, אוֹת שֶׁאֵין נִיכֶּרֶת י] בָּהּ, מִפְּנֵי שׁוּרוֹת הַבְּקַעַת שֶׁמַּפְסִיקוֹת בָּהּ הַפְסָקוֹת הַרְבֵּה. לָשׁוֹן אַחֵר: הַשּׁוּרוֹת עַצְמוֹ קָרֵי לְהוּ וָוִי"ן, שֶׁדּוֹמִין לָהּ. כְּלוֹמַר, אֵין זֶה טַעַם, דְּאִיכָּא לְאַקְשׁוּיֵי: א"כ – אֲפִילּוּ קִדּוּשׁ שֶׁל שַׁחֲרִית יא] [שֶׁל יוה"כ] נָמֵי לָא לְעַכֵּב בֵּיהּ, דְּהָא אִימְעוּט בְּיוֹם הַכִּפּוּרִים מִ"וּלְבֵשָׁם". וְהָיְתָה לָהֶם (ב) לְחָק עוֹלָם. בְּקִידּוּשׁ כְּתִיב. בְּזַרְעוֹ. בְּכֹהֲנִים הֶדְיוֹטִים, דְּהַיְינוּ קִידּוּשׁ שֶׁבִּשְׁעַת כְּנִיסָה שֶׁנּוֹהֵג בְּכָל הַכֹּהֲנִים – מְעַכְּבָא יב] בְּאַהֲרֹן בְּיוֹם הַכִּפּוּרִים, דְּהָא "חוּקָּה" כְּתִיב. לְדוֹרוֹת הוּא דִּכְתִיב. אַזְהָרָה לִנְהוֹג חוּקָּה זוֹ לְזַרְעוֹ אַחֲרָיו, וְלָאו לְהֶיקֵּשָׁא אֲתָא. שֶׁאֵין בּוֹ. שֶׁאֵין מַחֲזִיק מַיִם כְּשִׁיעוּר אַרְבַּע קִידּוּשִׁין. *מֹשֶׁה וְאַהֲרֹן. תְּרֵין, וּבָנָיו תְּרֵין. שֶׁאַף מֹשֶׁה כֹּהֵן הָיָה בְּשִׁבְעַת יְמֵי הַמִּילּוּאִים. וְאע"ג דְּלָא כַּהֲנוּ בְּבַת אַחַת, מִיהוּ קְרָא לְהָכִי מִידְרִישׁ. מַנִּיחַ יָדָיו כו'. דְּבָעֵינַן יָדָיו וְרַגְלָיו (ג) יג] כְּאֶחָד יִרְחֲצוּ, כִּדְכְתִיב קְרָא. הִפְלַגְתָּה. דְּבָרִים מִמִּדַּת כָּל אָדָם, דְּאִי אֶפְשָׁר לוֹ שֶׁלֹּא יִפּוֹל. אָמַר רַב יוֹסֵף. הָא דְּרַבִּי יוֹסֵי בְּרַבִּי יְהוּדָה – כְּשֶׁחֲבֵירוֹ מְסַיְּיעוֹ, מַחֲזִיק בּוֹ שֶׁלֹּא יִפּוֹל. מַאי בֵּינַיְיהוּ. בְּמַאי פְּלִיגֵי? עֲמִידָה מִן הַצַּד. כְּגוֹן זוֹ, שֶׁאֵינוֹ בְּלֹא סִיּוּעַ. לְרַבָּנַן לָא הָוְיָא עֲמִידָה, וַאֲנַן עֲמִידָה בָּעֵינַן כִּדְמְפָרֵשׁ לְקַמָּן. אָמַר קְרָא לְשָׁרֵת. "אוֹ בְגִשְׁתָּם אֶל הַמִּזְבֵּחַ לְשָׁרֵת" – אִיתְקַשׁ קִידּוּשׁ לְשֵׁירוּת. (ד) אֵינוֹ צָרִיךְ לְקַדֵּשׁ בַּלַּיְלָה. אִם לֹא יָצָא וְלֹא הִסִּיחַ דַּעְתּוֹ. צָרִיךְ לְקַדֵּשׁ בַּיּוֹם. כִּדְמְסַיֵּים מִילְּתֵיהּ: שֶׁהַלִּינָה פּוֹסֶלֶת בְּקִידּוּשׁ. וְעַמּוּד הַשַּׁחַר הוּא הָעוֹשֶׂה לִינָה, לְקַמָּן בְּפֶרֶק "הַמִּזְבֵּחַ מְקַדֵּשׁ" (דף פז.). מִתְּחִילַּת עֲבוֹדָה. כְּשֶׁהִתְחִיל לַעֲבוֹד עֲבוֹדוֹת *הַלָּלוּ וְלֹא הִסִּיחַ שׁוּב דַּעְתּוֹ יד] *[עַד עֲשָׂרָה יָמִים, וּבִלְבַד שֶׁיְּהֵא עוֹמֵד וְעוֹבֵד]. דִּפְסַק לֵיהּ מִן הָעֲבוֹדָה. אֶלָּא שֶׁלֹּא הִסִּיחַ דַּעְתּוֹ. דְּלָא תָּנֵי בָּהּ "הָיָה עוֹמֵד וּמַקְרִיב" כִּי הָכָא. דִּכְתִיב בְּגִשְׁתָּם. טו] וְגִישָׁה דְּשַׁחֲרִית גִּישָׁה אַחֲרִיתִי הִיא, שֶׁהֲרֵי יֵשׁ כָּאן מַעֲרָכָה חֲדָשָׁה. דִּכְתִיב בְּבוֹאָם. וַהֲרֵי [זֶה] לֹא יָצָא. טז] אֲבָל גִּישָׁה וְגִישָׁה. וַאֲפִי' שְׁתֵּיהֶן בּוֹ בַּיּוֹם. אַבִּיאָה רֵיקָנִית. נִכְנַס שֶׁלֹּא לַעֲבוֹד. דְּרַב אַחָא בַּר יַעֲקֹב. בְּסֵדֶר יוֹמָא. הַכֹּל מוֹדִים. ר"מ וְרַבָּנַן, דִּפְלִיגֵי *בְּקִידּוּשׁ שֶׁלִּפְנֵי כָּל טְבִילָה שֶׁל יז] טְבִילוֹת [כ"ג, רַבָּנַן אָמְרֵי]: קִידֵּשׁ יָדָיו וְרַגְלָיו וּפָשַׁט, רַבִּי מֵאִיר אוֹמֵר: פָּשַׁט, קִידֵּשׁ יָדָיו וְרַגְלָיו – מוֹדִים הֵם בְּקִידּוּשׁ שֶׁל אַחַר טְבִילָה, שֶׁלּוֹבֵשׁ הַבְּגָדִים שֶׁהוּא מַחֲלִיף וְאַחַר כָּךְ מְקַדֵּשׁ, וְאֵינוֹ מְקַדֵּשׁ כְּשֶׁהוּא עָרוֹם, דִּכְתִיב "בְּגִשְׁתָּם יִרְחֲצוּ" – מִי שֶׁאֵינוֹ מְחוּסַּר אַחַר קִידּוּשׁ אֶלָּא גִּישָׁה. לְהַקְטִיר אִשֶּׁה. דִּכְתִיב גַּבֵּי קִידּוּשׁ, לָמָּה לִי? פְּשִׁיטָא דְּבָעְיָא קִידּוּשׁ, דְּהָא גִּישַׁת מִזְבֵּחַ הִיא!

מַהוּ

מסורת הש"ס

[יבמות עד: סנהדרין פג:]

יומא ל: תוספתא דמנחות פ"א ע"ש תוספתא דיומא פ"א

[יומא יט. ל. לא. עא.]

חולין טז.

נ"א שאין מחזיק כדי רש"ק

פסחים ב: תוספתא דמנחות פ"א תוספתא דיומא פ"א

יומא לב:

הלילה נ"ק *ס"א

גי' הנ"ק בקידוש שלפני כל טבילה וטבילה דרבנן סברי קידש ידיו וכו' כנ"ל ועיין במסכת יומא דף לב ע"ב

הגהות הב"ח

(א) גמ' ששם מניח תפילין: (ב) רש"י ד"ה והיתה להם חק עולם: (ג) ד"ה מניח וכו' כאחת כדכתיב קרא ירחצו הס"ד: (ד) ד"ה אינו. נ"ב ע"ל בדף כ ע"ב:

גליון הש"ס

גמ' הוה אמינא אפילו אביאה ריקנית. עיין סנהדרין דף פג ע"א תוס' ד"ה ולא משום טומאה:

שיטה מקובצת

א] אי הכי דצפרא נמי ואפשר דצפרא מרבינן מגז"ש דמחוסר בגדים א"כ מיעט דולבשם לאו דוקא מאותו דצפרא כמו כן לא יהיה דוקא מן האחריני. מהר"פ: ב] דבר המעכב בזרעו כגון תמיד של שחרית שבכל יום שנוהג בכהנים הדיוטים אבל עבודת יה"כ שאינו נוהג אלא בכה"ג אין מעכב בו: ג] משה ואהרן ובניו. אע"ג דמשה היה לוי מ"מ היה משמש בז' ימי המילואים וא"ת ליבעי שיתא דד' בנים הוו לאהרן וי"ל דכבר מתו נדב ואביהוא וא"ת והרי ארבע נמי לא שימשו ביום אחד דבז' ימי המילואים ששימש משה לא שימש אהרן ואח"כ ששימש אהרן שוב לא שימש משה ואפ"ה קחשיב להו ד' כמו כן ליבעי שיתא אע"פ שנדב ואביהוא לא שימשו וי"ל דמיעוט בניו שנים והר"ם תירץ דבשמיני למילואים נמי שימש משה שמה שהובחרה העבודה באהרן כדכתיב קרב אל המזבח היינו דוקא עבודת היום כגון עגל וכבש ושאר עבודות דשייכי (לשמיני) (לשמינית) [ליום השמיני של] ימי המילואים אבל עבודות שהיו עושין בכל יום כגון תמידין וקטורת זה עשה משה כדכתיב ויהי באחד לחודש הוקם המשכן ואח"כ כתיב ויעל את העולה אלמא משמע מי (שהוקם) [שהקים] את המשכן דהיינו משה העלה את העולה ובאותו יום שהוקם את המשכן היה שמיני למילואים ונטל עשר עטרות. מהר"פ: ד] עמידה מן הצד כו'. וא"כ צריך ליזהר בכל מקום שצריך עמידה כגון בתפילה והקורא בתורה שלא יסמוך כדאיתא בירושלמי כו' ור' יחיאל מפריש היה אומר דדוקא שלא היה יכול לעמוד בלי סמיכה לא שמה עמידה אבל היכא שהיה יכול לעמוד בלי סמיכה אף כי עושה סמיכה שמה עמידה ומורי אומר אם הוא סומך כל כך בחוזק שאם תנטל הדבר שהוא סומך עליו יפול לא שמה עמידה ואם לאו שמה עמידה. מהר"פ: ה] לאורה. גליון פי' לעמוד השחר: ו] לאשמועינן ולפי' השני שפי' לעיל מטעם חציצה צריך לפרש דהיא גופא קמ"ל דשערו היה נראה (שום) [וליכא משום] חציצה ומהכא משמע שהיה הציץ נתון על גובה הראש ולא על מצחו ממש אלא במקום שיער [דהא] מזכיר בין ציץ למצנפת ואע"ג דכתיב מצחו בציץ [לא היה] על מצחו ממש אלא במקום השיער בגובה הראש [ודלא] כתרגום [על] בין עינוהי ומזה מיישב ריב"א הא דשואלין מאי שנא של כה"ג דקרי ליה מצנפת ושל כהן הדיוט קורין ליה מגבעות אלא משום דשל כה"ג היתה קטנה לפי שהיה מניח הציץ על שערו אבל של כהן הדיוט היתה גדולה ומכסה כל הראש ואע"ג דביומא קרו לשל הדיוט מצנפת לשון חכמים לחוד ולשון תורה לחוד. מהר"פ: ז] ולהכי כתיב עכובא הכא למעוטי ולומר דעכובא דחוקה לא קיימא: ח] תיבת שני נמחק: ט] שבפסוק זה: י] תיבת בה נמחק: יא] שחרית של יה"כ: יב] מעכבא בו: יג] ורגליו בחדא רחיצה כדכתיב בקרא הס"ד: יד] דעתו עד עשרה ימים ובלבד שיהא עומד ועובד: טו] בגישתם וגישת שחרית גישה: טז] מה"ד על כל גישה וגישה: יז] של ה' [טבילות] ותיבת כה"ג רבנן אמרי ל"ש ונמחק: יח] אלא בדברים הנעשים: יט] מסייעו לקדש: כ] הולך יחידי ושמא ההיא פליגא: כא] ונראה דצריך להזהיר בשעה שקורין בתורה: כב] תיבת האי נמחק: כג] יעקב קסבר אות ד' נמחק:

מהו דתימא, א] הני מילי – עבודה דמעכבא כפרה, אבל עבודה דלא מעכבא כפרה – לא, קמ"ל. כי אתא רב דימי אמר רבי יוחנן, בעי אילפא: לדברי האומר אין לינה מועלת בקידוש ידים ורגלים, מי כיור מהו שיפסלו? מי אמרינן: הני למאי – לקידוש ידים ורגלים, קידוש ידים ורגלים גופייהו לא ב] פסול בהו לינה. או דלמא: כיון ג] דקידוש להו בכלי שרת, מיפסלי? כי אתא רבין אמר רבי ירמיה, אמר רבי אמי אמר ר' יוחנן: הדר פשיט אילפא – כמחלוקת בזו כך מחלוקת בזו. אמר לפניו ר' יצחק בר ביסנא: רבי, אתה אומר כן? ד] *אלא הכי אמר (א) ר' אסי אמר ר' יוחנן [משמיה דאילפא]: כיור שלא שקעו מבערב – מקדש ממנו לעבודת לילה, ולמחר אינו מקדש; והוינן בה: ה] למחר אינו מקדש – דלא צריך לקידוש, או דלמא איפסלו בלינה? ולא פשיט לן, ומר קא פשיט ליה מיפשיט. ת"ש: *בן קטין עשה אשנים עשר דד לכיור. אף הוא עשה במוכני לכיור שלא יהיו מימיו נפסלין בלינה; מאי לאו רבי אלעזר ברבי שמעון היא? לא, רבי היא. והא מדרישא רבי אלעזר ברבי שמעון, סיפא נמי רבי אלעזר ברבי שמעון! דקתני רישא: *גבא לו אצל פרו, (ג) ופר היה עומד בין האולם ולמזבח, ראשו לדרום ופניו למערב, והכהן עומד במזרח ופניו למערב. מאן שמעת ליה דאמר: בין האולם ולמזבח – צפון, רבי אלעזר ברבי שמעון. *דתניא: איזהו צפון – מקיר מזבח צפוני ועד כותל עזרה צפוני, וכנגד כל המזבח כולו – צפון, דברי *רבי יוסי ברבי יהודה. רבי אלעזר ברבי שמעון מוסיף: *דאף בין האולם ולמזבח. רבי מוסיף: האף מקום דריסת רגלי הכהנים ומקום דריסת רגלי ישראל. אבל מן החליפות ולפנים – הכל מודים שפסול. ותסברא, רבי אלעזר ברבי שמעון היא ולא רבי? ו] *[השתא רבי] אדרבי יוסי ברבי יהודה מוסיף, אדרבי אלעזר בר' שמעון לא מוסיף? אנן הכי קאמרינן: אי ס"ד רבי היא – לוקמה במקום דריסת רגלי כהנים ובמקום דריסת רגלי ישראל. אלא מאי, רבי אלעזר ברבי שמעון היא? לוקמה מקיר מזבח צפוני עד כותל עזרה צפוני! אלא מאי אית לך למימר – משום חולשא דכהן גדול, הכא נמי משום חולשא דכהן גדול.§ *אמר רבי יוחנן: יקידש ידיו ורגליו לתרומת הדשן – למחר אינו צריך לקדש, שכבר קידש מתחילת עבודה. למאן? *אי לרבי – האמר: פסלה לינה, אי לרבי אלעזר בר"ש – האמר: ז] אין צריך לקדש אפי' מיכן ועד עשרה ימים! אמר אביי: לעולם לרבי, ולינה דרבנן היא, ומודי ח] דמקרות הגבר ועד צפרא לא פסלה לינה. רבא אמר: לעולם רבי אלעזר ברבי שמעון ט] [היא, וראה ר"י דבריו] בתחילת עבודה ולא בסוף עבודה. מיתיבי: *יראוהו אחיו הכהנים שירד, והן רצו ובאו, מיהרו וקידשו ידיהם ורגליהם מן הכיור. בשלמא

רש"י

מהו דתימא ה"מ. דבעינן קידוש שחרית – בעבודה דמעכבת כפרה, כגון דם וקמיצה. אבל כל הקטרת אימורין, דלא מעכבא – אימא לא תיבעי קידוש. מהו שיפסלו. בלינה אם לא שקעה *בבור. י] *(בני הגולה) דאמרי' בסדר יומא (דף לז.) דמשקע להו. או דילמא כיון יא] דקידוש (ג) בכלי שרת איפסלו. דלא דמי לקידוש ידים, שהמים יגבו ואין לינה על מי לחול. ה"ג: כי אתא רבין אמר כו' ול"ג ת"ש (ד). אמר לפניו רבי יצחק בר ביסנא. לפני ר' (ה) אמי. וכולה רבין אמר לה. שלא שקעו. בבור. לעבודת לילה. להקטיר חלבים. והוינן בה. קמייה דרבי (ו) *אסי, ולא יב] פשט לן. דלא צריך לקדושי. וכרבי אלעזר בר' שמעון דלא פסל לינה בקידוש. או דילמא אין ראויות לקדש – יג] דאיפסלו להו בלינה ואפי' לר' אלעזר. דאי לרבי יד] ליכא למיבעי *אין צריך, דהא אפילו בקידוש פסל. ולא פשט. ר' (ז) *אסי הך בעיא, למימר דאין צריך לקדש קאמר ולא לפוסלה בלינה, כדקאמרת כמחלוקת בזו כך מחלוקת בזו. ומר סבר ר' אלעזר לא פסלה בלינה. שנים עשר דד. שמוציאין מימיו, ואמרינן בסדר יומא שיהו שנים עשר כהנים העסוקים בתמיד מקדשים בבת אחת. מוכני. מפרש התם: טו] גלגלים, שמעלין אותו בגלגלין מן הבור שחרית שלא יהא מימיו נפסלים בלינה. לפיכך משקעין אותו ערבית בבור – שיהו מימיו מחוברים למי המעין, ובטלה טז] לינתן. מאי לאו. אפילו ר' אלעזר קאמר לה, דאף על גב דפליג בקידוש שניגב – מודה יז] במים? בא לו. כהן יח] אצל פרו להתוודות עליו ביום הכיפורים, יט] דכתיב: "וכפר בעדו" וגו' (ויקרא טז). ראשו לדרום ופניו למערב. *)מצפון לדרום היה עומד ופניו למערב. והתם מפרש לה בעוקם את ראשו. והתם פריך: לוקמיה להדיא ממזרח למערב! ומשנינן לה. והכהן עומד. אחוריו למזרח המזבח ופניו למערב כלפי ההיכל, ואמרינן טעמא התם.

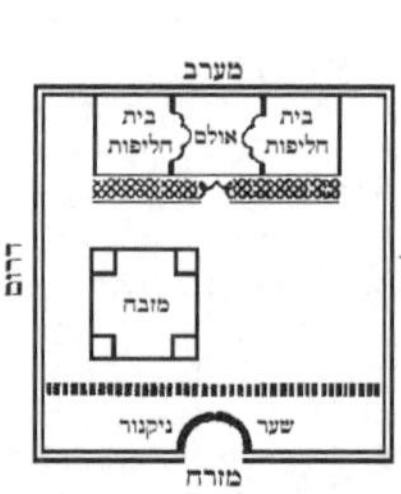

מאן שמעת ליה [דאמר] כו'. דקתני בפירקא דבתרייה (דף מג:): שחטו וקיבל כ] במזרק את דמו סמוך לוידויו מיד. אלמא בין האולם ולמזבח צפון הוא לשחיטת קדשי קדשים, דהא פר חטאת הוא. כנגד כל המזבח. כנגד צפונו. ולא מן המזבח והלאה, לא לצד מזרח ולא לצד מערב. ואע"פ שהוא בחלי חלק כא] עזרה הצפוני – לאו כשר הוא לשחיטת חטאת, דבעינן "על ירך המזבח" וליכא. ר' אלעזר מוסיף אף בין האולם ולמזבח. שהוא מערבו של מזבח, ובלבד שיהא כב] (כל) חלק צפונו של עזרה. אבל מזרחו של מזבח לצד שער נקנור שבו נכנסין לעזרה – לא מכשר אפי' חלק צפוני, דקילא קדושתיה, דהוא מקום דריסת ישראל וכהנים, י"א אמה מקום דריסת ישראל מן השער ולפנים, וי"א אמה כג] עד לצד המזבח מקום של *דריסת רגלי הכהנים. רבי מוסיף. אף צפון שבאותן עשרים ושתים אמה של צד מזרח שהן דריסת ישראל וכהנים. ה"ג: אבל מן החליפות ולפנים הכל מודים שפסול. **)ומיהו בית כד] חליפות האולם עודף רוחבו על רוחב ההיכל ט"ו אמה לצפון וט"ו לדרום. והוא נקרא בית החליפות, כה] שהיה בכותל האולם מאחריו חלונות שהכהנים מגניעין שם את סכיניהם, [וסכין קרי חילוף בלשון ערבי]. הכי תנן לה במסכת מדות. ואשמועי' דמאחורי האולם לאו צפון הוא לשחיטת קדשי קדשים, דכיון דלא מתחזי מזבח התם לא קרינן כו] "על ירך". אע"ג דמכשרינן ליה לקמן (דף כו.) לשחיטת קדשים קלים, לקדשי קדשים פסול. ותסברא דר' אלעזר היא ולא רבי. דלא מודה רבי בבין האולם ולמזבח דליהוי צפון. כז] השתא רבי כו'. האי מוסיף דקתני אדר' יוסי קאי, אדר' אלעזר לא קאי. והא [ע"כ] אדר' אלעזר [נמי] אמרה למילתיה, כח] דעל כרחך כיון דמכשר מקום קדושה קלה לשחוט שם – מקום קדושה חמורה לכ"ש. אנן הכי קאמרי'. הא (ח) דשקליה ליה מרבי – לאו משום דרבי לא מכשיר בין האולם ולמזבח לשחיטת חטאת. אלא הכי קשיא לן: כיון דרבי נמי מכשיר (לצפון) לצפון שבמזרח, למה לו לשוחטו אצל האולם? לוקמיה בצפון המזרחי סמוך לכניסתן לעזרה, דהא לאו אורח ארעא לאקרובי להיכל. אלא מאי ר"א היא. ומשום דלא מכשר מקום דריסת ישראל וכהנים, כט] ושחיטת חטאת מטי ליה להתם – אכתי תקשה לך, דהוה מצי לאוקמי מקיר מזבח צפוני עד כותל עזרה צפוני, דהוי צפון לדברי הכל! אלא מאי אית לך למימר. עליה. משום חולשה דכ"ג. שכל עבודות ל] (פנים) של יום הכיפורים עליו ותש כחו, להכי ממטינן ליה להתם, לפי שהוא צריך להכניס דמו להיכל ולהזות ולא יכבד עליו משוי המזרק והדם. ה"נ. כי מוקמת ליה כרבי, הא טעמא איכא. תרומת הדשן. דכתיב: "והרים את הדשן". בכל בקר היה נוטל לא] מחתה מן הגחלים המאוכלות הפנימיות, ויורד ונותנה במזרחו של כבש בדרומו של מזבח, כדכתיב: "ושמו אצל המזבח", ושם היה נבלע במקומו. והיא היתה בכל יום ראשונה לכל העבודות. מתחילת עבודה. שזו תחילת עבודת יום לב] הוא. הא אמרת פסלה לינה. ולינה בעמוד השחר תליא, דכתיב "עד בקר". הא אמר מכאן ועד י' ימים. ואת תלית טעמא משום דקדיש בתחלת עבודת יום זה. ולינה דרבנן. לינה זו שמועיל בקידוש, שאין המים בפניו – מדרבנן הוא דגזור בה שלא תזלזל בלינה. ומודה רבי שכשהעלו לכיור מן הבור מקרות הגבר שהוא זמן תרומת הדשן כדאמרינן בפרק קמא דיומא (דף כ.), דמשום האי פורתא לא פסלה לינה בקידוש, דלא מפקי אינשי אדעתייהו לג] דדמי כמה שקידש ביום. וראה רבי יוחנן דבריו. של ר' אלעזר נכונים במקדש ידיו בתחלת עבודת היום דלא פסל בה לינה, ולא במי שקידש בלילה להקטיר חלבים שהוא סוף עבודת יום אתמול. ראוהו אחיו שירד. משנה היא במסכת תמיד (פרק ב מ"א) בתורם את הדשן שירד מן המזבח והמחתה של תרומת הדשן בידו. מיהרו וקידשו כו'. להוציא את הדשן שבמקום המערכה, או לסלקו לתפוח שבאמצע המזבח. והכי תנן בה התם: החלו מעלין באפר על גבי התפוח. וקא סלקא דעתך בכהנים שעבדו כל הלילה קאי, ומקודשי ידים ורגלים היו, וצריכין לחזור ולקדש עכשיו, לד] *שתמשך עבודה זו עד היום ויפסל קידוש הלילה בלינת עמוד השחר, *ויועיל להם קידוש זה של אחר קרות הגבר. בשלמא

*) כין נפון ולדוס נ"ק **) נ"ל ומהו נ"ק

תוספות

מיתיבי ראוהו אחיו הכהנים כו'. למאי דס"ד לה] דלא מיירי בכהני חדתי, יש תימה: דלא פריך מרישא, דתני לו] קידוש בתורם את הדשן! ויש לומר דפשיטא דההוא דתרומת הדשן הוי בכהני חדתי. *וקשה קשה: דלמאי ס"ד *דלא הוו חדתי, דבמתניתין דתמיד (דף לג.) משמע דכולהו הוו חדתי, שהעזרה היתה ננעלת והם היו בחוץ ממקום שהיו ישנים שם בבית לז] המוקד! [הגה"ה: ויש לומר, דסלקא דעתיה דמאן דלא פסיל בלינה לא פסיל בהיסח הדעת, ומאן דפסיל בהאי – פסיל בהאי. והני כהני הוה להו היסח הדעת, שהיו ישנים בבית המוקד. ע"כ הגה"ה].

בִּשְׁלָמָא לְאַבַּיֵי דְּמוֹקֵים לָהּ כְּרַבִּי, וּמוֹדֵי רַבִּי דְּמִקְּרוֹת הַגֶּבֶר עַד צַפְרָא לָא פָּסְלָה לִינָה, הָא מַנִּי? רַבִּי הִיא. אֶלָּא לְרָבָא, דְּמוֹקֵים לָהּ כְּרַבִּי אֶלְעָזָר בְּרַבִּי שִׁמְעוֹן, אֲבָל לְרַבִּי – מִקְּרוֹת הַגֶּבֶר עַד צַפְרָא פָּסְלָה לִינָה, הָא מַנִּי? אִי רַבִּי – א] פָּסְלָה לִינָה, אִי רַבִּי אֶלְעָזָר בְּר"ש – הָא אָמַר: אֲפִי' מִיכָּן וְעַד עֲשָׂרָה יָמִים אֵינוֹ צָרִיךְ לְקַדֵּשׁ! לְעוֹלָם כְּרַבִּי אֶלְעָזָר בְּרַבִּי שִׁמְעוֹן, וְהָכָא בְּמַאי עָסְקִינַן – בְּכָהֲנֵי חֲדָתֵי.§ אִיבַּעְיָא לְהוּ: יְצִיאָה מַהוּ שֶׁתּוֹעִיל בְּקִידּוּשׁ יָדַיִם וְרַגְלַיִם? אִם תִּימְצֵי לוֹמַר לִינָה לָא פָּסְלָה – דְּלָא פָּרֵישׁ, אֲבָל יְצִיאָה דְּפָרֵישׁ – אַסּוּחֵי מַסַּח דַּעְתֵּיהּ, אוֹ דִלְמָא כֵּיוָן דִּבְיָדוֹ לַחֲזוֹר – לָא מַסַּח? ת"ש: אקִידֵּשׁ יָדָיו וְרַגְלָיו וְנִטְמְאוּ – מַטְבִּילָן, וְאֵין צָרִיךְ לְקַדֵּשׁ. יָצְאוּ – הֲרֵי הֵן בִּקְדוּשָּׁתָן. ביָצְאוּ יָדָיו לָא קָמִיבָּעֲיָא לָן, כִּי קָמִיבָּעֲיָא לָן יָצָא כָּל גּוּפוֹ, מַאי? ת"ש: *גשֶׁלֹּא רָחוּץ יָדַיִם וְרַגְלַיִם *מְקַדֵּשׁ בִּכְלֵי שָׁרֵת בִּפְנִים. דקִידֵּשׁ בִּכְלֵי שָׁרֵת בַּחוּץ, אוֹ בִּכְלֵי חוֹל בִּפְנִים, *האוֹ שֶׁטָּבַל בְּמֵי מְעָרָה וְעָבַד – עֲבוֹדָתוֹ פְּסוּלָה. טַעְמָא, דְּקִידֵּשׁ בִּכְלֵי שָׁרֵת בַּחוּץ, הָא קִידֵּשׁ בִּפְנִים וְיָצָא – עֲבוֹדָתוֹ כְּשֵׁרָה. דִּלְמָא קִידֵּשׁ בִּכְלֵי שָׁרֵת בַּחוּץ הֵיכִי דָּמֵי – כְּגוֹן דְּאַפֵּיק יָדָיו לְבַר וְקִידֵּשׁ; (הָא קִידֵּשׁ בִּפְנִים וְיָצָא, דְּאַפֵּיק יְדֵיהּ לְבַר – ב] כְּשֵׁרָה.) אֲבָל יָצָא כָּל גּוּפוֹ תִּיבָּעֵי לָךְ! א"ל רַב זְבִיד לְרַב פַּפָּא: ת"ש, ויָצָא חוּץ ג] לִמְחִיצַת חוֹמַת הָעֲזָרָה, אִם לִשְׁהוֹת – טָעוּן טְבִילָה, אִם לְפִי שָׁעָה – טָעוּן קִידּוּשׁ יָדַיִם וְרַגְלַיִם! א"ל: הָכָא בְּמַאי עָסְקִינַן – כְּגוֹן שֶׁיָּצָא לְהָסֵךְ רַגְלָיו וּלְהַטִּיל ד] מַיִם. הָא בְּהֶדְיָא קָתָנֵי לָהּ: *זכָּל הַמֵּסֵךְ רַגְלָיו – טָעוּן טְבִילָה, וְכָל הַמַּטִּיל מַיִם – טָעוּן קִידּוּשׁ יָדַיִם וְרַגְלַיִם! תָּנֵי וַהֲדַר מְפָרֵשׁ. ות"ש: פָּרָה, רַבִּי חִיָּיא בַּר יוֹסֵף אָמַר: מְקַדֵּשׁ בִּכְלֵי שָׁרֵת בִּפְנִים וְיוֹצֵא, וְרַבִּי יוֹחָנָן אָמַר: אֲפִי' בַּחוּץ, וַאֲפִי' בִּכְלֵי חוֹל, וַאֲפִי' בִּמְקֵידָה שֶׁל חֶרֶס. אָמַר רַב פַּפָּא: שָׁאנֵי פָּרָה, הוֹאִיל וְכָל מַעֲשֶׂיהָ בַּחוּץ לָא פָּסְלָה בָּהּ יְצִיאָה. אִי הָכִי, לָמָּה לִי דִּמְקַדֵּשׁ? כְּעֵין עֲבוֹדָה *פְּנִים. אִיבַּעְיָא לְהוּ: טוּמְאָה מַהוּ שֶׁתּוֹעִיל לְקִידּוּשׁ יָדַיִם וְרַגְלַיִם? אִם תִּימְצֵי לוֹמַר יְצִיאָה לָא פָּסְלָה – דְּגַבְרָא חֲזֵי, אֲבָל הָכָא דְּגַבְרָא לָא חֲזֵי – אַסּוּחֵי מַסַּח דַּעְתֵּיהּ. אוֹ דִלְמָא כֵּיוָן דַּהֲדַר חֲזֵי – ה] [דָּק לֵיהּ] וְלָא מַסַּח דַּעְתֵּיהּ? ת"ש: קִידֵּשׁ יָדָיו וְרַגְלָיו וְנִטְמְאוּ – מַטְבִּילָן, וְאֵין צָרִיךְ לְקַדֵּשׁ. נִטְמְאוּ יָדָיו – לָא מִיבָּעֲיָא לָן, [כִּי ו] מִיבָּעֲיָא לָן] נִטְמָא כָּל גּוּפוֹ, תֵּיפוֹק לִי כֵּיוָן דְּבָעֵי לְמֶעֱבַד הַעֲרֵב שֶׁמֶשׁ – אַסּוּחֵי מַסַּח דַּעְתֵּיהּ! חכְּגוֹן דְּאִיטַּמֵּי סָמוּךְ לִשְׁקִיעַת הַחַמָּה. ת"ש: פָּרָה, רַבִּי חִיָּיא בְּרַבִּי יוֹסֵף אָמַר: מְקַדֵּשׁ בִּכְלֵי שָׁרֵת בִּפְנִים וְיוֹצֵא, וְרַבִּי יוֹחָנָן אָמַר: אֲפִילּוּ בַּחוּץ, וַאֲפִילּוּ בִּכְלֵי חוֹל, וַאֲפִילּוּ בִּמְקֵידָה שֶׁל חֶרֶס.

רש"י

בִּשְׁלָמָא לְאַבַּיֵי דְּמוֹקֵי לָהּ. לְהָא דְּר' יוֹחָנָן כְּרַבִּי, וּמוֹדֶה רַבִּי דְּמִקְּרוֹת הַגֶּבֶר וְעַד לְצַפְרָא לֹא פָּסְלָה לִינָה בְּקִידּוּשׁ – הָא מַנִּי (א) נַמִי דְּקָתָנֵי דְּקִידּוּשׁ זֶה לֹא יִפָּסֵל בְּעַמּוּד הַשַּׁחַר, אֲבָל קִידּוּשׁ הַלַּיְלָה יִפָּסֵל – רַבִּי הִיא. אֶלָּא לְרָבָא כו' הָא מַנִּי. שֶׁמַּצְרִיכִין קִידּוּשׁ עַל קִידּוּשׁ, וּמַתִּיר קִידּוּשׁ הַשֵּׁנִי בִּקְרוֹת הַגֶּבֶר. אִי רַבִּי הָא אָמַר פָּסְלָה לִינָה. אַף בָּזֶה שֶׁבִּקְרוֹת הַגֶּבֶר. וְאִי ר' אֶלְעָזָר. אַף הָרִאשׁוֹן לֹא יִפָּסֵל. וְשֵׁנִי זֶה לָמָּה? בְּכָהֲנֵי חֲדָתֵי. שֶׁלֹּא שִׁימְּשׁוּ בַּלַּיְלָה, וְלֹא הָיוּ רְחוּצֵי יָדַיִם וְרַגְלַיִם. יְצִיאָה. חוּץ לָעֲזָרָה, מַהוּ שֶׁתּוֹעִיל, כְּדֶרֶךְ שֶׁפּוֹסֵל בְּכָל הַקֳּדָשִׁים שֶׁקִּדְּשׁוּ בִּכְלִי שָׁרֵת, שֶׁאִם יָצְאוּ נִפְסָלִין בְּיוֹצֵא. דְּלָא פָּרֵישׁ. (ב) לֹא נִבְדַּל ז] מֵעֲבוֹדָה. וְנִטְמְאוּ. הַיָּדַיִם בְּדָבָר שֶׁאֵין טוּמְאָתוֹ מִן הַתּוֹרָה, שֶׁיִּטְמָא גּוּפוֹ, אֶלָּא בְּפִיגּוּל אוֹ בְּנוֹתָר, שֶׁשָּׁנִינוּ בִּפְסָחִי' (דף קכ:) שֶׁמְּטַמְּאִים אֶת הַיָּדַיִם. מַטְבִּילִין. אֶת הַיָּדַיִם ח] לְבַדָּן. יָצְאוּ יָדָיו. שֶׁהוֹשִׁיטָן לַחוּץ. מְקַדֵּשׁ בִּכְלֵי שָׁרֵת. אוֹ כִּיּוֹר אוֹ כְּלִי שָׁרֵת אַחֵר, דִּמְרַבִּינַן לְקַמָּן בִּשְׁמַעְתִּין כָּל כְּלֵי שָׁרֵת לְקִידּוּשׁ. בִּפְנִים. שֶׁהֲרֵי ט] הוּקְבְּעוּ לוֹ מָקוֹם בָּעֲזָרָה, דִּכְתִיב: "וְנָתַתָּ אֶת הַכִּיּוֹר" וגו', וְהָתָם כְּתִיב "וְרָחֲצוּ מִמֶּנּוּ". בִּכְלֵי חוֹל פָּסוּל. דְּ"רָחֲצוּ מִמֶּנּוּ" כְּתִיב, וְכִי אִיתְרַבּוּ שְׁאָר כֵּלִים לְקַמָּן – דּוּמְיָא דִּידֵיהּ אִיתְרַבּוּ. אוֹ שֶׁטָּבַל בְּמֵי מְעָרָה. שֶׁהֵן כְּשֵׁרִין לִטְבִילָה. וְה"ה לְמַיִם חַיִּים, אֶלָּא שֶׁרוֹב טְבִילוֹת בְּמַיִם מְכוּנָּסִין י]. עֲבוֹדָתוֹ פְּסוּלָה. וְלָא אָמְרִי': טְבִילָה דָּבָר חָשׁוּב הוּא, וּמְהַנְּיָא לֵיהּ בִּמְקוֹם קִידּוּשׁ. הָא קִידֵּשׁ בִּפְנִים וְיָצָא יא] כְּשֵׁרִין. דְּאִי ס"ד פְּסוּלָה, הַשְׁתָּא קִידֵּשׁ בִּפְנִים וְיָצָא פְּסוּלָה – קִידֵּשׁ בַּחוּץ מִיבָּעֲיָא? וְכִי יֵשׁ יְצִיאָה גְּדוֹלָה מִזּוֹ? וּמְשַׁנֵּי: דִּילְמָא קִידֵּשׁ בַּחוּץ. דְּאִיצְטְרִיךְ לֵיהּ לְתַנָּא לְמִיתְנֵי *דִּפְסוּלָה. כְּגוֹן דְּאַפֵּיק יְדֵיהּ לְבַר. וְגוּפֵיהּ בִּפְנִים, וְקִידֵּשׁ. דְּאִילּוּ קִידֵּשׁ בִּפְנִים וְהוֹצִיא יָדָיו – תַּנְיָא לְעֵיל: הֲרֵי הֵן בִּקְדוּשָּׁתָן. אֲבָל יָצָא גּוּפוֹ לֹא תִּידוֹק מִינָּהּ. אִם (ג) יב] לְהַשְׁהוֹת טָעוּן טְבִילָה. קס"ד מִשּׁוּם הֶיסַּח הַדַּעַת. הָכָא בְּמַאי עָסְקִינַן. דְּקָתָנֵי: אִם לִשְׁהוֹת טָעוּן טְבִילָה. שֶׁיָּצָא לְהָסֵךְ רַגְלָיו. לִגְדוֹלִים. וּדְכַוָּותֵיהּ סֵיפָא, דְּקָתָנֵי: אִם לְפִי שָׁעָה טָעוּן קִידּוּשׁ – שֶׁיָּצָא לְהַטִּיל מַיִם. דְּאָמְרִינַן בְּסֵדֶר יוֹמָא (דף ל.): מִצְוָה לְשַׁפְשֵׁף בְּיָדוֹ נִיצוֹצוֹת שֶׁעַל גַּבֵּי רַגְלָיו, שֶׁלֹּא יֵרָאֶה כִּכְרוּת שָׁפְכָה, לְפִיכָךְ צָרִיךְ לְקַדֵּשׁ יָדָיו וְרַגְלָיו. בְּהֶדְיָא קָתָנֵי לָהּ. בְּסֵיפָא דְּהַהִיא. פָּרָה. בַּעֲבוֹדַת פָּרָה אֲדוּמָּה, יג] שֶׁהָיָה חוּץ לִירוּשָׁלַיִם בְּהַר הַמִּשְׁחָה. וְיוֹצֵא. אַלְמָא לֹא פָּסַל יְצִיאָה בְּקִידּוּשׁ יָדַיִם וְרַגְלַיִם. יד] כְּעֵין עֲבוֹדָה. שִׁינּוּיָ' הוּא. טוּמְאָה. קס"ד טו] נִטְמְאוּ יָדָיו וְלֹא גּוּפוֹ קָמִיבָּעֲיָא לֵיהּ. את"ל יְצִיאָה לֹא פָּסְלָה. הָתָם הוּא מִשּׁוּם דְּגַבְרָא חֲזֵי לַחֲזוֹר וְלִיכָּנֵס – לָא מַסַּח דַּעְתֵּיהּ, וְלָא מִיפְסַל קִידּוּשׁ בְּהֶיסַּח הַדַּעַת. אוֹ דִלְמָא כֵּיוָן דַּהֲדַר חֲזֵי. עַל יְדֵי *)הַטְּבִילָה, **)דָּק לֵיהּ – מְדַקְדֵּק (ד) טז] בְּקִדּוּשִׁין וְנִזְהָר מִלִּיגַּע יָדָיו בִּדְבַר טִינּוּף, וְלָא מַסַּח דַּעְתֵּיהּ. וְהָא

*) הטבילה הס"ד ואח"כ מ"ה דק ליה כו' נ"ק **) נ"א דקיל

תוספות

יציאה מהו שתועיל בקידוש ידים ורגלים. פירש בקונטרס: כדרך שפוסלת בכל הקדשים שקדשו בכלי, שאם יצאו – נפסלין ביוצא. ואי אפשר לומר כן, אלא כדמפרש טעמא. משום דכיון דפריש – אסוחי מסח דעתיה *מיניה. דמשום קידוש כלי לא מיפסל ביוצא במידי שלא נעשה בו עבודה עדיין, כדמוכח בפ"ק דמנחות (דף ט.) ובפ' "התודה" (שם דף עח) *דאמר: בללה חוץ לחומת העזרה, רבי יוחנן אמר: פסולה, וריש לקיש אמר: כשרה. אלמא *לרבי יוחנן לא פסיל אלא משום יז] (*דס"ד דמאן דלא פסיל בלינה לא פסיל בה הסח הדעת, ומאן דפסיל פסיל בהאי. והני כהני הוו להו הסח הדעת, שהיו ישנים בבית המוקד. הג"ה) עבודה בחוץ, אבל משום יציאה לא. יח] [וכן משמע] בפרק "התכלת" (שם מז.) גבי שתי הלחם, דלא קדוש ליפסל ביוצא אלא בשחיטת הזבח, אע"ג דכבר נתקדש בכלי, דרבי סבירא ליה דתנור מקדש, בפרק "רבי ישמעאל" (שם עב:). ומיהו, יש לדחות: דבאין עם הזבח שאני, דהא נסכים הבאין עם הזבח לא מיפסלי בלינה כי אם בשחיטת הזבח, כדאמר זעירי בפרק "התודה" (שם עט.), ואילו באין בפני עצמן – תנן: קדשו בכלי – נפסלין בלינה. ויש עוד ראיה יט] מהא דתנן במעילה פרק ב' (דף ט.) גבי מנחות ושתי הלחם: קרמו בתנור – הוכשרו ליפסל במחוסר כיפורים ובלינה. כ] אבל יוצא לא קתני. ואע"ג דגבי עופות וזבחים הוה מלי למיתני יוצא אגב כא] *אחרים, לא תני, אגב שתי הלחם ולחם הפנים ומנחות. כב] והא דאמר בפרק "כל שעה" (פסחים לו.) גבי לישה דמנחות: נהי דזריזין ליתא, במקום זריזין איתא – אורחא דמילתא נקט, שדרך לעשותם במקום זריזין. והא דאמר פרק "המזבח מקדש" (לקמן פח.): כלי שרת אין מקדשין ליקרב, אבל מקדשין ליפסל – היינו בטבול יום ובמחוסר כיפורים ובלינה, אבל לא ביוצא. ול"ע *מה שפירש בקונטרס פ' "שתי מדות" (מנחות פז:) גבי שלחן: אבל מקדשין ליפסל בלינה וביוצא. ולקמן בסוף "המזבח מקדש" (דף פח.) פירש בקונט': אבל מקדשין ליפסל ביוצא – אם יצא חוץ לקלעים, או נגע בו טבול יום. והא כג] *דאמר פרק "שתי הלחם" (מנחות לה:): [א' שתי הלחם וא'] לחם הפנים, לישתן ועריכתן בחוץ, אלמא מדת יבש לא נתקדשה. וכן בסוף "כל המנחות באות מצה" (שם סג.) דריש ר"ש: "תנור" "תנור" שתי פעמים, שתהא אפייתן בתנור ושיהא הקדשן בתנור. ופריך, והתנן, ר"ש אומר: לעולם הוי רגיל לומר שתי הלחם ולחם הפנים כשרות בעזרה וכשירות בבית פאגי – לאו משום דאי נתקדשה הוה מיפסלא ביוצא, אלא משום דדבר מכוער להוציא לחוץ לאחר שנתקדשה. ואם תאמר: וכיון דבקדושת כלי לא מיפסלא ביוצא, מנחת כהנים וחביתי כ"ג דלית בהו קמילה אימתי מיפסלי ביוצא? ושמא באותן מועיל קידוש כלי. כד] ומהאי טעמא יתכן פי' הקונט' דהכא.

קידש בכלי שרת בחוץ כו'. כה] תימה: דמשמע הא הכניס בכלי שרת בפנים וקידש – עבודתו כשרה. אלמא לא מיפסלא ביציאת המים! כו] וי"ל: דלא שייך הסח הדעת במים כמו בידים. ועוד: דאין כלי מקדש ליפסל ביוצא אלא בפנים, *)כדמשמע בההיא דסוכה (דף נ.). דפריך: וניתי במקודשת. ועוד: כדפירשנו, כז] דאין כלי מקדש ליפסל ביוצא עד שנעשית מלוותו, והיינו הקידוש, כמו מנחה עד שעת קמילה. כח] ולכן מיבעיא ליה בקידוש ידים ורגלים טפי מבמים. **כל** המטיל מים בעי קידוש ידים ורגלים. תימה: דתיפשוט מהכא דאין יציאה מועלת, דמשמע: כט] הא בחנם לא פסלה יציאה! וי"ל: דודאי אי נפיק בשעת עבודה לא מיפסל בהכי, כיון דאין שוהא אלא מעט. מי

*) ועיין נ"ק

עין משפט נר מצוה

מו א מיי' פ"ה מהלכות ביאת מקדש הלכה ו:
מז ב מיי' שם הלכה ה:

גי' הל"ק מיניה וס"ד דמאן דלא פסיל בלינה פסיל בהסח הדעת אבל משום קידוש כלי כו'

ליתא שם ובאמת בסוכה נ. ד"ה ואי לא מייתי אלא האי דפ"ק דמנחות

דבכל בחוץ ולא משום יוצא רש"ק. וגי' הל"ק אלא משום עבודה בחוץ אבל משום יציאה לא וכפ' התכלת גבי שתי הלחם נמי משמע דלא כו' והג"ה זו קיימא על כל כאן ושייך לעיל קידוש כלי כו'

מח ג ד מיי' שם הל' י:
מט ה מיי' שם הל' יח:
נ ו ז מיי' שם הל' ה:
נא ח מיי' שם הלכה ו:

הגהות הב"ח

(א) רש"י ד"ה בשלמא וכו' הא מני נמי הוא דקתני ושני יפסל הס"ד: (ב) ד"ה דלא פריש לא נבדל. נ"ב ופירוש לקמן דף יט ע"ב מבואר באריכות דר"ש פליג אף בחוץ מקריב רק בלא יצא ממקדש אינו פוסל בלינה ולא פריש לכהן היינו לא פריש ממקדש וק"ל ול"ע: (ג) ד"ה אם להשהות טעון: (ד) ד"ה דק ליה כו' מדקדק בקידוש ונזהר:

תוספתא דמנחות פ"א

נ"ל כיצד וכו"ה בתוספ' שם [לקמן כח.]

דפסולה כגון כו' הס"ד נ"ק

אחרינא לא נ"ק

יומא כח. [מנחות ק.]

ורש"י שלפנינו שם לא פי' כלום ואפשר שכך היה הגירסא לפני התוספות

נ"ל דלייק פ' שתי הלחם אמרת לישתן כו' נ"ק

ר"ל אפילו

רש"ק מ"ז

גליון הש"ס

גמרא ת"ש פרה. עיין פ"ד דפרה משנה א בהרע"ב ותוס' יו"ט:

נ"א בעינן

שיטה מקובצת

א] רבי הא אמר פסלה: ב] לבר עבודתו כשרה: ג] חוץ לחומת העזרה: ד] ולהטיל מימיו: ה] חזי דק ליה: ו] כי קא מבעיא לן: ז] נבדל מן העבודה: ח] הידים לבד הס"ד: ט] שהרי הוקבע לו: י] מכונסין וקמ"ל דעבודתו פסולה והד"א: יא] ויצא כשרה: יב] לשהות: יג] אדומה שהיתה: יד] כעין עבודה הס"ד ומה"ד למה לי דמקדש. לקדש בכלי חול ובכלי שרת למה לי דמקדש הס"ד: טו] קס"ד שנטמאו: טז] מדקדק בקידושו: יז] מתיבת הס"ד עד תיבת עבודה שייך לע"א אחר הג"ה נמחק: יח] לא

כן משמע: יט] ראיה וכן משמע בפ"ב דמעילה גבי מנחות כו' עד לא קתני ויש דוחין ראיה זו שהרי גבי חטאת קתני ומועלין בהן משהוקדשו (קדשו בכלי) [נמלקו] הוכשרו לפסול בטבול יום ולא קתני יוצא אע"ג דאמת הוא דמיפסל ביוצא ומיהו מ"מ יש להביא ראיה מדלא תניא במנחות ש"מ דלא פסלה בהו קדושת כלי ליפסל ביוצא דאי אמרת בשלמא במנחות דוקא איכא למימר אגב דלא תניא במנחות לא תניא בחטאת אע"ג דמיפסלא ביוצא אלא אי מיפסלא ביוצא אמאי משייר הכא והכא אלא ודאי קדושת כלי לא מהני ליפסל ביוצא: כ] ובלינה ואילו יוצא: כא] אגב אחריני: כב] ומנחות אלא אי פסלא ביוצא במנחות אמאי משייר ליה הכא והכא. מהר"פ: כג] והא דדייק פרק שתי הלחם אמרת לישתן ועריכתן: כד] כלי. כדאמרינן בפ"ב דמעילה ושאין לו מתירין משיקדש בכלי: כה] תימה הכא משמע הא הכנים הכלי שרת בפנים כו' אלמא לא פסלא יציאה במים וכ"ש בקידוש דהא לעיל איבעיא לן לר' אלעזר בר' שמעון דאמר אין לינה מועלת בקידוש אם מועלת במי כיור: כו] וי"ל כו' וא"ת מ"מ דייקינן מיניה דווקא דקידש בחוץ אבל (הכנים) [הוציא] הכלי והמים מבחוץ (מבחוץ) [לחוץ] וחזר והכניסו וקידש מבפנים שפיר דמי אלמא לא פסיל יציאה במים וכ"ש קידוש דהא לעיל מבעיא לן לר' אלעזר דאמר אין לינה פוסלת בקידוש אם מועלת במי כיור וי"ל דשאני יוצא לפי שקדושת הכלי לא מהני ליפסל ביוצא כדמוכח בפ"ק דמנחות דאמרינן בללה חוץ לחומה כשרה ור' יוחנן פוסל כו' כמו שכתבו התוס' לעיל והא דקא בעי הכא אי יציאה פסלה בקידוש אי לא משום היסח הדעת הוא אבל במים לא שייך טעם זה וקשה דהטעם של היסח הדעת לא איצטריך אלא לר"א אבל לרבי דאמר לינה פוסלת אם כן יציאה פסלה נמי בקידוש כמו לינה בלא טעמא דהיסח הדעת מדקאמר בבעיא דלעיל ואת"ל דלא פסלה משום דלא פריש יציאה דפריש אסוחי מסח דעתיה אלא למ"ד לינה לא פסלא ואם כן תימה השתא אמאי פסול יוצא מטעם קדושת כלי הא (הוכרחנו) [הוכחנו] דקדושת כלי לא מהניא למפסיל ביוצא כדפרישנא וי"ל דוודאי בקידוש ידים ורגלים מהני קדושת ביוצא משום דכיון דקידש ונעשית מצותו מהניא קדושה בכלי שרת ליפסל ביוצא מידי דהוי אמנחה לאחר קמיצה שפסולה ביוצא אבל מי כיור לא פסלא ביוצא כדמשמע מדיוקא כדפרשינן משום דעדיין לא נעשית מצותו שלא נעשה מהם עדיין קידוש ידים ועוד יש לפרש דוודאי במי כיור מהני קדושת כלי ליפסל מיד ביוצא כמו במנחות שאינן נקמצות והא דמשמע הכא מדיוקא דאם הכנים בפנים וקידש כשר היינו משום דקדשינהו בחוץ לא מיפסלא ביוצא עד דקלטינהו מחיצות כדמוכח בסוכה. עכ"ה מהר"פ: כז] כדפרשנו לעיל: כח] קמיצה ולהכי מבע"ל: כט] דמשמע דוקא משום הטלת מים הא בחנם כו' וי"ל דלאוקמי בשעת עבודה דוודאי אי נפיק כו' אלא מעט כיון דעסיק בעבודה לא מסח דעתיה וכי קא מבעיא לן בין עבודה לעבודה אבל אין לאוקמי באמצע העבודה דזה לא תמצא שיצא לשהות זמן מרובה בתוך העבודה:

תיבת

נב א מיי' פ"ה מהלכות פרה הלכה יד:
נג ב מיי' פ"ה מהלכות ביאת מקדש הלכה יח:

תגיגה כג: ע"ש יומא ב. פרה פ"ג מ"ז ע"ש

וְהָא פָּרָה, דְּטַמּוּיֵי מְטַמְּינַן לֵיהּ, דִּתְנַן: *אמְטַמְּאִין הָיוּ הַכֹּהֵן הַשּׂוֹרֵף אֶת הַפָּרָה וּמַטְבִּילִין אוֹתוֹ, לְהוֹצִיא מִלִּבָּן שֶׁל צְדוֹקִין, שֶׁהָיוּ אוֹמְרִים בִּמְעוֹרָבֵי שֶׁמֶשׁ הָיְתָה נַעֲשֵׂית; ש"מ, לָא פָּסְלָה בָּהּ א] (מַחֲשֶׁבֶת) טוּמְאָה! שָׁאנֵי פָּרָה, הוֹאִיל ב] דִּטְבוּל יוֹם לָא פָּסֵיל בָּהּ. אִי הָכִי, לָמָּה לִי דִּמְקַדֵּשׁ? כְּעֵין עֲבוֹדָה [בָּעֵינַן] אִיבַּעְיָא לְהוּ: מַהוּ לְקַדֵּשׁ יָדָיו ג] [וְרַגְלָיו] בַּכִּיּוֹר? °"מִמֶּנּוּ" אָמַר רַחֲמָנָא — וְלֹא בְּתוֹכוֹ, אוֹ דִּלְמָא אֲפִילּוּ בְּתוֹכוֹ? אָמַר רַב נַחְמָן בַּר יִצְחָק, תָּא שְׁמַע: *אוֹ שֶׁטָּבַל בְּמֵי מְעָרָה וְעָבַד — עֲבוֹדָתוֹ פְּסוּלָה. הָא מֵי כִּיּוֹר דּוּמְיָא דְּמֵי מְעָרָה וְעָבַד — עֲבוֹדָתוֹ כְּשֵׁרָה. בלָא, מֵי מְעָרָה אִיצְטְרִיכָא לֵיהּ, שֶׁלֹּא תֹּאמַר: כָּל גּוּפוֹ טוֹבֵל בָּהֶן, יָדָיו וְרַגְלָיו לֹא כָּל שֶׁכֵּן? אָמַר רַבִּי חִיָּיא בַּר יוֹסֵף: מֵי כִיּוֹר נִפְסָלִין לְמַתִּירִין כְּמַתִּירִין, ד] לְאֵבָרִים כְּאֵבָרִים. רַב חִסְדָּא אָמַר: אַף לְמַתִּירִין אֵין נִפְסָלִין אֶלָּא בְּעַמּוּד הַשַּׁחַר, כְּאֵבָרִין. ה] וְרַבִּי יוֹחָנָן אָמַר: כִּיּוֹר, כֵּיוָן שֶׁשִּׁקְעוּ — שׁוּב אֵין מַעֲלֵהוּ. לְמֵימְרָא דְּלַעֲבוֹדַת לַיְלָה נַמִּי לָא חֲזֵי? *וְהָאָמַר רַבִּי אַסִּי אָמַר רַבִּי יוֹחָנָן מִשְּׁמֵיהּ דְּאִילְפָא: כִּיּוֹר שֶׁלֹּא שִׁקְעוּ מִבָּעֶרֶב — מְקַדֵּשׁ מִמֶּנּוּ לַעֲבוֹדַת לַיְלָה, וּלְמָחָר אֵינוֹ מְקַדֵּשׁ! מַאי "אֵינוֹ מַעֲלֵהוּ" נַמִּי דְּקָאָמַר — לַעֲבוֹדַת יוֹם, אֲבָל לַעֲבוֹדַת לַיְלָה חֲזֵי. [אִי הָכִי] הַיְינוּ דְּרַבִּי חִיָּיא בַּר יוֹסֵף! אִיכָּא

(שמות ל) (לעיל כ:) (לעיל כ.)

רש"י

וְהָא פָּרָה דְּטַמּוּיֵי מְטַמְּאִינַן לֵיהּ. אַחַר קִידּוּשׁ זֶה, ו] כִּדְתְנַן כו'. וּטְבִילָה זוֹ בְּהַר הַמִּשְׁחָה הָיְתָה, וְהָכִי תְּנַן לָהּ בְּמַסֶּכֶת פָּרָה (פ"ג מ"ו), וְאַחַר טְבִילָתוֹ מִיָּד הוּא מְסַדֵּר מַעֲרַכְתָּהּ וְשׂוֹרְפָהּ. אַלְמָא, אַחַר הַקִּידּוּשׁ הַזֶּה הָיְתָה, וש"מ לָא פָּסְלָה ז] לָהּ טוּמְאָה. יֵ"שׁ חִסָּרוֹ"ן בַּסְּפָרִי"ם, וְנִרְאֶה לִי הַגִּירְסָא הָכִי: שָׁאנֵי פָּרָה הוֹאִיל וּטְבוּל יוֹם כָּשֵׁר בָּהּ ח] טוּמְאָה לֹא פְּסָלָהּ בְּקִידּוּשִׁין שֶׁלָּהּ. אִי הָכִי לָמָּה לִי דִּמְקַדֵּשׁ. הוֹאִיל וְאֵין קִידּוּשׁ כִּשְׁאָר (א) קִידּוּשׁ עֲבוֹדָה. בְּכִיּוֹר. שֶׁיַּכְנִיס יָדָיו וְרַגְלָיו בְּתוֹכוֹ. הָא כִּיּוֹר דּוּמְיָא דִּמְעָרָה. וְהֵיכִי דָּמֵי — כְּגוֹן שֶׁנִּכְנַס לְתוֹכוֹ. מֵי מְעָרָה אִיצְטְרִיךְ לֵיהּ. כְּלוֹמַר, לְעוֹלָם דִּכְוָותֵיהּ בְּכִיּוֹר נַמִּי פָּסוּל. וְהַאי דְּנָקַט מֵי מְעָרָה — אִיצְטְרִיךְ, סד"א: הוֹאִיל וּטְבִילָה מְעַלַּיְיתָא הִיא — עֲדִיפָא הִיא מִכִּיּוֹר, שֶׁהֵן שְׁאוּבִין, וְקִידּוּשׁ אֵין כָּאן וּטְבִילָה אֵין כָּאן. אֲבָל הָכָא — טְבִילָה אִיכָּא, קָמַשְׁמַע לָן. ה"ג: אָמַר רַבִּי חִיָּיא בַּר יוֹסֵף מֵי כִיּוֹר נִפְסָלִין לְמַתִּירִין כְּמַתִּירִין לְאֵבָרִים כְּאֵבָרִים וְרַב חִסְדָּא אָמַר אַף לְמַתִּירִין אֵין נִפְסָלִין אֶלָּא בְּעַמּוּד הַשַּׁחַר כְּאֵבָרִים. מֵי כִיּוֹר. לְפִי זְמַן ט] עֲבוֹדָה שֶׁהַקִּידּוּשׁ צָרִיךְ לָהּ הָוֵי זְמַן מֵימָיו לִיפָּסֵל. אִם עֲבוֹדַת [מַתִּיר הוּא, כְּגוֹן עֲבוֹדַת] דָּם אוֹ קְמָצִים שֶׁנִּפְסָלִים בְּבֹא הַלַּיְלָה עֲלֵיהֶם, כִּדְאָמְרִי' בְּ"אֵיזֶהוּ מְקוֹמָן" (לקמן דף נו.): מִנַּיִן לְדָם שֶׁנִּפְסָל בִּשְׁקִיעַת הַחַמָּה וכו' — מֵי כִיּוֹר נִפְסָלִין בִּשְׁקִיעַת הַחַמָּה, אִם לֹא נִשְׁקַע הַכִּיּוֹר בַּבּוֹר לִפְנֵי שְׁקִיעַת הַחַמָּה — נִפְסָלִים מֵימָיו לְקַדֵּשׁ עוֹד י] מֵהֶם לְצוֹרֶךְ עֲבוֹדַת יוֹם מָחָר. אֲפִי' שִׁיקְעוּ קוֹדֶם עַמּוּד הַשַּׁחַר הָעוֹשֶׂה לִינָה בְּכָל מָקוֹם — אֵינוֹ מוֹעִיל לוֹ, שֶׁלְּפִי עֲבוֹדָתוֹ הוּא חֲשׁוּבוֹ. וְכֵן אִם שִׁקְעוּ לִפְנֵי שְׁקִיעַת הַחַמָּה וְהֶעֱלֵהוּ בַּלַּיְלָה, מִכֵּיוָן שֶׁמִּלְּאוּ הַלַּיְלָה שָׁעָה אַחַת חוּץ לַבּוֹר — נִפְסְלוּ מֵימָיו לַעֲבוֹדַת הַיּוֹם. לְאֵבָרִים כְּאֵבָרִים. לְקַדֵּשׁ מֵהֶן לַעֲבוֹדַת הֶקְטֵר חֲלָבִים — נִפְסָלִין בְּעַמּוּד הַשַּׁחַר, כְּמוֹ יא] שֶׁאֵבָרִים נִפְסָלִין בְּלִינַת עַמּוּד הַשַּׁחַר, כִּדְכְתִיב: "עַד בֹּקֶר". אֲבָל כָּל הַלַּיְלָה כְּשֵׁרִין לְקַדֵּשׁ מֵהֶן לַעֲבוֹדַת[א] לַיְלָה. יב] וְאִם שִׁיקְעוּ קוֹדֶם עַמּוּד הַשַּׁחַר מְעַט — כְּשֵׁרִין מֵימָיו לְקִידּוּשׁ עֲבוֹדַת [הַיּוֹם: אַף] לְמַתִּירִין כו' כְּאֵבָרִים. כְּשֵׁם שֶׁאֵין הָאֵבָרִים נִפְסָלִין אֶלָּא בְּעַמּוּד הַשַּׁחַר, אַף כָּל יג] לִינוֹת אֵין פּוֹסְלוֹת מִשּׁוּם קְדוּשָּׁה אֶלָּא בְּעַמּוּד הַשַּׁחַר. וְר' יוֹחָנָן אָמַר כִּיּוֹר כֵּיוָן שֶׁשִּׁקְעוֹ. בַּבּוֹר כְּדֶרֶךְ מִנְהָגוֹ, סָמוּךְ לִשְׁקִיעַת הַחַמָּה. שׁוּב אֵין מַעֲלֵהוּ. כָּל הַלַּיְלָה. וְקס"ד דַּאֲפִי' לַעֲבוֹדַת הַלַּיְלָה יד] קָאָמַר ר' יוֹחָנָן דְּמִיפְּסֵל בָּהּ הַעֲלָאָתוֹ, וְאַתַּרְוַיְיהוּ פָּלֵיג. לַעֲבוֹדַת לַיְלָה. הֶקְטֵר חֲלָבִים. וּלְמָחָר אֵינוֹ מְקַדֵּשׁ. קס"ד דְּאָסוּר לְקַדֵּשׁ הֵימֶנּוּ קָאָמַר, שֶׁנִּפְסָל בִּשְׁקִיעַת הַחַמָּה לַעֲבוֹדַת יוֹם. אַלְמָא כּוּלָּהּ כְּרַבִּי חִיָּיא סְבִירָא לֵיהּ. מַאי אֵינוֹ מַעֲלֵהוּ נַמִּי דְּקָאָמַר. רַבִּי יוֹחָנָן לְעֵיל — לַעֲבוֹדַת יוֹם. מִשּׁוּם פְּסוּל עֲבוֹדַת יוֹם קָאָמַר לָהּ, שֶׁלֹּא יִפָּסְלוּ מֵימָיו לַעֲבוֹדַת יוֹם. וְקָא סָלְקָא דַּעְתָּךְ הַשְׁתָּא [ב]שֶׁהַעֲלָאַת הַלַּיְלָה תְּפָסְלֵם לַעֲבוֹדַת טו] מַתִּיר, כְּר' חִיָּיא. אִי הָכִי הַיְינוּ דְּרַבִּי חִיָּיא. [ג] מַאי "אֵינוֹ מַעֲלֵהוּ" דְּקָאָמַר רַבִּי יוֹחָנָן עֲלָהּ דְּר' חִיָּיא וּדְרַב חִסְדָּא? מַאי אֲתָא לְמֵימַר? הָא רַבִּי חִיָּיא נַמִּי ה"ק! אִיכָּא

תוספות

מי כיור נפסלין למתירין כמתירין. פי': לדם וקומץ נפסלים מימיו בשקיעת טז] [החמה], כמו שהמתירין נפסלין בשקיעת החמה, כדאמר ב"איזהו מקומן" (לקמן דף נו.). כיור כיון ששקעו אין מעלהו. למאי דס"ד השתא דהעלאת לילה יז] פוסלן לכל עבודות, יש תימה: דתיקשי ליה כמה משניות דמסכת תמיד (דף כח.) שהיה מקדש לתרומת הדשן, ואחיו הכהנים שהיו מקדשים כמו כן בלילה! ומיהו, איכא לאוקמינהו כר' אלעזר בר"ש, וכמאן דפשיט לעיל: כמחלוקת בזו כך מחלוקת בזו, יח] והא כרבי. אבל קשה: אכתי היאך היו עושין תרומת הדשן לרבי? וי"ל: בכהנים ישנים, שניעורו כל הלילה ואין צריכין לקדש. ומתני' דיומא (דף כב.) דמוכחא שהיה תרומת הדשן בכהני חדתי, דקאמר עלה דלכך לא יט] הוה פייס בתחילה בתרומת הדשן, משום אונס שינה — כר' אלעזר בר"ש. אי נמי י"ל: שהיה להם מים בכלי שרת אחר כדי קידוש של תרומת הדשן. ועוד יש לומר: דמקידוש תרומת הדשן לא קשיא מידי, דפסול עבודת לילה דרבנן. ויש עוד טעם להכשיר בתרומת הדשן טפי[ד] מבכולה לילה, כדפירש בקונטרס בסמוך. עוד יש לומר: דניחא ליה למיפרך מדר' יוחנן אדר"י טפי ממתניתין דתמיד, משום דאיכא לדחויי דסבירא ליה למתני' דמקרות הגבר עד לפרא לא פסלה לינה אפי' במים, אע"ג דסוגיא דשמעתין ודאי לאו הכי סבירא. ולהאי פירוש ניחא השתא דלא מצי לאקשויי מברייתא דלעיל דפליגי בה רבי ורבי אלעזר בר"ש, דקתני: קידש בלילה — צריך לקדש ביום, דמשמע: הא בלילה — מיחזי חזי. כיור כיון ששקעו. פירוש: האי דמהני שיקוע למים — היינו קודם שנפסלו. דלאחר שנפסלו אמרי' בפ' "כל שעה" (פסחים לד.) דאין זריעה להקדש. כיור שלא שקעו. השתא ס"ד דלאו דוקא, כ] אלא אפילו שקעו מעלהו [ומקדש] לעבודת לילה. אלא רבותא נקט הכי, אע"פ שלא היה משוקע כא] בשקיעת החמה — כשר לעבודת לילה. אבל לבסוף דמשני ומסיק דאיכא בינייהו גזירת שיקוע — ניחא דנקט שלא שקעו, דאם איתא דשקעו — אין מעלהו עד תרומת הדשן. מאי אין מעלהו דקאמר לעבודת היום. פי': שיהא כשר לקדש, לענין שיועיל לו קידוש לעבודת יום, כגון קומץ ודם. אבל לעבודת לילה, כגון לאיברים — חזי. ופריך: היינו דר' חייא בר' יוסף! ומשני: איכא בינייהו גזרת שיקוע. כלומר, כב] לר"י אסור להעלותו, גזירה שמא יפשע ולא יחזור וישקיענו, דר' יוחנן אית ליה גזירת שיקוע. ולהכי נקט שלא שקעו, דאם שקעו — לא יעלהו עד תרומת הדשן, דלמא פשע. אבל אם לא שקעו, או שקעו והעלהו — מקדש ממנו. ור' חייא בר יוסף לא גזר, וסבירא ליה דמעלהו כל שעה שירצה, ולא חיישינן דלמא פשע. וא"ת: ולמה היו משקעין אותו כלל בערב? כג] היה להם להמתין עד סמוך לעמוד השחר,[ה] כיון שהיו יכולין כד] [להעלות] כל הלילה לקדש לאברים! וי"ל: (דלמא) לא רצו להמתין זמן שיקועו עד סמוך לזמן פסולו, דלמא פשע ולא משקע ליה בעמוד השחר. וה"ה שהיו יכולין לקבוע זמן שיקוע בתחילת הלילה או באמצעה, כה] *) דכדי שיהא זכור בעמוד השחר. אלא לפי שהוא זמן פסול מתירים של דם וקומץ — קבעו זמנו בערב. ולר' יוחנן, אע"פ שעל כו] כרחן יש להן להעלותן לתרומת הדשן — לא דמי, כדפי' בקונטרס [לקמן. וז"ל]: דלא סגיא ליה בלאו קידוש זה שזכה לפיס של תרומת הדשן. ולגזירת שיקוע ליכא למיחש, דכיון שמלאו שקוע והעלהו, ועכשיו הגיע זמן הסמוך לפסולו — לא פשע כז] ליה, והדר משקע ליה. ולא דמי למעלהו בלילה, שמניחו לקדש כהנים הבאין תמיד להקטיר, ואתי למיפשע. וא"ת: ויפסול מימיו, ומה בכך? והא השתא נמי כשמשקעו בעמוד השחר וחוזר ומעלהו ביום — לא היה יכול לקדש במימיו למתירין, דכבר נפסלו, ולא מהני להו זריעה, אלא לאברים היה יכול לקדש, ומי הוא שוטה שיכול לקדש ביום קידוש גמור שיועיל לכל העבודות, והוא עומד ומקדש קידוש שאינו מועיל אלא לאברים? וי"ל: דכיון כח] דקידש להו המים בכלי שרת — מצוה לשומרן כשאר קדשים, שלא יפסלו, כדפי' בקונטרס בהך דשמעתין. אי נמי: כדי שלא יבואו כט] לידי נותר ויטמאו את הידים. וכשמעלין את הכיור ביום — היו מערין מימיו בכלי שרת, דפעמים שמקדשין הרבה כהנים בכל דין, ומי שיש לו לקדש לאברים — מקדש מן המים שבכלי שרת. ושנים עשר כהנים[ו] שהיו מקדשין בבת אחת מן הכיור לצורך התמיד, אף על פי שהיה פייס של תמיד קודם ע"ה כדמוכח במסכת תמיד (פ"א) מ"מ לא היו מקדשין בלילה עד שהיה יום, ומעלין הכיור ונותנים מימיו בכלי שרת, וממלאין אותו מים חדשים ומקדשים מהם, שהרי היה זורק דם התמיד, ונפסלו מימיו למתירין ולא מהני להו זריעה. ל] והא דפסלה להו לינה במים בכולה שמעתין — היינו כרבי ולא כרבי אלעזר בר"ש, למאי דפשיט אילפא לעיל כמחלוקת בזו כך מחלוקת בזו. [וכולהו אמוראי דלעיל מודו דלכל הפחות ספיקא הוי, והכא מפשט פשט. ועוד צריך לומר: דהא דאמר אביי לעיל דמקרות הגבר עד לפרא לא פסלא לינה — היינו קידוש, אבל במים — פוסלת. לא] והאי דפסלה נמי לינה במים — אינו אלא מדרבנן, דכיון דלא פסיל בקידוש — לא פסיל במים, דהכל [אחד], כדאמר לעיל: כמחלוקת בזו כך מחלוקת בזו]. ורבינו פי' בענין אחר, וזה לשונו: ומאי אינו מעלהו דקאמר — משום חשש עבודת היום, שאם יעלהו לעבודת לילה קודם תרומת הדשן — יהיו סבורים העולם לב] שמשקעין אותו בשקיעת החמה שלא יפסלו המים למתרין, וקודם השחר — שלא יפסלו לאברים, לג] ויבא לקדש ממנו למחר למתירין אף על פי שלא היה משוקע כל

*) נ"ל וכלבד שיהא זכור כו'

שיטה מקובצת

[א] תיבת מחשבת נמחק: [ב] הואיל וטבול יום כשר בה לא פסיל בה טומאה בקידוש שלה א"ה: [ג] ידיו ורגליו בכיור: [ד] לאברים כאברים. וא"ת והיכא דשקעו בעמוד השחר למה נפסלים למתירין...

הגהות הב"ח

(א) רש"י ד"ה הואיל כו' וכו' כשאר קידוש הס"ד ואח"כ מ"ה ומקני כשנן עבודה:

שיטה מקובצת

היכי דלשמעו כהנים וליתו...

יד] הלילה. היינו אברים ופדרים קאמר ר"י דמפסל בהעלותו דס"ל דלאברים כמתירין וצריך שיהא משוקע כל הלילה ואתרוייהו: טו] לעבודת מחר כר"ח: טז] בשקיעת החמה: יז] לילה פוסלת: יח] בזו. ורבי יוחנן סבר לה כרבי אבל קשה וכו' לשון מהר"פ במה היו מקדשין בתרומת הדשן והיכא משכחת לה תרומת הדשן לרבי כו' עד ולדידיה המוכני שעשה לכיור לא היה בשביל שלא יפסלו מימיו אלא כדי להשמיע את הקול כדמסיק בסוף שמעתין ואע"ג דאכתי לא ידעינן טעמא דקלא היינו דוקא בשעת שיקוע בראשון דקאמר שלא היו משקעין אותו עד תרומת הדשן והוא היה סבר דבשיקוע לא הוי קלא אבל השתא נאמר לראב"ש שהיה משוקע עד תרומת הדשן והיו מעלין אותו לקדש ממנו ושקיעה משום קלא דהעזרה כי נצטרך בכהני עתיקי ע"כ: יט] לא היה: כ] דלאו דוקא שלא שקעו אלא אפילו שקעו מעלהו: כא] משוקע קודם: כב] כלומר אי שקעו אסור ותיבות לר"י ל"ש ונמחק: כג] בערב ולא היו עד סמוך: כד] שהיו יכולין כל הלילה לקדש לאברים וי"ל דלא רצו: כה] באמצעה בכדי כו] פשע ביה והדר משקע כו' לקדש כל כהנים כו' למיפשע עכ"ל וא"ת: כח] דכיון דקדש יבואו ויטמאו את: ל] זריעה והאי דפסלא בהו לינה: לא] פוסלת ומאי דפסלה נמי לינה מדרבנן וכיון דלא פסיל בקידוש לא פסיל במים דהכל אחד כדאמרן לעיל כמחלוקת בזו כך שלכך משקעין: לג] לאברים ויבואו:

א) נראה דל"ל ומ"מ קשה אם אסרו להעלותו משיקעו כל הלילה תקשה מברייתא לעיל דף יט. דקתני קידש בלילה צריך לקדש א"כ היה מעלהו וכו'.

הגהות צ"ק [א] לילה הס"ד ואח"כ ד"ה אף למתירין כו' בעמוד השחר ואם שיקעו קודם עמוד השחר מעט כשרים מימיו לקידוש עבודת מתירין הס"ד וכל"ל וכן הוא בס"י: [ב] שבהעלאת: [ג] נ"ל ומאי איתו: [ד] מבכולהו כדפי' בקונט' [ה] נ"ל כדי שיהיו יכולין כל הלילה: [ו] היו:

נד א מיי' פ"ה מהל' ביאת מקדש הל' יג:
נה ב מיי' שם הל' יח:

א] אִיכָּא בֵּינַיְיהוּ: גְּזֵירַת שִׁיקּוּעַ. *וְהָאָמַר רַבִּי יוֹחָנָן: קִידֵּשׁ יָדָיו לִתְרוּמַת הַדֶּשֶׁן – לְמָחָר אֵין צָרִיךְ לְקַדֵּשׁ, שֶׁכְּבָר קִידֵּשׁ מִתְּחִילַּת עֲבוֹדָה! ב] בִּשְׁלָמָא לְרָבָא דְּמוֹקֵים לְהַהִיא כְּרַבִּי אֶלְעָזָר בְּרַבִּי שִׁמְעוֹן – הָא כְּרַבִּי. ג] אֶלָּא לְאַבַּיֵי דְּמוֹקֵים לָהּ כְּרַבִּי – קַשְׁיָא דְּרַבִּי אַדְּרַבִּי: מַאי שְׁנָא הָתָם דְּמִשְׁקַע לֵיהּ, וּמַאי שְׁנָא הָכָא דְּלָא מְשַׁקַּע לֵיהּ? ד] דִּמְסַלֵּק לֵיהּ וַהֲדַר מְשַׁקַּע לֵיהּ. ה] אִי הָכִי, לְמָחָר אֵינוֹ מְקַדֵּשׁ, [*אַמַּאי? אֵין צָרִיךְ לְקַדֵּשׁ]. ו] לְמֵימְרָא, דִּלְמַתִּירִין מִיחֲזָא חָזֵי – הַיְינוּ דְּרַב חִסְדָּא! אִיכָּא בֵּינַיְיהוּ: מִצְוַת שִׁיקּוּעַ. מֵיתִיבֵי: *לֹא הָיוּ רוֹאִין אוֹתוֹ וְלֹא שׁוֹמְעִין אֶת קוֹלוֹ, עַד שֶׁשּׁוֹמְעִים קוֹל שֶׁל עֵץ שֶׁעָשָׂה בֶּן קָטִין מוּכְנִי לַכִּיּוֹר, וְהֵן אוֹמְרִים: הִגִּיעַ [עֵת] קִידּוּשׁ יָדַיִם וְרַגְלַיִם מִן הַכִּיּוֹר; מַאי לָאו דִּמְסַלֵּק לֵיהּ? אַלְמָא מְשַׁקַּע לֵיהּ! ז] לָא, דִּמְשַׁקַּע לֵיהּ. אִי דִּמְשַׁקַּע לֵיהּ, מִי מִשְׁתַּמַּע קָלֵיהּ? מְשַׁקַּע לֵיהּ בְּגִילְגְּלָא. לִישָּׁנָא אַחֲרִינָא: דִּמְשַׁקַּע לֵיהּ בְּחוּמְרָתֵיהּ, כִּי הֵיכִי דְּלִישְׁתַּמַּע קָלֵיהּ וְלִשְׁמְעֵי וְלֵיתֵי. וְהָא הֲוָה *גְּבִינִי כָּרוֹז! בֵּי תְרֵי הֵיכְּרֵי הָווּ עָבְדִי, דְּשָׁמַע מֵהַאי – אָתֵי, וְשָׁמַע מֵהַאי – אָתֵי.§ גּוּפָא, *אָמַר רַבִּי יוֹסֵי בְּרַבִּי חֲנִינָא: כָּל אכִּיּוֹר שֶׁאֵין בּוֹ כְּדֵי לְקַדֵּשׁ אַרְבָּעָה כֹּהֲנִים מִמֶּנּוּ – אֵין מְקַדְּשִׁין בּוֹ, שֶׁנֶּאֱמַר: °"וְרָחֲצוּ מִמֶּנּוּ מֹשֶׁה וְאַהֲרֹן וּבָנָיו" וגו'. (שמות מ) מֵיתִיבֵי: בכָּל הַכֵּלִי' מְקַדְּשִׁין, בֵּין שֶׁיֵּשׁ בָּהֶן רְבִיעִי',

בֵּין

רש"י

אִיכָּא בֵּינַיְיהוּ גְּזֵירַת שִׁיקּוּעַ. כְּלוֹמַר, הָא דְּאוֹקִים "אֵין מַעֲלֵהוּ" דְּרַבִּי יוֹחָנָן מִשּׁוּם פְּסוּל עֲבוֹדַת יוֹם – לָא כִּדְקס"ד שֶׁיְּהֵא הַלַּיְלָה פּוֹסְלוֹ לַעֲבוֹדַת הַיּוֹם כְּרַבִּי חִיָּיא. אֶלָּא שֶׁמָּא לֹא יַחֲזוֹר וִישַׁקְּעֶנּוּ, וְנִמְצָא עַמּוּד הַשַּׁחַר פּוֹסְלוֹ לַעֲבוֹדַת מָחָר. [א] וּלְעוֹלָם (אִם שִׁקְּעוֹ קוֹדֶם עַמּוּד הַשַּׁחַר כָּשֵׁר). וְהַיְינוּ דְּלָא נָקַט רַבִּי יוֹחָנָן לִישָּׁנָא דִּפְסוּלָה אֶלָּא לְשׁוֹן אִיסּוּר הַעֲלָאָה, שֶׁלֹּא יִגְרְמוּ לָהֶן לִיפָּסֵל, דְּכֵיוָן דְּקַדֵּשׁ לְהוּ בִּכְלֵי שָׁרֵת – מִצְוָה לְשָׁמְרָן כִּשְׁאָר קָדָשִׁים. וּמִיהוּ בְּהַעֲלָאָה לָא מִיפְסִיל. וּלְקַמָּן פָּרֵיךְ: הַיְינוּ דְּרַב חִסְדָּא, דְּאָמַר: לַיְלָה לָא פָּסֵיל, אֶלָּא עַמּוּד הַשַּׁחַר פּוֹסֵל. וְרַבִּי חִיָּיא לָא אָסַר לֵיהּ לְהַעֲלוֹתוֹ מִשּׁוּם גְּזֵירַת שִׁיקּוּעַ, אֶלָּא ח] דִּבְהַעֲלוֹתוֹ נִפְסָל מִיָּד לַעֲבוֹדַת מַתִּיר, הִלְכָּךְ נָקַט לְשׁוֹן נִפְסָלִין. וְהָאָמַר רַבִּי יוֹחָנָן כו'. אַלְמָא (א) אָמַר שֶׁמַּעֲלֵהוּ לְקַדֵּשׁ לִתְרוּמַת הַדֶּשֶׁן, ט] וְלֹא הִצְרִיךְ לַחֲזוֹר וּלְשַׁקְּעוֹ. וּבִשְׁלָמָא הַעֲלָאָתוֹ לָא קַשְׁיָא לָן, דְּלָא סַגִּי י] בְּלָאו קִידּוּשׁ זֶה שֶׁזָּכָה לְפַיִיס שֶׁל תְּרוּמַת הַדֶּשֶׁן. וְלִגְזֵירַת שִׁיקּוּעַ לֵיכָּא לְמֵיחַשׁ, דְּכֵיוָן שֶׁמְּצָאוֹ מְשׁוּקָּע וְהֶעֱלָהוּ וְעַכְשָׁיו הִגִּיעַ הַזְּמַן הַסָּמוּךְ לִפְסוּלוֹ – לָא פָּשַׁע בֵּיהּ, וַהֲדַר מְשַׁקַּע לֵיהּ. וְלָא דָּמֵי לְמַעֲלֵהוּ בַּלַּיְלָה שֶׁמַּנִּיחוֹ לְקַדֵּשׁ בּוֹ כֹּהֲנִים הַבָּאִים תָּמִיד לְהַקְטִיר, וְאָתֵי לְמִיפְשַׁע בֵּיהּ. אֶלָּא הָא קַשְׁיָא יא] לָךְ: דְּלָא אַיְירֵי בֵּיהּ רַבִּי יוֹחָנָן בְּמִצְוַת שִׁיקּוּעַ, וְנֵימָא דְּנִישְׁקְעֵיהּ! בִּשְׁלָמָא לְרָבָא דְּמוֹקֵי. לְעֵיל הָא מִילְּתָא דְּר' יוֹחָנָן אַלִּיבָּא דְּרַבִּי אֶלְעָזָר, דְּאָמַר אֵין לִינָה מוֹעֶלֶת בְּקִידּוּשׁ – אִיכָּא לְמֵימַר דְּמִשּׁוּם הָכִי לָא חָשׁ יב] לְשִׁיקּוּעוֹ, דְּקָסָבַר רַבִּי אֶלְעָזָר דִּבְמֵי כִּיּוֹר גּוּפַיְיהוּ נַמִּי לָא פָּסְלָה [ב] לִינָה. הָא. דְּאָמַר ר' יוֹחָנָן לְעֵיל אֵין מַעֲלֵהוּ. כְּרַבִּי. אַמְרָהּ, דְּאָמַר לִינָה מוֹעֶלֶת בְּקִידּוּשׁ, וְכָל שֶׁכֵּן בְּמֵי כִּיּוֹר. אֶלָּא לְאַבַּיֵי. יג] דְּאוֹקִים לְעֵיל כְּרַבִּי, קַשְׁיָא דְּרַבִּי אַדְּרַבִּי: לְעֵיל א"ר יוֹחָנָן אַלִּיבָּא דְּרַבִּי לִגְזֵירַת שִׁיקּוּעַ חָיֵישׁ, [ג] וְהָכָא נַמִּי נִשְׁקְעֵיהּ! וְהָכָא לֵיכָּא לְמִיתְלֵי טַעְמָא בְּמוֹדֶה רַבִּי דִּמְקוּרוֹת הַגֶּבֶר עַד נַפְרָא לָא פָּסְלָה לִינָה. דְּבִשְׁלָמָא גַּבֵּי קִידּוּשׁ דִּפְסוּל לִינָה דִּידֵיהּ דְּרַבָּנַן, שֶׁהֲרֵי אֵין הַמַּיִם בָּעוֹלָם – הוּא דְּאִיכָּא לְמֵימַר הָכִי. אֲבָל מֵי כִּיּוֹר דְּהָווּ קָמָן, וּקְדוּשַּׁת כְּלִי עֲלֵיהֶם, וְלִינָה דִּידְהוּ דְּאוֹרַיְיתָא – עַמּוּד הַשַּׁחַר הוּא דְּגָרֵים לֵיהּ. מַאי שְׁנָא הָתָם דִּמְשַׁקַּע לֵיהּ. כְּלוֹמַר, מַאי שְׁנָא גַּבֵּי אֵין מַעֲלֵהוּ דְּחָשׁ לִגְזֵירַת יד] שִׁיקּוּעוֹ, ומ"ש כו'? דִּמְסַלֵּק לֵיהּ וַהֲדַר מְשַׁקַּע לֵיהּ. לְאַחַר קִידּוּשׁ תְּרוּמַת הַדֶּשֶׁן. וְרַבִּי יוֹחָנָן הוּא דְּלָא אַיְירֵי בְּתַקָּנַת מֵי כִּיּוֹר, אֶלָּא בְּהִלְכוֹת קִידּוּשׁ, לְאַשְׁמוּעִינַן דְּמוֹדֵי רַבִּי מְקוּרוֹת הַגֶּבֶר עַד נַפְרָא לָא פָּסְלָה לִינָה. הָכִי גָּרְסִי': אִי הָכִי לְמָחָר אֵינוֹ מְקַדֵּשׁ אֵין צָרִיךְ לְקַדֵּשׁ הַיְינוּ דְּרַב חִסְדָּא כו'. אִי הָכִי, דְּלר' יוֹחָנָן אוֹקְמָא דְּלַיְלָה לָא פָּסֵל, וּלְמָחָר אֵינוֹ מְקַדֵּשׁ, [ד] בִּתְמִיָּה. אַמַּאי. א"ר יוֹחָנָן מִשְּׁמֵיהּ דְּאִילְפָא מְקַדֵּשׁ מִמֶּנּוּ לַעֲבוֹדַת לַיְלָה, וּלְמָחָר אֵינוֹ מְקַדֵּשׁ, דְּשָׁמְעִי' מִינֵּיהּ דְּמִשּׁוּם דְּלָא שִׁיקְּעוֹ טו] בָּעֶרֶב קָא פָּסַל לְהוּ קִידּוּשׁ מָחָר? וּמְשַׁנֵּי: אֵין צָרִיךְ לְקַדֵּשׁ. קָאָמַר, דְּכֵיוָן שֶׁקִּידֵּשׁ לַעֲבוֹדַת לַיְלָה אֵין צָרִיךְ טז] לְמָחָר. וְאַשְׁמְעִי' דְּאֵין לִינָה מוֹעֶלֶת בְּקִידּוּשׁ, וְכִדְרַבִּי אֶלְעָזָר. הַיְינוּ דְּרַב חִסְדָּא. הַשְׁתָּא יז] דְּאוֹקְמָא אֵין מַעֲלֵהוּ דְּר' יוֹחָנָן מִשּׁוּם פְּסוּל עַמּוּד הַשַּׁחַר, אֲבָל לַיְלָה לָא פָּסֵיל – הַיְינוּ דְּרַב חִסְדָּא! אִיכָּא בֵּינַיְיהוּ מִצְוַת שִׁיקּוּעַ. לְר' יוֹחָנָן מִצְוַת שִׁיקּוּעַ מִבָּעֶרֶב, כְּדֵי שֶׁיִּמְצָאֶנּוּ מְשׁוּקָּע בְּקִידּוּשׁ תְּרוּמַת הַדֶּשֶׁן, וִיהֵא נִזְכָּר לַחֲזוֹר וּלְשַׁקְּעוֹ. וְהַיְינוּ דְּקָאָמַר (ג) "כֵּיוָן שֶׁשִּׁקְּעוֹ", אַלְמָא מִבָּעֶרֶב הוּא מְשַׁקַּע לֵיהּ. וּלְרַב חִסְדָּא לָא הֶחֱמִירוּ בּוֹ כָּל כָּךְ, וְאֵין מִצְוַת שִׁיקּוּעוֹ אֶלָּא סָמוּךְ לִזְמַן פְּסוּלוֹ, קוֹדֶם עַמּוּד הַשַּׁחַר. לֹא הָיוּ רוֹאִין אוֹתוֹ כו'. יח] [בְּמִי שֶׁזָּכָה] בִּתְרוּמַת הַדֶּשֶׁן קָמַיְירֵי בְּמַסֶּכֶת תָּמִיד. כְּשֶׁהָיָה נִכְנָס לָעֲזָרָה לְקַדֵּשׁ יָדָיו וְרַגְלָיו לֹא הָיָה מַכְנִיס בְּיָדוֹ לֹא נֵר וְלֹא אֲבוּקָה, אֶלָּא מְהַלֵּךְ לְאוֹר הַמַּעֲרָכָה, וְלֹא הָיוּ רוֹאִין אוֹתוֹ אֶחָיו יט] [הַכֹּהֲנִים] שֶׁהָיוּ בְּבֵית מוֹקֵד, עַד שֶׁשּׁוֹמְעִין כו'. וְהֵן אוֹמְרִים הִגִּיעַ. לַכִּיּוֹר. מְזָרְזִין אֶת עַצְמָן לִהְיוֹת נְכוֹנִים לְהַעֲלוֹת אֵפֶר לַתַּפּוּחַ לְאַחַר שֶׁיָּרַד זֶה מִן הַמִּזְבֵּחַ. כִּדְתְנַן לְעֵיל גַּבֵּי רָאוּהוּ אֶחָיו הַכֹּהֲנִים שֶׁיָּרַד. מַאי לָאו. הַאי שְׁמִיעַת קוֹל הָעֵץ דְּקָתָנֵי – כ] דְּסָלֵיק לֵיהּ לַכִּיּוֹר מִן הַבּוֹר. אַלְמָא מְשׁוּקָּע הֲוָה, וְקַשְׁיָא לֵיהּ לְרַב חִסְדָּא דְּאָמַר לָא מְשַׁקַּע לֵיהּ עַד נַפְרָא! לָא דִּמְשַׁקַּע כא]. הַשְׁתָּא. מִי מִשְׁתַּמַּע קָלֵיהּ. הֲלֹא אֵין מוּכְנִי צָרִיךְ לְשׁוֹקְעוֹ אֶלָּא לְהַעֲלוֹתוֹ, אֲבָל שִׁיקּוּעוֹ – מְשַׁלְשְׁלוֹ לַבּוֹר וְהוּא נוֹפֵל מֵאֵלָיו! וּמְשַׁנֵּי: דִּמְשַׁקַּע לֵיהּ בְּגִלְגְּלָא. כִּי הֵיכִי דְּלִישְׁתַּמַּע קָלֵיהּ וְיִשְׁמְעוּ [ה] הַכֹּהֲנִים הַיְּשֵׁנִים בָּעִיר, וְיֵיתוּ לְפַיֵּיס. דִּתְנַן בְּמַסֶּכֶת תָּמִיד (פרק ג מ"ח): מִירִיחוֹ הָיוּ שׁוֹמְעִין אֶת קוֹל הָעֵץ שֶׁעָשָׂה כו'. בְּחוּמְרָתֵיהּ. = גַּלְגַּלָּא. וְהָא כב] גְּבִינִי כָּרוֹז. שֶׁהָיָה מַכְרִיז: עִמְדוּ הַכֹּהֲנִים לַעֲבוֹדַתְכֶם וּלְוִיִּם לְדוּכָנְכֶם וְיִשְׂרָאֵל לְמַעֲמַדְכֶם. גְּבִינִי. שֵׁם הָאִישׁ. בֵּי תְרֵי הֵיכְּרֵי הָווּ עָבְדִי. שְׁתֵּי הֶיכֵּרוֹת עוֹשִׂין לַדָּבָר. כָּל הַכֵּלִים מְקַדְּשִׁים. מַיִם שֶׁנִּתְקַדְּשׁוּ בָּהֶן, לְקַדֵּשׁ אֶת הַיָּדַיִם וְרַגְלַיִם.

בֵּין

תוספות

כל הלילה, רק בשקיעת החמה ובעמוד השחר. והיינו גזירת שיקוע דקאמר בסמוך, דגזרינן שיהא משוקע כל הלילה עד תרומת הדשן, כדי שידעו העולם שלא שקעוהו מבעוד יום כי אם להיות זכורים על ידי כך שיקוע דסוף כל הלילה, כג] שכשמצאוהו משוקע בשעת תרומת הדשן – יחזרוהו וישקעוהו קודם היום. כי אם יעלוהו לאחר שקיעת החמה – יש לגזור שמא יאמרו כד] שלהכשירו לעבודת מתירין למחר שיקעוהו בשקיעת החמה, וכשר למתירין אף על פי שיעלוהו לאחר שקיעת החמה. ופריך: אי הכי, היינו דרבי חייב ברבי יוסף, שפוסל למתירין בשקיעת החמה! כי לרב חסדא שאינו פוסל למתירין אלא בעמוד השחר – לא איכפת לן במה שיכשירוס למחר למתירין, כי בשיקוע דעמוד השחר מתכשר אפי' למתירים. ומשני: איכא בינייהו גזירת שיקוע דרבי יוחנן גזר [ו] להשהותו בשיקוע משום שיקוע דשקיעת החמה, שאנו צריכין אז לשקעו כדי להזכיר שיקוע דסוף הלילה, שלא יאמרו שאינו להזכיר אלא להכשיר למתירין, ולכך צריך להשהותו עד תרומת הדשן, כדפרישית. ורבי חייא בר יוסף לא גזר. [ז] והא"ר יוחנן קידש ידיו לתרומת כו'. בשלמא לרבא דמוקי ליה להיא כרבי אלעזר בר' שמעון – הא כרבי. *)איכא למימר דסבירא ליה לרבא דלרבי אלעזר ברבי שמעון לא פסלה לינה במי כיור, כמאן דאמר לעיל כמחלוקת בזו כך מחלוקת בזו, ולא כההיא דלא פשיט ליה לעיל. "ולמחר אינו מקדש" דבמילתיה דאילפא – אינו צריך לקדש קאמר, כרבי אלעזר ברבי שמעון. ולא קאי אמי כיור לפוסלם למחר, כי כשרים הם לרבי אלעזר בר"ש. אלא לאביי דמוקי לה כרבי, קשיא דרבי אדרבי: דמאי שנא בהא דכיון דשקעו שוב אינו מעלהו – דמצריך לשקעו כדי להזכיר שישקעוהו בסוף הלילה. ומאי שנא בהא דקאמר דכבר קידש מתחילת עבודה, דמשמע דתרומת הדשן תחלת עבודת היום, שמשם ואילך עסוקים בעבודת היום בלא הפסק, וכל שעה מקדש ועובד כל הבא לעבוד. משם ואילך משמע דלא משקע ליה אחר שהעלהו לתרומת הדשן, שאם כן יש הפסק בדבר! ומשני: הא דקרי ליה תחילת עבודה – לאו משום דלא משקע ליה, דודאי מסלק ליה והדר משקע ליה, וקצת יש תימה בין לפי' זה בין לפירוש אחר לישנא דמסלק ליה, דהא נמי היה יודע דמסלק ליה, ואין קשה לו אלא משיקוע (דבתרא) מאי שנא הכא דמשקע ליה, ומאי שנא התם דלא משקע ליה. אי משקע ליה. שהיה למעלה וכרב חסדא, כה] ומורידין לבור – הלא אין קולו נשמע. וא"ת: ליפני דנשמע קולו דקתני – היינו בהעלותו! וי"ל: היינו [ח] כו] דקא אמר דמשקע ליה בגלגלא (כגון) לבור, והקול שנשמע – היינו בהוליאו מן הבור ומעלהו. ואי בעית אימא: דמשקע [ט] בחומרתיה, דהיה בגלגלא אף השיקוע, כדי להשמיע קול הרבה בהורידו ובהעלותו. **הגה"ה** איכא בינייהו גזירת שיקוע. פירש רש"י: משקעו בערב, שלא ישכח לשקעו בעמוד השחר. אבל לילה אינו פוסלו כלל לעבודת דם למחר אם משקעו בעמוד השחר, ולרבי חייא לילה פוסלו. וקשה: אם כן איכא בינייהו טובא, דלרבי יוחנן לילה אינה פוסלת, ולרבי חייא פוסלת! ועוד, דליפרך מיד: היינו דרב חסדא! ועוד: דבסמוך פריך מכח למחר אינו צריך לקדש, אלמא למתירין חזי, היינו דרב חסדא. משמע דבלאו ההיא דלמחר וכו' לא הוה מצי למפרך מידי! לכך נראה לי: גזירת שיקוע – ואם לא שיקעו יהא פסול מדרבנן לעבודת דם משום כז] לילה, אפילו שקעו בעמוד השחר. ולר' חייא יהא פסול מן התורה. ולכך פריך: למחר אינו צריך לקדש, אלמא אפילו מדרבנן כשרה לעבודת דם, ואין לילה פוסלן – ואם כן היינו דרב חסדא! וקאמר: איכא בינייהו מצות שיקוע. ברו"ך.

*) דאיכא דס"ל דלראב"ש לא פסלה לינה אפילו במי כיור

בין

דהרואים אותו משוקע בעמוד השחר יאמרו משוקע היה כל הלילה וחזי אף למתירין [ונפיק] מיניה חורבא לכך אינו מעלהו כלל והשתא ניחא דמוכח שפיר ממילתיה מדקאמר שוב אינו מעלהו דאית ליה למתירין כמתירין ומהאי טעמא נפיק מיניה חורבא דאי סבירא ליה לאברים כאברים איזה חורבא נפיק אבל ודאי בדיעבד אם העלהו בלילה וקדשו לאברים מהני הקידוש גם השתא ניחא נמי האי דנקט לשון גזירת כיון דמשום שמא יבא לידי חורבא הוא וי"מ דהטעם [הוא] שאם היה מעלהו למחר לאחר שיקוע ויקדשו לאברים אתי לקדושי אף למתירין משום דאמרי כשם ששיקוע עמוד השחר מועיל לאברים אע"ג דפסול לינה עמוד השחר פוסל בו ושוב לא [תיפסל] בלינה מאחר ששקעו כמו כן כששיקעו בשקיעת החמה הפוסל במתירין שוב לא תפסל בלינה אף כי העלהו בלילה אבל עתה דמצרכינן שיקוע תו ליכא למיגזר והאי פי' לא נהירא דאיך יטעו בזה שידעו ששקיעת החמה גופיה אינו אלא משום פסול לילה וכ"ש דפסול לילה גופיה פוסלתן למתירין

למה משקע ליה הרי מיד יבאו אחיו הכהנים שיהו צריכין להעלותו כדי לקדש ידיהן אלא ודאי היה משקע כדי להשמיע קול. סליק שמעתתא דמי כיור. מהר"פ ז"ל: ח] אלא דבהעלאתו: ט] הדשן אין צריך לחזור: י] סגי ליה בלא קידוש: יא] קשיא לן דלא כו' שיקוע. ס"א ולא אמר לאחר תרומת הדשן חוזר ומשקעו: יב] לא חש למיתני וחוזר ומשקעו דקסבר: יג] לאביי דאוקמא לעיל כרבי כו' אליבא דרבי דחייש לגזירת שיקוע והכא לא אמר דנשקעיה והכא ליכא למימר דטעמא דמודה רבי דמקרות כו' לא פסלה בה לינה: יד] לגזירת שיקוע: טו] שיקעו מבערב: טז] אין צריך לקדש למחר: יז] השתא דאוקמת: יח] כו'. במי שזכה: יט] הכהנים שהיו בבית המוקד: כ] דקתני דמסלק: כא] דמשקעי ליה: כב] והא הוה: כג] דסוף כל הלילה שכשימצאהו: כד] יאמרו שלא הכשירו לעבודת מתירין למחר אלא כשישקעהו: כה] חסדא ומורידו: כו] דקאמר. ס"א משקע ליה בגלגל לבור: כז] משום לינה אפילו:

הגהות צ"ק [א] ולעולם והיינו כו' והשאר יש למחוק: [ב] לינה והא דאמר ר"י הד"א: [ג] ס"א והכא לא אמר דלישקעיה והכא וכו' וגי' הל"ק והכא נמי נימא דנישקעיה: [ד] בתמיה אמאי אמר הד"א: [ה] הכהנים בעזרה וניתו לפייס: [ו] להשהותו בשיקוע דשקיעת החמה משום שיקוע שאנו צריכין כו': [ז] ופריך: [ח] היינו דקא משני ליה בגילגלא והקול שנשמע כו': [ט] בחומרתיה בגילגלא ואף השיקוע היה כדי כו':

הגהות הב"ח (א) רש"י ד"ה והאמר רבי יוחנן כו' דלאחר שמעלהו לקדש לתרומת הדשן לא הצריך: (ב) ד"ה איכא בינייהו וכו' והיינו דקאמר כיור ששקעו:

בין שאין בהן רביעית, ובלבד שיהו כלי שרת! אמר רב אדא בר א] אחא: אבקודח בתוכו. והא "ממנו" אמר רחמנא. "ירחצו" — בלרבות כלי שרת. אי הכי, כלי חול נמי! אמר אביי: כלי חול לא מצית אמרת, מקל וחומר מכנו: ומה כנו שנמשח עמו — אינו מקדש, כלי חול שאינו נמשח עמו — אינו דין שאינו מקדש? וכנו מנלן? דתניא, ר' יהודה אומר: יכול יהא כנו מקדש כדרך שהכיור מקדש — תלמוד לומר: °"ועשית כיור נחשת וכנו נחשת" — לנחשת הקשתיו ולא לדבר אחר. אמר ליה מר זוטרא בריה דרב מרי לרבינא: מה לכנו — שאין עשוי לתוכו, תאמר בכלי חול שעשוי לתוכו! אלא: "ממנו" — גלמעוטי כלי חול. אי הכי, כלי שרת נמי! הא רבי רחמנא "ירחצו". ומה ראית? זה טעון משיחה עמו, וזה אין טעון משיחה כמוהו.§ אמר ריש לקיש: דכל המשלים למי מקוה משלים למי כיור, לרביעית — אינו משלים. למעוטי מאי? אילימא למעוטי טיט *הנדוק; היכי דמי? האי דפרה שוחה ושותה ממנו — אפי' לרביעית נמי, ואי אין פרה שוחה ושותה ממנו — אפילו למקוה נמי אין משלים! ב] אלא למעוטי יבחושין אדומין — אפילו בעינייהו נמי, דהא תניא, רשב"ג אומר: וכל שתחילת ברייתו מן המים — מטבילין בו; ג] ואמר רב יצחק בר אבדימי: זמטבילין בעינו של דג! אמר רב פפא: חלמעוטי נתן סאה ונטל סאה. *דתנן: טמקוה שיש בו מ' סאה מכוונות, נתן סאה ונטל סאה — הרי זה כשר. ואמר רב יהודה בר שילא אמר רב אסי א"ר יוחנן: יעד רובו. אמר רב פפא: אם קדח בו רביעית — מטבילין בו מחטין וצינוריות, הואיל ומהכשירא דמקוה אתיא. א"ר ירמיה אמר ריש לקיש: מי מקוה כשירים למי כיור. למימרא, דלא מים חיים נינהו? והתניא: °"במים" — *כולא ביין, "במים" — ולא במזוג, "במים" — לרבות שאר מים, וק"ו למי כיור. מאי ק"ו למי כיור? לאו דמים חיים נינהו? לא, ד] (לקדוש) דקדיש. וקדישי מעליותא היא? והא תנא ה] *רבי שמואל: מים שאין להם שם לוי, יצאו

רש"י

בין שאין בהן רביעית. הלוג מים. ואע"ג ו] *דליכא שיעורא (א) גבי נטילת ידים — לגבי קידוש לא בעינן שיעור. בקודח (ב) בתוכו. קודח דופנו של כיור, ותוחב בתוכו כלי קטן ומקלחו לחוץ, ויוצק מימי הכיור ומוציא. ז] *אבל בחפיה נפשיה בעינן שיעור ארבעה כהנים. והא ממנו כתיב. אמתני' פריך, דקאמר: כל כלי שרת ראויין הם לקדש ח]. ירחצו. "ובקרבתם אל המזבח ירחצו". קרא יתירא הוא האי "ירחצו", דהא כתיב לעיל מיניה "ורחצו ממנו" וסמיך ליה "בבואם אל אהל מועד ובקרבתם אל המזבח", לא לכתוב "ירחצו" דהא א"ורחצו" הסמוך קאי. שנמשח עמו. ונתקדש במשיחתו כמותו — אינו מקדש ידים ורגלים. לנחושת הקשתיו. לא בהיקשא יליף לה, אלא כלומר: [דימיתיו לכיור] להיות של נחשת הכן כמו הכיור (דימיתיו לכיור). ולא לדבר אחר. לא היקשתי שניהם בפסוק אחד ללמוד שאר דברים, ולומר שכנו מקדש כמותו. דמדאיצטריך למיכתב נחשת גבי כנו זימנא אחריתי — שמע מינה לאו לאקשינהו בעי, דאי איתקוש — נחשת נמי ניתי בהיקשא. אלא שמע מינה: למאי ט] דדמיא — פריש בהדיא, ולמאי דלא פריש — לא דמיא. לנחשת. לענין נחשת י] הקשתיו. הקשתיו. דימיתיו. כל המשלים למקוה. במסכת מקואות (פ"ז מ"א) תנן: יש מעלין ולא פוסלין. מעלין — משלימין לארבעים סאה. והתם יא] מפרש להו. משלים למי כיור. לשיעור ד' כהנים. לרביעית. של נטילת ידים אינו משלים. למעוטי מאי. אתא, דאין משלים לרביעית? אילימא למעוטי טיט הנדוק. שהוא מן המעלין את המקוה, כדקתני התם. נדוק. יב] דק, שראוי להריקו מכלי אל כלי. אי דפרה שוחה ושותה ממנו. שאינו עב ליפסל משתיית בהמה. אפי' לרביעית נמי. דכל זמן יג] *שנפסלו משתיית בהמה, בין בכלי בין בקרקע — פסולין, הא לא נפסלו — כשרין. אפי' למקוה נמי לא. דלא נדוק הוא. יבחושין אדומין. כמין יתושין בלא כנפים, כדרך שגדל בשולי חביות של יין שלנו מבחוץ. יבחושים דקין אף הן נבראים מן המים. אפי' בעינייהו נמי. אם כל המקוה נעשה מהן — כשר. וריש לקיש נקט לישנא דהשלמה. בעינו של דג. דג גדול שנימוק שומן עינו בחורו. למעוטי נתן סאה ונטל סאה. למעוטי הנך מינים דתנן בהן לגבי מקוה: פעמים מעלין ופעמים אין מעלין — מי פירות וכל משקה שאינו מים, ואמד משהחמיץ. וקתני התם: פעמים מעלין פעמים אין מעלין, כיצד? מקוה שיש בו ל"ט סאין ונפלה יד] סאה מהן לתוך — לא העלתהו, פירוש: לא השלימתהו ואף לא פסלתו. פעמים דמעלין, כיצד? היו בתוכו ארבעים סאה מכוונות, נתן סאה מאלו המינים ונטל סאה אחר הנתינה — כשר, דבטלו להנך קמאי במקוה השלם, הילכך, כי חזר ונטל — לא מיפסיל. נמצא שהמקוה הזה נשלם על ידיהם לכשנטל סאה. ודכוותיה בנטילת ידים לא משלמי, שאם היתה טו] בו רביעית מים, ונתן ממינים הללו לתוכו רובע רביעית ונטל כנגדם — פסולה, דלא חשיבא שיעור טז] זוטרא דרביעית לבטולינהו. עד רובו. אם עירב בו ממינין הללו עד רובו של מקוה, ולא רובו בכלל, ע"י נתינת ונטילת סאה — כשר. אם קדח רביעית. בדופן המקוה, והמים נמשכין שם. ואף על פי שנתמעטו המים ואין מעורבין מי המקוה באותה קדיחה. מטבילין בו מחטין כו'. ציוריות = מזלגות קטנות של טווי זהב. מי מקוה. אף על פי שאינן חיין. כשרים. להשאיב הכיור יז] בתוכו, למלאות מהן ולתת לתוכו. למימרא. דלא בעי מים חיים? והתניא. בת"כ: "והקרב והכרעים ירחץ במים" — ולא במזוג, מים ויין מזוגים יחד, שני חלקי מים ואחד יין. שאר מים. ואפילו מכונסין. מאי קל וחומר למי כיור לאו יח] [למימרא דמים חיים נינהו. וה"ק: ק"ו] למים חיים הראויין לכיור, שכשרין לרחילת קרבי קדשים. לא דקדשי. ומי כיור ממש קא יליף בק"ו שרוחצין במימיו קרבים, וק"ו שלהן דקדשי הוא. והא תנא רבי שמואל. לא ידענא אהיכא קאי. ומיהו שמעינן מיניה דהיכא דכתיב "מים" סתמא אין מי כיור כשרין לו. יכול — לרבות שאר מים]. *) יכול שאני מרבה אף מי תותין? תלמוד לומר: "מים" — מים שאין להם שם לווי, יצאו מי תותים שיש להם שם לווי **).

תוספות

בין שאין בהן רביעית. למאי דקס"ד בלא קודח, יש תימה: דגרע מנטילת ידים? ויש לומר: דנטילת ידים נמי, כשיש בו רביעית נוטלין אפילו לשנים, והכא בדהוה ביה רביעית מעיקרא.

והא ממנו אמר רחמנא. פי' בקונטרס: דאמתניתין יט] (פריך) דאמר: כל כלי שרת ראויין לקדש פריך. וקשה: תיקשה ליה מתניתין [דיומא] (דף מג.), דקתני: דכהן גדול מקדש בקיתון של זהב! ונראה דקאי אהא דשני: בקודח מתוכו. כ] [ופריך]: והא "ממנו" אמר רחמנא, דאין לקדש אפי' קודח, אלא אם כן יהא כמוהו, שיהא בו כשיעור. קודח מתוכו. פי': שנוטל כא] ממימיו בכלי קטן. וכשירה לקדש, כיון דבאין מכלי גדול. וכה"ג לקמן: אם קדח בו רביעית — מטבילין בו מחטים וצנוריות, כב] דמהכשירות דמקוה אתו. ובקונטרס לא פירש כן. ק"ו מכנו. משמע שיש לו תוך, ועשוי כמין תיבה פרוצה למעלה והכיור יושב עליו. כג] *ורבי' פי': כעין יורה כפוייה על חיה ותחתיו [illegible] [illegible].

לרביעית אינו משלים. פי' בקונטרס: לרביעית — לנטילת ידים. וקלא כה] תימה. והיה נראה לפרש: לרביעית — היינו להטביל מחטין וצנוריות, דבהכי מיירי בסוף שמעתא. ומיהו, נראה כפירוש הקונט', דבימי ר"ל כבר בטלו רביעית דמקוה, כדמוכח בנזיר בפרק "שלשה מינים" (דף לח.). למעוטי טיט *הנדוק. אע"ג דמשלים למי מקוה — אין מטבילין בו. כדאמר בפרק קמא דסוכה (דף יט.) גבי אויר מצטרף ואין ישיבים תחתיו, ופריך: מי איכא מידי דאיהו לא חזי ומצטרף? וקאמר: טיט הנדוק יוכיח. ולא כמו שפירש שם בקונטרס, דאע"ג דמשלים, כדתנן במסכת מקואות פ"ז: אלו מעלין ולא פוסלין: מי השלג והברד וטיט הנדוק, מכל מקום אם עשה מקוה שלם מטיט הנדוק לא עלתה לו טבילה. דלפירושו אין זה יוכיח, דטיט הנדוק בשעה שהוא משלים חזי לטבילה, ולא דמי כו] [לאויר] דאין ישיבים תחתיו אפי' בשעה שהוא משלים. לפיכך נראה [דטיט הנדוק נמי], אפי' בשעה שמצטרף — אין מטבילין בו. והכי תנן במסכת מקואות פ"ב (מ"י): מקוה שיש בו מ' סאה כז] וטיט, רבי אליעזר אומר: מטבילין במים ואין מטבילין בטיט, רבי יהושע אומר: בטיט ובמים. באיזה טיט אמרו — בטיט שהמים צפין על גביו. ואם היו המים מצד אחד — מודה רבי יהושע שמטבילין במים ואין מטבילין בטיט. באיזה טיט אמרו — בטיט שהקנה יורד מאליו כח] בתוכו, דברי רבי מאיר. רבי יהודה אומר: מקום שאין קנה המדה עומד. אבא כט] אליעזר [בן דילאי] אומר: מקום שהמשקולת יורדת. רבי אליעזר אומר: היורד בפי חבית. רבי שמעון אומר: ל] היורד בשפופרת הנוד. רבי אליעזר ברבי צדוק אומר: הנמדד בלוג. והיינו טיט הנדוק דסוכה (דף יט:) דאמר יוכיח, לא] [דכשהטיט מצד א' מצטרף לכ"ע, ואין מטבילין בו].

אפילו לרביעית. כאן פי' בקונטרס: דאמרינן פרק "כל הבשר" (חולין דף קו.): מים שנפסלו משתיית בהמה, בין בכלים בין בקרקע — פסולין, הא לא נפסלו — כשירים. ואינו כן, דהתם תניא בהדיא: בקרקע כשירים. ופליגי התם באפסקא בבת בירתא, אבל במקומן — כשירין לכולי עלמא, ואפי' מקוה. והא דקאמר הכא: אי אין פרה שותה ושותה ממנו אפילו למקוה נמי אינו משלים — לא קשיא מידי, דהתם במים צלולים מיירי בלא טיט, אלא שהם סרוחים ונפסלו משתיית בהמה, והכא מיירי במים עבים שנפסלו על ידי טיט המעורב בהן. ויש תימה: מנא ליה האי שיעורא? דכל הני תנאי דמסכת מקואות (פ"ב) לא מיירי בשתיית פרה לב].

נתן סאה כשר. במי פירות מיירי, כדפי' פרק "הערל" (יבמות דף פב:). אבל מים שאובין אפי' כל היום כולו לג] [כשר, דראשון ראשון בטל. ויש תימה: דגבי קרב וכרעים דרשינן: "במים" — ולא במזוג, והכא גבי לד] *כיור כתיב "במים" ומכשרינן במזוג!

והא תנא *רבי שמואל. פי' בקונטרס: לא ידענא אהיכא קאי. ומיהו, בתורת כהנים תניא: לה] ["והקרב והכרעים ירחץ במים" — ולא ביין ולא במזוג, "במים" — לרבות שאר מים]. *) יכול שאני מרבה אף מי תותין? תלמוד לומר: "מים" — מים שאין להם שם לווי, יצאו מי תותים שיש להם שם לווי **).

*) [בת"כ שלפנינו לא נמצא עדיין] **) [ע' בהרא"ש ריש פי"ד דנגעים ד"ה מים חיים כו' ושמא אהך מתניא וכו' ע"ש דגם הת"כ שהעתיק בזה"ל מים חיים ולא מלוחים ולא פושרים ולא המכזבים וכו' לא נמצא עדיין בת"כ שלפנינו]

עין משפט נר מצוה

נו א מיי' פ"ה מהל' ביאת מקדש הל' יא בהשגה וסמג עשין קעה:
נז ב ג מיי' שם הל"י:
נח ד מיי' שם הלי"ב:
נט ה מיי' שם ומיי' פ"ח מהל' מקוואות הל"ט סמג עשין רמח טוש"ע או"ח סי' קסב סעי' ט:
ס ו ז מיי' שם הלכה יא טוש"ע יו"ד סי' רא סעי' לג וטוש"ע או"ח סי' קס סעי' י:
סא ח מיי' פ"ז שם הלכה ו:
סב ט י מיי' פ"ד שם הלכה ז טוש"ע יו"ד סי' רא סעי' כד:
סג כ מיי' פ"ו מהל' מעה"ק הל"ו:

שיטה מקובצת

א] בר אהבה תיבת אחא נמחק: ב] אלא למעוטי. פי' קושיא היא ותירוצא דקושיא זו מיתרצא לקמי' אמר רב פפא למעוטי נתן סאה וכו' וק"ל: ג] ואמר. וא"ת והלא שלג וברד משלימין למקוה אבל בעינייהו לא וי"ל דשלג וברד אין תחילתו מן המים הילכך לא מהני בהו בעינייהו וברד היינו גריילא ולא גרילילא. תו"א: ד] תיבת לקדוש נמחק: ה] תנא. דבי תיבת ר' ל"ש: ו] ואע"ג. דבעינן שיעורא: ז] ומוציא. ס"א ואותו כלי אינו מחזיק רביעית אבל הכיור עצמו בעינן: ח] לקדש. והא ממנו כתיב דמשמע דוקא ממש מן הכיור: ט] למאי. דדמי: י] נחשת. הס"ד ומה"ד הקשתיו. דימיתיו הס"ד: יא] מפרש. מאן נינהו הס"ד: יב] נדוק רך שראוי: יג] זמן. שלא נפסלו משתית בהמה ולא נעשה בהם מלאכה כשרים לידים דהכי תנן התם ומייתי לה בפ' כל הבשר מים שנפסלו משתית בהמה: יד] (ונפלה) [ונפל] (בה) סאה תיבת מהן נמחק: טו] תיבת בו נמחק: טז] שיעור. זוטרתא: יז] הכיור. לתוכו או למלאות: יח] לאו. למימרא דמים חיים נינהו בתמיה וה"ק ק"ו: יט] דאמתניתין. פריך דאמר כל כו' ראוין לקדש וקשה תקשה ליה מתניתין דיומא: כ] מתוכו. אבל לעולם ידע שפיר דאם יש שיעור בבלי שרת דמקדשין בו כמו בכיור אבל קשיא ליה למאי דשני בקודח מתוכו דמשמע דלית בה כשיעור ומש"ה פריך: כא] ממימיו לשון הר"פ פרש"י שנוקב בכיור נקב מצדו ומדבקין שם כלי אחד קטן שמקלח מים לקדשו ולא נהירא דפשיטא דהוי כמו כיור גופיה ומאי פריך ממנו אמר רחמנא. לכן נראה שנוטל אותו בכלי קטן ונותן אותו תוך הכיור ונוטל מימיו ומקדש בו וכה"ג כשרים לקדש כיון דמכלי גדול קא אתי וכה"ג כו': כב] דמהכשירא: כג] ורבינו. ש"י פי' בחומש: כד] שולים. גליון ולא נראה דא"כ לא היה יכול לקדש ממנו. תו' מהר"פ: כה] וקצת היה נראה לפרש: כו] דמי. לאויר: כז] סאה. מים וטיט: כח] תיבת בתוכו נמחק: כט] אלעזר בן דולעי: ל] ר"ש אומר הנכנס בשפופרת: לא] יוכיח. דכשהטיט מצד אחד מצטרף לכ"ע ואין מטבילין בו: לב] פרה. גליון ונראה התם דלא איירי אלא לענין הטבילה במים מפליג בין קנה יורד ואינך חילוקים כדמפרש התם אבל הכא איירי בהטבלה בטיט עצמו ובקנה יורד עצמו איכא לאפלוגי ולא משכחת ליה אלא בין שוחה ושותה הפרה לאין שוחה ושותה. תו' חיצוניות: לג] כולו. כשר דראשון ראשון בטל: לד] גבי טבילה ותיבת כיור ל"ש ונמחק: לה] תניא. כה"ג:

סד א מיי' פ"ה מהל' ביאת מקדש הל"ב:
סה ב מיי' פ"ד שם הלכה ט:
סה ג מיי' פ"ד שם הלכה ט: [שייך לעיל במשנה טו:]
סו ג ד מיי' פ"ב שם הלכה יב:

יָצְאוּ מֵי כִיּוֹר שֶׁיֵּשׁ לָהֶם שֵׁם לֵוִי! אֶלָּא לָאו — דִּרְאוּיִין לְמֵי כִיּוֹר; אַלְמָא מַיִם חַיִּים נִינְהוּ! תַּנָּאֵי הִיא, *דְּאָמַר ר' יוֹחָנָן: מֵי כִיּוֹר, ר' יִשְׁמָעֵאל אוֹמֵר: מֵי מַעְיָן הֵן, וַחֲכָמִים אוֹמְרִים: אשְׁאָר מֵימוֹת הֵן.§ "עָרֵל". מְנָלַן? *אָמַר רַב חִסְדָּא: דָּבָר זֶה מִתּוֹרַת מֹשֶׁה רַבֵּינוּ לֹא לָמַדְנוּ, מִדִּבְרֵי יְחֶזְקֵאל בֶּן בּוּזִי לָמַדְנוּ: °"כָּל בֶּן נֵכָר עֶרֶל לֵב וְעֶרֶל בָּשָׂר לֹא יָבֹא אֶל מִקְדָּשִׁי (לְשָׁרְתֵנִי".) וּמְנָלַן דִּמְחַלֵּי עֲבוֹדָה? דִּכְתִיב: °"בַּהֲבִיאֲכֶם א] (אֶת) בְּנֵי נֵכָר עַרְלֵי לֵב וְעַרְלֵי בָשָׂר לִהְיוֹת בְּמִקְדָּשִׁי לְחַלֵּל אֶת בֵּיתִי". תָּנוּ רַבָּנַן: "בֶּן נֵכָר" — ב] יָכוֹל בֶּן נֵכָר מַמָּשׁ? תַּלְמוּד לוֹמַר: "עֶרֶל לֵב". אִם כֵּן, מַה תַּלְמוּד לוֹמַר "בֶּן נֵכָר" — שֶׁנִּתְנַכְּרוּ מַעֲשָׂיו לְאָבִיו שֶׁבַּשָּׁמַיִם. וְאֵין לִי אֶלָּא עֶרֶל לֵב, עֶרֶל בָּשָׂר מִנַּיִן? תַּלְמוּד לוֹמַר: "וְעֶרֶל בָּשָׂר". *וּצְרִיכִי, דְּאִי כָּתַב רַחֲמָנָא "עֶרֶל בָּשָׂר" — מִשּׁוּם דְּמָאִיס, אֲבָל עֶרֶל לֵב דְּלָא מָאִיס — אֵימָא לָא; וְאִי אַשְׁמְעִינַן עֶרֶל לֵב — מִשּׁוּם דְּאֵין לִבּוֹ לַשָּׁמַיִם, אֲבָל עֶרֶל בָּשָׂר דְּלִבּוֹ לַשָּׁמַיִם — אֵימָא לָא, צְרִיכִי.§ "טָמֵא פָּסוּל".§ אָמְרוּ זִקְנֵי דָרוֹם: לֹא שָׁנוּ אֶלָּא טְמֵא שֶׁרֶץ. אֲבָל טְמֵא מֵת, ג] מִתּוֹךְ שֶׁמְּרַצֶּה בְּצִיבּוּר — מְרַצֶּה נַמִי בְּיָחִיד. אִי הָכִי, טְמֵא שֶׁרֶץ נַמִי לֵיתֵי בְּקַל וָחוֹמֶר מִטְּמֵא מֵת: מַה טְּמֵא מֵת שֶׁטָּעוּן הַזָּאָה שְׁלִישִׁי וּשְׁבִיעִי — מְרַצֶּה, טְמֵא שֶׁרֶץ שֶׁאֵינוֹ טָעוּן הַזָּאָה ג' וּשְׁבִיעִי — אֵינוֹ דִּין שֶׁמְּרַצֶּה? קָסָבְרִי זִקְנֵי דָרוֹם: מְכַפְּרִין כְּמִתְכַּפְּרִין, מַה מִּתְכַּפְּרִין — בטְמֵא מֵת אִין, טְמֵא שֶׁרֶץ לָא, אַף מְכַפְּרִין — טְמֵא מֵת — אִין, טְמֵא שֶׁרֶץ — לָא. מַאי קָסָבְרִי? אִי קָסָבְרִי: *אֵין שׁוֹחֲטִין וְזוֹרְקִין עַל טְמֵא שֶׁרֶץ — אַמַּאי לָא עָבְדִי צִיבּוּר בְּטוּמְאָה? הָא כָּל שֶׁבְּיָחִיד נִדְחֶה — צִיבּוּר עָבְדִי בְּטוּמְאָה! אֶלָּא קָסָבְרִי: שׁוֹחֲטִין וְזוֹרְקִין עַל טְמֵא שֶׁרֶץ. אָמַר עוּלָּא, תְּקַע לְהוּ (א) ר"ל לְדָרוֹמָאֵי: וְכִי אֵיזֶה כֹּחַ מְרוּבֶּה, כֹּחַ מְכַפְּרִין אוֹ כֹּחַ מִתְכַּפְּרִין? הֱוֵי אוֹמֵר — כֹּחַ מִתְכַּפְּרִין; וּמָה בְּמָקוֹם גשֶׁנִּטְמְאוּ בְּעָלִים בְּשֶׁרֶץ ד] מְשַׁלְּחִין קָרְבְּנוֹתֵיהֶן — כֹּהֵן שֶׁנִּטְמָא בְּשֶׁרֶץ אֵינוֹ מְרַצֶּה, ה] מָקוֹם שֶׁנִּטְמְאוּ בְּעָלִים בְּמֵת, דשֶׁאֵין מְשַׁלְּחִין קָרְבְּנוֹתֵיהֶן — כֹּהֵן שֶׁנִּטְמָא בְּמֵת אֵינוֹ דִּין שֶׁאֵינוֹ מְרַצֶּה? ו] קָסָבְרִי זִקְנֵי דָרוֹם: טְמֵא מֵת [נַמִי] מְשַׁלֵּחַ קָרְבְּנוֹתָיו. וְהָכְתִיב: °"אִישׁ אִישׁ כִּי יִהְיֶה טָמֵא וְעָשָׂה פֶסַח בַּחֹדֶשׁ הַשֵּׁנִי" וגו'! לְמִצְוָה. וְהָא כְּתִיב: °"אִישׁ לְפִי

תורה אור | יחזקאל מד | שם | במדבר ט | שמות יב

רש"י

יָכוֹל בֶּן נֵכָר מַמָּשׁ. גּוֹי. תַּלְמוּד לוֹמַר עֶרֶל לֵב. אֵינוֹ נִפְסָל אֶלָּא מֵחֲמַת עַרְלוּת לִבּוֹ. אַלְמָא דְּכֹהֵן קָאָמַר. שֶׁנִּתְנַכְּרוּ מַעֲשָׂיו. נֶחְשָׁבִים לְנָכְרִים לַמָּקוֹם. עָרֵל בָּשָׂר. וְהוּא לַדִּיק, מִנַּיִן? טָמֵא פָּסוּל. וְהוּא לְמַתְנִי' קָאֵי, ז] דִּתְנַן בְּמַתְנִי': טָמֵא מְחַלֵּל עֲבוֹדָה. וְעַל כָּרְחֵיךְ בְּקָרְבַּן יָחִיד קָאָמַר, דְּאִילּוּ קָרְבַּן לִבּוּר קָרֵב בְּטוּמְאָה. מִתּוֹךְ שֶׁמְּרַצֶּה בְּצִבּוּר. לְכַתְּחִילָּה. מְרַצֶּה בְּיָחִיד. דִּיעֲבַד, עַל יְדֵי ח] שֶׁהַפִּיךְ מְרַצֶּה עָלָיו. וְהַאי דִּבְטוּמְאַת מֵת פְּשִׁיטָא לָן — דִּכְתִיב "בְּמוֹעֲדוֹ" וַאֲפִי' בְּטוּמְאָה, מַשְׁמַע בֵּין ט] שֶׁכֹּהֵן (נַמִי) טָמֵא, בֵּין שֶׁהַלִּבּוּר טְמֵאִין. וּמִדְּגַלֵּי בְּדוּכְתָּא אַחֲרִיתִי גַּבֵּי טוּמְאַת בְּעָלִים דְּכִי אִישְׁתְּרַאי טוּמְאָה בְּלִבּוּר בְּמֵת אִישְׁתְּרַאי, דִּכְתִיב: "אִישׁ (ב) כִּי יִהְיֶה טָמֵא לָנֶפֶשׁ", יָלְפִינַן מִינָּהּ: אִישׁ נִדְחֶה, וְאֵין לִבּוּר נִדְחִין — אַף גַּבֵּי כֹּהֵן הַמְרַצֶּה נַמִי, בְּמֵת אִישְׁתְּרַאי. אִי הָכִי ל"ג. טָמֵא שֶׁרֶץ נַמִי לֵיתֵי בְּקַל וָחוֹמֶר. דִּמְרַצֶּה בְּלִבּוּר לְכַתְּחִילָּה, בְּק"ו מִטְּמֵא מֵת. קָסָבְרִי זִקְנֵי דָרוֹם. דְּאָמְרִי מֵת דַּוְוקָא. מְכַפְּרִין בְּמִתְכַּפְּרִין. כְּשֶׁהוּתְּרָה טוּמְאָה בְּלִבּוּר שְׁנֵיהֶם הָיוּ בְּמַשְׁמַע, הַכֹּהֵן וְהַלִּבּוּר, דְּהָא י] מִ"מּוֹעֲדוֹ" נָפְקָא לָן (פסחים דף עז.). הִילְכָּךְ, כֹּהֵן כְּלִיבּוּר: מַה כְּשֶׁהוּתְּרָה טוּמְאָה אֵצֶל רוֹב לִבּוּר שֶׁנִּטְמְאוּ — טְמֵא מֵת הוּתַּר וְלֹא טְמֵא שֶׁרֶץ, יא] [אַף כְּשֶׁהוּתַּר לְכֹהֵן בְּקָרְבַּן לִבּוּר מֵת הוּתַּר וְלֹא שֶׁרֶץ]. מַאי קָסָבְרִי. זִקְנֵי דָרוֹם, דִּפְשִׁיטָא לְהוּ דְּלֹא הוּתְּרָה טוּמְאַת שֶׁרֶץ אֵצֶל רוֹב לִבּוּר וְתֵיתֵי בְּקַל וָחוֹמֶר. אִי קָסָבְרִי אֵין שׁוֹחֲטִין וְזוֹרְקִין. אֶת הַפֶּסַח עַל יָחִיד טְמֵא שֶׁרֶץ, יב] וְאַף ע"ג דְּיָכוֹל לִטְבּוֹל וְלֶאֱכוֹל לָעֶרֶב. וְאִיכָּא לְמ"ד בִּפְסָחִים (דף צ:) [דס"ל] הָכִי, וְיָלֵיף לָהּ מֵ"אִישׁ אִישׁ כִּי יִהְיֶה טָמֵא לָנֶפֶשׁ" — וַאֲפִילּוּ חָל שְׁבִיעִי שֶׁלּוֹ עֶרֶב הַפֶּסַח בְּמַשְׁמַע, דַּהֲוָה לֵיהּ כִּטְמֵא שֶׁרֶץ יג]. אַמַּאי לָא עָבְדִי צִיבּוּר בְּטוּמְאָה הָא כָּל שֶׁבְּיָחִיד נִדְחֶה צִבּוּר עָבְדִי בְּטוּמְאָה. דְּאִישׁ וְלֹא לִיבּוּר קָאָמַר רַחֲמָנָא. אֶלָּא סָבְרִי (ג) יד] לָן כְּמ"ד הָתָם שׁוֹחֲטִין וְזוֹרְקִין עַל טְמֵא שֶׁרֶץ. הוֹאִיל וַחֲזֵי לְאוֹרְתָּא. הִילְכָּךְ, לִבּוּר טְמֵאֵי שֶׁרֶץ — אַף הֵן לֹא הוּתַּר לָהֶן לִיכָּנֵס לָעֲזָרָה טְמֵאִין, אֶלָּא יְשַׁלְּחוּ קָרְבְּנוֹתֵיהֶם לָעֲזָרָה טו] וְיַקְרִיבוּהוּ כֹּהֲנִים טְהוֹרִין, וְיִטְבְּלוּ וְיֹאכְלוּ לָעֶרֶב. דְּלֹא הוּתְּרָה לָהֶם טוּמְאָה אֶלָּא בְּמָקוֹם שֶׁאִילּוּ לֹא הוּתְּרָה הָיוּ נִדְחִין. הִילְכָּךְ, טְמֵא מֵת שֶׁאֵינוֹ מוּתָּר לֶאֱכוֹל לָעֶרֶב — טז] הוּתַּר לָהֶן, אֲבָל טוּמְאַת שֶׁרֶץ לֹא. וְאֵין כָּאן ק"ו, שֶׁהֲרֵי יְכוֹלִין לַעֲשׂוֹתוֹ בְּטָהֳרָה. תָּקַע לְהוּ. נָעַק לָהֶם קוֹל גָּדוֹל. אֵיזֶה כֹּחַ מְרוּבֶּה. לִדְחוֹת אֶת הַטּוּמְאָה. הֱוֵי אוֹמֵר כֹּחַ מִתְכַּפְּרִין. כִּדְמְפָרֵשׁ וְאָזֵיל, (ד) שֶׁהַיָּחִיד טְמֵא שֶׁרֶץ מְשַׁלֵּחַ קָרְבָּנוֹ לָעֲזָרָה, כִּדְקָאָמְרִיתוּ: שׁוֹחֲטִין וְזוֹרְקִין עַל טְמֵא שֶׁרֶץ. וְהַכֹּהֵן הַמְרַצֶּה בּוֹ, אִם נִטְמָא בְּשֶׁרֶץ — פָּסוּל לוֹ, כִּדְמוֹקְמִיתוּ מַתְנִי' דְּקָתָנֵי טָמֵא פָּסוּל בִּטְמֵא שֶׁרֶץ. מָקוֹם שֶׁאִם נִטְמְאוּ בְּעָלִים כו'. יָחִיד שֶׁנִּטְמָא בְּמֵת אֵין מְשַׁלֵּחַ פִּסְחוֹ לָעֲזָרָה לִשְׁחוֹט עָלָיו, יז] [אֶלָּא נִדְחֶה לְפֶסַח שֵׁנִי] כְּדִכְתִיב: "אִישׁ אִישׁ כִּי יִהְיֶה" וגו', וְאע"ג דְּכֹחוֹ מְרוּבֶּה מִשֶּׁל כֹּהֵן אֵצֶל שֶׁרֶץ. כֹּהֵן שֶׁנִּטְמָא בְּמֵת אֵינוֹ דִּין שֶׁאֵינוֹ מְרַצֶּה. שֶׁהֲרֵי כֹּחוֹ רַע מִשֶּׁל בְּעָלִים אֵצֶל שֶׁרֶץ. וְאַמַּאי אָמְרֵי זִקְנֵי דָרוֹם מְרַצֶּה בְּיָחִיד מִגּוֹ דִּמְרַצֶּה בְּלִבּוּר? טָמֵא מֵת נַמִי. יָחִיד טְמֵא מֵת נַמִי מְשַׁלֵּחַ קָרְבְּנוֹתָיו. כְּלוֹמַר, אִם שִׁילַּח פִּסְחוֹ לָעֲזָרָה וּשְׁחָטוֹ וּזְרָקוֹ עָלָיו — פָּטוּר מִלַּעֲשׂוֹת פֶּסַח שֵׁנִי, וְאַף עַל פִּי שֶׁלֹּא יֹאכַל יח] מִמֶּנּוּ, דְּקָסָבְרִי: אֲכִילַת פְּסָחִים לֹא מְעַכֶּבֶת. וּמִיהוּ, לְכַתְּחִילָּה אָמַר רַחֲמָנָא (ה) נִדְחֶה לְפֶסַח שֵׁנִי. וְלִבּוּר עָבְדִי בְּטוּמְאָה, הִילְכָּךְ כֹּהֵן הַמְכַפֵּר בְּקָרְבַּן יָחִיד, מִתּוֹךְ שֶׁמְּרַצֶּה [בְּלִבּוּר] לְכַתְּחִילָּה — מְרַצֶּה בְּיָחִיד דִּיעֲבַד. וְהָכְתִיב אִישׁ אִישׁ וגו' וְעָשָׂה פֶסַח בַּחֹדֶשׁ הַשֵּׁנִי. אַלְמָא מִידְחֵי! לְפִי

תוספות

יצאו מי כיור שיש להם שם לווי. הא דאמרינן בסוכה (דף יג.) ובחולין (דף סב:): כל שנשתנה שמו קודם מתן תורה ובאה תורה והקפידה עליו זהו שם לווי — לא קשיא מידי, דכך שמו "מי כיור" בשעת מתן תורה. *ערל. מפרש *רבינו שלמה יט] בכל מקום: שמתו אחיו מחמת מילה. ור"ת מפרש: דמומר לערלות. וקרי ליה לבו לשמים — לפי שאינו עושה אלא מדאגת לער המילה. ובריש הערל (יבמות דף ע.) פירשתי*. משום דאין לבו לשמים. אפילו שב בשעת עבודה אמרינן בסוף מנחות (דף קט.) דאין קרבנו ריח ניחוח. ואע"ג דהשתא לבו לשמים — מתחילה לא היה לבו *לשמים.

אבל טמא מת. פירוש: קודם שביעי, מרצה אפי' בקרבן יחיד על ידי ציץ, מתוך שמרצה בלא ציץ. והא דאמר: עון הקדשים ולא עון מקדישים — מוקמינן להו בטומאת שרץ. וכן כל טומאת מת דשמעתין — היינו קודם שביעי שלו. אבל בשביעי — היינו כמו טמא שרץ, דאינו מרצה ביחיד לפי ששוחטין וזורקין עליו, וגם אינו מרצה בצבור טמא מת בשביעי [נמי], לפי שיכולין לעשות ע"י שלוחין טהורים, ולאורתא מצו אכלי הפסח בטהרה, כדמוכח. אי הכי טמא שרץ נמי. בקונטרס לא גרס "אי הכי", כ] דאפי' לית לן מתוך שמרצה כו' מצי לאקשויי הך פירכא: טמא שרץ לירצי בצבור מקל וחומר מטמא מת. ויש ליישב: אי הכי דקאמרת מתוך שמרצה וכו' וילפת יחיד בדיעבד מצבור לכתחילה — א"כ טמא שרץ נמי לירצי ביחיד, דהא מרצה הוא בציבור מק"ו דטמא מת. אבל אי לאו "מתוך" — לא הוה קשיא מידי, דאמינא דמתני' דפסלה טמא מיירי בין בטמא מת בין בטמא שרץ. ועוד יש לפרש: כי נמי אמרינן "מתוך" הוה לכו לאוקמי מתני' בזב ומצורע, מי שטומאה יוצאת מגופו, אבל טמא מת ושרץ — לא, דמרצו ביחיד בדיעבד הואיל ומרצו בצבור לכתחילה, ושרץ מקל וחומר. ומשני: טמא שרץ אינו מרצה בציבור לכתחילה, שהרי מכפרין כמתכפרין. ובמתכפרין טמאי שרץ אינן עושים פסח בטומאה, שהרי שוחטין וזורקין על טמא שרץ, וכל שאין היחיד נדחה — אין צבור עושין בטומאה, אלא שולחין שלוחיהן הטהורים ועושים פסחיהן בשבילם. וא"כ איכא למיפרך: מה לטמא מת שכן מרצה בצבור, מה שאין כן בטמא שרץ. [הגה"ה]. ורבינו תם גרס "אי הכי", ומפרש ד"במועדו" אפי' בטומאה — היינו בין במת בין בשרץ, בין דפסח בין דתמיד. והא דקאמרי זקני דרום: לא שנו אלא טמא שרץ, אבל טמא מת מתוך שמרצה בצבור — מיירי ברילוי של אכילה בטומאה. כלומר, מתוך שמרצה רילוי גדול שנאכל בטומאת בעלים במת — מרצה נמי ביחיד ששימש בטומאת מת. אבל טמא שרץ, נהי דיש לו רילוי בצבור, כגון היכא דנטמאו הכהנים או הסכינים בשרץ, דעבדי בטומאה, ד"במועדו" אמר רחמנא ואפילו בטומאה, וכל שביחיד נדחה — בצבור עבדי בטומאה, מ"מ אין לו רילוי גדול כמו מת, ואילו נטמאו לבור בשרץ — כא] אין להם לאכול בטומאה, כמו שאמר לבסוף. ופריך: אי הכי טמא שרץ נמי, כיון דאמרת דבטומאת מת מרצה ביחיד מטעם דמרצה בצבור, דאכלי בטומאת מת — א"כ טמא שרץ נמי בקרבן יחיד לירצי, מקל וחומר מטמא מת כב] דיחיד! ומשני, קסברי זקני דרום: מכפרין, פירוש: דיחיד — כמתכפרין, דטמא מת אין, טמא שרץ לא. *) ואם תאמר: ומנ"ל ד"במועדו" איירי אף בטומאת שרץ? אי ממשמעותא ד"מועדו" — אם כן אפילו זב ומצורע. אי מקל וחומר דמת, שטעון שלישי ושביעי — מה לטומאת מת שכן אישתראי לאכול בטומאת בעלים, תאמר בשרץ דאם נטמאו בעלים בשרץ לא אכלי! כג] [ויש לומר: דהאי דלא אכלי] — לאו משום חומר דשרץ, אלא משום דשוחטין וזורקין עליו [ולא] איפטר ליה מפסח. וכה"ג במת בשביעי שלו, אם היו רוב לבור טמאים בשביעי שיכולים ליטהר לערב — לא הוו אכלי בטומאה. וקשה לפירוש ר"ת: כי היכי דאמר מכפרין כמתכפרים כד] [למעוטי טומאת שרץ, דלא לירלי ביחיד] — הכי נמי נימא בליבור, ודווקא טמא מת ולא טמא שרץ! ואי משום דאתי קל וחומר ומפיק מהיקישא — הכא

*) עיין ל"ק בדיבור זה שהאריך

[יבמות דף ע.] | [וע"ע תוס' חגיגה ד: ד"ה דמרכבה] | עיין בחילופי גירסאות

שיטה מקובצת

א] תיבת את נמחק: ב] יכול בן נכר ממש. תימה תיפוק ליה שהוא זר וי"ל דשמא פסול דורות לא שייך אלא מבני ישראל. ת"א: ג] עי' בהשמטות בסוף המסכת: ד] בשרץ. שמשלחין: ה] מקום שנטמאו בעלים במת כו'. וקשה דמה לשרץ שאינו מרצה בצבור כלל לפ"ה תאמר במת שמרצה בצבור ואף לפר"ת איכא למיפרך מה לשרץ שכן אינו מרצה לענין אכילת בעלים בטומאה כדפי' לעיל תאמר במת שכן מרצה לענין אכילת בעלים בטומאה נמי ואומר הר"ם דאין זה ק"ו אלא סתירת דברים בעלמא על מה שאמרו זקני דרום דלענין מכפרים בטמא מת אין חילוק בין צבור ליחיד ואע"ג דלענין מתכפרים יש חילוק בין צבור ליחיד כדפרישית וע"ז פריך דאדרבה יש לי לדון ק"ו אחר דמשמע דאיכא הרצאה לבעלים יותר מלגבי כהן שהרי גרע טפי מבעלים דבעלים משלחין קרבנותיהן וכהן לא מרצה וא"כ כ"ש שיש לנו לומר דגריעותא שהוא בבעלים דטמא מת שאינו משלח שיהיה בכהן שנטמא במת שלא ירצה ולהשוות כהן לבעלים לענין מת ביחיד וכמו דבבעלים יש חילוק בין צבור ליחיד כמו כן בכהנים נחלק בין צבור ליחיד כיון דבשרץ הורע כח כהן מכח בעלים וא"כ בקל יש לנו לומר דלא אמרינן מתוך. הר"פ: ו] קסברי [זקני דרום] טמא מת נמי כו' וא"כ הו"ל אינו נדחה ביחיד וכל שאינו נדחה ביחיד אין צבור מביא (טומאה) [בטומאה] כדאמרי' בפסח שני וא"ת א"כ טומא' דהורצה במת היכי משכחת לה וי"ל כיון דאם בא יחיד לימלך אמרינן ליה תמתין עד פסח שני כדמסיק הכא למצוה (נדחה) [קרינא] שפיר [נדחה] [קרינא] כיון דאינו מרצה לכתחילה: ז] קאי. כלומר דקתני במתני' ותיבת דתנן ל"ש ונמחק: ח] ידי. הציץ שמרצה: ט] בין. שהכהן: י] מבמועדו: יא] שרץ. אף כשהותר לכהן בקרבן צבור מת הותר ולא שרץ: יב] שרץ. ונדחה לפסח שני וא"ג כו' לערב. דאיכא מ"ד בפסחים: יג] שרץ. שאינו מחוסר אלא טבילה והזאה ויכול ליטהר כדי לאכול הפסח בלילה והכי משמע קרא דכתיב ולא יכלו לעשות הפסח ביום ההוא דמשמע הא למחר יכולין לעשותו. הס"ד: יד] להו. כמ"ד: טו] לעזרה. ויקריבו: טז] לערב. אם אינו בשביעי שלו הותר: יז] עליו. אלא נדחה לפסח שני: יח] יאכל. הימנו דקסברי אכילת פסחים לא מעכבי ומיהו כו' רחמנא. יחיד נדחה לפסח שני וצבור עבדי בטומאה כו' שמרצה. בצבור לכתחלה: יט] שלמה. ז"ל: כ] מתיבות דאפילו כו' עד תיבות משא"כ בטמא שרץ מוקף חצי לבנה ואח"כ צ"ל ע"כ הג"ה: כא] בשרץ. אינו נאכל בטומאה: כב] מטמא מת. בקרבן: כג] לא אכלי. וי"ל דהאי דלא אכלי בצבור לאו: כד] כמתכפרים. למעוטי טמא שרץ דלא לירצי ביחיד ה"נ נימא בצבור דמכפר בצבור כמתכפר בצבור ולא יהא כהן מרצה בצבור בטומאת שרץ ולא ידחה במועדו אלא דוקא טמא:

הגהות הב"ח

(א) גמ' תקע להו וריש לקיש. תא"מ ונ"ב ס"א אלא איש: (ב) ד"ה אלא סברי להו כמ"ד: (ג) ד"ה הוי אומר כח וכו' ואזיל ומה במקום שנטמאו וכו' שהיחיד טמא: (ה) ד"ה טמא מת וכו' אמר רחמנא יחיד נידחי:

סוטה טו. | לעיל יח: [וש"נ] | פסחים ע. יבמות עח. | ל"ק | [פסחים סט. וש"נ]

לפי אכלו"! למצוה. ולעכובי לא? *והתניא: °"במכסת נפשות" – מלמד אשאין הפסח נשחט אלא למנוייו. שחטו שלא למנוייו יכול יהא כעובר על המצוה? א] תלמוד לומר: "תכוסו", הכתוב *שנה עליו לעכב; ואיתקש אוכלין למנויין! זקני דרום לא מקשי. ב] וכי לא מקשי נמי, (א) מהא נמי אית להו פירכא: ומה במקום שנטמאו בעלים בשרץ, שמשלחין קרבנותיהם לכתחילה – כהן שנטמא בשרץ אינו מרצה, ג] מקום שנטמאו בעלים במת, שאין משלחין קרבנותיהן לכתחילה – כהן שנטמא במת אינו דין שאינו מרצה? מיתיבי: *במפני שאמרו: נזיר ועושה פסח, הציץ מרצה על טומאת דם ואין הציץ מרצה על טומאת הגוף. ד] במאי? אילימא בטומאת שרץ – האמרת: שוחטין וזורקין על *טומאת שרץ! אלא טומאת מת, וקתני: אין הציץ מרצה, אלמא: נטמאו בעלים במת – אין משלחין קרבנותיהם! לא, אי דאיטמו בעלים במת – ה"נ. הכא במאי עסקינן – כגון שנטמא כהן בשרץ. אי הכי, ה] אימא סיפא: גניטמא טומאת התהום – הציץ מרצה; הא תני רבי חייא: *לא דאמרו טומאת התהום אלא למת בלבד, למת – ו] למעוטי מאי? לאו למעוטי טומאת התהום דשרץ? לא, למעוטי טומאת התהום דזיבה. ואלא הא *דבעי רמי בר חמא: כהן המרצה בקרבנותיהם, הותרה לו טומא' התהום או לא ז] הותרה לו טומאת התהום? תפשוט דטומאת התהום הותרה לו, דהא הכא בכהן קיימינא! דרמי בר חמא ודאי פליגי. תא שמע: °"ונשא אהרן את עון הקדשי'", *וכי איזהו עון נושא? אם

שמות כח | שם כח * פסחים טז: יומא ז. מנחות כה.

רש"י

לפי אכלו. הראוי לאכילה תכוסו עליו, דהיינו שחיטה. במכסת. לשון מנין, כמו "מכסת ערכך" (ויקרא כז). ואיתקש אוכלין למנויין. מה מנויין מעכבי – אף אוכלים מעכבי, שאם שחטו לטמאים ולערלים ח] וחולה וזקן שאין יכולין לאכול כזית – פסול, ואפי' הן מנויין, דהא "לפי אכלו" בהאי קרא כתיב, ט] לגבי מנויין. תורה אור

וכי לא מקשי נמי. וסברי: טמא מת משלח קרבנותיו בדיעבד – אית להו הך פירכא גופא דפרכינן לעיל אמילתייהו, י] דמוקמינן מתניתין בכהן טמא שרץ אבל כהן טמא מת הציץ מרצה, דהא מודה מיהא דלכתחילה אמר רחמנא טמא מת ידחה לשני, וטמא שרץ אמרינן לעיל דשוחטין עליו לכתחילה. ומה במקום כו' בעלים. יחיד. מיתיבי. לזקני דרום. מפני שאמרו. משנה היא ב"כילד צולין" (פסחים דף פ:) שהנזיר ועושה פסח כו'. קס"ד יא] האי טומאת הגוף – בבעלים קאמר. ולהכי נקט נזיר ועושה פסח, דאילו שאר קרבנות – אין טומאת בעלים פסול בהן, אבל עושה פסח אכילתו מעכבת, ונזיר נמי [illegible] שסותר נזירותו וצריך לחזור ולמנות, כדכתיב (במדבר ו): "וכי ימות מת עליו" וגו', ואין ראוי לקרבנות תגלחתו עד שיטהר ויביא תחילה קרבנות (ב) נזירות יב] טומאתו שתי תורים ואשם, וימנה את נזירתו, ואחר כך יביא קרבנות נזירות טהרה. וקתני: אין הציץ מרצה, בדיעבד. אלמא נטמאו כו'. כלומר, אם שלח קרבנו ושחטו וזרקו עליו – לא נפטר מפסח שני. הכי נמי. דמרצה ליך. כגון שנטמא כהן בשרץ. כדתנן: טמא פסול, ואוקימנא בשרץ. ותנן נזיר ועושה פסח, וה"ה לכל קרבנות יחיד. והא דנקט הני – משום סיפא נקט, דבעי מיתני: נטמא טומאת התהום הרי זה מרצה, וכי גמירי היתר טומאת התהום – בנזיר ועושה פסח גמירי לה ב"כילד צולין". וטומאת התהום – טומאת ספק, והתם מפרש איזוהי טומאת התהום כו'. והילכתא גמירי לה דהותרה בנזיר ועושה פסח, כדאמרי' ב"כילד צולין" (פסחים דף פ:). לא אמרו. דהותרה טומאת התהום בנזיר ועושה פסח – אלא בטומאת המת בלבד. מאי לאו למעוטי טומאת התהום דשרץ. דלא הותרה. ומק"ו לא אתיא, שאין דנין ק"ו מהלכה. טומאת התהום דזיבה. כגון ראה בין השמשות, ספק כולה מן היום או כולה מן הלילה ואין כאן אלא ראייה אחת, ספק חלייה מן היום וחלייה מן הלילה והוי לה כשתי ראיות, דזב מטמא בימים ובראיות. והך טומאת התהום הוא דממעט, משום דחמירא, דיולדה עליו מגופו. דבעי רמי בר חמא. ב"כילד צולין". כהן המרצה בקרבנותיהן. של נזיר ועושה פסח – הותרה לו טומאת התהום, אם נטמא בה. יג] והא הכא בכהן אוקמא לה. לרישא דקתני: אין הציץ מרצה על טומאת הגוף, ועלה קתני: נטמא טומאת התהום – הרי זה מרצה. יד] דרמי בר חמא פליג הוא. אדזקני דרום. הוא מוקים להיא בטומאת בעלים, וסבירא (ג) דאין יחיד טמא מת משלח קרבנותיו, דאכילת פסחים מעכב. תא שמע. תיובתא לרמי בר חמא. ונשא אהרן. בציץ כתיב. את עון הקדשים. פסול קרבנות ירצה בציץ. אם

תוספות

הכא נמי נייתי ק"ו ליפוק מהיקשא! ועוד קשה: היכי יליף טמא שרץ דיחיד בק"ו מטמא מת דיחיד! הא טמא טו] גופיה דיחיד יליף על ידי "מתוך", וכי האי גוונא חשיב בבנין אב בפרק "איזהו מקומן" (לקמן דף נא.), דקאמר: לן בדם כשר הואיל ולן טז] כשר באימורין. ודבר הלמד בבנין אב אינו חוזר ומלמד בקל וחומר! וי"ל: דבעיא היא ב"איזהו מקומן", והכא – אם יז] נאמר דילפי' קאמר. ועוד י"ל: דהאי "מתוך" אינו בבנין אב, דאי הוי בבנין אב – א"כ יאכל ביחיד כבציבור. **זקני** דרום לא מקשי. וזקני דרום תנאי הוו, ופליגי אמתני' ד"תמיד נשחט" (פסחים דף סא.) דתנן: השוחט לערלים ולטמאים – פסול. יח] אי נמי, סבירא להו כר' נתן, ולית להו הא דקאמר התלמוד יט] ב"כילד צולין" (שם דף עח:) דמודה ר' נתן היכא דגברא לא חזי. **מפני** שאמרו נזיר ועושה פסח. אע"ג כ] דפרש"י זקני דרום תנאי היא – אפירכא דסיפא סמיך, דנטמא טומאת התהום מרצה [ו] (וכולי עלמא אית כא] להון טומאת התהום מרצה) דהילכתא גמירי לה, כדאיתא פרק "כילד צולין" (פסחים פ:). וכן ברייתא דר' חייא לא אמרו טומאת התהום אלא למת בלבד, דפריך מינה התם לרבי יוסי. **אלא** בטומאת מת כב] בבעלים וקתני אין הציץ מרצה. וקשיא לזקני דרום, דאמרו "איש איש" למצוה. **לא** למעוטי טומאת התהום דזיבה. וא"ת: מ"מ קשיא ברייתא דר' חייא, דלא אמרו טומאת התהום אלא למת בלבד, הא כג] איטמי כהן טומאה ידועה – לא מרצי! ותירץ ה"ר חיים: דמיירי במת בשביעי, והוי כטומאת שרץ דשוחטין וזורקין, ולא מרצי – משום דמכפרין כמתכפרין. והשתא חמיר בשביעי דלא מרצי, וטמא מת בראשון מרצי. והיינו טעמא: דבשביעי יכול לעשות בטהרה על ידי שליח, וחזי למיכל לאורתא, אבל בראשון – לא אפשר לתקנו ולעשותו בטהרה, לכך בדיעבד כשר. ומיירי ברייתא דר' חייא כד] [בטומאת התהום, דאי איטמי] כהן בטומאת ודאי של שרץ, או במת בשביעי שלו – אינו מרצה ביחיד אפי' בדיעבד, (שהרי אינו מרצה בציבור בתמיד) דהא מכפרין כמתכפרין, וציבור טמאי שרץ או בשביעי של מת לא עבדי בטומאה, אלא שולחים קרבנותיהם על ידי טהורין, כיון דחזו לאורתא. אבל בטומאת התהום – מרצה כהן ביחיד. אבל בבעלים לא מתוקמא ברייתא דר' חייא, דכיון דשוחטין וזורקין על טמאי שרץ ושולחים קרבנותיהם ביד טהורים – איזה ריצוי צריך שייך? וגם טומאת התהום נמי לא שריא להו למיעבד אינהו גופייהו, כיון דשוחטין וזורקין עליהן, ומצו למיעבד ע"י טהורין. ועוד יש לפרש: דמיירי בכהן שקיבל הדם בטומאת התהום דמת, שמרצה לכתחילה לזרוק, ולא מהדרי' אטהורין אפי' איכא כהן טהור. הא טומאה ידועה – לא מרצה לכתחילה, אלא מהדרינן אטהורין, דטומאה דחויה היא בציבור. וכי האי גוונא צריך לפרש בפרק "כילד צולין" (שם פא.) דבעי התם: כהן המרצה בתמיד, הותרה לו טומאת התהום או לא הותרה? ומאי קמיבעיא ליה! הא קיימא לן "במועדו" אפי' בטומאה! אלא אי יכול לזרוק בטומאה לכתחילה קמיבעיא ליה, כדפרישית, ואפי' איכא טהורין. **טומאת** התהום דזיבה. פ"ה: כגון ראה בין השמשות כה] של י"ג, ספק כולה מן היום או מן הלילה ואין כאן אלא ראייה אחת, ספק חליה מן היום וחליה מן הלילה ויש כאן שתי ראיות, דזב מטמא בימים ובראיות. וקשה: דבפרק "כילד צולין" (נ"ז שם) לא מצי משכח לרבי יוסי טומאת התהום, כו] ולימא כי האי גוונא! ונראה לי ברו"ך דבעינן שהספק לא יהא נודע עד לאחר שחיטה, [ב] ואם אמרו לו לאחר שחיטה: ראית בין השמשות סוף יום שלשה עשר – הא בעינן כז] טומאת התהום שלא יהא אחד מכיר בסוף העולם. לכך בעי התם: בשלמא לרבנן משכחת לה דשחטו על זב בשביעי שלו, דשוחטין וזורקין על טמא שרץ, ואח"כ ראה – וסותר. אבל לר' יוסי דאמר מקצת היום ככולו, ומכאן ולהבא מטמא, ולא סתר מידי כח] – [היכי משכחת ליה]? ורבינו הקשה: לימא שראה לפני שחיטה ושחטו עליו, וחזר וראה שניה, דסבר אפי' לר' יוסי, וצריך למנות שבעה, דזב תלוי בראיות, וליכא לא תחילת היום בטהרה ולא סוף היום! ולדידי אתי שפיר, דכיון דראה בצפרא – מיד היה ספק אולי יראה עוד כט] ביום, והוי כנודע הספק קודם ל] שחיטה. ורבינו מתרץ בזה: דכיון דראייה ראשונה אינה מטמאה במשא – א"כ מועיל לו מה ששחטו וזרקו עליו. אע"ג דראייה שנייה מצטרפת לראשונה לחייבו מנין שבעה – מכל מקום לעולם היה קרוי טמא שרץ בשעת עשיית הקרבן, וגם אחר כן לא פקע שמו, ויצא ידי פסחו. וקשה [ג] על לא] פירושו משמעתין *) (כהן המרצה [ד] בציבור היא)! וי"ל: כגון שראה אחת בי"ג וטבל והעריב שמשו, ושחט למחר הפסח, ואחרי כן ראה שנייה ומצטרפת. ואין זה קרוי נודע הספק קודם שחיטה – כיון שטהור גמור בשעת שחיטה. וליכא למימר אולי יראה [ה] לשני ימים ומצטרפין – דלר' יוסי אינה מצטרפת לראשונה. ברו"ך. אם

*) רש"ק מ"ז

עין משפט נר מצוה

סז א מיי' פ"ב מהל' קרבן פסח הל"ח:
סח ב ג מיי' פ"ד מהל' קרבן פסח הל"ב ופ"ז שם הל"ב ופ"ד מהל' ביאת מקדש הל' ז ופ"ז מהל' נזירות הל' טו:
סט ד מיי' פ"ו מהל' נזירות הל' יח:

מסורת הש"ס

פסחים סא. עח: ע"ש
[פסחים סא. עח: יומא לט: נח: יבמות מ. שבועות יד. מנחות יט:]
פסחים פ: תוספת' דפסחים פ"ו תוספתא דנזיר פ"ו תוספתא דמנחות פ"ק
נזיר סג. [פסחים פ: פא:]
פסחים פ:

הגהות הב"ח

(א) גמ' לא מקשי נמי מיהא אית כצ"ל ותיבת נמי נמחק: (ב) רש"י ד"ה מפני וכו' קרבנות נזיר טמא שתי תורים: (ג) ד"ה דרמי וכו' וסבירא ליה דאין:

שיטה מקובצת

א] המצוה. וכשר: ב] מקשי. אמר רב אשי וכי לא מקשי נמי אית להו פירכא: ג] מקום שנטמאו בעלים במת כו' תימה דדיו לבא מן הדין להיות כנדון בסוף דינא מה בעלים לכתחלה לא מרצה אבל בדיעבד ...

... שהביא קרבנותיו של נזירות ראה וסתר וזהו טומאת התהום שנתברר לבסוף אבל בשעת שהביאו קרבנותיהן נזיר ועושה פסח לא היה יודע אם יראה יומים ומיירי ע"כ בבעלים דאי בכהן לא היה נכנס בעזרה אם היה זב ואפי' בעל ב' ראיות דהא מחוסר הערב שמש וכ"ש בזב בעל (שתי) [שלש] ראיות דהא מחוסר כפרה וא"כ אפילו קודם שראה איך היה נכנס מתחלה [בעזרה] להקריב קרבנות (בעזרה) והך דר' חייא לא הוי דומיא דרישא דהא אוקמינא רישא בכהן שנטמא והך דר' חייא איירי בבעלים ואל תתמה על זה דהא בלאו הכי נמי לא הוי דומיא דרישא ממש דהא אוקמינא רישא בטומאת שרץ ומילתא דרבי חייא איירי [במת] והתם אפי' בדיעבד אין הציץ מרצה ובמילתא דר' חייא הוי אפי' לכתחילה כך פי' מורי [ע"כ]:
לא] על. פירושנו דשמעתין בכהן המרצה בצבור איירי וי"ל:

אילימא

הגהות צ"ק [א] מיהו אלו מן דכולי עד מרלה נמחק: [ב] ואפילו אמר לן לאחר שחיטה ראיתי בה"ש של י"ג הא כו': [ג] וקשה על פירושי: [ד] נ"א ודור דהא לא שוחטים טומאת שרץ: [ה] ב' ימים:

אִם עֲוֹן פִּיגּוּל — הֲרֵי כְּבָר נֶאֱמַר: "לֹא יֵחָשֵׁב", אִם עֲוֹן נוֹתָר — הֲרֵי כְּבָר נֶאֱמַר: "לֹא יֵרָצֶה", הָא אֵינוֹ נוֹשֵׂא אֶלָּא עֲוֹן טוּמְאָה שֶׁהוּתְּרָה מִכְּלָלָהּ בְּצִבּוּר; מַאי טוּמְאָה? א] אִילֵימָא (א) מִטּוּמְאַת שֶׁרֶץ — הֵיכָא אִישְׁתְּרֵי? אֶלָּא טוּמְאַת מֵת, וְלָאו כְּגוֹן שֶׁנִּטְמְאוּ בְּעָלִים בְּמֵת? אַלְמָא: נִטְמְאוּ בְּעָלִים בְּמֵת מְשַׁלְּחִין קָרְבְּנוֹתֵיהֶן. וּבְמַאי? אִי בְּנָזִיר — "וְכִי יָמוּת מֵת עָלָיו" אָמַר רַחֲמָנָא! אֶלָּא לְעוֹשֶׂה פֶּסַח (וְלָאו כְּגוֹן שֶׁנִּטְמְאוּ בְּעָלִים בְּמֵת?). לְעוֹלָם בְּשֶׁרֶץ, וְשֵׁם טוּמְאָה בָּעוֹלָם. וְאִיכָּא דְּדָיֵיק וּמַיְיתֵי הָכִי: עֲוֹן הַקֳּדָשִׁים — אִין, עֲוֹן מַקְדִּישִׁין — לָא; ב] מַאי טוּמְאָה? אִילֵימָא טוּמְאַת שֶׁרֶץ — מִי אִישְׁתַּרְיָא בְּצִיבּוּר? אֶלָּא לָאו טוּמְאַת מֵת, וַעֲוֹן קֳדָשִׁים — אִין, ג] עֲוֹן מַקְדִּישִׁים — לָא! לְעוֹלָם טוּמְאַת שֶׁרֶץ, וְשֵׁם טוּמְאָה בָּעוֹלָם.§ "יוֹשֵׁב". מְנָלַן? *אָמַר רָבָא אָמַר רַב ד] נַחְמָן: אָמַר קְרָא: "לַעֲמוֹד לְשָׁרֵת" — לַעֲמִידָה בְּחַרְתִּיו וְלֹא לִישִׁיבָה. ת"ר: "לַעֲמוֹד לְשָׁרֵת" א) — מִצְוָה, כְּשֶׁהוּא *אוֹמֵר: "הָעוֹמְדִים" ג) — שָׁנָה עָלָיו הַכָּתוּב לְעַכֵּב. א"ל רָבָא לְרַב נַחְמָן: מִכְּדֵי יוֹשֵׁב כְּזָר דָּמֵי, וּמַחֵיל עֲבוֹדָה, אֵימָא: מָה זָר בְּמִיתָה — אַף יוֹשֵׁב בְּמִיתָה; אַלְּמָה *תַּנְיָא: אָבֵל בעָרֵל, גאוֹנֵן, דיוֹשֵׁב — אֵינָן בְּמִיתָה אֶלָּא בְּאַזְהָרָה? מִשּׁוּם דַּהֲוֵי מְחוּסַּר בְּגָדִים וְשֶׁלֹּא רְחוּץ יָדַיִם וְרַגְלַיִם ה] שְׁנֵי כְתוּבִין הַבָּאִין כְּאֶחָד, וְכָל

א) [עי' תוס' לעיל טז. סד"ה מיושב] ב) [פסחים סא. וש"נ]

אִם עֲוֹן פִּיגּוּל הֲרֵי כְּבָר נֶאֱמַר לֹא יֵרָצֶה וְאִם עֲוֹן נוֹתָר הֲרֵי כְּבָר נֶאֱמַר לֹא יֵחָשֵׁב. ה"ג לָהּ בְּת"כ, וְכֵן הַלָּעָתָהּ בְּכָל מָקוֹם. וְה"ק: אֵיזֶה פְּסוּל קָרְבָּן ו] מְרַצֶּה הוּא? אִם עֲוֹן פִּיגּוּל דְּמַחֲשֶׁבֶת חוּץ לִמְקוֹמוֹ, דְּאִיקְּרֵי פִּיגּוּל, כִּדְאָמַר לְקַמָּן בְּפִירְקִין (דף כח.): "פִּיגּוּל הוּא לֹא יֵרָצֶה", אִם אֵינוֹ לְעִנְיַן חוּץ לִזְמַנּוֹ תְּנֵיהוּ לְעִנְיַן חוּץ לִמְקוֹמוֹ — הֲרֵי כְּבָר נֶאֱמַר "לֹא יֵרָצֶה". אִם עֲוֹן נוֹתָר. פְּסוּל מַחֲשֶׁבֶת נוֹתָר, שֶׁחִישֵּׁב לְאוֹכְלוֹ לְאַחַר שֶׁנַּעֲשָׂה נוֹתָר, דְּהַיְינוּ מַחֲשֶׁבֶת חוּץ לִזְמַנּוֹ. הֲרֵי כְּבָר נֶאֱמַר הַמַּקְרִיב אוֹתוֹ לֹא יֵחָשֵׁב. וְהַאי קְרָא בְּחוּץ לִזְמַנּוֹ מִיתּוֹקְמָא בְּפִירְקִין. וּבַסְּפָרִים שֶׁלָּנוּ גִּירְסָא זוֹ מְשׁוּבֶּשֶׁת בְּכ"מ בַּתַּלְמוּד, וּמַחֲלִיפִין הַמִּקְרָאוֹת. וְלָאוֹתָהּ הַגִּירְסָא אֵינָךְ יָכוֹל לְפָרֵשׁ "נוֹתָר" זֶה בְּמַחֲשֶׁבֶת חוּץ לִזְמַנּוֹ וְהַ"פִּיגּוּל" בְּמַחֲשֶׁבֶת חוּץ לִמְקוֹמוֹ, דְּ"לֹא יֵחָשֵׁב" בְּחוּץ לִזְמַנּוֹ כְּתִיב. וְצָרִיךְ אַתָּה לְפָרֵשׁ נוֹתָר מַמָּשׁ, וְאִי אֶפְשָׁר לוֹמַר כֵּן, שֶׁאֵין הַקָּרְבָּן שֶׁקָּרְבוּ מַתִּירָיו בְּהֶכְשֵׁר ז] נִפְסָל מִלְּרַצּוֹת וְלַעֲלוֹת לְשֵׁם חוֹבָה אִם הוֹתִיר מִמֶּנּוּ ח]. הָא אֵינוֹ נוֹשֵׂא כו'. ט] הָא, כְּלוֹמַר *הִנֵּה מָלִינוּ שֶׁאֵינוֹ נוֹשֵׂא אֶלָּא עֲוֹן הַטּוּמְאָה. וְיֵשׁ טַעַם לַדָּבָר לִיתֵּן י] נְשִׂיאַת פְּסוּל קָדָשִׁים זֶה עַל טוּמְאָה, הוֹאִיל וּמָלִינוּ לָהּ הֶיתֵּר אַחֵר, שֶׁהוּתְּרָה מִכְּלָלָהּ בְּצִבּוּר לְכַתְּחִילָּה, הִילְכָּךְ יָחִיד שֶׁלֹּא הוּתְּרָה אֶצְלוֹ — יָבֹא הַצִּיץ וִירַצֶּה בְּדִיעֲבַד. אִילֵימָא טוּמְאַת שֶׁרֶץ. יא] מִתּוֹקְמָא, בְּכֹהֵן אוֹ בִּבְעָלִים, וּלְמֵימַר דְּהַאי דְּשׁוֹחֵט וְזוֹרֵק עַל טְמֵא שֶׁרֶץ — צִיץ הוּא דִּמְרַצֶּה. הֵיכָא אִישְׁתְּרַאי. בְּצִבּוּר? כֵּיוָן דְּאֵין יָחִיד נִדְחֶה — לְצִבּוּר לָא עָבְדֵי בְּטוּמְאָה. לָאו כְּגוֹן שֶׁנִּטְמְאוּ בְּעָלִים בְּמֵת. בִּתְמִיָּה: וּמִי לָא מַיְירֵי בְּטוּמְאַת בְּעָלִים? וְקָתָנֵי: מְשַׁלְּחִין! וְכִי יָמוּת מֵת עָלָיו אָמַר רַחֲמָנָא. יב] דְּטָמֵא רֹאשׁ נִזְרוֹ וְסוֹתֵר, וְאֵין רָאוּי לְקָרְבָּנוֹת טׇהֳרָה עַד שֶׁיַּעַבְרוּ יְמֵי טוּמְאָה וְיָבִיא כַּפָּרַת טוּמְאַת נְזִירוּתוֹ שְׁתֵּי תוֹרִים וְאָשָׁם, וְיִמְנֶה וְיַשְׁלִים וְיָבִיא קָרְבְּנוֹת תִּגְלַחְתּוֹ! אֶלָּא בְּעוֹשֶׂה פֶּסַח. וש"מ: טְמֵא מֵת מְשַׁלֵּחַ פִּסְחוֹ, וְקַשְׁיָא לְרָמִי בַּר חָמָא. לְעוֹלָם. טוּמְאַת שֶׁרֶץ קָאָמְרִינַן (ג) יג] מְהַכָּא, דְּצִיץ מְרַצֶּה לִשְׁחוֹט וְלִזְרוֹק עַל טְמֵא שֶׁרֶץ. וּדְקַשְׁיָא לָךְ: הֵיכָא אִישְׁתְּרַאי בָּהֶן? וְשֵׁם טוּמְאָה בָּעוֹלָם. אַשְׁכַּחַן דְּאִישְׁתְּרַאי יד] בָּהֶן. וְטַעְמָא גָּדוֹל בָּהוּ לְהַטִּיל רִיצּוּי צִיץ עַל טוּמְאַת שֶׁרֶץ. וְאִיכָּא דְּדָיֵיק. לִישָּׁנָא דִּקְרָאֵי, טו] וּמַיְיתִינָא לְהַךְ תְּיוּבְתָּא דְּבָרַיְיתָא לְזִקְנֵי דָרוֹם, וְסַיַּיעְתָּא לְרָמִי בַּר חָמָא. עֲוֹן מַקְדִּישִׁים לֹא. טוּמְאַת הַגּוּף, בֵּין דְּכֹהֲנִים בֵּין דִּבְעָלִים — לֹא מְרַצֶּה. בְּמַאי טוּמְאָה קָאֵי דְּקָא מְמַעֵט טוּמְאַת הַגּוּף? אִילֵימָא טוּמְאַת שֶׁרֶץ. וְנוֹקְמָא זִקְנֵי דָרוֹם בְּכֹהֵן. דְּאִילּוּ גּוּף דִּבְעָלִים לָא בָּעֵי צִיץ, שֶׁהֲרֵי אֵין נוֹגֵעַ בּוֹ בְּטוּמְאָה, וְלָאוֹרְתָּא — בְּטׇהֳרָה אָכֵיל לֵיהּ. הֵיכָא אִישְׁתְּרַאי בְּצִבּוּר. הָא כֵּיוָן דְּאִית לְהוּ שׁוֹחֲטִין וְזוֹרְקִין עַל טְמֵא שֶׁרֶץ, וְיָחִיד אֵין נִדְחֶה — לְצִבּוּר לָא עָבְדֵי בְּטוּמְאָה! אֶלָּא לָאו טוּמְאַת מֵת. טז] *) שֶׁאֵינוֹ מְשַׁלֵּחַ קָרְבָּנוֹת, וְלֹא כֹּהֵן טְמֵא מֵת מְרַצֶּה בְּקָרְבַּן יָחִיד. לְעוֹלָם בְּטוּמְאַת שֶׁרֶץ. קָאֵי, וְקָמְמַעֵט כֹּהֵן טְמֵא שֶׁרֶץ מִלְּרַצּוֹת, יז] כִּדְאוֹקְמֵי זִקְנֵי דָרוֹם פָּסוּל דְּמַתְנִיתִין אַטְּמֵא שֶׁרֶץ. וְטוּמְאַת בְּעָלִים אֵין צְרִיכִין צִיץ, שֶׁהֲרֵי קָרְבָּן בְּטׇהֳרָה קָרֵב. וּדְקַשְׁיָא לָךְ: הֵיכָא אִישְׁתְּרַאי בְּצִבּוּר — שׁוּם טוּמְאָה בָּעוֹלָם אִישְׁתְּרַאי בְּהוּ. לַעֲמוֹד לְשָׁרֵת. רֵישֵׁיהּ דִּקְרָא: "כִּי בוֹ בָּחַר ה' אֱלֹהֶיךָ מִכׇּל שְׁבָטֶיךָ יח] לַעֲמוֹד [א] לְשָׁרֵת" וגו'. יט] לֹא לִישִׁיבָה. א) וְכֵיוָן דְּלֹא נִבְחֲרוּ — הָווּ לְהוּ זָרִים, וְזָר מַחֵיל עֲבוֹדָה. הָעוֹמְדִים שָׁם. *) [לְעֵיל מִינֵּיהּ כְּתִיב] "וְשֵׁרֵת כְּכׇל אֶחָיו הַלְוִיִּם" וגו'. [אֵימָא מַה זָּר וכו'. וְנִיגְמַר בְּ"מָה מָּלִינוּ" בְּזָר שֶׁמֵּיחֵל עֲבוֹדָה וְחַיָּיב מִיתָה — אַף יוֹשֵׁב שֶׁמְּחַלֵּל עֲבוֹדָה בְּמִיתָה]. שְׁנֵי

* ס"א אלמא אין טמא משלח קרבנות מהרש"ק *) נ"ל רישיה דקרא רש"ק

אם עון פיגול הרי כבר נאמר לא ירצה ואם עון נותר הרי כבר נאמר לא יחשב. כך כ] פי' הקונטרס, משום דאמרי' לקמן בפירקין (דף כח.) דאיסור רבה דחוץ לזמנו שהוא בכרת — מקרא רבה ופרשה רבה ב"לו את אהרן", ואיסורא זוטא דחוץ למקומו דליכא כרת — מקרא זוטא ופרשתא זוטא בפרשת "קדושים תהיו". והביא ראייה מתורת כהנים. ורבינו תם מקיים גירסת הספרים, דגרסינן איפכא: בפיגול — "לא יחשב" ובנותר "לא ירצה", דלקמן בפירקין מסקינן דתרווייהו [ב] מקרא אחרינא נפקי, דכתיב ביה "לא ירצה ולא יחשב". ומה שנזכר פיגול קודם לנותר אף ע"ג דבקרא כתיב כא] נותר ברישא, דהיינו חוץ לזמנו — משום דלשון פיגול כתיב בקרא בהדיא. **אם** עון נותר הרי כבר נאמר כו'. לאו נותר ממש [קאמר], כדאמרי' לקמן בפירקין (דף כט.): לאחר שהוכשר יפסל? אלא במחשבת נותר, דהיינו מחשב לאוכלו חוץ לזמנו. **הא** אינו נושא אלא עון טומאה שהותרה מכללה. וא"ת: תיפוק לי דלא משכחת מידי דמיתוקם ביה קרא אלא בטומאה! ואומר רבינו תם: משום דכתיב גבי ציץ: "לרצון להם" — דמשמע דבר שהוא לרצון במקום אחר, ולהכי דחיק לאשכוחי הותר מכללן מכל הני דפריך מינייהו (במנחות דף כה.): יוצא, ושמאל, ובעל מום. כב] [וא"ת:] (א"כ) נותר ופיגול היכן הותרו מכללן, דאיצטריך ליה "לא ירצה" ו"לא יחשב"? ואומר רבינו תם: דפיגול הותר מכללו בבמה, דלא שייך שם מחשבת חוץ למקומו. והא דפריך ב"הקומץ רבה" (מנחות דף כה.): אימא עון יוצא שהותר מכללו בבמה? כג] אמר קרא: "לרצון להם לפני ה'", עון דלפני ה' אין, עון דיוצא לא — חוץ למקומו חשיב שפיר "לפני ה'", שהמחשבה בפנים. ואין לומר דבבמה לא קרינן ליה הותר מכללו כיון דהכשירו בכך כדקאמר התם גבי שמאל, דכיון דאסור בפנים — אין זה קרוי הכשירו בכך. ונותר כדי נסבה, ואגב פיגול נקט נותר הואיל ומשכח ביה קרא, אע"ג דלא צריך. אי נמי: נותר הותר מכללו בראשו של מזבח, דאיכא למאן דאמר אין לינה מועלת בראשו של מזבח בריש "תמיד נשחט" (פסחים ד' נט.) ובפ' "המזבח מקדש" (לקמן ד' פז.). ומיהו, פלוגתא דאמוראי היא, וקשיא [ג] למ"ד [דאית ליה] לינה מועלת מהך ברייתא. ונראה דנותר יש ללמדו "עון" "עון" מריצוי ציץ, ופגול נמי מלינן למילף כד] ואפי' לא משכחת בהו הותר מכללן. ו"לרצון להם" איכא לאוקמי כדדרשי' בפ' "הבא על יבמתו" (יבמות דף ס:): כה] [להם לרצון ולא לפורעניות], אבל לגוים אפי' לפורענות. ועוד י"ל: דנותר הותר מכללו במנחת כהנים ומנחת כהן משיח וקומץ, וכל דבר שאין לו מתירים כו] אין חייבים עליהן משום פיגול, כדתנן פ' "ב"ש" (לקמן דף מג:). ואפי' פסולא נמי נראה דליכא, מדאמר לעיל בסוף פ"ק (דף יד.) דמודה ר' שמעון בהולכת חטאות הפנימיות. ופריך, והא"ר שמעון: כל שאינו על מזבח החיצון אין חייבין עליו משום פגול! ומשני: מודה ר' שמעון דפסול מק"ו, ומה שלא לשמו הכשר בשלמים פסול בחטאת, חוץ לזמנו הפסול בשלמים — א"ד שיפסל בחטאת? משמע דאי לאו ק"ו כז] הוה אמינא דאפי' פסולא ליכא. א"כ במנחת כהנים ובמנחת נסכים דליכא ק"ו, דלא מיפסל בזו שלא לשמן — ליכא פסולא כלל. אלמא אשכחן נותר דהותר מכללו לגמרי. **לאו** כגון שנטמאו בעלים במת. תימה: מאי קשיא ליה? לוקמה בטומאת הדם, שנטמא הדם הציץ מרצה דגבי טומאת דם מייתי לה בכולי התלמוד (לקמן מה.) דדם שנטמא וזרקו בשוגג — הורצה. ותנן נמי בפסחים (דף עח:) נטמא כח] *הדם והבשר קיים — זורק הדם! וי"ל: דס"ל להאי לישנא דלית ליה למימר דנושא עון טומאה אלא בכי האי גוונא שהותרה בצבור, דהיינו בטומאת בעלים דהותרה לאכול בטומאת הגוף, למאי דלא מסיק אדעתיה השתא עון קדשים ולא עון מקדישים. **אי** נימא טומאת שרץ בבעלים היכא אישתראי. דאי סבר שוחטין וזורקין על טמא שרץ, וכן טמא מת בשביעי שלו דחשיב כטמא שרץ — הא לא עבדי לצבור בטומאה. כיון דאין יחיד נדחה — לצבור נמי לא עבדי בטומאה, אלא עושין שליח לשחוט בעבורם, כיון דאינהו אכלי לאורתא. ואי סבר אין שוחטין וזורקין על טמא שרץ, דהשתא לצבור עבדי בטומאה — א"כ אין הציץ מרצה על היחיד, דהא אין שוחטין וזורקין עליו, כט] אלא נטמאו בעלים במת, וקודם שביעי מרצה ליחיד שהביא פסחו, וסייעתא לזקני דרום דאמרי: "איש איש" למעוט. וקשה: מאי פריך היכא אישתראי? לוקמה בכהן שנטמא בשרץ, דמרצה בצבור מק"ו דלעיל, לרמי בר חמא, דלית ליה כמו זקני דרום מכפרים כמתכפרין? ועוד, כי משני: לעולם בשרץ, ושם טומאה בעולם — הא כיון דשוחטין וזורקין על טמא שרץ, א"כ ריצוי ציץ ל"ל? הא קרב בטהרה, כדפירש רבינו שלמה בסמוך. ואי סבר אין שוחטין על טמא שרץ — א"כ לא יועיל ציץ, *כדפירש ל] לעיל אי בשרץ היכא אישתראי! וי"ל: למעיקרא בעי לאוקומה בטומאת בעלים בשרץ, והוה מצי למפרך ל"ל ריצוי ציץ. אלא שפיר פריך היכא אישתראי. וכי משני לעולם בשרץ — רוצה לומר ולא בטומאת בעלים, אלא בטומאת כהן גרידא, וכ"ש בטומאת מת. וסבר רמי בר חמא טומאת מת מרצה בכהן ביחיד. וקצת קשה: דלא ה"ל למימר שם טומאה בעולם, משמע דטומאת מת בצבור קאמר — והלא טומאת שרץ נמי הותרה לכהן מק"ו דלעיל. אלא משום דעיקר היתר לצבור בטומאת מת כתיבא, להכי נקט ליה. כרו"ך. **אימא** מה זר במיתה אף יושב במיתה. פי' בקונטרס: דניגמר במה מלינו, מה זר מחלל עבודה וחייב מיתה — אף יושב שמחלל עבודה במיתה. וקשה: דגבי ערל ואונן נמי היה לן להקשות כמו כן ליהוי במיתה מבנין לא] אב! ונראה דפריך משום דדרשי' לעמידה בחרתיו ולא לישיבה, שלא בחר בכהנים יושבים, אלא נחשבים כמו ישראלים זרים — לכך מחלל עבודה לב] כזר, [ומש"ה גם במיתה להוי כזר]. ומשני: דמשום דהוי מחוסר בגדים ושלא רחוץ ידים ורגלים לג] [שני כתובים הבאים כאחד, דבמחוסר בגדים כתיב ביה מיתה: "ולא ישאו עון ומתו", ובשלא רחוץ ידים ורגלים] נמי כתיב ביה מיתה: "ולא ימותו". ובחנם נכתבה, דהא ילפי' "חוקה" "חוקה" לגזירה שוה, אלא למימרא דלא ילפי' מיתה דקרי' רחמנא זר. וניחא השתא, דהלא

א) מדברי התוס' ד"ה אימא מה זר נראה דצריך למחוק מן וכיון עד מחיל עבודה וה"ג ה"ג ולא לישיבה ומהכא נפיק לן אזהרה בסנהדרין (דף פד.) באלו הן הנשרפין לעיכוב כדקתני לקמן העומדים שם לשרת כו'

ד] א) רב. הונא אמר רב: ה] שני כתובין. פ"ה וה"ה כו' אלא משום דמחוסר בגדים כו' שייך למיפרך דטעם דידהו לא הוי משום פיסול זר ומשני: לג] ורגלים. שני כתובים באים כאחד ולפי מה שפירשתי [לעיל בהא] דמטעם זרות פסלינן ליושב כמו כן מחוסר בגדים ושלא דמחוסר בגדים פסול מטעם זרות וכתיב ביה מיתה בפרשת ואתה תצוה ולא ימותו ושלא רחוץ ידים ורגלים:

...ל אמר רבא רק רב הונא אמר רב.

הגהות צ"ק [א] לשרת כו' וגו' ולא לישיבה וכיון דלא נבחרו ה"ל זרים וזר מחיל עבודה כדילפינן מושרת ככל אחיו הלוים העומדים שם הס"ד וכצ"ל: [ב] נ"ל מקרא אריכא: [ג] נ"א למ"ד דלינה מועלת כו':

עין משפט נר מצוה

ע א מיי' פ"ד מהל' ביאת מקדש הל"ז ופ"א מהל' פה"מ הל' לד ופי"א הלכה יט:

עא ב מיי' פ"ו מהל' ביאת מקדש הל"ח:

עב ג מיי' פ"ב שם הל"ח:

עג ד מיי' פ"ה שם הל' יז:

שיטה מקובצת

א] אילימא טומאת שרץ. פ"ה ותוקמא בין בכהן בין בבעלים ולא דק...

הגהות הב"ח

שיטה מקובצת

עין משפט נר מצוה

עד א מיי' פ"ה מהל' ביאת מקדש הלי"ח:
עה ב מיי' שם הלי"ט:
עו ג מיי' פ"א מהל' בית הבחירה הל"י:

נ"א ולפירוש הקונטרס דיליף במה מצינו קשה כו' וגי' רש"ק ולפירוש הקונטרס דיליף מחדא וכו'

גמרא

תורה אור

*וְכָל שְׁנֵי כְתוּבִים הַבָּאִין כְּאֶחָד אֵין מְלַמְּדִין. וּלְמַאן דְּאָמַר מְלַמְּדִין, א] שְׁתוּיֵי יַיִן הֲוָה לֵיהּ שְׁלִישִׁי, וּשְׁלֹשָׁה ב] לְדִבְרֵי הַכֹּל אֵין מְלַמְּדִין.§ "עוֹמֵד עַל גַּבֵּי כֵלִים, עַל גַּבֵּי בְהֵמָה, עַל גַּבֵּי רַגְלֵי חֲבֵירוֹ – פָּסוּל".§ מְנָלַן? דְּתָנָא דְּבֵי רַבִּי יִשְׁמָעֵאל: הוֹאִיל וְרִצְפָּה מְקַדֶּשֶׁת וּכְלֵי שָׁרֵת מְקַדְּשִׁים, מַה כְּלֵי שָׁרֵת – לֹא יְהֵא דָּבָר חוֹצֵץ בֵּינוֹ לְבֵין כְּלֵי שָׁרֵת, אַף רִצְפָּה – לֹא יְהֵא דָּבָר חוֹצֵץ בֵּינוֹ לְבֵין הָרִצְפָּה. וּצְרִיכָא, דְּאִי אַשְׁמְעִינַן כְּלִי – מִשּׁוּם דְּלָאו מִינָא דְּבָשָׂר ג] נִינְהוּ, אֲבָל בְּהֵמָה דְּמִינָא דְּבָשָׂר הוּא אֵימָא לָא; וְאִי אַשְׁמְעִינַן בְּהֵמָה – דְּלָא מִינָא דְּאָדָם הוּא, אֲבָל חֲבֵירוֹ דְּאָדָם הוּא אֵימָא לָא, צְרִיכָא. *תַּנְיָא, רַבִּי אֱלִיעֶזֶר אוֹמֵר: רַגְלוֹ אַחַת עַל הַכְּלִי וְרַגְלוֹ אַחַת עַל הָרִצְפָּה, רַגְלוֹ אַחַת עַל הָאֶבֶן וְרַגְלוֹ אַחַת עַל הָרִצְפָּה – רוֹאִין, כָּל שֶׁאִילּוּ ד] יִנָּטֵל הַכְּלִי וְתִנָּטֵל הָאֶבֶן יָכוֹל לַעֲמוֹד עַל רַגְלוֹ אַחַת וְיַעֲבוֹד – עֲבוֹדָתוֹ כְּשֵׁירָה, וְאִם לָאו – עֲבוֹדָתוֹ פְּסוּלָה. בָּעֵי רַבִּי אַמִי: נִדַּלְדְּלָה הָאֶבֶן וְעָמַד עָלֶיהָ, מַהוּ? הֵיכָא דְּאֵין דַּעְתּוֹ לְחַבְּרָהּ – לָא תִּיבָּעֵי לָךְ, דְּוַדַּאי חָיְיצָא, כִּי תִּיבָּעֵי לָךְ – דְּדַעְתּוֹ לְחַבְּרָהּ, מַאי? כֵּיוָן דְּדַעְתּוֹ לְחַבְּרָהּ – כְּמָה דִּמְחַבְּרָ' דָּמְיָא, אוֹ דִילְמָא הַשְׁתָּא מִיהָא הָא תְּלִישָׁא? רַבָּה זוּטֵי בָּעֵי לָהּ הָכִי, בָּעֵי רַבִּי אַמִי: נֶעֶקְרָה הָאֶבֶן וְעָמַד בִּמְקוֹמָהּ, מַהוּ? מַאי קָא מִיבַּעְיָא לֵיהּ? כִּי קַדֵּישׁ דָּוִד – רִצְפָּה עֶלְיוֹנָה קַדֵּישׁ, אוֹ דִילְמָא עַד לְאַרְעִית דִּתְהוֹמָא קַדֵּישׁ? וְתִיבָּעֵי לֵיהּ כָּל הָעֲזָרָה כּוּלָּהּ! לְעוֹלָם פְּשִׁיטָא לֵיהּ דְּעַד אַרְעִית דִּתְהוֹמָא קַדֵּישׁ, וְהָכִי קָמִיבַּעְיָא לֵיהּ: דֶּרֶךְ שֵׁירוּת בְּכָךְ, אוֹ אֵין דֶּרֶךְ שֵׁירוּת בְּכָךְ? תֵּיקוּ.§ "קִיבֵּל בִּשְׂמֹאל – פָּסוּל, וְר"ש מַכְשִׁיר".§ ת"ר: *"בְּאֶצְבָּעוֹ וְלָקַח" – *מְלַמֵּד שֶׁלֹּא תְּהֵא קַבָּלָה אֶלָּא בְּיָמִין, °"בְּאֶצְבָּעוֹ וְנָתַן" – מְלַמֵּד שֶׁלֹּא תְּהֵא נְתִינָה אֶלָּא בְּיָמִין. אָמַר ר"ש: וְכִי נֶאֶמְרָה יָד בְּקַבָּלָה? אֶלָּא "בְּאֶצְבָּעוֹ וְנָתַן" – שֶׁלֹּא תְּהֵא נְתִינָה אֶלָּא בְּיָמִין; הוֹאִיל וְלֹא נֶאֶמְרָה יָד בְּקַבָּלָה, קִיבֵּל בִּשְׂמֹאל – כָּשֵׁר. וְר"ש, מִמָּה נַפְשָׁךְ? אִי אִית לֵיהּ גְּזֵירָה שָׁוָה – כִּי לֹא נֶאֶמְרָה יָד בְּקַבָּלָה מַאי הָוֵי? וְאִי לֵית לֵיהּ גְּזֵירָה שָׁוָה – כִּי נֶאֶמְרָה יָד בְּקַבָּלָה מַאי הָוֵי? אָמַר רַב יְהוּדָה: לְעוֹלָם לֵית לֵיהּ גְּזֵירָה שָׁוָה, וְהָכִי קָאָמַר: וְכִי נֶאֱמַר יַד יָמִין בְּקַבָּלָה? הוֹאִיל וְלֹא נֶאֱמַר יַד יָמִין בְּקַבָּלָה, קִבֵּל בִּשְׂמֹאל – כָּשֵׁר. א"ל רַבָּה: א"ה, אֲפִילּוּ נְתִינָה נַמִי! וְעוֹד, וְכִי לֵית לֵיהּ לְר"ש ג"ש? *וְהָתַנְיָא, ר"ש אוֹמֵר: כָּל מָקוֹם שֶׁנֶּאֱמַר "יָד" – אֵינָהּ אֶלָּא יָמִין, "אֶצְבַּע" – אֵינָהּ אֶלָּא יָמִין! אֶלָּא אָמַר רָבָא: לְעוֹלָם אִית לֵיהּ ג"ש, וְהָכִי קָאָמַר: וְכִי נֶאֶמְרָה יָד בְּקַבָּלָה? הוֹאִיל וְלֹא נֶאֶמְרָ' יָד בְּקַבָּלָה אֶלָּא אֶצְבַּע, וְאִי אֶפְשָׁר לְקַבָּלָה בְּאֶצְבַּע, קִיבֵּל בִּשְׂמֹאל – כָּשֵׁר. אֲמַר לֵיהּ רַב סַמָּא בְּרֵיהּ דְּרַב אַשִׁי לְרָבִינָא: אֶפְשָׁר דְּעָבֵיד לֵיהּ אוֹזֶן לִשְׂפַת מִזְרָק וּמְקַבֵּל (א) בָּהּ! אֶלָּא אָמַר אַבַּיֵי:

בְּמִקְרָא

רש"י

*שְׁנֵי כְתוּבִין הַבָּאִין כְּאֶחָד. ה] דְּבִתְרַוַיְיהוּ כְּתִיב קְרָאֵי לְמִיתָה, בְּסַנְהֶדְרִין בְּ"אֵלּוּ הֵן הַנִּשְׂרָפִין". וְטוּבָא קַשְׁיָא לִי בְּגַוַּהּ: חֲדָא, דְּמַה לּוֹ לִלְמוֹד מֵהֶן? הָא מִיתָה בְּגוּפָהּ כְּתִיב, דְּכֵיוָן דְּזָר הוּא – "וְהַזָּר הַקָּרֵב יוּמָת". דְּהָא מְחוּסַּר בְּגָדִים נַמִי הָכִי יָלְפִינַן לֵיהּ בְּסַנְהֶדְרִין: אֵין בִּגְדֵיהֶן עֲלֵיהֶן – אֵין כְּהוּנָּתָן עֲלֵיהֶן, וְהָווּ לְהוּ זָרִים. וְעוֹד: א"כ חִילּוּל עֲבוֹדָה לָא נֵילַף מִינֵּיהּ, דִּבְחִילּוּל נַמִי קְרָאֵי טוּבָא אִיכָּא. הוֹאִיל ו] וְרִצְפָּה מְקַדֶּשֶׁת. לַעֲמוֹד לְשָׁרֵת. שֶׁהֲרֵי דָּוִד קִידְּשָׁהּ בִּשְׁתֵּי תוֹדוֹת וּבְשִׁיר שֶׁל פְּגָעִים, כִּדְאָמְרִינַן לְקַמָּן בִּשְׁמַעְתִּין: כִּי קַדֵּישׁ דָּוִד כו'. וּכְלֵי שָׁרֵת מְקַדְּשִׁין. כְּדִכְתִיב: "וַיִּמְשָׁחֵם וַיְקַדֵּשׁ אוֹתָם" (במדבר ז). לֹא יְהֵא דָּבָר חוֹצֵץ בֵּין כֹּהֵן לִכְלִי שָׁרֵת. בְּקַבָּלַת הַדָּם, כְּדִכְתִיב: "וְלָקַח הַכֹּהֵן" (ויקרא ד) – שֶׁתְּהֵא לְקִיחָה בְּעַצְמוֹ שֶׁל כֹּהֵן. וּצְרִיכָא. לְמִיתְנֵי בְּמַתְנִי' חֲלִילַת כֵּלִים וּבְהֵמָה וְרֶגֶל חֲבֵירוֹ לְפִי הַסֵּדֶר שֶׁשְּׁנָאוּ בָּהּ. דְּלָאו מִינָא דְּבָשָׂר אָדָם הוּא. וְכֵיוָן דְּאֵינוֹ מִמִּין אָדָם כְּלָל – הָוֵי מִין בְּשֶׁאֵינוֹ מִינוֹ, וְחוֹצֵץ. רַגְלוֹ אַחַת עַל הָאֶבֶן. שֶׁמּוּטֶּלֶת עַל הָרִצְפָּה, וְאֵינָהּ מִן הָרִצְפָּה. נִידַּלְדְּלָה. *אֶבֶן אַחַת ז] מֵאַבְנֵיהָ מִקְּבִיעוּתָהּ, וּמִתְנַעְנַעַת בָּרִצְפָּה. נִידַּלְדְּלָה. לְכָאן וּלְכָאן. נֶעֶקְרָה. לְגַמְרֵי, וְהַגּוּמָּא נִרְאֵית שָׁם, וְעָמַד בַּגּוּמָּא וְעָבַד. כִּי קַדֵּישׁ דָּוִד. ח] שֶׁהָיָה מְקַדֵּשׁ אוֹתָהּ בִּשְׁתֵּי תוֹדוֹת וּבְשִׁיר שֶׁל פְּגָעִים, כִּדְתְנַן בְּמַסֶּ' שְׁבוּעוֹת (דף יד. טו:). תִּיבָּעֵי לֵיהּ כָּל הָעֲזָרָה כּוּלָּהּ. שֶׁנִּטְּלָה רִצְפָּה שֶׁלָּהּ. דֶּרֶךְ שֵׁירוּת בְּכָךְ. מִי הָוֵי אוֹרַח אַרְעָא, וּמִיקְרֵי שֵׁירוּת, אוֹ לָא? בְּאֶצְבָּעוֹ וְלָקַח. דִּכְתִיב: "וְלָקַח הַכֹּהֵן מִדַּם הַחַטָּאת בְּאֶצְבָּעוֹ וְנָתַן עַל קַרְנוֹת" – הֶטִּילוֹ הַכָּתוּב לְאֶצְבַּע בֵּין קַבָּלָה לִזְרִיקָה. ט] דּוֹרְשֵׁהוּ לְפָנָיו וּלְאַחֲרָיו, לוֹמַר שֶׁלֹּא יִהְיוּ אֶלָּא בְּיָמִין, דְּיָלְפִינַן לְקַמָּן בִּשְׁמַעְתִּין: כָּל מָקוֹם שֶׁנֶּאֱמַר אֶצְבַּע – אֵינוֹ אֶלָּא יָמִין. וְכִי נֶאֶמְרָה יָד בְּקַבָּלָה. קס"ד דְּאִם נֶאֶמְרָה בָּהּ יָד הֲוָה ר"ש מוֹדֶה בָּהּ, אֲבָל בְּאֶצְבַּע לָא יָלֵיף בָּהּ יָמִין. לְקַמָּן בָּעֵי לָהּ וּמְשַׁנֵּינַן לָהּ. אֶלָּא בְּאֶצְבָּעוֹ וְנָתַן כו'. בְּהָא מוֹדֵינָא לָךְ דִּזְרִיקַת חַטָּאת בָּעְיָא יָמִין. וְר"ש. דְּאָמַר: אִי הֲוָה כְּתִיב בָּהּ יָד הֲוָה יָלֵיף לָהּ יָמִין, וּמֵאֶצְבַּע לָא יָלֵיף. מִמָּה נַפְשָׁךְ אִי אִית לֵיהּ ג"ש י]. דְּיָלְפִינַן יָד יָד דִּקְמִיצָה מִמְּצוֹרָע דִּכְתִיב בֵּיהּ "עַל בֹּהֶן יָדוֹ הַיְמָנִית" – אַף כָּל מָקוֹם שֶׁנֶּאֱמַר יא] יָד אֵינָהּ אֶלָּא יָמִין. כִּי לֹא נֶאֱמַר יָד בְּקַבָּלָה מַאי הָוֵי. הֲרֵי נֶאֱמַר בָּהּ "אֶצְבָּעוֹ", וְנֵילַף "אֶצְבַּע" "אֶצְבַּע" נַמִי מֵהָתָם, דִּכְתִיב בִּמְצוֹרָע "וְטָבַל הַכֹּהֵן אֶת אֶצְבָּעוֹ הַיְמָנִית"! יב] ה"ג: לְעוֹלָם לֵית לֵיהּ ג"ש וְה"ק וְכִי נֶאֱמַר יָד יְמָנִית כו'. אֶלָּא אָמַר רָבָא לְעוֹלָם אִית לֵיהּ ג"ש וְה"ק וְכִי נֶאֱמַר יג] בָּהּ יָד בְּקַבָּלָה. אִי הֲוָה כְּתַב יָד, שֶׁהָיָה רְאוּיָה לֶאֱחוֹז בִּכְלִי וּלְקַבֵּל הַדָּם – *הוּא יד] אִיכָּא לְמִידְרַשׁ נַמִי הַקַּבָּלָה. וְהוֹאִיל וְלֹא נֶאֱמַר כָּאן יָד אֶלָּא אֶצְבַּע, וְאִי אֶפְשָׁר לְקַבֵּל דָּם בִּכְלִי בְּאֶצְבַּע לְבַדָּהּ – ע"כ מִשּׁוּם נְתִינָה הוּא דִּכְתִיב טו] בָּהּ, שֶׁהוּא רָאוּי לָהּ, וְלֹא מִשּׁוּם קַבָּלָה. נִמְצָא שֶׁאַף אֶצְבַּע לֹא נֶאֱמַר בּוֹ, לְפִיכָךְ קִיבֵּל בִּשְׂמֹאל כָּשֵׁר. אוֹזֶן. כְּמוֹ שֶׁעוֹשִׂים לְכַדִּים שֶׁל חֶרֶס, שֶׁקּוֹרִין *מאניק"ו. וּמְקַבֵּל בֵּיהּ. בְּהַהוּא אוֹזֶן מְקַבֵּל אֶת הַדָּם בְּאֶצְבַּע, שֶׁאוֹחֵז אֶצְבָּעוֹ לְתוֹכָהּ וְנוֹשֵׂא אֶת הַמִּזְרָק, וּמְקַבֵּל.

נִדְרָשׁ

תוספות

זר הוי קרא שלישי, וא"כ ליהוו שלשה כתובין הבאין כאחד! ולמאי דפרישית אתי שפיר, דמיתה דמחוסר בגדים לא טז] מיתורא, אלא משום דאשכחן דזר הוי במיתה, ולכך אמרינן דלא ילפינן מיתה מהא דקרייה רחמנא זר. *ולפירוש הקונטרס דיליף מבינייא קשה: דהוה ליה שלשה כתובים הבאין כאחד! ובקונטרס פירש: וה"ה נמי דמצי למימר משום דהוי זר ושלא רחוץ ידים ורגלים שני כתובים הבאין כאחד, דהא מחוסר בגדים גופיה לא כתיבא ביה מיתה אלא משום דזר הוא, וחדא מינייהו נקט. ואי איפשר לומר כן, דבהדיא אשכחן מיתה במחוסר בגדים בפרשת "ואתה תצוה". ומיהו, פירוש הקונטרס על כרחין עיקר, דבסנהדרין סוף פרק "הנשרפין" (דף פג: ושם ד"ה אין) יליף בהדיא מחוסר בגדים במיתה משום דהוו להו זרים, דאין בגדיהם עליהם – אין כהונתן עליהן. ומיתה דכתיבא בפרשת "ואתה תצוה" אחרה"ר יעקב מאורלינש דבמכנסים כתיב. וקרא ד"וחגרת" דדריש מיניה בריש פירקין בסנהדרין: אין בגדיהם עליהם אין כהונתן עליהם, והוו להו זרים – איצטריך לשאר בגדים, ומיניה לא הוה ילפינן מכנסים, דלא כתיבא בההיא פרשתא. ומיהו, למאן דמרבי ביומא (דף ה:) מכנסיים מ"וזה הדבר" [וי"ו מוסיף על ענין ראשון], קשה: מיתה דכתב רחמנא גבי מכנסים למה לי? ועוד קשה לפירוש הקונטרס: דליהוי זר ומכנסים ושלא רחוץ שלשה כתובים.

הואיל ורצפה מקדשת. דוד קידשה, כדפירש בקונטרס. ואע"ג דשלמה בנה הבית – דוד קידשה, כדאמר לקמן בשמעתא: כי קדיש דוד וכו'. ובירושלמי דפרק ב' דשבועות אמרינן: דוד – זה מלך, גד – זה נביא, יז] ומה שפירש בקונטרס שקידשה בשתי תודות ובשיר – אינו כן, דעזרה אינה מקדשה בשתי תודות, אלא בשירי מנחה, כדאיתא בשבועות (דף טו.) יח].

הואיל ורצפה מקדשת. פירוש: דמקדשת האדם לעבוד עבודה שם, דאינו יכול לעבוד במקום אחר. וכלי שרת – פירוש: בגדי כהונה, מקדשין האדם לעבוד עבודה. מה כלי שרת לא יהא דבר חוצץ בינו לבין כלי שרת, דהא כתיב "על בשרו" כדאמרינן לעיל (דף יט.), ובגדי כהונה קרי להו כלי שרת, כדאמר לעיל (דף יג.) שתהא בכהן כשר ובכלי שרת. ובקונטרס פי': שבכלי שרת ממש, שלא יהא דבר חוצץ בין כהן לכלי שרת יט] בקבלת הדם, כדכתיב: "ולקח הכהן" – שתהא לקיחה בעצמו של כהן. ואם תאמר: מדאחשיב ליה הכא חצילה, ולעיל נמי דפריך: ותיפוק לי משום חצילה, וגבי ההוא דכריך ידיה בשיראי (פסחים דף נז.): אלמא לקיחה ע"י ד"א לא שמה לקיחה. ובפ' "לולב הגזול" (סוכה דף לז.) קאמר רבא דלקיחה ע"י דבר אחר שמה לקיחה! ויש לומר: דהתם (ב) כ] [לא] איירי כגון דכריך ידיה בסודר ונוטל לולב, דהא ודאי לא הוי לקיחה, אלא דכריך ליה ללולב בסודרא ונוטלו, ובאותו ענין מייתי רבא ראיה מאזוב. וכן צריך לומר מתוך שמעתא דהתם, *דקאמר רבא גופיה: מין במינו אינו חוצץ, הא בשאינו מינו – חוצץ. ואמאי? והא לקיחה ע"י דבר אחר שמה לקיחה! ושמא חד מינייהו "רבה". ולמאי דפרישית ניחא, דכי כריך ליה ללולב בסודר, אף על פי שאינו חיבור חשיב ליה לקיחה. וקצת קשה מההיא דיומא (דף נח.), דקאמר: הניח מזרק בתוך מזרק מהו? מאי קא מיבעיא ליה? הא כי האי גוונא הויא לקיחה על ידי ד"א שמה לקיחה, דליהוי חילון בית יד לפנימי! ויש לומר: דאי אחיז ליה חילון בדופניו, שמטלטל הפנימי על ידו – הכי נמי דהויא לקיחה מטעם בית יד. אלא הכא במאי עסקינן – כגון שנושא החילון מתחתיו, דלא מהני כלל לפנימי*).

במקרא

*) [וע"ע תוס' פסחים נז. ד"ה דכריך ותוס' יומא נח. ד"ה מין ותוס' סוכה לז. ד"ה כי היכי]

מסורת הש"ס

נ"א שני כתובין הבאין כאחד כו' דתרווייהו מחלי עבודה וכתיב בהו מיתה בסנהדרין וה"ה דהוה מצי למימר דהוי זר ושלא רחוץ ידים ורגלים שני כתובין הבאין כאחד דהא מחוסר בגדים לא כתיב ביה מיתה אלא משום דזר הוא וחדא מינייהו נקט

שבת לג:

נ"א אבן אחת מאבני הרצפה מקביעותה ומתנענעת לכאן ולכאן נ"ק

[ע' תוס' יומא נב: ד"ה שאן]

מנחות י.

[מנחות יט. ע"ש]

צ"ל הוי

הגהות הב"ח

(א) גמ' ומקבל ביה אלא:
(ב) תוס' ד"ה הואיל וכו' וי"ל דהתם מיירי כגון דכריך לולב בסודרא ונוטל הסודר בידו דהא ודאי לא הוי לקיחה אלא היכא דכריך ליה ללולב:

שיטה מקובצת

א] מלמדין מאי איכא למימר הא איכא שתויי יין נמי והוי: ב] ושלשה כתובים הבאים כאחד: ג] תיבת נינהו נמחק: ד] שאילו נטל הכלי ותנטל האבן ויכול לעמוד: ה] דבתרווייהו. ס"א מחלי עבודה וכתיב בהו מיתה כדאיתא בסנהדרין וה"ה נמי דהוי מצי למימר משום דהוי זר ושלא רחוץ ידים ורגלים שני כתובים הבאים כאחד דהא מחוסר בגדים גופיה לא כתיב ביה מיתה אלא משום דזר הוא וחדא מינייהו נקיט: ו] ורצפה. מקודשת ס"א מקדשת האדם לעבוד עבודה שם דאינו יכול לעבוד במקום אחר ויש גורסין הואיל ורצפה מקודשת כלומר לעמוד כו': ז] אחת מאבני הריצפ' מקביעות' ומנענעת לכאן ולכאן הס"ד ומה"ד נעקרה: ח] שהיו מקדשין אותה בשתי תודות: ט] לזריקה ולדורשו: י] ג"ש דלקמן: יא] שנאמר בו: יב] (הימנית). לעולם לית ליה ג"ש גרסי' ותיבות ה"ג נמחק: יג] תיבת בה נמחק:

יד] הוא דאיכא: טו] דכתיב. (ביד שהשבו) [ביה שהוא]: טז] לא מייתרא אלא משום כו' ולפירוש הקונטרס דיליף מבנין אב קשה: יז] נביא. אבל מה: יח] בשבועות. וי"מ הואיל והד"א: יט] שרת. בשעת קבלת הדם כדכתיב כו' וא"ת מ"ש דחשיב ליה כו' וגבי ההוא נמי דכריך ידו בשיראי. בשילהי מקום שנהגו: כ] דהתם לא איירי כו' ללולב בסודרא ונוטל שני ראשי הסודר ובאותו ענין:

*בְּמִקְרָא נִדְרָשׁ לְפָנָיו וּלְאַחֲרָיו קָמִיפַּלְגִי. אָמַר אַבַּיֵי: הָא דְּרַבִּי אֶלְעָזָר בְּרַבִּי שִׁמְעוֹן, מַפְּקָא מִדַּאֲבוּהּ, וּמַפְּקָא מִדְּרַבָּנַן. דְּתַנְיָא, רַבִּי אֶלְעָזָר בְּרַבִּי שִׁמְעוֹן אוֹמֵר: כָּל מָקוֹם שֶׁנֶּאֱמַר אֶצְבַּע בְּקַבָּלָה, שִׁינָּה בְּקַבָּלָה — פָּסוּל, בִּנְתִינָה — כָּשֵׁר. וְכָל מָקוֹם שֶׁנֶּאֱמַר אֶצְבַּע בִּנְתִינָה, שִׁינָּה בִּנְתִינָה — פָּסוּל, בְּקַבָּלָה — כָּשֵׁר, וְהֵיכָן נֶאֱמַר אֶצְבַּע בִּנְתִינָה — דִּכְתִיב: °"וְלָקַחְתָּ מִדַּם הַפָּר וְנָתַתָּ עַל קַרְנוֹת הַמִּזְבֵּחַ בְּאֶצְבָּעֶךָ". וְקָסָבַר: *מִקְרָא נִדְרָשׁ לְפָנָיו וְלֹא לִפְנֵי פָנָיו (א) א] וּלְאַחֲרָיו.§ *אָמַר רַבָּה בַּר בַּר חָנָה אָמַר ב] רַבִּי יוֹחָנָן: כָּל מָקוֹם שֶׁנֶּאֱמַר אֶצְבַּע וּכְהוּנָּה — אֵינָהּ אֶלָּא יָמִין. קָא סָלְקָא דַּעְתִּין תַּרְתֵּי בָּעֵינַן, כִּדְכְתִיב: °"וְלָקַח הַכֹּהֵן מִדַּם הַחַטָּאת בְּאֶצְבָּעוֹ", וְיָלֵיף מִמְּצוֹרָע, דִּכְתִי': °"וְטָבַל הַכֹּהֵן אֶת אֶצְבָּעוֹ הַיְמָנִית". ג] וַהֲרֵי קְמִיצָה דְּלָא כְּתִיב בַּהּ אֶלָּא כְּהוּנָּה, *וּתְנַן: אקָמַץ בִּשְׂמֹאל פָּסוּל! ד] אֶלָּא אָמַר רָבָא: אוֹ אֶצְבַּע אוֹ כְּהוּנָּה. א"ל אַבַּיֵי: *הֲרֵי הוֹלָכַת אֵבָרִים לַכֶּבֶשׁ, דִּכְתִיב בְּהוּ כְּהוּנָּה, דִּכְתִיב: °"וְהִקְרִיב הַכֹּהֵן אֶת הַכֹּל [וְהִקְטִיר] הַמִּזְבֵּחָה", וְאָמַר מָר: זוֹ הוֹלָכַת אֵבָרִים לַכֶּבֶשׁ, *וּתְנַן: בהָרֶגֶל שֶׁל יָמִין בִּשְׂמֹאלוֹ, וּבֵית עוֹרָהּ לַחוּץ! ה] [כִּי אָמְרִינַן] אוֹ אֶצְבַּע אוֹ כְּהוּנָּה — בְּדָבָר הַמְעַכֵּב כַּפָּרָה, דּוּמְיָא דִּמְצוֹרָע. וַהֲרֵי קַבָּלָה, ו] דִּכְתַב בְּהוּ כְּהוּנָּה, וְדָבָר הַמְעַכֵּב בְּכַפָּרָה הוּא, וּתְנַן: קִבֵּל בִּשְׂמֹאל — פָּסוּל, וְר"ש מַכְשִׁיר! ר"ש תַּרְתֵּי בָּעֵי. מִי בָּעֵי ר"ש תַּרְתֵּי? וְהָתַנְיָא, רַבִּי שִׁמְעוֹן אוֹמֵר: כָּל מָקוֹם שֶׁנֶּאֱמַר יָד — אֵינוֹ אֶלָּא יָמִין, אֶצְבַּע — אֵינוֹ אֶלָּא יָמִין! אֶצְבַּע לָא בָּעֲיָא כְּהוּנָּה, כְּהוּנָּה בָּעֲיָא אֶצְבַּע. וְאֶלָּא כֹּהֵן לָמָּה לִי? ז] בְּבִיהוּנָּן. וַהֲרֵי זְרִיקָה, דְּלָא כְּתַב בְּהוּ אֶלָּא כְּהוּנָּה, וּתְנַן: זָרַק בִּשְׂמֹאל — פָּסוּל, וְלָא פָּלֵיג רַבִּי שִׁמְעוֹן! אָמַר אַבַּיֵי: פָּלֵיג בְּבָרַיְיתָא, דְּתַנְיָא: קִיבֵּל בִּשְׂמֹאל — פָּסוּל, וְרַבִּי שִׁמְעוֹן מַכְשִׁיר. זָרַק בִּשְׂמֹאל — פָּסוּל, וְרַבִּי שִׁמְעוֹן מַכְשִׁיר. אֶלָּא הָא *דְּאָמַר רָבָא: ◦"יָד" "יָד" לִקְמִיצָה, "רֶגֶל" "רֶגֶל" לַחֲלִיצָה, "אֹזֶן" "אֹזֶן" לִרְצִיעָה, לָמָּה לִי? מִדְּרַבָּה בַּר בַּר חָנָה נָפְקָא! חַד לְקוֹמֶץ, וְחַד לְקִידּוּשׁ קוֹמֶץ. וּלְר"ש

נִדְרָשׁ (ג). ר"ש סָבַר: ח] מִקְרָא נִדְרָשׁ לְאַחֲרָיו וְלֹא לְפָנָיו. הִילְכָּךְ, אֶצְבַּע אַ"וְנָתַן" דִּכְתִיב בַּתְרֵיהּ קָאֵי, וְלֹא אַ"וְלָקַח" דִּכְתִיב לְקַמֵּיהּ. וְרַבָּנַן סָבְרִי: מִקְרָא נִדְרָשׁ לְפָנָיו וּלְאַחֲרָיו. מַפְּקָא מִדַּאֲבוּהּ. מוֹצֵאת מִכְּלַל דִּבְרֵי אָבִיו וּמִכְּלַל דִּבְרֵי חֲכָמִים. כָּל מָקוֹם שֶׁנֶּאֱמַר אֶצְבַּע בְּקַבָּלָה. וְלֹא בִּנְתִינָה. כְּגוֹן הַאי קְרָא דִּלְעֵיל. דְּר' אֶלְעָזָר בְּר"ש דָּרֵישׁ אֶצְבַּע אַ"וְלָקַח", דְּהַיְינוּ לְפָנָיו, וְלֹא אַ"וְנָתַן". שִׁינָּה בְּקַבָּלָה. שֶׁקִּיבֵּל בִּשְׂמֹאל. (ג) וְקָאָמַר לָךְ: בְּמָקוֹם שֶׁנִּכְתַּב — שָׁם תִּתְּנוּ, וְלֹא ט] בַּמֶּה שֶׁלֹּא נִכְתַּב בּוֹ. וְלָקַחְתָּ מִדַּם הַפָּר. בְּפַר הַמִּילּוּאִים כְּתִיב. וְלֹא לִפְנֵי פָנָיו. דְּלָא דָּרֵישׁ לְהַאי בְּאֶצְבַּע דְּמִילּוּאִים אַ"וְלָקַחְתָּ", וְלֹא לְאַחֲרָיו — דְּלָא דָּרֵישׁ לְהַאי "בְּאֶצְבָּעוֹ" דְּחַטָּאת יָחִיד (ויקרא ד) אַ"וְנָתַן" וְהַיְינוּ פָּלֵיג אַדַּאֲבוּהּ, דַּאֲבוּהּ סָבַר לְאַחֲרָיו וְלֹא לְפָנָיו, וְאַדְּרַבָּנַן — דְּאִינְהוּ סָבְרִי בֵּין לְפָנָיו בֵּין לְאַחֲרָיו. וּכְהוּנָּה. כְּגוֹן "הַכֹּהֵן" אוֹ "הַכֹּהֲנִים". תַּרְתֵּי בָּעֵינַן. אֶצְבַּע וּכְהוּנָּה. כְּגוֹן הַאי קְרָא דִּכְתִיב גַּבֵּי זְרִיקַת חַטָּאת "וְלָקַח הַכֹּהֵן מִדַּם הַחַטָּאת בְּאֶצְבָּעוֹ", וְקָאָמַר י] רַבִּי יוֹחָנָן דְּהָכָא יָמִין בָּעֵי, דְּגָמַר מִמְּצוֹרָע עָשִׁיר דִּכְתִיב בֵּיהּ אֶצְבַּע וּכְהוּנָּה, וּמְפָרֵשׁ יא] בֵּיהּ יְמָנִית. הָרֶגֶל שֶׁל יָמִין. נוֹשֵׂא בְּיַד שְׂמֹאל לַכֶּבֶשׁ. מִשּׁוּם דְּרֶגֶל יָמִין יב] קְרֵבָה תְּחִילָּה עִם הָרֹאשׁ, כִּדְקַיְימָא לָן בְּפ"ב דְּסֵדֶר יוֹמָא (דף כה.). וְהִילְכָּךְ מוֹלִיךְ הָרֹאשׁ בְּיָמִין שֶׁהוּא חָשׁוּב, וְהָרֶגֶל בִּשְׂמֹאל. וּבֵית עוֹרָהּ לַחוּץ. כְּלַפֵּי הָעָם, וּמְקוֹם הַחֲתָךְ כְּלַפֵּי הַמּוֹלִיךְ, דְּהָכִי שַׁפִּיר שֶׁלֹּא יֵרָאֶה הַחֲתָךְ. הַמְעַכֵּב כַּפָּרָה. דּוּמְיָא דְּהַזָּאָה שֶׁל מְצוֹרָע, יג] כְּגוֹן קְמִיצָה. אֲבָל הוֹלָכַת אֵיבָרִים דְּלָא מְעַכְּבָא כַּפָּרָה, דְּהוּא עַצְמוֹ שֶׁלֹּא הוּקְטְרוּ אֵימוּרִין כָּשֵׁר — לָא בָּעֲיָא יָמִין. קַבָּלָה כְּתַב בָּהּ כְּהוּנָּה. דִּכְתִיב: יד] "וְהִקְרִיבוּ בְּנֵי אַהֲרֹן הַכֹּהֲנִים", וְאָמַר מָר: זוֹ קַבָּלַת הַדָּם. וְאֶלָּא כֹּהֵן לָמָּה לִי. בְּקַבָּלָה? הָא כְּתִיב "בְּנֵי אַהֲרֹן", טו] אִי לָאו לְאַגְמוּרֵי אַיָּמִין אָתָא. בְּבִיהוּנּוֹ. בְּבִגְדֵי כְהוּנָּה. זָרַק בִּשְׂמֹאל פָּסוּל וְר"ש מַכְשִׁיר. אַשְּׁאָר כָּל הַזְּבָחִים (ד) דְּלָא כְּתַב בְּהוּ אֶצְבַּע, אֶלָּא "וְזָרְקוּ הַכֹּהֲנִים". אֲבָל בִּזְרִיקַת חַטָּאת מוֹדֶה ר"ש, כִּדְקָאָמַר לְעֵיל: "בְּאֶצְבָּעוֹ וְנָתַן" — שֶׁלֹּא תְּהֵא נְתִינָה אֶלָּא בְּיָמִין. וְאֶלָּא הָא דְּאָמַר רָבָא. בִּמְנָחוֹת בְּפ"ק (דף י.): "יָד" "יָד" לִקְמִילָה, בְּפָרָשַׁת מְצוֹרָע עָשִׁיר כְּתִיב: "עַל תְּנוּךְ אֹזֶן הַיְמָנִית וְעַל בֹּהֶן יָדוֹ הַיְמָנִית וְעַל בֹּהֶן רַגְלוֹ הַיְמָנִית", וּקְרָא יְתֵירָא הוּא, כִּדְמְפָרֵשׁ הָתָם. וְקָאָמַר רָבָא: יָד דִּמְצוֹרָע אָתֵי לְג"ש לְמִיגְמַר יָד דִּקְמִילָה מִינָּהּ שֶׁתְּהֵא בְּיָמִין. וְהֵיכָא טז] כְּתַב יָד בִּקְמִילָה — "וַיִּמַלֵּא כַּפּוֹ מִמֶּנָּה". לַחֲלִיצָה. שֶׁתְּהֵא בְּיָמִין. לָמָּה לִי. יָד בִּקְמִילָה. מִדְּרַבָּה בַּר בַּר חָנָה נָפְקָא. דְּהָא כְּהוּנָּה כְּתִיב יז]. לְקִידּוּשׁ קוֹמֶץ. בִּכְלִי שָׁרֵת, שֶׁיְּהֵא בְּיָמִין, שֶׁיֹּאחַז הַכְּלִי שֶׁהוּא מְקַדֵּשׁ בּוֹ בְּיָדוֹ הַיְמָנִית. וּלְרַבִּי

במקרא נדרש לפניו ולאחריו קמיפלגי. הא דפליגי אמוראי בפרק "השואל" (ב"מ דף צה.) במקרא נדרש לפניו ולא לפני פניו, ופריך ממתני' ד"השואל" – לא מצי למימר דהיא ר"ש דלא דריש קרא לפניו. דהתם הוי מטעמא דהוי"ו מוסיף על ענין ראשון, ומודה ר"ש, כדאמר ב"הקומץ רבה" (מנחות דף יט.): היינו טעמא דר"ש – "והביא" וי"ו מוסיף על ענין ראשון. וגבי "ולקח ונתן" לא אמרינן וי"ו *מוסיף על ענין ראשון, וא"כ לילף קבלה מנתינה בימין, כדפי' התם בקונטרס ד"אצבעו" הפסיק הענין בין "ולקח" ל"ונתן". יח] ופ' קמא דקדושין (דף טו:) משמע דכולי עלמא יט] דרשינן מקרא לפניו בלא וי"ו מוסיף כ] על ענין, [וא"כ איכא] למילף קבלה מנתינה, דפריך: ונקיש מזוזה לתלמוד תורה. ובפ"ק דראש השנה (דף ט:) דרשי כולי עלמא מקרא לפניו, ובלפני פניו ולאחריו פליגי. ובסמוך קשה טפי, דקאמר רבי אלעזר בר"ש: כל מקום שנא' אצבע בנתינה, שינה בנתינה – פסול, בקבלה – כשר, כגון "ולקחת מדם הפר ונתת על קרנות המזבח באצבעך", וקסבר: מקרא נדרש לפניו ולא לפני פניו כא] ולאחריו – נימא וי"ו מוסיף על ענין ראשון! ושמא רבי אלעזר בר"ש לית ליה וי"ו מוסיף. א"נ לא דרשינן וי"ו מוסיף כדי לדרוש המקרא לפני פניו. **והרי** זריקה ותנן זרק בשמאל פסול. אפילו בשאר זבחים, ולא פליג ר"ש. אמר אביי: פליג בברייתא. ופרש"י: זרק בשמאל – בשאר קרבנות. אבל בחטאת מודה ר"ש דבעי ימין, כדאיתא בברייתא לעיל. והקשה הרב ר' יעקב מאורלינש: מאי קושיא? ואמאי כב] פליג ר"ש בברייתא? נהי דלא כתב אלא כהונה – מ"מ אתיא מהיקשא ד"זאת התורה" דאמר לקמן סוף "דם חטאת" (דף צח.) ובמנחות סוף "התודה" (דף פג.): מה חטאת אינה באה אלא מן החולין וביום ובידו הימנית – אף כל וכו'. ופריך: ידו הימנית מדרבה בר בר חנה נפקא, דכל מקום שנאמר אצבע וכהונה אינה אלא ימין! ומשני: כדי נסבה. אי נמי: סבר לה כר"ש דכהונה בעיא אצבע. משמע בהדיא דר"ש יליף שאר קרבנות כג] מחטאת! והשיב לו ר"ת: דלא גרסינן "והרי זריקה", דאינה, משנה בשום מקום. אלא גרסינן והרי מליקה ומשנה היא לקמן בפרק "חטאת העוף" (דף סח.), דתנן: כל הפסולין שמלקו – מליקתן פסולה, ואין מטמאין בגדים אבית הבליעה. מלק בשמאל או בלילה כד] כו'. והתלמוד הביאה בקוצר, שכן דרך התלמוד לקצר כמה משניות, והסופרים טעו וכתבו במקום מליקה זריקה. ועופות לא אתו בהיקשא ד"זאת התורה". אבל זריקה בשאר קרבנות פסול שפיר בשמאל, דיליף בהיקשא ד"זאת התורה" כדמשמע שילהי "דם חטאת" (לקמן דף צח.). ובסמוך נמי גרסינן בברייתא: מלק בשמאל פסול ור"ש מכשיר. ועוד אומר ר"ת: דאפילו גרסינן זרק, מצינו למימר דההוא תנא ד"זאת התורה" דמפיק ימין מחטאת סבר לה כר"ש דכהונה בעיא אצבע, אבל ר"ש לא סבר לה כוותיה כה] למילף ימין בזריקה בשאר קרבנות מחטאת, משום דזריקה לא ילפינן מהזאה. וקשה על זה: מעיקרא, כי פריך: והרי זריקה, דלא פליג ר"ש – כו] דילמא היינו משום דיליף מהיקשא! ויש לומר: דעדיפא משני פליג בברייתא. וקשה לפר"ת: דאפילו גרס בברייתא מלק – על כרחיך אמת הוא דמכשיר ר"ש זריקה בשמאל, כדמוכח בסמוך, ובפ"ק (לעיל דף יא.) דאמר: ומאי טעמא דר"ש, בא לעובדה בכלי – עובדה בשמאל, כאשם והיינו בזריקת אשם, כז] דבקבלה לא איירי, דאפי' חטאת נמי לא בעי ימין בקבלה לר"ש, דאמר לעיל: וכי נאמרה יד בקבלה (לר"ש) כו'. וצריך לתרץ: דהאי תנא סבר לה כוותיה בחדא. ואם תאמר: לפירוש רבינו תם נמי, דגרסינן מלק, הא מליקה נפקא לן בפ"ק דחולין (דף כב.) ימין אפילו לר"ש, מדכתיב: "ואת השני יעשה עולה כמשפט", דרשינן: *כמשפט חטאת בהמה, כח] דאינה באה אלא מן החולין וביום ובידו הימנית. והתם נמי פריך: ימנית מדרבה בר בר חנה נפקא. ומשני: כר"ש דכהונה בעיא אצבע! וי"ל: דמליקה שהיא כנגד שחיטה – לא נפקא, והתם בהזאה מיירי דבעיא ימין, אבל מהיקשא לא ילפינן עופות מחטאת בהמה, ולכך איצטריך נמי "כמשפט" התם. א"נ: ההוא תנא סבר כתנא דפליג עליה דר"ש לעיל, ופוסל קבלה בשמאל, משום דמקרא נדרש לפניו ולאחריו, ומוקי "אצבעו" דכתיב גבי חטאת גם על קבלה. ולדידהו ילפינן שפיר מליקה בימין מחטאת, דקבלה לא שייך למילף, דליתיה בעוף, וילפינן מליקה. אבל ר"ש דאמר קבל בשמאל כשר, ולית ליה ימין בחטאת בהמה, אלא בהזאה לחודה – בעולת העוף

עין משפט נר מצוה

עז א מיי' פי"א מהל' פסה"מ הל"ב:
עח ב מיי' פ"ו מהל' מעשה"ק הל"א:

נ"א מוסיף על ענין ראשון למילף קבלה כו' נ"ק

מסורת הש"ס

[שבת לב: וש"נ]
[שבת לב: וש"נ]
לקמן לח. מנחות י. [ג] הסוגיא עד סופו פג. חולין כב.
מנחות ו. י.
שם ולעיל יד: וש"נ חגיגה יא.
תמיד לה: [מנחות י. יומא מח:]
מנחות י.
נ"ק
נ"ל כמשפט חטאת בהמה מה חטאת בהמה אינה כו' נ"ק

שיטה מקובצת

א] פניו ולא לאחריו: ב] אמר ריש לקיש כל מקום: ג] והרי קמיצה כו' וא"ת ולישני הכא דשאני קמיצה דכתיב בה יד וילפינן יד יד לקמיצה כדאמר בסמוך אבל בעלמא בעינא כהונה ואצבע וי"ל דמקידוש קומץ בכלי שרת פריך דהתם ליכא ג"ש דיד יד ואפ"ה אמרינן קמץ בשמאל פסול וסמיך אברייתא דמנחות דפסל בקומץ ובקידוש קומץ: ד] תיבת אלא נמחק: ה] לחוץ כי אמרינן: ו] דכתיב בה כהונה: ז] לי בביהונו: ח] דמקרא נדרש: ט] במקום שלא: י] וקאמר ריש לקיש דהכא: יא] ומפרש בה: יב] ימין קרב: יג] מצורע או כגון: יד] דכתיב בה: טו] הא כתיב בני אהרן וא"כ אמאי כתיב ביה כהן (הא) [אי] כו': טז] והיכא כתיב: יז] כתיב בה: יח] לונתן ובפ"ק: יט] עלמא דרשי מקרא: כ] מתיבת על עד תיבת דפריך נמחק: כא] ולא לאחריו: כב] ואמאי משני אביי דפליג ר"ש כו' דלא כתיב בה אלא כהונה כו' דאמר לקמן בסוף דם חטאת: כג] מחטאת. דכי היכא דמתן דם דידיה הוי בימין דכתיב ביה אצבע ה"ה בשאר קרבנות: כד] כו'. ואם היתה המליקה כשירה פשיטא דאינו מטמא אבית הבליעה ולא חשבינן ליה פסולו בקודש הר"פ: כה] כוותיה ולא יליף ימין: כו] ר"ש. מאי קשיא ליה דלמא כו' משני דפליג וקשה לפר"ת: כז] אשם שהיא בשמאל דבקבלה לא איירי כו' לר"ש כדקאמר לעיל וכי נאמרה יד בקבלה וצריך לתרץ כו' כוותיה. ס"א [סבר לה] כר"ש ור"ש לא סבר ליה כוותיה: כח] בהמה מה חטאת בהמה דאינה באה כו' והתם נמי פריך ידו הימנית מדרבה בר בר חנה כו' בעי אצבע. גליון מהיקשא דזאת התורה נפקא כמאן דאית ליה היקשא בפ"ק דחולין ובריש מנחות. ע"כ:

הגהות הב"ח

(א) גמ' ולא לפני פניו ולא לאחריו: (ב) רש"י ד"ה נדרש לפניו ולאחריו קמפלגי ר"ש סבר: (ג) ד"ה שינה וכו' בשמאל פס וקאמר: (ד) ד"ה זרק וכו' כל הזבחים קאי דלא:

גליון הש"ס

גמ' יד יד לקמיצה. עי' לקמן סג ע"ב תוס' ד"ה מה חטאת בהמה:

וְלִר"ש דְּלָא בָּעֵי קִידּוּשׁ קוֹמֶץ, וּלְמַאן דְּאָמַר: לְר"ש נַמִּי בָּעֵי קִידּוּשׁ קוֹמֶץ — בִּשְׂמֹאל אַכְשׁוּרֵי מַכְשַׁר, "יָד" "יָד" דְּרַבָּא לָמָּה לִי? אִי לִקְמִיצָה עַצְמָהּ — א] מִדְּרַב יְהוּדָה בְּרֵיהּ דְּרַבִּי חִיָּיא נָפְקָא, *דְּאָמַר ר"י בְּרֵיהּ דְּרַבִּי חִיָּיא: מַאי טַעְמָא דְּרַבִּי שִׁמְעוֹן? [דְּאָמַר קְרָא:] °"קוֹדֶשׁ קָדָשִׁים הִיא כַּחַטָּאת וְכָאָשָׁם", בָּא לְעוֹבְדָהּ בַּיָּד — עוֹבְדָהּ בְּיָמִין כְּחַטָּאת, בָּא לְעוֹבְדָהּ בִּכְלִי — עוֹבְדָהּ בִּשְׂמֹאל כְּאָשָׁם! לָא נְצְרְכָא ב] [אֶלָּא] לְקוֹמֶץ מִנְחַת חוֹטֵא; סד"א: *הוֹאִיל וְאָמַר ר"ש: *שֶׁלֹּא יְהֵא קָרְבָּנוֹ מְהוּדָּר, כִּי קָמַץ לָהּ בִּשְׂמֹאל נַמִּי תִּיתַּכְשַׁר — קָא מַשְׁמַע לָן.§ **מתני'** *אנִשְׁפַּךְ הַדָּם עַל הָרִצְפָּה וַאֲסָפוֹ — פָּסוּל.§ **גמ'** תָּנוּ רַבָּנַן: °"וְלָקַח הַכֹּהֵן הַמָּשִׁיחַ מִדַּם הַפָּר" מִדַּם הַנֶּפֶשׁ, וְלֹא מִדַּם הָעוֹר, וְלֹא מִדַּם הַתַּמְצִית. "מִדַּם הַפָּר" — דָּם מֵהַפָּר יְקַבְּלֶנּוּ. דְּאִי סָלְקָא דַּעְתָּךְ מִדַּם הַפָּר כִּדְכְתִיב: "מִדַּם" — וַאֲפִילּוּ מִקְצָת דָּם — *וְהָאָמַר רַב: (א) ג] הַשּׁוֹחֵט צָרִיךְ שֶׁיְּקַבֵּל אֶת *כָּל דָּמוֹ שֶׁל פָּר, שֶׁנֶּאֱמַר: °"וְאֶת כָּל *דָּמוֹ יִשְׁפּוֹךְ". אֶלָּא "מִדַּם הַפָּר" — דָּם מֵהַפָּר יְקַבְּלֶנּוּ, וְקָסָבַר: *גּוֹרְעִין וּמוֹסִיפִין וְדוֹרְשִׁין. גּוּפָא, אָמַר רַב יְהוּדָה אָמַר רַב: בהַשּׁוֹחֵט צָרִיךְ שֶׁיְּקַבֵּל אֶת כָּל דָּמוֹ שֶׁל פָּר, שֶׁנֶּאֱמַר: °"וְאֶת כָּל דַּם הַפָּר יִשְׁפֹּךְ". וְהָא בִּשְׁיָרַיִים כְּתִיב! אִם אֵינוֹ עִנְיָן לִשְׁיָרַיִים, דְּהָא לֵיתֵיהּ לְכוּלֵּיהּ דָּם — תְּנֵיהוּ עִנְיָן (ב) ד] בְּקַבָּלָה. אָמַר רַב יְהוּדָה אָמַר שְׁמוּאֵל: גהַשּׁוֹחֵט צָרִיךְ שֶׁיַּגְבִּיהַּ סַכִּין לְמַעְלָה, שֶׁנֶּאֱמַר: °"וְלָקַח מִדַּם הַפָּר" — וְלֹא מִדַּם הַפָּר וְדָבָר אַחֵר. וְדַם סַכִּין בְּמַאי מְקַנַּח לֵיהּ? אָמַר אַבַּיֵי: *דבִּשְׂפַת מִזְרָק, כִּדְכְתִיב: °"כְּפוֹרֵי זָהָב". אָמַר רַב חִסְדָּא אָמַר רַב יִרְמְיָה בַּר אַבָּא: ההַשּׁוֹחֵט צָרִיךְ שֶׁיִּתֵּן וְרִידִין

רש"י

וּלְרַבִּי שִׁמְעוֹן דְּלָא בָּעֵי קִידּוּשׁ קוֹמֶץ. כִּדְקָאָמַר בְּ"הַקּוֹמֵץ רַבָּה" (מנחות דף כו.) שֶׁלֹּא בִּכְלִי שָׁרֵת פְּסוּלָה, וְרַבִּי שִׁמְעוֹן מַכְשִׁיר. וּלְמ"ד נַמִּי ר"ש בָּעֵי קִידּוּשׁ קוֹמֶץ. דְּאִיכָּא אֲמוֹרָאֵי דִּפְלִיגֵי הָתָם בְּמִילְּתֵיהּ דְּר"ש, וְאִיכָּא לְמ"ד הַכֹּל מוֹדִים בְּקוֹמֶץ שֶׁטָּעוּן קִידּוּשׁ, וְכִי קָאָמַר *ר"ש כְּשֵׁרָה — בְּהַקְטָרָה קָאָמַר, אִם נְטָלוֹ מִתּוֹךְ כְּלִי שָׁרֵת לְאַחַר שֶׁקִּידְּשׁוֹ, וְהִקְטִירוֹ בְּיָדוֹ. בִּשְׂמֹאל אַכְשׁוּרֵי מַכְשַׁר. לַקֹּדֶשׁ, דְּלָא עֲדִיף קִידּוּשׁ הַקּוֹמֶץ מִקַּבָּלַת הַדָּם דְּמַכְשַׁר לָהּ רַבִּי שִׁמְעוֹן בִּשְׂמֹאל. אִי לִקְמִיצָה גּוּפָהּ. שֶׁתְּהֵא בְּיָמִין, דִּלְר"ש לָא נָפְקָא לֵיהּ מִ"וְקָמַץ הַכֹּהֵן", דְּהָא ה] אָמְרוּ לְעֵיל דְּבָעֵינַן לְרַבִּי שִׁמְעוֹן אֶצְבַּע — מִדְּר' יְהוּדָה נָפְקָא. מַאי טַעְמָא דְּר' שִׁמְעוֹן. דְּמַכְשַׁר הַקְטָרַת קוֹמֶץ שֶׁלֹּא בִּכְלִי, אִם ו] הֶעֱלָן לַמִּזְבֵּחַ בְּיָדוֹ? אָמַר קְרָא בְּמִנְחָה "קֹדֶשׁ קָדָשִׁים הוּא", (ג) לְהָכִי אִיתְקַשׁ מִנְחָה לְחַטָּאת וְאָשָׁם, לוֹמַר לָךְ: בָּא לְעוֹבְדָהּ בַּיָּד — עוֹבְדָהּ בְּיָמִין כַּחַטָּאת, שֶׁזְּרִיקַת דָּמָהּ ז] בְּיָמִין בְּמַתַּן אֶצְבַּע וְלֹא בִּכְלִי, וּבָעֵיָא יָמִין, דִּכְתִיב בָּהּ אֶצְבַּע וּכְהוּנָּה. בָּא לְעוֹבְדָהּ בִּכְלִי עוֹבְדָהּ בִּשְׂמֹאל כְּאָשָׁם. שֶׁזְּרִיקָה בִּכְלִי, (ד) וְהִיא כְּשֵׁרָה בִּשְׂמֹאל לְר"ש, כִּדְאָמַר לְעֵיל: זָרַק בִּשְׂמֹאל פָּסוּל, וְר' שִׁמְעוֹן מַכְשִׁיר. אַלְמָא, אִי בָּעֵי בְּיָד — עָבֵיד, אִי בִּכְלִי — עָבֵיד. וּמִמֵּילָא נָפְקָא קְמִיצָה בְּיָמִין, דְּהָא עֲבוֹדַת יָד הִיא וְלֹא עֲבוֹדַת כְּלִי. לְקוֹמֶץ דְּמִנְחַת חוֹטֵא. שֶׁתְּהֵא קְמִיצָתוֹ בְּיָמִין (ה). דְּהוֹאִיל וְא"ר שִׁמְעוֹן. בְּפ"ק דִּמְנָחוֹת (דף ו.): בְּדִין הוּא שֶׁתְּהֵא מִנְחַת חוֹטֵא טְעוּנָה שֶׁמֶן וּלְבוֹנָה, שֶׁלֹּא יְהֵא חוֹטֵא נִשְׂכָּר, וּמִפְּנֵי מָה לֹא הִטְעִינָהּ — שֶׁלֹּא יְהֵא קָרְבָּנוֹ מְהוּדָּר. ח] סד"א: קְמִיצַת שְׂמֹאל תִּתְכַּשַּׁר בָּהּ, קמ"ל "יָד" "יָד" דְּרָבָא. כּוּלָּהּ שְׁמַעְתִּין בִּמְנָחוֹת. **מתני'** נִשְׁפַּךְ עַל הָרִצְפָּה. מִצַּוַּאר בְּהֵמָה, שֶׁלֹּא נִתְקַבֵּל בִּכְלִי. **גמ'** מֵהַפָּר יְקַבְּלֶנּוּ. שֶׁאִם נִשְׁפַּךְ מִן הַצַּוָּאר עַל הָרִצְפָּה וַאֲסָפוֹ — פָּסוּל, שֶׁהֲרֵי לֹא נִתְקַבֵּל מֵהַפָּר.* דְּאִי ס"ד דְּהַאי מֵ"ם דִּכְתִיבָא בְּ"מִדַּם" דָּרְשִׁינַן לֵיהּ כִּדְכְתִיב, דְּמַשְׁמַע: מִקְצָת הַדָּם יְקַבֵּל — וְהָאָמַר רַב ט] כו'. גּוֹרְעִין. אוֹת מִתֵּיבָה זוֹ, וּמוֹסִיפִין אוֹתָהּ עַל חֲבֵירְתָּהּ, וְדוֹרְשִׁים י] *כְּר"ש בְּסֵדֶר יוֹמָא. יא] בִּשְׁפִיכַת שִׁירַיִים כְּתִיב. וְלֹא בְּקַבָּלָה. דְּהָא לֵיתֵיהּ לְכוּלֵּיהּ דָּם. שֶׁכְּבָר נִיתַּן מִמֶּנּוּ עַל הַקְּרָנוֹת. סַכִּין לְמַעְלָה. שֶׁלֹּא יִפּוֹל יב] דַּם הַסַּכִּין עַל הַמִּזְרָק. וְדָבָר אַחֵר. סַכִּין. בִּשְׂפַת מִזְרָק. וְלֹא יג] לְתוֹכָן. כְּפוֹרֵי זָהָב. קָרֵי לַמִּזְרָקִין בְּסֵפֶר עֶזְרָא, עַל שֵׁם קִינּוּחַ. כִּדְאָמַר בְּמַסֶּכֶת חוּלִּין (דף ח:): אִי אִיכָּא גְּלִימָא דְּפָרִיסָא לְמִכְפְּרֵיהּ. א"נ: וּבָעֵי לְכַפּוּרֵי יְדֵיהּ בְּהַהוּא גַּבְרָא, גַּבֵּי נִירוֹן קֵיסָר (גיטין דף נו.). צָרִיךְ שֶׁיִּתֵּן וְרִידִין

תוספות

הָעוֹף נמי לא יד] הוה בעי ימין במליקה, אלא בהזאה דווקא. וא"ת: וכיון דר' שמעון פליג במליקה, א"כ מתני' דפרק "חטאת העוף" (לקמן דף סח.) דמלק בשמאל כו' — לא אתיא כרבי שמעון. טו] והא על כרחין כרבי שמעון אתיא, מדקתני סיפא: או בלילה — אינו מטמא בגדים אבית הבליעה, ומפרש טעמא — משום דכל שפסולו בקדש אינו מטמא בגדים אבית הבליעה. ומפרש בגמרא: דכיון דהך שחיטה מתרת את האיסור, פי': שאם עלה לא ירד. והיינו כרבי שמעון, דלרבי יהודה נשחטה בלילה תרד, דממעט לה מ"זאת היא העולה" בפירקין! וי"ל: דההוא תנא סבר לה כוותיה בחדא ופליג עליה בחדא. אי נמי: אפי' רבי יהודה מודה בעופות דלא ירדו משום טז] לילה, דכיון דהוה פסולן בקודש, דלא כתיב שלשה מיעוטי אלא בבהמה. וא"ת: דבריש "מזבח מקדש" (לקמן דף פג.) מפקי רבי עקיבא ורבי יוסי הגלילי מעולה וכבשים דמזבח מקדש את הראוי לו, ומאן דדריש מכבשים — פוסל הרבה בעוף יותר מבבהמה! וי"ל: דרבי יהודה סבר כמאן דדריש מעולה ולא מהכבשים, או משאר דרשות דהתם. ורבינו שמואל מיישב גירסת הספרים, ומפרש: והרי זריקה דלא כתיב אלא כהונה, ותנן: זרק בשמאל פסל, ולא פליג רבי שמעון. דמכיון דתנן: יז] כל הזבחים שקיבל בשמאל פסל — כל שכן זריקה, שהיא עיקר כפרה. ולא פליג רבי שמעון כי אם על קבלה, ואי הוה פליג אזריקה — הוה ליה לאשמועינן כח דהיתירא, דמכשיר ר' שמעון בזריקה, וכ"ש בקבלה. יח] ול"ע אי יט] מצי לפרש הכי לשון "ותנן זרק בשמאל פסל". כ] *והא דאמרי' בפרק "כל הפסולין" (לקמן דף לב.): קבל בימין ונתן בשמאל יחזור לימין — והיינו משום הזריקה דבעי ימין. דאי משום הולכה* — כא] מפני מה? הא לא כתיב בה אצבע, ואמאי פסל? ותו: דרבי שמעון הוה ליה לפלוגי ולהכשיר, משום דעבודה שאפשר לבטלה הוא. כב] ושמא לכתחילה קאמר יחזור לימין, שלא יעשה זריקה בשמאל. אבל בדיעבד, זרק בשמאל — כשר. כג] א"נ: משום הולכה נמי קאמר, דלכתחילה יחזור לימין, אבל בדיעבד כשר. *א"נ: מיירי בחטאת, דמודה ר' שמעון דבעי ימין בזריקה. וא"ת: וכיון דילפינן אצבע דחטאת בגזירה שוה מאצבע דמצורע דהויא בימין, היכי ילפינן ימין בשאר קרבנות מחטאת בהיקישא ד"זאת התורה"? הא פלוגתא דאמוראי היא בריש "איזהו מקומן" (לקמן דף נ.) אי דבר הלמד מגזירה שוה חוזר ומלמד בהיקש, או לא! ונראה מתוך כך דלכל שכן דניחא הכא טפי, דהכי פריך: והרי זריקה דלא כתיב בה אצבע, ולא פליג ר' שמעון. ואע"ג דדרשי' ימין מהיקישא דחטאת — הניחא למאן דאמר דבר הלמד בגזירה שוה חוזר ומלמד בהיקש, אלא למאן דאמר אין חוזר ומלמד בהיקש — אמאי לא פליג ר' שמעון? והשתא הא דמשני כד] בפ"ק דחולין (דף כב.): סבר לה כרבי שמעון דכהונה בעיא אצבע — היינו כמאן דאמר חוזר ומלמד בהיקישא. כה] *אבל רבי שמעון דמכשר בברייתא הכא שמאל בזריקה — לא בעי למילף ימין בהיקישא ד"זאת התורה" מחטאת, דסבר דזריקה מהזאה לא ילפינן. ואידך שינויא דמשני בפרק "התודה" (מנחות דף פג.): כדי נסבה — הוי כמאן דאמר אין חוזר ומלמד בהיקישא. ומיהו, בפרק קמא דחולין (דף כב.) לית שינויא דכדי נסבה. אבל בסוף "דם חטאת" (לקמן דף לח.) משני תרוייהו. ומיהו, אפשר דהכא מודו כולי עלמא דחוזר ומלמד בהיקישא, כיון דמצורע כו] חול דהוא מלמד ראשון. ותירוץ זה אנו צריכין בסמוך, [דדריש]: בא לעובדה ביד עובדה בימין כחטאת, והיינו היקש, וחטאת גופיה מגזירה שוה דמצורע ילפינן לה. ואם תאמר, מאי פריך: והרי זריקה, דלא כתיב אצבע אלא כהונה ופסולה, ולא פליג רבי שמעון? כז] [מת"ק] נמי הוה ליה למיפרך: אמאי פסל? שהרי בחטאת בעי אצבע בברייתא כדאמר "באצבעו ולקח". וגם אמרו דתנא קמא סבר מקרא נדרש לפניו, אבל מכהונה לא יליף. ואי פסול בזריקת שמאל בשאר קרבנות מהיקישא ד"זאת התורה" — א"כ מאי פריך כח] מר' שמעון? ונראה לי: דמדרבנן לא הוה בעי למיפרך, דהוה מצי למימר דטעמא דרבנן לאו משום דאצבע נדרש לפניו, וברייתא דתני "באצבעו ולקח" — לדברי ר' שמעון נקטיה. וטעמא דרבנן דפסלי שמאל בקבלה — משום דכתיב: "ולקח הכהן מן הדם", וסברי רבנן כהונה לא בעיא אצבע. וכן משמע פרק "דם חטאת" (לקמן דף לח.) דפריך: ימין מדרבה בר בר חנה נפקא! ומשני: ימין כדי נסבה. ואיבעית אימא: כר' שמעון דאמר כהונה בעיא אצבע — מכלל דלרבנן כהונה לא בעיא אצבע, ולכך הוצרך לשנויי כדי נסבה. כט] ולרבנן דכתיב בהו בזריקה בשאר קרבנות — כהן משמע ימין, ולא צריך למילף מאצבע דחטאת. ל] ברו"ך.

גורעין ומוסיפין ודורשין. לא שייך למיפרך: "סכינא חריפא אפסקא קראי", אלא כשמחסר תיבה אחת, כי ההיא ד"יש נוחלין" (ב"ב דף קיא:). ואם תאמר: תיפוק לי מדממעטינן דם סכין — כל שכן שעל הרצפה! ויש לומר: דדילמא דם סכין גרע, משום דנתקבלה בפסול. אי נמי: אי לאו טעמא דגורעין ומוסיפין ודורשין, הוה אמינא ד"מדם הפר" ולא מדם הפר ודבר אחר אתא למעוטי שעל הרצפה, אבל דסכין שפיר דמי.

בשפת מזרק. לא] [פירש"י]: בתוך, ולא שיפול [לתוכו, פי']: בתוך המזרק, דאם כן הוה ליה דבר אחר. [ואין להקשות], דגבי הזאה דפרה אמרינן: גמר להזות — מקנח לב] ידיו בגופה של פרה, בפרק קמא דמנחות (דף ז:). אבל הכא לא מקנח ליה לסכין בגופה של פרה, לפי שאז היה הסכין מלא נימין ולא היה עוד נאה לשחוט. ומיהו, בההיא שמעתא גופה גבי פרה אמרינן: בשלמא ידו מקנח לה בגופה של פרה, אלא אצבעו במאי מקנח? אמר אביי: בשפת מזרק. והשתא ידו נמי ליקנח בשפת מזרק

עין משפט נר מצוה

עט א מיי' פ"א מהל' פסולי המוקדשין הלכה כה:

פ ב ג ד ה מיי' פ"ד מהל' מעה"ק הל"ח:

מסורת הש"ס

נ"א ר"ש שלא בכלי שרת כשירה בהקטרה כו' כצ"ל

לעיל יח. וש"נ

[מנחות ו.]

יומא מח. לעיל טו. נזכר במנחות כו:

[יומא מח. ע"ש ט: ע"ש דאיתא והאמר רב יהודה המקבל וכו']

יומא מח. [בכורות מד:] ב"ב קיח:

[לקמן לג: מנחות ז:]

הס"ד נ"ק

נ"א כך שמעתי

ואידך שנויא דמשני כו' כצ"ל ומתיבת אבל ר"ש כו' עד לא ילפינן שייך לסוף הדבור נ"ק

[סוטה טז. מנחות ז:]

[ע' תוס' לקמן לג: ד"ה למעוטי]

[נ"ל ודם הפר ישפך וכ"א בסמוך וביומא מח.]

נ"א דבפרק כל הפסולין תנן קיבלו בימין כו'

נ"א מ"מ קשה הא לא כתיב כו' כצ"ל

נ"א ולאו

הגהות הב"ח

(א) גמ' והאמר רב יהודה אמר רב השוחט צריך: (ב) שם תניהו ענין לקבלה: (ג) רש"י ד"ה מאי טעמא וכו' קדשים הוא כחטאת וכאשם להכי איתקש: (ד) ד"ה בא לעובדה וכו' בכלי הוא וכשרה וכו' אי בעי בכלי: (ה) ד"ה לקומץ וכו' בימין סד"א דהואיל כצ"ל והד"א:

שיטה מקובצת

א] מדרב יהודה. האי סוגיא אליבא דמ"ד דבר הלמד בג"ש חוזר ומלמד [בהיקש] ולעיל דקאמר ולא פליג ר"ש [מקשה] אליבא דמ"ד אין חוזר ומלמד דרוצה ליישב אליבא דכ"ע הר"פ: ב] לא נצרכא. אלא: ג] והאמר. רב יהודה אמר רב: ד] ענין לקבלה: ה] דהא. אמרי' לעיל כו' אצבע וכהונה (בעי) מדר' יהודה ב"ר חייא [נפקא]: ו] אם. העלו למזבח כו' קדש קדשים הוא. כחטאת וכאשם להכי: ז] דמה. ביד ימין במתן: ח] מהודר. אימא קמיצת ותיבות סד"א ל"ש ונמחק: ט] רב יהודה א"ר: י] ודורשין. כך שמעתי ותיבות כר"ש נמחק: יא] מה"ד והא בשפיכת: יב] יפול מן הסכין: יג] ולא לתוכו הס"ד: יד] לא בעי ימין כו' וא"ת כיון: טו] שמעון. והיכי מצי למימר הכי: טז] משום. בלילה דכיון כו' דלא כתיב גבי מליקה מיעוטי: יז] תיבות כל הזבחים נמחק: יח] בקבלה. דאינו עבודה כל כך ואע"ג דאכתי קשה נילף מחטאת הניחא למ"ד כו' אמאי לא פליג ר"ש דמסברא יש ליישב מילתיה דר"ש אליבא דכ"ע. לשון מהר"פ: יט] אי מצינו לפרש גירסת ספרים הכי ותיבת לשון ל"ש ונמחק: כ] פסל דבפ' כל כו' ותיבות והא דאמרי' ל"ש ונמחק: כא] הולכה. מכל מקום הא לא ותיבות מפני מה ל"ש: כב] הוא. כי היכא דהוה מכשיר לעיל בשילהי פ"ק הולכה בזר אי לאו משום דיליף מק"ו: כג] כשר. או משום: כד] דמשני. בשילהי דם חטאת ותיבות בפ"ק דחולין נמחק: כה] בהקישא ואידך שנויא כו' והשאר בס"א אינו: כו] דמצורע. חולין דהוא כו' בסמוך דדריש בא: כז] שמעון. את"ק דר"ש דלעיל נמי הוה ליה כו' וגם אמרי' דת"ק: כח] פריך. לר"ש: כט] נסבה. דכהן ותיבת ולרבנן נמחק: ל] דחטאת: הס"ד ומתחיל הדבור חד לקידוש קומץ. אע"ג דקידוש קומץ במקום קבלת דם אתיא מדרבה בר בר חנה קידוש קומץ לא אתיא מהקישא דזאת התורה: כי קמץ לה נמי בשמאל נמי תיתכשרי אע"ג דמחטאת ילפינן לה דשייך טעמא דשלא יהא קרבנו מהודר בפ"ק דרוחות: תו"חו לא] מוע"ק. פי' משיפול בחוץ ולאו משיפול בתוך המזרק: לב] מקנח. ידו:

פא א מיי' פ"ד מהל' מעשה"ק הל"ט:
פב ב מיי' פ"ו מהל' פרה אדומה הל"ט:
פג ג מיי' פ"ד מהל' מעשה"ק הל"ט:
פד ד מיי' פ"ו מהל' מקוואות הלכה טו סמג עשין רמח טוש"ע יו"ד סי' רא סעיף לח:
פה ה מיי' פ"א מהל' פסה"מ הל' כט:
פו ו מיי' שם הל' כט:
פז ז מיי' פ"ו מהל' מעשה הקרבנות הלי"ג:
פח ח מיי' פ"א מהל' פסה"מ הל' טו:
(וע' תוס' מנחות: ד"ה אלא)

ורידין לתוך הכלי, איתמר נמי, אמר רב אסי אמר רבי יוחנן: ורידין צריך שיראו אויר כלי. בעא מיניה רבי אסי מרבי יוחנן: היה מקבל, ונפחתו שולי מזרק עד שלא הגיע דם לאויר, א] מהו? *אויר שאין סופו לנוח כמונח דמי, או [א]לא כמונח דמי? אמר ליה, תניתוה: חבית שמונחת תחת הזינוק – מים שבתוכה ושבחוצה לה פסולין; צירף פיה לזינוק, מים שבתוכה – פסולין, ושבחוצה לה – כשירין. האי מאי? בעי מיניה אויר שאין סופו לנוח, וקא פשט ליה אויר שסופו לנוח! תרתי קא בעי מיניה, אם תימצי לומר: אויר שאין סופו לנוח לאו כמונח דמי, אויר שסופו לנוח מאי? רב יוסף מתני הכי. רב כהנא מתני: חבית בעא מיניה, ופשט ליה חבית. רבה מתני: חבית בעא מיניה, ופשט ליה מזרק, אי אתה מודה במזרק שאי אפשר לו בלא זינוק? *תנן התם: [ב]נתן ידו או רגלו או עלי ירקות כדי שיעברו מים לחבית – פסולין, עלי קנים ועלי אגוזים – ב] כשירה. זה הכלל: דבר המקבל טומאה – פסולין, דבר שאינו מקבל טומאה – כשירין. מנא הני מילי? דאמר רבי יוחנן משום רבי יוסי בר אבא: אמר קרא °"אך מעין ובור מקוה מים יהיה טהור" (ויקרא יא), הוייתן על ידי טהרה תהא. אמר רבי *חייא אמר רבי יוחנן: זאת אומרת [ג]אויר כלי ככלי דמי. א"ל רבי זירא לרבי חייא בר אבא: ודילמא בשותת? א"ל: *תרדא, "כדי שיעברו מים לחבית" תנן! ואמר רבי חייא בר אבא אמר רבי יוחנן: מעדותו של רבי צדוק נישנית משנה זו, *דתנן: העיד רבי צדוק [ד]על הזוחלין שקילחן ג] בעלי אגוזין – שהן כשירין, זה היה מעשה באוהלייא, ובא מעשה לפני חכמים בלשכת הגזית, ד] והכשירו. *אמר רבי זירא אמר רבי: (א) [ה]הצורם אזן הפר ואח"כ קיבל דמו – פסול, שנאמר: °"ולקח מדם הפר" (שם ד), פר שהיה כבר. אשכחן קדשי קדשים, קדשים קלים מנלן? אמר רבא: תניא, °"שה תמים זכר בן שנה" (שמות יב) – שיהא תמים ובן שנה בשעת שחיטה; בקבלה, בהולכה, בזריקה מנין? ת"ל "יהיה" – כל הוויותי' לא יהיו אלא תם ובן שנה. איתיביה אביי: *רבי יהושע אומר: [ו]כל הזבחים שבתורה, שנשתייר מהן כזית בשר או כזית חלב – זורק את הדם! *תרגומא אבן שנה. ומי איכא מידי דבשעת שחיטה בן שנה, בשעת הולכה וזריקה בן שתים? אמר רבא: *[ז]זאת אומרת ה] שעות פוסלות בקדשים. אמר רבי אמי אמר רבי אלעזר: [ח]היא בפנים ורגליה בחוץ, חתך ואח"כ שחט – כשירה.

שחט

רש"י

ורידין לתוך כלי. ו] דנהוי קבלה מהספר שפיר. והאי "תוך" – לאו דווקא, דהא לא אפשר, אלא על אוירו של תוך כלי. שולי מזרק. קרקעיתו, *פיני"ו בלע"ז. עד שלא הגיע דם לאויר מזרק. לבין דופני ז] מזרק, בעוד הדם למעלה מהן. ומיהו על כנגד אוירו הן, דהא ורידין רואים אויר ח] כלי [בעינן]. אויר שאין סופו לנוח. כגון האי, שעתידים שוליו ליפול עד שלא ינוח דם לתוכו – כמונח דמי, והוה ליה כמי שנתקבל ט] ונשפך, דכשר לאוספו. או לא כמונח דמי, והוה ליה כנשפך מן הצואר לרצפה, דפסול. וכשהגיע דם לאויר דופנותיו עד שלא נפחתו שוליו – לא מיבעיא ליה, דמשנכנס לתוכן הויא קבלה. חבית שמונח תחת הזינוק. לכור המקלח מים מהר זקוף, והקילוח מקלח למרחוק ונופל לחבית, וחבית זו אינה מונחת שם לשם קידוש מי חטאת י]. מים שבתוכה ושבחוצה לה פסולין יא]. כלומר, שלא יתן כלי לתוך אוירה ויאחזנו בידו לקבל בו הקילוח לקידוש, יב] ואף לא חוצה לה למעלה מאוגניה כנגד אוירה. דכיון שהגיעו מים כנגד אוירה – הרי הן כמונחים בתוכה, *ופסק לה חיותייהו, ואנן "מים חיים אל כלי" יג] בעינן לקדוש. אלמא, אויר כמונח דמי. ולקמיה פריך: האי אויר שסופו לנוח הוא! צירף פיה לזינוק. שאין אויר מפסיק בין פיה לזינוק. שבתוכה. כלומר, שבאו לתוך אויר דופנותיה – פסולים. שבחוצה לה. אע"פ שכנגד אוירה – (ב) כשירין, שעדיין לא פירשו מן הצינור, ואפי' אויר אין כאן. וקא פשיט ליה אויר שסופו לנוח הוא. כגון הא דקתני רישא שבחוצה לה פסולין, דילמא האי דחשיב ליה כמונח – משום דראוי היה לנוח, שהרי חבית זו שלימה, וראוי היה לנוח אי לא שבא זה וקלט. אבל נפחתו שולי מזרק – לא היה עתיד יד] ראוי לנוח! תרתי בעא מיניה. ופשט ליה חדא מינייהו. חבית בעא מיניה. לא הוה שמיעא ליה הא מתניתין, ובעא מיניה: חבית שמונחת תחת הזינוק, מים שבחוצה טו] [לה] כנגד אוירה, מהו לקלוט אותן למי חטאת? ופשט ליה מהא מתני' דפסולין. ופשט ליה מזרק. לא ולמד מקבלת דם. אי אתה מודה במזרק שאי אפשר לו בלא זינוק. כששוחט על אויר הכלי – אין הדם שותת טז] במקומו, אלא מקלח לרוחב הכלי עד להלן. ואי אויר שסופו לנוח לאו כמונח דמי, נמצא כשהוא יורד לכלי – מן האויר הוא בא ולא מן הפר, והתורה אמרה דם מהפר יקבלנו. *וגבי חבית נמי, אויר שסופו לנוח הוא, וכמונח דמי ופסולין. נתן ידו או רגלו. קילוח היורד מהר מעוקם, שמשפע ועולה, ואין הקילוח יורד לחבית, ונתן ידו למעלה יז] מראש הצינור [לעשות כעין מרזב], כדי שיעברו המים דרך ידו לחבית של קידוש. ובן עלי ירקות. הראויין לאכילה, ומקבלין טומאה יח]. פסולין. [המים], כדיליף לקמיה. הוייתן. של מים המטהרים, ע"י טהרה תהא. כשאתה מהווה אותם להיות מקוה או קדוש – הוי מהווה אותם על ידי דבר שאין מקבל טומאה. זאת אומרת אויר כלי ככלי דמי יט]. מדקתני: נתן ידו כו' פסל, דהא אין המים שותתין כ] מידו לכלי בשתיתה אלא בהעברה, כשיוצאין מידו מקלחין להם על פני רחב פי החבית, ואפי' הכי פסול. אלמא, משיצאו מידו לקלח על פני אויר – הוה ליה כאילו שתתו מידו לכלי, שהרי ידו על כנגד שפת הכלי מונחת, ומשיצאו מידו מקלחים באו כנגד אוירו. דאי לאו ככלי דמי – אמאי פסול? הלא מן האויר באין לו, והוה ליה כנותן ידו בצינור משוך מן הקילוח עשר אמות. דילמא בשותת. מידו לכלי, ולא באו מן האויר. תרדא. = שוטה, בהול. שיעברו תנן. והעברה בקילוח משמע. הצורם. *אקרני"ר, דהוי מום, דתנן (בכורות דף לז.): נפגמה אזנו גבי מום. ואחר כך קיבל דמו. דהוה כא] ביה מום בין שחיטה לקבלה. שהיה כבר. צריך שיהא שלם בשעת קבלה כבשעת שחיטה. אשכחן קדשי קדשים. כב] דהאי בפר (*העלם דבר של צבור) כתיב. בשעת שחיטה. דכתיב (שמות יב): "תכוסו על השה", דהיינו שחיטה, וסמיך ליה "שה תמים" וגו'. שנשתייר מהן. בשעת זריקה, כג] *אם נטמא כל הבשר והחלב או שאבד – לא יזרוק. רבי יהושע לטעמיה, דדריש: "ועשית עולותיך הבשר והדם", אם אין בשר אין דם, *במנחות (דף כו). קתני מיהא זורק, ואין לך בעל מום גדול מזה, קשיא לרבה דאמר בעינן תם בשעת זריקה. אבל לרבי זירא לא קשיא, כד] דהא לא בעי תם אלא בשחיטה וקבלה. תרגומה אבן שנה. אביי אמר ליה לרבא: תרגומא אבן שנה כה] למתניתך, דבעי כל הוויותיו *בשעת שחיטה – אבן שנה קאי דסליק מיניה, "בן שנה יהיה" – כל הווייתו יהיה בן שנה. אבל אם נכנס בשנה שניה בין שחיטה לזריקה – פסול, דשעות פוסלות בקדשים כו] כדפירש ואזיל. אבל תם לא תילף מיניה, דהאי "יהיה" לאו אתמים קאי. וקבלה בקדשים קלים בתמימות, הואיל וגלי בקדשי קדשים גלי. שעות פוסלות בקדשים. דשנה האמורה בקדשים קיימא לן בפרק "יוצא דופן" במסכת נדה (דף מז:) דאין מונין לה מתשרי כשאר ראשי שנים, אלא מיום שנולד מעת לעת לשנה הבאה, וילפינן לה מקרא דכתיב בהו "בן שנתו" – שנתו שלו ולא (ג) שנתו של מנין עולם. ואשמעינן הכא דלא תימא מיום ליום הוא דבעינן, ולא משעה לשעה. אלא אף משעה לשעה שאם נולד בניסן בי"ד ובט' שעות, ושחטו לשנה הבאה בי"ד בניסן בט' שעות – אסור לזרוק דמו בעשירית, שכבר עברה שנתו. הוא בפנים. בעזרה. חתך. כז] רגליה, ואחר כך שחט – כשרה. שלא נתערב דם פסול יוצא עם דם שבמזרק שנתקבל בו הדם. ולקמיה פריך: הא שויה בעלת מום! *שחט ואחר כך חתך פסולה. כח] שמשנשחטה נפסל דם הרגלים ביוצא, וכל דמי בהמה יונקים זה מזה, ועלה ויצא דרך בית שחיטה ונתערב בדם המזרק, ופסלו.

ה"ג

תוספות

מזרק – נראה לפי שצריך לשרוף לכוליה דם. אבל אצבעו לא אפשר לקנח בגוף הפרה – שהיה מזה בהר המשחה אל נכח פני אהל מועד, וכי בין כל הזאה והזאה ירד מן ההר לקנח ידיו בגוף הפרה? אי נמי, כדפי' בקונטרס לקמן בפרק "דם חטאת" (דף צג:): שלא יתלכלך אצבעו בנימין בין ההזאות. דהכי נמי חיישינן לנימין בפ' "כל כתבי" (שבת דף קטו:) גבי מפשיטין את הפסח עד החזה. וכן נראה, דשחיטתה והזייתה במקום אחד היו, כדאיתא בפרק "פרת חטאת" (לקמן דף קיג.) וכן במסכת מדות (דף לה.) תנן: כל הכתלים שהיו שם גבוהין עשרים אמה, חוץ מכותל מזרחי שהכהן השורף רואה פתחו של היכל בשעת הזייה*. ע"כ.

זאת אומרת אויר כלי ככלי דמי. מהכא הוה מצי למיפשט לעיל. וע"ע פרק "המזבח מקדש" (לקמן דף פז:) גבי אויר כבש ככבש דמי.

קדשים קלים מנין. ותימה: דלעיל גבי "מדם הפר" [ולא מדם העור] לא קאמר קדשים קלים מנין! ויש לומר: דכיון דגלי הכא – ה"ה התם. שחט

גליון הש"ס

גמ' תרגומא אבן שנה. ע' יומא דף סב ע"ב תוס' ד"ה שלא: שם זאת אומרת שעות פוסלות. ע' טורי אבן ר"ה דף ט ע"ב ד"ה פתח מלי יום: רש"י ד"ה מים שבתוכה ושבחוצה לה כו' ופסק לה חיותייהו. עיין כר"ש פ"ט מ"ג דפרה.

הגהות הב"ח

(א) גמ' אמר ר' זירא אמר ר' יוחנן הצורם: (ב) רש"י ד"ה שבתוכה וכו' אוירה הן כשירין: (ג) ד"ה שעות וכו' ולא שנה של מנין עולם:

מסורת הש"ס

[ב"מ יב. קכ.]
פרה פ"ו מ"ד
[צ"ל ר' חייא בר אבא]
[ב"ק קט: כריתות יח. וע' בכל המקומות מה שפירש"י אבן כענין שנה]
[עדיות פ"ז מ"ד]
בכורות לט: [לקמן כו. ע"ש]
[בכורות שם תוספתא דזבחים פ"ד תוספתא דפסחים פ"ו פסחים עט. מנחות ט. כו. מעילה טו. (לקמן קט.)]
[צ"ל אלא ע"כ אויר שסופו לנוח כמונח דמי וגבי חבית סי' ג"כ]
[צ"ל כהן מעיה וכו' רש"י בכורות לט:]
[צ"ל אם נטמא לשם לקמן קד. ופסחים עז.]
[צ"ל בשעת]
שייך לדף כו.

שיטה מקובצת

א] לאויר מזרק. פי' קודם שהגיע לאויר המחיצות המזרק שאם לא נפחתו עד שהיה כנגד המחיצות פשיטא דכמונח דמי: ב] אגוזים. כשירין: ג] שקילחן: ד] הגזית. והכשירוהו: ה] שעות פוסלות בקדשים [illegible]

לא מבעיא שבתוכה שכבר ידו בתוך החבית אלא אפי' שבחוצה לה פסולין: יב] לקידוש דכיון שהגיעו כו' והשאר בס"א אינו: יג] כלי של קידוש בעינן: יד] וראוי לנוח: טו] שבחוצה. לה: טז] שותת כו' ואי אמרת שסופו לנוח: יז] למעלה. בראש הצינור לעשות כעין מרזב: יח] טומאה: הס"ד ומה"ד [כדי שיעברו מים] לחבית. האי חבית מיירי כשנתנה שם לשם מי חטאת: מלשון הר"פ פירש"י: יט] דמי. ש"מ אויר כלי ככלי דמי שהרי על עובי שפת הכלי מונחת ואין המים שותתין ונופלים מידו לכלי כדמסיק [כדי שיעברו] דמשמע כשיצאו המים מידו הם מקלחין להלן רחוק מידו קצת הכלי ואח"כ נופלים בכלי וכיון שהם מקלחין א"כ הקילוח גבוה קצת למעלה [באויר] שכנגד המחיצות לכל הפחות כשיעור עובי ידו ואותו אויר שהוא קצת למעלה מן האויר שכנגד המחיצות קורא אויר כלי ככלי דמי ומים שיוצא [מידו והולכים] באויר הכלי כדפי' הרי הם כמונחים תוך הכלי ומאז חשובה נתינת מים אל הכלי שהזכיר הכתוב גבי מי חטאת דכתיב ונתן מים חיים אל כלי ולכך לא [חשיבא] [illegible]

שָׁחַט וְאַחַר כָּךְ חָתַךְ — פְּסוּלָה. חָתַךְ וְאח"כ שָׁחַט — כְּשֵׁרָה? בַּעַל מוּם קָא מַקְרִיב! אֶלָּא אֵימָא: א] [אחָתַךְ וְאח"כ קִיבֵּל — כְּשֵׁרָה], קִיבֵּל וְאח"כ חָתַךְ — פְּסוּלָה. (א) חָתַךְ וְאח"כ קִיבֵּל כְּשֵׁרָה? וְהָא *א"ר זֵירָא: הַצּוֹרֵם אֹזֶן ב] *בִּבְכוֹר וְאח"כ קִיבֵּל דָּמוֹ — פָּסוּל, שֶׁנֶּאֱמַר: "וְלָקַח מִדַּם הַפָּר", פַּר שֶׁהָיָה כְּבָר! א"ר חִסְדָּא אָמַר אֲבִימִי: ג] בחוֹתֵךְ בָּאֵבֶר עַד שֶׁמַּגִּיעַ לָעֶצֶם. קִיבֵּל וְאח"כ חָתַךְ — פְּסוּלָה; שָׁמְעַתְּ מִינָּהּ: דָּם הַמּוּבְלָע בָּאֵבָרִים — דָּם הוּא? דִּלְמָא מִשּׁוּם שַׁמְנוּנִית. שָׁמְעַתְּ מִינָּהּ: בְּשַׂר קָדָשִׁים קַלִּים שֶׁיָּצָא לִפְנֵי זְרִיקַת דָּם — פָּסוּל? דִּלְמָא בְּקָדְשֵׁי קָדָשִׁים. ת"ר: גקָדְשֵׁי קָדָשִׁים שְׁחִיטָתָן בַּצָּפוֹן וְקִיבּוּל דָּמָן בִּכְלִי שָׁרֵת בַּצָּפוֹן. דעָמַד בַּדָּרוֹם וְהוֹשִׁיט יָדוֹ לַצָּפוֹן וְשָׁחַט — שְׁחִיטָתוֹ כְּשֵׁרָה. הקִיבֵּל — קַבָּלָתוֹ פְּסוּלָה, והִכְנִיס רֹאשׁוֹ וְרוּבּוֹ — כְּאִילּוּ נִכְנַס כּוּלּוֹ. *זפִּרְכְּסָה, וְיָצְתָה לַדָּרוֹם, וְחָזְרָה — כְּשֵׁרָה. חקָדָשִׁים קַלִּים — שְׁחִיטָתָן בִּפְנִים וְקִיבּוּל דָּמָן בִּכְלִי שָׁרֵת בִּפְנִים. עָמַד בַּחוּץ וְהִכְנִיס יָדוֹ לִפְנִים וְשָׁחַט — שְׁחִיטָתוֹ כְּשֵׁרָה. טקִיבֵּל — קַבָּלָתוֹ פְּסוּלָה, הִכְנִיס רֹאשׁוֹ וְרוּבּוֹ — כְּאִילּוּ לֹא נִכְנַס. יפִּרְכְּסָה וְיָצְתָה לַחוּץ וְחָזְרָה — פְּסוּלָה. שְׁמַע מִינָּהּ: בְּשַׂר קָדָשִׁים קַלִּים שֶׁיָּצָא לִפְנֵי זְרִיקַת ד] דָּמִים — פְּסוּלִים! דִּילְמָא בְּאַלְיָה וְיוֹתֶרֶת הַכָּבֵד וּשְׁתֵּי כְלָיוֹת. בְּעָא מִינֵּיהּ אֲבוּהּ דִּשְׁמוּאֵל מִשְּׁמוּאֵל: הִיא בִּפְנִים וְרַגְלֶיהָ בַּחוּץ, מַהוּ? א"ל, כְּתִיב: °"וֶהֱבִיאוּם לַה'" — כעַד שֶׁתְּהֵא כּוּלָּהּ לִפְנִים. תְּלָה וְשָׁחַט, מַהוּ? א"ל: כְּשֵׁרָה. א"ל: **לאִישְׁתַּבַּשְׁתְּ, בָּעֵינַן שְׁחִיטָה עַל יָרֵךְ, וְלֵיכָּא. נִתְלָה וְשָׁחַט, מַהוּ? אֲמַר לֵיהּ: פְּסוּלָה. אֲמַר לֵיהּ: אִישְׁתַּבַּשְׁתְּ, שְׁחִיטָה עַל יָרֵךְ מוְלֹא שׁוֹחֵט עַל יָרֵךְ. נִתְלָה וְקִבֵּל, מַהוּ? אֲמַר לֵיהּ: כְּשֵׁרָה. אֲמַר לֵיהּ: אִישְׁתַּבַּשְׁתְּ, אֵין דֶּרֶךְ שֵׁירוּת בְּכָךְ. תְּלָה וְקִיבֵּל מַהוּ? אֲמַר לֵיהּ: פְּסוּלָה. אֲמַר לֵיהּ: אִישְׁתַּבַּשְׁתְּ, שְׁחִיטָה עַל יָרֵךְ וְלֹא קַבָּלָה עַל יָרֵךְ. אָמַר אַבַּיֵי: בְּקָדְשֵׁי קָדָשִׁים כּוּלָּן פְּסוּלוֹת, בַּר מִנִּתְלָה וְשָׁחַט. בְּקָדָשִׁים קַלִּים — כּוּלָּן כְּשֵׁרוֹת, בַּר מִן נִתְלָה וְקִיבֵּל. אָמַר רָבָא: מַאי שְׁנָא תָּלָה וְקִיבֵּל בְּקָדָשִׁים קַלִּים דִּכְשֵׁרָה — דַּאֲוִיר פְּנִים כִּפְנִים דָּמֵי, בְּקָדְשֵׁי קָדָשִׁים נַמִי — אֲוִיר צָפוֹן כְּצָפוֹן דָּמֵי! אֶלָּא אָמַר רָבָא: בֵּין בְּקָדְשֵׁי קָדָשִׁים בֵּין בְּקָדָשִׁים קַלִּים — כְּשֵׁרוֹת, נבַּר מִן תָּלָה וְשָׁחַט בְּקָדְשֵׁי קָדָשִׁים, סנִתְלָה וְקִיבֵּל — בֵּין בְּקָדְשֵׁי קָדָשִׁים בֵּין בְּקָדָשִׁים קַלִּים. בְּעָא מִינֵּיהּ רַבִּי יִרְמְיָה מֵרַבִּי זֵירָא: הוּא בִּפְנִים וְצִיצִיתוֹ בַּחוּץ, מַהוּ? אֲמַר לֵיהּ: לָאו אָמְרַתְּ "וֶהֱבִיאוּם לַה'" — עַד שֶׁתָּבֹא כּוּלָּהּ לִפְנִים? עהָכָא נַמִי, °"בְּבוֹאָם אֶל אֹהֶל מוֹעֵד" — עַד שֶׁיָּבֹא כּוּלּוֹ לְאֹהֶל מוֹעֵד.§ **מתני'** פנִתְּנוּ עַל גַּבֵּי הַכֶּבֶשׁ, שֶׁלֹּא כְּנֶגֶד הַיְסוֹד, נָתַן אֶת הַנִּיתָּנִין לְמַטָּה לְמַעְלָה, וְאֶת הַנִּיתָּנִין לְמַעְלָה לְמַטָּה, וְאֶת הַנִּיתָּנִין בִּפְנִים בַּחוּץ, וְאֶת הַנִּיתָּנִין בַּחוּץ בִּפְנִים — פָּסוּל, וְאֵין בּוֹ כָּרֵת.§

גמ'

(ויקרא יז) (שמות כח) (חולין ד"ב)

רש"י

*ה"ג: ה] שָׁחַט וְאַחַר כָּךְ חָתַךְ פְּסוּלָה בַּעֲלַת מוּם קָמַקְרִיב אֶלָּא אֵימָא חָתַךְ וְאַחַר כָּךְ קִיבֵּל. שֶׁחֲתָכוֹ בֵּין שְׁחִיטָה לְקַבָּלָה - כְּשֵׁרָה. וְהָא א"ר זֵירָא הַצּוֹרֵם כו'. אַלְמָא הַמּוּם פּוֹסֵל בְּקַבָּלָה. וּמְשַׁנֵּי: אָמַר רַב חִסְדָּא אָמַר אֲבִימִי חוֹתֵךְ בָּאֵבֶר עַד שֶׁמַּגִּיעַ לָעֶצֶם. דְּלָאו מוּם הוּא, וְהַדָּם מְעוּכָּב ע"י חֲתִיכָה ו] מִלַּעֲלוֹת וְלִיכָּנֵס לִפְנִים. תורה אור קִבֵּל וְאַחַר כָּךְ חָתַךְ פְּסוּלָה. מִילְּתֵיהּ דְּרַבִּי אֶלְעָזָר הָדַר וְנָקֵיט, כְּמוֹ "אָמַר מָר". ש"מ דָּם הַמּוּבְלָע בָּאֵבָרִים דָּם הוּא ז] *וְכָרֵת נַמִי לְחַיֵּיב. דְּאִי לָא הָוֵי דָּם — הֵיכָא חָיֵיל פְּסוּל יוֹצֵא, אַמַּיָּא בְּעָלְמָא? דִּלְמָא מִשּׁוּם שַׁמְנוּנִית. דַּחֲזָיָא לַאֲכִילָה, וַחֲשִׁיבִי כְּבָשָׂר לְאִיפְּסוּלֵי בְּיוֹצֵא, כִּדְכְתִיב (שמות כב): "וּבָשָׂר בַּשָּׂדֶה טְרֵיפָה", וּמִיבְּלַע בְּדַם הָרֶגֶל, וְנָפְקָא דֶּרֶךְ בֵּית שְׁחִיטָה, וּפָסְלָה לֵיהּ לַדָּם שֶׁבַּמִּזְרָק. ש"מ בְּשַׂר קָדָשִׁים קַלִּים שֶׁיָּצָא מִן הָעֲזָרָה לִפְנֵי זְרִיקָה פָּסוּל. וְאַעַ"פ שֶׁסּוֹפוֹ לָצֵאת אַחַר זְרִיקָה וְלִהְיוֹת נֶאֱכָל בְּכָל הָעִיר — הַשְׁתָּא מִיהָא לָא מְטָא זִמְנֵיהּ. וְתֶיהְוֵי הָךְ דְּרַב אַמִּי אָמַר ר' אֶלְעָזָר ח] דְּלָא כְּדְרַבִּי יוֹחָנָן, דְּמַכְשַׁר לֵיהּ לְקַמָּן בְּפֶרֶק "כָּל הַתָּדִיר" (דף פט:). דִּלְמָא. כִּי אֲמָרָהּ ט] רַבִּי [אַמִּי אָמַר ר' אֶלְעָזָר]. בְּקָדְשֵׁי קָדָשִׁים. אָמַר, דְּמִיפְּסַל לִפְנֵי זְרִיקָה בְּיוֹצֵא לְדִבְרֵי הַכֹּל, שֶׁאֵין סוֹפוֹ לָצֵאת. וְקִיבּוּל דָּמָן בִּכְלִי שָׁרֵת בַּצָּפוֹן. לְקַמָּן יָלְפִינַן לָהּ בְּ"אֵיזֶהוּ מְקוֹמָן" (דף מח.) דְּסָמַךְ קַבָּלָה לִשְׁחִיטָה. עָמַד. בְּחֵלֶק דְּרוֹמִי שֶׁל עֲזָרָה, סָמוּךְ לְאֶמְצָעָהּ. הוֹשִׁיט יָדוֹ לַצָּפוֹן וְשָׁחַט שְׁחִיטָתוֹ כְּשֵׁרָה. לְקַמָּן יָלְפִינַן לָהּ: "אוֹתוֹ" בַּצָּפוֹן וְאֵין הַשּׁוֹחֵט בַּצָּפוֹן. אֲבָל הַמְקַבֵּל צָרִיךְ לִהְיוֹת בַּצָּפוֹן, הִלְכָּךְ, קִיבֵּל - קַבָּלָתוֹ פְּסוּלָה. הִכְנִיס רֹאשׁוֹ וְרוּבּוֹ. בַּצָּפוֹן, וְקִיבֵּל - כְּאִילּוּ נִכְנַס כּוּלּוֹ, כִּדְקִי"ל בְּכָל הַתּוֹרָה: רוּבּוֹ כְּכוּלּוֹ. פִּרְכְּסָה. לְאַחַר שְׁחִיטָה, וְיָצְתָה לַדָּרוֹם, וְחָזְרָה - כְּשֵׁרָה, דְּאֵין פְּסוּל יוֹצֵא י] אֶלָּא מִתּוֹךְ הַמְּחִיצוֹת. וְהַאי "וְחָזְרָה" - לָאו דַּוְקָא. אֶלָּא, אַיְּידֵי דְּבָעֵי לְמִיתְנֵי סֵיפָא גַּבֵּי פְּנִים וָחוּץ "וְחָזְרָה", לְאַשְׁמוּעִינַן רְבוּתָא דְּאַעַ"ג דְּחָזְרָה פְּסוּלָה - תָּנָא רֵישָׁא נַמִי "וְחָזְרָה". שְׁחִיטָתָן בִּפְנִים יא]. דִּכְתִיב (ויקרא ג) בִּשְׁלָמִים: "וּשְׁחָטוֹ פֶּתַח אֹהֶל מוֹעֵד", דְּהַיְינוּ תּוֹךְ הָעֲזָרָה. וְקִיבּוּל דָּמָן בִּכְלִי שָׁרֵת בִּפְנִים. קַבָּלָה בִּפְנִים נָפְקָא לָן מִ"לַעֲמוֹד לִפְנֵי ה' לְשָׁרְתוֹ" (דברים י), אַלְמָא כָּל שֵׁירוּת לִפְנֵי ה' הוּא. עָמַד בַּחוּץ וְהוֹשִׁיט יָדוֹ בִּפְנִים וְשָׁחַט שְׁחִיטָתוֹ כְּשֵׁרָה. לְקַמָּן בְּפֶרֶק "כָּל הַפְּסוּלִין" (דף לב:) יָלְפִי' לָהּ: "בֶּן הַבָּקָר לִפְנֵי ה'" וְלֹא הַשּׁוֹחֵט לִפְנֵי ה'. קִבֵּל קַבָּלָתוֹ פְּסוּלָה. כִּדְפָרִישִׁית. הִכְנִים רֹאשׁוֹ וְרוּבּוֹ כְּאִילּוּ לֹא נִכְנַס. כִּדְיָלְפִינַן לְקַמָּן בִּשְׁמַעְתִּין: "בְּבוֹאָם אֶל אֹהֶל מוֹעֵד" — עַד שֶׁיָּבֹא כּוּלּוֹ. וְגַבֵּי עֲזָרָה יב] דִּכְתִיב: "לַעֲמוֹד לִפְנֵי ה'" - בָּעֵי נַמִי כּוּלּוֹ, דְּכֵיוָן דְּגַלֵּי בַּחֲדָא - גַּלֵּי בְּכוּלְּהוּ, וְהָכִי אָמַר בִּשְׁמַעְתִּין*. פִּרְכְּסָה. לְאַחַר שְׁחִיטָה, וְיָצְאָה לַחוּץ, וְחָזְרָה - פְּסוּלָה, דְּאִיפְּסַלָּא בְּיוֹצֵא. כִּדְגָמְרִי' פְּסוּל יוֹצֵא בִּפְסָחִים בְּ"כֵּיצַד צוֹלִין" (דף פב.) מֵ"הֵן לֹא הוּבָא אֶת דָּמָהּ אֶל הַקּוֹדֶשׁ פְּנִימָה" (ויקרא י) וּמִ"בָּשָׂר בַּשָּׂדֶה טְרֵיפָה" (שמות כב). דִּילְמָא. הָא דְּקָתָנֵי פְּסוּלָה - בְּאַלְיָה וְיוֹתֶרֶת כו', דְּאֵימוּרִין נִינְהוּ, וְאֵימוּרֵי קָדָשִׁים קַלִּים קָדְשֵׁי קָדָשִׁים הֵן. הִיא בִּפְנִים כו' מַהוּ. לְשׁוֹחֲטָהּ לְכַתְּחִילָּה יג]. תָּלָה. הַבְּהֵמָה בַּאֲוִיר הָעֲזָרָה. עַל יָרֵךְ. מַשְׁמַע יד] אֶצְלוֹ. נִתְלָה. הַשּׁוֹחֵט בַּאֲוִיר הָעֲזָרָה, מַהוּ? אֲמַר לֵיהּ פְּסוּלָה. מִינֵּיהּ קָגָמַר לָהּ, דְּשָׁמַע דְּקָא"ל: תָּלָה וְשָׁחַט פָּסוּל, וְסָבַר: ה"ה לְנִתְלָה. אֲמַר לֵיהּ כְּשֵׁרָה. כִּדְאָמַר לֵיהּ לְנִתְלָה וְשָׁחַט. טו] [א"ל פְּסוּלָה. מִינֵּיהּ גָּמַר, כִּדְאָמַר לֵיהּ בְּתָלָה וְשָׁחַט, וּבְנִתְלָה וְקִבֵּל, וְסָבַר: ה"ה לְתָלָה וְקִיבֵּל]. בְּקָדְשֵׁי קָדָשִׁים. דִּכְתִיב בְּהוּ: "עַל יֶרֶךְ". כּוּלָּן פְּסוּלִין בַּר מִן נִתְלָה וְשָׁחַט. דְּבְשׁוֹחֵט לָא כְּתִיב יֶרֶךְ אֶלָּא בְּנִשְׁחָט, כִּדְכְתִיב: "אוֹתוֹ עַל יֶרֶךְ". אֲבָל תָּלָה וְקִבֵּל - פְּסוּלָה, דַּאֲוִיר צָפוֹן לָאו כְּצָפוֹן דָּמֵי, וּבָעֵינַן קַבָּלָה בַּצָּפוֹן, כִּדְגָמְרִי' בְּ"אֵיזֶהוּ מְקוֹמָן" (לקמן מח.). וְאַף עַל גַּב דְּלָא כְּתִיב יֶרֶךְ בְּקַבָּלָה — צָפוֹן מִיהָא כְּתִיב בָּהּ. בְּקָדָשִׁים קַלִּים. טז] לָא כְּתִיב בְּהוּ "עַל יֶרֶךְ" וְלָא כְּתִיב בְּהוּ צָפוֹן - כּוּלָּן כְּשֵׁרִים, בַּר מִנִּתְלָה וְקִבֵּל, דְּאֵין דֶּרֶךְ שֵׁירוּת בְּכָךְ. דַּאֲוִיר פְּנִים כִּפְנִים דָּמֵי. דְּהָא עַל כָּרְחָךְ פְּנִים יז] מִיהוּ כְּתִיב בְּהוּ, וּמוֹדֵית דַּאֲוִיר פְּנִים כִּפְנִים. אַמַּאי פְּלִגְתְּ אַהֲלָכוֹת דִּשְׁמוּאֵל בְּתָלָה וְקִבֵּל? לֵימָא נַמִי: אֲוִיר צָפוֹן כְּצָפוֹן דָּמֵי! אֶלָּא אָמַר רָבָא. כּוּלָּהּ כְּהִלְכוֹת דִּשְׁמוּאֵל קָאָמַר לָהּ. אֶלָּא דְּהִלְכוֹת דִּשְׁמוּאֵל לָא אַיְירֵי בְּקָדָשִׁים קַלִּים. בַּר מִן תָּלָה וְשָׁחַט בְּקָדְשֵׁי קָדָשִׁים. דְּבָעֵינַן "עַל יֶרֶךְ". אֲבָל בְּקָדָשִׁים קַלִּים, דְּלָא כְּתִיב "עַל יֶרֶךְ" — כְּשֵׁרָה. תָּלָה וְקִבֵּל - כָּשֵׁר בְּכוּלָּן, דְּדֶרֶךְ שֵׁירוּת בְּכָךְ, וַאֲוִיר צָפוֹן כְּצָפוֹן דָּמֵי, וּבְקַבָּלָה לָא כְּתִיב "עַל יֶרֶךְ". וְנִתְלָה וְקִבֵּל בֵּין בְּקָדָשִׁים כו'. נַמִי פָּסוּל, דְּקַבָּלָה שֵׁירוּת הִיא, וְאֵין דֶּרֶךְ שֵׁירוּת בְּכָךְ. אֲבָל נִתְלָה וְשָׁחַט — כְּשֵׁרָה, דִּשְׁחִיטָה לָאו שֵׁירוּת הִיא. וְ"עַל יֶרֶךְ" נַמִי לָאו בְּשׁוֹחֵט כְּתִיב אֶלָּא בִּבְהֵמָה. צִיצִיתוֹ. צִיצִית רֹאשׁוֹ, דְּהַיְינוּ שְׂעָרוֹ. **מתני'** נִתְּנוּ. לְמַתַּן דָּמוֹ. עַל גַּבֵּי הַכֶּבֶשׁ. שֶׁאֵינוֹ מְקוֹם מַתַּן דָּמִים. אוֹ בַּמִּזְבֵּחַ שֶׁלֹּא כְּנֶגֶד הַיְסוֹד, וְיָלְפִינַן לְקַמָּן דְּעוֹלָה טְעוּנָה מַתַּן דָּמִים כְּנֶגֶד הַיְסוֹד, שֶׁהָיָה יְסוֹד הַמִּזְבֵּחַ לְמַטָּה מִמַּתַּן דָּמָהּ. לְמַעוּטֵי קֶרֶן מִזְרָחִית דְּרוֹמִית דְּלָא הָוֵה לָהּ יְסוֹד, כִּדְאָמְרִינַן בְּ"אֵיזֶהוּ מְקוֹמָן" (לקמן דף נג:). לְמַטָּה. מֵחוּט הַסִּיקְרָא. וְאֵין בּוֹ כָּרֵת. אֵין בַּאֲכִילָתוֹ כָּרֵת. וּבַגְּמָרָא מְפָרֵשׁ לְמַאי אִיצְטְרִיךְ לְמִתְנְיֵיהּ.

תוספות

שחט ואח"כ חתך פסולה. דדם פסול אינו בטל ברוב, כדמוכח פ' "התערובת" (לקמן דף עט:) יח] דגזרי' גזירה במקדש.

חתך ואח"כ שחט כשרה. ובסמוך דקאמר: "והביאום" כתיב, שתהא כולה לפנים – היינו לכתחלה. ע"כ. **שמע** מינה דם המובלע באברים דם הוא. פי' בקונט': ונפקא מינה שחייבין כרת על אכילתו. ואי אפשר לומר כן, דהא קי"ל בכריתות (דף כא:) דדם האברים בלאו. ואין לפרש דמיירי הכא להתחייב עליו משום דם קודש שנפרש מן האבר, דפשיטא דשרי באכילה, כדפירשנו בחולין (דף יד.*) מכמה ראיות. ונראה לפרש: דאיירי הכא ליפסל ביוצא. ואפי' למ"ד אין יוצא בבשרי] בקדשים קלים – היינו משום דסופה לצאת. אי נמי: לענין דאין מועלין בו, ואין חייבין עליו משום פיגול. או לענין דם חטאת שניתז על הבגד. **דילמא** באליה ויותרת הכבד. וא"ת: מ"מ תיפשוט דאימורי קדשים קלים שיצאו לפני זריקה פסולין. ולקמן בפרק "כל התדיר" (דף פט:) רוצה לומר דכשרין! וי"ל: דמכאן אין ראיה, דדלמא כר' אליעזר ס"ל דפסיל כ] ביוצא התם. (תוספות) דא"ר אליעזר: אימורי קדשים כא] שיצאו לפני זריקה – פסולים ביוצא, ואין חייבין עליהן משום פיגול וכו', אבל רבי עקיבא מחייב. *וקשה: לרב פפא דאמר התם בדעיילינהו לגואי בשעת זריקה לא פליגי, פירוש: דאינם פסולין, הלא הכא קאמר פסולה! וליכא לפרושי הכא דחזרה לאחר זריקה, דדומיא דלעיל בכשרה הוי, דמיירי בחזרה קודם קבלה. וי"ל, דה"פ: עיילינהו לגואי לא פליגי. פירוש: דודאי חייבין עליהם משום פיגול, דזריקה מועלת לחייב משום פיגול על יוצא כי האי, דלפני זריקה, והיה לפנים בשעת זריקה. אבל מכל מקום – נפסל ביוצא לכולי עלמא, כדאיתא בשמעתין: כי פליגי – בעיילינהו בתר זריקה, אי חייבין משום פיגול דהא עיילינהו, או לאו כב].

עין משפט נר מצוה

פט א ב מיי' פ"א מהל' פסה"מ הלכה טו:
צ ג מיי' שם הלכה ז:
צא ד מיי' שם הל' ח:
צב ה מיי' שם הל' ט:
צג ו מיי' שם הלכה י:
צד ז ח מיי' שם הל' יא:
צה ט מיי' שם הל' יב:
צו י מיי' שם הלכה יג:
צז כ מיי' שם הל' יד:
צח ל מיי' שם הל' טו:
צט מ נ מיי' שם הלכה יז וע"ש בכ"מ:
ק ס מיי' שם הלכה יט:
קא ע מיי' שם הל' יב:
קב פ מיי' פ"ב שם הלכה ו:

[לעיל כה: ע"ש בסוגיות לט: ע"ש]
נ"א הפר [וכ"ה בתוס' יומא נ. ד"ה ולא]
נ"א כפיגול ונותר וטמא משום דלא מפסל ביוצא ומיהו קשה

שיטה מקובצת

א] תיבות חתך ואח"כ קיבל כשרה נמחק: ב] אזן הפר: ג] חותך באבר עד שמגיע לעצם והשתא לא הוי בעל מום דאין נעשה בעל מום [עד] שמגיע לעצם וא"ע א"כ אמאי הדר ביה מהא דקאמר חתך ואח"כ שחט וי"ל דמ"מ מום עובר הוי קודם שיגיע נמי לעצם ולא מצי מקריב ליה עד שיעבור המום אבל בקבלה לא הוי פסול מום עובר וקרינא ביה שפיר (מום) [מדם הפר] שהיה בו כבר כך פי' מורי. הר"פ: ד] דמים פסול: ה] ה"ג חתך ואח"כ שחט כשרה: ו] חתיכה זו מלעלות וליכנס לפנים והשתא אפילו חתך ואח"כ שחט כשרה והאי דלא אמר אלא לפי שלא אמרו [אמורא] בתירוץ ראשון. גליון: ז] הוא ודם נפסל ביוצא בין בקדשי קדשים בין בקדשים קלים וג"מ שחייב עליו כרת על אכילתו דאי לאו דם הוא ובשר נמי לא הוי אהיכא: ח] אלעזר פליגא אדרבי יוחנן: ט] רב אמי אמר רבי אלעזר: י] יוצא בתוך המחיצות והאי וחזרה לאו דוקא דמאי מהניא חזרה בצפון ודרום והא לאו יוצא הוא: יא] בפנים בעזרה: יב] עזרה נמי דכתיב לעמוד לפני ה' דבעינן נמי כולו דכתיב כו' והכי אמר בשמעתין אבל לגבי הכנסות צפון לא בעינן כולו שהרי הוא עומד בעזרה הס"ד: יג] לכתחלה ולעיל דקאמר חתך ואח"כ שחט כשרה היינו בדיעבד: יד] אצלה כלומר שהוא אצלה בקרקע: טו] ושחט הס"ד ומה"ד אין דרך שירות בכך וקבלה שירות הוא הס"ד ומה"ד תלה הבהמה וקבל הדם מהו הס"ד ומה"ד א"ל פסולה כדקאמרת לי בתלה ושחט הס"ד: טז] קלים דלא: יז] פנים מיהא: יח] התערובת בההיא שמעתתא דגזרינן: יט] בבשר קדשים קלים: כ] דפסיל התם ביוצא הג"ה ותיבת תוספת נמחק: כא] קדשים קלים שיצאו כו' עיי"ש ויהיו קשה: כב] לאו ברוך עפ"ח:

מסורת הש"ס

נ"ל ה"ג חתך ואחר כך שחט כשרה בעלת מום קמקריב כו' ס"י

נ"א ודם נפסל ביוצא בין בקדשים קלים ובין בקדשי קדשים וג"מ שחייב כרת על אכילתו דאי לאו דם הוא ובשר נמי לא הוי אהיכא דאי

[לקמן לב:]

[שבועות כח:]

נ"א אבל גבי הכבשן לפון לא בעינן כולו דהא בעזרה הוא

הגהות הב"ח

(א) גמ' אלא אימא חתך ואח"כ קיבל כשרה קיבל ואח"כ חתך פסולה והא אמר וכו' הס"ד ואח"כ:

גמ' אָמַר שְׁמוּאֵל: א] פָּסוּל בָּשָׂר, אֲבָל בְּעָלִים נִתְכַּפְּרוּ. מַאי טַעְמָא? דְּאָמַר קְרָא: °"וַאֲנִי נְתַתִּיו לָכֶם עַל הַמִּזְבֵּחַ לְכַפֵּר", כֵּיוָן שֶׁהִגִּיעַ דָּם לַמִּזְבֵּחַ – נִתְכַּפְּרוּ בְּעָלִים. אִי הָכִי, בָּשָׂר נַמִּי! אָמַר קְרָא: "לְכַפֵּר" – °לְכַפָּרָה נְתַתִּיו, וְלֹא לְדָבָר אַחֵר. אַלְמָא קָסָבַר: בשֶׁלֹּא בִּמְקוֹמוֹ – כִּמְקוֹמוֹ דָּמֵי. תְּנַן בְּאִידָךְ פִּירְקִין: *נְתָנוֹ עַל הַכֶּבֶשׁ שֶׁלֹּא כְּנֶגֶד הַיְסוֹד, נָתַן אֶת הַנִּיתָּנִין לְמַטָּה לְמַעְלָה, וְאֶת הַנִּיתָּנִין לְמַעְלָה לְמַטָּה, וְאֶת הַנִּיתָּנִין בִּפְנִים בַּחוּץ, וְאֶת הַנִּיתָּנִין בַּחוּץ בִּפְנִים, אִם יֵשׁ דַּם הַנֶּפֶשׁ – יַחֲזוֹר הַכָּשֵׁר וִיקַבֵּל; וְאִי ב] ס"ד שֶׁלֹּא בִּמְקוֹמוֹ כִּמְקוֹמוֹ, לָמָּה לִי יַחֲזוֹר הַכָּשֵׁר וִיקַבֵּל? וְכִי תֵּימָא: לְהַתִּיר בָּשָׂר בַּאֲכִילָה – מִי אִיכָּא זְרִיקָה דְּלָא מְכַפֶּרֶת וְשַׁרְיָא בָּשָׂר בַּאֲכִילָה? אִי דִּיהֲבֵיהּ כָּשֵׁר – ה"נ, גהָכָא בְּמַאי עָסְקִינַן – דִּיהֲבֵיהּ פָּסוּל. וְלֶיהֱוֵי דָּחוּי, *דִּתְנַן: וְכוּלָּן שֶׁקִּיבְּלוּ חוּץ לִזְמַנּוֹ וְחוּץ לִמְקוֹמוֹ, אִם יֵשׁ דַּם הַנֶּפֶשׁ – יַחֲזוֹר הַכָּשֵׁר וִיקַבֵּל; קִיבְּלוּ – אִין, זְרָקוּ – לָא; מ"ט? לָאו מִשּׁוּם דְּהָוֵי דָּחוּי? לָא, מִשּׁוּם דְּפָסִיל בְּמַחֲשָׁבָה. אִי הָכִי, קַבָּלָה נַמִּי! וְעוֹד: מִי פָּסְלָה מַחֲשָׁבָה? *וְהָאָמַר רָבָא: דאֵין מַחֲשָׁבָה מוֹעֶלֶת אֶלָּא בְּמִי שֶׁרָאוּי לַעֲבוֹדָה, וּבְדָבָר הָרָאוּי לַעֲבוֹדָה, ג] וּבְמָקוֹם הָרָאוּי לַעֲבוֹדָה! לָא תֵּימָא: זְרָקוּ לָא, אֶלָּא אֵימָא: שְׁחָטוּ לָא. מַאי קמ"ל, דְּפָסְלָה מַחֲשָׁבָה? תְּנֵינָא: *לְפִיכָךְ הֵן פּוֹסְלִין בְּמַחֲשָׁבָה! הָא קמ"ל: הדְּמִקַּבָּלָה וְאֵילָךְ לָא פָּסְלָה מַחֲשָׁבָה; מ"ט – כִּדְרָבָא. מֵיתִיבֵי: *חִישֵּׁב לִיתֵּן אֶת הַנִּיתָּנִין לְמַעְלָה לְמַטָּה, לְמַטָּה לְמַעְלָה, לְאַלְתַּר – כָּשֵׁר ד] (לְמָחָר – פָּסוּל) חָזַר וְחִישֵּׁב

חוּץ

רש"י

גמ' אמר שמואל פסול. דקתני מתני', אבשר קאי, אבל בעלים נתכפרו. **על המזבח.** (א) כל המזבח שוה לענין כפרה. **לכפרה נתתיו** ה]. הקשיתי (ב) כל מקומות המזבח שוין. **ולא לדבר אחר,** שתהא זריקה חשובה להתיר בה בשר. דזריקה הוא דשריא לה, דכתיב: "ודם זבחיך ישפך", והדר: "והבשר תאכל" (דברים יב). **יחזור הכשר ויקבל.** יחזור כהן הכשר לקבלה, ויקבל כדי מתן (ג) ו] מן הבהמה, ויחזור ויתן במקומו. וקס"ד השתא דעד השתא בכהן כשר נמי איירי, והאי "הכשר" דקתני – כדי נסבה. **למה לי יחזור.** הלא נתכפרו! **וכי תימא להתיר בשר באכילה.** דזריקה הוא דשריא לה. **ומי איכא זריקה דלא מיכפרא.** כגון הך בתרייתא, דלאו לכפרה אתיא, דהא איכפר בקמייתא. **אי דיהביה.** שלא במקומו כהן כשר – הכי נמי דלא בעי יחזור ויקבל. **הכא במאי עסקינן דיהביה פסול.** דהא דקתני: נתנו על גבי הכבש – ארישא קאי, דקתני: כל הפסולים ששחטו כו', וכולן שקיבלו את הדם כו', ועלה קאי: נתנו על גבי הכבש כו' בפ"ג. **וליהוי דחוי.** כיון דאמרי' שלא במקומו כמקומו דמי ובלבד שיהא במזבח, כי יהביה פסול – ז] הויא לה זריקה פסולה כאילו נתנו פסול במקומו. וניהוי כל הדם דחוי, ולא תיהוי ליה תו תקנתא! **דהא תנן.** בהאי. **וכולן שקבלו.** את הדם. ואפסולין קאי, שקבלו את הדם במחשבת אכילת בשר חוץ לזמנו או חוץ למקומו. **אם יש דם הנפש.** עוד בצואר בהמה – יחזור הכשר ויקבל מן הדם, ויתן שלא במחשבה, וכשר. דמחשבה דחשיב עלה קמא לא ח] נפסל, דכיון דאינו ראוי לעבודה – אין מחשבתו מחשבה. **קבלו אין.** הוא דאית ליה תקנתא* ט]. **מאי טעמא לאו משום.** דזריקה פסולה משויא ליה דחוי, משום דגמר י] כפרתו? **לא.** הא דדייקינן זרקו לא – יא] משום דמיפסיל במחשבה, דהא בעושה מחשבה קיימינא, ודכוותה דייקינן זרקו לא. **א"ה.** דמחשבת פסולין פסלה – מקבלה שקיבל במחשבה ליפסיל! **ועוד, מי פסל** (ד) יב] במחשבת כהן פסול? **במי שראוי לעבודה.** כהן כשר. **ובדבר הראוי לעבודה.** מנחת חטים. לאפוקי מנחת יג] [העומר שהיא של] שעורים, דלא חייל עלה פגול ליענש כרת באכילתה. **ובמקום הראוי לעבודה.** לאפוקי נפגם המזבח. הכי מפורש במנחות (דף ה:). **לא תימא זרקו לא.** דודאי איכא תקנתא, ואפי' זרקו פסול במחשבה. **אלא אימא שחטו לא.** שאם שחטו פסול במחשבה – תו ליכא תקנתא. דכיון דכל הפסולין כשירין לשחוט – יד] פוסלין (ה) מחשבתן. **תנינא.** בההיא משנה גופה: כל הפסולין ששחטו – שחיטתן כשרה, לפיכך הן (ו) פוסלין במחשבה. **הא קמ"ל.** הא דקתני וכולן שקיבלו את הדם כו': טו] [אע"ג] דבשחיטה תנן פוסלין במחשבה, אבל בקבלה ומקבלה ואילך – לא פסלי. ולא למידק מיניה זרקו לא, דה"ה לזרקו. אלא קמייתא דכולהו נקט, דכיון דפסול אינו ראוי לה – לא פסלה מחשבתו. **כדרבא.** דאמר: אין מחשבה מועלת אלא בראוי לעבודה. **חישב.** כהן כשר. **ליתן את הניתנין כו'.** ששחט או קיבל או הוליך על מנת לזרוק הזריקה שלא במקומו. **לאלתר כשר.** אם חישב על מנת לזרוק שלא במקומו היום – כשר. (ז) ואי נמי זריקה פסולה היא, ונמצא שעבד שאר העבודות על מנת לזרוק את הדם בפסול – כשר הוא בזריקה הוגנת במקומו, כדאמרינן במשנה "כל הפסולין" (לקמן לו.): אין המחשבה פוסלת אלא חוץ לזמנו וחוץ למקומו, ופסח וחטאת שלא לשמן. **חזר וחישב.** בעבודה שניה על מנת לאוכלו חוץ למקומו – פסול, ואין חייבין כרת על אכילתו.

חוץ

תוספות

אמר שמואל טז] **פסול בשר אבל בעלים נתכפרו.** נראה דלקאי אניתנין למעלה שנתנן למטה ולמטה שנתנן למעלה. אבל אניתנין על גבי הכבש – לא קאי, דבהא כולי עלמא מודו יז] בשלא במקומו לאו כמקומו דמי. אע"ג דבפ' "המזבח מקדש" (לקמן פז.) מרבה כבש כמזבח לענין קידוש דאם עלו לא ירדו, ובפ' "כל המנחות" (מנחות נז:) לענין הקטרה דהמעלה מכולן ע"ג הכבש לר' יוחנן חייב, מ"מ לענין דמים לא מצינו בשום מקום כבש כמזבח, דלקמן בפ' "קדשי קדשים" (דף סד:) גבי עולה וגבי חטאת, ממעטינן מדכתיב "קיר המזבח" ולא קיר הכבש. ועל כרחין שמואל לאו אכולה יח] *מילתיה קאי, דניתנין בפנים שנתנן בחוץ, ובחוץ שנתנו בפנים – לכ"ע לאו כמקומן דמי, כדמוכח פ' "כל הפסולין" לקמן בסופו (דף לה:) דא"ר יהודה: חישב להניח דמו למחר פסול, דסבר מחשבה כמעשה. ופריך (שם לו.): וליפלוג בסיפא, על ניתנין למטה שחשב ליתנן למעלה שיהא פסול! ומשני: קסבר ר' יהודה שלא במקומו כמקומו דמי. יט]* (תוספות) והשתא אמאי הדר פריך: וליפלוג ר' יהודה בנתן הניתנין בפנים בחוץ ובחוץ בפנים? אלמא *דהני [לכ"ע] שלא במקומו כ] מיקרי (ע"כ). ומיהו, לקמן פירש בקונטרס דמהניתנין בחוץ שחישב ליתן בפנים דוקא קמקשי. דהתם ודאי אי הוה יהיב חטאת חיצונה בפנים מיפסלא, דכתיב: "וכל חטאת אשר יובא" וגו', אבל מחישב ליתן הניתנין בפנים בחוץ – לא פריך. וכן *מוכיח מדקמשני: קסבר רבי יהודה בעינן מקום כא] שהוא משולש בדם ובבשר ובאימורים. פירוש: דגבי מחשבת חוץ למקומו כתיב "שלישי", ודרשינן: שיהא אותו כב] (שלישי) חוץ למקומו משולש בדם ובשר ואימורים שהיה מותר בו, דהיינו חוץ לעזרה ממש, שבשעת היתר הבמות נשתלש בכל אלה (תוספות) והותר שם, לאפוקי פנים שלא הותרו מעולם ליכנס שלשתן, דדם חטאת אסור, דכתיב: "וכל חטאת אשר יובא מדמה", וכן אימורין כתיב: "ועולה לא יעלו עליו" (ע"כ). ואניתנין בפנים שנתנן בחוץ – לא שייך האי שינויא. ומיהו, מצינו למימר דבעי' נמי שיהא המחשבה במקום משולש. תדע, דאי כג] לאו הכי, למ"ד שלא במקומו לאו כמקומו דמי – מאי הוה משני מבפנים אחוץ? מיהו, ר' יהודה אית ליה כמקומו דמי. ונראה (תוס') ור' יוחנן דאמר בסמוך שלא במקומו לאו כמקומו דמי – היינו דוקא לרבנן, אבל לר' יהודה אית ליה כמקומו דמי אפי' לר' יוחנן, כדמשני פרק "כל הפסולין" (גם זה שם) על ניתנין למטה למעלה ולמטה למעלה. וה"ה דסבר כן בניתנים בפנים שנתנן בחוץ. והתם לא פריך אלא מניתנים בחוץ שנתנן בפנים דוקא, כדפי' רש"י: משום דנפסל בשעה כד] שהובא בהיכל. וא"כ מצי שמואל קאי אכולהו. אבל לא מצי למימר כמקומו דמי על בחוץ שנתנו לפנים, שנפסל בביאתו בהיכל קודם שנתנן על מזבח הזהב (ע"כ). (הגה"ה): ועוד נראה, דעל כרחין כבש נמי כמקומו דמי, מדלא פריך לקמן דליפלוג ר' יהודה אחישב ליתנו על גבי כבש. וכי תימא משום דיאספנו, ואין כאן בית מיחוש כה] מחשבה, דהרי בחשב לשפוך מן הכלי על הרצפה יאספנו לכ"ע – הא לקמן אמרי' דלר' יהודה לא יאספנו היכא דקלטי' מזבח, וא"כ מהאי טעמא לא יאספנו מעל גבי כבש, דכבש מקדש פסולין כמזבח. ומיהו, כיון דפרישית לעיל דלענין דמים לא הוי כבש כמזבח – לא קלטיה, ויאספנו. ומיהו, על כרחיך אכבש נמי קאי שמואל, דלקמן בשמעתין פריך: ור' יוחנן, אי שלא במקומו לאו כמקומו דמי – א"כ זריקתו אינה כלום, ליהוי כנשפך מן הכלי על הרצפה ויאספנו! משמע: לשמואל ולריש לקיש דאמרי שלא במקומו כמקומו דמי – ניחא. ואמאי? לדידהו נמי תיקשי מניתנין על גבי הכבש, ומניתנין בפנים שנתנן בחוץ! כו] אבל על ניתנין בחוץ שנתנן בפנים, דמודו כולהו דשלא כמקומו דמי – לא שייך למיפרך אמאי (לדידהו נמי תיקשי מניתנין על גבי כבש ומניתנים בפנים בחוץ. תוס') פסול, נימא יאספנו. שהרי בלא ניתנין על מזבח הזהב כבר נפסל בביאתו בהיכל, ואפי' נשפך שם – לא יהא כשר כז] לאספנו. ע"כ הג"ה. **לכפרה** נתתיו ולא לדבר אחר. בעלמא (לקמן דף מו.) דרשינן: לכפרה נתתיו ולא למעילה. **ואי** שלא במקומו כמקומו דמי למה לי יחזור הכשר ויקבל. תימה: דלקמן בפ' "התערובת" (דף עט:) תנן: הניתנין למטה שנתערבו בניתנין למעלה, ר' אליעזר אומר: יתן למעלה, ורואה אני את *הניתנין למטה כאילו הן מים, ויחזור ויתן למטה. דייק מינה בגמרא דר' אליעזר סבר יש בילה. והשתא, אמאי יחזור ויתן למטה? הרי כבר נתכפר! וי"ל: כיון דאית ליה רואים כאילו הן מים – לא הוי כמכופר, כח] ולא יהיב ליה לשם כפרת התחתון. ומיהו, קשה לרבנן דלית להו רואין, ומשמע התם דלרבנן יחזור ויתן למטה, דקתני: נתן *למעלה ולא נמלך (כשר). **הכא** במאי עסקינן דיהביה פסול. כט] תימה: אם כן, אפילו נתן במקומו נמי! וי"ל: דהאי פסול – היינו טמא דאיירי ביה לעיל. ל] ואי יהביה במקומו – כולי עלמא מודי דהוי דחוי, ולא יחזור כשר ויקבל, כדאמר בפ"ק דמעילה (דף ה:) דאין לך עושה שיריים ופסול אלא טמא – הואיל ומרצה בקרבן ציבור, וחוץ לזמנו וחוץ למקומו – הואיל ומרצה לפיגולו לא].

ואי

עין משפט נר מצוה

קג א ב ג מיי' פ"כ מהלכות פסה"מ הלכה י וע"ש:

קד ד ה מיי' פי"ד מהל' פסה"מ הלכה כ:

מסורת הש"ס

ויקרא יז | נ"א מתניתין | נ"א ופריך תו וליפלוג בניתנין בפנים שנתנן בחוץ והשתא כו' | דבהני שלא במקומו מודה כו' ל"ק | לקמן לב. | ג"ז שם | מנחות ה: | לקמן לג: | לקמן לו: | נ"א הא דזרקו הפסולין לא אית ליה תו תקנתא | מנחות נ"ק | רש"ק מ"ז | נ"א ל"ג ומהרש"ק מוחק מן מניתנין עד נימא | [במשנה שם אותה ורואה אני את התחתונים כאלו כו'] | ס"א למעלה ולא נמלך אלא ואלו מודים שיחזור ויתן למטה

שיטה מקובצת

א] שמואל בשר פסול: ב] ואי ס"ד שלא במקומו כו'. [illegible]

הגהות הב"ח

(א) רש"י ד"ה על המזבח לכפר כו': (ב) ד"ה לכפרה וכו' דלכל: (ג) ד"ה יחזור וכו' כדי מתן דמו וכו' הבהמה: (ד) ד"ה מי פסל במחשבת וכו' מי פסל מחשבה בכהן פסול: (ה) ד"ה אלא אימא וכו' הן פוסלין במחשבתן: (ו) ד"ה תנינא וכו' הן פוסלין במחשבה: (ז) ד"ה לאלתר וכו' ולאי נמי וכו' במשנה דכל:

גליון הש"ס

גמ' אבל בעלים נתכפרו. עי' לקמן דף כב ע"ב ובתוס' שם ד"ה אותה: שם לכפרה נתתיו. עיין לקמן לח ע"א תוספות ד"ה וכיפר:

טז] שמואל בשר פסול: יז] דשלא במקומו: יח] אכולה מתני': יט] תיבת תוספת נמחק: כ] במקומו הוי ומיהו ותיבות מיקרי ע"כ נמחק: כא] מקום שהוא: כב] שיהא אותו חוץ למקומו כו' ואימורים דהיינו חוץ [illegible] תר שם (והשאר נמחק): כג] דאי לא תימא הכי אם כן מצינו למימר כפי' הקונטרס דמחוץ (בפנים) [אבפנים] קא פריך אבל (מחוץ בפנים) [מבפנים אבחוץ] לא [illegible] ואל נמי קאי אכולהו ועוד דע"כ כבש נמי כמקומו דמי [ע"כ]: כד] בשעה דהובא בהיכל: כה] מחשבת פסול דהרי הוא כחשב לשפוך כו' על הרצפה דיאספנו: כו] מתיבת אבל כו' [illegible] שיאספנו: כח] כמכופר דלא יהיב: כט] פסול תימה פסול מאן דכר שמיה ופ"ה דקאי ארישא דקתני כו' ותימה א"כ אמאי קתני הניתנים למטה שנתנם מלמעלה אפילו: ל] לעיל אי יהביה במקומו כו' דהוי דחוי כל הדם ולא יחזור הכשר ויקבל: לא] לפיגולו אבל השתא ששינה את מקומו דאיכא דחוי [אחר] דחוי דהוי טמא ושלא במקומו וכיון דתרי דחוי [illegible]

א חוּץ לִמְקוֹמוֹ — פָּסוּל; וְאֵין בּוֹ כָּרֵת, חוּץ לִזְמַנּוֹ — פִּיגּוּל וְחַיָּיבִין עָלָיו כָּרֵת. ב לְמָחָר — פָּסוּל; חָזַר וְחִישֵּׁב, בֵּין חוּץ לִזְמַנּוֹ בֵּין חוּץ לִמְקוֹמוֹ — פָּסוּל וְאֵין בּוֹ כָּרֵת. וְאִי שֶׁלֹּא בִּמְקוֹמוֹ כִּמְקוֹמוֹ דָּמֵי, הַאי פָּסוּל? פִּיגּוּל הוּא! אָמַר מָר זוּטְרָא: ג זְרִיקָה דְּשַׁרְיָא בָּשָׂר בַּאֲכִילָה — מַיְיתָא לִידֵי פִּיגּוּל, זְרִיקָה דְּלָא שַׁרְיָא בָּשָׂר בַּאֲכִילָה — לָא מַיְיתָא לִידֵי פִּיגּוּל. א"ל רַב אַשִׁי לְמָר זוּטְרָא: מְנָא לָךְ הָא? א] דִּכְתִיב: °"וְאִם הֵאָכֹל יֵאָכֵל מִבְּשַׂר זֶבַח שְׁלָמָיו פִּיגּוּל יִהְיֶה" — מִי שֶׁפִּיגּוּלוֹ גָּרַם לוֹ, יָצָא זֶה שֶׁאֵין פִּיגּוּלוֹ גָּרַם לוֹ, אֶלָּא אִיסּוּר דָּבָר אַחֵר גָּרַם לוֹ. ב] אִי הָכִי, אִיפְּסוּלֵי נַמִי לָא לִיפָּסֵל! אָמַר רַב נַחְמָן בַּר יִצְחָק: מִידֵי דַּהֲוָה אַמַּחֲשֶׁבֶת הִינּוּחַ, וְאַלִּיבָּא *דְּרַבִּי יְהוּדָה. ג] רֵישׁ לָקִישׁ אָמַר: לְעוֹלָם פָּסוּל מַמָּשׁ, וְשֶׁלֹּא בִּמְקוֹמוֹ כִּמְקוֹמוֹ דָּמֵי. וְלָא קַשְׁיָא: כָּאן — שֶׁנְּתָנַן בִּשְׁתִיקָה, כָּאן — שֶׁנְּתָנַן בַּאֲמִירָה. ד] תְּנַן: חִישֵּׁב לִיתֵּן אֶת הַנִּיתָּנִין לְמַטָּה לְמַעְלָה, לְמַעְלָה לְמַטָּה, ה] עַד: מִידֵי דַּהֲוָה אַמַּחֲשֶׁבֶת הִינּוּחַ וְאַלִּיבָּא דְּרַבִּי יְהוּדָה ו] כו'. רַבִּי יוֹחָנָן אָמַר: אִידִי וְאִידִי שֶׁנְּתָנַן בִּשְׁתִיקָה, וְשֶׁלֹּא בִּמְקוֹמוֹ לָאו כִּמְקוֹמוֹ דָּמֵי. וְהָא — דְּאִיכָּא דַּם הַנֶּפֶשׁ, הָא — דְּלֵיכָּא דַּם הַנֶּפֶשׁ. תְּנַן: פָּסוּל וְאֵין בּוֹ כָּרֵת; בִּשְׁלָמָא לְרֵישׁ לָקִישׁ — הַיְינוּ דְּקָתָנֵי פָּסוּל וְאֵין בּוֹ כָּרֵת, אֶלָּא לְרַבִּי יוֹחָנָן מַאי אֵין בּוֹ כָּרֵת? קַשְׁיָא. וְלִשְׁמוּאֵל מַאי אֵין בּוֹ כָּרֵת? ה"ק: אִם נָתַן בְּמַחֲשָׁבָה — פָּסוּל וְאֵין בּוֹ כָּרֵת. וְרַבִּי יוֹחָנָן, אִי שֶׁלֹּא בִּמְקוֹמוֹ לָאו בִּמְקוֹמוֹ דָּמֵי, לֶיהֱוֵי כְּמִי נִשְׁפַּךְ מִן הַכְּלִי עַל הָרִצְפָּה, וְיַאַסְפֶנּוּ! סָבַר לָהּ כְּמ"ד: לֹא יַאַסְפֶנּוּ. דְּאָמַר רַב יִצְחָק בַּר יוֹסֵף א"ר יוֹחָנָן: הַכֹּל מוֹדִים בַּנִּיתָּנִין לְמַעְלָה שֶׁנְּתָנָן לְמַעְלָה, לְמַטָּה שֶׁנְּתָנָן לְמַטָּה, שֶׁלֹּא כְּמִצְוָתָן — לֹא יַאַסְפֶנּוּ. לֹא נֶחְלְקוּ אֶלָּא בַּנִּיתָּנִין לְמַעְלָה שֶׁנְּתָנָן לְמַטָּה, לְמַטָּה שֶׁנְּתָנָן לְמַעְלָה, שֶׁרַבִּי *יוֹסֵי אוֹמֵר: ז] לֹא יַאַסְפֶנּוּ, וְרַבִּי שִׁמְעוֹן אוֹמֵר: יַאַסְפֶנּוּ, וּמִשְׁנָתֵינוּ

רש"י

חוּץ לִזְמַנּוֹ פִּיגּוּל וְחַיָּיבִין עָלָיו כָּרֵת. שֶׁהֲרֵי קָרְבוּ מַתִּירָיו. דְּהָכִי תְּנַן בְּמַתְנִי' (לקמן כט:): חוּץ לִמְקוֹמוֹ – פָּסוּל, חוּץ לִזְמַנּוֹ – פִּיגּוּל, שֶׁהֲרֵי קָרְבוּ מַתִּירָיו, מֵהֶן ח] פִּיגּוּל מֵהֶן שְׁתִיקָה, וְאֵין כָּאן פְּסוּל מַחֲשָׁבָה אַחֶרֶת לְהוֹצִיאוֹ מִיַּד פִּיגּוּל. לְמָחָר פָּסוּל. אֲבָל אִם אוֹתָהּ מַחֲשָׁבָה שֶׁחִישֵּׁב בַּעֲבוֹדָה רִאשׁוֹנָה, לִיתֵּן אֶת הַנִּיתָּנִין לְמַטָּה לְמַעְלָה, חִישֵּׁב לִזְרוֹק אוֹתָהּ זְרִיקָה לְמָחָר – פָּסוּל, כִּדְמוֹקְמִינַן לְקַמָּן: מִידֵי דַּהֲוָה אַמַּחֲשֶׁבֶת הִינּוּחַ, שֶׁהֲרֵי שָׁחַט ע"מ לְהַנִּיחַ דָּמוֹ לְמָחָר – פָּסוּל, וְרַבִּי יְהוּדָה הִיא דְּפָסֵיל לֵיהּ בְּפ"ג (לקמן לה:). חָזַר וְחִישֵּׁב. בַּעֲבוֹדָה שְׁנִיָּיה, בֵּין חוּץ לִזְמַנּוֹ בֵּין חוּץ לִמְקוֹמוֹ – פָּסוּל וְאֵין בּוֹ כָּרֵת. דְּהָא אִיפְּסִיל לֵיהּ בְּמַחֲשָׁבָה קַמַּיְיתָא, וְתוּ לָא חָיֵיל עֲלֵיהּ פִּיגּוּל, דְּלָא קָרְבוּ כָּל מַתִּירָיו. וְאִי שֶׁלֹּא בִּמְקוֹמוֹ. דְּמִזְבֵּחַ, כִּמְקוֹמוֹ דָּמֵי. הַאי פָּסוּל. בִּתְמִיָּה. אַמַּאי קָרֵי לֵיהּ פָּסוּל לְהַאי דְּחִישֵּׁב לִיתֵּן שֶׁלֹּא בִּמְקוֹמוֹ לְמָחָר? פִּיגּוּל הוּא, שֶׁהֲרֵי חִישֵּׁב בִּשְׁחִיטָה ע"מ לִזְרוֹק דָּמוֹ לְמָחָר, דְּהִיא אֲכִילַת מִזְבֵּחַ *אֶלָּא ט] לָאו כִּמְקוֹמוֹ דָּמֵי, וְלָא חֲשִׁיבָא אֲכִילָה. זְרִיקָה דְּשַׁרְיָא בָּשָׂר בַּאֲכִילָה כו'. כְּגוֹן בִּמְקוֹם מַתַּן הַדָּם – מַיְיתֵי לִידֵי פִּיגּוּל, בֵּין שֶׁחִישֵּׁב בָּהּ ע"מ לְהַקְטִיר אֵימוּרִים לְמָחָר, בֵּין שֶׁחִישֵּׁב בִּשְׁחִיטָה לִזְרוֹק לְמָחָר י]. וּזְרִיקָה דְּלָא שַׁרְיָא בָּשָׂר בַּאֲכִילָה. יא] אִי הֲוָה עָבֵיד לָהּ בִּזְמַנָּהּ, כְּגוֹן זְרִיקָה שֶׁלֹּא בִּמְקוֹמוֹ – לָא מַיְיתֵי לִידֵי פִּיגּוּל. בֵּין שֶׁחִישֵּׁב בָּהּ ע"מ לְהַקְטִיר אֵימוּרִים לְמָחָר, בֵּין שֶׁחִישֵּׁב בִּשְׁחִיטָה לְמֶיעֱבַד הַךְ זְרִיקָה לְמָחָר – לָא מַיְיתֵי לִידֵי פִּיגּוּל. פִּיגּוּל יִהְיֶה. "וְהַנֶּפֶשׁ הָאוֹכֶלֶת" וגו'. מִי שֶׁפִּיגּוּלוֹ גּוֹרֵם. שֶׁלֹּא יֵאָכֵל, הוּא דְּקָאֵי בַּ"עֲוֹנָהּ תִּשָּׂא". יָצָא בָּשָׂר שֶׁנִּזְרַק הַדָּם שֶׁלֹּא בִּמְקוֹמוֹ, דְּאִיסּוּר זְרִיקָה שֶׁלֹּא בִּמְקוֹמוֹ גָּרַם לוֹ שֶׁלֹּא יֵאָכֵל – הִלְכָּךְ אֵין חַיָּיבִין עַל פִּיגּוּלוֹ כָּרֵת. וְנָפְקָא לָן מֵהָכָא דְּאִי חִישֵּׁב בִּזְרִיקָה שֶׁלֹּא בִּמְקוֹמוֹ ע"מ לֶאֱכוֹל אוֹ לְהַקְטִיר לְמָחָר – לָא הָוְיָא מַחֲשֶׁבֶת זְרִיקָה לְעִנְיַן פִּיגּוּל. וּמִינָּהּ, כִּי חִישֵּׁב בִּשְׁחִיטָה ע"מ לַעֲשׂוֹת זְרִיקָה זוֹ חוּץ לִזְמַנּוֹ – לָא הָוְיָא מַחֲשָׁבָה בִּזְרִיקָה הַמְפַגֶּלֶת. אִי הָכִי. דְּלָא הָוְיָא זְרִיקָה לְעִנְיַן מַחֲשָׁבָה – אִיפְּסוּלֵי נַמִי לָא נִפְסוֹל! אַמַּחֲשֶׁבֶת הִינּוּחַ. דְּהָא חָשֵׁיב מִיהָא לְהַנִּיחוֹ לְמָחָר. וְאַלִּיבָּא דְּר' יְהוּדָה. לְקַמָּן בְּפ' "כָּל הַפְּסוּלִין" (דף לה:) תְּנַן: לְהַנִּיחַ מִדָּמוֹ לְמָחָר – כָּשֵׁר, וְר' יְהוּדָה פּוֹסֵל. וְרֵישׁ לָקִישׁ אָמַר כו'. אַמַּתְנִיתִין קָאֵי, וּפָלֵיג אַדִּשְׁמוּאֵל. לְעוֹלָם פָּסוּל מַמָּשׁ. דְּלָא תֵּימָא פָּסוּל אַבָּשָׂר לְחוּדֵיהּ, אִי לָא פָּרֵישׁ בְּהֶדְיָא. וּמַתְנִי' פָּסוּל לְגַמְרֵי קָאָמַר, שֶׁאַף בְּעָלִים לֹא נִתְכַּפְּרוּ. וְשֶׁלֹּא בִּמְקוֹמוֹ. כִּשְׁמוּאֵל סְבִירָא לֵיהּ, דְּכִמְקוֹמוֹ דָּמֵי לְעִנְיַן כַּפָּרָה, וְלֹא לְהַתִּיר בַּאֲכִילָה, כִּדְדָרֵישׁ לֵיהּ שְׁמוּאֵל לִקְרָא דִּלְעֵיל "וַאֲנִי נְתַתִּיו לָכֶם" וגו'. וְלָא קַשְׁיָא יב] אַמַּתְנִי'. כָּאן שֶׁנְּתָנַן בִּשְׁתִיקָה. דְּרָשָׁא דִּקְרָא, דְּמַשְׁמַע בְּעָלִים נִתְכַּפְּרוּ – כְּשֶׁנְּתָנַן יג] בְּשֶׁלֹּא בִּמְקוֹמוֹ בִּשְׁתִיקָה. וּמַתְנִי' דְּקָתָנֵי פָּסוּל – בִּנְתָנַן בְּמַחֲשֶׁבֶת לֶאֱכוֹל בָּשָׂר חוּץ לִזְמַנּוֹ. וְאַשְׁמְעִינַן דְּפָסוּל וְאֵין בּוֹ כָּרֵת, דְּמַחֲשֶׁבֶת זְרִיקָה זוֹ מַחֲשָׁבָה הוּא לִפְסוֹל, דְּכִמְקוֹמוֹ דָּמֵי. וְלָא לְפַגֵּל, דִּזְרִיקָה דְּלָא שַׁרְיָא בָּשָׂר בַּאֲכִילָה לָא מַיְיתֵי לִידֵי פִּיגּוּל. תְּנַן כו'. כָּל הָנָךְ תְּיוּבְתָּא דְּאוֹתְבִי' יד] לִשְׁמוּאֵל מוֹתְבִי' נַמִי לְרֵישׁ לָקִישׁ, דְּהָא כְּוָותֵיהּ סְבִירָא לֵיהּ, דְּשֶׁלֹּא בִּמְקוֹמוֹ כִּמְקוֹמוֹ דָּמֵי. וְרַבִּי יוֹחָנָן אָמַר אִידִי וְאִידִי. מַתְנִיתִין דְּקָתָנֵי פָּסוּל וְלֵיכָּא תַּקַּנְתָּא, וּמַתְנִיתִין דְּכָל הַפְּסוּלִים דְּתָנֵי תַּקַּנְתָּא – שֶׁנְּתָנַן בִּשְׁתִיקָה. בִּשְׁלָמָא לְרֵישׁ לָקִישׁ. דְּאוֹקֵי מַתְנִי' כְּשֶׁנְּתָנַן בְּמַחֲשָׁבָה, אִיצְטְרִיךְ לְמִיתְנֵי אֵין בּוֹ כָּרֵת לְאַשְׁמוּעִינַן דְּאַע"ג דְּחָשֵׁיב בְּהַךְ זְרִיקָה חוּץ לִזְמַנּוֹ – אֵינוֹ פִּיגּוּל, וּכְדַאֲמָרַן: (א) טו] דְּלָא שַׁרְיָא בָּשָׂר בַּאֲכִילָה – לָא מַיְיתֵי לִידֵי פִּיגּוּל. אֶלָּא לְרַבִּי יוֹחָנָן. דְּמוֹקֵי בִּשְׁתִיקָה, וְהַאי טז] פָּסוּל מִשּׁוּם דְּלָא בִּמְקוֹמוֹ הוּא – פְּשִׁיטָא דְּאֵין בּוֹ כָּרֵת! קַשְׁיָא. וְלִשְׁמוּאֵל מַאי אֵין בּוֹ כָּרֵת. דְּאִיהוּ נַמִי מוֹקֵי לָהּ בִּשְׁתִיקָה. הָכִי קָאָמַר וְאִם נָתַן בְּמַחֲשָׁבָה. דְּחוּץ לִזְמַנּוֹ – פָּסוּל וְאֵין בּוֹ כָּרֵת. וְאִיצְטְרִיךְ לְאַשְׁמוּעִינַן, יז] אַע"ג דִּלְעִנְיַן כַּפָּרָה כִּמְקוֹמוֹ דָּמֵי – מַחֲשֶׁבֶת פִּיגּוּל לָא חָיְילָא, הוֹאִיל וְלָא שַׁרְיָא בָּשָׂר בַּאֲכִילָה. אֲבָל לְרַבִּי יוֹחָנָן לָא מָצֵי לְשַׁנּוּיֵי הָכִי, דְּכֵיוָן דְּאַשְׁמְעִינַן תַּנָּא דִּידַן פָּסוּל וּמִשּׁוּם דְּשֶׁלֹּא בִּמְקוֹמוֹ (הוּא אַלְמָא) לָאו כִּמְקוֹמוֹ דָּמֵי – פְּשִׁיטָא דְּאִם נָתַן בְּמַחֲשָׁבָה לָא הָוְיָא מַחֲשָׁבָה, דַּהֲוֵי כְּאִילּוּ נְתָנוֹ עַל הָרִצְפָּה דְּלָא קָרְבוּ כָּל מַתִּירָיו. וְרַבִּי יוֹחָנָן. כֵּיוָן דְּלָאו זְרִיקָה הוּא כְּלָל, נֶיהֱוֵי כְּמִי שֶׁנִּשְׁפַּךְ מִן הַכְּלִי עַל הָרִצְפָּה וְיַאַסְפֶנּוּ. וַאֲפִי' לֵיכָּא דַּם הַנֶּפֶשׁ אַחֲרִינָא – אַמַּאי פָּסוּל? יח] יֶאֱסוֹף אֶת זֶה מִן הַמִּזְבֵּחַ וְיַחֲזוֹר וְיִתְּנֶנּוּ בִּמְקוֹמוֹ! בִּשְׁלָמָא לִשְׁמוּאֵל וּלְרֵישׁ לָקִישׁ, כֵּיוָן דִּזְרִיקָה הִיא לְכַפָּרָה – אִידַּחֵי לֵיהּ מִלְּאָסְפוֹ, שֶׁהֲרֵי כִּיפֵּר, אֶלָּא לְר' יוֹחָנָן יַאַסְפֶנּוּ! סָבַר לָהּ. תַּנָּא דְּמַתְנִיתִין. כְּמ"ד לֹא יַאַסְפֶנּוּ. יט] כֵּיוָן דְּהִגִּיעַ לַמִּזְבֵּחַ, וְאַע"ג דְּשֶׁלֹּא כְּהִילְכָתוֹ הוּא – קְלָטֵיהּ מִזְבֵּחַ, לְאַפּוּקֵי מִתּוֹרַת כַּפָּרָה אַחֲרִיתִי. הַכֹּל מוֹדִים בַּנִּיתָּנִין לְמַעְלָה שֶׁנְּתָנָן לְמַעְלָה שֶׁלֹּא כְּמִצְוָתָן. כְּגוֹן בְּמַחֲשָׁבָה, אוֹ בִּשְׂמֹאל. שֶׁלֹּא יַאַסְפֶנּוּ. לַחֲזוֹר וְלִיתְּנוֹ כְּמִצְוָתוֹ. דְּכֵיוָן דְּנִיתַּן בִּמְקוֹמוֹ – חָזְיָא לֵיהּ תּוֹרַת זְרִיקָה מִינֵּיהּ. לֹא נֶחְלְקוּ. הָנָךְ תַּנָּאֵי דְּבָעֵינַן לְמֵימַר. כ] שֶׁרַבִּי יוֹסֵי אוֹמֵר לֹא יַאַסְפֶנּוּ, וְאַף עַל גַּב דְּלָאו כִּמְקוֹמוֹ דָּמֵי. וְרַבִּי שִׁמְעוֹן אוֹמֵר כו'. וְעַ"כ לֵיכָּא לְמֵימַר דְּטַעְמָא

תוספות

ואי שלא במקומו כמקומו דמי כו'. תימה: ואי לאו כמקומו דמי, לאלתר אמאי כשר? וי"ל: דהוה מצי למימר "וליטעמיך". והשתא ניחא הא דקאמר לקמן בסוף "כל הפסולין" (דף לו.): ר' יהודה לטעמיה דקאמר שלא במקומו כמקומו דמי. ופירש שם בקונטרס: דשמעינן ליה כא] *דהכא בברייתא דמוקמינן כוותיה בשמעתין (תוספות). ומנא ליה לקמן דר' יהודה סובר כן בעלמא, דקאמר "ר' יהודה לטעמיה"? אי *ברייתא דשמעתין – דלמא סוברת דלאו כמקומו דמי! אלא דסמיך אהא דקתני: לאלתר כשר, א"כ על כרחין כמקומו דמי. וסיפא דלמחר פסולא – אתיא כרבי יהודה, כמו מחשבת הינוח (ע"כ). **יצא** זה שאין פיגולו גרם לו. וא"ת: אמאי איצטריך לקמן (דף כט:) "לא יחשב" לומר שמחשבות מוליאות זו מזו? תיפוק ליה מהכא: מי שפיגולו גרם לו, יצא זה שאין פיגולו גרם לו! כב] ועוד קשה: לרבא דמסיק בסוף פ"ק דמנחות (דף יב.): לדברי האומר שירים שחסרו בין קמילה להקטרה מקטיר קומץ עליהן, וקיי"ל דאותן שירים אסורים באכילה *דמהניא להו הקטרה למיקבעינהו בפיגול ולאפוקי מידי מעילה! וי"ל: דהא דמיתסר באכילה אין מחמת כג] מיעוט ההקטרה של קומץ, הלכך לא ממעטי ליה מ"אם האכל יאכל". כד] "מי שפיגולו גרם לו" משמע דאי לא הוי המחשבה – הוי הזריקה מעלייתא, ומשתריא בשר. יצא זה שאין פיגולו גרם לו, דאפי' לא הוי המחשבה – לא הויא זריקה מעלייתא, דהא לא שריא בשר *באכילה. (תוספות) וי"ל: דמי שפיגולו גרם לו, משמע באותה עבודה עצמה, דאי לא הויא מחשבה – הויא הזריקה מעלייתא, ומשתריא בשר באכילה. יצא זה שנתן למטה למעלה, שאין פיגולו גרם לו, ואפילו לא הויא המחשבה – לא הויא זה זריקה מעלייתא, דהא לא שרייא בשר באכילה. אבל אם שחט חטאת שלא לשמה, או במחשבת חוץ למקומו, והדם קיבל או זרק חוץ לזמנו – סד"א ליהוי פיגול ובכרת, דכיון דבאותה עבודה דפיגול ליכא מחשבה אחרת, קמ"ל "לא יחשב". אי נמי, אימא: הני מילי כי נפסל תחלה לא הדר תו מיקבע בפיגול בעבודה שאחריה, אבל כי נקבע בפיגול בעבודה כה] אחת, ובעבודה שניה שאחריה חשב שלא במקומו לא פקע שם כרת מיניה, קמ"ל "לא יחשב", וקשה לר' יהודה דאזיל בתר מחשבה שקדמה, כדתנן בפירקין. כו] ולאלתר דכשר – במסקנא אתיא כרבי יהודה, דסבר שלא במקומו כמקומו דמי. ותימה: כיון דמחשבה כמעשה לרבי יהודה, *א"כ לאלתר כשר – היינו בעלים נתכפרו, אבל בשר פסול, כדאמר שמואל לעיל. וא"כ חזר וחישב חוץ לזמנו בעבודה שניה, אמאי פיגול להתחייב כרת? הא זריקה דלא שריא בשר באכילה לא מייתי לידי פיגול, כמו בסיפא: למחר – פסול ולא פיגול, מהאי טעמא! ונראה כז] דר' יהודה לא עביד מחשבה כמעשה אלא היכא דבמעשה פסול גמור, ולא נתכפרו בעלים. ואם כן לאלתר כשר – היינו כשר גמור, ושריא בשר באכילה. דאי לאו הכי – ליפלוג בניתנין למעלה למטה שיהא פסול בשר באכילה כמו במעשה. ברו"ך ע"כ. **אלא** דבר אחר גרם לו. והקשה ה"ר חיים: מידי "דבר אחר" כתיב? כדאמר בבבא קמא (דף כה.): מי שקרויו גרם לו, יצא זה שאין קרויו גרם לו, אלא דבר אחר גרם לו. ופריך: מידי דבר אחר כתיב! וי"ל: דסמיך אקרא ד"לא יחשב" – לא יערב בו מחשבות אחרות. אע"ג דלריכי תרוייהו, מ"מ סברא הוא שדבר אחר *יגרום לו כח] [פיסול להפקיע מידי פיגול], כיון דאשכחן מחשבות שמוליאים זו את זו. אי נמי: קרא יתירא קדריש הכא. והא דאמר פרק "גיד הנשה" (חולין קא.): מי שגידו אסור ובשרו מותר, יצא זה שגידו ובשרו אסור – לא דמיא להכא. **ור"ש** לקיש אמר כו'. אע"ג דלר"ש לקיש צריכי לשנויי כדרבא, ובפ"ק דמנחות (דף ה:) משמע דלא סבר ליה כוותיה בדבר הראוי לעבודה – מ"מ בהאיך סבר ליה כוותיה שפיר. לאו

שיטה מקובצת

א] הא א"ל דכתיב: ב] אי הכי איפסולי כו'. תימה מאי אמרת בשלמא איכא הכא הא אפילו אי אמרינן לאו כמקומו דמי קשיא אמאי למחר פסול אי לאו משום מחשבת הינוח ותירץ השר מקוצי דה"ק אי אמרת בשלמא לאו כמקומו דמי ניחא דלמחר פסול משום מחשבת הינוח משום דליכא אכילת מזבח אבל השתא דאמרינן כמקומו דמי והוי שפיר אכילת מזבח ומ"מ גלי קרא אם האכל יאכל דליכא פיגול אם כן יש לנו לומר דמעטיה קרא לגמרי דאף מחשבת הינוח לא הוי כיון דלאו במקומו הוא דחישב ומשני דלהכי לא מהני קרא להוציאו ממחשבת הינוח. תו"ח: ג] ר"ל (אומר) [אמר לעולם] פסול ממש. כלומר הא מתני' דקתני פסול פסול לגמרי משמע אף לענין שלא נתכפרו בעלים ושלא במקומו כמקומו דמי ודרשינן שפיר כיון שהגיע דם לאויר המזבח נתכפרו הבעלים ולא קשיא מן המקרא דמשמע כמקומו דמי ובמתני' אמרינן פסול ממש דמתני' מיירי (במחשבת) [במחשבה] שנתן (במחשבת) [במחשבה] לאכול בשר חוץ לזמנו והויא מחשבה לפסול דכמקומו דמי והלכך הוי פסול לגמרי ומ"מ אין בו כרת דזריקה דלא שריא בשר באכילה לא מייתא לידי פיגול ואפ"ה פסול מידי דהוה אמחשבת הינוח כך שיטת הקונטרס והא דנקט לאכול בשר חוץ לזמנו לא דק דהא אם הניח הבשר עד למחר לא מיפסלא קרבן ומחשבה בדם לא מצינן למימר דהא כיון דכמקומו דמי לא מיפסל אם הניח שאר הדם למחר ולא מצי למינקט א) מחשבת אימורין עד למחר דפסול מיהא מדרבנן הוא ואומר רבינו פרץ דאיכא לאוקמי במחשב ע"מ לשפוך שירים למחר ואע"ג דשירים לא מעכבי מ"מ איכא למימר (איכא) דגזרינן אטו להניח דם: ד] באמירה במחשבה תנן הניתנין והשאר נמחק: ה] למטה כו' עד. ס"א כל הני תיובתא ושנינן כדשנינן: ו] תיבת כו' נמחק: ז] שר' יוסי אומר יאספנו ור"ש אומר לא יאספנו: ח] מהן בפיגול ומהן בשתיקה: ט] אלא ש"מ לאו: י] למחר דזריקה דשריא בשר באכילה אי הוי עביד לה בזומנה מייתי לידי פיגול הס"ד: יא] כי עביד כו' ותיבות אי הוה ל"ש ונמחק: יב] ולא קשיא קרא: יג] כשנתן שלא במקומו כו' בנתן הניתנין למעלה למטה במחשבת: יד] דאותבינן לעיל: טו] וכדאמרן דכיון: טז] והאי דתני פסול: יז] לאשמועינן דאע"ג: יח] יאסף מן המזבח: יט] לא יאספנו דכיון: כ] למימר קמן הס"ד ומה"ד אלא שר' יוסי אומר יאספנו ור"ש אומר לא יאספנו ותיבות ור"ש אומר כו' נמחק: כא] ליה בברייתא דהכא: כב] לו לשון הר"פ וי"ל דאי לא כתיב לא יחשב [הו"א] במחשבה בעלמא לא ואי כתיב לא יחשב הו"א ב) דוקא התם [הוא דאינו פסול] לגמרי [שפיר] מכפר אבל הכא דפסול לגמרי (שיכפר) אימא לא [יכפר] קמ"ל: כג] מחמת גריעות הזריקה ולא מחמת גריעות ההקטרה: כד] דמי שפיגולו: כה] בעבודה ראשונה ובעבודה: כו] כדתנן בפרקין הס"ד ומה"ד לאלתר כשר והוא דבור בפני עצמו ושייך לדף כו ע"ב: כז] ונראה לי: כח] לו פיסול להפקיע מידי פיגול ואין זה אלא גילוי מילתא בעלמא דכיון דאשכחן:

תורה אור: א] ויקרא ז

עין משפט נר מצוה: קה א מיי' פט"ז מהל' פסה"מ הלכה ה: קו ב ג מיי' שם הל' ו:

נ"ל הכי

נ"א מברייתא נ"ק

הגהות הב"ח

(א) רש"י ד"ה בשלמא וכו' וכדאמרן זריקה דלא שריא:

ומהגיה נ"ק

נ"א באכילה ומי שפיגולו כו' כל"ל והשאר נמחק נ"ק

יש מהפכים הגירסא מר"י לר"ש ור"ש מקיים הגירסא

[לקמן לו.]

נ"א אלא לאו דלאו כמקומו כו'

[לקמן לה:]

א) אולי צ"ל ולא מצי למנקט כך במחשב באימורין דאם הניח האימורין עד למחר פסול דרבנן מיהא הוי ועי' היטב בתוספות לקמן (דף לו) ד"ה שיאכלוהו. ב) אולי צ"ל דוקא התם דפסיל לגמרי שפיר מוציא מידי פיגול אבל הכא דאינו פסיל לגמרי דהא מכפר אימא דאינו מוציא מידי פיגול קמ"ל:

קז א מיי' פ"ג מהל' פסה"מ הלכה ו:
קח ב מיי' שם הל' ז:
קט ג ד מיי' שם הלכה יח:
קי ה מיי' פי"ח מהל' פסה"מ הלכה י:
קיא ו ז מיי' פי"ג מהלכות פסה"מ הלכה א ופט"ז הל' ה:

עיין ל"ק דקאמר האי דכחוץ ונתנן בפנים הוא טעות גמור דהיאך שייך זה יאספנו הלא כבר איפסלה קודם הזריקה בביאתו בהיכל כמ"ש תוס' לעיל כו: בד"ה אמר שמואל ול"ע

קיב ח מיי' פי"ח מהל' פסה"מ הלכה ו:
קיג ט מיי' פי"ד מהל' פסה"מ הלכה ז:

ומשנתינו כדברי האומר: לא יאספנו. ורב חסדא אמר אבימי: הכל מודין בניתנין למטה שנתנן למעלה – שלא יאספנו, וכל שכן בניתנין למעלה שנתנן למטה, הואיל ודמים העליונים למטה הן באין. לא נחלקו אלא בניתנין לפנים שנתנן בחוץ, *בחוץ שנתנן לפנים, שר' יוסי אומר: יאספנו, ור"ש אומר: לא יאספנו. אמר רב נחמן בר יצחק: אף אנן נמי תנינא, *רבי יהודה אומר: °"זאת היא העולה" – הרי אלו *מיעוטין, [א]פרט לנשחטה בלילה, ושנשפך דמה, ושיצא דמה חוץ לקלעים, אם עלתה – תרד. ר"ש אומר: "עולה", אין לי אלא עולה כשרה, מנין לרבות שנשחטה בלילה, ושנשפך דמה, ושיצא דמה חוץ לקלעים, [ב]והלן, והיוצא, והטמא, ושנשחט חוץ לזמנו וחוץ למקומו, ושקיבלו פסולין וזרקו את דמה, והניתנין למעלה שנתנן למטה, והניתנין למטה שנתנן למעלה, והניתנין בפנים שנתנן בחוץ, והניתנין בחוץ שנתנן בפנים, והפסח והחטאת ששחטן שלא לשמן – מנין? ת"ל: "תורת העולה" – ריבה תורה אחת לכל העולין, שאם עלו לא ירדו. יכול שאני מרבה אף הרובע והנרבע, והמוקצה והנעבד, והאתנן, והמחיר, והכלאים, והטריפה, ויוצא דופן? ת"ל: "זאת". ומה ראית לרבות את אלו ולהוציא את אלו? א] *מרבה אני את אלו – שהיה פסולן בקודש, ומוציא אני את אלו – שלא היה פסולן בקודש. קתני מיהא: הניתנין למטה שנתנן למעלה ולמעלה שנתנן למטה, ולא פליג רבי יהודה, מ"ט? לאו משום דקלטיה מזבח? ושמע מינה: לא יאספנו. א"ר ב] *אליעזר: [ג]מזבח הפנימי מקדש פסולין. מאי קמ"ל? תנינא: הניתנין בפנים כו'! אי מהתם, הוה אמינא: ה"מ דם, דחזי ליה, אבל קומץ דלא חזי ליה – אימא לא, קמ"ל. מיתיבי: קטרת זרה שעלה לגבי מזבח – תרד, שאין לך מקדש פסולין אלא מזבח החיצון בראוי לו; חיצון – אין, פנימי – לא! תריץ הכי: [ד]קטרת זרה שעלתה למזבח החיצון – תרד, שאין מזבח החיצון מקדש פסולין אלא הראוי לו, והפנימי – בין ראוי לו בין שאין ראוי לו. מאי טעמא? האי – רצפה, ג] והאי – כלי שרת.§

מתני' [ה]השוחט את הזבח לזרוק דמו בחוץ או מקצת דמו בחוץ, להקטיר אימוריו בחוץ או מקצת אימוריו בחוץ, לאכול בשרו בחוץ או כזית מבשרו בחוץ, או לאכול כזית מעור האליה בחוץ – [ו]פסול, ואין בו כרת. לזרוק דמו למחר, מקצת דמו למחר, להקטיר אימוריו למחר או מקצת אימוריו למחר, לאכול בשרו למחר או כזית מבשרו למחר, או לאכול כזית מעור האליה למחר – [ז]פיגול, [ח]וחייבין עליו כרת.§ **גמ'** סברוה: [ט]עור אליה כאליה

תורה אור: ויקרא ו

דטעמא ד] דר' יוסי משום דס"ל דשלא במקומו כמקומו דמי. דאם כן, אדמיפלגי באסיפה – ליפלגי בכפרה, ונימא רבי יוסי כיפר ור' שמעון לא כיפר. אלא לרבי יוסי נמי לאו כמקומו דמי, ואפ"ה לא יאספנו. ומשנתינו כדברי האומר לא יאספנו, ומשום הכי תנא פסול במתני'*. ורב חסדא אמר אבימי הכל מודים. ר' יוסי ור"ש. בניתנין למטה שנתנן למעלה שלא יאספנו. דהואיל וניתן במזבח הראוי לו – לא הוי כנשפך על הרצפה, דקלטיה מזבח, לאפוקי מכלל זריקה במקום אחר. וכל שכן בניתנין למעלה שנתנן למטה. דקרובה היא למתנה גמורה, שהרי דמים העליונים למטה הן שותתין ויורדין, הלכך האי דם סופו לירד למטה היה ראוי, וכי יהביה ולמטה *קלטיה מזבח מלאוספו ולחזור וליתנו למעלה. שרבי יוסי אומר יאספנו. דכיון דלמזבח זה לא היה ראוי – לא קלטיה כלל. ורבי שמעון אומר לא יאספנו. שהרי לשם מזבח היה ראוי, והרי בא לשום מזבח. אף אנן נמי תנינא. דאיתיה לדר' יוחנן דאמר דאיכא דאית ליה לא יאספנו. ואע"ג דשלא במקומו לאו כמקומו דמי לענין כפרה – לענין אסיפה ה] מיהו קלטיה מזבח. זאת היא העולה. הרי אלו ג' מיעוטין. לפי שבא המקרא הזה ללמדנו על הפסולין ו] למזבח שעלו דלא ירדו, דילפינן מ"עולה על מוקדה על המזבח כל הלילה" – משעלה על מוקדה תהא שם כל הלילה, לפיכך מיעט לך בו ג' ז] [מעוטין, למעט בו ג'] פסולין. זאת. היא מיעוטא: זאת ולא אחרת. "היא" – הוי מיעוטא. ה"א ד"העולה" הוי מיעוטא, כלומר העולה המיוחדת ולא כולן. פרט לנשפך דמה ולשנשחטה בלילה ושיצא דמה. אבל שאר פסולין אם עלו לא ירדו. ולקמן בפרק "המזבח מקדש" (דף פד:) מפרש טעמא דרבי יהודה דמרבי שאר פסולין ומפיק הנך. אין לי אלא עולה כשרה. תהא על מוקדה כל הלילה עד הבקר. והלן. שלן בשרה חוץ למזבח. והיוצא. שיצא בשרה. והטמא ושנשחט. ע"מ להקטיר חוץ לזמנו כו'. מנין. שכיון שעלו לא ירדו? רובע ונרבע. על פי עד אחד, שמותר להדיוט ואסור לגבוה. ונפקי לן מקראי במסכת תמורה בפ' "כל האסורין" (דף כח.). וכן מוקצה ונעבד וטריפה. מוקצה – שהקצהו לתקרובת עבודה זרה. נעבד. שהשתחוה לבהמה. כלאים. "שור או כשב" – פרט לכלאים, "כי יולד" – פרט ליוצא דופן (חולין דף לח:). מאי ראית. אחר שריבה הכתוב ומיעט, ולא פירש לך הכתוב מה ריבה ומה מיעט. אמרת. ומעצמך מרבה אני את אלו שהיה פסולן בקדש משבאו לעזרה נפסלו. קתני מיהת כו'. ולא פליג רבי יהודה לשוויגהו כנשפך על הרצפה, וניגמא ירדו כדאמר ר' יהודה פרט לנשפך דמה. ואלמא, לאו כנשפך דמה קשיב ליה. מאי טעמא לאו משום דקלטיה מזבח. לקדושי. ושמע מינה: לענין אסיפה – לא יאספנו. והא ליכא למימר: משום דקסבר שלא במקומו כמקומו דמי ומשום דכיפרה הוא, דהא דומיא דשאר זריקות פסולות קתני ליה. ומדרבי שמעון היינו טעמא דלא מייתי ליה, ח] דאיכא למימר: טעמא דרבי שמעון – משום ד"תורת העולה" ריבה, ואפילו נשפך דמה נמי קאמר דלא ירדו. מקדש פסולין. שאם עלו לא ירדו. ואף על גב דלא כתיב קרא אלא בחיצון. תנינא הניתנין בחוץ שנתנן בפנים לא ירדו. אבריהם ממזבח, ולא פליג ר' יהודה. מאי לאו דקלטיה פנימי לדם זה ט] שניתנו עליו? ואע"פ שנפסל בכניסתו להיכל משום "וכל חטאת אשר יובא מדמה" (ויקרא ו), א) הוה ליה כנשפך דמה. הני מילי דם. י] שפסול, הוא דמקדש, הואיל וחזי ליה דם בעלמא כגון דמים הפנימיים. אבל קומץ דלא חזי יא] כלל. דכתיב (שמות ל): "לא תעלו עליו קטרת זרה ועולה ומנחה", אימא אם עלה עליו ירד, קמ"ל. קטרת זרה. קטרת נדבה. שלא התיר הכתוב אלא קטרת של ציבור שחרית וערבית. שעלתה לגבי מזבח. קסלקא דעתך דמזבח הקטרת קאי. בראוי לו. לאפוקי קמצים שלא קידשו בכלי, הכי מפרש לקמן בפרק "המזבח" (דף פג:). האי רצפה. יב] כבנין אבנים שלא נמשח, לפיכך אין קדושתו בזה חמורה. והאי כלי שרת. ונמשח עם המשכן. **מתני'** את הזבח. שלמים או שאר הנאכלין. פסול ואין בו כרת. והאוכלו, ואפילו בחוץ – אין ענוש כרת. לאכול את בשרו למחר. ליכא לאוקומה בשלמים אלא בתודה יג] וחטאת ואשם, דאילו בשלמים – מחר זמנו הוא. אבל לזרוק דמו או להקטיר אימוריו – אפילו בשלמים הוי למחר חוץ לזמנו. פיגול וחייבין עליו כרת. האוכלו אפילו בזמנו ענוש כרת. ובגמרא יליף לה. **גמ'** כאליה

א) נ"א לא הוה

לאו משום דקלטיה מזבח וש"מ לא יאספנו. פי' בקונטרס: יד] והא ליכא למימר משום דסבר שלא במקומו כמקומו דמי, ומשום דכיפרה הוא, דהא דומיא דשאר זריקות פסולות קתני לה. וקשה: דהא בסוף "כל הפסולין" (לקמן לו.) מסקינן דר' יהודה אית ליה שלא במקומו כמקומו דמי! טו] ונראה לפרש דהאי דקא"ר יהודה כמקומו דמי – לא לענין דנתכפר, אלא לענין מחשבה דווקא הוי כמקומו. כיון דמהניא הזריקה לענין דאם עלו לא ירדו – מהניא נמי שלא לפסול במחשבה, ולכך טז] מיד לאלתר כשר. ומיהו, קשה: דא"כ בתר דשני כמקומו דמי, מאי קפריך התם מחישב ליתן הניתנין בחוץ בפנים ובפנים בחוץ? הא התם נמי קלטי' מזבח, דאם עלו לא ירדו! וה"ר יוסף מפרש דהכי מייתי סייעתא: מ"ט לאו משום דקלטיה מזבח, דאפי' בפנים וחוץ קאמר רבי יהודה דקלטיה מזבח, אע"ג דפני' ודחוץ לכ"ע לאו כמקומו, ואפי' הכי קאמר רבי יהודה דקלטיה מזבח לענין דאם עלו לא ירדו – הכי נמי קלטיה מזבח לענין דלא יאספנו. ומיהו, לא יתכן פי' זה למאי דפרישי' לעיל דמאן דאית ליה כמקומו דמי – אפי' בפנים וחוץ קאמר, מדפריך לר' יוחנן: ואי שלא במקומו לאו כמקומו להוי כנשפך מן הכלי ויאספנו, ולשמואל ולריש לקיש לא פריך. (תוספות) ורבי חיים בה"ר מרדכי מפ': דמוכח יז] מנתנו בחוץ שנתנו בפנים, ולכולי עלמא לאו כמקומו דמי ואין זריקתו כלום לפי שנפסל מקודם שנכנס להיכל, ונהי דאין תקנה באסיפה לפי שנפסל קודם הזריקה – כ"ש דהוה לן למימר דהוי כנשפך הדם מן הכוס על הרצפה דאמר ר' יהודה תרד, דכל זבח שלא נזרק כלל, אם עלו אימורין ירדו לר' יהודה, ואפי' הכי אמר דקלטיה המזבח לזריקתו, ואמרינן לא ירדו. ה"ה בניתנין למטה למעלה, דאמר ר' יוחנן דלא כמקומו דמי ולא כיפר כלל, דנימא דמהניא הזריקה, וקלטיה מזבח שלא יאספנו עוד להועיל זריקה אחרת. ברו"ך ע"כ. **האי** רצפה והאי כלי שרת. ועדיף יח] מכלי שרת, דלא מקדשי פסולין ליקרב, ומזבח מקדש.

אמר

ע"כ שייך לע"א

נדה מ. ע"ש לקמן פד. הוריות ג: קלטי' מזבח לאפוקי מלאוספו כו' כצ"ל ג"ק

נ"א אחר שריבה הכתוב ומיעט מרבה אני כו' ג"ק

[נ"ל אלעזר]

שיטה מקובצת

א] אלו אחר שריבה הכתוב ומיעט אמרת מרבה אני את כו' ומוציא אני את אלו שאין פסולן בקודש. פי' רובע ונרבע ופרש"י דאותם פסולים קודם שבאו לעזרה ולא נהירא דהא פסיק ותני רובע ומי לא עסקינן (דנרבע) [דרבע] אחר שבא לעזרה לכ"נ לפרש שהיה פסולן בקודש דיש הכשר במקום אחר בקודש וה"פ שלא לשמו יש לו הכשר בשלמים בפנים שנתנן בחוץ [יש לו הכשר] כל אחד כמשפטו ושקבלו פסולים פי' טמא בצבור (והלן בבמה) והלן בדם שכן כשר באברים (באברים משום בשר) והיוצא (בבמה טמא פי') [דמה] חוץ לקלעים [שכן כשר] בבמה ושנשחט בלילה משום אברים ופדרין דקריבין בלילה [אך מנשפך] דמה קשיא וי"ל דכיון דשחיטה שהיא עבודה ראשונה עשויה בהכשר הכשר במקום אחר קרינא ביה וה"ה לכולם שייך טעם זה משום הכשר שחיטה אבל [בנשחט] בלילה צריך לומר משום אברים ופדרים: ב] אמר ר' אלעזר מזבח הפנימי מקדש פסולים. שאם עלו לא ירדו ואע"ג דלא כתיב קרא אלא בחיצון: ג] והאי כלי שרת. אע"ג דאמרינן כלי שרת אינו מקדש [אלא הראוי לו] הכא שאני דאית ביה תרתי שהוא מזבח וכלי שרת הלכך מקדש פסולים ליקרב הקשה הר"ר שמואל מאיברא וכי יפה כח מחמת פסולן הא בכשרים לא מקדש דכתיב מנחה ונסך לא תסכו עליו וכיון דכשרים לא (רמו) [מקרבי] עליה היאך יקדש פסולים להקריב עליו וי"ל דקרא מיירי לכתחלה אבל דיעבד יקדש עוד תירץ דהא דמקדש פסולים לאו לענין לא ירדו דודאי ירדו מעל מזבח הפנימי אלא לומר שאם עלו אחר כן על מזבח החיצון שלא ירדו ומיירי בקמצים שלא קדשם בכלי שהעלה על מזבח הפנימי ואח"כ העלה על מזבח החיצון ומזה [מיירי למה] שהמזבח הפנימי מקדשם דאי לאו דמזבח הפנימי מקדשם מזבח החיצון לא היה מקדשם דאינו מקדש כי אם הראוי לו [ופי'] הראוי לו (הוי) [היינו] דנתקדשו בכלי והלכך מיירי כמו כן שלא נתקדשו דאי נתקדשו בכלי דל מהכא מזבח הפנימי מזבח החיצון מקדשם. תר"ח: ד] דטעמא דר"ש משום דס"ל כו' ונימא ר' יוסי לא כיפר ורבי שמעון כיפר אלא לר' שמעון נמי לא: ה] אסיפה מיהא: ו] הפסולין שעלו למזבח דלא: ז] ג' מיעוטין למעט ג' פסולין הס"ד ומה"ד זאת. הוי מיעוט: ח] ליה לא כיפר כלל דאיכא: ט] זה שניתן: י] דם פסול: יא] דלא חזיא ליה כלל: יב] רצפה בנין אבנים שלא קדושתו חמורה כזה שהוא כלי שרת המטלטל הס"ד: יג] בתודה ובחטאת: יד] בקונטרס דאי לאו דקלטיה מזבח הו"ל כנשפך דמה דפליג ר' יהודה והאי: טו] דמי וא"כ מאי מייתי הכא לכך נ"ל הא דמייתי הכא סייעתא [מהא דקלטיה] מזבח משום דאף בפנים וחוץ קאמר ר"י דאם עלו לא ירדו ואע"ג דמפנים לחוץ לכ"ע לאו כמקומו דמי כדמשמע בסוף כל הפסולים ומיהו קשה לעיל כי פריך לר"י דאמר לאו כמקומו דמי ליהוי כנשפך כו' אמאי [לא] קשה כמו כן לשמואל מנתן [הניתנים] בפנים בחוץ דקתני במתני' [דפסול דהא] דפנים לחוץ דכ"ע שלא כמקומו דמי ושמא מר"י ניחא ליה [טפי] להקשות משום דלר"י קשיא ליה מכל המתני' וריב"א פירש דניתנים בחוץ שנתן בפנים דוקא הוא דקאמר דשלא כמקומו דמי איבעית אימא סברא משום דדמים של חוץ לא שייכי כלל בפנים אבל של פנים שייכי בחוץ כגון דם השירים ואיבעית אימא טעמא משום דגלי קרא דכל חטאת אשר יובא מדמה וגו' אבל בניתנים בפנים שנתנם בחוץ א) לא דנימא כמקומו דמי והשתא ניחא הכל דהכא מוכח דלא יאספנו מן בחוץ שנתנם בפנים דהתם ודאי [לאו] כמקומו דמי ואפ"ה קתני ר"י לא יאספנו אלמא משום דקלטיה מזבח ולעיל לר"י דוקא פריך דלשמואל לא קשיא אפילו מבחוץ שנתנם בפנים דמאי פרכת ליהוי כנשפך ויאספנו הואיל ולאו כמקומו דמי לכ"ע [דהא] גלי קרא בהדיא דלא יאספנו דכתיב וכל אשר יובא מדמה אל אהל מועד באש תשרף [אבל הכא] מוכח שפיר מדקלטיה מזבח ש"מ לא יאספנו ומינה שמעינן גם בנתן למעלה ולמטה למ"ד לאו כמקומו דמי דליכא למימר דשאני חוץ בפנים דגלי קרא אבל חטאת [מנ"ל] דנהי דגלי לענין דלא כיפר ואין לו תקנה כי [אם באחרת] מ"מ לענין קליטת מזבח דלא ירדו שייך למילף מחוץ [שאם עלה לא ירדו] כגון למעלה ולמטה למ"ד שלא במקומו לאו כמקומו דמי וכיון דקלטה מזבח לענין דלא ירדו ממילא שמעינן נמי לא יאספנו תדע מדפליג ר"י גבי ניתז דמה מן הצואר על הרצפה ואמר התם ירדו וגבי חוץ בפנים מודה דלא ירדו. לשון מהר"פ ז"ל: טז] תיבת מיד נמחק: יז] מהניתנין בחוץ שנתנן בפנים דלכולי עלמא: יח] ועדיף משאר כלי שרת:

הא

כְּאַלְיָה דָּמֵי, וְהָא קָא מְחַשֵּׁב מֵאֲכִילַת מִזְבֵּחַ לְאָדָם! אָמַר שְׁמוּאֵל: א] הָא מַנִּי — *ר' אֱלִיעֶזֶר הִיא, דְּאָמַר: מְחַשְּׁבִין מֵאֲכִילַת מִזְבֵּחַ לַאֲכִילַת אָדָם, וּמֵאֲכִילַת אָדָם לַאֲכִילַת מִזְבֵּחַ. *דִּתְנַן: הַשּׁוֹחֵט אֶת הַזֶּבַח לֶאֱכוֹל דָּבָר שֶׁאֵין דַּרְכּוֹ לֶאֱכוֹל, לְהַקְטִיר דָּבָר שֶׁאֵין דַּרְכּוֹ לְהַקְטִיר — כָּשֵׁר, וְר"א פּוֹסֵל. בְּמַאי אוֹקִימְתָּא — כְּר"א. אֵימָא סֵיפָא: *זֶה הַכְּלָל, כָּל הַשּׁוֹחֵט, וְהַמְקַבֵּל, וְהַמּוֹלִיךְ, וְהַזּוֹרֵק, לֶאֱכוֹל דָּבָר שֶׁדַּרְכּוֹ לֶאֱכוֹל, וּלְהַקְטִיר דָּבָר שֶׁדַּרְכּוֹ לְהַקְטִיר; דָּבָר שֶׁדַּרְכּוֹ לֶאֱכוֹל — אִין, שֶׁאֵין דַּרְכּוֹ לֶאֱכוֹל — לָא, אֲתָאן לְרַבָּנַן. רֵישָׁא ר' אֱלִיעֶזֶר וְסֵיפָא רַבָּנַן? אֲמַר לֵיהּ: אִין. ב] רַב הוּנָא אָמַר: עוֹר אַלְיָה לָאו כְּאַלְיָה דָּמֵי. אָמַר ג] רָבָא: מ"ט דְּרַב הוּנָא? (ויקרא ג) °"חֶלְבּוֹ הָאַלְיָה" — וְלֹא עוֹר הָאַלְיָה. רַב חִסְדָּא אָמַר: לְעוֹלָם עוֹר הָאַלְיָה כְּאַלְיָה דָּמֵי, וְהָכָא בְּמַאי עָסְקִינַן — בְּאַלְיָה שֶׁל גְּדִי. כּוּלְּהוּ כִּשְׁמוּאֵל לָא אָמְרִי — רֵישָׁא ר"א וְסֵיפָא רַבָּנַן לָא מוֹקְמִי. כְּרַב הוּנָא לָא אָמְרִי — עוֹר אַלְיָה כְּאַלְיָה דָּמֵי קָא מַשְׁמַע לְהוּ. כְּרַב חִסְדָּא מַאי טַעְמָא לָא אָמְרִי? מַאי קמ"ל, עוֹר אַלְיָה כְּאַלְיָה דָּמֵי? ד] תָּנֵינָא: *וְאֵלּוּ שֶׁעוֹרוֹתֵיהֶן כִּבְשָׂרָן — [א]עוֹר שֶׁתַּחַת הָאַלְיָה! וְרַב חִסְדָּא? אִיצְטְרִיךְ, סד"א: ה"מ לְעִנְיַן טוּמְאָה, דְּרַכִּיךְ מִצְטָרֵף. אֲבָל הָכָא אֵימָא: (במדבר יח) °"לְמָשְׁחָה" — *לִגְדוּלָּה, כְּדֶרֶךְ שֶׁהַמְּלָכִים אוֹכְלִין, וְלָא עֲבִידִי מְלָכִים דְּאָכְלִי הָכִי — אֵימָא לָא, קמ"ל. מֵיתִיבִי: *הַשּׁוֹחֵט אֶת הָעוֹלָה לְהַקְטִיר כְּזַיִת מֵעוֹר שֶׁתַּחַת הָאַלְיָה חוּץ לִמְקוֹמוֹ — פָּסוּל וְאֵין בּוֹ כָּרֵת, חוּץ לִזְמַנּוֹ — פִּיגּוּל וְחַיָּיבִין עָלָיו כָּרֵת. אֶלְעָזָר בֶּן יְהוּדָה אִישׁ אֲבֵלִ' אוֹמֵר מִשּׁוּם רַבִּי יַעֲקֹב, וְכֵן הָיָה רַבִּי שִׁמְעוֹן בֶּן יְהוּדָה אִישׁ כְּפַר עִיכּוֹס אוֹמֵר מִשּׁוּם ר' שִׁמְעוֹן: אֶחָד עוֹר בֵּית הַפְּרָסוֹת בִּבְהֵמָה דַּקָּה, וְאֶחָד עוֹר הָרֹאשׁ שֶׁל עֵגֶל הָרַךְ, וְאֶחָד עוֹר שֶׁתַּחַת הָאַלְיָה, וְכָל שֶׁמָּנוּ חֲכָמִים גַּבֵּי טוּמְאָה וְאֵלּוּ שֶׁעוֹרוֹתֵיהֶן כִּבְשָׂרָן, לְהָבִיא עוֹר שֶׁל בֵּית הַבּוֹשֶׁת, חוּץ לִמְקוֹמוֹ — פָּסוּל וְאֵין בּוֹ כָּרֵת, חוּץ לִזְמַנּוֹ — פִּיגּוּל וְחַיָּיבִין עָלָיו כָּרֵת; עוֹלָה — אִין, אֲבָל זֶבַח — לָא. בִּשְׁלָמָא לְרַב הוּנָא — הַיְינוּ דְּקָתָנֵי עוֹלָה, אֶלָּא לְרַב חִסְדָּא — מַאי אִירְיָא דְּתָנֵי עוֹלָה? לִיתְנֵי זֶבַח! אָמַר לָךְ רַב חִסְדָּא: אִיבָּעֵית אֵימָא בְּאַלְיָה שֶׁל גְּדִי, וְאִיבָּעֵית אֵימָא: תְּנֵי זֶבַח.§ "פָּסוּל וְאֵין בּוֹ כָּרֵת" כו'.§ מנה"מ? אָמַר שְׁמוּאֵל: תְּרֵי קְרָאֵי כְּתִיבִי. מַאי הִיא? אָמַר רַבָּה: (ויקרא ז) °"שְׁלִישִׁי" — *זֶהוּ חוּץ לִזְמַנּוֹ, "פִּיגּוּל" — זֶהוּ חוּץ לִמְקוֹמוֹ, "וְהַנֶּפֶשׁ הָאוֹכֶלֶת מִמֶּנּוּ", אֶחָד וְלֹא שְׁנַיִם — ה] זֶהוּ חוּץ לִזְמַנּוֹ, וּלְמַעוּטֵי חוּץ לִמְקוֹמוֹ. וְאֵימָא: "וְהַנֶּפֶשׁ הָאוֹכֶלֶת מִמֶּנּוּ" — זֶהוּ חוּץ לִמְקוֹמוֹ, וּלְמַעוּטֵי חוּץ לִזְמַנּוֹ! מִסְתַּבְּרָא חוּץ לִזְמַנּוֹ עָדִיף, דִּפְתַח בֵּיהּ. אַדְּרַבָּה, חוּץ לִמְקוֹמוֹ עָדִיף, דִּסְמִיךְ לֵיהּ! אֶלָּא אָמַר אַבָּיֵי: כִּי אֲתָא רַב יִצְחָק בַּר אַבְדִּימִי ו] *[אֲמַר רַב] סָמֵיךְ אַדְּתָנֵי תַּנָּא: כְּשֶׁהוּא אוֹמֵר "שְׁלִישִׁי" בְּפָרָשַׁת "קְדוֹשִׁים תִּהְיוּ" — שֶׁאֵין ת"ל, שֶׁהֲרֵי כְּבָר נֶאֱמַר: (שם) °"וְאִם הֵאָכֹל יֵאָכֵל מִבְּשַׂר זֶבַח (א) ז] הַשְּׁלָמִים בַּיּוֹם הַשְּׁלִישִׁי", אִם

תורה אור

כְּאַלְיָה דָּמֵי. וַאֲפִילּוּ לְעִנְיַן הַקְטָרָה. וּבִשְׁלָמֵי כֶּבֶשׂ שֶׁאַלְיָיתוֹ קְרֵיבָה נַמִּי הָעוֹר ח] קָרֵב, כִּי הֵיכִי דִּלְעִנְיַן אֲכִילָה חָשֵׁיב לֵיהּ בָּשָׂר — לְעִנְיַן מִצְוַת הַקְטָרָתוֹ נַמִּי בָּשָׂר הוּא. וְקָתָנֵי מַתְנִי' דְּכִי שָׁחֵיט שְׁלָמִים לֶאֱכוֹל עוֹר הָאַלְיָה בַּחוּץ אוֹ לְמָחָר — הָוְיָא מַחֲשָׁבָה, וְאַע"ג דְּחִישֵּׁב מֵאֲכִילַת מִזְבֵּחַ לְאָדָם. רַבִּי אֱלִיעֶזֶר הִיא. לְקַמָּן בְּפֶ' "כָּל הַפְּסוּלִים" (דף לה.). לֶאֱכוֹל דָּבָר שֶׁאֵין דַּרְכּוֹ לֶאֱכוֹל. כְּגוֹן אֵימוּרִים, אוֹ חוּץ לִזְמַנּוֹ, אוֹ חוּץ לִמְקוֹמוֹ. וּלְהַקְטִיר. חוּץ לִזְמַנּוֹ אוֹ חוּץ לִמְקוֹמוֹ. דָּבָר שֶׁאֵין דַּרְכּוֹ לְהַקְטִיר. כְּגוֹן בָּשָׂר. לֶאֱכוֹל דָּבָר שֶׁדַּרְכּוֹ לֶאֱכוֹל. בָּשָׂר. שֶׁדַּרְכּוֹ לְהַקְטִיר. אֵימוּרִין. אֲבָל אִם חִישֵּׁב לְהַקְטִיר בָּשָׂר לְמָחָר, אוֹ לֶאֱכוֹל אֵימוּרִין לְמָחָר — כָּשֵׁר, שֶׁאֵין מְחַשְּׁבִין מֵאֲכִילַת אָדָם לַמִּזְבֵּחַ וּמֵאֲכִילַת מִזְבֵּחַ לְאָדָם. לָאו כְּאַלְיָה דָּמֵי. לְעִנְיַן מִצְוַת הַקְטָרָתוֹ הוּא, דְּמַעֲטֵיהּ קְרָא, כִּדְמְפָרֵשׁ *רַבָּה: "חֶלְבּוֹ הָאַלְיָה תְמִימָה" גַּבֵּי הַקְטָרַת אַלְיָה כְּתִיב, וּפָרֵישׁ בְּהֶדְיָא: חֵלֶב וְלֹא עוֹר. וְהָכָא בְּמַאי עָסְקִינַן. מַתְנִי' דְּחָשֵׁיב לֵיהּ אֲכִילַת אָדָם בְּאַלְיָה שֶׁל גְּדִי, שֶׁאֵינָהּ קְרֵיבָה, כִּדְאָמְרַן בְּפ"ק (לעיל דף ט.): לִימֵּד עַל הָעֵז שֶׁאֵינָהּ טְעוּנָה אַלְיָה. מַאי קמ"ל. תַּנָּא דְּמַתְנִי', אִי בְּאַלְיָה שֶׁל גְּדִי קָאֵי. אִי אָמְרַתְּ בִּשְׁלָמָא בְּשֶׁל כֶּבֶשׂ — קמ"ל לִשְׁמוּאֵל דִּמְחַשְּׁבִין מֵאֲכִילַת אָדָם ט] לַמִּזְבֵּחַ וּמֵאֲכִילַת מִזְבֵּחַ לַאֲכִילַת אָדָם, כְּרַבִּי אֱלִיעֶזֶר. וּלְרַב הוּנָא דְּמוֹקֵי לָהּ כְּרַבָּנַן — אַשְׁמַעִינַן תַּנָּא דִּידַן דְּעוֹר אַלְיָה לָאו כְּאַלְיָה דָּמֵי לְהַקְטִירוֹ. אֶלָּא לְרַב חִסְדָּא לָמָּה לִי לְמִתְנְיֵיהּ? אִי לְאַשְׁמוּעִינַן דְּעוֹר אַלְיָה לְעִנְיַן אֲכִילַת אָדָם כְּאַלְיָה דָּמֵי, וְכִי חָשֵׁיב עֲלֵיהּ לְאוֹכְלוֹ לְמָחָר כְּאִילּוּ חִישֵּׁב עַל כְּזַיִת מִבְּשָׂרוֹ, הוֹאִיל וְרַכִּיךְ וַחֲזֵי לַאֲכִילָה. תָּנֵינָא. בִּשְׁחִיטַת חוּלִּין. וְאֵלּוּ שֶׁעוֹרוֹתֵיהֶן כִּבְשָׂרָן. לְטַמֵּא טוּמְאַת נְבֵילוֹת, וְקָחָשֵׁיב עוֹר הָאַלְיָה. מִצְטָרֵף. לְטַמֵּא טוּמְאַת אוֹכָלִין בְּכַבֵּיצָה, אוֹ טוּמְאַת נְבֵילוֹת בְּכַזַּיִת. אֲבָל הָכָא. לְעִנְיַן קָדָשִׁים, כְּתִיב גַּבֵּי מַתְּנוֹת כְּהוּנָּה "לְכָל קָדְשֵׁי בְּנֵי יִשְׂרָאֵל לְךָ נְתַתִּים לְמָשְׁחָה" (במדבר יח) — וְהַיְינוּ לִגְדוּלָּה, כִּדְמְתַרְגְּמִינַן "לִרְבוּ" לְלַמֵּד שֶׁיְּהוּ אוֹכְלִין אוֹתָן דֶּרֶךְ אֲכִילַת מְלָכִים הַמְּשׁוּחִים, וְלָא עֲבִידִי מְלָכִים דְּאָכְלִי עוֹר, אֵימָא לָא תְּהֵא מַחֲשָׁבָה י]. עֵגֶל הָרַךְ. מְפָרֵשׁ בְּ"הָעוֹר וְהָרוֹטֵב" — כָּל שְׁנָתוֹ. לְהָבִיא עוֹר בֵּית הַבּוֹשֶׁת. שֶׁל נְקֵבָה. וְזֶה לְבַדּוֹ יֵשׁ לְךָ לְהָבִיא עוֹד אֵצֶל קָדָשִׁים מִכָּל הַשְּׁנוּיִים שָׁם. יא] עוֹר בֵּית הַפְּרָסוֹת. מִן הָאַרְכּוּבָּה וּלְמַטָּה. חוּץ לִמְקוֹמוֹ. אִם שָׁחַט ע"מ לֶאֱכוֹל מֵאַחַת מֵאֵלּוּ חוּץ לִמְקוֹמוֹ. עוֹלָה אִין. גַּבֵּי עוֹלָה הוּא דְּתָנָא מַחֲשֶׁבֶת הַקְטָרַת עוֹר אַלְיָה דְּפָסְלָה. אֲבָל זֶבַח. סְתָמָא לָא קָתָנֵי. שְׁמַע מִינָּהּ: אֵין מַחֲשֶׁבֶת הַקְטָרָה מוֹעֶלֶת בְּעוֹר הָאַלְיָה בִּשְׁאָר זְבָחִים. לְרַב הוּנָא. דְּאָמַר: בְּהֶדְיָא מַעֲטֵיהּ קְרָא גַּבֵּי אַלְיָה דְּנֶהֱוֵי אֵימוּרִין, אֲבָל גַּבֵּי עוֹלָה לָא אִימְעִיט, דִּכְתִיב: "הַנְּתָחִים", (שם) וְעוֹר הָאַלְיָה בָּשָׂר הוּא. אֶלָּא לְרַב חִסְדָּא. דְּאָמַר: גַּבֵּי אַלְיַית אֵימוּרִין עוֹר נַמִּי קָרֵב — לִיתְנֵי זֶבַח סְתָמָא! אִיבָּעֵית אֵימָא. הַךְ מַתְנִי' נַמִּי בְּאַלְיָה שֶׁל גְּדִי, וְלָא מִיתְנֵי לֵיהּ זֶבַח בְּאַלְיָה בְּמַחֲשֶׁבֶת הַקְטָרָה אֶלָּא בְּמַחֲשֶׁבֶת אֲכִילַת אָדָם, כִּי מַתְנִי'. מִנָּהָנֵי מִילֵּי. דְּמַחֲשֶׁבֶת יג] *חוּץ לִזְמַנּוֹ וְחוּץ לִמְקוֹמוֹ פּוֹסֶלֶת, וְעָנוּשׁ כָּרֵת בַּאֲכִילָה זֹאת שֶׁחִישֵּׁב עָלָיו חוּץ לִזְמַנּוֹ. תְּרֵי קְרָאֵי כְּתִיבִי. חַד חוּץ לִזְמַנּוֹ וְחַד חוּץ לִמְקוֹמוֹ. שְׁלִישִׁי. "אִם הֵאָכֹל יֵאָכֵל מִבְּשַׂר זֶבַח (ב) יד] הַשְּׁלָמִים בַּיּוֹם הַשְּׁלִישִׁי" (ויקרא ז) וּמוֹקֵי' לֵיהּ תַּנָּא לְקַמָּן: בִּמְחַשֵּׁב בִּשְׁעַת עֲבוֹדָה לֶאֱכוֹל מִזִּבְחוֹ בַּיּוֹם הַשְּׁלִישִׁי הַכָּתוּב מְדַבֵּר. זֶה חוּץ לִזְמַנּוֹ. דִּשְׁלִישִׁי חוּץ לִזְמַן אֲכִילַת שְׁלָמִים הוּא. פִּגּוּל. דִּכְתִיב בְּסֵיפֵיהּ דִּקְרָא: "פִּגּוּל יִהְיֶה" — קְרָא יְתֵירָא הוּא, לְרַבּוֹת חוּץ לִמְקוֹמוֹ. וּמִסְתַּבְּרָא דְּמַחֲשֶׁבֶת חוּץ לִמְקוֹמוֹ מוֹקְמִינַן לָהּ, וְלָא מַחֲשֶׁבֶת שְׁאָר פְּסָלוֹת, כְּגוֹן לִשְׁפּוֹךְ דָּמוֹ טו] [עַל הָרִצְפָּה אוֹ] ע"מ לְעָרְבוֹ בְּדַם הַפְּסוּלִין. דְּדָמֵי לְחוּץ לִזְמַנּוֹ קָמְרַבֵּי בְּהַאי קְרָא, וְחוּץ לִמְחִיצָּה דָּמֵי לְחוּץ לַזְּמַן. מִמֶּנּוּ. מַשְׁמַע דְּלָא קָאֵי אַ"עֲוֹנָהּ תִּשָּׂא" דְּנָפְקָא לָן מִינֵּיהּ כָּרֵת, אֶלָּא אַחַד מִינַּיְיהוּ. דְּאֶחָד מַשְׁמַע וְלֹא שְׁנַיִם, מִדְּלָא כְּתִיב "הָאוֹכֶלֶת" וְלִשְׁתּוֹק טז]. לְמַעוּטֵי. דְּ"מִמֶּנּוּ" מִיעוּטָא הוּא. עָדִיף. לְאוֹקוּמֵי כָּרֵת עֲלֵיהּ. דִּסְמִיךְ לֵיהּ. דְּהַאי "מִמֶּנּוּ" סָמוּךְ לְ"פִגּוּל יִהְיֶה" דִּמְרַבִּינַן בֵּיהּ חוּץ לִמְקוֹמוֹ. כְּשֶׁהוּא אוֹמֵר שְׁלִישִׁי. בְּפָרָשַׁת "קְדוֹשִׁים תִּהְיוּ" קְרָא זוּטָא: "וְאִם הֵאָכֹל יֵאָכֵל בַּיּוֹם הַשְּׁלִישִׁי פִּגּוּל הוּא לֹא יֵרָצֶה" (ויקרא יט). תְּנֵהוּ לְחוּץ לִמְקוֹמוֹ. דְּבְאוֹכֵל מַמָּשׁ בַּיּוֹם הַשְּׁלִישִׁי לֵיכָּא לְאוֹקְמָא, דְּהָא כְּתִיב "לֹא יֵרָצֶה", וְאָמְרִינַן לְקַמָּן (דף כט.): וְכִי אַחַר שֶׁהוּכְשַׁר יַחֲזוֹר וְיִפָּסֵל? אֶלָּא עַל כָּרְחָךְ בִּמְחַשֵּׁב בִּשְׁעַת עֲבוֹדָה ע"מ כֵּן קָאָמַר. אִם

אמר שמואל הא מני ר' אליעזר היא. וסבר לה כההוא תנא דאמר בריש "הקומץ רבה" (מנחות דף יז.) דלר' אליעזר הוי בכרת. ולא סבר לה כרבי ירמיה דמוקי בסוף פירקין (דף לא:) סיפא כרבי אליעזר, דלא תיקשי: רישא וסיפא כר' אליעזר ומליעתא כרבנן. וא"ת: לרבי אליעזר מאי איריא עור האליה? אפילו אליה נמי. ואי לאשמועינן יז] עור האליה כבשר — תנינא: ואלו שעורותיהן כבשרן, כדפריך בסמוך! וי"ל: כיון דעיקרה אתא לאשמועינן כר' אליעזר, אין לחוש אי אגב אורחיה אשמועינן דעור כבשר, אע"ג דתנינא. יח] דאשכחן בשמעתא קמייתא דברכות (דף ב.) דפריך: וליתני צאת הכוכבים, ומשני: מילתא אגב אורחיה קמ"ל, דכפרה לא מעכבא, אע"ג דתנינא במסכת נגעים (פ' י"ד מ"ג): העריב שמשו — אוכל בתרומה, הביא כפרתו — אוכל בקדשים*.

תנינא אלו שעורותיהן בבשרן. הקשה ה"ר יעקב מאורליינש: טובא קמ"ל, דבפ' "העור והרוטב" (חולין דף קכב:) אמרינן: אל תקניטוני שבלשון יחיד אני שונה אותה, גבי עור הראש של עגל הרך, דפליגי רבנן משום דסופו *להקשות. ועור האליה הוי לכ"ע כבשר! ועוד קשה: היכי דייק מעור הראש דיחידאה היא מברייתא דאלעזר בן יהודה? יט] *הא פשיטא לן מדפריך "תנינא" הא *קחשיב עור האליה, דהוי לכולי עלמא כבשר.

להביא עור של בית הבושת. פי' בקונטרס: וזה לבדו יש לך עוד להביא אצל קדשים מכל השנוים שם. ותימה: הא איכא נמי עור השליל! ופי' בקונטרס בחולין (דף נו.) דלא חשיב שליל משום דאינו נוהג בעולה. ותימה: והרי כ] בית הבושת דאין נוהג בעולה! ונראה דלא קתני שליל משום דאמר פרק "כל הפסולין" (לקמן דף לה.) דפיגל בשליל לא נתפגל הזבח, כא] ולא קאמר להביא כב] אלא *דבר שאינו לגמרי בעולה. ומשום דמיירי ברייתא בעולה לא תנא בית הבושת בהדיא, וקאמר "להביא"*.

בשלמא לרב הונא היינו דקתני עולה. תימה: דבתוספתא קתני זבח! וי"ל: דרב הונא הוה מוקי לה כרבי אליעזר, דאמר מחשבין מאכילת מזבח לאדם.

אלא לרב חסדא מאי איריא דקתני עולה ליתני זבח. לשמואל לא מקשה: כג] למה לי למיתני עולה ליתני זבח. דאי תני זבח — הוה מוקמינן ליה כרבי אליעזר. מסתברא

שיטה מקובצת

א] הא מני ר' אליעזר היא. וא"ת א"כ מאי איריא עור האליה אפי' האליה עצמה נמי ואי לאשמועינן דעור האליה כאליה דמי תנינא ואלו שעורותיהן כבשרן כדפריך בסמוך ונראה לפרש הואיל ועיקר בבא אתא לאשמועינן כר"א אגב אורחיה אשמועינן דעור האליה כאליה דמי אע"ג דשמעינן לה במקום אחר. תו"ח: ב] אין רישא ר' אליעזר וסיפא רבנן: ג] אמר רבה: ד] תנינ' ואלו שעורותיהן כבשרן. הקשה הר"ר יעקב מאורליינש מאי מייתא מאותה משנה הא אמרינן בחולין אל תקניטני בלשון יחיד (שונה) אני [שונה] אותה וי"ל דהא דקאמר התם דהוי כיחידאה קאי על עור הראש של עגל הרך דפליגי רבנן עליה משום שסופה להקשות אבל עור האליה לכ"ע הוי כבשר. תו"ח: ה] שנים איזה זה: ו] אבדימי אמר רבה: ז] זבח שלמיו: ח] העור נמי קרב: ט] אדם לאכילת מזבח ומאכילת: י] מחשבה הס"ד ומה"ד עור בית הפרסות בבהמה דקה מן הארכובה ולמטה הס"ד ומה"ד עגל הרך: יא] ד"ה עור בית כו' ולמטה נמחק: יב] עור האליה: יג] דמחשבת ס"א [חוץ לזמנו] פוסלת וענוש כרת באכילתו ואת שחשב עליו חוץ למקומו פוסלת ואין בו כרת. זו גירסת הר"פ ברש"י שלו: יד] זבח שלמיו: טו] דמו על הריצפה או ע"מ כו' הפסולין דמסברא דומיא דשלישי דהיינו חוץ לזמנו: טז] ולשתוק ולמעוטי אתא והד"א: יז] לאשמועינן דעור: יח] דתנינא כדאשכחן בריש יבמות ובשמעתא קמייתא: יט] תיבות הא פשיטא לן מדפריך תנינא נמחק: כ] והרי חשיב בית: כא] הזבח והואיל ולא הוי פיגול לגמרי כשלמים שיריה אבל בית הבושת דינו ממש כשלמים דאם נתפגל בית הבושת נתפגל הזבח. מהר"פ: כב] להביא א) דרך שאינו לגמרי בשלמים ומשום דמיירי בעולת: כג] נקשה דלמה לי:

קיד א מיי' פ"א מהל' שאר אבות הטומאה הלכה ט:

[וע"ע תוס' מנחות נג. ד"ה הכל ביתר ביאור]

להקשות וקמ"ל הכא דעור כו' כל"ל וכ"ה בס"י נ"ק

נ"ל הא קחשיב עור האליה ופשיטא לן מדפריך תנינא דהוי לכולי עלמא כבשר

נ"א דבר שהוא פיגול לגמרי בשלמים

[וע' היטב תוס' חולין נו. ד"ה להביא]

לקמן לה.

לקמן לה.

לקמן כט:

נ"ל רבא

חולין נה: קכב. נדה נה.

[לקמן לא. סוטה טו. חולין קלב.]

[תוספתא פ"ב מ"ע חולין נה:]

הגהות הב"ח

(א) גמ' מבשר זבח שלמיו ביום השלישי: (ב) רש"י ד"ה שלישי וכו' זבח שלמיו ביום:

[לעיל יד.]

[דלא גרסינן אמר רבה מוכח כמה דוכתי עיין יבמות ג. ובתוספות שם ד"ה אמר ובחולין קי. וכתוב' שם ד"ה איכא דמוכח כן ממנם אחר העיון בכל הנהו תוספות הנ"ל מוכח דגם אמר רב לא הוה גרסינן ע"ש]

נ"א חוץ לזמנו פוסלת וענוש כרת עליו וחוץ למקומו פוסלת ואין בו כרת

(א) נ"ל להביא תנא דבר שהוא פיגול לגמרי כשלמים וכו' וכ"ה הג"ק.

קטו א ב מיי' פי"ג מהלכות פסה"מ הל' ב סמג לאוין שלז:
קטז ג מיי' פי"ח מהל' פסה"מ הלכה טז:
קיז ד מיי' פי"ג מהל' פסה"מ הלכה ג:

אִם אֵינוֹ עִנְיָן לְחוּץ לִזְמַנּוֹ — תְּנֵהוּ לְעִנְיַן חוּץ לִמְקוֹמוֹ; וּמִיעֵט רַחֲמָנָא גַּבֵּי נוֹתָר °"וְאוֹכְלָיו עֲוֹנוֹ (ויקרא יט) יִשָּׂא" — לְמַעוּטֵי חוּץ לִמְקוֹמוֹ. וְאֵימָא: "וְאוֹכְלָיו עֲוֹנוֹ יִשָּׂא" — זֶהוּ חוּץ לִמְקוֹמוֹ, א] וּלְמַעוּטֵי נוֹתָר מִכָּרֵת! ב] מִסְתַּבְּרָא נוֹתָר הֲוָה לֵיהּ לְאוֹקְמֵי בְּכָרֵת, לְמִגְמַר "עָוֹן" "עָוֹן" לְחוּץ לִזְמַנּוֹ דְּדָמֵי לֵיהּ בְּז"ב. אַדְּרַבָּה, חוּץ לִמְקוֹמוֹ הֲוָה לֵיהּ לְאוֹקְמֵי בְּכָרֵת, לְמִגְמַר "עָוֹן" "עָוֹן" לְחוּץ לִזְמַנּוֹ דְּדָמֵי לֵיהּ בְּמקד"ש! אֶלָּא אָמַר רַבִּי יוֹחָנָן, *תָּנֵי זַבְדִּי בַּר לֵוִי: אָתְיָא "קוֹדֶשׁ" "קוֹדֶשׁ"; כְּתִיב הָכָא: (א) °"אֶת קֹדֶשׁ ה' חִילֵּל וְנִכְרְתָה", (שם) וּכְתִיב הָתָם: °"וְשָׂרַפְתָּ אֶת הַנּוֹתָר בָּאֵשׁ" ג] וגו', (שמות כט) מַה לְהַלָּן נוֹתָר — אַף כָּאן נוֹתָר. וּמִיעֵט רַחֲמָנָא גַּבֵּי נוֹתָר "וְאוֹכְלָיו עֲוֹנוֹ יִשָּׂא" — לְמַעוּטֵי חוּץ לִמְקוֹמוֹ מִכָּרֵת. וּמַאי חָזֵית דִּקְרָא אֲרִיכָא בְּחוּץ לִזְמַנּוֹ, וּשְׁלִישִׁי דְּפָרָשַׁת "קְדוֹשִׁים תִּהְיוּ" חוּץ לִמְקוֹמוֹ? אֵיפּוּךְ אֲנָא! מִסְתַּבְּרָא, אֲרִיכָא בְּחוּץ לִזְמַנּוֹ, דְּגָמַר "עָוֹן" "עָוֹן" מִנּוֹתָר דְּדָמֵי לֵיהּ בְּז"ב. אַדְּרַבָּה, אֲרִיכָא בְּחוּץ לִמְקוֹמוֹ, וּשְׁלִישִׁי דִּ"קְדוֹשִׁים תִּהְיוּ" בְּחוּץ לִזְמַנּוֹ, מִשּׁוּם דְּדָמֵי לֵיהּ סַמְכֵיהּ, וְקָא מְמַעֵט לֵיהּ! אֶלָּא אָמַר רָבָא: ד] כּוּלְּהוּ מִקְּרָא אֲרִיכָא אָתְיָין. דִּכְתִיב: °"הֵאָכֹל יֵאָכֵל" — (ויקרא ז) *אבִּשְׁתֵּי אֲכִילוֹת הַכָּתוּב מְדַבֵּר, אֶחָד אֲכִילַת אָדָם וְאֶחָד אֲכִילַת מִזְבֵּחַ. "מִבְּשַׂר זֶבַח שְׁלָמָיו" — *מַה שְּׁלָמִים מְפַגְּלִין וּמִתְפַּגְּלִין, אַף כֹּל מְפַגְּלִין וּמִתְפַּגְּלִין. ב"שְׁלִישִׁי" — זֶה חוּץ לִזְמַנּוֹ; "לֹא יֵרָצֶה" — *כְּהַרְצָאַת כָּשֵׁר כֵּן הַרְצָאַת פָּסוּל, וּמַה הַרְצָאַת כָּשֵׁר עַד שֶׁיִּקְרְבוּ כׇּל מַתִּירָיו — גאַף הַרְצָאַת פָּסוּל עַד שֶׁיִּקְרְבוּ כׇּל מַתִּירָיו. "הַמַּקְרִיב" — בְּהַקְרָבָה הוּא נִפְסָל, דוְאֵינוֹ נִפְסָל בַּשְּׁלִישִׁי. "אוֹתוֹ" — בְּזֶבַח הַכָּתוּב מְדַבֵּר, וְאֵינוֹ מְדַבֵּר ה] בְּכֹהֵן. "לֹא יֵחָשֵׁב" —
לא

[עי' כריתות ה.]
[לעיל יג: מנחות יז. חולין פא:]
לקמן לח. מנחות פג.
[לקמן מב: מנחות טז:]
נ"ל הזמן
[נ"ל בזמן קרב]

אם אינו ענין לענין מחשבת חוץ לזמנו תנהו לענין חוץ למקומו. ופיגול דקרא אריכא ד"צו את אהרן" לא תידרשיה לחוץ למקומו, אלא כוליה קרא בחוץ לזמנו. הלכך "ממנו" אחוץ לזמנו קאי. וכ"ת: הכא נמי כרת כתיב, דסמיך ליה "ואוכליו עונו ישא" וגו'! ההוא בנותר ממש מיתוקם, כדמפרש ואזיל. תורה אור וכדי שלא תאמר שניהם במשמע – מיעט רחמנא "ואוכליו" דהיינו מיעוטא, מדלא כתיב "והאוכל", למעוטי חוץ למקומו דלעיל מיניה. ואימא ואוכליו עונו ישא אחוץ למקומו. דסליק מיניה קאי. וכדי שלא תאמר: אין מקרא יוצא מידי פשוטו, ואף נותר במשמע, ונהי דב"לא ירצה" ליתא, אבל בכרת איתיה – להכי מיעט "ואוכליו" דמשמע אחד ולא שנים, למעט נותר מכרת. ה"ג: מסתברא נותר אית לך לאוקומי בכרת למיגמר "עון" "עון" לחוץ לזמנו ו] דדמי ליה בז"ב אדרבה חוץ למקומו הוה ליה לאוקומי בכרת ז] דמיגמר "עון" "עון" לחוץ לזמנו דדמי ליה במקד"ש. והכי פירושא: נותר הוה ליה לאוקומי בכרת ח] דמיגמר "עון" "עון" כו' – שמלמד כרת על חוץ לזמנו, שאין כרת מפורש בו אלא נשיאות עון אמורה בו, ולימד מכאן בגזירה שוה, דהכא כתיב "נשיאות עון" ומפרש כרת. הלכך, אי מוקמת ליה להאי ט] בנותר – איכא למילפיה לג"ש שפיר, דדמו אהדדי בשני דברים הללו: ששניהן נפסלים בזמן, זה בזמן ממש וזה במחשבת זמן, ושניהם נוהגים בבמה, כדתנן בפרק בתרא י] (לקמן דף קיג.). דכי פרכת: ונילף "עון" "עון" מטומאת בשר, דכתיב "ונשא אהרן את עון הקדשים", מה להלן לאו ולא כרת אף כאן לאו ולא כרת – אמרינן: מנותר הוה ליה למילף, יא] דדמי ליה בז"ב. אבל אי מוקמת ליה להאי כרת בחוץ למקומו, כי גמרת ליה חוץ לזמנו מיניה בג"ש, ופרכינן ליה: ונילף "עון" "עון" מטומאה – ליכא לתרוצי: מחוץ למקומו הוה ליה למילף, דדמי ליה בז"ב. דהא אין פסולו בזמן, ואינו נוהג בבמת יחיד, שאין שם מחיצות יב]. במקד"ש.

מ' – מחשבה, ק' – קלת, ד' – דם, ש' – שלישי. חוץ לזמנו וחוץ למקומו שניהם פסולין במחשבה, ואם חישב במקלתו נפסל כולו, ושניהם נפסלין בעבודת הדם, ובשניהם נאמר "שלישי". לאפוקי טומאה דאינה פסול מחשבה, ואם נטמא מקלתו לא נטמא כולו, וישנה לאחר זריקת דמים, ולא נאמר בו "שלישי" יתירא. אבל בחוץ לזמנו וחוץ למקומו "שלישי" מיותר לג"ש דלעיל, דבכל חד מינייהו כתיב: "והנותר ביום השלישי באש ישרף" וסמיך ליה "ואם האכל יאכל", ולא בעי למכתב "שלישי". אתיא קודש קודש. דהאי "ואוכליו" בנותר כתיב. קרא אריכא. "ואם האכל יאכל" ד"צו את אהרן" אריכא הוא. איפוך אנא. ואימא דאריכא בחוץ למקומו, וכתיב ביה נשיאות עון. ו"שלישי" ד"קדושים תהיו" – חוץ לזמנו, ואימעוט מכרת! מסתברא אריכא בחוץ לזמנו. דכיון דלא פריש ביה כרת בהדיא, אלא בג"ש ד"עון" מנותר יליף, מסתברא דדמי מדדמי יליף, דדמי ליה בז"ב. דאי יג] מוקמן ליה בחוץ למקומו – תו לא יליף כרת מנותר, דלא דמי ליה במידי. אדרבה. מסתברא משום דדמי ליה חוץ לזמנו לנותר סמכיה לנותר, וקא ממעט ליה מ"אוכליו", דלא תימא: משום דדמי ליה ניגמר מיניה. כולהו מקרא אריכא אתיין. זה לחיוב וזה לפטור, כדיליף ליה רבה בריש שמעתין. בשתי אכילות כו'. שמחשבת שתיהן פוסלת. דהא לקמן במחשבה מוקי ליה תנא, ולא באוכל ביום השלישי. אחד אכילת אדם כו'. דלא שנא חישב לאכול למחר, ל"ש חישב להקטיר אימורין למחר – פגול. מבשר זבח שלמיו. הקיש זבחים לשלמים, מה שלמים יש בהן מפגלין ויש בהם יד] מתפגלין, שהדם הוא המפגל והבשר והאימורין המתפגלין. אף כל. שיש בו מפגלין ומתפגלין פיגול נוהג בו. יצאו מנחת כהנים ומנחת כהן משיח ומנחת נסכים, שהם מתירין את עצמם ואין בהם שיריים להתפגל מחמת עבודות מתיריהם, שאין פיגול נוהג בהן. לא ירצה טו] המקריב. משמע (ג) אזריקה, לא תהא זריקה זו מרצה. שמע מינה דעד שיזרק הדם מחשבת פיגול תלויה ועומדת, נזרק הדם – הוקבע הפיגול, לא נזרק הדם, כגון שנשפך – בטל הפיגול, דכתיב ביה הרצאה כדכתיב גבי כשר. מה הרצאת כשר. לא קרי ליה הרצאה אלא בזריקה, שהוא סוף ארבע עבודות המתירות – אף פיגול אינו קבוע עד שיזרק הדם, שהיא סוף כל מתיריו. בהקרבה הוא נפסל. השתא יליף (ג) טז] (פסול) דבמחשבה הכתוב מדבר, שמחשב בשעת הקרבה לאוכלו בשלישי. ואינו נפסל בשלישי. אם בהקרבה לא חישב ע"מ כן ואכל ממנו בשלישי – אין הקרבן נפסל למפרע. דהכי מידריש: "לא ירצה המקריב" – לא תהא זריקתו מרצה אם ע"מ כן הקריבו. אותו בזבח הוא מדבר ואינו מדבר בזובח. כלומר, (ד) ושלא תאמר דהאי המקריב לאו להכי הוא דאתא, אלא לומר לך שהכהן המקריבו לא יחשב עוד בכהונה ויפסל מלכהן. לכך נאמר "אותו" – הזבח בלא יחשב, ואין הכהן בלא יחשב.
לא

מסתברא נותר אית לן לאוקומי בכרת למיגמר עון עון לחוץ לזמנו דדמי ליה בז"ב. פי' בקונטרס: אי מוקמת ליה להאי יז] בנותר – איכא למילפיה לגזירה שוה שפיר, דדמו אהדדי בשני דברים הללו, ששניהם נפסלים בזמן, זה בזמן ממש, וזה במחשבת זמן. ושניהם נוהגין בבמה, כדתנן בפ' בתרא (לקמן דף קיג.). יח] וכי פרכת: ונילף "עון" "עון" דטומאת בשר, דכתיב "ונשא אהרן את עון הקדשים" מה להלן לאו ולא כרת אף כאן לאו ולא כרת – אמרינן: מנותר הוה ליה למילף, דדמי ליה בז"ב. אבל אי מוקמת להאי כרת לחוץ למקומו, כי גמרת [ליה] חוץ [לזמנו] מיניה בגזירה שוה, ופרכת ליה: ונילף "עון" "עון" מטומאה – ליכא לתרוצי: מחוץ למקומו הוה ליה למילף, דדמי [ליה] בז"ב, דהא אין יט] נפסלים בזמן, ואינו נוהג בבמת יחיד, שאין שם מחילות. (עד כאן לשונו). ופירוש זה תימה גדול: דמה סברא היא זו? ומנין לנו דנוקי קרא בנותר כדי ללמוד ממנו חוץ לזמנו מ"עון" "עון", כ] כדי שלא נלמוד מטומאה? ועוד: הא לענין במה שוה נמי נותר לטומאת בשר, כדאמרינן בסוף מכילתין (גם זה שם): אבל *הפיגול והנותר והטמא שוין כא] זה בזה. וכן טמא שימש ליכא למימר, דהוא נמי לא הותר בבמה, כדאמר לעיל: מה להלד השוה שבהן שכן לא כב] הותרו בבמה. ועוד, כשמקשה: אדרבה חוץ למקומו הוה ליה לאוקומי כו' דדמי במקד"ש – בלאו כג] דומיא דמקד"ש אית לן למילף חוץ לזמנו מחוץ למקומו טפי מטומאה, כדאמרינן בפ' "בית שמאי" (לקמן דף מה:): שכן הותר ליך טהור כד] (*בקרא), חוץ לזמנו וחוץ למקומו לא הותרו מכללם ואין ליך מרצה. ושניהם טהורין, ושניהם כה] [לא] עשה קרב כמקריב. מה שאין כן בטומאה. דמאי דחוץ למקומו הותר מכללו בבמה – אין זה קרוי הותר כו] מכללו! על כן נראה לפרש דגזירה שוה זו ניתנה בסיני, למילף "עון" "עון" הנך קראי דהכא זה מזה. ולכך מסתברא לן לאוקומי טפי בנותר מבחוץ למקומו, משום דדמי לחוץ לזמנו בז"ב – דאית לן לאוקומי קרא במילתא שיהיו דומין זה לזה מה שאנו למידין בגזירה שוה. ולא משום שלא נלמוד מטומאה, כדפירש כז] [רש"י]. ופריך: אדרבה, חוץ למקומו דמי ליה במקד"ש. וכי האי גוונא הויא סוגיא דלעיל בריש פירקין (דף יז.) דפסיל בתרומה מחיל עבודה, דלא פסיל בתרומה לא מחיל עבודה. וא"ת: דמוקמינן קרא בדדמי טפי לג"ש, טומאת בשר תיהוי בכרת בג"ש ד"עון" "עון"! וי"ל: דממעט כח] ליה קרא מכרת, כדאמר לקמן פרק "ב"ש" (דף מג:): "וטומאתו עליו" – מי שטומאתו פורחת ממנו כט] (יוצא עליו מגופו), יצאת טומאת בשר שאין טומאה פורחת ממנו. **ואיפוך** אנא. תימה: ל] הא כתיב קרא "שלישי"! והא דמוקמינן ליה בחוץ למקומו – בהם אינו ענין לחוץ לזמנו מוקמינן ליה בחוץ למקומו. א"כ קרא קמא, לא] היינו קרא אריכא – אית לן לאוקומי בחוץ לזמנו! לב] ודוחק לומר דסבר המקשה אין מוקדם ומאוחר בתורה. **מה** שלמים מפגלין ומתפגלין. תימה: מהיקישא ד"זאת התורה" נפקא לן לקמן בפ' "דם חטאת" (דף לח.) ובמנחות פרק "התודה" (דף פג.). וכמה דרשות דרשינן מההוא היקישא, אע"ג דנפקי מקראי אחריני.
למקום

הגהות הב"ח

(א) גמ' כתיב הכא כי את וכו' את הנותר באש כי קדש הוא מה להלן: (ב) רש"י ד"ה לא ירצה וכו' משמע לאזריקה קאי לא: (ג) ד"ה בהקרבה וכו' יליף דבפסול מחשבה: (ד) ד"ה אותו וכו' כלומר שלא כצ"ל ואות ו' נמחק:

שיטה מקובצת

א] ולמעוטי נותר מכרת. פ"ה דס"ד דאית ביה כרת מדכתיב [ונכרתה הנפש] והנפש ההיא גבי פיגול דנהי דע"כ לא איירי בנותר מדכתיב לא ירצה מ"מ אין מקרא יוצא מידי פשוטו והייתי אומר דהכרת קאי אנותר ולא ירצה אחוץ למקומו לכך אצטריך ואוכליו למעוטי נותר מכרת. מהר"פ: ב] מסתברא כו' פרש"י כו' ולא נהירא חדא דכל זה מבחוץ בא דאמרינן דלא תקשי מטומאה דהוי ליה לפרש בהדיא ועוד היכי מצי למילף מטומאה התם איכא פירכא דלא מצי למילף ועוד הא אמרינן לקמן הפיגול והנותר והטמא שוה בזה ובזה פי' בבמה גדולה ובבמה קטנה ונראה לפרש א) כו'. לשון הר"פ: ג] וגו' לא יאכל כי קדש הוא: ד] אלא אמר רבא כו' כל זה שהביא רבא לא אצטריך לן לבעיין אלא מפרש הוא כל הפסוק: ה] מדבר בזובח ותיבת בכהן נמחק: ו] לזמנו לענוש כרת: ז] בכרת למגמר עון: ח] בכרת למגמר עון: ט] להאי כרת: י] בתרא וכ"ת למה איצטריך טעם זה דדמי ליה בז"ב איצטריך דכי מוקמת: יא] למילף טפי דדמי: יב] מחיצות ואין ראוי לומר ביה חוץ למקומו: יג] דאי מוקמת אות ן' נמחק: יד] בהם שהם מתפגלין שהדם כו' והאימורין הם המתפגלין הס"ד: טו] ירצה משמע ותיבת המקריב נמחק: טז] יליף דבפסול מחשבה: יז] להאי כרת בנותר איכא למילפה בג"ש שפיר: יח] בתרא דכי פרכת: יט] אין פסולו בזמן: כ] מעון עון ולא נלמוד: כא] שוין בזה ובזה וכן טמא ששימש נמי ליכא: כב] לא הותר: כג] בלאו טעמא ותיבת דומיא נמחק: כד] טהור בזמן קרב דחוץ לזמנו: כה] ושניהם לא: כו] הותר בבמה ותיבת מכללו נמחק: כז] כדפי' רש"י: כח] תיבת ליה נמחק: כט] תיבות יוצא עליו מגופו נמחק: ל] תימה דהא כתיב בקרא: לא] קמא דהיינו: לב] לזמנו דמסברא קרא קמא לעולם בחוץ לזמנו:
א) ר"ל ונראה לפרש כמו שכתבו התוס' בד"ה מסתברא ונראה לפרש דג"ש זו ניתנה וכו'.

קיח א מיי' פי"ד מהל' מעשה"ק הלכה טו סמג לאוין שלה:

לא יערב בו מחשבות אחרות. מכאן למחשבות שמוציאות זו מזו, שמחשבת פסול מוציאה מידי פיגול. כדתנא מתני': כיצד לא קרב המתיר כמצותו כו'. **יהיה.** עשאן הכתוב לחוץ למקומו ולחוץ לזמנו הויה אחת, מלמד שמצטרפין חצאי שיעוריהן לפסול את הקרבן, כדתנן במתני': לאכול כחצי זית בחוץ כחצי זית למחר — פסול. **דדמי ליה בז"ב.** ולא (א) שבקיה חוץ לזמנו דדמי לנותר, דאתיא ג"ש מיניה, ונגמר חוץ למקומו דלא דמי לנותר במידי. והא דלא שנייה רבה בריש שמעתא הכי, כי פרכינן: אדרבה חוץ למקומו עדיף דסמיך ליה — משום דאכתי לא קמה ליה ג"ש דתני לוי בר זבדי ו] דכרת בנותר כתיב, דנימא דנשיאות עון דגבי מחשבה בדדמי לנותר משתעי הואיל ומיניה גמר. **שיהא משולש כו'.** ולימד על מחשבת חוץ למקומו שאינה מועלת אלא או בקדשי קדשים שחישב עליהם לאוכלם חוץ לעזרה, או בקדשים קלים לאוכלם חוץ לעיר — שיש לנחשב (ב) לאכול בהיכל דלא פסיל, דבעינן ז] שחישב על מקום המשולש. **בדם בבשר ואימורין.** היינו חוץ לעזרה בשעת היתר הבמות. לאפוקי היכל, שאין בו הקטרת אימורין ולא אכילת בשר. **תיפוק לי מקרא קמא.** מדאפקיה רחמנא בלשון "שלישי" לחוץ לזמנו, וכתיב בההוא קרא חוץ למקומו. **שלישי פרט.** מקום משולש ולא פנים. **מאחר שהוכשר.** בעבודת דמו ח] כתקונו. **בזב וזבה.** שפסקו, והתחילו למנות ימי ספורן ומנו ד' או ה' ימים, ואם ראו — סתרו על הנייעס, כדאמרינן במס' נדה (דף סז:): "ואחר תטהר" — אחר אחר לכולן, שלא תהא טומאה מפסקת ט] בהן. **ושומרת יום כנגד יום.** הרואה תוך אחד עשר יום שבין נדה לנדה, וטבלה למחר י] שחרית — הרי היא טהורה, דמקצת היום ככולו. וטבילתה ביום, ואם תראה היום — סתרה טהרתה, ואדם וכלים שנגעו בהן היום טמאין למפרע. כדתנן בפ"ב דנדה (דף עב.): ושוין ברואה תוך אחד עשר יום כו' וטבלה ביום של אחריו ושמשה — הרי זו תרבות רעה, ומגעה ובעילתה תלויין, וזו היא תלייתן: אם תראה היום — יהיו טמאין למפרע, וחייבין בקרבן. **הרי הוא אומר המקריב.** (ג) בהקרבה נפסל. והכי מידרש: "לא ירצה המקריב" — אין הקרבתו מרצה. **אלא זה כהן המקריב.** ואמר לך הכתוב שלא יהא כשר יא] לכהונה. ושמע מינה תרתי: שעת הקרבה ופסול (ד) יב] כהן. **אותו.** דא"כ ליכתוב "המקריב לא יחשב". השתא דכתיב "אותו" — הזבח ב"לא יחשב", ואין המקריב ב"לא יחשב". **במחשבה הוא נפסל.** (ה) זה מפורש מן הראשון, ד"המקריב" לא משמע להו שעת הקרבה, עד דגמר קרא למילתיה ואמר "המקריב אותו לא יחשב" — במחשבה זאת. דהאי "לא יחשב" יג] לדרשא הוא, דהא כתיב "לא ירצה". **נפקא ליה מדאחרים.** מדאיצטריך קרא למימר ואינו נפסל בשלישי — שמע מינה בזבח הכתוב מדבר, דאי בזובח — למה יפסל בשלישי? הלא הוא לא חטא כי אם האוכל. **מדכתיב לישנא דלא ירצה ולא ירצה זיבחא הוא.** דאין לשון "לא ירצה" נופל בפסול כהן. **שעיברה שנתו.** וזהו איחור, דכתיב: "לפני ה' תאכלנו שנה בשנה".

[לקמן לו. פב:]

תורה אור

לא יערב בו מחשבות אחרות; "פיגול" — זה חוץ למקומו; "יהיה" — מלמד שמצטרפין זה עם זה; "והנפש האוכלת ממנו" — אחד ולא שנים, ואיזה זה — חוץ לזמנו, דגמר "עון" "עון" מנותר, דדמי ליה בז"ב. אמר ליה רב פפא לרבא: לדידך, "שלישי" דפרשת "קדושים תהיו" מאי דרשת ביה? ההוא מיבעי ליה *למקום שיהא משולש, בדם בבשר ובאימורין. תיפוק לי מקרא קמא "אם האכל יאכל", מדאפקיה רחמנא בלשון "שלישי"! אמר רב אשי: אמריתה לשמעתא קמיה דרב מתנה, א"ל: אי מהתם, הוה אמינא: "שלישי" — פרט, "פיגול" — כלל, ונעשה כלל מוסף על הפרט, ואיתרבו שאר מקומות, קמ"ל. ת"ר: (ויקרא ז) "ואם האכל יאכל מבשר זבח שלמיו", אמר רבי אליעזר: כוף אזנך לשמוע: במחשב לאכול מזבחו ביום השלישי הכתוב מדבר. או אינו אלא באוכל מזבחו ליום שלישי? אמרת: א] אחר שהוא כשר — יחזור ויפסל? אמר לו רבי עקיבא: הן! מצינו בזב וזבה ושומרת יום כנגד יום, שהן בחזקת טהרה, וכיון שראו — סתרו. אף אתה אל תתמה על זה, שאע"פ שהוכשר — שיחזור ויפסל! אמר ב] ליה: הרי הוא אומר "המקריב" — בשעת הקרבה הוא נפסל, ואינו נפסל בשלישי. ג] או אינו אומר "המקריב" — אלא זה כהן המקריב? כשהוא אומר "אותו" — בזבח הוא מדבר, ואינו מדבר בכהן. *בן עזאי אומר: "אותו" מה ת"ל? לפי שנא': (דברים כג) "לא תאחר לשלמו", יכול אף מאחר נדרו ב"לא ירצה"? ת"ל: "אותו" — אותו ב"לא ירצה", ואין המאחר נדרו ב"לא ירצה". אחרים אומרים: "לא יחשב" — במחשבה הוא נפסל, ואינו נפסל בשלישי. ובן עזאי, דבזבח הכתוב מדבר ואינו ד] בכהן, מנא ליה? אי בעית אימא — נפקא ליה מדאחרים. ואיבעית אימא: מדכתיב "לא ה] *ירצו" ו"לא ירצה" — זיבחא הוא. ובן עזאי, אותו ב"לא ירצה" ואין מאחר נדרו ב"לא ירצה", מהכא נפקא? מדאחרים נפקא! *דתניא, אחרים אומרים: יכול יהא בכור שעיברה שנתו כפסולי

למקום שיהא משולש בדם ובבשר ואימורים. פירש בקונטרס: פרט למחשב לאכול בהיכל דלא פסול. דבעינן יד] שחישב על מקום המשולש בדם ובשר ואימורים, דהיינו חוץ לעזרה בשעת היתר הבמות, לאפוקי היכל שאין בו הקטרת אימורים ולא אכילת בשר. וזה לא דק בקונטרס, דאכילת בשר מצי משכחת בהיכל, כדאמר לקמן (דף סג.): שאם הקיפו גוים את כל העזרה שכהנים נכנסים בהיכל ואוכלין שם ק"ק. ועוד קשה לפירוש הקונטרס, מאי קפריך: תיפוק לי מקרא קמא מדאפקיה רחמנא בלשון "שלישי"? הא האי "שלישי" לאו בחוץ למקומו כתיב אלא בחוץ לזמנו, ומקום משולש לא שייך בחוץ לזמנו אלא בחוץ למקומו! ועוד, דקמשני: *הוה אמינא "שלישי" פרט, הא האי "שלישי" בחוץ לזמנו טו] [כתיב, ופיגול] במקום משולש כתיב! ויש מפרשים: דמקום משולש — היינו דלא פסלה מחשבה אלא במזבח החיצון שמלאחן הזירין בו, לאפוקי מזבח הפנימי שאין נותנין בו רק דם וזה אי אפשר, דמתנות הפנימיות פלוגתא דר' שמעון ורבנן, דרבנן מחייבין בפיגולן כרת. וכן ר"מ ורבנן סברי בפ' "בית שמאי" (לקמן דף מב:) גבי ארבעים ושלש של יום הכיפורים. ולעיל בפ"ק (דף יג:) גבי טבילת אצבע בחטאות הפנימיות דאמרינן דפסול מק"ו. טז] ואמר נמי בגיטין (דף נד:): כהן גדול ביום הכפורי' יוכיח, דכי אומר פגול — מהימן. ובמקום שאינו משולש — אפילו פסול ליכא, כדמוכח לקמן בפ' "כל הפסולים" (דף לו.). וי"מ: דמקום משולש — היינו דבעינן שיעמוד יז] *המחשבה במקום משולש, פרט לעומד חוץ בעזרה ושוחט בסכין ארוכה. ולפירוש זה יח] קשה ממתנות הפנימיות, דלאו מקום משולש הוא והוי פיגול. (תוספות) ויש לומר: חוץ לעזרה אין שלשתן כשרין, שהרי דם ואימורין נפסלין שם. אבל היכל — יש דם שלא נפסל שם, כגון דם פנימי, ואימורין אם הכניסן שם — לא נפסלו בכך. מיהו, אין נראה, דשילהי "כל הפסולין" (לקמן דף לו.) קאמר: מחשב לניתנין בחוץ שנתנו בפנים דאינו פסול, משום דאינו מקום משולש. הג"ה ע"כ. והרב ר' יום טוב מפרש: דמקום משולש — היינו שיחשוב לזרוק במקום שדם ובשר ואימורין פסולין, כגון מחשב לזרוק יט] קדשים קלים חוץ לירושלים. אבל מחשב לזרוק בירושלים — לא, דאין שום פסול בבשר. וקדשי קדשים אפילו בירושלים, כיון דבזה כ] *המקום שלשתן פסולין שם. ולהאי פירושא ניחא הא דקשיא לן לעיל אברייתא דחישב ליתן את הניתנין למטה למעלה למטה לאלתר כשר, דמשמע דאי שלא במקומו לאו כמקומו דמי — ניחא. ויתיישב לפי' זה, משום דלאו מקום משולש הוא. ומיהו, קשה: כא] אם כן למחר פסול, אמאי? לאו מקום משולש הוא! וכי תימא: מידי דהוי אמחשבת הינוח ואליבא דר' יהודה — הא משמע לעיל דלא צריך להאי טעמא אלא למאי דמסקינן שלא במקומו כמקומו דמי. וי"מ: ד"שלישי" בחוץ לזמנו איירי, ובעינן שיחשוב לזרוק ליום שלשתן פסולין, אפילו לאכול הבשר — היינו ליום שלישי. דאם חישב לזרוק דם שלמים למחר — לא פיגל, עד שיהא משולש באכילה, דהיינו לשלשה ימים. והוא הדין בקדשי קדשים לזרוק דמן למחר כב] — פיגול, דזמן אכילתו נמי למחר, אלא דקרא בשלמים כתיב, דזמנו ליום שלישי. והכי קאמר: ההוא מיבעי ליה למקום משולש, דאם חישב לזרוק דם שלמים בחוץ ליום הג' — פיגל, אבל קודם השלישי — לא פיגל. והא דאמר בפ' "איזהו מקומן" (לקמן דף נו:) דקדשים הנאכלין ליום ולילה מחשבים בדמן משתשקע החמה — ההוא כמאן דלית ליה מקום משולש. דפלוגתא דתנאי היא בפ' "כל הפסולין" (לקמן דף לו:). ופי' זה לא יתכן כלל, דכולה שמעתא כג] מיירי במקום שיהא משולש. **וכיון** שראו סתרו. פי' הקונטרס: דזב וזבה שפסקו והתחילו למנות ימי ספורן, ומנו ארבעה או חמשה ימים. וקשה: דאין זה קרוי חזקת טהרה! כד] אלא נראה: דמיירי בשביעי שלהן לאחר שטבלו. (תוספות) דזב וזבה טבילתן ביום, ואם טבלו בשביעי ואחר כך נגעו בטהרות, או שמשו וראו לאח"כ (או) קודם הערב שמש — טמאים למפרע. ואם המתינה לשמש עד הלילה ואח"כ ראתה — אינה טמאה אלא מכאן ולהבא. (הג"ה ע"כ). ומיהו, כה] רבי יוסי דאמר פ' "כילד צולין" (פסחים דף פא.) דלא מטמא למפרע — לא יתכן. **ואין** מאחר נדרו בלא ירצה. יש תימה: דלמה לן קרא? דמהיכא תיתי לן דהוי ב"לא ירצה" דאיצטריך קרא כו] ד"לא ירצה" למעוטיה? **נפקא** לן מדאחרים. תימה: הא רבי אליעזר נמי דריש שאינו נפסל בשלישי, ואפילו הכי צריך פסוק שאין כז] כהן נפסל! וי"ל: דרבי אליעזר, כיון דלא דריש "לא יחשב" לומר במחשבה הוא נפסל

ה"א שלישי פרט למקום משולש הא האי שלישי בחוץ לזמנו כתיב כל"ל וכ"ה בס"י נ"ק

[נ"ל המחשב]

נ"ל ירצה

שם ה: תמורה כה: [תוספתא סנהדרין פ"ג]

שיטה מקובצת

א] אמרת מאחר שהוכשר יחזור: ב] אמר לו הרי הוא אומר המקריב בהקרבה ותיבת בשעת נמחק: ג] או אינו [אומר המקריב] אלא [זה] כהן המקריב. פ"ה האי או אינו אינו כמו כל או אינו שבתלמוד דאינו ר"ל או אינו דכולה לכהן הוא דאתא ולא למידרש דאין הקרבן נפסל בשלישי (בשלישי) אלא בשעת הקרבה ובהא קאמר דהכהן לא ירצה אצל זה דמה פשע הכהן במה שהותירו לאוכלו אלא ודאי המקריב משמע בשעת הקרבה כלומר דאם חישב בשעת הקרבה (גם) הזבח והכהן לא ירצה והכי משמע קרא משמע בהקרבה הוא נפסל בשלישי וכמו כן משמע נמי דמיירי בכהן שחישב מדכתיב מחשבה בלשון המקריב משמע דקאי נמי [אכהן] דליכא למימר דכוליה לכהן הוא דאתא דאין לו לפסול במה שהותירו כיון דלא פשע. העתקת לשון רש"י של מהר"פ ז"ל: ד] ואינו מדבר בכהן: ה] לא ירצה: ו] זבדי דאשמועינן דכרת: ז] דבעינן שיחשב: ח] כתקונן הס"ד: ט] מפסקת ביניהם הס"ד: י] למחר ס"א ביום של אחריו: יא] כשר עור לכהונה: יב] כהן דאי אכהן קאי ע"כ מהקרבה קאמר והאי או אינו משונה מכל או אינו שבתלמוד שפירושו או אינו בא לדרשא זו אלא לדרשא אחרת והכא אי אפשר לומר כן דלמה הכהן נפסל אם אכלו הבעלים מבשר זבח ביום השלישי אלא ע"כ במחשבת הכהן הוא עצמו נפסל וגם הזבח נפסל מדכתיב והנפש האוכלת ממנו עונה תשא: יג] יחשב יתירה הוא לדרשא דהא: יד] דבעינן שיחשב: טו] בחוץ לזמנו כתיב. וי"מ והשאר נמחק: טז] מק"ו ואמרינן נמי בגיטין בהניזקין כה"ג ביוה"כ כו' אמר פיגול: יז] שיעמד המחשב: יח] זה נמי קשה ממתנות כו' הוא ולא יהא פיגול. הג"ה. וי"ל: יט] לזרוק דם קדשים: כ] הקרבן שלשתן כו' ניחא. לשון מהר"פ דגבי חוץ לזמנו [מתוקם] זמן משולש כגון חטאת שחישב למחר שאינו [ראוי] אף לאכילת בשר [ע"כ]: כא] קשה דאם כן למחר אמאי פסול הא לאו מקום: כב] למחר פיגל דזמן אכילתן לאו למחר אלא דקרא בשלמים כתיב כו' בחוץ לזמנו ליום הג' פיגל אבל: כג] שמעתא לא מיירי אלא במקום: כד] טהרה עד שימנו ז' ימים לשון הר"פ ז"ל וי"ל שמנה שבעת ימים אבל לא גמר היום דמקצת היום ככולו: כה] ומיהו לרבי יוסי: כו] קרא למעוטי חס"ד גליון וי"ל דסד"א שיפסל באיחור חטאתו כמו באיחור זמן גופו כמו קרבן הבא כבש והביאו לאחר שנתו: כז] שאין הכהן נפסל כדקאמר או אינו:

הגהות הב"ח

(א) רש"י ד"ה דדמי וכו' ולא שבקינן לחוץ וכו' ונגמר לחוץ וכו' שנייה רבה: (ב) ד"ה שיהא משולש וכו' לאכלן בהיכל דלאו פסול הוא דבעינן: (ג) ד"ה הרי הוא אומר המקריב בשעת הקרבה: (ד) ד"ה אלא זה וכו' כהן הפסול ואח"כ מ"ה כשהוא אומר אותו: (ה) ד"ה במחשבה הוא נפסל מקרא זה וכו' לדרשא הוא לאתא דהכי:

קיט א מיי' פ"ו מהל' בכורות הלכה יג:
קכ ב מיי' פי"ד מהל' פסה"מ הלכה ח:
קכא ג מיי' פט"ז מהל' פסה"מ הל' ח:
קכב ד ה מיי' שם הלכה ב:
קכג ו מיי' פי"ד מהל' פסה"מ הלכה י:

תורה אור

כפסולי המוקדשין ויפסל? ת"ל: °"ואכלת לפני ה' אלהיך מעשר דגנך" א] וגו', מקיש בכור למעשר, מה מעשר אינו נפסל משנה לחבירתה – אאף בכור אינו נפסל משנה לחבירתה! איצטריך, סלקא דעתך אמינא: הני מילי – בכור דלאו בר הרצאה הוא, אבל קדשים דבני הרצאה נינהו – אימא לא לירצו, קמ"ל. ואכתי, מהתם נפקא: °"והיה בך חטא" – ולא בקרבנך חטא! (א) ב] ובן עזאי: ההוא מבעי ליה: "והיה בך חטא" – ולא באשתך חטא; סלקא דעתך אמינא: הואיל ואמר *רבי אלעזר, ואיתימא רבי יוחנן: אין אשתו של אדם מתה אא"כ ג] מבקשין ממנו ממון ואין לו, שנאמר: °"אם אין לך לשלם למה יקח משכבך מתחתיך" – בהאי עון דבל תאחר נמי מתה, קמ"ל.§ אחרים אומרים: ד] במחשבה הוא נפסל, ואינו נפסל בשלישי. ורבי אליעזר, ה] "לא יחשב" מאי עביד ליה? מיבעי ליה לכדרבי ינאי, דאמר רבי ינאי: מנין למחשבות שמוציאות זו מזו – שנאמר: "לא יחשב", לא יערב בו מחשבות ו] אחרות. ורב מרי מתני, אמר רבי ינאי: מנין למחשב בקדשים שהוא לוקה – ת"ל: °"לא יחשב". א"ל רב אשי לרב מרי: לאו שאין בו מעשה הוא, וכל לאו שאין בו מעשה אין לוקין עליו! אמר ליה: רבי יהודה היא, *דאמר: לאו שאין בו מעשה לוקין עליו.§ מתני' *זה הכלל: בכל השוחט, והמקבל, והמהלך, והזורק, לאכול דבר שדרכו לאכול, ולהקטיר דבר שדרכו להקטיר, ז] כזית, חוץ למקומו – פסול ואין בו כרת, חוץ לזמנו – פגול וחייבין עליו כרת. גובלבד שיקריב המתיר כמצותו. כיצד קרב המתיר כמצותו? שחט בשתיקה, קבל והלך וזרק חוץ לזמנו; ח] או ששחט חוץ לזמנו, וקבל והלך וזרק בשתיקה; או ששחט וקבל והלך וזרק חוץ לזמנו – זהו שמקריב המתיר כמצותו. כיצד לא קרב המתיר כמצותו? שחט חוץ למקומו, קבל והלך וזרק חוץ לזמנו; או ששחט חוץ לזמנו, קבל והלך וזרק חוץ למקומו; או ששחט וקבל והלך וזרק חוץ למקומו ט] (ולזמנו) הפסח והחטאת ששחטן שלא לשמן, וקבל והלך וזרק חוץ לזמנו; או ששחט חוץ לזמנו, קיבל והלך וזרק שלא לשמן; או ששחט וקבל והלך וזרק י] דמן שלא לשמן – זהו שלא קרב המתיר כמצותו. *דלאכול כזית בחוץ כזית למחר, כזית למחר כזית בחוץ, כחצי זית בחוץ כחצי זית למחר, כחצי זית למחר כחצי זית בחוץ – פסול ואין בו כרת. אמר רבי יהודה: זה הכלל, כל שמחשבת הזמן קדמה למחשבת המקום – פגול וחייבין עליו כרת, ואם מחשבת המקום קדמה למחשבת הזמן – פסול ואין בו כרת. *וחכמים אומרים: הזה וזה פסול, ואין בו כרת. *)לאכול וכחצי זית להקטיר כחצי כזית – כשר, שאין אכילה והקטרה מצטרפין.§ גמ' אמר אילפא: *מחלוקת בשתי עבודות, אבל בעבודה אחת – דברי הכל עירוב מחשבות הוי. ורבי יוחנן אמר: אף בעבודה אחת מחלוקת. בשלמא לאילפא, מדרישא בשתי עבודות – סיפא נמי בשתי עבודות. אלא לרבי יוחנן, רישא בשתי עבודות וסיפא בעבודה אחת?
אין

(דברים יד; שם כג; משלי כב; ויקרא ז; מעילה ז.)

*) מנחות יז. [וש"נ]

כפסולי המוקדשין. כאילו נפל בו מום. מה מעשר אינו נפסל משנה לחבירתה. שהרי בשלישי יא] זמן ביעור לבער כל המעשרות מן הבית ולהתוודות, כדכתיב: "מקצה שלש שנים תוציא" (דברים יד). דלאו בר הרצאה הוא. אינו בא לכפר. אבל קדשים, כגון עולה שמכפרת על עשה, ושלמים שמביאין לדורון ליתן שלום בין ישראל לאביהם שבשמים, ואימא: הואיל ואיחרו – יב] *פסול בעבודה הוא ולא לירצו, קא משמע לן. ולא בקרבנך חטא. שאם איחרו אינו נפסל. "והיה בך חטא" סיפיה דקרא ד"לא תאחר לשלמו" *הוא. הא אוקימנא. במס' (ב) ר"ה. מבקשין ממנו יג]. ממונו שגזל. משכבך. אשתו. שמוציאות זו מזו. מחשבת פסול מוציאה מיד פיגול. לא יד] יחשב. קרי ביה (ג) לא יחשב, להזהיר כהנים על כך. רבי יהודה היא. במס' שבועות (דף ג:): "והנותר ממנו עד בקר באש תשרפו" – בא הכתוב ליתן עשה אחר לא תעשה, לומר שאין לוקין עליו. דטעמא דבא הכתוב, הא לא בא הכתוב – לוקה המותיר, ואע"ג דאין בו מעשה. מתני' זה הכלל כל השוחט ומקבל כו'. או זו או זו. לאכול דבר שדרכו לאכול. בשר. או להקטיר דבר שדרכו להקטיר. אימורין. כדילפינן לעיל דשתי אכילות מפגלות, ובלבד דליחשיב עלייהו להאכילו למחר לראוי להן, אימורין – למזבח, בשר – לאדם. ובלבד שיקריב המתיר כמצותו. טו] הדם הוא המתיר. כמצותו – שלא יהיה בו פסול אחר. אם יש בו פסול מחשבה אחרת – יצא מידי פיגול, כדילפינן לעיל דמחשבות מוציאות זו מזו. הפסח והחטאת ששחטן שלא לשמן. מוציאן מידי פיגול. אבל שאר זבחים – אין שלא לשמן מוציאן מידי פיגול, דהא כשרים הן שלא לשמן. לאכול כזית בחוץ כזית למחר. היינו הך דאמרן, אלא דרישא איירי בב' עבודות וכאן בעבודה אחת, ששחט על מנת לאכול כזית למחר טז] כזית בחוץ. ולמאן דמוקי לה בגמרא להא נמי בשתי עבודות – משום כחצי זית נקט לה, לאשמועינן דמצטרפין זה עם זה. רבי יהודה אומר כו'. אכולה מתני' פליג, דלית ליה מחשבות מוציאות זו מזו אלא אם כן קדם פסולו לפיגולו, דתו לא קרינן ביה כהרצאת כשר. ובעבודה אחת נמי פליג, דאית ליה תפוס לשון ראשון. לאכול כחצי זית ולהקטיר כחצי זית. ושניהם חוץ לזמנו או חוץ למקומו – כשר, שאין אכילה והקטרה מצטרפין לפוסלו. דהכא ליכא שיעורא, והכא ליכא שיעורא. גמ' בשתי עבודות. דהא דתני סיפא: כזית למחר כזית בחוץ, דפליג ר' יהודה עלה – בשתי עבודות מיירי כי רישא ששחט על מנת לאכול כזית למחר וקבל על מנת לאכול כזית בחוץ – אהא הוא דפליג רבי יהודה, שהרי הוקבע בפיגול ותו לא אתא מחשבת פסול ומפקע לה. אבל בעבודה אחת – אפילו ר' יהודה מודה דלא הוקבע בפיגול במחשבה מעורבת. אף בעבודה אחת מחלוקת. דאית ליה לר' יהודה תפוס לשון ראשון. מדרישא בשתי עבודות. דקתני בהדיא: כיצד לא קרב המתיר כמצותו – שחט חוץ לזמנו וקבל והלך יז] חוץ למקומו. סיפא נמי. כזית למחר כזית בחוץ דפליגי בה ר' יהודה ורבנן. בשתי עבודות. קא מיירי. והאי דהדר נקיט ליה – לאשמועינן צירוף כחצי זית, דלא אשמועינן ברישא.
אין

נפסל – איכא למימר יח] שהוא לשון חשיבות, ואתא למימר שאף הכהן נפסל, אי לאו דמעטיה קרא בהדיא אבל בן עזאי דדריש "לא יחשב" לשון מחשבה – יט] ממילא שמעינן דלאו בכהן מיירי. אלא אם כן מבקשין ממנו ממון ואין לו. פי' בקונטרס: ממון שגזל. ונראה דמיירי בנדר, כדאמר בפ' שני דשבת (דף לב:): דבעון נדרים אשתו של אדם מתה, שנאמר: "למה יקח משכבך מתחתיך". והא דדריש הכא: בך חטא ולא באשתך חטא – מיירי בשלם אחר כן, אלא שעבר על בל תאחר.

מחלוקת בשתי עבודות. פי' בקונטרס: כגון שחיטה והולכה. והא דקאמר בתר הכי: מדרישא בשתי עבודות סיפא נמי בשתי עבודות, פי' בקונטרס דהאי דהדר נקיט ליה – לאשמועינן צירוף בחצי זית, דלא אשמועינן ברישא. וזהו כ] דוחק. והיה נראה לפרש: שתי עבודות – כי ההוא דפ"ק דמעילה (דף ד.) דמפרש: סימן ראשון חוץ לזמנו וסימן שני חוץ למקומו, כעין שתי עבודות. ועבודה אחת – היינו סימן אחד. וצריך לומר לפירוש זה דאילפא ס"ל ישנה לשחיטה מתחילה ועד סוף, ומפגלין בחצי מתיר. כא] דאי אינה לשחיטה אלא לבסוף – כך (יש) לי מחשב בשני סימנים כמו מחשב בסימן אחד, כיון דאין המחשבה חלה אלא בגמר רוב שחיטה. אבל ר' יוחנן יכול לסבור כאביי, דאמר בלחצות מודה רבי מאיר דתרוייהו חיילי, דלא שייך ביה הקדמה. אבל כזית למחר כזית בחוץ – אפילו בסימן אחד פליגי, ושייך ביה הקדמה בתחילת סימן ובסופו. ולקמן דאמר אביי סימן ראשון וסימן שני – נקט דבר המסוייס, ואליבא דאילפא. אבל לר' יוחנן הוי מצי למנקט בסימן אחד בתחילתו ובסופו, דהא ר' יוחנן סבר ישנה לשחיטה מתחילה ועד סוף פ' "השוחט" (חולין כט:), כב] א"כ סובר הכא בסימן אחד נמי מחלוקת. ויכול לסבור ר' יוחנן נמי כרבא כג] בלחצות נמי פליגי, וכל שכן בסימן אחד דפליג, דשייך ביה הקדמה, דסבר רבי יוחנן ישנה לשחיטה מתחילה ועד סוף. הג"ה.
אמר

כ"א בה בעבירה

גי' ל"ק הוא והכי אוקימנא במס' ר"ה וכל"ל והד"ה

סנהדרין כב. ר"ה ו.

הגהות הב"ח

(א) גמ' ולא בקרבנך חטא הא אוקימנא לבן עזאי ההוא: (ב) רש"י ד"ה הא וכו' ר"ה הס"ד ואח"כ מ"ה מבקשין ממנו ממון: (ג) ד"ה לא יחשב קרי בי' לא יחשב:

[ב"מ לא. סנהדרין סג. שבועות ג: תמורה ג. מכות ד: טז. כ:]

[מנחות יב. לקמן סה.]

[ל"ע חכמים היינו ת"ק וכו' הקשה התוי"ט והגיה בכ"י ולפמ"ש תוספות מנחות יב ד"ה וחכמים וכו' ע"ש וכו' לייסב]

יעב"ץ מ"ז

מנחות יב. [לעיל כח.]

שיטה מקובצת

א] דגנך ובכורות בקרך: ב] חטא הא מוקמינן והיה בך כו' והשאר ל"ש: ג] מבקשים כו' כלומר מבקשים ממנו ואומר שאין לו שהכל משועבדים לכתובת אשתו והיא אומרת גם כן שאין לו. גליון בגמ' ישנה: ד] אומרים לא יחשב במחשבה: ה] אליעזר האי לא: ו] תיבת אחרות נמחק: ז] תיבת כזית נמחק: ח] או ששחט כו' פי' או או קתני אם עשה אחד מאלה ע"מ לאכול חוץ לזמנו וכל השלשה חוץ לזמנו לא קרב המתיר כמצותו וכן פי' רש"י ז"ל במנחות בפ"ק (דף י"ב ע"ב) על משנה הקומץ את המנחה לאכול שיריה בחוץ כו' שהיא דומה למשנה זאת. גליון: ט] תיבת ולזמנו נמחק: י] תיבת דמן נמחק: יא] זמן הביעור: יב] ואיחרו בא בעבירה: יג] ממנו ממון: יד] לא יַחשב קרי ביה לא יֵחשב: טו] דמתיר הדם הס"ד ומה"ד כמצותו שלא יהיה בו פסול אחר אבל אם יש: טז] למחר וכזית בחוץ: יז] וקבל והלך וזרק חוץ: יח] למימר לא יחשב הוא לשון חשיבות לשון הר"פ ז"ל והילכך אע"ג דבזבח מיירי לומר שיהא נפסל מ"מ מדכתיב המקריב הייתי אומר שאף הכהן נפסל אי לאו דמעטיה קרא בהדיא אבל בן עזאי כו': יט] מחשבה ולומר דבמחשבה אינו נפסל ממילא: כ] דוחק לשון מהר"פ דליפלוג בחדא וישמיענו דמצטרפין ולמה לי תרי בבא לכך נראה דמיירי בב' עבודות ממש ברישא ובסיפא מיירי בעבודה אחת כעין ב' עבודות כגון בין סימן לסימן ולא נהירא חדא דבמעילה מוקי לה בסימן ראשון לסימן שני וע"ק דקאמר אח"כ מיד מדרישא בשתי עבודות וקשה תרתי בשתי עבודות למה לי ואי לאשמועינן צירוף דחצי חצי מ"מ הו"ל למיפרך [לימא הך] רישא (ומימרא) [ולימרא] (דרב) [דרבי] יהודה פליג עליה לחודה לכך נ"ל דהכל בשחיטה איירי בעבודה אחת כעין שתי עבודות קאמר כדאמרינן במעילה בפ"ק בסימן ראשון לסימן שני וקסבר ישנה לשחיטה מתחילה ועד סוף ומפגלין בחצי מתיר וא"כ חלה שפיר הפיגול בסימן ראשו כמו בעבודה שלימה והשתא סיפא אשמועינן דכה"ג חשיב שתי עבודות [ע"כ] ונראה לפרש. ותיבת והיה נמחק: כא] מתיבת דאי כו' עד סוף הדבור מוקף בחצי לבנה: כב] השוחט וגם סובר ותיבות א"כ נמחק: כג] כרבא דאמר

אין, רישא בשתי עבודות, סיפא בין בעבודה אחת בין בשתי עבודות.§ תנן, אמר רבי יהודה: זה הכלל, אם מחשבת הזמן קדמה למחשבת המקום – פיגול, וחייבין עליו כרת. בשלמא לרבי יוחנן – היינו דקתני "זה הכלל", א] אלא לאילפא מאי "זה הכלל"? קשיא.§ *תנן התם: "הרי זו תמורת עולה תמורת שלמים" – הרי זו תמורת עולה, דברי רבי מאיר. אמר רבי יוסי: אאם לכך נתכוון תחילה, הואיל ואי אפשר להוציא שתי שמות כאחת – דבריו קיימין. ואם משאמר: "הרי זו תמורת עולה" (א) ב] ונמלך ואמר: "הרי זו תמורת שלמים" – הרי זו עולה. איבעיא להו: "הרי זו ג] תמורת עולה ושלמים", מהו? ד] "לחצות", מהו? אמר אביי: בהא ודאי מודה רבי מאיר. רבא אמר: עדיין היא מחלוקת. אמר ה] רבא לאביי: לדידך, דאמרת: בהא ודאי מודה רבי מאיר, ו] הרי שחיטה, דלכי לחצות דמי, ופליגי! אמר ליה: *מי סברת אינה לשחיטה אלא לבסוף? ישנה לשחיטה מתחילה ועד סוף, ומשנתינו – דאמר: "סימן ראשון חוץ לזמנו, סימן שני חוץ למקומו". הרי קמיצה, ז] דלכי לחצות דמי, *ופליגי! ח] התם נמי, ט] שהקטיר קומץ מנחה חוץ לזמנו, י] *קומץ לבונה חוץ למקומו. הרי קומץ דמנחת חוטא, דליכא לבונה בהדיה, ופליגי! לא פליגי. אמר רב *אשי: אם תימצי לומר פליגי – פליגי בפסיעות. רב שימי בר אשי מתני כדאביי, רב הונא בר נתן מתני כדרבא. כי אתא רב דימי אמר: רבי מאיר בשיטת רבי יהודה אמרה, דאמר: תפוס לשון ראשון. דתנן, אמר רבי יהודה: זה הכלל, אם מחשבת הזמן קדמה את מחשבת המקום – פיגול, וחייבין עליו כרת.

אמר

א) [נ"ל בתמורה בפרק כילד מערימין כי הוא פרק שם] ב) היום אמר אביי כו' הד"א נ"ק ג) נ"א וכי הוליא ד) נ"א הוי כאילו נ"ק ה) למקומו ומשני ישנה לשחיטה מתחלה ועד סוף ודאמר סימן ראשון כו' ודווקא סימן שלם דהוי דבר כו' והד"א כצ"ל נ"ק

רש"י

אין רישא בשתי עבודות. דהא מפרש בהדיא. סיפא איכא לאוקמא דבתרווייהו פליגי. היינו דקתני זה הכלל. לאיתויי עבודה אחת. תנן התם. במסכת תמורה. הרי זו תמורת עולה תמורת שלמים. שהעמיד בהמת חולין אצל שתים, אחת עולה ואחת שלמים, ואמר: "הרי זו תמורת עולה תמורת שלמים" – הרי זו תמורת עולה. תפוס לשון ראשון, ואין קדושה חלה על קדושה. הואיל ואי אפשר לקרות שתי שמות כאחת. והוצרך להקדיש זה אחר זה. דבריו קיימין. ותרעה יא] ותימכר, ויביא בדמי חציה עולה ובדמי חציה שלמים. וכן מפרש בתמורה. ה"ג איבעיא להו הרי זו תמורת עולה ושלמים מהו. מי אמרי': הא דפליג ר' מאיר ואמר תפוס לשון ראשון – משום דאמר יב] "תמורת" "תמורת" תרי זימני, והוה ליה כנמלך. אבל הכא דאמר "תמורת עולה ושלמים" – חד דיבורא הוא ותרווייהו חיילי, או דלמא: תפוס לשון ראשון לעולם, ופשטה קדושת עולה בכולה, ותו לא אתו שלמים וחיילי. לחצות מהו. את"ל יג] פשטה קדושת עולה בכולה, אמר: "הרי יד] (זו) בהמה זו לחצות לעולה ושלמים" מאי הא? טו] חד דיבורא הוא ואין זה חל בלא זה, או דלמא: כיון דפשטה בפלגא – פשטה בכולה, ולא אתו שלמים וחיילי. והרי שחיטה. דקתני מתני': לאכול כזית למחר כזית בחוץ. דכי לחצות דמי. דלאו מיהדר אימלוכי, טז] שהרי כמה זיתים יש בה וחד דיבורא הוא, ופליגי, וקאמר ר' יהודה: תפוס לשון ראשון! ור' מאיר דתמורה בשיטת רבי יהודה דמתניתין קאי, דאמרינן בשמעתין: ר"מ בשיטת רבי יהודה אמרה. אמר ליה מי סברת אינה לשחיטה אלא לבסוף. יז] דלהוי הך תרתי מחשבות (ג) בסוף שחיטה, יח] וחד דיבורא הוא, ואפי' הכי נימא ר' יהודה: תפוס לשון ראשון. ישנה לשחיטה מתחילה ועד סוף. וכי היכי דמהניא מחשבה בסוף – יט] מהניא בתחילתה. ומתוקמא מתני' כגון דאמר: כ] שחיטת סימן ראשון חוץ לזמנו, ובשחיטת סימן שני חוץ למקומו. ואית ליה לרבי יהודה מפגלים בחצי מתיר, דהיינו חד סימן, ותרי דבורי נינהו, ואיפגל ליה מדבורא קדמאה. אבל לחצות, דחד דבור הוא – מודי. כא] (ומהכא שמעינן דרבא אליבא דר"מ סבירא ליה אינה לשחיטה אלא בסוף, מדקאמר עדיין היא מחלוקת *מתני'. והיינו דאמר ב"תמיד נשחט" (פסחים דף סג.): נימא קסברי אחרים אין לשחיטה אלא לבסוף, וכדרבא, דאמר רבא: עדיין היא מחלוקת – (ג) מתני' דתמורת עולה ושלמים כלחצות. ד"אחרים" היינו רבי מאיר, ורבא מוקי דלרבי מאיר אינה לשחיטה אלא לבסוף). הרי קמיצה. דפליגי רבי יהודה ורבנן בה בפרק קמא דמנחות (דף יב.) כי מחשב לאכול כזית למחר כזית בחוץ כו'. דכי לחצות דמי. דחד דיבורא הוא, וזיתים הרבה יש, ולאו מיהדר אימלוכי הוא. והכא ליכא לפלוגי בתרי דבורי כדפלגא בשחיטה בב' סימנין. דאמר קומץ כב] מנחה כו'. שהמנחה יש לה שני מתירין, הקומץ והלבונה. וכי פליגי רבי יהודה ורבנן – לאו בקמיצה פליגי, דאין קמיצה בלבונה, אלא בהקטרה פליגי, כג] שהיא עבודה בכל אחת ואחת. וכגון שהקטיר קומץ כד] מנחה על מנת לאכול כזית למחר, *וקומץ כה] לבונה על מנת לאכול כזית בחוץ, ואית ליה לרבי יהודה מפגלין בחצי מתיר, וכיון כו] דהיינו תרי דבורי נינהו – מקמא איפגלא לה. אבל בקמיצה, דחד מתיר הוא – לא פליג רבי יהודה. מנחת חוטא. מטמא מקדש או שמיעת הקול – מביא מנחה בדלי דלות, דכתיב: "לא יתן עליה לבונה" (ויקרא ה). פליגי בפסיעות. ובמחשבת הולכה, דאמר בפסיעה ראשונה חוץ לזמנו, ובפסיעה שניה אמר חוץ למקומו, דהוו להו תרי דבורי. מתני כדאביי. תני מתנייתא כדאביי, דב"לחצות" מודי רבי מאיר. מתני כדרבא. תני מתנייתא כדרבא, דבלחצות נמי פליג רבי מאיר.

כי

תוספות

אמר רבי יוסי אם לכך נתכוון מתחילה. פרק "מרובה" (ב"ק דף עג:) אמרינן: תרי תוך כדי דיבור הוו, חד כדי שאילת רב לתלמיד דזוטר, וחד כדי שאילת תלמיד לרב דנפיש. ותוך כדי דיבור קטן מודה רבי יוסי דמועיל דיבורו, והכי קאמר: אם אמר "תמורת שלמים" בתוך כדי דיבור קטן של "תמורת עולה", דהשתא דומה כז] דנתכוון מתחילה לכך, ואפי' עומד ולוח שלא נתכוון, הואיל ואי אפשר להוציא שתי שמות כאחת – דבריו קיימין. ונמלך קרי ליה תוך כדי דיבור גדול כשאמרו לאחר כדי דיבור קטן, שדומה לנמלך. ואפי' אומר שנתכוון מתחלה לשניהם – לא אמר כלום. דבריו קיימים. וא"ת: והא אמרינן בפ"ב דקדושין (דף נ:) ובעירובין פרק "מי שהוליאוהו" (דף נ.) כח] ובפ' "נערה המאורסה" (נדרים סט:): כל שאינו בזה אחר זה – כט] בבת אחת אינו! וי"ל: דכיון *דמשכחת בזה אחר זה, כגון דאמר "חליה לדמי עולה וחליה לדמי שלמים", ואפילו בקדושת הגוף משכחת לה, כגון בבהמה של שני שותפין. ועוד: דכל שאינו בזה אחר זה בבת אחת אינו – מיירי בדבר שאי אתה יכול לקיים את שניהם, שסותרים זה את זה, כגון מקדש אשה ובתה, דהי מינייהו מפקת. וכן "קיים ליכי ומופר ליכי" דנדרים, וכן ארבע אמות דעירובין (דף מט:). אבל הכא מקיימי תרווייהו וכן בפרק "השולח" בגיטין (דף מב.): הכותב כל נכסיו לשני עבדיו – קנו ומשחררין זה את זה, ולא אמרינן כל שאינו בזה אחר זה אפי' בבת אחת אינו, משום דהתם בזה אחר זה א"א לקיים את שניהם, דבזה אחר זה קמא קני נפשיה וקני חבריה, ובתרא לא קני כלל. אבל בבת אחת – אפשר לקיים את שניהם, ואמרי' קנו ומשחררין זה את זה. והא דאמרינן בפ"ק דקדושין (דף ז:): "חלייך בחלי פרוטה וחלייך בחלי פרוטה" דאינה מקודשת, וקמבעיא ליה: "שני חלייך בפרוטה" מהו – לא שייך למימר: תפשוט מדרבה דאמר כל שאינו בזה אחר זה אפי' בבת אחת אינו. דכל שאינו בזה אחר זה – מיירי בדבר שאין השני יכול לחול מחמת שחל הראשון תחלה, כגון שתי אחיות ושתי תרומות ושתי מעשרות, הלכך בבת אחת אינו, משום דהי מינייהו ל] מפקת. אבל גבי קדושין, בזה אחר זה אינו לא זה ולא זה, אבל בבת אחת תפסי תרווייהו. והא דאמר בסוף פ"ק דמנחות (דף יא.): היכי דמי ריבה שמנה – כגון שהפריש לה שני לוגין, ומשמע קלת מתוך הסוגיא שיש בהן קדושת הגוף. וגבי חסר לבונתה לא] דדייק התם: הא יתר כשרה, [והתניא: יתר פסולה]. ומפרשי שם: כגון שהפריש לה שני קמלים, ואכשרה קאי לב] כדפרישית התם. והשתא היכי קדשי? הא אמרי' כל שאינו בזה אחר זה בבת אחת אינו! ונראה לפרש: כגון דאמר "יקדש קומץ אחד מתוך שני קמלים", כדאמר בפרק "התודה" (שם עח:) ובפ"ב דקדושין (דף נא.) גבי תודה ששחטה על שמונים חלות: הכל מודים היכא דאמר "ליקדשו מ' מתוך שמונים" דקדשי. **לחצות** מהו. פי' בקונט': דאמר "הרי בהמה זו לחלותה לעולה לג] ושלמים" ואין זה דומה לחליה עולה וחליה שלמים דפליגי בהדיא לד] א) בתמורה (דף כו.) ובפרק "כילד מערימין" (דף נט). אבל בפ' "תמיד נשחט" (פסחים סג.) לא דקדק בקונטרס, שהביא הך דשמעתין ופי': לחלות – כגון דאמר "חליה תמורת עולה וחליה תמורת שלמים". ור"ח מפרש: לחלות – כגון דאמר "לחלי היום תיהוי עולה ושלמים". א"נ: "עולה ושלמים תהוי לחלי ב) היום". **אמר** אביי בהא ודאי מודה ר"מ. ופריך: והרי שחיטה דכי לחלות דמי, דכיון דאינה לשחיטה אלא לבסוף – לה] ג) היכי הוליא שני הדיבורים קודם שיהא סוף שחיטה? ד) והוי כאילו אמר לו] "לבסוף שחיטה יהא כזית חוץ לזמנו וכזית חוץ ה) למקומו" לז]. [**סימן** ראשון חוץ לזמנו.] ודווקא סימן אחד, דהוי דבר המסויים, ומפגלין בחלי מתיר. אבל אם אמר: "משהו ראשון חוץ לזמנו ומשהו שני חוץ למקומו" – לא הוי פיגול אע"ג דמפגלין בחלי מתיר, כיון דלא הוי דבר המסויים, ולא דמי לפסיעות. וא"ת: דמשמע הכא דרבא סבירא ליה אינה לשחיטה אלא לבסוף, והיינו כריש לקיש דפרק שני דחולין (דף כט:). ושמעינן ליה לרבא בפרק "החולץ" (יבמות לו.) דבכולי התלמוד הלכתא כרבי יוחנן לגבי ר"ל בר מתלת! ויש לומר: דשאני לח] הכא, מדקאמר לה ר"ל משמיה דלוי סבא. ויש לתמוה: רבא דפריך ליה לאביי, וס"ד דס"ל אינה לשחיטה אלא לבסוף – תיקשי ליה לט] מתני' דהקדים מולים לערלים – כשר, ערלים למולים – פסול, הרי בסוף שחיטה חל דיבור ראשון ולא שני, דאי הוו חיילי תרווייהו – הא קיימא לן דמקלת ערלה לא פסלה. **והרי** קמיצה דכי לחצות דמי ופליגי. תימה: דלא פריך ממליקה דחטאת העוף דפליגי. מ] דחטאת העוף הכשירו בסימן אחד וליכא שני מתירין! ויש לומר: דאיכא שתי מתירין, כגון מפרקת וסימן אחד.

עין משפט נר מצוה

קכד א מיי' פ"ב מהל' תמורה הלכה ד:

נ"א דמשכחת לתלאין כגון דאמר כו' נ"ק וכ"ה הגירסא בהרא"ש דמס' נדרים דף סט ע"ב ע"ש

מסורת הש"ס

ב"ק עג: תמורה כה: נדרים סט:

פסחים סג. חולין כט: וש"נ

מנחות יב.

נ"א קורט

נ"א אסי

נ"א וקורט

הגהות הב"ח

(א) גמ' ואם משאמר הרי זו תמורת עולה ונמלך: (ב) רש"י ד"ה א"ל מי וכו' דלהוי הך תרתי מחשבות כל חד בסוף שחיטה וחד: (ג) ד"ה ישנה וכו' במתניתין דתמורה:

גליון

גי' הגי"ק בתמורת עולה ושלמים כלחצות מתמני' כו' עדיין הוא מחלוקת ואחרים היינו כו' וכו"ה בכס"י

שיטה מקובצת

ברגע אחד ולא שייך כאן טעמא דתפוס לשון ראשון או דלמא מ"מ איכא למימר שדעתו היה שיחולו הקדושה כדרך סדר דבורו וע"כ שייך כמו כן תפוס לשון ראשון. מהר"פ ז"ל: ה] אמר ליה רבא: ו] עיין בהשמטות בסוף המסכת: ז] קמיצה דכי: ח] התם נמי כגון דאמר קומץ דמנחה כו'. פ"ה בשעה שהקטיר קומץ [מנחה ע"מ לאכול כזית למחר וקומץ] הלבונה אמר חוץ למקומו ולא מיירי בקמיצה כי אם בהקטרה דיש שני מתירין קומץ ולבונה ולא מצי לשנויי גבי מנחת חוטא כגון שהקטיר חצי קומץ חוץ לזמנו וחצי קומץ חוץ למקומו דכיון דלא הוי מסויים לא מהני אפילו למ"ד מפגלין בחצי מתיר וא"ת מ"ש מחטאת העוף (משום) דאין בו אלא סימן אחד אמרינן דשייך ביה תפוס לשון ראשון למ"ד מפגלין בחצי מתיר וי"ל דכיון (דרוב בני אדם חולקין) [דחולקין] עמו המפרקת הוי ליה כשני סימנים. מהר"פ ז"ל: ט] תיבת שהקטיר נמחק: י] וקומץ דלבונה: יא] ותרעה עד שיסתאב ותימכר: יב] תמורה תמורה תרי: יג] את"ל בתמורת עולה ושלמים פשטה: יד] הרי בהמה זו לחצותה לעולה ולשלמים: טו] האי ודאי חד: טז] אימלוכי הוא שהרי: יז] דניהוי הנך תרתי: יח] שחיטה יחד וחד: יט] בסוף שחיטה מהניא: כ] דאמר בשחיטת סימן: כא] מתיבת ומהכא עד תיבות הרי קמיצה נמחק: כב] קומץ דמנחה: כג] שהיא. ס"א שנוהגת בשניהם וכגון שהקטיר: כד] קומץ המנחה: כה] וקומץ הלבונה: כו] דהני תרי: כז] דומה לנתכוון: כח] ובנדרים פ' נערה: כט] זה אפילו בב"א אינו וי"ל דהכא משכחת. ותיבת דכיון ואות ד' נמחק: ל] מינייהו מייתת והי מינייהו מפקת: לא] לבונתה נמי דייק התם: לב] קאי כדמוכח התם ותיבת כדפרישית נמחק: לג] לעולה ולשלמים: לד] בתמורה בפרק כיצד מערימים דהתם שמא מתחלה לא היה דעתו אלא לעולה אבל הכא כיון דאמר בלשון (זה) לחצות ודאי לתרווייהו איכוין מיהו אם כן צריך להגיה הספרים לחצותה ובכל הספרים גרסינן לחצות ור"ח כו'. לשון הר"פ ז"ל: לה] לבסוף הרי הוציא תיבת היכי נמחק: לו] אמר לסוף אות ב' נמחק: לז] למקומו דדמי לחצות היום ומסיק ישנה לשחיטה מתחלה ועד סוף ומיירי דאמר שתהא סימן ראשון כו' והד"א: לח] התם תיבת הבא נמחק: לט] ליה דמתני' בפרק תמיד נשחט דהקדים: מ] דפליגי וחטאת כו' אות ד' נמחק:

והא

שיטה מקובצת

א] אלא לאילפא מאי זה הכלל. דליכא למימר דנקיט ליה משום עבודה כעין שתי עבודות כיון דאינו מראה טעם חדש אבל לר"י ניחא דמראה לנו טעם חדש דאמרי' תפוס לשון ראשון ובעבודה אחת נמי וא"כ הכלל דקאמר ר"י בכל ענין הוא אמת דהיכא דמחשבת הזמן קדמה הוי פיגול משום דתפוס לשון ראשון אבל לאילפא לא הוי כלל בכל ענין דהיכי דהוי בעבודה אחת הוי עירוב מחשבות אפילו קדמה מחשבת הזמן וא"כ מאי זה הכלל: ב] נמלך ואמר: ג] ע' בהשמטות בסוף המסכת: ד] לחצות מהו פי' הקונטרס כו' א) עד לכך פי' ר"ח דה"ק לחצות היום תהיה בהמה זו חציה תמורת עולה וחציה תמורת שלמים מהו. פי' מי אמרינן דדוקא כי אמר תמורת עולה ושלמים דלא היה זמן לחלות הקדושה א"כ דעתו שיחול מיד הקדושה מיד שהוציא הדבור וא"כ כיון שהקדיש עולה ושלמים מיד פשטה עליה [קדושת עולה] בכולה אבל כי אמר לחצות היום (יחצו) [יחולו] שניהם אפי' כי אמר תמורה ב' פעמים מ"מ אין דעתו שתחול הקדושה [אלא] עד אותה שעה ממש וא"כ אין לאחת הקדמה לחברתה כלל והוא בזמן שחלות הקדושה עליה כבר יצא הדבור מפיו גם דבור שני דשלמים וא"כ תרווייהו חיילי

א) כוונתו לציין על דברי התוספות בד"ה לחצות.

אמר ליה אביי: והא א] רבה בר בר חנה א"ר יוחנן: כי מגעת להו, ב] רבי מאיר ורבי יוסי בהדי הדדי לא פליגי! ולא פליגי? והא מיפלג פליגי! א"ל: פליגי במאי דפליגי, ולא פליגי במאי דלא פליגי. דאמר *רבי יצחק בר יוסף א"ר יוחנן: הכל מודים היכא דאמר "תחול זו ואחר כך (אמר) תחול זו" — דברי הכל לא חיילא; "לא תחול זו אלא א"כ חלה זו" — דברי הכל חיילא; כי פליגי — דאמר: "תמורת עולה תמורת שלמים", רבי מאיר סבר: ג] מדהוה ליה למימר "תמורת עולה ושלמים", ואמר: "תמורת עולה תמורת שלמים" — שמע מינה מיהדר קא הדר ביה. ד] ור' יוסי: אי אמר "תמורת עולה ושלמים", הוה אמינא: פלגא תמורת עולה ופלגא תמורת שלמים — להכי אמר "תמורת עולה תמורת שלמים", למימרא דכולה עולה וכולה שלמים הויא. אמר ליה: הוא אמר לא פליגי, ואנא אמינא פליגי. אמר עולא ואיתימא רב אושעיא: *אפשר ידעין חברין בבלאה "כזית" "כזית" תנן, או "כזית וכזית" תנן? "כזית" "כזית" תנן, אבל "כזית וכזית" — דברי הכל עירוב מחשבות הוי. או דלמא: "כזית וכזית" תנן, דלרבי יהודה פרטא הוי, וכל שכן "כזית כזית"? תא שמע, דבעא מיניה לוי מרבי: חישב ה] לאכול כזית למחר בחוץ, מהו? א"ל: *זו שאלה! עירוב מחשבות הוי. אמר לפניו רבי שמעון ברבי: לא משנתינו היא? לאכול כזית בחוץ כזית למחר, כזית למחר כזית בחוץ, כחצי זית בחוץ כחצי זית למחר, כחצי זית למחר כחצי זית בחוץ — פסול ואין בו כרת; הא אידך — עירוב מחשבות הוי! א"ל: הוא ו] שאל בי דבר חכמה, ואת אמרת משנתינו. לדידך דאתניתך תרתי — לא קשיא לך. לדידיה דלא אתניתיה אלא חדא, ושמעינהו לרבנן דקא גרסי תרתי, ז] וסבר: דידי דווקא, ודידהו עירוב מחשבות הוי. או דלמא דידהו דווקא, ולדידי שיורי שייר לי, ומדשייר לי לדידי הא — שייר להו לדידהו נמי בהך. והי אתנייה? אילימא "כזית ח] וכזית" אתנייה — האי לאו שיורא הוא! אלא "כזית כזית" אתנייה. ותיבעי ליה "כזית וכזית"? סבר: *איבעי מיניה חדא דשמענא תרתי. דאי בעינא "כזית וכזית", הא ניחא אי אמר לי כללא — כ"ש "כזית למחר בחוץ". אלא אי אמר לי פרטא — אכתי "כזית למחר בחוץ" קא מיבעיא לי. אי הכי, השתא נמי, התינח אי אמר ליה "כזית למחר בחוץ" פרטא — כ"ש "כזית וכזית". אלא אי א"ל כללא — אכתי "כזית וכזית" מיבעי ליה! ט] אם כן מרתח רתח:

השתא

רש"י

כי מגעת להו. אם תרצה לקרב את דבריהם — קרובים הם להיות שוים, דתרווייהו לית להו תפוס לשון ראשון, כדמפרש לקמיה. והלכך, אפילו רבי מאיר דתמורה בשחיטה לא סבר לה כר' יהודה. ול"פ. בתמיה. והא שמעי' להו דפליגי ואמר ליה פליגי במאי דפליגי. כדמפרש ואזיל. ול"פ במאי דלא פליגי. והאי "ל"פ" דקאמר הכי קאמר: ל"פ בתפוס לשון ראשון, י] אלא כדעתיה דגברא, בהוכחת דיבורו על מחשבתו. אבל תרווייהו אית להו דבתר כוונתו אזלינן. הכל מודים היכא דאמר תחול תמורת עולה ואח"כ תחול תמורת שלמים דברי הכל לא חיילא. דאין קדושה חלה על (א) קדושה. חיילא. הואיל ונתכוון לכך. ותרעה, ויהא דמי חציה עולה ודמי חציה שלמים. מיהדר קהדר ביה. ולחזור אי אפשר יא]. ורבי יוסי. אמר לך: האי גברא לא מיהדר קהדר, אלא לכך נתכוון. וסבר: אי אמינא יב] (תורת) "תמורת עולה ושלמים" — משתמע פלגא עולה פלגא שלמים, וקדושה ואינה קריבה, דאי אפשר להקריב לחצאין. אימא "תמורת עולה תמורת שלמים" כי היכי דתפשוט קדושת עולה בכולה וקדושת שלמים בכולה. וטעי, דסבר השתא קריבה. הלכך לתרווייהו איכוין, ודבריו קיימין, ותימכר. ה"ג: להכי אמר תמורת עולה תמורת שלמים למימרא דכולה עולה כולה שלמים. וכ"ך קבלת"י בתמור"ה. שמעינן מיהא מדרבה בר בר חנה, דהיכא דאמר "תמורת עולה ושלמים" מודה רבי מאיר, אלמא לאו כרבי יהודה סבירא ליה. דמתני' להא דמיא, דלכך נתכוון תחלה, והא דאמר "כזית" "כזית" תרי זימני — משום דבעא למיחשב בשני זיתים, ועל כרחך לאו מיהדר הוא, דכמה זתים יש בה. אמר ליה. רב דימי לאביי: ומדרבה בר בר חנה מותבת לי? איהו אמר לא פליגי, ואנא אמינא פליגי. אף באומר "תמורת עולה ושלמים" שנתכוון לשניהם — אית ליה לרבי מאיר תפוס לשון ראשון כר' יהודה. כזית כזית תנן. דלרבי יהודה הוי פרטא, וכשתי מחשבות נינהו ואפילו בעבודה אחת, ותפוס לשון ראשון. אבל "כזית וכזית" חד דבורא הוא — עירוב מחשבות, ואינו פגול. ת"ש. ד"כזית וכזית" תנן, וכ"ש "כזית כזית". דבעא מיניה לוי מרבי כזית למחר בחוץ. חישב על זית יג] לאכלו למחר חוץ למקומו, לר' יהודה מהו? מי אמרי': בהא יד] מודי רבי יהודה, (ב) ואחדא מחשבה מעורבת היא, דאההוא גופיה דקחשיב לאכול למחר טו] חשיב בחוץ, וכחדא אכילה או דלמא תפוס לשון ראשון לעולם. זו שאילה. בניחותא, שאילה גדולה שאלת. עירוב מחשבות הוי. אפי' לר' יהודה. לא משנתינו היא זו. ואמאי קלסת ליה? הא מתניתין היא דעירוב מחשבות הוי, מדנקט פלוגתייהו ב"כזית למחר כזית בחוץ" דהוי שתי אכילות — בהא הוא דפליג ר' יהודה. הא "כזית למחר בחוץ", דבחדא אכילה טז] קחשיב לאוכלו למחר חוץ למקומו — מודי! הוא שאלני דבר חכמה. לפוס מאי דאתנייה. לדידך יז] (ג) הוא דאתניתך במתניתין תרתי. לך יח] שניתים במחלוקתם, דבין "בכזית כזית" בין "בכזית וכזית" פליגי. לא קשיא לך. דאמרת: מדתנינן הך תרתי ולא תנן הך, שמע מינה: בהא מודי רבי יהודה. לדידיה דלא אתניתיה אלא חדא. ללוי, שלא שניתי לו במחלוקתם אלא אחת מהם, ולקמן מפרש ד"כזית כזית" אתנייה. יט] ושמעינהו להו לרבנן. דבי מדרשא, שאר תלמידיי דקא (ד) גרסינן תרתי, כמו ששניתי לך. ולא ידע לוי אם מעצמם הוסיפוה או אני שניתיה להם, ומשום הכי מספקא ליה הך שלישי, דסבר: הי דווקא, כ] משנתו או משנתיהם? דידי דווקא. ד"בכזית כזית" הוא דפליגי, ודידהו ד"כזית וכזית" — עירוב מחשבות הוי. ולא קבלוה מרבי, אלא הם טעו והוסיפוה. וכ"ש "כזית למחר בחוץ" הוי עירוב מחשבות. או דלמא דידהו דווקא, ומפיו שמעוה, ולדידי שיורי שייר לי ולא שנאה, ולעולם אף בה נחלקו, ואע"פ שלא היה לי ללומדה כא] מגד ששנה לי. וכי היכי דשייר לי. הך ד"כזית וכזית" שייר להו נמי הך ד"כזית למחר בחוץ" ולא שנאה להם, ולעולם אף בה נחלקו. הילכך דבר חכמה שאל. והי אתנייה. דלא הוה ליה למילף הך מיניה. אילימא כזית וכזית אתנייה. ולרבי יהודה פרטא הוי — האי לאו שיורא הוא, דממילא מצי למילף דכל שכן "כזית כזית". וכיון דלא שייר ליה מידי, הוי ליה למשמע דאי בהא ד"כזית למחר בחוץ" נמי איפלוג הוה מתני לה ניהליה, ודווקא אתנייה כב] כדהנך הוא דפליגי, אבל בהא מודה רבי יהודה. אלא כזית כזית אתנייה. דלא הוה ליה למילף מינה ההיא ד"כזית *כזית", וכי שמעינהו לרבנן דתנו לה — איסתפק ליה אי אתנינהו רבי לדידהו ולדידיה שיירה, אי לדידיה דווקא אתנייה ואינהו כג] הא דאוסיפו. ותיבעי ליה כזית וכזית. הואיל ומספקא ליה אי רבי אתנינהו כד] לה אי לא. ה"ג: הניחא אי אמר לי כללא כל שכן כזית למחר בחוץ, אלא כה] אמר לי פרטא אכתי כזית למחר בחוץ תיבעי לי. אי הכי השתא נמי הניחא אי א"ל כזית למחר בחוץ פרטא כל שכן כזית וכזית, אלא אי א"ל כללא אכתי כזית וכזית מיבעיא ליה. א"כ מירתח רתח, השתא כזית וכזית כללא כזית למחר בחוץ מיבעיא. א"כ מירתח קא רתח. כלומר, הכי סבר לוי: איבעי מיניה הך דאישמע מיניה תרתי, דאי אמר לי בה פרטא — כ"ש "כזית וכזית" דתרי אכילות נינהו ואיכא לפלוגינהו בתרי דיבורי. ואי אמר לי כללא, בניחותא בלא רתיחה — איִשמע מיניה דהך הוא דהוי כללא, אבל "כזית וכזית" — פרטא, וכדאתנינהו לרבנן. דאם סבירא ליה ב"כזית וכזית" נמי כללא — מירתח רתח, ומהדר לי בריתחא מאי

תוספות

אמר ליה אביי והאמר רבה בר בר חנה כו'. כו] לתרווייהו לית להו תפוס לשון ראשון, כדמפרש לקמן. והלכך, רבי מאיר דתמורה בשחיטה לא כרבי יהודה סבירא ליה, כז] דשחיטה הויא כמו לאכות, דאמר אביי דמודה רבי מאיר, ולא כרבי יהודה. ותימה: דמאי מקשי ליה רבא לאביי לעיל: והרי שחיטה דכי לאכות דמי ופליגי? הלא ר' יהודה ודאי הוא דאית ליה תפוס לשון ראשון, אבל רבי מאיר — לא, דלית ליה לאביי רבי מאיר בשיטת רבי יהודה, אלא מדאמר *תמורה כו' — שמע מינה מהדר קהדר ביה, ואפילו אמר מתחלה נתכוונתי לומר שניהם — לא מהימנינן ליה!

כזית כזית תנן אבל כזית וכזית דברי הכל עירוב מחשבות הוי. מכאן הגי"ה רבינו תם הספרים, דגרסינן בשבועות בסוף "שבועת הפקדון" (דף לח.) ד"לא לך לא לך" — אינו חייב אלא אחת, דכללא הוי. ואילו "לא לך ולא לך" — חייב על כל אחת ואחת, דהוי פרטא. והכא משמע איפכא, דטפי הוי עירוב מחשבות "כזית וכזית" מ"כזית כזית". וכן משמע התם בירושלמי, דמדמי שאילת שלום בגט ל"לא לך ולא לך" וגבי שאילת שלום אמרינן בגיטין (דף פו.): "שאילו" — פסול, "ושאילו" — כשר, ברוך. *קשה לי: מ"למחר בחוץ" דאמר רבי מודה רבי יהודה בעירוב מחשבות, והיינו כמו לאכות. ולעיל דאמר רבא כח] דלאכות פליגי, ומייתי ראיה לאביי משחיטה דרבי יהודה. ומאי ראיה? הא רבי יהודה מודה! ועוד: דסבר רבא אינה לשחיטה אלא לבסוף, וכיון דאין המחשבה חלה עד משהו אחרון — כך שוה "כזית למחר כזית בחוץ" כמו "כזית למחר כט] וכזית בחוץ", ופליגי לרבא. ועוד: "תמורת עולה ושלמים" דפליגי לרבא. ברו"ך. א"כ מרתח רתח. שלא היה לו להניח "כזית וכזית" ולשאול מ"כזית למחר בחוץ", דמשמע דמדשבקיה — דפשיטא ליה דפרטא הוא.

ויקן

נ"א תמורת עולה תמורת שלמים כו' הס"ד ואח"כ מה"ד ש"מ

[נ"א מתחיל הדיבור עירוב מחשבות הוי קשה לי כו'] ל"ק

[תמורה כו. ע"ש]

[פסחים פט: גיטין עח: חולין מה.]

שבועות לח. קדושין מז.

[לקמן לב: ב"ק קטז.]

(שבועות לג קדושין מז) [חולין נב.]

נ"ל וכזית נ"ק

שיטה מקובצת

א] והא אמר רבה כו': ב] להו לר"מ: ג] מדהוה ליה למימר כו'. ואע"ג דתוך כדי דבור יכול לחזור ודאי אי הוי חזר ביה רשאי אבל הכא דנמלך [והוי] כמו דאמר תחול זו ואח"כ תחול זו ולא חיילא. מהר"פ: ד] עיין בהשמטות בסוף המסכת: ה] לאכול כזית למחר בחוץ מהו א"ל [זו שאילה] עירוב מחשבות הוי תימה דכיון (דכזית) [דבחר כזית] קא מחשב הויא ליה כתמורת עולה וכתמורת שלמים דאמרי' לעיל תפוס לשון ראשון ובחדא מילתא קא מחשב וי"ל דלא דמי דהתם אי אפשר לקיים שניהם דאין קדושה חלה על קדושה והלכך אמרינן תפוס לשון ראשון אבל למחר בחוץ בידו לעשות איסור זה וכיון דיכול לעשות כן תפסה המחשבה בשניהם והוי עירוב מחשבה. כפ"ה מהר"פ: ו] הוא שאלני דבר ותיבת בי נמחק: ז] תרתי מספקא ליה ואמר דידי ותיבת וסבר נמחק: ח] וכזית אתנייה דלרבי יהודה פרטי הוי כ"ש כזית כזית אלא כו' ותיבות האי לאו שיורא הוא ל"ש: ט] אם כן מרתח קרתח כו'. וקשה דמהכא משמע דשיך ריתחא אף כשדעת השואל להחמיר שהיה סבור דכזית וכזית הוי פיגול והוי פרטא וכרת [וקרתח] להורות לו שהוא כללא וליכא חיוב כרת ובפרק אלו טרפות גבי נעקרה הצלע וחוליא פ"ה דלא שייך ריתחא אלא כשטעה השואל להקל בהוראה א) ועוד קשה דלבעי מיניה כזית וכזית ואי אמר ליה פרטא ש"מ דכזית למחר בחוץ כללא דאי הוי פרטא א"כ מירתח קא רתח השתא כזית למחר בחוץ פרטא כזית וכזית מבעיא וי"ל דהכא לאו איסור והיתר הוא דלהוי שייך ריתחא להוציא השואל מטעותו אלא קרתח לפי שמעצמו היה לו להבון מדאתנייה במתניתין כזית כזית דהוי פרטא משמע כזית וכזית הוי כללא מדלא אתנייה נמי בהדי כזית וכזית אבל אי בעי מיניה כזית וכזית ואי"ל פרטא אכתי כזית למחר בחוץ מספקא דשמא הוי כללא ב) כי למה יכעוס (עמו) [עליו] אם בשביל שלא שנה לו במשנה כזית למחר בחוץ מש"ה משמע דהוי כללא דדוקא כזית כזית הוי פרטא הא כזית וכזית הוי כללא ועוד הרי אפילו כזית וכזית לא שנה לו שהוא פרטא וכן משמע מתוך פ"ה ולפי מה שפי' הר"ר יהודה מקורביל שם ניחא דמרתח קרתח היכא שמבין מתוך השואל שאין דעתו לשאול לו השאילה שהלכך דרך השואלים לשאול תחלה כזית וכזית ואח"כ כזית למחר בחוץ אבל אי הוי שואל מתחלה מכזית למחר בחוץ או יבין שאין בדעתו לשאול כלל מכזית וכזית וטועה הוא בכזית וכזית ולכך אינה שואלה שאם היה דעתו לשאלה שהיה מסופק ממנה היה שואל תחלה ממנה וקא רתח להוציאו מטעותו. מהר"פ: י] ראשון דכולהו לית להו תפוס לשון ראשון אלא: יא] אי אפשר. גליון משום דאין מוציא דבריו לבטלה הלכך הויא תמורה ולא שלא יוכל לחזור מדבורו הראשון דקא מהדר הדר ביה בתוך כדי דבור אלא כלומר שהוא כנמלך וכמ"ד תחול זו ואח"כ תחול זו. ע"כ: יב] תיבת תורת נמחק: יג] זית אחד לאכלו: יד] מודה ר' יהודה: טו] למחר חישב בחוץ: טז] אכילה היא קחשיב דחשב לאוכלו: יז] לדידך דאתנייתך ותיבת הוא נמחק: יח] לך ששניתי: יט] ושמעינהו לוי לרבנן ותיבת להו נמחק: כ] דוקא משנתי או משנתם הס"ד מזו ששנה ותיבת מצד נמחק: כב] אתנייה דבהנך: כג] ואינהו הוא: כד] אתנינהו ליה: כה] אלא אי אמר: כו] כו'. משמע דתרווייהו לית: כז] מתיבת דשחיטה כו' עד תיבת ותימה דמאי כו' בס"א אינו: כח] רבא דלאכות: כט] תיבת וכזית ל"ש ונמחק:

הגהות הב"ח

(א) רש"י ד"ה הכל וכו' קדושה הס"ד ואח"כ מ"ה ד"ה חיילא: (ב) ד"ה דבעא מיניה וכו' דאחדא מחשבה: (ג) ד"ה לדידך דאתניתך כצ"ל ותיבת הוא נמחק: (ד) ד"ה ושמעינהו וכו' דקא גרסי תרתי:

א) לכאורה נראה דהכא ג"כ קילא לענין חטאת אם אכל בשוגג דאם אינו חייב כרת הוי חולין בעזרה. ב) נראה דצ"ל דשמא הוי ג"כ פרטא כי למה יכעוס עליו דשמא בשבילו כו' משמע ליה דהוי.

הַשְׁתָּא "כְּזַיִת וּכְזַיִת" כְּלָלָא, "כְּזַיִת לְמָחָר בַּחוּץ" מִיבַּעְיָא? א] (לִישָּׁנָא אַחֲרִינָא: "כְּזַיִת לְמָחָר בַּחוּץ" פְּרָטָא, "כְּזַיִת ב] כְּזַיִת" מִיבַּעְיָא?) אִיתְּמַר: חֲצִי זַיִת חוּץ לִזְמַנּוֹ חֲצִי זַיִת חוּץ לִמְקוֹמוֹ וַחֲצִי זַיִת חוּץ לִזְמַנּוֹ — אָמַר רָבָא: א"וַיִּקַץ כְּיָשֵׁן" הַפִּיגּוּל, וְרַב הַמְנוּנָא אָמַר: עֵירוּב מַחֲשָׁבוֹת הָוֵי. אָמַר רָבָא: מְנָא אָמִינָא לָהּ? דִּתְנַן: *בכְּבֵיצָה אוֹכֶל רִאשׁוֹן וּכְבֵיצָה אוֹכֶל שֵׁנִי שֶׁבְּלָלָן זֶה בָּזֶה — רִאשׁוֹן. חִלְּקָן — זֶה שֵׁנִי וְזֶה שֵׁנִי; הָא חָזַר וְעֵירְבָן — רִאשׁוֹן הָוֵי, מִמַּאי? מִדְּקָתָנֵי סֵיפָא: *גנָפַל זֶה ג] בְּעַצְמוֹ וְזֶה בְּעַצְמוֹ עַל כִּכַּר שֶׁל תְּרוּמָה — פְּסָלוּהָ, נָפְלוּ שְׁנֵיהֶן כְּאַחַת — עֲשָׂאוּהָ שְׁנִיָּה. וְרַב הַמְנוּנָא אָמַר: הָתָם אִיכָּא שִׁיעוּרָא, הָכָא לֵיכָּא שִׁיעוּרָא. אָמַר רַב הַמְנוּנָא: מְנָא אָמִינָא לָהּ? דִּתְנַן: *דהָאוֹכֶל שֶׁנִּטְמָא בְּאַב הַטּוּמְאָה וְשֶׁנִּטְמָא בִּוְלַד הַטּוּמְאָה — מִצְטָרְפִין זֶה עִם זֶה לְטַמֵּא בַּקַּל ד] שֶׁבִּשְׁנֵיהֶם; מַאי לָאו, אע"ג דַּהֲדַר מַלְיֵיהּ? דִּלְמָא דְּלָא הֲדַר מַלְיֵיהּ! ה] כִּי אֲתָא רַב דִּימִי אֲמַר: חֲצִי זַיִת חוּץ לִמְקוֹמוֹ וַחֲצִי זַיִת חוּץ לִזְמַנּוֹ וַחֲצִי זַיִת חוּץ לִזְמַנּוֹ — תָּנֵי בַּר קַפָּרָא: פִּיגּוּל, אֵין חֲצִי זַיִת מוֹעִיל בִּמְקוֹם כְּזַיִת. כִּי אֲתָא רָבִין אֲמַר: חֲצִי זַיִת חוּץ לִזְמַנּוֹ וַחֲצִי זַיִת חוּץ לִזְמַנּוֹ וַחֲצִי זַיִת חוּץ לִמְקוֹמוֹ — תָּנֵי בַּר קַפָּרָא: פִּיגּוּל, אֵין חֲצִי זַיִת מוֹעִיל בִּמְקוֹם כְּזַיִת. רַב אַשִׁי מַתְנֵי הָכִי: החֲצִי זַיִת חוּץ לִזְמַנּוֹ, וּכְזַיִת חֶצְיוֹ חוּץ לִמְקוֹמוֹ וְחֶצְיוֹ חוּץ לִזְמַנּוֹ — תָּנֵי בַּר קַפָּרָא: פִּיגּוּל, אֵין חֲצִי זַיִת מוֹעִיל בִּמְקוֹם כְּזַיִת. אָמַר רַבִּי יַנַּאי: ו] וחִישֵּׁב שֶׁיֹּאכְלוּהוּ כְּלָבִים לְמָחָר — פִּיגּוּל, דִּכְתִיב: °"וְאֶת אִיזֶבֶל יֹאכְלוּ הַכְּלָבִים בְּחֵלֶק יִזְרְעֶאל". מַתְקִיף לָהּ רַבִּי אַמִּי: ז] אֶלָּא מֵעַתָּה, זחִישֵּׁב שֶׁתֹּאכְלֵהוּ אֵשׁ לְמָחָר, דִּכְתִיב: °"תְּאָכְלֵהוּ אֵשׁ לֹא נוּפָּח", ה"נ דְּפִיגּוּל? וְכִי תֵּימָא הָכִי נַמִי — וְהָתְנַן: לֶאֱכוֹל כַּחֲצִי זַיִת וּלְהַקְטִיר *חֲצִי כְּזַיִת — כָּשֵׁר, שֶׁאֵין אֲכִילָה וְהַקְטָרָה מִצְטָרְפִין! חאִי דְּאַפְּקָהּ בִּלְשׁוֹן אֲכִילָה — ח] ה"נ, הָכָא בְּמַאי עָסְקִינַן — דְּאַפְּקָהּ בִּלְשׁוֹן הַקְטָרָה, דִּלְשׁוֹן אֲכִילָה לְחוּד וּלְשׁוֹן הַקְטָרָה לְחוּד. בָּעֵי ט] *רַב אַשִׁי: חִישֵּׁב לֶאֱכוֹל כְּזַיִת בִּשְׁנֵי בְּנֵי אָדָם, מַהוּ? בָּתַר מַחֲשָׁבָה אָזְלִינַן י] דְּאִיכָּא שִׁיעוּרָא, אוֹ בָּתַר אוֹכְלִין אָזְלִינַן וְלֵיכָּא שִׁיעוּרָא? אָמַר אַבָּיֵי, ת"ש: לֶאֱכוֹל כַּחֲצִי זַיִת וּלְהַקְטִיר כַּחֲצִי זַיִת — כָּשֵׁר, שֶׁאֵין אֲכִילָה וְהַקְטָרָה מִצְטָרְפִין; הָא

מלכים ב ט — איוב כ

רש"י

מַאי תִּיבָּעֵי לָךְ? הָשְׁתָּא "כְּזַיִת וּכְזַיִת" הֲוָה לָךְ לְמֵידַק דְּהָוֵי כְּלָלָא, מִדְּלָא אַתְנִיתָא אֶלָּא "כְּזַיִת כְּזַיִת" לִפְרָטָא — הָא "כְּזַיִת וּכְזַיִת" כְּלָלָא, כְּזַיִת לְמָחָר בַּחוּץ מִיבַּעְיָא לָךְ? וּבַעְיָין אִיפְּשִׁיט, דְּבָעֵינַן לְעֵיל: "כְּזַיִת כְּזַיִת" תְּנַן אוֹ "כְּזַיִת וּכְזַיִת" תְּנַן — ש"מ דִּ"כְזַיִת וּכְזַיִת" תְּנַן. וּמֵהָכָא אָמְרִינַן בַּגְּמָ' דְּ"הָאוֹמֵר לַחֲבֵירוֹ" בְּקִדּוּשִׁין (דף מו.) וּבַגְּמָרָא דִּ"שְׁבוּעַת הַפִּקָּדוֹן" (שבועות לח.): רַבִּי הִיא דְּאָמַר ל"ש "כְּזַיִת כְּזַיִת" ל"ש "כְּזַיִת וּכְזַיִת" פְּרָטָא הָוֵי. לִישָּׁנָא אַחֲרִינָא יא] [לָא] גָּרְסִינַן. וַיִּקַץ כְּיָשֵׁן (א) פִּיגּוּל. כֵּיוָן שֶׁמָּלָא חֲצִי יב] זַיִת רִאשׁוֹן חֲצִי זַיִת אַחֲרוֹן שֶׁהוּא מִינוֹ — נֵיעוֹר מִשְּׁנָתוֹ וּמִבִּטּוּלוֹ *שֶׁנִּצְטָרֵף עִם יג] חוּץ לִמְקוֹמוֹ לִפְסוֹל וְלֹא לְפַגֵּל, וְחוֹזֵר מִצְטָרֵף עִם זֶה לְפַגֵּל. וּבָטֵל לוֹ חֲצִי זַיִת דְּחוּץ לִמְקוֹמוֹ מִלְּהוֹצִיאוֹ מִידֵי פִּיגּוּל, דְּאֵין חֲצִי זַיִת מוֹעִיל בִּמְקוֹם כְּזַיִת, וְלָא אָמְרִי': כְּבָר נִצְטָרֵף עִם שֶׁאֶצְלוֹ לִפְסוֹל וְלֹא יַחֲזוֹר וְיִפָּרֵד מִמֶּנּוּ. עֵירוּב מַחֲשָׁבוֹת הָוֵי. מִכֵּיוָן שֶׁנִּצְטָרֵף שׁוּב לֹא יד] יֵרֵד. רִאשׁוֹן. הַתַּעֲרוֹבוֹת הַזֶּה תּוֹרַת רִאשׁוֹן עָלָיו לַעֲשׂוֹת מַגָּעוֹ שֵׁנִי, דְּהָא אִיכָּא שִׁיעוּרָא דְּרִאשׁוֹן בְּגַוֵּיהּ לִיתֵּן טוּמְאָה. חִלְּקָן זֶה שֵׁנִי וְזֶה שֵׁנִי. שֶׁהֲרֵי בְּכָל אֶחָד חֲצִי שִׁיעוּר דְּרִאשׁוֹן וַחֲצִי שִׁיעוּר דְּשֵׁנִי, וּתְנַן לְקַמָּן בְּמַתְנִיתָא: רִאשׁוֹן וְשֵׁנִי מִצְטָרְפִין לְטַמֵּא בַּקַּל שֶׁבִּשְׁנֵיהֶם. הָא חָזַר וְעֵירְבָן רִאשׁוֹן. כִּדְמְסַיֵּים וְאָזֵיל מִגּוּפָא דְּמַתְנִי'. אַלְמָא, כְּשֶׁחָזַר וּמָלָא אֶת מִינוֹ נֵיעוֹר מִצֵּירוּף דְּשֶׁאֵינוֹ מִינוֹ. נָפַל זֶה טו] בְּעַצְמוֹ וְזֶה בְּעַצְמוֹ. כְּשֶׁנִּסְתַּלֵּק הָרִאשׁוֹן נָפַל חֲבֵירוֹ עָלֶיהָ — טז] פְּסָלָהּ, וְלֹא טִימְּאָהּ לַעֲשׂוֹת שְׁנִיָּה. שֶׁכְּשֶׁנָּפַל הָאֶחָד — לֹא הָיָה בּוֹ כְּבֵיצָה רִאשׁוֹן, וּכְשֶׁנָּפַל חֲבֵירוֹ — כְּבָר נִסְתַּלֵּק זֶה. נָפְלוּ שְׁנֵיהֶם כְּאֶחָד. וְה"ה בָּזֶה אַחַר זֶה, אִם נָפַל הַשֵּׁנִי בְּעוֹד הָרִאשׁוֹן עָלֶיהָ — שְׁנֵיהֶם כְּאֶחָד קָרֵי לֵיהּ. עֲשָׂאוּהָ שְׁנִיָּה. אַלְמָא הָדְרִי וּמִצְטָרְפִי רִאשׁוֹן שֶׁבָּזֶה וְשֶׁבָּזֶה. הָתָם אִיכָּא שִׁיעוּרָא. מֵעִיקָּרָא יז] שָׁלֵם הוּא וְנֶחְלָק, הִלְכָּךְ כְּשֶׁחָזַר וְעֵירְבוֹ — חָזַר שְׁמוֹ עָלָיו. אֲבָל הָכָא מֵעִיקָּרָא חֲצִי זַיִת פִּגּוּל וַחֲצִי זַיִת פָּסוּל לֹא נִקְרָא שֵׁם פִּגּוּל עָלָיו, כִּי אִם שֵׁם פָּסוּל, הִלְכָּךְ כִּי הֲדַר אָתֵי חֲצִי יח] [זַיִת] דִּזְמַן — לָא פָּקַע שֵׁם פְּסוּל לְמֵיחַל שֵׁם פִּגּוּל. ה"ג: הָאוֹכֵל חֲצִי בֵּיצָה שֶׁנִּטְמָא בְּאַב הַטּוּמְאָה יט] וַחֲצִי בֵּיצָה אַחֶרֶת שֶׁנִּטְמָא בִּוְלַד הַטּוּמְאָה מִצְטָרְפִין כ] זֶה עִם זֶה לְטַמֵּא בַּקַּל שֶׁבִּשְׁנֵיהֶם מַאי לָאו אַף עַל גַּב דַּהֲדַר מַלְיֵיהּ לָא דְּלָא הֲדַר מַלְיֵיהּ. לְטַמֵּא בַּקַּל שֶׁבִּשְׁנֵיהֶם. אִם נָגַע בִּתְרוּמָה — פְּסָלָהּ וְלֹא טִמְּאָהּ, דְּלֵיכָּא כְּשִׁיעוּר מִן הָרִאשׁוֹן. מַאי לָאו אֲפִי' חָזַר וְהִשְׁלִים מֵאוֹכֵל רִאשׁוֹן אַחֵר עַל זֶה עַד שֶׁהָיָה בּוֹ כְּבֵיצָה אוֹכֶל רִאשׁוֹן, כא] דְּאֵינוֹ עוֹשֶׂה עוֹד רִאשׁוֹן, הוֹאִיל וְלֹא הָיָה בּוֹ מֵעוֹלָם שִׁיעוּר קוֹדֶם שֶׁנִּתְעָרֵב עִם אוֹכֶל שֵׁנִי. אַלְמָא, כִּי לָא הָוֵי בֵּיהּ שִׁיעוּרָא מֵעִיקָּרָא — אֵין חוֹזֵר וְנֵיעוֹר. וְא"ת: אִי (ב) כב] בְּלָא הָוֵי בֵּיהּ שִׁיעוּרָא מֵעִיקָּרָא, הֵיאַךְ קִיבֵּל טוּמְאָה מֵאַב הַטּוּמְאָה מִתְּחִילָּתוֹ? תְּשׁוּבָה לִדְבָרֶיךָ: שֶׁהָאוֹכֶל מְקַבֵּל טוּמְאָה בְּכָל שֶׁהוּא, אֲבָל לְטַמֵּא אֲחֵרִים צָרִיךְ כְּבֵיצָה. וּבְרַיְיתָא שְׁלֵימָה כג] בְּת"כ: "כָּל אֲשֶׁר בְּתוֹכוֹ יִטְמָא מִכָּל הָאוֹכֶל" — מְלַמֵּד שֶׁמִּטַּמֵּא בְּכָל שֶׁהוּא. יָכוֹל יְטַמֵּא אֲחֵרִים בְּכָל שֶׁהוּא? ת"ל: "אֲשֶׁר יֵאָכֵל", דְּהַיְינוּ כְּבֵיצָה, כִּדְלְקַמָּן בְּפ"ח דְּיוֹמָא (דף פ.): אוֹכֶל הַנֶּאֱכָל בְּבַת אַחַת, וְשִׁיעֲרוּ חֲכָמִים אֵין בֵּית הַבְּלִיעָה מַחֲזִיק יוֹתֵר מִכְּבֵיצַת תַּרְנְגוֹלֶת. ה"ג: בְּדְרַב דִּימִי: חֲצִי זַיִת חוּץ לִמְקוֹמוֹ וַחֲצִי זַיִת חוּץ לִזְמַנּוֹ וַחֲצִי זַיִת חוּץ לִזְמַנּוֹ תָּנָא בַּר קַפָּרָא כו'. דְּכֵיוָן דַּהֲוֵי לְהוּ הָנָךְ תְּרֵי דִּזְמַן גַּבֵּי הֲדָדֵי מִצְטָרְפִי, וְלָא אָמְרִינַן: מִכִּי כד] חָשֵׁיב חֲצִי זַיִת דִּזְמַן קַמָּא נִצְטָרֵף עִם חֲצִי זַיִת דְּמָקוֹם שֶׁקְּדָמוֹ. דְּהָא כה] דְּאָמְרַתְּ (לעיל כט.): "יִהְיֶה" מְלַמֵּד שֶׁמִּצְטָרְפִין — (ג) הֵיכָא דְּלֵיכָּא מִינוֹ לְצָרוּפֵי בַּהֲדֵיהּ. כִּי אֲתָא רָבִין אֲמַר. לָאו הָכִי תָּנֵי בַּר קַפָּרָא, דְּכֵיוָן שֶׁקְּדָמוֹ חֲצִי זַיִת דְּמָקוֹם — אָתֵי חֲצִי זַיִת קַמָּא דִּזְמַן וְאִיצְטְרִיף, כו] וְשׁוּב אֵין חוֹזֵר וְנֵיעוֹר. אֶלָּא הָכִי תְּנָא: חֲצִי זַיִת חוּץ לִזְמַנּוֹ וַחֲצִי זַיִת חוּץ לִזְמַנּוֹ וַחֲצִי זַיִת חוּץ לִמְקוֹמוֹ — פִּיגּוּל, אֵין חֲצִי זַיִת דְּמָקוֹם מוֹעִיל לְבַטֵּל זְמַן דַּהֲוֵי כְּזַיִת. רַב אַשִׁי כו'. כְּרַבָּא סְבִירָא לֵיהּ, דְּאָמַר לְעֵיל: וַיִּקַץ כְּיָשֵׁן. הַפִּיגּוּל, וַאֲפִילּוּ אַפְסְקֵיהּ בְּמַחֲשֶׁבֶת מָקוֹם. וַעֲדִיפָא דְּרַב אַשִׁי מִדְּרָבָא, דְּאַשְׁמְעִינַן רְבוּתָא: כז] אע"ג דְּחַשְׁבִינְהוּ לִזְמַן וּמָקוֹם בְּחַד דִּבּוּרָא וְלֵירָפֵן בִּשְׂפָתָיו לִכְזַיִת אֶחָד, וַאֲפ"ה מִצְטָרֵף לְמִינוֹ. יֹאכְלוּ הַכְּלָבִים. אַלְמָא שְׁמֵיהּ אֲכִילָה. אֶלָּא מֵעַתָּה חִישֵּׁב. עַל הַבָּשָׂר כח] לֶאֱכוֹל בְּאֵשׁ הֶדְיוֹט לְמָחָר. הָכִי נַמִי. דַּהֲוֵי פִּיגּוּל? וְכִי תֵּימָא הָכִי נַמִי וְהָא אֲנַן תְּנַן. דַּאֲפִי' אֵשׁ כט] גָּבוֹהַּ, בְּמִידֵי דַּחֲזֵי לָהּ וְאוֹרְחָהּ — לָא מִצְטָרְפָא אִם חִישְּׁבָהּ עִם אֲכִילַת אָדָם, וְאע"ג דַּאֲכִילָה שְׁמָהּ. אַלְמָא לָא מְדַמֵּי אֲכִילוֹת לַהֲדָדֵי, דְּכָל חֲדָא וַחֲדָא לְמִילְּתֵיהּ הוּא דַּהֲוָיָא אֲכִילָה. בָּתַר אוֹכְלִין. שְׁנַיִם הָאוֹכְלִין אֶת הַזַּיִת. הָא

א) [לקמן לו: ד"ה שיאכלוהו כו' כתבו הטעם ע"ש] ב) [עיין תוספות מנחות יז: ד"ה דלא שנא וכו' התעוררת רב בסוגיא דהכא]

תוספות

ויקץ כישן הפיגול. לא שייך הכא "מלא מין את מינו וניעור" לן. עירוב מחשבות הוי. לא] שאין הפסול מניח הפיגול ליפרד מעליו לב]. הא חזר ועירבן ראשון הוי. תימה: מה ענין זה אצל זה? דגבי קרבן כשאמר חצי זית חוץ למקומו וחצי זית חוץ לזמנו — הרי כבר נפסל הקרבן, ואינו חוזר ונעשה פיגול. אבל חצי ביצה ראשון וחצי ביצה שני שנתערבו, דנעשה שני — אין הטעם לפי שנתבטל חצי ביצה הראשון, אלא משום דאין לו כח לטמאות לג] בפני עצמו. הלכך, כשילטרף עמו חצי ביצה ראשון למה לא יהא ראשון?

נפלו שניהם כאחד עשאוה שניה. למ"ד: יש נוגע חוזר ונוגע.

התם איכא שיעורא. פי' בקונט': מעיקרא שיעור שלם הוה ונחלק, הלכך כשחזר וערבו — שמו חזר עליו. אבל הכא, מעיקרא חצי זית פיגול וחצי זית פסול — לא נקרא שם פיגול עליו כי אם שם פסול, הלכך כי הדר אתי חצי זית דזמן — לא פקע שם פסול למיחל שם פיגול. ולפירוש זה הוה ליה למימר: התם הוה ביה שיעורא, הכא לא הוה ביה שיעורא. ומפרש ר"ת: לד] איכא שיעורא — שיש מן השני כשיעור, לפיכך מניח לו לראשון להפרד מעליו, לה] והלך לו להתחבר אצל ראשון אחר. הכא ליכא שיעורא מן הפסול, ואין מניח לו לפיגול להפרד מעליו. אמר רב המנונא מנא אמינא לה דתנן האוכל שנטמא באב הטומאה. שהיה בו כביצה. ושנטמא בולד הטומאה — שהיה בו כמו כן כביצה. מלטרפין זה עם זה — אם יש חצי ביצה מן הראשון וחצי ביצה מן השני מלטרפין לטמא בקל שבשניהם. מאי לאו אע"ג דהדר מלייה — שלקח מן הראשון ושם עליו? אלמא, כיון דליכא שיעורא מן השני — אין מניח לו לראשון להפרד מעליו לילך לו אצל ראשון חבירו. ומשני: דלמא דלא הדר מלייה. ואין לדמות זה לטומאה שבטלה לו] חזרה וניעורה, דהכא לא בטלה, והכא טעמא משום דאין לז] להפרד ממנו. ולפי' רבינו תם שפירשתי לא לריכא למה שפירש בקונטרס דאוכל מקבל טומאה בכל שהוא, והארכתי בפרק "המלניע" [שבת דף לא. ד"ה אי לענין].

חישב שיאכלוהו כלבים למחר פיגול. בסוף "כל הפסולין" (לקמן דף לו.) אמרינן דחישב שיאכלוהו טמאים — לא הוי פיגול. ולריך לפרש טעם אמאי גרע מאכילת כלבים א).

ואת איזבל יאכלו הכלבים. לח] הא פשיטא ליה דשייכא ליה גבי בהמה בדבר הראוי לה, כדכתיב: "תהיה כל תבואתך לאכול". אלא מאכילת בשר מייתי ראיה לט].

דכתיב תאכלהו אש לא נופח. תימה: דלא מייתי קרא ד"אש האכל יאכל" דבשתי אכילות הכתוב מדבר, אחת אכילת אדם ואחת אכילת מזבח (לעיל יג:), וכתיב (ויקרא ו): "אשר תאכל האש את העולה"! וי"ל: דאש דגבוה פשיטא ליה דשמה אכילה, מ] ובכל מקום אין אכילה והקטרה מלטרפין. ב) אבל השתא דאמרת דכל אכילת אש שמה אכילה — קשיא ליה אמאי אין מלטרפין.

שאין אכילה והקטרה מצטרפין. מרישא הוה מא] מלינא למידק, דקתני: להקטיר דבר שדרכו להקטיר, הא דבר שאין דרכו להקטיר — לא, אלמא אכילת אש לא שמה אכילה. הא

קכה א מיי' פט"ז מהל' פסה"מ הלכה ד:
קכו ב ג מיי' פ"ד מהל' טומאת אוכלין הלכה יג:
קכז ד מיי' שם הלכה יב:
קכח ה מיי' פט"ז מהל' פסה"מ הלכה ד:
קכט ו ז ח מיי' פי"ד מהלכות פסה"מ הלכה י:

שיטה מקובצת

א] מתיבת לישנא עד תיבת איתמר לא גרים רש"י: ב] כזית כזית מיבעיא בס"י כזית וכזית מיבעיא: ג] זה לעצמו וזה לעצמו: ד] שבשניהם מאי לאו אע"ג דהדר מלייה. פ"ה לפי שיטתו אפי' כו' אבל קשה לר"ת על הא דפי' דאוכלים מקבלים טומאה בכל שהוא מהא דאמרינן באהלות (פי"ג מ"ה) אלו ממעטין בחלון וחשיב פחות מכביצה אוכלים ואי מקבלים טומאה היאך חוצצין (דקיי"ל) [דהא קיי"ל] דכל דבר המקבל טומאה אינו חוצץ בפני הטומאה ולפי' ניחא דלעולם היו בו כשיעור מעיקרא [עד] שנטמא באב הטומאה שחלקן ועירבן עד חצי ביצה מ"מ מייתי שפיר א) דכי הדר מליה שלקח חצי ביצה מן הראשון ושם עם השני דליכא שיעורא כיון דהשני אין מניחו לראשון להפרד ממנו ולילך לו אצל הראשון חבירו ודחי דלא הדר מליית. לשון הר"פ ז"ל: ה] כי אתא רב דימי כו'. כרב המנונא ס"ל מיהו הכא דהוו הני דדמי גבי אהדדי מצטרפין ולא אמרינן מכי חשיב אחצי זית זמן קמא מצטרף בהדי חצי זית חוץ שקדמו דכתיב יהיה מלמד שמצטרף דה"פ כי ליכא זמן בהדיה לאצטרופי ורבין אמר דלאו להכי תני בר קפרא דהם בענין זה אינו חוזר וניעור דכיון שהפסול נקבע בחצי זית דזמן קמא אלא להכי תני חצי זית חוץ לזמנו [וחצי זית חוץ לזמנו] וחצי זית חוץ למקומו כו'. מהר"פ ז"ל: ו] חישב שיאכלוהו כלבים כו'. וא"ת והלא בפ' כל הפסולים כו' וי"ל דשאני טמאים שפוסלים ב) קודם אכילה בנגיעה ואע"פ שיכול חבירו לתוחבו בבית הבליעה שלו אין דרך אכילה בכך וריב"א פי' דלקמן אינו בא רק לדחות ראייתו של רבא שהביא לרב חסדא אבל דברי רב חסדא לא נדחו ועוד דשיאכלוהו טמאים אין זה בידו הלכך לא הוי מחשבה והוי כאילו לא אמר כלום אבל אכילת כלבים הויא בידו. מהר"פ ז"ל: ז] אלא מעתה חישב כו' פ"ה דאף בשר הדיוט כו' אבל תימה הגבי מזבח נמי אשכחן אכילה דכתיב בפיגול גופיה ואם תאכל כו' עד אין ג) מצטרפין ואפי' כי מפקה להקטרה

הגהות הב"ח

(א) רש"י ד"ה ויקץ כישן הפיגול וכו' ומתבטל לגירוף שמלטרף וכו' וחוזר ומלטרף: (ב) ד"ה לטמא וכו' וא"ת אי דלא וכו' כתוכו: (ג) ד"ה ה"ג וכו' מלמד שמלטרפין היינו דוקא היכא:

מסורת הש"ס

רש"ק מ"ז וה"ק מקיימו
נ"א ואינו מלטרף טהרות פ"א מ"ה
ג"ז שם
ג"ז שם מעילה יז:
כתלי זונן ל"ק
נ"ל רב אסי

בלשון אכילה (דהא) [דלא] מקרייא אכילה לפי שאין אכילה לגבוה אלא אכילת אש אבל השתא (כי) [כו' אמאי] אין מצטרפין. דהא גם הקטרה לא פקע ממנה שם אכילת אש כמו בהדיוט ומשני דהיינו [טעמא] לפי שהלשון חלוק ... שמה אכילה. מהר"פ ז"ל: ח] הכי נמי. גליון דהוי פיגול ומצטרף הב"ע כלומר מתניתין דאין אכילה והקטרה מצטרף מיירי דאפקה כו' ע"כ: ט] בעי רבא תיבות רב אשי נמחק: י] והא ... זית ראשון את חצי הזית אחרון: יג] עם של חוץ: יד] לא יעיר הס"ד: טו] זה לעצמו וזה לעצמו: טז] עליה פסלוה ולא טמאוה לעשות אות י' נמחק: יז] מעיקרא שיעור שלם: יח] חצי זית: יט] ... אחרת נמחק: כ] מצטרפין. גליון כלומר וחצי ביצה אחרת נגע בולד הטומאה: כא] אוכל ראשון קאמר דאינו נעשה עוד: כב] אי בדלא הוה ביה: כג] שלימה היא בתו"כ: כד] מכי אחשיב: כה] דהא דאמרת ...

קל א ב מיי' פי"ד מהלכות פסה"מ הלכה י:
א ג מיי' פ"א מהלכות פסה"מ הלכה א ופ"ט מהלכות ביאת מקדש הל' ו ופ"ה מהלכות מעה"ק הלכה א:
ב ד מיי' פי"ד מהלכות פסה"מ הלכה ב:

א] הָא לֶאֱכוֹל וְלֶאֱכוֹל דּוּמְיָא דְּלֶאֱכוֹל וּלְהַקְטִיר, וְהֵיכִי דָּמֵי – בִּשְׁנֵי בְנֵי אָדָם – מִצְטָרֵף, אִשְּׁ"מ. בָּעֵי רָבָא: חִישֵּׁב לֶאֱכוֹל כְּזַיִת בְּיָתֵר מִכְּדֵי אֲכִילַת פְּרָס, מַהוּ? לַאֲכִילַת גָּבוֹהַּ מְדַמֵּינַן לֵיהּ, אוֹ לַאֲכִילַת הֶדְיוֹט מְדַמֵּינַן לֵיהּ? אָמַר אַבַּיֵי, ת"ש: לֶאֱכוֹל כַּחֲצִי זַיִת וּלְהַקְטִיר כַּחֲצִי זַיִת – כָּשֵׁר, שֶׁאֵין אֲכִילָה וְהַקְטָרָה מִצְטָרְפִין. טַעְמָא דְּלֶאֱכוֹל וּלְהַקְטִיר, הָא לֶאֱכוֹל וְלֶאֱכוֹל – ב] מִצְטָרֵף; וְהָא הַקְטָרָה בְּיוֹתֵר מִכְּדֵי אֲכִילַת פְּרָס הוּא! דִּלְמָא בְּהֶיסֵּק גָּדוֹל.§ "לֶאֱכוֹל כַּחֲצִי זַיִת וּלְהַקְטִיר כַּחֲצִי זַיִת – כָּשֵׁר" ג] .§ *טַעְמָא דְּלֶאֱכוֹל וּלְהַקְטִיר, הָא לֶאֱכוֹל וְלֶאֱכוֹל דָּבָר שֶׁאֵין דַּרְכּוֹ לֶאֱכוֹל – מִצְטָרֵף. הָא קָתָנֵי רֵישָׁא: לֶאֱכוֹל ד] אֶת שֶׁדַּרְכּוֹ לֶאֱכוֹל (מִצְטָרֵף) אֶת שֶׁדַּרְכּוֹ לֶאֱכוֹל – אִין, שֶׁאֵין דַּרְכּוֹ – לָא! אָמַר רַבִּי יִרְמְיָה: הָא מַנִּי – *רַבִּי אֱלִיעֶזֶר הִיא, דְּאָמַר: מְחַשְּׁבִין מֵאֲכִילַת אָדָם לַאֲכִילַת מִזְבֵּחַ וּמֵאֲכִילַת מִזְבֵּחַ לַאֲכִילַת אָדָם. *דִּתְנַן: הַשּׁוֹחֵט אֶת הַזֶּבַח לֶאֱכוֹל דָּבָר שֶׁאֵין דַּרְכּוֹ לֶאֱכוֹל, וּלְהַקְטִיר דָּבָר שֶׁאֵין דַּרְכּוֹ לְהַקְטִיר – כָּשֵׁר, וְרַבִּי אֱלִיעֶזֶר פּוֹסֵל. אַבַּיֵי אָמַר: אֲפִי' תֵּימָא רַבָּנַן; וְלָא תֵּימָא: הָא לֶאֱכוֹל וְלֶאֱכוֹל דָּבָר שֶׁאֵין דַּרְכּוֹ לֶאֱכוֹל, אֶלָּא אֵימָא: הָא לֶאֱכוֹל וְלֶאֱכוֹל דָּבָר שֶׁדַּרְכּוֹ לֶאֱכוֹל. מַאי קמ"ל? אִי דָּבָר שֶׁדַּרְכּוֹ לֶאֱכוֹל קמ"ל – מֵרֵישָׁא ש"מ: כַּחֲצִי זַיִת בַּחוּץ כַּחֲצִי זַיִת לְמָחָר – פָּסוּל, *(הָא כַּחֲצִי זַיִת לְמָחָר – ה] *פִּיגּוּל! אֶלָּא) אִי לֶאֱכוֹל וּלְהַקְטִיר – מִדּוּקְיָא דְּרֵישָׁא ש"מ: לֶאֱכוֹל דָּבָר שֶׁדַּרְכּוֹ לֶאֱכוֹל – אִין, שֶׁאֵין דַּרְכּוֹ לֶאֱכוֹל – לָא; הַשְׁתָּא וּמַה לֶאֱכוֹל וְלֶאֱכוֹל דָּבָר שֶׁאֵין דַּרְכּוֹ לֶאֱכוֹל – לָא מִצְטָרֵף, לֶאֱכוֹל וּלְהַקְטִיר מִבָּעֵי? לֶאֱכוֹל וּלְהַקְטִיר אִיצְטְרִיךְ; ס"ד אָמִינָא: הָתָם הוּא דְּלָאו כִּי אוֹרְחֵיהּ קָא מְחַשֵּׁב, אֲבָל הָכָא דִּבְהַאי כִּי אוֹרְחֵיהּ וּבְהַאי כִּי אוֹרְחֵיהּ – אֵימָא לִיצְטָרֵף, קָא מַשְׁמַע לָן.§

הדרן עלך כל הזבחים שקבלו דמן

כָּל *גהַפְּסוּלִין שֶׁשָּׁחֲטוּ – שְׁחִיטָתָן כְּשֵׁרָה. שֶׁהַשְּׁחִיטָה כְּשֵׁרָה בְּזָרִים, וּבְנָשִׁים, וּבַעֲבָדִים, וּבִטְמֵאִים, וַאֲפִילּוּ בְּקָדְשֵׁי קָדָשִׁים, וּבִלְבַד שֶׁלֹּא יִהְיוּ טְמֵאִים נוֹגְעִין בַּבָּשָׂר. *דלְפִיכָךְ הֵן פּוֹסְלִין בְּמַחֲשָׁבָה. וְכוּלָּן

הָא לֶאֱכוֹל וְלֶאֱכוֹל. לִשְׁנַיִם, דּוּמְיָא דְּלֶאֱכוֹל וּלְהַקְטִיר, שֶׁאֵין זַיִת שָׁלֵם לְאוֹכֵל אֶחָד – מִצְטָרֵף. בְּיָתֵר מִכְּדֵי אֲכִילַת פְּרָס. לִשְׁהוֹת בֵּין תְּחִילַּת אֲכִילָתוֹ לְסוֹפָהּ יוֹתֵר מִכְּדֵי אֲכִילַת פְּרָס. דְּאִילּוּ גַּבֵּי כָּל אִיסּוּרִים שֶׁבַּתּוֹרָה קַיְימָא לָן דְּלָא הָוְיָא אֲכִילָה, הָכָא מַאי? לַאֲכִילַת גָּבוֹהַּ מְדַמֵּינַן לָהּ. דְּהָא אִיתְקוּשׁ לְעִנְיַן מַחֲשָׁבָה אֲכִילַת גָּבוֹהַּ וַאֲכִילַת אָדָם כַּהֲדָדֵי, וַאֲכִילַת גָּבוֹהַּ אַף בְּיוֹתֵר מִכְּדֵי אֲכִילַת פְּרָס הִיא, פְּעָמִים שֶׁאֵינוֹ מְמַהֵר לִשְׂרוֹף. ה"ג: ו] לֶאֱכוֹל וְלֶאֱכוֹל דּוּמְיָא דִּלְהַקְטִיר מִצְטָרֵף. וְהֵיכִי דָּמֵי – יוֹתֵר מִכְּדֵי אֲכִילַת פְּרָס. לֶאֱכוֹל חֲצִי זַיִת וְלַחֲזוֹר וְלֶאֱכוֹל חֲצִי זַיִת, וּבֵין זֶה לָזֶה יוֹתֵר מִכְּדֵי אֲכִילַת פְּרָס, דּוּמְיָא דְּהַקְטָרָה – מִצְטָרֵף. דִּלְמָא. הַאי לְהַקְטִיר דְּקָתָנֵי – בְּהֶיסֵּק גָּדוֹל קָאָמַר, וְדִכְוָותֵהּ דַּוְקָא לֶאֱכוֹל וְלֶאֱכוֹל דְּמִצְטָרֵף. ה"ג: מַתְנִי' לֶאֱכוֹל כַּחֲצִי זַיִת כו' טַעְמָא דְּלֶאֱכוֹל וּלְהַקְטִיר כו'. דָּבָר שֶׁאֵין דַּרְכּוֹ לֶאֱכוֹל כִּי הַאי לְהַקְטִיר דְּמַתְנִי', דְּקָמַיְירֵי (הָא) בְּאֵימוּרִים. הָא קָתָנֵי רֵישָׁא זֶה הַכְּלָל כָּל הַשּׁוֹחֵט וְהַמְקַבֵּל לֶאֱכוֹל דָּבָר שֶׁדַּרְכּוֹ לֶאֱכוֹל כו'. אַלְמָא מֵאֲכִילַת ז] מִזְבֵּחַ לְאָדָם לָאו מַחֲשָׁבָה הִיא! הָא מַנִּי הַךְ סֵיפָא. דְּאִיצְטְרִיךְ לְמִיתְנֵי אֵין אֲכִילָה וְהַקְטָרָה מִצְטָרְפִין – רַבִּי אֱלִיעֶזֶר הִיא. לֶאֱכוֹל דָּבָר שֶׁאֵין דַּרְכּוֹ לֶאֱכוֹל. ח] [דְּהַיְינוּ] אֵימוּרִין, וְחִישֵּׁב עָלָיו חוּץ לִמְקוֹמוֹ אוֹ חוּץ לִזְמַנּוֹ. אֶלָּא אֵימָא הָא לֶאֱכוֹל וְלֶאֱכוֹל דָּבָר שֶׁדַּרְכּוֹ לֶאֱכוֹל. הָכִי דּוּק מִינֵּיהּ: אֲכִילָה וְהַקְטָרָה אֵין מִצְטָרְפִין לְפַגֵּל, ט] הָא לֶאֱכוֹל וְלֶאֱכוֹל דָּבָר שֶׁדַּרְכּוֹ לֶאֱכוֹל – מִצְטָרֵף, וְאַע"ג דְּחָשֵׁיב לַחֲלָאִין. וּמַאי קמ"ל. הַךְ סֵיפָא, אִי לָאו לְמֵידַק מִינֵּיהּ: הָא לֶאֱכוֹל וְלֶאֱכוֹל דָּבָר שֶׁאֵין דַּרְכּוֹ לֶאֱכוֹל, דּוּמְיָא דִּלְהַקְטִיר, י] מַאי קַמַּשְׁמַע לָן? לָמָּה לִי לְמִתְנְיֵיהּ? אִי לֶאֱכוֹל וְלֶאֱכוֹל דָּבָר שֶׁדַּרְכּוֹ לֶאֱכוֹל קָא מַשְׁמַע לָן, כִּדְקָאָמְרַתְּ דְּמַחֲשֶׁבֶת חֲלָאִין מִצְטָרֶפֶת – מֵרֵישָׁא שָׁמְעַתְּ מִינָּהּ. וְאִי לֶאֱכוֹל וּלְהַקְטִיר. כְּלוֹמַר, וְאִי הִיא גּוּפָהּ קָא אָתָא לְאַשְׁמוּעִינַן, דְּאֵין אֲכִילָה וְהַקְטָרָה מִצְטָרֶפֶת, וְלָאו לְדִיוּקָא דִּילָהּ אָתְאִי. מִדִּיוּקָא דְּרֵישָׁא שְׁמַע מִינָּהּ. דְּקָתָנֵי: לֶאֱכוֹל דָּבָר שֶׁדַּרְכּוֹ לֶאֱכוֹל הָוְיָא מַחֲשָׁבָה, אֲבָל לֶאֱכוֹל דָּבָר שֶׁאֵין דַּרְכּוֹ לֶאֱכוֹל – לָא הָוֵי מַחֲשָׁבָה. ש"מ דְּאִם חִישֵּׁב לֶאֱכוֹל חֲצִי זַיִת בָּשָׂר וַחֲצִי זַיִת יא] אֵימוּרִים – לָא מִצְטָרְפִי, וְכָל שֶׁכֵּן לֶאֱכוֹל חֲצִי זַיִת בָּשָׂר וּלְהַקְטִיר חֲצִי זַיִת אֵימוּרִין, דְּלָא מִצְטָרְפִי יב]. הַשְׁתָּא וּמַה לֶאֱכוֹל וְלֶאֱכוֹל לָא מִצְטָרְפִי. בָּשָׂר וְאֵימוּרִים, לֶאֱכוֹל וּלְהַקְטִיר מִיבַּעְיָא? יג] הָתָם. כִּי חִישֵּׁב לֶאֱכוֹל אֵימוּרִים הוּא דְּלָא מִצְטָרֵף בַּהֲדֵי אֲכִילַת בָּשָׂר – מִשּׁוּם דְּלָאו כִּי אוֹרְחֵיהּ קָמְחַשֵּׁב אֲבָל לֶאֱכוֹל בָּשָׂר וּלְהַקְטִיר אֵימוּרִין, דִּבְהַאי כִּי אוֹרְחֵיהּ קָמְחַשֵּׁב כו', קמ"ל.

הדרן עלך כל הזבחים שקבלו דמן

כָּל הַפְּסוּלִין שֶׁשָּׁחֲטוּ שְׁחִיטָתָן כְּשֵׁרָה. כִּדְיָלֵיף בַּגְּמָ'. וּבִטְמֵאִים. בִּטְמֵא שֶׁרֶץ קָאָמַר, שֶׁאֵינוֹ מְטַמֵּא כְּלִי, דְּלָאו אַב הַטּוּמְאָה הוּא. אוֹ בִּטְמֵא מֵת, וּכְגוֹן שֶׁבָּדַק קְרוּמִית שֶׁל קָנֶה וְשָׁחַט בָּהּ. אֲבָל בְּסַכִּין – לֹא, שֶׁהוּא מְטַמֵּא אֶת הַסַּכִּין וְהַסַּכִּין מְטַמֵּא אֶת (א) הַבָּשָׂר. וּכְגוֹן דְּעָבֵיד סַכִּין אֲרִיכָא וְשָׁחֵיט. לְפִיכָךְ הֵן פּוֹסְלִין. אֶת הַקָּרְבָּן בְּמַחֲשָׁבָה, אִם שְׁחָטוּהוּ (ב) בְּמַחֲשָׁבָה. הוֹאִיל וּרְאוּיִין לַעֲבוֹדָה זוֹ – מַחֲשַׁבְתָּן מַחֲשָׁבָה. וְכוּלָּן

הא לאכול ולאכול דומיא דלאכול ולהקטיר מצטרף. וא"ת: דלמא לעולם לא יד] יצטרף, ואתא למידק דלאכול ולאכול בחד גברא מצטרף ואפי' ביתר מכדי אכילת פרס. וכן בתר הכי, דדייק אביי דלאכול ולאכול ביתר מכדי אכילת פרס מצטרף, מדקתני לאכול ולהקטיר – דלמא אתא למידק דלאכול ולאכול בשני בנ"א מצטרף! ויש לומר: דדייק מדתלי טעמא שאין הקטרה ואכילה מצטרפין, משום דהאי אכילה והאי הקטרה. הא אי חשיבא הקטרה כאכילה – הוה מצטרף טו] (אי חשיבא הקטרה), אע"ג דהוי כעין שני בני אדם, וביתר מכדי אכילת פרס. ביתר מכדי אכילת פרס מהו. וא"ת: לוכח מדתנן: חצי זית בחוץ חצי זית למחר פסול! וי"ל: דדלמא בלהקטיר. אע"ג דרישא קתני: לאכול כזית בחוץ כזית למחר – שמא בבא דחצי זית מיירי בלהקטיר דווקא. ומאי קמ"ל אי לאכול ולאכול טז] שדרכן לאכול כו'. תימה: טובא קמ"ל – כדדייק אביי גופיה לעיל: לאכול ולאכול בשני בני אדם, וביתר מכדי אכילת פרס!.

הדרן עלך כל הזבחים שקבלו דמן

כל הפסולין ששחטו. שהשחיטה כשרה בנשים. בגמרא מוכח דנשים שוחטות אפי' לכתחלה. יז] *הא דתנן ששחטו דיעבד – משום דבעי למיתני טמאים דלכתחילה לא, ולא קאמר: משום דבעי למיתני נשים דקתני ברישא. יח] מיכן תשובה למה שכתבו בהלכות א"י דנשים לא ישחטו מפני שדעתן קלה. ועוד כתוב בהן: שחט ולא בירך, וערום ששחט – שחיטה פסולה. ונראה שהם חומרות בעלמא שהיה אומר אותו החכם יט] שכתב הלכות ארץ ישראל. ובטמאים. מפרש בגמרא דלכתחילה אין שוחטין, שמא יגעו בבשר. ואע"ג דדם קדשים אינו מכשיר – חיבת הקודש מכשרת. או כשהעבירה בנהר ועדיין משקה טופח עליה, כדאמר בפ"ק דפסחים (דף כ.). וא"ת: תיפוק ליה דלמא אתיא לאימשוכי בפנים. כ] ואפי' טהור גמור, לבן זומא דאמר (יומא ל.): הנכנס למקדש טעון טבילה – כא] אין יכול לשחוט בסכין ארוכה, דלמא אתי לאמשוכי, כב] כדאמר בפ' "אמר להם הממונה" (שם דף לא.)! וי"ל: דבטהור שייך למיגזר טפי דלמא אתי לאימשוכי, אבל טמא מיזהר זהיר ומידכר. ומשום הכי לא נקט נמי שמא יכניס ידו לפנים, אע"ג דאיכא איסורא כג] למאן דאמר (לקמן לג:) ביאה במקצת שמה ביאה. ומיהו, איכא למימר דנקט טעמא דהוי לכולי עלמא. והקשה ה"ר אפרים: כד] והיאך במוקדשין שוחט? דאע"ג דמוקי לה בגמ' בסכין ארוכה – איך יתכן שיהא כל כך ארוכה כה] מהר הבית עד עזרת ישראל, כדתנן במסכת כלים (פ"א מ"ח): החיל מקודש כו] מהר הבית, שאין גויים וטמאי מתים נכנסין לשם. עזרת נשים מקודשת כז] הימנה שאין טבול יום נכנס לשם. ואפי' כח] אי האי סוגיא בטמא שרץ ומותר ליכנס בחיל – מ"מ עזרת נשים ארוכה קל"ה אמה,*) והיאך יתכן שתהא סכין ארוכה כל כך? כט] וי"ל: דהיכא דנטמא בעזרת נשים לא החמירו

*) [מדות פ"ב מ"ה]

מנחות יב: כל הסוגיא

[לעיל כח.]

לקמן לה. [לעיל כח.]

חולין ב:

לעיל כו:

ל"ק מ"ז

[נ"ל מדקאמר הא דתנן כו']

כ"א ל"ג

כ"א וכחצי זית למחר

הגהות הב"ח

(א) רש"י ד"ה ובטמאים וכו' את הבשר הס"ד ואח"כ מ"ה ובלבד שלא יהיו טמאים נוגעין בבשר וכגון דעביד סכין: (ב) ד"ה לפיכך וכו' שחטוהו במחשבה חוץ לזמנו וחוץ למקומו דהואיל וראויין:

שיטה מקובצת

א] הא לאכול ולאכול כו'. א) ואם תאמר כו' וי"ל דסברא הוא כיון שיש לדקדק כל הני רבותות אית ליה דדייקינן כל [מה] דאפשר לדייק דאם לא בא כי אם לדקדק הא ביתר מכדי אכילת פרס מצטרף ליתני לאכול בשני בני אדם דלא מצטרף וכ"ש לאכול ולהקטיר וכן אם לא בא כי אם לדקדק הא בשני בני אדם מצטרף ליתני לאכול באדם אחד ביותר מכדי אכילת פרס דלא מצטרף וכ"ש אכילה והקטרה. מהר"פ ז"ל: ב] ולאכול דומיא דלהקטיר מצטרף והא הקטרה דביותר מכדי: ג] כשר כו': ד] לאכול דבר שדרכו לאכול דבר שדרכו תיבות את מצטרף נמחק: ה] למחר וכחצי זית למחר פיגול אי תיבת אלא נמחק: ו] ה"ג הא לאכול: ז] מאכילת אדם למזבח ומאכילת מזבח: ח] לאכול אימורין אין דרכו לאכול וחישב ותיבת דהיינו ל"ש ונמחק: ט] לפגל אבל אכילה ואכילה מצטרפין לפגל מתיבת הא עד תיבות ואף על גב ל"ש ונמחק: י] תיבות מאי קמשמע לן נמחק: יא] זית אימורין למחר לא מצטרפי: יב] דלא מצטרפי דהשתא ומה והוא דבור אחד: יג] מבעיא הס"ד ומה"ד לאכול ולהקטיר איצטריך פי' לעולם לגופיה ורבנן היא כדאמרן ואע"ג דמדוקיא שמעינן לה איצטריך סד"א התם כי כו': יד] לא מצטרף: טו] תיבות אי חשיבה הקטרה נמחק: טז] ולאכול דבר שדרכו לאכול: יז] דמפרש דהא דתנן: יח] ברישא מכאן תשובה: יט] החכם מדעתו: כ] דאפילו טהור: כא] טבילה איבעיא לן בפרק אמר להם הממונה אי יכול לשחוט בסכין ארוכה אי לא דלמא: כב] תיבות כדאמר בפרק אמר להם הממונה נמחק: כג] איסורא דאורייתא למאן: כד] אפרים וטמא היאך שוחט במוקדשין דאע"ג: כה] ארוכה מעזרת נשים עד כו' ותיבות מהר הבית נמחק: כו] מקודש ממנו שאין תיבות מהר הבית נמחק: כז] מקודשת ממנו תיבת הימנה נמחק: כח] ואפילו הוי האי טמא בטבול יום והלא עזרת נשים כו' והשאר נמחק: כט] וי"ל דמיירי בטמא מת שנטמא בפנים ומותר מן התורה ליכנס במחנה לויה ואפילו מת עצמו כדכתיב ויקח משה את עצמות יוסף עמו ודרשינן עמו במחיצתו וכיון שאינו אסור אלא מדרבנן לא גזור וכ"ש בטומאה שאירעה בפנים דליכא איסור שהיה או שמא מיירי בהיתר הבמות. לשון מהר"פ ז"ל:

א) כוונתם לדברי התוס' בד"ה הא.

*אוְכוּלָּן שֶׁקִּיבְּלוּ אֶת הַדָּם חוּץ לִזְמַנּוֹ וְחוּץ לִמְקוֹמוֹ, אִם יֵשׁ דַּם הַנֶּפֶשׁ — יַחֲזוֹר הַכָּשֵׁר וִיקַבֵּל. *בקִיבֵּל הַכָּשֵׁר וְנָתַן לַפָּסוּל — יַחֲזִיר לַכָּשֵׁר. גקִיבֵּל בִּימִינוֹ וְנָתַן לִשְׂמֹאלוֹ — יַחֲזִיר לִימִינוֹ. דקִיבֵּל בִּכְלִי קֹדֶשׁ וְנָתַן לִכְלִי חוֹל — יַחֲזִיר לִכְלִי קֹדֶשׁ. *הנִשְׁפַּךְ מִן הַכְּלִי עַל הָרִצְפָּה וַאֲסָפוֹ — כָּשֵׁר. *ונְתָנוֹ עַל גַּבֵּי הַכֶּבֶשׁ שֶׁלֹּא כְּנֶגֶד הַיְסוֹד, נָתַן אֶת הַנִּיתָּנִין לְמַטָּה לְמַעְלָן, וְאֶת הַנִּיתָּנִין לְמַעְלָן לְמַטָּה, וְאֶת הַנִּיתָּנִין בִּפְנִים בַּחוּץ, וְאֶת הַנִּיתָּנִין בַּחוּץ בִּפְנִים, א] אִם יֵשׁ דַּם הַנֶּפֶשׁ — יַחֲזוֹר הַכָּשֵׁר וִיקַבֵּל.§ **גמ'** ב] "שְׁחָטוּ", דִּיעֲבַד — אִין, לְכַתְּחִלָּה — לָא. וּרְמִינְהוּ: "וְשָׁחַט" — שְׁחִיטָה בְּזָר כְּשֵׁרָה, שֶׁהַשְּׁחִיטָה כְּשֵׁרָה בְּזָרִים וּבְנָשִׁים וּבַעֲבָדִים וּבִטְמֵאִים, וַאֲפִילּוּ בְּקָדְשֵׁי קָדָשִׁים. אוֹ אֵינוֹ אֶלָּא בְּכֹהֲנִים? אָמַרְתָּ: וְכִי מֵאַיִן בָּאתָה — מִכְּלַל שֶׁנֶּאֱמַר: °"וְאַתָּה וּבָנֶיךָ אִתְּךָ תִּשְׁמְרוּ אֶת כְּהוּנַּתְכֶם לְכָל דְּבַר הַמִּזְבֵּחַ", יָכוֹל אַף בִּשְׁחִיטָה? ת"ל: °"וְשָׁחַט אֶת בֶּן הַבָּקָר לִפְנֵי ה' ג] *וְהִקְרִיבוּ" וגו' — מִקַּבָּלָה וְאֵילָךְ *מִצְוַת כְּהוּנָּה, לִימֵּד עַל הַשְּׁחִיטָה שֶׁכְּשֵׁרָה בְּכָל אָדָם! הוּא הַדִּין זדַּאֲפִי' לְכַתְּחִילָּה נַמִי, וּמִשּׁוּם דְּקָא בָּעֵי לְמִיתְנָא טְמֵאִים דִּלְכַתְּחִילָּה לָא, גְּזֵירָה שֶׁמָּא יִגְּעוּ בַּבָּשָׂר — תָּנָא: "שֶׁשְּׁחָטוּ". וְטָמֵא דִּיעֲבַד שַׁפִּיר דָּמֵי? וּרְמִינְהוּ: "וְסָמַךְ וְשָׁחַט" מַה סְּמִיכָה בִּטְהוֹרִים — אַף שְׁחִיטָה בִּטְהוֹרִים! חמִדְּרַבָּנַן. מ"ש סְמִיכָה — טדִּכְתִיב: "לִפְנֵי ה'", שְׁחִיטָה נַמִי — הָכְתִיב: "לִפְנֵי ה'"! אֶפְשָׁר דַּעֲבִיד סַכִּין אֲרוּכָּה וְשָׁחֵיט. סְמִיכָה נַמִי, אֶפְשָׁר דִּמְעַיֵּיל יְדֵיהּ וְסָמֵיךְ! קָסָבַר: *בִּיאָה בְּמִקְצָת שְׁמָהּ בִּיאָה. רַב חִסְדָּא מַתְנֵי אִיפְכָא: "וְסָמַךְ וְשָׁחַט", מַה שְׁחִיטָה בִּטְהוֹרִין — אַף סְמִיכָה בִּטְהוֹרִין. מַאי שְׁנָא שְׁחִיטָה — דִּכְתִיב: "לִפְנֵי ה'" סְמִיכָה

רש"י

וְכוּלָּן. הַפְּסוּלִין. שֶׁקִּיבְּלוּ הַדָּם. עַל מְנָת לֶאֱכוֹל ד] וּלְהַקְטִיר חוּץ לִזְמַנּוֹ אוֹ חוּץ לִמְקוֹמוֹ. אִם יֵשׁ דַּם הַנֶּפֶשׁ. עוֹד בַּבְּהֵמָה, יַחֲזוֹר הַכָּשֵׁר וִיקַבֵּל וְיִזְרוֹק הַכָּשֵׁר. שֶׁאֵין מַחֲשַׁבְתָּן שֶׁל אֵלּוּ פּוֹסַלְתָּן בְּקַבָּלָה, לְפִי שֶׁאֵין רְאוּיִין לָהּ, וְאֵין מַחֲשָׁבָה פּוֹסֶלֶת אֶלָּא בְּמִי שֶׁרָאוּי לַעֲבוֹדָה, דִּכְתִיב: "הַמַּקְרִיב אוֹתוֹ לֹא יֵחָשֵׁב" (ויקרא ז) — בָּרָאוּי לְהַקְרָבָה הַכָּתוּב מְדַבֵּר. יַחֲזִיר לַכָּשֵׁר. דְּלָא מִיפְסִיל בְּהָכִי. וּבְפֶרֶק ה] [רִאשׁוֹן] (דף יד:) שָׁנִינַן לָהּ לְמַאן דְּאִית לֵיהּ הוֹלָכָה שֶׁלֹּא בְּרֶגֶל שְׁמָהּ הוֹלָכָה, לְמַר כִּדְאִית לֵיהּ וּלְאִידָךְ כִּדְאִית לֵיהּ. נְתָנוֹ ו]. הַפָּסוּל, עַל גַּבֵּי הַכֶּבֶשׁ אוֹ שֶׁלֹּא כְּנֶגֶד הַיְסוֹד כו'. יַחֲזוֹר הַכָּשֵׁר וִיקַבֵּל. אִי סְבִירָא ז] לָן דְּפָסוּל עוֹשֶׂה שִׁירַיִים, אַשְׁמְעִינַן הַאי תַּנָּא דְּשֶׁלֹּא בִּמְקוֹמוֹ לָאו כִּמְקוֹמוֹ דָּמֵי, לְפִיכָךְ לֹא עֲשָׂאָן שִׁירַיִים. וְאִי סְבִירָא לֵיהּ דְּשֶׁלֹּא בִּמְקוֹמוֹ כִּמְקוֹמוֹ דָּמֵי, וַהֲוָיָא לָהּ זְרִיקָה גְּמוּרָה בְּאָדָם פָּסוּל — אַשְׁמְעִינַן דְּאֵין פָּסוּל עוֹשֶׂה שִׁירַיִים. **גמ'** ה"ג: וּרְמִינְהוּ וְשָׁחַט שְׁחִיטָה בְּזָר כְּשֵׁרָה. מִדְּלָא כְּתִיב "וְשָׁחַט הַכֹּהֵן". וְכִי מֵאַיִן בָּאתָ. לוֹמַר שֶׁצְּרִיכָה כְּהוּנָּה? וַהֲלֹא לֹא נֶאֱמַר בָּהּ כֹּהֵן! וְהִקְרִיבוּ הַכֹּהֲנִים. וּמִדִּכְתִיב בְּקַבָּלָה כְּהוּנָּה, וּבִשְׁחִיטָה לָא כְּתִיב — לִימֵּד עַל הַשְּׁחִיטָה שֶׁכְּשֵׁרָה בְּזָר. מַה סְּמִיכָה בִּטְהוֹרִים. כִּדְמְפָרֵשׁ לְקַמֵּיהּ. מִדְּרַבָּנַן. שֶׁמָּא יִגְּעוּ בַּבָּשָׂר. מַאי שְׁנָא סְמִיכָה. דִּבְטְהוֹרִים מִדְּאוֹרַיְיתָא. דִּכְתִיב לִפְנֵי ה'. וְשָׁחַט

תוספות

החמירו עליו לצאת, כמו שמפרש רבינו תם, משום דקשיא ליה דהתם אסר ליה לטבול יום ליכנס בעזרת נשים משום דסמוך למחנה ח] [שכינה]. ואמרינן נמי בגמ' שחידשו דברים ואמרו: טבול יום אל יכנס למחנה לויה, פירוש: לא בכל מחנה לויה, ט] דמפתח הר הבית עד שער ניקנור מחנה לויה, כדתנא בתוספתא ובסיפרי. ובפרק בתרא דמכילתין (דף קטז:) ובכלים (פ"א מ"ח) משמע דשרי בכולהו חוץ מעזרת נשים, ואפי' טבול יום דזבין וזבות. אלא במחנה לויה — כגון עזרת נשים דסמוך למחנה שכינה קאמר. ובמסכת תמיד משמע דשרי בכל מחנה לויה, גבי בית המוקד שזקני בית אב ישנים שם, וקתני: י] כשאירע קרי לאחד מהן — הולך וטובל וחוזר לאחיו הכהנים עד שהשערים נפתחין, והולך לו. ואין לך סמוך למחנה שכינה יותר מבית המוקד, שחציה בקודש וחציה בחול. ובסוטה פרק "היה נוטל" (דף כ:) יא] (הא) דקתני: והם אומרים הוציאוה שלא תטמא העזרה. ופריך עלה מהא דדרשינן דטמא מת מותר ליכנס במחנה לויה ואפי' מת עצמו, כדכתיב: "ויקח משה את עצמות יוסף עמו" — עמו במחיצתו. ואי דרבנן אסור מאי קושיא? ומתוך כך מחלק רבינו תם דלא גזור היכא דנטמא בעזרה. ומורי מתרץ: דבעזרת נשים החמירו יותר משאר מקומות, אע"פ שסמוכים ממש למחנה יב] לויה — לפי שהוא מקום כניסה ויציאה לכל אדם יותר, שדרך שם נכנסין לעזרת ישראל דרך שער נקנור, שהוא שער העליון המשמש הכניסה והיציאה. והא דפריך בסוטה על מה שאמר "הוציאוה" — משום דקתני "הוציאוה" תרי זימני, דמשמע שהיו נבהלים להוציאה וממהרין מאד. ואי לאו דאיכא איסורא דאורייתא — לא היו דוחקין כל כך למהר. והא דאמר בפרק "אלו הן הנשרפין" (סנהדרין דף פא:): כהן המשמש בטומאה אין אחיו הכהנים מביאין אותו לב"ד, אלא מוציאין אותו חוץ לעזרה ומפצעין את מוחו בגיזרין — לאו דווקא חוץ לעזרת ישראל, אלא אף חוץ לעזרת נשים וחוץ לחיל. וכי ה"ג נמי הוי ההיא דסוטה דקתני: שלא תטמא העזרה, יג] והיו זקוקין להוציאה אף חוץ לחיל להר הבית, דהא מפרש טעמא התם שמא תפרוס נדה. וא"ת: וכיון דטבול יום מותר בשאר העזרה כדפרישית, אמאי איצטריך לו למצורע בערב הפסח לחות עשה? ילך בשאר הלשכות ויכניס שם ידיו לבהונות! וי"ל: דלא אפשר, משום דכתיב: "פתח אהל מועד" — והיינו בשער נקנור שהוא מכוון כנגדו. ומיהו, בקדשי קדשים לא אפשר ליה לטמא לשחוט בצידי העזרה, [דשחיטתן] בצפון, ולא משכחת פתח מכוון לצד הצפון, כדמוכח בגמ' למ"ד מרחק לפון, דפריך: וליעבד פשפש, ומשני: הכל בכתב. ולפירוש רבינו תם נמי, דמפרש דנטמא בעזרת נשים לא גזור — מ"מ למ"ד מרחק לפון יד] ושחיט בסכין ארוכה עשרים ושתים אמה. ואין לחוש בכך [הא דקאמר] דשחיטה כשירה בדיעבד, ושמא יגעו בבשר נקט משום קדשים קלים. וה"ר אפרים היה מפרש דמשכחת לה דשחיט טמא דרך גגין ועליות דלא נתקדשו, ובסכין ארוכה, למ"ד ביאה במקצת שמה ביאה שאין יכול להכניס שם ידו. ומיהו, התינח בקדשים קלים שיכול לתלות הבהמה ולשחטה. אבל בקדשי קדשים לא אפשר, דבעינן שחיטה על ירך, כדאמר לעיל בפרק שני (דף כו.), אם לא נאמר דעביד טו] בסכין ארוכה מן העליה והגג עד הרצפה. ולהאי פירושא לא תקשי לו מיניה ממצורע שיכניס ידיו לבהונות דרך גגין ועליות, ולא איצטריך לדחות עשה, דהיאך יעלה לגגין דרך הר הבית והחיל?*. ת"ל והקריבו מקבלה ואילך מצות כהונה. ואם תאמר: תיפוק ליה מהיקישא דסמיכה ושחיטה, דמה סמיכה בזרים — אף שחיטה בזרים, כדדריש ר"ש בריש "הקומץ רבה" (מנחות יט.)! וי"ל: דאי לאו דרשא דהכא הוה ממעטינן שחיטה מדכתיב: "תשמרו את כהונתכם", דמשמע אפי' שחיטה בכלל. ואע"ג דאיצטריך לן לעיל ספ"ק (דף יג.) "והקריבו בני אהרן הכהנים" לגז"ש, שתהא בכהן כשר ובכלי שרת — מ"מ דריש מיניה שפיר: מקבלה ואילך מצות כהונה. **מאי** שנא סמיכה דבטהורים דכתיב לפני ה'. פי' בקונטרס: דהיינו מדכתיב "ושחט את בן הבקר לפני ה'", וכיון דבעינן תיכף לסמיכה שחיטה — אין סמיכה מבחוץ ושחיטה מבפנים, אלא אף הסמיכה מבפנים, ואין טמא נכנס לעזרה. והקשה הרב רבי יעקב דאורלינ"ש: דבפ' בתרא (דף*) משמע דכתיב בסמיכה גופה "לפני ה'". דקאמר: דאין סמיכה בבמה, משום דכתיב "לפני ה'". ואי לא כתב בה "לפני ה'", אלא מקרא דשחיטה — הא שחיטה גופה ישנה בבמה. והתם פירש בקונטרס דהיינו קרא דכתיב בפר כהן משיח "לפני ה' וסמך". ומיהו, לקמן בשמעתין (דף לג.) משמע כפירוש הקונט' דהכא. דפריך למאן דאמר תיכף לסמיכה שחיטה לאו דאורייתא, מדתניא: "וסמך ושחט", מה סמיכה בטהורים אף שחיטה בטהורים, ואי אמרת לאו דאורייתא — בטמאין נמי משכחת לה. משמע בהדיא דלא ידעינן סמיכה לפני ה' אלא משום דתיכף לסמיכה שחיטה. וצריך לדחוק ההוא דלקמן דפ' בתרא (גם זה שם). ומיהו, יש ליישב ההיא דלקמן בשמעתין, משום טז] דההיא סוגיא כמאן דאמר ביאה במקצת לאו שמה ביאה. דאי משום "לפני ה'" — אפשר דמעייל ידיה וסמיך, אבל אי אמרת תיכף לסמיכה שחיטה — לא אפשר, יז] דמרחק לפון. מיהו, "וסמך ושחט" דכתיב גבי עולה דטעונה לפון דריש בתורת כהנים בפרשת ויקרא: מה סמיכה בטהורים — אף שחיטה בטהורים. ובהדיא דריש התם מקרא דלעיל, דכתיב: "יקריב אותו לרצונו לפני ה' וסמך", יח] מדכתיב ממש "וסמך" אגל "לפני ה'" דריש "לפני ה'". ולא כפי' הקונטרס דפרק בתרא, דדריש לה מקרא אחרינא דפר כהן משיח. תדע דמפר כהן משיח היכי מצי למילף שאר סמיכות לפני ה'? יט] שאני התם, דקדושה חמורה היא חטאות הפנימיות.

ורבי

מסורת הש"ס

לעיל כו: | [לעיל יד:] | יומא מח. לעיל טו. | לעיל כו. | [יומא כז.] | במדבר יח | ויקרא א | נ"ל והקריבו בני אהרן הכהנים וגו' | [ברכות לא: וש"נ] | [לקמן לג:] | [יומא לח.] | רש"ק | וע"ע תוספות חולין ב: ד"ה שמא יגעו | קיט: וע"ש ברש"י ד"ה לפני ה' וסמך לרצונו לפני ה' וסמך ליה וסמך את ידו ויקרא א]

עין משפט נר מצוה

ג א מיי' פי"ד מהלכות פסה"מ הלכה ב:
ד ב מיי' פ"א מהלכות פסה"מ הלכה כז:
ה ג ד מיי' שם הלכה כד ופי"א שם הל' ב:
ו ה מיי' שם פ"א הלכה כה:
ז ו מיי' פ"ב מהלכות פסה"מ הלכה י:
ח ז מיי' פ"א מהלכות פסה"מ הלכה א:
ט ח ט מיי' פ"ג מהל' מעה"ק הלכה יא:

שיטה מקובצת

א] אם יש דם הנפש כו'. האי תנא אי ס"ל דפסול עושה שיריים א"כ צריך לפרש דחוץ למקומו לאו כמקומו דמי ולכך יחזור הכשר ויקבל ואי ס"ל כמקומו דמי (אינו) צריך לפרש [אינו] עושה שיריים. כפ"ה. ואגב חורפיה לא דק דמאן דאית ליה לאו כמקומו דמי לא קאי אפסול כלל כדמוכח לעיל מיהו ודאי (כמ"ד) [למ"ד] כמקומו דמי ע"כ אפסול קאי וא"ת א"כ מאי איבעי ליה לר"ל מר"י אי פסול עושה שיריים אי לא והא אית ליה לר"ל לעיל כמקומו דמי וא"כ תפשוט מהא דפסול אינו עושה שיריים וי"ל דאיכא למימר משום דדוקא שנתנו למעלה או למטה אבל אם נתנו בהכשירו לא יחזור הכשר ויקבל ומיהו קשה דא"כ תפשוט דפסול עושה שיריים מדנקט פסול [שנתן שלא בהכשירו] משמע משום פסול לחוד עושה שיריים לכך נ"ל כדפי' לעיל בפ' קבלה דאי קאי אפסול היינו אטמא דבהא מיהא כ"ע מודו דעושה שיריים הואיל ומרצה בצבור כדאיתא במעילה [עי' תוס' דף כו ע"ב ד"ה הכ"ע עכ"ה]: ב] ששחטו דיעבד: ג] והקריבו הכהנים וגו' מקבלה ואילך מצות כהונה. תימה תיפוק ליה מהיקשא דסמיכה לשחיטה כדדריש ר"ש בפ' הקומץ רבה וי"ל דאי לאו דרשא דהכא הוי ממעטינן שחיטה נמי בכלל כהונה מדכתי' כהונתכם ואף על גב דאיצטרך בפ"ק והקריבו בני אהרן הכהנים לג"ש שתהא בכהן כשר ובכלי שרת מ"מ דריש נמי מקבלה ואילך מצות כהונה. מהר"פ: ד] לאכול או להקטיר חוץ: ה] ראשון מפרש לה: ו] נתנו פסול זה על גבי: ז] סבירא ליה דפסול: ח] שכינה אמרי': ט] לויה קאמר דמפתח הר הבית כו' מחנה לויה כדתניא: י] וקתני אירע קרי לאחד כו' וחוזר ויושב אצל אחיו הכהנים וכו' נפתחין ויוצא והולך לו:

יא] נוטל אחא דקתני כו' תטמא העזרה פריך עלה: יב] למחנה שכינה לפי: יג] שהרי היו זקוקין להוציאה אף חוץ להר הבית כו' מותר בשארי צידי העזרה כדפרישית כו' למצורע שחל שמיני שלו בערב הפסח כו' דיו לבהונות ויקיים את שתיהן וי"ל: יד] צפון היכי שחיט בסכין: טו] דעביד סכין ארוכה מן כו' תקשי ממצורע שיכנים כו' דהיאך יעלה לגגין ועליות אם לא דרך הר הבית: טז] משום דההיא סוגיא: יז] דמרחק דסמך ושחט גבי עולה כתיב דטעונה צפון ועלה דריש בת"כ בפ' ויקרא: יח] ה' וסמך ולא: יט] ה' דלמא שאני התם דקדושה דחטאות הפנימית חמורה היא הס"ד:

סְמִיכָה נַמִי כְּתִיב: "לִפְנֵי ה'"! אֶפְשָׁר דִּמְעַיֵּיל יְדֵיהּ וְסָמֵיךְ. שְׁחִיטָה נַמִי, אֶפְשָׁר דְּעָבֵיד סַכִּין אֲרוּכָּה וְשָׁחֵיט! הָא מַנִּי – שִׁמְעוֹן הַתִּימְנִי הִיא. דְּתַנְיָא: "וְשָׁחַט אֶת בֶּן הַבָּקָר לִפְנֵי ה'" – א] וְלֹא הַשּׁוֹחֵט לִפְנֵי ה'. שִׁמְעוֹן הַתִּימְנִי אוֹמֵר: מִנַּיִן שֶׁיְּהוּ יָדָיו שֶׁל שׁוֹחֵט לִפְנִים מִן הַנִּשְׁחָט – ת"ל: "וְשָׁחַט אֶת בֶּן הַבָּקָר לִפְנֵי ה'", שׁוֹחֵט אֶת בֶּן הַבָּקָר יְהֵא ב] לִפְנֵי ה'. אָמַר עוּלָּא אָמַר רֵישׁ לָקִישׁ: אטָמֵא שֶׁהִכְנִיס יָדוֹ לִפְנִים – לוֹקֶה, שֶׁנֶּאֱמַר: °"בְּכָל קֹדֶשׁ לֹא תִגָּע" ג] וגו', מַקִּישׁ בִּיאָה לִנְגִיעָה, מַה נְּגִיעָה בְּמִקְצָת שְׁמָהּ נְגִיעָה, אַף *בִּיאָה בְּמִקְצָת שְׁמָהּ בִּיאָה. אֵיתִיבֵיהּ רַב הוֹשַׁעְיָא לְעוּלָּא: *במְצוֹרָע שֶׁחָל שְׁמִינִי שֶׁלּוֹ לִהְיוֹת בְּעֶרֶב הַפֶּסַח, וְרָאָה קֶרִי בּוֹ בַּיּוֹם וְטָבַל, אָמְרוּ חֲכָמִים: אע"פ שֶׁאֵין טְבוּל יוֹם אַחֵר נִכְנָס – זֶה נִכְנָס, ד] מוּטָב יָבוֹא עֲשֵׂה שֶׁיֵּשׁ בּוֹ כָּרֵת וְיִדְחֶה עֲשֵׂה שֶׁאֵין בּוֹ כָּרֵת. *וְרַבִּי יוֹחָנָן אָמַר: דְּבַר תּוֹרָה אֲפִי' עֲשֵׂה אֵין בּוֹ, שֶׁנֶּאֱמַר: °"וַיַּעֲמֹד יְהוֹשָׁפָט בִּקְהַל יְהוּדָה וִירוּשָׁלַםִ בְּבֵית ה' לִפְנֵי הֶחָצֵר הַחֲדָשָׁה". מַאי "חָצֵר הַחֲדָשָׁה"? ה] אָמַר ר' יוֹחָנָן: שֶׁחִידְּשׁוּ בָּהּ דְּבָרִים (הַרְבֵּה) וְאָמְרוּ: *גטְבוּל יוֹם אַל יִכָּנֵס לְמַחֲנֵה לְוִיָּה. וְאִי אָמְרַתְּ בִּיאָה בְּמִקְצָת שְׁמָהּ בִּיאָה – הֵיכִי מְעַיֵּיל יְדֵיהּ (א) בַּבְּהוֹנוֹת? אִידִי וְאִידִי עֲשֵׂה שֶׁיֵּשׁ בּוֹ כָּרֵת הוּא! א"ל: *מְטוּנָּף, שָׁאנֵי מְצוֹרָע, הוֹאִיל וְהוּתַּר לְצָרַעְתּוֹ הוּתַּר לְקִירְיוֹ. אָמַר רַב יוֹסֵף, קָסָבַר עוּלָּא: רוּבָּן זָבִים וְנַעֲשׂוּ טְמֵאֵי מֵתִים, הוֹאִיל וְהוּתְּרוּ לְטוּמְאָתָן – הוּתְּרוּ לְזִיבָתָן. אֲמַר לֵיהּ אַבַּיֵי: מִי דָּמֵי? טוּמְאָה אִישְׁתְּרַאי, זִיבָה לָא אִישְׁתְּרַאי! (ב) אֲמַר לֵיהּ: דִּלְמָא הָכִי קָאָמַר מָר: רוּבָּן טְמֵאֵי מֵתִים וְנַעֲשׂוּ זָבִים, הוֹאִיל וְהוּתְּרוּ לְטוּמְאָתָן – הוּתְּרוּ לְזִיבָתָן? אֲמַר לֵיהּ: אִין. (ג) וְאַכַּתִּי לָא דָּמֵי, מְצוֹרָע הֶיתֵּירָא הוּא, הוֹאִיל וְאִישְׁתְּרֵי – אִישְׁתְּרֵי. טוּמְאָה דְּחוּיָה הִיא, לְהָא אִידְחַאי, לְהָא לָא אִידְחַאי! אֲמַר לֵיהּ רָבָא: אַדְּרַבָּה, אִיפְּכָא מִסְתַּבְּרָא: מְצוֹרָע הֶיתֵּירָא הוּא, לְהָא אִישְׁתְּרַאי וּלְהָא לָא אִישְׁתְּרַאי. טוּמְאָה דְּחוּיָה הוּא, מַה לִּי חַד דִּחוּיָא מַה לִּי שְׁתֵּי דְּחִיּוֹת.

מִכְּלָל

"וְשָׁחַט אֶת בֶּן הַבָּקָר לִפְנֵי ה'", וְכֵיוָן דְּבָעֵינַן תֵּיכֶף לִסְמִיכָה שְׁחִיטָה – אֵין סְמִיכָה מִבַּחוּץ וּשְׁחִיטָה מִבִּפְנִים, אֶלָּא אַף הַסְּמִיכָה בִּפְנִים, וְאֵין טָמֵא נִכְנָס לָעֲזָרָה. וְאֵין הַשּׁוֹחֵט לִפְנֵי ה'. שֶׁאִם רָצָה, עוֹמֵד חוּץ לָעֲזָרָה וְשׁוֹחֵט בְּסַכִּין אֲרוּכָּה. לִפְנִים מִן הַנִּשְׁחָט. לִפְנִים מִן הַבְּהֵמָה. ה"ג: שׁוֹחֵט אֶת בֶּן הַבָּקָר יְהֵא לִפְנֵי ה'. [מַה] נְגִיעָה. סְתָם בְּמִקְצָת הִיא. שֶׁחָל שְׁמִינִי שֶׁלּוֹ. וְהָיָה לוֹ הַיּוֹם לִיכָּנֵס לְהַר הַבַּיִת לַחֲלַל שַׁעַר נִקָּנוֹר, שֶׁלֹּא נִתְקַדֵּשׁ, לְהַכְנִיס יָדָיו לִבְהוֹנוֹת. וְרָאָה קֶרִי, וּבַעַל קֶרִי אֵין נִכְנָס לְהַר הַבַּיִת, כִּדְאָמְרִי' בְּ"אֵלּוּ דְּבָרִים" (פסחים דף סז:): "זָב" "וְכָל זָב" – לְרַבּוֹת בַּעַל קֶרִי שֶׁמִּשְׁתַּלֵּחַ חוּץ לִשְׁתֵּי מַחֲנוֹת, כִּדְאָמְרִינַן הָתָם. אע"פ שֶׁאֵין טְבוּל יוֹם אַחֵר. שֶׁל טוּמְאַת קֶרִי נִכְנָס לְהַר הַבַּיִת, דְּקָסָבַר: טְבוּל יוֹם דְּזָב כְּזָב דָּמֵי ו] – זֶה נִכְנָס, וּמַכְנִיס יָדָיו לָעֲזָרָה לִיתֵּן מִדַּם הָאָשָׁם וּמִלּוֹג הַשֶּׁמֶן עַל בְּהוֹנוֹתָיו כְּדֵי שֶׁיִּטָּהֵר לֶאֱכוֹל פִּסְחוֹ לָעֶרֶב. וְהוּא יְשַׁלְּחֶנּוּ לָעֲזָרָה הַיּוֹם לִשְׁחוֹט וְלִזְרוֹק עָלָיו, אֲבָל הוּא לֹא יִכָּנֵס לָעֲזָרָה, ז] (וְשׁוֹחֵט בְּסַכִּין אֲרוּכָּה) דִּטְבוּל יוֹם שֶׁנִּכְנָס לָעֲזָרָה בְּכָרֵת, כִּדְאָמְרִי' בְּ"הַקּוֹמֵץ רַבָּה" (מנחות כז:). מוּטָב יָבוֹא עֲשֵׂה. שֶׁל פֶּסַח. שֶׁיֵּשׁ בּוֹ כָּרֵת וְיִדְחֶה עֲשֵׂה. דְּשִׁילּוּחַ טְמֵאִים מֵהַר הַבַּיִת שֶׁאֵין בּוֹ כָּרֵת. שֶׁאֵין עָנוּשׁ כָּרֵת אֶלָּא מְחוֹמַת הָעֲזָרָה וְלִפְנִים. אֲפִי' עֲשֵׂה אֵין בּוֹ. בְּהַר הַבַּיִת לְגַבֵּי טְבוּל יוֹם. דְּקָסָבַר: טְבוּל יוֹם דְּזָב לָאו כְּזָב דָּמֵי. *נֹכַח הֶחָצֵר הַחֲדָשָׁה. הַר הַבַּיִת, שֶׁחִידְּשׁוּ בָּהּ בְּהִלְכוֹתֶיהָ. אִידִי וְאִידִי. עֲשֵׂה שֶׁל כָּרֵת! טְבוּל יוֹם לְגַבֵּי עֲזָרָה בְּכָרֵת הוּא, וְהָא קָא מְעַיֵּיל ח] לָעֲזָרָה, שֶׁהֲרֵי אִי אֶפְשָׁר לְהוֹצִיא דַּם הָאָשָׁם לַחֲלַל הַשַּׁעַר, דְּמִיפְסַל בְּיוֹצֵא. מְטוּנָּף. מְמַשָּׁחָךְ ט] שֶׁבָּאתָה עָלַי לְהַכְבִּיד – אַכְבִּיד עָלֶיךָ. מִמְּצוֹרָע הֶשִׁיבוֹתָ, שֶׁגְּזֵירַת הַכָּתוּב הִיא אֶלָּא שֶׁהוּתְּרָה לוֹ בִּיאָה בְּמִקְצָת, שֶׁהֲרֵי מְחוּסַּר כִּיפּוּרִים הוּא, וְהוּא מַכְנִיס יָדָיו לִבְהוֹנוֹת. הוֹאִיל וְהוּתְּרָה. בִּיאָה י] מִקְצָת לְצָרַעְתּוֹ. הוּתְּרָה. אַף לִטְבוּל יוֹם שֶׁל קֶרִי שֶׁלּוֹ. אָמַר רַב יוֹסֵף. שְׁמַע מִינָּהּ מִדְּעוּלָּא דְּאָמַר: הוֹאִיל וְאִישְׁתְּרֵי לְהָא אִישְׁתְּרֵי לְהָא. רוּבָּן. שֶׁל צִיבּוּר זָבִין בְּפֶסַח, וְלֹא נִדְחֵית טוּמְאַת זִיבָה אֶצְלָן, וְנַעֲשׂוּ טְמֵאֵי מֵתִים בּוֹ בַּיּוֹם, הוֹאִיל וְהוּתְּרוּ לְטוּמְאַת הַמֵּת שֶׁנִּדְחָה אֶצְלָן – הוּתְּרוּ יא] לְזִיבָתָן. טוּמְאָה אִישְׁתְּרַאי. שֶׁבָּאָה אַחֲרוֹנָה, זִיבָה רִאשׁוֹנָה עוֹמֶדֶת בִּמְקוֹמָהּ. וְלָא דָּמֵי לִמְצוֹרָע, דְּהָתָם אִיכָּא לְמֵימַר: מִיגּוֹ דְּקַמַּיְיתָא לָא הָוֵי אֲסִירָא לֵיהּ – בַּתְרַיְיתָא לָא חֲמִירָא לָךְ מִקַּמַּיְיתָא, שֶׁהֲרֵי טָמֵא הָיָה וּמוּתָּר. אֲבָל הָכָא, כִּי הֲוָה זִיבָה גְּרֵידְתָּא – הָווּ אֲסִירֵי, הַשְׁתָּא דְּאִיתּוֹסְפָא טוּמְאָה עֲלַיְיהוּ *אִישְׁתְּרוּ לְהוּ. הוֹאִיל וְהוּתְּרוּ לְטוּמְאָתָן. הַקּוֹדֶמֶת, אֵינָן נֶאֱסָרִין מֵחֲמַת הָאַחֲרוֹנָה. שֶׁהֲרֵי אַף הָרִאשׁוֹנָה טוּמְאָה שֶׁל כָּרֵת הָיְתָה, וְהָיוּ מוּתָּרִים הַיּוֹם. הֶיתֵּירָא הֲוַאי. בְּהֶיתֵּר גָּמוּר, יב] גְּזֵרָה עָלָיו תּוֹרָה בִּיאָה בְּמִקְצָת.

טוּמְאָה

ורבי יוחנן אמר דבר תורה אפי' עשה אין בו. לפרושי ברייתא קאתי, ולאו לאיפלוגי. דר' יוחנן לאו תנא הוא, כדמוכח בפ"ק דכתובות (דף ח.) גבי מתניס מן המנין, ומשני: רב תנא ופליג, ואר' יוחנן לא משני הכי. תדע, דאי דאורייתא – אם כן היה לנו לאסור מפתח הר הבית, שכל זה מחנה לויה, כדאיתא בסוף מכילתין (דף קטז:). ובהדיא תנן במס' כלים (פ"א מ"ח): עזרת נשים מקודשת הימנו, שאין טבול יום נכנס לשם, אבל בהר הבית ובחיל מותר. יג] ותני נמי בתמיד (דף כו.) דבא וישב לו אצל אחיו הכהנים. ומיהו, מתוך פירכות הללו מיתרצא פירכא קמייתא, דאע"ג דר' יוחנן לאו תנא הוא – דלמא סבר לה כמתני' דתמיד יד] וכלים. ולמאי דפירש בקונט' טעמא דברייתא דאין טבול יום של טומאת קרי נכנס להר הבית, משום דקסבר טבול יום דזב כזב דמי, ואמרינן פ' "אלו דברים" (פסחים סז:): "זב" ו"כל זב" לרבות בעל קרי. ור' יוחנן דאמר אפילו עשה אין בו, משום דקסבר טבול יום דזב לאו כזב דמי – אתי שפיר, דפלוגתא דתנאי היא, טו] ואיכא למ"ד טבול יום דזב לאו כזב דמי. ומיהו קשה: דאי קסבר האי תנא טבול יום דזב כזב דמי – אם כן איכא לאו ד"לא יטמאו את מחניהם", ואין עשה דוחה את לא תעשה ועשה! ועוד קשה: מדאמרינן פרק "ג' מינין" (נזיר דף מה.): "טמא יהיה" – לרבות טבול יום, "עוד טומאתו בו" – לרבות מחוסר כיפורים. ואי טבול יום אסור טז] למחנה לויה, למה לי קרא לרבות במחנה שכינה? ומיהו, מצי למימר משום כרת איצטריך, דאיירי ביה קרא, שאין ענוש כרת אלא מחומת העזרה ולפנים. ועוד קשה: דאי טעמא דרבי יוחנן משום דקסבר דטבול יום דזב לאו כזב דמי, והא רבא אית ליה הך דרבי יוחנן בפסחים פרק "האשה" (דף צב.), ושמעינן ליה לרבא בכריתות פרק שני (דף י.) דמחוסר כיפורים דזב כזב דמי! יז] אלא ודאי הא דאמר דטבול יום דזב כזב דמי – לאו לענין ביאת מקדש קאמר, אלא לענין פסח הבא בטומאה לא יאכלו ממנו זבים וזבות, כדפי' לעיל בריש פרק שני (דף יז:) בשם ה"ר חיים. ומיהו, סוגיא דנזיר (דף מה.) קשה למה שפי' דטבול יום שרי במחנה לויה, דמשמע התם דאפי' נאמר דטבול יום דזב לאו כזב דמי – אסור ליכנס למחנה לויה. דקאמר התם: מה אהל מועד מחוסר כיפורים לא עייל – אף התם נמי במחנה לויה מחוסר כיפורים לא עייל. ומקרא דריש יח] התם, דקתני התם בברייתא: "ובא לפני ה' אל פתח אהל מועד" – לשער נקנור, אימתי הוא בא – בזמן שטבל ועשה הערב שמש! ונראה, דדווקא בטבול יום דזב יט] שלש ראיות, שהוא טבול יום ומחוסר כיפורים, דאיכא תרתי, קאסר במחנה לויה. וכי מסיק התם: אלא אמר אביי, טבול יום דזב לאו כזב דמי, ואפי' הכי כיון דמחוסר כיפורים לא עייל – כלומר, דאיכא תרתי כ] ולאו מלשון זבא דריש, דאם כן גבי נזיר דכתיב "יביא שתי תורים" וגו' הוה לן למידרש הכי כדאמר התם. אבל טבול יום דזב בעל שתי ראיות, ודבעל קרי – שרי, דלאו מחוסר כפרה. והא דאמר הכא כשראה קרי בו ביום וטבל, דנכנס, אע"פ שהוא טבול יום וגם מחוסר כיפורים – אין אלו שני הדברים על טומאה אחת, אלא טבול יום משום קרי, ומחוסר כפרה משום לרעתו. ולפי' הקונטרס ניחא דנקט בברייתא "וראה קרי" ולא טמא שרץ ונבילה, דטמא שרץ ואפילו טמא מת נכנסין להר הבית, כדדרשינן בפסחים פ' "אלו דברים" (דף סז.) ובסוטה פרק "היה נוטל" (דף כ:): "ויקח משה את עצמות יוסף עמו" – במחיצתו. אבל לפי מה שפירשתי, דרבי יוחנן לא פליג כא] אברייתא, ולא אסור אלא מדרבנן – כולהו טמאים נמי אסירי, כדתנן בפ"ק דכלים: החיל מקודש הימנו שאין גוים וטמאי מתים נכנסין לשם. וכל שכן בעזרת נשים, כדתני התם: שאין טבול יום נכנס לשם. כב] וכולהו *טבול יום, אפילו דטמאי מת דשרץ ונבילה [איירי], דאיירי ביה לעיל. ונראה לפרש דלרבותא נקט וראה קרי, דאף על גב דמשתלח חוץ לשתי מחנות – התירו לו משום פסח. **שחידשו** בה דברים ואמרו טבול יום אל יכנס למחנה לויה. וא"ת: מנלן שחידשו מטבול יום? אימא שחידשו ממת עצמו, או מטמא מת! ויש לומר: דמשמע דלא חידשו אלא על אגר, ואגר היינו עזרת נשים, כדמוכח ביחזקאל. (מ) ואילו מת וטמא מת – מצינו דאסורין אפילו בחיל. **א"ל** מטונף. פירוש: ממשאך, שבאת להכביד עלי – אכביד עליך. דאדרבה, משם סייעתא לדברי, כג] דשאני מצורע וכו'. מדנקט "וראה קרי בו ביום" – משמע דווקא בו ביום, דילא בשעת היתר דלרעת, ואיכא למימר מתוך שהותר לצרעתו הותר לקיריו, אבל כד] מאתמול – לא. ואי ביאה במקצת לא שמה ביאה – אפי' מאתמול נמי. והשתא אתי שפיר הא דאמר בפ"ק דיבמות (דף ח.): מי לא מודה עולא שאם ראה קרי בליל כה] (שלישי) [שמיני] שאינו מכניס ידיו, שלא יצא בשעה שהיא ראויה להביא קרבן. מנא ליה דמודה עולא? אלא מדנקט "בו ביום" דייק דטעמא דעולא משום דהואיל והותר לצרעתו הותר לקיריו. ובענין זה יש לפרש "מטונף" דפ' "הזרוע והלחיים" (חולין דף קלג.). דקאמר התם: עולא יהיב מתנתא לכהנתא, אלמא דקסבר עולא כהן ואפילו כהנת. כו] והכתיב "וכל מנחת כהן כליל תהיה"! ואמר ליה: רבי, מטונף, אהרן ובניו כתובים בפרשה. כלומר, משם אכביד עליך.

שהיא

י א מיי' פ"ג מהלכות ביאת מקדש הלכה יח:

יא ב מיי' פ"ו מהלכות קרבן פסח הלכה ה:

יב ג מיי' פ"ג מהלכות ביאת מקדש הל' ו:

שיטה מקובצת

א] ה' בן הבקר לפני ה' ולא: ב] לפני ה'. ס"א שיהא שוחט ובן הבקר לפני ה': ג] לא תגע ואל המקדש לא תבא וגו': ד] מוטב יבא עשה שיש בו כרת וידחה עשה שאין בו כרת. פרש"י שאין ענוש כרת אלא מן החומה ולפנים משמע (הכי) [הכא] דטבול יום דקרי בקרי דמי וקשה טובא חדא דאיך פליג ר"י על ההיא ברייתא [ועל מתני' דתמיד] דתני אירע קרי לאחד מהם הולך וטובל במסיבה ההולכת תחת הבירה וירד וטבל וישב לו אצל אחיו הכהנים במדורת בית המוקד ומדורת בית המוקד היתה חציה בקדש וחציה בחול אלמא בעל קרי דזב לאו כזב דמי דאי כזב דמי היאך יכול לישב אצל אחיו לכך נראה דר"י אתא לפרושי הברייתא ועתה ניחא האי דתמיד דכיון דליכא אלא טומאה דרבנן לא הזקיקוהו חכמים לצאת וה"ק יבא עשה כו' שאין בו כרת אלא איסור מדרבנן משום דלאו כזב דמי. מהר"פ: ה] החדשה שחדשו בה דברים ואמרו (והשאר נמחק): ו] דמי וה"ה לטבול יום דקרי. גליון ואין להקשות לפירוש הקונטרס דבפרק שלשה מינין אמרינן טמא יהיה לרבות טבול יום עוד טומאתו בו לרבות מחוסר כפורים ואי טבול יום אסור במחנה לויה למה צריך לרבות טבול יום במחנה שכינה [מיהו אפשר לומר] דאיצטרך משום כרת דאין כרת אלא מחומת עזרה ולפנים מיהו קשה אי טבול יום דזב כזב דמי א"כ לאו נמי איכא ולא יטמאו את מחניהם כמו שהקשו בתוספות ועוד מאי קאמר רבא יבא עשה שיש בו כרת כו' תיפוק ליה הואיל והותר לצרעתו הותר נמי לקירויו אלא ע"כ אינו עשה גמור ורבי יוחנן מפרש הברייתא כדפי' לעיל ויבא עשה כו' לאו דוקא אלא כלו' לא העמידו דבריהם במקום כרת. ע"כ: ז] תיבות ושוחט בסכין ארוכה נמחק: ח] מעייל ידיה לעזרה: ט] שבאת להכביד עלי: י] ביאה במקצת: יא] הותרו אף לזיבתן: יב] גמור התירה עליו תורה: יג] מותר ותנן נמי במס' תמיד: יד] דתמיד אבל דוחק הוא לומר דפליגא הך ברייתא אמתניתין דתמיד וכלים: טו] היא ס"א וקי"ל כמ"ד לאו כזב דמי ותיבת לאו נמחק: טז] אסור במחנה לויה כו' מצי למימר דמשום כרת: יז] דמי וכ"ש טבול יום: יח] דריש ליה התם: יט] דזב בעל שלש: כ] מלשון ובא דריש: כא] אברייתא ס"א אלא קמפרש אליבא דברייתא דאפילו עשה אין בו ומדרבנן מיירי כולהו כו': כב] לשם ובכולהו טבולי יום קאמר אפילו: כג] לדברי דביאה במקצת שמה ביאה דדוקא משום דהואיל דהותר לצרעתו הותר לקירויו וא"ת מנא ליה האי דיוקא וי"ל מדקתני וראה קרי כו'. לשון מהר"פ: כד] אבל בלילה או מאתמול: כה] בליל שמיני שאינו מכניס ידיו לבהונות שלא יצא כו' דייק עולא דטעמא משום: כו] כהנת איתיביה רבה לעולא מנחת כהנת נאכלת והכתיב: קורא

[יומא לח.]

פסחים לב. יבמות ז:

רש"ק מ"ז

הוריות ה: ע"ש יבמות ז: ע"ש פסחים לב. ע"ש

כלים פ"א מ"ח

נ"ל לפני

[ר"ה ל: חולין קלב.]

נ"ל לא אישתרו

ויקרא יב

דה"ב כ

נ"א טמאים נ"ק

הגהות הב"ח

(א) גמ' ידיה לבהונות: (ב) שם זיבה לא אישתראי דלמא כצ"ל ותיבות אמר ליה נמחק: (ג) שם אמר ליה אין אמר ליה ואכתי:

גליון הש"ס

גמ' אף ביאה במקצת. עיין לקמן דף לה ע"א תוס' ד"ה מכניסו: **שם** במקצת שמה ביאה. עיין שבועות דף יז ע"א תוס' ד"ה תלה:

מִכְּלָל דְּתַרְוַיְיהוּ סְבִירָא לְהוּ: *אטוּמְאָה דְּחוּיָה הִיא בְּצִבּוּר. לֵימָא מְסַיַּיע לֵיהּ: *כָּל בהַסְּמִיכוֹת שֶׁהָיוּ שָׁם, קוֹרֵא א] *עֲלֵיהֶן אֲנִי: תֵּיכֶף לִסְמִיכָה שְׁחִיטָה, גחוּץ מִזּוֹ שֶׁהָיְתָה בְּשַׁעַר נִקָּנוֹר, שֶׁאֵין מְצוֹרָע יָכוֹל לִיכָּנֵס לְשָׁם עַד שֶׁמַּזִּין עָלָיו מִדַּם חַטָּאתוֹ וּמִדַּם אֲשָׁמוֹ; וְאִי אָמְרַתְּ בִּיאָה בְּמִקְצָת לָא שְׁמָהּ בִּיאָה — לִיעַיֵּיל יְדֵיהּ וְלִסְמוֹךְ! אָמַר רַב יוֹסֵף: הָא מַנִּי *ר' יוֹסֵי בְּרַבִּי יְהוּדָה הִיא, דְּאָמַר: מְרַחֵק צָפוֹן. וְלִיעֲבֵד פִּישְׁפָּשׁ! אַבַּיֵּי וְרָבָא דְּאָמְרִי תַּרְוַיְיהוּ: °"הַכֹּל בִּכְתָב מִיַּד ה' עָלַי הִשְׂכִּיל (אֶת) כֹּל מַלְאֲכוֹת הַתַּבְנִית". אִיכָּא דְּאָמְרִי, אָמַר רַב יוֹסֵף: כָּל הַסּוֹמֵךְ — רֹאשׁוֹ וְרוּבּוֹ מַכְנִיס, מַאי טַעְמָא — דכָּל כֹּחוֹ בָּעֵינַן, הִלְכָּךְ לָא אֶפְשָׁר. מַאי קָסָבַר? אִי קָסָבַר סְמִיכַת אֲשַׁם מְצוֹרָע דְּאוֹרַיְיתָא, *וְתֵיכֶף לִסְמִיכָה שְׁחִיטָה דְּאוֹרַיְיתָא — לֵיעוּל וְלִסְמוֹךְ לְהֶדְיָא, דְּרַחֲמָנָא אָמַר! אָמַר רַב אַדָּא בַּר מַתְנָה: גְּזֵירָה שֶׁמָּא יַרְבֶּה בִּפְסִיעוֹת. אִיכָּא דְּאָמְרִי, אָמַר רַב אַדָּא בַּר מַתְנָה: סְמִיכַת אֲשַׁם מְצוֹרָע דְּאוֹרַיְיתָא, וְתֵיכֶף לִסְמִיכָה שְׁחִיטָה לָאו דְּאוֹרַיְיתָא. מֵיתִיבֵי: "וְסָמַךְ וְשָׁחַט" — מַה סְּמִיכָה בִּטְהוֹרִין — אַף שְׁחִיטָה בִּטְהוֹרִין; ב] וְאִי אָמְרַתְּ לָאו דְּאוֹרַיְיתָא, בִּטְמֵאִין נַמִי מַשְׁכַּחַתְּ לָהּ! אֶלָּא, אֵיפוֹךְ: סְמִיכַת אֲשַׁם מְצוֹרָע לָאו דְּאוֹרַיְיתָא, וְתֵיכֶף לִסְמִיכָה שְׁחִיטָה דְּאוֹרַיְיתָא.
רָבִינָא

רש"י

*ג] [טוּמְאָה] דְּחוּיָה הִיא. כְּלוֹמַר, בְּקוֹשִׁי נִדְחֵית הֲלָכָה, דִּיחוּי בְּעָלְמָא עַל יְדֵי נְשִׂיאוּת עָוֹן שֶׁהַצִּיץ מְרַצֶּה וְלֹא בְּהֶיתֵּר גָּמוּר, ד] לְטוּמְאַת מֵת חִידַּשְׁתִּי וְלֹא לְטוּמְאַת זִיבָה. דְּתַרְוַיְיהוּ. אַבַּיֵּי וְרָבָא סְבִירָא לְהוּ טוּמְאָה דְּחוּיָה הִיא בְּצִבּוּר. וְנ"מ לְמֵיהֱוֵי (א) מַאן דְּאָמַר בְּפ"ק דְּיוֹמָא (דף ו:) דְּאָמַר הוּתְּרָה הִיא בְּצִיבּוּר, יָחִיד בִּמְקוֹם רַבִּים. תורה אור

לֵימָא מְסַיַּיע לֵיהּ. לְעוּלָּא, דְּאָמַר: בִּיאָה בְּמִקְצָת שְׁמָהּ בִּיאָה. תֵּיכֶף לִסְמִיכָה שְׁחִיטָה. כִּדְכְתִיב: "וְסָמַךְ וְשָׁחַט". חוּץ מִזּוֹ. שֶׁל אֲשַׁם מְצוֹרָע. שֶׁהָיְתָה בְּשַׁעַר נִקָּנוֹר. הוּא שַׁעַר ה] הַמִּזְרָחִי, כִּדְתְנַן בִּשְׁקָלִים (פ"ו מ"ג): שֶׁבַּמִּזְרָח שַׁעַר נִקָּנוֹר. וַחֲלָל ו] שַׁעַר לֹא נִתְקַדֵּשׁ בִּקְדוּשַּׁת הָעֲזָרָה, כִּדְאָמְרִי' בְּ"כֵּיצַד צוֹלִין" (פסחים פה:), לְפִי שֶׁהַמְּצוֹרָע עוֹמֵד שָׁם וּמַכְנִיס יָדָיו ז] לַעֲזָרָה. וְשָׁם מוֹצִיאִין לוֹ אֶת הָאָשָׁם וְסוֹמֵךְ עָלָיו, וְחוֹזֵר וּמַכְנִיסוֹ לִמְקוֹם שְׁחִיטָתוֹ וְשׁוֹחֲטוֹ, מִפְּנֵי שֶׁאֵין ח] מְצוֹרָע יָכוֹל לִיכָּנֵס בָּעֲזָרָה וְלִסְמוֹךְ. עַד שֶׁמַּזִּין עָלָיו מִדַּם חַטָּאתוֹ. לָאו עָלָיו מַמָּשׁ קָאָמַר, שֶׁאֵין נוֹתְנִין עַל בְּהוֹנוֹת אֶלָּא מִדַּם הָאָשָׁם. אֶלָּא שֶׁזּוֹרְקִין בִּשְׁבִילוֹ דַּם חַטָּאתוֹ וְדַם אֲשָׁמוֹ. לִיעַיֵּיל יְדֵיהּ. (ב) לְתוֹךְ הַפֶּתַח וְלִסְמוֹךְ, וְלִישְׁחֲטֵיהּ אֵצֶל הַפֶּתַח. דְּהָא כָּל הַפְּתָחִים שֶׁהָיוּ שָׁם רָחְבָּן עֶשֶׂר אַמּוֹת, וְחָמֵשׁ מֵהֶן בַּצָּפוֹן וְחָמֵשׁ מֵהֶן בַּדָּרוֹם, שֶׁהַפֶּתַח מְכוּוָּן כְּנֶגֶד פִּתְחוֹ שֶׁל הֵיכָל בְּאֶמְצַע הָעֲזָרָה, וְיָכוֹל לִשְׁחוֹט ט] לִפְנֵי צְפוֹנוֹ שֶׁל פֶּתַח דַּהֲוָה לֵיהּ צָפוֹן. וְקס"ד י] רַבִּי הִיא, דְּאָמַר: כָּל צְפוֹן הָעֲזָרָה כָּשֵׁר יא] לִשְׁחִיטַת קָדָשִׁים, וְאַף צָפוֹן שֶׁבִּמְקוֹם דְּרִיסַת רַגְלֵי כֹּהֲנִים וְיִשְׂרָאֵל כִּדְאָמַר יב] לְעֵיל. מְרַחֵק צָפוֹן. צָפוֹן הַכָּשֵׁר יג] (מֵהֶן) לִשְׁחִיטַת קָדְשֵׁי קָדָשִׁים רָחוֹק מִן הַפֶּתַח יוֹתֵר מִכ"ב אַמָּה, מְקוֹם דְּרִיסַת יִשְׂרָאֵל וּמְקוֹם דְּרִיסַת כֹּהֲנִים, דְּכָל אַחַת מֵהֶן י"א אַמָּה, בְּמַסֶּכֶת מִדּוֹת (פ"ה), [וּכְר"י בְּרַבִּי יְהוּדָה], דְּאָמַר (יומא דף לו.): אֵיזֶהוּ צָפוֹן — מִקִּיר מִזְבֵּחַ וְעַד כּוֹתֶל הָעֲזָרָה כְּנֶגֶד צְפוֹנוֹ שֶׁל מִזְבֵּחַ, וְתוּ לָא. הִילְכָּךְ, צָרִיךְ לְהַחֲזִירוֹ בִּצְפוֹן הַמִּזְבֵּחַ, וְלֵיכָּא תֵּכֶף לִסְמִיכָה שְׁחִיטָה. הָכִי גָּרְסִינַן: וְלִיעֲבֵד פִּישְׁפָּשׁ. וּפֵירוּשׁוֹ: פֶּתַח קָטָן, כִּדְתְנַן בְּמַסֶּכֶת שְׁקָלִים: שֶׁבַּמִּזְרָח יד] בְּשַׁעַר נִקָּנוֹר, וּשְׁנֵי פִשְׁפָּשִׁין הָיוּ לוֹ, אֶחָד מִימִינוֹ וְאֶחָד מִשְּׂמֹאלוֹ. וְהֵן מֵחֶשְׁבּוֹן טו] פְּתָחִים, שֶׁהָיוּ מִשְׁתַּחֲוִים כְּנֶגֶד הַפְּתָחִים. וְהָכָא פָּרְכִינַן: וְנִיעֲבִיד פֶּתַח קָטָן בְּכוֹתֶל צְפוֹנִי שֶׁל עֲזָרָה כְּנֶגֶד הַמִּזְבֵּחַ, וְיַעֲמוֹד מְצוֹרָע בַּחֲלָלוֹ וְיַכְנִיס יָדוֹ וְיִסְמוֹךְ, אִי לָאו דְּבִיאָה בְּמִקְצָת שְׁמָהּ בִּיאָה. הַכֹּל בִּכְתָב. כָּךְ אָמַר דָּוִד: כָּל פֶּתַח הָעֲזָרָה וּמִדּוֹתֶיהָ וּבִנְיַן כָּל הַבַּיִת נִמְסַר לִי מִיַּד ה', וְאֵין לְהוֹסִיף עַל הַחֶשְׁבּוֹן. טז] וּבִיאָה בְּמִקְצָת לֹא שְׁמָהּ (ג) בִּיאָה. אָמַר רַב יוֹסֵף. לְעוֹלָם רַבִּי הִיא, וּדְקָאָמְרַתְּ: לֵיעוּל וְלִיסְמוֹךְ — כָּל הַסּוֹמֵךְ כו'. מַאי קָסָבַר. הַאי תַּנָּא דְּאָמַר: כָּל הַסְּמִיכוֹת צְרִיכוֹת תֵּכֶף לִסְמִיכָה שְׁחִיטָה חוּץ מִזּוֹ? לֵיעוּל וְלִיסְמוֹךְ יז] בְּהֶדְיָא. דְּרַחֲמָנָא אָמַר לוֹ שֶׁיִּכָּנֵס וְיִסְמוֹךְ. שֶׁמָּא יַרְבֶּה בִּפְסִיעוֹת. לְאַחַר שֶׁסָּמַךְ, אִם יִכָּנֵס פְּסִיעָה לְצַד פְּנִים יוֹתֵר מִשֶּׁהָיָה צָרִיךְ — נִמְצָא עָנוּשׁ כָּרֵת. סְמִיכַת אֲשַׁם מְצוֹרָע דְּאוֹרַיְיתָא. כִּשְׁאָר אֲשָׁמוֹת, דְּגָמְרִינַן לְהוּ סְמִיכָה מֵהֶיקֵּשָׁא דְ"כַחַטָּאת כָּאָשָׁם" בְּפ"ק (לעיל יא.). (ד) תֵּיכֶף לִסְמִיכָה שְׁחִיטָה לָאו דְּאוֹרַיְיתָא. דְּלָא מַשְׁמַע לֵיהּ: "וְסָמַךְ וְשָׁחַט" בַּמָּקוֹם יח] *שֶׁסּוֹמֵךְ יִשְׁחוֹט. מֵיתִיבֵי וְסָמַךְ וְשָׁחַט. הַאי דְּסַמְכִינְהוּ קְרָא — לְהֶיקֵּישָׁא סַמְכִינְהוּ, כִּדְאָמְרִי': מַה סְּמִיכָה בִּטְהוֹרִים כו'. יט] וּסְמִיכָה דִּפְשִׁיטָא לָן בָּהּ — מִשּׁוּם דִּכְתִיב "לִפְנֵי ה'" בִּשְׁחִיטָה דִּצְרִיכָה שֶׁתְּהֵא לִפְנִים, וּמִשּׁוּם דְּתֵכֶף לִסְמִיכָה שְׁחִיטָה צָרִיךְ שֶׁיִּכָּנֵס הַסּוֹמֵךְ לִפְנִים. וְלַעֲמוֹד טָמֵא מִבַּחוּץ וְלִסְמוֹךְ בִּפְנִים אִי אֶפְשָׁר, כְּדַאֲמָרַן לְעֵיל שֶׁרֹאשׁוֹ וְרוּבּוֹ מַכְנִיס. וְאִי אָמְרַתְּ לָאו דְּאוֹרַיְיתָא. הֵיכִי פְּשִׁיטָא לֵיהּ סְמִיכָה בִּטְהוֹרִין? בִּטְמֵאִין נַמִי אִיתָא. שֶׁסּוֹמֵךְ בַּחוּץ, וּמַכְנִיסָהּ טָהוֹר לִפְנִים וְשׁוֹחֵט. סְמִיכַת אֲשַׁם מְצוֹרָע לָאו דְּאוֹרַיְיתָא. קָסָבַר שֶׁאֵינוֹ בִּכְלַל כ] אֲשָׁמוֹת, שֶׁהֲרֵי אֵינוֹ בָּא אֶלָּא לְהַכְשִׁיר.
רָבִינָא

תוספות

שהיא ראייה לדברי, כא] מדלא שנה התנא חילוק זכרים מנקבות היכא דכתיב כהן סתם, כגון גבי מתנות כהונה, אלא גבי מנחה, דכתיב "אהרן ובניו", שמע מינה היכא דכתיב כהן סתם — לא שנא כהן ולא שנא כהנת. ואם תאמר: ואי מטעם הואיל והותר לצרעתו הותר לקרויו, למה לי יצא עשה שיש בו כרת וידחה עשה שאין בו כרת? בלאו הכי נמי! כב] ויש לומר: כג] דעל מחנה לויה שנכנס טבול יום שבבעל קרי, הוצרך לומר עשה דפסח דבכרת דחי עשה וכו', דטבול יום כד] אינו נכנס, אי מן התורה — אי טבול יום דזב כזב דמי, אי מדרבנן — מגזירת יהושפט. והתם לא שייך למימר מתוך שהותר לצרעתו — שהרי בשמיני קאי, ואינו אלא מחוסר כפורים דלא נאסר מעולם במחנה לויה, ומה שייך שם לומר שהותר? אבל על מחנה שכינה, שמכניס ידיו לבהונות והוא טבול יום של קרי — על זה קאמר: מתוך שהותר מחוסר כיפורים של מצורע, דבעלמא אסור בעזרת שכינה והכא כה] הותר — הותר נמי לטבול יום דקרויו כו].

הגה"ה: מכלל דתרוייהו סבירא להו טומאה דחויה היא בציבור. והא דאמר רב תחליפא משמיה דרבא: זאת אומרת הותרה היא בציבור בפ"ק דיומא (דף ו:) — זאת אומרת, ולא סבירא ליה*. **וליעבד** פשפש כז] הכל בכתב כו'. והא דמוסיפים על העיר ועל העזרות — *היינו היכא דאיכא למימר קרא אשכחו ודרוש, כי ההיא דסוכה (דף נא:). ומיהו קשה: דהכא נמי אין לך קרא גדול מזה, דניעביד פשפש לקיים מצות סמיכה, דרחמנא אמר "וסמך". כח] ולמאי דמסיק דסמיכת אשם מצורע לאו דאורייתא — ניחא. אבל לטעמא דשמא ירבה בפסיעות — קשה, דניעבד פשפש, דליכא למיחש! ומיהו כט] דשמא ירבה בפסיעות גזירה דרבנן בעלמא היא, וקרי כאן "הכל בכתב". והא דאמר בריש "כיסוי הדם" (חולין פג:) דכיסוי הדם אינו נוהג במוקדשין משום דלא איפשר, דהיכי ליעביד? לבטליה — קא מוסיף אבניין, וכתיב "הכל בכתב" — אין זה חשוב כמו קרא, דכיון דלא כתב בהדיא בקרא שינהוג כיסוי הדם במוקדשין.

ל] **ניעול** וניסמוך. כיון דלא איפשר בענין אחר, ולא מקיימין סמיכה בטהרה. *)ולא דמי לשאר [טמאים] שמשלחין קרבנותיהם, ולא אמרינן ניעול וניסמוך — דמקיימא סמיכה דידהו בטהרה. **סמיכת** אשם מצורע לאו דאורייתא לא]. ואמרינן: *אקפו ידייכו, דלא תיהוי עבודה בקדשים. ומתוך הך שמעתא אתי שפיר הא לב] דאמר בריש "התערובת" (לקמן דף עו.) גבי ספק מצורע שמביא אשמו ולוגו עמו, ואומר: אם מצורע הוא — זה אשמו כו', ואותו אשם טעון סמיכה לג] ובהונות. והשתא למה לי למיתני סמיכה? בין יהא אשם בין לא יהא [אשם] בעי סמיכה! אלא משום דסמיכת אשם מצורע לאו דאורייתא, לד] וקאתי לאשמועינן דטעון סמיכה (דאורייתא) משום ספיקא דשלמים. וכן לעיל בריש מכילתין (דף ד:) גבי אשם, דפריך: מה לשלמים שכן טעונין סמיכה — משום אשם מצורע נקט סמיכה. ולא כפי' הקונטרס דלא גרים סמיכה, כדפרישית בפ"ק. והא דתנן בפ' "כל התדיר" (לקמן צ:): כל אשמות לה] באין בני שתי שנים ובכסף שקלים, חוץ מאשם נזיר ואשם מצורע — לא מצי למיתני: כל אשמות טעונין סמיכה חוץ מאשם נזיר ואשם מצורע, כיון דמדרבנן מיהא טעון סמיכה. והא דתנן בפ' "כל המנחות באות" (מנחות דף סא.): רבי שמעון אומר, שלשה מינים טעונין שלש מצות, שתים בכל אחד ואחד והשלישית אין בהן: אשם מצורע טעון סמיכה ותנופה חי, ואין בו תנופה שחוט — לאו משום שתהא סמיכה דאורייתא. והא דפריך בגמ': ויהא אשם מצורע טעון תנופה שחוט מקל וחומר, ומה זבחי שלמי יחיד שאין טעונין תנופה חיים טעונין תנופה כו' — *לא שייך למיפרך: מה לשלמי יחיד שכן טעונין סמיכה דאורייתא — כיון דמתנופה אתנופה עביד קל וחומר. ומיהו קשה, דפריך התם: ויהיו שלמי ציבור טעונין סמיכה לו] מקל וחומר, ומה שלמי יחיד שאין טעונין תנופה חיים טעונין סמיכה מקל וחומר כו'. אמאי לא קאמר: אשם מצורע יוכיח, שטעון תנופה מחיים ואין טעון סמיכה! ובתורת כהנים בפרשת "לו את אהרן" עביד נמי קל וחומר כי האי גוונא, א) וקאמר: אשם מצורע יוכיח. ודבר תימה הוא, ב) אמאי? לז]. **איפוך** סמיכת אשם מצורע לאו דאורייתא. לח] לעיל בפ"ק (דף יא:) ילפינן שאר אשמות מדכתיב "כחטאת כאשם", מה חטאת טעון סמיכה — אף אשם טעון סמיכה. ואם כן מ] קשה: אפילו אשם מצורע נמי! ומה שפירש בקונטרס, דקסבר אינו בכלל שאר אשמות משום דאינו בא אלא להכשיר — קשה: הא אמרינן פרק קמא דיבמות

א) נ"א ולא קאמר ב) גירסת הג"ק אמאי סמיכת אשם לאו דאורייתא דהא לעיל פ"ק כו' והד"א *) [עי' לעיל כח: וברמב"ם פ"ג מהלכות ביאת מקדש]

יז א מיי' פי"ח מהל' פסה"מ הלכה יב:

ל"ל האשם

יח ב מיי' שם הלכה יג:

ס"א דביאה

[עי' היטב תוס' חולין עח. ד"ה מנין וכו']

גי' הג"ק כרת הס"ד ואח"כ מה"ד הכי גרסינן

רבינא אמר: לענין מלקות איתמר. כי אתא רבין, אמר רבי אבהו: לענין טמא שנגע בקודש איתמר. דאיתמר, טמא שנגע בקודש, ריש לקיש אמר: לוקה, רבי יוחנן אמר: [א]אינו לוקה. ריש לקיש אמר: לוקה — °"בכל קודש לא תגע". (ויקרא יב) ורבי יוחנן אמר: אינו לוקה — א] ההוא בתרומה כתיב. וריש לקיש, האי קרא להכי הוא דאתא? האי מיבעי ליה אזהרה לאוכל בשר קודש. *דאיתמר, אזהרה לאוכל בשר קודש מנין? ריש לקיש אמר: "בכל קודש לא תגע". רבי יוחנן אמר, תני בר דלא: אתיא "טומאתו" "טומאתו" מביאת מקדש, מה להלן ענש והזהיר — אף כאן ענש והזהיר! טמא שנגע בקודש — מדאפקה רחמנא בלשון נגיעה, אזהרה לאוכל — מדאיתקש קודש למקדש. *תניא כוותיה דריש לקיש: [ב]"בכל קודש לא תגע" — אזהרה לאוכל. אתה אומר: אזהרה לאוכל, או אינו אלא לנוגע? תלמוד לומר: "בכל קודש לא תגע ואל המקדש לא תבא", מקיש קודש למקדש, מה מקדש דבר שיש בו נטילת

רש"י

רבינא אמר. הא דאמר עולא לעיל משמיה דריש לקיש בביאה ב] מקלת. לענין מלקות אמרה. כדקאמר לוקה בהדיא. אבל לא לענין כרת, דתותביה ג] מצורע שראה קרי. דכי איתקש ביאה לנגיעה — לאזהרה איתקש, כדכתיב "לא תבא", אבל לעונש לא איתקש, דאין עונש בנגיעה. לטמא שנגע בקדש איתמר. לא יליף ריש לקיש מלקות מההוא קרא אלא לטמא שנגע בקדש, ולא איירי בביאת מקדש כלל. בתרומה כתיב. כדמוכח סיפיה דקרא: "עד מלאת ימי טהרה", שיעריב שמשה. שהיא טבולת יום ארוך, שטובלת בשביעי ללידתה וכל ימי טוהר שלה [הרי] היא כטבולת יום, ד] וביום מ' ואחד מביאה קרבנה. (ל"ק) ומדכתיב: "לא תגע עד מלאת", ה] אבל משימלאו ימיה תגע, ואפי' מחוסרת כפרה — ע"כ בתרומה כתיב, דלענין קדש — עד שתביא כפרתה. והכי מוקמינן להאי קרא ביבמות ב"הערל". (מכות יז: ע"ש) וכיון דבתרומה כתיב — לא ילפינן מלקות דקדש ו] ואפילו בק"ו, דאין מזהירין מן הדין. לאוכל בשר קדש. בטומאת הגוף. בכל קדש לא תגע. (שם ויבמות עה.) ודרשינן לקמן אזהרה לאוכל. טומאתו טומאתו. כתיב ז] בכרת באוכל קדש בטומאת הגוף "וטומאתו עליו", וכתיב בביאת מקדש "עוד טומאתו בו", מה ביאת מקדש איכא אזהרה "ולא יטמאו את מחניהם" — אף טומאת הגוף דאוכל קודש, תיפוק ליה אזהרה מהכא! ומשני: טמא שנגע נפקא לן מדאפקיה בלשון נגיעה. אזהרה לאוכל. עיקר קרא ח] מידריש. מדאיתקש קדש למקדש בהאי קרא, דדרשינן: מה ביאת מקדש דבר שיש בו כרת — אף אזהרת קודש דבר שיש בו כרת, והיינו אכילה, דאילו בנגיעה לא אשכחן כרת. ומיהו, אזהרה לנוגע נפקא לן מיניה, מדאפקיה בלשון נגיעה. תניא כוותיה דריש לקיש. דאזהרה לאוכל קדש מהכא. נטילת

תוספות

דיבמות (דף ז.), ולקמן בריש "איזהו מקומן" (דף מט.): לפי שיצא אשם מצורע לידון בדבר החדש, בבהן יד ובבהן רגל, יכול לא יהא טעון מתן דמים ואימורים לגבי מזבח? ת"ל: "כחטאת ט] *כאשם הוא לכהן", מה חטאת טעונה וכו'. ואם כן נימא: י] מה חטאת טעונה סמיכה ומתן דמים ואימורים לגבי מזבח — אף אשם כו'!

לענין מלקות איתמר. פירש בקונטרס: אבל לא לענין כרת, דתותביה יא] מצורע שראה קרי. והקשה ה"ר חיים: דאכתי איכא לאקשויי, דאין עשה יב] דוחה לא תעשה ועשה — לאו יג] *דנגיעה במקצת, "וטמא יהיה" לרבות טבול יום! ועוד קשיא ליה: אפילו לאו גרידא, היכי דחי ליה? הא בעידנא דמיעקר לאו לא מיקיים עשה! יד] ויש לומר: דעשה שיש בו כרת חמור *ודחי טו] להו, כדאשכחן בפרק "תמיד נשחט" (פסחים נט.) דעשה שיש בו כרת דוחה עשה דהשלמה, אע"ג דבעלמא אין עשה דוחה עשה. ואם תאמר: והלא גבי עשה דמצורע, דחמיר משום שלום בית ודחי עשה, אפילו הכי לא דחי לא תעשה בהדי עשה, כדקאמר גבי שילוח הקן (חולין קמא.): לא צריכא טז] שנטל' ע"מ לשלחה, דלאו ליכא! וי"ל: דעשה דמצורע, אף ע"ג דחמיר — כיון דליכא כרת לא דחי לתרוייהו, אבל בפסח איכא *כרת. יז] הכי גרסינן: רבי יוחנן אומר אינו לוקה גבי אומרות דתרומה, דקאמר שכן מתפ"ז, הוה מצי למיחשב נמי נגיעת קודש דלוקה בתרומה ולא בקודש לרבי יוחנן. ועוד יש אומרות הרבה כדפירש' ביבמות. **ההוא** בתרומה כתיב. הקשה ה"ר חיים: מכל מקום לילקי בקודש, כדאשכחן בפ"ק דכריתות (דף ד:) דאוכל חלב המוקדשין לוקה שלש, משום "וכל זר לא יאכל קודש", אע"ג דבתרומה כתיב, כיון דכתיב לשון קודש! יח] ותירץ: דהתם איכא מעילה שהוא נהנה, ילפי' "חטא" "חטא" מתרומה כדאמר גבי הזיד יט] במעילה, ובכל דוכתא ילפינן מעילה "חטא" "חטא" מתרומה. אבל לענין שאר לאוין — לא ילפינן ללקות על קודש כמו על תרומה, כ] ד"חטאה בשגגה" במעילה כתיב, ובנוגע בקודש ליכא מעילה. וה"ר יעקב דאורלינ"ש לא גרים "וכל זר לא יאכל קודש", אלא "וזר לא יאכל כי קודש הם" [דכתיב גבי קודש עצמה, ומתרומה לא ילפינן]*.

*[עיין לעיל דף טו ע"ב ד"ה אלא למעוטי]

ל"ק [ועי' בתוס' מסכ' מכות יז: דמתרלו בע"ל]

***אזהרה** לאוכל בשר קודש מנין. תימה: תיפוק ליה מ"לא תוכל לאכול בשעריך", כי היכי דנפקא לן בפ' "הערל" (יבמות דף עג:) מעשר וביכורים דאוכלן בטומאת עצמן לוקה, מדכתיב: "לא תוכל לאכול בשעריך", ולהלן הוא אומר: "בשעריך תאכלנו הטמא והטהור יחדו יאכלנו" דאפי' טמא וטהור אוכלין בקערה אחת, וקאמר רחמנא כא] לך: *בשעריך תאכלנו, הכא לא תוכל לאכול, ובין בטומאת הגוף ובין בטומאת עצמן איירי קרא! ובההוא שמעתא גופה קשה: דקאמר גבי מעשר וביכורים טומאת הגוף בהדיא כתיב ביה: "לא יאכל מן הקדשים כי אם רחץ", ואמאי איצטריך? והלא מהאי קרא תיפוק לן תרוייהו, טומאת הגוף וטומאת בשר! ויש מפרש: דלא מצי לאפוקי מהאי קרא אלא טומאה הנוהגת במעשר כב] דכתיבי בקרא, הילכך צריך קרא בטבול יום שמותר במעשר, שמוזהר על אכילת קדשים. וקשה, מדאמרינן בפרק "כל שעה" (פסחים כד.): "והבשר אשר יגע בכל טמא לא יאכל" למה לי? מ"לא תוכל לאכול בשעריך" נפקא. הא לא נפקא לן מהתם אלא טומאה הנוהגת במעשר, ואיצטריך "והבשר" לטמאים, דטהורים במעשר! ושמא קרא ד"לא תוכל" הוה מוקמינא כג] לדיוקא בטמא האוכל דחמיר טפי, אי לאו דכתביה קרא בעלמא, ואזהרה לטומאת בשר לא הוה ידענא.

לך התם ל"ק

תניא כוותיה דריש לקיש בבל קדש לא תגע. תימה: דהכא משמע דהך ברייתא מוקמא להאי קרא בקודש ולא בתרומה. ובפ' "הערל" (יבמות עה.) אמרינן: ואיבעית אימא נגיעה דתרומה מהכא נפקא, דתניא "בכל קדש לא תגע", ומייתי הך ברייתא! ויש לומר: דהתם קאי אקראי דנגיעה דמעשר ותרומה. כד] דלעיל מיניה מקשי: ואיפוך אנא, צריך לחלק בין נגיעה לאכילה דתרומה, ולהכי מייתי ראייה מהך ברייתא דגבי קודש נגיעה כאכילה, והוא הדין בתרומה. ועוד קשיא: דבהיא שמעתא דהתם ובפרק קמא דשבועות (דף ז.) אמרינן: "בכל קודש לא תגע" — לרבות את התרומה, וברייתא היא בתורת כהנים. ובאכילה דתרומה מיירי, כדמוכח שמעתא דהתם, דקאי אהא דקאמר: אי סלקא דעתך לתרומה — גיורת ושפחה בנות מיכל תרומה נינהו? ואי במגע — הא ודאי בנות מגע נינהו. אלא באכילה מיירי. והשתא ההיא דרשא כמאן? לא כריש לקיש כה] דמוקי ליה לאזהרה לטמא שאכל את הקדש מדאיתקש קודש למקדש, ומדאפקיה כו] בלשון נגיעה אפקיה לאזהרה לנוגע בקודש, ומרבויא ד"בכל" אזהרה לאוכל לפני זריקה. אבל כז] לתרומה לא מוקי ליה כלל, אלא נפקא ליה כח] לאזהרה לאוכל תרומה מ"איש איש". ורבי יוחנן מוקי "לא תגע" אזהרה לנוגע בתרומה, אבל לאוכל — לא מוקי ליה! ותירץ ה"ר אפרים: האי דמוקי ליה ביבמות [דף עה. ושם ד"ה והכתיב] אזהר' לאוכל תרומה — היינו למאן דמוקי קרא ד"איש איש מזרע אהרן" בזב בעל שלש ראיות, "ולא יאכל עד אשר יטהר" — עד דמייתי כפרה, ולקודש, כדקאמר התם. ואם כן אזהרה לאוכל תרומה מנא ליה? אלא מ"בכל קודש לא תגע". אע"ג דהתם פריך לתנא דמוקי ליה בזב בעל שתי ראיות — מכל מקום פריך שפיר, דהא איכא מאן דמוקי ליה בתרומה, אע"ג דגיורת ושפחה לאו בנות מיכל תרומה נינהו. אף על גב דבאכילת קדשים מצרכינן תרי קראי, חד בזב וחד ביולדת —כט] [גבי תרומה לא] צריכי, כיון דחזינן כבר באכילת קודש דזב ויולדת שוין — ה"נ גבי אכילת תרומה. ועוד יש לומר, דבתרומה דלא תליא בכפרה — לא בעי תרי קראי לזב ויולדת, אלא דווקא *למקדש שצריך להמתין הכפרה.

והבשר

נ"א לקודש ל"ק

לוקה

שיטה מקובצת

א] ההוא בתרומה. פ"ה כו' והקשה הר"ר חיים כו' וי"ל כו' עד נהנה וילפינן חט חט מתרומה כדאמרינן בעלמא אבל בנגיעה לא ילפינן דליכא מעילה וי"ס דלא גרסי שם [אלא] וזר לא יאכל (קדש שנאמר) כי קדש [שנאמר] גבי קדש אבל קרא דהכא משמע בתרומה כדכתיב עד מלאת ימי טהרה ואי בקדש אפילו לאחר מלאת לא כדפי' רש"י עד שתביא כפרתה והקדוש [ר"ש] מדריוש פי' דההיא בתרומה ליפסל תרומה בנגיעתה הוא דאתא דודאי בנגיעת תרומה ליכא מלקות ולפסול קודש לא איצטריך דאפילו לאחר מלאות נמי פסלה וניחא הכל: ב] במקצת הס"ד: ג] דתותביה ממצורע שראה: ד] יום ארוך: ה] מלאת משמע אבל: ו] דקדש מיניה ואפילו: ז] תיבת בכרת נמחק: ח] קרא ביה מידריש: ט] כחטאת האשם הוא: י] נימא נמי מה: יא] דתותביה ממצורע שראה: יב] עשה דפסח דוחה: יג] לאו דואל המקדש לא תבא אי ביאה במקצת שמה ביאה ועשה דהכא וטמא יהיה: יד] ויש לומר כו'. ועי"ל דכי היכא דלא איתרבאי ביאה במקצת לענין כרת כמו כן לא איתרבאי ביאה במקצת לענין עשה דטמא יהיה דכי היכי דלא איתרבאי לענין כרת לא איתרבאי לענין עשה. מהר"פ: טו] ודחי לאו ועשה כדאשכחן: טז] צריכא דעקר ושקליה לאם דלאו ליכא ועשה הוא דאיכא וי"ל: יז] כרת עכ"ה ותיבות הכי גרסינן נמחק: יח] קודש ולא אמרינן אין מזהירין מן הדין ותירץ: יט] הזיד ס"פ הנשרפין ובפרק כל שעה (פסחים דף לג.): כ] מתיב דחטאה כו' עד תיבת וה"ר יעקב כו' נמחק: כא] רחמנא ההיא דאמרי התם לך: כב] הנוהגת במעשר. ס"א בכל הנהו דכתיבי: כג] מוקמינא דוקא בטמא: כד] ותרומה דלמה דמקשה ואיפוך. ותיבות דלעיל מיני' מקשי ל"ש ונמחק: כה] ולא כר"י דר"ל מוקי ליה אזהרה לטמא: כו] ומדאפקיה ללא תגע בלשון נגיעה אפיק לאזהרה: כז] אבל אזהרה לאוכל תרומה לא: כח] ליה מאיש איש מזרע אהרן ותיבות לאזהרה לאוכל תרומה נמחק: כט] ביולדת גבי תרומה לא צריך כיון:

נְטִילַת נְשָׁמָה, אַף קוֹדֶשׁ – דָּבָר שֶׁיֵּשׁ בּוֹ נְטִילַת נְשָׁמָה; וְאִי בְּנוֹגֵעַ – נְטִילַת נְשָׁמָה מִי אִיכָּא? אֶלָּא בַּאֲכִילָה. וְאַכַּתִּי מִיבָּעֵי לֵיהּ לְטָמֵא שֶׁאָכַל בְּשַׂר קוֹדֶשׁ לִפְנֵי זְרִיקָה. דְּאִתְּמַר, טָמֵא שֶׁאָכַל בְּשַׂר קוֹדֶשׁ לִפְנֵי זְרִיקָה, רֵישׁ לָקִישׁ אָמַר: לוֹקֶה, וְרַבִּי יוֹחָנָן אָמַר: אאֵינוֹ לוֹקֶה. רֵישׁ לָקִישׁ אָמַר: לוֹקֶה – "בְּכָל קוֹדֶשׁ לֹא תִגָּע", לָא שְׁנָא לִפְנֵי זְרִיקָה, וְלָא שְׁנָא לְאַחַר זְרִיקָה. רַבִּי יוֹחָנָן אָמַר: אֵינוֹ לוֹקֶה א] – כִּדְתָנֵי בַּרְדְּלָא: אָתְיָא "טוּמְאָתוֹ" "טוּמְאָתוֹ", וְכִי כְּתַב הַהוּא – לְאַחַר זְרִיקָה. אִם כֵּן, לֵימָא קְרָא "בְּקוֹדֶשׁ", מַאי "בְּכָל קוֹדֶשׁ"? ש"מ תַּרְתֵּי. גּוּפָא, טָמֵא שֶׁאָכַל בְּשַׂר קוֹדֶשׁ לִפְנֵי זְרִיקָה, ר"ל אָמַר: לוֹקֶה, רַבִּי יוֹחָנָן אָמַר: אֵינוֹ לוֹקֶה. אָמַר אַבַּיֵּי: מַחֲלוֹקֶת בְּטוּמְאַת הַגּוּף, אֲבָל בְּטוּמְאַת בָּשָׂר – דִּבְרֵי הַכֹּל לוֹקֶה, דְּאָמַר (א) קְרָא: °"וְהַבָּשָׂר" – לְרַבּוֹת עֵצִים וּלְבוֹנָה דְּלָאו בְּנֵי אֲכִילָה נִינְהוּ, וַאֲפִילּוּ הָכִי רַבִּינְהוּ קְרָא. וְרָבָא אָמַר: במַחֲלוֹקֶת ב] בְּטוּמְאַת הַגּוּף, אֲבָל בְּטוּמְאַת בָּשָׂר – דִּבְרֵי הַכֹּל אֵינוֹ לוֹקֶה, מַאי טַעְמָא? כֵּיוָן דְּלָא קָרֵינָא בֵּיהּ °"וְטוּמְאָתוֹ עָלָיו וְנִכְרְתָה" – לָא קָרֵינָא בֵּיהּ °"וְהַבָּשָׂר אֲשֶׁר יִגַּע בְּכָל טָמֵא לֹא יֵאָכֵל". *וְהָאָמַר מָר: "וְהַבָּשָׂר" – לְרַבּוֹת געֵצִים וּלְבוֹנָה! הָכָא בְּמַאי עָסְקִינַן – כְּגוֹן שֶׁקִּדְּשׁוּ בִּכְלִי, דְּנַעֲשָׂה כְּמִי שֶׁקָּרְבוּ כָּל מַתִּירָיו. *דִּתְנַן: דכָּל שֶׁיֵּשׁ לוֹ מַתִּירִים – מִשֶּׁקָּרְבוּ מַתִּירָיו, כָּל שֶׁאֵין לוֹ מַתִּירִין – מִשֶּׁקָּדַשׁ בִּכְלִי. אִיתְּמַר, הַמַּעֲלֶה אֶבְרֵי בְהֵמָה טְמֵאָה ע"ג הַמִּזְבֵּחַ, רֵישׁ לָקִישׁ אָמַר: לוֹקֶה, רַבִּי יוֹחָנָן אָמַר: אֵינוֹ לוֹקֶה. רֵישׁ לָקִישׁ אָמַר: לוֹקֶה, טְהוֹרָה – אִין, טְמֵאָה – לָא, וְלָאו הַבָּא מִכְּלַל עֲשֵׂה – לוֹקִין עָלָיו. וְרַבִּי יוֹחָנָן אָמַר: אֵין לוֹקִין עָלָיו, לָאו הַבָּא מִכְּלַל עֲשֵׂה – ג] אֵין לוֹקִין עָלָיו. מוֹתִיב רַבִּי יִרְמְיָה: °"אוֹתָהּ תֹּאכֵלוּ" – וְלֹא בְּהֵמָה טְמֵאָה, *וְלָאו הַבָּא מִכְּלַל עֲשֵׂה – עֲשֵׂה! א"ל רַבִּי יַעֲקֹב לְרַבִּי יִרְמְיָה בַּר תַּחְלִיפָא: אַסְבְּרָא לָךְ, הבְּאֶבְרֵי בְהֵמָה טְמֵאָה – דְּכוּלֵּי עָלְמָא לָא פְּלִיגִי, כִּי פְּלִיגִי – בְּחַיָּה. וְהָכִי אִיתְּמַר, רַבִּי יוֹחָנָן אָמַר: ועוֹבֵר בַּעֲשֵׂה, רֵישׁ לָקִישׁ אָמַר: אֵינוֹ עוֹבֵר בְּלֹא כְלוּם. רַבִּי יוֹחָנָן אָמַר: עוֹבֵר בַּעֲשֵׂה, בְּהֵמָה – אִין, חַיָּה – לָא. רֵישׁ לָקִישׁ אָמַר: אֵינוֹ עוֹבֵר ד] עָלָיו בְּלֹא כְלוּם, הַהוּא לְמִצְוָה. מוֹתִיב רָבָא: אִילּוּ נֶאֱמַר °"קָרְבָּן לַה' בְּהֵמָה" – הָיִיתִי אוֹמֵר: חַיָּה בִּכְלַל בְּהֵמָה, כְּעִנְיָן שֶׁנֶּאֱמַר: °"זֹאת הַבְּהֵמָה אֲשֶׁר תֹּאכֵלוּ שׁוֹר שֵׂה כְשָׂבִים וְשֵׂה עִזִּים אַיָּל וּצְבִי" וגו' – תַּלְמוּד לוֹמַר: °"בָּקָר וְצֹאן", בָּקָר וְצֹאן אָמַרְתִּי לְךָ, וְלֹא חַיָּה. יָכוֹל לֹא יָבִיא, וְאִם הֵבִיא כָּשֵׁר? הָא לְמָה זֶה דּוֹמֶה – לְתַלְמִיד שֶׁאָמַר לוֹ רַבּוֹ: "הָבֵא לִי חִטִּים" וְהֵבִיא לוֹ חִטִּים וּשְׂעוֹרִים, ה] שֶׁאֵינוֹ כְּמַעֲבִיר עַל דְּבָרָיו אֶלָּא מוֹסִיף עַל דְּבָרָיו, וְכָשֵׁר? תַּלְמוּד לוֹמַר: "בָּקָר וְצֹאן" – זבָּקָר וְצֹאן אָמַרְתִּי לְךָ, וְלֹא חַיָּה. הָא לְמָה זֶה דּוֹמֶה – לְתַלְמִיד שֶׁאָמַר לוֹ רַבּוֹ: "אַל תָּבִיא לִי אֶלָּא חִיטִּין" וְהֵבִיא לוֹ חִיטִּין וּשְׂעוֹרִים, שֶׁאֵינוֹ כְּמוֹסִיף עַל דְּבָרָיו אֶלָּא כְּמַעֲבִיר עַל דְּבָרָיו, וּפָסוּל

(ויקרא ז) (שם) (שם) (שם יא) (שם א) (דברים יד) (ויקרא א)

רש"י

נְטִילַת נְשָׁמָה. כָּרֵת. וְאַכַּתִּי מִיבָּעֵי לֵיהּ כו'. וְכֵיוָן דִּלְאַחַר זְרִיקָה נָפְקָא לָן ו] מִינֵּיהּ, הֵיכִי יָלֵיף מִינֵּיהּ תַּרְתֵּי? אָתְיָא טוּמְאָתוֹ טוּמְאָתוֹ. אַזְהָרַת טָמֵא שֶׁלֹּא יֹאכַל קֹדֶשׁ. אַלְמָא אַזְהָרָתוֹ מֵעוֹנְשׁוֹ יָלְפָא, וְעוֹנְשׁוֹ לְאַחַר זְרִיקָה הוּא וְלֹא לִפְנֵי זְרִיקָה, כִּדְקָתָנֵי בְּגְמָ' דְּ"הַקּוֹמֵץ רַבָּה" (מנחות כה:): יָכוֹל יְהוּ חַיָּיבִין עָלָיו מִשּׁוּם טוּמְאָה לִפְנֵי זְרִיקַת דָּמִים – תַּלְמוּד לוֹמַר: "כָּל טָהוֹר יֹאכַל בָּשָׂר וְהַנֶּפֶשׁ אֲשֶׁר תֹּאכַל בָּשָׂר" וגו' (ויקרא ז), הַנִּיתָּר לִטְהוֹרִים – חַיָּיבִין עָלָיו מִשּׁוּם טוּמְאָה, שֶׁאֵין נִיתָּר לִטְהוֹרִים – אֵין חַיָּיבִים עָלָיו מִשּׁוּם טוּמְאָה. אִם כֵּן. דִּלְאוֹכֵל לְאַחַר זְרִיקָה ז] אֲתָא קְרָא – לִכְתּוֹב "בְּקֹדֶשׁ", וַאֲנָא אָמֵינָא: לְאַחַר זְרִיקָה הוּא, דּוּמְיָא דְּעוֹנֶשׁ. מַחֲלוֹקֶת בְּטוּמְאַת הַגּוּף. כְּהַהוּא קָאָמַר ר' יוֹחָנָן אֵינוֹ לוֹקֶה, דְּנָפְקָא לֵיהּ אַזְהָרָה מֵעוֹנֶשׁ. אֲבָל טוּמְאַת בָּשָׂר. טָהוֹר שֶׁאָכַל אֶת הַטָּמֵא, דְּאַזְהָרָה דִּידֵיהּ בְּהֶדְיָא ח] כְּתִיבִי: "וְהַבָּשָׂר אֲשֶׁר יִגַּע בְּכָל טָמֵא לֹא יֵאָכֵל" (שם) – דִּבְרֵי הַכֹּל לוֹקֶה. דְּאָמַר מָר וְהַבָּשָׂר. יְתֵירָא, דִּכְתִיב בְּסֵיפֵיהּ "וְהַבָּשָׂר כָּל טָהוֹר" וגו'. לְרַבּוֹת עֵצִים וּלְבוֹנָה. לְטוּמְאַת עַצְמָן, דְּחִיבַּת הַקֹּדֶשׁ מַכְשַׁרְתָּם לְשַׁוּוֹיְנְהוּ אוֹכְלָא, וְאַע"ג דְּהָנֵי לָאו בְּנֵי אֲכִילָה נִינְהוּ. וּבָשָׂר לִפְנֵי זְרִיקָה לָא גָּרַע מִינַּיְיהוּ. ה"ג: וְרָבָא אָמַר ט] בְּטוּמְאַת הַגּוּף אֲבָל טוּמְאַת בָּשָׂר אִיתְקִישׁ לְעוֹנֶשׁ, דִּסְמִיךְ לֵיהּ "וְהַנֶּפֶשׁ אֲשֶׁר תֹּאכַל בָּשָׂר" י] דְּאוֹקִימְנָא בִּלְאַחַר (ב) *(זְרִיקַת בָּשָׂר). שֶׁקִּדְּשׁוּ בִּכְלִי. עֵצִים שֶׁחָתָה אוֹתָן בְּמַחְתַּת כְּלִי שָׁרֵת מֵעַל הַמִּזְבֵּחַ עִם גֶּחָלִים, וּלְבוֹנָה שֶׁקִּידְּשָׁהּ בְּבָזִיכִין, דַּאֲפִי' כָּרֵת בְּטוּמְאַת הַגּוּף נַמִּי אִית בְּהוּ. דִּתְנַן. לְקַמָּן בְּפֶרֶק "בֵּית שַׁמַּאי" (דף מג.) גַּבֵּי טוּמְאַת הַגּוּף. כָּל שֶׁיֵּשׁ לוֹ מַתִּירִין. הַמַּתִּירִין אוֹתוֹ בַּאֲכִילָה – חַיָּיבִין עָלָיו מִשּׁוּם טוּמְאָה מִשֶּׁקָּרְבוּ מַתִּירָיו. וְשֶׁאֵין לוֹ מַתִּירִין – מִשֶּׁקָּדַשׁ בִּכְלִי. בְּהֵמָה טְמֵאָה. סוּסִים וּגְמַלִּים. יא] טְהוֹרִים אִין. "מִן הַבָּקָר וּמִן הַצֹּאן תַּקְרִיבוּ". אוֹתָהּ תֹּאכֵלוּ. "מַפְרֶסֶת פַּרְסָה וּמַעֲלַת גֵּרָה". וְלָאו הַבָּא מִכְּלַל עֲשֵׂה. כָּךְ *שְׁנוּיָה בְּתוֹךְ יב] הַבָּרַיְיתָא. וּמַסְקִינַן: בְּלֹא תַעֲשֶׂה מִנַּיִן? תַּלְמוּד לוֹמַר: "אַךְ אֶת זֶה לֹא תֹאכְלוּ". אַלְמָא, מִדְּאִיצְטְרִיךְ לֹא תַעֲשֶׂה אַחֲרֶיהָ – לָאו אַזְהָרָה הוּא. דְּכ"ע ל"פ. דַּעֲשֵׂה הוּא דְּאִיכָּא, וְתוּ לָא. כִּי פְּלִיגִי בְּחַיָּה. וְלֹא לְעִנְיַן מַלְקוּת אֶלָּא לַעֲשֵׂה, יג] וְאֵימוֹר נַמִּי אֵיפוּךְ דְּרַבִּי יוֹחָנָן לְרֵישׁ לָקִישׁ. °וְהָכִי הֲוָה שְׁמִיעַ לֵיהּ לְרַבִּי יַעֲקֹב. הַהוּא לְמִצְוָה. בְּהֵמָה מִצְוָה לְהַקְרִיב, וְחַיָּה רְשׁוּת. וּמִיהוּ טְמֵאָה וַדַּאי לֹא, דִּכְתִיב: "מִמַּשְׁקֵה יִשְׂרָאֵל" – מִן הַמּוּתָּר לְיִשְׂרָאֵל, בְּפֶרֶק קַמָּא דִּמְנָחוֹת (דף ו.), גַּבֵּי טְרֵיפָה. אִילּוּ נֶאֱמַר קָרְבָּן לַה' מִן הַבְּהֵמָה. וְלֹא פֵּירֵשׁ בָּקָר וָצֹאן. הָיִיתִי אוֹמֵר כו'. כְּעִנְיָן שֶׁנֶּאֱמַר "זֹאת הַבְּהֵמָה" וּכְתִיב בַּתְרֵיהּ "אַיָּל וּצְבִי". (ג) תְּרֵי בָּקָר וָצֹאן כְּתִיבִי הָתָם: "מִן הַבָּקָר וּמִן הַצֹּאן תַּקְרִיבוּ", וַהֲדַר כְּתִיב: "אִם עוֹלָה קָרְבָּנוֹ מִן הַבָּקָר וְאִם מִן הַצֹּאן קָרְבָּנוֹ מִן הַכְּשָׂבִים".

פָּסוּל

תוספות

והבשר לרבות עצים ולבונה. מהכא נפקא לן דחיבת הקודש מכשרת. ומקשים: הא דאמר בפ' קמא דפסחים (דף טז.): משקי בי יד] מדבחיא דכן, כגון יין ושמן, אמאי? ליתכשרו בחיבת הקודש כמו עצים ולבונה! י"ל: דחיבת הקודש מהניא לשווי אוכל *מוכשר מידי דדמי לאוכל, כגון עצים ולבונה שהוא דבר עב וקשה כעין אוכל, אבל לשווי המשקה כאוכל מוכשר – לא מהניא חיבת הקודש. ואם תאמר: הא דאמר בפ' "כל שעה" (פסחים כד.): "והבשר אשר יגע בכל טמא לא יאכל" למה לי? אם אינו ענין לגופו, דנפקא ליה מ"לא תוכל לאכול בשעריך", תנהו ענין לכל איסורין שבתורה – הא איצטריך לגופיה, דלקי אעצים ולבונה! ויש לומר: כיון דאיתרבאי עצים ולבונה מייתורא ד"והבשר" – ממילא טו] אשמעינן דלקי מ"לא תוכל לאכול בשעריך". ודברי תימה הוא: מנלן דאתא לרבות עצים ולבונה? דילמא דווקא לבשר קאתי, דמהניא ליה חיבת הקדש ולא טז] בעיא הכשר! **ואפי'** הכי רבינהו קרא. משמע שהיא דרשא גמורה ולא אסמכתא. וכן משמע בפרק שני דחולין (דף לו:): חיבת הקודש דאורייתא. ולא כפירוש הקונט' דלקמן בסוף פ' "בית שמאי" (דף מו:) דקאמר, והאמר מר: "והבשר" – לרבות עצים ולבונה! ומשני: לפסולא בעלמא. ופי' בקונטרס: מדרבנן. וכן בפסחים בפרק "כל שעה" (דף לד:) דקרי ליה "מעלה", פירש בקונטרס: מעלה דרבנן. ואי אפשר לומר כן, דהכי נמי הביא כפרתו אוכל בקדשים קאמר התם "מעלה" – יז] דאורייתא הוא, דמקראי נפקא לן בפ' "הערל" (יבמות עד:). והא דקאמר לקמן פסולא בעלמא – היינו דליכא מלקות אלא איסור *דאורייתא. וצריך לדקדק אי אתיא מילתא יח] דאביי דהכא כהני תרי לישני דלקמן פרק "ב"ש" (דף מו:).

שקדש בכלי. תימה: מה קידוש כלי יש בעצים? דאי מה שמבקעין אותו בקורדום כשהיו מתליעים אותו – הא קורדום אינו כלי שרת כדמשמע בתוספתא, כדתניא: השואל קורדום של הקדש, בקע בו ובא חבירו ובקע בו – כולן מעלו. נתנה לחבירו וחבירו לחבירו – הראשון מעל והשני לא מעל. ובעולה אינו כן, נתנה לחבירו וחבירו לחבירו – כולן מעלו. ובקונטרס פירש דמיירי הכא בעצים שחתה יט] במחתת כלי שרת מעל המזבח עם גחלים. ואין משמע, דבמס' תמיד (דף כח:) משמע שהיה חותה מן המאוכלות הפנימיות. כ] ומיהו, י"ל: לא בתרומת הדשן מיירי, אלא ביוה"כ שחותה גחלים לקטרת. ונראה דקידוש כלי דעצים היינו כא] *דמשפי להו לגיזרין, אע"ג דקורדום לאו כלי שרת הוא, כדאמר בפרק י"ב דמנחות (דף קא.): עצים כמה דלא *משפי להו לגיזרין – לא מיתכשרי. והא דאמר ב"הקומץ רבה" (שם כא.): יצאו עצים שאין מקבלים טומאה, היינו קודם קידוש כלי א).

אותה תאכלו. כב] אסיפא סמיך, ב) דקתני בתורת כהנים: אין לי אלא בעשה, בלא תעשה מנין. **שאינו** כמעביר על דבריו. אע"פ שאין זה מביא אלא חיה לבדה, כיון דמרצונו מביא הקרבן – אין זה מעביר, שהרי תלה בדעתו. **אלא** כמעביר על דבריו. ל"ע במעילה (דף כ:) ובפ' "אלמנה ניזונת" (כתובות לח:) גבי "זבן לי ליתכא" ואזיל וזבן ליה כורא.

פסול

א) [וע"ע תוספות מנחות קא. ד"ה אע"ג] ב) [ועי' מכות יח: ול"ע]

עין משפט נר מצוה

יט א ב מיי' פי"ח מהל' פסה"מ הלכה יב:

מוהכשר וכן לקמן ל"ק

כ ג מיי' פ"ו מהלכות איסורי מזבח הל' ח:

כא ד מיי' י"ח מהל' פסה"מ הלכה טז:

כב ה ו מיי' פ"ה מהל' איסורי מזבח הל' ו [דלוקה ועיין כ"מ מפרש טעמו דהא דמסיק הש"ס דכ"ע לא פליגי היינו דכ"ע ס"ל דלוקה ודלא כפרש"י ע"ש]:

כג ז מיי' פ"א מהלכות מעה"ק הלכה א:

מסורת הש"ס

חולין לו: [לקמן מו: פסחים כד: לה.] | מעילה י. | [מכות יח: ע"ש] | [וע"ע תוספו' פסחים יט. ד"ה אלמא ותוס' חגיגה כג: ד"ה והא ותוספות מנחות כא. ד"ה יצאו ותוס' חולין לה. ד"ה אין] | [פסחים מח: יבמות נב: נו: סח. עג: חולין פא.]

הגהות הב"ח

(א) גמ' דברי הכל לוקה דאמר מר והבשר: (ב) רש"י ד"ה דאוקמינא וכו' בלאחר זריקה הס"ד ותיבת בשר נמחק: (ג) ד"ה הייתי אומר וכו' וכתיב בתריה איל וצבי הס"ד ואח"כ מ"ה ת"ל בקר וצאן תרי בקר.

גליון הש"ס

רש"י ד"ה כי פליגי בחיה וכו' והכי הוה שמיעא ליה. וכזה שבת דף טו ע"א נדה דף כד ע"ב.

שיטה מקובצת

א] לוקה רבי יוחנן לטעמיה דאמר דתני ברדלא: ב] ס"א בטומאת בשר אבל בטומאת הגוף ד"ה אינו לוקה מאי טעמא כו': ג] אינו לוקה עליו: ד] אינו עובר ולאו כלום. הקשה בקונטרס בהמה טמאה נמי ותירץ א) וקשה דחיה טהורה נמי מי גרע ממפריש נקבה לעולה דאמרינן לקמן דהויא כבעלת מום ובבעלת מום יש שני לאוין משום בל תקריבו ומשום בל תשחטו וי"ל דדוקא בנקבה לעולה דהויא מין הקרבה כמו בעל מום אבל חיה דלאו בת הקרבה היא כמו חולין לא שייך בה לאוין כמו בבעל מום וגם לא הוי מקריב חולין לעזרה כיון שאינם ראוים לזבוח בקירוב מקום במקדש דחולין בעזרה נפקא לן מוכי ירחק ממך המקום וזבחת: ההוא למצוה. פרש"י להקדים בהמה לחיה דבהמה מצוה וחיה רשות ולא רצה לפרש למצוה שמצוה לכתחלה להביא בהמה ולא חיה דא"כ היינו עשה ממש ומה שמהפך האמוראים הכי הוי שמיע ליה לרבי יעקב מקבלה וכיוצא בזה אשכחן בכמה מקומות: ה] שאינו כמעביר על דבריו אלא מוסיף על דבריו. וא"ת הא אין הנדון דומה לראיה שאינו מביא רק חיה לבדה והוי כמעביר שאין מביא מה שאמר לו רבו וי"ל דאם נצטוה להביא קרבן הדין עמך שהיה כמעביר [על דבריו] אבל הוא מביא מרצונו ובדעתו תלה ולא הוי העברה: ו] לן ג) אלא מינה: ז] זריקה לחודא אתא: ח] בהדיא כתיב והבשר: ט] אמר מחלוקת בטומאת הגוף אבל בטומאת בשר ד"ה אינו לוקה בטומאת הגוף הוא דאמר ריש לקיש לוקה דנפקא ליה מבכל קודש לא תגע אבל: י] בשר וגו' דאוקמנא לאחר זריקה הס"ד: יא] מה"ד טהורה אין: יב] בתוך המשנה ומסקינן בברייתא אין לי אלא בעשה בלא: יג] לעשה ואמוראי נמי איפוך דר"י לדריש לקיש: יד] בי מטבחיא: טו] ממילא שמעינן דלקי: טז] ולא בעי הכשר: יז] מעלה ומדאורייתא: יח] דאביי ס"א דרבא: יט] שחתה במחתה שהיא כלי שרת כו' ואין משמע כן דבמס': כ] הפנימיות ולא היה חותה עצים כלל ומיהו לא בתרומת: כא] היינו דמשפי להו כו' לאו כלי שרת הוא מ"מ חתוכו ותיקונו חשיב להו כלי שרת כדאמר בפרק המנחות והנסכים (דף קא ע"א) עצים כמה דלא משפי להו: כב] תאכלו ולא בהמה טמאה ולאו הבא מכלל עשה עשה. פ"ה שכך לשון המשנה ומסיים עוד בה לא תעשה מנין ת"ל אך את זה כו' ולא דק שהרי בהך ברייתא אינו כן בת"כ והכי איתא התם ולא בהמה טמאה אין לי אלא בעשה בלא תעשה מנין כו' והתלמוד הביא בקיצור ע"כ תוס' מהר"פ זצ"ל:

ורבנן

א) נראה דצ"ל ומה"ט משום דכתיב ממשקה ישראל וכו'. ומיהו עדיין קשה. ב) נראה דגרס כרש"י לאחר זריקה לא נפקא לן אלא מיניה וכו'.

כד א מיי' פ"א מהלכות פסה"מ הלכה כח:
כה ב מיי' פ"ב מהלכות פסה"מ הלכה כא:

וּפָסוּל. תְּיוּבְתָּא דְּרֵישׁ לָקִישׁ! תְּיוּבְתָּא.§ "וְכוּלָּן שֶׁקִּיבְּלוּ" כו'.§ *בְּעָא מִינֵּיהּ רֵישׁ לָקִישׁ מֵרַבִּי יוֹחָנָן: פָּסוּל מַהוּ שֶׁיַּעֲשֶׂה שִׁירַיִם? אֲמַר לֵיהּ: אאֵין (א) עוֹשֶׂה שִׁירַיִם אֶלָּא חוּץ לִזְמַנּוֹ וְחוּץ לִמְקוֹמוֹ, הוֹאִיל וּמְרַצֶּה לְפִיגּוּלוֹ. רַב זְבִיד מַתְנֵי הָכִי: בְּעָא מִינֵּיהּ רֵישׁ לָקִישׁ מֵרַבִּי יוֹחָנָן: כּוֹס פָּסוּל מַהוּ שֶׁיַּעֲשֶׂה שִׁירַיִם? אֲמַר לֵיהּ: פָּסוּל גּוּפֵיהּ מַאי סְבִירָא לָךְ? אִי פָּסוּל מְשַׁוֵּי שִׁירַיִם — כּוֹס פָּסוּל נַמִי מְשַׁוֵּי שִׁירַיִם, אִי פָּסוּל לָא מְשַׁוֵּי שִׁירַיִם — כּוֹס פָּסוּל נַמִי לָא מְשַׁוֵּי שִׁירַיִם! רַב יִרְמְיָה מִדִּיפְתִּי מַתְנֵי הָכִי: בְּעָא מִינֵּיהּ אַבַּיֵי (מֵרָבָא) [מֵרַבָּה] כּוֹס מַהוּ *שֶׁיַּעֲשֶׂה אֶת חֲבֵירוֹ, דָּחוּי אוֹ שִׁירַיִם? אֲמַר לֵיהּ: פְּלוּגְתָּא דְּרַבִּי אֶלְעָזָר בְּרַבִּי שִׁמְעוֹן וְרַבָּנַן. א] *דְּתַנְיָא: לְמַעְלָה הוּא אוֹמֵר: °"אֶת דָּמוֹ יִשְׁפֹּךְ", לְמַטָּה הוּא אוֹמֵר: °"וְאֶת כָּל דָּמָהּ יִשְׁפֹּךְ"; מִנַּיִן בלְחַטָּאת שֶׁקִּיבֵּל דָּמָהּ בְּאַרְבָּעָה כּוֹסוֹת וְנָתַן מַתָּנָה אַחַת מִזֶּה, וּמַתָּנָה אַחַת מִזֶּה, שֶׁכּוּלָּן נִשְׁפָּכִין לַיְסוֹד — תַּלְמוּד לוֹמַר: "וְאֶת כָּל דָּמָהּ יִשְׁפֹּךְ". יָכוֹל נָתַן אַרְבַּע מַתָּנוֹת מִכּוֹס אֶחָד יְהוּ כּוּלָּן נִשְׁפָּכִין לַיְסוֹד? תַּלְמוּד לוֹמַר: "וְאֶת דָּמוֹ". הָא כֵּיצַד? הוּא נִשְׁפָּךְ לַיְסוֹד, וְהֵן נִשְׁפָּכִין לָאַמָּה. רַבִּי אֶלְעָזָר בְּרַבִּי שִׁמְעוֹן אוֹמֵר: מִנַּיִן לְחַטָּאת שֶׁקִּיבֵּל דָּמָהּ בְּאַרְבָּעָה כּוֹסוֹת וְנָתַן ד' מַתָּנוֹת מִכּוֹס אֶחָד, שֶׁכּוּלָּן נִשְׁפָּכִין לַיְסוֹד — תַּלְמוּד לוֹמַר: "וְאֶת כָּל דָּמָהּ יִשְׁפֹּךְ". וְהָכְתִיב: "וְאֶת דָּמוֹ יִשְׁפֹּךְ"! א"ר אַשִׁי: הַהוּא לְמַעוּטֵי שִׁירַיִם שֶׁבְּצַוַּאר בְּהֵמָה.§ "קִיבֵּל הַכָּשֵׁר וְנָתַן לְפָסוּל" כו'.§ וּצְרִיכָא, דְּאִי אַשְׁמְעִינַן פָּסוּל, הֲוָה אָמִינָא: מַאי פָּסוּל — טָמֵא, ב] דַּחֲזֵי לַעֲבוֹדַת צִיבּוּר, אֲבָל שְׂמֹאל — לָא. וְאִי אַשְׁמְעִינַן שְׂמֹאל — דְּאִית לֵיהּ הֶכְשֵׁירָא בְּיוֹם הַכִּיפּוּרִים, אֲבָל כְּלִי חוֹל — לָא. וְאִי אַשְׁמְעִינַן כְּלִי חוֹל — מִשּׁוּם דַּחֲזוּ לְקַדּוּשִׁינְהוּ, אֲבָל הָנָךְ — אֵימָא לָא, צְרִיכָא. וְלֶיהֱוֵי ג] לֵיהּ דָּחוּי! אֲמַר לֵיהּ רָבִינָא לְרַב אַשִׁי, הָכִי אָמַר רַב יִרְמְיָה מִדִּיפְתִּי מִשְּׁמֵיהּ דְּרָבָא: הָא מַנִּי — *חָנָן הַמִּצְרִי הוּא, דְּלֵית לֵיהּ דִּחוּיִין. דְּתַנְיָא, חָנָן הַמִּצְרִי אוֹמֵר: אֲפִי' דָּם בַּכּוֹס — מֵבִיא חֲבֵירוֹ וּמְזַוֵּוג לוֹ. *רַב אַשִׁי אָמַר: כָּל שֶׁבְּיָדוֹ לָא הָוֵי דָּחוּי. אָמַר רַב שַׁיָּיא: כְּוָותֵיהּ דְּרַב אַשִׁי מִסְתַּבְּרָא; מַאן שָׁמְעַתְּ לֵיהּ דְּאִית לֵיהּ דִּחוּיִין — רַבִּי יְהוּדָה, *דְּתְנַן: וְעוֹד אָמַר רַבִּי יְהוּדָה: נִשְׁפַּךְ הַדָּם — יָמוּת הַמִּשְׁתַּלֵּחַ, מֵת הַמִּשְׁתַּלֵּחַ — יִשָּׁפֵךְ הַדָּם. וְשָׁמְעִינַן לֵיהּ דְּאָמַר: כָּל שֶׁבְּיָדוֹ — לָא הָוֵי דָּחוּי, *דְּתַנְיָא, רַבִּי יְהוּדָה אוֹמֵר: כּוֹס אֶחָד הָיָה מְמַלֵּא מִדַּם הַתַּעֲרוֹבֶת וְזוֹרְקוֹ זְרִיקָה אַחַת כְּנֶגֶד הַיְסוֹד. ש"מ: כָּל שֶׁבְּיָדוֹ לָא הָוֵי דָּחוּי, ש"מ. גּוּפָא, תַּנְיָא, רַבִּי יְהוּדָה אוֹמֵר: כּוֹס אֶחָד הָיָה מְמַלֵּא מִדַּם הַתַּעֲרוֹבֶת, שֶׁאִם יִשָּׁפֵךְ אֶחָד מֵהֶם נִמְצָא שֶׁהוּא מַכְשִׁירוֹ. אָמְרוּ לוֹ לְרַבִּי יְהוּדָה: וַהֲלֹא לֹא נִתְקַבֵּל בִּכְלִי! מְנָא יָדְעִי? אֶלָּא, שֶׁמָּא לֹא נִתְקַבֵּל בִּכְלִי! אָמַר לָהֶן:
אַף

תורה אור: ויקרא ד; שם

פסול מהו שיעשה שירים. יז] לדם שבצואר בהמה, ולא יהיה עוד תקנה, או יחזור הכשר ויקבל ויזרוק. בפסול שקבל לא מיבעיא, יח] דהתנן: יחזור הכשר ויקבל. אלא בפסול שזרק מיבעיא ליה, כדפירש בקונטרס. וממתני' ליכא למידק: קבלו – אין, זרק – לא, דאיכא לדחויי כדאמרינן בפירקין דלעיל: לא תימא זרקו לא, אלא אימא: שחטו לא. יט] ⊕ומיהו, למאן דאמר שלא במקומו כמקומו דמי – מוכח לעיל דהוא הדין ⊕בזרק הפסול שיחזור הכשר ויקבל. וה"ר אפריס מפרש: דהך בעיא כ] אמתני' דכל הפסולין שעלו לא ירדו קאי, דלכתחלה לא יעלו. וקמיבעיא כא] אם זרק פסול, מהו שיעשה שירים להיות נשפכין לכתחלה ליסוד כמו בכל שירי הדם. או לא, ואסור לזורקם לכתחלה, וישפכו לאמה. וקשה לפי' זה, דהוה ליה למימר: מה שיעשה שירים או דחוי, כדקאמר באידך בעיא: כוס מהו שיעשה את חבירו שירים או דחוי. ועוד: אמרינן בהדיא בריש מסכת מעילה (דף ה.) גבי חטאת פסולה אין דמה טעון כיבוס: הא קמ"ל, דאע"ג דקיבל פסול וזרק וקבל כשר וזרק – לאו כלום כב] (פסול), מאי טעמא – שירים נינהו. ופריך: והא בעי מיניה ר"ל מר' יוחנן פסול מהו שיעשה שירים, כג] וא"ל: אין עושה שירים כי אם חוץ לזמנו. כד] מאי לאו, אבל שאר פסולין אינן עושים שירים? ומאי קשיא ליה? הא מודה ריש לקיש דלכל כה] היותר שירים הוי, אבל מיבעיא ליה דשמא אפילו דחוי הוי. ואם כן, ממה נפשך אין טעון כיבוס! ול"נ דלא קשיא מידי, דאי שירים הוי – א"כ הוי כשאר דמים כשרין, שהשירים נשפכין ליסוד. אבל שירים דקאמר התם דאין דמה טעון כיבוס – היינו שירים ופסול. אבל קשה, כו] (בסיפא) דקאמר: מאי לאו בר משאר פסולין? ומאי פריך? אי שאר פסולין אינן עושים שירים – א"כ ליהוי דחוי, וכל שכן דאין דמה טעון כיבוס! אבל לפי' רש"י אתי שפיר, דאי אינו עושה שירים – יחזור הכשר ויקבל, והוי דם כשר וטעון כיבוס. ברו"ך.

למעוטי שירים שבצואר בהמה. כז] והא דאמר (לעיל כה.) דצריך שיקבל כל דמו של פר – היינו למצוה.

ולהוי דחוי. כח] תימה: אם נתן לפסול מה בכך? מעשה איצטבא הוא! מי גרע מנתן על האבן? שהרי לא פריך הכי אמתניתין דאמר פרק "הוציאו לו" (יומא נג:) דקתני: יצא והניחו על כן הזהב שבהיכל! ועוד תיקשי ליה קרא דמייתי לעיל בפרק קמא (דף יד.) "ויזרקו הכהנים" כט] (את הדם)! ונראה, דהא דפריך וליהוי דחוי – לא קאי אונתן לפסול, דאין זה אלא מעשה איצטבא בעלמא. אלא פריך אנתן לכלי חול, ואנשפך מן הכלי על הרצפה. **כל** שבידו לא הוי דחוי. ל] *ענפיו מרובין מעליו דסוכה (דף לג.) אין זה בידו, כיון דאין ממעטין ביום טוב. וגבי כסוי הדם (חולין דף פז.) דקרי ליה דחוי כשכיסהו הרוח ונתגלה, כיון דאין מלוה לבטל הדחוי – לא] לא חשיב בידו, ולא דמי להכא דמלוה לאוספו. והפריש קרבן והמיר דת דלעיל לב] בפרק קמא (דף יב:) אין זה קרוי בידו, כיון דאין דעתו לחזור*.
אין

פָּסוּל מַהוּ שֶׁיַּעֲשֶׂה שִׁירַיִם. מִי שֶׁהוּא פָּסוּל לַעֲבוֹדָה. מַהוּ שֶׁיַּעֲשֶׂה שִׁירַיִים. אִם קִבֵּל וְזָרַק, מַהוּ שֶׁיַּחֲזוֹר הַכָּשֵׁר וִיקַבֵּל וְיִזְרוֹק וְיַכְשֵׁר הַקָּרְבָּן? מִי אָמְרִינַן: כֵּיוָן דְּזָרַק פָּסוּל — שַׁוְיֵיהּ לַדָּם שֶׁבַּצַּוָּאר ד] שִׁירַיִים, וְתוּ לָא מִיחֲזֵי לִזְרִיקָה. אוֹ דִּלְמָא: לָא אַלִּימָא זְרִיקַת פָּסוּל לְשַׁוְיֵיהּ לַדָּם שֶׁבְּצַוַּאר בְּהֵמָה שִׁירַיִם, וְיַחֲזוֹר הַכָּשֵׁר וִיקַבֵּל. אֵין לְךָ זְרִיקָה פְּסוּלָה שֶׁעוֹשָׂה אֶת הַשְּׁאָר שִׁירַיִם. אֶלָּא זְרִיקָה בְּמַחֲשֶׁבֶת חוּץ לִזְמַנּוֹ וְחוּץ לִמְקוֹמוֹ. הוֹאִיל וּמְרַצֶּה לְפִיגּוּלוֹ. הוֹאִיל וַהֲוָיָא זְרִיקָה מִן הַתּוֹרָה לְמִיקְבְּעֵיהּ ה] פִּיגּוּל. וּפָסוּל. כּוֹס פָּסוּל. כְּגוֹן שֶׁיָּצָא, מַהוּ שֶׁיַּעֲשֶׂה לַדָּם שֶׁבַּצַּוָּאר ו] שִׁירַיִם אִם זְרָקוֹ כֹּהֵן כָּשֵׁר לָזֶה, וְלֹא יְהֵא תַּקָּנָה לַקָּרְבָּן שֶׁיַּחֲזוֹר וִיקַבֵּל. פָּסוּל גּוּפֵיהּ מַאי סְבִירָא לָךְ. אָדָם פָּסוּל שֶׁזָּרַק, מַאי סְבִירָא לָךְ בַּשִּׁירַיִם שֶׁבְּצַוַּאר בְּהֵמָה, דְּלָא קָמִיבַּעְיָא לָךְ? כּוֹס מַהוּ שֶׁיַּעֲשֶׂה אֶת חֲבֵירוֹ דָּחוּי אוֹ שִׁירַיִם. כְּגוֹן חַטָּאת שֶׁקִּבֵּל דָּמָהּ בִּשְׁנֵי כוֹסוֹת, וְנָתַן כָּל מַתְּנוֹתָיו מֵאֶחָד מֵהֶן — חֲבֵירוֹ שִׁירַיִם הוּא, וְנִשְׁפָּךְ לַיְסוֹד, ז] דִּכְתִיב: "וְאֶת כָּל הַדָּם יִשְׁפֹּךְ" וגו' (ויקרא ד). אוֹ דָּחוּי הוּא. ח] דְּחִיָּיה בְּיָדַיִם, שֶׁלֹּא נִיתַּן מִמֶּנּוּ עַל הַקְּרָנוֹת. וְיִשָּׁפֵךְ לָאַמָּה שֶׁבָּעֲזָרָה הַמּוֹלִיכָה דָּמִים לְנַחַל קִדְרוֹן. לְמַעְלָה. בַּפָּרָשָׁה, הוּא אוֹמֵר בִּשְׂעִיר נָשִׂיא בְּשִׁירֵי הַדָּם: "וְאֶת דָּמוֹ יִשְׁפֹּךְ", וְלָא כְּתִיב "כָּל דָּמוֹ". לְמַטָּה. בְּחַטָּאת יָחִיד, הוּא אוֹמֵר "וְאֶת כָּל דָּמָהּ יִשְׁפֹּךְ". וְהֵן נִשְׁפָּכִין לָאַמָּה. דְּכוֹס עוֹשֶׂה אֶת חֲבֵירוֹ דָּחוּי. לְמַעוּטֵי שִׁירַיִם שֶׁבְּצַוַּאר בְּהֵמָה. שֶׁהֵן נַעֲשִׂין שִׁירַיִם עַל יְדֵי הַדָּם ט] הַמִּתְקַבֵּל, וְיִשָּׁפְכוּ לָאַמָּה. וּצְרִיכָא. לְאַשְׁמוּעִינַן י] דְּאִית לְהוּ תַּקָּנָה בַּחֲזָרָה. דַּחֲזֵי לַעֲבוֹדַת צִיבּוּר. כְּגוֹן טָמֵא, דַּחֲזֵי יא] לְכַתְּחִלָּה בְּצִיבּוּר, הִלְכָּךְ גַּבֵּי יָחִיד אִיכָּא תַּקַּנְתָּא בַּחֲזָרָה. בְּיוֹם הַכִּיפּוּרִים. נָטַל אֶת הַמַּחְתָּה בִּימִינוֹ וְאֶת הַכַּף בִּשְׂמֹאלוֹ. וְנֶיהֱוֵי דָּחוּי. דְּהָא נִרְאָה וְנִדְחָה, וְאַמַּאי אִית לֵיהּ תַּקַּנְתָּא בַּחֲזָרָה? אֲפִילּוּ דָּם. שָׂעִיר הַנַּעֲשֶׂה בִּפְנִים. בְּכוֹס. וּמֵת הַמִּשְׁתַּלֵּחַ — לֹא נִדְחֶה הַדָּם, אֶלָּא מֵבִיא שָׂעִיר אַחֵר וּמְזַוֵּוג יב] לְהַדָּם, וְכָשֵׁר הַדָּם לְמַתְּנוֹתָיו, וְזֶה יִשְׁתַּלַּח. וּלְשׁוֹן "אֲפִילּוּ" דְּנָקַט — מִשּׁוּם דִּשְׁלֹשָׁה מַחֲלוֹקוֹת בַּדָּבָר, אִיכָּא לְמַאן דְּאָמַר: אֲפִילּוּ בַּעֲלֵי חַיִּים נִדְחִים, דְּקָתָנֵי: וְאִם מִשֶּׁהִגְרִיל מֵת אֶחָד מֵהֶן — יָבִיא שְׁנַיִם וְיַגְרִיל עֲלֵיהֶם כְּבַתְּחִלָּה, וְהַנִּשְׁאָר יִדָּחֶה. וְאִיכָּא לְמַאן דְּאָמַר: מֵבִיא חֲבֵירוֹ שֶׁלֹּא בְּהַגְרָלָה, דְּבַעֲלֵי חַיִּים אֵין נִדְחִין, וְהַגְרָלָה לָא מְעַכְּבָא. אֲבָל דָּם בַּכּוֹס וּמֵת הַמִּשְׁתַּלֵּחַ — יִשָּׁפֵךְ הַדָּם, דִּשְׁחוּטִין נִדְחִין וְאֵין חוֹזְרִין וְנִרְאִין. וְאָתָא חָנָן הַמִּצְרִי לְמֵימַר: אֲפִילּוּ דָּם בַּכּוֹס יג] מְזַוֵּוג לֵיהּ אַחֵר. שֶׁבְּיָדוֹ. לְתַקֵּן לְהַחֲזִיר כִּי הָנָךְ דְּמַתְנִיתִין. אֲבָל הַהוּא דְּמִשְׁתַּלֵּחַ — אֵין בְּיָדוֹ, מִי יֵימַר דְּיָהֲבֵי לֵיהּ אַחֲרִינֵי? יָמוּת הַמִּשְׁתַּלֵּחַ. דְּאִידַּחֵי לֵיהּ, וְיָבִיא שְׁנַיִם אֲחֵרִים. מִדַּם יד] הַתַּעֲרוֹבֶת. שֶׁל פְּסָחִים. זוֹרְקוֹ זְרִיקָה אַחַת. כְּדִין פֶּסַח. כְּנֶגֶד הַיְסוֹד. לְאַפּוּקֵי קֶרֶן דְּרוֹמִית מִזְרָחִית, כִּדְאָמְרִי' לְקַמָּן. *שֶׁאִם נִשְׁפַּךְ דָּמוֹ שֶׁל אֶחָד מֵהֶן עַל יְדֵי שֶׁהֵן רַבִּים וְנִבְהָלִים לַעֲשׂוֹת — נִמְצָא כּוֹס זֶה מַכְשִׁירוֹ, שֶׁהֲרֵי טו] כּוּלָּם מְעוֹרָבִים בּוֹ. וְאִי מִשּׁוּם דְּאִיעֲרוּב בְּדַם הַתַּמְצִית — אָמְרִינַן לְקַמָּן: רַבִּי יְהוּדָה לְטַעְמֵיהּ דְּאָמַר אֵין דָּם מְבַטֵּל דָּם, וְלָא אָמְרִינַן אִידַּחֵי לֵיהּ בְּהִתְעָרְבוֹ, הוֹאִיל וּבְיָדוֹ לְאוֹסְפוֹ. וַהֲלֹא. זֶה שֶׁנִּשְׁפַּךְ. לֹא נִתְקַבֵּל בִּכְלִי. טז] הֵיאַךְ יִהְיֶה כָּשֵׁר? הָא קַיְימָא לָן: נִשְׁפַּךְ מִן הַצַּוָּאר עַל הָרִצְפָּה וַאֲסָפוֹ — פָּסוּל! מְנָא יָדְעִי. רַבָּנַן שֶׁלֹּא נִתְקַבֵּל? וַהֲלֹא לֹא מַעֲשֶׂה הִיא, אֶלָּא סְבָרָא הִיא בְּעָלְמָא, דְּחָיֵישׁ לְשֶׁמָּא נִשְׁפַּךְ דָּמוֹ שֶׁל אֶחָד מֵהֶן! שֶׁמָּא לֹא נִתְקַבֵּל. וְנִמְצָא זוֹרֵק דָּם פָּסוּל.
אַף

שיטה מקובצת

א] ורבנן היא דתניא למעלה הוא אומר ואת דמו: ב] טמא. ס"א הנך פסולים דחזי כו' דחזי לעבודת צבור. ואע"ג דמהאי טעמא מסיק במעילה דאדרבה עושה שיריים שאני הכא שלא עשה כלום והרי מעשה איצטבא הוא ושייך לומר איפכא: ג] וליהוי דחוי ותיבת ליה נמחק: ד] שבצואר הבהמה שירים: ה] בפיגול ופסול: ו] שבצואר בהמה שירים: ז] ליסוד כדכתיב ואת: ח] דדחיה בידים שלא נתן: ט] הדם שנתקבל וישפכו לאמה: י] לאשמועינן בכולהו ראית: יא] דחזי לעבודה לכתחלה: יב] ומזווג לו וכשר: יג] בכוס מביא חבירו ומזווג לו ויהיה כשר הדם הס"ד: יד] מדם התערובות: טו] שהרי מכולם מעורבים: טז] והיאך כשר ותיבת יהיה נמחק: יז] שירים. פ"ה כו' ולא רצה לפרש בקבלה פסול ולא זרק דהא תנן בהדיא יחזור הכשר ויקבל וליכא למדחי דהתם משום פסול מחשבה דמחשבה לא פסלא אלא בראוי לעבודה וא"ת זרק נמי תפשוט מדתנן קבלו כו': יח] מיבעיא ליה דהתנן יחזור כו' בפסול שקבל וזרק מיבעיא: יט] לא וכיון דשחיטה כשרה בפסולין מהניא מחשבתו: כ] בעיא קמייתא אמתני': כא] וקמיבעיא ליה אם זרק פסול כו' שיריים מותר הדם להיות נשפכין: כב] כלום הוא מ"ט: כג] מתיבת וא"ל כו' עד תיבות ומאי קשיא ליה מוקף בשני חצאי לבנה: כד] לזמנו כו' מאי לאו אבל ס"א אפי' שאר פסולים ומאי קשיא: כה] דלכל הפחות שיריים הוי: כו] בסיפא. ס"א מספרים דקאמרי כו': כז] בהמה. אם לא נתקבל כל הדם שלא יהיה השירים הנשאר בצואר הבהמה לשפוך ליסוד אלא ישפוך לאמה: כח] דחוי. פ"ה דהא נראה ונדחה הוא משמע דאכולהו פריך ותימה: כט] הכהנים מידם תיבות את הדם נמחק: ל] דחוי וענביו מרובים מעליו דהדם דמס' סוכה דפסול דאמר דהיכא דאשחור מע"ש הוי דחוי מעיקרא אע"ג דבידו לתקנו אין זה: לא] הדיחוי דאין מצוה לגלותו. לשון הר"פ: לב] דפרק קמא כו' בידו אע"ג דבידו לעשות תשובה כיון דאין:

[נ"ל ענביו]

[ועיין היטב תוס' סוכה לג. ד"ה נקטס ותוספות לקמן נט. ד"ה על]

מעילה ה:

[יומא נז: לקמן קיב תמורה כב:]

יומא נז:

יומא סג: תמורה ו: [לקמן עד. מנחות נט:]

[מנחות מט: ע"ש]

יומא סב. [מנחות נט:]

פסחים סה. ע"ש [תוספתא שם פ"ד לקמן ס. ע"ש מנחות נט:]

לקמן

הגהות הב"ח

(א) גמ' אמר ליה אין לך זריקה עושה שיריים:

גליון הש"ס

תוס' ד"ה פסול וכו' ומיהו למ"ד שלא במקומו לעיל טו ע"ב: **בא"ד** בזרק הפסול שיחזור הכשר ויקבל. עי' לקמן דף ל' ע"א תוס' ד"ה וקיבלו:

אף אני לא אמרתי אלא כשנתקבל בכלי. והוא גופיה מנא ידע? *כהנים זריזין, א] ועבדין הייא ומשתפכין. והלא דם התמצית מעורב בו! רבי יהודה לטעמיה, דאמר: דם התמצית קרי דם. דתניא: *אדם התמצית באזהרה, רבי יהודה אומר: בכרת. *והאמר ר' אלעזר: ב] מודה רבי יהודה לענין כפרה שאינו מכפר, שנאמר: °(״כי *הדם הוא ג] הנפש״,) דם שהנפש יוצאה בו — קרוי דם, שאין הנפש יוצאה בו — אין קרוי דם! אלא *רבי יהודה לטעמיה, דאמר: אין דם מבטל דם. *אמר להם רבי יהודה: לדבריכם, למה פוקקין העזרה? אמרו לו: שבח הוא לבני אהרן שיהלכו עד ארכובותיהן בדם. והא ד] דם הוי חציצה! לח הוא, ולא הוי חציצה. *דתנן: *בהדם, והדיו, והדבש, והחלב, יבישין — חוצצין, לחין — אין חוצצין. והא קא מיתווסי מאנייהו, *ותנן: *היו בגדיו מטושטשין ועבד — עבודתו פסולה! וכי תימא דמדלו להו — *והתניא: °״מדו״ — גכמדתו, שלא יחסר ושלא יותיר! בהולכת אברים לכבש, דלאו עבודה היא. ולא? *והתניא: °״והקריב הכהן את הכל״ — ה] זו הולכת אברים לכבש. אלא בהולכת עצים למערכה, דלאו עבודה היא. ולעבודה היכי אזלי? אאיצטבי.§

מתני' *דהשוחט את הזבח לאכול דבר שאין דרכו לאכול, ולהקטיר דבר שאין דרכו להקטיר — כשר, ורבי אליעזר פוסל. לאכול דבר שדרכו לאכול, ולהקטיר דבר שדרכו להקטיר פחות מכזית — כשר. *ולאכול כחצי זית ו] ולהקטיר כחצי זית — כשר, שאין אכילה והקטרה מצטרפין. יהשוחט את הזבח לאכול כזית מן העור, ומן הרוטב, ומן הקיפה, ומן האלל, ומן העצמות, ומן הגידין, ומן הקרנים, ומן הטלפים, חוץ לזמנו וחוץ למקומו — כשר, חואין חייבין עליהן משום פיגול, ונותר, וטמא. השוחט את המוקדשין טלאכול שליל או שליא בחוץ — לא פיגל. המולק את התורין ז] ילאכול ביציהן בחוץ — לא פיגל. חלב מוקדשין כוביצי תורין — אין חייבין עליהן משום פיגול ונותר וטמא.§

גמ' אמר רבי אלעזר: ח] לפיגל בזבח — נתפגל השליל, בשליל — לא נתפגל הזבח. ט] פיגל באלל — נתפגלה מוראה, במוראה — לא נתפגל אלל. פיגל באימורין — נתפגלו פרים, בפרים — לא נתפגלו אימורים. לימא מסייע ליה: *ושוים, משאם חישב באכילת פרים ובשריפתן — לא עשה ולא כלום. מאי לאו, הא חישב באימורים — נתפגלו פרים? לא, הא

הא

רש"י

אף אני לא אמרתי. שיאסף, אלא בנתקבל בכלי. **והוא גופיה** מנא ידע שנתקבל בכלי? זריזין הן. ומקבלי י] לכולהו. **דם התמצית** באזהרה. ה' לאוין כתיבי בדם, חד לדם התמצית כדאמרינן בכריתות בפ"ק (דף ד:). **ר' יהודה אומר בכרת.** התם יליף טעמא. **אין דם מבטל דם.** דמין במינו לרבי יהודה לא בטיל. ולקמן תנן לה בפ' "כל הזבחים שנתערבו" (דף עח.). **למה פוקקין את העזרה.** יא] ערבי פסחים, שלא יצאו הדמים דרך אמה לנחל קדרון. **והא קא הויא חציצה.** בין רגליהם לרצפה, ותנן: עומד על גבי כלים כו' — פסול (לעיל דף טו:)! **היו בגדיו מטושטשין** יב]. לעיל בפרק ב' תניא לה. **בהולכת אברים לכבש.** הא דקתני: שבח הוא לבני אהרן כו' — בהולכת אברים קאמר. ולקמן פריך: ובהולכת דם היכי אזלי? **אאיצטבי.** איצטבאות גבוהין היו שם, בנין אבנים, ואינן חוללין, דמן הרצפה הן. **מתני' לאכול דבר שאין דרכו לאכול.** חוץ למקומו או חוץ לזמנו. היתה מחשבה ב"העור והרוטב" (חולין דף קכ.): **תבלין** ודקדקת הבשר השוכנת בשולי קדרה. **אלל.** גיד הצואר, שהוא קשה ואין ראוי לאכילה. **ואין חייבין עליהן משום פיגול.** אם היה הזבח פגול, שחישב על בשרו או על אימוריו חוץ לזמנו, ונתפגל — האוכל מאלו פטור. **וטמא.** אם אכל בטומאת הגוף מאחת מאלה — יג] **הזבח כשר. את המוקדשין.** כל היכא דנקיט האי לישנא מיירי בנקבות. **לאכול שליל.** שבמעיה. **לא פיגל.** את הזבח, דלאו גופיה דזיבחא הוא. **חלב המוקדשין.** חלב שבדדיה. **אין חייבין עליהן** משום פיגול. אם פיגל בזבח ואכל מחלבה — לא מחייב כרת, דלאו זיבחא הוא. **גמ' פיגל בזבח.** שחטו ע"מ לאכול או להקטיר חוץ לזמנו. **נתפגל השליל.** האוכל מהשליל חייב. **בשליל.** ששחט את הזבח ע"מ לאכול מן השליל חוץ לזמנו. **לא נתפגל הזבח.** קסבר רבי אלעזר: שליל גופיה דזיבחא יד] הויא, דעובר ירך אמו הוא. ומיהו, אין מחשבתו מפגלת הזבח, דדבר שאין דרכו לאכול הוא, דרובא דאינשי לא אכלי ליה. ושליל עצמו (א) לא נתפגל, מדקתני מתני': לאכול שליל או שליא בחוץ — לא פיגל. **אלל.** של עוף. ראוי לאכילה הוא, דרכיך. **מוראה.** לא חזי לאכילה, דפירשא בעלמא הוא. הלכך, מחשבה דידה לא מפגלא. ומיהו היכא דנתפגל העוף ע"י דבר אחר, כיון דאיכא אינשי דאכלי — חייב עליו כרת. **פיגל באימורין.** שחט פרים הנשרפים ע"מ להקטיר אימוריהן חוץ לזמנן. **נתפגלו פרים.** והאוכל מבשרן חייב. **חישב בפרים.** ששחט ע"מ לאכול מבשרן חוץ לזמנו. **לא נתפגלו אימורי'.** להתחייב כרת האוכל מכליות או מיותרת הכבד שלהם, וכל שכן דלא נתפגלו פרים עצמן, שהרי חישב לאכול דבר שאין דרכו לאכול, ואיידי דנקט פיגל באימורין — נקט נמי לא נתפגלו אימורין. **לימא מסייע ליה.** לר' אלעזר, דאמר: מתפגל ואע"פ שאין מפגל, כגון שליל ומוראה ובשר הפרים. **ושוין.** ר"ש וחכמים, שנחלקו בפ' "ב"ש" (לקמן מג.), דרבנן אמרי: פיגול נוהג בפרים הנשרפים, ור"ש אמר: כל שאינו על מזבח החיצון טו] אין חייבין עליו משום פיגול. ושוין שאם חישב באחת מעבודות הדם לאכול מן הפרים למחר או לשורפן בבית הדשן כהילכתו למחר — לא עשה כלום, דמחשבת אכילה לא מהניא בהו, דדבר שאין דרכו לאכול הוא. ומחשבת שריפה *)נמי לא, דאמחשבת אכילת מזבח קפיד רחמנא, אבל שריפה לאו לשון אכילה הוא. ואע"ג דאמרן בפירקין דלעיל חישב שתאכלהו אש למחר פיגול — ה"מ דחשיב בלשון אכילה, כדאוקי התם. **מאי לאו.** הא דפליגי רבנן דאמרי פיגול נוהג בהם — בבשר דפרים עצמו קאמר, דאם חישב באימורין להקטירם למחר, דחשיב כי אורחייהו (ב) טז] ואכילת מזבח — נתפגל בשר הפרים ליענש כרת על אכילתו?

אימורים

*) נ"ל נמי לא מהניא בהו לאמחשבת נ"ק

תוספות

אין דם מבטל דם. ודם התמצית זרק ליה לשם מים, כרבי אליעזר דפ' "התערובות" (לקמן דף עז.) דאית ליה רואין. אי נמי: סבר לה כרבי אליעזר דאמר: *נתערב בדם התמצית — כשר. **והתניא** מדו כמדתו יז]. הך פירכא אליבא דמ"ד אבנט מיגז גייז, לעיל בפרק שני (דף יח.).

פיגל בזבח נתפגל שליל. כיון דאיכא אינשי דאכלי ליה — חייב כרת, דירך אמו יח] *הוא כו', שאין דרכו לאכול כו'. כך פי' בקונטרס. וכענין זה יט] גבי מוראה, דלא חזיא לאכילה דפירשא בעלמא היא, הלכך מחשבה דידה לא מיפגלא. ומיהו, היכא דנתפגל העוף ע"י דבר אחר, כיון דאיכא אינשי דאכלי — חייב עליו כרת. ושם דחק בחנם, דאפילו חזיא כשאר בשר אינה מפגלת את העוף, דמוראה כ] אבית הדשן, ואין בה לא אכילת אדם ולא אכילת מזבח. והיינו טעמא דחישב בפרים לא נתפגלו אימורים. אבל בשליל לא אפשר לומר כך, דאע"ג דבפ' "כילד מערימין" (תמורה דף כה.) גבי [illegible] בה בן ארבעה חי, תני חדא: נאכל לכל אדם ובכל מקום ולעולם. וא"כ הייתי יכול לומר דהיינו טעמא דלא פסלא ביה מחשבה — משום דלאו גופיה דזיבחא הוא. אבל ע"כ ר"א סבירא ליה דגופה דזיבחא הוא, דהא אמר: פיגל בזבח — נתפגל שליל, וסבר לה כאידך ברייתא דתניא התם: דאין נאכל אלא לזכרי כהונה כא] ליום ולילה לפנים מן הקלעים, והתם נמי משני להו, הלכך צריך לפרש הטעם כמו שפי' בקונט'. ויש דוחקים כאן כב] לפרש: משום דדרשינן בתורת כהנים בפרשת "צו" גבי נותר: "הזבח" — פרט לשליל ולשיליא. *ועל כרחין שייך נותר בשליל, כדאיתא בתמורה בפרק "כילד מערימין" (גם זה שם) גבי שליל שבחטאת, דאין נאכל אלא ליום ולילה. הילכך, אם אינו ענין לנותר — תנהו ענין למחשבת נותר. ואין נראה פירוש זה, דמנא ליה לתנא הא? דלמא איצטריך לגופיה למעוטי שליא כג] מנותר! ונראה דמדין שריפה קממעט שליל ושיליא, דשריפה כתיבא כד] בקרא.

פיגל באלל נתפגלה מוראה. בפ' "העור והרוטב" כה] (חולין דף קכא.) מודו כו"ע דפלטתו סכין היינו אלל, *בההוא מיירי הכא. כו] *ודעולה איירי, שקודר להסיר המוראה בנוצתה, דאי אפשר שלא יקח מן הושט עם המוראה.

באכילת פרים ובשריפתן לא עשה ולא כלום. דמחשבת אכילה לא מהניא בהו, דדבר שאין דרכו לאכול הוא. ומחשבת שרפה נמי לא, דלמחשבת אכילת מזבח קפיד רחמנא, אבל שרפה — לאו לשון אכילה הוא. ואע"ג דאמרינן בפירקין לעיל (דף לא.): חישב שתאכלהו אש למחר — כז] הני מילי דחישב בלשון אכילה, כדאוקימנא התם. כך פירש בקונטרס. ובחנם דחק, דלעיל מיירי במידי דראוי לאכילת אדם ומחשב שתאכלהו האש, דהוי פיגול. אבל האי — לא שייך ביה לא אכילת אדם ולא אכילת מזבח.

וש"מ

מסורת הש"ס

[שבת כ. וש"נ] [תוספתא פ"ב דכריתות פסחים סה. חולין עב: כריתות ד:] [כריתות כב. פסחים סה. ע"ש] נ"ל כי הדם הוא בנפש יכפר ויקרא יז [לקמן לו. עח. ע"ש. פסחים סה: מנחות כב. חולין פז: נדה עא:] [נ"ל דתניא] מנחות כח. שבת קב: פסחים סה: [תוס' מקוואות פ"ו] [נ"ל והתניא] פסחים סה: לעיל יח. יומא כג: נ"ל בזבח יומא כז. לעיל ד. וש"נ לעיל כח: לח: [לעיל כט: לקמן סה. מנחות יב: יז.] [לקמן קז:]

דברים יב | ויקרא ו | שם א

[לקמן עח.] נ"ל הוא ומיהו אין מחשבתו מפגלת הזבח דדבר שאין דרכו לאכול הוא כו' נ"ק [פסחים סה:] תוספתא דפסחים פ"ה [נ"ל ובההוא] נ"א ובעולת העוף איירי כו' נ"ק

עין משפט נר מצוה

כו א מיי' פ"ו מהלכות מאכלות אסורות הלכה ז:
כז ב מיי' פ"ב מהלכות מקוואות הל' ב סמג לאוין קיא טוש"ע יו"ד סי' קצח סעיף טו:
כח ג מיי' פ"ח מהל' כלי המקדש [illegible]
כט ד מיי' פי"ד מהל' פסה"מ הלכה כב:
ל ה ו מיי' שם הל' י:
לא ז מיי' פי"ח שם
לב ח מיי' פי"ד מהל' פסה"מ הלכה כב:
לג ט מיי' פי"ד שם הלכה ו:
לד כ מיי' פי"ח שם הל' כב:
לה ל מיי' שם הל' כג ועי' כס"מ:
לו מ מיי' שם פרק יד הלכה ח:

הגהות הב"ח

(א) רש"י ד"ה לא נתפגל וכו' ושליל עצמו נמי לא: (ב) ד"ה מאי לאו וכו' כי אורחייהו באכילת:

גליון הש"ס

תוס' ד"ה פיגל בזבח וכו' ועל כרחין שייך נותר בשליל. קשה לי הא להדיא קתני בברייתא דשמעתין ואין חייבים עליהם משום נותר והרמב"ם פסק דחייב משום נותר. ומצאתי במרכבת המשנה להתירץ דסבירא ליה להרמב"ם דכמה דאמר רבה אף אנן נמי תנינא וכו' הא שליל ושליא חייבים. ה"ה דחייב משום נותר וטמא. ומוכח דמתני' פליג אברייתא. אבל תוס' בשמעתין ד"ה הא שליל לא פ"כ. גם אם נימא כך למאי הוצרך לדחוק ברייתא דת"כ הא י"ל דהך ברייתא סברה כתנאי וברייתא דסוגיין דאין חייבים משום נותר. וגם פשטא לדברי תוס' דא"א לומר כלל דליכא חיוב בנותר. ולא הזכירו כלל מברייתא דסוגיין וצ"ע:

שיטה מקובצת

א] זריזין הן אי זריזין הן אשתפוכי נמי לא משתפיך אגב דזריזין עבדין: ב] רבי אלעזר משום רבי יוחנן מודה: ג] הוא בנפש יכפר דם שהנפש: ד] והא קא הוי חציצה: ה] הכל והקטיר המזבחה זו: ו] לאכול כחצי זית. עיין רש"י ריש פ' הקומץ רבה: ז] התורין בפנים לאכול: ח] פיגל בזבח נתפגל השליל [בשליל לא נתפגל הזבח] (ואע"ג דרובא דאינשי לא קא אכלי ליה (מ"מ) [מש"ה] הוי ליה כמחשב בדבר שאין דרכו לאכול כפ"ה והדין עמו שכך צריך לפרש גבי פיגל במוראה ולא כמו שפי' בקונטרס במתני' דמש"ה אם פיגל בשיליא לא נתפגל הזבח משום דלאו גופיה דזבח הוא: ט] פיגל באלל נתפגל מוראה. וא"ת הא אלל עצמו לא נתפגל והאוכלו אינו חייב כרת וי"ל כדפי' הקונטרס דהכא איירי באלל של עוף דרכיך טפי וכדנקט מוראה אבל פיגל במוראה לא נתפגל האלל ולא שאר העוף ואפילו בחטאת העוף דאכלי כהני (מוראה) ואיכא אינשי דאכלי לי' כדפי' גבי שליל אבל בעולת העוף אפי' תהיה המוראה ראויה לאכול לא פיגל דהא אין בה לא אכילת אדם ולא אכילת המזבח ולבית הדשן אזלי: י] הן. ומקבלי להו לכולהו: יא] העזרה. בערבי פסחים שלא יצא הדמים דרך האמה: יב] מטושטשין כו' לעיל: יג] מאלה בזבח כשר: יד] דזיבחא הוא דעובר: טו] החיצון כשלמים אין: טז] אורחייהו באכילת המזבח נתפגל כו' על אכילתו אלמא בבשר פרים אע"פ שאינו מפגל מתפגל ע"י מחשבת אימורים והיינו כר' אלעזר דאמר פיגל כו': יז] כמדתו. וא"ת ודילמא דעביד להו ע"י אבנט וי"ל הך כו': יח] אמו וגופא דזיבחא הוא ומ"מ פיגל בשליל לא נתפגל זבח כיון דרובא דאינשי לא אכלי ליה הוי כמחשב בדבר שאין דרכו לאכול כך: יט] זה פירש גבי: כ] דמוראה לבית אות א' נמחק: כא] כהונה ואינה נאכלת אלא ליום ולילה: כב] כאן הטעם דפיגל בשליל לא נתפגל הזבח לפרש: כג] שליא ושליל מנותר: כד] כתיבא בההוא קרא הס"ד: כה] והרוטב אמרינן מודו: כו] ובעולה מיירי אות ד' נמחק: כז] למחר דהוי פיגול הני מילי:

לז א ב מיי' פ"ב מהל' מעילה הלכה ד:
לח ג מיי' פי"ג מהל' פסה"מ הל' ח:

הָא חִישֵּׁב בָּאֵימוּרִין — נִתְפַּגְּלוּ אֵימוּרִין עַצְמָן.§ *ת"ש: אפָּרִים הַנִּשְׂרָפִים וּשְׂעִירִים הַנִּשְׂרָפִים — מוֹעֲלִין בָּהֶן מִשֶּׁהוּקְדְּשׁוּ, נִשְׁחֲטוּ — הוּכְשְׁרוּ לִיפָּסֵל בִּטְבוּל יוֹם, וּבִמְחוּסַּר כִּיפּוּרִים, וּבְלִינָה; מַאי לָאו — לִינַת בָּשָׂר? וש"מ: א] מִגּוֹ דְּפָסְלָה בְּלִינָה — פָּסְלָה בָּהּ מַחֲשָׁבָה! לָא, לִינַת אֵימוּרִים. הָא מִדְּקָתָנֵי סֵיפָא: כּוּלָּן במוֹעֲלִין בָּהֶן עַל בֵּית הַדֶּשֶׁן עַד שֶׁיּוּתַּךְ הַבָּשָׂר, מִכְּלָל דְּרֵישָׁא לִינַת בָּשָׂר! מִידֵי אִירְיָא? הָא כִּדְאִיתָא וְהָא כִּדְאִיתָא, רֵישָׁא אֵימוּרִים, וְסֵיפָא בָּשָׂר. מוֹתִיב (רָבָא) [רַבָּה], וְאֵלּוּ שֶׁאֵין מְפַגְּלִין וְאֵין מִתְפַּגְּלִין: ב] צֶמֶר שֶׁבְּרָאשֵׁי כְבָשִׂים, וְשֵׂעָר שֶׁבִּזְקַן תְּיָישִׁים, וְהָעוֹר, וְהָרוֹטֶב, וְהַקִּיפָה, וְהָאָלָל, וְהַמּוּרְאָה, וְהָעֲצָמוֹת, וְהַגִּידִין, וְהַקַּרְנַיִם, וְהַטְּלָפַיִם, וְהַשָּׁלִיל, וְהַשִּׁלְיָא, וַחֲלֵב הַמּוּקְדָּשִׁין, וּבֵיצֵי תוֹרִין — ג] [כּוּלָּן] לֹא מְפַגְּלִין וְלֹא מִתְפַּגְּלִין, וְאֵין חַיָּיבִין עֲלֵיהֶן מִשּׁוּם פִּיגּוּל נוֹתָר וְטָמֵא, וְהַמַּעֲלֶה מֵהֶן בַּחוּץ — פָּטוּר; מַאי לָאו לֹא מְפַגְּלִין — הַזֶּבַח, וְלֹא מִתְפַּגְּלִין — מֵחֲמַת זֶבַח? לָא, לֹא מְפַגְּלִין אֶת הַזֶּבַח, וְלֹא מִתְפַּגְּלִין — מֵחֲמַת עַצְמָן. א"ה, הָא דְּקָתָנֵי סֵיפָא: כּוּלָּן לֹא מְפַגְּלִין וְלֹא מִתְפַּגְּלִין, הָא תּוּ לָמָּה לִי? וְלִיטַעֲמִיךְ, אֵין חַיָּיבִין עָלָיו מִשּׁוּם פִּיגּוּל, הָא תּוּ לָמָּה לִי? אֶלָּא, אַיְּידֵי דְּבָעֵי לְמִיתְנָא נוֹתָר וְטָמֵא — תְּנָא פִּיגּוּל; הָכָא נַמִי, אַיְּידֵי דְּבָעֵי לְמִיתְנֵי הַמַּעֲלֶה מֵהֶן בַּחוּץ — תְּנָא נַמִי: וְכוּלָּן לֹא מְפַגְּלִין וְלֹא מִתְפַּגְּלִין. ד] רָבָא אָמַר, אַף אֲנַן נַמִי תְּנֵינָא: הַשּׁוֹחֵט אֶת הַמּוּקְדָּשִׁים לֶאֱכוֹל שָׁלִיל אוֹ שִׁלְיָא בַּחוּץ — לֹא פִּיגֵּל, וְהַמּוֹלֵק אֶת הַתּוֹרִים לֶאֱכוֹל בֵּיצֵיהֶם בַּחוּץ — לֹא פִּיגֵּל. וַהֲדַר תָּנֵי: חֲלֵב הַמּוּקְדָּשִׁין וּבֵיצֵי תוֹרִים — אֵין חַיָּיב עֲלֵיהֶן מִשּׁוּם פִּיגּוּל נוֹתָר וְטָמֵא; הָא שָׁלִיל וְשִׁלְיָא — חַיָּיבִים. אֶלָּא לָאו ש"מ: כָּאן — מֵחֲמַת הַזֶּבַח, כָּאן — מֵחֲמַת עַצְמָן, ש"מ.§ *תְּנַן הָתָם: וּבַעֲלֵי מוּמִין. ר"ע מַכְשִׁיר בְּבַעֲלֵי מוּמִים. א"ר חִיָּיא בַּר אַבָּא *א"ר יוֹחָנָן: לֹא הִכְשִׁיר ר"ע אֶלָּא בְּדוּקִין שֶׁבָּעַיִן, הוֹאִיל וּכְשֵׁירִים בְּעוֹפוֹת. וְהוּא שֶׁקָּדַם הֶקְדֵּישָׁהּ אֶת מוּמָהּ. ס] *(א"ר חִיָּיא בַּר אַבָּא) וּמוֹדֶה רַבִּי עֲקִיבָא בְּעוֹלַת נְקֵבָה, דִּכְמַאן דְּקָדַם מוּמָהּ לְהֶקְדֵּישָׁהּ דָּמֵי. מְתִיב רַבִּי זֵירָא: הַמַּעֲלֶה מֵהֶן בַּחוּץ — פָּטוּר, הָא מֵאִימָּן — חַיָּיב, וְהֵיכִי מַשְׁכַּחַתְּ לַהּ — בְּעוֹלַת נְקֵבָה; אִי אָמְרַתְּ בִּשְׁלָמָא קָסָבַר רַבִּי עֲקִיבָא עוֹלַת נְקֵבָה אִם עָלְתָה לֹא תֵּרֵד, הָא מַנִּי — ר"ע הִיא. אֶלָּא אִי אָמְרַתְּ אִם עָלְתָה תֵּרֵד — הָא מַנִּי? אֵימָא: הַמַּעֲלֶה מֵהֶן בַּחוּץ — פָּטוּר, הָא מֵאֵימוּרֵי אִימָּן — חַיָּיב. וְהָא "מֵהֶן" קָתָנֵי, וְאִימָּן דּוּמְיָא דִּידְהוּ! אֶלָּא אֵימָא: הַמַּעֲלֶה מֵאֵימוּרֵיהֶן בַּחוּץ — פָּטוּר, הָא מֵאֵימוּרֵי אִימָּן — חַיָּיב.§

מתני' שְׁחָטוֹ עַל מְנָת לְהַנִּיחַ אֶת דָּמוֹ אוֹ אֵימוּרָיו לְמָחָר, אוֹ לְהוֹצִיאָן לַחוּץ *רַבִּי יְהוּדָה פּוֹסֵל, גוַחֲכָמִים מַכְשִׁירִין. ע"מ לִיתְּנָן עַל גַּבֵּי הַכֶּבֶשׁ שֶׁלֹּא כְּנֶגֶד הַיְסוֹד, וְלִיתֵּן אֶת הַנִּיתָּנִים לְמַטָּה לְמַעְלָן, וְאֶת הַנִּיתָּנִים לְמַעְלָן לְמַטָּה, וְאֶת הַנִּיתָּנִים בִּפְנִים

אֵימוּרִין עַצְמָן. יוֹתֶרֶת הַכָּבֵד וְהַכְּלָיוֹת. אֲבָל לֹא בָּשָׂר, שֶׁאֵין מִתְפַּגֵּל כְּדָבָר שֶׁהוּא גּוּפוֹ ו] [שֶׁל] זֶבַח אֶלָּא דָּבָר הַמְפַגֵּל, דְּכֵיוָן דְּלָא חָשִׁיב אֲכִילָה לְעִנְיַן פִּיגּוּל — לָא חָשִׁיב נַמִּי אֲכִילָה לְעִנְיַן אִיפְגּוּלֵי. הוּכְשְׁרוּ. *נִתְקְנוּ ז] לִקְבּוֹעַ פְּסוּלִין הַלָּלוּ. בִּטְבוּל יוֹם וּבִמְחוּסַּר כִּיפּוּרִים. אִם נָגְעוּ בָּהֶן. ח] מִדְּפָסְלָה לִינָה. פָּסְלָה נַמִּי מַחֲשֶׁבֶת לִינָה. מַאי לָאו לִינַת בָּשָׂר. קָתָנֵי שֶׁאִם לָן נִפְסָל? וְה"ה לְמַחֲשֶׁבֶת לִינָה שֶׁפּוֹסֶלֶת בַּבָּשָׂר. וּנְהִי נַמִּי דְּהֵיכָא דְּחִישֵּׁב אַבָּשָׂר עַצְמוֹ לָא תָּדוּק מִינָּהּ, דְּהָא מַחֲשָׁבָה בְּדָבָר שֶׁדַּרְכּוֹ לֶאֱכוֹל בָּעֵי, וּבָרַיְיתָא לְעֵיל נַמִּי תַּנְיָא כְּהֶדְיָא: וְשָׁוִין שֶׁאִם חִישֵּׁב ט] לֶאֱכוֹל פָּרִים לֹא עָשָׂה כְּלוּם, אֲפִילּוּ לִפְסוּל, מִיהוּ, הָא דַּיְיקִינַן מִינָּהּ דְּמַחֲשֶׁבֶת לִינַת י] אֵימוּרִים מְפַגֶּלֶת הַבָּשָׂר, כְּרַבִּי אֶלְעָזָר. לֹא לִינַת אֵימוּרִים. *דְּקָתָנֵי דְּפָסְלָה — הָאֵימוּרִים נִפְסָלִים בְּלִינָה קָתָנֵי, וְדִכְוָותַהּ *פְּשׁוֹט מִינָּהּ דְּמַחֲשֶׁבֶת לִינַת אֵימוּרִים מְפַגֶּלֶת בָּאֵימוּרִין. עַד שֶׁיִּתִּיךְ יא] אֶת הַבָּשָׂר. גָּרְסִינַן בְּמַסֶּ' מְעִילָה. וְל"ג "מִשֶּׁיּוּתַּךְ", דְּא"כ הֲוָה לֵיהּ דָּבָר שֶׁנַּעֲשֵׂית מִצְוָתוֹ וְאֵין מוֹעֲלִין בּוֹ. אֲבָל עַד שֶׁיִּתִּיךְ, דַּאֲכַתִּי אִית בְּהוּ צוֹרֶךְ עֲבוֹדַת גָּבוֹהַּ — קָרֵי יב] בְּהוּ "מִקָּדְשֵׁי ה'". וְלֹא מִתְפַּגְּלִין. לְקַמֵּיהּ מְפָרֵשׁ לֵיהּ. צֶמֶר שֶׁבְּרָאשֵׁי כְבָשִׂים וְשֵׂעָר שֶׁבִּזְקַן תְּיָשִׁים. אִיצְטְרִיךְ לְאַשְׁמוּעִינַן דְּלָא מְהַנְּיָא מַחֲשָׁבָה בְּהוּ, מִשּׁוּם דְּעוֹר הָרֹאשׁ קָרֵב עִם הָרֹאשׁ, שֶׁאֵינוֹ בִּכְלַל הֶפְשֵׁט, כִּדְתַנְיָא בְּ"הַשּׁוֹחֵט" (חולין דף כז.): מִנַּיִן לְרַבּוֹת הָרֹאשׁ שֶׁכְּבָר הוּתַּז, וּמְהַנְּיָא בֵּיהּ מַחֲשֶׁבֶת הַקְטָרָה — בְּהָנָךְ מִיהָא לָא מְהַנְּיָא מַחֲשָׁבָה אִם חִישֵּׁב לְהַקְטִיר לְמָחָר, דְּלָאו דַּרְכּוֹ לְהַקְטִיר הוּא. דְּגַבֵּי אִם עָלוּ יֵרְדוּ קָא תָּנֵי לְהוּ בְּפֶ' "הַמִּזְבֵּחַ" יג] (לקמן דף פה:). וְהַמּוּרְאָה. שֶׁל עוֹף, וְהָאָלָל שֶׁל בְּהֵמָה. "וְהָעוּבָּר" ל"ג, דְּהַיְינוּ שָׁלִיל. וַחֲלֵב הַמּוּקְדָּשִׁין. חָלָב שֶׁבְּדַדֵּי נְקֵבָה. הָכִי גָּרְסִי' יד] לְבָרַיְיתָא הָכָא. וּבַתּוֹסֶפְתָּא כָּךְ שְׁנוּיֶיהָ: כּוּלָּן לֹא מְפַגְּלִין וְלֹא מִתְפַּגְּלִין וְאֵין חַיָּיבִין עֲלֵיהֶן מִשּׁוּם פִּיגּוּל נוֹתָר וְטָמֵא וְהַמַּעֲלֶה מֵהֶן בַּחוּץ פָּטוּר. ה"ג לַגִּירְסָא דִּגְמָ': מַאי לָאו לֹא מְפַגְּלִין אֶת הַזֶּבַח וְלֹא מִתְפַּגְּלִין מֵחֲמַת הַזֶּבַח לֹא לֹא מְפַגְּלִין אֶת הַזֶּבַח וְלֹא מִתְפַּגְּלִים מֵחֲמַת עַצְמָן. אִי הָכִי הָא דְּקָתָנֵי סֵיפָא כּוּלָּן לֹא מְפַגְּלִים וְלֹא מִתְפַּגְּלִין הָא תּוּ לָמָּה לִי. וְלִיטַעְמִיךְ אֵין חַיָּיבִין עֲלֵיהֶן מִשּׁוּם פִּיגּוּל תּוּ לָמָּה לִי אֶלָּא אַיְּידֵי דְּבָעֵי לְמִיתְנֵי נוֹתָר וְטָמֵא תָּנָא פִּגּוּל ה"נ אַיְּידֵי דְּבָעֵי לְמִיתְנֵי הַמַּעֲלֶה מֵהֶן כו'. אֵין חַיָּיבִין עֲלֵיהֶן מִשּׁוּם פִּיגּוּל – אִם טו] חִישֵּׁב בַּזֶּבַח פִּיגּוּל וְאָכַל מֵאֵלּוּ. וְהַמַּעֲלֶה מֵהֶן בַּחוּץ פָּטוּר – דְּאֵין רְאוּיִין לְפֶתַח אֹהֶל מוֹעֵד. [וה"פ]: מַאי לָאו אֵין מְפַגְּלִין אֶת הַזֶּבַח – אִם זָרַק ע"מ לֶאֱכוֹל אוֹ לְהַקְטִיר מֵאֵלּוּ חוּץ לִזְמַנּוֹ – הַזֶּבַח כָּשֵׁר. וְלֹא מִתְפַּגְּלִין מֵחֲמַת הַזֶּבַח. אִם חִישֵּׁב לֶאֱכוֹל מִבְּשַׂר הַזֶּבַח, אוֹ לְהַקְטִיר טז] (*מֵחֲמַת) אֵימוּרִין חוּץ לִזְמַנּוֹ – וְלֹא נִתְפַּגְּלוּ אֵלּוּ לֵיעָנֵשׁ בַּאֲכִילָתוֹ כָּרֵת. וּתְיוּבְתָּא דר"א, דְּהָכָא שָׁלִיל וּמוּרְאָה תְּנַן! מֵחֲמַת עַצְמָן. אִם זָרַק ע"מ לֶאֱכוֹל לְאֵלּוּ חוּץ לִזְמַנּוֹ – אֵין מִתְפַּגְּלִין, שֶׁאֵין מַחֲשַׁבְתּוֹ מַחֲשָׁבָה. הָא תּוּ לָמָּה לִי. לָאו לְאִיתּוּיֵי דְּאַף מֵחֲמַת זֶבַח אֵין מִתְפַּגְּלִין? וְלִיטַעְמִיךְ אֵין חַיָּיבִין עֲלֵיהֶם מִשּׁוּם פִּיגּוּל. פַּעַם שְׁלִישִׁית, לָמָּה לִי לְמִיתְנֵי הָא? מַאי תֵּיתֵי לְאַשְׁמוּעִינַן לְדִידָךְ? אֶלָּא עַל כָּרְחָךְ מִשְׁנָה (א) יז] לָאו דַּוְקָא, אֶלָּא אַגְּרָרָא דְּטָמֵא וְנוֹתָר נַסְבָהּ. לְרַבִּי אֶלְעָזָר נַמִּי מִשְׁנָה שְׁנִיָּה לָא תִּיקְשֵׁי, דַּאֲגְרָרָא דְּהַמַּעֲלֶה מֵהֶן בַּחוּץ נַסְבָהּ. אַף אֲנַן נַמִּי תְּנֵינָא. כְּרַבִּי אֶלְעָזָר, דְּשָׁלִיל וְשִׁלְיָא מִתְפַּגְּלִין וְלֹא מְפַגְּלִין. לֹא פִּיגֵּל. מַשְׁמַע: לֹא אֶת עַצְמָן וְלֹא אֶת הַזֶּבַח. הָא שָׁלִיל וְשִׁלְיָא חַיָּיבִין. עֲלֵיהֶן מִשּׁוּם פִּיגּוּל. אַלְמָא, מִתּוֹרַת מְפַגֵּל אַפְּקִעִינְהוּ, מִתּוֹרַת מִתְפַּגֵּל לָא אַפְּקִעִינְהוּ. מֵחֲמַת זֶבַח. מִתְפַּגְּלִין, מֵחֲמַת מַחֲשֶׁבֶת עַצְמָן לֹא מִתְפַּגְּלִין. תְּנַן הָתָם. גַּבֵּי אִם עָלוּ לֹא יֵרְדוּ בְּפֶרֶק "הַמִּזְבֵּחַ" יח]. מַכְשִׁיר. אִם עָלוּ שֶׁלֹּא יֵרְדוּ. וּכְשֵׁרִין בְּעוֹפוֹת. לְכַתְּחִלָּה. שֶׁאֵין פּוֹסֵל בָּהֶן אֶלָּא חֶסְרוֹן אֵבֶר, כְּגוֹן יָבַשׁ גַּפָּהּ נִסְמֵית עֵינָהּ *(וְיָלֶאת) אוֹ נִקְטְעָה רַגְלָהּ, מִשּׁוּם "הַקְרִיבֵהוּ נָא לְפֶחָתֶךָ", כִּדְמְפָרֵשׁ בִּבְכוֹרוֹת. דּוּקִין = *טייל"א בְּלַעַ"ז, לְשׁוֹן "אוֹ דַק" (ויקרא כא), כְּמוֹ "הַנּוֹטֶה כַדּוֹק" (ישעיה מ). [אֲבָל] דּוּקִין שֶׁבָּעַיִן לָא פָּסְלֵי בְּהוּ. וְאע"ג דְּמוּם גָּמוּר הוּא – לֹא נֶאֶמְרוּ מוּמִין אֶלָּא בִּבְהֵמָה, דִּכְתִיב: "תָּמִים זָכָר בַּבָּקָר בַּכְּשָׂבִים וּבָעִזִּים" (ויקרא כב), מִינֵּיהּ דָּרְשִׁי' (מנחות דף כה.): תַּמּוּת וְזַכְרוּת בִּבְהֵמָה, וְאֵין תַּמּוּת וְזַכְרוּת בְּעוֹפוֹת. הוֹאִיל וּכְשֵׁרִין בְּעוֹפוֹת לְכַתְּחִלָּה – בִּבְהֵמָה אִם עָלוּ לֹא יֵרְדוּ. וְהוּא שֶׁקָּדַם הֶקְדֵּשָׁן אֶת מוּמָן. אֲבָל קָדַם מוּמָן אֶת הֶקְדֵּשָׁן – לֹא חָלָה עֲלֵיהֶן קְדוּשַּׁת מִזְבֵּחַ מֵעוֹלָם, אֶלָּא קְדוּשַּׁת דָּמִים. וְאֵין הַמִּזְבֵּחַ מְקַדֵּשׁ פְּסוּלִין אֶלָּא שֶׁנִּרְאוּ לוֹ, כִּדְמְפָרֵשׁ בְּפֶ' "הַמִּזְבֵּחַ". וּמוֹדֶה ר"ע בְּעוֹלַת בְּהֵמָה נְקֵבָה. שֶׁתֵּרֵד, וְאע"פ שֶׁכְּשֵׁרָה בְּעוֹפוֹת לְכַתְּחִלָּה. מ"ט – דִּכְמַאן דְּקָדַם מוּמָהּ לְהֶקְדֵּישָׁהּ הוּא, שֶׁאֵין לְךָ מוּם בְּעוֹלָה גָּדוֹל מִזֶּה, דְּכָל עוֹלָה זָכָר הוּא. הַמַּעֲלֶה מֵהֶן בַּחוּץ. בַּבָּרַיְיתָא דִּלְעֵיל תְּנַן לָהּ, וְקָתָנֵי בָּהּ שָׁלִיל. וּמַעֲלֶה מֵהֶן – מַשְׁמַע מִבְּשָׂרוֹ – פָּטוּר, דְּלָאו גּוּפֵיהּ דְּזִיבְחָא הוּא וְלָא חֲזֵי לְהַקְרָבָה, כִּדְתַנְיָא בִּ"בְהֵמָה הַמַּקְשָׁה" (חולין דף עה.): מָה יוֹתֶרֶת כָּבֵד וּכְלָיוֹת הָאֵמוּרִים בְּאָשָׁם – מוּלָּא מִכְּלַל שָׁלִיל, אַף כָּל מוּלָּא מִכְּלַל שָׁלִיל. הָא מִבְּשַׂר אִימָּן חַיָּיב. וְהֵיכִי מַשְׁכַּחַתְּ לָהּ בְּעוֹלַת נְקֵבָה. דְּאִילּוּ בִּשְׁלָמִים, הַמַּעֲלֶה מִבָּשָׂר בַּחוּץ פָּטוּר, דְּלָא מִתְקַבֵּל בִּפְנִים הוּא, כִּדְתְנַן בְּפֶרֶק בַּתְרָא (לקמן דף קיב:): הַמַּעֲלֶה מִבְּשַׂר חַטָּאת כו'. הָא מַנִּי ר"ע הִיא. דְּכֵיוָן דְּבִפְנִים אִם עָלְתָה לֹא תֵּרֵד – מִיחַיֵּיב עֲלָהּ בַּחוּץ. הָכִי גָּרְסִינַן: אֵימָא הַמַּעֲלֶה מֵהֶן בַּחוּץ פָּטוּר הָא מֵאֵימוּרֵי אִימָּן חַיָּיב וְהָא מֵהֶן קָתָנֵי וְאִימָּן דּוּמְיָא דִּידְהוּ אֵימָא הַמַּעֲלֶה מֵאֵימוּרֵיהֶן בַּחוּץ פָּטוּר הָא מֵאֵימוּרֵי אִימָּן חַיָּיב. לָא תֵּימָא: הָא מֵאִימָּן חַיָּיב, אֶלָּא אֵימָא: הָא אֵימוּרֵי אִימָּן חַיָּיב. וּבִשְׁלָמִים אוֹ בְּחַטָּאת עָסְקִינַן, שֶׁבָּאִין נְקֵבוֹת. וְהָא מֵהֶן קָתָנֵי. דְּמַשְׁמַע מִבְּשָׂרָן, וְאִימָּן דּוּמְיָא דִּידְהוּ, וְדָיְיקִינַן מִינָּהּ: הָא מֵאִימָּן – חַיָּיב, ע"כ דּוּמְיָא דִּידֵהּ דָּיְיקִינַן – מִן הַבָּשָׂר, ע"כ בְּעוֹלָה קָאֵי. **מתני'** רַבִּי יְהוּדָה פּוֹסֵל. אַף עַל פִּי שֶׁאֵין כָּאן לֹא אֲכִילָה וְלֹא הַקְטָרָה. וּבַגְּמָרָא מְפָרֵשׁ טַעְמָא. שֶׁלֹּא כְּנֶגֶד הַיְסוֹד. אוֹ עַל הַמִּזְבֵּחַ שֶׁלֹּא כְּנֶגֶד הַיְסוֹד.
גמ'

וש"מ מיגו דפסלה בה לינה פסלה בה מחשבה. תימה: דלישני יט] כדמשני לקמן פרק "טבול יום" (דף קד:): דלמא מחשבה לא פסלה, לינה פסלה! וי"ל: משום דלא בעי למפשט הא דבעי ר' ירמיה פ' "טבול יום" לינה מהו שתועיל בפרים הנשרפים. כ] ועוד י"ל: דקסבר התלמוד דאי לינה מועלת – מועיל כא] פיגול לענין דאם פיגל באימורים פיגל הבשר לכל הפחות.
*לאכול שליל או שיליא בחוץ לא פיגל. הוא הדין למחר.
הא שליל ושליא חייבין אלא ש"מ כאן מחמת זבח כו'. וא"ת: אכתי נותר וטמא קשיא, דמשמע הכא כב] (דוקא) [דיוקא] דאשליל ושיליא חייבין משום נותר וטמא, וברייתא דלעיל קתני: ואין חייבין עליהם משום פיגול ונותר וטמא! וי"ל: דלעולם אין חייבין אשליל ושיליא משום נותר וטמא, והאי כג] (דשירייה) [דשיירינהו] – משום פיגול. אלא בדוקין שבעין הואיל וכשרים בעופות. לאו דוקא דוקין שבעין, דה"ה שאר מומין שאינן מחוסרי אבר, כדאמר בפרק קמא דקדושין (דף כד:) דוקא יבש גפה כד] ונסמית עינה. *אי נמי, שאר מומין פסלי מדרבנן. ומה שפי' בקונטרס דמחוסר אבר פסול בעוף משום "הקריבהו נא לפחתך" – בחנם פירש, דבהדיא דריש לה בקדושין (ג"ז שם) מדכתיב "מן העוף" ולא כל העוף.
תרי

שיטה מקובצת

א] מגו דפסלה בה לינה פסלה בה מחשבה. פי' אם חישב לינה באימורים פסל נמי הבשר עצמה דמחשבה בדבר שדרכו לאכול בעינן (וחישבת) [ומחשבה] באכילת פרים ובשריפתן לאו כלום היא אלא ש"מ דלענין לינת אימורין קאמר דמפגלין הבשר. מהר"פ: ב] צמר שבראשי כבשים איצטריך לאשמועינן דלא מהני בה מחשבה ואע"ג דעור הראש קרב עם הראש שאינו בכלל הפשטה אפ"ה לא מהני בה מחשבה משום דלא קרינא ביה בצמר אכילת מזבח לפי (שהוא) [שהעור] בטל אגב הראש. מהר"פ: ג] תורין כולן לא: ד] מתפגלין אמר רבא: ה] תיבות א"ר חייא בר אבא נמחק: ו] גופו של זבח אלא דבר המפגל אבל פרים עצמן כיון דלא חשיב: ז] נתקנו לידי קבול פסולין: ח] בהן הס"ד ומה"ד בלינה מדפסלה לינה: ט] באכילת פרים: י] תיבת אימורים נמחק: יא] תיבת את נמחק: יב] קרי ביה מקדשי: יג] המזבח מקדש: יד] גרסי' לה לברייתא הכא ובתוספתא כך היא שנויה: טו] אם פיגל בזבח ואכל: טז] להקטיר מאימוריו חוץ לזמנו: יז] משנה שלישית לאו: יח] המזבח מקדש: יט] דלשני ליה כדמשני: כ] י"ל כו'. ועוד י"ל דלקמן ר"ל דלינה פסלא בבשר ומחשבה לא פסלא כשחשב בבשר עצמו אבל כשחשב באימורים דין הוא שיועיל לפגל הבשר כיון דשייכא לינה בבשר. מתוס' הר"פ ז"ל: כא] מועיל נמי פיגול: כב] הכא מהאי דיוקא: כג] והאי דשיירינהו משום דשייר פיגול דשייך בהו פיגול משום זבח וטעמא משום דבנותר איכא מיעוטא הזבח כדפי' לעיל ופיגול וטמא ילפי' מנותר אבל חישב בזבח לא ילפינן מנותר למעוטי מכרת לאכילת שליל ושליא ופשיטא דבלאו מיעוטא יש לחלק בין נותר לפיגול מידי דהוי אפרים דאמר לעיל פיגל באימורים כו'. מהר"פ: כד] גפה ונקטע רגלה ונסמית: תיבת

[שייך למשנה דלעיל פ"ח]
[ע' תוס' לקמן עז: ד"ה הכא בדוקין]
ג"ק
ס"א נתקנו לידי פסולין
מעילה ט. לקמן קד:
נ"ל הא נ"ק
ס"א דייק
לקמן פד.
לקמן פה: ע"ש
[שם ליתא]
[לעיל כז.]
נ"א מקצת נ"ק
*יעב"ץ מ"ז

הגהות הב"ח

(א) רש"י ד"ה ולטעמיך וכו' משנה שלישית לאו דוקא:

בפנים בחוץ ואת הניתנין בחוץ בפנים, שיאכלוהו טמאים, שיקריבוהו טמאים, *שיאכלוהו ערלים, ושיקריבוהו ערלים, לשבר עצמות הפסח, לאכול הימנו נא, ולערב דמו בדם הפסולים – אכשר, שאין מחשבה פוסלת אלא בחוץ לזמנו וחוץ למקומו, בוהפסח והחטאת שלא לשמן.§ **גמ'** מ"ט דרבי יהודה? אמר רבי אלעזר: תרי קראי כתיבי בנותר, כתוב אחד אומר: °"לא תותירו ממנו עד בקר", וכתוב אחד אומר: °"לא יניח ממנו עד בקר", אם אינו ענין להניח – תנהו לענין מחשבת הינוח. ורבי יהודה, האי קרא להכי הוא דאתא? האי מיבעי ליה לכדתניא: °"ובשר זבח תודת שלמיו" – גלמדנו לתודה שנאכלת ליום ולילה. חליפין דוולדות התמורות מנין? ת"ל: "ובשר". *וחטאת ואשם מנין? ת"ל: "זבח". א] ומנין לרבות זשלמי נזיר *חושלמי פסח? ב] ת"ל: "שלמיו". לחמי תודה, וחלות ורקיקים שבנזיר מנין? ת"ל: "קרבנו" – כולן קורא אני בהן "לא יניח". ג] א"כ לימא קרא ד] "לא תותירו", מאי "לא יניח"? אם אינו ענין להינוח – תנהו ענין למחשבת הינוח. התינח להניח, להוציא מאי איכא למימר? ועוד, טעמא דר' יהודה סברא הוא. דתניא, *אמר להם רבי יהודה: ה] אי אתם מודים שאם הניחו למחר שהוא פסול? אף חישב להניחו ו] למחר – פסול!* אלא, טעמא דרבי יהודה סברא הוא? וניפלוג נמי ר"י בכולהו! בהי ניפלוג? בשובר עצמות הפסח ולאכול ממנו נא – זיבחא גופיה מי מיפסיל? ע"מ שיאכלוהו טמאים ושיקריבוהו טמאים – זיבחא גופיה מי מיפסיל? שיאכלוהו ערלים ושיקריבוהו ערלים – זיבחא גופיה מי מיפסיל? לישנא אחרינא: כל כמיניה? לערב (א) ז] דמן בדם הפסולין – *רבי יהודה לטעמיה, דאמר: אין דם מבטל דם. ליתן את הניתנין למעלה למטה, למטה למעלה – ח] *רבי יהודה לטעמיה, דאמר: שלא למקומו נמי מקומו קרינא ביה. ט] וליפלוג בניתנין בפנים שנתנן בחוץ, והניתנין בחוץ שנתנן בפנים! קסבר רבי יהודה: בעינן *מקום שיהא משולש, בדם בבשר ובאימורין. ומי אית ליה לרבי יהודה האי סברא? והתניא, רבי יהודה אומר: °"דבר רע" – ריבה כאן חטאת ששחטה בדרום. וחטאת שנכנס דמה לפנים – פסולה! *ולית י] לרבי יהודה שלישי? *והתנן, אמר רבי יהודה: הכנים בשוגג – כשר; הא במזיד – פסול, וקי"ל בשכיפר; השתא, ומה התם יא] עיילי עיילא, אי כיפר – אין, אי לא כיפר – לא, הכא דחשיב חשובי – לא כל שכן? תרי תנאי ואליבא דרבי יהודה. וסבר ר' יהודה, חטאת ששחטה בדרום יב]

יהא

שמות יב | ויקרא ז | שם | דברים יז | תורה אור

רש"י

גמ' תרי קראי כתיבי בנותר. חד בפסח וחד בתודה. חליפין. מפריש תודתו ואבדה, והפריש אחרת תחתיה, ונמצאת הראשונה – הויא שניה חליפי תודה, וקריבה. וולדות יג] תמורה. ולד תודה ותמורת תודה. וכולן קרינן, כדאמרי' בבכורות (דף יד:): "רק קדשיך" – אלו התמורות, "אשר יהיה לך" – אלו הוולדות, בכולן אני קורא בהן "תשא ובאת" וגו'. ת"ל ובשר. דהוה ליה למכתב "ותודתו ביומו יאכל", הוה ליה יד] קרא יתירא לדרשא. שלמי נזיר. איל נזיר הטעון לחם כמותה. ושלמי פסח. חגיגת ארבעה עשר. אבל שלמים בעלמא – לא מצי לרבויי, דהא כתיב בהדיא בהו שני ימים, "ביום זבחכם יאכל וממחרת". ה"ג: א"כ לימא קרא לא תותירו. כדכתיב בכל שאר הנותרים לשון נותר. ועוד טעמא דר' יהודה ע"כ סברא הוא. ולא מריבויא דקרא. אלא ס"ל דהואיל ומיפסיל בהולכה ובהינוח – מיפסיל נמי במחשבת הולכה והינוח. שאם הניח למחר שהוא פסול. דדם נפסל בשקיעת החמה טו]. ונפלוג נמי ר' יהודה בכולהו. הואיל וטעמא מהאי סברא הוא – נפלוג בכולהו הנך דמתני' דקתני כשר! ומשנינן: בהי מינייהו נפלוג? מי קא מיפסיל. אם היה שובר את העצמות או אוכל נא. שיקריבוהו טמאים מי קמיפסיל. טז] והאי "יקריבוהו" באימורין קאמר, דומיא ד"יאכלוהו" בבשר. *וכן אם יאכלו טמאים או ערלים זבח שנזרק דמו כהלכתו – מי פסיל הקרבן למפרע מלרצות? ה"ג: לישנא אחרינא כל כמיניה. מי ישמע לו להקריבו בפסול? הכהנים טמאים לא ישמעו לו, וכן הערלים להקריב למזבח בעבירה, או לאכול קדש בעבירה. הלכך, אין מחשבתו מחשבה בדבר התלוי באחרים. לערב (ב) דמן בדם כו'. כולי האי משיוויא. כלומר, ואי איפליג בלערב דמה כו' – אין דם מבטל דם, וכיון דעירוב לא פסיל – מחשבת עירוב [נמי] לא פסיל. ליתן את הניתנין כו'. (ג) ליפלוג יז] במחשבה שלא במקומו. ר' יהודה לטעמיה. דאמר: אפילו יהביה חוץ למקומו לא מיפסיל זיבחא מלרצות, דשלא במקומו כמקומו דמי. בפ"ב (לעיל כו.), דאוקימנא מתניתין דחישב ליתן את הניתנין למטה למעלה כו', דס"ל לתנא דשלא במקומו כמקומו דמי, יח] דמסקנא: מידי דהוה אמחשבת הינוח, ואליבא דר' יהודה. (ד) ולפלוג בליתן את הניתנין בפנים בחוץ. יט] והניתנין בחוץ שחשב ליתן בפנים קא מקשי, דהתם ודאי אי הוה יהיב חטאת החיצונה בפנים – מיפסלא, דכתיב: "וכל חטאת אשר יובא" וגו' (ויקרא ו). קסבר רבי יהודה. מחשבה ליתן את הניתנין בחוץ בפנים לא פסלא, דגבי מחשבת חוץ כ] *לזמנו כתוב "שלישי" ודרשינן שיהא אותו חוץ משולש בדם ובשר ואימורין, דהיינו חוץ לעזרה ממש, שבשעת היתר הבמות נשתלש בכל אלה. כא] הלכך, גזירת הכתוב דפסול חוץ למקומו, אבל להכניסו לפנים – לאו מחשבה היא. דבר רע. "לא תזבח לה' אלהיך שור ושה אשר יהיה בו מום" וגו', ריבה כאן אזהרה שלא ישחוט החטאת בדרום. וחטאת שנכנס דמה לפנים כו'. כלומר, כב] לא תזבחנו ע"מ להכנים דמה לפנים. ולאו בהכנסה ממש קמזהר ליה, אלא במחשבת הכנסה, דהא בזביחה קאי. וקא קרי ליה "דבר רע", אלמא מיפסיל! הכנים בשוגג כשר. בפרק "כל הזבחים שנתערבו". וקיימא לן התם בגמרא בשילהי פירקין דהא דדייקינן: הא מזיד פסול – בשכיפר, בשנתן ממנו על כג] מזבח הפנימי הוא דקפסיל רבי יהודה, ולא מיפסל בהכנסה. והשתא ומה כו'. דאיכא למשמע מיניה, דכל שכן דמחשבת הכנסה לא פסיל.

יהא

תוספות

כד] תרי קראי כתיבי בנותר. חד בפסח וחד בתודה, ותימה: דדריש ב"אם אינו" כה] דמפסח, היכי ילפי' שאר נותר? שלמי פסח. פירשתי בפ"ק סמוך כו] לתחילתו (לעיל ט.). שיאכלוהו טמאים ויקריבוהו טמאים זיבחא גופיה מי מיפסל. פי' בקונט': דהאי יקריבוהו באימורין קאמר, ולא בדם, דומיא דיאכלוהו כז] בבשר, דאם אכלו טמאין או ערלים זבח שנזרק דמו כהלכתו – מי מפסיל קרבן כח] מלרצות? וא"ת: חישב להניח אימורים למחר או כט] בחוץ, אמאי פסול? הלא אם הניח אימורים עד למחר או בחוץ, כיון שנזרק דמו כהלכתו – לא נפסל קרבן מלרצות! וי"ל: דלא דמי. דלהניח אימורין למחר, אי עביד ל] *במחשבתו – מיפסיל כוליה קרבן בקדשים הנאכלים ליום ולילה. דכיון דהוו אימורין בעין, כל כמה דלא מיקטרי – לא משתרי בשר באכילה, וכי מטי למחר – מפסיל בשר משום נותר. אבל שיקריבוהו טמאים לא מיפסיל בשר, חדא, דהקריבוהו טמאין – אם עלו לא ירדו. ועוד: נטמאו אימורים או אבדו – משתרי בשר באכילה כיון דנזרק הדם כהלכתו. לא] אכתי קשה מלהוציאו לחוץ, אי קאי אאימורין – אמאי פסיל ר' יהודה? הלא אם עשה כן לא נמנע הדם בכך מלרצות, וגם בשר מישתרי באכילה. דכיון שהוציא אימורים בחוץ – הוה ליה כנטמאו אימורים או אבדו, לב] והבשר שרי לאכול! ואי לא קאי להוציאו רק אדם – אתי שפיר לג] הכי. **קסבר** ר' יהודה בעינן מקום שיהא משולש בדם ובבשר ובאימורין. תימה: לאמאי דלא ידע טעמא דמקום משולש, תיקשי ליה לרבנן, אמאי לא חשיב [הניתנין בחוץ בפנים] חוץ למקומו? דמהאי טעמא ממעטינן ליה בפירקין דלעיל, ולקמן בפ' "התערובות" (דף פב:)! וי"ל: דס"ד דרבי יהודה הוא, דלא בעי, לד] משום דמסקינן טעמא מסברא. **ומי** אית ליה לרבי יהודה כו'. צריך ליישב סוגיא זו לכל הלשונות שפי' בפירקין דלעיל (דף כט.) מקום משולש. **וחטאת** שנכנס דמה לפנים פסולה. פי' בקונטרס: שלא תזבחנה ע"מ להכניס דמה לפנים. ולא בהכנסה ממש קמזהר ליה, אלא במחשבת הכנסה, דהא בזביחה קאי, וקא קרי ליה "דבר רע" אלמא מיפסיל. ועוד יש לפרש: ד"דבר רע" משמע ליה לה] ע"י דבור, דהיינו מחשבה, ולאו הכנסה ממש. **וקי"ל** בשכיפר. וא"ת: למ"ד שלא במקומו לאו כמקומו דמי, אמאי פסיל רחמנא טפי בחטאות משאר קרבנות? לו] וי"ל: דבשאר דמים כשנתן ממנו על הפרכת ובין הבדים – איכא למימר דיאספנו, לז] *ואם יש עוד דם – יזרוק במקומו, וכשר. ובחטאת אין תקנה לדם *הנשאר. א"נ תנא דסבר לאו כמקומו דמי – יסבור בחטאת דפסול אף בלא כיפר. כרו"ק. **הכא** דחשובי חשיב לא כל שכן. תימה: א"כ בטלה תורת פיגול, דזרק מקצת דם בחוץ או אוכל כזית בחוץ – לא מיפסיל, ומחשב לח] מחשבה פוסל. הכי נמי, נהי דמכנים בלא מכפר לא מיפסיל, מחשב *)להכנים ולכפר לט] פוסל! וי"ל: "דבר רע" משמע: דבר שהוא רע במקום אחר, מ] דהוא בכיפר – זה אסרתי במחשבה בשעת זביחה. הכא דחישב – לא כל שכן דכשר, דאפילו חישב ליתן בפנים על מזבח הזהב על מנת להתכפר – כשר, כיון דבמחשבה לא שייכא כפרה כלל. אבל נתינה ממש – ראויה לכפר בשום מקום.

שיאכלוהו

*) נ"א להכנים בלא מכפר נ"ק

עין משפט נר מצוה

לט א מיי' פ"י מהל' פסה"מ הלכה ח:
מ ב מיי' פט"ו מהלכות פסה"מ הלכה ה:
מא ג מיי' פ"י מהל' מעה"ק הל' ז:
מב ד מיי' פ"ד מהל' תמורה הל' ו:
מג ה מיי' פ"ג שם הלכה ה:
מד ו מיי' פ"י מהל' פסה"מ הלכה ז:
מה ז מיי' שם ופ"ח מהל' נזיר הל' יב:
[נ"ל כמחשבתו]
מו ח מיי' פ"י מהל' קרבן פסח הלכה טו ודלא כמתני' כמתניתין דפסחים דנאכל לב' ימים ולילה אחד:
[עי' תוס' פסחים עא. ד"ה לימד וכו']
[מנחות יח.]
[עי' תוס' לעיל כז. ד"ה ולאו]

מסורת הש"ס

תוספתא דמנחות פ"ה
[מנחות נה: נזיר מה:]
נ"א שיאכלוהו ערלים ושיקריבוהו ערלים
נ"א ואי אתם מודים שאם הוציאו בחוץ שפסול אף חישב להוציאו בחוץ פסול
ל"ק
[לעיל לה. וש"נ]
[לעיל כט. לקמן פב:]
נ"א ולית ליה לרבי יהודה האי סברא והתנן כו' ועי' בכסף משנה פ"ב מהלכות פסה"מ ובכ"מ נ"א לגמקשין

שיטה מקובצת

א] תיבות ומנין לרבות ל"ש: ב] פסח מנין ת"ל: ג] א"כ לימא קרא לא (תותירו) [יניח] מאי לא (יניח) [תותירו] אם אינו ענין (לנותר) [להינוח] תנהו ענין למחשבת (נותר) [הינוח] וא"ת אימא איפכא דלא תותירו אתיא למחשבת נותר ואם אינו ענין לנותר דמלא יניח נפקא תנהו ענין למחשבת נותר וי"ל דלא תותירו לא מצינו למידרש דמשום מחשבת נותר אתיא ויש לגמגם מאי טעמא (דמאם) [לא אמרינן דאתיא מאם] אינו ענין ואמר מהר"פ משום דלא תותירו משמע לעולם שמזהיר לאכול שלא יביאנו לידי נותר הלכך באם אינו ענין לא הוי (מדריש) [דריש] מחשבת נותר אלא למחשבת לאכול חוץ לזמנו (הלכך א) למחשבת הינוח לא (מדריש) [מידרש] כלל דאוקימנא ע"י אם אינו ענין מעטה)

הגהות הב"ח

(א) גמ' כל כמיניה לערב דמו וכו' שלא במקומו נמי: (ב) רש"י ד"ה לערב דמו בדם כו' האי טליה משיטיה כלומר ואי ליפליג: (ג) ד"ה ליתן את הניתנים וכו' ואי ליפלוג: (ד) ד"ה ר"י לטעמיה וכו' וליפלוג בליתן. נ"ב עי' זה בתוס' דף כו ע"ב:

שמשמע מתוך הפסוק והיינו אכילה כמו שמצינו גבי דתן ואבירם ויותירו אנשים ממנו עד הבוקר שלא אכלו כל המן שלקטו ובלשון המשנה נמי נותר הוי אכילה כדאמר לעיל אם עון נותר הרי כבר נאמר לא יחשב פי' עון נותר ממש לאכול חוץ לזמנו אבל לא יניח משמע לשון הצנעה מתוך הפסוק כמו ויניחוהו במשמר אלמא משמע לשון הצנעה הילכך באם אינו ענין מוקמינן ליה למחשבת הינות. מהר"פ ז"ל: ד] קרא. בספרים ישנים [גרסינן לימא קרא] לא יניח מאי לא תותירו אם אינו ענין (לנותר) [להניח] תנהו ענין למחשבת (נותר) [הינוח] וכך הוא גירסת מהר"פ ז"ל: ה] אי אתם מודים כו' וא"ת להניח אימורים מאי איכא למימר למה אם הניחם [עד] למחר שיהא פסול דהא הוא עצמו שלא נקטרו אימוריו כשר וי"ל דגזרינן להניח אימורין אטו להניח דמו א"נ כיון דבהנחת אימורין [עד] למחר נפסל הבשר כדאמרינן דכל כמה דלא מתקטרי אימורין לא מתאכלי בשר א"כ אפי' מחשבת הינוח נמי. מהר"פ: ו] למחר פסול. ואי אתם מודים שאם הוציאו בחוץ שפסול אף חישב להוציאו בחוץ פסול: ז] לערב דמו בדם אות ן' נמחק: ח] ר' יהודה לטעמיה דאמר (למקומו) [שלא במקומו] כמקומו דמי פי' מדתניא לעיל לאלתר כשר והיינו כר"י מדקתני למחר פסול וא"כ הא דמכשר לאלתר היינו משום דכמקומו דמי כיון דלא ידע דרשא דמקום משולש. מהר"פ: ט] וליפלוג. עיין תוס' (דף כו ע"ב) ד"ה אמר שמואל: י] ולית ליה לר' יהודה האי סברא והתנן: יא] התם דעיילי עיילי: יב] בדרום פסולה: יג] וולדות ותמורות ולד: יד] ליה כוליה קרא: טו] בשקיעת החמה הס"ד: טז] קמיפסיל דהאי יקריבוהו באימורין כו' דיאכלוהו דהוי בבשר ואם יאכלו טמאים או ערלים כו' כהלכתא מי מיפסיל הקרבן: יז] במחשב ליתן דם שלא במקומו: יח] דמי ומסקנא מידי דהוה: יט] בחוץ כו' מהניתנין: כ] חוץ למקומו: כא] אלה לאפוקי היכל שאין בו הקטרת אימורין ואכילת בשר הלכך גזרת הכתוב דפסול חוץ למקומו: כב] כלומר שלא תזבחנה ע"מ להכנים כו' וקא קרי' ליה דבר רע אלמא בדיבורא מיפסיל הס"ד: כג] על גבי מזבח: כד] תרי קראי כתיבי. פ"ה חד גבי פסח וחד גבי נותר וקשה דא"כ מאי שייך לומר אם אינו ענין האי לגופיה איצטריך והאי לגופיה איצטריך לכן נ"ל דתרווייהו בתודה כתיבי חד בפרשה צו וחד בפרשה אמור. מהר"פ ז"ל: כה] אינו ענין ומפסח: כו] סמוך לסופו (דף ע ע"א): כז] דיאכלוהו דהוי בבשר ואם יאכלו טמאין: כח] מלרצות והלא הוא עצמו שלא נקטרו אימוריו כשר וא"ת בלהניח דמיו למחר אמאי פסול וי"ל דגזרינן מקצת דם אטו כולו דם. מהר"פ: כט] למחר או להוציאו לחוץ אמאי כו' למחר או הוציאו לחוץ כיון: ל] כמחשבתו: לא] כהלכתו אבל אכתי: לב] אבדו דהבשר: לג] שפיר טפי הס"ד וי"ל דטעמא דלהניח אימורים או להוציאו כולהו כדפי' לעיל משום דגזרינן אטו להניח כל דמו או להוציאו ובהכי מיפסל הקרבן אבל שיקריבהו טמאים לא שייך למגזר כאן כיון דאין בידו לעשות. מהר"פ ז"ל: לד] בעי מקום משולש: לה] ליה ס"א דבור רע דהיינו כו': לו] קרבנות דבשאר קרבנות נמי פסול: לז] דיאספנו ובחטאת פסול ואם: לח] תיבת מחשבה נמחק: לט] ולכפר ס"א שלא לכפר נמי ליפסיל: מ] תיבות דהוא בכיפר נמחק:

והתניא

א) נראה דל"ל אבל למחשבת הינוח לא מדרש כלל דלא אוקימנא ע"י אם אינו ענין רק כמו הענין שמשמע מתוך כו': ב) אולי נ"ל למה פסול דהא אם הניחם עד למחר ג"כ אינו פסול וכו'.

מז א מיי' פי"ד מהל' פסה"מ הלכה ט:
מח ב מיי' פי"ח מהל' פסה"מ הלכה יט:
מט ג מיי' שם הל' יח:
א ד ה מיי' פי"ה מהל' פסה"מ הל' ...
ב ו מיי' פי"ה מהלכות פסה"מ הל' ח:
ג ז מיי' פ"ב שם הל' ג:
ד ח מיי' פי"ז שם הל' א:

[לעיל לא.] **שיאכלוהו** טמאים. לא דמי לאכילת כלבים. *דבטמאים מיפסיל קודם אכילה משעת נגיעה. ואפי' תחב לו חבירו, מ"מ בהך כב] *(מחשבה אכילת) [נ"ל מחשבת אכילה] דבר אחר גורם לו, שבלא אכילה יכול לפוסלו בנגיעה. **בשר** פסח שלא הוצלה. הא דתניא ב"הקומץ רבה" (מנחות דף כה:) דשאין ניתר לטהורים אין חייבין עליו משום טומאה – היינו בדבר שצריך היתר מזבח, כגון בשר שנטמא לפני זריקה. ולא דמי לבשר פסח שלא הוצלה, ולחמי תודה שלא הורמו. וצריך לדקדק: דהכא דרשינן "אשר לה'" לרבות אימורי קדשים קלים לטומאה, והתם מוקמינן ליה לרבות לן ויוצא.

הדרן עלך כל הפסולין

מנין לניתנין על מזבח החיצון שנתנן מתנה אחת כיפר כו'. לכאורה אתיא כבית שמאי. דבית הלל, כג] *כיון דמכשרי בחטאת לקמן: "וכפר" אע"פ שלא נתן אלא אחד – לא צריך קרא לשאר קרבנות. וכן משמע בסוף שמעתין, דקאמר: וכל הנך תנאי דמנפקי ליה להאי "ודם זבחיך ישפך" לדרשא אחרינא, כל הניתנין על מזבח החיצון שנתנן במתנה אחת שכיפר מנא להו? סברי לה כבית הלל, דאמרי: אף חטאת שנתנה במתנה אחת כיפר, וילפי כולהו מחטאת. ונראה דאתיא אפי' כב"ה, וקסבר האי תנא דלא ילפינן מחטאת, משום דשתי מתנות שהן ארבע דשאר קרבנות ילפי' בפ' "איזהו מקומן" (לקמן דף נג:) מדכתיב "סביב", כד] *והוה אמינא שתים עשאן הכתוב כמתנה אחת ולא כיפר, אי נמי: משום דטובא "סביב" כתיבי, כה] ושנה לעכב. ולקמן נמי אמרי' "וכפר" ו"כפר" מפני הדין כו', מה דמים האמורים למטה שנתנן מתנה אחת – כיפר, אף דמים שלמעלה כן

נ"א כיון דמכשרי אף בחטאת וליליף לקמן מוכפר כו'. ג"ק

גי' ל"ק וטו"א עשאן הכתוב כו'

יְהֵא חַיָּיב? א] וְהָתַנְיָא, רַבִּי יְהוּדָה אוֹמֵר: יָכוֹל חַטָּאת שֶׁשְּׁחָטָהּ בַּדָּרוֹם יְהֵא חַיָּיב? ת"ל: °"לֹא תִזְבַּח לַה' אֱלֹהֶיךָ שׁוֹר וָשֶׂה וגו' כֹּל דָּבָר רָע" – עַל ב] דָּבָר רַע אַתָּה מְחַיְּיבוֹ, וְאִי אַתָּה מְחַיְּיבוֹ עַל חַטָּאת שֶׁשְּׁחָטָהּ בַּדָּרוֹם! תְּרֵי תַּנָּאֵי אַלִּיבָּא דְּרַבִּי יְהוּדָה. אָמַר ג] רַבִּי אַבָּא: וּמוֹדֶה רַבִּי יְהוּדָה, שֶׁחוֹזֵר וְקוֹבְעוֹ לְפִיגּוּל. ד] אָמַר רָבָא: תֵּדַע, דְּפִיגּוּל לִפְנֵי זְרִיקָה לֹא כְּלוּם הוּא, וְאָתְיָא זְרִיקָה וְקָבְעָה לָהּ בְּפִיגּוּל. וְלָא הִיא, הָתָם הוּא חֲדָא מַחֲשָׁבָה הִיא, הָכָא – תְּרֵי מַחֲשָׁבוֹת. אֵיתִיבֵיהּ רַב הוּנָא ה] לְרַבִּי אַבָּא: *לִיתֵּן אֶת הַנִּיתָּנִין לְמַעְלָה לְמַטָּה, לְמַטָּה לְמַעְלָה, לְאַלְתַּר – כָּשֵׁר; חָזַר וְחִישֵּׁב חוּץ לִמְקוֹמוֹ – פָּסוּל וְאֵין בּוֹ כָּרֵת, חוּץ לִזְמַנּוֹ – פִּיגּוּל וְחַיָּיבִין עָלָיו כָּרֵת. לְמָחָר – פָּסוּל; חָזַר וְחִישֵּׁב, בֵּין חוּץ לִזְמַנּוֹ בֵּין חוּץ לִמְקוֹמוֹ – פָּסוּל, וְאֵין בּוֹ כָּרֵת. תְּיוּבְתָּא ו] דְּרַבִּי אַבָּא! תְּיוּבְתָּא. אָמַר רַב חִסְדָּא אָמַר רָבִינָא בַּר סִילָא: אחִישֵּׁב שֶׁיֹּאכְלוּהוּ טְמֵאִים לְמָחָר – חַיָּיב. אָמַר רָבָא: תֵּדַע, דְּבָשָׂר לִפְנֵי זְרִיקָה לָא חָזֵי, וְכִי מְחַשֵּׁב בֵּיהּ – מִיפְּסִיל. וְלָא הִיא, הָתָם – זָרֵיק וּמִיחֲזֵי, הָכָא – לָא מִיחֲזֵי כְּלָל. אָמַר רַב חִסְדָּא, *מַרְגְּלָא בְּפוּמֵיהּ דְּרַב דִּימִי בַּר חִינָּנָא: בבְּשַׂר פֶּסַח שֶׁלֹּא הוּצְלָה, וְלַחְמֵי תוֹדָה שֶׁלֹּא הוּרְמוּ – חַיָּיבִין עֲלֵיהֶן מִשּׁוּם טוּמְאָה. אָמַר רָבָא: תֵּדַע, *דְּתַנְיָא: °"אֲשֶׁר לַה'" – גלְרַבּוֹת אֵימוּרֵי קָדָשִׁים קַלִּים לְטוּמְאָה; אַלְמָא, אע"ג דְּלָאו בְּנֵי אֲכִילָה נִינְהוּ – חַיָּיבִין עֲלֵיהֶן מִשּׁוּם טוּמְאָה. הָכָא נַמִי – אע"ג דְּלָאו בְּנֵי אֲכִילָה נִינְהוּ – חַיָּיבִין עֲלֵיהֶן מִשּׁוּם טוּמְאָה. וְלָא הִיא, הָתָם – אֵימוּרֵי קָדָשִׁים קַלִּים חֲזוּ לְגָבוֹהַּ, לְאַפּוּקֵי בְּשַׂר פֶּסַח שֶׁלֹּא הוּצְלָה וְלַחְמֵי תוֹדָה שֶׁלֹּא הוּרְמוּ, דְּלָא חֲזוּ לֹא לְגָבוֹהַּ וְלֹא לְהֶדְיוֹט. (א) ז] (לִישָּׁנָא אַחֲרִינָא: הָא אֵימוּרִין לָא חֲזוּ. וְלָא הִיא, הָנָךְ חֲזוּ לְמִילְּתַיְיהוּ, וְהָנֵי לָא חֲזוּ כְּלָל).§ ס"א ל"ג

דברים יז | ויקרא ז

תורה אור

יְהֵא חַיָּיב. מַלְקוּת. דָּבָר רָע. מוּם בְּגָלוּי שֶׁהוּא מְגוּנֶּה קָרֵי "דָּבָר רָע", בִּבְכוֹרוֹת בְּפֶרֶק "עַל אֵלּוּ מוּמִין" (דף לז.). וּמוֹדֶה רַבִּי יְהוּדָה. בְּחִישֵּׁב עַל מְנָת יא] לְהַנִּיחַ – (ב) שֶׁחוֹזֵר וְקוֹבְעוֹ לְפִיגּוּל אִם חָזַר וְחִישֵּׁב בַּעֲבוֹדָה שְׁנִיָּה עַל מְנָת לֶאֱכוֹל חוּץ לִזְמַנּוֹ, וְלָא אָמְרִי' כְּבָר נִפְסַל בְּמַחֲשֶׁבֶת הִינּוּחַ. אָמַר רָבָא תֵּדַע. דְּמַחֲשֶׁבֶת הִינּוּחַ לְרַבִּי יְהוּדָה לָאו כְּמַחֲשֶׁבֶת חוּץ לִמְקוֹמוֹ וְשֶׁלֹּא לִשְׁמוֹ הִיא, לְאַפּוּקֵי מִידֵי פִּיגּוּל. דְּהָא פִּיגּוּל, דְּשׁוֹחֵט עַל מְנָת לִזְרוֹק אֶת דָּמוֹ לְמָחָר – לִפְנֵי זְרִיקָה לָאו כְּלוּם הִיא, וְאֵין הַמַּחֲשָׁבָה מוֹעֶלֶת עַד שֶׁיִּזָּרֵק הַדָּם הַיּוֹם, דְּבָעֵינַן יב] קָרַב כָּל מַתִּירָיו. וּמִיהוּ, מַחֲשָׁבָה קַמַּיְיתָא מַחֲשֶׁבֶת הִינּוּחַ הָוֵי, וְכִי זָרֵיק לֵיהּ – אָתְיָא זְרִיקָה יג] וְקָבְעֵי לֵיהּ, (ג) וְלָא אָמְרִי': הוֹאִיל וּמֵעִיקָּרָא פִּיגּוּל לָא חָיְילָא – אִיפְּסִיל לֵיהּ בְּמַחֲשֶׁבֶת הִינּוּחַ, וְכִי זָרֵיק לֵיהּ אוֹ בְּפִיגּוּל אוֹ בִּשְׁתִיקָה לָא לֵיחוּל פִּיגּוּל. הָתָם חַד מַחֲשָׁבָה. דְּלָא שִׁינָּה יד] מַחֲשַׁבְתּוֹ הָרִאשׁוֹנָה, וְהִיא הָיְתָה לְשֵׁם פִּיגּוּל. תְּרֵי מַחֲשָׁבוֹת. וְהָאֶחָד שֵׁם פָּסוּל לָהּ וְלֹא שֵׁם פִּיגּוּל. כָּשֵׁר. כִּדְאָמְרִינַן בְּמַתְנִי' לְדִבְרֵי הַכֹּל. לְמָחָר פָּסוּל. חִישֵּׁב לִיתֵּן לְמָחָר אֶת הַנִּיתָּנִין לְמַטָּה לְמַעְלָן. וְאוֹקֵי בְּפֶרֶק שֵׁנִי מִשּׁוּם מַחֲשֶׁבֶת הִינּוּחַ, כְּרַבִּי יְהוּדָה, וְלֹא מִשּׁוּם מַחֲשֶׁבֶת נְתִינַת מָחָר, דְּא"כ – פִּיגּוּל מִיבָּעְיָא לֵיהּ. טו] אַלְמָא לָא הָוֵי פִּיגּוּל, דִּזְרִיקָה דְּלָא כָּשֵׁר בַּאֲכִילָה לָא אָתְיָא לִידֵי פִּיגּוּל. וְקָתָנֵי: חָזַר וְחִישֵּׁב בּוֹ, אַלְמָא לָא מִיקְבַּע בּוֹ טז] פִּיגּוּל. חִישֵּׁב שֶׁיֹּאכְלוּהוּ טְמֵאִים לְמָחָר. פִּיגּוּל. וְלָא אָמְרִינַן לָאו מַחֲשָׁבָה הִיא, דַּאֲכִילַת טְמֵאִים לָא חָזְיָא, וְהָוֵי כִּמְחַשֵּׁב מַחֲשֶׁבֶת פָּסוּל. תֵּדַע. דְּמַחֲשֶׁבֶת אֲכִילַת פָּסוּל לָא מַפְקָא מִידֵי פִּגּוּל, בַּר יז] מַחֲשֶׁבֶת חוּץ לִמְקוֹמוֹ (וְלִזְמַנּוֹ). דְּהָא בָּשָׂר לִפְנֵי זְרִיקָה לָא חֲזֵי לַאֲכִילָה, וְכִי מְחַשֵּׁב בֵּיהּ בִּשְׁחִיטָה ע"מ לְאוֹכְלָהּ לְמָחָר – מִפְגִּיל, יח] דְּהַשְׁתָּא אֲכִילָה פְּסוּלָה הִיא בְּלָא שׁוּם פִּיגּוּל. הָתָם זָרֵיק וּמִיחֲזֵי. וְאִשְׁתַּכַּח דִּלְמָחָר, אִי לָאו מִשּׁוּם פִּיגּוּל, הֲוָה יט] חַזְיָא לַאֲכִילָה. שֶׁלֹּא הוּרְמָה. ד' חַלּוֹת הַנִּתְרָמוֹת לְכֹהֵן מֵאַרְבָּעָה מִינִין שֶׁבָּהּ, דִּכְתִיב: "וְהִקְרִיב מִמֶּנּוּ אֶחָד מִכָּל קָרְבָּן תְּרוּמָה" וגו' (ויקרא ז). מִשּׁוּם טוּמְאָה. אִם אֲכָלָן בְּטוּמְאַת הַגּוּף. וְאע"ג דְּקי"ל* כ] שֶׁאֵין נִיתָּר לִטְהוֹרִים אֵין חַיָּיבִין עָלָיו מִשּׁוּם טוּמְאָה, הַאי כֵּיוָן דְּאִיזְּרַק דָּם – נִיתָּר לִטְהוֹרִין קָרֵינַן בֵּיהּ, וְאע"ג דְּאֵין פֶּסַח נֶאֱכָל אֶלָּא צָלִי, וְחַלּוֹת הַתּוֹדָה עַד שֶׁיּוּרְמוּ. ה"ג אֲשֶׁר לַה' לְרַבּוֹת אֵימוּרֵי קָדָשִׁים קַלִּים לְטוּמְאָה. "וְהַנֶּפֶשׁ אֲשֶׁר תֹּאכַל" מִבְּשַׂר זֶבַח הַשְּׁלָמִים אֲשֶׁר לַה'". לְטוּמְאָה. לְהִתְחַיֵּיב כָּרֵת הָאוֹכְלָן בְּטוּמְאַת הַגּוּף. דַּ"אֲשֶׁר לַה'" יְתֵירָא הוּא, לְמִידְרַשׁ בֵּיהּ דָּבָר שֶׁהוּא עוֹלֶה לַגָּבוֹהַּ.

לעיל כו: [שם איתא חישב ליתן כו']
[עי' פירש"י בסנהדרין נג: ד"ה מרגלא]
פסחים כב: [עו.] כריתות כג:
פסחים לה: מנחות כה:
[מנחות מח:]

הדרן עלך כל הפסולין

הדרן עלך כל הפסולין

סנהדרין ד. פסחים פט:

בֵּית שַׁמַּאי אוֹמְרִים: *דכָּל הַנִּיתָּנִין עַל מִזְבֵּחַ הַחִיצוֹן, שֶׁנְּתָנָן ח] בְּמַתָּנָה אַחַת – כִּיפֵּר, וּבְחַטָּאת – שְׁתֵּי מַתָּנוֹת. וּבֵית הִלֵּל אוֹמְרִים: האַף חַטָּאת שֶׁנְּתָנָהּ מַתָּנָה אַחַת – כִּיפֵּר. ולְפִיכָךְ, אִם נָתַן אֶת הָרִאשׁוֹנָה כְּתִיקְנָהּ וְאֶת הַשְּׁנִיָּה חוּץ לִזְמַנָּהּ – כִּיפֵּר, וְאִם נָתַן אֶת הָרִאשׁוֹנָה חוּץ לִזְמַנָּהּ וְאֶת הַשְּׁנִיָּה חוּץ לִמְקוֹמָהּ – פִּיגּוּל וְחַיָּיבִין עָלָיו כָּרֵת. זכָּל הַנִּיתָּנִין עַל הַמִּזְבֵּחַ הַפְּנִימִי ט] שֶׁאִם חִיסֵּר אַחַת מִן הַמַּתָּנוֹת – כְּאִילּוּ לֹא כִּיפֵּר. לְפִיכָךְ, חנָתַן כּוּלָּן כְּתִיקְנָן וְאַחַת שֶׁלֹּא כְּתִיקְנָהּ – פְּסוּלָה וְאֵין בּוֹ כָּרֵת.§ **גמ'** תָּנוּ רַבָּנַן: *מִנַּיִן לַנִּיתָּנִין עַל מִזְבֵּחַ הַחִיצוֹן שֶׁנְּתָנָן י] בְּמַתָּנָה אַחַת, שֶׁכִּיפֵּר? תַּלְמוּד לוֹמַר: °"וְדַם זְבָחֶיךָ יִשָּׁפֵךְ". וְהַאי לְהָכִי הוּא דַּאֲתָא? הַאי מִיבְּעֵי לֵיהּ לְכִדְתַנְיָא: דברים יב

מִנַּיִן

בֵּית שַׁמַּאי אוֹמְרִים. מַתָּנָה אַחַת. זְרִיקָה אַחַת – כִּיפֵּר, אע"פ שֶׁרוּבָּן טְעוּנִים שְׁתֵּי מַתָּנוֹת שֶׁהֵן אַרְבַּע. וּבְחַטָּאת שְׁתֵּי מַתָּנוֹת. מַתָּנוֹת אַרְבַּע מִמֶּשׁ. וּבַגְּמָרָא יָלֵיף טַעְמָא. לְפִיכָךְ. חַטָּאת וְכָל הַזְּבָחִים לְבֵית הִלֵּל, וּלְבֵית שַׁמַּאי שְׁאָר זְבָחִים חוּץ מֵחַטָּאת. נָתַן אֶת הָרִאשׁוֹנָה בְּתִקְנָהּ. בִּשְׁתִיקָה, וְאֶת הַשְּׁנִיָּה בְּמַחֲשֶׁבֶת אֲכִילַת בָּשָׂר חוּץ לִזְמַנּוֹ – כִּיפֵּר, וְכָשֵׁר הַקָּרְבָּן. שֶׁכְּבָר נִיתַּר הַקָּרְבָּן לִיקָּרֵב עַל יְדֵי מַתָּנָה רִאשׁוֹנָה, וְאֵין הַשְּׁנִיָּה מַתֶּרֶת אֶת הַבָּשָׂר – לְפִיכָךְ אֵינָהּ מְפַגֶּלֶת. פִּיגּוּל וְחַיָּיבִין עָלָיו כָּרֵת. שֶׁאֵין מַחֲשֶׁבֶת חוּץ לִמְקוֹמוֹ דִּשְׁנִיָּה מוֹצִיאָתוֹ מִידֵי פִּיגּוּל, שֶׁכְּבָר הוּקְבַּע בָּרִאשׁוֹנָה, שֶׁכְּבָר קָרְבוּ כָּל מַתִּירָיו. שֶׁחִיסֵּר אַחַת מִכָּל הַמַּתָּנוֹת לֹא כִּיפֵּר. כִּדְיָלֵיף בַּבָּרַיְיתָא בַּגְּמָרָא. לְפִיכָךְ. הוֹאִיל וְכוּלָּן מַתִּירוֹת אֵין זוֹ מַתֶּרֶת בְּלֹא זוֹ, וְאֵין זוֹ מְפַגֶּלֶת בְּלֹא זוֹ. וְאִם נָתַן כּוּלָּן כְּתִקְנָן בִּשְׁתִיקָה, וְאַחַת שֶׁלֹּא כְּתִקְנָהּ, כְּגוֹן שֶׁנְּתָנָהּ בְּמַחֲשֶׁבֶת חוּץ לִמְקוֹמוֹ אוֹ חוּץ לִזְמַנּוֹ – פָּסוּל, שֶׁלֹּא נִיתַּר בָּרִאשׁוֹנוֹת, וְאֵין בּוֹ כָּרֵת – שֶׁאֵין הָאַחֲרוֹנָה מְפַגַּלְתּוֹ, דְּקָסָבַר: אֵין מְפַגְּלִין בַּחֲצִי מַתִּיר. **גמ'** יִשָּׁפֵךְ. שְׁפִיכָה אַחַת מַשְׁמַע, כא] דְּלָא כְּתִיב "סָבִיב" דְּיָלְפִינַן מִינֵּיהּ שְׁתֵּי מַתָּנוֹת שֶׁהֵן אַרְבַּע בְּפֶרֶק "אֵיזֶהוּ מְקוֹמָן".

מִנַּיִן

הגהות הב"ח

(א) גמ' לישנא אחרינא ולא היא הני אימורים חזו למילתייהו הני לא חזו כלל כנ"ל: (ב) רש"י ד"ה ומודה וכו' על מנת להניח את דמו או אבריו שחוזר וקובעו: (ג) ד"ה אמר רבא וכו' וקבעי ליה בפיגול ולא:

שיטה מקובצת

א] והתניא בספרי בפרשת שופטים מייתי קצת בע"א (ותיבת חיי' נמחק): ב] על כל דבר: ג] אמר רבא ומודה ר"י: ד] אמר רבא תדע כו'. תימה א"כ אפי' במחשבת חוץ למקומו ושלא לשמו בפסח וחטאת לא תוציא מפיגול מטעמיה דרבא ואי משום דגלי קרא לא יערב בו מחשבות אחרות א"כ אפי' מחשבת הינוח נמי וי"ל דהא דקאמר הכא שהוקבעו לפיגול לא קאי לכולהו מחשבות דלעיל במתני' אלא אלהניח דמו למחר כיון שחזר וחשב לזרקו למחר אין זה עירוב מחשבות אלא עירוב מחשבתו ראשונה דלהניח ולזרוק דמו קאמר וקצת קשה דמשמע דקאי אכוליה מתני' גם אלהוציאו [לחוץ או להניחו] למחר (בחוץ) כמו שהזכיר בקונטרס לכך נראה למהר"פ דהא דגלי דעירוב מחשבות מוציא מידי פיגול היינו דוקא במחשבות הכתובות בפסוק דהיינו חוץ למקומו או שלא לשמו אבל מחשבת הינוח דמיפסלא מסברא לא וא"ת א"כ אמאי איצטריך להאי תדע דקאמר רבא וי"ל שלא תלמוד אותו פסול מחשבת הינוח משאר עבודות דכתיב בקראי ועוד שלא תאמר כהרצאת כשר: ה] הונא לרבא: ו] תיובתא דרבא: ז] מכאן ועד סוף הפרק נמחק: ח] החיצון שנתן מתנה: ט] הפנימי שחיסר אחת מן המתנות לא כפר: י] שנתנן מתנה אחת: יא] מנת להוציאו לחוץ או להניחו למחר שחזר: יב] דבעינן קרבו כל: יג] זריקה וקבעא: יד] שינה ממחשבתו: טו] ליה אלא לא הוי פיגול דזריקה דלא שריא בשר באכילה לא מייתי לידי: טז] תו בפיגול הס"ד: יז] בר ממחשבת חוץ למקומו: יח] מפגיל אע"ג דהשתא: יט] הוה חזי לאכילה: כ] שאם אין ניתר: כא] משמע מדלא כתיב: כב] בהך מחשבת אכילה דבר: כג] כיון דמכשרי בחטאת ומכפר אע"פ ומתיבת ומכפר עד תיבת לא בס"א אינו: כד] והו"א שעשאן מתנה אחת לא כיפר: כה] כתיבי דשנה לעכב ולקמן נמי אמרי' לב"ה וכפר:

My Notes

My Notes